AMERICAN FOREIGN POLICY:

FORMULATION, PRINCIPLES, AND PROGRAMS

AMERICAN

FORMULATION

BY

RICHARD C. SNYDER

Associate Professor of Politics

AND

EDGAR S. FURNISS, Jr.

Associate Professor of Politics

PRINCETON UNIVERSITY

FOREIGN POLICY

RINCIPLES, AND PROGRAMS

RINEHART & COMPANY, INC.

Publishers in New York, N. Y.

PREFACE

It seems particularly important at the outset that the readers of this book understand what the authors are trying to do. We assume we do not need to argue the significance of American foreign policy as a subject for study. Recent events have convinced us all that an area of national behavior which used to be the special preserve of a few interested citizens and experts must now be given systematic attention by the whole society. While it is always a temptation for scholars to exaggerate the social importance of the things they are interested in, one can scarcely doubt that the future of American security rests squarely upon the collective ability of our people to manage successfully their relations with the rest of the world. This is not to say, of course, that the American people and their officials can control all of the factors which bear on their well-being in the present situation, but unless we are prepared to surrender national destiny to some vague force called "fate" or to cling to magical formulas in the hope we shall be saved, everything socially possible should be done to ensure rational conduct and thought. A faith in some measure of control over human fortunes would appear to be implicit in the democratic way of life.

Therefore the question is not whether to study American foreign policy but how. We have tried to write an analytical volume built around various topics bearing on the substantive side of policy and various organizational aspects of policy making. The analytical approach has necessitated development of a frame of reference within which factual materials can be organized and made meaningful. We have tried to provide the reader with a basis for making some sense out of developments in the current period.

Historical trends and factors as well as contemporary events are employed as means to larger ends, not as ends in themselves. The chapter on the historical background of American foreign policy does not purport to contain a blow-by-blow account. Rather, it analyzes how and why policy developed as it did and how America arrived where it was by 1941—all this as a preliminary to the assessment of America's new international position in Chapter 2. Factual developments, both recent and current, are presented as examples or illustrations for the general points made throughout the analysis. Our reason for this approach is to avoid if possible a major depreciation of the value of the book as events move forward. We have attempted to provide a framework which will continue to be useful for an understanding of future as well as past developments in American foreign policy.

We have undertaken this approach with the knowledge that it poses certain difficulties for the reader as well as for us. It is not necessarily the easiest way to study American foreign policy in the present period. Much has happened since 1941, and the meaning of recent events cannot be entirely clear now and may not be for years to come. Yet some judgments must be made, although they must perforce be *tentative*. Such a warning does not automatically eliminate all the pitfalls, but we should be able to walk around some of them. This book deliberately underscores a basic theme: we are studying American policy in *transition*. This theme makes for trouble too. Not only has a great deal happened, but it has happened quickly and it is still happening. A phase of rapid transition may be likened to a pressure chamber, speeding up change, and altering or distorting the factors normally at work. Change brings its own peculiar problems, chief among which is the adaptation of policy and policy making to constantly shifting conditions.

We are trying, therefore, to do a big job within the covers of a single volume. Any one of the chapters could be expanded into a monograph. We have had to be selective. A social science treatise—or any treatise for that matter—will be the result of a number of conditioning factors: the age in which it is written, the state of knowledge in its particular branch of learning, the intellectual capacity and value judgments of those who write it. This one is no exception. We have deliberately simplified—we hope without distorting—and we have avoided being encyclopedic in our coverage. To make a subject manageable does not require "seeing everything at once," even if that were possible. In addition to risking possibly serious omissions, we have had to come face to face with trying to spell out complex relationships—always a risky, difficult enterprise where human behavior is concerned. The relationship between domestic social factors and policy making, between the substance of policy and the process of formulation, and between national behavior and the international environment is complex indeed. Yet without such analysis the full richness of the subject might be missed and important questions ignored.

If the table of contents of this book is compared to those of other works in the field of American foreign policy and international relations generally, the task to which we have set ourselves will be clearer. One can find valuable, comprehensive studies of American Government, International Organization, Diplomatic History, International Politics, and Comparative Government which deal respectively with the workings of American federal government, the operations of the United Nations, the detailed development of the external relations of the American people, the nature of interstate relations in the modern world, and the institutions and behavior patterns of nations which interact with the United States—particularly Great Britain, France, and the Soviet Union. Naturally all these subjects are related, directly or indirectly, to American foreign policy. But we cannot be as intensive as these works are or use the materials in quite the same way. We have tried to analyze essentially the same materials on a more restricted basis but within a much larger frame of reference.

Consequently we were confronted with two types of problem in organizing our presentation. First, should major developments like the North Atlantic Alliance and Treaty Organization be discussed in full at one special place in the text? We decided against such a procedure and have discussed major events, factors, and problems wherever they were relevant. Whatever is sacrificed by way of neatness and convenience is more than compensated for by the fact that we are able accordingly to emphasize that great developments and policies have more than one kind of significance. There are not just one thing or four things to be said about the Atlantic Alliance; there are an indefinite number of things to be said depending on how skillful we are at establishing criteria of relevance. The Atlantic Alliance is commented on either briefly or in detail in Chapters 1, 2, 3, 5, 7, 8, 9, 10, 11, 12, 14, 17, 20. So it is with other matters of equivalent magnitude. Second, we soon realized the need for an unusual amount of cross reference—backward and forward. Reminders of connecting links between what is at hand and what has gone before or is to come subsequently are generously sprinkled throughout the text and in the footnotes. "As was noted previously . . ." and "As will be shown later . . ." are recurrent phrases. This device can be overused, of course, but on balance we would rather err on the side of excess. If it appears to the reader that we are going in the same doors twice and that we are always meeting ourselves coming out, let him be reminded that one of the primary characteristics of the total contemporary American foreign policy picture is the relatedness of its parts to each other and to the whole.

It must be emphasized that we have left much for the reader to do on his own. Some will like this treatment, some not. Be that as it may, we have— again deliberately—left questions unanswered, problems unsolved, and implications only suggested. We have done this partly because we do not know the answers and partly because we believe it is sound intellectually for the reader to wrestle with problems himself, relying on such help as we and other scholars can give and seeking further help from our bibliographical notes. Some items of great importance we have been able barely to mention. We included them for the sake of whatever comprehensiveness we aspired to, and in the hope that, depending on their inclinations and resources, the users of the book would explore further. Some may argue that we should have tried to set the universe in order for the reader. It is always somewhat upsetting to be challenged to difficult mental exercise in an age of crisis. We do not believe, however, that the universe can be set in order by scholars or even by scientific investigation. What we do believe is that investigators (including the authors) can and must develop techniques which enable them to make their examination and interpretation of the universe and its problems more reliable, more orderly, more fruitful.

Let us, finally, state what we hope the reader will find in the succeeding pages: first, some basis for understanding what has happened to American foreign relations and foreign policy since 1941; second, some paths to an awareness of the complex foreign policy problems and issues confronting the American people in the present period; third, a framework of analysis which will help provide meaning for current events and criteria for judging both events and policy problems; and fourth, bibliographical suggestions for further study and for correcting errors or omissions which the authors may unwittingly have made.

Naturally, we owe many debts for the generous and substantial help we have received in the preparation of this volume. We appreciate the careful reading which Professor Arnold Wolfers of Yale University gave to part of the manuscript. To Dean Lawrence Chamberlain of Columbia College we are deeply indebted for the time and effort which he devoted to giving the authors the advantage of his insight and experience. Margaret Sprout gave unselfishly of her editorial skills and substantive competence in the field—we cannot really thank her. To Harold Sprout we owe many intellectual debts; his encouragement and accommodation as we needed them lightened our task considerably. We have dedicated this book to our wives, as a token of the important part they played in its development.

Richard C. Snyder

Edgar S. Furniss, Jr.

Princeton, New Jersey
July, 1954

TABLE OF CONTENTS

► PART TWO: POSTWAR AMERICAN FOREIGN POLICIES

Fourteen

Fifteen

INTRODUCTION

CHAPTER ONE

THE HISTORICAL BACKGROUND, 1898-1939

► INTRODUCTION

Americans, looking back at their country's history, are in danger of being deluded by the long shadows cast by the first hundred years of the nation. This was a period of phenomenal growth: growth in territory, in population, in resources, in technological organizations, in political and social maturity. At the dawn of the present century the United States had become a great power, with world-wide interests and responsibilities, although they were frequently unrecognized. Distorted perspective has made American expansion appear inevitable and governed by easily recognizable principles and policies of contemporary relevancy and applicability. While the circumstances surrounding our involvement in World War II and the postwar crisis in relations with the Soviet Union have done much to disillusion us about any "immutable" foreign policies, these later events have unfortunately strengthened rather than weakened the view that nineteenth-century progress was simple, effortless, and foreordained. Such an interpretation, however, does not do justice to the early leaders of American statecraft. Re-examination of the foreign relations of the United States should go far toward demonstrating its falsity.

There is no law of international politics that says a new nation must come into existence, that it must continue to exist, to enhance its stability, and to expand its base. History is littered with the corpses of states, many of them small, some of them noble in conception and enlightened in practice. During the first thirty years of its existence the United States could have become one of the corpses. Its early demise could have taken place either as a result of serious errors in leadership or as a result of changes in the inter-

3

national environment over which it could not exert any control. Independence was achieved in part because of the determination, wisdom, stubbornness, and foolhardiness of the continental leaders, and in part because of the involved quarrels among European states, which placed France and Spain on the side of the American colonies for the protection of their mutual interests. As a result of its European involvement, Great Britain did not choose to make the military commitment necessary to win that part of the conflict which from the British point of view took place in a subordinate theater.

CONTRAST OF AMERICAN AND EUROPEAN EXPANSION

Following the attainment of independence, a combination of American and European difficulties succeeded by 1820 in removing the United States from direct entanglement in the complex skein of European politics. Continental expansion thenceforth could take place over largely empty territory with a minimum of international conflict. Contrast this situation with that in Europe, where nations by the nineteenth century already had a heritage of a millenium of hostility, suspicion, and war. The attempts of one nation to move its frontier a few kilometers could come to fruition only after years of intrigue and preparation for the clash of armed forces that usually resulted, while in North America peacefully negotiated treaties with Spain and France, plus a short war with weak Mexico, could expand the domain of the United States from the Appalachians to the Pacific coast, a distance of over two thousand miles. The Indians seemed to believe the land was theirs, but who could let even "noble" savages, nomads without a settled home, stand in the way of advancing "civilization"?

EVILS OF EUROPEAN "POWER POLITICS"

Certain compelling conclusions were evident in these events for all "right-thinking" Americans of the time to see. It was the European "system" which was bad. As Monroe proclaimed, the nature of European governmental relations seemed to lead inevitably to chaos and war. Given the inability and unwillingness of European monarchy to reform, the United States should have as little as possible to do with that whole wretched continent. In its own policies the United States should abjure the contemptible politics of power until the time that peace, as America pursued it, should have entered into the hearts and minds of all men. The classic statement of American abstention from European affairs and predominance of interest in the Western Hemisphere was, of course, the statement of President Monroe. As the nineteenth century progressed, what had been a pronunciamento without power behind it became a doctrine in the name of which the United States was prepared to employ force if necessary. These twin attitudes of hostility toward Europe and expansion in the Western Hemisphere laid the groundwork for Wilsonian idealism and interwar isolationism.

A LACK OF INTEREST IN FOREIGN AFFAIRS

Nineteenth-century experience was reflected in a lack of general interest in foreign affairs. Separated by the great expanse of the Atlantic Ocean, the American and his government did not need to know much about Europe. The United States could afford to do without a foreign policy, since its primary objective—continental expansion—could be attained in an international vacuum. Such a balance of priorities between affairs foreign and domestic seemed generally justifiable until 1898, with possible exceptions relating to American interests in the Western Hemisphere and in the Far East. When the United States developed in the twentieth century the interests of a great power and, with tragic belatedness, the commitments and responsibilities of one, its foreign office, significantly known as the "State" Department, was without the trained personnel, the size, and the intragovernmental prestige to serve the nation abroad. Americans were so long accustomed to label one long list of items "domestic policy" and another, much shorter, list "foreign policy," that the close relationship between the two lists was obscured, and the mere fact that any relationship existed was often indignantly denied. The tragic consequences of this point of view were magnified by the historically oriented belief that the first list was not only longer but intrinsically of so much greater value that if any incompatibility could be demonstrated, it was the items on the list labeled "foreign policy" which should be sacrificed.

The preoccupation of the average citizen with so-called "domestic" matters was not affected by the development undergone by nineteenth-century American political institutions. Only two national political parties emerged, both composed of such amalgamations of sectional groupings that it was frequently difficult to distinguish their orientation toward domestic issues, let alone toward foreign policy. The separation of executive from legislative functions which had been imposed by the Founding Fathers made party responsibility impossible to enforce. Even should the average citizen desire to record through his vote strong sentiments regarding his nation's foreign relations, he had no means of doing so.

BRITISH CONTRIBUTIONS TO AMERICAN SECURITY UNRECOGNIZED

Because of its strategic geographic position, the United States was able to take advantage of European turmoil, and the real implications of the strategic distance between North America and Europe were not recognized. Just as Great Britain at times sought to continue to play a lone hand after the basis for such a policy had vanished, so did American statecraft seem to regard the remote and secure position of the United States in the world as immutable. Only after the situation had changed did Americans recognize that the luxury of noninvolvement was dependent on British command of the seas, which hemmed in the European state system and rendered it incapable of expressing itself with full force beyond the European shore of the

Atlantic Ocean. By the end of the nineteenth century, however, the British foundations of American security had vanished. New powers had arisen in Europe and Asia which could not be controlled by Great Britain. In physical extent the Atlantic and Pacific were as wide as ever; in strategic geographic terms they had rapidly narrowed. American foreign policy was then developing interests and consequent commitments on the other side of the Pacific at the very time that British determination to protect its own security—and hence, incidentally American security—through maintenance of the balance of state power was no longer matched by its ability to do so.

AMERICAN COLONIZATION

The experiences derived from this continental expansion led Americans to equate imperialism with colonialism but not with other forms of territorial aggrandizement. Because colonialism in turn was identified with the behavior of European states, similar behavior on the part of this country was difficult to recognize. As a result of the war with Spain the United States became an empire in fact. Policies adopted toward the small states of Central America and the Caribbean exhibited many of the aspects of imperialism. In its heart and in the pronouncements that issued from its government, however, the United States was never an empire and consequently saw nothing incongruous in continuing to point an accusing finger at the mote (or beam) in the eyes of other countries.

HIGH IDEOLOGICAL CONTENT OF AMERICAN FOREIGN POLICY

In general it may be said that in the nineteenth-century foreign-policy expressions of the United States the moral and ideological content was relatively high. Proclivity for preachment came easily to a nation which had been fortunate enough not to have to reconcile the dictates of conscience with the imperatives of "sacred egotism." That Great Britain should pursue democratic principles at home, yet clearly label them "not for export" to overseas possessions, frequently was condemned in the United States as sharp practice or worse. That France or Italy (as after World War I) should recognize no higher obligation than the advancement of its own interest seemed to Americans indicative of the base origin of the foreign policies and the statecraft of these countries.

There is nothing unusual in the pursuit of ideological objectives or the use of ideology as an instrument of statecraft. Quite the contrary, as the present state of relations between the United States and the Soviet Union demonstrates. Nineteenth-century America, however, viewed its ideological principles as undeviating absolutes, not as guideposts and mentors of finite state action. Moreover, these absolutes were thought to reflect some inherent virtue of the United States, and thus this country not only was absolved from further efforts at self-improvement but also was entitled to serve as judge of the performance of other states. To make the same point in other terms, the

United States reached the twentieth century prepared to insist verbally on its rights and privileges as a great power but unprepared to admit of any concomitant duties and responsibilities. (It should be recognized that such a national practice could and did gain friends among foreign peoples oppressed by the power of other states.) In the long run the imbalance between privileges and responsibilities would be corrected. Pending recognition of this uncomfortable fact, however, the United States was content in the nineteenth century to permit the initiation of international action to remain where it had been when the United States was small and weak—in London and in the capitals of continental Europe.

► THE DEVELOPMENT AND EXPLOITATION OF AMERICAN
   HEGEMONY IN THE CARIBBEAN AREA

THE ACQUISITION OF CUBA

By 1900 the United States had achieved a permanent settlement with Great Britain and had restricted the activities of other European powers to the point where for practical purposes an American hegemony prevailed in the Caribbean area. In previous decades the nation had been profoundly disturbed by the deteriorating relationship between Spain and its island possession of Cuba. Periodic uprisings, and the bungling ineptitude with which the mother country dealt with them, made it probable that within the foreseeable future Cuba would attain a measure of autonomy or complete independence. The United States preferred not to wait for this outcome, however. Aroused by the jingoist press,* the American people were prepared to follow their intransigently belligerent government into war. Important in the thinking of prominent Americans, however, were more rational elements leading to the same conclusion. Influenced by the writings of Captain A. T. Mahan, who had been stressing the need for American control over the sea approaches to the projected Isthmian canal, such eminent Republicans as Senator Henry Cabot Lodge and Assistant Secretary of the Navy Theodore Roosevelt wished to see Cuba wrested from Spain so that its strategic position might be utilized to protect American dominance within the Caribbean.

For such a policy, independence of Cuba from *any* foreign control was obviously not enough. United States control had to be substituted for Spanish ownership. To be sure, the joint resolution of Congress had declared via the Teller Amendment that the United States had no "disposition or intention to exercise sovereignty, jurisdiction, or control over said Island" and that when its "pacification" had been completed, this country would "leave the govern-

---

* To his photographer in Cuba who had reported, "Everything is quiet. There is no trouble here. There will be no war. I wish to return," Hearst had replied, "You furnish the pictures and I'll furnish the war." Quoted in Samuel Flagg Bemis, *A Diplomatic History of the United States* (New York, Henry Holt and Company, 1950), p. 442.

ment and control of the Island to its people." At the conclusion of the war with Spain, however, the United States acquired extraterritorial base rights to Guantánamo and excluded from Cuban jurisdiction the Isle of Pines. In addition, the Congress appended to the 1901 Army Appropriations Bill the famous Platt Amendment, which severely limited Cuban sovereignty. Article III stated that "the Government of Cuba consents that the United States may exercise the right to intervene for the preservation of Cuban independence, the maintenance of a government adequate for the protection of life, property, and individual liberty, and for discharging the obligations with respect to Cuba imposed by the Treaty of Paris on the United States, now to be assumed and undertaken by the government of Cuba." Since the United States was obviously to be the judge of the efficacy of Cuban governments in maintaining their "independence," that island became in fact an American protectorate under which the United States felt free to utilize periodically the interventionary power conferred upon it by the Platt Amendment. Not until 1934 was the amendment officially abrogated as part of the comprehensive alteration in the relationship of the United States with Latin America.

AMERICAN STRENGTH MEETS BRITISH WEAKNESS IN VENEZUELA

Whereas Spain was driven from the Caribbean, British power was induced to withdraw from the area through a combination of intimidation and diplomatic negotiation. From the British point of view, recognition of American paramountcy had become a necessity because of the increasing difficulty in fulfilling imperial commitments elsewhere. A unified Germany rapidly increased its national power in the last decades of the nineteenth century and, together with France and other nations, entered the colonial scramble in competition with England to establish title to choice portions of non-European real estate all over the globe. As a result of this challenge to its position, Great Britain narrowly avoided war with France over the division of Africa and watched with anxious eyes the intrusion of Russia, Germany, and Japan into China. Of immediate moment was the eruption of war in South Africa in 1898, into which the German Kaiser seemed determined to project his government. His telegram to President Kruger, referring to British forces as "armed bands" and congratulating the Boer leader on his success "in maintaining the independence of your country against foreign aggression," forced British statecraft to recognize the serious unbalance between its commitments and its capabilities.

To meet the German threat three things had to be done. British armed might, particularly naval strength, had to be increased, even though England could no longer hope to maintain its old standard of superiority over the next two national navies. Britain had to abandon its position as manipulator of the balance of European power and instead to join that side of the balance arrayed against Germany. Even this policy would be dangerous unless more allies could be brought into the anti-German camp. Finally Great Britain had to cut down its commitments where it could and attempt to transfer them to friendly hands. In retrospect it can be seen that the position of Britain in 1898 was a portent of the even more serious situation which that nation confronted in 1946.

It was the last policy which dictated British attitudes toward American power in the Caribbean and also its attempts, to be examined below, to induce the United States to play a larger role in the Far East. British willingness to withdraw from the Caribbean therefore coincided with American determination to bring about such a withdrawal. The conclusion of controversy between the two countries over the Venezuelan boundary indicated the changing relationship, and the Hay-Pauncefote Treaty formally ratified it. In dealing with Venezuela over the disputed Guiana border region, England had been acting in the characteristic manner of strong states embroiled with weaker ones. It refused to submit the question to arbitration unless Venezuela would previously concede Britain's claim to part of the territory, and Venezuela had broken off diplomatic relations by the time the Cleveland Administration decided to interpose American power between the two contestants. The manner adopted lacked the tact customary in official diplomatic correspondence. In direct contrast to earlier American practice, Secretary of State Richard Olney specifically mentioned the Monroe Doctrine. His forceful restatement of that principle in fact opened the door for its future enlargement, which was to prove highly distasteful to the Latin-American republics. "The rule in question," Secretary Olney declared, "has but a single purpose and object. It is that no European power or combination of powers shall forcibly deprive an American state of the right and power of self-government and of shaping for itself its own political fortunes and destinies."

SECRETARY OLNEY'S DEFINITION OF THE MONROE DOCTRINE

On what foundation, then, did the Monroe Doctrine rest? Olney's answer was a remarkable combination of ideological principle with practical power politics. The former represented a continuity of thought with President Monroe and Secretary of State Daniel Webster, whereas the latter was the self-confident effusion of a young and newly strong empire. "The people of the United States," Great Britain was reminded, "have a vital interest in the cause of popular self-government. They have secured the right for themselves and their posterity at the cost of infinite blood and treasure. They have realized and exemplified its beneficent operation by a career unexampled in point of national greatness or individual felicity. They believe it to be for the healing of all nations, and that civilization must either advance or retrograde accordingly as its supremacy is extended or curtailed." The same applied as well to Latin America. "The states of America, South as well as North, by geographical proximity, by natural sympathy, by similarity of governmental constitutions, are friends and allies, commercially and politically, of the United States."

Even were Latin-American countries not disposed to accept this interpretation of their common interests with those of the United States, the words "geographic proximity" delicately suggested the power which the North American state could employ to induce other American republics to accept a status of "friends and allies." In case British statesmen missed the allusion to the advantage of geography, Secretary Olney spelled it out for them. While the Monroe Doctrine "does not establish any general protectorate by the United States over other American states," on the other hand, "today the United States is practically sovereign on this continent, and its fiat is law upon the subjects to which it confines its interposition . . . . because, in addition to all other grounds, its infinite resources combined with its isolated position render it master of the situation and practically invulnerable against any or all other powers."

If American fiat was law within the hemisphere and if it desired to keep European nations aloof, then it was just a short step to the Theodore Roosevelt thesis of American hegemonical responsibility. In 1895 Olney was denying that the Monroe Doctrine could be construed so as to "prevent any European power directly interested from enforcing such obligations [as fixed by international law] or from inflicting merited punishment for the breach of them." A scant nine years later President Roosevelt was telling Congress that "chronic wrongdoing or an impotence which results in a general loosening of the ties of civilized society, may in America, as elsewhere, ultimately require intervention by some civilized nation, and in the Western Hemisphere the adherence of the United States to the Monroe Doctrine may force the United States, however reluctantly, in flagrant cases of such wrongdoing or impotence, to the exercise of an international police power."* It was clear that foreign countries were to look for relief from Latin-American practices not to their own legally justifiable measures of self-help, but to the power of the United States.

To return to the Venezuela dispute—President Cleveland supported his secretary of state with a statement to Congress that should an investigatory committee, for which he was requesting authorization, find that some of the disputed territory belonged to Venezuela, the United States had the "duty" "to resist by every means in its power" any subsequent move by Great Britain to take the territory. For reasons mentioned earlier, however, Britain exhibited a mature recognition of its own interests in ignoring the gage of battle. In their responses, furthermore, British statesmen cleverly sought to identify American interests with their own. Lord Salisbury, the prime minister, compared the position of the United States in the Caribbean to that of Britain with respect to Holland and Belgium. The Conservative leader, Joseph Chamberlain, told a Birmingham audience that "the two nations are allied

* Annual Message to Congress, December 6, 1904, quoted in Ruhl J. Bartlett, ed., *The Record of American Diplomacy* (New York, Alfred A. Knopf, Inc., 1947), p. 539.

and more closely allied in sentiment and in interest than any other nations on the face of the earth . . . . I should look forward with pleasure to the possibility of the Stars and Stripes and the Union Jack floating together in defense of a common cause sanctioned by humanity and justice." The young man beating on the door, shouting disparaging comments, and threatening to tear down the house was ushered into the parlor, invited to look around and join a very respectable club of only one other member. The invitation was declined until 1917 and its acceptance repudiated after 1920, but the opening of the door had catapulted the young man inside, willy-nilly.

THE ACQUISITION OF PANAMA AND EXCLUSIVE RIGHTS TO AN ISTHMIAN CANAL

The manner in which the United States acquired title to the Panama Canal is indicative of its determination to expand its interests with newly won power. As in the Venezuelan question, the United States was here dealing with a retreating Britain and a weak Latin-American country. After the Spanish-American War, American interest called for early construction of an Isthmian canal and for its control when built. This involved revision of the Clayton-Bulwer Treaty, signed a half century previously with Great Britain, which had provided for joint ownership and the absence of fortification. By 1902 this treaty had been replaced by the Hay-Pauncefote Treaty, which gave exclusive authority to the United States and removed by silence the prohibitions against fortification. The constitutional requirement of a two-thirds Senate vote for treaty ratification, which has frequently been deplored by historians and political scientists, fortunately in this instance had forced revision of an earlier draft that would have continued the barrier to fortification and left the Panama Canal open at all times to all vessels of all nations, as was the Suez Canal.

The two great powers by negotiation had thus succeeded in defining their relationships to projected developments in territory which belonged to neither of them. The site of the canal by this time was narrowed to a choice between Nicaragua and Colombia, with the former favored by most investigators. Agreements had been negotiated with both countries which ensured their sovereignty over any canal built on their property. The American Congress authorized negotiations first with Colombia and with Nicaragua only if the Colombian negotiations should fail. They did fail because of the unwillingness of the Colombian Senate to sell complete control over a six-mile strip for an annuity of a quarter million dollars and a lump sum of ten million. But the decision as to whether to transfer attention to the proposed Nicaraguan route was opportunely taken out of the hands of American policy makers by the officials of the French-controlled and bankrupt New Panama Canal Company, who were reluctant to see their chances of collecting a once-proffered forty million dollars for their rights go a-glimmering. In a politically unstable land, in an area never under effective Colombian control, a revolution was organized.

International law is clear on the obligation of every state, large or small, strong or weak, to refrain from interference in the internal affairs of another. This obligation was incumbent upon the administration of President Theodore Roosevelt, whatever enlarged interpretation that devotee of the vigorous life might place on the Monroe Doctrine. Yet interfere in Panama Roosevelt did. It became known that insurrectionists would attempt to seize the Colombian government or detach part of its territory. Before the revolution ever began, American warships were sent to patrol both the Atlantic and Pacific sides of the Isthmus. Three days after the outbreak of the revolt, the United States recognized *de facto* the new Panamanian government, this precipitous action being itself an illegal intervention. Because of the absence of overland communications, Colombian attempts to reassert its sovereignty depended on ability to transport troops by sea. Knowing this fact and with its warships standing by, the United States now informed Colombia that it would not permit any Colombian troops to debark. "I took Panama," Theodore Roosevelt is supposed later to have boasted. The record shows the alleged statement to have been an exaggeration, but a small one. The carefully protected revolution was a success. Two weeks later a canal treaty was signed with the Panamanian envoy, who, significantly enough, was construction engineer for the now-defunct New Panama Canal Company. Under terms of the treaty the United States, for the same amount it had previously offered Colombia, acquired rights indistinguishable from sovereignty to a ten-mile strip. Indication of the relationship between the new republic and its foster parent was the inclusion in the treaty of the right of the United States to intervene if necessary to protect the canal, which ran through the middle of Panamanian territory. In both Cuba and Panama the United States now had the right to intervene to protect its own interests, however it might define them.

BASES OF AMERICAN POLICY IN THE CARIBBEAN: PRESTIGE

Difficulties naturally arise from geographic propinquity of a large state and several weaker ones. For the former, three courses of action might in theory be pursued. The large state might seek to disclaim any interest in the weaker states, consciously adopting policies to keep its interest at a minimum. Such a course, however, would create a power vacuum which would be dangerous to the stability of the world community since it would constitute an invitation to other great states to meddle in the area. Second, the great state can positively assert its power in the unilateral protection of its interests. Such a course would produce unfortunate resentment and hostility on the part of the small countries which are unwilling subjects of neighborly solicitude. Finally, multilateral arrangements for joint responsibility might be worked out as a formal and legalistic cover to protect the rights and sensibilities of both parties as far as possible where great disparity in power exists. Policies of this nature demand a high degree of political maturity in all parties, the large state and the smaller neighbors.

The third course now characterizes inter-American relations, but the second was its predecessor during the first three decades of the twentieth century. It could be plausibly argued that the second course was the only one open at the time, given existing circumstances in the United States, in the nations of Central America and the Caribbean, in the European state system including Great Britain, and in the international community. Self-abnegation is not one of the normal characteristics of a great power, particularly of a newly great power which has achieved with unparalleled rapidity a vast territorial expansion. It was to be expected that the expansive forces which had been at work in the nineteenth century would eventually push American power outward from the continental limits, and this is precisely what happened in the Pacific as well as in the Caribbean. Denying vociferously the traditional motivations of other large nations, the United States nonetheless exhibited many of their characteristics in its behavior.

The record indicates that, as with other newly arrived great powers, the United States was determined to force recognition of its recently acquired status upon the other important members of the international community. Since self-esteem, moreover, is an important ingredient of national as well as individual behavior, the exhibition of American power would also serve the purpose of showing to both Americans and outsiders that such power existed.

If the behavior of the United States in the Caribbean seems unduly crass to mid-century Americans, it should be recalled that the diplomacy of *arriviste* states is not likely to have the finesse, smoothness, and polish of longer established, more experienced nations. Carefully cultivated aloofness from Europe, the vaunted uniqueness of American development, the absence of any need for artistry in diplomatic maneuver and expression combined to give the muscular behavior of the United States in expansionist policies beyond the confines of North America a crudeness and tactlessness which wounded the delicate sensibilities of small nations unfortunate enough to lie in its path.

When all due weight has been given to irrational and crude elements in American Caribbean policy, however, it is important to bear in mind that this policy did not produce as disruptive and explosive results as did similar actions of other newly powerful states. Germany during this same period and Japan three decades later carried self-importance, pressure on other nations large and small, and violations of diplomatic usage down the long dark path to war. Only strength and skill in the West can prevent the present policies of the Soviet Union from producing the same disastrous result.

BASES OF AMERICAN POLICY: SECURITY

The proliferation of interventions in the internal affairs of Central American and Caribbean republics was in addition motivated by more rational concerns than the pressure of expansionist forces. After the war with Spain the strategic position of the United States in both the Pacific and the Caribbean was greatly altered. The Monroe Doctrine had recognized three quarters of a century earlier that activities of European powers in the American neighborhood were a potential threat to the security of the United States. Now the United States was taking steps to limit and remove that threat. Although the Monroe Doctrine banned further colonization and expansion of existing dependencies, the intrusion of European states could still be justified by political and economic chaos in independent American countries. Moreover, such direct action was sanctioned by international law and precedent.

In 1902, when Germany took steps to force the Venezuelan dictator Castro to honor his debts, it was joined in the blockade of Venezuelan ports by Great Britain and Italy. It was Germany that the United States most feared by reason of its provocative international behavior. Secretary of State John Hay admitted the right of European governments to chastise the recalcitrant republic but not, under the Monroe Doctrine, to the extent of occupation of territory. The United States moved further to persuade the blockading powers to accept arbitration, after Castro himself had suggested this procedure. Such a disquieting settlement was made by the Hague Court of Arbitration, however, that further significant changes seemed necessary in American policies designed to protect its strategic position.

The Hague Permanent Court of Arbitration decided that the allocation of Venezuelan debt payments should give priority to Germany, Great Britain, and Italy, the blockading powers. This amounted to an invitation to European states to intrude themselves forcefully into the financial affairs of other American republics in the Caribbean area, none of which were noted for the stability of their political or economic institutions. To be sure, the Hague Convention later adopted the so-called Drago Doctrine, which forbade recourse to force for the collection of debts *unless* the debtor refused to follow arbitral procedure to the end and was unwilling to accept the final award. The exception was important, since the recalcitrance of Dictator Castro might be duplicated elsewhere. Furthermore the United States was not disposed to await or rely on the processes of international law. The result was a series of American interventions—in Santo Domingo (the Dominican Republic), Haiti, and Nicaragua, justified by the Roosevelt "corollary" to the Monroe Doctrine, referred to earlier. The policies of the United States thus had the effect of forestalling opportunities for establishment of European power in an area of great sensitivity, a sensitivity heightened by the beginning of work on the Panama Canal.

BASES OF AMERICAN POLICY: ECONOMIC INVESTMENT

So far interventionist policies have been discussed in connection with two objectives: the development of a new American strategic position in the Caribbean (Cuba and Panama) and the prevention of economic conditions which could provide pretexts for the reintrusion of European powers (Santo

Domingo, Haiti, and Nicaragua). Two other motivations, intimately connected with those just mentioned, also lay behind American actions in this area. As the United States approached economic maturity, Americans began to invest money abroad, in Latin America as well as in Europe and Canada. Political unrest and economic irresponsibility in Latin America brought American creditors to the doors of the State Department seeking protection. Some of the interventions referred to were motivated, then, by the American as well as by the European stake in the Caribbean area. The opprobrious term "dollar diplomacy" came to be applied to customs receiverships, and "economic imperialism" to the direct action of North American businesses throwing their weight about in small, unstable Latin-American republics.

BASES OF AMERICAN POLICY: PROMOTION OF DEMOCRACY

Finally at this point should be included the Wilsonian or moralistic justification for American intervention, which follows logically from the rationale previously developed. The Wilsonian credo may be stated as follows: Political instability in weak countries creates situations dangerous to American security. Such instability is caused by the immaturity of governmental institutions. Progress toward maturity can be measured by the degree of popular sovereignty attained by various countries. The United States leads all others in this respect and, as pronouncements mentioned earlier indicate, has always served as a shining example for others to follow. Now, by virtue of its position in the Western Hemisphere, the United States should assume a more active responsibility for the welfare of Latin-American peoples. Strategic and ideological interests thus coincide; in fact the latter is a steppingstone on the way to the protection of the former.

One method of promoting political stability entailed revision of the customary American practice with regard to the recognition of new governments. The classical policy had been enunciated by Thomas Jefferson and followed naturally from the revolutionary and "illegitimate" origins of the United States itself. Periodically during the nineteenth century, American statemen had reiterated this idea. President Pierce in 1856 made one of the clearest statements: "It is the established policy of the United States to recognize all governments without question of their source or their organization, or of the means by which the governing persons attain their power, provided there be a government *de facto* accepted by the people of the country." As in the case of neutral rights, the United States as a great power of the twentieth century proceeded to alter the principles endorsed by the United States as a small state of the nineteenth century. *Declaration* of intent to fulfill international commitments was supplanted by the necessarily subjective judgment as to the new government's *ability* to carry out its promises, with especial emphasis laid on those obligations which involved financial contracts, public and private.

Examples of United States pressure to obtain compliance with this new standard for recognition include the Dominican Republic and Haiti prior to World War I and the Obregón regime in Mexico immediately after. The Wilsonian doctrine set up a test of "constitutionality," likewise unilaterally determined by the United States, as a standard to measure the international responsibility of the new government. Recognition on this basis was used as a diplomatic weapon to guide Latin-American regimes on the road to democracy in the case of the Huerta regime in Mexico and those appearing in the Dominican Republic and Costa Rica. Two standards of applicability apparently existed, however, depending on the relative proximity of the government in question to the United States. During this same period the Wilson Administration did not withhold diplomatic recognition from two Peruvian governments of revolutionary origin, a fact which would tend to support the thesis that the attainment by Latin America of democratic institutions was an objective of American policy closely related to its economic and security interests in the Caribbean area.

After World War I the United States announced adherence to the so-called Tobar Doctrine, originally put forward by the Ecuadoran foreign minister in 1907. The Central American governments embodied this doctrine in a treaty binding them not to recognize "any other government which may come into power in any of the five republics as a consequence of a *coup d'état*, or of a revolution against the recognized government." This test of constitutionality was applied during the twenties to Honduran and Nicaraguan regimes and broke against the ability of Martínez to maintain himself in power in El Salvador despite collective nonrecognition. In actual fact, of course, there could be no guarantee that the orderly succession of governments in Latin-American countries would increase the democratic nature of such governments. Under modern conditions, which have increased tremendously the weapons of popular coercion in the hands of any government, the willingness of dictatorial regimes to use their guns and armies against the people may make revolution the only, though a dangerous, avenue by which popular responsibility can be enforced.

► THE FAR EASTERN POLICY OF THE OPEN DOOR

During the years after 1898 the foreign policy of the United States in the Caribbean clearly reflected the expanded commitments commensurate with its big-power status. In this arena was achieved a balance between power and commitments capable of protecting the declared interests of the country. No such pattern can be discerned in the pre–World War I foreign policy of the United States in the Pacific and in the Far East.

THE UNITED STATES BECOMES A FAR EASTERN POWER

In 1898, many years after American power had first made itself felt in the area, the Spanish-American War transformed the United States into an imperial power in the Pacific. American statecraft had taken a leading part in opening Japan to Western influence and was manifesting an increasing economic interest in China, founded on hopes for large-scale trade which were to prove illusory. Tripartite arrangements were made with Germany and Great Britain for the government of Samoa, and support was growing for the annexation of the Hawaiian Islands to the United States.

The foundation had thus been laid for the expanded commitments which the United States assumed upon the defeat of Spain. United States naval forces occupied both Wake and Guam as part of their operations against the Spanish in the Philippines, but the essential question was the disposition of the Philippines. A combination of economic interest and expansionist ideology provided the answer. The former caused Americans to look with distrust on the rapid encroachments which Japan, Russia, Germany, and Great Britain were making on China. Naval stations, leaseholds, and spheres of influence seemed to forecast a situation in which the United States would be effectively excluded from commercial privileges on the Asiatic mainland. Furthermore, "manifest destiny," as interpreted by the same figures leading the United States toward a protectorate over Cuba, seemed to argue that the United States could not shirk its responsibility for the welfare of the Filipinos, particularly since to cast them adrift would only waft them into the hands of another foreign power. The Philippines became American upon payment of twenty million dollars to Spain, a clear example of the American proclivity to penalize itself financially for having won a war. President McKinley proclaimed sovereignty over the islands, a precipitate action which the Senate ratified in the peace treaty by a margin of only two votes above the requisite two thirds. Sufficient Democratic votes to carry the measure were found at the urging of the head of the anti-imperialist party, William Jennings Bryan, who wished to subordinate the issue of imperialism to the domestic platform of free silver in the forthcoming presidential election.

THE ATTEMPT AT LEADERSHIP WITHOUT POWER: THE OPEN DOOR

Economic and political interest thus led the United States to adopt a foreign policy of sorts without the power to implement it. Even so the policy there achieved a fair measure of success despite the hesitancies and inconsistencies which appeared. Secretary of State John Hay's Open Door notes of September 6, 1899, constituted another attempt to gain objectives without the presence of power or even the inclination to develop it. As in the case of the Monroe Doctrine, American action coincided with British interest, though here again the United States deliberately chose to move independently. Throughout the previous half century Great Britain had taken the lead among European states in forcing Western commerce on the unwilling Chinese. The United States followed along behind with its "me-too" policy of equality of treatment. Whatever privileges other countries wrested from China, the United States insisted on obtaining also, in some instances with the support of the Chinese themselves, who hoped that one great power could be played off against another and that the United States, which had no territorial ambitions on the Asiatic mainland, would act as a barrier to the imperial appetites of the European intruders. Because Great Britain possessed world industrial leadership, trading advantages, and colonies in the area, it also was interested in seeing that China was not divided into closed political or economic spheres.

By the end of the nineteenth century, however, it was clear that British power alone could not for much longer prevent the dismemberment of China at the hands of Germany, Japan, and Russia. The first was acting with a belligerent aggressiveness characteristic of its world-wide search for colonies and a "place in the sun." The second engaged China in war and was only prevented by the European states from acquiring the Liaotung Peninsula. The last was pushing southward in an almost unconsciously inspired drive for warm-water ports and for economic advantages in Manchuria. British policy in China was to draw from the United States a commitment which would go far beyond its formerly passive attitude. John Hay responded by seeking declarations from "all the great powers" interested in China that the Chinese tariff, harbor dues, and railway charges within their vested areas would apply equally and without discrimination among themselves. This was the "Open Door" all right, but of a particular sort. It did not seek to preserve or increase Chinese sovereignty over territory under its theoretical control, nor did it preclude the possibility that Chinese independence itself might disappear. Even in this form, however, European response was mixed. Great Britain excluded Hongkong and Kowloon from application of Open Door principles, Russia evaded any commitment, and Germany accepted only on condition that all other powers did. France, Japan, and Italy, which were then largely on the outside looking in, responded in the same way as Germany.

How was the United States to keep open the door to China? Time had only just demonstrated that, despite Hay's pronouncement that his proposed principles were "final and definitive," the other powers were not prepared to do the job for the United States when this country enormously enlarged the size of the door it sought to keep open. During the joint intervention of the European states and Japan in the Boxer Rebellion against all foreigners, the secretary stated that "the policy of the Government of the United States is to seek a solution which may bring about permanent safety and peace to China, preserve Chinese territorial and administrative entity, protect all rights guaranteed to friendly powers by treaty and international law, and safeguard for the world the principle of equal and impartial trade with all parts of the Chinese empire." Later, during the Russo-Japanese War, Hay defined American policy as the maintenance of "the integrity of China and the 'Open Door' in the Orient."

Here was no self-implementing policy. On the contrary it recurrently presented the United States with the difficult choice of giving ground and compromising principle, or taking a stand which the ultimate arbiter of American military force could not sustain. This unpleasant alternative has repeatedly confronted American statecraft since 1900, and, as events since World War II indicate, the end is not yet in sight.

THE AMERICAN HAND IN THE RUSSO-JAPANESE SETTLEMENT

Although it was not clear at the time, the main challenge to Chinese integrity was to come from the newly great Asiatic power nearest the mainland. Germany came late into the field, and its lack of command of the seas made its control of territory in the Far East dependent on the maintenance of peace. Russian power moved glacierlike, slowly and inexorably from the north, to engulf China until the acquisition of warm-water ports, not international politics, should dictate a halt. To the surprise of many, however, small Japan was able to inflict on Russia a defeat whose reverberations were *and Asia* felt in Moscow and throughout Europe, and whose effects are with us today. Japan, however, was willing to support equality of opportunity for foreign exploitation in China only so long as it did not have the power to carve out exclusive spheres of influence on its own. As early as the 1870's Japan had undertaken to detach Korea from Chinese sovereignty and transfer it to Japanese protection. Its success was recognized by the American treaty of 1883, which did not refer to Korea's status as a Chinese dependency. Attempts by China to regain control resulted only in the further loss to Japan of Formosa, the Pescadores, and the Liaotung Peninsula, although the last-named was disgorged under European pressure. Once again the United States came to terms with reality, through the medium of the Taft-Katsura memorandum, signed during the Russo-Japanese War, under which Japan agreed to keep hands off the Philippines in return for American recognition of its free hand in Korea.

The Russo-Japanese War confronted the United States with a dilemma in the maintenance of its newly expounded principles. Should Russia win, much of Manchuria would vanish from even nominal Chinese jurisdiction, and augmented Russian power would be able to push on further south. Japan seemed to be fighting America's battle in preventing this development, and American public opinion gave its traditional applause to the small boy who knocks down the big bully (David and Goliath). But unfortunately for the United States, the successful David seemed prepared to adopt the giant's oppressive role. It could hardly suit American interests to see Japan substituted for Russia on the Asiatic mainland. In laying the groundwork for the Treaty of Portsmouth, Theodore Roosevelt was seeking to prevent either belligerent from attaining its maximum objectives. Although the conditions of peace temporarily preserved a precarious balance in Manchuria, most of the advantage went to Japan, despite widespread Japanese resentment at American interference. In addition to the southern half of Sakhalin Island, Japanese power encompassed "predominant political, military, and economic interests in Korea." Russian concessions in the Liaotung Peninsula, which had been returned from Japan to Russia in 1895, now, ten years later, were transferred once more to Japan.

AMERICAN POLICY TOWARD JAPAN'S ADVANCE IN ASIA

The war with Russia marked the achievement of great-power status by Japan in the same manner as the war with Spain had done for the United States only half a decade earlier. Just as the United States had immediately thereafter solidified its expansionist position in the area adjacent to it (the Caribbean), so did Japan seek to confirm its position in Manchuria. The United States had the advantage of previous pronouncement and practice (the Monroe Doctrine), which could be broadened into a moral sanction for hegemony. Japan, on the other hand, was still confronting European interests and American principle (the Open Door) and had to move more warily. In the circumstances its accomplishments were substantial and were at least partially recognized by other countries. For the United States the recognition of Japanese "rights" in Manchuria signified a tactical retreat from, or repudiation of, the stands taken in 1899 and 1900.

The same desire on the part of Great Britain to limit its commitments and make friends in the face of Germany's challenge that had caused Britain's withdrawal from the Caribbean also prompted Britain to come to terms with Japan in the Anglo-Japanese Alliance of 1902, revised in 1905, and renewed in 1911. Assurance of Japanese neutrality permitted Britain to concentrate its power in India and the Near and Middle East. After Britain's settlement with Russia in 1907 added Russia to the United States, France, and Japan on the roster of friends or allies, Great Britain was free to maximize its naval strength closer to home waters. On its side Japan gained the valuable assurance that Britain would not assist its enemy, Russia, or oppose its activities in Korea. The 1905 edition of the alliance listed among its objectives "the preservation of the common interests of all powers in China by insuring the independence and integrity of the Chinese Empire and the principle of equal opportunities for the commerce and industry of all nations in China." These high-sounding words were immediately followed, however, by "the maintenance of the territorial rights of the high contracting parties in the regions of eastern Asia and of India, and the defense of their special interests in the said regions." As interpreted by subsequent Japanese action, the alliance permitted Japanese economic penetration of Manchuria, an area in which British interests did not conflict.

With Russia defeated and Britain aloof, Japan began after 1905 to consolidate its successes and push even further its penetration of Manchuria. Recognition of its special rights was sought from and granted by France and Russia in treaties. For its part the United States signed the Root-Takahira Agreement of 1908, which supported in language similar to the Anglo-Japanese Alliance the "independence and integrity of China and the principle of equal opportunity for commerce and industry of all nations in that Empire." Two potentially contradictory principles were again linked, for the search for commerce might well lead to the violation of China's independence and integrity. Secretary of State Knox and President Taft next attempted to reverse the tide of Chinese disintegration by proposing a joint loan to China with which to buy up or build railways in its territory, including Manchuria. The net effect of the proposal was the formulation of agreements by French, German, British, and American banking houses, to which Japanese and Russian groups were admitted, for joint supervision of all loans to China. This was a further step toward economic exploitation without conflict among the exploiters. The agreement terminated with the withdrawal of the United States after the election of Woodrow Wilson and the advent of World War I. By 1914, however, Japan had reached an agreement with Russia, which marked out the Manchurian area for Japanese penetration.

AMERICAN ATTEMPTS TO LIMIT JAPANESE OPPORTUNITIES CREATED BY WORLD WAR I

On the heels of Japan's successes in Manchuria, the outbreak of World War I provided new dangers to Chinese integrity. The attempts by China to preserve its territorial integrity and political independence by playing off one intruder against another were fast foundering on the traditional ability of great powers to come to terms with one another at the expense of a defenseless state. Only a resurgence of national determination could save China. This had been the goal of the Boxer Rebellion in 1898. It was also the goal of Sun Yat-sen and his followers, who succeeded after some false starts in overthrowing the Manchus and establishing a republic in 1911. World War I, following so soon afterward, temporarily focused elsewhere the attention of most of the foreign powers intruding in China. Only Japan and the United States remained, and the United States as a neutral in the European War could be expected to lend China only diplomatic assistance in accordance with American precepts of the Open Door.

In removing Russia, Germany, France, and Great Britain from the scene, the war gave Japan an opportunity to establish an unchallengeable position in China. Although not bound by its alliance with Britain to do so, Japan joined the war on the side of the Allies. The Allies hoped for naval assistance in the Mediterranean; the Japanese hoped to acquire German holdings in China. This objective of Japan was speedily accomplished, along with occupation of German islands north of the equator. The basis for future Western difficulties with the Oriental ally was thus laid. Japan then turned its attention to the rest of China, which was technically independent. In a secret ultimatum it presented the Chinese government with the so-called Twenty-one Demands, which would have gone far toward establishing a Japanese protectorate. China was asked to acknowledge Japanese rights in Manchuria and to former German holdings. China was to agree to cede or lease none of its coast to any power other than Japan. But Japan wanted far more than this. It asked for joint control with China of the industrially important iron mines near Hankow and the appointment of Japanese "advisers" to the Chinese government.

China, being powerless by itself to resist the Twenty-one Demands, did what it could to mobilize outside support by making them public. The European Allies, deeply engaged with Germany, could not check their Eastern member. Only the United States was free to take steps in this direction if it were so inclined. The principle involved was obviously that of the Open Door, a principle on which the United States had been forced to compromise in the past. Lacking the capacity or the inclination to use force, the United States undertook once more to see what it could do by negotiation. Secretary of State Bryan told the Japanese that his government "could not regard with indifference the assumption of political, military, or economic domination over China by a foreign power," but, and a significant *but* it was, regarding Manchuria, "territorial contiguity creates special relations between Japan and these districts." This American interposition did secure the verbal toning down of the demands and the temporary abandonment of those in the fifth group calling for Japanese advisers to the Chinese government. The rest China was forced by another ultimatum to accept.

During the course of the war Japan succeeded in binding the Western Allies to support its postwar claims, but the entrance of the United States into the war was destined to bring to the peace conference an uncommitted, even hostile nation with augmented military power. After the Chinese capitulated to the second Japanese ultimatum, Secretary Bryan in a note to Japan expressly reserved American rights. He stated his government's refusal to agree to any arrangement that would lead to "impairing . . . the political or territorial integrity of the Republic of China, or the international policy relative to China commonly known as the open door policy." This pronouncement put Japan on notice that some arrangement must be made with the United States. The Japanese therefore attempted to secure American recognition of Japan's "paramount interests" or "special influence" in China. The best that could be done, however, was the Lansing-Ishii Agreement, signed on November 11, 1917, exactly one year before the end of the war.

The terms of this agreement reveal rather than conceal the basic opposition of American and Japanese interests in the Far East. Its effect was to record two opposing principles, and to leave the future balance of power in the area to determine which would emerge on top. The United States acknowledged that "territorial propinquity creates special relations between countries, and, consequently, . . . that Japan has special interests in China, particularly in that part to which her possessions are contiguous." The rest of the agreement was a denial of the implications inherent in this statement. "The territorial sovereignty of China nonetheless remains unimpaired. . . ." Both countries declared themselves opposed to the intrusion of third powers into China and for themselves denied "any purpose to infringe in any way the independence or territorial integrity of China." Furthermore, both governments reiterated their adherence "to the principle of the so-called 'open door' or equal opportunity for commerce and industry in China." By a protocol remaining secret at Japanese insistence, Japan further bound itself not to take advantage of the war to upset the principles to which it publicly subscribed.

The agreement gave each nation ample room to interpret the terms as it saw fit. For the United States it meant only that Japan was naturally acutely sensitive to Chinese developments by reason of its closeness to that area but would not seek to use its position to destroy the independence of China. For the Japanese the agreement meant that the United States recognized with regard to Japan and China roughly the same relationship as between itself and the Caribbean, and that Japan could now exploit China to the full, provided it stopped short of actual annexation. Japanese intrusion into Manchuria, and the purely nominal ties between this area and China, made Manchuria a test of the Japanese interpretation of the ability of China to resist and of the extent to which the United States was prepared to back by force its commitment to the Open Door and the territorial integrity of China.

► THE FAILURE OF THE AMERICAN POLICY OF NEUTRALITY DURING WORLD WAR I

TRADITIONAL ALOOFNESS FROM EUROPE

If the American position with respect to the Caribbean between 1898 and 1914 may be roughly characterized as that of expanding commitment and expanding power, and the position in the same period with respect to the Far East as that of expanding commitment without a commensurate expanse in power, American policy toward Europe before World War I was one of an absence of commitment and a positive denial of power. Loosely labeled by publicists as "isolation," the American relation to Europe in reality was deeply grounded in historical tradition and represented an interpretation of interest valid at the time. The European state system was far more fully developed than either the Latin American or the Asiatic and thus left little room for the intrusion of power from outside the Continent. The power of each of its leading components, Great Britain, France, Austria-Hungary, Russia, and Germany, during most of the nineteenth century exceeded that of the United States. But as long as the European states remained internally preoccupied, the disentanglement of the United States so successfully negotiated between 1789 and 1820 could be maintained. It was logical, moreover, that as the European countries moved into Africa and the Near East, the American policy of aloofness from Europe should be extended to those areas also. After President Theodore Roosevelt took a hand in the 1906 Algeciras Conference, the Senate added to its ratification of the act the clear statement that "the traditional American foreign policy . . . forbids participation by the United States in the settlement of political questions which are entirely European in their scope."

It is always easier to follow day-to-day precedent than to engage in the thorough analysis necessary to produce significant changes in policy. Particularly is this human tendency true where following previous practice involves a minimum of effort and when preceding policy has been very successful. American statecraft may therefore be forgiven its failure to discern after 1898 the growing cracks and fissures in the nineteenth-century European state system, especially the deteriorating relationship between Britain and Germany. Americans also remained blissfully unaware that an important consequence of the world-wide expansion of the European state system would be the transformation of any conflict among its members into a world conflict.

EUROPEAN RELATIONS AT THE OUTBREAK OF WAR

There had been many world wars before, notably the colonial struggles among Britain, France, Spain, and Portugal. Limited military technology, however, made these affairs tame in comparison with the war that broke out in July, 1914. European statesmen were very much like Americans in their underestimate of the nature of the war and of its duration. Austria-Hungary thought it saw a chance to strengthen the Dual Monarchy by turning back the Balkan, pan-Slavic ambitions of Russia at the minor cost of a quick punishment of Serbia. Germany thought it was assisting its ally Austria-Hungary in this endeavor, and that its support would force the other powers to remain aloof. Russia did not wish to see the eclipse of its Balkan interests which would follow Serbian defeat; and France was tied to Russia. Germany wanted to fight France first if it had to take on both powers at once. The extent of British commitments to France and Russia was obscure, even to the British, who had been hoping to reach some kind of settlement with Germany and in 1914 still believed the conflict could be isolated and settled quickly by the European system itself. Even when France and Russia became involved, no *casus belli* as yet existed for Britain, whose leaders had been moving slowly, hesitantly, and incompletely toward a division of military and naval responsibility with France. When Britain did enter the war, it did so to protect its traditional interest in the Dutch and Belgian coasts against a hostile power and to prevent the single-power hegemony over Europe which would result from further enlargement of the initial German successes against France.

THE AMERICAN RESPONSE TO EUROPEAN WAR: NEUTRALITY

The automatic reaction by the United States to a formerly valid concept of its own interests was embodied in President Wilson's declaration of neutrality. The United States did not realize that the concept and practice of neutrality had undergone changes as a result of alterations in the nation-state system, nor had examination of its own Civil War experience been intensive enough to suggest the difficulties of maintaining a policy of neutrality under twentieth-century conditions. For this country neutrality still meant a particular legal and economic relationship which could keep the country out of war and enable it to grow prosperous at the same time. Legally neutrality meant the right to trade with both belligerents in all materials except a restricted number directly related to the conduct of military warfare. President Wilson, however, was aware that a long conflict would imperil American neutrality. He used his position to urge at strategic intervals that the belligerents quit fighting on a "peace-without-victors" basis. To his interpositions both sets of combatants remained cool, Germany because it expected to win the war and impose a conqueror's peace, the Allies because a mere reversion to the *status quo ante* would leave them in constant danger of renewed German attack.

In destroying the economic rights of the neutral United States the belligerents finally made it impossible for this country to cling to the legal concept and still behave like a great power. Norway remained neutral during the war because it was willing to abandon all its rights as a neutral. The United States, by a revival of Jeffersonian policy, could have done likewise and might have chosen this course had it been, like Norway, a small power with few resources.*

BRITISH VIOLATIONS OF AMERICAN NEUTRALITY

Both Great Britain and Germany violated what the United States regarded as the basic principles of its neutrality. The former undertook a type of blockade which was of questionable legality under the rules adopted at Paris in 1856, and ultimately sought to establish its control of all commerce between the United States and neutral countries. As the struggle continued, Great Britain expanded the list of articles it deemed contraband to include almost every normal article of commerce. Its use of the black list against neutral firms suspected of trading with the enemy went far beyond an invasion of neutral rights. These and other practices, such as detaining vessels for long periods in England rather than stopping them on the seas for thorough search, and the censorship of American mails, were offensive to American commercial interests and caused official protest.

The protests by the United States came to be less and less seriously regarded by Great Britain for four reasons. First, the stagnation of the war into one of trench positions placed added emphasis on the indirect weapon of economic blockade through which the Allies thought they could drive

---

* It should be noted that Bryan's efforts as secretary of state were based on his belief that the United States, like Norway, should abandon legal rights to preserve its neutrality.

Germany to a defeat by attrition. In the second place, manipulation of the contraband list was so cleverly attuned to the growth of lucrative Anglo-American wartime trade that the right of the United States to trade with other neutrals and with the Central Powers became a principle for which it was hardly worth risking the burgeoning American prosperity. In the third place, Allied violations of American neutrality paled into insignificance in comparison with the use which Germany made of its submarine. Finally, American Ambassador Walter Hines Page, in presenting American notes, not infrequently exceeded his instructions in suggesting to the British ways in which they could be answered without costing Great Britain any substantial advantage while at the same time soothing American sensibilities.

MORE SERIOUS GERMAN VIOLATIONS OF AMERICAN NEUTRALITY: THE SUBMARINE

There were several things wrong with the submarine from the American point of view. It was German and successful at a time that most Americans were becoming more and more sympathetic with the Allied side. It was a radically new weapon of warfare and hence startling in its manifestations. Radical departures are always difficult to assimilate into the traditional framework of man's thinking, and this was especially true of the submarine. Not only was it new; it was by nature incapable of operating according to the principles of international law, i.e., like a surface vessel. It could not appear and stop merchant vessels without danger of being outgunned and rammed. It could not convoy seized vessels to shore. Finally, and most important, it could not see to the safety of passengers before sinking a vessel, whether belligerent or neutral. In the face of Allied and ultimately American insistence on arming merchant vessels the submarine could only lurk in the darkness of the ocean and torpedo indiscriminately such ships as it sighted.

The adoption by all belligerents in World War II of indiscriminate submarine warfare may perhaps render it difficult to appreciate the shock which this weapon produced on Americans, private citizens and governmental officials alike, during World War I. After the war was over, international lawyers engaged in the highly fruitless occupation of attempting to turn back the clock with respect to both the submarine and the airplane to a time when the depths of the sea and the heights of the air were not traversed by man bent on killing man.

If Germany had quickly won the war or quickly lost it, American efforts to force modifications in German submarine practices might have succeeded and thereby preserved American neutrality. Because German violations of principles of neutrality involved loss of American lives as well as property, the United States was disposed to take them more seriously than the violations of Great Britain, which affected American property alone. It would have taken a passionate addiction to impartiality between the belligerents to have remained neutral in thought and deed in the face of the loss of American life through German torpedoing of American, other neutral, or belligerent vessels, particularly when the ominous words "without advance warning" were included in reports of the attacks. By insisting on the right of Americans to travel with impunity on belligerent and other neutral vessels as well as on its own, the United States government lost 223 of its citizens, all but 28 on non-American vessels. For all these deaths the United States maintained that Germany was solely responsible.

TEMPORARILY SUCCESSFUL AMERICAN EFFORTS TO MODIFY GERMAN SUBMARINE PRACTICE

More than half the Americans lost went down on the *Lusitania,* the disaster which initiated American diplomatic attempts to alter German sub-marine practices. For almost a year Germany responded with denials, eva-sions, and justifications. The patience of the United States ended with the sinking of the French-owned *Sussex;* a virtual ultimatum was delivered to Germany that "unless the Imperial Government shall now immediately declare and effect an abandonment of its present methods of submarine war-fare against passenger and freight carrying vessels, the Government of the United States can have no choice but to sever diplomatic relations with the German Empire altogether."

It should be noted that, in accordance with the existing concepts of international law, the United States was seeking to throw a diplomatic blanket of immunity not only over its own ships but over all merchant vessels, whether neutral or belligerent, on which Americans happened to be traveling. It was this policy which had caused the resignation of Secretary of State Bryan after the sinking of the *Lusitania.* Postwar study indicated that the insistence on this point was a crucial factor leading to the involvement of the United States in the conflict. Upon the outbreak of World War II, therefore, President Roosevelt proclaimed certain "war zones" where Americans as well as American ships traveled at their own risk and without the support of their government.

In actuality, however, German submarine activity was only symptomatic of the changed nature of warfare, which compelled both sets of contestants to resort to any practice, without regard for its legality, which might attain victory or at least save them from defeat. Upon receipt of the *Sussex* note, Germany had to balance the advantages of submarine warfare against the disadvantages of potential American participation on the side of the Allies. For the time being the German government decided to placate the United States, and a breathing spell ensued, lasting from May, 1916, to January, 1917. It was marked by the efforts of President Wilson to negotiate a com-promise peace. These efforts failed, as they were bound to, given the situa-tion existing at the time. Germany still held a decided territorial advantage and had expanded its original war aims to include domination over most of the area, including Belgium, which it had conquered. To this the Allies could not agree unless they were prepared to accept a partial defeat. On the contrary it appeared to them reasonable to believe that Germany, having failed to win a quick victory, could not win at all.

FINAL ACTS LEADING TO AMERICAN INVOLVEMENT: RESUMPTION OF SUBMARINE WARFARE, THE ZIMMERMANN NOTE, THE RUSSIAN REVOLUTION

The Allied analysis of the military situation faced by Germany was correct. The German government itself came to fear that, unless a convulsive effort were made, a prolonged war of attrition might bring defeat. An integral part of this decisive effort naturally would be use of the submarine, and Germany accordingly announced at the end of January, 1917, that unrestricted warfare with this weapon would be resumed. The United States, as it had threatened eight months earlier, broke off diplomatic relations.

President Wilson still did not believe that this action was the inevitable prelude to American entrance into the war. Two events which intervened between the rupture of relations and the declaration of war in April led the United States to take the last, short step. The first was the infamous Zimmermann note, politely turned over to the American government by the British, who had intercepted and deciphered it. The note aroused both American officials and the American public on two counts: the message had been sent by Berlin through the diplomatic facilities of the United States itself, and the note instructed the German ambassador in Mexico to propose to that government that, should the United States not remain neutral, an alliance be made with Germany by which Mexico could recover its "lost territory" north of the Rio Grande. Germany clearly was using the official communication machinery of the United States in an attempt to force upon it a two-front war. The second event, in long-range retrospect far more significant, was the deposition of the Russian czar by the revolution of March, 1917. The successor regime was recognized only eight days later, because it seemed to the United States to be (1) more stable than its predecessor, (2) more democratic, and (3) more able to continue the war on the Central Powers than the corrupt, inefficient, bankrupt Czarist regime. If the United States should now enter, it would be fighting a war for democracy against tyranny; the specter of the Czar of all the Russias in the Allied camp had conveniently been removed. On April 6, 1917, the House and Senate overwhelmingly recorded that a state of war existed with the Imperial German Government.

The irony

But what if the sequence of events had been different? Winston Churchill in *The World Crisis* indulges in this speculation: "If the Russian Revolution had occurred in January instead of March, or if, alternatively, the Germans had waited to declare unlimited U-boat war until the summer, there would have been no unlimited U-boat war and consequently no intervention of the United States. If the Allies had been left to face the collapse of Russia without being sustained by the intervention of the United States, it seems certain that France could not have survived the year, and the war would have ended in a peace by negotiation or, in other words, a German victory."* The quoted remarks do not seem at all farfetched when one remembers the narrow margin of Allied strength in the face of the German summer offensive of 1918.

THE ABSENCE OF STRATEGIC INTEREST IN AMERICAN ENTRANCE INTO WORLD WAR I

The United States did not enter the war to save the Allies, however, nor did it do so in the belief that by saving the Allies it would be saving itself. To be sure, Colonel House has quoted President Wilson as far back as 1915: "He said he had never been sure that we ought not to take part in the conflict and, if it seemed evident that Germany and her militaristic ideas were to win, the obligation upon us was greater than ever."† American essayists, notably Walter Lippmann and the other editors of the *New Republic,* were pointing out in rather precise terms what it would mean to the United States if a benevolent British power standing between Europe and the United States should be replaced by an imperialistic German hegemony over the Continent, including France, Belgium, and Holland. There is no evidence, however, that such thoughts actually motivated American official policy.

The American public was initially disposed to favor the Allies. This feeling naturally increased after the invasion of Belgium, with the exaggerated, not to say untrue, reports of what happened in the conquered part of that small country, and with each German violation of American neutral rights. These attitudes undoubtedly led the United States to take a harsher stand toward Germany than toward Great Britain, but they certainly did not lead and in all probability could not have led the United States to declare war. It has previously been pointed out that the extent of American dependence for its own greatness and prosperity on the greatness and prosperity of Great Britain (a thesis espoused by Walter Lippmann and recurrently popular in World War II exegesis) was not generally recognized. Nor can it be conclusively demonstrated that the reverse was true—that the security of the United States would have been severely endangered by a limited German victory. There is no valid historical analogy between the European state system of 1917 and German objectives therein, and the European state system of 1939 and Hitler's egomaniacal ambitions. Even with the tremendous advantages of hindsight it would be difficult to make a convincing case for the argument that the United States could have moved to war in a manner other than that which it actually followed—unwilling, hesitant, piecemeal, erratic, above all unplanned.

* Winston Churchill, *The World Crisis* (New York, Charles Scribner's Sons), III, p. 215.
† Charles Seymour, *Intimate Papers of Colonel House* (Boston, Houghton Mifflin Company, 1926), II, p. 84.

WHAT THE UNITED STATES DID NOT FIGHT FOR

Although the United States had previously engaged in war, it did not believe in war or the goals which war could attain. In typically American fashion the United States simply became entangled in the conflict. Once committed, it did what it could to ensure victory for its side in the quickest possible time, but its definition of victory was never that of the Allies. The United States in fact never assumed the status of Ally at all, but insisted on being regarded as an "Associated Power." Translated into more precise political terms, this meant that the United States was not bound to win the same kind of peace as that desired by Britain and France. There can be no doubt that President Wilson knew of the existence and terms of the network of secret treaties which committed the other major nations fighting Germany to certain settlements in Europe, but his refusal to recognize them officially or to commit the United States to their contents enabled the leader of the United States to proclaim far different objectives.

The United States did not fight to restore the *status quo,* for that was impossible. What was the 1914 *status quo* after all but an attractive jumping-off-point for German power? Nor could all the American and Allied horses and men, even had they so desired, put the Austro-Hungarian and Russian Humpty Dumpties back on their walls. Events born of war had moved onward the clock of Europe, and it could not be set back.

Nor did the United States fight for a new balance of power in Europe. In the second decade of the twentieth century the United States did not believe in the balance of power system any more than it did in the fifth. This "system" was not a real system at all; it could not maintain peace, it could only start wars; it could not sustain the weak and defenseless, it could only hand them over to the greedy and strong; it could not promote the happiness and evolution of man, it could only hold him back and dehumanize him.

Finally, the United States was not fighting for a victor's peace, for the destruction of Germany, and for its "unconditional surrender." When General Pershing opposed an armistice and wanted to continue the march on to Berlin, it was only because he believed that the Allies and the United States would thereby be less handicapped in the reconstruction of an enduringly stable Europe.

AMERICAN WAR AIMS AS DEFINED BY WILSON

The war aims of the United States, as President Wilson defined them, embodied the politico-ideological principles for the attainment of a new and a better world which American thought had traditionally espoused. If they sounded on many occasions like unrealistic, idealistic balderdash to European statesmen, so much the worse for them. The foreign policy of the United States had, because of the experiences of the previous century, reflected idealistic and not infrequently unrealistic views of international relations. Now this country was to bring its idealism backed by its power to Europe in order to achieve a peace of principle, the only type of peace that could last, so Americans believed. As developed by President Wilson, the bases of peace—and the objectives of the war—were fourfold and interrelated: the right of national self-determination of peoples, the enlargement of the field of popular sovereignty, the rights of states large and small to increase through unhampered trade their own prosperity, and a concert of nations to maintain the peace. If any of the principles were unrealized, all were endangered.

On the right of self-determination, Wilson declared: ". . . . no right anywhere exists to hand peoples about from sovereignty to sovereignty as if they were property. What we demand in this war, therefore, is nothing peculiar to ourselves. It is that the world be made fit and safe to live in; and particularly that it be made safe for every peace-loving nation which, like our own, wishes to live its own life, determine its own institutions, be assured of justice and fair dealing by the other peoples of the world as against force and selfish aggression." ". . . . the nations should with one accord adopt the doctrine of President Monroe as the doctrine of the world: that no nation should seek to extend its polity over any other nation or people, but that every people should be left free to determine its own policy, its own way of development, unhindered, unthreatened, unafraid, the little along with the great and powerful."

On the enlargement of the scope of popular sovereignty: "No peace can last or ought to last, which does not recognize and accept the principle that governments derive all their just powers from the consent of the governed . . . ." "Our object . . . . is to vindicate the principles of peace and justice in the life of the world as against selfish and autocratic power and to set up amongst the really free and self-governing peoples of the world such a concert of purpose and of action as will henceforth insure the observance of these principles." "Cunningly contrived plans of deception or aggression, carried it may be from generation to generation, can be worked out and kept from the light of day only within the privacy of courts or behind the carefully guarded confidences of narrow and privileged class. They are happily impossible where public opinion commands and insists upon full information concerning all the nation's affairs."

On the right of trade: "With a right comity of arrangement no nation need be shut away from free access to the open paths of the world's commerce. And the paths of the sea must alike in law and in fact be free. The freedom of the seas is the *sine qua non* of peace, equality, and cooperation."

On a concert of nations: "It will be absolutely necessary that a force be created as a guarantor of the permanency of the settlement, so much greater force than the force of any nation now engaged in any alliance hitherto formed or projected that no nation, no probable combination of nations could face or withstand it." "A general association of nations must be formed under specific covenants for the purpose of affording mutual guarantees of political independence and territorial integrity to great and small states alike." "I am proposing that all nations henceforth avoid entangling alliances which would draw them into competitions of power, catch them in a net of intrigue and selfish rivalry, and disturb their own affairs with influences intruded from without. When all unite to act in the same sense and with the same purpose, all act in the common interest and are free to live their own lives under a common protection." *

These brief quotations illustrate two points important to the development of American relations with Europe. First was the primacy in Wilson's mind of the League of Nations as the only instrument capable of maintaining the peace. This led him, during the course of negotiations in Paris over the peace settlement, to rationalize his compromise with other principles by the belief that injustices could be remedied and the valuable parts of Versailles saved if only the League be established. It led him to claim—correctly and without boasting—that the League and the peace were so intertwined that the Senate could not separate them. Second, the concept of the League was for Wilson but the embodiment of traditional American policies. "Neutrality," as he told Congress in his war message, "is no longer feasible or desirable . . . ." That being the case, the safety of the United States as well as of the rest of the world lay in a concert of nations which was far more than an alliance and had both the power and the right to act on behalf of the international community.

▶ AMERICAN REJECTION OF THE LEAGUE OF NATIONS

DIFFICULTIES IN APPLYING WILSONIAN PRINCIPLES

That the League did not assume the stature envisioned for it by President Wilson was due to a combination of factors inherent in the frailty of man and of his works. Wilson sometimes forgot that he was, in addition to being titular head of the state, a politician and a party leader, as when he composed the list of Americans to accompany him to Paris and failed to prepare the way for the treaty at home. Wilson sometimes acted as though he alone possessed a monopoly of truth and could sit in judgment on the motives and morality of other statesmen. Moreover, one of his principles was extremely faulty, given the nature of Europe and of the world as it was: nationalism, national self-determination, and popular sovereignty were all destructive as well as constructive forces, a fact which is now well recognized. The *right* of people to choose their own government did not necessarily assure their *ability* to make it operate or to live under it. In the hodgepodge that was the ethnic map of Europe it was impossible to apply the right to all peoples at the same time. Then there were the Germans, whose government was the

---

* This and the foregoing quotations were taken from Address of President Wilson to the Senate, January 22, 1917; President Wilson's War Message; Address of President Wilson to the Congress, January 8, 1918 ("Fourteen Points"). Quoted in Bartlett, *op. cit.,* pp. 452–461.

defeated enemy and whose rights could only be returned by the victorious Allies.

Both the British and the French had developed national projects looking toward a league of nations, but their concepts were different from Wilson's, and for neither country did a league have the same primacy in the scale of priorities. Wilson talked of nationalism and sovereignty but did not recognize the heritage which those principles had left in Europe. European states had been created by conflict, nurtured or destroyed by conflict, and now were at the end of the latest in a series of wars stretching back a thousand years. European tradition demanded that any peace treaty embody in it the simple fact that some states had won and others had lost. In writing a punitive peace the victorious statesmen were demonstrating loyalty to one of the principles Wilson talked so glibly about—national sovereignty.

What was this League, anyway? Was it an instrument to ensure the supremacy of the victors over the vanquished? Was it a system to enhance the arts of diplomatic negotiation and compromise? Was it perhaps a device for insinuating the guilty into the councils of the innocent? Was it a means whereby the United States might arbitrate the destinies of Europe? Or was it perchance a figment of the Wilsonian imagination? Clemenceau wanted answers first and the League afterward; Wilson could only argue that the League came first and dictated the answers. It was not enough.

REJECTION OF THE LEAGUE COVENANT

The United States Senate rejected the League of Nations and the Versailles Treaty of which it was a part. Instead, the American government separately concluded peace with the Central Powers in July and August, 1921. In so doing the United States entered upon the twenty-year interwar period of what has erroneously been described as a state of "isolation." This term does justice neither to the situation as it existed in fact nor to the ideas and attitudes of those Americans who repudiated Wilsonian idealism. It should be noted that most of the American people and the majority of their representatives favored the League when the small, hostile majority of the Senate Foreign Relations Committee set out to deliberate and talk it to death. Furthermore, the League, with the accompanying Lodge Reservations, which the European members of the League would have perforce accepted, was turned down by a Senate vote of 49 for and 35 against, reflecting a favorable percentage of almost 60 per cent or only 8 votes less than the required two-thirds majority. This defeat was directly attributable to the intransigence of Wilson himself, who wanted *his* League, not Lodge's, and of his die-hard followers in the Senate, who refused to vote for the amended version.

Most of the subsequent repudiation of the Democratic party, whose presidential candidate, Governor James Cox, campaigned with vice-presidential nominee Franklin Roosevelt for the League, had nothing to do with the League at all, or with anything else more serious than that the American people in their sovereign majesty were glad the war was over and voted for the man who was telling them that it was and that their responsibilities were at an end. Warren G. Harding, certainly one of the weakest figures to attain the presidency, declared himself in favor of "an association of nations," when he was allowed by his campaign managers to say anything at all, and a group of prominent Republicans believed or said they believed that this meant in actuality American participation in the existing League of Nations. Only when he was inaugurated was Harding ready to say that "the Administration which came into power in March, 1921 definitely and decisively put aside all thoughts of entering the League of Nations. It doesn't propose to enter now, by the side door, back door, or cellar door."

In turning its back on the League of Nations, the United States was returning to principles and attitudes which had been historically tested. The fault did not lie with the principles themselves but with people of such limited insight that they could believe, because they wished to believe, that particular principles of foreign policy could be regarded as immutable. A set of principles may fit precisely a particular set of relationships between states existing at a certain time, but at some other point in time they may have limited relevancy or no relevancy at all. There is no such thing as an exact historical analogy.

THE EVOLUTION OF THE LEAGUE OF NATIONS

Some sound reasoning lay behind the flight from the League, although it is difficult to discover it amidst the numerous statements of the twenties and thirties repudiating American responsibilities and in the retrospective investigations by thesis-ridden scholars. A brief attempt will be made here to separate wisdom from fancy in order that the interwar role of the United States in world politics may more clearly be seen.

Despite President Wilson's claim that neutrality was no longer possible for this country, there were eminent historians and international lawyers who believed the contrary. Particularly when Versailles emerged as just another settlement, incomplete, transitory, and carrying within itself the seeds of future conflict, did they argue that America had needlessly and to its own loss abandoned a basic policy which was responsible for its growth to greatness. Since the articles of the League of Nations enforced on members a legal commitment incompatible with neutrality, they pointed out, the United States was pursuing the right course in remaining aloof. It should be remembered that even some European powers, such as Switzerland, Belgium, and Norway, later became aware of the same incompatibility. Implicit in this reasoning, of course, was the assumption that the United States could and should continue to act as these three states did, i.e., like a small power.

Opponents of the League could also with some justice claim that the political commitments assumed by members were greater than either the peoples of the various countries or their governments were as yet ready to assume. This argument was especially leveled against Articles X and XVI, the former guaranteeing the "territorial integrity and existing political independence of all Members of the League," and the latter binding the members to consider themselves at war with, and to take sanctions, including, under certain circumstances, military ones, against any member violating the Covenant by going to war.

The United States was not alone in its view that these clauses went too far. A Canadian attack was launched on Article X at the very first session of the Assembly, and only the rule of unanimity and the lone vote of Persia prevented it from being wiped out. Other British dominions, removed as they were from Europe, agreed with Canada, while Great Britain itself, because of its own geographical position and its relation to the Commonwealth, shied away from a rigid interpretation of the Covenant. Successive British governments vetoed two French proposals to "put teeth" into the Covenant by providing a mechanism for enforcing its provisions, and the substitute arrangement of Locarno was, significantly, completed outside the formal framework of the League. Moreover, the League members themselves interpreted Article XVI in such a way as to destroy its automatic character and thereby to assert their freedom of action in case of aggression and nonunanimity of the Council. In the end, of course, the League could neither apply sanctions against Germany or Japan nor employ effective coercion against Italy. The cause of the League's failure, then, certainly did not rest altogether or even in large part at the door of American nonparticipation. There was a failure of will also among the members.

The League was, generally speaking, an instrument to preserve the *status quo,* as may be seen in the contrast between the articles for the protection of the *status quo* previously cited and the final weak provision which only *permitted* the Assembly to *advise* the members to reconsider in appropriate treaties any existing situations which they might deem dangerous to peace. This last provision was the door through which peaceful change was to enter; a small door it was and one which led only into a blind alley. If the League was primarily the victors' instrument to perpetuate their victory, most change would obviously be unwelcome, although it should be remembered that Italy, while nominally a victor, actually became one of the foremost revisionist powers. However, the League purported to be far more than a large Holy Alliance to enforce the *status quo.* It was to be a "concert of powers" dealing out justice to all states impartially. As such it found itself unable either to promote changes sufficient to satisfy the revisionists, particularly Germany, Italy, and Japan, or to enforce a rigidly defined *status quo,* even after the other great nonparticipant, Soviet Russia, entered the Council in 1934. Fear that the League would founder on the Scylla and Charybdis of *status quo* and peaceful change was not confined to the United States; it permeated the foreign offices of Britain, France, and Russia as well.

Reduced to its essentials, the League was designed as an instrument to permit peaceful operation of the post–World War I European state system. The Covenant placed in the hands of Great Britain and France the power necessary to maintain that system as established by the Treaty of Versailles. While the nonparticipation by the United States and the late entry of the Soviet Union are important elements in this situation, it did not alter the basic fact that the preponderance of power rested at that time with Great Britain and France. The irresponsible manner in which these two countries frittered away their power and permitted Hitlerite Germany eventually to dominate the Continent cannot be disguised even by according all due weight to the contemporary irresponsibility of the United States. Geographic propinquity inevitably placed on their shoulders the primary task of preventing a new European conflict which would engulf the world. The United States could have lightened this burden. Even without the aid of this country, however, their own selfish interests still dictated that the job should be done. These interests were not recognized; the full implications of the task were not grasped, and the interrelationships of European states for the second time in the twentieth century speedily deteriorated.

► AMERICAN FOREIGN POLICY IN THE ERA OF "NORMALCY"

AMERICAN ALOOFNESS FROM EUROPE

Despite its nonparticipation in the League, the United States in the interwar period did not remain completely aloof from Europe and was extremely active in its relations with the Far East and Latin America. Although a sharp division is impossible, the American government did confine its European relations mainly to the spheres of economics and military disarmament. Immediately after the war, Herbert Hoover organized relief activities for European countries, and to them Americans contributed generously. The prestige of the United States as a humanitarian nation was thereby enhanced, especially because this country refused to endow its relief activities with political connotations. Although the United States officially denied the existence of any connection between reparations due to the Allies from Germany and the war debts due to the United States from the Allies (Coolidge: "They hired the money, didn't they?"), Americans officially and unofficially acted as though the intimate relationship did in fact exist. Charles G. Dawes and Owen D. Young headed international commissions which studied the reparations problem, reduced the amounts to be wrested from Germany, and drew up a schedule of payments. It was the American secretary of state who suggested the employment of these Americans. In their private capacities Americans poured money into Germany and Austria, money essential to the functioning of the entire European economy. Upon these loans were based what reparations payments Germany did make and the recovery it did attain. It was not, after all, the United States which had formulated the fundamentally unworkable scheme of forcing Germany to pay for the war. The intimate connection between American economic power and the health of the European state system was starkly revealed later when depression struck the United States.

The United States took the lead or participated fully in each of the various disarmament conferences, beginning with the Washington Naval Conference in 1921–1922 and ending with the failure of the League's Geneva Conference in 1934. The premises on which American policy was based stemmed from the historically rooted belief that armaments were an unnecessary drain on the economic resources of any country and were deeply dangerous to the peace of the world. That this belief was validly applicable only to certain states at certain times lent an aura of unreality to American action. It was difficult for the American people to understand what appeared to be the intransigence of France and Italy in respect to naval disarmament and almost impossible for them to sympathize with France's insistence on maintaining a large standing army. In the trilogy of objectives—disarmament, security, and arbitration—the United States tended to make the first a pre-requisite for the others, France the second, and the British, at times, the third. In the end none was attained. This failure did not prevent the United States from carrying the policy of aloofness from European problems to its logical conclusion in the form of unilateral disarmament both on land and on sea, once its right to parity with Great Britain in capital ships had been recognized at the Washington Naval Conference.

THE UNITED STATES BEGINS TO LIQUIDATE ITS INTERVENTIONS IN LATIN AMERICA

The term "isolation" could never be applied to the interwar policies of the United States toward Latin America. During the decade of the twenties economic ties multiplied in the form of trade, private investment in private concerns, and private investment in Latin governments. The economic power of the United States placed the American government and certain private businesses in the position of virtual arbiters of the destinies of small, weak states in the Central American and Caribbean area. The United States continued its policy of intervention, which had placed it in control of the Dominican Republic, Haiti, and Nicaragua. Against a rising tide of criticism both in Latin America and in the United States, Secretary of State Charles Evans Hughes passionately defended American practices at the Havana Inter-American Conference in 1928 as a right and duty justified under international law. The year 1928 marked, however, the high point of American interventionism. The administration of Herbert Hoover began the liquidation process and that of Franklin Roosevelt succeeded in substantially changing the entire relationship between the Colossus of the North and the other American republics.

The essentials of the Good Neighbor policy in the period preceding

World War II should here be briefly summarized.* The components of that policy, as carried out by Secretary of State Hull and Under Secretary Sumner Welles, were political, economic, and administrative. Not only did the Democratic administration complete the liquidation of Caribbean imperialism; American representatives at the Montevideo and Buenos Aires conferences, in 1933 and 1936, abandoned the position of Secretary Hughes in favor of a nonintervention declaration admitting of no exceptions, not even those supposedly justifiable under international law.

After wholesale Latin-American default on debt obligations in the early years of the depression, a substantial shift took place in the nature of United States investment in the area. Branches of American businesses were established in most countries, encouraged to do so by the possibility of avoiding high Latin-American tariff barriers. Private American loans to Latin-American governments were replaced by governmental loans made by the Export-Import Bank, which was established in 1934. The United States, furthermore, carried the implications of its nonintervention policy into the economic field. American business was warned not to interfere in Latin-American elections, and discriminatory taxation levied against American firms was handled by the United States government in an informal and lenient manner if at all. The United States admitted the right of Latin-American governments to expropriate American business interests altogether, and its manner of settling the Mexican oil expropriation issue indicated a generous looseness in applying the principle of "prompt and full compensation for such expropriation." Cordell Hull's Trade Agreements Program resulted in successful negotiations with most of the American republics for the mutual enlargement of trade, the significant exception being Argentina.

Action in accordance with Good Neighbor principles permitted the growth of the Inter-American System, which had previously been confined to elaboration of largely unused treaties of pacific settlement and compilation of technical data under the auspices of the Pan American Union. Now the System began to concern itself with the problem of hemisphere security in the face of the rapidly deteriorating situation in Europe. Notwithstanding the recalcitrance of the inveterate nonratifier, Argentina, the twenty-one American republics had by 1939 formally agreed that a threatened or actual attack from without the hemisphere on any of the twenty-one should be met by concerted action.

Mention finally should be made of the program of scientific and cultural cooperation initiated in 1938 by the Department of State and an interdepartment committee, following adoption of an authorizing convention at Buenos Aires. Although just begun by the time war broke out, the program laid the groundwork for the substantial exchange of personnel in the scientific and cultural fields which followed. The objectives were greater knowledge, hence greater understanding between Latin-American and United States

---

* See Chapter Nineteen.

societies, and the provision by the United States of technical assistance in diverse fields ranging from agriculture to tax policy.

AMERICAN WEAKNESS IN THE FACE OF A DETERIORATING FAR EASTERN SITUATION

The United States continued after World War I, as it had in the period 1898–1914, to assume a position in respect to the Far East somewhere between its policy toward Latin America and its policy toward Europe. By 1931 the chickens hatched from the policy of commitment without power and willingness to use power were coming home to roost. Upon the United States now rested primary responsibility for the maintenance of Chinese independence and the balance of power in the area of the Pacific. Increasingly this became a problem of restraining Japan, which had taken advantage of its opportunities during World War I. First, Japan was induced at the Versailles Peace Conference to relinquish her political hold on Shantung. Next, the entrance of large numbers of Japanese troops into Russian Pacific territory for the announced purpose of aiding the Czech military prisoners in Russia on their crosscontinental hegira was countered by American participation in the enterprise in order, despite what Soviet propaganda now asserts, to keep watch on the Japanese, frustrate their ambitions, and liquidate as soon as possible the entire operation. As part of the over-all settlement of Pacific problems at the Washington Conference in 1921–1922, the Anglo-Japanese Alliance was ended. The Japanese were granted a ratio of naval power which was deemed sufficient to protect their home islands but not enough for them to engage in aggressive operations. Security for the possessions of other powers was further enhanced by the Four-Power Treaty, under which Japan supposedly agreed not to fortify the former German Pacific islands, then under Japanese mandate from the League of Nations. Finally, all the Pacific nations signed the Nine-Power Treaty, embodying the principles of the Open Door and the territorial and administrative independence of China. Japan thereupon renounced the incompatible group of its Twenty-one Demands which, it will be remembered, had called for Japanese political tutelage of China.

This system of security proved in 1931 to rest on documentary paper and nothing more. The United States did not maintain its navy at treaty strength, thus altering to Japan's advantage the actual balance of power in the Pacific, nor did the United States maintain in a state of preparedness the fortifications of Guam, Wake, and the Philippines, the first of which was located in the midst of the Japanese-mandated islands. For its part Japan continued secretly to militarize its mandates and did not change its mental interpretation of what constituted the Open Door. Two triggers only, both readily apparent as early as 1925, needed to be pulled to complete the dissolution of this paper system. One was growth in the determination and ability on the part of the Chinese Nationalists to recapture control over all of China, including Manchuria. The second was the deterioration in the state of Japanese political institutions to the extent that governmental policy could be controlled by military groups bent on the further expansion of Japanese power, notwithstanding the existence of diplomatic commitments to the contrary.

▶ AMERICAN POWER AND RESPONSIBILITY IN THE EVENTS LEADING TO WORLD WAR II

After 1930 both the European state system and the Asiatic balance of power distintegrated with increasing rapidity, while the United States watched with a mixture of incomprehension, incredulity, and impotency. Not only the Germans, but the entire complex of interwar relationships among the nations helped to produce Adolf Hitler. Neither Britain nor France chose to stop his systematic destruction of the Versailles settlement when they could, and with the outbreak of the Spanish Civil War and the German invasion of the Rhineland it was too late. The pillars of Versailles— German disarmament, German military inferiority, and an alliance of states ringing Germany—all vanished.

CONFLICTING AMERICAN VIEWS OF THE EUROPEAN SITUATION

In the United States the existence of counteracting trends of thought prevented the adoption of policies which would either have strengthened British and French resolve to alter the course of events, or have confronted Hitler with a coalition of overpowering strength. The concern of the Roosevelt Administration with the march of totalitarianism was matched by its preoccupation with domestic recovery from the greatest depression the most prosperous nation in the world had ever known. In some instances, such as the 1933 London Economic Conference, cooperation with Western European democracies was consciously sacrificed to the exigencies of national financial policy.

The record is clear that Roosevelt himself regarded totalitarianism as evil, war as evil, and the former as destined to lead to the latter in a holocaust from which the United States would not be able to remain aloof without immeasurable sacrifice of its principles and its interests. Roosevelt was, however, president of a democratic republic, a position subject to powerful and complex pressures. He was elected to office by a people conditioned by experience and history to regard with profound pessimism and skepticism the course of European events, a people whose natural ignorance about foreign affairs and equally natural preoccupation with where their next meal was coming from (this was during the depression) precluded their exercising enlightened influence on their country's foreign policy. In addition to being president, Roosevelt was the leader of a political party internally divided on both domestic and foreign issues. Some Democrats were New Dealers at home and opposed to intervention in European affairs (Wheeler). Others were profoundly skeptical of, or outright antagonistic to, measures of domestic reform but wanted the United States to assume a position in international affairs which the existing state of its military power could not have maintained (Southern Democrats). In evaluating his diverse political support, Roosevelt had to take care not to advance at any time beyond the point to which the American people would follow. When that point was passed, as in the Chicago quarantine-the-aggressors speech, political sensibility plus a recognition of responsibility to the public dictated a hasty retreat. Historical examination of the role of the United States as a World War I neutral, inspiring and inspired by the Nye Committee investigations, focused popular and official attention, not on ways in which the new threat of German hegemony over Europe might be thwarted, but on specific devices to prevent entanglement of the United States in Europe's future wars.

Thus did the internal situation of the United States in the 1930's result in disastrous weakening of its foreign policies, both as to method and as to power, to the point where they were quite inadequate to protect the national security against German expansionism.

An awakening of the American people to the need for power was requisite to the use of power in the advancement of United States foreign policy. This awakening the Roosevelt Administration increasingly attempted to produce between 1936 and 1939. In addition to public indifference on foreign-policy issues and the political difficulties mentioned above, two factors, one American and one European, largely frustrated these efforts. Because of the interpretation placed on their past experience, Americans were prone to condemn the very words "national power" or "power politics." Those who sought to demonstrate what is now, after World War II, self-evident— that both phrases can be used, not as value judgments, but simply as recognition of the fact that the presence or absence of the attributes of national strength plays a great role in the relationships between sovereign states—were bitterly assailed from both flanks, by idealists who wanted the United States to lead the world toward Utopia by the strength of its moral position, and by those who wanted to retain for their country the inherently contradictory luxury of a powerful nation behaving like a small, weak state. Abnegation and denial of power had characterized American foreign policy after World War I, and many wished to continue this role of irresponsibility.

EUROPEAN RESPONSIBILITY FOR THE ADVENT OF WORLD WAR II

As for the European factor, it was difficult for the United States seriously to consider saving the democracies of Western Europe when those democracies seemed bent on suicide as soon as possible. After the German occupation of the Rhineland doomed France's Central and Eastern European allies, France, racked by such serious economic, social, political, and ideological cleavages as to place it on the edge of revolution, did not find it possible to build up its own military strength and to reach a firm under-

standing with the only great power at Germany's back, the Soviet Union.*
The weakness of Britain's "arm on the Continent" was masked by its previous reputation for power. Britain itself, guided by men who were for the
most part ignorant of the workings of international politics, failed to equip
itself or even to recognize the connection between British security and events
in Central Europe, despite the Cassandra-like warnings of Winston Churchill.
If Hitler was actually encouraged by Chamberlain to take more than he
hoped for in Czechoslovakia provided that it be done peacefully, if the Men
of Munich were prepared to sacrifice the last democratic bastion in Eastern
Europe and actually to glory in the murder as bringing "peace in our time,"
how could the United States be expected to augment its own military strength
for the avowed purpose of stopping Hitler? Given the supposed security of its
geographic position, the failure of the United States to rearm was not incom-
parable to the too-little, too-late measures of Britain and France.

WEAKNESSES OF AMERICAN FOREIGN-POLICY TECHNIQUE: THE NEUTRALITY ACTS AND THE STATE DEPARTMENT

Along with the lack of power on the part of the United States went
consequent weaknesses in technique for accomplishing American foreign-
policy objectives. When President Roosevelt combined warning with appeal
to Mussolini and Hitler, the latter gentlemen could safely ignore the appeal
because they knew the United States could not and would not make good
on the threat. Investigation of the munitions industry and of loans granted
to the Allies, reinforced by reflections on the horrors of war, resulted in the
Neutrality Acts of 1935 and 1937. Under the 1935 act the President was to
ban the shipment of arms to both belligerents and to prohibit the granting
of loans and credits in case of *inter-* or *intra*national conflict. After signing
the measure with some misgivings, Roosevelt applied it to the Italian attack
on Ethiopia and to the Spanish Civil War. In both instances the effect of the
act was to promote fascist aggression. Hitler could well believe that American
neutrality would assist him in any war with Britain and France by cutting
off from the Allies American economic, financial, and military assistance,
which Germany would not have been able to obtain in any event. The
United States was officially declaring that it did not care whether or not
Britain and France fell and German hegemony was established in Europe.

Another serious weakness of technique, which still haunts the United
States, was the inadequate training and organization of experts in the field
of international relations.† The State Department and the Foreign Service as
institutions in part reflected the moods and attitudes of the American people.
Since foreign affairs ranked low on the scale of American preoccupation, not
many qualified persons sought employment in the field. Nor was the State

---

* The Franco-Russian Alliance of 1935 did not create that understanding, as
Munich and the Nazi-Soviet pact showed.

† This subject will be treated in detail in Chapter Seven.

Department anxious to seek out the few qualified people available. Representation of the United States abroad was regarded as a highly complex art, the technicalities of which were more important than the definition, planning, and advancement of the broad political interests of the country. Would-be initiates were carefully examined with a view to keeping the organization (the private club, as it were) small and of like-minded membership. The personality of the Secretary of State and his belief in the panacea of reciprocal trade agreements further weakened the State Department by widening the gap between the tasks it should have assumed and the resources, physical and intellectual, which it saw fit to mobilize. Much of the area of foreign-policy activity consequently passed by default under the control of other agencies of government, including the White House itself.

AMERICAN IDEOLOGICAL CONFUSION

Efficiency of technique was hampered further by the moral and ideological confusion which permeated the American twilight between peace and war. What was actually meant by the value-loaded words "democracy," "fascism," and "communism"? Was Great Britain, the ancient enemy and erstwhile friend, a democracy in the American sense? Could Léon Blum and his Socialist party, governing France with the active assistance of the Communists in a so-called Popular Front, be called a democrat at all? Would not American aid to these *foreign* countries weaken the only democracy most Americans believed in—American democracy? What if Mussolini were labeled a fascist; had he not rescued Italy from the Communists, made the trains run on time, and restored a measure of that country's former greatness? Was not the fact that Hitler had saved his country from decadence and chaos and created an efficient and increasingly powerful government more important than the fact that he was a National Socialist, whatever that meant? The fifteen years' rupture of relations with Russia and the inherent secretiveness of the Russian totalitarian regime did not help to clarify American views concerning the nature of communism. Was not the Soviet Union the chief enemy to civilization, as Hitler so often said? And yet were not the Soviet Union (until August, 1939) and communists everywhere in the forefront of the fight against fascism, in the League of Nations and outside? Or were all these ideological terms meaningless in the face of the fascist-communist, German-Russian peace? Was the ensuing war, as Lindbergh argued, merely another in the long series of conflicts which had bedeviled Europe from the beginning of time?

AMERICAN INABILITY TO DETER JAPAN IN THE FAR EAST

After invoking the Neutrality Act in the Spanish and Ethiopian cases, President Roosevelt refused to find any war in Japan's resumption of aggression against China in 1937, precisely because, as mentioned above, application of the act would have hurt the victim. Instead, the Roosevelt Administration continued the policy embarked upon by former Secretary of State Stimson of making moral condemnations and technical charges of treaty violations. When Japan first moved into Manchuria to establish the puppet regime of Manchukuo, Stimson had made clear the attitude of the United States. His government could not condone the Japanese action; it claimed the applicability of the Nine-Power Pact; it would refuse to recognize any alteration in the *status quo* achieved by force of arms. The United States was not prepared, however, to act in conjunction with the League of Nations or to apply any sanctions against Japan. But it did take its position first, and the position was more strongly stated than that of the League. The members of the League also proved unwilling to apply sanctions and used the lengthy investigations of the Lytton Commission to cover their hesitancy in antagonizing Japan. Remember that this was the first case in which the League of Nations confronted a determined aggression by a major power. The legally phrased commission report, which still sought an area of diplomatic maneuver between the contestants, was nonetheless too strong to suit Japan, which announced its withdrawal from the League and continued with the conquest of Manchuria.

► CONCLUSION: THE WORLD SITUATION IN 1939— THE INDIVISIBILITY OF SECURITY

The attack on China, following three years of relative calm, was part of the same Japanese design for hegemony over a vaguely defined "Greater East Asia," under policies and principles libelously likened to America's Monroe Doctrine. If German and Italian intervention made the Spanish Civil War the first battle of World War II, Japan's attack on China provided the first continuing thread of conflict. From 1937 until 1945 China fought the aggressor in the Far East, for four long years alone. Japan's signature to the Anti-Comintern Pact of 1935–1936 formally linked Asiatic and European aggression. Once more was demonstrated the fact which had existed since the beginning of the twentieth century: that the European state system had become world-wide and that in consequence peace was truly indivisible. It was hopeless to dream of settling the conflict in the Far East without removing the causes of conflict in Europe. Hitler's attack in Poland in 1939, Mussolini's attack on Greece, the anti-Comintern, anti-American pact of both dictators with Japan resulted in the global encirclement of the two remaining great neutrals. Their neutrality was subject to destruction at the whim of the aggressor. Both the Soviet Union, which had attempted to buy its way out by unleashing war upon the detested democracies, and the United States, which wished somehow to reconcile its determination to see the Allies triumph, with its determination to stay out of war, would eventually be forced willy-nilly to throw their full military power against the would-be conquerors of the world.

► SELECTED BIBLIOGRAPHY

For detailed studies of American diplomatic history see Samuel F. Bemis, *A Diplomatic History of the United States* (New York, Henry Holt & Company, 1950), and Dexter Perkins, *The Evolution of American Foreign Policy* (New York, Oxford University Press, 1948). Both authors have special works in the Latin-American field: Bemis, *The Latin American Policy of the United States* (New York, Harcourt Brace & Company, 1943); Perkins, *Hands Off: A History of the Monroe Doctrine* (Boston, Little, Brown & Company, 1941). The intimate relationship between foreign and domestic policy is revealed in such general American histories as Charles and Mary Beard, *The Rise of American Civilization* (New York, The Macmillan Company, 1927) and S. E. Morison and H. S. Commager, *The Growth of the American Republic* (New York, Oxford University Press, 1950–1951), and in such special studies as Julius W. Pratt, *Expansionists of 1812* (New York, The Macmillan Company, 1925), and *Expansionists of 1898* (Baltimore, Johns Hopkins University Press, 1937). A useful documentary collection is Ruhl Bartlett, *The Record of American Diplomacy* (New York, Alfred A. Knopf, Inc., 1947). On American Far Eastern policy, see A. Whitney Griswold, *The Far Eastern Policy of the United States* (New York, Harcourt, Brace & Company, 1938). Amidst the flood of literature on American entrance into World War I, such works stand out as Charles Seymour, *American Neutrality, 1914–1917* (New Haven, Conn., Yale University Press, 1935); Walter Millis, *The Road to War* (Boston, Houghton Mifflin Company, 1935); and Charles C. Tansill, *America Goes to War* (Boston, Little, Brown & Company, 1938)—the last two being critical of American policy in this period. Much of the flavor of the interwar United States is recaptured in Karl Schriftgeisser, *This Was Normalcy* (Boston, Little, Brown & Company, 1948). For European developments, see William Rappard, *Quest for Peace* (Cambridge, Mass., Harvard University Press, 1940); and Arnold Wolfers, *Britain and France between Two Wars* (New York, Harcourt, Brace & Company, 1940). A highly adverse view of Rooseveltian policy is taken by Charles Beard, *American Foreign Policy in the Making, 1932–1940* (New Haven, Conn., Yale University Press, 1946) and *President Roosevelt and the Coming of the War* (New Haven, Conn., Yale University Press, 1948), and by Charles C. Tansill, *Back Door to War* (Chicago, Henry Regnery Company, 1952). More dispassionate accounts are rendered by Basil Rauch, *Roosevelt: From Munich to Pearl Harbor* (New York, Creative Age Press, Inc., 1950), and by William L. Langer and S. Everett Gleason, *The Challenge to Isolation, 1937–1940* (New York, Harper & Brothers, 1952), and *The Undeclared War* (New York, Harper & Brothers, 1953). For re-examination of American foreign policy, see E. M. Earle, "A Half Century of American Foreign Policy: Our Stake in Europe, 1898–1948," *Political Science Quarterly,* June, 1939; Frank Tannenbaum, "The American Tradition in Foreign Relations," *Foreign Affairs,* October, 1951; Dexter Perkins, "Where the United States Stands Today," *Foreign Policy Bulletin.*

September, 1951; Dexter Perkins, *The American Approach to Foreign Policy* (Cambridge, Mass., Harvard University Press, 1952); Frank Klingberg, "The Historical Alteration of Moods in American Foreign Policy," *World Politics*, January, 1952; Walter Lippmann, *U.S. Foreign Policy: Shield of the Republic* (Boston, Little, Brown & Company, 1942); and George Kennan, *American Diplomacy, 1900–1950* (Chicago, The University of Chicago Press, 1951).

CHAPTER TWO

THE REVOLUTION IN AMERICAN FOREIGN POLICY: SOME BASIC FACTORS AND IMPLICATIONS

Introduction • Generalization Based upon the History of American Foreign Policy • Some Aspects of World War II and Its Aftermath • The New Security Position of the United States • The Capabilities of the United States • The Nature of the Transition through Which American Foreign Policy Is Passing • Summary • Selected Bibliography

► INTRODUCTION

American foreign policy is now in a period of revolutionary transition. Since the entrance of the United States into World War II, traditional patterns of policy have been abandoned or reshaped, new policies have been instituted, new underlying assumptions and principles have been replaced or reinterpreted, and new techniques for implementing foreign-policy objectives have been developed. It is an important theme of this book that *all* the subjects to be analyzed in ensuing chapters must be viewed against this backdrop of dynamic change. The way foreign policy is formulated and executed is just as much affected by the transition as are the content and direction of policy.

As can be seen from the previous chapter the process of reorientation had already begun before 1941. Nevertheless, the new framework of American foreign policy was not clearly visible until the latter half of the decade 1941–1951. The period of change is not yet over and probably will not be for an indefinite time, but enough of the broad outline of the new order has taken shape to be identified and tentatively analyzed.

This chapter will present a general summary of the current international situation of the United States and certain of its implications. The kinds of elements to be considered are some basic factors which influence American foreign policy—either new factors or old factors in new guise; the commitments and responsibilities accepted by the American people since 1945; and some thorny problems thrust upon the United States as a result of recent developments.

Naturally, there is a marked contrast between the present situation and the situation on the eve of World War II. As a preliminary step, therefore, it will be helpful to recall a few of the interpretations and conclusions implicit in the historical survey presented in the previous chapter.

► GENERALIZATIONS BASED UPON THE HISTORY OF AMERICAN FOREIGN POLICY

1. Relative geographical isolation, room for continental expansion, the absence of any nation of equal power potential in this hemisphere, and above all, European rivalries and distresses which prevented the great powers of the world from undertaking major operations in the American domain determined consequently the form and effectiveness of the specific policies which implemented the fundamental traditions of American foreign policy. The United States was largely freed from the burdens of international conflict, and national growth proceeded without costly overseas ventures and without substantial involvement in conflicts of rights or interests of other states.

2. Historically, American foreign policy has been largely negative. No positive global foreign policy program beyond our frontiers was necessary. The Far East, Europe, and Latin America could be treated as separate compartments with specially designed policies for each. Genuine threats to national security were, for the most part, minor, sporadic, indirect, and hence could be reasonably well defined and predicted. No real planning was necessary and the military establishment could be small and unbalanced. America neither wanted nor needed economic privilege abroad or additional territory. America was under no compulsion to regard any one nation as "the enemy."

3. Until 1939, except in a few specific periods, foreign affairs directly affected only a small segment of the people. Momentous decisions were infrequent. On balance, national resources were never heavily committed to foreign relations. Domestic issues were primary and not basically and continuously affected by international developments. The day-to-day business of foreign affairs was carried on by a small group of experts working in relative obscurity on highly technical matters. Occasionally the general public was aroused, but citizen attitudes normally reflected apathy and ignorance. This traditional noninvolvement in foreign affairs, combined with a rather conscious pacifism, necessitated a slow "re-education" of the public after 1935.

4. The role of ethical or democratic principles, missionary zeal, and moral idealism in American foreign policy cannot be overestimated. American

reactions to international politics and to the use of American power abroad have been heavily influenced by a strong sense of right and wrong, a dislike for exploitation and tyranny, a distrust of "power politics," a belief in individual liberty and equality, and a dedication to the rule of law among nations and its corollary of peaceful settlement of international disputes.

5. One of the most significant characteristics of American foreign policy was the peculiar combination of assumptions and expectations upon which it was based. The United States assumed that the following conditions prevailed and would continue to prevail: (a) a nonthreatening balance of power buttressed by British resources and commitments; (b) a relatively stable, unchanging international order based on agreed rules of conduct; (c) a liberal world economic system in which trade moved primarily in response to price and quality differentials; and (d) a stable military technology which gave the advantage to defense. It was expected that (a) a major war would always be of long duration, thus giving the United States a choice of whether and how it would participate; (b) the United States would never have to fight simultaneously both in Europe and in Asia; and (c) the affairs of Europe would never be of great concern to the United States.

6. During the period 1900 to 1939, America continued to pursue its national objectives according to the patterns set forth in the previous chapter. It is now apparent in perspective that, slowly and surely, the assumptions underlying foreign policy became invalid, the techniques became inappropriate, and America's view of the world and of its position in it became ever more illusory. The climax came with the essentially involuntary involvement of the United States in a two-front war under much less than optimum conditions. America had changed and so had the world, but the significance of these changes had been apparently omitted from American calculations of the national interest.

7. The most significant change was America's loss of relative immunity from international conflict and politics. The nineteenth century's delicate power balance underwritten largely by British seapower had been gradually undermined after 1900. Germany and Japan had become great powers, the realization of whose aims depended on major alterations of the *status quo.* America had also become a great power. Given the total nature of modern war and the potential strength of the American economy, American power automatically had become a factor in any large-scale struggle. Neutrality, therefore, became first difficult, then impossible. Technology altered the defensive value of ocean frontiers and made possible the domination of the European heartland by one power. Such developments should have prompted a re-evaluation of America's international position. It should have been apparent that the essential result of World War I was to restore only temporarily the more desirable balance of power upon which American security was thought to rest.

8. America gave hostages and accepted political commitments in the Far East in the form of the acquisition of the Philippines and an insistence upon the territorial integrity of China. Japanese aspirations were to be kept within limits by a series of somewhat ambiguous paper agreements and concessions. America did not, however, effectively underwrite these commitments by military or political power. By remaining aloof from Europe the United States sacrificed additional power leverage. The attitudes and policies of European states toward the Far East were primarily the results of their rivalries and other relationships on the continent of Europe. Therefore, it became increasingly improbable that substantial collective support to thwart Japanese moves could or would be mobilized.

9. The failure to balance American commitments and objectives with adequate application of national power in its concrete forms was evident in other ways. Heavy emphasis on sheer moral exhortation and high principles as exemplified in Woodrow Wilson's Fourteen Points, in the League Covenant, in the Kellogg Pact, in the Hoover-Stimson Doctrine of Nonrecognition of the fruits of aggression, and in tongue-lashings directed at the European dictators, helped to create the impression that America was a nation of words, not deeds. Aggressive states thus tended to base their policies on erroneous appraisals of American behavior and strength.

10. The period between the two world wars, 1919 to 1939, was one in which some powers clung tenaciously to the *status quo* while others wanted to overthrow it. In the absence of an agreed international process which would facilitate peaceful change and which would harness national power to the maintenance of a system capable of satisfying minimum national needs or interests, war was bound to be the ultimate instrument of national power. International law, antiwar declarations, the outlawing of aggression and disarmament—techniques relied on by the United States—were by themselves doomed to failure.

11. Finally, long-range historical forces were at work from 1900 to 1939. The intensification of nationalism, the steady increase of government intervention in economic life in all countries, and the revolt against the concepts and institutions of liberal democracy and laissez-faire capitalism were symptomatic of the collapsing economic and political stability of the later nineteenth century. The Russian Revolution of 1917, the dislocations resulting from World War I, and the depression of 1929–31 were interwoven in these trends and added strength to them. International politics were bound to be affected. The conditions which directly and indirectly permitted and encouraged new ideologies and totalitarianism, which weakened the imperial power of Great Britain, and which blocked the establishment of a true international community during the hopeful days of Woodrow Wilson's influence, had existed long before the outbreak of war in 1939 but unfortunately were not well understood.

► SOME ASPECTS OF WORLD WAR II AND ITS AFTERMATH

No proper understanding of the new conditions underlying American policy is possible without the realization that the United States fought World War II in alliance with other major powers (France, Great Britain, China, and the Soviet Union) whose war aims were not the same. True, they all wanted the military defeat of the enemy but defeat of the enemy is more than an end in itself; it is a means to other ends—the political conditions to follow victory. Given the manner in which the Allies became embroiled, there could be no beforehand agreement on basic objectives. The result was that the later declarations of war and peace aims—the Atlantic Charter, 1941, the United Nations Declaration, 1942, the Moscow Declaration, 1943, the Yalta Declaration, 1944—were all *general* in both language and content. It was almost inevitable that when the time came to implement these less specific aspirations, disagreements would arise over the meaning of words and over how to carry out obligations. Changing conditions had altered the impact of previous agreements. Such difficulties are inherent in coalition warfare. When the shooting ceases, the partners tend to revert to purely individual aims because each has gained the one most important thing he wanted from the others, namely, help in overcoming a common enemy.

Some of the knottiest of current problems are due in part to the effects of the war itself and its unforeseen consequences. It is not entirely a question of diplomatic blundering or willful deceit. When people speak of "losing the peace" they illustrate one of the ramifications of modern war. Wars are begun with one balance of international strengths and weaknesses and end with another. War aims are set under one, must be carried out under another. World War II solved one problem: the defeat of German and Japanese aggressive designs. It created a whole host of other problems, among them the rise of two giants who soon became mortally suspicious of each other. War as a "solution" to political conflict thus breeds its own special problems. It changes the world in which it is fought.

War is a part of a political process which does not begin with the first shot nor end with the last. This fact becomes all the more meaningful when it is realized that the United States had two kinds of objectives in fighting World War II. One was the defeat of an immediate threat to American security; the other was the building of a new world order—in a sense the resumption of Woodrow Wilson's plans but with a more realistic foundation. The war tended to confuse and obscure these two quite different purposes. They were not always compatible. The war itself produced changes which were bound to affect the search for a durable peace. The process of establishing a new world order was not identical with that of subduing an enemy, though the two were related. There is abundant indication that people did not keep the two separate in their minds. The resulting confusion was clear. Building a new international system through the United Nations necessitated reliance upon certain restraints on national behavior: agreement to submit differences to approved processes, agreement to take a much broader view of national security, willingness to accept political limitations on national aims—all of which presume a measure of trust, some common values, common security situations, in short, a minimal community of interest. Fighting a successful coalition war on the other hand, especially since the coalition was an accidental one, increased the opportunities for intensification of purely national desires. In the muddled period of armistice the temptation was overwhelmingly great to take individual national measures. But above all, in the carrying on of common military efforts decisions were made, on a military basis, which later turned out to have far-reaching political consequences. A gigantic military campaign which covered almost the entire continent of Europe, the Mediterranean, the Middle East, and the Far East and which saw armies overriding local cultures with consequent disruption of civil societies was bound to produce decisions with far-reaching political implications. The Soviet Union seems to have been more conscious of this factor than the United States.

The way the war ended is in point here. Russian troops were in control of most of Eastern Europe (except Greece) and part of the Far East; Western troops controlled North Africa, Greece, Italy, Japan, western Pacific islands, and Western Europe. In view of the fact that no immediate formal peace was forthcoming for many of these territories, de facto military control became immensely significant. It provided the basis of a new power alignment which could have been different only if the original lines of attack had been different or if prompt formal peace had resulted in troop withdrawal. A further complication was the unequal effect of World War II on the victorious partners. The Russians took a more severe physical beating and, generally speaking, the impact on Russia internally was much greater than on the United States. Furthermore, the view the Russians had of their own role in Europe was so different from the traditional attitudes of the United States that, all in all, the two nations were bound to take completely different views of the postwar situation. In all likelihood, the collapse of the Axis Powers in 1945 signified much more to the Soviet Union than just the defeat of the enemy. It provided an opportunity to strike a blow for future security and for spreading Communism.

These various considerations, plus the evolving enmity of Russia and the United States, have produced two major areas of adjustment for American foreign policy. One concerns the United Nations. The latter was set up and put into operation before World War II was ended; that is, before the new international power alignment became formalized. As a result, nearly every concrete question which confronted the new organization after 1945 was an occasion for direct or indirect maneuvering for position among the victorious

Allies. Such issues would have been difficult to meet in any case. Under such circumstances they could seldom be decided on their merits. In 1948 the United States referred the Soviet blockade of Berlin to the Security Council, charging the Russians with a violation of the Charter. The Berlin question was of course a part of the unfinished business of the war. The move actually resulted in taxing the United Nations with a difficult task of peacemaking, a function intended to be kept separate from the building of a new world order until final treaties could be intrusted to the United Nations for enforcement.

The failure to make immediate peace altered the significance of the occupation of the former enemy states, chiefly Japan and Germany. Instead of being a device whereby agreed Allied aims could be carried out, occupation soon became an individual national enterprise with the French, British, Russian, and American forces, whether by compulsion or by deliberate decision, pursuing different and sometimes opposed objectives. Once again incompatible sets of interests arose from the unstable over-all power balance. The first United States objective of disarming and rehabilitating the defeated enemy was one thing; the later aim, incorporating the former enemy into the uneasy pattern of collaboration among the victors, was another. These two sets of objectives were not necessarily incompatible. The point is that reconstruction in, say, Japan, would have been carried out differently if there had been a general agreement between Russia and the West. In any uncertain security situation one of the aims of occupation will be stability. Stability could be more easily achieved by slowing up the reform of the basic conditions which supposedly produced German and Japanese aggression. Certain leaders were tolerated and used who might not otherwise have been, and a contest ensued for the goodwill of the defeated peoples. Occupation without a peace settlement in fact provided these occupied peoples with opportunities for a subtle kind of blackmail.

For the United States, occupation has lasted much longer than anticipated, and has been more complicated and expensive. One of the new arenas of American foreign policy is the deep, continuous involvement in the domestic politics of occupied areas. Occupation is not just a matter of policing a country while it goes about its business. Occupation is an exercise in government—the enforcement of certain rules of conduct by the application of military and political force. For this task America was not well equipped. It had had no extensive experience and by tradition was unsympathetic to the kinds of activities required for ruling others. Often occupation forces vacillated between the role of the naïve candy-bearing liberator and the role of the imperator who brings with him habits which belie his official statements or irritate and confuse the local populace. To this disability was added the further debilitating effect of the American desire for normalcy at home and for a quick return of the regular draft army. To be successful, occupation requires special skills, long training, patience, and single-mindedness of purpose. Though their record may compare favorably with others in the past, the American occupation forces have, generally speaking, gone about their business with less than adequate understanding of the institutions of the defeated enemy. Apart from the problem of gaining a minimum of cooperation from the defeated enemy—a process which requires knowledge of his culture and behavior traits—the United States has faced the necessity of replacing crumbled political machinery in Germany and a disintegrating social system in Japan, as well as shattered economies in both. Nor was the task of rebuilding, difficult in itself, simply an economic matter. It was necessary to make decisions on delicate questions of industrial monopoly, labor relations, public education, private property, and freedom of political activity which have not been fully resolved in the United States.

The German problem, as will be shown later, exemplified the complexity of the situation created by the deterioration of Russo-American relations. Western German manpower and resources had to be kept out of Russian hands and at the same time made available for the protection of the Atlantic rimland. A healthy outlet for German energies and capabilities was also required. Yet all this had to be accomplished in such a way as to alleviate French fears and to prevent any German attempt to dominate Western Europe.

► THE NEW SECURITY POSITION OF THE UNITED STATES

A combination of historical forces—particularly the lessons and results of two world wars and radical changes in military technology—has imposed a new security position upon the United States. What is meant by "a new security position"? It means, in the first instance, that certain *conditions which affect* American security have been basically altered. It means, second, that traditional *thinking about* American security has had to be thoroughly revised. Accordingly, it is necessary to consider the major premises which now underlie national security and to review briefly the factors which influence the search for security under the present pattern of international politics.

MAJOR PREMISES UNDERLYING AMERICAN SECURITY THINKING

There appear to be five premises, among others, now consciously accepted by the United States in determining policy: (1) no one hostile or potentially hostile nation (or group of nations) can be permitted to dominate both the Atlantic and the Pacific rimlands; (2) no hostile or potentially hostile nation (or group of nations) can be permitted to integrate into its economy those presently free areas where large-scale industrial production is possible; (3) peace must be enforced in the last resort by the responsible use of armed force; (4) security cannot be preserved by unilateral action alone and hence permanent alliances and arrangements must be entered into with nations whose security interests are akin to its own; and (5) national means must be commensurate with national aims and objectives if policy is to be effective.

Implicit in all of these is a further assumption that security depends upon what has been called by Edward Mead Earle "grand strategy": "The highest type of strategy is that which so directs and integrates the policies and armaments of the nation that the resort to war is either rendered unnecessary or is undertaken with the maximum chances of victory."* Implicit, too, is the notion of "total diplomacy," which means a general policy that is designed to produce those external political conditions most conducive to the security needs of the nation and that is supported by the mobilization of all necessary national resources. This last point will be treated again in a later section of this chapter.

THE BIPOLAR DISTRIBUTION OF NATIONAL CAPABILITIES

Among the new factors which affect American security is the redistribution of national strength which has taken place since 1939. From the standpoint of total capability the number of really great powers has been reduced to two, the United States and the Soviet Union.† While Great Britain still retains a not inconsiderable influence and has access to the diffused resources of the British Commonwealth, it has fallen to a position of inferiority relative to the two superpowers. Former great powers, France, Japan, Italy, and Germany, seem destined to achieve little more than second rank in the immediate future. America and Russia are truly world powers because their capacity to influence the action of other states can be made effective in both Eastern and Western Hemispheres. Areas lying uneasily between the Big Two—notably Western Europe, the Middle East, and the Pacific Islands—have tended to become "low-pressure" zones which are more vulnerable to superior capabilities and to become also "outer security" zones in which anything either Russia or America does or tries to do is of vital importance to the other. Thus national capability is not only much more highly concentrated, but has shifted away from its former European center.

However, the real significance of the bipolar distribution of national strength lies not in the fact itself, but in its consequences. The United States has been compelled to adopt a global strategy, to use its military power on a world-wide basis. There is no longer, as there was from 1815 to 1914, a sufficient number of strong independent nations whose interrelationships can be relied on to preserve a balance which is not dependent on a commitment of American power. Whereas internal rivalries among European states once prevented any European state from challenging the United States in this

---

* E. M. Earle, "Political and Military Strategy for the United States," *Proceedings of the Academy of Political Science,* January, 1941.

† This generalization is, of course, subject to the qualification that Communist China may emerge as a first-rate military power. Though aided by the Soviet Union in the Korean conflict, China has given evidence of growing military proficiency.

hemisphere, now it is American power which stands athwart the potential hegemony of Europe by one power, i.e., the Soviet Union. In addition, no effective mediation is possible, given the concentration of power in two nations. It is far easier to achieve compromise and mediation when there are six or seven great powers of roughly equal rank. Since 1945 no nation or even a group of nations has had sufficient power or prestige to act as a balancing force between the United States and the Soviet Union.

RUSSIAN-AMERICAN RIVALRY AND CONFLICT

Nearly all the serious international disputes and conflicts of the present period involve, directly or indirectly, the two hostile superpowers. Indeed, this has been, and still is, the central fact of international politics in the post–World War II era. After a war in which both nations were somewhat accidental and reluctant allies, mutual fear and distrust have come to dominate Soviet-American relations. The motives and actions of each are either misinterpreted or distrusted by the other. Each believes, or acts as though it believed, that its survival is menaced by the power of the other, each feels it would be intolerable to live in a world where the values and institutions of the other prevailed, and each fears that the other will or must eventually attack it. There seems to be a conviction on both sides that uncontrollable forces drive the other's policymakers, and that while there are some individuals on each side who are rational and can be "dealt with," it is the over-all political system in each case which determines policy. A succession of moves and countermoves has developed into a vicious circle: the more security America has, the less Russia has, and vice versa. Both nations emerged from periods of relative isolation without substantial experience in international diplomatic maneuvering and without having had substantial dealings with each other. Ideological factors have further complicated the impasse. Hostility is supported and intensified by the fact that Russia and America interpret the world and each other in terms of different historical experiences, different cultures, and different sets of beliefs and assumptions about human behavior. Each of the two nations has built up a set of expectations about the policies and conduct of the other. Foreign-policy action based on these expectations in turn tends to produce reactions which appear to fulfill the original prophecy whether it was valid or not.

TECHNOLOGY AND NATIONAL SECURITY

Developments in military technology (the applied science of weapons of warfare) have altered the traditional role of sea power, increased the mobility and fire power of land troops, given new functional importance to air power, and provided atomic bombs, guided missiles, and germicidal and other weapons. The implications of these developments are far-reaching and run in several directions, at least some of which lead beyond the purely military field.

In effect, the new alignment of national power mentioned above plus technological changes has forced the United States to face a new geostrategic situation. Land masses have assumed changed significance; areas which were of little consequence militarily are now of strategic importance. The Arctic (if not the Antarctic) regions have become bases which must be prevented from falling into the hands of an enemy and which must figure in the continental defense of the United States. Other areas, like Turkey and Iran, have almost become security outposts.

From a military standpoint, the whole globe is viewed as a series of defense rings. It is readily apparent that a global strategy requires the establishment of air bases and interceptor stations, radar nets, supply depots, and assignment of key military personnel to all kinds of places, some of which must be made habitable by artificial means. The technical problems are enormous. But since many strategic facilities must be erected and maintained within the territory of other states, there are complicated diplomatic and political problems as well. More or less continuous friction has prevailed between the citizens of Great Britain and France on the one side and United States military personnel on the other. Gangs in Manchester, England, once attacked two United States Air Force patrols. In France one source of animosity has been the allocation of very scarce housing to American officers and men. Even the renewed consideration of statehood for Alaska and Hawaii in 1953–1954 could be attributed in part to the fact that air power has brought the Soviet and United States homeland very close together along the great-circle route and in part to defense needs in the Pacific.

The security problem has been complicated in other ways. Security planning is necessary and is one of the new bases of foreign policy. Time-space-power realities require that the United States anchor its military strength on a core of "readiness potential"*—an offensive striking power ready for action at a moment's notice. Military capabilities and specific commitments (exemplified by the armed intervention in Korea) must be balanced so far as possible; yet exactly what kinds of tasks may be forced upon the military establishment cannot always be foreseen. Military strength can only be relative—relative, that is, to the strength of an enemy—because science is constantly altering the face of war. A very considerable degree of mobilization for war must be maintained in peacetime because by its very nature the American military machine cannot be assembled overnight. The new weapons of war present what seem to be almost unlimited risks. They are costly to produce, may be even more costly to use—particularly in view of the skilled manpower required—and the results may be uncertain. It is no longer possible to calculate total armed forces needed in simple terms of a clear and proportionate means, except in case of limited military situations.

The foregoing suggests the necessity of security planning which in turn

---

* The phrase is from Hanson Baldwin, military editor of the New York *Times*. See his *The Price of Power* (New York, Harper & Brothers, 1948), Chap. 16.

must evolve from a number of decisions. There are obvious technical aspects of military planning, of course—among them how to develop the most fire power in the most usable form at the lowest cost. But such decisions have foreign and domestic social, economic, and political repercussions. In addition they must be based on a series of calculations. As noted, the rapid increase in the numbers, cost, complexity, and destructiveness of weapons complicates the whole problem. A series of questions will amplify the range of difficulties. What kinds of war under what conditions at what time should military planning be geared to: an all-out, atomic war twenty years hence or a foot-soldier war à la Korea, or both? Shall the industrial mobilization base of the military preparedness program be broad or narrow—i.e. shall there be a large number of plants with stand-by idle equipment or a small number of plants producing arms at a modest rate as a part of normal operations? The Truman Administration favored the former; the Eisenhower Administration, the latter. Should defense spending be geared to a minimum plateau for, say, ten to thirty years or should it be geared to a crisis year? For the Democratic administration which made policy until 1952, 1954 was the crisis year and defense goals were timed to that year. Republican successors in January, 1953, abandoned the crisis-year approach. What weapons should be stockpiled: those which, though they become quickly obsolescent, nonetheless satisfy immediate needs, or only the more durable items? Shall more emphasis be placed on defensive weapons or on offensive weapons or equally on both? Should reliance be placed on one weapon or concept such as air power or "Fortress America" or on balanced forces and multiple strategies? What should be the absolute size of combat forces at any particular time?

To answer these and related questions, estimates must be made and calculated risks assumed. A serious ammunition shortage in the Korean conflict was directly related to a decision to use stored surpluses during the first year of fighting on the assumption that it would be over by June, 1951. When the new Republican administration recommended a cutback from President Truman's military budget of 5 billion dollars, the economy was justified on the grounds that the Soviet Union did not appear to be concentrating on offensive weapons and that the proposed reductions would not reduce the existing size of the armed forces. But at the time when this reduction was being considered the usual information on Soviet production for the first quarter of 1953 was missing and civilian and military estimates of Soviet military strength were conflicting. The cutback definitely was a calculated risk: 1954 was *not* to be a year of crisis. Indeed, there was a major shift from a "crisis-year" approach to a "long-haul" approach. In August, 1953, however, the United States government officially and publicly recognized that the Soviets had exploded a hydrogen bomb. Apparently this news did not reopen the program of long-term strategic military planning already decided upon.

Security planning also requires hard-choice priorities and balancing. In a real sense, the various branches of the Armed Forces (Army, Navy, Air Force, Marines) are continuous rivals for prestige, appropriations, and functional importance in the total preparedness program. The cutback mentioned above hit the Air Force hardest, a fact which stimulated a vigorous debate over the desirable strength of the Air Force and its role in national security. Hence balance among the armed forces is both a technical and political question. Choices must be made on the strategic deployment of military forces. The priority assigned to Europe as against the Far East was called into question during the Congressional hearings which followed the removal of General MacArthur as United Nations Commander by President Truman in April, 1951. A balance must be struck between defensive and offensive weapons and strategies, between arms-producing plants and stockpiles, between continental and overseas defenses, and between domestic needs and foreign aid. Awkward choices arise from relationships with allies: what effect will military build-up have on their economic well-being? What effect will insistence on defense have on internal political opposition?

The relationships between the military establishment and other domestic institutions are affected by planning. Can a free economy survive under ever-increasing armament and mobilization? Has military expenditure made impossible any substantial long-range reduction in the federal budget and hence in taxes? Can the United States maintain a stable, indefinite "military posture" in the face of traditional American resentment against regimentation and discipline? Can the military establishment compete effectively for leaders? How can civilian and military voices in security planning be coordinated and reconciled?

IDEOLOGICAL COMPLICATIONS

Thus far emphasis has been placed on purely strategic factors in the security position of the United States and in the conflict between the two superpowers. Stress must also be laid on the contemporary role of beliefs and ideas in international politics and their relation to the bipolar struggle.

Ideological cleavages are not peculiar to the present age, but, for reasons which cannot be explored fully here, they are probably more serious. Today, rival social systems and political ideas are backed by formidable national power. Differences in belief have become another source of international tension. One nation is pitted against another not only for all the reasons which normally set group against group—clashes of interest, diverse personalities, or transferred hostility—but because the particular form of economic and social organization of each one is a menace to the other.

It appears clear that the Russian-American impasse consists in part of a mutual mistrust of each other's ideas. Neither feels it could live in a world dominated by the other's system of political and social thought. From the point of view of Russia, the spread of Western democratic ideology with its emphasis on individual rights, representation, multiparty practice, and majority rule not only would violate Soviet beliefs about how politics should operate but would open the door to anti-Russian policies and to antiproletarian activities by the decadent *bourgeoisie* in countries dominated by this ideology. On the other hand, the spread of the Moscow-brand communist governmental technique with its emphasis on one party, minority rule, unchallenged power of officials, and socialized economic life would confront the United States on every side with totalitarian regimes whose appetites for further political encroachment would be insatiable.

Ideologies contribute to conflict in another way: they function as frames of reference for the interpretation of national behavior. The Russians charge that American participation in the Korean war was due to the dictates of "Wall Street bankers" might have been a deliberate political lie; yet it might also reflect the fact that Russian beliefs require this kind of interpretation of American behavior.

Ideological conflict in the present situation is particularly serious because Russia is a relatively "closed" society and America is a relatively "open" society. There is little opportunity for a reconciliation of the conflict of ideas or values or for mutual understanding when one of the parties steadfastly resists normal intercourse with the rest of the world.

Ideologies influence the selection and formulation of national objectives in two ways. The spread of a system of beliefs and the destruction or weakening of an opposing system of beliefs have themselves become foreign-policy objectives. A nation's ideology also constitutes a source of significant clues as to why that nation wants what it does. Both processes are apparent in the rivalry of Russia and America. Each tries, by different means and for different reasons, to extend the practice or influence of its own political values. In the United Nations majority rule is consonant with and reflects American political values, whereas it is contrary to the precepts of the Soviets and is therefore opposed by them.

Ideas, furthermore, have become techniques of foreign policy, serving a variety of functions. The development of mass communications in many forms and new methods of political warfare have made it feasible to attempt to control national groupings for specific purposes. By 1952, Russia and America were reaching into each other's inner and outer security zones via short-wave broadcasts, pamphlets, magazines, newspapers, organizers of resistance cells, and political agents. Ideological techniques are aimed at weakening a potential enemy, both on his home ground and in his zones of influence, by creating or supporting dissent and resistance. Under modern conditions, waging war or otherwise taking effective political action requires a high degree of cooperation and morale, a solid agreement that the group's beliefs and ways of doing things are worth dying for if necessary. A fifth column—highly organized local minorities who pay allegiance to the ideas and interests of a government other than that in whose jurisdiction they dwell—can be an effective dissolver of morale. The Germans skillfully and successfully capitalized on splits in

French opinion before, during, and after the fall of France in 1940, a fact which helped make it impossible for the French nation to resist invasion and which eased the problems of occupation for the invader.

Ideological appeals also serve to mobilize a society beforehand against real or imagined external enemies. There is no better way to close ranks internally and to strengthen morale than to stress the threat to values and institutions from outsiders.

Finally, ideological appeals, i.e., propaganda, may help to attract friends and allies and to persuade potential enemies to remain neutral. Information programs—so-called "truth" or "education" campaigns—may explain one nation's motives and actions and thus alter favorably the interpretation and reception of such motives and actions by others.

This brief sketch suggests that a new element has been added to international politics. It is conceivable that if a total global conflict is avoided in the near future, the "cold war" may become a normal pattern. Subversion, proaganda, sabotage, and infiltration may tend to replace, or to become as important as, traditional diplomatic methods. The impact on the security position and foreign policy of the United States is significant. To put the matter bluntly, the United States has been compelled to recognize the necessity of carrying on political warfare in the broadest sense, including all its branches. This necessity has been one direct result of the fact that the Soviets have waged such warfare in deadly earnest and as an integral part of their over-all foreign-policy strategy. National security must, therefore, be defined not only in terms of the capacity to employ military and economic techniques but in terms of the capacity to influence attitudes and beliefs abroad and the strength to resist subversion, sabotage, and propaganda attacks at home. It has not been easy for the United States to accept the fact that political warfare is now deeply imbedded in the international political process and that ideas are as crucial as bullets, dollars, or material goods. For one thing, it has come as a shock to the American people that they could be subjected to a subtle, almost invisible internal attack. For another, the endowment of an already powerful federal government with techniques for controlling or influencing the minds of men is something they have traditionally abhorred.

▶ THE CAPABILITIES OF THE UNITED STATES

America's total capacity to achieve its aims is constantly shifting. It is impossible to draw up a balance sheet which will be accurate for very long. At any moment the production of a jet-propelled bomber, the refusal of Congress to appropriate funds for foreign economic aid, a great propaganda triumph, the invention of a new submarine by the Russians, or any similar development could alter the relative power position of this country. American capability, as broadly defined, is simply one of several fluid aspects of the international situation in which American foreign policy must operate. Nonetheless, an outline of the new role of the United States in world affairs would not be complete without reference to certain obvious ingredients—military, economic, and political—of its national capabilities. The term "position" simply refers to the capacity to employ the various forms of the foreign policy techniques grouped under the three major headings.

THE MILITARY POSITION

The military strength of the United States cannot be estimated by merely adding up men, tanks, ships, planes, and weapons. Military strength is determined and supported ultimately by the national economy. The American military machine, viewed in the large, is comprised principally of highly technical devices operated by highly skilled and trained personnel. Technology is really the key element. Nor can the possible demands on the military establishment be overlooked. Air power was adequate to enable the Western nations to stay in Berlin in 1948–1949, but it is doubtful that America could have prevented a successful land attack on Western Europe at that time. Apparently one of the reasons the United States tried so hard to limit the Korean conflict was that it was not prepared to carry the campaign beyond the peninsula under prevailing strategic conditions. To the military power equation must be added the strength of friends and allies. On balance, they constitute assets. Yet in some cases the actual realization of their power required an additional expenditure of resources by the United States. The necessity of sending four to six divisions to Western Europe under the North Atlantic Alliance put a visible though temporary strain on American manpower in 1951.

The United States is *potentially* the strongest military power on earth. Its military establishment is now backed up by an unmatched *productive capacity*. Temporarily at least it enjoys a substantial technological advantage (and hence strategic advantage) in the perfection and production of atomic bombs, guided missiles, and biological weapons. A large stockpile of atomic bombs has been built up, and tactical atomic weapons for use on the battlefield are being produced. A near monopoly on uranium is under American control. Even though the Soviets have exploded a hydrogen bomb, it is estimated that as of late 1953 the advantage in production remained with the United States temporarily. It is some distance (in time and engineering techniques) from a hydrogen explosion to bomb production. The United States enjoys clear superiority in forms of naval power, both ships and planes, except for submarines. In terms of having planes and the know-how to deliver atomic bombs to distant targets the United States has an advantage in strategic air power.

America's military position has been strengthened by other recent developments. Between June, 1950, and October, 1951, the armed forces were increased from 1,458,000 to 3,350,000 men and their equipment was modernized and expanded. The establishment of the North Atlantic Treaty

Organization also enhanced America's military security by providing, among other things, a friendly international army in Western Europe. Military aid to Greece, Turkey, Spain, Formosa, Latin America, and other countries further buttressed America's position. Security pacts binding the nations of the Western Hemisphere and certain nations of the Pacific (Australia, New Zealand, the Philippines, and Japan) have been negotiated. These and other arrangements give the United States access to, or actual control over, military bases at such strategic points as Spain, Greece, Turkey, North Africa, Greenland, Japan, the insular Pacific, and Western Germany.

These elements and developments are of course to a large extent dependent upon and underwritten by, partial industrial and military mobilization in the United States. The ability of the United States to improve its own armed forces and those of its friends and allies depends on American factories. As of early 1952, it appeared likely that defense plans would not be fulfilled until 1955 or 1956. Furthermore, American military strength now depends partially on the collective efforts of these same friends and allies whose capacity for carrying out quick, expensive rearmament is considerably inferior to that of the United States. Meanwhile, the Soviet Union and its satellites in Europe maintain a huge land army, have superior tanks and tactical air power, have produced the atom bomb, and are increasing their production of steel, coal, oil, and other ingredients of war. For these reasons, it is necessary to speak of the *relative* military capability of the United States, its *potential* nature and the importance of time in bringing present plans to fruition.

The outlines of the so-called New Look, which resulted from, and was accomplished by, the reductions in military expenditures carried out by the Eisenhower Administration, emerged in 1954. It is reported that the National Security Council made a basic decision sometime in 1953 which was reflected in important policy statements by President Eisenhower, Secretary of State Dulles, and Secretary of Defense Wilson. Dimensions of the new strategy are essential to an understanding of America's present military position. As noted later on in this chapter, the 1953–1954, and 1954–1955 budgets reveal the trend of security planning. The chief features appear to be these: (1) more reliance on a great military striking force carrying advanced atomic bombs and capable of instant retaliation on the home bases of aggressors whether they themselves are directly engaged or are supporting those who are so engaged; (2) more reliance on highly mobile and flexible air and sea forces armed with tactical atomic weapons; (3) stronger continental defenses; and (4) some reduction of military commitments abroad as exemplified by withdrawal of two American divisions from Korea. Responsible statements indicate that the greater emphasis on "massive retaliatory power" represented an effort to reduce the chances of involvement in local defensive conflicts requiring weapons and battlefields of an enemy's choosing and to develop a "long-pull" armaments plan which would pave the way for a balanced federal budget. In essence, this amounted to fewer men and more atomic weapons and a declaration that henceforth an aggressor would be punished on his home ground. However, a close analysis of the New Look suggests that the change is not as drastic as it appears at first glance. Basically, the present military budget reveals an uneasy marriage between the theory of strategic air attack with hydrogen bombs and the theory of surface strength (foot soldiers plus ships plus tactical air support) modernized by recent weapon developments. Together the two elements are aimed at the possibility of one type of large scale-war and at several smaller types which the nation may be forced into.

There is at this writing no known completely effective defense against an atomic attack on the continental United States. Therefore civil defense and plant location must be included in this appraisal. As the international crisis deepened, agencies were established on the local, state, and federal level to prepare for air raids. After several years, mock air raid drills had been held in some major cities, warning systems had been set up and specialized services (medical, fire fighting, and so on) had been mobilized, but in general by 1954 civil defense was still alarmingly inadequate. The same Congress which appropriated $60 billion for rearmament in October, 1951, slashed the federal civil defense appropriation from a requested $550 million to $69 million and eliminated money for air raid shelters altogether—a decision which left New York City to go on with its own $25 million fund for building shelters without the anticipated matching grant from Washington. A heavily populated state like Illinois had appropriated only $200,000 for all civil defense purposes. Governor Dewey announced that in New York State 16 counties and 15 cities were "shockingly delinquent" despite the state's Defense Emergency Act. By 1953 an air raid warning system for 191 target cities was only 50 per cent complete and Congress turned down a budget request which would have increased the speed of construction. An eighteenth-month survey (Project East River) undertaken by 88 scientists, educators, business leaders and government representatives under the auspices of Associated Universities, Inc., clearly demonstrated America's increased vulnerability.

So far as plant dispersal is concerned, well over half of America's industrial capacity is jammed into nineteen concentrated target areas. Sixty-five per cent of the new plants built after the Korean war started are in cities of 100,000 population or over and one third are in the nineteen target areas. Seventy-two per cent of America's steelmaking capacity is concentrated in four states. All aircraft production is centered in five large areas, and 75 per cent of the vital machine-tool industry is in vulnerable target areas.

Significant conclusions can be offered despite the crudeness of these estimates. First, the United States is capable of placing more emphasis on military techniques than at any other time in its history. Recovery of American military strength to something like its pre-1945 level is not complete, but is substantial enough to reduce the chances of an unprovoked attack and to make possible action in behalf of the system of collective security embodied in the United Nations Charter. Second, conscious preoccupation with military preparedness has opened the door to a possible "watering down" or neglect of other important techniques of foreign policy. Third, the growing military might of America differentiates the present international situation from the period following World War I when American disarmament and political withdrawal weakened the power balance which the Allied victory had established. Fourth, there seems little doubt that American military power and the willingness to use it have increased America's prestige and its drawing power in the contest for friends and allies. Finally, nonetheless, the United States appears vulnerable to air attack.

THE ECONOMIC POSITION

The economic power of the United States is imposing indeed. Its forms are manifold: loans, production, gifts, technical assistance, and market opportunities. In a period of no war–no peace, it probably constitutes one of America's most effective diplomatic weapons. To quote Professor Jacob Viner of Princeton University: "Since the beginning of nation-wide boundaries there probably has never been so great a proportionate concentration of the world's goods and of the world's capacity to produce them within the limits of any single country."* The accomplishments of the American economy are well known. Suffice it to say here that it supported a costly four-year war, provided postwar relief to other nations of approximately 17 billions in loans and gifts, and underwrote the recovery of Western Europe for about 5.5 billions annually from 1948 to 1951. It currently supports a huge military budget as well as substantial military aid to friends and allies. As was remarked earlier, it was the bold use of this tremendous economic power which enabled the United States to recapture diplomatic initiative after 1947. Meanwhile national income and national productivity have risen to unprecedented heights.

It would be a mistake, however, to assume that the United States is economically invulnerable and has unlimited resources, or that no potential difficulties counterbalance the imposing economic picture.

There are some fifty-three "strategic" minerals essential to the production of armaments—minerals for which there are no known substitutes and the domestic supply of which is not adequate in the light of defense needs. The United States is normally dependent on foreign sources for cobalt (3,729 short tons from the Belgian Congo), copper (553,000 short tons from Chile, Canada, and Mexico), lead (400,900 short tons from Mexico, Canada, Peru, Yugoslavia), manganese (1,544,526 short tons from India, South Africa, the

* Chamberlain and Snyder, *American Foreign Policy* (New York, Rinehart & Company, 1948), p. 739.

Gold Coast, Russia), nickel (91,471 short tons from Canada and Norway), tin (98,535 long tons from Bolivia, Malaya, Indonesia, and the Belgian Congo), tungsten (3,137 short tons from China, Brazil, Bolivia, Spain, Thailand, Korea), zinc (281,000 short tons from Canada and Mexico). If critical materials are added to the list, making a total of seventy-two, forty must be supplied from outside the United States. Because of stepped-up defense production and the gradual drying up of foreign sources—notably Russia and China—it was necessary to institute a large-scale national program of stockpiling these and other materials. By August of 1952, however, only 38 per cent ($3.5 billion) of the total amount of $8,870,000,000 worth of materials needed for relative safety over the next five years had actually been stockpiled. The goals for fourteen materials had been reached, but at a time when arms production was swinging into high gear, shortages of manganese, tungsten, and sulfur became very acute. In addition, other materials not usually thought of as strategic were in short supply because of new military requirements, materials such as waterfowl feathers, hog bristles, bauxite, wool, and long-staple cotton. Great strides were made in stockpiling; yet the demands of the crisis situation seemed to increase at an even faster rate.

A sobering report on this whole problem was issued by the President's Materials Policy Commission in June, 1952. After an eighteen months' study of raw material needs, the commission concluded that the United States was becoming increasingly a relatively have-not nation and that by 1975 would import 20 per cent of its industrial needs at an annual cost of 3 billions. American industry rests on one-hundred minerals (not all of them strategic or critical for armament production); one third are fully supplied from domestic sources, one third (including cobalt, columbium, high-grade quartz crystals) come entirely from outside sources, and one third (including iron ore, lead, zinc, bauxite, petroleum, copper) come from a combination of domestic and foreign sources. Despite the continued rapid exploitation of United States natural resources and the development of synthetics, the trend toward increasing dependence cannot be arrested. The commission was careful to point out that the problem confronting the United States was not one of raw materials literally drying up but rather one of constantly rising demand plus increasing costs—the number of hours of human labor and amounts of capital required to bring a pound of industrial material or a unit of energy to usable form. It was also pointed out by the commission that outdated federal laws, certain tariffs, and the Buy-American Clause (which forbids federal purchases overseas except where the domestic price is unreasonable or quality or quantity is insufficient) had become handicaps to a sound national policy on raw materials. Needless to say, certain other implications of the commission's findings are clear too. Control of strategic air lanes and seaways is essential to protect raw material sources abroad. Equally important is cooperation with the nations who own such supplies. If anything happened to the Belgian Congo source of cobalt, the production of jet engines would be immediately affected.

Another kind of weakness became evident as partial mobilization of the economy proceeded. A serious bottleneck developed in the machine-tool industry which slowed up the production of items like jet engines and which held up the desired mass production of tanks and infantry weapons. Roughly 54,000 highly skilled laborers are employed in this industry, which under ordinary circumstances could supply the needs of the economy. Machine tools were not being produced fast enough and the industry had in late 1951 a backlog of unfilled orders totaling one billion dollars. Rapid expansion of production in such an industry is difficult and is not achieved overnight. Over two years later, however, employment in the machine-tool industry had substantially increased and the backlog of orders had been substantially reduced.

American production is vulnerable to other disruptions and delays. The absence in the present period of a no-strike pledge such as prevailed in World War II and the lack of any real plan by industry and government to prevent or settle defense strikes mean that when they are most needed certain key activities may be subject to paralysis. One could list four unions which alone are capable of interrupting the defense effort and reducing America's efficiency in the cold war: the International Union of Mine, Mill and Smelter Workers, the longshoremen's and warehousemen's unions, the American Communications Association, and the United Electrical Workers. All of them are under leadership which has been characterized as "Left-Wing" and either are independent or have been expelled from the CIO for policies deemed detrimental to the best interests of labor and the nation. An example of how seriously strikes might menace the national security occurred in August, 1951. The first of the four unions mentioned called a strike in the copper mines which took fifty-eight thousand workers out of fifty plants in fifteen states and reduced the normal production of refined copper (3,000 tons a day) to 5 per cent; the same strike also affected workers in lead and zinc, two other strategic metals. During the period 1949–1951 costly interruptions were caused by strikes affecting dock workers and tugboat crews, coal miners, automobile workers, electrical equipment workers, and locomotive firemen. In August, 1952, three hundred defense contractors were shut down as a result of a long steel strike.*

Additional weaknesses are more deep-seated and are dependent on more than short-term remedies. Shortages of skilled personnel are serious. The United States has still no coherent, long-term policy for preserving and developing its land and water resources. There is steadily accumulating evidence that America may yet pay a heavy price for wanton wastage of soil and forest

---

* The authors intend no general indictment of the labor movement on the basis of the strikes mentioned nor do they imply that any strike is automatically illegitimate because it affects national security. Strikes, whether justified or not, may have these consequences.

resources. Important segments of the American economy are greatly dependent on foreign markets. A disruption of the world's grain market, for example, could cause hardships among large groups in the agricultural population. Despite the prosperity which currently accompanies the present expenditures on armaments, the economy is still subject to cyclical ups and downs of business activity and employment. When the Soviet government appeared to be making persistent peace overtures in March and April, 1953, there was a sharp drop in the price of stocks. At about the same time, business and labor leaders expressed great concern to the president lest the proposed cutback in military expenditures cause a recession or worse. Both incidents reveal the uncertainty and fear over the possible economic consequences of drastic changes in the state of world affairs. Given the piecemeal and inadequate application of wage, price, and other controls imposed after the start of the Korean war, it is not surprising that dislocations resulted from inflationary pressures. In the year 1950, inflation took two of every ten defense dollars.

There is little doubt that the American economy can produce and pay for both a heavy foreign-aid program and billions of dollars worth of defense production over and above ordinary consumer needs without collapsing under the strain, provided certain conditions are met. For while the economy has this capacity and while actual production is increasing, success and stability depend ultimately on tax and fiscal policies as well as other controls which will prevent a drop in the per capita consumption of the American people and which will prevent a decline in the amount of capital equipment per worker. The first would result obviously in a lower standard of living and the second would result in a lowering of the rate of production. Therefore policies are required which preserve productive incentive and per capita consumption rates and which avoid inflationary borrowing by the federal government. Such policies must be formulated on the political level and they involve hard choices. It is conceivable that for political reasons such policies will not be adopted or if adopted in part will not constitute a coherent control program geared to the problems of simultaneously mobilizing a great defense effort, maintaining present standards of living, and sustaining normal economic development. In this event, political and social contention might seriously slow up domestic rearmament and foreign aid.

This brief discussion of the American economic position suggests that in terms of all-round strength, America is potentially capable of underwriting its national security to the limit; its position is generally superior to that of its enemies. However, the fact that the economy is highly integrated and technologically complex means that constant threats of temporary paralysis arise from the kind of strategic shortages and bottlenecks cited. Also, the fact that unusual pressures—inflationary and otherwise—have been imposed on the economy means that control policies assume critical significance. America has in abundant supply most of the basic sinews of economic strength—raw materials, factories, skilled labor, technological know-how—necessary to underwrite foreign-policy needs and national security insofar as they depend on economic factors or techniques. The effectiveness with which these are employed depends on American ingenuity in overcoming shortages, in avoiding, or in minimizing the effects of, bottlenecks, in discovering substitutes, and in devising policies which will enable the economy to accommodate abnormal burdens without collapse.

THE HUMAN RESOURCES POSITION

The age distribution, birth and death rates, health, skills, efficiency, and differentiation of the population into specialized roles are major elements of national capability. Obviously the term "human resources" calls attention to more than mere numbers of people. The ultimate manpower pool available to the nation consists of 155 million Americans, but their training, recruitment, assignment, and effectiveness are far more important. It has been discovered that human, like natural, resources can be wasted and that strategic shortages can develop.

Despite the fact that the United States has only 6 per cent of the world's population as against the 35 per cent to which potential enemies have access, the general population picture is on balance a favorable one for several reasons. American industry produces half of the world's industrial goods. America produces its own food, using only one eighth of its people. Productivity per man-hour has increased steadily since 1909 and is still increasing at 2 per cent a year. The improvement of skills is indicated by the fact that only six million of a labor force of over 63 million are unskilled. Most important is the steady growth of the labor force in proportion to the total population—it was 39.5 per cent in 1950. Age distribution is favorable for continued production, there being a sizable bulge in the 20-40 bracket. A declining death rate makes available a growing pool of older workers. Therefore, while the United States cannot match its rivals in sheer numbers, productive efficiency and favorable age distribution provide a reasonably favorable basis for economic strength.

From 1951 to 1953, the need to mobilize industrial and military manpower revealed temporary shortages in both categories. Full employment due to plant expansion and arms production after 1950 and the demand for young soldiers caught the United States in a short-run population trend which saw a drop of nearly 100,000 in the annual number of males becoming eighteen years old. The normal rate of 1,200,000 will not be reached until 1959, but the leveling off of military production and the reduction of military personnel below the peak of 3.5 million originally planned on for the years after 1952 have eased the shortage considerably. However, so acute was the shortage while it lasted that civilian and military manpower officials were genuinely alarmed. A sudden need for more manpower during the years 1954 to 1959 might once again embarrass the nation, curb the full mobilization of its power, and slow up its responses to a crisis.

More enduring shortages—and more serious perhaps—concern certain types of skilled personnel essential to national security. There is a chronic shortage of *medical doctors*. It is generally agreed that the approximately 210,000 doctors are inadequate for the nation's needs. Increased military needs, whether abroad or as a result of attack at home, would intensify the shortage. The general shortage reinforces specific shortages of psychiatrists, medical researchers, and teachers for medical schools. Another critical weakness lies in the undersupply of *scientists*. The combination of increased demands and a declining number of science graduates is responsible. In 1950, 75,000 science majors were graduated, but it was estimated that in 1954 less than half that number would be graduated. Chemists have been particularly hard hit. The American Society of Chemists heard a report in September, 1952, that only half as many chemists would be turned out in the academic year 1953–1954 as were turned out in 1949–1950. There is abundant evidence that research scientists have begun to decline too. Most pure research is done in university laboratories, and yet the number of scientists working in such labs has been reduced by half between 1940 and 1951. On top of the shortage of candidates and graduates have come competing demands of civilian and military needs.

Engineers comprise a key group of technicians in America. It is the consensus of qualified opinion that America needs at least 30,000 new engineers each year. After graduating approximately 50,000 in both 1949 and 1950, engineering suffered a drastic drop in new enrollments. In 1951 only 35,000 were graduated. According to the Engineering Manpower Commission, the estimated shortage of engineers in January, 1953, was 40,000. Only 23,000 were graduated in 1953. Not until 1956 will the supply return to anywhere near the annual requirement.

Aside from scientists, it is clear that the nation lacks educated personnel generally. In 1953, the National Manpower Council reported the results of a sixteen months' study of the problem of more effective use of the nation's human resources and development of potential skills and capacities. The Council concluded that there were "serious shortages of brainpower involving danger to national security and social progress." The Council took particular note of the fact that there is a huge reservoir of intelligent young people who are not being educated beyond high school and are therefore lost to technical careers ranging from medicine to policy analysis. Columbia University's "Conservation of Human Resources Project" also has reported on its three-year study and has concluded that the uneducated constitute a serious loss to American manpower. Two and one-half million illiterates are unable to fill skilled jobs which require ability to read and interpret technical instructions. Since the armed forces must compete with the professions and business for a limited number of qualified young people, it is not surprising that there is a shortage of military officers and candidates for responsible military positions.

THE POLITICAL POSITION

Though its military and economic capabilities are closely related to a nation's political strength and may serve as bases for the latter, they are not identical with it. In general, political power, as the term is used here, refers to the use of influence and persuasion in the pursuit of national aims. The political capabilities of the United States are comprised of its capacity to win friends and attract allies, to accomplish its aims by persuasion, and to use effectively the nonmilitary, noneconomic techniques of foreign policy—particularly those of a psychological nature. The political position of the United States rests on all these things. For present purposes, only some general points indicating political strengths and weaknesses will be set forth.

One source of strength is American internal stability. Despite crises and economic ups and downs it is probably true that over the past twenty-five years American society has been less unstable than any other major society. This stability has been accompanied by an obvious material success which has underwritten an unparalleled standard of living. Neither of the two great wars produced the direct shocks on the pattern of living in the United States which were produced in England, Europe, the Mediterranean, and large areas of the Far East. To a world in which mere existence has become a desperate and tiring business, America appears to have fabulous wealth and strength. That America has been richly endowed by nature and that its relative achievements have not been entirely due to inherent virtues are irrelevant. The point is that if the appearance of success, certainty, and vigor constitutes one of the qualities of leadership, America has a potential, if only partially realized, source of political strength.

Whether the United States *can* or *will* use wisely all its available means and techniques is open to question, but the fact that it has the material resources to support more extensively a wider range of techniques than any other nation is of enormous political significance. For example, it is only the United States which is able at the moment to supply the requisite technological skills and capital necessary for the industrialization of backward areas.

A vital element of a nation's political strength lies in its capacity to attract allies for both peacetime and wartime objectives. During the postwar years the United States has shown considerable ability to win support for its views on major policy matters among the middle-sized and small states. Several obvious reasons for this are to be noted. The great military and economic capability of this country has acted as a magnet. In an age of uncertain peace, nations incapable of defending themselves by their own efforts alone naturally look for support where they can obtain it without losing a substantial portion of their independence as the price. In its United

Nations policy the United States has made a deliberate effort to throw its weight behind the causes of smaller powers—Iran, Syria, Lebanon, Greece. There were other reasons, of course, for this effort. Nonetheless the American attempt to build majority support in a manner calculated to provide reasonable justice and security for all states in the organization has undoubtedly enhanced our political prestige. The willingness of the United States to contribute considerable money and resources to postwar relief and reconstruction and to the United Nations, while it has been sometimes resented or misinterpreted, has provided strong evidence of distinterested generosity. Similarly, the waiving of reparations and the relatively restrained treatment of the former enemies Germany and Japan have helped to build up confidence in American motives.

It is of immense importance that the United States came to a position of international leadership with a relatively clean record in its international dealings. America has no traditional enemies in the usual sense. Nor has it been prominently identified by the world as an exploiter of humanity. Not that America has made no mistakes, made no "manifest destiny" claims, or made no attempts to let its power weigh too heavily in its foreign relations during the twentieth century (particularly with Latin-American countries before 1930). Yet America has conducted no grand imperialistic enterprises far beyond its frontiers. Though largely an unknown quantity in international politics, America had become accepted as a well-intentioned nation whose word could be trusted more often than not. The other countries which wielded international influence after World War II—particularly Russia and Great Britain—had been deeply involved in various parts of the world at one time or another in the not too distant past and had accumulated a reservoir of hostility and distrust. The case is not black or white, but America's relative lack of an unfortunate diplomatic past is a factor of consequence. In some areas (for example, the Near East and China) the United States had in 1945 a substantial reservoir of goodwill. Oriental nations also remembered that the United States had granted the Phillipines their independence in 1936.

Finally, the political power position of the United States has been given unintentional support by the heavy-handed blunders of the Soviet Union. America is not naturally attractive to many states, but to many of the nations with some freedom of choice it has appeared definitely as the lesser of two evils. On many international bodies, Great Britain and the United States have been thrown together by the persistent perverseness of Soviet diplomacy when they might otherwise have had no common interest. The unreasonable nature of some Soviet charges and the grossness of some Soviet techniques have made useful political counters for the United States. Even states like Australia and Belgium, anxious to play the role of mediator, have on occasion been forced to the American side in exasperation or fear.

One of the first things to be said about weaknesses of America's political position is that, given the present international situation, the factors which diminish the effectiveness of American persuasion and which disaffect friends and allies tend to be exaggerated. As will be seen in the next section of this chapter, the pitfalls confronting American policy are numerous. Errors are easy and are likely to be costly. Under different circumstances, American political strengths would mean relatively more and political weaknesses would mean relatively less. For example, while American aid abroad has been cited as creating prestige and influence, it is true that friction, resentment, and hurt feelings have also resulted. It seems unlikely that such reactions would have been so marked were it not for the fact that many nations are dependent on the United States whether they like it or not. Because America is the leader in the Western world, her actions unfold in a kind of fish bowl. Miscalculations and inconsistencies are quickly detected and pointed out. The fact that American leadership has not always been itself united has weakened its influence; nations dependent on the United States are often not sure which of two official pronouncements is to be accepted.

There continue to be some suspicion and uncertainty concerning American aims and intentions. This seems to be a rather generalized feeling that probably reflects several different factors. There is apparently still a fear in some quarters that the United States may one day withdraw from its deep participation in world affairs and revert to some form of isolation. American strength is not always trusted, not so much because of possible aspirations for conquest and dominion, but because it may not be used wisely. Many foreign statesmen have noted ruefully that despite great technological skills and great material wealth, the American government has not always shown an awareness of the limitations of these factors as bases of action or an appreciation of the more subtle aspects of human relations. The chasms of conflict and distrust between the United States and the Soviet Union cause fear among two groups: those who think America will blunder into war and those who are afraid that America may soften its "containment" policy. American strength and good health and prosperity are resented because they are viewed through the eyes of people short of food and fuel, and through the eyes of governments who wonder how much American aid is going to cost them in terms of going along with American policy views with which they disagree or which they resent. There seems little doubt that Communist propaganda, especially in Europe, has convinced some that there are imperialistic overtones to American foreign policy and the reckless recommendations of some United States leaders have unintentionally helped the Communist cause in this respect.

Fundamentally, much of this kind of difficulty would seem to stem from American failure to state aims clearly, from a failure to coordinate word and deed, from inexperience, from having to make too many adjustments in a short time. In the period after World War II the meager talents that America brought to its new tasks were spread pretty thin. Blunders and reversals have not helped much, understandable though they may be. By-passing the United

Nations with a program of 300 million dollars in aid to Greece and Turkey in March, 1947 (the Truman Doctrine), and withdrawing support from the General Assembly resolution of November 29, 1947, which projected a partition of Palestine, and for which America had almost singlehandedly garnered thirty-three affirmative votes, are cases in point. America's political position has been further embarrassed by its grant of tacit approval or support to such regimes as Franco's Spain and Perón's Argentina, although American officials are on record as unalterably opposed to many of their institutions and ideas. Governments which have supported American aims have often complained that the United States did not take adequate account of internal factors which made their position difficult.

By 1952 evidence had been steadily increasing to the effect that the United States was notably in a position of relative weakness with respect to political warfare.* America has not yet achieved the level of mobilization and effectiveness of its propaganda capabilities that it has achieved in its economic and military capabilities. In terms of the distribution of its national resources among the various techniques of foreign policy, America has been parsimonious in its expenditures for winning the "war of ideas" and undermining internal popular support for communist regimes. It is estimated that the Soviet Union and its satellites spend 1.5 billions a year on propaganda and that in the Soviet Union there are 6 million trained propagandists and agitators. The United States has not been idle in this direction, but neither has it established a counteroffensive on the scale of the Soviet program. Most propaganda victories in the postwar period went to the Communist bloc. Until quite late in 1951, there was no attempt in the United States to create an over-all psychological warfare strategy, but the Psychological Strategy Board was finally set up under the pressure of reverses to rectify previous omissions and mistakes. A Senate committee reported in 1953 that this board had failed to achieve its purposes.† During 1951 there appeared to be a clear shift of emphasis in the foreign-aid program of the United States from butter to guns, from economic reconstruction to military preparedness. Coupled with lack of much real success in the battle for men's minds, this move raised the criticism at home and abroad that American strength was being geared primarily to military techniques and was emphasizing military aspects of the cold war at the expense of other equally important considerations.

For many weeks in the spring of 1953, Senator McCarthy's permanent Senate investigating committee probed alleged disloyalty and subversion in the Voice of America and other aspects of the United States Information Program. Regardless of the general merits of this investigation or of its tactics, one result was to produce confusion and paralysis in America's propaganda efforts at a critical time. An attack on the books housed in United States

---

* See Chapter Sixteen for further comments on the substantive weaknesses of United States programs.

† Organizational aspects are reviewed briefly in Chapter Six.

Information Libraries abroad resulted in a great controversy over which authors and volumes were pro-Communist or un-American. Several books were actually burned and some were withdrawn from circulation. It appears generally agreed that such activities tended to lower American prestige, whatever else was accomplished.

The capacity of the United States to employ military, economic, and political techniques will assume further significance when viewed in the light of the transition through which American foreign policy as a whole is passing.

▶ THE NATURE OF THE TRANSITION THROUGH WHICH AMERICAN FOREIGN POLICY IS PASSING

NEW COMMITMENTS AND NEW PATTERNS OF POLICY

The contemporary crisis in international politics has suddenly thrust the United States into an unprecedented role. It is probably safe to say that no previous society in modern times has been confronted with a greater challenge or has made more far-reaching commitments to foreigners. American military, moral, economic, political, and ideological commitments may be generally summarized as follows:

1. To check as far as possible all direct and indirect thrusts of Soviet military power; to reduce, if possible, the monopoly of Soviet power where it prevails; and, where necessary, to fill the vacuum left by former great powers who once exercised political or strategic control in areas lying between the two superpowers. (The form of the checks may range from full-scale combat as in Korea to the dispatch of Air Force technicians as in the case of Indo-China in 1954.)

2. To prevent the further spread of Communist ideas and institutions, and to aid the cause of freedom wherever or whenever it is endangered, particularly in the non-Soviet world:

3. To use American money, goods, and technical skills in raising world living standards, in achieving a balanced international economy, and in strengthening the bases of democratic institutions.

4. To create a reasonably stable, orderly, unified, and peaceful community of free nations through unilateral action, regional alliances, and a strong United Nations.

5. To make clear what kind of country the United States is, what it wants and why, as part of the obligation inherent in its great power status and to refute Soviet attacks on American motives.

6. To assume and carry out positive moral leadership in the world, acting as chief standard-bearer for the values of Western civilization.

Two major lines of foreign policy grow out of these commitments. American power will be used to hold the Soviet Union at bay. And it will be employed to help create, in the course of time, those political, social, economic, and psychological conditions which will sustain peaceful and prosperous human relationships, domestic and international. While such commitments have been largely prompted by the Soviet attack on American interests, ideas, and institutions, some of the most trying problems and some of the conditions which affect American policy exist quite independently of anything the Kremlin has done or will do. Implicit in the obligations voluntarily or involuntarily accepted by the American people since 1945 is the acceptance of both the Soviet challenge and the challenge of mankind's unhappy state. True, America has said it will not and cannot by itself thwart aggression and aid humanity, and America has helped to create many international agencies dedicated to these tasks. True, the principle of self-help has been invoked as a price for American aid. But the hard fact remains that the United States has designated itself, or been designated, or been compelled by circumstances to become, the leader, the financier, the armed protector, and the moral fiber of the struggle for a free world.

It is to be noted that the six commitments listed above are expressed in very general terms. This is proper for the purposes of the present chapter. Nevertheless it should be emphasized that in response to the factors outlined so far, specific new means-ends patterns of American foreign policy have been evolved, such as participation in the United Nations and its many subsidiary organs, the Economic Assistance and Point Four Programs, the Inter-American System, the Military Aid Program, the North Atlantic Alliance and the Pacific Defense Pact, the International Trade Organization, the Big Three Foreign Ministers' Conference, regulatory bodies for the occupation of former enemy states, a huge military establishment, and such new devices of diplomacy as the Voice of America and the International Information and Education Program. These topics will be treated more extensively in Part II, Chapters Fifteen through Nineteen.

THE FOREIGN-POLICY BUDGET OF THE AMERICAN PEOPLE

A few selected figures will provide crude indexes of some of the costs paid by the United States for its foreign policies and for its assumption of its international responsibilities. From 1939 to 1949 America expended $72 billion on loans and gifts to other countries, $49 billion of this going for Lend-lease aid. During the postwar period—June, 1945, to June, 1952—America provided foreign aid totaling approximately $38 billion. Some ninety nations have received various types of economic or military aid or both. Through the Marshall Plan and the Mutual Defense Assistance Program, Western Europe was by far the largest recipient—$25.8 billion in economic aid and $3 billion in military aid. Asia and the Pacific area received combined aid of $7 billion, Latin America $800 million, and the Near East and Africa, $400 million. For the period mentioned, the United States expended 11.3 per cent of total federal revenues on foreign aid and such aid comprised 10.6 per cent of the total federal expenditures. After reaching a high annual rate of $7.3 billion in 1951–1952, aid to friends and allies leveled off at around $5 billion, divided almost equally between economic and military. Estimates covering 1952 to 1955 indicated that America would expend almost $32 billion, $26 billion for military aid and $6 billion for economic aid. By 1953 the defense of Europe was costing Americans $69 per capita a year.

The Korean conflict turned out to be one of America's relatively costliest military efforts. Two years and eight months of fighting cost 20 billions at an average annual rate of approximately $7 billion. Five hundred thousand American military personnel were directly or indirectly involved on a continuous basis. As of June, 1953, the casualties totaled 136,029: 24,281 dead, 98,851 wounded, 8,642 missing, and 2,675 captured.

On top of the foreign-aid program and the Korean war, the United States was pouring billions into its domestic defense establishment. By the end of 1952, the annual rate of military expenditures was $58.5 billion. While this rate dropped in the ensuing two years, it appeared likely that domestic rearmament alone would have cost the American people approximately $260 billion between July, 1950, and July, 1955. For the single fiscal year 1951–1952, the combined cost of foreign aid and domestic rearmament was $75 billion. Over one and one-half million members of the armed forces overseas required an annual expenditure of over $18 billion for maintenance and equipment. Nearly $8 billion had been invested in nuclear research and development by late 1953.

It must be remembered that these outlays were exclusive of the expenditures required for operation of the State Department and other agencies handling foreign relations, of interest on that portion of the national debt attributable to World War II, of payments to veterans, and of the American share of United Nations expenses. Worthy of note is the fact that from June, 1944, to July, 1951, $12.4 billion were spent for education and training of veterans. The federal budget in 1953 revealed that *86 cents of every tax dollar* was earmarked for foreign policy and foreign relations: 58.0 cents for the armed forces, 7.7 cents for foreign aid, 2.9 cents for stockpiling strategic materials, 2.7 cents for atomic energy, 6.0 cents for pensions and other aid to war veterans, and 8.7 cents for interest on the national debt (mostly due to war). Graphic illustration of the change which has taken place is seen in a comparison of the figures of 86 per cent with previous selected years: 44.27 per cent in 1933, 36.87 per cent in 1937, 31.70 per cent in 1939, 36.70 per cent in 1940.*

These figures give some idea of the tremendous drain on American resources imposed by the challenge and crisis discussed above. Specific categories of expenditures in dollars and manpower reveal some of the new patterns of American foreign policy: limited war, permanent stationing of American troops abroad, military alliances, large-scale military defenses

---

* Figures from James L. McCamy, *The Administration of American Foreign Affairs* (New York, Alfred A. Knopf, Inc., 1950), p. 5.

at home, long-term foreign economic aid programs, and participation in international organization. Finally, there has been a complete reversal of the relative distribution of the resources of the federal government between purely domestic and external needs.

IMPLICATIONS AND DIFFICULTIES

In the first place, it is a dangerous generalization to reduce contemporary international politics to a simple formula of a conflict of power and ideas between the Soviet Union and the United States. Even the phrase "East-West" is somewhat misleading if taken by itself. The external setting in which American foreign policy must operate is vastly more complex than these formulations suggest. Roughly 1,750,000,000 human beings are not under the direct control or influence of either superpower. Riven by the bipolar distribution of national capabilities, these people—particularly the populations of the Middle East, Africa, Latin America, India, and Southeast Asia—dwell in an awkward, uncertain, and even dangerous situation. Not only are their homelands potential or actual battlegrounds, but the techniques of propaganda, subversion, and sabotage almost automatically involve these areas in the two-power struggle. For the most part, the nations of the in-between world have no spontaneous affection for or affinity toward, either Western democracy American-style or Soviet-brand Communism. Their view of the total international situation is different: the world is not black or white; it is a mosiac of grays. To many of them—especially the so-called underdeveloped areas—it must appear that history is repeating itself. From their point of view, it must appear that once more their interests and problems are submerged in an external conflict over which they have little control. One very significant aspect of the bipolar struggle is, therefore, the relative skill, understanding, and success with which the Soviet Union and the United States handle their relations with such people. The fact that India, for example, does not interpret the Communist threat or how properly to deal with it as does the United States, and also disagrees with the latter on the most effective policies to be pursued in the United Nations, makes it very tempting to condemn the Indian government as foolish or traitorous or both. Even if these characterizations were true by some standard, it is poor tactics to tongue-lash India because her resentment provides a good talking point for the Russians and reduces the capacity of the United States to persuade others of the desirability of its program.

A conjunction of historical forces has produced in the mid-twentieth century a cultural crisis and multiple social revolution affecting men everywhere, particularly in the areas of importance in the cold war. Instability and unrest prevail. Traditional loyalties, habits, and institutions are crumbling, changing, or under direct attack. Poverty is universal. Individuals are subject to tension, insecurity, and fear. Ignorance, apathy, and intellectual confusion stand in the way of social progress as defined by the people themselves. In many cases, small groups rule by terror, exploitation, and by capitalizing on the weaknesses of the masses. Three types of interlocked revolutionary processes are at work: a revolution in the ownership of means of production and in the distribution of goods; an emergence of new leadership challenging older ruling elites, bringing with it a competitive struggle for the support of the masses; and a revolt against imperial control. Thus in the Far East, the key political words are "land" and "anti-landlordism," "nationalism" and "anti-imperialism." In one degree or another, most of the countries of the in-between world are moving either from democracy based primarily on an emphasis on individual rights to democracy based primarily on an emphasis on collective welfare or directly from feudalism to socialism. The absence of a sizable, effective middle class and adequate capital resources, as well as the lack of suitable institutional supports for industrialization in backward areas, means that some form of centralized political control is inevitable and that outside help will be needed.

Soviet policy exploits and intensifies this state of affairs but did not create it. American foreign policy now includes elements of a program of international social reconstruction and a battle for men's minds, but strengthening other societies against aggression and helping them develop free political institutions requires more than military aid, platitudes, and new constitutions. America faces the necessity of acquiring a sophisticated knowledge and understanding of these other societies. Given the nature of the political process in the United States, this basic knowledge of the international social environment in which objectives must be pursued must be shared by the general public, by nongovernmental leaders and interest groups, and by congressmen as well as by the State Department experts. Specifically, a practical distinction must be drawn between the general indigenous revolutionary ferment abroad in the world and the particular Moscow-inspired Communist revolution which seeks to capitalize on it. To repeat, there is much more going on in the present external setting of United States policy than the conflict with the Soviet Union and the extension of the Communist revolution.

A second implication is that the crisis and challenge have been imposed on the whole of American society. No important phase of American life has escaped. Partial or total mobilization of productive facilities for possible war is not enough. Several quotations from American leaders will illustrate various aspects of the point. President Truman, speaking to Congress on the state of the Union in January, 1950, said: "We must preserve our national strength. Strength is not simply a matter of force and arms. It is a matter of economic growth, and social health and vigorous institutions, public and private." Former Secretary of State Acheson, explaining what he meant by "total diplomacy," bemoaned the fact that America had not mobilized its "total resources" in the struggle for freedom and called for national self-discipline and unity. The secretary also stressed the fact that American society now dwells in a glass house: "Today the whole United States is acting before the world as its own representative. . . . Everything that we do or say enters into the picture of America which is seen abroad."*

George Kennan, former counselor of the State Department, former ambassador to Russia, and a distinguished foreign-policy analyst, has summarized one of the most important elements of national security in the face of the Communist danger in this way: "Few Americans are aware . . . of the beneficial effect produced on both our friends and enemies by evidence that we are seriously tackling the problems of our own society. This is not just a question of material prosperity. What the outside world is more eager to know is whether we are capable of coping with the sociological and spiritual strains placed upon us by all this abundance. It is eager to know whether we are going to be able to retain, in a mechanized environment, the individuality, the emotional tone and the civic vigor of earlier generations. . . . We will not convince others, or perhaps even ourselves, that we are protecting something precious unless we cultivate that something as assiduously as we are prepared to defend it.†" John Foster Dulles, President Eisenhower's first Secretary of State, wrote: "We cannot successfully combat Soviet Communism . . . unless we have a faith with spiritual appeal that translates itself into practices which, in our modern, complex society, get rid of the sordid, degrading conditions of life in which the spirit cannot grow."‡ In effect, one interpretation of the accumulation of broad official declarations of American foreign policy between 1945 and 1954 is that America claims to have an answer to the problems of modern man which is superior to anything Communism can offer. Therefore a basic question is, Can or will the American people practically demonstrate that they have an effective alternative to Communism both at home and abroad?

Most students of American policy agree that recent experience indicates that more is required abroad than a simple rebuttal of Soviet propaganda and praise of "the American way," important as these are. Not only must words be backed by deeds, as they were in the case of the Korean conflict and economic aid to Europe, but American values must somehow be adequately translated into terms meaningful to the daily lives of those whose life histories and situations are vastly different. On the domestic side, America is now compelled to juggle urgent internal and foreign-policy issues simultaneously. Often such issues must be handled separately by different agencies even though they are in most cases completely intertwined. Hence priorities must be set, consistency maintained, and attention paid to the adequacy and the distribution of policy-making resources. The dual task of providing an

---

* United States Department of State *Bulletin,* March 20, 1950, pp. 427–428.

† George Kennan, "Is War with Russia Inevitable?" *Reader's Digest,* March, 1950, p. 4.

‡ John Foster Dulles, *War or Peace* (New York, The Macmillan Company, 1950), p. 252.

example of real democratic living to the world and of mobilizing to fulfill foreign-policy commitments has raised extremely difficult problems for the American people. Three such problems will be discussed below.

A third implication concerns the policy-making process to which Part I of this book is devoted entirely. A reminder in the context of the present chapter is, however, necessary. As noted previously, the ultimate effectiveness of foreign policy will depend significantly on the adequacy of the machinery and of the processes by which it is formulated and executed. The burdens heaped upon policy-making resources from 1945 to 1951 are almost beyond measure. Many difficulties stem directly from the fact that America's role in international politics changed so quickly that the necessary adaptation of decision-making habits and agencies tended to lag behind policy needs. Thus full-scale reorganization of the State Department did not take place until 1949. Underlying the foreign policy-making process are certain basic elements of the American political system which were, of course, established when national requirements were quite different and when domestic affairs had top priority. It follows that every aspect of foreign-policy formation and execution must be reanalyzed now in the light of the changes outlined.

Finally, some potential dangers and pitfalls must be mentioned. An obvious one is the temptation to oversimplify and to misread the total nature of the international crisis. The foregoing analysis points up the fact that it is more than military. Another danger lies in the assumptions upon which American policy is based. It has already been suggested that assumptions are of fundamental importance and that one of the weaknesses in foreign policy prior to 1939 was the degree to which assumptions had become false or only half-true. Assumptions only partially valid open the door to a wider margin of error in national judgment. Some common assumptions relevant to current policy may be put in the form of the following selective questions. Is it to be assumed

that Communism's appeal is primarily material rather than spiritual?

that everyone who is anti-Communist or anti-Russian is prodemocratic, pro-American?

that non-Communist left-wing forces abroad are unreliable friends and allies?

that stability and recovery are more important than social reform in strategic areas?

that the chief threat to world peace is military aggression?

that the Soviet Union's behavior is aggressive rather than self-defensive?

that the phenomenon of Stalin was a repetition of the phenomenon of Hitler?

that nothing can be done to influence long-range Soviet expectations of what is going to happen in the world?

Another very subtle danger which confronts America is that its aims and motives will continue to be misunderstood and its capacity for world leadership doubted. Proposals to expel Russia from the United Nations and to wage a "preventive war," emanating from influential persons and even high government officials, have apparently lent credence to misinterpretation of American intentions. Some of the objectives of United States policy have not yet been made clear. Two possible misreadings are especially crucial: one is that the United States may inadvertently give, and occasionally has given, the impression that it is merely *using* other nations for its own purposes; the other is that the United States may *appear* to support the *status quo* in the face of legitimate need for change.

The mere possession of tremendous national strength as well as the opportunity to exercise leadership is an invitation for other nations to deliberately or otherwise distort American aims and actions. The line between playing what is commonly called "power politics" and the responsible use of power to promote international peace is neither as sharp nor as easy to draw as might be thought. Friends and enemies alike will judge American foreign policy in terms of its basic aims and its actual impact. Particularly where American economic and military power has been directly applied in areas like Western Europe, that power will be evaluated in part according to its effect upon local conditions and politics. In addition, the application of American power in the Far East will be viewed not as the American people view it, but against the backdrop of a hundred years of imperialism and culture conflict. The danger is, then, that vagueness of purposes or lack of proper self-restraint or both, may undermine the intended effects of American foreign policy.

Obvious disparity of capabilities among the Western nations has introduced a certain awkwardness in their relationships. Agreement with American policies may appear to be bought with superior influence, and domestic opposition groups in Great Britain, France, and West Germany are quick to harass their governments over real or alleged capitulations. This is particularly true because the United States has urged these nations to arm and has helped them do so, thus alienating those who fear the possible mistakes of United States policies and who wish to remain neutral in the American-Russian conflict. Though the United States bore the brunt of the Korean fighting, it had to be very careful not to offend any of its allies. In June, 1952, the United Nations Commander (an American, General Mark Clark) ordered a huge raid on Communist installations on the Korean side of the Yalu River. Evidently the move was ordered without consultation, and a storm of protest arose in the British Parliament, after which the prime minister won a test vote on the issue. Another example of the by-products of disparity in strength was provided in high-level talks between France and the United States in the spring of 1953, during which the American representatives assured the French that they were still considered a "great power."

▶ SUMMARY

Even on the basis of the preceding simplified analysis, full comprehension of the ramifications of the revolutionary change in America's international position is difficult. This chapter has suggested, however, only the major characteristics of the current transition and development of American foreign policy and has outlined some of the resulting problems and implications which will be discussed at greater length later on. The reader need not be overwhelmed by this complexity if he holds to the following main line of argument. America's entrance into World War II formally marked either the total obsolescence or the extensive alteration of traditional bases of policy. Given the nature of the war and the conditions which followed it, a redefinition of national security and of national interest was inevitable. When it became clear that the unity and cooperation of the winning coalition was not to continue intact through the peacemaking period, America's difficulties multiplied and its responsibilities became proportionately greater. The uncertainties which usually accompany the liquidation of international conflict were intensified. The unprecedented problems which had to be faced required new policies and techniques. In a very short time and despite inexperience as an active great power, America accepted an enormous challenge and pledged herself to heavy commitments. Costs have been high and choices hard.

Inconsistencies, painful dilemmas, and bewildering reversals of policy have been a national by-product. Within the space of seven or eight years it has seemed to many citizens of the United States that their foreign relations have turned upside down. America fought Japan in alliance with China; recently Japan has become an ally and American troops have fought Chinese troops in Korea. After spending four years, 589,000 casualties, and billions of dollars to defeat Germany, the United States was later urging the rearmament of Germany. Russia was an ally in World War II and received billions in Lend-Lease aid only to emerge as a threat to the United States. Yugoslavia, a Communist-controlled country which shot down American planes in 1946, was receiving American aid in 1951.

America has reacted positively, and has made certain adjustments to this period of crisis in its external relations. To understand how this has taken place and what its effect upon America and its foreign policy has been, this chapter considered three factors: first, the external setting—including the way in which American security is affected by the behavior of other states, the distribution of national capabilities, technological developments, ideology, and world-wide social trends; second, the response of the United States to this new setting as well as the impact of the United States upon it—including general objectives and an estimate of the capacity which can be brought to bear on these objectives as determined by the nature of American society and its decision-making mechanism; and third, the more obvious problems and implications which arise from the pursuit of new aims under new conditions.

► SELECTED BIBLIOGRAPHY

Chapters 1–4 of Nathaniel Peffer's *America's Place in the World* (New York, The Viking Press, 1945) provide a clear understanding of how America lost its immunity from world politics and what kinds of choices confronted it after World War II. The new international position of the United States is briefly and graphically portrayed in the following: William G. Carleton, *The Revolution in American Foreign Policy*, "Doubleday Short Studies in Political Science" (New York, Doubleday & Company, 1954); The Brookings Institution, *Major Problems of U.S. Foreign Policy 1952–1953* (Washington, D.C., The Brookings Institution, 1953), Chap. 2; Walter Lippmann, *Isolation and Alliances* (Boston, Little, Brown & Company, 1952), pp. 31 ff.; and Joseph Roucek and associates, *Introduction to Political Science* (New York, The Thomas Y. Crowell Company, 1950), Chap. 21. The critical survey of fifty years of foreign policy by George Kennan, in his *American Diplomacy, 1900–1950* (Chicago, The University of Chicago Press, 1951), should be read in conjunction with the generalization offered early in this chapter. Walter Lippmann's *The Cold War: A Study in U.S. Foreign Policy* (New York, Harper & Brothers, 1947) can still be read profitably along with "Sources of Soviet Conduct" by X (reputedly George Kennan), reprinted in Hamilton Fish Armstrong, editor, *The Foreign Affairs Reader* (New York, Council on Foreign Relations, 1947). Mr. Lippmann also spells out some of the points in this chapter in a provocative essay entitled "Break-up of the Two-Power World," *Atlantic Monthly*, April, 1950. William A. Williams, in *American-Russian Relations, 1781–1947* (New York, Rinehart & Company, 1952), argues that there has been a mutuality of interest between the United States and Russia since the earliest times, and he opposes the American policy of "containment" as too inflexible. Harold and Margaret Sprout, *Foundations of National Power* (2d ed.; New York, D. Van Nostrand Company, 1951), discuss aspects of American capabilities (pp. 915–944) and implications of atomic weapons (pp. 743–761). Two books, though somewhat dated, are still worth consulting: Hanson Baldwin, *The Price of Power* (New York, Harper & Brothers, 1948) and Robert Strausz-Hupé, *The Balance of Tomorrow* (New York, G. P. Putnam's Sons, 1945). A recent article by Mr. Baldwin, military analyst of the New York *Times*, "What Kind of Defense in the Atomic Age," *New York Times Magazine*, May 17, 1953, focuses attention on problems of security planning in the light of new weapons. W. G. Carleton discusses the role of ideology in foreign policy in "Ideology or Balance of Power," *The Yale Review*, June, 1947. Two thought-provoking articles by Raymond Fosdick, "We Are Living in Two Centuries," *New York Times Magazine*, November 24, 1946, and "We Must Not Be Afraid of Change," *New York Times Magazine*, April 3, 1949, explore the effects of the discrepancy between eighteenth-century thinking and twentieth-century reality and of social change on international politics and foreign policy. A very useful analysis of some implications of the ideological conflict between Russia and America is contained in G. T. Robinson, "The Ideological Combat," *Foreign Affairs,* July, 1949. A comprehensive analysis of the economic problems which have arisen because of the burdens of fighting aggression on a broad front is to be found in Jules Backman and others, *War and Defense Economics* (New York, Rinehart & Company, 1952).

PART ONE

STRUCTURE AND PROCESSES OF AMERICAN FOREIGN POLICY-MAKING

CHAPTER THREE

THE DECISION-MAKING PROCESS

Introduction • The Decision-Making Approach • Elements of the Decision-Making Process • Personality and Decision Making • Limitations on Decision Making • Some Outstanding Characteristics of Decision Making in the United States • Conclusion • Selected Bibliography

► INTRODUCTION

It is quite probable that the average citizen is more interested in whether a decision is "right" or "wrong" and in the way a decision affects him and his fellow citizens than he is in how it was made. This is, all things considered, understandable. The connection between *what is done* and *how it is done* in foreign policy is rarely obvious, and when it is, the full implications are likely to escape the casual observer. Furthermore, trying to find out *who* made a decision can be a frustrating experience indeed. In the present period, Americans have been treated to a rather constant bombardment of typical statements as that *the late President Roosevelt* "sold out" to the Russians at the Yalta Conference of 1944; that *a small group in the State Department* stabbed the Chinese Nationalist government in the back in favor of the Communist regime; that *former President Truman* sabotaged bipartisanship in the making of foreign policy after the 1948 election; that *a group of congressmen* undercut the State Department's policy by legislating a loan to Franco Spain; that *former Secretary of State Acheson* was responsible for the shedding of so much American blood in Korea; that *members of a group located in various executive agencies* were guilty of a "soft" policy toward the Soviet Union at critical points in the postwar period; and that General MacArthur was relieved of his United Nations command in Korea because *he* tried to make policy as well as execute it. These statements (they appeared in many forms and the themes were subject to wide variation) ranged from allegations of fact to "charges" and judgments of praise or blame. But the nature of such statements is of no relevance for the moment. Rather, the point is that the question of who was responsible for a decision tends to be widely discussed only when an argument rages over whether the decision was right or wrong, good or bad. Then it is that ignorance and misconceptions of policy making become particularly important. In the absence of

89

reasonably precise understanding and knowledge, explanations which are simple, handy, and superficially convincing carry great weight.

While the average citizen cannot be held entirely to blame for his confusion and lack of interest in the face of what must appear to him to be an elusive mixture of appearance and reality, order and disorder, the student of foreign policy cannot back away from the necessity of tackling this complicated subject. For decision making is a complex process and so is its analysis, especially when it must be done at long range. The study of decision making is difficult for several reasons. In the first place, examination of the formal machinery and the constitutionally prescribed allocation of power and duties is not enough. It provides only a skeleton of the *structure* of decision making. It will reveal who does what if all the rules and formalities are adhered to, but it is not always a reliable guide for determining how the system actually operates. A good many of the rules which are followed are the result of custom, of precedents; they are understood and obeyed but they are nowhere written down and they often function alongside of, or in place of, formal rules. Furthermore, patterns of decision-making practice develop which cannot be predicted from a knowledge of the formal structure alone. In the second place, particularly in crisis situations, important aspects of policy-making procedures are deliberately kept secret. Throwing up a screen to prevent vital information from falling into the wrong hands or to avoid misinterpretation inevitably conceals much which an observer needs to know in order to follow a line of foreign-policy action through from start to finish. Again, sometimes even the decision makers do not have a complete picture of what is going on. They do not all keep diaries, nor are they necessarily self-conscious about the procedural matters which would interest an outside student—being, of course, preoccupied with getting their jobs done. Memories cannot be trusted entirely. Moreover, only persons very strategically placed in the process are able to get anything like a total view of what happens. Finally, the process by which decisions are arrived at in any form of human endeavor is usually a subtle one and in an organizational setting is both subtle and complicated, partly because of the sheer number of factors involved. The very obscurity of what goes on constitutes, on one hand, a temptation to oversimplify, in which case crucial factors may be overlooked, or, on the other, an invitation to look into everything from personal gestures in a conference to the arrangement of offices, in which case it is difficult to say what factors are really crucial.

It has already been suggested that to focus attention on official decision makers and their activities is a convenient and fruitful way of approaching the study of state behavior and foreign policy. To ignore the substance of policy or the actions of states, however, would be absurd. The organization and process of decision making and the content of policy are inseparable. Each influences the other and each provides valuable clues in the analysis of the other. In addition, decision making is a basic factor in national capabilities in two respects. First, it is through the decision-making process that national capacity to achieve objectives is estimated, generated, and applied. Second, the strengths and weaknesses of a nation's policy formation and execution are vital ingredients in its total capability. At the present time, when the American people are debating the proper role of various agencies and are anxious about faulty policies, it is necessary that the student have some basis for judging the techniques which yield effective, responsible, mature decisions. The purposes of this chapter are therefore to explore what is involved in foreign-policy decision making and how decision making may appear to the decision makers themselves, and to comment in a preliminary way on the major characteristics of decision making in the United States. To the extent that these purposes are realized, the imposing array of structural features and processes to be presented in the next ten chapters may make more sense and may be somewhat easier to analyze.

Obviously, decisions are made by fallible human beings subject in their deliberations to many kinds of forces. Since the human behavior of concern here ranges from the statesmanlike acts of a Roosevelt or a Churchill to the routine functions of anonymous bureaucrats, two roads of description and analysis beckon: the humanistic and the deterministic. The former tends to stress the impact of the unique individual on history, the man of energy and genius who reroutes the stream of destiny. The latter tends to view men as prisoners of circumstances, as bound to a predetermined course of events, trapped by myths, processes, and institutions, and swept along by irresistible tides. Both are useful approaches, but the insistence upon either one or the other leads to the neglect of additional factors which are known to condition the lives of all men. Neither the Great Leader nor the unknown division chief in government escapes the influence of such factors. Though what follows must perforce be an abstraction from reality, let Harold Nicolson's warning be remembered: "Do not underestimate the influence of the incidental and fortuitous in the lives of men. As men perform their official functions, as they act out their roles as policy-makers they are affected by personal friction—vague dislikes of, and shades of incompatibility with, those with whom they must associate; by friendship and loyalties which transcend rules and color judgments of opinions; by ill health—bringing its distortions of perception and drain upon the reservoir of patience; by impulse—the momentary overwhelming of reason and experience; and by the alternating fluctuations of energy and passivity which may or may not coincide with need."* These factors, and others related to them, make it significant that, say, Mr. J. was at a conference while Mr. W. was not, that a meeting was held at night rather than in the morning, and that the order of items on some agenda was arranged in one way rather than in another.

The possible relevance of such factors becomes clearer if one asks

---

* See the stimulating article by this renowned scholar of diplomacy, Harold Nicolson. "Men and Circumstances." *Foreign Affairs,* April. 1945, p. 476.

searching questions about a given decision: Who made the decision? How many persons participated? By what method was it reached—conference, telephone conversation, or exchange of memoranda? What and how many alternatives were considered? How accurate and how complete was the information available? How was it interpreted? What values were operative? What expectations of consequences were entertained? Were limitations on knowledge and situations beyond control consciously faced? Who among the participants was most influential? Why? What patterns of interpersonal relationships conditioned the decision? Was the reaction of the participants to the decision one of shared doubt, certainty, satisfaction, or dissatisfaction? What was the attitude of those who had to execute the decision? Was there a common understanding of what had been decided?

► THE DECISION-MAKING APPROACH

WHO ARE THE DECISION MAKERS?

Clearly, it would be awkward and confusing to include *all* persons employed in any governmental agency or body which might make foreign-policy decisions or otherwise participate in the conduct of foreign affairs. If carried to the logical extreme, this would require calling file clerks and stenographers "decision makers." Nor is it necessary to include, automatically, those who perform other minor functions related to decision making—professional and technical personnel lower down in the civil service classification system. While it is impossible to draw a precise line which would be satisfactory indefinitely, the list of potential decision makers can be said to embrace those who are empowered to make or carry out decisions, who are held responsible for official acts; those whose duties require them to formulate policies and to plan for the execution of policies on behalf of those who are held responsible; and, finally, those whose functions directly or indirectly influence the other two groups. Hence the members of Congress, and members of Congressional committee staffs, and a large number of Executive Branch personnel from the President on down would be included. For the sake of completeness, the Supreme Court must also be added. These are the decision makers. But not all of these officials will participate in all decisions. Not all of them are daily engaged in the wide variety of foreign-policy functions. Therefore the answer to the question, Who are decision makers? is this: A group of officials as just specified who *may* be involved in a particular decision and who *may* be continuously occupied with some phase of foreign relations. Naturally a core of such officials in the Congress and particularly in the Executive Branch will always be directly or indirectly involved in matters of vital importance. The President, the Secretary of State, and other top officials of the State Department as well as key members of the Senate Foreign Relations Committee would be in this category. Furthermore, the performance of certain policy-related functions such as collection of information continues, whether a decision is under consideration or not.

Included in the core of officials who more or less constantly add to the total number of foreign-policy decisions in being or in process are those whose responsibilities appear to be relatively minor and routine. Generally these lower-level officials act on a daily basis, making spot decisions either on the basis of precedent or, perhaps, without any clear rules for guidance. Any one of these decisions may not be significant in itself, but an accumulation of day-to-day decisions could be very crucial in shaping the conditions under which a future top-level decision must be made. For example, suppose an extensive revolt breaks out in Bolivia. The official sitting at the Bolivian desk of the Inter-American Affairs Division of the State Department answers a request for instructions from the American embassy by ordering an expression of American sympathy and support for the incumbent government. In the event of a smashing victory by the rebels, the United States would be somewhat embarrassed in its dealings with the new government.

THE UNIT OF DECISION

In order to determine which officials are to be considered as decision makers and hence to be acting for the United States, it is helpful to think in terms of a separate unit for each decision. The unit may be the State Department or a subgroup thereof—a division, an office, or a committee, an interdepartmental committee, the National Security Council, an *ad hoc* group called together by the President, Congress as a whole or one of its committees. Thus the unit is comprised of the major participants and contributors for a particular decision. If the import duty on shoes were lowered, the unit would be the Trade Agreements Committee made up of representatives from the State Department, the Commerce Department, and several other interested agencies. If the amount of money to be spent on foreign aid were reduced as a result of Congressional action, the most likely unit would be the Senate Foreign Relations Committee, the House Foreign Affairs Committee, or the Appropriations Committee of either chamber.

Now in these and similar cases, the unit which made a decision is easily identifiable. In point of fact, however, major policies more often than not *evolve* essentially through a *series of units*. The Marshall Plan began in a small planning group in the State Department and ended as a complex statute following hours of Congressional hearings and debate. Any one unit could be chosen for study, or the evolution from unit to unit might be analyzed. In the latter instance, the end product could be viewed as resulting from a series of decisions. Within any unit, the final product could likewise be viewed as the result of a series of preliminary decisions. Whichever way is necessary or convenient—to speak of the decision of a single unit or of a decision which evolved through the contributory decisions of several units—

it is possible to lay down a few propositions about their nature which will apply to both.

THE SETTING OF THE UNIT OF DECISION

It should be made clear at this point that the decision makers carry on their activities in a *setting* which has an internal and an external aspect. When it is said that a unit of decision has internal and external settings, this is simply a way of alerting attention to those factors and conditions outside the relationships and activities of the decision makers themselves which are relevant to their behavior. Thus far, internal setting and external setting have been equated with, respectively, the society for which the decision makers act and the universe beyond the state's frontiers. Two qualifications now need to be added. First, American officials in the United Nations or any of its agencies as well as in various diplomatic establishments abroad can be regarded as part of the total government organization out of which units for particular decisions are formed. But the foreign decision makers with whom Americans negotiate should be regarded as part of the external setting, i.e., as acting for other states. Second, the notion of internal setting should be broadened to include for any single unit of decision in the federal government other units, agencies, or individual officials. To illustrate, suppose the unit is the State Department; only certain officials of that department constitute the unit. Yet other officials in the total list of decision makers may be very important. The President himself or one of his staff, the Defense Department, the Foreign Operations Administration, the Congress as a whole or any of its key foreign-policy committees or individual senators or representatives—these and others should be regarded as potentially significant factors in the internal setting in which the State Department makes its decisions. Such other units and individuals will constitute a source of limitations and cues as will be demonstrated later on in the chapter.

A DEFINITION OF DECISION MAKING

Decision making is a process in which the activities of duly authorized officials result in a selection of one from a number of possible or available courses of action, and also result in the application of selected possible or available means to the attainment of one or more selected ends. Several terms in the definition deserve a world of explanation. The emphasis on *process* is important. A decision is not an isolated act but is the climax of a whole set of interrelated acts, one supplementing the other. *Activities* include fact finding and reporting, evaluation and analysis, discussion and argument, negotiation and compromise, coordination and communication—subsuming, of course, all activities upon which these in turn depend. *Selection* points to the central ingredient of choice—not random, grab-bag choice, but choice following deliberation and calculation. *Possible or available* is inserted in the definition as a reminder that the range of alternative means and ends which comprise a course of action is never unlimited. Alternative goals may be desired yet not feasible; possible, yet not advisable; obvious to an outside observer, yet not perceived by the decision makers. Alternative means to an end or a cluster of ends may be effective, yet not available; available, yet not possible to employ.

It is necessary to differentiate the decision-making process from the "administration of foreign affairs," which in common usage includes the execution of policy, maintenance of routine functions, and performance of nondecisional tasks. One large section of the State Department, for instance, is concerned simply with the efficient operation of the organization, not with policy making per se. It is also necessary to take note of decision making which though it does not yield foreign policy has a direct bearing on how policy is made, namely, *the decisions about who is to decide*. Often the unit of decision and the decision makers in particular cases are the result of deliberate choices. Almost hourly in the State Department it is being decided who will handle certain matters. Congress has frequently been excluded from the decision-making process as the result of a Presidential decision to negotiate an executive agreement rather than a treaty which would require approval by the Senate. In 1951, John Foster Dulles was brought into the State Department and given sole responsibility for drafting and negotiating the Japanese Peace Treaty. Normally, the treaty would have been the responsibility of officers working under the direction of the Assistant Secretary of State for Far Eastern Affairs. While "who decides" is determined in part by formal rules, the unit which emerges for a particular decision or the series of units which emerge may be the result of considerable pulling and hauling, especially when the rules are not clear.

THE STAGES OF DECISION MAKING

For analytical purposes, five rough stages in the process can be noted. First, there is the occasion for decision when the need for a course of action is recognized by the appropriate officials. The occasion may arise from within a unit, that is, from planning and discussion. In this case, recognition of a problem or situation is largely spontaneous. Events, conditions, and the actions of other states may also provide the occasion for decision, in which case the necessity to decide is more or less forced on the decision makers. The most graphic illustration of the two cases can be seen in the contrast between the invasion of South Korea in June, 1950, which forced a choice on the United States, and the various military aid agreements negotiated with Latin-American republics in 1952–1953, which were not occasioned by any drastic change in the external setting but were basically anticipatory. Second, the question presented for decision will be further defined and analyzed, including some appraisal of the national interest involved and such predecisional planning as is undertaken. At the third stage, preliminary recommendations will be drafted and circulated to the responsible and interested officials both inside and outside the unit. The next stage is one in which criticisms, omitted considerations, and suggested modifications are filtered through the preliminary recommendations. Finally a decision is made. Naturally, decision making does not end here. To translate a general policy statement into a concrete program or to actually follow through when the type of action is specified in the decision requires that further choices be made all along the line. If it is decided, for example, to aid nations menaced by aggression, other questions remain: What kind of aid? Under what kinds of circumstances? How much aid? How can the aid be provided?

Stage five is the decision point, legally, because a recommendation by, say, the Secretary of State to the President is not officially a policy decision until the President or someone acting in his name formally approves and initials it. An agency or an individual may be said to have *originated* a recommendation or to have *initiated* a decision, but, strictly speaking, a decision is not officially taken unless it is backed up by governmental power or is ultimately accepted by the President. The President may or may not openly take a stand; even if he does not, presumably a decision may still become official. A decision, although not made by President or announced by him, will continue to prevail until he reverses or otherwise modifies it. This fact frequently causes newspapermen, congressmen, and foreign diplomats to inquire directly of the President whether a particular decision has been made and is the policy of the United States. In most cases decisions emanating from the Executive Branch will come from officials acting on authority granted to the President. Hence it is permissible to say that someone besides the President himself "made" a decision or that in the predecisional stages someone or some agency was primarily influential in shaping the content of a decision.

DECISION MAKING TAKES PLACE IN AN ORGANIZATIONAL CONTEXT

The units of decision referred to should be regarded as organizations regardless of how small the number of officials included. Thus the over-all foreing-policy decision-making organization of the United States consists of all the agencies and individuals who might participate in an actual decision, who carry on some phase of the activities which characterize the process, or who do both. Each unit is an organization in itself and each unit is a component of the total policy-making structure. However, the purpose in calling the unit of decision an organization is to highlight an important set of factors in foreign-policy making. Activities and relationships within any unit will be greatly conditioned by formal rules and precedent. For most of the officials, their membership in the unit constitutes a livelihood. Most of the functions essential to decision making will be performed by professionals, specialists who owe their membership to demonstrated competence. Division of labor and specialization will be highly developed. Regardless of individual whims and temporary departures, decision-making activities will be largely according to "system." To put all this another way: the decision-making process will be to a great extent "bureaucratized." Explanations of the behavior of states commonly minimize or ignore entirely the impact of organizational factors on decision makers. This is especially true when the "great man" theory is emphasized or when the head of the foreign office is discussed as though he were acting all by himself. Organization implies a high degree of formalized relationships among the members, which is one reason why decision making in governmental units is likely to be quite different from decision making in small, informal groups.

Organization can be ignored more or less

THE NATURE OF DECISIONS

Beyond saying that a decision is the result of a calculated choice among alternative objectives and techniques, it is not easy to be more specific. Yet if decision making is to be meaningfully analyzed, some effort at clarification is necessary. An official decision may be said to represent an authoritative cluster of expectations concerning the pattern and consequences of future action. The objective implicit in any action may be described as the decision makers' image of a future state of affairs. A future state of affairs will have several components. First, there will be a fairly specific target, to borrow a military term, i.e., a raising of the standard of living in France as a result of economic aid. Second, there will be a general orientation—a conviction that the achievement of the target will be in the direction of world peace and recovery and that the action supplements other foreign-policy plans such as the integration of Western Europe. Third, there will be expectations concerning other conditions and relationships in the external setting, such as heightened resistance to communist appeals inside France and greater immunity to Soviet pressures. Finally, there will be a time strategy—aid is projected for a five- or six-year period and concrete results will be evident within that period, while other beneficial results are hoped for ultimately at some unspecified time. Thus when decision makers decide on a course of action (whether it be a simple declaration or a complicated alliance) they will have some sort of mental picture of the actual changes to be brought about when the action is completed. The changes are not always precisely envisaged. In one sense a decision can be likened to a prediction by officials of what will happen when a pattern of future action has unfolded.

As already noted, decisions must be implemented. More often than not, those officials who help to make decisions do not participate extensively in the series of subsequent actions, each of which may involve new decisions. Actually, the execution of a decision represents a process whereby general objectives and policy guides become more and more specific and concrete. During this process, original aims may be reinterpreted, distorted, or otherwise altered. It is only by a succession of "how" decisions that a broad policy decision receives genuine substance. Viewed in this light, any distinction between "policy formation" and "administration" is artificial. Actions taken far down the line of authority from the point of original decision, though apparently of a routine nature, may have a great deal of influence on the concrete policy which emerges. Therefore, the preceding discussion of the elements of decision making would also apply to decisions concerning implementation. What may be called the "administration of decisions" will include allocation of power and responsibility, choice making, information, coordination, communication, and so on. The characteristics of decision making presented immediately below will also apply in large part to the subsequent decisions which comprise "execution."

KINDS OF DECISIONS

The process of decision making cannot be fully understood or evaluated without recognizing different types of decisions. Several types have already been implied: objectives—general or specific, short-term and long-term—and priorities among objectives; decisions on techniques and execution; decisions to act or not to act; and decisions forced or shaped by the accumulation of previous decisions (including precedent).

Those referred to by the term "policy decisions" are a very important class of decisions. Policy may be defined as action or rules, or both, to guide future action. A literal application of the definition here would make "policy decisions" a partially redundant phrase. To avoid confusion, it can be said that a policy decision is a special type wherein the course of action decided on by the decision makers is to agree on a set of rules for the interpretation of future events, for the solution of typical recurring problems, or for guidance in the selection of future objectives and techniques. Sometimes a policy declaration may embrace all three. For example, the now famous "containment policy" initially meant that certain acts of the Soviet Union would henceforth be regarded as aggressive and threatening, that when such acts occurred they were to be opposed, and that opposition was to take the form of positive acts on the part of the United States.

Another basic distinction is between *major* and *minor* decisions. The difference can be measured by the following standards: the extent to which the decision makers regarded a decision as crucial for national security and anticipated a high degree of change in the future situation; the cost of decision making in resources, money, and possibly lives; the amount of public interest and discussion aroused; the number of other nations affected by the action; the kind of risks involved; the length of time from initiation to execution; the number of top-level officials who participated. A major decision would not necessarily rank equally high in all these categories. If such criteria are applied to a concrete comparison of the North Atlantic Alliance with the Pacific Security Pact, it is clear that the former was a relatively major decision. The Atlantic Pact is a central core of security planning and strategy, it has cost the United States several billions in dollars and military supplies along with 400,000 troops to be stationed in Western Euorpe, at least six months of lively debate preceded the adoption of the policy and also accompanied its later implementation, eleven nations besides the United States are included in the alliance (the Pacific Pact includes only the United States, New Zealand, Australia, and the Philippines), and the obligations inherent in the North Atlantic Alliance confront the United States with the risk of war if any of the members are attacked.

Decisions can be classified on the basis of *who made them* or *who initiated them*. The decision to produce the hydrogen bomb was a presidential decision; the loan to Franco Spain (1950) was a Congressional decision. Closely related is the *level* on which the decision was made. The decision to intervene in Korea in July, 1950, was a top-level decision, while the program in 1942 for freezing German assets in Europe and Latin America was formulated far below the Cabinet level. Another possible distinction depends on the *number of units* drawn into a decision—how complicated the process was. The Mutual Defense Assistance Program of 1950 required the combined efforts of upward of a dozen important agencies or their subunits; the National Security Council alone recommended to the president that the United States stay in Berlin in 1948 despite the Soviet blockade. Some decisions require *subsequent decisions* of almost equal importance. The original European Recovery Program was such a decision. On the other hand, the decision to press for an enhancement of the power of the General Assembly of the United Nations in order to circumvent the exercise of veto in the Security Council stood by itself and required no further action. The *extent of planning* and the *time taken* to reach a decision provide a basis for further differentiation. Much planning went into the decision to establish a North Atlantic Alliance, while little preceded the intervention in Korea. Similarly, the evolution of the Soviet containment policy took several years, and the Truman Doctrine of 1947 was hastily decided upon over a week end. Finally, some decisions may be *highly political* and *highly controversial*. Decisions involving other nations, the powers of Congress, and sensitive "policy areas," such as China after 1949, fall into this category.

DECISION-MAKING PATTERNS

The unit of decision may be a single individual official. He may also initiate decisions. The President is probably more closely identified with this pattern than are any other officials, but the Secretary of State, the Secretary of Defense, the High Commissioner for the American Zone in Germany, and military field commanders may act individually. Individuals can make a "free decision" as an exercise of prescribed functions or as an act of mediation between several individuals or agencies. When the President makes a decision on his own—a rather rare occurrence—he will reflect the decision-making process in miniature form. When the President accepts a single recommendation, the process is already complete and he simply makes it official. When the President decides a question after listening to a group of high-level advisers discuss various alternatives, he chooses a recommendation which has itself been filtered through a process. As will be seen, policy announcements and interpretations usually come from individuals. Policy initiative often rests with individuals. However, as foreign policy issues become more numerous and complex, full-blown decisions by individuals are relatively rare.

Most major decisions are either evolved or actually decided by conference—by group discussion and personal interaction rather than by written memoranda or telephone conversations. The conference may consist of a Cabinet meeting, the President meeting with specially selected advisers, a meeting of the National Security Council, a meeting between the Secretary of State and his policy-making team, or a meeting of a special committee established to deal with particular problems. While a single individual may himself go through the decision-making process as defined, the conference pattern combines the elements of the process differently and may lead to different results. The fact that the major decisions of American foreign policy formulated in the Executive Branch during the last six years have been largely group products suggests that the conference may be a more thorough, deliberate, and generally safer method. It is also to be noted that conferences may be climaxed by a vote among the participants, by an agreement on "the sense of the meeting," Quaker style, or by a decision of the chairman (if he is a responsible official), choosing from or rejecting proposals submitted.

The diaries and memoirs of high-level officials have revealed how difficult it is to determine precisely what happens at a decision-making conference. Participants do not always agree on who said what with what effect, nor do they always agree on what was decided. In the absence of a recorded vote or a definite stand by the chairman, decisions may be subjected later to misinterpretation and second-guessing. For this reason (there are others, of course) decisions can come "unglued," especially in view of their composite nature. If the viewpoint of a key person is not in fact integrated into a decision, it may mean later withdrawal or weakening of an essential ingredient. "This is not what I agreed to" is a familiar response of conferees after they hear an official announcement of what they were supposed to have decided.

Another kind of pattern is a decision made or formulated by a single unit such as the State Department or the Economic Cooperation Administration. Within a unit several subpatterns may characterize decision making. If a decision is more or less routine and involves no peculiar problems, it may work its way up the hierarchy of authority, each official adding his contribution to the final product. The head of an agency or one of the top command may assign a problem to a subordinate unit for recommendations. When a decision requires the coordination of different agencies in the unit, a temporary committee may be created.

A fourth pattern is interunit collaboration, the number ranging from two to as many as are necessary. Again, the four elements of the decision-making process will operate, but with the likelihood of different problems and different results. Problems of communication, coordination, conflicts of viewpoints, and jurisdiction tend to be intensified. A great deal depends on the form of the collaboration. Thus interunit collaboration through the National Security Council will differ in many respects from collaboration through an interdepartmental committee. The former is undertaken by high-level officials (Cabinet members and presidential advisers), while the latter are staffed by subordinates who cannot always speak with authority. Inter-agency collaboration in the Executive Branch must be distinguished from interagency collaboration between the executive and legislative branches. In the latter case, problems of coordination and communication tend to be even more difficult, greater time is consumed, decisions are often more political in nature, and ordinarily more subsequent decisions are required.

Correlating the types of decisions with the patterns outlined, two generalizations can be made. Major decisions will tend to require interunit collaboration among a substantial number of units, heavy use of the conference method, extensive planning or predecisional preparation, decision at higher levels, and more delicate handling because of their political nature. Contrariwise, minor decisions tend to involve relatively more opportunity for individual initiative and decision making, less interagency collaboration, less planning, decision making at lower levels, and issues that are not highly political. Though these are broad generalizations, they serve to point up the connection between the content of a decision and how it is made and between the kind of decision and who made it.

► ELEMENTS OF THE DECISION-MAKING PROCESS

Decision making has been defined as a complex process. In the absence of a sufficient number of case histories from which the major components of the process can be derived, it is necessary to designate arbitrarily some rough categories which will identify the phenomena to be studied. Decision-making activity is determined by the following: formal allocation of power and responsibility, motivation, communication and coordination, and information and intellectual skills.

FORMAL ALLOCATION OF POWER AND RESPONSIBILITY

For decision making to take place, certain persons must be empowered to act and must act under certain conditions, duties and responsibilities must be assigned, and orders must be obeyed. Every unit of decision will thus have a "table of organization" which provides an answer to the general question, Who is supposed to do what, when and how? In short, every unit of decision will consist of officials who play various roles, role in this case including powers which are exercised, influence which is exerted, and functions which are performed according to rules. These roles will, of course, be related. The roles and their relationships give decision making a structure Thus the total structure of foreign-policy decision making in the United States is the total set of relevant roles and the way they are related to each other. One purpose of the next nine chapters is to sketch in the structure of decision making in this sense.

Allocation of power and responsibility prevails *among* units of decision as well as *within* them. Hence one speaks of the general role of Congress—the power it has, the influence it can exert, the functions it performs vis-à-vis other units. And one speaks of the role of key committees, chairmen, and individual congressmen in the decision-making process internal to Congress. Similarly, one may speak of the general role of the Executive Branch and also of the role of the President, the State Department, and so on. Within the State Department, to chose one particular unit of the Executive Branch, one may speak of the role of the secretary and other responsible officials. It is impossible to reconstruct the decision-making process within a unit or when participated in by two or more units without some knowledge of the way roles are related. For example, the Secretary of State may be relieved of all responsibility for certain kinds of decisions by delegating power to subordinates, who then will act in the expectation that the secretary will not, and that he will accept their judgment and will concentrate on certain matters knowing that they will act on others. If the State Department and the Congress are jointly involved in a decision, the exercise of power and the discharge of functions by each will be conditioned by the other. To take an extreme case, Congress could cut off all funds from the State Department but would be unable itself to take over the responsibilities. There are expectations on both sides concerning the continued discharge of functions.

Evidence of the formal allocation of power and responsibility—the structure of decision making—is found in constitutional prescriptions (written and unwritten or customary), court decisions, statutes, executive orders from the White House, civil service job descriptions, administrative rulings, and operating codes adopted by Congress and individual executive agencies. Two things must be said about these rules of procedure which constitute the structure of decision making. First, not all the rules are written down anywhere. What the decision makers in the State Department do and how they interact with each other to accomplish the missions of the department will be explained only in part by reference to the original Congressional act which created this agency, to the successive amendments to the act, to the accumulation of presidential directives, and to the department's periodically revised administrative manual. Other explanations must be sought in custom—behavior based on precedent, on the fact that officials assume they must fulfill certain functions in certain ways and that their colleagues expect them to so conduct themselves. Many of the most crucial relationships among decision makers will depend on well-established habit, but will nonetheless be just as binding as written rules. George Washington met once with the Senate Foreign Relations Committee in its chambers and never did thereafter; nor has any President since. No written rule prevents it; it simply is not done.

Second, written provisions are often quite general in form and therefore are inadequate guides to behavior in specific situations. One result is that more precise allocations are spelled out as these situations arise. As noted, decisions on who will decide what help to shape the decision-making process. Such decisions also stand as interpretations of the general rules which guide the exercise of power and discharge of functions. For example, the Constitution speaks of the "advice and consent" of the Senate with respect to many matters; yet what this means and the form it is to take depend on negotiation among the Senate Foreign Relations Committee, the President and the Secretary of State. Articles 5 and 11 of the North Atlantic Treaty (approved by a two-thirds vote in the Senate) can be viewed as evidence of a more precise allocation of power and responsibility between Congress and the President in a particular case. Again, to take the example of the Japanese Peace Treaty, the Defense Department by its officially prescribed responsibilities naturally had an important share in the decisions which finally emerged because the treaty was closely bound up with national security and because arrangements had to be made concerning the stationing of American troops in Japan. But the division of responsibility which emerged during the course of the treaty's development resulted from agreement between officials of the Defense and State Departments.

It follows from the nature of the rules which constitute the formal structure of decision making within and between units that the various roles are subject to different interpretations by the persons who occupy them. That is, while there will be basic functions typical of any role, functions may be added or subtracted and methods of discharging functions may be altered, depending on what person is involved. One chairman of the Senate Foreign Relations Committee may regard himself primarily as a spokesman for the President, whereas another may feel he has to protect Congress from inroads by the Executive Branch. One Secretary of State may interpret his role as distinctly subordinate to that of the President, but another may attempt to act as a check upon the President. Roles in a particular unit of decision or among decision makers generally will vary greatly in the extent to which they can be altered by interpretation; moreover, whether or not opportunities for discretionary action are taken advantage of will depend in part on the personalities of individual officials. An aggressive (in the best sense), dynamic, imaginative type of personality, for example, will tend to interpret broadly the rules governing a position.

The concept of a formal structure of decision making based on the allocation of power and responsibility directs attention to factors which may be highly significant in determining the behavior of decision makers. Are allocations clear-cut or ambiguous? If ambiguous, greater negotiation and conflict among decision makers can be expected. Are assignments of responsibility general or specific? Presumably, the more general the character of allocations (which really means that roles are not well defined in all respects), the more opportunity there will be for discretionary action, and therefore uncertainty in decision making will be more likely. Do allocations permit overlapping jurisdictions? The conditions under which power and responsibility are divided and shared will be one of the important clues to possible conflict in any decision-making unit and between units. Do allocations tend to support relatively centralized or decentralized decision-making processes? A relatively decentralized structure is one in which power is rather widely diffused instead of being exercised at the top of the hierarchy. In such a structure, presumably more voluntary coordination is required and conflicts are settled less quickly.

A serious problem arises when there is a discrepancy between power and responsibility—a situation in which an agency or an individual has been assigned responsibilities which cannot be fully discharged for lack of adequate power. This situation exists with reference to certain aspects of the role of the President. Under some conditions, the President may have legal power but be unable to use it; under others, he may not have legal power but can achieve his ends through political power or influence. In any event, if there is a discrepancy, real or imagined, between responsibility and power, it will condition the behavior of policy makers. It intensifies the difficulties which the executive agencies face of having to estimate whether they can act and how far they can go. This is a characteristic of a relatively decentralized system.

MOTIVATION

Why do states behave as they do? Answers to this general question depend in part on an inquiry into the motivation of the duly constituted individuals who carry on the decision-making process and hence act for the state. Probing motivation is one of the trickiest aspects of observing human behavior generally. There is a good deal of so-called common-sense knowledge of what moves people to act as they do, but it is not always complete or reliable. Much of the discussion of the motives of policy makers is on a similar plane. One hears it said, for example, that a particular group of policy makers is driven by an insatiable desire for power. It may be alleged that a given individual is motivated mainly by personal ambition. Again, an agency is said to be moved by the need to survive or to expand its operations. A senator is believed to be governed by a desire to be re-elected. A diplomatic representative's behavior is explained by his having been an army officer or a businessman. Party affiliations, domestic and foreign, are believed to transcend allegiance to the nation in some instances. All of these kinds of explanations may be true in particular cases at particular times, and this list falls far short of exhausting the wide range of factors which may determine motivation.

The term "motivation" as used here refers to a set of tendencies on the part of decision makers to approach the need for state action in a certain way—to define their situation by selecting certain conditions and factors as relevant, by making evaluative judgments, by expending proportionate energy and resources on various programs, by establishing objectives and priorities among objectives, and by selecting appropriate means. There is obviously no simple, foolproof method for accounting for such tendencies. What can be done is to set forth several categories of factors which might throw some light on the motives of those who act for the nation.

1. *The functions and goals of the unit of decision making.* A decision maker will be influenced by his organizational affiliation. Organization functions relevant to motivation might range from the general (i.e., foreign-policy making in the case of the State Department or the maintenance of national defense in the case of the Defense Department) to the specific (i.e., rendering of some specialized service such as intelligence reports, diplomatic representation, or advice on economic matters). To take a somewhat different case, the congressman will be moved in part by what Congress conceives to be its role in the foreign-policy-making process, and by the need to represent constituents and organized groups. It appears likely that the lower a decision maker is in the hierarchy, the less significant organizational goals will be. Particular plans and projects of the unit also exert motivational pull. Thus the "containment of Soviet power," once accepted, became a crucial factor in the future tendencies of decision makers.

2. *Other factors internal to the unit of decision making.* By the same token, decision makers may be motivated by factors which have nothing to do with organizational goals per se, but arise from the rules and values accepted with organizational membership. An individual official may respond to the rewards appropriate to his position, to his particular role in the organization, to the expectations of his colleagues, to the necessity to "buck for promotion," to pressures to conform and appear knowledgeable, and a host of similar influences. A senator on the Foreign Relations Committee will be governed somewhat by committee procedures and its interpersonal relations as well as by the committee's staff. The military officer and the Foreign Service officer will be subject to the close associations of close-knit professional groups.

Tradition—the cumulative effect of a unit's decision-making activities over time—must be included under this heading. The formation of traditional outlooks or ways of viewing things which is imputed to bureaucracy is a case in point. It could be said of the State Department before 1941 that it viewed itself as an agency apart—isolated from the hurly-burly of the political process. Clustered around the tradition of isolation were several tendencies which undoubtedly motivated its staff. One was a resistance to basic changes in administrative procedures which in turn shaped the substance of decisions. Only in the late 1930's was the vital importance of economic factors recognized in structural changes of the department's organization. Organizations have memories in the form of personnel whose long employment makes them repositories of precedent which can never quite be disregarded. Precedent is a strong motivational force. An organization learns from experience and in some manner reviews the progress of its courses of action. There is little doubt that American officials who had to negotiate in person with Soviet officials from 1947 to 1951 were motivated somewhat differently toward Soviet policy than were officials who did not share the experience. Neither is there any doubt that the motives of State Department officials changed under the impact of continuous charges of disloyalty after 1950. In order to avoid such charges, officials shifted their judgment of certain factors in the external setting, and their tendencies toward certain kinds of action were altered accordingly. The motives of congressmen have been conditioned by years of experience with administrative agencies. It is proper to speak of organizational experience because resulting motivational changes spread throughout to affect even members who did not share the experience directly. In a very real sense, the change in American foreign policy from support of peace by exhortation to peace by force if necessary reflected a change in American motives which grew out of reconsideration of ends and means and awareness of the discrepancy between expectations and consequences in past policy action by decision-making agencies.

3. *Norms and values shared by decision makers with other members of the society.* Each individual decision maker is a product of the national culture. To his official role, he brings preferences, beliefs, and ways of looking at things which were "built into" his personality through the process of growing up and being educated. When the Secretary of State speaks eloquently of free elections, a free press, and the rule of law he is expressing values shared generally by Americans. The extremely high value placed on human life by American society certainly motivates all American decision makers, as was demonstrated by the insistence on voluntary repatriation of North Korean and Communist prisoners in the Korean truce in July, 1953. Cultural biases—i.e., stereotyped views of foreigners—may enter into decision making via the individual policy maker. A drive for competitive achievement and success—a widely approved motive in the United States—may reinforce the decision maker's role in the decisional system or it may counterbalance his desire to make a substantive contribution to policy. Social values not shared by the majority of citizens may be absorbed by the decision makers before they become government officials. Thus an official who was a lawyer, or a businessman, or an economist before taking on responsibilities as a policy maker, and particularly if he continues his professional affiliations outside office hours, will be influenced by the ways such groups look at policy problems. A lawyer, for example, might be expected to stress legal norms,

such as strict interpretation of written agreements, verbal compromise, and precedent.

Beliefs, goals, hopes, ethics, ideas, and moral principles are subtle factors in decision making. It is not as easy to "see" the transfer of these cultural factors from their general social setting to the utterances and attitudes of the decision maker as it is to "see" the government protecting the interests of American business abroad. More often than not, decision makers will not be conscious of the values which shape their judgments. The fact that common value orientations shared by a majority of Americans do affect national choices can be deduced from the recent criticism concerning the unfortunate impact of legalistic-moralistic considerations on the conduct of American policy officials.*

4. *Material needs and values of the society or any segment thereof.* It seems useful for analytical purposes to preserve a distinction between the norms and values brought into a unit of decision as part of the decision maker's make-up on the one hand, and on the other hand the needs and values which are accepted consciously by the decision maker after his entrance into a unit. The range of factors here is wide and need only be suggested briefly. Several million Americans depend on foreign trade, and the American economy would suffer what many consider to be a mortal blow if it were lost. Certain strategic materials vital to American industry must be obtained from outside the United States. These two examples represent what might be called functional necessities for the whole society (since the collective prosperity and well-being are involved) and must be recognized by the decison makers. Again, the decision makers may not share certain common values, yet feel duty bound to see to it that these are expressed in official action. Finally, of course, all of the various interest groups which make demands on policy makers must be included in the key motivational influences to which the latter are subject. Factors referred to in this category appear to enter into decisions in two ways: first, through *estimates* of social needs and *voluntary representation* of values by the decision makers; second, through *expectations* of rewards or punishments which might result from deciding to respond or not respond to various demands. The two will be related but should be kept separate because not every motive of the decision makers is forced on them by pressure from individuals and groups outside the unit of decision.

A combination of estimates, expectations, and representation is one of the crucial ways in which the internal setting conditions the behavior of decision makers. In general, there would seem to be no other way to account for the familiar influence of public opinion and interest groups on policy making than to assume that the decision makers take over the expressed demands, needs, and values to the extent that these considerations define the

---

* See George F. Kennan, *American Diplomacy, 1900–1950* (Chicago, University of Chicago Press, 1951), pp. 91–103.

decision makers' orientation to a situation or problem. This ties in with the theory of access* applied to the political process as a whole, though motivation of policy makers is only one channel through which such influences can enter policy formation.

The foregoing formulation suggests that factors relevant to motivation in a unit of decision should be sought in the organizational nature of the unit, in the setting of the unit, and in the decision-maker himself. Clearly the motives of those who make policy will be mixed. It is difficult to imagine a case where only one of the above motivational components of decision making would be operative.

COMMUNICATION AND COORDINATION

The necessity for communication and coordination is implicit in the existence of a division of labor and specialization of function as well as in the transmission of motivational influences. General policy directives and specific decisions must be communicated to the participants in the decision-making process. If the broad purposes and directions of American foreign policy are not clearly transmitted to those engaged in decison-making activities, their work may become ineffective or it may lead to inconsistencies. If specific decisions are not communicated, others making decisions may act on the wrong assumptions. The values, objectives, and plans of the decision-making unit which constitute motivation for the members and so contribute to organizational efficiency must be communicated throughout.

In many ways, the decision-making process may be likened to a mobilization process. Orders and requests must be communicated if functions are to be performed and action carried out. Information, cast in the appropriate form, must be made available to the unit of decision and then circulated to the individuals and groups who need it and when it is needed. In one year, the State Department receives some 350,000 reports from its representatives in the field which must be routed to the proper places. Special studies and memoranda must be available to those located at decision points. Finally, decision makers must communicate with each other, not only in a physical sense but in the sense of being able to understand each other. A policy analyst or a technical expert must have both the opportunity and the ability to communicate his ideas and findings to appropriate persons. For example, the advice of an economist on a decision regarding aid to an underdeveloped area may be ineffectual for one of two reasons. Those who have to decide may not know what he thinks because his views have not been circulated properly, or he may be unable to translate complicated economic analysis into everyday terms.

Communication takes place via channels which connect the participants in the decision-making process. Different mediums—telephone, memoranda,

---

* See David Truman, *The Governmental Process* (New York, Alfred A. Knopf, Inc., 1951), for a definitive analysis. This theme runs throughout the whole study.

policy papers, cables and telegrams, conference, personal conversation, and so on—characterize the channels. Rules govern mediums and channels. Normally, the decision makers will prepare written communications in certain ways, cast them in certain forms, and will follow formal procedures with respect to "with whom" and "to whom" communication is possible. As will be shown in Chapter Seven, many policy papers in the State Department do not become official until a requisite number of decision makers have affixed their signatures.

Needless to say, the nature and effectiveness of the communication system in a unit of decision have a very important bearing on the results of the decison-making process. The system should provide, for example, some way for policy-making officers in the State Department to be kept informed of pertinent research studies available in that department's Office of Intelligence Research or in the Central Intelligence Agency. If new information about the external setting does not get into the communication system, or if it does but is not circulated to the appropriate officials, decisions may be made without adequate and full information. For many months, American officials operated on the assumption that the Israeli army was an inferior fighting force when the war between Israel and the Arab countries was being carried on in 1947–1948—this despite repeated field reports to the contrary. Information being circulated in a communication system is always classified in some way—"secret," "routine," "background," "urgent" and so on. Security classifications have been known to hide information from those who need it. Furthermore, data marked "routine" may suddenly become very significant and unless the classification is changed, the significance may be lost. It is more than likely that when the summary of a policy problem reaches the Secretary of State, it will be one page in length and hence the route it has followed will partially determine the contents.

Channels of communication serve to inform the decision makers about each other's activities. No great imagination is required to realize the great mischief which can be caused by a failure of communication among policy makers. The United States took part in a conference of American states in the capitol of Colombia in 1948 and was embarrassed considerably by a Communist-inspired riot which hampered the conference. Warnings of the intended riot were in possession of authorities in the Central Intelligence Agency. Congressmen have been known to make statements which were very ill-advised in view of delicate negotiations under way between the United States and another country. In July, 1948, the State Department thought, and announced publicly, that the Air Force was no longer able to provide supplies for the Western sector of Berlin under Soviet blockade; yet at the same time an air trip for this very purpose had already been completed. While the State Department was assuring the recipients of European aid that they could continue to expect aid, a representative of the Economic Cooperation Administration was threatening withdrawal. As will be shown in Chapter Seven, difficulties of communication can delay important decisions by adding to the time necessary to produce consensus and by encouraging "buck passing."

Coordintion will become a familiar theme in this part of the book. It is dependent on communication, and some degree of it is necessary for two reasons. First, because the allocation of power and responsibility to different agencies and individuals requires for many decisions the views and agreement of separate authorities. When a decision relates in some way to the functions of both the State Department and the Department of Defense, the decision or recommendation to be authoritative must be based on their joint consultation. The same type of thing would be true between the executive and legislative branches or between divisions within a department. Coordination reconciles different powers and duties when that becomes necessary for decision and action. Coordination is also needed when two or more kinds of skills and information must be fed into decision making. The large issues of foreign policy no longer fit neat labels: economic, political, or military. As issues become more complicated, as foreign affairs embrace more varieties of human experience, the technology of policy formation becomes increasingly specialized. As specialization grows, the number of individuals and agenices required multiplies. The informational and analytical contributions of many must be woven into a single decision. Coordination and communication are, to repeat, closely connected. In one sense, coordination would be impossible without communication in some form—conference, memoranda, reports, or personal conversation. But there is another sense in which communication facilitates coordination. Coordination is, after all, the taking of joint actions and the merging of diverse points of view of those whose functions cannot or should not be carried on in isolation. For example, the coordination of area specialists (Far Eastern and other area experts) and subject-matter experts (economists, political scientists, and so on) is primarily a task of making it possible or likely that they will perceive problems or decisions within a common frame of reference so that they can understand each other and can pool their respective contributions. The same process must be carried on between civilian and military experts in the National Security Council or between congressmen and State Department officials in a committee hearing.

INFORMATION AND INTELLECTUAL SKILLS

What has been said so far may be summarized thus: In order for decision making to take place, there must be officials empowered to decide and to perform various functions related to deciding; these officials must be motivated to decide and to perform functions in certain ways; and these officials must communicate with each other and their functions must be coordinated. Two further elements are necessary—the appropriate skills and resources, i.e., *information* and *intellectual skills*. Without the mobilization of appropriate skills and resources, decison making in any real sense would be impossible. It is not necessary to catalogue all the kinds of skills and resources needed by the agencies which formulate policy. Some of the important needs of the State Department, for example, are for skilled negotiators, diplomats, economists, linguistic experts, political analysts, drafters of documents, legal advisers, trained reporters, area specialists, intelligence experts, communications experts, and public relations counselors. A similar list could be drawn up for all the other agencies involved.

To cast the point in a larger context, it can be asked, What are the *intellectual ingredients* required by the decision-making process? Knowledge is required—knowledge of the national interest, knowledge of alternative objectives and techniques, knowledge of consequences. Knowledge would seem to rest upon adequate information of many sorts. Also required is the *capacity* to organize and interpret the information, including ability to estimate the effects of policy alternatives and to formulate objectives clearly as well as to devise effective means to achieve them. Two primary intellectual ingredients emerge, then, as vital: information and the capacity for policy analysis.

How are these to be supplied? Information pours in from literally hundreds of technical operations and investigations designed to yield the facts which decision makers must bear in mind as they deliberate on particular problems or issues. Capacity for policy analysis must be provided in the persons of those who perform specialized functions at various stages in the process and of those who finally make the decisions. Both ingredients obviously require the recruitment and training of skilled personnel. Skills and resources must be located or bought to bear at strategic points in the process and, above all, at the points of decision. It does little good for an organization to have information buried in its files and highly skilled analysts at work on various problems if the structure and functioning of the organization do not permit efficient use of such resources when and where needed.

Accordingly, the technological aspects of the decision-making process will include those activities concerned with the provision of the intellectual ingredients of decision—that is, the skills and resources required; cultivation of the sources of such ingredients; and the effective distribution and use of ingredients throughout the process. Clearly the manner in which these three technological functions are performed will affect the content and effectiveness of decisions. From the point of view of the decision makers, a primary task in making foreign policy is the determination of what is really significant in the external environment for purposes of the decision to be considered. If the environment is imperfectly or erroneously perceived—if information is lacking or inaccurate or misinterpreted—the decision will probably be different from what it otherwise would be and its consequences will be different from those anticipated.

Suppose it is imagined for the moment that the State Department is confronted with the problem of preventing the acquisition of some strategic raw material by a potential enemy who is putting pressure on a smaller nation that controls the supply. Basically, the problem involves a choice of intervening in what is essentially the domestic affairs of another nation or of letting the potential enemy acquire the raw material. The range of questions which immediately confront the State Department is enormous. How vital is the material to the enemy? How much would it enhance his war-making capacity? Could it be used by him right away or are there technical difficulties in the way of his realizing a short-run gain? Would the enemy retaliate or would he take more forceful measures to achieve his end? What form might this action take? The knowledge of the enemy implied in just these six questions is extensive. What would be the general effect of American intervention in the smaller country? Would it upset the tenuous balance of political power there? Would it strengthen the hand of local anti-American forces or foment distrust of America? Would there be serious social consequences which might create instability? How would the neighbors of the smaller country react? Would the American move be regarded as "imperialistic"? The answers to this list would depend upon a knowledge of the social structure and process of the smaller country along with an understanding of the region and international relationships within the region.

Other questions—in some respects no less difficult—would arise concerning the internal setting in which the decision is to be taken. What will be the attitude or reaction of the military establishment to a proposal not to intervene? What do other executive agencies have at stake in the choice? What other decisions have been made or are in process of being made which would be affected by this one? Would Congress support the intervention if it cost money? What reactions could be expected from key senators and congressmen? How would the general climate of opinion be affected? Would powerful groups support or oppose one of the choices?

These questions do not exhaust the logical inquiries which decision makers would have to make about the alternatives presented nor do they include questions of implementation. But the list is sufficient to indicate the types of information and analytical skills which would be necessary in the hypothetical case. As soon as the problem was recognized as requiring decision, the technological (as defined here) procedures of the decision-making process would begin to function. If they could be tracked down systematically it would be found that the mobilization of policy-making resources rested on immediate factors such as the latest cables from representatives in the countries involved and on long-range factors such as the kind of experts available to and selected by the State Department.

What factors will affect the way a decision maker's mind works when he comes to grips with a problem? To put the question differently, What are the sources of the intellectual skills which will be applied by decision makers? An immediate answer would be the cumulative life experience of the individual official and his total personality. In the broadest sense this answer would be correct, but it would make the task of investigation almost impossible. To focus the point somewhat more narrowly, it may be suggested that two factors be singled out for special attention. First, there is the past professional training and experience of the decision maker which might be relevant to his present policy-making function. From this training and experience will be derived certain perspectives. The decision maker who has been trained as an economist will view things differently from the decision maker who has been trained as a lawyer or a political scientist. A career in government will induce different perspectives from a career in university teaching and research. An official who has spent most of his professional life in a staff job (i.e., primarily advisory) will be likely to assess problems differently from an official who has had "line" experience where he has been called upon to make decisions and to be responsible for them. Similarly, an area specialist's approach will differ from that of a functional expert such as a banker or an engineer or a military officer. A generalist—a man with many kinds of experience and a broad education—may react one way; a specialist, another.

These distinctions are sometimes referred to by shorthand expressions: the "military mind," the "legal mind," the "Congressional mind," the "Foreign Service mind," and so on. What is implied, of course, is a rather loosely defined set of typical thinking habits. More will be said about these characterizations in later chapters. For present purposes, it can be said that professional training and experience will be among the key factors which determine the way an individual decision maker defines and analyzes problems, what he regards as important, and how he judges various events.

A second factor to be considered consists of the working theories of knowledge employed by the decision makers. All decision makers will from time to time use certain theories, formulas, and proverbs which are more or less common to the culture or to particular subcultures. For examples, some decision makers do not believe scientific knowledge of human behavior is possible, nor do they believe that human behavior is predictable. Therefore such officials prefer to rely on intuitive judgments and are very mistrustful of what the social sciences can do to improve the analysis which is so crucial in decision making. A great deal of attention has been paid to the nature and adequacies of the estimate, say, of Soviet capabilities by American policy makers, but relatively little attention has been paid to the impact of unquestioned ideas about reliable knowledge. It is easy for persons living in a comparatively free society to make assumptions about dictatorships which may or may not be true. Since policy officials are constantly dealing with foreign nations, it would not be surprising to find that they have theories about them based upon personal experience—the Germans are too energetic to be kept subdued, the French care too much for living to sacrifice for national security, the Arabs are untrustworthy, and so on. Some decision makers apparently insist that intelligence reports contain only "facts"—which supposedly have an objective existence and can be gathered without anything happening to them in the process. Some decision makers believe they can learn more about the state of public opinion in country X by frequenting leading bars and restaurants than by using elaborate attitude surveys and polling devices. Other decision makers believe that a United States information program in Italy can be run according to American advertising practices. These are simply hypothetical examples and no criticism is intended. Perhaps intuition and educated guesses are all that is possible, given the condition of knowledge. However, the point being made here is that to insist on intuitive judgments as a matter of principle when other judgments are available, or to refuse to admit the verifiability of theories, will have a definite effect on the intellectual operations which go into foreign-policy choices.

Are the intellectual ingredients of decision making different when the process is carried on by a group rather than by an individual? Aside from the rather obvious advantage of having more opportunities to exploit alternate sources of information and ideas, it would appear that shared responsibility for decision may permit the assumption of greater risks because there is a group consensus to help counterbalance individual doubts. Probably a group deliberation encourages a more thorough exploration of a wider range of alternative courses of action. Nevertheless, a large group may lead to more disagreement and hence to delay. The group process undoubtedly puts a great premium on intellectual leadership, on the ability to explain and reconcile differences in viewpoint.

Decision makers, then, analyze situations, define problems, establish a range of alternatives, assign meaning to events and conditions in the setting, and interpret information. On the basis of all this, a conclusion is reached. But the process is not a mechanical one. Ingredients are not placed in a machine which grinds out policy solutions. It is necessary to emphasize this again and again because the outside observer is tempted to assume that the process is automatic, completely formalized, and results mostly from adding, subtracting, or weighing data; or else he is tempted to assume that the process is disorderly, manipulative, and whimsical, and that attempts to conceptualize the process grace it with a form it does not in fact have. Either extreme should be avoided. One way to do so is to remember that structural elements and formal rules of the unit of decision are modified by other factors, among them the interpretations, choices, and strategies of the officials working at various points in the process. Another is to remember the highly evaluative character of the ingredients of decision mentioned above. The term "information," referring to one of the ingredients, means more than raw "facts." Facts, particularly social facts, are usually selected and can be interpreted in various ways. Definition of national interest, formulation of objectives, and selection of means—all are matters of judgment. The assumptions and expectations of some officials constitute information or knowledge for other officials which is used in analyzing and interpreting facts.

There is likely to be, therefore, a substantial amount of intellectual pulling and hauling in the reaching of any decision. Policy officials must argue, must be convinced, must justify, and must develop strategies to accomplish their purposes. The intellectual activities of decision making include tactics employed to make action or proposed action "acceptable." Such tactics are evident while a decision is being made, that is, the decision makers use them on each other with the result that their attitudes and choices are affected. Such tactics are also evident after a decision is made. Tactics operate both within the decision-making group and outside the decision-making group.

What forms do tactics take? First, appeals to past experience—previously successful policies and tradition—or to mistakes. Second, appeals to principle. Third, appeals based on the personality and reputation of the decision makers as individuals. Fourth, appeals to alleged consequences. All four types of justification were employed in the case of the North Atlantic Alliance. It was pointed out that the absence of firm collective commitments to resist aggression had been costly prior to 1939. "An attack on one is an attack on all" and mutual help for preparedness were two principles invoked. The appointment of General Eisenhower as the first NATO commander served to convince many of the worth-whileness of the project. One of the consequences anticipated was a waning of communist influence in Western Europe.

The major purposes of these tactics—perhaps they can be called "legitimation" tactics—are to explain the meaning of a decision, to enhance its acceptability, and to minimize the reprisals or maximize the rewards bestowed by individuals and groups who can hold the decision makers responsible. Every decision is the embodiment of an official consensus, consensus being defined as the common acceptance of an action and its meaning. There will be an official version of the meaning of the decision which is binding so far as the decision makers of a particular unit are concerned. This does not imply that all of them necessarily agree with the decision or are equally convinced of its soundness, but only that the decision is authoritative once it is official. If a decision starts with a small group, say in the State Department, and ends as a piece of major legislation in Congress, it can be said that an ever-broadening consensus was achieved, eventually embracing the American public. Even when Congress does not participate in the making of a decision, it must usually be "sold." Policies also have to be sold to those who must carry them out and often to other nations affected. Foreign policy in a democratic society must rest on a minimum consensus among officials and the public. The need to avoid or minimize reprisals and maximize rewards is simply a reflection of the fact that decisions result in action which is in turn followed by approval, opposition, confidence or the decline of it, enthusiasm, substantiation of expectations, or disillusionment. External to the unit of decision, the decision makers must do all they can to gain approval and support—the rewards which are necessary to a continuing delegation of authority and discharge of responsibilities. This is especially true in a case where the State Department formulates policy but must rely on the Department of Defense or the Foreign Operations Administration to help carry it out.

Very often a policy must be sold to Congress and to the public on a quite different basis from that on which the decision makers convince themselves. Consequently the legitimation tactics which help carry the day within the unit of decision are obscured. For example, policy officials may accept a course of action because of its immediate consequences; yet they may feel it necessary to make the action acceptable to the public by means of an appeal to principle. There is danger in this not only because the motives of the decision makers may be distorted but because false expectations may be aroused in those who did not participate in the decision. In all fairness it must be said that the decision makers may find it very awkward to reveal fully why they accepted a course of action. Apart from the necessity to conceal vital secrets which may be required in a limited number of cases, the main reason is that congressmen, State Departments experts, and the mass public do not all view problems in the same way. It is therefore considered easier— particularly by officials in the Executive Branch—to try to make a decision fit existing mental processes than to try to alter the processes to fit the problem. Suppose the National Security Council decided suddenly to withdraw all American military personnel from Western Europe on the ground that one consequence of leaving them there would be to expose them to destruction by enemy forces. Whatever else might be said publicly, it seems hardly likely that this argument would be prominently featured.

▶ PERSONALITY AND DECISION MAKING

It may appear that personality factors have been slighted in the foregoing analysis. If there is an omission, it is more apparent than real. In the discussion of the formal roles of decision makers it was suggested that an individual's personality might well be the determinant of whether he conducted himself on the basis of a broad interpretation of his prescribed duties. As will be observed later, the role of the president is par excellence a role in which interpretation by the occupant is important. The late President Franklin Roosevelt, for example, was evidently a person of supreme self-confidence and therefore was not averse to deciding many things himself. By his own admission, former President Truman leaned heavily on advice, especially during the early years of his tenure. Such factors as ambition, beliefs, judgment, strict conformity to rules, and so on, discussed under motivation are, of course, intimately bound up with personality. Similarly, intellectual skills are very much a part of a person's total make-up.

Controversy has long been rampant over the relative influence of role and personality. Does the man make the role or vice versa? Senator Borah (an imposing figure in the field of foreign policy) was Senator Borah, regardless of whether he was chairman of the Senate Foreign Relations Committee—so it has been argued. Senator Vandenberg grew in stature, became a responsible leader as a result of his experience in the same role—again, so it has been argued. Trite though it may sound, personality and role interact, albeit with different results in different situations. The controversy can be avoided. Certainly a man will have to accommodate himself to the requirements of a role and certainly no two men will perform a role in exactly the same way even with "all other things equal." Generally speaking, in view of the fact that personality may be a very loose concept and therefore difficult to appraise accurately, it may be better to try first to explain the behavior of decision makers in terms of role, motivation, communication, information, and intellectual skills. This would leave individual differences and other aspects of action not explainable by these factors to be accounted for by reference to unique personal factors. Even then, the student of decision making will not be interested in all facets of personality but only those which are relevant to behavior in a decision-making context. An official may have an unhappy home life or he may suffer from some neurosis; yet there is no way, short of complete investigation, of knowing whether such conditions are relevant to his conduct in government.

Two other points in connection with personality are worthy of note. Since one's organizational position will have an effect on his personality, he may in the course of a lengthy career absorb certain habits which are not necessarily decreed by his job description. Habits of this type became inseparable from the individual's total patterns of behavior. There is evidence which suggests that some career officials tend to become cautious, unimaginative, and too prone to pay attention to ritual and precedent. In view of the significance of the roles of those who are loosely termed "bureaucrats," their personality traits may assume major proportions in the decision-making process.

Given the importance of coordination and intellectual skills, leadership becomes an obvious ingredient in the decision-making process. From the president on down, the capacity to formulate issues, to compromise differences, to anticipate needs, to induce cooperation, and to build consensus is essential. This capacity rests on understanding, sensitivity, popularity, powers of expression, patience, balance, tact, and many other attributes of personality. All top decision makers are in a sense leaders. Though the qualities of leadership are not always agreed upon, everyone seems to know when they are lacking. In the absence of presidential leadership, Congress may overstep its authority; in the absence of a strong Secretary of State, factions may seriously weaken the State Department's efficiency. Without an effective chairman, an interdepartmental committee may be paralyzed; without a foreign-policy leader, the Senate may become a barrier to any decision at all.

▶ LIMITATIONS ON DECISION MAKING

Having discussed the nature of decisions and decision making, it is necessary to remind the reader of the importance of limitations. It seems reasonable to assume that decision makers consider their operations and freedom of choice limited in a number of ways. For one thing, time is often a limiting factor. Major decisions sometimes must be made in a matter of hours. There is not enough time to consider a wide range of alternatives and to analyze each one carefully, nor is there enough time for gathering together all the available reports and memoranda for thorough study. Again, the members of one decision-making unit will have to be very careful about what other decision makers will think about a given course of action, how they will react to it. In an age of combined military-political foreign-policy problems, civilian policy makers must consider the way in which the military establishment will be affected by certain proposals. Decisional units in the Executive Branch, of course, are constantly limited by the estimated reception of policies by members of Congress. Furthermore, when a major move in foreign policy is contemplated—a treaty or an aid program or an occupation or a conference—it will be necessary to know whether the appropriate officials having the appropriate skills can be freed from what they are doing in order to take on the new project. This is another way of saying that the resources of a decision-making organization will always be scarce relative to the demands upon them.

Other limitations arise from the nature of the particular society, its resources, technology, and geographical position. The objectives and techniques which the decision makers can properly consider as feasible will be limited by the nation's economic, political, and military capabilities and its human resources. Reliance on a mechanized army may be dictated by population trends. Economic aid to other countries may not be possible because of the lack of domestic surpluses. Technicians may be lacking for a successful propaganda effort. Or the means may be available and cheap enough, but public opinion may be unreceptive. Thus some limitations are material; and some are due to the inability of decision makers to count on or to gain a national consensus behind a course of action. Some of the domestic limitations are subject to control or change by the decision makers, but some are not. Public opinion can be educated or swayed—sometimes quickly—but minerals cannot be replaced nor the number of males between eighteen and twenty-five doubled except over a long-time period. In any event, the range of alternatives may be severely contracted.

Friends and allies, world social conditions, and potential enemies are sources of limitation. Most decisional units are caught between domestic public opinion and the opinion of foreign governments and peoples. What is acceptable at home may be entirely out of the question abroad. Allies and friends are sensitive and may see problems quite differently. To the extent that a nation is dependent on the help and cooperation of others, its decision makers must be ready to make concessions. Much of the international environment in which foreign policies must be effective is not under the direct control of decision makers. Racial tensions, ancient hostilities, poverty, disease, civil strife, and ideological conflcits cannot be abolished; they may be improved slowly, but for the most part they must be accepted and made the most of. If the decision makers are confronted by an "enemy" state, every action must be calculated in terms of its effects on that state. Either there will be a whole range of influences on the behavior of the enemy state unavailable to the decision makers, or every action which might promote full-scale conflict must be avoided, or both.

All the foregoing comprise external limitations that may narrow the action which can be considered, may reduce the effectiveness of action, and may affect the timing of action. These are external in the sense that their source lies outside the decision unit. However, on the basis of the analysis presented above, limitations may also be related to the decision-making process itself, i.e., to factors internal to the unit. Action may be limited to what the particular decision makers are able to agree on despite the existence of means and a favorable environment. The motivations of the decision-making groups may lead them to overemphasize, say, military techniques. Adequate skills may be lacking for the planning and execution of a propaganda program. Coordination may be faulty, thus dividing energies and making inconsistencies possible. The decision makers may lack sufficient information. Lack of information—and partciularly verifiable information (i.e., subject to agreed interpretations)—seems to be a chronic limitation. Failures in communications may prevent the circulation of information to all the decision makers who ought to have it.

Such examples could be multiplied. The next section in this chapter is devoted to a consideration of certain limitations to which American decision makers are subject.

SUMMARY

In brief, decisions result from the activities of certain officials who fulfill key roles in the decision-making system. These roles are based on prescribed powers and functions whose exercise is subject to formal rules and to convention. The officials influence, and are influenced by, each other. They are linked together by channels of communication and their activities are coordinated. Decision makers view the setting in which they must act and establish alternative courses of action in accordance with judgments and preferences derived from their membership in the unit of decision and inter-action with other members, from their membership in the society, and from their estimate of the desires and needs of individuals and groups external to the unit. During the process of reaching a decision, several kinds of required information are circulated and interpreted. To this information are applied the intellectual skills of the decision makers. An important part of the intellectual activity will consist of the ways in which the decision makers render a decision acceptable to themselves and to others.

Such are the elements of the decision-making process. Through the process, a group of responsible officials define the situation in which a decision must be made. Some factors are found to be relevant, some not. Some factors are found to be subject to their control, some not. Some factors are found to be favorable, some not. Alternatives are evaluated in terms of probable consequences. A choice is made and it embodies at least a general outline, a program of action, and an ultimate state of affairs desired.

► SOME OUTSTANDING CHARACTERISTICS OF DECISION MAKING IN THE UNITED STATES

Having in mind generally what the decision-making process is and what its key elements are, some observations on concrete conditions which affect the process in the United States are in order. Perhaps these conditions are not peculiar to this nation, but they are certainly different in degree and often in kind. The selected items presented below should be looked upon as sources of complications which affect the deliberations and other activities of decision makers—particularly those in the Executive Branch. Naturally, the conditions mentioned simultaneously affect the quality and effectiveness of the nation's foreign policy and therefore should be regarded as potential limitations.

THE MULTIPLICITY OF AGENCIES AND VOICES

One of the striking features of decision making in America is the large number of agencies and individual officials who may potentially play a role in foreign-policy formation—that is, who may constitute a given unit of decision. Even when they are not actually participants in the decision-making process, these agencies and individuals may try to influence predecisional activities and to influence the execution of decisions. In addition, there are constant attempts to influence the official interpretation of policies already in effect. Some officials deal directly with the representatives of other states on a daily basis; others who never come in personal contact with foreign diplomats may nonetheless seriously affect America's external relations by their words and actions. There are an estimated fifty-eight separate executive agencies along with the many subdivisions of the United Nations and the members and committees of the two houses of Congress. Former Secretary of State Acheson thus put the matter succinctly: "What a nation should do, if it were one person with one will and one mind, is often very different from what it actually can do, and does do, when those in charge of its government resolve the multiplicity of thrusts into a single decision."* The number of individual officials who—on a self-appointed basis or otherwise—can and do speak on foreign policy is almost unbelievable. To the sum total of officials must be added the growing list of private citizens—opinion leaders and others—who try to affect the decision-making process.

One result of the allocation of power and responsibility among a potentially large number of decision makers is the possibility of open disputes over policy and diverse interpretations of national action. Secretary of State Acheson carried on a public conflict with General Douglas MacArthur (Supreme Commander of the Allied Powers) over the substance of occupation policy toward Japan and over the respective jurisdictions of the Army and the State Department. In 1949, the Economic Cooperation Administration fought with the Maritime Commission over the freight rates to be charged on American goods shipped under the foreign-aid program. Throughout 1950–1951, General MacArthur disagreed with the Joint Chiefs of Staff and the Secretary of Defense over the conduct of the Korean war. During the same period members of the Senate Foreign Relations Committee feuded with members of the State Department over United States policy on Communist China. The general direction of American foreign policy was the subject of a long controversy between Secretary of State Acheson and Secretary of Defense Louis Johnson. Conflict of viewpoints is natural; indeed it is indispensable to decision making, but these few examples from among many were public, were of fairly long duration, and were often of the jurisdictional type which carries over from one issue to another and which leaves behind a residue of resentment.

Closely allied to the above are the rivalries for power, prestige, and appropriations. Some of the more enduring ones have been Foreign Service officers vs. non-Foreign Service officers within the State Department; the Air Force vs. the Navy; the State Department vs. the Defense Department; the Senate vs. the House of Representatives; the State Department vs. any agency which dispenses foreign aid; and the appropriations committees in Congress vs. those dealing with foreign affairs. When John McCloy was appointed United States High Commissioner to Germany, he insisted upon being also named ECA administrator for Germany because the Army and ECA both had money to spend in Germany and therefore might outrank the State Department in prestige. It was necessary for the late James Forrestal, when he was Secretary of Defense in 1948 to order the three armed services not to take their budget and policy disputes to Congress without clearing with the Defense Department's Director of Legislative Liaison.

During one single week in 1950, the American people were treated to somewhat contradictory speeches by General MacArthur, Secretary of the Navy Mathews, Secretary of State Acheson, and Major General Orvil Ander-

* United States Department of State *Bulletin,* October 31, 1949, pp. 668–669.

son of the Air Force. All the speeches were widely publicized in the mass mediums. All concerned American policy toward the Soviet Union, war and peace, and the relation between European policy and Far Eastern policy. With the exception of the remarks of the Secretary of State, the views set forth were known to be contrary to the officially understood position of the government. This "Tower of Babel" had to be followed by a presidential attempt to clarify American policy. One of the results of the hearings on the dismissal of General MacArthur in the spring of 1951 was the variety of interpretations of what America's China policy had been and should be from the Secretary of State, Assistant Secretary Dean Rusk, MacArthur himself, the Joint Chiefs of Staff, the Secretary of Defense, and a dozen prominent senators. At one point, there was a lengthy controversy over whether a speech of Dean Rusk did or did not represent a change in American foreign policy. Paul Hoffman, when ECA administrator, speculated with reporters, in Shanghai in 1949 just before China fell to the Communists, that American aid might continue despite the Communist success, and the State Department had to explain that Mr. Hoffman spoke only for himself.

This kind of thing has happened over and over again. Similar examples could be recited at length. What conclusions are justified with respect to the decision-making process? First, the State Department is not a "foreign office" in the European sense. It shares important decision-making functions with other agencies. Second, policy is often made, or appears to be made, in a casual, off-the-cuff basis. Impetuous public statements must be followed by public and private disclaimers. Poorly coordinated announcements convey an impression of uncertainty and inconsistency. It would be difficult to overestimate the effect of carelessness in this respect. People at home and abroad are able to read into American actions and decisions, choices and intentions which are not really there. Third, the multiplicity of agencies and voices connected with the policy process requires maximum attention to coordination and planning in order to avoid confusion and to prevent undue reliance upon improvisation. An indefinite number of voices of indeterminate authority tends to reduce public confidence at home and abroad. A constant parade of individuals across the policy-making stage either causes, or is symptomatic of, instability in foreign policy.

The internal setting of decision making in the United States has become increasingly one of argument and confusion. As the number of agencies grows, as the number of people who assume or are accorded policy-making roles increases, and as foreign policy is increasingly ensnared in domestic politics, debating tactics and the meaning of words take on larger significance. Differences over details or means appear as differences over principles or major objectives. Controversies which rage while a decision is being reached may overshadow the action taken. Attention tends to focus on a handful of key individuals as personalities and performers without reference to their legitimate position in the structure of decision making. The sheer outpouring of words muddies fundamental issues.

Illustrations are to be found in the "great debates" which accompanied the Senate acceptance of the Atlantic Alliance, its implementation, and the MacArthur hearings. When the Atlantic Treaty was accepted in 1949, the far-reaching implications were thrust aside in the wake of an acrimonious argument over the one billion in military aid to America's new allies. Later, in the winter of 1950–1951, the "troops to Europe" conflict between the chief executive and Congress covered up the fact that the Senate took the revolutionary step of putting American soldiers in an international army and of agreeing to leave them permanently in Western Europe. The dramatic circumstances surrounding the recall of General MacArthur and the hearings which followed obscured the basic policy issue: Was Europe or Asia to be America's first and chief line of defense? Almost as important were the sharp differences of opinion over the intentions and motives of the Soviet Union which were never clarified. The diametrically opposed premises underlying the arguments of the administration, certain congressmen, and General MacArthur, were never spelled out.

With the multiplication of the number of decision makers involved in major issues, arguments take place at long range, the participants jousting at one another indirectly through the newspapers and over the radio. The intellectual process which is the core of decision making then takes place under circumstances most conducive to misunderstanding and to verbal gymnastics. Coordination and communication, so essential to decision making, must be achieved via the weakest mediums. For example, in May, 1951, after the speech mentioned above by Dean Rusk, Assistant Secretary of State, Senators Taft and Douglas claimed that the State Department had reversed or shifted its policy toward Chiang Kai-shek's deposed China regime. The department announced that Rusk's speech was only a mere restatement. What had happened was that Rusk had tried to use strong language to assure Congress and the public that no "deal" would be made with Communist China and more was read into his remarks than he intended.

UNCERTAIN FOUNDATIONS OF POLICY

Many policy makers must feel themselves on a perpetual tightrope because of the delicate problems with which they must cope. To use a different metaphor, in his last address as Secretary of Defense, General George Marshall, who had served his country also as Secretary of State and Chief of Staff, spoke of the need for enduring policy protected from "fluctuations of public opinion." He recalled that in September, 1950, he requested a $17 billion military budget which was turned down, and in December "people were clamoring" for his resignation on the ground that he was derelict in his responsibilities for defense. His successor as Secretary of Defense, Robert

Lovett, who had been Under Secretary of State, once lamented that he bore "scar tissue" as a result of "swings of feeling." It is almost impossible for decision makers to predict when the consensus which appears to undergird a line of foreign-policy development will crumble, or how soon the public mood will change. Such changes may be focused directly on decision making via Congressional control over appropriations. Needed funds may be withheld or a program already in operation may be starved to death.

Other unknown quantities enter into decision making. One is the difficulty of assessing the intentions of other countries.* Policy must often be based on "guesses." Half the world is cloaked in official censorship. The iron curtain distorts information and makes necessary the use of policy techniques such as propaganda which are unfamiliar and whose effects are uncertain. It must also be said that the capacity for policy analysis referred to above as essential in decision making has not been adequate during the past six years to establish reliable assumptions about Soviet behavior. To a certain extent such assumptions can never be absolutely infallible, but policy makers have simultaneously entertained both widely variant assumptions about Soviet power and logically incompatible assumptions about Soviet motives and actions. The heated debate over America's Far Eastern policy in 1951 revealed that different officials at the same time believed that Communist China was trying to eject the United States from the region, that the Soviet Union was trying to pin American forces down in the region, and that the foreign policies of China and Russia were closely coordinated.

Elements of uncertainty are introduced by the behavior and attitudes of allies and friends. Great Britain and India have made their own, and different, guesses about China and Russia. The will of Western Europe to arm itself with American help has vacillated. Just when the effort appears to be going forward, it sags visibly and further delays ensue. After the United States has quietly notified its allies of an intended act which has not been opposed by them, domestic political factors in those countries apparently prompt them publicly to chastise the United States when the act is ultimately carried out. British troubles in Iran and Egypt in 1951 put the United States in the situation of having to watch from the side lines dangerous developments over which at the time it had little if any control but which turned out to greatly affect its interests and policies.

PROBLEMS OF STRATEGY CONNECTED WITH THE DOMESTIC LEGISLATIVE PROCESS

The range of problems in this category is great indeed and they constitute the subject of much of the analysis in Part II of this book. Only a few typical problems will be noted here. There is evidence that many decision makers in the Executive Branch operate on the principle that Congress should not be approached on a major issue without a specific program surrounded by an atmosphere of crisis. An example in point is the Greek-Turkish Aid

* See also Chapter Fourteen on the international environment.

Bill (to implement the Truman Doctrine) which was suddenly presented to Congress in March, 1947. The haste and "all or nothing" spirit of the proponents of the proposal tended, among other things, to produce a swing to extremes on both sides. Congress stressed the cost ($350,000,000) and the dangers of intervention; administration spokesmen ignored the cost and emphasized the dangers of nonintervention. One result was that, even though the program was approved, the implications of the new policy were never explored for the benefit of the nation's future policy.

It is easy to understand why executive decision makers are dismayed over the effects of the legislative process on foreign policy formation. The two-months debate over "troops of Europe" in the winter of 1950 and the six-week debate over General MacArthur's dismissal in the spring of 1951 measurably slowed down policy planning at a time when decisions were essential in both Europe and the Far East. When the Marshall Plan was first conceived it was designed primarily to promote long-term economic and political stabililty in Europe; yet the emphasis in the presentation to Congress had to be primarily on its usefulness as a short-term anticommunist weapon.

Strategy enters the picture in other ways. In February, 1951, the President's top foreign-policy advisers had to decide whether or not to reveal to the Senate the exact number of troops which were to be sent to Europe under the Atlantic Alliance. The arguments against the move were that it would tell the Russians too much; Congress would seize on the figure to the exclusion of major issues; and it would commit the United States to an allocation of troops to Europe before Europe had done its part. The chief argument for it was that if the figure were not revealed, Congress might erroneously believe the exaggerated reports which were rife in Washington at the time. The decision was to tell Congress how many troops would be sent   200,000 or 6 divisions. If the figure had been given in confidence earlier, it would not have been public knowledge, the Europeans would not have felt let down, and perhaps Congress would not have taken such an extreme position. The lack of coordination between Congress and the White House—a failure in strategy—had other consequences. The issue of a future voice for Congress in the sending of troops to Europe (opposed by the administration) was lost by only a few votes, thus leaving Europeans with what might be a wrong impression and doubts. One of the basic objectives of the administration was to encourage Europe to abandon its limited approach to its own rearming. A footnote to the whole episode was the announcement by the Defense Department in July, 1951, that 400,000 men would be stationed in Western Europe —an announcement which gave rise to the phrase "rubber division." Additional complications are likely when Congress and the presidency are controlled by different political parties.

Another example of the significance of strategy occurred in the summer of 1951. Over a billion dollars was cut from the amount requested for foreign military and economic aid, mostly from the latter item. At least part of the explanation lay in the fact that administrative decision makers failed to demonstrate clearly to two key Senate committees that general American aid was an inextricable factor in the domestic politics of Europe and was not solely a military question. Again, it appears that the State Department reversed its previous policy in order to enter into an aid agreement with Spain, partly for the reason that a powerful pro-Franco bloc in Congress could substantially interfere with the Mutual Aid Program (just mentioned) which was due to come up for consideration.

These selected examples suggest that when the legislative process becomes part of the decision-making process as a whole, executive officials are confronted with four kinds of problems in strategy. First, how should a policy be presented to Congress? This requires an assessment of the mood of Congress, the choice of arguments to be used, and close attention to the effects of legislative procedures on the content of the policy. Second, how can policy planning be accommodated to legislative delays? Third, how much can be safely revealed to Congress? Fourth, how is the strategy on one issue related to strategy on other issues being taken up by Congress or about to be taken up by Congress?

PRESSURES ON DECISION MAKING AND DECISION MAKERS

One thing which can be said immediately is that "the pressure to decide" never lets up. And in the present period the decisions pressing for attention are usually basic. Basic decisions call for study and reflection that high-level policy makers rarely have time to give them. Therefore reliance must be placed on the information and recommendations of subordinates who do not bear political responsibility and who cannot provide the means for implementation. A related pressure stems from a fact already noted: administrative officials having formulated a policy cannot actually reach a final decision unless they alone have clear power to act and to provide means to execute the policy. Often they do not know when or if they can follow through on a proposed course of action.

As a result of the intensification of Congressional investigations into all aspects of American foreign policy during 1949–1954, a new set of pressures was generated. At a time when extremely difficult questions had to be faced, those responsible for the day-to-day handling of foreign affairs were under a Congressional searchlight and microscope. They were under both legitimate, responsible criticism and irresponsible criticism, as well as charges ranging from holding pro-Communist sympathies to treason. Cabinet officers and high-level foreign-policy advisers spent thousands of hours on the witness stand before many Congressional committees and subcommittees undergoing nerve-racking cross-examination. The point being made here is not that Congress does not have the right of criticism and investigation, or that administrators are always right and congressmen are always wrong, or that respected, competent individuals were abused. The question arises as to the effect of such tactics, and the way they were used, on decision making and decision makers.

Secretary of State Acheson probably spoke for many when he once said: "Anyone in public life, of course, must bear all sorts of criticism, just, unjust, perhaps outrageous. One thing which is irritating is to be charged with an attitude that is directly contrary to one's entire public life. The things I read about myself as an appeaser seem to me so incredible that I cannot believe that even disinterested malevolence could think them up." * The psychological impact of a constant stream of charges upon the mental processes of men who must be in full possession of their wits to carry out their responsibilities is something to be pondered.

In the course of investigations personal diaries and minutes of top-secret discussions of decisions among high policy officials have been exposed to public view. Keeping in mind the definition of decision making as an intellectual process in which problems must be thoroughly dissected and alternatives fully explored with no insight, judgment, and data left unconsidered, the question arises as to the inhibitions put upon decision makers at a critical stage in their operations. As President Grayson Kirk of Columbia University—a distinguished student of international politics—has said, "It's much harder to make decisions . . . if you feel that your innermost thoughts are going to be made public within a very short time with a partisan or at least a searching scrutiny."† When officials have been publicly accused of saying, thinking, or recommending something in a supposedly off-the-record exchange of ideas on possible policy alternatives, it follows that there is likelihood that decision makers will pay as much attention to how their views will appear to someone whose position and responsibilities are quite different as to the business of arriving at sound conclusions after policy analysis.

Policy makers now dwell for the most part in glass houses. This is not the place to discuss how *open* diplomacy should be or how *democratic* policy formation can be, but it is beyond argument that additional strains have resulted from the increasing demand for publicity at every stage of decision making. One of the great changes in procedures of international negotiation in the modern era is that preconference planning and conferences now take place in public. Officials are no longer free to change their minds or alter their policies without loss of face. The attempts to negotiate a truce in the Korean conflict in the summer and fall of 1951 were somewhat strait-jacketed because proposals and counterproposals, being widely known, were bound to be judged in the light of public pressure on American officials to avoid anything bordering on "appeasement."

In addition, the heated controversy over America's Far Eastern policy led to attempts to apportion blame for past "mistakes" in policy and for the generally unfortunate position of the United States in that part of the world.

---

* Before the Senate Foreign Relations Committee, January 13, 1949, as reported in the New York *Times,* January 14, 1949, p. 1.

† New York *Times,* May 18, 1951, p. 10.

One result was public assignment of complete responsibility for certain events and conditions to men whose control over such events and conditions could have been only partial at best. Moreover, this re-examination of foreign policy —a healthy thing for any nation to do—led to a *reinterpretation* of things done in the past but on the basis of different criteria, assumptions which were not held when the action was taken, and information which was not then available. The decisions and recommendations of the men involved were judged not simply in terms of contemporary needs but also in terms of a reconstructed past. The necessity to defend themselves against charges of pro-Communist views or of being "soft" toward the Communist regime in China compelled officials to say things which were bound to introduce an element of rigidity into their weighing of future alternative. Thus Ambassador-at-Large Philip C. Jessup, defending himself before a Senate Foreign Relations subcommittee in October, 1951, emphasized over and over again that he and others in the State Department had never seriously entertained a decision to recognize Communist China or to urge its admission to the United Nations nor would such action ever be considered in the future. Now, suppose that circumstances change abruptly and radically and these courses of action become appropriate for reasons of national security. Policy makers are clearly on record as denying themselves this alternative in a new situation.

Beginning in June, 1951, after months of charges by Senator McCarthy that there were Communists in the State Department and after numerous Foreign Service officers had been investigated partly through exposure of their reports from the field, for their alleged pro-Communist leanings, officials of the State Department began to notice a reticence on the part of diplomatic personnel (particularly in the Far East) to express themselves freely in their reports or to continue personal contacts with Communists as sources of intelligence data. It became increasingly difficult to get experienced diplomats to accept important assignments in "politically sensitive" posts. John Carter Vincent and Walton Butterworth, who held responsible policy-making positions in the department, were long under fire. The latter ended up in the relatively minor post of Stockholm, while John Service, reputedly a very skilled diplomatic observer in China, was cleared of formal charges of being a bad security risk, but was put to work doing accounting in the State Department.

Two other kinds of pressures on decision making and decision makers may be mentioned. One concerns the need to pursue conflicting purposes. It is necessary to keep the door open for negotiation and settlement with the Soviet Union, but it is necessary, too, to avoid anything which might erode the nation's determination to make sacrifices for, and support, a total security policy. It is necessary to apply economic sanctions to Communist China, but it is necessary to have continued access to China's tungsten and tin. It is necessary to implement the North Atlantic Alliance as quickly as possible, but it is necessary also to take account of the demand for equal votes and autonomy by less powerful members of the Treaty Organization. The second kind of pressure concerns the awkward choice between secrecy and security requirements on the one hand, and the desirability of public understanding and support on the other. A considerable amount of time and money are spent to conceal information from enemies, yet Congressional investigations and debates, plus injudicious "leaks" by officials have provided enemies with vital intelligence material. However, if security regulations are tightened, as they were by President Truman's ruling in October, 1951, the press charges censorship.

THE DEMANDS ON HUMAN RESOURCES

The variety of skills needed throughout the decision-making process puts a heavy premium on available human resources. Since 1945, there has been a shortage of high-level personnel and a rapid turnover in key agencies. From 1945 to 1949, there were five Secretaries of State, six Under Secretaries, and twenty-six Assistant Secretaries. The President has had a difficult time recruiting experienced men for responsible positions. Heavy reliance on military officers and business executives is testimony not only to their specialized contributions in an age of violence and industrial mobilization, but to the fact that few others could be chosen or would accept. The Foreign Service has not provided many officers who could move out into the broader arena of decision making. One of the outstanding features of the past decade is that America came to rely on a handful of men for foreign-policy leadership. Consequently, in the words of Anne O'Hare McCormick, writing in the *New York Times,* May 28, 1951, "Top level officials everywhere are harassed and overworked men." Currently, responsible personnel are required to direct departments (particularly Defense and State), testify before Congress, attend foreign ministers' conferences, act as delegates to the many agencies of the United Nations, keep an eye on the development of the North Atlantic Treaty Organization, handle the diplomatic problems of the Korean war, and to be trouble shooters in special cases. These people cannot be everywhere at once and do everything at once. For example, in October, 1951, President Truman had to shift his trusted foreign policy adviser, Averell Harriman, from the Iranian oil dispute to the NATO rearmament program—both problems needed his experience and ability. The State Department ran a risk of stirring up the China policy debate by nominating Philip Jessup to be a delegate to the United Nations Assembly, where his dialectical skill and diplomatic know-how were essential. At a somewhat lower level, staff must be found for roughly six thousand international conferences to which the United States sends representatives each year.

The scarcity of human resources raises several problems for decision making in this country. Unfortunately, the capacity for policy analysis mentioned above is not easily come by, being rooted in a combination of natural gifts, experience, and specialized training. Sidney Souers, the important

Executive Secretary of the National Security Council, once remarked that his job required of its occupant that he be a nonpolitical confidant of the President, that he be objective and subordinate his personal views in order to coordinate the views of the council's members, and that he forgo personal publicity and aggrandizement. Such qualities are not always found in the same person.

The shortage and misuse of human policy-making resources are due to a number of factors, notation of which will in turn define some of the problems involved. American institutions of higher learning are not, in general, devoting themselves to the training of policy analysts who combine intellectual talents with political sophistication, attributes which are required by the nature of decision making in the United States. Many of the small number of persons who have these skills are not working in government but are attached to research agencies from which their contributions are fed into policy making on a hit-or-miss basis. It is also probable that the government's recruitment and in-service training programs are not geared to supply needs at the top levels. Some capable men undoubtedly are kept in relatively minor positions because they would not be acceptable to Congress. Finally, there is no doubt that other capable men are unavailable to government because the pressures outlined make such careers unattractive.

The demands on human resources in the decision-making process suggest two needs: the development of new resources and the husbanding of existing ones. No one knows how many good men are doing third-rate tasks.

THE FACTOR OF TIME

The time consumed between the first stages of the decision-making process and actual implementation of decisions—especially major ones—is usually considerable, and slowness constitutes a basic characteristic of policy formation in the United States. In the case of the original European Recovery Program (1948), the legislative process alone took four months, to say nothing of the administrative process which preceded it. Every decision of this magnitude has to be handled in the following cycle: hearings by both House and Senate committees on broad policy issues; floor debate and approval in both chambers; hearings by the Appropriations Committee of each chamber; and another floor debate and vote. In the case of the Mutual Defense Assistance Program (1950) to implement the Atlantic Alliance, the President approved the recommendations of the National Security Council in July, 1948, and Congress finally acted in October, 1949.

Time enters policy formation in another way. There is nearly always a time lag between the expert's conviction that a particular course of action is necessary and the acceptance of this view by citizens. Consensus is fundamental to a durable foreign policy and consensus does not form overnight. This time lag helps to encourage improvisation on the part of policy leaders.

Improvisation, which has been evident in American policy during critical periods, implies a time strategy. The tendency is to postpone big decisions until a crisis is reached. It leads to piecemeal policies, constant revisions, and the continuing necessity for new decisions. Policy planning, on the other hand, puts time in a different perspective. It tries to anticipate problems and needs. As noted, planning has become increasingly evident in American policy. The Truman Doctrine (1947) illustrates the pattern of facing up to the implications of the decline of British power bit by bit instead of meeting the large issue head on. In 1947 the problem involved Greece and Turkey. In 1951, the same problem involved Iran and Egypt, confronting the United States with the necessity of acting quickly under unfavorable circumstances. Economic aid to Europe, on the other hand, represented an attempt to forestall certain developments by a long-term decision.

But both improvisation and planning are complicated by another kind of time factor—a dual time lag between international events and the unfolding of their inner meaning, and between a policy decision and the unfolding of its consequences. George Kennan has estimated that upward of ten years may be required in the first time lag. An example would be the decline of British power alluded to above. It was perfectly clear that Great Britain would emerge from World War II a less than first-class power; yet the kinds of problems this would raise were not evident all at once. As a matter of fact, the picture is still not complete.

The fact that time alone reveals the effects of a decision enhances the difficulties which beset the administrative policy maker. Assessment of probable policy results becomes vital. Not only is it inherently difficult, but much depends on the expectations of the policy makers. If they assume that a decision can bring about certain changes, their assessment will be directed accordingly. If they assume that a decision cannot change certain things, their assessment will be different. Hence experts may feel that a policy which has a negative result is a success, that is, their expectations were fulfilled. However, defending policies which are negative is difficult, for Congress and the people have a tendency to expect positive results or solutions. The mounting impatience over the apparent stalemate of the Korean conflict exemplifies this. Some critics of American policy pointed to it as evidence of policy failure and demanded that America either get out or push the military action to its logical conclusion. Since one of the objectives of official policy was to limit the Korean war, administration spokesmen could point only to negative results. As for other objectives, only a passage of time could determine success or failure. Meanwhile it was possible for critics to insist there was "no policy."

Time puts a triple squeeze on policy makers. They must await developments to test their expectations. They must evaluate the significance of changes which are partly the result of the decision and partly not, in order to modify original estimates. They must also, under the American system, "show results." The first requires a degree of patience—which not all those participating in the decision-making process share in equal amount. The second requires a subtle intellectual exercise which differs considerably from a give-and-take argument over the success or failure of policy. The third requires strategy. If results cannot in the nature of things be shown immediately, policy leaders must preserve the consensus by making it very clear why this is so, which is hard to do in view of the factors discussed above. Or they must contrive something which can be made to appear as a result—a hazardous undertaking because it may jeopardize objectives through misunderstanding and through setting up a new chain of consequences.

DECISION MAKING IN A PERIOD OF TRANSITION

An outstanding feature of the transition which presently characterizes American foreign policy is the mixture of improvisation and planning. Essentially this means that emergency decisions must be correlated with long-term or permanent policies. After the Atlantic Alliance was established with twelve members who proceeded to work out a permanent defense system, it was found necessary to enlarge the program to include Greece, Turkey, and Egypt. Each addition to the original group necessitated some reconsideration of such problems as the allocation of military and economic resources among the member nations. In 1951, the United States decided to impose trade penalties on Czechoslovakia for the immediate purpose of forcing concessions from the Czech government, only to find that this action raised awkward questions concerning the long-term objectives of the International Trade Organization, one of which is the elimination of discriminatory trade restrictions.

Even more important is the fact that the transition is accompanied by a restructuring and reinterpretation of decision-making functions and responsibilities. Therefore, the "great debates" about the content and direction of foreign policy also take the form of controversies about the relations of the chief policy-making agencies to one another. The decision-making process is currently called upon to accommodate the additional burden of decisions about decision making itself. One must ask: Does a policy debate *obscure* a struggle for the power to decide? Does an argument over who is to decide obscure policy issues? How do the two interact upon each other?

▶ CONCLUSION

The description and analysis presented in this chapter were designed to accomplish three purposes: first, to give some indication of the structure and process of decision making as the source of action by the state in its relations with other states; second, to suggest the wide range of factors which affect the behavior of decision makers and which they must take into account; and third, to make preliminary mention of particular institutional arrangements and conditions which affect the decision-making process in the United States and give it distinctive characteristics. Chapters to follow will amplify all three themes.

► SELECTED BIBLIOGRAPHY

Among the limited number of general books which deal explicitly and directly with the nature and related elements of decision making are Chester Barnard, *Functions of the Executive* (Cambridge, Mass., Harvard University Press, 1938), Chaps. 12, 13, 14; Herbert Simon, *Administrative Behavior* (New York, The Macmillan Company, 1951), Chaps. 1, 2, 12; Robert Merton, *et al., Reader in Bureaucracy* (Glencoe, Ill., The Free Press, 1952), pp. 18–26, 51–59, 180–193, 233–241, 361–371; Robert Dubin, *Human Relations in Administration* (New York, Prentice-Hall, Inc., 1951), pp. 199–205, 212–228; Harold Stein, *Public Administration and Policy Development* (New York, Harcourt, Brace & Company, 1952), pp. ix–xlv. Perhaps the most valuable general analysis of foreign-policy making in the United States is Arthur Macmahon's *Administration in Foreign Affairs* (University, Ala., University of Alabama Press, 1953). A sound, thorough bird's-eye view of the many executive agencies concerned with foreign-policy making is available in James L. McCamy, *The Administration of American Foreign Affairs* (New York, Alfred A. Knopf, Inc., 1950); the Brookings Institution, *The Administration of Foreign Affairs and Overseas Operations* (Washington, D.C., Government Printing Office, 1951); Harvey A. Bundy and James G. Rogers, *The Organization of the Government for the Conduct of Foreign Affairs,* Task Force Report on Foreign Affairs (Washington, D.C., Government Printing Office, 1949); and Commission on Organization of the Executive Branch of the Government (The Hoover Commission), *Foreign Affairs: A Report to Congress* (Washington, D.C., Government Printing Office, 1949). The most thorough essay on the literature concerning American foreign-policy formation and execution is Arthur Macmahon's "The Administration of Foreign Affairs," *American Political Science Review,* September, 1951. An excellent analysis of Congressional decision making is Stephen Bailey's *Congress Passes a Law* (New York, Columbia University Press, 1950). Daniel Cheever and Field Haviland, in *The Separation of Powers and American Foreign Policy* (Cambridge, Mass., Harvard University Press, 1952), present a series of decisions involving Congress and the Executive Branch. Treaty-making procedure is summarized in Elmer Plischke, *The Conduct of American Diplomacy* (New York, D. Van Nostrand Company, 1950), Chap. 10. Another phase of policy formation is discussed briefly in Francis B. Sayre, *How Trade Agreements Are Made* (New York, The Macmillan Company, 1939), Chap. 8. Program formulation is portrayed by a series of cases in Stein, *op. cit.,* pp. 199–362 and the *Foreign Service Act Case,* pp. 661–739. Former Secretary of State and of War Henry L. Stimson describes a crucial choice in "The Decision to Drop the Atom Bomb," *Harper's Magazine,* February, 1947. A sample problem paper, reputedly quite similar to those commonly employed at the administrative level, is available in the Brookings Institution, *Major Problems of U.S. Foreign Policy 1952–1953* (Washington, D.C., The Brookings Institution, 1953), pp. 313–372. In a valuable contribution, Roger Hilsman, Jr., discusses an important aspect of decision making in "Intelligence and Policy Making in Foreign Affairs," *World Politics,* October, 1952. Illuminating essays on diplomatic aspects of policy formation are to be found in Raymond Dennett and Joseph E. Johnson, eds., *Negotiating with the Russians* (Boston, World Peace Foundation, 1951). Finally, numerous insights and concrete information can be obtained from the memoirs, biographies, and diaries of the decision makers themselves: Cordell Hull, *Memoirs* (2 vols., New York, The Macmillan Company, 1948); Robert E. Sherwood, *Roosevelt and Hopkins* (New York, Harper & Brothers, 1948); Arthur H. Vandenberg, Jr., *The Private Papers of Senator Vandenberg* (Boston, Houghton Mifflin Company, 1952); Henry L. Stimson and McGeorge Bundy, *On Active Service in Peace and War* (New York, Harper & Brothers, 1947); Samuel L. Rosenman, *Working with Roosevelt* (New York, Harper & Brothers, 1952); Walter Millis, ed., *The Forrestal Diaries* (New York, The Viking Press, 1951); William Hillman, *Mr. President* (New York, Farrar, Straus & Young, 1952); Lucius D. Clay, *Decision in Germany* (New York, Doubleday & Company, 1950); and Dwight D. Eisenhower, *Crusade in Europe* (New York, Doubleday & Company, 1948).

CHAPTER FOUR

THE CONSTITUTIONAL FRAMEWORK

► INTRODUCTION

The constitutional framework within which American foreign policy is formulated and executed is comprised of the written Constitution, Congressional statutes, judicial interpretations as expressed in cases decided by the Supreme Court and by other federal courts, custom or usage, and "understandings." Together these elements form a constitutional system which allocates power and responsibility for foreign-policy decision making. A broad conception of the constitutional bases for the conduct of foreign relations is essential because the written Constitution says *relatively little of a specific nature* and what it does say may be variously interpreted. Furthermore, certain provisions of the Constitution which apparently have nothing to do with foreign affairs per se do affect the conduct of foreign affairs. Thus the division of powers between the federal government and the several states, along with the separation of powers between the Congress and the President, constitutes a kind of bedrock limit within which delicate adjustments must be made. However, the written Constitution does not provide answers to questions which arise in concrete cases, for example: Does the national government have greater power over foreign affairs than over domestic affairs? Are there special limitations on the powers of the states vis-à-vis foreign affairs? In the event of a head-on clash between the states and the national government involving control over international relations, which is paramount? What is the actual balance of power between the President and the Congress in particular instances?

It is therefore in the "living constitution"—the working arrangements and continuous interpretations based on the written document—that answers are found. Usage, for example, has decreed that Congress is not compelled to pass supplementary legislation for a treaty despite the fact that the "supreme law of the land" proviso (Article VI, Section 2) would seem to make this

135

automatic. Neither presidential agents nor executive agreements are directly authorized by the written Constitution. Originally it was intended that the "advice and consent" of the Senate in treaty making should truly reflect the late eighteenth-century practice of genuine collaboration between a small upper legislative chamber and the chief executive; actually nothing of the sort has developed, negotiation being solely in the hands of the President. Usage and Supreme Court decisions have combined to make the President a towering figure in foreign-policy matters despite the weak chief executive envisaged by the Founding Fathers.

Because of the vagueness of the written Constitution, the changing interpretations by the political organs of the national government, and the lack of comprehensive pronouncements by the Supreme Court, a large, settled body of constitutional law governing the exercise of the foreign-relations power has not emerged. Further complications have arisen from the so-called "dual" position of the foreign-relations power. This power is granted by the Constitution, but it is also inherent in the sovereignty of the nation as a member of the international community. If the Constitution said nothing at all about power over foreign relations, the United States would still possess it. Therefore, both constitutional and international law apply. International law requires that a treaty formally entered into be executed in good faith by the parties; yet the execution may depend upon Congressional action and may involve trespassing on the police powers of the states. Hence two points of view as to the nature and extent of the foreign-relations power are possible: interpretations based on domestic constitutional law, and interpretations based on international law. If either is pushed to an extreme, difficulties are multiplied. The result is, as will be seen below, that, where necessary, reconciliation is accomplished through a combination of "constitutional understanding" and "international understandings."

So far as foreign affairs are concerned, then, the constitutional system is being interpreted and reinterpreted more or less continuously within the limits imposed by provisions which can only be changed by formal amendment. The system is adaptable and flexible in the light of circumstances and necessities. It is characterized by areas of uncertainty because of the requirements of federalism and of separation of powers, the potential conflict between domestic constitutional processes and international obligations, and the need to convert general allocations of power into actual operations in concrete situations. Consequently, "the Constitution," as broadly defined, at once conditions the way in which foreign-policy decisions are made or implemented and provokes debate. A senator or group of senators may under the constitutional system challenge the exercise of some power by the President, but the specific arguments used may or may not be sound in the light of accepted doctrine and previous practice and may or may not be effective in determining the outcome of the controversy. The importance of habit, practical necessity, and political opportunity cannot be overestimated. Relatively few of the distinguishing features of the present system were the result of a deliberate plan or a great constitutional ruling. Rather, a problem had to be faced or a policy had to be decided and some agency of government had the vigor or opportunity to go ahead in the absence of a constitutional blueprint.

It follows that in addition to the influence of the constitutional system on policy formation, a second focal point of interest in this chapter is the effect of America's new international position on this system. For it is the interaction of the system and the changing character of foreign relations which produces significant constitutional issues. During this period of transition such issues have occurred and have had considerable effect upon decision making.

► THE NATURE OF THE FOREIGN-RELATIONS POWER

The power to conduct foreign relations is lodged exclusively in the national government.* No residuum of power is left to the several states. Apparently the fear on the part of the drafters of the written Constitution that the powers of the national government over domestic affairs might overrun the powers of the states did not carry over into the realm of foreign affairs. Article I, Section 10 says: "No state shall enter into any treaty, alliance or confederation; grant letters of marque and reprisal; . . . No State shall, without the consent of the Congress, lay any imposts or duties on imports or exports, . . . No state shall, without the consent of Congress, lay any duty of tonnage, keep troops, or ships of war in time of peace, enter into any agreement or compact . . . with a foreign power, or engage in war, unless actually invaded, or in such imminent danger as will not admit of delay." Coupled with explicit grants of power to the national government, these prohibitions render the monopoly complete. "This constitution, and the laws of the United States which shall be made in pursuance thereof; and all treaties made, or which shall be made, under the authority of the United States, shall be the supreme law of the land; and the judges in every state shall be bound thereby, any thing in the constitution or laws of any state to the contrary notwithstanding"—so reads the supremacy clause. Within the range of its prescribed powers, the federal government is supreme.

This constitutional grant of exclusive power to the national government really only confirms the fact that the capacity to control its external relations inheres in the United States as a sovereign entity.† Both doctrines are expressed by Mr. Justice George Sutherland in his book *Constitutional Power* *and World Affairs* (New York, Columbia University Press, 1919): "Where the powers claimed for the general government are to be subtracted from the mass of orignal state powers, that is, where they relate to domestic and internal affairs, the claim must be justified by the express grants of the Constitution,

---

* *Missouri v. Holland,* 252 U.S. 416 (1920).
† *United States v. Curtiss-Wright Export Corporation,* 299 U.S. 304 (1936); *Chinese Exclusion Cases,* 130 U.S. 581 (1889).

or by the implications arising therefrom; but where the powers claimed are among those originally acquired and always exclusively held by the Nation, that is, where they relate to external affairs, the claim is justified unless the powers are prohibited by the Constitution, or unless contrary to the fundamental principles upon which it was established."*

A second major characteristic of the federal power follows from the first: the foreign-relations power and the domestic power of the federal government are quite different in nature and extent. Congress cannot legislate on matters within state control in the absence of a treaty but it can do so if a treaty exists and requires such legislation. After so stating, Mr. Justice Holmes went on to say in the Supreme Court's ruling in *Missouri* v. *Holland: "We do not mean to imply that there are no qualifications to the treaty-making power, but they must be ascertained in a different way*. It is obvious that there may be matters of the sharpest exigency for the national well being that an act of Congress could not deal with but that a treaty followed by such an act could, and it is not lightly to be assumed that, in matters requiring national action, 'a power which must belong to and somewhere reside in every civilized government' is not to be found." Moreover, working together the President and Congress can do almost anything;† certainly they can do things in the field of foreign policy which they cannot do in the field of domestic policy. Even private rights can be seriously curtailed without the due process ordinarily guaranteed. Thus some American citizens were denied claims against the Russian Insurance Company as a result of a Supreme Court decision in 1942.‡ Moreover, so long as the President and Congress operate within their proper functions, powers may be delegated in legislation and treaties virtually without limit—a clear departure from constitutional practice in purely domestic matters where the content and the method of delegation are subject to close scrutiny by the Court. All this is reinforced by the fact that the Supreme Court leans heavily toward the view that its competence with respect to foreign relations is quite limited as compared with its competence on internal political questions. Foreign-policy questions are, generally speaking, for the nonjudicial organs of the federal government to decide.

THE POSITION OF THE STATES

It is clearly established that the states have no independent powers regarding foreign relations which can substantially impede the exercise of the power of the national government in this realm. Nor do the "police powers" of the states, that is, the broad powers over their own internal affairs, restrict the control of the national government over foreign policy. The Tenth Amendment, which reserves to the states the powers not delegated to the

---

* From Chapter 3, as quoted in L. H. Chamberlain and R. C. Snyder, *American Foreign Policy* (New York, Rinehart & Company, 1948), p. 16.
† It is generally agreed that this is the purport of the Curtiss-Wright decision.
‡ *United States* v. *Pink,* 315 U.S. 203 (1942).

United States, gives way before Article VI—the supremacy clause—which provides that all treaties shall be "the supreme law of the land" state laws notwithstanding. Therefore, the dual federal principle "does not limit in any way the power of the National Government in treaty-making or in the governance of foreign commerce, the operation of the Supremacy Clause being as regards these powers complete and unqualified."* When state laws and state action clearly within the powers reserved to the states conflict with a treaty or with other federal action taken within the express powers of the central government and implemented under the necessary and proper clause (Article I, Section 8), the latter prevails. Perhaps the most celebrated case is *Missouri v. Holland* (1920). Here the issue was the constitutionality of a Congressional statute passed in 1917 to implement an agreement between the United States and Great Britain to protect birds which migrated between this country and Canada. The state of Missouri brought suit against the federal government in the Supreme Court, insisting that the statute was an invasion of the state's right to the regulation of wild life within its borders. Justice Holmes upheld the statute on behalf of the Court in an opinion already quoted. But the practice of declaring state legislation void in the face of treaties had begun long before. Shortly after the formation of the republic, Virginia† and Maryland‡ statutes were held to conflict with the terms of the treaty of peace with Great Britain which concluded the American Revolution. Federal treaties with Indian tribes were also upheld against contrary provisions of local legislation.§ In *Chirac v. Chirac* (1817)‖ even state control of the inheritance of property was required to give way before provisions of a treaty with France. Not only treaties but federal legislation bearing on foreign relations have resulted in state statutes being declared unconstitutional. A Pennsylvania law regulating the activities of enemy aliens was so declared for conflicting with the federal Alien Registration Law of 1940.# All this has happened—these cases are only a small sample—despite the fact that the reserved powers of the states are reserved against the treaty power just as much as against the federal tax and commerce power. While the treaty power is not without limit, it is not clear from the cases involving state action just what its limits really are. However, the written Constitution obligates the national government to guarantee the territorial integrity of each state and its republican form of government and this provision does limit the treaty power. In sum, it does not appear that *legally* state rights interfere in any substantial way with the making and carrying out of national decisions on foreign affairs.

Nonetheless, within these agreed propositions there is ample room for

---

* Edward S. Corwin, *The Constitution and World Organization* (Princeton, N. J., Princeton University Press, 1944).
† *Ware v. Hylton,* 3 Dallas 199 (1796).
‡ *Clerke v. Harwood,* 3 Dallas 342 (1797).
§ *Worcester v. Georgia,* 6 Wheaton 264 (1821).
‖ 2 Wheaton 259. See also, *Havenstein v. Lynham,* 100 U.S. 483 (1880).
Hines v. Davidowitz, 312 U.S. 52 (1941).

varying interpretations and for "understandings" which do draw the line between the foreign-relations power and the power of the states on a more flexible, less black-or-white basis. Professor Quincy Wright has written: "The practice of the Senate, the opinions of statesmen and dicta of the courts indicate that, except for the most cogent reasons, the treaty power ought to exercise its powers in such way as not to interfere with the control by the states of their own land, natural resources, and public services and not to interfere unnecessarily with the enforcement by the state of its own policy with reference to the protection of public safety, health, morals and economic welfare."* This point becomes all the more significant when it is realized that the United States has become in recent years a party to many multilateral agreements inside or outside the United Nations which involve the protection of human rights and the regulation of social relations. International legislation of this type represents a much more important aspect of American foreign policy than it did prior to World War II. The outstanding Supreme Court decisions bearing on the foreign-relations power were decided in an era of comparative national isolation when treaties which deeply penetrated the traditional domain of the states were exceptional.

In May, 1950, the California Court of Appeal decided, in effect, that the United Nations Charter superseded a California statute. The case involved the validity of the California Alien Land Law which prohibits Japanese and other "aliens" from owning and occupying land in the state. In taking this position, the court cited Articles 55 and 56 of the United Nations Charter. Article 55 says in part: ". . . the United Nations shall promote: . . . universal respect for, and observance of, human rights and fundamental freedoms for all without distinction as to race, sex, language, or religion." Article 56 says, in toto: "All Members pledge themselves to take joint and separate action in cooperation with the Organization for the achievement of the purposes set forth in Article 55." If it set an accepted pattern, this decision could pave the way for the contention that all discriminatory legislation on the state level is automatically invalid. It seems unlikely that the case will reach the Supreme Court, however, because in April, 1952, the Supreme Court of the State of California upheld the unconstitutionality of Alien Land Law, but refused to accept the lower court's reasoning on the applicability of the United Nations Charter. Judge Gibson, speaking for a majority of the Supreme Court of California, argued that the provisions of the charter cited by the plaintiff did *not* constitute a self-executing treaty and therefore did not automatically supersede local law. In view of the bitter opposition to Fair Employment Practice legislation in Congress, such a development could be of far-reaching political and social importance. This case differs from the famous *Missouri v. Holland* ruling, which laid down the principle that a treaty can accomplish anything

---

* Quincy Wright, *The Control of American Foreign Relations* (New York, The Macmillan Company, 1922), p. 93.

of a national character so long as it is plausibly related to the general welfare. But in the latter, a treaty with Canada regulating migratory birds was backed up by an act of Congress and the subject matter did not touch upon funda- mentals of the social order or the sanctity of private property.

Essentially the same kind of issue was raised by the Genocide Treaty (a multilateral international agreement outlawing the planned extinction of whole national, racial, or religious groups) discussed by the Senate in 1950.* If the same construction were applied, many discriminatory statutes and social practices conceivably might be interpreted as subject to repeal and punishment under the treaty. However, the most interesting feature of the treaty was the four "understandings" drawn up by a subcommittee of the Senate Foreign Relations Committee to obviate constitutional difficulties. The first one asserted that the treaty did not disturb the traditonal jurisdictional division between the federal government and the states. As a matter of fact, a "federal-state clause" is now a fairly common feature of treaties touching on domestic social matters.

Both of these examples point up a subtle, difficult distinction which may have an increasingly important bearing on the way in which the line between state rights and the federal foreign-relations power is drawn. The distinction is between self-executing and non-self-executing treaties or agreements. A self- executing treaty is one which requires no Congressional action to implement it and which automatically replaces domestic federal or state law. It is not certain whether or not there is a moral obligation on Congress to legislate international commitments which are not self-executing. Presumably, the Genocide Treaty is a clear case of a non-self-executing treaty because Article 5 obligates the signatories to supply needed legislation "in accordance with their respective constitutions." To the extent that treaties and agreements which ultimately embrace matters within the police power of the states are treated as non-self-executing, state rights will be protected in Congress—particularly in the Senate. In view of the increasing sensitivity over federal civil rights legis- lation, it appears unlikely that, insofar as senators and representatives speak for states per se, any large-scale invasion of local control of social relations will be permitted. On the other hand, if the decision of the California court is upheld, Congressional protection of state rights might be by-passed. Be this as it may, the *Missouri v. Holland* principle, the "understanding" noted by Professor Wright above, and new types of international agreements have been

---

* The Genocide Treaty was sent to the Senate for "advice and consent" to ratification on June 16, 1949. Hearings were held by the Senate Foreign Relations Committee from January 23 to February 9, 1950. Indifference and opposition froze the treaty for the next four years. Testifying before a Senate Judicial Subcommittee in April, 1953, Secretary of State Dulles stated that the administration would not press for Senate acceptance "at this time." In view of the general agitation over treaties of this sort and the pressure of supporters of the Bricker amendment, it would appear that the Genocide Convention is a dead issue indefinitely.

thrown together in a new situation likely to produce controversies in the Senate or before the Supreme Court.*

The determination of the Eisenhower Administration to improve relations between the states and the federal government and to encourage more political control and responsbility at the state and local level had its implications for foreign policy. In May, 1953, the President and other high officials gave forty-four state and territorial governors a secret briefing on foreign-policy moves. Writing to the governors, President Eisenhower said: "It is my earnest conviction that you will find this conference a worth-while occasion. The program will give consideration, among other matters of national concern, to current developments in the field of international relations, the American defense effort, the problems of national security and an analysis of our fiscal policies as related thereto." When he opened the conference, the President said further: "The conduct of foreign affairs and the business of war and peace are, under our Constitution, the responsibility of the Federal Government. But in times like ours the danger to our country involves the civilian populations in the cities and towns and on the farms of our states. The responsibility of all local governments is immense."† Reports of the secret conference indicate that the governors were called upon for their views and advice.

No extended treatment of the complicated tidelands oil issue is possible here. Suffice it to say that the Republican administration came to power in January, 1953, pledged to the general principle of supporting the claims of coastal states to ownership of submerged lands adjacent to their shores. By March of that year, bills had been introduced in the Senate which would give Texas and Florida rights to lands exceeding ten miles from shore. Mr. Jack B. Tate, deputy legal adviser of the State Department, told the Senate Interior Committee: "If the nation should recognize the extension of the boundaries of any state beyond the three-mile limit, its identification with the broader claim would force abandonment of its traditional position. At the same time, it would renounce the grounds of protest against claims of foreign states to greater breadths of territorial waters."‡ Mr. Tate spoke only with reference to ownership of submerged lands, not exploitation of oil and other national resources. He added, later in his testimony, that maintenance of the nation's traditional position on the three-mile limit was "vital at a time when a number of foreign states show a tendency unilaterally to break down the principle of freedom of the seas by attempted extensions of sovereignty over high seas."

SEPARATION OF POWERS

There is little doubt that important as are the broad grant of power to the national government and the duality of the federal system as constitutional

* See the discussion of the Bricker amendment below. It is interesting to note that at its annual meeting (December 10, 1952) the Association of Attorneys General of the several states adopted a resolution calling for modification of the treaty power.
† New York *Times,* April 12, 1953, p. 1.
‡ New York *Times,* March 4, 1953, p. 11.

bases of foreign-policy making, the separation of power between the executive and legislative branches probably constitutes an even more fundamental conditioning factor. While together the President and Congress have a very wide area of discretionary power, the important point is that they must collaborate if decision making is not to break down altogether or limp badly. Such collaboration is necessary for those major aspects of foreign policy involving appropriations, appointments, war making, and international agreements. The proper coordination of presidential and Congressional power is an unavoidable yet thorny problem.

The nature of this problem will be analyzed more fully in Chapters Eleven and Twelve but one important point must be made here. While the separation of powers results almost inevitably in "built-in" conflict at the heart of the American political process, the conflict has definite limits. Strangely enough, the limits are not primarily constitutional in the narrow sense. There is, obviously, plenty of room for effective Congressional challenge of the interpretations of the foreign-relations power by the Executive Branch and vice versa, paving the way for all the potentialities of the "irresistible force–immovable object" situation. If pressed too far, chaos could result. Actually no constitutional conflict of this type has been pushed to its logical conclusions and for very practical reasons.

An example will illustrate. During the Senate hearings on the removal of General MacArthur in the spring of 1951,* General Bradley, Chairman of the Joint Chiefs of Staff (created by an act of Congress), refused to divulge the contents of his conversation concerning the matter with President Truman. The refusal caused a furor in the Senate, some members arguing that General Bradley was subject to the regulatory and investigatory power of Congress and should therefore be compelled to testify. What courses of action were open? First, the general could have been cited for contempt of the Senate. If the citation were upheld by the Supreme Court, it would ultimately have to be enforced by the Department of Justice, an executive agency which could have been stopped from enforcing the ruling by order of the President. Second, the Senate could have threatened to withhold appropriations, but if it had stood firm on this the wheels of the federal government, including defense activities, would have been slowed to a halt. Third, the Senate could have instituted impeachment proceedings against the President, an extreme measure requiring the cooperation of the House of Representatives. Apart from other difficulties, there was insufficient support for this move. To all intents and purposes, the Congress and the Supreme Court could not have enforced a ruling compelling General Bradley to testify unless the President acquiesced. Neither had any direct control over the President short of impeachment, which would not have pried loose the particular conversation anyway. Conversely,

* Eighty-second Congress, 1st Session, "The Military Situation in the Far East," Hearings before the Committee on Armed Services and the Committee on Foreign Relations, United States Senate, Parts I–V, 1951.

neither the President alone, or with the cooperation of the Supreme Court, can force Congress to do anything it is determined not to do.

It is worth noting that the problems arising from the separation of powers are complicated by the fact that there have been no definitive Supreme Court decisions bearing directly on the relationship between the powers of Congress and the powers of the President. Until 1935, there were few cases involving the separation of powers generally and these did not concern foreign affairs.* Furthermore, there have been very few instances when the Court has either agreed to, or been forced to, rule on the powers of the President not based on a legislative act.† No one knows what the result would be if Congress did formally authorize or tacitly approve some action by the President if it were submitted for judicial review. To take a famous example, Lincoln's blockade of Southern ports was upheld by the Supreme Court, which appeared to lean rather heavily on the fact that eventually Congress had given its assent.‡ The *Curtiss-Wright Case* contains authoritative pronouncements on aspects of the foreign-relations power, but it yields little light on the question of the "cognate powers"§ of the other two branches of the federal government. Professor Corwin holds the opinion that these powers "are so broad, so indefinite, so overlapping, that the Court could not disentangle them if it wished to . . ."‖ Thus it is not surprising that there is an area between the clear, unshared powers of Congress and the clear, unshared powers of the President which is a kind of no man's land regarding which the ground rules are unsettled.

CONCLUSION

A very broad interpretation has been given to the foreign-relations power of the national government. The most effective checks on the federal power have been *political, not legal.* Unless the President and Congress act in complete harmony, the full limit of this power will probably not be exercised. As noted, the several states do not, constitutionally, have substantial rights against the foreign-relations power of the national government; yet for political reasons caution tends to curb the extent to which the police powers of the states are invaded. There are other checks on the federal power. Any treaty is superior to existing state or federal law but not to the Constitution itself. The treaty power cannot authorize what the Constitution forbids.# In 1870, the Supreme Court said: "It need hardly be said that a treaty cannot change the Constitution or be held valid if it be in violation of that instrument."¶

---

* Benjamin F. Wright, *The Growth of American Constitutional Law* (New York, Reynal & Hitchcock, 1942), p. 139.

† *Ibid.*

‡ *The Prize Cases,* 2 Black 635 (1863).

§ The Supreme Court's phrase.

‖ Edward S. Corwin, *Total War and the Constitution* (New York, Alfred A. Knopf, Inc., 1947), p. 154.

Geofroy v. Riggs, 133 U.S. 267 (1889).

¶ *Cherokee Tobacco Case,* 11 Wallace 620 (1870).

Furthermore, a treaty is subordinate to later statutes: ". . . it is well settled that in the case of a conflict between an act of Congress and a treaty . . . the last one in date must prevail . . ."* No treaty can amend the written consti- tution. No unconstitutional methods can be employed in conducting foreign relations. Presumably the general outline of the balance of power established in the constitutional system cannot be modified. However, no treaty or impor- tant act of the President has been declared unconstitutional and there is, to reiterate, a continuing, flexible interpretation of the foreign-relations power.

The relatively free hand given to the federal government in the control of external relations stands in rather stark contrast to the more restricted inter- pretations of its power over domestic matters. An interesting irony is that Justice Sutherland—a most vocal and influential proponent of the "limited government" concept on the Supreme Court bench from 1895 to 1937—was the spokesman in one of the two significant cases which established the present doctrine. In the *Curtiss-Wright Case* he declared: "Not only . . . is the federal power over external affairs in origin and essential character different from that over internal affairs, but participation in the exercise of the power is significantly limited." Again, ". . . congressional legislation which is to be made effective through negotiation and inquiry within the international field must often accord to the President a degree of discretion and freedom from statutory restriction which would not be admissible were domestic affairs alone involved." Two assumptions seem to underlie this opinion: one is that a restriction on the foreign-relations power would impair the right of a united people to perform the necessary functions of statehood—a right they held independently of any constitution; the second is that there is no inconsistency between a broad interpretation of one segment of the federal power and a narrower interpretation of the other segment—in other words, the distinction between foreign and domestic affairs is real as well as apparent.

However this may be, Sutherland helped mightily to lay the groundwork for a doctrine which may in the end add to the federal government's power in the domestic sphere. The federal power over foreign affairs is virtually un- limited and so long as the purpose is legitimate the means can be found. Now when this concept is joined with the recognition emphasized in an earlier chapter that there is no longer any real distinction between foreign and domes- tic policy, it is clear that by means of treaties, agreements, and Mutual Aid Programs the way is open at least for necessary actions which might be forbidden were domestic policy alone under consideration. Foreign-policy expenditures have already required economic planning in peacetime beyond even that sanctioned by a more liberal post-Sutherland Supreme Court. It seems safe to predict that, as the adjustment to the new international situation becomes more and more specific and far-reaching, adversely affected domestic interests will sooner or later petition the Supreme Court for redress. Unless previous rulings are upset completely, such interests probably have little to

* *Hijo v. United States,* 194 U.S. 324 (1904).

hope for. To repeat, these rulings were made at a time when American foreign relations were "primitive" and were quite overshadowed by domestic considerations.

► THE POWERS OF THE PRESIDENT*

This discussion of presidential and Congressional powers does not by itself explain what either branch will do or should do in any particular instance. Nor is it sufficient to account for the broad role of each in the formation of foreign policy or to provide reasons why each does or tries to do certain things. The constitutional system in a general way *formally* allocates power and responsibility for the conduct of foreign relations and the following suggests the nature of the division of labor worked out through time.

THE GENERAL CONSTITUTIONAL POSITION

The constitutional powers of the President—available to him personally or to the agencies responsible to him—are imposing indeed. They rest, as has been argued, on several foundation stones: explicit grants having to do with foreign affairs in the written Constitution, implicit grants in the written Constitution not specifically directed to foreign affairs, legislative statutes, Supreme Court decisions, and custom and understandings. It is a combination of these which provides the legal underpinning for the great discretion any power which can be exercised by the President.

Article II (the executive article) states in Section 1: "The executive power shall be vested in a president of the United States of America"—phraseology which omits the words "herein granted" found in Article I (the legislative article). Actually, the President has powers in addition to those set forth in the other clauses of Article II. "He has vague and vast 'executive power' which have never been enumerated or defined."† Section 3 of Article II reads: "He shall take care that the laws be faithfully executed . . ." Together the two articles are an indefinite reservoir of permissiveness for the President to take action to preserve the Constiution, to defend the nation, and to protect American lives and property abroad. They are reinforced by the more specific powers listed below. It must also be remembered that the President as head of state is recognized as having certain prerogatives under international law; he must, for example, uphold international law binding upon the United States as a member of the community of nations and must prevent or punish violations of treaties. All this has been admitted by the Supreme Court, which said in the *Curtiss-Wright Case* that the President must be granted "a degree of

* The powers of the President and Congress are described briefly in this chapter to serve as background for the later discussion of the general role of each in foreign affairs.

† Edward S. Corwin and Jack W. Peltason, *Understanding the Constitution* (New York, William Sloane Associates, 1949), p. 40.

discretion and freedom from statutory restriction which would not be admissible were domestic affairs alone involved." Article II, Section 2, Paragraph 1 of the Constitution provides that the President ". . . may require the opinion, in writing, of the principal officer in each of the executive departments, upon any subject relating to the duties of their respective offices, . . ." Although Congress creates executive departments (and ordinarily defines their duties) by law and appropriates the money for their operation, the President's powers over the official acts of the heads of executive departments are *complete* and have always gone beyond the mere request for reports.* Insofar as the foreign-relations power is exercised through the Executive Branch, the total legal responsibility rests with the President. It is noteworthy that while Congress directs all federal departments to supply information, in the case of the State Department, Congress *requests* the President to furnish it.

A SUMMATION OF THE PRESIDENT'S LEGAL POWERS

1. The President has the power to make treaties (Article II, Section 2). He alone *negotiates* treaties. "Into the field of negotiation the Senate cannot intrude; and Congress itself is powerless to invade it."† He controls every phase of the treaty-making process except at the point where the Senate must give approval. He can withdraw a treaty from consideration by the Senate and he is not compelled to accept Senate amendments or other modifications. He can refuse to exchange ratifications with other parties to a treaty or to formally proclaim a treaty which the Senate has approved. While a treaty is in operation, the President retains the initiative with respect to interpretation and implementation. Acting through the State Department he can terminate a treaty—an act which can have considerable significance as in the case of the 1911 commercial treaty with Japan which was denounced by the United States in July, 1939 as a sanction against Japanese foreign policy.

2. Article II, Section 2 specifies that the President "shall nominate, and by and with the advice and consent of the Senate, shall appoint ambassadors, other public ministers and consuls . . ." and Article II, Section 3 specifies that "he shall receive ambassadors and other public ministers. . . ." There are two significant consequences of these provisions. First, the President is the sole organ of official communication with foreign governments, a position which gives him, legally, a monopoly over information relating to external affairs. A Congressional statute acknowledges these facts by forbidding any member of the legislature from communicating with a foreign government. Second, the power to send and receive diplomatic representatives makes available an important policy technique: "recognition" of foreign governments or states. Full or *de jure* recognition through the establishment of formal diplomatic relations is tantamount to saying that a new state or a new regime has been admitted to the rights and duties shared by other members of the international

---

* *Ibid.*, pp. 48–49.

† *United States v. Curtiss-Wright Export Corporation,* 299 U.S. 304 (1936).

community. Nonrecognition has come more and more to mean disapproval of new states and governments regardless of whether in fact they are capable of maintaining normal diplomatic intercourse. Formerly recognition, was a purely legal and factual matter so far as the United States was concerned—that is, if a new government was actually exercising sovereign power in a territory or if a new state was willing and able to fulfill its rights and duties toward other states it was accorded recognition. Now the element of approval–disapproval has become paramount. Nonrecognition may even constitute a form of sanction against policies and practices which are opposed for one reason or another. The political implications of American recognition of Soviet Russia in 1933 and of the new state of Israel in 1948 were far-reaching. One need only note the bitter opposition in the United States to the recognition of the Communist regime which came to power in China in 1949 to realize that recognition is no longer simply a legal technicality. In a divided world, recognition carries with it the possibility of American aid and support over and above the ordinary by-products of diplomatic intercourse.

3. Special statutes confer other powers on the President. There are approximately one hundred statutes which provide him with a variety of emergency powers related to foreign affairs in one way or another. A proclamation of national emergency or threat of war would be necessary to invoke most of these. President Truman proclaimed such an emergency on December 16, 1950, and cited some sixty-one statutes which yielded him new powers as a result. Even without such a proclamation, there is a long list of powers the President could use to mobilize the economy, and so on. The Defense Production Act of 1950 placed broad authority in the hands of the President without the need for a national emergency. In addition, many well-known legislative enactments confer extensive powers: the Reciprocal Trade Agreements Act (1934), the Bank Conservation Act (1933), the Silver Purchase Act (1934), the Gold Reserve Act (1934), the Greek-Turkish Aid Bill (1947), the Foreign Relief Act (1948), and the Mutual Aid Bill (1951).

4. The President can declare policy and interpret previous declarations of policy. Several of the country's most important foreign policies have been formulated by presidential messages: Washington's doctrine of "no entangling alliances," the Monroe Doctrine, the Good Neighbor policy of Franklin Roosevelt, the Truman Doctrine of 1947. Declarations of this type may simply codify existing thought and practice, they may constitute "trial balloons," or they may indicate new directions in policy. They may be announced in special messages or annual messages to Congress, in radio broadcasts or public addresses, in letters to some distinguished person or group, or in press conferences. They are generally accepted as official by the nation and the world. Through such mediums a persistent and skillful President can shape public opinion. So sensitive is the line of communication between the President and the public that even the most casual, offhand remarks of the former are seized upon and analyzed. Early in 1949 President Truman informally remarked at

a luncheon in Washington that there were "some men in the Kremlin" who wanted to end the conflict between the United States and Russia. These words became headlines immediately, giving rise to speculation as to a shift in American policy.

5. Special agents have become an important presidential device in foreign affairs. Two types may be noted. One consists of presidential agents who hold no official position in the federal government. Outstanding examples are Colonel House, who served and influenced Woodrow Wilson during World War I, and Harry Hopkins, who served and influenced Franklin Roosevelt during World War II. Men like House and Hopkins exercised tremendous power. This fact has led to suspicion and criticism, for, although these men were neither elected nor approved by any public body, they were in a position to influence the destiny of the whole country. However, these men rendered valuable service without any real reward, occasionally under great abuse, a fact not always recognized by a sometimes puzzled public. Special agents of this type are responsible only to the President—they are personal agents. Yet their activities become presidential activities and can therefore be held to account. The necessity for personal agents is admirably summed by Robert E. Sherwood in his brilliant study *Roosevelt and Hopkins:* "Roosevelt deliberately educated Hopkins in the arts and sciences of politics and of war and then gave him immense powers of decision for no reason other than that he liked him, trusted him, and needed him."* The second type of agent is the person who already holds some federal office and is chosen for a particular mission. In 1940 Franklin Roosevelt sent Under Secretary of State Sumner Welles to Europe to investigate confidentially the possibilities of bringing World War II to a quick conclusion. President Truman proposed to send Chief Justice of the Supreme Court Vinson to Moscow in 1948 for special talks with Stalin. When necessary, presidential agents can do nearly everything regular diplomats can do: negotiate agreements, talk confidentially with heads of state, collect information, attend conferences, or open diplomatic relations. Often they can do more. The chief significance of the special agent is that he has all the stature of the regular diplomat but, from the President's point of view, none of the liabilities. Ambassadors and ministers are often "political" appointees and for one reason or another the President may wish to circumvent them. Information may be more readily accessible to a purely personal emissary of the chief executive. The special agent can concentrate on one task instead of being burdened with duties which normally confront the head of a mission. The man can be picked for the particular job with due regard for such factors as specialization and flexibility.

In the light of developments since 1940, two powers of the President deserve particular emphasis: his control over the nation's armed forces and his ability to negotiate executive agreements.

---

* Robert F. Sherwood, *Roosevelt and Hopkins* (New York, Harper and Brothers, 1948), p. 1.

THE PRESIDENT AS COMMANDER IN CHIEF

Article II, Section 2, Paragraph 1 of the written Constitution states: "The President shall be commander in chief of the army and navy of the United States and of the militia of the several states, when called into actual service of the United States. . . ." This power is reinforced by the "executive power" already mentioned, by the President's being the "sole organ of the nation," and by statutes. In this clause, incidentally, the framers guaranteed the important principle of civilian supremacy over the military. In time of war, the President's power over the armed forces is complete. "The power to use an army is coextensive with the power to make war; . . . and it is for the President as Commander-in-Chief to direct the campaigns of that war wherever he may think they should be carried on."* Subjugated territories can be governed by the President until they are disposed of by formal agreement.† Under conditions of total war, the aggregate of power available to the President is great indeed and includes more than purely military prerogatives. As a result of a presidential order during World War II, 112,000 Japanese on the West Coast —most of them American citizens—were taken from their homes and forced to live in relocation centers. Lincoln freed the slaves as a "war measure" during the Civil War. Even in peacetime, the President is the ultimate authority on questions of "grand strategy." If he wishes, he can ignore his military advisers. His control of all military personnel is complete. There is no doubt whatever that under the Constitution President Truman had the legal right to relieve General MacArthur of his command in April, 1951.

What are the constitutional grounds for the use of the Armed Forces by the President in peacetime as a general instrument of foreign policy? First, the Armed Forces—especially the Navy—have been used on some 150 different occasions to protect American lives and property in the absence of Congressional authorization or declaration of war.‡ Exercise of this authority has been challenged only once in the courts and in that case the trial judge of the Second Circuit Court of Appeals upheld the authority saying, in part:

> As the executive head of the Nation, the President is made the only legitimate organ of the general Government to open and carry on correspondence or negotiations with foreign nations. . . . It is to him, also, the citizens abroad must look for protection of person and property. . . . For this purpose, the whole executive power of the country is placed in his hands, under the Constitution. . . . Now as it respects the interposition of the Executive abroad, for the protection of the lives or property of the citizen, the duty must, of necessity, rest in the discretion of the president. . . . The question whether it was the duty of the President to interpose . . . was a public political question . . . which belonged to the Executive to determine . . . §

* Former Chief Justice Hughes, *War Powers under the Constitution*, Senate Document No. 105, 65th Congress, 1st Session (1917).

† *Fleming v. Page*, 9 Howard 615 (1850).

‡ James Grafton Rogers, *World Policing and the Constitution* (Boston, World Peace Foundation, 1945). The incidents are listed on pp. 92–123.

§ *Durand v. Hollins*, 4 Blatchford, 451, 454–455 (1860).

Second, the President has employed the Armed Forces to avenge an alleged insult to the United States.* Third, the President has, in his capacity as commander in chief, acted to defend the national interest or to serve some larger aspect of foreign policy. Examples of the latter are the intervention in Texas in 1845, in Mexico in 1917, and in Panama in 1903–1904, and the stationing of American troops in Iceland in 1941. In *The Prize Cases,* the Supreme Court upheld a whole series of acts by President Lincoln to deal with the outbreak of war between the North and the South. Justice Grier said: "If a war be made by invasion of a foreign nation, the President is not only authorized but bound to resist force by force. He does not initiate the war, but is bound to accept the challenge without waiting for any special legislative authority."†

Congressional authorization for presidential use of the Armed Forces began very early in constitutional history when Congress gave George Washing the power to enforce the embargo of 1794 with military force. In its capacity as war-declaring power Congress has been solicited by various presidents for approval of the use of the Armed Forces. President Buchanan, for example, asked in vain for authority to protect Americans on the way to the California gold fields via Panama, Nicaragua, and Mexico. Other presidents have justified their actions to Congress on the basis of legislative policy as did Franklin Roosevelt when he invoked the Lend-Lease Act as one reason for sending troops to Iceland. Sometimes, Congressional authorization comes ex post facto, appropriations to implement the destroyer-bases deal of 1940 being a case in point. Strictly speaking, none of these approving procedures is *legally* necessary, whatever may be deemed good politics in a specific situation. It is also true that most of the 150 cases mentioned could be fitted into the rubric of self-defense rather than classified as political intervention. Neither can the President declare war. There is, in fact, a strong presumption that he ought not to deliberately create a state of war. Yet the President can take—and has taken—steps ranging from punitive action against the Barbary pirates under Jefferson, through Woodrow Wilson's arming of American merchant ships, to the "shoot on sight" order of Franklin Roosevelt, all of which may make a declaration of war by Congress perfunctory. Needless to say, acts or policies of the President unrelated to his powers as commander of the Armed Forces may lead to the same result. Franklin Roosevelt's refusal to accede to Japanese demands in November, 1941, probably helped to seal the issue of war with Japan.

Fourth, the President may send troops abroad to execute a treaty. The doctrine was set forth by John Marshall (later Chief Justice) while he was still a member of the House of Representatives: "He [the President] is charged to execute laws. A treaty is declared to be a law. He must then execute a treaty where he, and he alone, possesses the means of executing it."‡ Under the Platt

---

* Clarence A. Berdahl, *War Powers of the Executive in the United States* (Urbana, Ill., University of Illinois, 1921), p. 51.

† *The Prize Cases,* 2 Black 668 (1863).

‡ 5 Wheaton, appendix, Note I, 26.

Amendment (giving the United States the right to intervene in Cuba after the Spanish-American War) and under the Colombia Treaty of 1846 (giving the United States the right to protect the Isthmus of Panama) the President sent troops to execute treaties—that is, to guarantee that the expected results of the agreements would be fulfilled. Neither treaty said anything about troops per se; the President simply took the action he thought would be most effective. Fifth, as commander in chief, the President can perform functions required or authorized by international law, notably the occupation of a defeated enemy nation.* There has been no direct statutory authorization, nor is there explicit permission in the written Constitution for the occupations of Germany and Japan, but Congress has acquiesced in and supported the administration of those areas. Naturally, the Preisdent can protect occupation forces if they are menaced by a hostile force.

President Truman's decision to intervene in Korea in 1950 would appear to rest, constitutionally, on a combination of several facets of his power as commander in chief: defense of the strategic interests of the United States; protection of American occupation forces in Japan; implementation of recommendations by the Security Council in accordance with the Charter of the United Nations—a treaty to which America is a party; and protection of American property and persons. Not since the days immediately prior to the outbreak of World War II has there been such a graphic illustration of the magnitude and importance of the President's power in this regard.

There are, however, limitations on this power. The President may not use it to subvert the Constitution or destroy the laws of the United States or commit American forces to the defense of any national interests save those of the United States. Congress *could,* if it wished, hamper the employment of the Armed Forces, as will be seen. Finally, the President cannot *augment* his power at the expense of Congress through a treaty or agreement.†

EXECUTIVE AGREEMENTS

The Constitution does not say a word about executive agreements any more than it says that the President may use military forces to promote American foreign policy. Yet executive agreements have been entered into since 1800. Important steps in foreign policy have been accomplished by such agreements rather than by regular treaty. The purchase of Louisiana, the annexation of Texas, the establishment of a Permanent Joint Defense Board with Canada, the famous destroyer-bases exchange with Great Britain in 1940, the Lend-Lease Program begun in 1941, the Atlantic Charter declared jointly by Winston Churchill and Franklin Roosevelt, as well as the significant Allied conferences at Moscow (1943), Yalta (1944), and Potsdam (1945), which resulted in general commitments to govern the postwar settlement, were

---

* *Cross v. Harrison,* 16 Howard 164 (1853).
† See Corwin, *Total War and the Constitution,* pp. 152–153.

all embodied in agreements of this type. By 1939, 1,182 out of a total of 2,000 international engagements to which the United States was then a party were executive in nature.

Executive agreements do not require the approval of two thirds of the Senate. They are just as binding as treaties and, like them, are the supreme law of the land unless countermanded by Congressional legislation. In practice there has been no differentiation between the subject matter of treaties on the one hand and executive agreements with or without prior or subsequent Congressional authorization. To all intents and purposes, treaties and executive agreements have the same status under both constitutional and international law.*

Two kinds of executive agreement must be distinguished. One is characterized by the formal legislative authorization of both Senate and House—notably the Reciprocal Trade Agreements Act which permits the President to negotiate up to a 50 per cent reduction in selected items of the American tariff. Sometimes Congressional approval is forthcoming after an executive agreement, as in the case of the Havana Declaration of 1940 in which the United States declared, along with its Latin-American neighbors, that it would not permit the transfer of territories in the Western Hemisphere then controlled by European powers who were at that time engaged in war. Congressional authorization has been the rule in those matters which require supplementary legislative action and which are designated in the Constitution as being within the specific powers of Congress: tariffs and commerce, immigration, extradition, and postal regulation. Executive agreements of this type are akin to the non-self-executing treaties mentioned earlier. It is here that the almost unlimited delegation of power in foreign relations, also mentioned earlier, takes place. The Supreme Court has ruled that the treaty power is not exclusive and that the cognate powers of the President and Congress jointly applied permit such agreements—and this decision came after years of usage. The other kind of executive agreement requires no Congressional action. It is called the "pure" type and is akin to the non-self-executing treaties. Apart from cases where supplementary legislation is required, the President is limited only by political, not by legal, considerations. So long as the President is within his proper functions, the Supreme Court has upheld the validity of "pure" executive agreements the few times the question has been before it. Constitutionally, the President's power in this instance stems from his general executive power, his power as the official spokesman to declare foreign policy, and his power to send and receive diplomatic representatives.

Executive agreements have, then, become firmly entrenched. Nevertheless, the regular treaty is still employed in major foreign-policy decisions made in collaboration with other nations, two oustanding examples in the postwar

---

* *United States v. Belmont*, 301 U.S. 324 (1937), where the phrase "equal dignity" is used.

period being the United Nations Charter (1945) and the North Atlantic Alliance (1949). Actually, in these two cases, a combination of the regular treaty form and the Congressionally authorized executive agreement was worked out. The contribution of American armed forces and other military aid to implement both treaties, respectively, was to be accomplished through executive agreements authorized in advance and not subject to later sanction by Congress.

► THE POWERS OF CONGRESS

Point for point, Congress alone probably does not have the number of powers which are at the disposal of the President alone. Until 1941, Congress's powers in the field of foreign relations were used less often and were, on the whole, less well developed. Historically, Congress has had much less room within which to act on its own. But its constitutional prerogatives are extensive nonetheless. For reasons to be analyzed later, Congress has recently enlarged its influence and control without anything being added to its reservoir of legal powers. Notice must be taken again of the fact that Congress shares with the President *potential source of power* which go beyond the Constitution per se. The power to acquire territory, the power to make international agreements, which are not treaties, and the power to *wage war* are not granted explicitly; rather they derive from the sovereignty inherent in nationhood itself. Thus, so far as foreign affairs are concerned, the grant of "all legislative powers" in Article I, Section 1, Paragraph 1 is not limited to those enumerated or which can be implied reasonably therefrom. It is significant, too, that several of Congress's basic powers can be exercised only in collaboration with the President, and that others held independently relate to matters over which the President has his own particular jurisdiction. Therefore the respective powers of Congress and the President are at once separated, mixed, and mutually interdependent.

THE LEGISLATIVE POWER

In many respects legislative power is the core of Congressional control over foreign relations. Any legislation required for foreign policy must be passed in identical form by both houses and signed by the President. The core within the core, so to speak, is the appropriations power: Article I, Section 9, Paragraph 7 states that "no money shall be drawn from the treasury but in consequence of appropriations made by law. . . ." A presidential veto can be overridden by a two-thirds vote in each house (Article I, Section 7, Paragraph 2). Veto arrangements endow Congress with a substantial advantage because the President must approve or disapprove a bill *in toto*—he cannot veto parts of it. "Riders," especially those attached to appropriations bills, become very important. Foreign-policy riders have become increasingly frequent.* More specifically, "the Congress shall have power To . . . provide for the common defence. . . ." (Article I, Section 8, Paragraph 1). Accompanying this is an imposing grant of power summarized in ten words: "To raise and support armies" (Article I, Section 8, Paragraph 12) and "To provide and maintain a navy" (Article I, Section 8, Paragraph 13). In the view of some authorities these clauses "plus the inherent powers of the national government in the field of foreign relations confer greater powers than the entire remainder of the Constitution."† Upon these foundation stones, the mobilization of American power rests. Without the exercise of this combination of provisions, the material bases of American foreign policy would disappear. Few policy pledges made by the President have been refused Congressional support, but in a very real sense he must come to Congress "hat in hand." Through appropriations and through provision for the Armed Forces, Congress can gain access to the policy-making process.

CONTROL OVER THE ARMED FORCES

The power to declare war resides solely in Congress (Article I, Section 8, Clause 11). This power cannot be delegated, though as has been noted, some powers can be delegated, and the President can exercise powers which seriously intrude on Congress's real freedom in the matter. In addition, Congress has other leverage on the armed forces. Military appropriations must be reviewed every two years (Article I, Section 8, Clause 12). To Congress is given the power "To make rules for the government and regulation of the land and naval forces (Article I, Section 8, Clause 14) and "To provide for organizing, arming and disciplining the militia and for governing such part of them as may be employed in the service of the United States . . ." (Article I, Section 8, Clause 16). Congress can call forth the militia (i.e., National Guard) "To execute the laws of the union, suppress insurrections and repel invasions" (Article I, Section 8, Clause 15) and shares with the several states the maintenance of the militia (Article I, Section 8, Clause 16).

At first glance it may appear that these powers, together with those mentioned in the preceding section, are sufficient to call into question the strong power position of the President with respect to the Armed Forces. One direct control available to Congress which might inhibit the President is the power to limit the over-all size of the military establishment. In March, 1951, Congress did impose a ceiling of four million men to be under arms. Conceivably such a limitation might ultimately restrict the President's ability to deploy the Armed Forces for foreign-policy purposes. And it is true that because Congress must raise and support them, it has an opportunity to inject its views on the nature of the balance among the Army, the Navy, and the Air Force. However, the powers of Congress have not been so construed nor have

* See Chapter Ten.
† Corwin and Peltason, *op. cit.,* p. 29.

they operated in practice to curb or cripple the powers of the President as commander in chief. As the Court of Claims has said:

> Congress may increase the Army, or reduce the Army, or abolish it altogether; but so long as we have a military force Congress cannot take away from the President the supreme command. It is true that the Constitution has conferred upon Congress the exclusive power "to make rules for the government and regulation of the land and naval forces"; but the two powers are distinct; neither can trench upon the other; the President cannot under the disguise of military orders, evade the legislative regulations by which he in common with the Army must be governed; and Congress cannot in the disguise of "rules for the government of the Army" impair the authority of the President as Commander-in-Chief.*

Congress has tried, without too much success, to limit the power of the President to move the Armed Forces where and for the purposes he sees fit. Neither the provisions of the Selective Service Act of 1940 nor the Lend-Lease Act of 1941 nor even the Neutrality Act of 1939 prevented President Franklin Roosevelt from using the Navy in the North Atlantic area or from sending troops to Iceland, Greenland, and other places. During the debate in the Senate on the Selective Service Act, Senator Ashurst commented on the provision designed to keep the President from sending armed forces outside the Western Hemisphere as follows: ". . . though it is a provision which should be in this bill . . . the expression of our opinion that drafted troops should not be sent to Europe . . . is not legally binding on the Executive."† Senator Wiley agreed because "under our form of government, the Executive is given constitutional powers with which the Legislature cannot interfere. . . . We have had example after example of the Executive power in the use of the Army . . .‡ President William Howard Taft was even more blunt when he wrote: ". . . it is clear that Congress may not usurp the functions of the Executive . . . by forbidding or directing the movements of the Army and Navy."§ When in 1922 Senator Reed suggested that Congress could compel the President to bring home troops then stationed abroad, Senator Borah replied: "We could not make the President do it. He is Commander-in-Chief of the Army and Navy of the United States; and if in the discharge of his duty he wants to assign them there, I do not know of any power that we can exert to compel him to bring them home."‖ Experience with such attempts and with restrictive legislation points to three kinds of results. First, the President may accept the advice as binding only if he chooses to so regard it. Second, the President may have sufficient constitutional power to do what he thinks

---

* *Swaim v. United States,* 28 Court of Claims 173, 221. Affirmed by the Supreme Court, 165 U.S. 553 (1897).

† *Congressional Record* (August 26, 1940), LXXXVI, 10896.

‡ *Ibid.*

§ William Howard Taft, "The Boundaries between the Executive, the Legislative, and the Judicial Branches of the Government," *Yale Law Journal* (1916), p. 599.

‖ *Congressional Record* (December 27, 1922), LXIV, 933.

must be done. Third, as in the case of the Neutrality Act, Congress is forced to leave a large area of discretion for the President.

It is sometimes argued that in view of Congress's power to declare war and its control over the Armed Forces, sending troops abroad or taking other belligerent action under circumstances which would raise the danger of war is an unconstitutional exercise of presidential prerogative. This reasoning was rejected by a majority of the Court in *The Prize Cases* (1863), which said that war can legally exist on the basis of hostile acts against the United States. The Constitutional Convention was aware of the problem. By a vote of eight to one, it was agreed to alter the original draft which gave Congress the power "to make war," substituting "declare" for "make." A convincing argument was that Congress would be too slow to make war. Thus the chief executive was deliberately left the power to repel sudden attack. To quote President Taft again:

> The President is the Commander-in-Chief of the Army and Navy. . . . Under this he can order the Army and Navy anywhere he will. . . . Of course the instrumentality which this power furnishes, gives the President an opportunity to do things which involve consequences that it would be quite beyond his power under the Constitution directly to effect . . . with the Army and the Navy the President can take action such as to involve the country in war and to leave Congress no option but to declare [war] or to recognize its existence.*

TREATIES AND INTERNATIONAL AGREEMENTS

Two thirds of the Senate must approve treaties (Article II, Section 2, Paragraph 2). Congress as a whole may participate in executive agreements via statutes authorizing the President to negotiate on certain matters. Doubtless the executive agreement has not added powers to Congress which it does not derive from the treaty power specifically granted, but the participation of Congress has been broadened to the extent that both houses act on the former. A very important aspect of Congress's power over treaties and agreements is the enactment of legislation to implement treaties. Mr. Justice Iredell in *Ware v. Hylton* held that a treaty "is valid and obligatory, in point of moral obligation, on all, as well as on the legislative, executive and judicial departments (so far as the authority of either extends . . .)."† Thus a treaty is binding on the various organs of government in accordance with their respective powers and duties. Professor Corwin points out that treaties differ in that some are "addressed to" Congress, others to the President for execution.‡ The phrase "addressed to" means either that the responsibility for execution

---

* William Howard Taft, *Our Chief Magistrate and His Powers* (New York, Columbia University Press, 1916), pp. 94–95.

† *Ware v. Hylton*, 3 Dallas 199 at p. 272 (1796).

‡ E. S. Corwin, *The President, Office and Powers* (3d ed., New York, New York University Press, 1948), p. 237.

is clearly spelled out or that the execution requires the exercise of congressional or presidential power or both. The power to execute or implement is almost as significant as the power to approve agreements in the first place, since the chances of influencing the actual course of policy are greater at the later stage. There is a limit beyond which Congress cannot be excluded from implementation, for "it is the overwhelming verdict of practice, at least, under the Constitution, that no treaty provision which deals with subject matter falling to the jurisdiction of Congress by virtue of its enumerated powers can have the force of 'law of the land' until Congress has adopted legislation to give it effect." *

OTHER CONSTITUTIONAL PREROGATIVES

Further provisions of the constitutional system, some related to foreign relations, some not, should be set forth briefly here for future reference. The Senate must approve nominations of diplomatic representatives and "all other officers of the United States . . ." (Article II, Section 2, Paragraph 2). Congress also has the power "To regulate commerce with foreign nations . . ." (Article I, Section 8, Clause 3) and "To establish a uniform rule of naturalization . . ." (Article I, Section 8, Clause 4). To regard these three powers as substantially routine would be correct but misleading. All provide Congress with potent weapons for influencing foreign policy and relations, especially in a period of executive-legislative conflict and cold war.† Thus the naturalization power confers on Congress the right to regulate the admission of persons into the United States and the conditions of their stay in this country—a power which looms large in the control of subversive activities.

Despite the fact that Section 7 of Article I of the Constitution specifies, "Every order, resolution, or vote to which the concurrence of the Senate and House of Representatives may be necessary (except on a question of adjournment) shall be presented to the President . . .," Congressional interpretation has produced the so-called "concurrent resolution" which is not really legislation but is an expression—sometimes a loud expression—of Congressional will and when written into legislation delegating power to the President can operate to withdraw original grants without risk of presidenital veto. The concurrent resolution has become part of Congress's repertoire in the field of foreign-policy making. Separation of powers requires that no member of Congress shall at one and the same time hold "any office under . . . the United States" (Article I, Section 6, Paragraph 2); however, congressmen can serve on temporary diplomatic missions for the United States, as several of them did at the San Francisco Conference of 1945, since such activities do not constitute officeholding in the technical sense. An ultimate weapon in a showdown with the President is impeachment. The Senate has sole power

---

* Corwin, *Total War and the Constitution*, p. 153.

† Examples of Congressional action based on these powers are presented in Chapter Ten.

to try the case after charges are brought in either chamber; a two-thirds concurrence is necessary to sustain conviction (Article I, Section 3, Paragraphs 6–7). The power of impeachment does not, though, extend beyond "treason, bribery, or other high crimes and misdemeanors"; unfitness, bad judgment, or incompetence are not proper grounds (Article II, Section 4). A derived power of fundamental importance is the power of investigation. Congressional hearings and special investigations have emerged as a primary vehicle of Congressional activity in foreign affairs. In view of this, a short phrase in the Constitution regarding members of Congress deserves special notice: ". . . and for any speech or debate in either house, they shall not be questioned in any other place" (Article I, Section 6, Paragraph 1). Previous comment concerning the psychological pressures on policy makers should be recalled in this connection.

► SOME CONSTITUTIONAL ISSUES

The selected issues reviewed in this section will serve several purposes. First, they will provide some indication of the kind of question relating to the allocation of decision-making power and responsibility which has arisen out of the change in America's international position. Second, the issues will illustrate the way in which the constitutional system is always being shaped by a process of redefinition growing out of specific needs, actions, and problems. Third, the discussion should serve to emphasize the subtle way in which legal arguments shade off into political arguments and vice versa. The nature of the constitutional system is such it generates arguments which cannot be permanently settled except within very broad limits. Often the judgment as to whether the President or Congress is right on a particular issue will depend on nonlegal criteria. When it does not, the judgment must often be, "Six of one, half a dozen of the other." The issues which follow are analyzed in terms of their constitutional ramifications. Needless to say, they have other aspects which have already been referred to or will be referred to in succeeding chapters.

THE UNITED NATIONS CHARTER

When the United States joined the United Nations it accepted as a new base of its foreign policy the principle of "peace by force if necessary." The importance of coercion in the Charter can be appreciated by quoting from the relevant articles:

> *Article 39*—The Security Council shall determine the existence of any threat to the peace, breach of the peace, or act of aggression and shall make recommendations, or decide what measures shall be taken in accordance with Articles 41 and 42, to maintain or restore international peace and security.

Article 40—In order to prevent an aggravation of the situation, the Security Council may, before making the recommendations or deciding upon the measures provided for in Article 39, call upon the parties concerned to comply with such provisional measures as it deems necessary or desirable.

Article 41—The Security Council may decide what measures not involving the use of armed force are to be employed to give effect to its decisions, and it may call upon the Members of the United Nations to apply such measures. These may include complete or partial interruption of economic relations and of rail, sea, air, postal, telegraphic, radio, and other means of communication, and the severance of diplomatic relations.

Article 42—Should the Security Council consider that measures provided for in Article 41 would be inadequate or have proved to be inadequate, it may take such action by air, sea, or land forces as may be necessary to maintain or restore international peace and security. Such action may include demonstrations, blockade, and other operations by air, sea, or land forces of Members of the United Nations.

Article 43—1. All members of the United Nations, in order to contribute to the maintenance of international peace and security, undertake to make available to the Security Council, on its call and in accordance with a special agreement or agreements, armed forces, assistance, and facilities, including rights of passage, necessary for the purpose of maintaining international peace and security. 2. Such agreement or agreements shall govern the numbers and types of forces, their degree of readiness and general location, and the nature of the facilities and assistance to be provided. 3. The agreement or agreements shall be negotiated as soon as possible on the initiative of the Security Council. They shall be concluded between the Security Council and Members or between the Security Council and groups of Members and shall be subject to ratification by the signatory states *in accordance with their respective constitutional processes.**

Article 45—In order to enable the United Nations to take urgent military measures, Members shall hold immediately available national air-force contingents for combined international enforcement action. The strength and degree of readiness of these contingents and plans for their combined action shall be determined, within the limits laid down in the special agreement or agreements referred to in Article 43, by the Security Council with the assistance of the Military Staff Committee.

A basic issue here was how America could fulfill the obligations inherent in these articles within the requirements of the constitutional system. It was clear that a formal agreement in advance to make all-out war on an aggressor was impossible because such action would amount to a delegation of the power to declare war. At the same time, it was also agreed that to wait for a formal declaration of war by Congress might defeat the aim of the United Nations to throttle aggression at its inception. Clearly, here was a familiar

---

* Italics by the authors.

dilemma: prompt security action vs. the Constitution. *How* could armed forces be put at the disposal of the international organization on less than total war terms and *who* under the American system would decide on the forces to be so used? The course chosen was to make available to the Security Council a limited force at the discretion of the President on the basis of the agreements mentioned in Article 43 after approval by the Senate. When the Charter was discussed in the Senate, it was apparently agreed by both the President and the Senate Foreign Relations Committee that the agreements envisaged under Aritcle 43 could *not* be entered into solely by executive action.

It is of considerable consequence that the terms of American participation in the United Nations were not set by a supplementary international agreement approved by the Senate nor by presidential prerogative but were set by the United Nations Participation Act of 1945* passed by both houses. This procedure represented an effort on the part of Congress to restrict somewhat the President's control over the Armed Forces. However, the attempt was directed only to the agreements specified under Article 43 of the Charter. By careful wording, Congress avoided requiring the President to come to Congress for approval in *every* instance of the use of Armed Force at the request of the Security Council. Section 6 of the Participation Act authorizes the President to negotiate the special agreements subject to congressional approval and then states:

> The President shall not be deemed to require the authorization of the Congress to make available to the Security Council on its call in order to take action under Article 42 of said charter and pursuant to such special agreement or agreements the armed forces, facilities, or assistance provided for therein: *Provided* that nothing herein contained shall be construed as an authorization to the President by the Congress to make available to the Security Council for such purpose armed forces, facilities, or assistance *in addition to*† the forces, facilities, and assistance provided for in such special agreement or agreements.

The House Committee on Foreign Affairs and the Senate Committee on Foreign Relations, using identical language in their reports on this act, made clear the reasoning behind Section 6: Any attempt to compel the President to come to Congress for approval in each individual case involving the special agreements of Article 43 "would clearly violate the spirit of one of the most important provisions of the Charter"; preventive or enforcement action by the forces provided under this article would not be an act of war but would be international action for the preservation of peace, consequently "the provisions of the Charter do not affect the exclusive power of Congress to declare war"; and further restrictions on the President "would also violate the spirit

---

* Public Law 264, 79th Congress, 1st Session, c. 583 (December 20, 1945).
† Italics by the authors.

of the United States Constitution under which the President has well established powers and obligations to use our Armed Forces without specific approval of Congress." *

In the Senate there were two notable attempts to curb the President's power via amendments to the United Nations Participation Act. Senator Wheeler offered an amendment prohibiting the President from making available to the Security Council armed forces to be used in connection with action taken under Article 42. It was defeated by a vote of 65 to 9. Section 3 of the act makes the significant proviso that the United States representative on the Security Council shall be answerable to the President and shall "at all times act in accordance with the instruction of the President." Senator Taft wished to require that the American representative act in response to Congressional guidance when the use of force was contemplated under Articles 39, 41, or 42 of the Charter. This amendment was also defeated. Debate on both amendments centered on Article 42, which deals with the use of forces provided under Article 43. Neither the Participation Act nor the reports and debates which preceded its passage appear to have constituted an attempt on the part of Congress to curtail the President's power to act on general constitutional authority or to support the United Nations under Articles 39 and 40. Because of the deadlock between the Soviet Union (including its satellites) and the other members of the Security Council, Article 43 has never been implemented. When the Korean conflict broke out in June, 1950, the Security Council had no permanent contingents at its disposal. The Council took action under Articles 39 and 40, and when the resolution calling for cessation of hostilities was ignored, another resolution recommended that members of the United Nations provide assistance to the Republic of Korea to repel the attack and to restore peace. President Truman responded by using his constitutional powers to dispatch troops to Korea. Article 2 of the Charter, be it noted, obligates members to "give the United Nations every assistance in any action it takes in accordance with the present Charter. . . ." Insofar as it lies within the President's own powers to interpret and execute treaties, he was constitutionally justified in employing American armed forces in this situation though there was nothing legally to compel him to do so.

A number of conclusions may be drawn regarding possible United States action under the United Nations Participation Act. First, while the Charter does raise in a general way the fundamental question of the President's power to employ the Armed Forces as an instrument of foreign policy versus Congress's power to declare war, that issue did not have to be met directly. Second, the President and Congress collaborated in a legislative grant of power to use American armed forces on certain terms without an unconstitutional delegation of Congress's power to declare war. Third, the Participation Act explicitly implemented only one set of provisions in the Charter so far as the Armed Forces are concerned—those embodied in Articles 42 and 43.

---

* Exact language from Senate Report 717, pp. 6–8.

Fourth, Congress refused to limit the President's power to use the Armed Forces on other grounds even though it also refused positive approval of such use. Fifth, the American representatives on the Security Council are admitted to be essentially presidential agents.

THE NORTH ATLANTIC ALLIANCE

The revolutionary step taken by the United States in committing itself to a defensive alliance with other nations did raise in acute form a group of issues which had lurked beneath the surface of discussions regarding implementation of the United Nations Charter. It is the declared purpose of the Atlantic Alliance to make clear the determination of the members of the North Atlantic community to protect their independence and freedom by a collective exercise of their basic rights of self-defense in the event of an attack on any one of them. Key provisions for purposes of this discussion are these:

Article 2. "The Parties will contribute toward the further development of peaceful and friendly international relations by . . . promoting conditions of stability and well-being."

Article 3. "In order more effectively to achieve the objectives of this Treaty, the Parties, separately and jointly, by means of continuous and effective self-help and mutual aid, will maintain and develop their individual and collective capacity to resist armed attack."

Article 4. "The Parties will consult together whenever in the opinion of any of them, the territorial integrity, political independence or security of any of the Parties is threatened."

Article 5. "The Parties agree that an armed attack against one or more of them in Europe or North America shall be considered an attack against them all; and consequently they agree that, if such an armed attack occurs, each of them, in exercise of the right of individual or collective self-defense recognized by Article 51 of the Charter of the United Nations, will assist the Party or Parties so attacked by taking forthwith, individually and in concert with the other Parties, such action as it deems necessary, including the use of armed force, to restore and maintain the security of the North Atlantic area."

Article 11. "This treaty shall be ratified and its provisions carried out by the Parties in accordance with their respective constitutional processes. . . ."

Early in the debate which preceded senatorial approval of the treaty two crucial questions emerged: What was the nature of the obligation accepted by the United States? Who was to decide for the United States what action was to be taken in the event of an armed attack on any one of the parties? The first question stemmed directly from the "heart" of the treaty, Article 5. There is no denying the fact that Congress and the President accepted the *principle* that an attack on one party was an attack on all and the obligation to "restore and maintain the security of the North Atlantic area." But Senators Vandenberg and Connally, who led the debate, made it abundantly plain that there was no "moral obligation" to go to war; both insisted that they would approve no provision which *standing alone* would create "an antecedent state of things" depriving the United States of its freedom of action, and this view appears to have been shared by their colleagues. The Senate Foreign Relations Committee, in its report on the treaty, said of the action contemplated in Article 5: "The Committee emphasizes that this clearly does not commit any of the parties to declare war . . . there are numerous measures short of the use of armed force which might be sufficient to deal with the situation . . . each party remains free to exercise its honest judgment in deciding upon the measures it will take. . . . Article 5 carries with it an important and far-reaching commitment for the United States; what we may do to carry out that commitment, however, will depend upon our own independent decision in each particular instance reached in accordance with our own constitutional process."*

The second question, of course, revived an old dilemma and argument. If the members of the alliance are to be really protected from a full-scale aggressive assault under modern conditions, swift action would probably be necessary; to await a formal declaration of war might be fatal. One hundred and forty-eight years ago the issue was argued heatedly between Jefferson and Hamilton. Jefferson's view was that the President's power to use the Armed Forces was narrowly constricted to purely defensive acts unless or until Congress formally declared war. Hamilton, on the other hand, felt that it was the exclusive prerogative of Congress to take the nation into war, adding that if a foreign nation openly made war upon the United States, any declaration on the part of Congress would be unnecessary. Repeatedly during the hearings on the North Atlantic Treaty, the following queries were put to the Secretary of State and the Secretary of Defense: In view of the provision in Article 5 that an attack against one shall be considered an attack against all, would the United States be obligated to react to an attack on Paris or Copenhagen in the same way it would react to an attack on New York City? In such an event does the treaty give the President the power to take any action, without specific Congressional authorization, which he could not take in the absence of the treaty?

No direct answer was forthcoming. Discussing Article 5 in a public address, March, 1949, Secretary of State Acheson said: "This does not mean that the United States would be automatically at war if one of the nations covered by the pact is subjected to armed attack. Under our Constitution, the Congress alone has the power to declare war. We would be bound to take promptly the action which we deemed necessary to restore and maintain the security of the North Atlantic Area. That decision would be taken in accordance with our constitutional procedures. . . . That decision will rest where the

---

* United States Senate, Report of the Committee on Foreign Relations, *The North Atlantic Treaty,* Executive L, 81st Congress, 1st Session, June 6, 1949, pp. 13–14.

Constitution has placed it."* Throughout his testimony, Acheson drew a distinction, when pressed, between the President's power to *make* war and Congress's power to *declare* war. When Senator Donnell asked the secretary whether an attack on Norway by 500,000 Russians would require the United States to go to war under the treaty, Acheson replied: "My judgment would be that the only way to restore peace and security would be by the use of armed force. You might differ with me on that."† Secretary of Defense Lovett hinted that in his opinion the President would consult Congress before ordering the use of force under the treaty. Members of the Senate Foreign Relations Committee, however, were sure that the answer to both questions was no. The reasoning of the committee is worth noting: "In the event any party to the treaty were attacked the obligation of the United States would be to decide upon and take forthwith the measures it deemed necessary to restore and maintain the security of the North Atlantic Area. The measures which would be necessary to accomplish that end would depend upon a number of factors, including the location, nature, scale and significance of the attack. The decision as to what action was necessary, and the action itself, would of course have to be taken in accordance with established constitutional procedures . . . the President and the Congress, within their sphere of assigned constitutional responsibilities, would be expected to take all action necessary and appropriate. . . ."‡ Almost casually, it was added: "The Committee does not believe it appropriate in this report to undertake to define the authority of the President to use the armed forces." Commenting specifically on the distribution of power between the two branches, the committee insisted: "The treaty in no way affects the basic division of authority between the President and Congress as defined in the Constitution. In no way does it alter the constitutional relationship between them. In particular, it does not increase, decrease, or change the power of the President as Commander-in-Chief of the armed forces or impair the full authority of Congress to declare war."§

Constitutional factors were responsible for several recurrent fears on the part of Congress and the President as expressed in the deliberations over the North Atlantic Treaty. Senatorial fears centered on the possibility that the treaty might make the exercise of the war power by Congress purely perfunctory, that Congress might inadvertently take on an unlimited commitment which might tie its hands, that the power to interpret the treaty might rest in practice predominantly with the President, and that the President might carry the implications of the treaty to an extreme through executive agreements. For their part, administrative officials feared that in giving Congress assur-

---

* Printed in the United States Department of State *Bulletin,* March 27, 1949, pp. 384–388.
  † Hearings, *The North Atlantic Treaty,* Senate Committee on Foreign Relations, 81st Congress, 1st Session, April 27, 1949, p. 28.
  ‡ See the committee's Report cited above, p. 14.
  § *Ibid.,* p. 19.

ances the President might be handicapped in an emergency and that undue emphasis on constitutional procedures might slow up implementation of the treaty and convince America's allies that the commitment of the United States was indefinite or "watered down." The wording of Article 5 of the Treaty naturally had to be a compromise. European parties to the agreement wanted an unconditional guarantee of American support in the event of an attack on them; yet the Senate's interpretation of the Constitution would admit of no such prior commitment. Hence the phraseology had to satisfy both sides. Obviously the Secretary of State felt that there was danger in a purely legalistic approach to the difficulty: "This is not a legalistic question. It is a question we have frequently faced, the question of faith and principle in carrying out treaties. Those who decide it will have the responsibility for taking all appropriate action under the treaty. Such a responsibility requires the exercise of will—a will disciplined by the undertaking solemnly contracted to do what they decide is necessary to restore and maintain the peace and security of the North Atlantic Area."* It was a theme to which he was to return and to amplify in the "troops-to-Europe" debate.

There are three conclusions to be noted at this point. First, despite the fact that the treaty could add nothing legally to the President's powers, it did provide a substantially greater scope for their operation. Second, Congress definitely expressed, during the bitter debate over the billion-dollar military aid program to accompany the new alliance, its intention of keeping a close check on later developments of the policy set forth in the treaty. Third, the outcome of the continuing struggle over the meaning of presidential as against Congressional powers was once again inconclusive.

THE "TROOPS-TO-EUROPE" DEBATE 1950–1951

The sending of troops to Europe inspired the so-called "Great Debate," which amounted to a rather thorough discussion of certain critical aspects of American foreign policy, of which only the constitutional side is of concern here. The troops-to-Europe issue amply illustrates the fact that constitutional factors at one and the same time provide, first, a basis on which Congress can challenge the President on substantive matters of policy and, second, provide the ammunition for both the policy arguments and the legal arguments. Whereas the constitutional issues surrounding the North Atlantic Alliance related to the wording of the treaty and to future problems which might arise, the announcement by the administration in the fall of 1950 that it was going to send American troops to bolster the defenses of Western Europe represented a concrete expression of presidential power. The use of armed forces short of all-out-war, a hypothetical question during the legislative action on the United Nations Charter and the Atlantic Treaty, suddenly emerged as a real possibility. This was the central issue: Can the President pursuant to the Atlantic Alliance agree to bind the United States to send American divisions

* United States Department of State *Bulletin,* March 27, 1949, p. 388.

in any number to join in the defense of Western Europe and to engage in action in an international army?

Senate hearings and floor debate, together with the responses of officials of the executive branch, were punctuated by extreme claims. These claims did not prevail, but the fact that they were made serves to highlight once again the extensive no man's land which opens up when cognate powers of the President and Congress are explored in any specific instance. Senator Taft, who led the attack, insisted that a "constitutional crisis" had arisen. He charged on January 5, 1951, that the President "had no authority whatever to commit American troops to Korea without consulting Congress and without Congressional approval. . . . The President simply usurped authority, in violation of the laws and the Constitution. . . ."* Senator George argued that the North Atlantic Treaty had actually curtailed the President's right to deploy troops. A most persistent charge in the Senate was that the Secretary of State had grossly misinterpreted the treaty: there was no commitment by the United States to take any particular action by way of implementation and the secretary had implied that no troops would be sent. President Truman announced flatly in a press conference on January 11, 1951, that he had the legal right to send American troops anywhere in the world. Other administration spokesmen stressed the obligations imposed on the President by the United Nations Charter and the North Atlantic Treaty. It was the responsibility of the Executive Branch to implement the treaty, first by the military aid program already subscribed to by Congress and now by the commitment of ground forces to Western Europe.

Secretary of State Acheson summarized the constitutional position as he saw it: The President's power to send the Armed Forces abroad is not dependent on Congressional authorization; the President, acting as commander in chief, has employed the Armed Forces in the interest of American foreign policy generally; it is the President's duty under the Constitution to ensure that treaties be faithfully executed; the President's powers cannot be interfered with by Congress in the exercise of its powers under the Constitution.† Once again he went on to say:

> It seems to me that perhaps a little more is involved here, and that we are in a position in the world today where the argument as to who has the power to do this, that, or the other thing, is not exactly what is called for from America in this very critical hour. . . . I think that regardless of the question of power or a division of power or responsibility, it is . . . vitally necessary to the complete unity of the American people behind this most important program that the American people feel that the Congress itself has certain responsibility and certain powers. . . .

* New York *Times,* January 6, 1951, p. 1.

† Hearings, *Assignment of Ground Forces of the United States to Duty in the European Area,* Senate Committee on Foreign Relations and Committee on Armed Services, 82nd Congress, 1st Session, February 16, 1951, pp. 89–92.

> Now, of course, the mere power to make appropriations or to raise armies, which does reside in Congress, would be in effect a participation and a joint participation along with the Executive in carrying on the treaty. But to my mind . . . this particular treaty should be interpreted especially in the light of the admitted meaning of its terms and its conditions by the Executive when the Executive submitted the treaty to Congress for ratification. . . . We do not really solve this question by trying to split legal hairs as to what is the authority of the Executive, what is the authority of the Congress. They must act together and no strong policy which will carry out what is so necessary here can be done without the full unity of the Executive and the Congress. . . .*

But the secretary rejected the idea of cooperation in a rigid pattern which resulted from Congress's attempt to limit by law the President's power to use troops.

As a matter of fact, neither the President himself nor the Senate stood stubbornly by their extreme positions. President Truman softened his bald statement of prerogative and said he would welcome an expression of views by the Senate both as a Congressional right and as good policy strategy. The Senate did not finally insist that the President was acting unconstitutionally, but exercised its constitutional rights in an important resolution passed April 4, 1951, after the long debate was over. In the resolution the Senate said in part:

> 1. The Senate approves the action of the President of the United States in cooperating in the common defensive effort of the North Atlantic Treaty nations by designating, at their unanimous request, General of the Army Dwight D. Eisenhower, as Supreme Allied Commander, Europe, and in placing armed forces of the United States in Europe under his command; . . .; 3. It is the sense of the Senate that the President of the United States as Commander-in-Chief of the armed forces, before taking action to send units of ground troops to Europe under Article 3 of the North Atlantic Treaty, should consult the . . . Committee on Foreign Relations of the Senate, the Committee on Foreign Affairs of the House of Representatives and the Armed Services Committee of the Senate and the House of Representatives . . .; 5. . . . such units of the United States ground forces as may be assigned to the above command shall be assigned only after the Joint Chiefs of Staff certify to the Secretary of Defense that in their opinion such assignment is a necessary step in strengthening the security of the United States; and the certified opinions referred to . . . shall be transmitted . . . to the Senate Committees on Foreign Relations and Armed Services, and to the House Committees on Foreign Affairs and Armed Services as soon as they are received; 6. It is the sense of the Senate that, in the interests of sound constitutional processes . . . Congressional approval should be obtained of any policy requiring the assignment of American troops abroad when such assign-

---

* *Ibid.*, pp. 93, 99.

ment is an implementation of Article 3 of the North Atlantic Treaty; and the Senate hereby approves the present plans of the President . . . to send four additional divisions of ground forces to Western Europe, but it is the sense of the Senate that no ground troops in addition to such four divisions should be sent to Western Europe in implementation of Article 3 of the North Atlantic Treaty without further Congressional approval; 7. It is the sense of the Senate that the President should submit to the Congress at intervals of not more than six months reports on the implementation of the North Atlantic Treaty. . . .

These sentiments and strictures were passed in identical form by the House of Representatives, thereby becoming a concurrent resolution. Constitutionally, concurrent resolutions are not binding upon the President. The wording of the resolution represented—as had the wording of Article 5 of the Treaty—a compromise. The Executive Branch wanted cooperative support but no legal strait jacket. Friendly senators wanted to obtain a strong majority expression of Congressional sharing of policy without intruding on the powers of the President. Unfriendly senators wanted to go as far as they could in curbing presidential initiative. All sides claimed victory.

To summarize, in spite of the claims made about the respective powers of Congress and the President, no clear line was drawn between them. The President, without waiving his interpretation of his constitutional rights, gained the Congressional approval he thought desirable. Congress, while it did not succeed in imposing its interpretation of the division of power and while it did not repudiate presidential initiative, did nonetheless enforce its desire to be consulted. Both the President and Congress used constitutional arguments to justify what were essentially policy views. Aside from the question of who should make the decisions regarding implementation of the Atlantic Alliance, the main issues were concerned with how much aid should be given, when, and in what form. Insofar as administration and Congressional leaders were sharply in disagreement, it was over how many troops should be sent to Europe, how effective this move would be, and what relation such action would have to other aspects of foreign policy. As will be seen later on, each side was arguing for a limitation of the other's power because it was somewhat distrustful of the other's policy views.

THE PROPOSED AMBASSADOR TO THE VATICAN

In November, 1951, former President Truman announced that he had appointed General Mark Clark "Ambassador to the State of the Vatican." The appointment created an immediate furor and eventually the President withdrew the nomination.* Nevertheless, the controversy which took place uncovered a constitutional issue or what some students consider to be an issue

---

* Even if there had not been substantial domestic and foreign political opposition to the move, an amendment to an 1870 statute prohibiting active military officers from holding civilian positions would have been necessary. See Chapter Nine.

even though the withdrawal prevented full development and resolution. Did the President violate the First Amendment? At first glance, the provision "Congress shall make no law respecting an establishment of religion" would seem to have no relevance to the President's action. Edward S. Corwin argued in a letter to the New York *Times** that the executive's diplomatic powers are virtually unlimited so far as the establishment of advantageous diplomatic relations are concerned, that the First Amendment prohibits Congressional legislation, not nonlegislative acts by the President, and, finally, that there is no procedure for bringing a purely presidential act before the Supreme Court for review. Other constitutional experts† were inclined to view it as dangerous doctrine that the federal government (in this case the President) was permitted to do things at the international level which it could not do at the domestic level. Furthermore, to these experts the fact that the President might "get away with" an act which was unconstitutional was hardly justification for the violation. Even if there is no method of judicial review, or, indeed, any other check, the President is under moral restraint to abide by the Constitution. Those dubious about the President's appointment of an ambassador to the Vatican also quoted Justice Black in the *Everson Case:* "The 'establishment of religion' clause of the First Amendment means at least this: Neither a state nor the federal government can set up a church. Neither can pass laws which aid one religion, aid all religions, or prefer one religion over another. . . . Neither a state nor the federal government can, openly or secretly, participate in the affairs of any religious organizations or groups or vice versa."‡ In this case and others the Court appears to have interpreted the First Amendment in such a way as to bear directly on the Vatican issue.

THE BRICKER AMENDMENT

Senator John Bricker (Republican of Ohio) brought to a head another kind of issue when he introduced his amendment to the treaty-making power on February 7, 1952. The issue is this: Should the Constitution be amended to curb the treaty-making power of the federal government? No general discussion of the proposal took place until after Senator Bricker had reintroduced it in January, 1953. Following several months of argument and hearings, and several revisions under the advice of numerous experts (in particular the American Bar Association), Senate Joint Resolution 1 was reported favorably on June 4, 1953, by the Senate Judiciary Committee by a vote of 9 to 5.§ Sixty-three senators joined in signing the Bricker resolution when it was first proposed, though it is by no means certain that this group would all have voted affirmatively by the time the Judiciary Committee reported.

---

* New York *Times,* November 12, 1951.
† For example, Mark DeWolfe Howe, writing in the *Nation,* January 12, 1952.
‡ *Everson v. Board of Education,* 330 U.S. 1 (1947).
§ Senate Report No. 412, 82nd Congress, 2nd Session.

The last version of the Bricker resolution reads as follows:

> *Section 1.* A provision of a treaty which conflicts with this Constitution shall not be of any force or effect.
>
> *Section 2.* A treaty shall become effective as internal law in the United States only through legislation which would be valid in the absence of treaty.
>
> *Section 3.* Congress shall have power to regulate all executive and other agreements with any foreign power or international organization. All such agreements shall be subject to the limitations imposed on treaties by this article.
>
> *Section 4.* The Congress shall have power to enforce this article by appropriate legislation.
>
> *Section 5.* This article shall be inoperative unless it shall have been ratified as an amendment to the Constitution by the legislatures of three-fourths of the several states within seven years from the date of submission.

These proposed restrictions should be read in the light of the analysis of the treaty power earlier in the chapter. Taken as a whole, the effect of the amendment would be to eliminate pure, self-executing executive agreements, to prohibit non-self-executing agreements which would require legislation not otherwise within Congressional power, and to invite passage of a law which would make it impossible for the President and the Senate to commit the United States to treaties and agreements on certain subjects. Naturally the interests and sentiments which entered into the preparation, presentation, and support of this amendment were numerous and complex. Leaving out the desire of the Republican party for another foreign-policy issue prior to the presidential election of 1952 and the possible desire of Senator Bricker to make a reputation for himself, other general factors should be noted. Undoubtedly, the proposal symbolized Republican reaction against something called "the Roosevelt-Truman treaty policy"—allegedly the overly generous use of executive agreements for inappropriate subjects, particularly as exemplified in the Yalta and Potsdam agreements. Some persons in and out of Congress favored the Bricker idea because of a concern lest the vague yet far-reaching treaty power subvert the Constitution. Others saw in the measure further protection of Congress against the President's already well-developed discretionary power. Still others regarded the provisions quoted as curbing the power of the federal government vis-à-vis the states. It also seems probable that the Bricker move reflected the more nationalistic sentiments of the Republican party as against the Dewey-Eisenhower "one-world" wing.

The majority report of the Senate Judiciary Committee* summarizes pretty well the arguments for each section of the resolution. Section 1 is necessary, in part, because the United Nations and its affiliated agencies have

---

* Cited immediately above.

drafted, and are drafting, conventions "which seek to regulate internationally almost every conceivable facet of American life. . . ." Such covenants are inappropriate subjects for treaties, and would abridge or void the civil liberties of American citizens as well as give some international organ jurisdiction over these rights as exercised within the United States. It is also time, in the majority's judgment, to make explicit the basic rule that no treaty can override the Constitution. In view of the fact that the Supreme Court has never declared a treaty unconstitutional, this section would be a blunt reminder of the Court's duty. Section 2 is necessary because of Articles 55 and 56 of the United Nations Charter, which concern international social cooperation and human rights. If these articles of the Charter are regarded by United States courts as self-executing, many state statutes would be automatically void, as already seen in the case of the California Alien Land Law. The danger is a real one because the Supreme Court has not been clear on the distinction between self-executing and non-self-executing treaties. Self-executing agreements constitute a method of domestic social reform not sanctioned or foreseen by the Founding Fathers. By prohibiting self-executing treaties and by providing that any agreement or treaty must be accompanied by Congressional legislation which would only be valid in the absence of agreement or treaty, the proponents hope to solve the difficult question of the line between domestic and international jurisdiction. The so-called "which clause" of Section 2 is justified as preventing an expansion of Congressional power at the expense of the states and making impossible legislation by an international body which would affect matters over which the several states normally have control. This clause would clearly void the present doctrine as embodied in the *Missouri v. Holland* decision.

The argument for abolishing pure executive agreements is that the Congress should determine the conditions which an executive agreement must satisfy to be binding on the United States and should be able to prevent the President from making certain types of agreements. An assumption here is that the executive has abused this power and that Congress can be trusted equally with the President to protect the interests of the American people. Under this provision no secrets could be withheld from Congress.

Secretary of State Dulles, Under Secretary Smith, Mutual Security Director Stassen, and Attorney General Brownell all opposed the proposed amendment on behalf of the Eisenhower Administration. A minority of the Senate Judiciary Committee, including Senator Wiley, the chairman of the Senate Foreign Relations Committee, joined in much the same arguments. While being generally sympathetic with the fears and objectives of Senator Bricker and others, these officials felt the amendment was unnecessary. It is already settled law that no treaty can alter or subvert the Constitution. The Senate and the President can also be trusted not to impair the rights of American citizens by treaties or agreements. Besides, the Senate can refuse approval of such treaties and can insist that any treaty be non-self-executing. Because he Supreme Court has not declared any treaty unconstitutional does not mean that it would not in a clear case. If an objectionable treaty or agreement sneaks by, the Congress can supersede it by the simple procedure of passing a law which, coming after the former, replaces it in the constitutional system.

Perhaps the argument most vehemently advanced by those who opposed the Bricker amendment was that no matter what verbal formula was worked out, the cure would be worse than the disease. In their opinion, no text can be devised which will not from the standpoint of national security dangerously restrict the President's power to negotiate treaties. Such an addition to the Constitution would have prevented United States adherence to the United Nations Charter and would bar United States adherence to an international pact controlling atomic energy. The proposal would tie the President's hands and strip him of his historic control over foreign policy. Secretary Dulles testified that Section 3 meant that "the President shall be subject to regulation by Congress in the conduct of foreign affairs, and that is a pretty fundamental thing." Requirement of implementing legislation for all treaties and agreements would give the United States the most cumbersome procedure in the world—a majority vote in both houses on top of a two-thirds vote in the Senate. In some cases, forty-eight state legislatures would have to accept a given agreement.

At a later stage in the debate over the Bricker proposal, the administration pointed out that eleven of twenty-three treaties passed by the Senate during the Second Session of the 1953 Congress would have to be submitted to the states. Representatives of the Executive Branch constantly reiterated the necessity for flexibility and rapidity if the President was to be able to act effectively and to speak authoritatively for the United States. If the Bricker amendment were interpreted broadly, it would also impinge on the President's powers as commander in chief (under which Yalta and Potsdam agreements were concluded).

Clearly there are several kinds of constitutional questions involved in this controversy, but the basic one goes back to *Missouri v. Holland:* if a treaty can serve any national purpose so long as its content is logically related to the national welfare, what limits are there to federal authority if exercised in pursuance of the treaty-making power? The Missouri case, after all, dealt with migratory birds. Current United Nations conventions deal with delicate social problems and situations, with property rights, and with other fundamental human freedoms. The fear that the doctrine of *Missouri v. Holland* might be applied to United Nations covenants, thus permitting the federal government to invade further the jurisdiction of the states, motivates many Bricker supporters. They are not sufficiently persuaded by Secretary Dulles's promise not to press for a genocide treaty and not to sign the United Nations human rights conventions, nor by the fact that the United States, in negotiating five recent treaties of friendship and commerce, inserted a reservation in each one to protect those states having special legislation concerning the activities of aliens. Proponents also fear that human rights agreements may level downward existing protections in the United States because the standards of the worst nation will tend to set the pace. However, the United Nations Draft Covenant on Civil and Political Rights has a derogation clause which forbids any nation from reducing its own constitutional protections on the ground that they are superior to standards in the convention. Opponents of the Bricker proposal acknowledge the theoretical danger of an enlargement of the federal power through international conventions which deal with purely domestic matters, but point to existing checks and to the fact that *Missouri v. Holland* doctrine has not been applied so as to affect the whole social order. The Republicans in Congress and in the Executive Branch did not disagree with each other on the dangers of unwise social legislation "boot-legged" into the law of the land via treaties and agreements. Before he became Secretary of State, John Foster Dulles charged* the Democratic administration with a tendency to use treaties as a vehicle of social reform by agreeing to obligations which could cut across the Bill of Rights, and during his testimony on the Bricker resolution he reiterated that such a tendency had existed before the Republicans took over. But clearly, the members of President Eisenhower's official family were more perturbed over the nightmare of potential executive paralysis in dealing with other nations than over the unfolding of the logical implications of the *Missouri v. Holland* ruling under contemporary conditions.

At any rate, the whole issue was postponed until the 1954 session of Congress when an attempt to reach a compromise formula to replace the Bricker resolution failed in July, 1953. During the early days of the new Congress in January, 1954, the whole complicated legal and political problem was reopened. Arguments grew in number and intensity. For several weeks another "great debate" took place. Three related issues emerged clearly: (1) Should Congress make sure that the Constitution is really supreme over treaties? (2) Should Congress attempt to prevent possible abuse of executive agreements? (3) Should there be constitutional requirement for roll-call votes on treaties? When it became apparent that most senators felt the Bricker amendment was far too restrictive, Senator George introduced a resolution designed to compromise the views on the three issues. Section 2 of the George resolution replaced the famous "which clause" of Senator Bricker's resolution, but the former required only those executive agreements having internal effect to be subject to Congressional action, whereas the latter required the regulation of all executive agreements. This section of the George compromise became the center of attention.

President Eisenhower was drawn into the debate and numerous conferences were held at the White House in an effort to arrive at a formulation acceptable to Senator Bricker and to other senators who wanted clarification of the treaty power. The President agreed to several important changes in

---

* In a speech to the Louisville Bar Association in April, 1952.

Senate procedures which would guarantee thorough consideration of all international agreements: a roll-call vote on all agreements, a change in the formal treaty vote from two thirds of the senators present to two thirds of the total membership, and the right of the Senate to declare whether a given agreement was accepted as self-executing or not. The President also agreed to a provision saying, in effect, that treaties which violate the Constitution are invalid. However, the President would not accept any inhibition on his power to negotiate agreements with a vital bearing on national security. In the end it turned out that no compromise on the "which clause" was possible, either within the Senate or between the Senate and the White House. On February 26, 1954, the George resolution failed by *one vote* to gain the requisite two-thirds support for constitutional amendments, the final tabulation being 60 to 31. The question may or may not be dead, for, at this writing, a motion to reconsider is pending.

Given the closeness of the vote (it was a bipartisan vote, 32 Republicans and 28 Democrats for and 14 Republicans and 16 Democrats plus Independent Wayne Morse against) it can only be concluded that the one senator who might have tipped the scale apparently was convinced that to run the risk of paralyzing the President was too great a price to pay for closing a loophole in the Constitution.

IMPLICATIONS OF THE FOREGOING CASES

These five cases represent a progressive development through time from the original problem of implementing the general peace provisions of the United Nations Charter to definition of the nature of American obligations under the Atlantic Alliance and then to the specific issue of sending troops to Europe under the Atlantic Alliance in the absence of an attack on any of its members. Each succeeding step made the issues a little more specific. All three cases exhibit certain common elements. The question of who was to decide how the United States would fulfill its international commitments was raised in each instance. The particular type of implementation under discussion involved the potential employment of American armed forces in situations short of legal war in the traditional sense. The possible use of armed forces threw the constitutional question into an area where the President and Congress have "cognate powers"; the President has constitutionally exercised the power to deploy American troops for foreign-policy purposes and Congress definitely has the power to raise troops, determine their number, and appropriate funds for their maintenance. At no stage in the process were the basic issues settled though they were discussed over again and subjected to some reformulation.

It is precisely in this realm of cognate powers that clear, agreed-upon constitutional guides are lacking. Perhaps this is one of the chief reasons why in the examples reviewed, the end result was either "no decision" or a semantic compromise sufficiently ambiguous to accommodate future maneuvering.

One significant conclusion to be drawn is, therefore, that in the nature of things constitutional issues of this type are not susceptible to final settlement. Whatever uncertainty this situation may introduce into the decision-making process—and it is considerable—the fact that neither the President nor Congress has seen fit to insist upon a showdown between extreme positions suggests that the price of such a showdown would be too high. However, one of the by-products of semantic compromises is that the next time the issue comes up, the terms of the compromise must be reinterpreted. This reinterpreting process helps to account for the charge by certain senators that the Executive Branch had grossly misjudged what had been agreed to in the Atlantic Alliance when the President proposed sending troops to Europe and merely wanted a kind of automatic approval from Congress.

The whole problem is aggravated by another factor. Constitutional foundations for the exercise of the powers of Congress and the President over war making in general and the armed forces in particular were laid in times when national defense could be—and was—narrowly construed. In Chapter One it was demonstrated that national security in the present world is quite different from what it was before World War I or even before World War II. While it is perfectly true that the President's use of the Armed Forces may be coincident to, or contributory to, the entrance of the United States into war, it is also true that in the most of the 150 instances referred to earlier, the President deployed military forces to protect and defend the rights of American citizens and their property from acts of violence abroad. These were not acts of war in any true sense and were not dictated by larger political motives. While Congress has declared war only five times—there being four other occasions in addition to the Korean war which historians regard as wars*— it is also true that on previous occasions Congress has legislated control over the President's discretionary use of the Armed Forces, notably in the case of the Neutrality Act of 1939, which rigorously prohibited various kinds of action regarding belligerent nations. With self-defense now very broadly defined, the ability of the President to propel the United States into war operates within a much larger range of possibilities. Recognition of this fact largely accounts for increased Congressional sensitivity to the constitutional niceties involved.

In turn, the horns of the old dilemma of constitutional prerogative vs. speedy effectiveness in an emergency have become much more pointed. The more Congress becomes aware of the tremendous potential power in the hands of the President under the Charter and the Atlantic Alliance, the more it is tempted to circumscribe that power in order to preserve its own. To the extent that Congress succumbs to this temptation, the risk of paralysis emerges. Most enlightened congressmen are aware that under certain circumstances

---

* The Naval War with France (1798–1800), the Barbary War (1801–1805), The Second Barbary War (1815), and the Mexican hostilities of 1914–1917. Conflict was carried on without a Congressional declaration.

only a sudden retaliatory move by the President could prevent ultimate disaster. The necessity of living with such a dilemma without being impaled on one or both of its horns has led Congress to engage in a battle of words with the President on the issue of control of the Armed Forces and at the same time to insist upon a collaborative relationship in the field of foreign relations, the latter generally on quite different constitutional grounds.

Doubtless Congress can, using constitutional arguments and devices, make things embarrassing and difficult for the President, and it can "slow up" or canalize presidential action. But in the last analysis, the odds are that final discretion will lie with the President. As a matter of constitutional fact, Congress has not had conspicuous success in limiting the President's control over the Armed Forces. Despite the rather extensive prohibitions written into the Neutrality Act of 1939, Congress was compelled also to permit wide discretionary power to the chief executive. The provisions did not become operative until a presidential proclamation naming belligerents and recognizing a state of war was issued. Furthermore, the President was himself permitted to establish "combat areas" from which ships were barred by the statute. President Franklin Roosevelt exercised these powers in such a way as to guarantee the flow of vital materials to Great Britain and other democratic nations after the outbreak of World War II in September, 1939. As part of the Selective Service Act of 1940, Congress imposed a geographical limitation on the use of United States troops abroad: persons called under the act could not be employed beyond the Western Hemisphere except in American territories and possessions. On July 7, 1941, President Roosevelt notified Congress that pursuant to an executive agreement he had sent troops to Iceland, seven hundred miles from Europe and east of the Azores. The Lend-Lease Act of 1941 included this provision: "Nothing in this Act shall be construed to authorize or to permit the authorization of convoying vessels by naval vessels of the United States. . . ." Nevertheless, in the face of both the Neutrality Act of 1939 and the Lend-Lease Act of 1941 extensive convoying did take place before the United States was attacked in December, 1941. During the "troops-to-Europe" debate, Senator George (already quoted) admitted that, legal arguments aside, a strong President would probably react to all-out attack without waiting for a declaration of war by Congress. If the Congress thought that by the joint resolution just set forth, it was limiting the number of American troops in Europe to 200,000 men (six divisions and their complements) it was mistaken for in August, 1951, the announcement was made that there would be 400,000 men (still six divisions). In short, Congress has sometimes authorized the presidential use of troops and has sometimes tried to legislate against it, but whenever the President has gone ahead on his own, the national legislature has often protested without necessarily repudiating the action.

There is still another aspect of the armed forces issue. The administration seemed particularly anxious to convince America's allies in 1951 that the United States would stand by its commitment under the Atlantic Alliance. Controversy over the respective powers of the President and Congress during the debate raised anew a fear entertained by other nations that statements and promises by the Executive Branch might be weakened by "constitutional procedures." As pointed out above, the President's spokesmen were more interested in cooperative support for a long-term policy than with legal hair-splitting. That "constitutional procedures" might conceivably introduce a major note of uncertainty into the calculations of allies was tacitly recognized in the Senate Foreign Relations Committee's Report: "It has been questioned whether a treaty subordinating action to the constitutional process of 12 democratic nations offers sufficient certainty and immediacy of action effectively to deter aggression. The committee is convinced that it does. . . . The action of the democracies in the past great war is concrete evidence of their ability to act with the necessary speed in the event of an emergency."* However, the "troops-to-Europe" debate indicates that constitutional requirements are probably not as much of a bar in an outright emergency as they are in a "no peace–no war" period which hovers between the real thing and something short of it.

About the time that the vote was taken on the George substitute for the Bricker amendment, another incident was culminating which demonstrated the persistence of an issue which has loomed large in the preceding discussion. In an address on January 12, 1954, Secretary of State Dulles outlined the "New Look" in American strategy and security planning. Among other things, he said that the United States would henceforth depend on "a great capacity to retaliate, instantly, by means and at places of our choosing." He also made it clear that this might well be directed at an aggressor's home territory and that the formal declaration of war might have to come later. Such a declaration not only marked a new departure in strategy but once again opened up the question of whether the President shall decide when the United States shall go to war. On March 11, 1954, President Eisenhower said: "I will say this: there is going to be no involvement of America in war unless it is a result of the Constitutional process that is placed upon Congress to declare it. Now, let us have that clear and that is the answer." Shortly thereafter Secretary Dulles remarked that the Rio Pact (the Inter-American Defense Treaty) and the North Atlantic Treaty permitted the President to act in certain situations *without* consulting Congress. Asked about this during his press conference March 18, 1954, the President said that in the event of an immediate grave threat—in which there were only "two minutes" to act—he would certainly take action, but he reaffirmed the general proposition that he would consult Congress as quickly as possible. President Eisenhower's position seemed to be that the exercise of presidential constitutional prerogatives would depend primarily upon the situation, upon the kind of threat to

* United States Senate, Report of the Committee on Foreign Relations, *The North Atlantic Treaty,* 81st Congress, 1st Session. June 6, 1949, p. 19.

United States interests, and upon the amount of time available for the formal declaration of war. However, he did not clarify the implied threat by the Secretary of State to retaliate on an aggressor's home bases for wars started elsewhere than on American soil.

► THE IMPACT OF TOTAL DIPLOMACY
ON THE CONSTITUTION

It is important to note the fact that the new international position of the United States which has grown out of World War II and the crisis period in foreign policy since 1945 has intensified certain recent patterns of development in the constitutional system. In his excellent essay, *Total War and the Constitution* (1947), Professor Corwin has summarized them as follows: (1) tolerance of an indefinite legislative prerogative in the federal government; (2) recognition of the President's power and duty to constantly stimulate the positive exercise of this enlarged prerogative; (3) permission for Congress to make almost unhampered delegations of power to the President; (4) extension to the President of a broad prerogative to meet emergencies as defined by him; and (5) progressive replacement of the judicial process by the administrative process in the enforcement of law. As this distinguished scholar puts it: "Here, in outline, is the postwar constitution or a close approximation of it." * It would appear likely that as long as the cold war continues, the Constitution will take even clearer shape along these lines.

► SUMMARY

The basic function of the constitutional system is to provide a general allocation of power and responsibility for the conduct of foreign affairs. Except within very broad limits, the allocation is never final and never entirely clear. In actual practice, the exercise of the foreign-relations power requires a continuous definition, interpretation, and application of constitutional authorizations to specific situations. Because of the peculiarities of the sytsem, two kinds of adjustments are absolutely required: first, adjustments to the division of power between the federal government and the several states; and second, adjustments to the separation of power between the President and Congress. The latter is more significant and troublesome than the former. Both will be conditioned by "practical necessities," i.e., by the opportunity to act, by the capacity to act quickly and appropriately, and by the pressure of political considerations.

That the constitutional system compels some sort of mutual accommodation of the respective powers of the President and Congress cannot be overstressed. There are, of course, settled areas of jurisdiction where conflict and difficulty have seldom arisen. Yet even in these areas foreign-policy develop-

---

* Corwin, *Total War and the Constitution*, p. 179.

ments may at any time throw clearly assigned powers into an entirely new light. However, it is the overlapping and cognate powers which are most crucial to the new patterns of American foreign policy. Neither the President nor Congress can go it alone for very long, though each possesses potent exclusive powers. Because the Supreme Court has not generally provided regular clarification of issues left unsettled in the written Constitution, the system has developed for the most part on the basis of action taken jointly or separately by the two political arms of the federal government.

Adjustments of constitutional relationships between the President and Congress can take several forms. Their powers may be meshed perfectly or workably through a deliberate agreement on a particular problem, a procedure which would automatically constitute a legal interpretation of the Constitution. One or the other (especially Congress) may let an action or a series of actions go by default because of an unwillingness or inability to do anything about it. Traditions are often established in this way. An action may be protested for the record, but allowed to pass or perhaps ultimately approved. Finally, both the President and Congress may agree to waive constitutional clarification in order to get a job done. Obviously, these forms are not mutually exclusive. Whichever way the adjustment takes place, an observer can usually count on the operation of certain recurrent factors: the necessity to do something, the requirement of satisfactory rationalization to save face and legitimize authority, and the desire not to circumscribe freedom in future situations.

It would be an unfortunate mistake to view the materials in this chapter as an obscure game of legal hairsplitting. Many of the participants appear to behave as though this were the case. It is much more realistic to regard the constitutional system as the setting within which a kind of collective bargaining between the President and Congress takes place. Major constitutional issues such as those analyzed briefly above actually represent a struggle, not primarily over legal subtleties, but over the terms under which collaboration will proceed. Though there are bedrock conditions which neither party can escape— i.e., the separation of powers and the nontransfer of some powers—there is also an area of extensive maneuverability where neither party has anything approaching complete control of the action.

► SELECTED BIBLIOGRAPHY

Two general collections of readings and documents on the constitutional framework are L. Larry Leonard, *Elements of American Foreign Policy* (New York, McGraw-Hill Book Company, 1953), pp. 25–88, and L. H. Chamberlain and R. C. Snyder, *American Foreign Policy* (New York, Rinehart & Company, 1948), Chap. 1. E. S. Corwin, *Total War and the Constitution* (New York, Alfred A. Knopf, Inc., 1947), is an authoritative discussion by a distinguished scholar of the impact of war on the distribution of powers in the Constitution. J. G. Rogers inquires into the powers of the President and Congress through nine wars and one hundred military operations covering the period 1789 to 1945 in *World Policing and the Constitution* (Boston, World Peace Foundation, 1945). An enlightening analysis of the difficult problem of self-executing treaties is to be found in L. Preuss, "On Amending the Treaty-Making Power: A Comparative Study of the Problem of Self-Executing Treaties," *Michigan Law Review,* June, 1953. A thorough study of the Bricker amendment is presented by P. Perlman in his article, "On Amending the Treaty Power," *Columbia Law Review,* November, 1952. F. Sherwood takes a somewhat different line of argument from the one embodied in this chapter in "Foreign Relations and the Constitution," *Western Political Quarterly,* December, 1948.

CHAPTER FIVE

THE PRESIDENCY AND FOREIGN POLICY

The Pre-eminent Position of the President • Aspects of the American Presidency and Their Relation to Foreign Policy • Other Factors Which Condition the Role of the President • Great Presidential Power: Danger and Salvation • A Preface to the Study of the Executive Organization for Foreign Affairs • Selected Bibliography

► THE PRE-EMINENT POSITION OF THE PRESIDENT

More than a century and a half of American political and constitutional history have established the undoubted supremacy of the President's leadership in foreign affairs. The American presidency is a unique office in modern government. All things considered, it is probably the most powerful. A major reason for its uniqueness and power is the emergence of the President as the key foreign-policy maker. Certainly in the present era, the control of foreign relations is the most crucial phase of the President's job. Some of the most important problems and paradoxes of American national government arise from this control. Moreover, the political fate of the Western world is intimately bound up with the effectiveness with which the President of the United States discharges his enormous responsibility.

NATURE OF THE PRESIDENT'S POWER AND RESPONSIBILITY

It was demonstrated in the previous chapter that the President has at his disposal an imposing set of legal powers: to negotiate treaties and agreements, to recognize new states and governments, to declare policy, to act as commander in chief, to nominate or appoint officials, and to exercise authority granted in legislative statutes. These powers have been built up by custom and understandings, Congressional delegation and approval, and court decisions. The development of presidential power has not been due to deliberate planning or foresight, but to the interplay of the need for action, action itself, and approval of action. Experience and the lessons of experience have accumulated over time. Presidential power has grown simply because it has been exercised. Accompanying the exercise of power—sometimes preceding it, sometimes following it—has been the growth of responsibility. *Primary* responsibility for the conduct of foreign relations rests on the President.

182

Responsibility in this context means basically that there is a *sanctioned expectation* that the President will act, must act, and has the power to act for the nation. What began as the exercise of direct and implied powers in the written Constitution has now emerged as a recognized position of leadership.

All this is confirmed by a clear historical record which cannot be examined minutely here. The generalization can be made, however, that the nation's major foreign policies have been presidential rather than Congressional in origin and conception. Beginning with Washington's policy of nonentanglement, many policies have been associated with a particular President's name: Jefferson's Embargo, the Monroe Doctrine, Theodore Roosevelt's "Big Stick" policy, Wilson's Fourteen Points, the Hoover Moratorium, the Truman Doctrine, and so on. All of the so-called "strong President's" (Washington, Jefferson, Lincoln, Wilson, the two Roosevelts) have been so described, in part, because of their vigorous exercise of some aspect of the foreign-relations power.

Now the President does not, of course, enjoy a monopoly of the foreign-relations power. To reiterate, he *shares* power with Congress. However, even though the President's position is not beyond challenge and his range of action is not unlimited, the *initiative* is ordinarily his alone. Whether something is done, and to a large degree what is done, will depend upon the President. The exercise of Congress's own power will be subject to substantial presidential direction. Even if the President has not himself the power to do everything, the total foreign-relations power of the federal government cannot be properly employed without his guidance. It is difficult, though not impossible, for the President to follow slavishly Congress's wishes and public opinion. Whenever this has happened, there have been troublesome consequences for the nation's foreign policy. Under present circumstances, the failure of the President to lead would probably be regarded as an abdication of responsibility. Given the nature of the American political system, a lack of presidential leadership would mean no real leadership at all in foreign affairs.

In addition to the fact that the President shares prerogatives with Congress, other characteristics of the President's power should be noted. While many of his powers are clear and specific, there is a sense in which they are general and undefined. Actually, any President has a storehouse of power available to him, but no one knows how much the storehouse holds. Woodrow Wilson, a profound student of the presidency as well as one of its most important occupants, said: "The President's office is anything he has the sagacity and force to make it. . . ." True only within certain limits, the statement nonetheless points up a significant fact: the over-all power of the President is really defined in terms of specific, discretionary action under particular circumstances and conditions. It is an exaggeration to say that the President does not know what he can do until he tries, but in many respects the total dimensions of his ability to control foreign relations are indefinite. How presidential power is defined will depend, therefore, on a combination of resources available in the constitutional reservoir, the skills and initiative of a particular President, and the surrounding political environment.

The point becomes clearer if a distinction is drawn between *presidential power* and *presidential influence*. Not everything the President can accomplish derives its authority directly from his legal powers narrowly conceived. As noted above, the capacity of the President to bring the nation into actual, if not formally declared, war has been recognized. Congress has the power to make final peace terms; yet other decisions of the President enable him to influence those terms. Contrariwise, the President cannot always exercise his clear legal powers. Power is a subtle phenomenon. It may be available to the President in a technical sense, but it must be generated and applied. As the American political process operates, much can be done if conditions are "right"; little if conditions are not. During the months preceding the national election of 1948, when it was universally thought that President Truman would be overwhelmingly defeated, his control of foreign policy was visibly shaken. Obviously the legal reservoir of presidential power had not run dry. The President's general political influence may affect his ability to use his legal power or it may be sufficient to enable him to act in the absence of clear legal permission.

Finally, while the power of the President resides solely in himself, in effect it is delegated by him to the executive agencies concerned with foreign affairs. This splintering of the executive power does not mean that the President makes no decisions himself; it means that in the general exercise of his powers the President is aided by a large staff acting in his name. One of the important elements in the power position of the President is the manner in which the President divides and administers the authority centralized in his office. It goes without saying that the successful discharge of presidential responsibilities and the effective use of presidential powers will depend on an efficient division of labor and proper coordination of functions within the Executive Branch.

REASONS FOR PRESIDENTIAL PRE-EMINENCE

The growth of the power, responsibility, initiative, and influence of the President is attributable to several kinds of factors. To begin with, the administration of foreign affairs is essentially an executive function. A single responsible agent to speak for the nation and special facilities for action are required. This fact was discovered early in the American Revolution, when the Continental Congress tried vainly to conduct foreign relations through one of its own committees. The necessity for quick aciton, day-to-day decisions, access to technical information, secrecy, and formal communication with other governments makes it natural that the chief executive be responsible. Only he can perform such functions. The President is also in an ideal position to take the initiative. He is the truly national figure in the federal government. Citizens look to him for leadership. He appears to have, as an institutional figure, a poise and prestige which raise him above other political officials. He is able to speak out when the occasion demands. As head of a huge administrative organization he has an available staff and other weapons in the highly specialized business of policy making. The very essence of presidential leadership in foreign affairs is that only the head of state can provide potentially the political and emotional certainty and symbolic unity called for. An eminent writer on the presidency has summarized it this way: "By virtue of being a single individual and always Johnny-on-the-spot, by virtue of the constantly recurrent pressure of crises that would not admit of delay, by virtue of certain theories of executive power . . . added to the creative power of aggressive personalities . . . the President has come to claim, and has often been able to make the claim good, a quite indefinite prerogative in the sphere of foreign relations."*

THE IMPACT OF RECENT FOREIGN-POLICY COMMITMENTS ON THE PRESIDENCY

Two general influences of the new international position of the United States on the American presidency are noteworthy. In the previous chapter, it was pointed out that there has always been a broad conception of the foreign-relations powers which Congress may delegate to the President. As a result of developments since 1941, the conception has been noticeably broadened. The pattern set in the Lend-Lease Act of 1941 has been followed. That act gave the President power to give material aid to "any country whose defense the President deems vital to the defense of the United States." Later, the Greek-Turkish Aid Act of 1947 stated: "Notwithstanding the provisions of any other law, the President may from time to time when he deems it in the interest of the United States furnish assistance to Greece and Turkey upon request of their governments and upon terms and conditions determined by him." So it was with the Foreign Assistance Act of 1948, the North Atlantic Alliance, the Mutual Aid Act of 1951—all endowed the President, directly or indirectly, with enormous discretion. Clearly, presidential decisions have increased in number and importance. Moreover, the expenditure of billions through foreign-policy programs has enlarged greatly the number of executive agencies concerned with foreign policy and has complicated the problem of coordination. Given the nature of American policy at present, the President's specific, daily responsibilities for foreign relations are greater than they have ever been before in peacetime.

TECHNIQUES AVAILABLE TO THE PRESIDENT

Availability and vigorous use of certain techniques of leadership have in large part accounted for the development of presidential supremacy. Some stem from the Constitution; others from technological improvements scarcely imagined when the original document was written. Of major significance is the President's influence over public opinion. The President has almost unparalleled access to mass mediums of communication—a kind of right to a com-

* Edward S. Corwin, *Total War and the Constitution* (New York, Alfred A. Knopf, Inc., 1947), p. 157.

mand performance any time he wants it. He can reach millions through the newspapers and over the radio. His weekly press conference has become a primary source of information and declaration of policy. Press releases from the Executive Branch have a top priority among news items. Via these mediums the President can "educate" and persuade the public, mobilize support for existing policies, prepare the ground for new developments, raise hopes and expectations, release "trial balloons," and intensify the tendency of the people to lean on a single leader in foreign-policy matters. President Franklin Roosevelt was extremely effective as an opinion leader. Almost singlehandedly he gradually remolded Amercian attitudes to the point where radical departures in policy after 1940 were accepted. Both he and Woodrow Wilson also added to their prestige and power by effective appeals to worldwide opinion.

It is not too much to say that the President and his staff enjoy, when they wish to exert it, enough of a monopoly on the appropriate information to control substantially the "picture of reality" held by most of the population with respect to foreign relations. The President's access to, and control of, vital information is a weapon of great significance. He personally or his staff can obtain information not open to anyone else. The use to which the information is put is subject to presidential discretion. The general principle of presidential control of "security data" is well established. Some newsmen and congressmen do share confidential information, but by and large the President can classify and keep secret what he wishes. Besides having the information, the President has the analytical skills at his disposal to organize and interpret it. In any struggle with Congress, the President can bombard committees with the testimony of his experts, whose knowledge and command of the subjects Congress can hardly match.

Transoceanic telecommunications and the airplane have also strengthened the President's position. President Franklin Roosevelt had a direct telephone connection to Prime Minister Winston Churchill after 1940. "For many matters of diplomatic negotiation, the President, by use of the telephone, became his own ambassador in London."* The airplane made it possible for Churchill to be a frequent visitor in Washington during World War II. Since 1939, the President himself has become more and more a negotiator. Not only has diplomacy been speeded up, but science has provided the President with dramatic techniques for directly influencing international politics. A sudden personal visit, a telephone call, the sending of a special emissary by presidential plane—these tactics are available to the resourceful chief executive. When the President so acts, not only are his efforts likely to be more effective than regular diplomatic communications, but his prestige is also enhanced. At home and abroad, the personal role of the President is emphasized and his constitutional position is constantly illustrated. Domestic political opponents

---

* Louis W. Koenig, *The Presidency and the Crisis* (New York, Columbia University Press, 1944), p. 19.

of the President have recognized the importance of this fact by bitterly denouncing dramatic gestures in foreign policy. President Truman's sudden proposal in October, 1948, to send Chief Justice Vinson to talk to Stalin and his own flight to talk to General MacArthur at Wake Island in October, 1951, were condemned as attempts to add to his own prestige.

Other techniques are less spectacular and less well-known. In 1939–1940, when Congress refused to give the President the discretionary power to prohibit shipments of aviation gasoline and scrap metal to the Axis Powers then engaged in World War II, he appealed to business leaders for a "moral embargo" and was not unsuccessful. As suggested previously, a clever President can sometimes gain his own ends by a favorable interpretation of the laws he is bound by oath to execute. A good deal of leeway often reposes with the President as to when and how laws will be carried out. The powers of the President with respect to the Lend-Lease Act of 1941 were interpreted to permit him to use convoys to protect the shipments authorized despite the fact that such action was expressly prohibited by other legislation. President Truman, having told Congress he disapproved of the measure, delayed action on a legislative directive to lend $100,000,000 to Franco Spain until he had changed his mind about its advisability. The dispersal of the President's power throughout the Executive Branch may create situations where he is frustrated or opposed by members of his own family, so to speak. If it is not politically feasible to remove an official or reorganize a department, the President can employ other devices to accomplish his purposes. Franklin Roosevelt by-passed his ambassador in London in 1940 by sending a special emissary. He also by-passed the State Department on certain matters by establishing the Board of Economic Warfare during World War II.

The foregoing analysis of the sources of presidential supremacy indicates briefly the reasons for his supremacy and the types of techniques inherent in his unique position in foreign affairs. These techniques provide him with a relatively wide range of maneuverability and serve several purposes. They have developed logically from his power and help him to use his power more effectively. They testify to his prestige as well as enhance it. They partially explain why he is the leader and they are part of his capacity for leadership.

CONCLUSION

The foregoing analysis justifies certain conclusions and suggests a pattern of discussion for the remainder of this chapter. It is evident that the President has very great power in the field of foreign relations. Serious problems for democratic government arise from the sheer magnitude of this power. It is also evident that the President is charged with the full responsibility for foreign-policy initiative and leadership. One question to be kept in mind, therefore, is whether the President's power is commensurate with his responsibility. The President has greater power over foreign affairs than over domestic affairs but his respective roles in each are closely related. What are the implications of this relationship? Since the President does not have a monopoly of the foreign-relations power, he must enter into workable arrangements with Congress. Insofar as the President's power is undefined, its realization will depend on the personality of the chief executive himself, his skills, and the conditions under which he operates. Because the President cannot personally exercise his power, it must be delegated to administrative agencies effectively staffed, organized, and coordinated.

To explore these propositions more fully, it is necessary to consider, in order, the nature of the American presidency and its impact on the role of the President in foreign affairs; the effect of the characteristics of individual Presidents and the political environment on the exercise of presidential power; the problems connected with the President's extensive power and the enforcement of presidential responsibility; the President's staff, presidential decision making, and the problem of coordination in the Executive Branch.

► ASPECTS OF THE AMERICAN PRESIDENCY AND THEIR RELATION TO FOREIGN POLICY

No real understanding of the President as key foreign-policy maker is possible except in terms of what the presidency has become in the American governmental system. Senator Paul Douglas of Illinois once remarked on the ideal attributes of a President: "He should have the brooding qualities of Lincoln, the philosophic depth of Jefferson, the sturdiness of Cleveland and the daring of Franklin D. Roosevelt. He needs the patience of Job and must have the physique of a Sandow."* All of the outstanding Presidents have left behind ample testimony to the tremendous demands made upon them. Jefferson himself said the honeymoon period was fun "but the moments of ecstasy must be ransomed by years of torment and hatred." In at least two cases, Woodrow Wilson and Franklin Roosevelt, the man could be said to be a casualty of the office. Students of politics agree that it is the biggest, toughest political job of all.

THE MULTIPLE ROLES OF THE PRESIDENT

For one thing, the President really has several jobs, not one. He is the ceremonial head of the state, national spokesman and foreign-policy leader, chief administrative officer of the federal government, commander in chief, party leader, and the most important source of policy recommendations generally. As President Truman put it informally to some of his Democratic colleagues: "I wear a lot of hats." This fact is a source of continuing confusion and irritation in American politics because it is all but impossible for the President to separate his various roles even if he self-consciously tries to do so. The system will not allow him to say, "I am now wearing my hat as director

---

* Quoted by James Reston in "The Qualities a President Needs," *New York Times Magazine,* October 31, 1948, p. 48.

of foreign relations." Further complications are due to the fact that the momentary political strength or weakness of the President may differ from role to role. He may be riding the crest of a wave of favorable public opinion, yet be opposed by his own party's leaders. He may win in Congress on domestic issues, yet be defeated on foreign-policy issues. He may have to conduct high-level negotiations with other nations, yet be on shaky ground at home. He may have to pursue foreign-policy actions which make his party unpopular. His various roles are thus interrelated. What the President can do in one will be affected by what he has done in another. His power and influence may be strengthened, weakened, or neutralized accordingly.

However, the more serious consequences of the President's multiple roles flow from what they require of him. Inasmuch as leadership is so important, the President must have some sense of the currents of his era. He can buck these currents or ride with them—perhaps even guide them. But if he is to dramatize issues he will have to make some assessment of the general direction in which events are moving. He cannot, on the other hand, be too far ahead of his time. The demand to lead will always be great; yet if he leads there will always be opposing forces. Hence he must be something of an opportunist, adapting his course to reality, compromising, conceding to persons to preserve principles. Having made a decision he must learn when to abide by it, when to retreat. Obviously the President must be able to get along with people in a variety of difficult relationships. He must have a common touch, yet be a cut above the common man. Over some men he has authority, over others not. Intuitive judgment and political acumen are necessary. He must be able to think and make decisions rapidly. He should have a tough skin while being sensitive to criticism. Channels of communication to both friends and opponents must be kept open. He must be able to absorb and use a mass of both technical and general information. If he has not the information himself, he must know where to get it. He has to have the ability to recruit advisers. He has to delegate functions to others and see to it that those functions are coordinated. He cannot lose track of what is happening to major policies in either the developmental or the implementation stages.

THE PRESIDENT HAS ULTIMATE RESPONSIBILITY

Public opinion may inspire or hamper, Congress may push or restrain, aides may give advice, but in the last analysis, *the President must decide.* He can delegate authority but not responsibility. Delegating authority is not easy. It cannot be used as a subterfuge to protect the President from having to make decisions. Officials down the line will be able to sense when delegation is not genuine. Furthermore, the President must choose aides who will not be hurt by being overruled and repudiated. At the same time, the President must protect his staff as far as possible from irresponsible criticism and pressures which are, or should be, directed at him. To do so is not easy in a sprawling bureaucracy subject to direct public or Congressional attack at numerous points. At the same time the President cannot overprotect his staff on penalty of harboring incompetence or losing necessary political support.

THE "LONELINESS" OF THE PRESIDENT

Besides having to juggle several complex jobs, besides carrying tremendous power and responsibility, and besides having to master certain complex skills, the President has to endure a personal loneliness. Robert Sherwood has called his office "the loneliest box in the most colossal organization chart in all creation."* Herbert Feis says of American Presidents: "All learned the terrible isolation, in the struggle of mind and conscience for him who has to decide for the whole nation."† It is said of Franklin Roosevelt that he "became more and more suspicious of the people associated with him and kept more and more to himself."‡ He is reputed to have remarked to Wendell Willkie: "But—someday you may well be sitting here where I am now as President of the United States. And when you are, you'll be looking at the door over there and knowing that practically everybody who walks through it wants something out of you. You'll learn what a lonely job this is. . . ."§ Even the rather gregarious President Truman referred frequently to "this big white jail." The point here is that because of the nature of the office, Presidents feel exposed and vulnerable. This feeling leads directly to the need for trusted advisers, special agents, and a close personal friend or two. These individuals perform several functions for the President: they may undertake particular missions (as noted in the last chapter), offer different kinds of advice from that ordinarily given by regular Cabinet officers, and act as intermediaries between him and the outside world. The actual role of such men is obscure from the standpoint of the general public, but there is no doubting their strong influence. They attract much criticism and abuse because they stand in the shadow of the President's great power. Harry Hopkins, who essentially shared this kind of relationship with Franklin Roosevelt, was the target of extreme abuse and was also cited as one of the evil by-products of a bloated presidential power over foreign affairs. W. Averell Harriman performed some of the same functions for President Truman though he was not so widely attacked. The presidency being what it is, this phenomenon will continue in one form or another.

PRESSURES AND UNCERTAINTY SURROUNDING THE PRESIDENT

Comments made in Chapter Three regarding pressures and uncertainties operating on policy makers apply, of course, to the chief executive. The President's position of ultimate responsibility and leadership subjects him to

* *New York Times Magazine,* January 16, 1949, p. 7.
† *New York Times Magazine,* January 21, 1951, p. 11.
‡ Robert Sherwood, *Roosevelt and Hopkins* (New York, Harper & Brothers, 1948), p. 3.
§ *Ibid.*

additional pressures as well. Chief Justice John Marshall argued that the President is responsible "to the country in his political capacity and to his own conscience." In foreign policy, the President's responsibility appears to be virtually unlimited. He therefore has an unlimited commitment to a rather vague political master, "the country." Much of the time the President is not only under pressure "to lead," but he is under the necessity of defining his own responsibility—a difficult task in itself. As noted, the limits of his power are undefined. Therefore, the President may have his own doubts and others may have doubts as to whether he has properly conceived his responsibility and it is *not always certain* that his power will match his responsibility. It will be seen presently that there are potential roadblocks in the way of an effective discharge of presidential responsibilities over which he may have only partial control. James Reston, the distinguished commentator for the *New York Times,* summed up this point: "This is the difficulty about the Presidency: the people are clear enough about what they expect from the Chief Executive, but they are somewhat foggy about the duties and limitations placed upon him."*

The President must work out combinations of his power and his responsibility under continuing direct pressures and conditions of uncertainty. The White House is the focus of a constant struggle for influence and of a flow of what may be irresponsible criticism. To quote Cabell Phillips, an experienced political writer for the *New York Times:* "Influence is Washington's most treasured commodity. The next dearest is knowing, and having access to, people who have it." † No day goes by but what the President is besieged for an audience by a wide variety of persons. To be sure there is a screening process; yet the President is never really certain whether the information given him by such visitors is correct, whether they represent authentic pressures, or what he has risked by failing to see them. In addition, all Presidents who have exerted positive leadership have been vilified. Jefferson was called "liar"; Jackson, "murderer"; Lincoln, a "baboon"; Wilson, a "tyrant"; and Franklin Roosevelt, "traitor." As chief executive, the President literally sits on top of a huge administrative structure which he cannot completely control, whose sheer size keeps him from knowing more than the bare essentials of what is going on. He must rely on his staff to tell him what he needs to know. Nevertheless, he may at any time suddenly find himself confronted by and deeply involved in a controversy or other embarrassing circumstances not of his personal making.

Between November, 1950, and late January, 1951, President Truman was the target of an attempted assassination, lost his close friend and press secretary, Charles Ross, through a sudden heart attack, was misinterpreted in two news conferences, was attacked bitterly in Congress over the troops-to-Europe issue, had to report severe reverses in Korea, took part in discussions

---

* *New York Times Magazine,* October 31, 1948, p. 7.
† New York *Times,* December 21, 1951, p. 9.

with British Prime Minister Attlee which required patience, energy, and tact, and was assailed for policy disagreements with General MacArthur. The usually calm President reacted to the build-up of pressure by angered, intemperate acts and words which directly affected his leadership position and foreign policy generally. Without implying any judgment of the wisdom or unwisdom of Mr. Truman's reaction, the episode illustrates the exposed nature of the presidency and raises the question whether the President—aside from his personal capacity for self-control—has the minimum institutional protection which his difficult job requires. At any rate this is the kind of thing which may happen to any President any time in a critical period.

THE PRESIDENT'S PRESS CONFERENCE

The press conference is a device whereby the President once a week communicates news, plans, and policies to the public. It has been growing steadily in importance since its inception in 1912. It is one of the presidential techniques for foreign-policy leadership and control. The way it operates and some of its results throw significant light on the nature of the presidency. Dissatisfaction with the press conference has grown up recently, largely because of cases involving foreign policy.

At the press conference, the President meets face to face with about a hundred newsmen. They are permitted to fire questions. The President may try to answer or he may say, "No comment." A stenographic record is kept. Newsmen are not allowed to quote the President directly. In the rapid give-and-take, and in the process of translating the President's statements to the public, opportunities for misinterpretation, diplomatic blunders, and other difficulties are virtually unlimited. For the President to slip from genuine communication to a battle of wits with his questioners is relatively easy. One correspondent has declared that the conference is a "cross between a tribal sacrifice and boxing match."* The President is a prime target for "loaded" questions, of course, but other dangers are more deep-seated. Questions may be unclear without being deliberately so. Misunderstandings may not arise until after the conference. Often the President must deal with complex questions on complex issues in impromptu fashion. He may answer off the cuff without adequate briefing.

Two cases demonstrate the serious repercussions which arise from mismanagement of the press conference. On November 30, 1950, President Truman was quoted as saying that use of the atomic bomb in the Korean war was being considered. The announcement created a furor throughout the world and was heralded as a change in American policy. A "clarifying statement," issued three hours later, said that there had been no change in policy, that use of the bomb had *not* been decided upon, and that the military would determine whether and when the bomb was to be employed in battle. On January 11, 1951, the press reported that the President had "defied" Congress

---

* Douglas Cater in the *Reporter*, March 20, 1951, p. 12.

on the troops-to-Europe issue and had insisted he had the power to send troops without consulting Congress. The report intensified the growing hostility between the two branches of the government and tended to exaggerate domestic policy differences before the outside world. President Truman flatly accused the press of not reporting his willingness to consult with Congress on the sending of troops to Europe. A period of bad feeling ensued, disturbing one of the primary channels of communication on foreign affairs between the President and his public. In both cases, however, the reporters could cite the press conference record to justify their stories and the President could legitimately say his words had been given a meaning he never intended.

The two examples are instructive. At the first conference dealing with the atomic bomb, the President was inadequately briefed and he made some specific comments of whose general implications he was momentarily unaware. During the second conference, the President was piqued after being asked the troops-to-Europe question fourteen times and hence he spoke or acted in a way which could easily be interpreted as "defiant." Under other circumstances, his remarks on his power and his willingness to cooperate with Congress might have been put together in a context more befitting his intentions and interests. Useful as it is and important though it is as a presidential technique, in its present form the press conference presents a recurring pitfall. Within a brief time period under awkward conditions the President is steadily bombarded with searching questions to which he replies with spontaneous oral answers. He may be called upon to comment on a wide range of policy matters covering the whole federal bureaucracy. His replies might be different if he could give careful, quiet thought to each one. Added to this is the fact that the press in itself is a screening process by which verbal responses become the printed word. The printed word may have an entirely different impact. Without any malice intended on either side, meanings can be distorted and "firmness" can become "defiance."

► OTHER FACTORS WHICH CONDITION
   THE ROLE OF THE PRESIDENT

General institutional aspects of the presidency are not the only factors which affect the exercise of presidential power and influence and the discharge of presidential responsibilities.

CHARACTERISTICS OF INDIVIDUAL PRESIDENTS

It is a truism to say that what the presidency looks like at any moment in time will be partly due to the man himself—his personality, his competence, and his conception of the office. Nonetheless the statement has profound implications for this study. Personal characteristics provide some of the clues as to how much energy and initiative the President will put into his role as foreign-policy leader, the effectiveness of his effort, the techniques he will find congenial, how much of the job he will personally do, the basic ideas which he brings to foreign-policy problems, whom he will listen to, whether he will get the most out of his staff, and whether he himself will act as one of the checks on his power.

Vigorous, imaginative men like Washington, Jefferson, Jackson, Lincoln, Theodore Roosevelt, Woodrow Wilson, and Franklin Roosevelt were able to accomplish much through sheer personal magnetism and the effect they had on the people whose acquiescence was important. On the other hand, Warren Harding seems to have been an attractive person but not a strong person; leadership in foreign policy from 1921 to 1923 was therefore exercised by Senator Borah and Secretary of State Hughes. The view the President takes of his office is important. Presidents Harding, Coolidge, and Hoover—whatever their competence—all (for different reasons probably) took a restricted view of the presidency. His powers and functions must be broadly conceived if a President is to give full expression to the possibilities inherent in his office, especially because there is no blueprint of permissible action in the field of foreign policy. One of the observable phenomena in Franklin Roosevelt's four terms was the change in the way he conceived his function as the primary architect of foreign policy. His conception in 1939 was much broader than when he was inaugurated in 1933 and it grew steadily throughout World War II.

Harry Truman, who succeeded Franklin Roosevelt when the latter died in office in April, 1945, differed markedly from his predecessor in several respects. Roosevelt was much more inclined to take a direct hand in foreign-policy problems and to decide things himself. He appeared to have great confidence in his own knowledge and judgment of foreign affairs. Truman, on the other hand, relied much more heavily on his staff and had less confidence in his own judgment. Both men "played hunches," as any President must, but Roosevelt was probably more imaginative and sophisticated, whereas Truman's approach to policy problems was inclined to be more pragmatic and restricted. Roosevelt's leadership was, on balance, more dramatic and inspired, Truman's more matter of fact and less personal. Roosevelt's qualities of leadership bordered on the aristocratic and paternal. Truman seemed to be more comfortable in an image of himself as just another citizen, a brother to all. Both men relied heavily on their ability to mobilize favorable public opinion behind their policy views. Yet Roosevelt was more likely in critical situations to make a personal appeal via the radio and to let his personality work for him. Truman would rely on common-sense argument and factual presentation. Roosevelt generally avoided the kind of difficulty Truman ran into on occasion with the press, and his offhand statements were more skillfully made. Truman had somewhat more difficulty than Roosevelt in combining his role as party leader with his role as foreign-policy leader. Roosevelt had stronger personal control over the Democratic party and its key figures than Truman was able to muster despite the latter's unexpected victory in 1948. Roosevelt also managed to be more subtle in concealing his partisan feelings. Such crude comparisons are admittedly risky, but they do point up the relevance of certain personal factors to the presidential conduct of foreign relations.

THE POLITICAL ENVIRONMENT

Individual personal characteristics of the President do not function in a vacuum. It is the way they interact with the nature of the office and particular circumstances which is crucial. The superior position of the President in foreign affairs has resulted mainly from a combination of strong leadership, strategic opportunities and techniques inherent in the presidency, and a favorable environment in which leadership, opportunity, and techniques could operate. Domestic and foreign crises have therefore become very important. The periods of 1861–1867, 1898–1902, 1914–1919, and 1939 to the present were periods of emergency and war which required and accommodated vigorous executive leadership. Indecision and paralysis are politically and psychologically intolerable in time of crisis. Emergencies justify temporary measures which either become permanent or become precedents for later repetition. By and large, a President may lead or follow public opinion, but in any case he dare not be too far out of step with it. Wide latitude for the exercise of presidential initiative has been possible when public opinion has demanded it or would accept it. Similarly the state of public opinion may limit the range of permissiveness for presidential action.

The political environment is also centrally influenced by legislative-executive relations. Quite apart from the potential conflict between the two branches which is built into the constitutional system via the separation of powers, a general fear of executive domination has prevailed since 1789— a fear sometimes active, sometimes dormant. American politics has been characterized by alternating periods in which the rough balance of power has been held by either Congress or the President. There have been noticeable cycles of reaction from the relative dominance of one or the other. True, the presidency has grown steadily (partially at the expense of the national legislature) and the role of the President in foreign affairs has expanded further than his other roles. Nevertheless, the possibility of Congressional reaction is always real.* Even strong Presidents have exercised their power somewhat uneasily. A hostile Congress or Senate may check the President even when public opinion is favorable to the latter. Strong Presidents as well as weak have been hampered by legislative pretensions and activities. Because the President is elected by the nation as a whole, he is almost duty-bound to act for the whole nation. Generally speaking, a representative legislature is capable of only limited leadership because of the heterogenous nature of its composition and because the pressures upon it represent something less than the total national interest. Under the American system, the President initiates policy but does not and cannot fully control its development and implementation.

* Whether such a cycle is now manifest will be considered in Chapter Ten.

The capacity of Congress to check the President's power and condition his leadership will depend on a number of things. Congressional animosity probably matters less when foreign relations are largely routine and foreign policy is predominantly declaratory. With the exception of the Neutrality Acts, the period 1933 to 1941 fits this description. Much will depend on the unity of the President's party. If a segment of his party splits off on key issues he is more vulnerable. If the President is not in good rapport with his party's leaders in Congress, the same will be true. Congress may be in a mood to "show" the President just as a matter of principle. During an election year, opposition members may feel called upon to redouble their efforts to weaken or discredit the President and his party.

Clearly, the political environment in which the President performs his role is a mixture of elements. It is also clear that the environment is fluid, changing as issues and problems change, changing as the various elements change. It is fruitful to think of this in terms of what might be called an "ebb and flow" of permissiveness for the exercise of presidential power and initiative. The public confidence, Congressional support, and leadership strength which comprise the permissiveness are fragile items and may grow or perish quite quickly. Not all the elements are within the President's control. Nor can they be assessed by him with perfect accuracy. Major moves in foreign policy will aways involve a certain risk. Presidential victories may leave scars which will affect later action.

▶ GREAT PRESIDENTIAL POWER: DANGER AND SALVATION

Thus far this chapter has stressed the extensive power and responsibility of the President and the factors which limit and condition his role. The *responsibility* as constitutionally defined remains very broad, but the *power* as constitutionally defined or politically possible may fluctuate between wide limits in actual practice. It may amount almost to presidential dictatorship or it may be reduced to modest proportions. On balance, however, presidential discretion has tended to increase over time and most cases indicate that the President is free to operate at the expanded rather than contracted end of the continuum of his power. In recent years, criticism of the President's power has increased. The question has been raised whether a strong presidency, particularly in foreign affairs, menaces democracy and the constitutional system.

IS THE PRESIDENT TOO POWERFUL?

Criticism of the President's power by Congress and by certain writers has concentrated mainly on events since 1939: the involvement of the United States in World War II, the destroyer-bases deal with Great Britain (1940), the shoot-on-sight order and the sending of troops to Iceland and Greenland

(1941), the Yalta Agreement (1944), and the troops-to-Europe issue (1950–1951). In 1950–1951, there were three major assaults on the executive power: first, the Twenty-second Amendment, which now limits any one President to two terms; second, the attempt to limit the power of the President as commander in chief as outlined in the previous chapter; and third, the attempt to hamstring presidential control of foreign affairs through the "Acheson-must-go" movement in Congress and the proposed amendment by Representative Coudert of New York that would have the President resign after a no-confidence vote in Congress. These three onslaughts were rooted in hostility toward President Truman, in the search for party advantage, and in doctrinaire beliefs on the correct balance of power between President and Congress.

"MR. ROOSEVELT'S WAR" AND THE YALTA AGREEMENT

Charles A. Beard, one of America's great historians, devoted his last years to a long treatise designed to demonstrate the dangers of presidential dictatorship in foreign policy. In the second volume,* he asked two questions: How did the secret actions of the Roosevelt Administration from August 17 to December 7, 1941, square with official reports to the people? Did the official documents sustain the official thesis respecting relations with Japan as set forth in the President's message of December 8, 1941? Beard tried to prove that the answer to the first was that they didn't square at all; and to the second, that the documents did not sustain the official thesis. He thus interpreted this evidence: President Roosevelt made a promise in the campaign of 1940 not to send American boys overseas when he really knew that ultimate war with Japan was a foregone conclusion; Roosevelt and his advisers pressed a "no compromise" basis of agreement with Japan so far that the latter had no alternative but to attack America; and Roosevelt went his own way *despite* public opinion and was able to do so only by *ignoring and deceiving* public opinion. This virtually amounts to saying the President was guilty of deliberately and deceitfully maneuvering the United States into war, the direct result of an overweening power in the hands of the chief executive unintended by the framers of the Constitution.

Without discussing the merits of Beard's contention, a second example can be noted. The Yalta Agreement has been the subject of a great deal of controversy. What is of concern here is that its provisions have been the basis for continuing charges of the abuse of presidential power. Whether the decisions taken at the Yalta Conference were wise or unwise can be left aside at the moment. The point is that these decisions are cited to prove that President Roosevelt secretly made commitments he had no right to make. It is further charged that without consulting the Chinese Nationalist Government he "gave" to the Soviet Union control over territories formerly under the control of China, that he agreed to the exercise of the veto by the Russians

---

* Charles A. Beard, *President Roosevelt and the Coming of War, 1941* (New Haven, Conn., Yale University Press, 1948).

in the Security Council of the proposed world organization, that he permitted Polish territory to be handed over to Russia, and that the agreement also intrenched the Russians in East Germany. These specific charges add up to a general one to the effect that Roosevelt made so many vital concessions to the Soviet Union that the whole balance of power in the postwar world (especially in the Far East) was altered to the disadvantage of the United States and encouraged the Russians to embark on aggressive policies.

SIGNIFICANCE OF THE ARGUMENT

Both cases represent presidential negotiations which turned out to be extremely important, as subsequent developments have amply shown. In each, the power of the President reached its fullest expression. The analysis of the constitutional system presented above suggests, however, that the legal limits of presidential power were not exceeded. No respected body of opinion or court decisions say that Roosevelt's actions were unconstitutional in a strict sense. What Beard and other critics have really argued is either that the decisions were substantively wrong or that *the President should not have this much power.* To obtain perspective on this issue, a synthesis of points made in previous sections of this chapter is necessary.

The President's responsibility for foreign policy is undenied. Initiative can come from no other place in the government. His power is great, but at the outer limits is unclear and may not be proportionate to his responsibility. The President's general position is naturally strong for the reasons cited. Effective techniques as well as powers are available to him. However, he shares power with Congress and his own power is diffused among his staff. Foreign-policy leadership is only one phase of the President's office. The nature of the presidential office not only creates difficulties but requires a wide range of individual skills. Much will depend on whether a particular President has these skills. Much also will depend on his other personal characteristics. Finally, the President must define his responsibility, mobilize his power, employ his techniques, and adjust to the obstacles inherent in his office in a political environment over which he has only partial control. In major matters of foreign policy, therefore, a great deal will depend on luck and improvisation—luck that the President has the minimum skills and that these will be effective, and improvisation to enable the President to discharge his responsibilities under conditions where the range of permissiveness may fluctuate considerably.

Two dilemmas emerge from all this. *First,* if the President does his job well, if he improvises skillfully and effectively overcomes obstacles in the path of his leadership, overcentralization of power may result and policy tends to become undemocratic to the extent that decisions are being made by one man or a small group of men who at the moment of decision may be temporarily beyond the reach of constitutional and political checks. On the other hand, if the President's instincts are not sound, if improvisation fails or falters, if the job does not get done, valuable time may be wasted and national interests may be placed in jeopardy. *Second,* if the President fully informs the public of the facts upon which he is acting, he may be accused of warmongering, of "crying wolf," or of making a bid for power, and he risks the sacrifice of his own and his party's chances for continued public support. On the other hand, if the President goes ahead in what he thinks is the nation's best interest he may be accused of treason and malfeasance. Both dilemmas relate to a major problem: how to reconcile the American political process, including its peculiarities, its tendency to diffusion of power and responsibility, and its proneness to spasmodic action, with the need for discretionary powers, rapid action, and specialized knowledge in foreign-policy making. Another aspect of this problem was discussed in the last chapter, namely, how to achieve the appropriate application of military power without depriving Congress of its constitutional prerogative of declaring war.

The problem cannot be considered solely from a constitutional viewpoint. The fact that the exercise of presidential power is constitutionally sanctioned is no reason that it may not be dangerous on other grounds. Neither is a hypothetical constitutional argument in opposition to the discretion of the President to be considered valid per se. Fundamentally, the problem is one of power. It seems unlikely that the responsibilities of the President in foreign affairs can be reduced or shifted to Congress. Presidential power must be adequate for the discharge of responsibilities. Yet the power cannot be so great or exercised in such a manner as to undermine political democracy and the constitutional system. Presidential leadership requires control of the ingredients which enter into the formulation and execution of sound foreign-policy decisions. At the same time, sufficient power must be drawn from the reservoir of total power available, and it must be applied within the limits required by representative government. The presidency must not be too strong for liberty to survive or too weak to lead effectively. So put, the problem can be broken down into several questions: How can presidential power be exercised *responsibly?* How can discretionary presidential leadership be exercised so that it contributes to and expresses *a true national consensus?* How can presidential power and leadership be exercised *rationally* so as to minimize "the risk of disastrous fallability" at the point where they are concentrated?

THE ENFORCEMENT OF PRESIDENTIAL RESPONSIBILITY

Probably the only way a democratic society can live with the problem outlined here is by relying on various devices for keeping the exercise of the President's power responsible. In this connection, the concept of responsibility set forth in the very first chapter is relevant. Professor Lasswell's dichotomy of *formal* and *effective* devices for enforcing responsibility can now be modified to *formal* and *conventional* to avoid confusing implications. What have been called formal devices may, after all, be effective and those called effective may be just as regularized as the formal. The chief differences between the two types concern the frequency of application, the time required for effect, and whether or not the rules governing the devices are written or implicit or both. Formal methods applied to the presidency would include elections, court decisions, Congressional investigations, and impeachment. By and large, such methods operate indirectly and spasmodically, and require a substantial time period to be consummated. Impeachment, as noted, is an extreme measure. Its infrequent use suggests that it is not readily available. In any event, it could only be achieved some time after an irresponsible action was taken. The role of foreign-policy issues in national elections indicates that action by the voters is not a very efficient device either. Foreign-policy questions tend to be so interrelated with others that it is not easy to tell just what sort of mandate has been bestowed or what previous actions have been punished. This device is limited to four-year intervals, although presumably the President would not deliberately sabotage his party's candidates at Congressional elections. Federal court cases may take from three to five years or longer to come to a decision and even then there is no guarantee that the decision will be pinpointed on the question of the President's power. Special Congressional investigations have increased rapidly in number and scope. All in all, they may be the most potent of the formal devices, but for reasons to be reviewed later they are not as effective as they might be in direct challenges of the President. They buttress other devices and cannot do the job alone.

It is through the operation of what we have called conventional devices that some measure of continuous daily interplay of principal and agent is achieved. Conventional devices refer to certain practices which have grown up through custom, operate frequently and at irregular intervals, and the rules surrounding their use are generally not made explicit in any law. However, most citizens and political observers are quite familiar with a number of these practices which keep the President and his executive officers aware of sources of opposition and possible bases of agreement.

Praise and blame are bestowed on the President. Economic, political, and psychological pressures are exerted. Warnings are signaled. These cues reach the President via Congressional speeches, hearings and statutes, news reporting and editorial comment, letters to the White House, and visits from influential leaders. Day in and day out a free and responsible press is probably the number one instrument of accountability, partly because it serves as communicator for congressmen, interest groups, and nongovernmental opinion leaders. Despite the fact that the President can legitimately censor "security information," by and large little of significance to policy making escapes the probing eye of the American press. As noted, the press not only has access to various agencies and officials in the Executive Branch, but can regularly interrogate the President himself.

It will be recalled that there are two aspects of the responsibility equation:

first, a commitment of power from principal to agent within which the agent must operate, *and,* second, an effective discharge of responsibilities of the agent. The power of the President discussed above constitutes the commitment of power for foreign relations. The responsibilities include the duties of initiative and leadership as well as the specific functions assigned to the President. Therefore, the President is held accountable for what he does and how he does it. Obviously, the President may make "mistakes" or promote inadvisable policies, but if he acts within his power and is discharging his responsibility for policy initiative and leadership, this is not a power problem per se. However, the principals in this case—that is, the Congress, the opposition party, the press, interest groups, opinion leaders, and the public at large— must also be an integral part of the consensus which is essential for the formation and execution of policy under the American system. Thus enforcement of presidential responsibility and the achievement of consensus are interlocked. A delicate balance between them must be constantly maintained. If the attempt to keep the President "honest" is pushed too far, his vital contribution to consensus through effective policy leadership may be paralyzed. On the other hand, unless the President's exercise of power is responsive to the elements which must ultimately constitute a consensus, consensus may be impossible or, if attained, may be highly perishable.

The effective forms of accountability are one of the most important sources of the pressures operating on policy makers which were analyzed in Chapter Three. From the standpoint of the policy maker, particularly in the Executive Branch, these pressures are a handicap. They make his job more difficult. His power is always subject to check. He may not be able to discharge his responsibilities fully. Nonetheless, these pressures are a natural by-product of the necessity to enforce responsibility. In a democratic system they are among the unavoidable conditions under which the policy maker functions. Now it is also true that the effective devices may themselves operate irresponsibly. A capricious withdrawal of support and prerogatives of leadership from the President can be as damaging as irresponsible use of presidential power. An attempt to redefine the President's power by means other than the accepted political process or an attempt to prevent the President from acting within his constitutional grant of power would be irresponsible. It would interfere with the discharge of presidential responsibilities. Similarly, an attempt to hold the President responsible for acts or policies not definitely within his commitment would be irresponsible.

The enforcement of presidential responsibility is also dependent on the particular President and his staff. To a certain extent, the President self-enforces his responsibility. Indeed, such is the discretionary nature of his position that on major issues he must interpret his own duty. His interpretation may be narrow or broad and still be constitutionally correct. But in extreme cases, there is a twilight zone where he cannot be sure. The President is sworn to defend as well as to uphold the Constitution. Referring to the measures taken by the President in 1941 to strengthen the democratic nations against the Axis, Sherwood writes: "Roosevelt never overlooked the fact that his actions might lead to his impeachment."* It is a matter of historical record that the Presidents who have been compelled to make grave decisions for the United States have been acutely aware of the problem of their responsibility regardless of whether their judgment was right or wrong, good or bad.

To the extent that the President is aided by conscientious administrators with pride in the trust placed in them, accountability will be further strengthened. The more stable is the executive handling of foreign affairs, the more competent and efficient is the President's staff, the less chance there will be for flagrant abuse of power. When the Executive Branch skillfully keeps its finger on the public pulse and makes a continuous effort to achieve a genuine agreement, the cause of responsibility is served. The rationality and effectiveness with which presidential power is exercised are also related to the problem of responsibility. These aspects will be of concern throughout the rest of this chapter and the three which follow.

► A PREFACE TO THE STUDY OF THE EXECUTIVE ORGANIZATION FOR FOREIGN AFFAIRS

Thus far in Chapter Four and in the present chapter, attention has been focused on the broad allocation of power and responsibility for the conduct of foreign relations and on some of the typical problems which result from the nature of that allocation. Certain aspects of the presidency as an institution have been discussed. In so doing, the terms "President" and "chief executive" have been employed as abstractions for the sake of making description and analysis easier to handle. However, it is perfectly clear that the terms are misleading if one thinks of a single man, a single will, or a simple monolithic structure. Behind the abstractions lies a complex bureaucratic organization of activities and functions carried on by thousands of political officials and permanent career officials. The formal organization consists, basically, of nine Executive Departments—whose heads comprise the Cabinet—and about fifty federal agencies, some of which have Cabinet rank. These departments and agencies differ in their size, function, and relationship to the President. It is permissible for present purposes to regard this organization as a huge staff which exercises the power and responsibility vested in the Executive Branch of the government by the constitutional system. To various parts of the organization duties and functions have been assigned either by authority of the President in his constitutional capacity or by authority of Congress in its constitutional capacity.

---

* Robert Sherwood, *Roosevelt and Hopkins* (New York, Harper & Brothers, 1948), p. 274. Reprinted by permission of the publisher.

PRESIDENTIAL RESPONSIBILITY AND INITIATIVE VIEWED AS SPECIFIC FUNCTIONS OF THE EXECUTIVE BRANCH

An adequate, effective foreign policy must rest upon the performance of five general functions which may be viewed as the components of the role of the Executive Branch. First, high policy and policy issues must be formulated, major decisions taken, and future problems anticipated. When necessary, as it was in the case of Korea, the President's organization will alone decide on a course of action. Otherwise, concrete proposals will be made to Congress and the general public, or issues will be presented for discussion and debate. Second, decisions must be executed, or, to put it another way, policies must be administered. This may be called "policy operations" to distinguish it from decision making in the broad sense. It is exemplified by the overseas information program and the provision of military and economic aid to friends and allies. Third, "routine" foreign relations must be carried on, meaning the regulation of social intercourse between the United States and the rest of the world—particularly the movement of goods, services, and persons in and out of the country. Fourth, diplomatic negotiations must be carried on and the United States officially represented abroad. Finally, there is a whole cluster of important activities related to decision making and execution, namely, collection of information, its analysis, and the review of policy in action. Such is the very essence of the presidential responsibility and initiative discussed in the first part of this chapter. If these are the primary functions discharged by the Executive Branch, it is also clear that presidential leadership means "taking the lead" in shaping up policy issues, formulating proposals, guiding discussion, and providing the relevant information for national decisions. The structure and functioning of the Executive Branch in foreign affairs generally should be viewed as a response to the need for these functions to be performed, and the operation of the organization should be judged according to the effectiveness with which they are performed.

PERSPECTIVE ON THE EXECUTIVE BRANCH

The organization of the Executive Branch for foreign affairs can neither be understood nor judged properly without a certain perspective, elements of which have already been suggested in this book. In the remainder of this chapter and in the next three, executive agencies are separated out for detailed description and analysis. While these agencies do constitute the core mechanism of foreign-policy making, it is essential to bear in mind that this mechanism is imbedded in a total system of government and that foreign-policy decision making is inevitably linked to and often must accompany a larger political process. That process is not always orderly or predictable even within fairly wide limits. There are institutional links between the President and Congress, many different kinds of links between Congress and various executive agencies, and between segments of the organized public and executive agencies. Earlier a good deal of stress was put on the significance of the separation of powers, but it is equally important to note that the American governmental system is characterized by a series of checks and balances: between the House of Representatives and the Senate, between committees in the same legislative chamber, between political officials and career officials, between staff agencies and operating departments, and between departments themselves. To a certain extent the executive and legislative branches each have a leg in the other's back yard. Congress concerns itself deeply with matters of administrative organization, and executive agencies actually legislate. The agencies upon which the President depends must always look to Congress for money and often for power to act. As noted, the President and other executive policy makers are peculiarly exposed to pressures under the American system. As noted also, public attitudes and social values affect the recruitment of policy makers and the nature of the careers open to them. Political mores, the behavior of the national press, and other factors condition the way issues are shaped up for public discussion. If serious issues are brought up too often or in unwieldy form, if relatively unimportant issues are overstressed, and if lack of coordination is generalized throughout the political process, the organizational structure and operation of the Executive Branch is only partly to blame.

THE IMPACT OF DEVELOPMENTS SINCE 1941

The revolution in American foreign policy has altered substantially the structure and functioning of the executive organization. To a large extent, its present form has resulted from the necessities and experiences of World War II and the postwar crisis which followed. All executive agencies, whether their special province is foreign affairs or not, now have some part in the conduct of foreign relations. The burdens of agencies with long-standing responsibilities for policy formation and execution have increased greatly. New agencies have been established. Lend-Lease (1940) was succeeded by a series of relief, loan, and aid programs of many kinds, including the United Nations Relief and Rehabilitation Administration (1943–1947), the International Bank and International Monetary Fund operations, the British Loan (1945), the Greek-Turkish Aid Bill (1947), the Marshall Plan (1948–1951), the Mutual Defense Assistance Act implementing the North Atlantic Alliance (1949), and the Mutual Aid Act of 1951. The territories of former enemies have been occupied and administered. An international information program has been begun and expanded. These new programs and operations have required organizational changes, either the formation of new agencies or the adaptation of existing ones. The State Department was reorganized in 1944, 1945, and 1949. A new omnibus Department of Defense has been formed out of the old Navy and War Departments. Special staff agencies have been added to the Executive Office—the National Security Council, the National Security Resources Board, the Council of Economic Advisers, and others. A Joint Chiefs of Staff has been created. The diplomatic corps was somewhat reorganized and modernized in the Foreign Service Act of 1946. All in all, the executive organization for foreign affairs has become larger and more complex. The entire Executive Branch has, in varying degrees, been sensitized to America's new role in international politics.

Membership in the United Nations and its specialized agencies* along with participation in regional organizations such as the North Atlantic Treaty Organization has had its own particular impact. The work of the specialized agencies—which are autonomous within the general United Nations framework—usually touches on the functions of at least two federal departments, thus necessitating the creation of appropriate interdepartmental committees. New units and staffs have had to be set up in the interested departments and new methods for formulating the positions taken by American representatives have had to be developed. Economic and social work within the United Nations proper has also required interdepartmental committees. Constant participation in the activities of the General Assembly and the Security Council has added enormously to the work load of certain individual officials in the Department of State and has required new organizational units.

Limited war in Korea further complicated the structure and operations of the Executive Branch. A new, powerful, and probably temporary agency— the Office of Defense Mobilization—has been added to an already complex picture. Not only did the Korean conflict raise vital issues which affected a number of federal agencies; American operations and decisions had to be geared to the political arrangements made by the United Nations Security Council.

Clearly these developments are those of a period of transition and crisis. Aside from a greater total burden of work and the addition of new units and personnel, three other direct results should be mentioned. First, the President himself has to devote much more attention to high policy in consultation with his advisers. A greater number of significant decisions or formulations of policy are necessary and must be considered at high levels in the policy-making organization. Second, it has become increasingly difficult for the President to lead and oversee the activities of the Executive Branch with respect to foreign policy. Therefore the nature and effectiveness of his immediate staff assume major significance. Third, the organization of policy making and policy execution is undergoing continuous change and adaptation

---

* Universal Postal Union, International Telecommunications Union, World Meteorological Organization, International Refugee Organization (temporary), International Bank for Reconstruction and Development, International Monetary Fund, International Labor Organization, United Nations Food and Agriculture Organization, United Nations Educational, Scientific and Cultural Organization (UNESCO), World Health Organization, and the International Civil Aviation Organization.

to change. Hence the capacity of the organization to make a satisfactory adjustment to new demands and problems will be a source of strength or weakness in the nation's foreign policy.

SOME FUNDAMENTAL QUESTIONS

The Brookings Institution in its fine study, *The Administration of Foreign Affairs and Overseas Operations,** has raised questions concerning organization and administration worth repeating here:

1. Do they produce objectives and policies that generate acceptance and broad support?
2. Do they bridge the gap effectively between policy planning and program development?
3. Do they reduce delays in decision, execution, and re-examination to reasonable limits?
4. Do they achieve and maintain the requisite sense of direction and continuity?
5. Do they avoid the development of contradictions (1) between various stages of executing a course of action, (2) between various courses of action, and (3) between different levels on which action is being taken?

THE PRESIDENT HIMSELF AS CHIEF OF STAFF FOR FOREIGN AFFAIRS

Defining the President's own job is not easy. It goes without saying that he cannot do everything himself. He must delegate certain powers and responsibilities to Executive Departments and he must lean heavily on advisers and staff aides who do not execute policies or have operating responsibilities. Their assignment is to act in the name of President and to aid him in the discharge of his particular duties. While the President may make his own decisions on occasion, for the most part he will officially approve the decisions or policy formulations of others, settle jurisdictional disputes, see to it that the total responsibilities of the Executive Branch are met, act as general spokesman for the nation and the Executive Branch when necessary, and prepare and submit recommendations to Congress. His most significant function is one of leadership, of providing central coordination for the sprawling bureaucratic structure on top of which he sits as chief executive. This is by no means a simple task. For the Executive Branch is characterized by latent centrifugal tendencies, that is, some degree of political and administrative disintegration is always present and threatens to become greater. To the extent that such tendencies are actually realized, it becomes more difficult to enforce presidential responsibility either through the efforts of the President

---

* *The Administration of Foreign Affairs and Overseas Operations,* a Report Prepared by the International Studies Group for the Bureau of the Budget, Executive Office of the President, June, 1951 (Washington, D.C., U. S. Government Printing Office, 1951).

himself or by the other devices discussed in a previous section. One reason for the dispersal of strength and lack of discipline in the administrative organization is that its sheer size has lessened the influence of the President as an individual. Another is that party ties are less and less effective as a technique of achieving cohesion. The composition and operation of American parties are such that they are unwieldy as a means of enforcing responsibility. Finally, and perhaps most serious, the functional specialization of career officials makes it almost impossible for them to offer a unified leadership. Career officials do not constitute a single corps of individuals with similarity of outlook, common agreement on their role in the government, and dedication to professional values. Some career groups behave at times as though they were a private pressure group putting their own interests above those of the presidency and the nation at large. Some are closer to Congress than to the President. In sum, though it is appropriate for analytical purposes to regard the Executive Branch as a huge staff which helps the President carry out his constitutional responsibilities, it would be an error to assume that it is an integrated unit which "supports" the President in the full sense of the word.

The nature of the presidency and the federal bureaucracy obviously affect the ability of the President to act as foreign-policy leader, but, conversely, the President's personal behavior will affect the decision-making process. He may himself take charge of a policy problem or make a decision. It appears that President Franklin Roosevelt alone decided on the "unconditional surrender policy" accepted by the Allies at the Casablanca Conference of January, 1943. For several months before the election of 1948, President Truman controlled American policy on the Palestine question. On the other hand, the President may allow himself to be overruled by his advisers or allow decisions to be pressed on him. Whether the President boldly delegates power or whether he has a tendency to keep his finger on all major issues will condition both the way in which decisions are reached as well as their content. The President's relationship to his advisers may be one in which the influence of *individual* advisers is relatively great or it may be one in which the President accepts as authoritative the collective opinion of all major advisers. Franklin Roosevelt listened to Harry Hopkins and Henry Morgenthau (Secretary of the Treasury) on many major issues, while evidence suggests that Harry Truman had no one man he listened to exclusively on foreign policy. When meeting with his immediate advisers, the President may act as arbiter or referee rather than as leader or coordinator. In the latter case, the President may introduce his own views into the deliberations and try to reconcile differences of viewpoint among his advisers. President Truman apparently was reluctant to have problems "dumped in his lap" without his staff having done all the preliminary work and having made recommendations. President Eisenhower apparently likes to have his advisers unanimously behind a recommendation. Naturally, Presidents will differ in the amount of foreign-policy documentation they personally read and will differ in the kind of policy matters in which they will be primarily interested. Much will depend on whether the President has a well-developed sense of personal mission with respect to his responsibilities of foreign affairs. Strong presidential leadership and courageous facing of major decisions could exist without it, but it is a significant coincidence that Woodrow Wilson, Franklin Roosevelt, and Harry Truman—though they differed widely in other respects —each had a conviction about his contribution to foreign policy in his particular era. Wilson tried to be the architect of a new world order after 1918. Roosevelt had a vision of America's rendezvous with destiny as the savior of the free world. Truman was dedicated to the task of maintaining peace in the uneasy, divided postwar world. Eisenhower was also dedicated to peace, but he apparently viewed his task—at least up until the end of 1954—as primarily one of cementing the unity of the American people behind the broad program of security already developed and of financing this program at minimum cost to the taxpayer and the economy in general.

► SELECTED BIBLIOGRAPHY

A good general view of the President's role can be found in the following: James J. McCamey, *The Administration of Foreign Affairs* (New York, Alfred A. Knopf, Inc., 1950), Chap. 7; Harold Laski, *The American Presidency—An Interpretation* (New York, Harper & Brothers, 1940), Chap. 4; Edward S. Corwin, *The President: Office and Powers* (3rd ed., New York, New York University Press, 1948), Chaps. 5, 6; Dexter Perkins, *The American Approach to Foreign Policy* (Cambridge, Mass., Harvard University Press, 1952), Chap. 8; and L. H. Chamberlain and R. C. Snyder, *American Foreign Policy* (New York, Rinehart & Company, 1948), Chaps. 2, 3. Wallace McClure, "The Presidency and World Affairs," *Journal of Politics,* February, 1949, examines the problem of staffing the presidency for greatly increased burdens in the realm of foreign affairs. Valuable insights into some of the topics treated in this chapter are to be found in a careful reading of Robert Sherwood, *Roosevelt and Hopkins* (New York, Harper & Brothers, 1948). A more recent statement of Laski's opinions is "The American President and Foreign Relations," *Journal of Politics,* February, 1949.

CHAPTER SIX

THE EXECUTIVE ORGANIZATION FOR FOREIGN AFFAIRS: MAIN STRUCTURE AND FUNCTIONS*

Introduction • The President's Personal Staff and Individual Advisers • Staff Agencies in the Executive Office • The National Security Council • The Central Intelligence Agency and the Organization of Intelligence Generally • The State Department • The Department of Defense • Other Departments and Agencies Concerned with Foreign Affairs • Interdepartmental Committees • The Administration of Foreign Economic and Military Aid • The Organization of "Psychological Warfare" • The Problem of Coordination in the Executive Branch • Summary • Selected Bibliography

► INTRODUCTION

An exploration of every nook and cranny of the executive organization for foreign affairs would overwhelm the reader with details. No one observer or group of observers knows *all* there is to know about the operations of the Executive Branch in the field of foreign policy. An overloading of details would only make a somewhat confusing picture more so. On the other hand, to take a bird's-eye view introduces a certain artificiality—some life is bound to be lost from the data, and the analysis will give the impression of more order than probably exists in reality. With this warning in mind, this chapter may be regarded as an attempt to outline the policy-making organization at the executive level. Emphasis will be placed on the main structural features, on the most important agencies and their functions. Emphasis will also be placed on relationships, on the mediums of coordina-

---

* Unfortunately, two of the most important agencies treated in this chapter—the National Security Council and the Central Intelligence Agency—operate largely in secrecy. The authors suggest that allowances be made for the fact that detailed information is relatively scarce. Some of the conclusions are based on deduction from such evidence as exists and hence are tentative.

tion, and on the problems which an era of transition has brought to the machinery of foreign-policy formulation and execution.

This chapter carries one step further the analysis of the formal allocation of power and responsibility which was discussed first as an essential element in the decision-making process in Chapter Three and then in terms of the broad constitutional distribution in Chapters Four and Five. Throughout the discussion which follows, the rest of the general analysis of decision making presented in Chapter Three should be kept in mind. The decision-making process should be viewed as flowing within and among the various Executive Departments and agencies. Hence the elements of the decision-making process—the structure of authority (formal allocation of power and responsibility), motivation, information and intellectual skills, and communication and coordination—will be found in the role, structure, functioning, and interrelationships of the decision makers who comprise departments and agencies. Certain agencies or units have as their sole function the collection and dissemination of information and the application of intellectual skills to that information—the Central Intelligence Agency and the Office of Intelligence Research in the State Department, for example. The general structure of authority in the Executive Branch will largely determine the units of decision which emerge for particular decisions and the units which execute decisions as well as who communicates with whom. Certain units can make decisions, others can only recommend, though the decision-making process operates in the latter case too. Motives of officials in, say, the meetings of the National Security Council, will be related to their organizational affiliation with the Defense Department or any of the other agencies represented. The allocation of power among various agencies will affect motives too—the values of some officials being accepted as authoritative under particular circumstances. So far as coordination is concerned, the amount and kind required for various types of decisions will depend on the allocation of power and responsibility—the number of functions and agencies involved. In short, what follows is a description and analysis of the structural factors which affect the elements of decision making in the Executive Branch. Naturally the analysis applies not only to decisions and the formulation of policies for decision but to the execution or administration of decisions as well. Certain of the characteristics of decision making in the United States outlined in Chapter Three, such as the multiplicity of agencies, the impact of change, and so on, will be very much in the background of the present discussion.

It is not possible to make a general description of the executive organization as dynamic as it should be. To do so would require a verbatim record of, say, the National Security Council's deliberations or a detailed case study of how an interdepartmental committee actually functioned on a given afternoon, or agreed on a certain policy. Such material is nonexistent or not available. Therefore the reader will have to imagine for himself at many points that these are human beings acting and interacting in particular situations. When one says it is the function of the State Department to do so and so, this is a statement abstracted from reality—a statement symbolizing a system of activities by which the function is actually carried out in the course of daily routine. In this connection it seems especially advisable to reiterate a rather obvious point: organizational structure and function in the formal sense are primary determinants of the nature and flow of the decision-making process, but the significance of the attitudes toward these factors held by the participants should not be underestimated. It is one thing to say that there are four official functions charged to the State Department and quite another to say that all State Department personnel are agreed on what these mean in practice or, even if they are, that other agencies would share their interpretation. Accordingly, it must be remembered that imbedded in the decision-making process will be a set of decisions about who is to decide. Sometimes these will be routine and peaceably arrived at; sometimes they will arouse conflict and have to be settled by unusual measures. This factor introduces an element of flexibility and uncertainty which belies the impression of rigidity conveyed by the account which follows. The decisions on how decisions are to be made will be more noteworthy in a period when organization must adapt to new burdens and changing needs. Serious weaknesses in policy formation can and do arise from this source and must be taken into account for evaluating purposes. However, capacity for adaptation and flexibility must be built into any organization; else it would break down. At the present time, these decisions have caused great wrenches in the organization for foreign affairs simply because patterns of adaptation have not yet become regularized. Obviously this is partly due to bad management but it is also due to the kind of international setting in which American policy must operate.

Differences of opinion over how decision making should be organized are not confined to executive units themselves. The President and Congress engage in almost continuous guerrilla warfare over the same issue. Staff help that the President would like or need is not always what Congress will permit insofar as it has a voice. Lately there have been differences over the roles of the Joint Chiefs of Staff and the State Department and their relationship to the President. As will be seen, the long arm of Congressional influence has had its effect on the structure of decision making.

► THE PRESIDENT'S PERSONAL STAFF
   AND INDIVIDUAL ADVISERS

A substantial portion of the help which the President receives comes from a relatively small group that comprises his personal staff. Known officially as the White House Office, this group generally consists of three secretaries, six administrative assistants, three military aides, and five personal assistants. The secretaries handle presidential appointments, correspondence, and press relations. In view of what was said previously about the press conference, the secretary in charge of it is of prime importance; it is he who must try to save the President from blunders and try to keep the flow of foreign-affairs information accurate and smooth. Administrative assistants and personal assistants meet together with the President daily and perform functions assigned to them by the President. Usually each will have a special area of responsibility connected with various phases of the President's complex job, such as administrative management, Congressional liaison, liaison with executive agencies, and contacts with the general arena of politics. In addition, each will take on spot tasks as the need arises. As a group, they help the President draft messages, addresses, policy statements, and legislative proposals. Usually one or two will be "idea" men, providing the President with advice on substantive matters of policy. Probably one or two will be responsible for drafting the initial versions of presidential speeches. When an important foreign-policy speech is discussed by the whole group sentence by sentence, there is opportunity for subtle changes which constitute a shaping influence on the general framework of American policy. President Truman once said, "It's funny how a pending speech will clear the air on policies."*

The President's decision to make a major foreign-policy speech is not taken lightly; it is in itself the result of a decision-making process. Once this decision is made, the speech—if it is regarded as important—will evolve through a series of drafts which express the general ideas the President had in mind. Somewhere along the line, other presidential staff members besides the ones primarily responsible for the original draft as well as the Secretaries of State and Defense (and their staffs) will be consulted. Such an address will usually emerge from the pulling and hauling by various groups of advisers not only over words but over aims and strategy as well. In the case of a speech which covers many subjects, basic questions of United States foreign-policy objectives and the specific purposes of the speech will come up for review and discussion.

Presidential aides also help to enforce executive responsibilities by following up on decisions to see that they are carried out and by acting as trouble shooters for the President. They may consult with others on the President's behalf. Through them the President tries to keep track of what is going on in the Executive Branch.

Members of this staff are closer to the President officially than any others. They are loyal to him and retain his faith and trust. Their assignments are flexible and they are not specialists in the usual sense. They have no power of their own and can act only in the President's name. Ordinarily, their activities are clothed in anonymity so far as the public is concerned, though their relationship to the President is well known in the official family itself. Because of their close personal contact with each other and with the President they constitute one of the central ways in which coordination is

---

* John Hersey, "Mr. President" (5th in a series), *New Yorker,* May 5, 1951, p. 40.

achieved at the top level in the Executive Branch. The great value to the President from this kind of staff arrangement goes far beyond mere clerical and routine matters and is due to the fact that the group is free enough, trusted enough, and flexible enough to perform tasks for the President which could not in the nature of things be performed by anyone else. During a period in which foreign-policy problems transcend all others, it is natural that the White House staff will have a greater direct and indirect influence on the discharge of presidential responsibilities in that direction.

An important new addition to the President's personal staff is the office of Special Assistant to the President established in 1950. This unit is to help the President with matters which require "the integration of the various interests of the departments and agencies concerned with the development of government-wide policies related to our international responsibilities." The Special Assistant has a small staff to help him. While technically a part of the White House Office, he differs from the other members discussed above in that he is permanently assigned to a functional area—foreign affairs—and can tackle problems on his own initiative without necessarily waiting for a presidential directive. It is too early to tell whether this is the beginning of a pattern in which high-level coordination will become the primary responsibility of a particular member of the President's staff. However, the number and variety of the burdens carried by Averell Harriman, the first occupant of the post, again illustrates the importance of having someone on intimate terms with the President to whom extraordinary and *ad hoc* foreign-policy jobs can be informally delegated. In addition to being a special trouble shooter—he intervened in the British-Iranian oil dispute in 1951 on President Truman's behalf—Mr. Harriman was coordinator of all foreign-aid programs, administrator of the Battle Act (controlling aid to nations which trade with nations behind the iron curtain), and American representative on the Temporary Council Committee of NATO (a group charged with trying to bridge the gap between the military requirements of the Atlantic Alliance and the capacities of individual members to meet their commitments). He also led the fight in Congress for new foreign-aid appropriations in 1952. His broad governmental and diplomatic experience as Secretary of Commerce and as Lend-Lease Administrator during World War II enabled him to serve as a link between President Truman and Winston Churchill, who had not had much personal contact with each other before the latter became Prime Minister again in 1951.

Supplementing the White House inner circle are other close advisers—"close" in the sense that they are intimate with the President, see him often, carry out special missions, or are looked to for general as well as specific advice. Such advisers may or may not hold official positions and may or may not be personal friends. Consultation with the President may be regular or irregular, and topics of conversation are usually at the President's discretion. The structure and function of this group of advisers will vary with the individual President and with circumstances. Therefore the President's relations with the group and the size of the group will be somewhat fluid and only partly defined by law. Heads of Executive Departments and other agencies of Cabinet rank are of course principal advisers to the President by statutory provision. But some members of the Cabinet will be closer to the President than others and may be consulted on matters beyond the realm of their official responsibilities. So far as foreign affairs are concerned—particularly in a crisis period—the President will tend to lean rather heavily on the Secretaries of State, Defense, and Treasury quite apart from regular meetings of the Cabinet. If this were a book on the national government generally, more attention would have to be paid to the Cabinet. For the most part, the Cabinet has not served in recent years as a board of directors on general policy to which problems—among them foreign-policy problems—have been submitted for group decision. After six months of the Eisenhower Administration, however, it began to appear as though this situation is changing. Rather than using the weekly Cabinet meeting as a source of information as President Truman seemed to do for the most part, President Eisenhower reportedly employs such meetings for a "sounding of group opinion." In other words, the Cabinet may be emerging as a genuine policy-making body. Yet in view of the role of the National Security Council, it would not seem likely that foreign-policy issues would loom very large on the Cabinet's agenda except under extraordinary circumstances.

Advisers on foreign policy who hold no official position are of two types. They may be to all intents and purposes permanent residents of the White House as were Colonel House in the Wilson Administration and Harry Hopkins in the Roosevelt Administration. Although Averell Harriman held several official positions under President Truman, and did not meet regularly with the White House staff, off and on he acted as special emissary for the President and performed numerous other functions for which there was no legal authorization. Advisers of the other type visit the White House periodically to consult the President. After he had resigned as executive secretary of the National Security Council, Sidney Souers saw President Truman rather regularly. General Lucius Clay, who served as American commander in occupied Germany before a civilian high commissioner was appointed, visits President Eisenhower as a private consultant. It is not uncommon for the President to appoint his own commission of distinguished private citizens, experts, or even members of Congress to help him formulate policy recommendations on subjects pertaining to foreign relations. President Eisenhower early in his tenure appointed two very important commissions. To examine the whole question of America's trade relations with the rest of the world and to propose legislation to replace the Reciprocal Trade Agreements Act renewed in 1953 by Congress for a one-year period, he created a bipartisan *Commission on Foreign Economic Policy,* consisting of five senators, five representatives, and seven private citizens under the chairmanship of Clarence Randall, chairman of the board of the Inland Steel Corporation. The *National Security Training Commission* was charged with responsibility for considering compulsory military training as a substitute for the draft. While the President is not, of course, obligated to accept recommendations from these and like groups, President Eisenhower is known to take their conclusions very seriously if they are unanimous.

▶ STAFF AGENCIES IN THE EXECUTIVE OFFICE

In addition to his personal staff and individual advisers, the President's general staff for foreign affairs also includes certain special agencies. While these are established by Congressional legislation and in some cases their chairmen or directors must be approved by the Senate, they stand outside the formal chain of command which runs directly from the President to Executive Departments and other operating agencies. With one or two recent exceptions these offices and bodies do not have power to act or to direct any other government unit to act. Although better known than the White House staff, their personnel share with the former a quality of anonymity; their purpose is to assist the President in fulfilling his responsibilities without much fanfare and without having to assume any responsibility themselves. They, too, cannot act except in the President's name and only at his direction. It might be said that staff agencies comprise a kind of nonpolitical permanent technical staff at the disposal of the President.

Although the *Joint Chiefs of Staff** is administratively located in the Defense Department, it seems logical for present purposes to include it among the staff agencies. The Joint Chiefs are comprised of the chiefs of staff of the Army, Navy, and Air Force, together with a nonvoting chairman. In 1952, Congress legislated an equal voice for the Commandant of the Marines on questions directly affecting the Corps. This group, supported by a joint staff of 120 officers, serves by law as principal military adviser to the President, the National Security Council, and the Secretary of Defense. Its advice is crucial because it has sole responsibility for strategic and logistic planning and strategic direction of the Armed Forces. In addition, the JCS provides the American representative on the Military Staff Committee of the United Nations Security Council, is represented on the subordinate bodies of the North Atlantic Treaty Organization, and advises the Secretary of State on various aspects of the military aid program. The chairman of the Joint Chiefs is in close touch with the President at all times through regular visits. Its role in policy making has become more and more important. Since its inception in 1942 (it was regularized by statute in 1947), the President has relied on it almost exclusively for military advice rather than on the Secretary of

---

* The problem of the organization and role of the JCS is given further attention in Chapter Nine. President Eisenhower's reorganization proposal of April 20, 1953 is also discussed.

Defense or on the individual armed services. After careful research and preliminary analysis by its own staff, the JCS issues policy papers which express its corporate opinion on strategic problems.

The *Bureau of the Budget* exerts indirect influence on foreign-policy formation because of its key position in budget planning and administrative supervision. Its chief functions are to review departmental requests for funds, to prepare the budget for Congress, to review legislative proposals from the departments and coordinate their views on legislation, and to handle problems of organization and administrative management. The bureau is a powerful agency through which the President can exert some control on the way policy is made at the lower levels of government. Cutting across all agencies, it is inevitably involved in plans and operations everywhere in the Executive Branch. If the State Department wishes to increase its funds for the overseas information program, the bureau may approve it, deny it, or propose a different amount. Changes were suggested by the bureau in the Foreign Service Act of 1946. When new interdepartmental committees are established, the bureau is consulted. It was at the direction of the bureau that the Brookings study, already cited, was undertaken. Implementation of the recommendation of that study will depend largely on this agency.

Another unit in the Executive Office is the *Office of Defense Mobilization* established after the Korean conflict began in 1950. Although it was originally a temporary agency, Reorganization Plan No. 3 submitted by President Eisenhower to Congress in April, 1953, makes it permanent and assigns to it the functions formerly assigned to but not really performed by the National Security Resources Board, along with the stockpiling functions of the Munitions Board. From the beginning, the director of this office has been delegated rather extensive authority by the President to direct, control, and coordinate mobilization activities. Not only does the office have great power; it has major responsibility for coordinating foreign and domestic economic policy. On the one hand it must mobilize the national economy—a most complicated task in a democratic society not working under full mobilization conditions—and on the other it must gear the details of mobilization to the needs of the military establishment and to the various aid programs. Its role in the success of a foreign policy based on armed strength and mutual aid is therefore crucial. The various subdivisions of the ODM must reconcile domestic needs with foreign-policy needs and must see to it that weapons and other materials are available to agencies in charge of defense or mutual aid. Since it has power to act, whereas the other staff agencies do not, its operations must be carried on in close cooperation with other related operating units. Such coordination determines whether strategic materials are stockpiled effectively, whether weapons are produced in sufficient quantity on time and are routed where needed, and whether steel or other materials are ready for shipment abroad. Naturally, with the cessation of hostilities in Korea, the major concerns of the ODM shifted from immediate industrial and military mobilization to other, more long-range problems. The division of labor among six assistants to the director suggests the present pattern of responsibilities a little more precisely. One assistant director is in charge of each of the following policy areas: (1) financial policy; (2) nonmilitary defense—continuity of government and industry in case of attack; (3) manpower—industrial and military; (4) production requirements and programing—for the National Military Establishment and foreign-aid programs; (5) stockpiling—strategic materials for civilian and military use; and (6) economic stabilization—stand-by price and wage controls to accommodate mobilization pressures.

The *Council of Economic Advisers* has no direct effect upon foreign affairs. Because of the interlocking between domestic and foreign affairs, however, it may have an important indirect effect upon foreign policy through its advice to the President on national economic policy. Under the Employment Act of 1946, the President is required to survey the general economic state of the nation and to make recommendations on maintaining maximum production, employment, and purchasing power. There is evidence that the President's policies on taxation and other economic matters reflect his reliance upon the council. To the extent that the council offers wise counsel which is accepted by the President and Congress, the economic bases of foreign policy will be stronger. The semiannual and annual reports, prepared by the council and issued under the President's name, provide the nation with a broad view of how the American economy is withstanding the impact of the foreign-policy budget. As remarked in Chapter Two, only sound public policies can enable America to endure the many heavy demands on its economic life without severe dislocations and perhaps collapse. Insofar as national power rests on sound planning and control of unusual strains, the Council of Economic Advisers contributes indirectly to the management of foreign policy. That the role of the council may loom even larger in the future is indicated by the fact that after Congress had allowed appropriations for this agency to lapse in January, 1953, President Eisenhower continued operations on a skeleton basis and requested that regular appropriations be resumed. He reorganized the council, bringing it into a clearer relationship with the White House, and generally let it be known that he would rely on it to help maintain a stable economy.

Two other units in the Executive Office deserve special emphasis: the *National Security Council* and the *Central Intelligence Agency*.

▶ THE NATIONAL SECURITY COUNCIL

Created by the National Security Act of 1947 and transferred from the National Military Establishment to the Executive Office in 1949, the National Security Council has emerged as one of the most powerful, least publicized agencies engaged in foreign-policy formation. The council itself now consists of the President, as chairman, the Vice-President, the Secretary of State, the Secretary of Defense, the director of the Office of Defense Mobilization, and the director of the Foreign Overseas Administration. Under President Eisenhower, the Secretary of the Treasury, the Chairman of the Joint Chiefs of Staff, the director of the Central Intelligence Agency, and the President's special assistants for psychological warfare and national security affairs all attend the meetings of the council. Sometimes the chiefs of staff for each of the armed services as well as the director of the Bureau of the Budget attend. The council meets once a week for two to three hours, usually presided over by the President himself. When convened as a formal body, the council is thus composed of the most important high officials who bear responsibility for the country's foreign affairs. It is, in effect, a Cabinet committee and as a formal body is not, strictly speaking, a staff agency like the ones discussed above. The two basic tasks of the council were set forth in the statute creating it: (1) to assess and appraise the objectives, commitments, and risks of American foreign policy in the light of the nation's actual and potential military power; and (2) to advise the President on the integration of domestic, foreign, and military policies relating to national security and on the coordination of the agencies concerned.

Since 1947 the role of the Security Council has been further clarified. It does not itself make binding decisions for the government. In this sense it does not "determine" foreign policy. However, it has been, as will be shown presently, a major influence in shaping the decisions which have become binding. Neither does the council supervise any operations, with the exception of the Central Intelligence Agency and the International Information Agency, which report to it. Nor does it execute or implement decisions. Actually the council does three things. First, it formulates national security policy for the consideration of the President. Second, it serves as a crucial channel for collective advice on major developments. Third, it deliberates only on matters where a presidential decision is required. The President has complete freedom to accept or reject the council's recommendations. One of its outstanding features is that it serves as the *principal point of coordination* between the State and Defense Departments below the level of the President himself. By 1953, under President Eisenhower, the council was devoting itself to what might be called a resolution of the executive will on key problems—to seeking out and reconciling interagency conflict. But also by this time, a great deal more emphasis was placed on discovering the neglected aspects of foreign policy and on anticipating future problems. In September, 1953, there were signs that the council might become the place where an attempt would be made to balance the defense budget with the rest of the federal budget.

The council differs from ordinary *ad hoc* Cabinet committees in that it has a Career Staff, a Planning Board, and an executive secretary. Daily contact between the President and the work of the council is maintained by the visits of the executive secretary, who provides the chief executive with brief intelligence digests and answers any questions he may have. Between them, they work out the agenda for the weekly meetings of the council members. The Planning Board is comprised of the head of the State Department's Policy Planning Committee, Assistant Secretaries of Defense and Treasury, the assistant director of the Central Intelligence Agency, the director of the International Information Agency, and representatives from the Office of Defense Management, the Joint Chiefs of Staff, and the Foreign Overseas Administration. Members of the Planning Board thus rank high enough in their respective agencies to be familiar with plans and policies and to be able to speak for their chiefs. The chairman of the board is the special assistant for national security affairs of the President's staff. A Career Staff of twenty-eight members drawn from the agencies mentioned perform research and administrative tasks for the board. Thus the Security Council has three levels of organization.

It took the United States a decade to develop an organizational feature which was a logical outcome of the crumbling of traditional bases of American foreign policy. What appeared to be separate foreign-policy issues turned out to be parts of the nation's total national security problem. The role of the military grew more significant. Military, economic, and political policies were intermixed. Decisions could no longer be made by single departments or agencies. Need for coordination was recognized with the establishment of the State-War-Navy Coordinating Committee in 1944, the purpose of which was to improve "existing methods of obtaining for the State Department advice on politico-military matters and of coordinating the views of the three departments on matters in which all have a common interest, particularly those involving foreign policy and relations with foreign nations." Later, SWNCC, as it was called, was defined in a memorandum signed by the Secretaries of War, Navy, and State as the agency "to reconcile and coordinate the action" to be taken by the three departments and was to operate "under the guidance" of the three secretaries. This committee was a step forward, but apparently did not meet the problems of coordination. It did not take the place of other forms of liaison and therefore competed with them. The members of the committee itself represented only the assistant secretary level, and the staff of the committee was not always composed of personnel who really knew what was going on in their respective departments and could speak with authority. Even the assistant secretaries had no power to act. Furthermore, they had full-time responsibilities in addition to the committee assignment. Policy memoranda were drawn primarily in military form and there is evidence to suggest that the influence of military representatives was inordinate. Until V-J Day real coordination tended to rest in an *ad hoc* committee of the three secretaries. But SWNCC did set a pattern and some of the lessons of its experience were reflected in the creation of the National Security Council.

The idea for the Security Council was apparently first made explicit in the Eberstadt report prepared for the Secretary of the Navy in 1945. As a matter of fact, it is interesting to note that chief support for the new body came originally from the military agencies of the government which had experienced success with committees of the Joint Chiefs of Staff and were impressed by the fact that the British chiefs of staff reported directly to the War Cabinet and were therefore better able to cope with economic and political issues. As provided in the National Security Act of 1947, the tone of the Security Council's constituency was predominantly military because the Secretaries of War, Navy, and Air Force were members along with the Secretary of Defense and the Secretary of State. Also, the council was administratively placed in the National Military Establishment. The Hoover Commission criticized these arrangements and, when Congress amended the Security Act in 1949, the Secretaries for Army, Navy, and Air Force were dropped; the Vice-President was added; the President was given power to add other members from time to time for special purposes; and the council was shifted to the Executive Office.

The council began meeting in September, 1947. From then on, it was involved in one way or another in major foreign-policy decisions—the Berlin Blockade, the return of Trieste to Italy, the North Atlantic Alliance, the Mutual Defense Assistance Program, intervention in Korea, and so on. However, during the period from late 1948 to mid-1950, the council did not function harmoniously or effectively. Though conceding that the council performed quite well in emergencies, the Hoover Commission reported that the functions of anticipation and long-term planning had been neglected. The commission concluded that the council "does not yet measure up fully to needs of the time." One of the basic difficulties during this period was the conflict between Secretary of State Acheson and Secretary of Defense Johnson—a personal and jurisdictional feud which was not liquidated until Mr. Johnson left the Cabinet in 1950. He was replaced by General Marshall, who previously had been Secretary of State and therefore had worked closely with Acheson. Later General Marshall was succeeded by Mr. Lovett, who also had worked with Acheson. Council meetings had become somewhat unwieldy because members brought small personal staffs with them, a procedure which added to the factors inhibiting free discussion. Furthermore, work at the council's staff level was not efficient. Distinguished, competent men like George Kennan and Philip Jessup, who served as staff consultants in the early days of the council, were harassed by the pressure of other duties and by organizational defects at the departmental level which prevented their being able to get quick and authoritative action. President Truman reorganized the council's operations in July, 1950. Meanwhile, reorganization in the State Department and elsewhere improved the effectiveness of what was then called the Senior Staff.

By 1952, a general pattern of procedures had been developed. The pattern may be varied somewhat in individual cases, but its outline will indicate how the council operates. (1) A major decision will originate as a preliminary policy paper usually drawn up in the secretariat of the council by the representatives of the department chiefly concerned. In most cases, this will be the State Department. The first draft will usually be drawn up in consultation with the appropriate subdivision in the department. (2) The preliminary policy paper is then discussed with other specialists in the secretariat for their criticisms, comments, and additions. At this point, the first injection of the views and contributions of the military, Central Intelligence, the Mutual Security Agency, Treasury, National Security Resources Board, or Office of Defense Mobilization takes place. (3) Next the Senior Staff goes over the paper, concentrating mostly on the crucial issues presented. Major changes may be made and a final draft is approved for presentation at a regular session of the council itself. (4) Council members then sit down to discuss the recommendation. The final draft will generally consist of a three- or four-paragraph recommendation buttressed by a few pages summarizing the factual data and reasoning upon which the recommendation is based. Thus the brief document is broken down into a statement of the problem, analysis, and conclusion. Unless some issue arises which has not been foreseen at earlier stages, only minor modifications will be made by the council itself, although the recommendation and its implications will be thoroughly aired. By and large the background analysis of the recommendation will not be challenged. (5) The council does not take a formal vote but concludes its deliberation by reaching a sense of the meeting. (6) The final policy paper is signed by the President, either then and there or after necessary drafting changes have been made. Only with the President's signature does the recommendation become a decision of the government. It is unlikely that the President will overrule a recommendation at this stage except under unusual circumstances. If no consensus could be reached, he might decline to act, but it appears doubtful that he would act in the face of a severe disagreement among council members. The President is able to exercise control over the agenda of the Council and he is at liberty to exclude an item, as President Truman did in the case of the Palestine problem in 1948. Furthermore, in his daily meetings with the executive secretary of the council, the President can and does keep track of policy recommendations as they develop. (7) Action is taken by the appropriate department, again in most cases by the State Department. If the agreement of other governments is required, it is secured through diplomatic channels. (8) The fact that action has been taken is supposedly reported back for the council's official notice, together with any available evaluation of results.

As a rule, the council will concern itself only with major decisions which are fairly clear-cut or which are broad policy directives requiring implementation by operating agencies. The former are illustrated by the decisions to stay in Berlin in 1948 despite the Russian blockade and to give Trieste back to Italy and by the recommendation of an increase in the American contribution to the French campaign against Communism in Indo-China. The latter is illustrated by the decision to implement the Atlantic Alliance by a mutual defense assistance program. In this latter case, after the President approved the Security Council's recommendation in July, 1948, the Defense Department and the Economic Cooperation Administration translated the program into a specific request for funds, which was presented to Congress in July, 1949. When a major problem is presented suddenly, as was true of the North Korean attack on South Korea in June, 1950, the rather elaborate procedures of the Security Council cannot yield advice quickly enough. From what can be reconstructed regarding the decision to intervene in the Korean conflict, it appears that a series of quick *ad hoc* conferences took place at the White House in which a series of decisions were made leading to the final one to send ordinary American ground forces into South Korea. At the first two conferences, the President, the Secretaries of State and Defense, and the Joint Chiefs of Staff were present. The National Security Council met several days later for an intensive discussion without arriving at a decision. At this meeting the council did not have the amount of distilled information and analysis which characterizes its regular policy papers. Following this meeting, the Secretaries and Joint Chiefs met with Congressional leaders and the President announced his intentions. There was no dissent and the President later announced the decision. One way or another the council's members figured in the decision, but the council as a continuing staff agency did not make its usual contribution. This was hardly the fault of the council unless it be assumed that such a problem should have been foreseen so that its usual preparatory work would have been completed when the emergency arose.

Two basic characteristics of the council's normal procedures are to be noted. First, the flow of policy papers is upward through three stages from lower staff levels, each representing a more authoritative influence, each moving closer to the point of decision. Second, political, economic, and strategic considerations can be fed in and integrated at each stage, the council itself being a kind of final check on the adequacy of coordination. It is probably accurate to say that policy ideas still originate largely in the State Department and are drafted mostly by State Department personnel. The council's procedures constitute a filter through which the department's policies must pass. On occasion, policy initiative may be taken elsewhere, as it was on the Berlin Blockade question. Secretary of Defense Forrestal started that question through the council's filtering process and military personnel did the drafting of the recommendation.

That the council has become as effective as it has is due in great measure to President Truman, who relied heavily upon it, did not try to dominate it, and brought about procedural improvements; and to President Eisenhower, who reorganized the council in March, 1953. This reorganization can be regarded as recognition that the council's role is to become even more important in the decision-making process. These observations suggest an important point. The council's all-round usefulness and effectiveness depend heavily on the President. If he circumvents the council, or if he allows one of its members to go beyond his proper functions, the consequences may seriously distort the council's purpose. President Truman is known to have remarked that he didn't know how his predecessors ever got along without this kind of agency. Obviously his attitude did much to invest the council's work with prestige and significance. Moreover, in a crisis period, when military techniques of foreign policy and limited armed conflict loom large, the leading participants in the council's discussions will be the Secretaries of State and Defense and the chairman of the Joint Chiefs of Staff. Potentially this represents a situation wherein the military viewpoint might be overweighted by sheer numbers because the Vice-President and Secretary of Treasury will make minor contributions. That Secretary of State Acheson was able in most cases to maintain his position of true policy leadership during 1951–1952 was a tribute not only to his skill but to the clearly expressed confidence of the President.

Aside from the key influence of the President, it is to be noted that much depends upon the personal relations among the members of the council. Animosity and mistrust can hamstring the council's work. No device of government can completely overcome the inability of top policy leaders to work in reasonable harmony. Chronic disharmony will again require either skillful presidential leadership or courage in making personnel changes. However, assuming that the President throws his support in the direction of making the council the key agency it is capable of being, and assuming minimum cooperation among its members, the degree to which the council is able to offer sound recommendations to the President will depend entirely on the technical competence of the staff at both lower levels. The determining influence of the preliminary drafting process can scarcely be exaggerated. What the members of the council finally discuss represents only the top of the iceberg, so to speak. A few pages are the end product of a series of related operations by which the intellectual ingredients of decision making discussed in Chapter Three are fed in appropriate form to the final stage of the decision-making process. The adequacy of the information and analysis will therefore condition the rationality of the decision which emerges. If the Career Staff of the council has inadequate or erroneous information and if the Planning Board does not throughly consider the basic alternatives presented by a foreign-policy problem, policy papers will suffer thereby. If departmental organization is such that the council's staffs cannot obtain the authoritative viewpoint of the State Department and Defense Department and other interested agencies, coordination will be faulty. On major policy issues, then, the drafting and analysis of the council's staffs will be of vital importance in themselves, but these will in turn be dependent on the efficient performance of functions at other points in the total process.

When the National Security Council was first established in 1947, the London *Economist* wrote that it "may mark a milestone in America's development as important, say, as Washington's Farewell Address." While this statement may be an exaggeration, the Brookings Institution concluded in 1951 that "the Council has become established as a necessary institution of the government and appears to be functioning with increasing success as a place for teamwork under the President,"* and that the council was "a true innovation in American governmental practice."† Naturally, the council does not operate perfectly nor is it a cure-all for many problems in foreign-policy making. John Fischer, in his revealing article on the Security Council, has summarized five kinds of criticism.‡ First, there is need for better personnel at the lowest level of the council's operations. Second, the Senior Staff (later the Planning Board) serve the council only part time; their talents are hard to come by and hence their competence is spread rather thinly. Third, the council does not check often enough and thoroughly enough on policy execution. Fourth, the executive secretary does not, the way his position has been defined, add his own contribution to the Council or add real consistency to the council's activities through time. Finally, the council does not sufficiently anticipate major policy developments and shape public opinion accordingly— which it should do under presidential leadership. Other suggestions concerning the council will be mentioned in connection with the problems of coordination. These criticisms were made in 1951. They should be considered in the light of changes made by President Eisenhower in 1953. The executive secretary now functions as chairman of the Planning Board. Members of the Planning Board concentrate their efforts exclusively on the needs of the council instead of dividing their time as was formerly the case. The board's staff was increased from fifteen (under Truman) to twenty-eight, thus providing more help for the board. President Eisenhower also set up a panel of seven advisers drawn from business, industry, education, journalism, and labor to serve the council on an individual basis. One of the major purposes of this reorganization was to equip the council for more attention to anticipation.

► THE CENTRAL INTELLIGENCE AGENCY AND THE ORGANIZATION OF INTELLIGENCE GENERALLY

THE NATURE OF INTELLIGENCE

It would be difficult indeed to overestimate the vital contribution of intelligence agencies to the formation of policy. As noted in Chapter Three, at the heart of the decision-making process is an intellectual process consisting

---

* The Brookings Institution, *The Administration of Foreign Affairs and Overseas Operations* (Washington, U.S. Government Printing Office, 1951), p. xviii.

† *Ibid.,* p. 362.

‡ John Fischer, "Mr. Truman's Politburo," *Harper's Magazine,* June, 1951, pp. 34–36.

essentially of acquisition of information (knowledge) and policy analysis (manipulation of knowledge in the determination of courses of action). One indispensable kind of information obviously concerns the external setting which stimulates reactions and the need for action on the part of the United States and in which its objectives must be sought. The Central Intelligence Agency and related agencies have primary responsibility for gathering, interpreting, and circulating the knowledge upon which national security in the broadest sense must be founded and which top-level decision makers must have to formulate sound policies. In the words of Sherman Kent, ". . . intelligence work remains the simple, natural endeavor to get the sort of knowledge upon which a successful course of action can be rested. And *strategic intelligence* we might call the knowledge upon which our nation's foreign relations, in war and peace, must rest."* This is deliberately a broad conception of intelligence. Therefore it should be distinguished on the one hand from military† or economic intelligence or other specialized forms which are only particular aspects, and, on the other hand, from domestic intelligence (knowledge of the *internal* environment) and from counterespionage (internal security). The focus of this section thus is on "high level foreign positive intelligence."‡

What is involved in intelligence so defined? Certainly it is a far more complicated and routine enterprise than is suggested by "secret agents" and romanticized "cloak and dagger" operations. The average citizen probably has a distorted notion of the essence of the intelligence function. It is larger in scope and less hush-hush than he thinks. Ninety per cent of intelligence consists of highly skilled research and anaysis based on "open" sources; hence the name "overt" intelligence. "Covert" intelligence, based on the activities of secret agents who try to acquire information held secret by foreign governments, is very important, but only a small percentage of any country's intelligence resources are devoted to it. Covert intelligence sources may be cut off at any time. Usually it is most effective in turning up specific data—movement of troops, new weapons, and so on—which is necessary but cannot answer some of the more general questions vital to foreign policy generally. It is difficult and expensive to camouflage covert operations. If they are performed unskillfully, they can be a downright liability—as they were when inexperienced American agents were caught with written records which provided the Russians with a tailor-made case against the leader of anti-Soviet forces in Hungary in 1947. In any event, covertly gathered information must be checked against the overt. Interestingly enough, captured German documents show that the Germans considered only 5 per cent of their covert intelligence reliable and in effect maintained two secret services, one to check on the other.

---

* Sherman Kent, *Strategic Intelligence for American World Policy* (Princeton, N. J., Princeton University Press, 1949), p. viii. Italics by the present authors.

† Tactical or combat intelligence narrowly defined is excluded.

‡ Kent, *op. cit.*, p. 3.

Overt intelligence sources are manifold, spanning almost the entire range of ways in which a foreign nation reveals itself. Much information is found in government statistical reports, edicts, speeches, and routine releases to diplomatic representatives. Budget figures, production figures, import and export figures, domestic sales figures—all are usually available and rich in information. Even official propaganda releases are useful. Newspapers, mass periodicals, professional and scientific journals, radio broadcasts, data supplied to international technical organizations, and miscellaneous pubications of private social agencies are also important. Of special significance is the knowledge to be gained from interviews with refugees and interrogation of prisoners. From these sources, official and unofficial, are derived a continuous picture of what is going on in a particular country, a report of trends and developments. Naturally, this material is supplemented, and must be, by basic descriptions of the geography, resources, population, technology, and political, economic, and social institutions of foreign nations. Much of such description results from just plain library work. At this point in the process data must be accurate and complete. Overt intelligence, then, is based on observation and research.

But so far, intelligence consists primarily of the collection and vertification of factual data. Left in this form, little use could be made of it. Next comes analysis—the sorting, ordering, and interpreting of the information. No matter how thorough the collection or reporting, analysis is the point at which information is shaped into meaningful patterns through evaluation and prediction. Analysis should yield two different kinds of intelligence. First, an assessment of general strengths and weaknesses of other nations with a view to judging the possible effects of an American policy or action, including their capacity for retaliation and for correcting their own vulnerabilities. Second, an estimation of the aims and objectives, available techniques, expectations, and future policy moves of other states, with a view to predicting the conditions with which American countermoves will have to cope. Analysis is a process whereby information is transformed into a statement of possibilities and probabilities, of predictions as to future events and behavior. Needless to say, this is not a mere routine research operation. For the most part, though not exclusively, intelligence at the analysis stage deals with human behavior in certain forms and contexts. It requires a wide variety of skills and a high level of sophistication in those skills. Not just anyone can draw the significant implications from a vast array of production figures. Not everyone can interpret a foreign scientific journal article. Not everyone can understand the possible meanings of a shift in religious practices or in family relationships in an alien culture. Nor can just anyone judge whether an outburst of riots is a temporary, surface phenomenon or a manifestation of a deeper social movement. Nor can everyone look at another country's top leaders and draw reliable conclusions from the manner in which they are recruited and function. Nor can just anyone select the proper inferences from foreign newspapers and official propaganda. In short, trained and experienced social and physical scientists with a sensitive grasp on the techniques of social and scientific analysis are required. Their skills must include an awareness of the state of knowledge in both the social and natural sciences, of where existing techniques do and do not yield reliable answers or predictions. Scientists with a feel for theoretical research must participate as well as those whose competence lies in empirical research. For intelligence is more than the processing of documents containing momentary summaries of facts and interpretations. Such documents become dated. Conditions change. Trends and developments cannot be projected or foreseen except in terms of a theoretical framework. Clearly, intelligence is a group endeavor representing teamwork in the assembly and interpretation of information. There has to be a proper division of labor and coordination among intelligence personnel.

However, let it be assumed that all the above requirements are present and that adequate intelligence analysis results. The next vital step *is the circulation of intelligence to the users in usable form.* Two things are, of course, involved—both twin aspects of communication. One is a translation and writing problem. The intelligence material must be translated from the language of the expert and written up with clarity and precision. It is unlikely that even an experienced top-level decision maker would fully understand a complicated content analysis of West German newspapers expressed in technical phraseology. Nor will it be very helpful if intelligence reports are vague, inconclusive, or not clearly focused on the problem at hand. A report which leaves a policy maker largely on his own resources simply subverts the whole purpose of skilled interpretation of relevant information. The user of intelligence should receive a statement of the relevant factual material ("raw" facts plus interpretation) which reduces the uncertainty surrounding the choice of alternatives to the lowest possible point. He must ultimately make the choice, but he must know about the causes and expected trends of various conditions he is dealing with and he must know about probable consequences of various alternatives as well as possible future action by other nations. Second, intelligence *must be communicated to the appropriate place in the decision-making structure when and as needed.* To put the matter tritely, the most perfect prediction of Russian behavior will be useless policywise unless the officials making decisions based on that behavior have it and have it on time. If processing of information—the latest and best—lags behind a policy evolving through the formulation process, an essential ingredient will be lacking at the point of final decision. If information reaches some but not all the policy makers concerned, they may discuss the issue at cross-purposes or effort will be wasted.

It is clear that the relationship between intelligence producers and consumers is crucial and is yet another example of the need for coordination in the decision-making process. But the relationship is also a two-way street. The consumers of intelligence can be of enormous help in making clear to the producers what is needed and in what form. Producers must determine *how* their responsibilities are to be fulfilled. Consumers must cooperate in *defining* those responsibilities. "We don't know what 'they' want, but we'll have to send them something" has probably been a frequent complaint among the producers. Dangers and tensions may arise if either side is left to control the relationship on its own. Consumers may exert pressure to minimize the contribution of the producers, to get them to confine themselves to the "simple facts" unadorned by analysis. Producers may either underestimate their responsibilities or overestimate it by trying, directly or indirectly, to make recommendations. Each side must understand the other's role and there must be mutual respect. Lack of respect for intelligence agencies, for example, was costly to national security during the 1940's and was aggravated by the fact that these agencies did not always know what was expected of them.

Of greater importance is the necessity that intelligence agencies be kept informed of the general direction of American foreign policy and of major policy developments or problems. The choice of large research projects and the sifting and ordering of data must always be done on the basis of such criteria. Intelligence cannot contribute to the solution of a policy problem unless it knows how policy makers conceive the problem. Neither will it have on hand estimates with respect to the consequences of American policy in a given area unless it knows what is contemplated there. This means that the work of intelligence must be integrated into policy making at both the planning stage and the decision stage. It also means that intelligence officials must have access to the highest levels of consultation. Like any organization, intelligence operates in a situation of scarce resources. Skills and time are not unlimited. Priorities must be set on the basis of urgency. The degree of urgency is determined by the nature of existing problems and proposed action.

Collection and collation of data—the reporting and descriptive phase of intelligence—goes on in many government agencies. Not all of it is crucial to strategic intelligence as defined above. But the kind of analysis which undergirds strategic intelligence must be performed at one central place by a special staff. No one agency could possibly acquire all the necessary information. Intelligence analysis therefore must have made available to it all the bits and pieces to be assembled for estimate and prediction. The Department of Agriculture may have what seems to be a routine piece of data on Chinese farm production. The State Department may have information on internal migration in China. Military intelligence may have figures on the size and age structure of Chinese divisions. By themselves, scraps of this kind may have little policy significance. Woven together and evaluated in the light of additional material, they may suggest a pattern which will eventually reveal a great deal about the trend of the manpower pool in China. It is at the point of general analysis, and only at that point, that comprehensive assembly and interpretation of data are possible. Therefore, coordination is once again paramount. Duplication must be minimized and yet all possibly relevant data must be fed from collection points to the headquarters of analysis. This is not to say that analysis will not take place among various agencies. Rather, the data at any one place will not necessarily be complete and hence the analysis will not necessarily constitute strategic intelligence in the broad sense although it may be perfectly adequate for the function of the individual agency.

In light of the foregoing factors, it is obvious that strategic intelligence requires a complex organization of interrelated parts, highly specialized personnel, a central staff for analysis, coordination of specialized activities, and communication, understanding, and respect between producers and consumers. At its base the system rests on hundreds of well-known routine reporting activities not usually called intelligence, but at its apex it must rest on the special talents of a team of analysts who do nothing except apply their skills to the selection and interpretation of features of the external environment relevant to the maintenance of national security. Out of the process comes knowledge which is circulated, or should be, throughout the decision-making process. Such knowledge is no guarantor of sound decisions. However, they are not possible without it.

THE BACKGROUND OF THE PRESENT ORGANIZATION

On the eve of Pearl Harbor the United States had no strategic intelligence system worthy of the name. Only three million dollars a year was spent on intelligence of all types. A handful of people, working in the Army and Navy, concentrated mostly on combat intelligence. Foreign Service reports were the only other major source of foreign-policy intelligence. The tragedy of December 7, 1941, illustrated graphically the price a nation must pay for not having a central agency to estimate the intentions of potential enemies and to impress the information on the top policy-making level. Information concerning the Japanese attack was available but was not impressed upon those who should have acted on it. During World War II, America relied heavily on the highly successful British Secret Service, so much so that in 1947, General Vandenberg remarked bitterly to the Senate Armed Services Committee: "The United States should never again have to go hat in hand, begging any foreign government for eyes with which to see." However, an important development did take place during the war period: the establishment of the Office of Strategic Services. This organization, consisting of ten thousand assorted scientists, professors, lawyers, Wall Street brokers, ministers, and others performed many intelligence functions not undertaken by the military services. Though geared primarily to the war itself, the OSS engaged in some strategic intelligence as already defined. Without passing judgment on its success in the latter field, it should be noted that OSS operations *did* train a sizable group of individuals in overt intelligence research as well as in cloak-and-dagger techniques. Its vigorous, imaginative director, Colonel William Donovan, became a key leader in the drive to create a central agency of some sort after the war.

Shortly after V-J Day, OSS was disbanded. Many valuable personnel were permanently lost to further intelligence duty but some went to a new intelligence unit established in the State Department in October, 1945, under Colonel McCormack, an experienced military intelligence officer. The Office of Research and Intelligence immediately ran into rough sledding. For six months, Congressional opposition and internal opposition in the department kept the new agency from functioning effectively or from emerging into a clearly defined role. In April, 1946, Congress withheld appropriations, Colonel McCormack resigned, and the Intelligence Office was abolished, its functions being transferred to the Division of Political Affairs. Meanwhile, the President had created the National Intelligence Authority embodied in the Central Intelligence Group, which was to coordinate intelligence activities and carry on some independent functions with a relatively small staff. This unit in turn limped along, feuding with the FBI and the Army's intelligence staff, G–2.

The Central Intelligence Agency succeeded the Central Intelligence Group by the terms of the National Security Act of 1947. This shift was not accomplished without a struggle. The campaign waged against Colonel McCormack's original efforts was renewed and there was opposition from existing military intelligence agencies. As finally constituted, the CIA represented a concept that there had to be a fully backed, centralized responsibility for coordination of intelligence under presidential authority at the staff level of the federal government. Hence the new unit was given adequate financial support and attached to the National Security Council. However, the CIA immediately ran into difficulties of the sort which seems to confront all new agencies in Washington. It inherited feuds going back to the days of the OSS. Over the next three years, the CIA and G–2 clashed over which was to control secret agents abroad. The former finally won. A running battle raged between the State Department and the CIA over the question of whether CIA personnel attached to diplomatic establishments abroad were to be under the jurisdiction of the heads of missions. Bitterness broke out between the FBI and the CIA when the latter took charge of foreign field operations; the CIA claimed that the FBI agents did not coperate in the change-over and the FBI claimed that CIA personnel were rank amateurs, careless about security. The Atomic Energy Commission refused for a long while to share its scientific information with CIA personnel, who were deemed unable to interpret it properly. Eventually this conflict was solved by appointment of a scientist acceptable to the commission to act as liaison.

Internally, the new agency was inefficiently organized. Duplication of function, lack of communication, empire-building tendencies, and inferior personnel handicapped it from the start. Meanwhile the number of agencies carrying on intelligence activities mushroomed. By 1947, the Atomic Energy Commission had its own unit, as did the new Air Force, and the State Department shortly revived its Office of Intelligence Research. All these units were in addition to the existing facilities of the Foreign Service and the Army and Navy. Thus competition became the rule. The muddled situation which resulted was due to failures on the part of the CIA and to the hostile attitude of other groups. Often when the CIA was right, it was not listened to, and when it was wrong the fact tended to justify the lack of respect usually accorded it. Opposition was strengthened by the fact that the CIA was either unwilling or unable (or both) to take a positive, aggressive role in the coordination of intelligence. It took a very limited view of its function, largely contenting itself with a mere presentation of "facts" accompanied by little analysis or interpretation. Often it simply repeated the judgments of other agencies.

Until 1950, the vital job of correlating and evaluating intelligence touching upon national security was poorly done if at all. There was no small, continuous high-level group of experts in the CIA freed of everything else except this job. Information was withheld from the CIA. Lines of responsibility among the many intelligence groups were unclear. At a time when strategic intelligence and accurate estimates of the relative power position of the United States in relation to its own objectives and the possible behavior of foreign nations were most needed, the system operated ineffectively and at cross-purposes. Not one but three or four official estimates of Russian strength were circulated. Apparently little attention was paid to the distinction between the *capabilities* of a nation and its *intentions*. In 1948, the various branches of the intelligence system could not agree on the meaning of Russian military activity in Eastern Europe, one insisting it meant an attack on Czechoslovakia, another insisting it meant action in the eastern zone of Germany. The latter view was correct for this activity proved to be a prelude to the Russian blockade of Berlin, but the United States came close to accepting the wrong assumption. Again, in 1948, an anti-American political riot took place in Bogotá, Colombia, timed to coincide with the Inter-American Conference which Secretary of State Marshall was attending. The riot was an unfortunate backdrop for the conference and might have menaced the lives of the American delegation. Congress reacted at once by an investigation to "learn whether the Secretary of State and other high officials were promptly warned that a revolution was impending in Colombia." The Central Intelligence Agency claimed that it had discovered the projected plot and had sent the information to the State Department. Regardless of where the fault lay, the episode demonstrated serious weaknesses in the intelligence process. The Director of the CIA testified on June 23, 1950, before the House Foreign Affairs Committee—one day before the North Korean attack on South Korea —that the agency knew of the concentration of troops above the thirty-eighth parallel. Yet the government seems to have been taken by surprise. When called back a week later to explain, the director said the information had been turned over to the Army. Once more, the exact location of blame was less important than that the failure occurred at all.

The Eberstadt task force of the Hoover Commission expressed its alarm over, and dissatisfaction with, the intelligence pattern set up in 1949 in these words: ". . . the Committee is convinced that too many disparate intelligence estimates have been made by individual departmental intelligence services; that these separate estimates have often been subjective and biased; that the capabilities of potential enemies have frequently been interpreted as their intentions; and that a more comprehensive collection system, better coordination, and more mature and experienced evaluation are imperative."* If this pithy indictment is compared to the general requirements of strategic intelligence summarized above, it can be seen how far short the American system fell in the critical years after the war.

General Walter Bedell Smith, former Ambassador to Moscow, well known as a good administrator, became director of the CIA in 1950. The situation had deteriorated to the point where it was necessary to appoint a civilian committee of experienced intelligence leaders, headed by Mr. Allen Dulles (who had worked with OSS and is now director of the CIA) to study the organization and functioning of the CIA and make recommendations. The committee worked for one year, and its suggestions for reorganization are now being carried out. There have been extensive changes in personnel, compartmentalization and rivalry within the agency have been reduced, and a top-level evaluating staff has been created. Some of the agency's bitterest critics served on the afore-mentioned committee and now participate regularly in its work either as full-time members or as private consultants. The new director and his deputies commanded increasing respect from other intelligence groups. Under General Smith, the CIA cast itself in a positive role for the first time. A "Joint Watch Committee" was established to detect day-to-day indications of Communist aggression. An Office of National Estimates was also created. Little by little, suggestions were made to others regarding kinds of information which were required at top levels. One of the most important changes since 1950 has been a shift away from preparation of mere factual data toward provision of a genuine basis for decision. In contrast to the agency's previous philosophy, an effort is now made to analyze the consequences of alternative courses of foreign policy. In sum, during its first three years, the CIA concentrated on covert intelligence and on collecting information other intelligence units did not have; during the next few years it became more of a central evaluation agency.

Before 1941, a comprehensive foreign intelligence service for the United States was not felt to be necessary, though in retrospect it is apparent that it would have strengthened American foreign policy during the interwar years. Once the need was realized, it took ten years, at a very critical time, to bring about the conditions under which such a service is now finally beginning to emerge. The foregoing account suggests certain lessons. The failures of the

* *Task Force Report on National Security Organization, Appendix G,* Prepared for the Commission on Organization of the Executive Branch of the Government, January, 1949, p. 76.

period were chiefly those of evaluation of data and communication of estimates. Competent personnel and effective coordination were lacking. The mere existence of organizational mechanisms and experts, however, is not enough. The central agency and its director must be respected. Leadership must be exercised. Finally, the attitudes of all the participants in various branches of the system are crucial. Rivalry, competition, and bad performance often result from lack of understanding and hostility. No matter how good it looks on paper, no intelligence system will completely fulfill its role in the policy-making process unless the attitudes of the personnel are appropriate to the nature, significance, and requirements of the intelligence process.

THE FUNCTIONS OF THE CENTRAL INTELLIGENCE AGENCY

According to the National Security Act of 1947, the CIA is under the direction of the National Security Council and has five functions: (1) to advise the council on the intelligence activities of government departments and agencies which relate to national security; (2) to make recommendations to the council for the coordination of such activities; (3) to correlate and evaluate national security intelligence and to circulate the results; (4) to perform services for existing agencies which are best done centrally; and (5) to perform any other duties and functions assigned to it by the Security Council. The CIA does not replace regular intelligence units; departments and agencies continue to collect, correlate, evaluate, and disseminate *departmental* intelligence. Neither does the CIA have any internal security or counterintelligence functions. It is not an operating agency in the usual sense; it confines itself only to those limited operations which can be most efficiently performed centrally, such as monitoring foreign radio broadcasts and supervising secret agents abroad. Beyond this, any original or creative work is confined to that which is required for coordinating and supplementing departmental efforts.

The basic function of the CIA is to see to it that all intelligence activities relating to national security result in the production of national intelligence estimates which can become the basis of foreign-policy decisions. This task requires not just correlation of data but coordination of activities. The coordination for which the CIA is responsible has several sides to it.* Various intelligence agencies must have clearly defined areas of work for which they are responsible. Unnecessary duplication must be avoided, and the agencies must be policed to see that their work is of proper quality and suitably oriented for interdepartmental correlation. What is suitable for one department's needs will not always lend itself to coordination with the information of other departments. Trouble must be diagnosed and suggestions offered for the correction of weaknesses from the standpoint of the end product expected from the sum total of intelligence activities. If an agency is not fully exploring its area of work it must be urged to do so. If one agency is better equipped

* Kent, *op. cit.,* pp. 91–94.

than another to collect and evaluate a certain kind of data, a shift may be suggested. All interdepartmental projects must be supervised by the central agency. Finally, it requires a central organization to guarantee that intelligence shall be interpreted from the standpoint of the *whole* government. Given the departmental rivalry for appropriations, it is not unnatural that at least some estimates are in the nature of "promotional bids" designed to enhance the significance of a particular agency's operations.

Strictly speaking, the director of the CIA does not have clear power to "order" departments and agencies to do all these things. The ability of the CIA to successfully "live off" the work of other units and the successful performance of their functions will be a major determinant of the effectiveness of its efforts to coordinate. Subsection (e) of Section 101 of the National Security Act states that the intelligence files of departments and agencies shall be open to the inspection of the director of the CIA and that such data "shall be made avaiable to" him. The one exception to this is the FBI, in which case there is no inspection power and the director must make a written request to that agency. Section 101(e) provides little else by way of positive power for the CIA. Thus it would appear that successful coordination is dependent on several factors: the respect accorded the director and his deputies; the ability of the director to influence and persuade departments and agencies toward the objectives of the national intelligence program; and the ultimate sanction of the Security Council and the President himself.

National intelligence estimates are probably the core of the strategic intelligence output. Here the CIA has the key role. Its high-level staff selects, correlates, and evaluates materials relevant to a particular estimate, which are then submitted for further analysis to the Interdepartmental Intelligence Advisory Committee (representing the CIA, the FBI, the Atomic Energy Commission, the State Department, and the Armed Forces) of which the director of the CIA is chairman. The draft estimate agreed to by the committee is later checked by a secret, private group which acts as a consultant to the director and becomes authoritative even though any one agency may dissent. It is not uncommon for the CIA to arrive at several "national estimates." No attempt is made for unanimous estimates. Rather the aim is the "best opinion." This document is naturally top secret and is circulated to only fifty or so top policy makers, including the members of the National Security Council. National estimates cover a wide range of subjects, from when or whether a potential enemy will attack to how a particular nation would react to an invasion by Communist China, from the strength of communism in France to the relative influence of East and West in Iran. If necessary, national estimates on most subjects can be produced on twenty-four hours notice.

OTHER DEPARTMENTS AND AGENCIES

Between twenty and thirty agencies, counting special units in six Executive Departments, make their own individual contributions to the flow of information necessary to the preparation of strategic intelligence. The Office of Intelligence Research in the State Department does some basic research and collects data from Foreign Service reports. In addition, there are intelligence attachés linked to the geographical divisions in the State Department. Military intelligence is gathered by permanent units in the Army, Navy, and Air Force, and by military, air, and naval attachés located in embassies and legations abroad. The Joint Chiefs of Staff has its own coordinating agency, the Joint Intelligence Committee representing the three services plus the Marines. A further source of military intelligence consists of the missions financed under the foreign-aid program. Though the FBI is technically in the field of counterintelligence, it constantly uncovers material relevant to strategic intelligence. The Atomic Energy Commission's secret program must be listed as a primary source of policy information. Other secondary agencies are the Bureau of Foreign Commerce (Commerce), the Office of Foreign Agricultural Service (Agriculture), the Office of International Finance (Treasury), the Foreign Operations Administration, and the Department of Labor.

Actually, all government agencies concerned with foreign affairs do a kind of intelligence work—directly or as a by-product of their regular duties. And, of course, private individuals, groups, and agencies contribute useful services. For example, the federal government may contract out research projects which bear closely on strategic intelligence. The Russian Research Center at Harvard did a study of the structure of Russian society for the Air Force. However, it is the Central Intelligence Agency, the Interdepartmental Intelligence Advisory Committee, and the member units of this committee dealing most closely with national security which comprise the organizational nucleus for direct, positive foreign itelligence. Some 25,000 persons are employed in these agencies and the total budget runs to $200,000,000 exclusive of secret funds. If the secondary agencies are included, some 35,000 persons are involved and the budget is $300,000,000. The figures do not include counterintelligence activities.

CRITICISMS AND POTENTIAL DANGERS

There is little doubt that the present intelligence process and its product represent a substantial improvement over the situation prior to 1950. After a decade of confusion and failure—marked, it is true, by some conspicuous successes such as the prevention of a blunder in 1948 concerning troop movements in the Soviet Zone of Germany and the discovery of the first Russian atomic explosion in 1949—the United States has laid the groundwork for a genuine foreign-intelligence system. Conditions are presently more favorable than unfavorable for this development. Much remains to be done and time alone can answer certain problems and alter certain conditions. Real and potential weaknesses still exist. The whole system is delicately balanced. A break in any link in the intelligence process could conceivably produce a national disaster. At this writing, there are still responsible critics—Hanson Baldwin, for example—who do not feel that the CIA has a reliable "best opinion" on "the $64 question" which has troubled the nation for eight years, namely, how strong is Russia? The CIA claims it had foreknowledge of the invasion of South Korea by North Korean forces in 1950; but no collective intelligence judgment was prepared. If top-level policy makers knew what the CIA knew, they did not or could not take it into account. As late as 1952, the Navy had advance warning of the Batista coup in Cuba but did not pass the information on. However, there are more checks and counterchecks than there were previously.

It takes more than ten years to develop a durable, effective intelligence system with sufficient built-in competence, continuity, confidence, and experience not to be shaken by political pressures, shifts in the attitudes of participants, and the vagaries of leadership. The lack of a relatively homogeneous, stable career service and the absence of high professional morale are general handicaps in the federal government which affect intelligence. Much depends on whether the recognition of foreign intelligence as a specialized function continues to spread. No one knows exactly how many skilled people were lost to this service in recent years because intelligence was not accepted as a respectable career—particularly in the military services. If competent personnel are to be attracted, there must be explicit acceptance by decision makers of the vital role of intelligence and a willingness to treat experts as more than mere research assistants. Nothing is worse for the morale of intelligence units than the feeling that they are so far removed from the main stream of policy making that what they do or whether they are more than routine clerks really doesn't matter. An equally important handicap is the general lack of qualified personnel. When he left his post as director in 1953, General Smith revealed, for example, that specialists were needed in no less than 115 languages and dialects and yet there are not teachers of these to train the men adequately. Of every one hundred applicants, only six can be counted as suitable for a professional career in intelligence.

Students of the intelligence problem still share some misgivings about the level of analytical techniques employed in the evaluation of data. A rather sizable corps of professional scientists, physical and social, would seem to be a required supplement to less sophisticated researchers and experienced generalists. Evidence suggests that major emphasis is still on rather crude techniques for constructing a reliable portrait of another society and what makes it tick. In some quarters there is marked resistance to any departure from conventional techniques and sources. Covert intelligence, newspapers, public opinion polls, and interviews with trusted friends or observers are all essential of course. But off-the-cuff interpretations and generalizations from long experience can be misleading. It is a long leap from a public attitude survey to a prediction of behavior, and the conclusions of single observers or informers may be open to question on a number of scores. Evaluation will be impaired to the extent that intelligence experts rely on techniques which demonstrably yield fallacious results under certain circumstances. Much economic reporting consists of recording inconsequential detail, with too much attention to commodities per se, and an overemphasis on daily occurrences at the expense of trend analysis. Much data gathered from abroad lacks cultural perspective and sociological depth.

Information is subject to other distortions. An intelligence evaluation can be used to defend a policy position or protect a departmental interest, rather than to establish a sound basis for decision. Data which run counter to existing patterns of thought can be suppressed. Political pressures can indirectly produce suppression of accurate reports. In January, 1952, President Truman refused to give the Senate permission to examine State Department papers relating to the loyalty of John Carter Vincent, a Foreign Service officer, on the ground that it would undermine objective reporting from the field. As noted in Chapter Three, tendencies in this direction have already been manifest. The functional value of intelligence research can also be limited by gearing it primarily to preconceived objectives. American strategic intelligence got its start during World War II, when specific goals and objectives of military and foreign policy were fixed in terms of the war and its outcome. Therefore strategic intelligence has had to outgrow the wartime state of mind. If grand strategy and major foreign policies are to be based on reliable information— reliable in the sense that it provides a basis for contingent predictions of the consequences of alternate courses of action—that information cannot be collected and evaluated as though one alternative had already been selected. Nor can information and analysis be tied to what someone would like to find or has to find to justify a policy already decided upon.

It is worth noting in this connection another dilemma of democracy. Since the intelligence process must be carried on largely in secret, suspicion, curiosity, and fear on the part of Congress and the public are to be expected. Influential political leaders and private groups—particularly if they have well-defined views on the external setting—naturally wonder what ingredients go into the bases of decisions. In their minds, the slip-over from objective analysis to pro-Russianism or anti-Francoism is easily accomplished. Charges are made that such and such an intelligence agency is saturated with pro-Communists. It is clear that strategic intelligence cannot be prepared under the klieg lights of public scrutiny. However, on the other hand, it is equally clear that responsible policy formulation will depend heavily on the effectiveness of the intelligence function properly conceived. The less distortion of the types mentioned above, the more likely it will be that policy formulations can be presented to Congress and the public with an adequate frame of reference for the discussion of alternatives and implications. During the presidential campaign of 1952, General Smith declared frankly that he supposed some Communist agents had infiltrated the CIA. He was only being realistic, but the furor caused by his statement was enormous. And it was only after a strong plea by him that the issue was kept out of the campaign. In the spring of 1953, Senator McCarthy threatened to subpoena William Bundy, employed by the CIA and a son-in-law of former Secretary of State Dean Acheson, to testify before his committee, but the director of CIA, Mr. Allen Dulles, refused and the threat passed.

Finally, two decisions have been made regarding the organization of intelligence, the wisdom and results of which cannot yet be judged. As in the case of other administrative problems, this is a period of trial and error. First, the intelligence function has been separated from decision making on the assumption that it is a distinct function deserving of the full-time attention of specialists. A related assumption was that intelligence could and would be fed back into decision making at appropriate points and used. Second, instead of concentrating all intelligence activities in one agency, decentralization among various departments and agencies has been preserved with coordination to be achieved by a staff agency and an interdepartmental committee. This is the prevailing pattern with respect to foreign-policy administration generally. Coordination and communication of strategic intelligence have improved. Whether they have achieved a level sufficient for preservation of the national security remains to be seen.

▶ THE STATE DEPARTMENT

A detailed analysis of the work of this important agency is presented in the next chapter. At this point it is necessary to take a broad look at the place of the State Department in the total executive structure for the conduct of foreign relations. As has already been hinted in previous pages, the structure of policy making has been altered in certain major respects since 1940 and this change has had its effect upon the State Department's general role and influence as well as on its relations with other agencies. The rise of military agencies to a significant place in policy making and the operation of huge aid programs have been among the major factors which have tended to unsettle the actual role of the department and to raise serious, complex problems and questions with respect to the structure of foreign-policy decision making and execution generally. Students of public administration have become increasingly concerned with this matter because of its practical bearing on the effectiveness of American foreign policy.* In addition, the Secretary of State has been compelled to enter controversies with Congress and with other departments to protect the traditional role and functions of his agency against encroachment. The fact that a continuous political struggle of this sort has been carried on since 1945 has enormously affected policy making in a very critical period.

On close examination, the "problem" of the role of the State Department is revealed as a mixture of related problems. One is the rather natural inter-

---

* See the bibliographical citations at the end of this chapter.

rganizational rivalry inherent in any complex bureaucracy. Another is the contemporary manifestation of Congressional distrust of the State Department. A third is the nature of the relationship between the President and the Secretary of State, i.e., between the chief executive and a regular department. A fourth is the presentation of unique situations resulting from America's new international position for which there was no administration blueprint and which produce genuine disagreement even among professional experts. Finally, there is the problem of the relationship of the State Department to functions of other agencies but which have now become very much a part of foreign affairs.

Until World War II, there was no real problem. The original prescription in the Congressional statute of 1789 which established the State Department was sufficient: "The Secretary of State shall perform such duties as shall from time to time be enjoined or entrusted to him by the President . . . and he shall conduct the business of the department in such manner as the President shall direct." Most of the nation's foreign relations could be conducted through normal diplomatic channels. There were no large-scale programs to be administered abroad. There were no special agencies dealing exclusively with foreign affairs, aside from the State Department itself. Other agencies and departments were not performing functions which seriously impinged on the nation's general foreign policy.

Some aspects of the problem which arose when these conditions were swept away can be clarified by asking certain questions: Should the State Department *operate* foreign-policy programs such as military and economic aid? If not, should all such programs be centralized in a single operating agency? Should there be one omnibus department of foreign affairs to handle all functions, similar to the Defense Department with program operations concentrated in a major subunit? If some functions relating to foreign affairs are to be left outside the Department of State, what power or control should the department have over them and how would such power or control be exercised? How are those purely domestic functions exercised by other agencies which ultimately bear on foreign-policy programs to be linked to the functions of the Department of State? Do the presidential staff agencies discussed above offer a possibility that the State Department will be circumvented? As will be seen, some of these questions have not been answered satisfactorily in practice, some have been answered by compromise, and some probably cannot be answered with any finality at this time. All are further complicated by the fact that no one knows how long extensive foreign aid will have to be continued.

THE PRESIDENT AND THE SECRETARY OF STATE

These questions go to the heart of the relationship between the President and the Department of State. The department is, in both fact and theory, the President's principal adviser on foreign policy. It is also legally an Executive

Department in the full constitutional and statutory sense, that is, it has been delegated powers by the President to carry on official relations with other governments, to represent the United States abroad, and to negotiate and speak for the President. The Secretary of State is politically responsible as a Cabinet member and is also personally responsible to the President. Thus the State Department has the characteristics of both a staff agency and an Executive Department. It is a staff agency in that its most important function is to provide *advice* to the President and in that it prepares an unusual amount of work for final action by the President. When it is realized that at the moment most foreign-policy *operations are not located within the department,* it becomes clear how crucial the relationship between the department and the President is and how important it is that the role of the former is clear.

Ultimately, the President must define the relationship, if for no other reason than that he alone can settle head-on jurisdictional disputes. However, there is more to the problem than this. While the State Department is presumably the President's chief adviser on foreign policy, it is not his only adviser, as has been shown. The nature and openness of the channels of communication between the department and the White House, as well as the gearing in of the department's advice to other sources of advice will depend on the President himself, on staff arrangements, and on coordination at the Cabinet level. The President must clarify the role of the department in both word and deed. If he does not do so, rivalry, uncertainty, and cross-purpose action will be intensified. The President can by judicious use of devices at his disposal create conditions under which the department can exercise its prerogatives effectively and under which the department's functions can be coordinated with those of other agencies. Congress and other executive agencies will always exert considerable pressure on the President to do these things one way rather than another. In particular, the President will be confronted, for an indefinite time, with the central issue of the degree of power of coordination to be given to the State Department over activities not in its immediate jurisdiction. Recently, the State Department has, not unnaturally, pressed for greater latitude in this direction. Congress and the affected agencies, on the other hand, have tended to insist on greater autonomy for the large operations outside the department. The issue is more easily stated than resolved. A distinction between policy making and operations as a means of defining the role of the State Department seems attractively logical, but constitutes an oversimplification and, in addition, ignores the fact that carrying on operations involves making decisions which may significantly determine the form of the policy which emerges. The issue is complicated because the potential rivals of the State Department have been granted by Congress and by the President powers to give financial assistance to other nations, to occupy enemy territory, to control foreign commercial and financial relations, and to regulate the movements of persons across the national frontier. For the most part, the powers of the State Department are limited to communication and negotiation with foreign nations. These are primarily ministerial rather than substantive powers.

Much depends on the relationship between a particular President and a particular Secretary of State. Some presidents—among them Franklin Roosevelt—have been accused of being their own Secretaries of State. It has been argued that when the President "usurps" the functions of the secretary, the prestige of the department suffers and men of stature will refuse to serve. A persuasive point is that if the President circumvents the Department of State, the latter's effectiveness in dealing with foreign nations is undermined. On the other hand, the President is by law the one responsible. The written Constitution clearly assigns executive power and treaty power to him. And the 1789 statute quoted above states that the secretary shall act according to presidential will. Yet a particular secretary may have been forced on the President by political necessity, may be a man who does not view the world as he does, a man who may knowingly or unknowingly block his aims. Constitutionally, the practice has been for the President to define his own relationship with the secretary. Adams dismissed Pickering for disloyalty, Lincoln put Seward in his place when necessary, and Wilson forced Lansing and Bryan out over policy clashes. Franklin Roosevelt often by-passed Cordell Hull. Henry L. Stimson's testimony that President Hoover "abstained from giving . . . any instructions whatever" when the secretary went to the London Naval Conference of 1930 and that "there was no time when he [the President] intervened with any instructions to us as to what we should or should not do,"* indicates another type of relationship which may exist but is not usual and certainly is not required by constitutional custom. Had President Truman acceded to the periodic insistence during 1950–1951 that he replace Secretary Acheson, he would have reversed a tradition of 150 years. However, the President does not, as already suggested, enjoy a free hand in the matter. Strong President though he was, Franklin Roosevelt had to appease the State Department to a certain extent simply because he could not afford to lose Secretary of State Cordell Hull's prestige in Congress.

The President would truly usurp the functions of the secretary only if he tried to administer or execute decisions as well as make them. Hence the secretary must be very much a part of the policy-making process. How well the President and secretary work together will be heavily influenced by how the two get along personally. If the President has geniune confidence in the secretary and if the President "understands" the secretary, then, other things being equal, the two can function as a team. Regardless of the personal equation, however, other factors enter the relationship. In a constitutional sense, the secretary is responsible to the President, but in terms of the sound

---

* Before the Senate Committee on Foreign Relations, 71st Congress, 2nd Session, May 12, 1930.

operation of the executive machinery for foreign-policy making the President also has a responsibility to the secretary. This point will be touched upon again in the next chapter.

In an era when events move rapidly and when the executive agencies are under rather constant pressure from Congress and other nations for statements of policy on a wide range of subjects, additional difficulties are introduced into the relationship between the President and the Secretary of State. Much state action consists of oral pronouncements by these two—in special messages to Congress, public addresses, and news conferences. Since not every utterance by one can be cleared with the other and since they cannot stand side by side whenever they speak, the possibilities of inconsistency, conflict, and inaccurate interpretations of what is said are ever-present. Very often a question arises as to whose words are authoritative and as to what the relationship is between two pronouncements. President Eisenhower's first major speech on foreign policy was given in April of his first year of office, 1953, and it has been described as a "peace" speech because it dealt frankly with Soviet-American tensions and outlined in general the conditions under which outstanding conflicts might be negotiated and settled. While firm, the President's tone was also conciliatory. For the next few weeks, Secretary of State Dulles made several statements on the President's general position which may be interpreted as a kind of tactical follow-up. By the middle of May there was considerable confusion evident in foreign capitals. Some felt the secretary's tone was much more "unconditional" than was the President's and therefore left much less leeway for genuine discussion and compromise. Were Mr. Dulles's remarks an emphasis within the boundaries set by the President or were they in excess of those boundaries? Were the secretary's remarks to be interpreted as amplification, clarification, or alteration? Apparently foreign statesmen had to come to their own conclusions. This is only one example, to be sure. But it must be remembered that the presidential speech was an important one and that it was very vital for European governments to discover the flexibility and direction of American policy toward the Soviet Union. Leaving out deliberate attempts to mislead and to misinterpret, there is still sufficient chance for verbal confusion to make it very essential that the President and the Secretary of State understand each other perfectly.

THE STATE DEPARTMENT AND OTHER AGENCIES: REORGANIZATION PLANS 7 AND 8, JUNE, 1953

With all this in mind, and supported by the recommendations of the Government Reorganization Committee headed by Nelson Rockefeller,* President Eisenhower evidently decided to strengthen the general position of the State Department. Reorganization Plans 7 and 8, which particularly concerned the department, were designed to divest it of functional tasks which

---

* This committee might be regarded as a follow-up to the Hoover Commission. It made nineteen studies of major agencies and reported to the President on April 23, 1953.

had involved it in political controversy—notably with Congress—in the post-war period, and to make the Secretary of State supreme next to the President in policy supervision of programs administered by other agencies. The presidential message which accompanied these two plans stated flatly that it was the intention to "confirm the historic responsibility of the Department of State as the agency responsible under the President for development and control of foreign policy and all relations with foreign governments," and to endow the secretary with "clear authority to provide guidance on our foreign policies to all other agencies. . . ." Details of the reorganization plans are discussed below, but two further points should be made here. The Secretary of State now advises the President concerning the appointment and tenure of the director of the Foreign Overseas Administration (successor to the Mutual Seurity Agency). Furthermore, the chief of each diplomatic mission abroad is to coordinate *all* United States government activity in that country.

► THE DEPARTMENT OF DEFENSE

The role of the military institutions and agencies has become so significant in the formulation and execution of American foreign policy that Chapter Nine will be devoted entirely to it. At this juncture it is necessary, however, to take note of the fact that the Department of Defense has emerged in the forefront among the key policy-making agencies. Aside from those of the State Department, the activities of no other agency now touch upon foreign policy and relations at so many points. This fact signifies a major redistribution of foreign-policy interest and influence in the Executive Branch. It can be seen clearly in the broad responsibilities of the Defense Department. First, the Defense Department advises the President, the National Security Council, and the State Department on the general military implications of the nation's over-all foreign policy and the military feasibility of specific foreign-policy programs or actions. Such advice is channeled largely, though not exclusively, through the Joint Chiefs of Staff. At the Cabinet level, it is the Secretary of Defense who advises the President, in addition to being responsible to him and to Congress for the administration of the military establishment. Second, the Defense Department prepares strategic plans for the support of national objectives. Third, it becomes an agency for the execution of foreign policy whenever this requires military operations and planning. Thus it carried out the Korean campaign and assists in the administration of military aid to friends and allies. The Department of Defense therefore has numerous and complex relationships with other agencies and with both regional and international organizations of which the United States is a member.

Military operations and considerations have loomed steadily larger in foreign relations, beginning with the effort to strengthen the anti-Axis coalition before 1941, during America's participation in World War II and the occupation of former enemy territories which followed it, and, finally, during the

period of increasing hostility between the Western world and the Soviet orbit
The Department of Defense provides two basic kinds of competence which
must be woven into the total fabric of policy formation and execution: highly
specialized advice and information at the formulation stage and operational
skills at the execution stage. A whole set of liaison devices is necessary to
accomplish these functions. Several important devices have already been
mentioned, namely, the National Security Council, direct contact between the
President and the Secretary of Defense, and direct contact between the President and the Joint Chiefs of Staff. Another important medium of coordination
is the interdepartmental committee to be discussed below. Needless to say, the
soundness of military advice together with the manner in which it is fed into
the policy-making process at appropriate points will be crucial to the success
of America's foreign policy.

The sheer size of the military establishment, apart from its functions,
makes it a force to contend with in the executive organization for foreign
affairs. Being a key agency with major responsibilities, the Department of
Defense naturally has its own ideas as to how it can best discharge those
responsibilities and also as to how the Executive Branch should be organized
for effective policy determination and execution. In addition to policy disagreements with the Department of State, the Defense Department has had
somewhat different ideas about how programs should be administered. The
result has been an intensification of controversy over the *how* of policy, i.e.,
over the way decisions are to be reached and carried out. It is sometimes
difficult to separate this aspect from the more general question of how
foreign affairs are administered in the Executive Branch, but in an era of
transition no reasonably comprehensive analysis of American foreign policy
can neglect this problem.

► OTHER DEPARTMENTS AND AGENCIES
CONCERNED WITH FOREIGN AFFAIRS

In addition to the core policy-making units already discussed, there
are seven Executive Departments along with many regulatory bodies and other
agencies which are involved in foreign affairs one way or another. It is not
necessary to catalogue the relevant functions of all these groups, but it is
necessary to mention some of them by name and to outline briefly the various
ways in which they become a part of foreign-policy organization. Most of the
secondary agencies have *no direct, regular connection with policy making
per se.* Of course, this does not mean that their activities do not have policy
implications, but only that their advice, information, and operating capacities
are not vital on every major issue. Their involvement in decision making is on
the whole limited and sporadic, despite their greater responsibilities in an era
of international economic collaboration and despite their control over matters
normally beyond the province of the State Department. They must obviously

be consulted whenever their official functions impinge on foreign policy. Many have specific statutory responsibilities which involve them in foreign relations and which require them to administer specific policy programs. Nearly all of them carry on domestic activities which ultimately bear on foreign-policy problems. Of utmost importance is the fact that in their normal attempts to serve purely domestic interests, these agencies may pursue policies which have repercussions for America's relations with other nations. Frequent clashes with the State Department arise because the latter is in a sense the protector of foreign interests in the United States. On the other hand, many of the permanent routine foreign relations performed by the peripheral agencies, particularly those of an economic nature, do not have to be integrated with general foreign policy.

Probably the most important of the Executive Departments is the *Treasury Department,* which has primary responsibility for all foreign trans-actions of a monetary and financial nature. With loans and economic aid play-ing such a central role in American policy, there is hardly a major issue or program which does not involve the skills and authority of this department. It takes the leading part in the negotiation of financial agreements, administers these agreements, and gives technical advice to other agencies. So extensive have become the foreign-affairs functions of Treasury that it has an Office of International Finance which advises and prepares the secretary for his duties and acts as liaison between Treasury and other federal units, international organizations, and foreign governments. In consequence, the Secretary of the Treasury is chairman of a very active interdepartmental body, the National Advisory Council, and is regularly invited to meetings of the National Security Council. The secretary also serves as governor of the International Bank for Reconstruction and Development. Potentially, the Treasury Department is a real rival of the State Department in certain areas of policy. During the last war, Treasury became a full-fledged operating agency through its Foreign Economic Administration and developed its own policy for postwar Germany. It negotiated, and still administers, the British Loan of 1945. Since Treasury administers customs regulations and tariff charges, its interpretations of the law have a direct impact on foreign economic relations. Next to the necessary coordination between the State Department and the Defense Department, teamwork between Treasury and State is most vital. It is almost impossible to distill out the purely financial aspects of general foreign policy, so the problem of jurisdiction and the balance between advising and policy-making functions arises again in acute form.

The *Department of Commerce* is sufficiently involved in foreign affairs to be represented on all interdepartmental committees working on economic problems. One of its most important functions, arising during the negotiation of trade agreements, is to offer reliable testimony on possible tariff reductions acceptable to domestic interests (exclusive of agriculture) and to make known what American businessmen want or need by way of trading conditions abroad. Collaboration with the State Department is required because Commerce is charged with protecting one large segment of the American public while State does the negotiating and must protect the total national interest. The Department of Commerce also collects, analyzes and publishes information about industrial and business conditions in foreign lands. Commerce, too, executes a segment of policy in its administration of the Export Control Program and the China Trade Act. A third executive department, also with vital functions in the realm of economic affairs, is the *Department of Agriculture*. Like Commerce, it has a statutory obligation to protect and serve domestic interests and therefore it has a dominant voice in the tariff rates for agricultural imports. Like Treasury, it has been the principal negotiator when international agreements were concerned solely with its substantive functions, as in the case of the International Wheat Agreement. The Department of Agriculture provides technical advice for foreign governments seeking to improve their production techniques. The economic aid programs of recent years have required huge shipments of food, fertilizer, and raw material; hence the Department has had a major voice in the determination of the amount and the allocation of such items abroad. It also helps in the procurement, storage, and shipment of agricultural materials. Finally, the department serves as America's major link to the Food and Agriculture Organization of the United Nations.

Generally speaking, the *Departments of Labor, Interior, Justice, and Post Office* are less deeply involved, though they perform important services for and are widely represented in policy-making agencies. Labor represents the United States in the International Labor Organization, has members on the interagency committees dealing with economic and social affairs, advises on labor questions in areas where American programs and policies must be geared into local politics. The role of labor attachés, nominated by the Labor Department and stationed at diplomatic outposts, is becoming increasingly significant. As the President's chief legal adviser, the *Department of Justice* is the major source of opinion on domestic legal aspects of foreign-policy problems, exemplified by the Attorney General's opinion on the Destroyer-Bases Agreement of 1940. The Antitrust Division has advised on cartel policy and other legal matters in occupied territories. The Department of Justice also administers the laws governing the movement of aliens in and out of the United States. The *Interior Department's* main involvement in foreign affairs stems from its administration of overseas possessions and territories and its responsibility for coordinating federal petroleum policy and administration at home and abroad. International postal relations are handled by the *Post Office Department*, which draws up all exchange of mails agreements and represents the United States in the Universal Postal Union.

In addition to the Executive Departments, numerous independent regulatory agencies also participate in the conduct of foreign relations. The *Atomic Energy Commission* collects and analyzes foreign atomic information, acquires fissionable materials abroad in behalf of the United States, and advises the State Department on policies to be pursued in the United Nations Atomic Energy Commission. Licenses for the operation of foreign air lines in this country are issued by the *Civil Aeronautics Board.* International loans are granted by the *Export-Import Bank.* The *Maritime Commission* builds, operates, and administers the American merchant marine. Foreign commerce via radio and telegraph is regulated by the *Federal Communications Commission.* An important agency in the field of economic foreign policy is the *Tariff Commission,* which recommends the rates to be granted by the United States in trade agreements, and in addition conducts research on competitive production costs throughout the world and the effects of barriers on foreign trade. The regulatory agency most squarely in the arena of foreign affairs is, of course, the *Foreign Operations Administration,* which replaced the Mutual Security Agency and will be discussed at length in the section on military and economic aid.

This brief outline gives some idea of the number of agencies having something to do with foreign policy and relations and the wide range of their functions. While they differ from each other in the nature and extent of their impact on policy, taken together their significance is great indeed, both organizationally and substantively. Quite apart from specific functions, every one of these departments and agencies—and their subunits—are actual or potential sources of information. Therefore in terms of the analysis of intelligence presented above, the communication network for relevant security information covers much more than the core decision-making agencies with primary responsibility for foreign policy. Furthermore, the sheer number of agencies means that some device is needed to coordinate functions and interests and to avoid conflict. The chances of conflict are enhanced because the independent regulatory agencies are normally subject to less presidential direction and control than are the Executive Departments. For example, in 1948 the Maritime Commission was almost successful in its refusal to carry out a request from the State Department to transfer certain ships to foreign countries. A Senate subcommittee on appropriations chastised the State Department for interfering with the work of the Maritime Commission. But the problem of coordination does not end here. Each of the Executive Departments and several of the other agencies have several foreign-relations functions and therefore more than one subunit within them concerned with an aspect of foreign affairs. Hence there are internal coordination problems. Departments differ considerably in the amount and methods of coordination and so differ considerably in the degree to which they speak with one voice and the ease with which coordination with other groups can be achieved. On occasion the State Department has had to act as coordinator of two separate units in another department. The Departments of Labor and Agriculture coordinate their foreign-affairs functions at the top level by an assistant secretary for International Labor Affairs and by a director of the Office of

Foreign Agriculture Relations, respectively. On the other hand, the Department of Commerce has three units dealing with foreign commerce, foreign air commerce, and with international cooperation programs, no one of which has full power of coordination. Nor does the Office of International Finance in the Treasury Department have authority to coordinate the various functions in the area of foreign affairs. The Federal Security Agency, however, has an advisory officer in charge of interagency and international relations and most of the regulatory agencies have a single staff officer advising on such matters. The danger of having diverse methods of coordination or lack of complete coordination in any one agency is that *all* the relevant information it has may not be available when and where needed and that the agency may not be able to speak authoritatively on interdepartmental committees.

► INTERDEPARTMENTAL COMMITTEES

The increased use of interdepartmental committees since World War II obviously reflects the need to coordinate the work of the many agencies whose operations relate in some way to foreign affairs. The existence of such committees also indicates the fact that the questions raised above concerning the role of the State Department have not been definitively answered as yet— the department has not been given a general directive to act as over-all policy guide or to exercise veto power over the activities of other agencies. Nor have presidential staff arrangements progressed to the point where all major coordination can be handled at that level. The National Security Council's work does not at the present time cover all the areas where coordination is needed, particularly with respect to economic matters. It is not likely that a single foreign-affairs department will be established in the foreseeable future. It is not surprising therefore that the number of committees increased from thirty-six to fifty between 1946 and 1950 and that they continue to thrive as essential links in the policy-making chain, despite general dissatisfaction with their organization and performance.

Interagency committees can be established by Congressional statute, by presidential order, or by agreement among interested departments. Probably more are created by the latter method, though there has been a trend recently toward Congressional action. The interagency committee is one of the devices whereby Congress seeks to direct the way the President coordinates the executive organization for foreign affairs and to control the sources of his advice. The fact that many committees arise spontaneously at the departmental level indicates a relative lack of attention to the problem of coordination on the part of the President himself. Diverse sources of origin, combined with a lack of systematic planning in the assignment of duties, have led to a certain disorder at this level of policy making. Some committees are permanent and some are *ad hoc;* hence there is a frequent turnover. Frequent jurisdictional disputes plague committee activities. Some operate with greater authority and influence than others.

In essence, committees are a device for voluntary coordination. Their chief function is to assist in the formulation of policy to be presented to Congress or to the President or to be negotiated with other nations. Ordinarily committees are established to handle policy problems which cannot be assigned to one agency and which need not go to the President or are not quite ready for the President's attention. Membership depends on the subject matter involved. The *Committee on Trade Agreements,* for example, which recommends to the President the detailed provisions of trade agreements to be negotiated by the United States, consists of top officials from the State Department, Treasury, Interior, Labor, Commerce, the Foreign Operations Administration (successor to the Mutual Security Agency), Agriculture, Defense, and the Tariff Commission. The *National Advisory Council on International Monetary and Financial Problems,* which provides instructions for the American directors on the International Fund and Bank as well as advice for operating agencies, consists of the Secretaries of State, Treasury, and Commerce, and the chairmen of the Federal Reserve Board and Export-Import Bank.

Thus, as a general rule, those agencies are represented which have a primary interest in a committee's work. Agencies with a secondary interest are invited to sit in when a particular problem involves them. Sometimes nonmember agencies balk at being omitted, claiming they are the best judges of what their primary interests are. For the most part, committee members are secretaries of departments, under secretaries, assistant secretaries, and office and agency directors. Since these are busy, responsible officials, the attendance at many committee meetings is irregular and alternates or substitutes often appear. Such an attendance pattern may be an indication of a committee's prestige or effectiveness as well as a cause of committee stagnation or inefficiency. Representatives of the so-called independent regulatory agencies may cause special difficulties because they are not subject to the same degree of presidential supervision as are the Executive Departments. Often they attend meetings unprepared to speak for their respective agencies. The Bureau of the Budget may send representatives who participate as unofficial observers. An important figure is the committee chairman, who will usually be the representative of the agency most centrally concerned with the problems handled by the committee. Thus the chairman of the *Committee on Trade Agreements* is the Secretary of State and the chairman of the *National Advisory Council* is the Secretary of the Treasury. Of the more than fifty such committees, the State Department member chairs well over half.

The organization and procedure of interdepartmental committees vary widely. However, it is customary in most cases to have a technical staff or

secretariat attached to the committee and to have subcommittees which discuss problems in greater detail, sift out irrelevant considerations, discover
areas of agreement and disagreement, and present formal policy papers to
the whole committee. Subcommittees meet regularly and more often than
the committee itself. There are in the neighborhood of two hundred subcommittees, and it is here that a great amount of duplication and overlapping
takes place. The tendency of the full committee to accept the subcommittee's
decision is strong. The competence of the staff and its relationship to subcommittees are very important. Organization and procedure are key determinants of a committee's effectiveness. Not all committees are equally successful. Some find it exceedingly difficult or even impossible to reach a
decision. Some manage to accomplish a steady output of reports and recommendations. Others labor slowly, become inactive, and eventually are abolished. Not all failures are due to procedural difficulties. Personality clashes,
skills of committee members, nature of the subject matter, length of the
committee's experience, refusal of one agency to cooperate—all these factors
will bear directly on effectiveness. But such things as inadequate staff preparation, failure to circulate documents before committee meetings, and lack
of clear agenda can be upsetting despite goodwill and cooperation.

In many ways, the interdepartmental committees can be viewed as
microcosms, as small decision-making bodies that are the focal point of
pressures and complexities which result from the number of agencies which
must be satisfied and from the fact that many problems cannot be neatly
broken down into component parts. Coordination does not take place simply
because personnel are brought together and talk among themselves. Most of
the major problems considered by the committees contain sets of potentially
conflicting values and organizational interests of varying intensity. A civil
aviation question coming before the Air Advisory Board, for example, will
be found to involve foreign vs. domestic interests, civil interests and military
interests, and the respective jurisdictional domains of the Civil Aeronautics
Board and the Civil Aeronautics Administration. To decide which agency
has the paramount interest is not always easy. It is often difficult to establish
criteria for deciding how much weight is to be given to the domestic responsibilities of an agency represented on a committee, or how much economic
considerations should yield to political. Clearly, hard choices and bureaucratic self-interest are thoroughly mixed up in the process.

Those interagency committees which have made major contributions to
the coordination of foreign policy have had identifiable characteristics: a
skilled, continuous leadership by the agency with paramount interest, i.e.,
the chairman; clear responsibilities unhampered by other committees whose
jurisdiction might overlap; an experienced secretariat located in and linked
to the subject-matter office of the chairman's agency; the high respect of
the members and Congress; and a history of consistent policy over time. The
Committee on Trade Agreements fits all these categories. On the other hand,

he *Executive Committee on Economic Foreign Policy* has not been as effec-
ive because of inferior procedures and because its particular functions could
ot be completely separated from those of other committees in the same
general field.

Formal and informal interdepartmental relations take place outside the
committee framework. Joint research, *ad hoc* conferences, letters, informal
conversations, joint replies to inquiries, preparations for international conferences all draw departments together in numerous day-to-day relationships.
These are mostly unregularized and take place without much planning or
supervision. Confusion results when agencies deal with each other on three
or four levels, each presuming to speak with authority. Opportunity exists
for officials to exceed their authority without it being discovered until commitments are brought to light. The existence of multiple informal communications between agencies may increase the difficulty of securing an exchange
of authoritative views unless such communications are geared to formal
communication.

► THE ADMINISTRATION OF FOREIGN
ECONOMIC AND MILITARY AID

The adoption of systematic, large-scale foreign-aid programs after
1948 sharply focused the issues concerning the organization of decision
making and the administration of foreign affairs which were mentioned above
in the section on the State Department. As the Brookings Institution has
pointed out: "The problem of how the executive branch can best be organized for the conduct of foreign economic aid and related foreign economic
activities involves a basic organizational dilemma . . . in due course it may
be necessary to decide between the permanent establishment of a Department
of Foreign Economic Affairs, which would have full status as an executive
department, and a concentration of foreign economic programs in the Department of State."* It is agreed that such a decision cannot now be made and
that for some time to come the responsibilities for foreign-aid programs must
be shared by several agencies.† This alternative has its difficulties, as experience since 1948 has shown. Though the present organization of foreign-aid
administration is quite different from what it was in 1948, several important
points can be highlighted by a brief history of developments prior to 1953.

ADMINISTRATION OF FOREIGN AID 1948–1953

During the debate which preceded the passage of the Foreign Assistance
Act of 1948 (the Marshall Plan), argument centered on the question of how
the European recovery program was to operate administratively as much as
on the substantive implications for American foreign policy. There appears

* Brookings Institution, *op. cit.,* p. xv.
† *Ibid.,* pp. xvi–xvii.

to have been little support for the idea of incorporating the aid program in the State Department, which was itself opposed to such a plan. But there was a good deal of discussion on the nature of the relationship between the State Department and the Economic Cooperation Administration, the new agency created to administer the billion-dollar program. Before Congressional committees, Secretary of State Marshall warned against the possibility of "two Secretaries of State" and he argued strenuously in favor of writing three propositions into the statute: first, that all members of ECA missions abroad be covered into the Foreign Service; second, that the Secretary of State should have the explicit power to veto any action of the director of the ECA deemed contrary to the general objectives of American foreign policy; and third, that communication between the new agency and its field staff should be routed through the State Department. Obviously the secretary proposed these measures in order to preserve the supremacy of the Department of State as a Cabinet agency and to retain control of broad foreign-policy questions. Congress rejected all three propositions. The Senate Foreign Relations Committee insisted that the program was a business enterprise and deserved business autonomy and argued that no man capable of filling the job of directing the ECA would accept status inferior to that of the Secretary of State. Consequently, the Foreign Assistance Act of 1948 created a separate agency headed by a person of Cabinet rank. The administrator of ECA was to "cooperate closely" with the Secretary of State, both were to mutually inform each other when either took action affecting the other's responsibilities, and each was to consult with the other when he felt an action inconsistent with his authority had been taken. Even though regular ambassadors and ministers were to outrank the heads of ECA missions attached to American diplomatic establishments abroad, the latter were to report directly to the ECA administrator in Washington. Settlement of head-on conflicts was left to the President.

While it is generally agreed that the ECA was administered successfully, experience from the 1948–1951 period demonstrated how difficult it was to draw a workable line between the ECA and the State Department with respect to their individual functions and responsibilities. There were more or less constantly open sores in the relationship of the two agencies, as will be shown in the next chapter. A few months before the statutory life of the ECA came to an end, President Truman was still trying to clarify the spheres of authority. On April 5, 1951, the President said in a letter to the Secretary of State and the ECA administrator, "The Secretary of State, under my direction, is the Cabinet officer responsible for the formulation of foreign policy and the conduct of foreign relations, and *will provide leadership and coordination among the executive agencies* in carrying out foreign policies and programs. The ECA, like other agencies engaged in administering specific overseas programs, will need to advise and consult with the Secretary of State and his staff to facilitate this responsibility for over-all foreign policy and program coordination."*

The ambiguous allocation of responsibilities undoubtedly injected some confusion into American relations with Western Europe at a time when maximum understanding and clarity of American policy would have been prime national assets. During this period, there was no single point, below the President himself, where American economic foreign policy as a whole could be coordinated. The result was that except for the Trade Agreements Program and matters of general commercial policy, the role of the State Department as coordinator was relatively weak. For that matter, there was no central coordination of domestic economic policy and foreign economic policy. Difficulties of meshing the respective roles of the ECA and the State Department indicate that the distinction between policy and operations or between policy and administration is illusory. Every time the ECA made a major decision on the nature, amount, and destiny of economic aid it was in fact giving specific substance to a general policy and therefore shaping general policy.

Although by 1951, the ECA was supervising aid not only to Western Europe, but to Greece, Turkey, and Korea (assigned in 1948), Germany (assigned in 1949), Austria and Southeast Asia (assigned in 1950), and the Philippine Rehabilitation Program (assigned in 1951), the Point Four Program legislated in the Act for International Development of 1950 was entrusted to the State Department. A Technical Cooperation Administration was established in the department and an Interdepartmental Advisory Council on Technical Cooperation was also created. Initial appropriations were small and did not approach the billions being handled by the ECA. However, Point Four turned out to be more significant than its appropriations would suggest and after a few years some of the operations of the ECA, too, looked very much like technical assistance. Yet the two related activities were carried on separately. The State Department also continues to administer the Institute of Inter-American Affairs, which engages in promoting economic development. Technical assistance programs later became increasingly important in stimulating the flow and stockpiling of scarce materials necessary for the American economy, an activity in which the ECA also participated.

Meanwhile, the military aid program begun in 1949 further complicated the administration of foreign aid. The Mutual Defense Assistance Act appropriated funds to the President for strengthening the members of the North Atlantic Alliance. Primary administrative responsibility was delegated to the Department of State with provision for the participation of the ECA and the Department of Defense. Until 1951, recommendations on the allocation of military aid were prepared by the Foreign Military Assistance Coordinating

---

* Italics by the authors. Reported in the New York *Times*, April 18, 1951, p. 18.

Committee, an interdepartmental committee consisting of representatives from State, Defense, and ECA. This committee acted as adviser to the Secretary of State and to his deputy, the director of Military Assistance, who was chairman of the committee. The chairman had no power of decision himself in the event of disagreements, which were to be settled by a steering committee composed of the Secretaries of State and Defense and the ECA administrator. It was agreed that the State Department would determine over-all policy and handle negotiations with other governments, and that economic and military aspects would be handled by the ECA and the Department of Defense, respectively. The committee's job was to decide how these responsibilities were to be actually carried out and thus was administrative as well as advisory.

In December, 1950, an interdepartmental agreement approved by the President created a new committee, the International Security Affairs Committee, and set up a director of International Security Affairs in the State Department who would act as chairman. According to the agreement the director was to "represent and speak for the Department of State on matters of policy and program relating to the North Atlantic Treaty, other similar international programs, and military and economic assistance for mutual defense." Further, the director was to "be responsible *for providing continuous leadership** in the interdepartmental coordination of policy and programs" and would be "exercising responsibility for the Government as a whole." The agreement also specified that "the Department of Defense has primary responsibility for determining the military character of international programs, for developing and implementing the end-item and military training programs, and for developing U.S. determinations as to military requirements in the formulation of programs for military production abroad." As for the ECA, it was to "have primary responsibility for developing and implementing plans for economic assistance required to support an adequate defense effort abroad, and for implementing approved programs for additional military production abroad." The new committee consisted of the members of the Foreign Military Assistance Coordinating Committee plus representatives from Treasury and the special assistant to the President.

Expanding the membership, changing the title, and creating a new agency in the State Department were designed to raise the level of authority on which coordination took place. But more important was the attempt to enhance the State Department's capacity for leadership in coordination by giving the chairman power of decision and by clarifying the roles of the ECA and the Defense Department. The interdepartmental understanding confirmed and strengthened the prevailing pattern. Actually, the Secretary of State could now control or at least exercise a veto over the recommendations of the committee. It is to be noted that in the case of economic aid alone, the ECA

---

* Italics by the authors.

retained relative autonomy, whereas in the case of the economic aspects of military aid, the ECA acted as an agent of the State Department. President Truman emphasized the major role of the State Department in the allocation of military and economic aid in April, 1951, saying that the "Secretary of State, after recommendation from the International Security Affairs Committee, where appropriate, should make the broad decisions concerning the use of the funds. . . ." This was precisely the type of arrangement rejected by Congress when it established the economic aid program in 1948. The emerging pattern of aid administration was to be the basis of President Truman's recommendation to Congress with respect to the question of legislation to supplant the Foreign Assistance Act of 1948. He favored a continuation of the ECA along existing lines, military assistance to be administered by the Defense Department with coordination by the State Department through an interdepartmental committee. Thus the President delegated authority to the Secretary of State for general foreign policy and program guidance and to the Secretary of Defense and the ECA for program formulation and operations. As the director of the Budget Bureau testified before the House Foreign Affairs Committee, the President's plan "recognizes the essential unity of our foreign policy and programs. . . . It retains ultimate control and direction of foreign-policy administration where they were placed by the Constitution—in the President." Partial decentralization and coordination at the departmental level with disputes decided by the President was the end result. It was all the more significant in view of the fact that American policy was reversing the relative positions of military and economic aid, the former growing larger at the expense of the latter.

Before Congress passed judgment in late summer, 1951, a number of groups studied the problem of foreign-aid administration. A report of the International Development Board, the Gray Report, the Committee for Economic Development, the Committee on the Present Danger, and the Brookings Institution all shared one recommendation in common: there should be a single agency (the ECA or a successor) in which would be centered the major responsibility for foreign economic aid. Congress probably did not need convincing, for its views of 1948 had, if anything, hardened. Congress differed with the President on the degree of centralization desirable, generally favoring the efficiency and orderliness it considered inherent in the omnibus agency idea. Congress also differed with the President on the method of coordination, being opposed to the "multi-headed command" of an interdepartmental committee. Indirectly, Congress expressed its distrust of the Department of State as *the* coordinating agency. The debates preceding the Mutual Security Act of 1951 suggest that Congress favored more autonomy and leadership responsibility for the central administrative agency than either the President or the Secretary of State found acceptable.

The Mutual Security Act replaced the ECA with the Mutual Security Agency, which had broader responsibilities than its predecessor. Approximately 7.5 billion dollars for economic and military aid was assigned to it for 1951–1952 and for 1952–1953. Not only was the director of the MSA in charge of the global economic aid programs; he exercised general supervision and coordinating authority over the military aid and technical assistance programs. Under the 1951 law, the Secretary of Defense retained the right to determine where planes, tanks, and guns are to be sent once manufactured. In all other respects, the director's authority was complete, subject, of course, to the powers or veto action of the President himself. The State Department continued to administer the technical assistance of the Point Four Program for underdeveloped countries. Congress explicitly abolished the interdepartmental committee on International Security Affairs. However, Mr. Harriman, the first director of MSA, quickly created an interdepartmental committee called the Mutual Assistance Advisory Committee, chaired this time not by a State Department official but by an assistant director of the MSA. Congress had omitted to include Treasury and the Office of Defense Mobilization in the new setup, so the Advisory Committee was constituted to include representatives from the MSA itself, and from State, Treasury, Defense, and the Office of Defense Mobilization.

It had become perfectly clear by this time that five agencies were interlocked in the foreign-aid program and that the line of demarcation between economic aid and military aid had become increasingly blurred. Foreign aid was squarely within the general framework of American foreign policy, which is the responsibility of the State Department. Loans and so-called counterpart funds of foreign currencies were involved; hence national monetary policy and Treasury had to be consulted. The Office of Defense Mobilization cannot be ignored since the civilian economy is affected by, and must provide, shipments of aid materials. Furthermore, the amount of military aid to be sent abroad depended on what Europe could produce for itself, which in turn depended on the economic aid programs of the MSA. The amount of military aid depended on what the Defense Department thought America could spare from its own military establishment, and its destination depended upon the points at which it was most needed. After European economic and military needs were determined, Treasury had to be consulted again on available national revenue. The purpose of the new interdepartmental committee was not so much to make decisions as to aid the director of MSA in his function of coordinator by participating in discussions leading up to decisions.

On paper at least, Congress had made an attempt to establish one-man responsibility for foreign-aid administration. It did not work out wholly on that basis, partly because during its first days—September to December, 1951—Mr. Harriman, the director, had to be in Europe to find out how much European nations were going to contribute to their own defense before he could begin to draw up estimates of American aid to be submitted to Congress in January, 1952. Though charged with central coordinating responsibilities, the director had operating responsibilities as head of the MSA. The quick return of an interdepartmental group was a tribute to the effectiveness of this device as a coordinating medium and an acknowledgment of the difficulties involved when one official or one agency is assigned sole responsibility for coordinating the interests and operations of five key agencies. In addition, the previous pattern of organization had been altered in that the State Department no longer had administrative responsibility for the military aid program as it had prior to the Mutual Security Act. Neither did it appoint the chairman of the interdepartmental committee. On the other hand, the first director of the MSA, Mr. Harriman, was also special assistant to the President for foreign affairs and sat regularly with the National Security Council. Coordination above the departmental level but just below the President was potentially possible, but it is doubtful whether the State Department retained fully its role as policy leader in the broad sense and also retained a check on how specific programs were coordinated with policy objectives.

SOME CONCLUSIONS FROM THIS EXPERIENCE

Obviously, the question of policy guidance versus operations or administration is continually troublesome. Once the function of formulating objectives is given to one agency while the function of executing directives is given to another, and once neither agency can control the other, there appears to be no neat formula for avoiding some serious conflict. This is even more true when policy-forming functions are divided on the same basis. Such formulas as "will provide leadership and coordination among the executive agencies" and provide "continuing leadership in the interdepartmental coordination of policy," employed to establish State Department superiority in foreign policy, simply do not create a structure of authority in which expectations and sanctions are clear. It seems clear from the foregoing history that one of the reasons for the "loose" structure of authority in the Executive Branch may be the attitude of Congress toward the agencies and agency heads involved. Creation of an almost autonomous agency (the ECA and Mutual Security) and a powerful director reflected Congressional mistrust of Dean Acheson and the Department of State, both as to policies and capacity to carry out a complex program. In any contest between a foreign-aid agency and the State Department, Congress will tend to favor the one whose values it shares at the moment. In the early days emphasis was on a business orientation which Congress felt the State Department could not supply. When a fairly long-term commitment is involved, as it was from 1948 to 1950, Congress will be more adamant on the subject of interagency relationships, desiring an arrangement which will facilitate its attempts to exert influence. Finally, Congress and the President tend to favor different coordination devices, the former leaning to the simplicity of one-man rule and the latter favoring interagency groups. One-man coordination makes Congressional oversight easier to achieve, while committees appeal to those who actually have to deal with several units on common problems—especially where lines of authority are not clear.

THE PRESENT ORGANIZATION OF FOREIGN AID ADMINISTRATION: THE FOREIGN OPERATIONS ADMINISTRATION

With the election of a Republican Congress and President, the way was paved for further changes. Conditions which had not been present for several years permitted a clarification of the role of the central foreign-aid agency and of its relationship to the State Department. President Eisenhower's Reorganization Plan 7, submitted to Congress in June, 1953, abolished the Mutual Security Agency and replaced it with the Foreign Operations Administration. The new agency discharges the functions and carries on the activities formerly assigned to the Mutual Security Agency, to the Technical Cooperation Administration, and to the Institute for Inter-American Affairs. Furthermore, the State Department also lost control of assistance to private relief organizations and arrangements for United States participation in United Nations Technical Assistance programs. Thus two trends noted above were continued: the State Department was stripped of all foreign-aid operations and all foreign-aid operations were finally consolidated in one unit. According to the reorganization decree, the Foreign Operations Administration is charged with "continuous supervision, general direction, and coordination of all foreign assistance programs, including the military assistance responsibilities vested in the Secretary of Defense," but the director would be mainly responsible for carrying out the policy decisions of three Cabinet officials— the Secretaries of Treasury, Defense, and, especially, State.

The new agency conducts global operations through a regional organization. Foreign aid to each of four areas is under a regional director. The four regions are the Far East; the Near East, South Asia, and Africa; Europe; and Latin America. Individual missions in particular nations report to the regional director, and the four regional directors report to the deputy director in Washington. Though consolidated, the military, economic, and technical aid programs are administered on a more decentralized basis. Most important, the director of this agency, though having the same title and salary as the director of Mutual Security, is *not* as powerful as was the latter. In effect, the Secretary of State can hire and fire the head of the Foreign Operations Administration. President Eisenhower's reorganization message made it clear that the director of FOA might have to take orders from "subordinate levels of the Department of State." Whereas the director of Mutual Security could speak authoritatively in the National Security Council, the Director of Foreign Operations can now only recommend. The regional directors work closely with regional officers in the State Department. Thus the Far Eastern regional director works with the Assistant Secretary of State for Far Eastern Affairs; the director for Near East, South Asia, and Africa works in liaison with the Assistant Secretary of State for Near Eastern, South

Asian, and African Affairs. The director for Europe will collaborate with the Assistant Secretary for Europe, and the director for Latin America will work with the Assistant Secretary of State for Inter-American Affairs. Plan 7 also abolished the office of Special Representative of the United States in Europe. The special representative was a powerful figure, combining under his jurisdiction the roles of chief of the Mutual Security Agency in Europe, United States Permanent Representative on the Council of NATO, and chief coordinator of all American diplomatic, military, and economic problems. He was responsible to the Secretaries of State, Defense, and Treasury and to the director of Mutual Security. Now there is a United States mission to NATO and European Regional Organizations. The chief of the mission reports to and receives instructions from the Secretary of State. It seems clear that, on paper at least, the reorganization provided for the distinctly superior voice of the State Department in the decision-making process. Thus the structure of authority for decisions on foreign aid was tightened and clarified. Coordination and communication were strengthened because of the greater control which can be exercised by the Secretary of State over the foreign-aid programs and because of the liaison between the regional directors of FOA and the regional Assistant Secretaries of State.

Reorganization does not necessarily accomplish all that is expected of it nor is it ever free of unwanted or unforeseen consequences. In June of 1953 Congress's mood was permissive and there was a will in the new executive leadership to make certain changes. Removal of all operating functions (except the exchange of foreign students) from the State Department implements a type of recommendation made by all groups which have studied executive organization from the Hoover Commission (1949) to the Rockefeller Committee (1953). However, the transfer of the Point Four Program to the new Foreign Operations Administration raised a question of the values and motives which would guide that program henceforth. Some critics felt that subsuming a technical, self-help program for underdeveloped areas under the general military-economic aid provided to America's allies would tend to destroy the spirit and techniques of the former. It was feared that the young technicians working for the Technical Cooperative Administration would be replaced by businessmen and military officials whose thinking and experience might be inappropriate. In particular, it was feared that the programs for improving living conditions in needy areas might be tied into or completely dominated by military considerations.

► THE ORGANIZATION OF "PSYCHOLOGICAL WARFARE"

THE OPERATIONS COORDINATING BOARD

The response of organizational developments to the increasing importance of what have been loosely termed "psychological techniques" of foreign policy illustrates once again the difficulties inherent in the proliferation of functions in the Executive Branch and also the close relationship between underlying policy assumptions and administrative structure.

In July, 1951, President Truman created the *Psychological Strategy Board*—henceforth to be responsible for the coordination of psychological warfare. What led to this move was the discovery of a familiar condition, namely, that while a number of agencies were engaged in activities closely related to psychological warfare, none had primary responsibility for developing a coherent program and for coordinating various operations. The State Department operated the Voice of America and an expanding international information program. The three armed services were engaged in psychological warfare geared to military functions. The Economic Cooperation Administration and other agencies had their own information programs. The Central Intelligence Agency was conducting secret operations abroad designed to undermine morale in nations behind the iron curtain and was otherwise carrying on activities essential to any over-all strategy employing essentially political techniques. Lack of coordination and duplication resulted. Operating programs were not effectively linked to foreign-policy objectives. When the question of a solution for this problem arose, a controversy ensued. Several high officials felt that a separate, powerful, independent operating agency was necessary. This was the counterpart of the argument for the same type of agency to administer foreign aid. Others, particularly State Department leaders, resisted this plan. The State Department wanted to continue to control its own operations and to be the chief coordinator of related programs via an interdepartmental committee chaired by one of its responsible officers. It is not surprising that a compromise was evolved.

The members of the board were the director of the Central Intelligence Agency (who is chairman), the Under Secretary of State, the Secretary of Defense, and the Senior Staff of the National Security Council. A delegate from the Joint Chiefs of Staff was assigned to the board to "insure that its objectives, policies and programs shall be related to approved plans for military operations." According to its directive, the board's mission was to report "on its evaluation of the national psychological operations, including implementation of approved objectives, policies, and programs by the departments and agencies concerned." Functions of the board were to be carried out by a director who was not a member of the board but who was responsible to it. He was aided by a staff of seventy recruited from the State Department, the Defense Department, and the Central Intelligence Agency. The Psychological Strategy Board had no operating responsibilities. These were retained separately by the agencies which comprised it. Neither the director nor the board had command authority over these agencies. Therefore coordination had to be achieved by voluntary means.

Apparently the Psychological Strategy Board was not completely successful. A Senate special committee investigating the information and propaganda activities of the United States government reported in June, 1953, that the board was not fulfilling its major purposes, that the State Department, the Defense Department, and the Central Intelligence Agency still went "their separate ways" and that conflicting approaches characterized the board's operations. Meanwhile President Eisenhower had appointed a Committee on International Information Activities to re-examine thoroughly the whole problem. This committee—named the Jackson Committee for its chairman William Jackson, an official with wide experience in political warfare generally and in the CIA in particular—began 250 hearings on January 30, 1953, and reported to the President early in July of the same year. As the committee began its study, the new Republican administration was putting great emphasis on psychological strategy and many of its high officials obviously believed in the possibility of great psychological victories cheaply bought.

One of the things which the Jackson group did was to inquire into the nature of psychological warfare to discover what could and could not be accomplished. In the end, the assumption that there was some simple magical formula for psychological triumphs was pretty well exploded. The committee openly criticized what it regarded as the misconception behind the creation of the Psychological Strategy Board: that "psychological strategy" exists apart from official policies and actions and should be handled by a separate agency. Rather, it was concluded, there is a psychological aspect or implication to every diplomatic, economic, or military policy or action. Every significant act of the state regarding other states has its psychological effect. Therefore the psychological aspect of foreign policy is the responsibility of all relevant departments or agencies and is very much bound up with the conduct and demeanor of the *whole* federal government. Except for propaganda, the committee felt there were no uniquely psychological techniques of foreign policy. Propaganda unsupported by various forms of national power was condemned as potentially ineffective. If propaganda is successful it does not always buy cheap victories: inciting the satellite of an enemy to revolt involves great risks.

The committee recommended the establishment of an *Operations Coordinating Board* to "coordinate the development by departments and agencies of detailed operational plans to carry out national security policies." In addition to ensuring that psychological aspects be given due consideration, the new board would attempt to bring together diplomatic, economic, and military facets of foreign policy, thus filling the gap between the formulation of general objectives and detailed actions. Hence the previous assumption of a separate, definable psychological strategy would be replaced by an assumption that the psychological function would be served if the critical functions of conceiving, developing, and implementing high national strategy were properly coordinated.

Following the Jackson recommendations, President Eisenhower directed the establishment of the *Operations Coordinating Board*. Several organizational differences between the new agency and its predecessor should be noted. It appears that the Operations Coordinating Board is an arm of the National Security Council in much the same way as the Central Intelligence Agency. Under the new setup, the Under Secretary of State is chairman, whereas the director of the CIA was chairman of the older board. There is now no special representative from the Joint Chiefs of Staff. Others on the present board include the Deputy Secretary of Defense, the deputy director of the Foreign Operations Administration, the director of the CIA, plus an executive officer and a small staff.

By September, 1953, it seemed evident that the psychological aspects of foreign policy were no longer completely in the hands of professional propagandists but had largely been made the explicit responsibility of every official involved in the formulation of policy. To make sure that this does not result in further confusion and omission is the task of the Operations Coordinating Board. It is too early to tell at this writing exactly what the precise duties of the board will be—partly because its activities will doubtless remain insulated from public view. But it appears likely that it will have responsibility for initiating new programs. For example, President Eisenhower's effective gesture of offering—and delivering—food parcels to a point on the border of the Soviet Zone of Berlin in the summer of 1953 might be a good example of what the new agency may do. Perhaps such an agency would also be concerned with anticipating and, if possible, counteracting, the adverse reaction abroad to such occurrences as the execution of the Rosenbergs, convicted atomic spies.

THE UNITED STATES INFORMATION AGENCY

By 1953, the United States had built up a sizable information and propaganda program. The Voice of America represented a heavy investment in a world-wide network of high-powered short-wave transmitters beamed to the Soviet Union, Eastern Europe, the Far East, and many other places. In addition, some two hundred information centers in sixty-three countries had been created to provide American motion pictures, books, periodicals, and official press releases for foreign peoples. These programs were conceived and executed under the International Information Administration within the State Department. However, information activities were also carried on by other units in the department as well as by what was then the Mutual Security Agency. Various Congressional investigating groups and the Jackson Committee were highly critical of the organizational setup of the government's information program. Apart from criticisms of the content of the various informational devices, a five-year history showed that there had been five different directors and, essentially, five different strategies employed, in addition to substantial amounts of duplication and to lack of coordination between propaganda experts and regular diplomatic officers. In April, 1953, the President's Government Reorganization Committee (under the chairmanship of Nelson Rockefeller) had made a strong recommendation—paralleling a later one by the Jackson Committee—for consolidation of all information and propaganda operations in a single agency independent of the State Department. Accordingly, President Eisenhower submitted to Congress Reorganization Plan 8, establishing the United States Information Agency. The new agency was given jurisdiction over the information-propaganda tasks formerly performed by the International Information Administration, the Technical Cooperation Administration, the Division of Occupied Areas (all in the State Department) and the Mutual Security Agency (now, of course, the Overseas Operations Administration).

The United States Information Agency is an appendage of the National Security Council and it reports to the President through the Council. When it was first established, President Eisenhower directed a member of the White House staff, Charles Jackson (a member of the Jackson Committee referred to above, not to be confused with William Jackson, the chairman) to oversee the functioning of this new unit. The wording of Reorganization Plan 8 also makes it clear that "the Secretary of State shall provide to the director of the new agency on a current basis full guidance concerning the foreign policy of the United States." In particular, any broadcasts and written materials which attempt to set forth the general position of the United States will be controlled by the Secretary of State.

Public Affairs Officers—as those with information and propaganda duties are called—will be attached to diplomatic missions abroad. Though such officers will receive their instructions from the director of the Information Agency in Washington, they will in fact be under the jurisdiction of the chief of mission. In cases of conflict, the latter's judgment will prevail. Information officers may appeal to the director of the Information Agency and presumably differences which cannot be reconciled will be submitted to the White House and the National Security Council. Principal advice on the use of psychological techniques in a particular country will come from the chief of the American diplomatic mission in that country and a "country team" of information experts working on the spot. In the case of regional and global ideological appeals, content and strategy will be largely controlled from Washington.

► THE PROBLEM OF COORDINATION IN THE EXECUTIVE BRANCH

In the preceding pages, the term "coordination" has appeared over and over again. It has been used to explain several kinds of relationships and problems, and its importance in decision making and execution has been stressed. There would seem to be no better way of drawing together some of the major organizational factors discussed in this chapter than by further analyzing the nature of coordination and viewing in retrospect the devices by which it is attempted in the Executive Branch. This may be regarded as an extension of the earlier discussion of coordination and communication (Chapter Three), in a more specific context.

THE NATURE OF COORDINATION

Basically, the reason that coordination assumes such overriding importance is that all foreign-policy functions and governmental functions relating to foreign policy cannot be centralized in one executive agency with a clear line of authority running from top to bottom. Instead, a rather complicated allocation of power and responsibility is required, accompanied by an elaborate division of labor among a large number of agencies which have a wide variety of functions. From this organization of activities is expected to come responsible formulation of policies, sound decisions, and effective, unified programs of implementation. Ideally, these results should be accomplished when and as needed, with the most efficient use of policy-making resources possible. If time were not significant and there were an inexhaustible supply of all policy-making resources available, such qualifications would be unnecessary. In essence, the foregoing means that foreign policy and foreign-policy problems are broken down into component aspects for special treatment. Given the nature of contemporary American policy, it is almost impossible to make the breakdown so neat that no frayed edges and overlapping occur. Often a clear division of function between two agencies is not possible. Furthermore, before sound decision and effective action can result, the component aspects and parts must be put back together again. Therefore, coordination, considered both as outcome and as process, is necessary to mobilize the requisite authority for the performance of functions at any point in the decision-making and execution process, to ensure that all relevant information (this would include the various aspects of policy, i.e., domestic, economic, and the like) is available and taken into account, to avoid or minimize waste and duplication of effort, and to avoid or minimize stoppages in the total policy process.

"Coordination" unfortunately is a word with many meanings. In practice, the term refers to a series of connecting links: from a simple exchange of information to the resolution of conflict between two agencies or points of view; from mere exercise of leadership in securing voluntary collaboration to the making of decisions. Voluntary coordination really involves the pooling of authority or agreement by two or more agencies of equal rank which are responsible in turn to a higher authority. All problems of coordination have their peculiar difficulties, but perhaps the most difficult situation exists when one agency has the primary interest in an area of policy, while other agencies of equal or superior rank perform functions related to that interest. Where an agency has clear command powers, the situation is not so troublesome. A basic fact about the Executive Departments in the American system is that for the most part they do not have command powers over each other. Matters are further complicated by the fact that presidential delegations of authority may be unclear and that Congressional delegations may be overlapping or conflicting. Jurisdictional disputes hence are due not only to bureaucratic rivalry and imperialism but to faulty verbal allocations of responsibilities. It is sometimes true that such ambiguities are deliberate, although the resulting confusion puts a heavy burden on decision making. At any rate, the real trouble comes when, for any reason, two agencies are given identical authority, status, and responsibility or when this is a reasonable interpretation by both sides. Competition automatically follows. Jurisdictional disputes can scarcely be avoided. Nonetheless, the absence of authority to settle disputes, or the absence of clear channels of appeal to this authority, intensifies the delay and conflict.

In this chapter, three general types of coordination in the Executive Branch have been discussed. First, coordination by the President himself, commonly called central coordination. This implies, of course, power of decision by the President as chief executive, commander in chief, head of state, director of foreign policy, and so on. The President may write a letter, issue an executive order, speak to someone personally, or have a member of his personal staff intervene. Second is staff coordination, a reflection of the President as an institution rather than as a person. Staff coordination is generally accomplished by agencies in the Executive Office without power of command. The Special Assistant to the President for National Security Affairs and the Bureau of the Budget are examples. The third type is line coordination at the departmental level where one agency assumes responsibility for coordination of policy matters in which it has primary interest. Implicit in the three types are two methods of achieving coordination, one by exercise of higher authority, the other by voluntary cooperation under the leadership of one among equals. It will be found in most cases that the two methods are mixed; authority rests more firmly on agreement and agreement must be provided by authority.

Coordination, as defined, is required when policies are being formulated for decision by the President or Congress and when programs are being drawn up and carried out. Coordination must take place on all levels from the lowest units in a department to the President. The various layers of coordination correspond more or less to the hierarchal pattern of decision-making authority mentioned in Chapter Three. It is precisely because authority is not centralized at its various layers that coordination is necessary. The layers of coordination are interdependent in that each will be more effective in proportion to the effectiveness of coordination below it. As already explained, for example, the State Department will be less able to act as coordinator of general foreign-policy formation if it cannot speak with a single voice, clarity of purpose, and proper mobilization of its internal resources.

When line coordination fails, staff and central coordination become difficult indeed, so much so that one of the chief tasks of the latter is to see to it that favorable conditions exist for the former.

THE DANGERS OF A LACK OF COORDINATION

There is little doubt that failures of coordination have been costly to the soundness of American foreign policy and to the nation's security in the postwar period. That they continue to crop up indicates both weaknesses in machinery and inadequate use of existing machinery.

In March, 1951, Secretary of Defense Marshall spoke publicly about his concern over the letdown in the national mobilization effort. The director of the Office of Defense Mobilization, Charles Wilson, publicly contradicted Marshall, saying that America was sufficiently rearmed to frighten any aggressor. After several days of controversy, the President tried to explain that there was really no conflict. Nine months later, Mr. Wilson differed, again publicly, with the Joint Chiefs of Staff as to the level of Russian military production and its relation to American military production. Assistant Secretary of State Dean Rusk had to fly to Tokyo in November, 1951, to iron out conflicts with the Defense Department over the administrative agreement concerning rights and obligations of United States military forces in Japan after the Japanese Peace Treaty took effect. Apparently in this case the National Security Council did not function as a coordinating device. Secretary of Treasury Snyder attended the Rome meeting of the North Atlantic Treaty Organization in November, 1951, to undo some of the damage done by American civil and military representatives of "varying degrees of authority" in promising to European nations varying amounts of aid. Apparently officials had secured production commitments from the Europeans based on the assumption that the bill for imported machinery would be footed by the United States. Some 1.5 billions in authorized foreign aid was bogged down at one time because while the director of the Mutual Security Agency was in Europe negotiating with the members of NATO, the deputy director of the agency could not act—for the simple reason that the director had designated the chairman of the Mutual Assistance Advisory Committee "to act in my behalf in coordination and general policy formation." Supposedly the committee was only advisory, yet the deputy director of the MSA could not act without a five-agency agreement.

One of the most dangerous by-products of lack of coordination has occurred in the acquisition and stockpiling of stategic materials. It will be remembered that, in Chapter Two, shortages of strategic materials were mentioned as a vulnerable point in the American economy. Under the Critical Materials Stockpiling Act of 1946 some sixteen executive agencies were given responsibilities for acquiring scarce resources and promoting the development of new and alternate sources of supply. The Munitions Board in the Defense Department was given a special assignment in planning and follow-up. Actual operations were placed under the jurisdiction of the Emergency Procurement Service of the General Services Administration. An interdepartmental committee on stockpiling was established to facilitate coordination. In July, 1951, a Senate preparedness subcommittee reported a "desperate" shortage of strategic tungsten among other items and accused the Department of the Army and the Munitions Board of playing blindman's buff with each other. This was only part of the problem. Things became bad enough by early 1952 so that a university research group was called in to review the entire program. Certainly one of the things which had happened was that some of the major agencies involved were making decisions in isolation, were working at cross-purposes, and were leaving crucial tasks undone. Several agencies were carrying on economic development operations abroad—the State Department, the ECA and the MSA, and the Export-Import Bank, for example—which were not apparently geared into a coherent, total picture of American needs. There was no central place where foreign needs under the aid program could be systematically reviewed and coordinated. The purchase of scarce materials abroad certainly had an important impact on the domestic economies of nations who were being given economic aid by the United States; yet the agencies responsible for the latter were not always consulted by the agencies making purchases. It has been difficult to carry out commitments to other states regarding strategic materials because export quotas are established in one set of agencies and export licenses are granted by the Department of Commerce, which has been in a position to delay this particular implementation of economic foreign policy. American agencies have competed against each other in the acquisition of strategic items, creating artificial shortages and high prices. Releases from the domestic stockpile have not always been allowed on the basis of the nation's total security position.

These few random examples suggest that coordination has at once become more difficult and more vital. The number of points at which it is essential have multiplied. More executive units are directly or indirectly concerned than ever before. Almost any problem of magnitude will be found to touch from five to twenty-five agencies. Foreign-policy programs require teamwork. So long as the time equation is significant, delays in execution will be costly. Six months can mean a marked change in the nation's political power position. Foreign policy and domestic policy must be coordinated. At the moment there is no central place where this is attempted. Economic and political aspects of foreign policy must be coordinated, but there is no central device for this. Military policy and foreign policy must be coordinated. Field operations and programs require meshing as in the case of rearming through NATO and economic recovery through mutual aid. The impact of multilateral relations and conference diplomacy has been tremendous.* Each year over

*A. Macmahon, "The Administration of Foreign Affairs," *American Political Science Review,* September, 1951, pp. 857–859.

four hundred meetings take place at which America's position must be officially stated. Twenty-four agencies besides the State Department have connections with permanent international bodies and the United Nations. The danger lies, of course, in "the tendency to express different views on related issues at different places."* All of these coordination points represent *potential* weaknesses in foreign-policy formation and execution.

DEVICES OF COORDINATION REVIEWED

Against this background on the nature of coordination and the dangers inherent in failure, a summary look at the coordination devices in the Executive Branch is in order. The President himself can directly and indirectly influence coordination. Directly he can enhance it in his role as chairman of the National Security Council, by calling *ad hoc* Cabinet committee meetings to break log jams, and by personally intervening promptly and vigorously in jurisdictional disputes. Indirectly, the President can influence favorably the conditions prerequisite to effective coordination. To the extent that he controls the relations between himself and Congress, he can facilitate the operation of coordination devices. The creation and abolition of interdepartmental committees may become a tactic in executive-legislative warfare. For example, the conflict over foreign-aid administration, which came to a climax in 1951, hardly made life easier for the International Security Affairs Committee. Dynamic presidential leadership can also contribute to unity in the Executive Branch itself and can strengthen the exercise of leadership coordination by Executive Departments. A minimum unity and leadership coordination tend to go together because Cabinet agencies of equal rank must be persuaded that it is both safe and necessary for them to accept the leadership of one of their number on certain aspects of public policy.

If the potentialities of the personal leadership of the President are to be even partially realized and if presidential functions are to be discharged, staff arrangements are of enormous importance. The job, to reiterate, has grown too big for the President to manage himself, no matter how capable he is. It seems clear that the placement of the National Security Council in the Executive Office as well as the establishment of the Office of Special Adviser (foreign affairs) has strengthened the President's over-all staff help. The role of the National Security Council is still evolving, and much depends on whether it continues to grow in stature and effectiveness. Clearly the council has moved beyond the original conception of its function in the National Security Act of 1947, which was that of a meeting ground for State Department–Defense Department coordination under direct presidential leadership. Fortunately, legislative modifications in 1949 restored greater presidential control over the membership. Nothing will subvert presidential power more quickly than the existence of staff agencies constituted and given special prerogatives by Congress. That the council has moved steadily toward

* *Ibid.*

a concern with general foreign-policy matters and with procedures which affect those matters can be seen in two recent examples. First, Congress in June, 1951, gave the Security Council the power to make exceptions to the so-called Kem clause, which prohibits the recipients of American aid from using the goods obtained to trade with nations in the Soviet orbit. Second, it was the council which drew up the President's order in September, 1951, creating more stringent controls on the release of security information by federal agencies. The order is administered by a subcommittee of the Inter-departmental Committee on Internal Security, which is under the council's jurisdiction.

However, the Security Council has apparently not served to coordinate adequately economic foreign policy or foreign policy, grand strategy, and national mobilization. An enlargement of the council's Planning Board may enable it to tighten the contacts between the Joint Chiefs, the Office of Defense Mobilization, and the Foreign Operations Administration at the staff level. Staff improvements for the council may also enable it to establish effective liaison with key interdepartmental committees. It has been suggested also that a permanent vice-chairman of the council might enhance continuity and assist the President in providing *genuine policy leadership*.* Until recently the executive secretary did not really function as a policy official but only as a go-between connecting the White House with the council. A go-between is an essential requirement, to be sure, yet an official having higher status as a policy representative of the President might enable the latter to exercise positive leadership when the council is deadlocked, as it was in 1951 1952 over a general policy on the Near East. President Eisenhower's appointment of his special assistant for national security affairs, Robert Cutler, as executive secretary of the council and chairman of the Planning Board may correct this situation. In addition, under present arrangements, another special assistant of the President, Charles Jackson, oversees the operations of the International Information Agency which now reports to the council.

While the President's staff help, personal and otherwise, has been strengthened since the creation of the Executive Office in 1939, it is still true that the Executive Office lacks unity, that relationships between the Executive Office staff and staff units at other levels of the government are frequently tenuous, and that even strong Presidents cannot provide sufficient positive policy leadership.† It has been repeatedly suggested that a chief staff secretary for the Executive Office is necessary—someone who could help bring about integration and who could stimulate effective interstaff contacts.‡ During President Eisenhower's first year, Sherman Adams, assistant to the

* Brookings Institution, *op. cit.,* p. xxv.
† George A. Graham, "The Presidency and the Executive Office of the President," *Journal of Politics,* November, 1950, pp. 604–606.
‡ See the review of such recommendations and the suggestive reformulation of the idea in Graham, *loc. cit.,* pp. 599–603, 606–612, 613–618.

President, emerged as a chief of staff for the White House. He functioned as organizer of *expertise* for the administration, overseer of non-Cabinet departments, and as primary presidential intermediary. Also on the President's staff are now several members devoted to liaison with Congress and various executive agencies. Professor George A. Graham of Princeton University has argued that improvement in positive presidential leadership could be achieved by clustering departments in major policy areas under an executive secretary, thus establishing a new echelon of command.* Existing arrangements would not appear to solve these difficulties. The new Office of Special Adviser could conceivably develop into a kind of chief of staff for foreign affairs, but it touches only part of the problem and violates the principle that staff agencies should not be functional specialists. Foreign-policy coordination now involves so many agencies, and is so intermixed with domestic policy, that some means of re-examining departmental assignments in the light of changing foreign-policy problems would seem to be necessary. In particular, to use the words of the Brookings report, the "lack of any central secretariat in the Executive Office of the President for the more important standing interdepartmental committees appears to be a gap in the governmental machinery of the United States."† Logically, such a secretariat should be in the Bureau of the Budget, which increasingly acts as a channel of appeal to the President and prepares administrative directives for foreign-affairs agencies. The director of Mutual Security in the Executive Office answered the need for coordination of foreign-aid programs at the executive staff level.‡ In the preceding administration, the fact that the special adviser to the President and the director of MSA were the same person undoubtedly aided integration, but it also lessened the chances of the special adviser's becoming a staff secretary as mentioned above. Conceivably, the special adviser and the directors of MSA and ODM working informally and through the National Security Council could have achieved effective coordination; yet this would have hardly been a long solution because of the temporary nature of the MSA and ODM. Ultimately, shifting responsibility for the coordination of domestic economic policy and foreign economic policy to the Council of Economic Advisers, together with a broadening of the functions of the Security Council, might suffice if buttressed by a staff secretary to enhance unity in the Executive Office and to cement interstaff relations.

From what has been said above, it is obvious that interdepartmental committees are a primary device for coordination in foreign policy. The success of these committees is uneven. There seems to be no agreed philosophy with respect to their organization and operation and no administrative

---

* *Ibid.*, pp. 618 ff. This is somewhat related to the Brookings discussion of a new executive department for foreign affairs modeled on the Defense Department Report, *The Administration of Foreign Affairs and Overseas Operations,* pp. 71–120.

† Brookings Institution, *op. cit.*, p. xxx.

‡ *Ibid.*, p. 231.

regulation of them from the top. Weaknesses have become evident: jurisdictional disputes have been allowed to fester or committees themselves have tried to arbitrate disputes; committees have given advice when they were supposed to decide, and vice versa; departmental control of policy may slip from politically responsible officials to career officials; there is a tendency to erect an intermediate body between the President and the executive agencies; it has been difficult to avoid duplication and competition; and areas of policy have been left uncovered by the committees as the nature of policy problems has changed. The coherent functioning of a real system of interdepartmental committees has probably suffered most from weaknesses in the internal organization of departments and from the fact that the President has lacked authority and staff to control their establishment, functions, and conflicts.

Interdepartmental committees require certain minimum conditions if they are to achieve effective coordination. Primarily, they must be given a clear assignment of subject matter. Normally, their chief function must be to advise the department whose interests and coordination responsibilities are paramount, but on occasion they may serve the National Security Council or the President directly. Jurisdictional disputes must be settled quickly and there must be prescribed methods of appeal to higher authority. Departmental organization should be geared to the committee system so that representatives can speak authoritatively and the department's resources are focused on the policy problems at hand. It will help greatly if the department's role is clearly specified. A troublesome factor in committees dealing with foreign policy has been that the State Department's relationship to other agencies has not been consistently, precisely defined by the President. The interdepartmental committee is essentially a device for helping the department with primary responsibility for an area of policy to create line coordination. Finally, there is no substitute for a skillful committee chairman and a competent staff. These conditions have not always prevailed or prevailed evenly through the interdepartmental structure.

Another coordination device is the single agency, but this may possess varying powers. First, the State Department is responsible for whatever coordination is necessary among line agencies in the formulation of general foreign policy. Second, the Foreign Operations Administration represents an attempt to centralize *related operations* in one agency with command powers. Third, the Central Intelligence Agency and the Operations Coordinating Board are staff agencies without command powers. Single-agency coordination, therefore, has its troublesome side. If no command power exists, there is risk of no enforcement of responsibilities. If an operating agency has command powers it may run into conflict with the agency which formulates general policy, as in the case of the ECA and the State Department. The problem then becomes twofold: to draw as practical a line as possible between the two, with effective mechanisms provided for joint decision when a given aspect of policy refuses to lend itself to such a separation, and to provide the general policy agency with information on day-to-day operations so it can judge whether further reconciliation is necessary. The Mutual Security Agency was a temporary answer to some questions raised earlier in this chapter on the role of the State Department.* It must be noted, however, that the MSA did not represent a full commitment even temporarily to the single-agency idea. Certain functions which are closely connected with the foreign-aid program were left for the most part to other agencies: the Point Four Program to the State Department, export controls to the Commerce Department, and procurement and development of strategic materials to the Munitions Board and others.† These forms of single-agency coordination once again emphasize the role of interdepartmental committees.

A WARNING ON COORDINATION AS A MAGIC CURE-ALL

Mere devices of government are never the whole story. It is comforting to think about "solving" organizational problems by tinkering, by adding an agency, or issuing a directive. And it is easy to blame policy failures entirely on a lack of coordinating methods or on inferior ones. Actually, coordination will never be any better or worse than the participants make it. A General Marshall as Secretary of Defense almost automatically enhances coordination with the Joint Chiefs and the State Department. Differences in personalities and attitudes can cause a given device to operate very differently. Then, too, most of the individuals who staff the agencies under discussion are experts or specialists who tend to resist general control of policy—which is one of the purposes of coordination—and who tend to resent having to defer to their equals. Specialists are likely to make a particular point of trying to maintain the utmost freedom in their future activities. Chapter Three stressed the fact that coordination requires an integration of perspective. One important aspect of this, having to do with smooth cooperation, is the necessity for participants to adopt certain attitudes toward others. Self-restraint, a broad view of the total policy-making process, a willingness to make concessions, and an ability to draw subtle distinctions are required. If voluntary coordination among agencies of equal rank is to work, the primary interests of one will have to be recognized and, conversely, no one agency can insist it has a primary interest in everything. This applies from the secretary down to the lowest departmental divisions.

Aside from organizational devices per se, a balance of forces working for and against coordination exists at any moment in time. The balance will be affected by the degree to which the centrifugal tendencies alluded to in the last chapter are kept under control. Psychological pressures operating directly on interdepartmental committees and departments are not always conducive

---

* For a fuller discussion of this problem, see the next chapter and Chapters 4 and 6 of the Brookings Report, *The Administration of Foreign Affairs and Overseas Operations.*

† Compare with the recommendation of the Brookings Report, p. xvi.

to cooperation. Every so often, problems will back up in the decision-making mechanism, thus inducing a desire to short-circuit routine processes. Budget uncertainties can weaken coordination because of reluctance to commit further time to an activity which may be discontinued. Factors working for coordination are harder to identify, but two may be singled out. First, the President's great power can be unleashed at any time to open up road blocks at points in the decision-making process. Second, foreign policy has become so complicated and risky that coordination has become a matter of individual agency self-interest and also a protective covering for the top-level, responsible policy makers. In the case of major decisions, collective agreement is easier to bear and to defend.

► SUMMARY

At the beginning it was stated that this chapter would consist of a brief sketch of the organizational setting for foreign-policy decision making in the United States—the structural boundaries within which the process flows in the Executive Branch. No such brief analysis can do justice to its magnitude and complexity. The number of agencies whose functions and contributions must be welded together before policy can be decided and implemented is greater than anyone would have imagined fifteen years ago. Perhaps the reader would do well to note certain basic features of the structure. Though large and in some respects unwieldy, it is delicate nonetheless, and when one remembers the heavily judgmental character of policy making it is easy to visualize the points of vulnerability. Part of the structure involves help to the President in his specific tasks, another part consists of repositories of delegations of authority from Congress and the President. The number, location, and clarity of these delegations are important. Huge operations such as foreign aid and political warfare must be carried out as well as policy planning and formulation. Communication and coordination at the executive staff level and departmental level must be achieved. The National Security Council, the Foreign Operations Administration, the Central Intelligence Agency, the Department of Defense, and the Department of State would appear to be the agencies of central significance.

Above all, the decision-making structure is in transition. The new roles and relationships of the core agencies illustrate the nature of this transition. Obviously the organization of policy making is in process of adapting to new circumstances. The tentative administrative solutions and the various patterns of coordination suggest a period of trial and error. In short, America is meeting new problems of policy and new problems of policy making. It has only been in the last five years that the Executive Branch has been questioned from the standpoint of its adequacy in a revolutionary international situation.

Thus far, the executive organization for foreign-policy making has been viewed from the top down, so to speak. In the next chapter, the view will be reversed: analysis will concentrate on the departmental level and below. A key question to be kept in mind is this: How do the organization and operation of the State Department square with its role in the Executive Branch generally and in the coordination mediums in which it participates?

▶ SELECTED BIBLIOGRAPHY

The following are indispensable background reading on problems of foreign-policy organization in the Executive Branch: H. H. Bundy and J. G. Rogers, *The Organization of the Government for the Conduct of Foreign Affairs*, Task Force Report on Foreign Affairs (Washington, D.C., Government Printing Office, 1949); Commission on the Organization of the Executive Branch of the Government (the Hoover Commission), *Foreign Affairs: A Report to Congress* (Washington, D.C., Government Printing Office, 1949); The Brookings Institution, *The Administration of Foreign Affairs and Overseas Operations* (Washington, D.C., Government Printing Office, 1951). A first-rate description and analysis of executive agencies involved in foreign policy is J. L. McCamy, *The Administration of American Foreign Affairs* (New York, Alfred A. Knopf, Inc., 1950), Chaps. 3, 5–7, 12, 13, 15. An excellent introduction to the problems of intelligence can be found in S. Kent, *Strategic Intelligence* (Princeton, N. J., Princeton University Press, 1949), which can be read profitably in conjuction with R. Hilsman, Jr., "Intelligence and Policy Making in Foreign Affairs," *World Politics*, October, 1952. The most adequate single volume on international information agencies is E. Barrett, *Truth Is Our Weapon* (New York, Funk & Wagnalls Company, 1953). A. Macmahon critically examines the literature concerning American foreign policy formation and execution in "The Administration of Foreign Affairs," *American Political Science Review*, September, 1951. Perhaps the wisest book on the general subject matter of this chapter is Macmahon's *Administration in Foreign Affairs* (University, Alabama, University of Alabama Press, 1953.)

CHAPTER SEVEN

THE ORGANIZATION AND FUNCTIONS OF THE STATE DEPARTMENT

Intradepartmental Communication • Communication within the Executive Branch • State Department Relations with Congress • State Department Communication with the American People • How Routine Work Is Done in the State Department • Conclusion • Selected Bibliography

It is safe to say that no more superficially clear or fundamentally ambiguous agency exists within the structure of American government than the Department of State. "I want to assure you," somewhat plaintively declared Loy W. Henderson, veteran Foreign Service officer, recently American Ambassador to Iran, "that we do have well-established foreign policies. We have long-term foreign policies which are as stable and as permanent as the traditions and way of life of the American people. We are also constantly formulating shorter-term policies in order to meet the ever-shifting world situation."*
On the other hand, New York *Times* reporter James Reston, describing the move of the department into its new building, felt it necessary to assure his readers that "Foggy Bottom . . . is not an intellectual condition but a geographical area down by the Potomac."† And Hugh Gibson, who filled many important diplomatic posts, noted that "the evil is that under our system the Department is unable to perform its essential mission. By any sane standard that mission is to look ahead, foresee developments, and plan for the future. Under existing conditions this cannot be done because there are no facilities for determining in advance what course the Department can take."‡

What, then, are the problems confronted by this department, whose head, personnel, and organizational structure have been subjected since the war to an almost continuous torrent of criticism and abuse from right and left, from official and nonofficial, from top and bottom, from home and abroad?

---

* State Department Publication 2651. (Nowhere in this pamphlet does Mr. Henderson explain just what either the "long-term" or "shorter-term" policies are.)
† New York *Times,* May 31, 1947.
‡ Hugh Gibson, *The Road to Foreign Policy* (New York, Doubleday & Company, 1944), p. 141.

Because the organization of the State Department and its relation to other governmental agencies dealing with foreign policy are so complex, the system of analysis deliberately chosen for this chapter is a series of problems of communication: communications within the department itself, within the Executive Branch of the government, between the department and Congress, with the public at large, and, finally, with foreign governments. From this focus should emerge clear conceptions of the pattern of power and responsibility operating within the department, a pattern which does not automatically emerge from the most detailed study of organizational charts and job descriptions. An accent on communications may also aid in placing in proper perspective the role of the State Department in the over-all formulation and execution of American foreign policy by the United States government.

▶ INTRADEPARTMENTAL COMMUNICATION

GEOGRAPHIC AND FUNCTIONAL DIVISIONS

Perhaps the most basic cleavage within the State Department has been between the group of offices set up on a geographic basis and those organized on a functional pattern. By the turn of the century the latter had begun to emerge alongside the traditional organization, which had been in terms of countries and areas with which the United States had relations. An Assistant Secretary of State for Economic Affairs appeared after World War I; two decades later he became an Under Secretary. Within these new economic functional units were located offices dealing with such matters as commercial and trade policy, economic planning, aviation, petroleum, telecommunications, and shipping.

The second functional branch, that of social relations, came into existence later—just before World War II—with the establishment of the Division of Cultural Relations, but its growth was even more spectacular. By the end of the war various units were dealing with exchange of persons, motion pictures, radio propaganda, health, scientific cooperation, and the like. In terms of units and personnel almost half the department had become functionally orientated.

The increase in the amount of activity outside the previously normal diplomatic pattern was an inevitable consequence of the augmented world position and responsibility of the United States. At the same time, relations between this government and other governments still demanded an organizational line from the embassy abroad, through the geographic divisions in the department to the secretary and his staff at the top. The geographic divisions had themselves added economic advisers, specialists on particular countries, at the very time that the functional offices were doing the same. How much autonomy, therefore, should the newer functional offices have? Should they have primary responsibility for planning the broad aspects of policy within a given field, leaving specific regional and national implementation to the political officers? Or should they serve as technical advisers to the political officers, who would have the final power of policy determination?

In the absence of definitive answers to these questions, coordination, communications, and cooperation were hesitant and faulty at the lower levels. As a result the ultimate reconciliation of conflicting points of view as to what the policy of the United States should be was forced upon the top-level desks or even into the secretary's office. Moreover, the problem in communications between the functional and geographic branches complicated relationships between the department as a whole and other agencies of the government, which also thought they were charged with the expression of American policy abroad within their own particularly defined provinces. The practice of the geographic divisions, within which Foreign Service officers naturally formed a high percentage, was to regard themselves as the center of power and responsibility in the determination of policy. Communication with the functional divisions was looked upon by them as largely a matter of courtesy, to provide information to these divisions on what decisions the geographic units had taken or were about to take.

After World War II the Hoover Commission entered this struggle. It was charged by law with examining the organization of the Executive Branch of the government and making recommendations for improvement. Its report on the State Department represented a fairly complete victory for the point of view of the geographic divisions. They were designated the "action units," while the function of the Assistant Secretary for Economic and Social Affairs was to furnish "staff" services and advice to the secretary and to serve as a coordinating point for other government departments. Recommendation 11 stated that "within the action units responsibility for decisions should be clearly fixed with adequate machinery by which the decision-maker *can consult but never be required to obtain the concurrence of staff advisory units or other action units."* In support of its recommendations the commission declared: "The present intolerable system of coordinate authority, whereby concurrences in different chains of command within the Department are required, should be eliminated."† The ensuing recommendation made the action units "the focal points of contact between the Department and overseas and international organization missions in both substantive and administive matters." The clear intent of the Hoover Commission was to decrease the functional units in both size and importance to small "staffs" furnishing "advice" but not empowered to make decisions or to execute policies.

However, the Hoover Commission's report is easier to read as a document in public administration than as a description of the actual operations of the department. On the one hand, the geographic divisions might in effect

---

* The Commission on Organization of the Executive Branch of the Government, *Foreign Affairs. A Report to the Congress,* February, 1949, p. 46. Italics added by the authors.

† *Ibid.,* p. 47.

ignore the unenforceable recommeadation for consultation with the functional divisions, and disregard their advice when given. On the other hand, the question still arises: How large is a "staff" and what is it to do? The natural bureaucratic tendency is to keep the functional divisions intact in terms of personnel. While the Hoover Commission did not make concrete proposals regarding the size which functional units should have in order to perform their staff duties adequately, these units were notably successful in resisting efforts toward any substantial reduction in personnel. Through their assistant secretary they are still in a position to press home to the secretary's office their point of view and thus try to obtain from the top a political decision which could then be enforced on the chain of command throughout the geographic divisions. Furthermore, a cogent argument can be made that staff advice must be based on complete information provided by a substantial body of experts who have access to the reports of the geographic division *before the latter take action upon them.*

WITHIN THE GEOGRAPHIC UNITS

Within the geographic unit itself there is a special problem of communication. Following the Hoover report, a departmental reorganization raised the regional offices to "bureaus," and put each one under the direction of an assistant secretary. Geographic bureaus encompass the world: European Affairs; Inter-American Affairs; Near Eastern, South Asian and African Affairs; Far Eastern Affairs. There is a sixth, a nongeographic bureau, that of United Nations Affairs. An effort has been made to reduce the number of regional units under the bureaus, although there has been little if any reduction in total staff. For example, the Bureau of Inter-American Affairs now contains three offices, replacing the six divisions that formerly existed. At the bottom of the hierarchical structure rest the country "desks." For the larger countries there is usually one officer in charge, but several smaller ones may be combined into one "desk."

Although the political problems of one entire region, therefore, are under the jurisdiction of one assistant secretary, the amount of communication within the bureaus cannot be effectively established by administrative edict. It is obviously desirable that political officers concerned with one country or a group of countries know what the others dealing with other countries in the same region are doing. Otherwise, foreign policy may emerge as a series of *ad hoc,* inconsistent actions which obstruct the attainment of over-all objectives. But several questions arise: Is this communication to aim at the broadest possible planning of policy in advance? Is it to be limited to consultation in the preparation of policy for which an individual office or desk officer is responsible? Or is it merely to be notification of policy decisions after the event? The natural tendency is for each desk officer and regional office to regard its problems as unique, its responsibility paramount, communication with outside offices as courtesy only. This viewpoint is especially typical of offices of long standing, which antedate the elaboration of relations with formerly unimportant countries, and which have only recently been forced by new lines on an administrative chart to give up their formerly autonomous position and become single units among several in a regional bureau. Just as the breakdown of geographic-functional communication may force problems of reconciliation upon the Secretary of State, so may the lack of effective coordination between country specialists place additional burdens on the four regional assistant secretaries. Increasing involvement of the United States in world affairs has resulted in steady pressure for the delegation of responsibility downward to the regional and desk experts in order to handle the growing work load. The unfortunate result may be to produce the very inconsistent and hand-to-mouth policies which the officers themselves individually deplore. Once again there is no effective solution by simply redrawing lines on an organizational chart. Each country's problems *are* unique, but effective foreign-policy making demands advance planning and the maximum amount of consistency. The emergence of effective patterns of communication, therefore, depends on the predisposition and ability of individual officers to distinguish between isolated problems and those requiring coordinated planning.

INITIATING UNIT AND INITIALING UNIT

Two additional problems in communication are suggested by the one just mentioned. Every item of American foreign policy has a point of initiation. While higher governmental officers not infrequently make policy themselves individually or in consultation, routine decisions invariably originate near the bottom of the administrative structure. From that point until final approval is obtained, suggested action follows a zigzag course from the bottom upward. The vertical path ↑ is the normal direction of the chain of responsibility: from the desk officer to his chief to the office director to the assistant secretary to the Secretary of State. Several additional steps may intervene in this vertical process, and whether the process culminates in issuance of a departmental paper obviously depends on the seriousness of the matter in question. Final action may be authorized by the office director without specific concurrence of the assistant secretary, or by the assistant secretary without consulting the Secretary of State.

No matter how far the vertical course of suggested policy operates prior to issuance, however, two kinds of communications problems are involved. The first is between stages on this vertical movement and other offices outside this line, whose concurrence it is deemed necessary or desirable to obtain. Thus, the problem may be diagrammed as ↑ vs. →. Formal papers of importance—memoranda, dispatches, telegrams, and airgrams—may need the initials of responsible officers in a number of different divisions outside the direct chain of command. These initials inscribed on the papers imply both notification and acceptance. But bringing in other units takes time. Papers must be routed properly, since some offices will not initial before others have been consulted. A decision is also involved on the part of the initialing officers as to how much responsibility and power they can and will permit the initiating office to assume. If additional problems of jurisdiction exist, as between political and functional divisions, or between units of a geographic area, the lateral movement may take on added importance as the prestige of various offices becomes involved. A tendency therefore exists to interpret initials as acceptance rather than merely as notification, a trend which frequently saddles the initiating office with the tasks of reconciling differing points of view which have appeared, or of testing its own strength against that of the initialing offices.

Any attempt on the part of the initiating office to avoid this cumbersome procedure of routing and initialing, any effort, that is, to adhere to vertical rather than horizontal routing, is doomed to failure by the existence of the Correspondence Review Staff, whose importance rests on the frequent discrepancy between the organizational chart and actual operational procedures. Located in the Executive Secretariat, which is a part of the Office of the Secretary, the Correspondence Review Staff has the responsibility of determining who shall see incoming messages, in what order, and where the initiative for response should lie. While other offices may alter the procedure later, once a paper has started on its rounds its course may be difficult to change, even its location at any particular moment difficult to determine. Outgoing messages are examined by the Correspondence Review Staff to determine whether the proper initials have been obtained, both quantitativly and qualitatively. It can send back for further lateral movement papers which have followed too closcly a vertical direction. While its power in this respect may be challenged and upset, the response of the initiating office interested in speed woud normally be to obtain the concurrences requested by the Review Staff. Not infrequently also the latter, by suggesting that papers signed by an office director should go to an assistant secretary or to the Secretary of State, or vice versa, may raise or lower the level which a given paper must reach before it issues from the department.

INITIATING UNIT AND DEPARTMENTAL COMMITTEE

The purpose of the lateral movement is, of course, coordination of policy. Now coordination may be achieved by individuals separately or by interested officers as a group. Thus a new problem in communication is introduced which may be diagramed as ↑ vs. O. The circle represents the intradepartmental committees, with which the department, searching for consistency in policy, abounds. But what is the function of such a committee? Is it to serve as a collective point of initiation or merely as the focus of information for policies originating in one office? The natural tendency of committees is to seek the former responsibility, while the tendency of initiating offices is to restrict them to the latter. Use of the committee device, therefore, reflects the desirability and also the difficulty of effective communication between the various geographic bureaus. As the problems and personnel of the department have increased, so have the number of departmental committees, to such a point that administrative practice becomes ambivalent under the conflicting pressure for speed and a clear chain of responsibility on the one hand, and the necessity for broad information and consistency on the other.

ACTION AND PLANNING

Traditional complaints about American foreign policy are that it is inconsistent and not anticipatory. Since the beginning of World War II the State Department has been organizationally wrestling with the second problem. In his book, *The Road to Foreign Policy,* Hugh Gibson tells of a "standard telegram" which was customarily sent to Foreign Service officers saying that "it is not the practice of the department to deal with hypothetical problems," words well calculated to stifle initiative. And when problems did arise, Gibson recalls this department reaction: "The Department is fully mindful of the difficulties of the situation with which you are faced. It is desired that you keep the Department fully informed as to developments and that you cooperate closely with your French and British colleagues. We are in close consultation with the interested governments, and, as occasion requires, shall be prepared to send you appropriate instruction for your guidance."* In addition to revealing a peculiar relationship between the department and overseas diplomatic establishments,† such instructions disclose an organization unable and unwilling to anticipate, to plan policy in advance.

One attempt to improve the situation was made in 1944 by the creation of a policy committee, consisting of top officials meeting with the Secretary of State. But this device merely gave administrative recognition to a type of staff meeting which was already taking place. Three years later the department announced the creation of a Policy Planning Staff in the Office of the Under Secretary. The new group, restricted to a few advisers under George F. Kennan as director, was charged with "the development, within the Department of State, of long-range policy which will serve as a framework for program-planning and a guide for current policy decisions and operations." It was explicitly stated that the "Policy Planning Staff has no operational responsibility and will not issue directives, instructions, etc., to the operational organization of the Department or to missions in the field." Rather was it given the formidable job of "formulating and developing . . . long-term programs for the achievement of American foreign-policy objectives . . . [and] anticipating problems which the Department may encounter in the discharge of its mission."

The existence of a group freed from day-to-day responsibility in order to concentrate on long-range planning sounds fine in theory. But obviously the

* Gibson, *op. cit.,* p. 151.
† This point is discussed in detail in Chapter Eight, "Representation of the United States Abroad."

Planning Staff could not plan in a vacuum; it had to have close communication with the various branches of the department in order to learn both what problems were arising and what the department was doing to meet them. This necessary information was easier to request than to control; it was easier to breach the wall than to stem the onrushing tide. No rigid definition could be laid down in advance as to what type of papers the Planning Staff should and should not see. To officers lower down in the hierarchy it seemed judicious to pass on all papers of remotest possible interest, both those which apprised the department of world developments and those which contained recommended action. Reciprocally, while the Planning Staff was to issue no directives, translating its planning into action necessarily entailed increasing contact, not only with the secretary and the under secretary, but with the geographic and functional divisions below as well. The authority and power of the Planning Staff over the policy of the department dictated that the divisions have as close contact as possible in order to present their respective, and possibly conflicting, recommendations.

The inevitable result of these pressures upon the Policy Planning Staff was to load its membership down with paper work, to increase the size of the Planning Staff, both in terms of formal membership and peripheral contacts, and to remove it further and further from its original purpose of long-range planning, while increasing its involvement in the day-to-day, specific operations of the department. So pronounced had this tendency become by the time the Hoover Commission conducted its investigations that its report recommended as part of the staff services to the secretary "a Planning Advisor supported by a broad-gauge staff to function as anticipator of the problems which will arise tomorrow because of today's policies." Specific Recommendation 17 went on to lay "special emphasis on freeing him [the Planning Advisor] and his staff of current problems, upon providing him with broad-gauge staff and upon utilization by him of competent advice from inside and outside the Government."

In line with the recommendation, the department took action to reduce the size of the Planning Staff and to fill it with planning advisers having direct access to the Secretary of State; in short, to return, as the Hoover Commission wished, to the original conception of the Policy Planning Staff.

However, the mere fact that the commission felt itself forced to recommend an administrative relationship which the department thought it was already following indicates the persistence of the problem, which has in fact taken on the proportions of a dilemma. There can be no solution in absolute terms. A planning staff cannot be totally divorced from communications with the other branches of the department. If it is, its judgment may rest on incomplete evidence and its recommendations may be based on faulty knowledge of what the department is actually doing. On the other hand, experience has aready indicated the danger of driving the Planning Staff too closely into the detailed operations of the department. Success in reconciling these two pressures will depend far less on lines on the administrative chart than on the judgment and skill of the members of the Policy Planning Staff, its director, and the Secretary of State.

DEPARTMENTAL AND FOREIGN SERVICE PERSONNEL

By all odds the most formidable problem in communications is that between the regular departmental personnel and the members of the Foreign Service. The existence of this bifurcation colors and complicates all relationships in the department, including the patterns of communication which have been mentioned. The significance of the cleavage has increased with the growth of the department and the enlargement of its operations during and after World War II. Professor Graham H. Stuart, in his recent biography of the State Department, writes: "When Marshall resigned [in 1800] the total personnel was only 10 and the total salary quota was $11,500. The office of Chief Clerk had become quite important, because in the absences of the Secretary he assumed all his routine duties. The other assistants, clerks, employees of no designated status and the messenger took care of recording and coping the correspondence, collating the laws, recording land patents, making out exequaturs for consuls, issuing passports, superintending and issuing patents and granting copyrights and performing any other functions assigned to the department. . . . Although by no means elaborate, the United States had adequate machinery both at home and abroad to carry on effectively a foreign policy aimed primarily at the maintenance of peace and neutrality."* By the outbreak of World War II the number of persons employed in the department had increased to 971, but the budget of the department was still the smallest of the ten Executive Departments—less than three million dollars.

During and immediately after the war, however, the department took on many new functions which it had neither the organization nor the personnel to handle. The addition of units in the economic field has already been pointed out. Other postwar responsibilities thrown on the department included informational and propaganda duties taken over, along with much of the personnel, from the former Office of War Information; intelligence duties and personnel from the Office of Strategic Services; supervision of the Institute of Inter-American Affairs, which had formerly been Nelson Rockefeller's Office of the Coordinator of Inter-American Affairs; disposal of surplus property through the Office of the Foreign Liquidation Commission; determination of political policy toward the defeated enemies, a staff for which was headed by an assistant secretary for occupied areas; determination and expression of policy in the United Nations, which rested with the Office of United Nations Affairs; and so on. By 1953 the personnel had increased tenfold, to about 10,000, with 15,000 more working under departmental supervision overseas. (Most of the overseas personnel were alien employees in subordinate posi-

---

* Graham H. Stuart, *The State Department* (New York, The Macmillan Company, 1950), p. 36.

tions.) While purely departmental expenses approximated $35 million, those of the Foreign Service were fifteen times as large as before World War II or about $300 million.

Listing of some of the new functions of the department points up the question, to be discussed later, whether the State Department was to become primarily a staff unit or remain a functional organization. It also demonstrates the dual nature of the problem in inter-personal relations with which the department has been plagued. The increased number of people in the department, reflected in the growing complexity of organizational procedures, replaced the traditional pattern of informality and personal relationships, which approached that of a private club, with the anonymity of any large governmental agency. Close personal relations and a consciously cultivated *esprit de corps* had been built up among members of the Foreign Service, who, to put it mildly, were not averse to keeping the personnel and appropriations of the department restricted. But a veritable tide of people had entered the Foreign Service with temporary wartime rank, people whose duties seemed destined to continue during peacetime. Even more non-Service personnel had found their way into the department itself during the war or immediately afterward with the absorption of various wartime agencies.

The new employees greatly outnumbered the old, and they and their operations threatened to engulf the Foreign Service and the units in which the Foreign Service officers were largely concentrated. Under the circumstances, protective devices naturally arose: emphasis on the paramount responsibility of the geographic divisions as against the functional, and on the vertical movement of action papers as against lateral concurrence.

AMALGAMATION OF FOREIGN AND DEPARTMENTAL SERVICES

Substantial improvement in interpersonal relations could not come so long as the rigid division existed between Foreign Service and departmental personnel, with the former seeking to retain their status as an elite corps, while the latter were left as hewers of wood and drawers of water. When the Hoover Commission studied the department, it recommended, as has been noted, improvements in structure which, if adopted without further changes would have greatly enhanced the disparity in power and responsibility between the Foreign Service and department employees. But the Hoover report went on in Recommendation 20 to state that "the personnel in the permanent State Department establishment in Washington and the personnel in the Foreign Service above certain levels should be amalgamated over a short period of years into a single foreign affairs service obligated to serve at home or overseas and constituting a safe-guarded career group administered separately from the general Civil Service.

As with other recommendations, it was one thing to point out what was wrong and baldly posit a solution. It was quite another to work out that solution in practice in such a way as not "to destroy the morale or spirit of either group," as James Forrestal noted in his reservation to the recommendation just quoted. It is no wonder that the practical problems of amalgamation have been plaguing the department ever since. If consolidation was to take place, the Foreign Service wished it to be done without jeopardizing the status its members had achieved by reason of their special training and varied assignments. On the other hand, departmental personnel could not be expected to show much enthusiasm for an amalgamation which would perpetuate their disadvantages and bar them from the upper echelons.

The department began with a twelve-hundred page report on the technical, personnel, and other problems which an attempt at consolidation would confront. Secretary of State Dean Acheson in December, 1949, then appointed a three-man committee to study the report and recommend procedures. The committee, following its intensive study, issued a report, dated August, 1950, in which the first recommendation was that "there should be a single, but flexible, personnel system for the Department of State and the Foreign Service instead of the separate systems that exist at present." Nineteen other recommendations, backed by supporting evidence, set forth a procedure which would, in the opinion of the committee, bring about amalgamation as speedily, successfully, and efficiently as possible.

The Department of State, however, was not prepared to accept the report of the Rowe Committee. Another directive came from the Secretary of State; another study was made. From all the mighty rumblings emerged a timid mouse. November 1, 1951, was set as the deadline for application by non-Foreign Service personnel who wished to enter the Foreign Service in the next three years. "Is there a definite plan to achieve ultimately a complete amalgamation, or integration, of the two Services?" the department asked itself in one of a hundred and two "Questions and Answers on Personnel Operations under the Secretary's Personnel Improvement Directive." Behind the bureaucratic jargon lurked a revealing answer: "Experience gained in implementing this limited program should provide a basis for determining *at some future date* what further steps, *if any,* it is practical or advisable to take."

It was no secret that departmental employees had avoided application to the Foreign Service like the plague prior to November 1, 1951. Asked how many economic positions could be classified as "dual service," i.e., capable of being filled by personnel subject to overseas assignment, that functional division had a simple answer—none. Notwithstanding the deadline, many departmental employees deliberately chose to resist the pressure and inducements and not to apply. Their reasons for holding out were readily apparent. Many did not desire overseas service. They were not satised that they could attain a class in the Foreign service under lateral entrance provisions which would carry the same salary they had previously commanded. Specialists were fearful that full use would not be made of them in fields in which they were expert. All applicants were required to take an oral examination upon which their grade in the Foreign Service would ultimately depend, regardless of their personnel record, and Class 5 applicants had to take a written examination as well.

The above record clearly indicates that, consciously or unconsciously, the department pursued from the issuance of the Hoover Commission's recommendation a backing and filling policy which would ultimately result in amalgamation, not through blanket administrative edict, but through the action of individual departmental employees. Non-Foreign Service personnel came to the reluctant conclusion that amalgamation was going to take place and that their own careers depended on their entrance into the Foreign Service. At the same time the department moved to alleviate the fears of departmental personnel that their entrance into the Foreign Service would entail acceptance of a perpetually subordinate status. The probem of communication between Foreign Service and departmental personnel, however, can only be satisfactorily solved when each group has completely accepted the other as an equal part of a true American foreign ministry.

RELATIONS BETWEEN THE TOP BRASS AND OTHER PERSONNEL

The subject of intradepartmental communication would not be complete without mention of the distinction between the top officials of the department and the rest of the personnel. The Secretary of State, being a member of the President's Cabinet, has traditionally been a political appointee, but few secretaries had as much previous experience in the department as Acheson, who had been assistant secretary in charge of economic affairs, assistant secretary supervising relations with Congress, and Under Secretary of State under General George Marshall. The selection by President Eisenhower of John Foster Dulles, while obviously political, brought to the department a man long conversant with American foreign affairs. In addition to being an adviser to the Republican party on international questions, Dulles had gained valuable experience in the formulation and execution of American foreign policy through his leadership in negotiating the Japanese Peace Treaty.

Not only is the head of the department usually outside both the Foreign Service and the departmental service, but he also brings with him a group of advisers personally chosen by him to become under secretary and assistant secretaries. This is true whether the new secretary is part of the same administration as his predecessor or enters with a new administration. Some of the secretary's immediate assistants may have had long experience in the department or in overseas diplomatic posts, but the criteria for selection include other than professional qualifications; they must include the ability to work in close harmony with the secretary. There is nothing, therefore, which approaches the British or continental position of a permanent, civil service under secretary. The incoming Secretary of State has on his desk the resignations of all the assistant secretaries, which he may accept if he chooses. That he sometimes does so choose was illustrated by the clean sweep of these positions made by Secretary Stettinius, who, when he replaced Cordell Hull, installed his own 'team" to the accompaniment of a mammoth rally of all employees, with a band playing patriotic airs.

The brief tenure of both the "team" and of Stettinius himself demonstrates another aspect of the problem of communication. The rapid turnover of secretaries and assistant secretaries of State even before the advent of the Eisenhower Administration could not but have impressed other departmental employees with the fact that their "superiors" might come and go, but that, barring accident, they could continue to a richly earned retirement. Although departmental personnel becoming assistant secretaries, like Foreign Service officers becoming ambassadors, no longer have to resign to take their new jobs and seek reinstatement when their indefinite period of tenure is ended, the present method of appointment naturally increases the difficulties of creating the close rapport necessary for the smooth operation of the department, in terms of either vertical or lateral communication.

► COMMUNICATION WITHIN THE EXECUTIVE BRANCH

DECLINE IN STATE DEPARTMENT PRESTIGE

The present position of the Department of State within the federal government reflects the severe decline in the prestige of that organization during the administration of Franklin Roosevelt. Neither the Truman Administration nor the Eisenhower Administration to date has been able to reverse this trend. Pending a full-scale study of this period, the basic elements in the decline can only be suggested. One was certainly the disparity in temperament and view of the Office of Secretary held respectively by the President and his Secretary of State. Roosevelt was noted for keeping in his own hands the responsibility for decision, even at the expense of organizational efficiency. His view of the role of the United States in international affairs was likewise dynamic and positive. Blunders were made but written off as the necessary price to be paid for action. On the other hand, writes Robert Sherwood in *Roosevelt and Hopkins,* "The State Department was compelled by twenty years of isolationism to operate on the principle that the Alpha and Omega of American foreign policy is to keep out of war. When this became impossible, the functions of the State Department, except in regard to neutral countries, became atrophied . . . Roosevelt was bound to become impatient with anyone whose primary concern was the maintenance of a personal record of 'no runs—no hits—no errors.' "* Granting that this view may be oversimplified and somewhat distorted, it reveals a mutual mistrust between the chief executive and his senior Cabinet officer.

Other factors also entered the picture. Because the State Department was both unwilling and unable to assume effective charge over new responsibilities of the United States in foreign relations, these went by default or by presiden-

* Robert Sherwood, *Roosevelt and Hopkins* (New York, Harper & Brothers, 1948), p. 135. This and the following quotation reprinted by permission of the publisher.

tial designation either to other agencies or to men in the President's personal entourage like Harry Hopkins. This procedure in turn aggravated the break-down of communications between the State Department and the rest of the government. Being in a state of increasing ignorance on matters of importance, the department was consulted less and less about the course of policy. It is significant that the *only* major wartime conference attended by Secretary Hull was the Moscow meeting of foreign ministers in 1943.

The break was personal and political as well as organizational. It was well known that Secretary Hull was out of sympathy with many New Deal measures and even more hostile to what he called the "extreme left fringe" of advisers close to the President. Picturing himself as occupying a position above partisan politics, Hull chose not to battle for the ear of the President. Neither did he actively fight for Rooseveltian policies, although, unlike James Farley, he did not desert Roosevelt in 1940. Roosevelt, on his part, regarded the department as peopled by ineffective reactionaries, or worse. Sherwood tells of a speech which the President sent to the State Department for clearance, a speech in which he proposed to say: "There are also American citizens, *many of them in high places,* who, unwittingly in most cases, are aiding and abetting the work of these [foreign] agents." Upon learning that the department wished to eliminate the *italicized* words, the President is reported by Sherwood to have remarked: "Oh, *do* they! Very well. We'll change it to read —'There are also American citizens, many of them in high places, especially in the State Department—and so forth.' "*

The man in the department with whom Roosevelt worked most closely was not Hull, but Under Secretary Sumner Welles. In *Seven Decisions That Shaped History* Welles relates how he appealed over the head of Hull to the President when the Secretary of State directed his nominal subordinate to reverse the position Welles had taken at the Rio meeting of foreign ministers in 1942. Not only was the appeal made; it was successful. Roosevelt told both men that he was supporting Welles. Inevitably such procedures, of which this is but one example, growing out of the close relationship between Welles and Roosevelt finally produced a crisis between the two top State Department officials which could only be resolved by the resignation of one. Removal of Hull, despite his age and recurrent ill-health, was too difficult for Roosevelt, who never faced such unpleasant situations when they could be avoided. Hull's dismissal would have been dangerous to the uneasy partnership of the liberal and conservative wings within the Democratic party and to executive-legislative relations, as well. It was therefore Welles who had to go, although his resignation in August, 1943, placed outside the government a man of exceptional experience and ability at the very time he was most needed. Whatever the merits of the personal quarrel between Hull and Welles, the manner of its resolution could not but weaken the structure

---

* *Ibid.*, p. 227.

of an organization whose morale was already low, and seriously impair its prestige among other departments.

Decline of the prestige of the Department of State continued after the war. Part of the reason lay in the rapid turnover at the top and the failure to achieve stability in administrative procedure. At the time of his appointment, Dean Acheson was the fifth Secretary of State in five years, and his relatively long tenure in office was due, in part at least, to the tenacious loyalty which President Truman habitually showed for his subordinates who came under fire. These Secretaries of State, moreover, had not been in Washington long enough to familiarize themselves with, and, more important, to control, the routine operations of the department. Acheson was a partial exception by reason of his previous experience and the decline of East-West conferences. The price of maintaining Acheson in office, however, was an increasing tempo of attacks on him and his department. One of the most serious problems confronting the Eisenhower Administration, therefore, was to restore to the department some of its prestige. As has been suggested, this problem was only in part a matter of personnel. Equally important was the re-examination of the role which the department could and should play within the federal government in the formulation and execution of American foreign policy.

THE STATE DEPARTMENT: STAFF OR LINE AGENCY?

One consequence of the decline in prestige of the department has been the failure to determine just what the State Department is to be. Should it be a functional operating agency, or an advisory agency—a line or a staff organization? It has been observed that the department acquired during 1945 and 1946 many wartime operating units which threw the bulk of its operations into the functional executory pattern at the same time that the old geographic units, imbued with the small, professional staff point of view were fighting hard to retain their traditional preponderance of responsibility. Secretary Byrnes believed that the department should be an advisory unit. "It must," he wrote in *Speaking Frankly,* "be a policy-making department. It cannot be run like one which is charged with conducting a variety of operations. The amount of time a Secretary of State must give to decisions on carrying out operating functions necessarily is taken away from the important questions of foreign policy."*

When the Hoover Commission studied the department, it found the same mixture of function and staff patterns. It also wanted to eliminate the former. Recommendation 6 was that "the State Department should concentrate on obtaining definition of proposed objectives for the United States in foreign affairs, on formulating proposed policies in conjunction with other departments and agencies to achieve those objectives, and on recommending

---

* James F. Byrnes, *Speaking Frankly* (New York, Harper & Brothers, 1947), p. 244.

the choice and timing of the use of various instruments to carry out foreign policies so formulated." The obverse side of the coin was made explicit in the recommendation which followed: "The State Department as a general rule should not be given responsibility for the operation of specific programs, whether overseas or at home."*

In the name of this principle Secretary Byrnes resisted the attempts of the War Department to turn over administrative responsibility for occupied countries to the State Department. On the other hand, Secretary Marshall only two years later argued before Congressional committees that the operations of the European Recovery Program should be centered in the State Department. Congress overrode Marshall's wishes, less because of the techniques of administration which were involved than because it did not like the department particularly and thought a separate agency created by legislative statute might be more subject to Congressional control. While President Truman later wished to increase the authority of the Secretary of State over foreign operations of the government, private study groups like the Brookings Institution, Gordon Gray's staff, and the staff headed by Nelson Rockefeller advised going even further in separating the operational aspects of economic policy from the department.

The stage was thus set for the recorganizations embarked on by President Eisenhower soon after he took office. Reorganization Plans 7 and 8, recommended to him by his Advisory Committee on Government Organization, went far toward removing operating activities from the direct control of the State Department. All information programs, with the sole exception of cultural exchange, were centralized in the new United States Information Agency. Although the Mutual Security Agency was the nucleus of the new Foreign Operations Administration, economic activities previously carried on by the Technical Assistance Administration and the Institute of Inter-American Affairs were transferred from the State Department to the Foreign Operations Administration.

At the same time an obvious effort was made to see that the Secretary of State continued to have a voice in the operations no longer under his administrative control. The President's message to Congress submitting the two reorganization plans said: "We are taking the necessary steps to confirm the historic responsibility of the Department of State as *the* agency responsible under the President for the development and control of foreign policy and *all* relations with foreign governments." (Italics added.) The measures alluded to were threefold. The Secretary of State was charged with the duty of giving policy guidance to the heads of the new agencies, and, reciprocally, the heads were told to seek such guidance. In the second place, the secretary was to advise the President on the appointment and tenure of the director of the Foreign Operations Administration, although Harold Stassen, hitherto head

---

* Commission on Organization of the Executive Branch of the Government, *op. cit.,* pp. 29, 32.

of the Mutual Security Agency, was to be the first director. Finally, and in specific recognition of the jurisdictional strife at lower levels inherent in the separation of planning and operating functions, the President's letter to executive agencies explaining the reorganization stated that "to the maximum feasible extent consistent with efficiency and economy, the internal organization of the new [Foreign Operations] agency should be designed to permit ready coordination with subordinate levels of the State Department."

It should be recognized, however, that proposals to make the department exclusively a staff, advisory agency entail an extreme resolution of a dilemma for which no decision can be completely satisfactory. There is much truth in the proposition that extensive preoccupation by the State Department with the details of operation handicaps that agency in the task of anticipating future issues on the foreign scene and planning programs which will not only meet the challenge of the Soviet Union wherever it occurs, but even wrest from Russia the initiative in international politics. On the other hand, an old adage may be paraphrased to read "administration is nine tenths of policy." If the department does develop a broad program, handing it to another agency for execution, it may see its ideas perverted or even reversed in the manner of their implementation without being able to exert sufficient control over personnel and administration to bring them back into line. Furthermore, much of what becomes general policy is nothing more than a compilation of precedents from day-to-day operation, which in time build up a pattern of procedure impossible to change or control. Finally, insofar as representation of the United States is concerned,* diffusion of power and responsibility over the actual conduct of day-to-day operations may lead foreign governments to conduct their relations, either at home or in Washington, not with the diplomatic officials nominally in charge, but with the people who are able to get them what they want.

As has been indicated, there is no pat solution to this problem. Delegation of operations in the field of foreign relations to other agencies has already seriously damaged the State Department's prestige. The retention of a broad range of functional powers has weakened its internal unity and its efficiency as a staff agency. It is reasonable to expect that the Eisenhower Administration has chosen to deal slowly and carefully with a problem of such complexity. Much of the form which the department takes in the Republican regime depends on the strength of opposing pressures, on its own ability to define its role and gain acceptance for it, and on the practical regard for the department exhibited by the presidential office, by the executive and legislative branches of government, and by the American people.

DECLINE IN PRESTIGE OF THE DIPLOMATIC TECHNIQUE

Not only have the foreign affairs of the United States increased in scope and volume, but a growing amount of activity has been carried on outside the

---

* See Chapter Eight, "Representation of the United States Abroad."

diplomatic field, particularly as defined by the State Department. This is not to say that international diplomacy is not important and has not itself increased in scope and amount—figures on departmental and Foreign Service personnel cited above reveal the contrary—but there has been a decline in the relative priority assigned to the diplomatic technique. This lower priority has resulted primarily from the breakdown of the wartime coalition with the Soviet Union. The failure of innumerable conferences to reach any lasting basis of understanding has forced the United States to make greater use of economic and military techniques. In these fields the State Department has played a minor role, both because of its own diminished prestige and because of the nature of the policies themselves. As an inevitable consequence, although cooperation between the agency concerned and the State Department may be legislatively or executively provided for, formal consultation does not result in the department having a controlling or even a coordinate voice in shaping policy.

Since the subject of the declining prestige of the diplomatic technique is more fully treated in another chapter, one obvious example will suffice at this point. In the relations of the United States with Western Europe between 1948 and 1950 no activity was more important than the effort to restore economic viability to Great Britain and that part of the Continent outside the grip of the Soviet Union. The decision of Congress to establish a separate agency for this purpose relegated the State Department to a very minor role in the process. It was the Economic Cooperation Administration, which discussed with Western European countries individually and collectively their needs under the Marshall Plan, saw that those needs were translated into Congressional appropriations, and supervised the disbursement of the funds. The ECA further provided the channel for the increasing American emphasis on "integration" of Western Europe, while the State Department remained quietly skeptical of concrete results and openly dubious about the desirability of giving the term any political meaning through such devices as the Council of Europe. As a result both in Washington and in Western Europe the Economic Cooperation Administration provided a more important channel of communication with foreign governments on the fundamental issues of survival than did the diplomatic missions and the State Department.

"We are attempting to build situations of strength," said Secretary Acheson, "from which successful negotiations with the Russians can be conducted." Two corollaries relative to the place of the department in United States foreign policy were implicit in his words. They indicated, on the one hand, the almost complete rupture in relations between the United States and the Soviet-controlled areas and, on the other hand, a reluctance by the United States to renew contacts until it had trumps in its own hands to match those of its adversary. Those trumps were to consist of military as well as economic power. The building of military strength in this country and in allied countries abroad was the obvious responsibility of the Defense Department. Even the incomplete unification of the various military services into one gigantic agency, which absorbed the bulk of the United States budget and which carried on operations approaching the sacrosanct because of their close relation to military security, placed unparalleled power in the hands of the Secretary of Defense and his supposedly subordinate secretaries and uniformed advisors. Consultation between the Defense and the State Departments was provided in such devices as the International Security Affairs Committee and the National Security Council, but it was only to be expected that the voice of authority would belong mainly to the possessor of responsibility. The fact that the Eisenhower Administration was well aware of the problem of interagency cooperation in the efficient use of American diplomatic, economic, and military techniques is revealed in its intensive study of United States establishments overseas and of domestic devices for coordination. His previous experience as leader of the Anglo-American political-military coalition assembled for the invasion of Western Europe made the new President personally sensitive to the importance of the problem.*

TYPES OF COMMUNICATION BETWEEN THE STATE DEPARTMENT AND OTHER EXECUTIVE AGENCIES

At least three patterns of communication exist between the State Department and other agencies of the federal government. Since there are close to half a hundred departments, offices, groups, and so on, whose operations are related directly to American foreign policy, the importance of these communications can readily be appreciated. The first type is that provided by legislative statute. There has been an increasing tendency for Congress to prescribe by legislation the manner in which particular policies shall be executed, in order that Congress may more readily exert influence and control over the operations of the government.† One example of communication established by legislation may be seen in the act setting up the Economic Cooperation Administration; it was stated that the administrator and the Secretary of State were to participate jointly in planning and executing assistance programs. Although three recommendations of the Hoover Commission studying foreign affairs deplored this tendency of Congress to enact into law a particular set of administrative relationships, the situation which has produced the tendency is easier to describe than to correct.

At the other end of the scale is the informal, largely unwritten pattern of communication which exists between the State Department and other agencies at all hierarchical stages but primarily at the lower, operating level. Each country specialist knows the names of people in other agencies with whom he can exchange information and advice, people to whom he can refer his country's diplomats as the occasion arises. A foreign representative seeking a

---

* For details on this point see Chapter Six, "The Executive Organization for Foreign Affairs," and Chapter Eight, "Representation of the United States Abroad."

† See Chapter Eleven, "The Problem of Executive-Legislative Relations and a Bipartisan Foreign Policy."

loan for his country from the United States would involve the State Department desk officer in conversations, telephonic or face to face, with members of the Export-Import Bank. Another seeking to purchase second hand military material would deal through the specialist with the Defense Department. Still another seeking the services of an American soil expert would occasion this type of informal communication between the State and Agriculture Departments. And so on ad infinitum.

Observers of the government from outside are inclined to see decision making in a bureaucracy as taking place in watertight compartments. In actuality, although the record of these communications may be only a hurriedly dictated memorandum of conversation, or indeed nothing at all, the bureaucrat at the lower, operating level, with his own self-interest at heart, would rather expand than decrease the area in which consultation takes place. In this manner he can avoid through diffusion sole responsibility for decision and thus not suffer alone from any mistakes which policy may subsequently make. He can also protect the interests of his department by avoiding little questions of jurisdiction which may become large issues of prestige. Since jurisdiction of two or more agencies so frequently overlap, this informal mode of communication is the most prudent and expeditious way of reaching decisions.

The third pattern of communication arises from State Department representation on most of the interdepartmental committees. Its role and voice naturally vary with the subject matter under discussion, but in general the function of State Department representation is threefold: protecting the State Department as one among many government agencies, giving advice on the probable impact of projected policies on the relationship between the United States and the countries involved, and working out channels by which the policy will be expressed vis-à-vis other nations. A few of the more important interdepartmental committees on which the department is represented are the National Security Council, the National Security Resources Board, the Air Coordinating Committee, the National Advisory Council on International Monetary and Financial Problems, the Executive Committee on Economic Foreign Policy, the Trade Agreements Committee, and the Committee on International Social Policy.

As has been observed, most issues of foreign policy involve several governmental agencies in addition to the State Department. Normally differences are ironed out and consistency is obtained through interdepartmental committees. These committees usually call for representation by the head of the agency invoved, such as the Secretary of State, "or his deputy." As the committees build up experience and precedent, the actual representative may be the deputy of the deputy or whoever happens to be around the office when the time of meeting comes. Since there are more and more committee meetings, both within and between departments, a large number of individuals may be acting at one time in the name of the Secretary of State. (An obvious exception is the National Security Council and a very few others of the highest level.)

Reduction in the status of representatives and increase in their number in turn make it impossible for the committees to perform their function of ✓ arriving at decisions binding upon various agencies. The committees may still serve as important informational and conciliatory centers, but the responsibility for decision gets thrown back again upon the individual departments for settlement at a higher level or for instructions to the representatives for expression at further meetings. Consequently the question arises: Who shall coordinate the coordinators? In any governmental apparatus as large as that of the United States the nature of the problem suggests a natural tendency to seek solutions through the pyramiding of committees and their ultimate focus on the White House and the Executive Office of the President. Thus the President and his immediate corps of advisers, including such organs as the Bureau of the Budget, are constantly involved in a two-way process: the downward delegation of authority and responsibility, usually carrying with it the requirement of effective communication between governmental agencies involved; and, on the other hand, the ratification or establishment of concrete decisions sent up from below. As has been noted in the case of interdepartmental committees, therefore, problems may be referred outward or downward from the presidency for solution, only to be returned to their starting point with the final decision still to be taken at the top. Part of the task of both Truman and Eisenhower has been to prevent the Office of the President from breaking down completely under this pressure through such devices as the appointment of personal foreign-policy coordinators and the use of the National Security Council.

▶ STATE DEPARTMENT RELATIONS WITH CONGRESS

CONGRESSIONAL FRUSTRATION

It is no secret that relations between the State Department and Congress became increasingly unsatisfactory after World War II. In the presidential campaign of 1952 the Republicans cogently argued that only the election of Eisenhower could restore harmony between the executive and legislative branches. Although the coming to responsibility of Congressional members of a party accustomed through eighteen years to last-ditch opposition has perhaps reduced some of the manifestations of friction, other underlying causes are inherent in the nature of Congress and of the State Department, and still others have arisen as divisive by-products of the cold war.

The postwar role of Congress in American foreign policy* has caused widespread individual and collective frustration. The rising cost of achieving American objectives abroad has led to heavy pressure upon Congress for

---

* See Chapter Eleven, "The Problem of Executive-Legislative Relations and a Bipartisan Foreign Policy."

huge appropriations to discharge commitments. This pressure is no longer seasonalized but operates the year around. Unavoidable federal deficits lead to demands for heavier taxes, and nothing is less attractive to a politician than to raise the levies on his constituents. Economy-minded Congressmen watch their painstaking efforts to save pennies brought to nothing by the hasty expenditure of billions. Part of the picture is the complexity of the appropriations requests, which defy detailed examination even if there were time. And there never is time, because the country is always rushing to plug a new breach in the dike against Soviet aggression. Yesterday Greece and Turkey; today Western Europe, Korea, and Indo-China; tomorrow who knows? Even an economy-minded Republican Congress has had to reconcile itself to the continuation of unwanted taxes to pay even partially for irreducible foreign commitments.

The discrepancy between what the Congress would like to do and what it must constantly do leads to harassment and frustration, which are increased by the unsuccessful efforts of Congress to hold its own against the Executive Branch in matters of foreign policy. The subsequent chapter on executive-legislative relations discusses the extent to which Congress has lost, in substance if not in theory, most of its important prerogatives in external affairs, while at the same time it is being asked to raise more and more money for executive disbursement. The very nature of American government ensures that strain will exist between the two branches, strain made greater by the absence of a responsible party structure. As its control over important areas of foreign policy slips away, all the greater is the effort by Congress to hold onto and exert the power which still remains.

CONGRESSIONAL FRUSTRATION AND THE STATE DEPARTMENT

Specific factors have focused congressional frustration on the State Department. The department's budget has been relatively easy to attack and not infrequently has been ineptly defended by representatives of the department who either are not qualified for the task or are not averse to congressional pruning, particularly of new units added since the war which have made more difficult the retention of power by a few old-line officers. Congressional axes are wielded either to save the money which cannot be wrung from other budgets or to vent frustration over the futility of the entire effort to save money. Although Senators Douglas and George, and the late Senator Taft, to name a few, called for closer Congressional attention to military budgets, a wholesale attack in that quarter might lead to politically dangerous charges of trifling with the nation's security. Much of the executive budget, furthermore, is secret, in other words, it is stated in large, round sums which are not broken down into detailed estimates. Congress does not wish to wield too heavy an ax on departments or administrations that directly serve its constituents, such as the Post Office, Veterans Affairs, Agriculture, Commerce, although it frequently trims where it can and where the political repercussions will not be too severe. In contrast, the State Department budget has neither the claim to a direct national security relationship nor sufficient political standing to exert influence on Capitol Hill or in individual states and Congressional districts. As the congressman wields the ax, he rationalizes his actions by loudly voiced attacks on the department in general or on particular sections of it. These rationalizations, whether justified or not, further poison the relationship between the two organizations.

Congress has other reasons to feel unhappy about the State Department in addition to the fact that it is part of the Executive Branch and always handy when the real sources of irritation are unavailable. Congress is displeased because the State Department has been unable to settle matters with the Soviet Union. If the State Department is unable to relieve East-West tension, Congress reasons, there must be something wrong with the State Department. The greater the power and success of the Soviet Union, the greater the ineptness attributed to the State Department. But Congress does not stop there. The failure, it is argued, is attributable not only to personal bungling, but also to bankruptcy of the particular technique for which the department by definition stands. The failure is one of diplomacy, and if that is so, then the diplomatic instruments are themselves faulty and must be replaced by others which, like economic or military coercion, more effectively employ the power of the United States. Thus has Congress consciously assisted in shifting the pattern of American foreign-policy making. With each failure of negotiation with the Soviet Union, with each extension of nondiplomatic techniques, Congress displays less and less willingness to listen sympathetically to the State Department's requests for additional authority, responsibility, and money.

Another assumption drawn by Congress from the failure of the State Department to settle the East-West conflict is that the department, in addition to being bungling and ineffective, is harboring disloyal personnel. The Department is not only unable to put right a world badly out of joint; it also refuses to recognize its incapacity. Diplomatic negotiation inevitably involves the possibility of compromise, but in a period of increasing rigidity and hostility any agency whose functioning involves compromise stands on dangerous ground indeed. It is likely to be charged with all the past failures of American policy, all the present successes of the Soviet Union, and any future reverses that may come along for the United States. This attack on the State Department is capable of extensive elaboration and, in addition, has a powerful emotional appeal to the American people. Congress, being composed, as the State Department is not, of representatives of the people, is naturally on the alert for issues readily translatable into language the man in the street can understand. The man in the street feels insecure. His prices and taxes are rising, and the dawn of a new world promised him during World War II is darkened by what seems to be the gathering storm of an even greater conflict. Who is responsible? Not only the Russian government for which no appellation, however low, does justice, but also insidious influences which are at work in the American government itself, especially in that branch whose manners, mores, and methods seem most foreign, least within the range of his experience. Thus the attack on the State Department becomes a political issue and mushrooms until the State Department is blamed ex post facto for all the events leading the United States to its present costly, unlimited, uncomfortable, unwanted world responsibility.

EFFECTS ON THE STATE DEPARTMENT OF CONGRESSIONAL ATTACKS ON ITS LOYALTY

The deleterious effects of charges of disloyalty leveled by individual congressmen against members of the State Department are visible at many points. It becomes more difficult to recruit for either the departmental or the Foreign Service and even harder to obtain the men of intelligence and understanding who are required. Young men searching for careers naturally prefer occupations where their personal integrity is not always open to underhanded attack launched from a privileged sanctuary. Men of established position and reputation hesitate to enter the government at all, let alone the State Department, where the financial returns may well be less, the work longer, and individual security nonexistent.

Personnel already in the department become less willing to take initiative and accept responsibility. Particularly in divisions which have been most criticized, safety lies in anonymity, in never volunteering, in passing the buck. Thus stagnation and immobility increase in a department already demonstrably unable and unwilling to assume effectively its share of the new burdens thrust on the United States. Individual is set against individual in an atmosphere of distrust, where one man's neighbor either may be storing up adverse allegations to "leak" to hostile congressmen or may be himself a "subversive influence" who ought to be reported.

Loyalty programs of the Executive Branch and of the department itself have been established to weed out disloyal personnel. The existence and functioning of these programs, however, have not relieved the pressure from Congress. An individual may at any moment be summarily dismissed without notice and told to prepare at his own expense to answer charges brought by people whose identity is not vouchsafed to him. He is guilty until he proves himself conclusively innocent, and proof is never regarded as permanent. The individual may be placed in double, triple, or quadruple jeopardy, depending on how many new tales are told or how many old ones are presented in new disguises. Once he is attacked, the cloud of suspicion may never be removed, particularly if the employee has only a modest status in the department. Higher officials, believing either that "where there is so much smoke, there must be just a little fire," or that "discretion is the better part of valor," may informally but nonetheless effectively bar the individual from better-paying positions of greater interest and responsibility, relegating him instead to routine assignments where "he can do no harm."

A department under constant surveillance and criticism gives under pressure, preferring to tell the critics what they want to hear rather than the exact and whole truth. Blanket whitewashes or lists of suspects and "moral cases" dismissed do not satisfy the critics nor do they protect honest individuals. Neither do such responses get to the core of the problem, which is simply to safeguard the nation against the infiltration of subversive influences into "sensitive agencies," while at the same time to enable those agencies to operate efficiently in an international situation which demands the full devotion of energy and ability on the part of their personnel. Congress has so far uncovered only one secret communicant with a foreign power, and that some eight years after the event. The Executive Branch of the government is now controlled by the party to which most of the loudest critics of the department belong. Nonetheless, it is only to be expected that Congress will continue indefinitely its view-hallooing at the State Department. After all, among the hundreds of characters being assassinated there may be another one that deserves his fate.

THE IMPORTANCE OF THE SECRETARY OF STATE

The deterioration of communications between the State Department and Congress may have been due in part to the personality and even to the outward appearance of former Secretary of State Acheson. Cordell Hull, a former congressman himself, was always popular on Capital Hill. For part of Stettinius' incumbency Roosevelt was to all intents and purposes his own Secretary of State, and in the last few months of Stettinius' tenure he was at the San Francisco Conference while President Truman was openly searching for his successor. Although Byrnes ran into some difficulties, he had two assets in his relationship to Congress. Like his chief, he had been himself a senator, and he also spent a good part of his time preparing for or attending conferences abroad. Marshall came to the position with the almost unassailable prestige of a general who had contributed much to the military victory of the United Nations.

By contrast Dean Acheson had none of the advantages enjoyed by his predecessors. He took the job when the aggressive course of Russian policy and the futility of diplomatic negotiation had become clear. To be sure, he had acquired a reputation of being able to work successfully with Congress in the days when he was Assistant Secretary of State for Congressional Relations. Since that time, however, the situation had changed for the worse. Congress was more intransigent than it had been. Acheson the Secretary of State could not run an entire department and deal with Congress on the same footing as Acheson the Assistant Secretary whose sole responsibility was Congressional liaison. The most important factor, however, was the deterioration of Russian-American relations. When Acheson took over, the negotiations with the Russians initiated under Byrnes had reached a stalemate, and the deadlock which had become manifest under Marshall had lengthened and deepened into the cold war. In these circumstances Acheson could offer no hope for an easy out, no course of action other than increased expense and increased effort to meet continued tension in international affairs. Acheson's personal appearance, manner, qualifications, and friendships only added to Congressional hostility. He looked like a typical diplomat, with quiet well-pressed clothes and a carefully cultivated mustache. At times, under the many pressures of his job, he was abrupt and impatient at Congressional questioning, which he appeared to regard as a waste of time. His very ability and experience made it seem at times as though he were lecturing to backward pupils on elementary facts and on Congress's manifest duty, whereas congressmen not unnaturally wanted to judge for themselves what the facts meant and where their own duty lay. Finally, the secretary had publicly declared his unwillingness to "turn his back" on Alger Hiss, a doubly unfortunate statement because Alger Hiss was the discovery of a Congressional committee. His critics never permitted Acheson to forget his unfortunate friend.

Congressional dissatisfaction with the personality of the Secretary of State worked to Republican advantage in the presidential campaign of 1952. The Republicans were able to promise three things the electorate desired. The first was an end to the Russian-American stalemate, equated in the popular mind with the unfortunately named policy of "containment" identified with Acheson. In its place would be substituted a more active, dynamic policy, the direction and extent of which was left vague, since only the new and Republican secretary could later give it form and content. The second promise was a reduction of expenditures on foreign affairs as the programs initiated by Democratic Secretaries of State, such as the Mutual Security Program, came to an end. And, finally, a new President and a new Secretary of State would be able to restore effective communication with Congress through common membership in the party whose Congressional representatives Acheson had so thoroughly antagonized.

The appointment of John Foster Dulles was not only an obvious one; it placed a man of diplomatic experience in charge of the department. But Acheson himself had had as much if not more acquaintance with all phases of State Department activity. The moral of the foregoing remarks is that the Secretary of State is important to the smooth functioning of the department and that there are other criteria for a successful Secretary of State which are just as important as, if more intangible than, those of experience and ability.

DEPARTMENTAL VIEWS OF CONGRESSIONAL RELATIONS

The Department of State has been devoting more of its energies to the problem of Congressional relations since the war than at any time previously. This is indicated by the appointment of an assistant secretary solely for Congressional liaison and by the enlargement of this office under subsequent reorganizations. Certain factors handicap the work of the office, however.

Most members of the department regard their primary responsibility as being the *foreign,* not the domestic, relations of the United States. As a result, personnel, already heavily burdened, are unwilling to make the necessary sacrifices of time and effort to deal with issues arising from the Congressional relationship. The office charged with this function may therefore find itself unable to obtain information readily. It is a standing departmental rule that letters of congressmen must be answered within three days, whereas normal correspondence, including replies to dispatches from the field, may take two to three weeks. This rule is not infrequently honored in the breach, either because the subject matter appears less important than other matters, or because the information requested is scattered through a number of divisions or may be of a sort which the department does not desire to make public. Congressmen, aware of the rule and desirous of doing their own jobs as members of the legislature satisfactorily representing their constituents, naturally resent the failure of the department to answer their requests promptly.

Strained relations here arise from the respective roles of the State Department and of Congress. The former is not and cannot be oriented primarily toward Congressional relations, while at the same time it is vulnerable to attack for failures in this field. Its position, so far as congressmen are concerned, contrasts unfavorably with that of other federal agencies which are organizationally more sensitive to Congressional requests and demands.

DIFFICULTIES OF A BIPARTISAN FOREIGN POLICY

Both a cause and an effect of the State Department's unsatisfactory relations with Congress was the deterioration of bipartisan foreign policy. Bipartisanship grew up during the war with the active support of Secretary Hull. Members of both parties in Congress and prominent Republicans outside Congress were given access to information on which policy was to be based, attended conferences where decisions were made, and participated in the execution of policy. But bipartisanship always operated more successfully in the execution of foreign policy than in the planning of policy, and in some areas, such as Latin America and Western Europe, than in others, such as the Far East. Its meaning and implications were never fully defined and never fully accepted.

Bipartisanship crumbled rapidly after the end of World War II. The breakdown of the international wartime coalition was accompanied by the rupture of internal unity. When the presuppositions on which American bipartisan policy in the postwar period began to fall apart, they did so at precisely those points at which bipartisanship had always been weakest—relations with the Soviet Union, Eastern Europe, China, and the Far East.* Increasingly, Republicans in Congress declined to associate themselves with unproductive policies in the adoption of which they had had little responsibility. At

---

* For a detailed account of the falsification of postwar assumptions see relevant chapters in Part II.

the same time the illness and death of Senator Vandenberg and the assignment of Senator Austin to the United Nations removed from Congress two of the most influential stalwarts of a bipartisan foreign policy. Perhaps the nadir of cooperation between the two parties came in 1950, when Senator Tom Connally, then chairman of the Foreign Relations Committee, declared angrily: "All this talk about 'bipartisanship' and 'you've got to consult the Republicans'—to hell with all that. . . . We will consult the Republicans, yes. But that doesn't mean that we are going to do just what they tell us to do. We are not going to do any such of [sic] an infernal thing."* The Texas senator went on to make it clear that by "bipartisanship" he meant only minority cooperation, that ultimate responsibility always rested with the majority.

After 1950 it became clear that foreign policy would be a major issue in 1952 and not just the target of sniping by individuals of both incoherent, undisciplined parties. The election of a Republican administration, however, did not make inevitable the speedy restoration of bipartisanship in American foreign policy. The task was easier in the sense that a major obstacle— Democratic control of the Executive Branch, including the State Department —had been removed. It was also easier to the extent to which the new administration followed the broad outlines of the course laid down by its predecessor and thus could command the support of influential Democrats as well as responsible members of the President's own party. On the other hand, bipartisanship has never been clearly defined. The term may have any one or a combination of five meanings: participation by members of both parties in the initial or planning stage of foreign policy, in the process of policy formulation as a series of specific programs, in the final stage of execution of those programs which have been drawn up and adopted. Two more limited meanings include bipartisan representation in any international negotiations which may take place among the Western Allies or with the East, and interparty agreement on vague goals of policy to be presented to the electorate. Finally separation of the executive and legislative branches, combined with the lack of party discipline, will plague any Republican, as it will any Democratic, administration in efforts to obtain commitment on foreign-policy issues from both parties as opposed to agreement by isolated individuals of each party.

▶ STATE DEPARTMENT COMMUNICATION
WITH THE AMERICAN PEOPLE

THE OFFICE OF PUBLIC AFFAIRS

As the direct involvement of the people in the issues of foreign policy has increased, their formal relationship with the State Department has become closer. It is basically a two-way relationship, with the department seeking to learn more about public attitudes and at the same time trying to

* New York *Times,* July 22, 1950.

explain to the public more about the role and activities of the department in the field of foreign policy. This concern with public opinion is fairly new and goes far toward reversing the formerly prevalent feeling that public interest in the department was something of a nuisance, and that the department's activities were such that little information could or should be divulged. The report of the Hoover Commission recommended (No. 16) that "the Assistant Secretary, Public Affairs, should concentrate on serving as a high-level staff adviser on domestic and foreign public opinion, and as chief of press relations and other media of public relations for the State Department." Recognized by the recommendation, as it is related to American attitudes, was the distinction, both in the incoming and the outgoing phases, between the body of public opinion and its so-called "leaders." This distinction is carried over into the actual operations of the department in this field.

One of the three offices under the Assistant Secretary for Public Affairs is the Office of Public Affairs, the other two being the International Information and Educational Exchange Program, and the UNESCO Relations Staff. Under the Office of Public Affairs two divisions are directly related to communication between the department and the American people; the Division of Public Liaison, and the Division of Public Studies. As the name of the former indicates, it is charged with supervision of the outgoing communications. According to the Organizational Manual of the department, the Division of Public Liaison, among other duties, "maintains relations with private groups and organizations and individuals interested in international affairs, providing information and consultative services and *arranging for the presentation of their views to the Department*." The italicized words reveal the close connection between the outgoing and incoming phases of the work. The Manual goes on to state that the Division of Public Liaison also maintains "relations with domestic information media, providing information concerning international affairs and assistance in the development of media materials and programs, except for news items released to the press. Analyzes and answers foreign policy comment and inquiry mail received by the Department and the President. Provides information *and advice* to Department officers based upon contacts with private organizations, groups and individuals interested in international affairs. Arranges public appearances and speaking engagements for Department officers."

Primarily concerned with the incoming communications between public and department, the Division of Public Studies "collects, analyzes, and interprets every available type of public expression on United States foreign affairs. Prepares periodic and special reports for the Department and the Foreign Service on public attitudes toward and opinions on important phases of United States foreign affairs. Advises policy officers regarding the attitudes, opinions, and state of information on the part of the American public concerning United States foreign policy. Makes recommendations, based upon its analyses, for the development of information policy."

LIMITATIONS ON THE OFFICE OF PUBLIC AFFAIRS

The foregoing official descriptions are perhaps more applicable to what these divisions should be doing and what they would like to do than to their actual functions, given the limitations which exist on the development of a satisfactory relationship between the department and the public. One such limitation arises from the difficulties of defining what is meant by "public opinion," finding out what opinion is, and deciding what to do with it when discovered. The Division of Public Studies follows closely the results of various polls on issues of foreign policy and circulates their results through the department. It does the same for "leadership" opinion: press editorials, radio commentators, newspaper columnists, influential groups interested in foreign policy, and so on. To say that department officers pay much attention to either type of report and that their own work is thereby affected would be to exaggerate unduly the impact of public opinion.

Much more meaningful are less formal contacts which exist with individual leaders of public opinion. These contacts are by no means limited to the Special Assistant to the Secretary for Press Relations, who, significantly, has no connection with the Office of Public Affairs, although, as one of his stated duties, he "plans, prepares, and releases information to news media on the activities and policies of the Department." Nor are contacts confined to the Secretary of State's own press conferences. Rather do they take place at all levels within the department. From such contacts officers can learn what the attitudes of influential people are, and these attitudes are more important to them than surveys of thousands of unidentified American citizens far from Washington.

Although the contrary is indicated from the quoted descriptions, advice is rarely given to policy makers by divisions maintaining contact with the public. This fact relegates these divisions to the role of interpreting and explaining American foreign policy after it has been established, since they have little or no actual influence over either the content or the method of application of that policy. But even in the realm of interpretation and explanation their function is more limited than might at first appear. There are the individual contacts just noted, which serve as outgoing as well as incoming channels of communication. Likewise, material for press and radio normally goes from the department via the Special Press Assistant. This leaves the Division of Public Liaison to deal mainly with the undifferentiated mass of the "public." It does draft replies to individual letters, or, as will be shown in a moment, at least most letters go out over the signatures of its officers "for the Secretary of State." It does arrange for speeches by other officers of the department and does on occasion prepare memoranda for general release. The primary decisions on what should go out to the general public through the Division of Public Liaison, however, are not reached in that office, but rather on the political level, mainly in the geographic divisions of the department or, if sufficiently important, in the Secretary's office.

The basic difficulty behind the inability of the Office of Public Affairs to discharge the extensive functions organizationally assigned to it results from the relatively low priority enjoyed by that office within the department itself. Earlier in this chapter it was noted that the geographic divisions have, in the main, been successful in maintaining their preponderance of power over the functional units. In power, prestige, and influence the divisions maintaining communications with the public rank lower than either of the afore-mentioned offices. This has been a situation of long duration and has continued despite efforts by the department and outside advisers such as the Hoover Commission to correct it. Correction cannot be had simply by drawing new lines and boxes on an organizational chart. The personnel in the Office of Public Affairs still lack intimate, informal contact with those on the political and functional levels, if only because the latter two groups are thrown together constantly as part of their everyday duties, while their relations with the Office of Public Affairs are more limited and regarded as less important. Few if any Foreign Service officers, the ruling elite in the department, are assigned to this office. It would be regarded as a demotion, a vote of no confidence, an "exile to Siberia."

As a consequence of the dearth of meaningful communication and the practical monopoly which the political divisions enjoy in relations with "leadership" opinion, it is frequently difficult for the Office of Public Affairs to obtain information either in advance of policy decision, in order to anticipate public response, or even to reply to specific public requests for information after policy decisions have been taken. It follows that specific requests are referred to the policy division most concerned for a suggested reply, which becomes the basis of fairly uniform answers to all future inquiries of a similar nature. While the Division of Public Liaison may try to operate on the theory that even the average American of no specific influence is entitled to full and prompt information, it cannot, by reason of lack of information of its own and because of a priority lower than that of the policy divisions, follow this practice if the policy divisions themselves do not cooperate. The latter determine what and how much will be told to the public, even if the letter to an inquiring John Doe finally goes out over the signature of an officer in Public Affairs.

It is clear that satisfactory communication between the public and the State Department is difficult even given the best will in the world by both parties. The foregoing paragraphs are not meant to imply that the political officers of the department deliberately and erroneously conspire to limit the department's contacts with the American people and thereby frustrate and negate the work of the Office of Public Affairs. Nor are they intended to leave the impression that the personnel in the Office of Public Affairs is inferior in ability to personnel in other sections of the department. The point is that the nature of the role of the Department of State in planning and executing American foreign policy and the *interpretation* which members of the department give to that role are such as to create barriers to easy understanding and communication between the department and the public.

The quantity of information and contact, both outgoing and incoming, has increased substantially since the war. In principle there is acceptance of the dual need for the public to be better informed on matters relating to foreign policy and for the department to take more active interest in aiding public enlightenment and in discovering, even if not being guided by, public responses. This acceptance is a recognition of the basic truth lying behind the cliché that upon the American people depends the long-range success of American foreign policy. Mutual understanding can only come slowly, as the people realize the full implications of the new world position of the United States. The attainment of this desired goal is not, however, aided by the increased public doubt and antipathy concerning the State Department arising out of suspicions of the loyalty of its personnel. Such an atmosphere only reinforces the traditional tendency of the department to talk to the public and its "opinion leaders" in meaningless generalities or even to withhold as much information as possible on subjects which might cause controversy.

► HOW ROUTINE WORK IS DONE IN THE STATE DEPARTMENT

A few words, finally, on the manner in which work is done in the department. The importance of the country desk officer has previously been stressed. Whether he happens to be a Foreign Service officer or a departmental employee, on him rests the burden for seeing that daily relations with "his" country proceed smoothly. While not himself normally responsible for the broader aspects of policy determination, in his hands rest the fundamentals out of which a broad policy emerges. In his daily routine the country desk officer is a reading, writing, and speaking individual. Early in the morning and periodically throughout the day material is brought to him to read: incoming telegrams, radiograms, dispatches from diplomatic establishments abroad, memoranda, newspapers, public opinion data; and outgoing messages (telegrams, radiograms, instructions) originating in the department. Most of this material requires no action other than initialing to indicate that he has been informed and, in some instances, concurs in what is proposed.

As a writing man, the desk officer drafts telegrams, radiograms, instructions to American embassies, usually after consultation with his immediate superior. These he sends on their circuitous and vertical route to pick up the requisite number of initials and ultimately the signature of someone acting for the Secretary of State or, far less frequently, of the Secretary himself. The desk officer also has the responsibility of keeping his superiors informed, either through separate memoranda or through short synopses attached to important incoming materials.

The country specialist spends much time talking, as well as reading and writing. The necessity of keeping in close touch with the embassy of "his" country puts him recurrently on the phone talking to the representatives of the foreign government, to others in the department, and to his opposite numbers in other agencies. The delays involved in consultation, collaboration, and clearance can frequently be minimized by the substitution of telephone conversations for face-to-face conferences or written memoranda. The country specialist's job pursues him at his office between and after hours, takes him to luncheons, cocktail parties, receptions, dinners, only part of whose functions are ceremonial and social. Like a physician, he must be always available, always on call. Crises which require speedy resolution take no account of Sundays and holidays. In his relations with his particular country the desk officer is a two-way channel of communication, explaining and frequently lobbying for that nation's needs and policies within the department, and expressing and interpreting for that country's representatives the policy of the United States, most of which he has helped to formulate himself.

The desk officer spends a good part of his time talking personally with others in the department and elsewhere within the government. He consults his immediate superiors to receive instructions on policy matters, to relay orally information of importance, to maintain proper coordination of action within the same geographic area. This last function may require formal staff meetings, but more likely it will be handled on an informal level without prior arrangement. Finally, the desk officer usually attends at least one but sometimes three or four committee meetings, either intra- or interdepartmental, possibly in his own right, but more often as representative of his office or bureau, or even of the Secretary of State.

Since each job within the department carries its own description and a salary fixed within rather narrow limits, the path toward greater individual responsibility and higher financial return involves frequent changes in positions. This constant shifting of personnel is augmented by the Foreign Service pattern of alternating overseas and departmental tours of duty. Because job descriptions must fit anyone who occupies the position and, as in any bureaucracy, because the relative prestige of an office or bureau is gauged in some measure by the job descriptions it includes, the descriptions themselves are couched in language which would be a grammarian's nightmare and carry an aura of unreality and omniscience. Their phraseology is an art to be acquired only after long practice.

Regardless of job descriptions, as the officer rises in the hierarchy, he becomes less of an actor and more of an administrator. He spends less time in reading incoming material in its original form and less also in writing material himself. Instead he functions as a director, handing out assignments to subordinates; as an editor, correcting their work; and as a manager, supervising the procedures of his office. More of his time also is spent in higher-level conversation and discussion, seeking guidance from or explaining policy to *his* superiors, representing his office at committee and staff meetings, when substitution of a subordinate is not advisable. Some, but only some, thought must go to anticipating developments and planning policies; more thought will go to the timing and methods by which policy and decisions will be implemented.

► CONCLUSION

Policy planning and decision take place in general only at the higher levels of the department. The "higher levels" would for most purposes include assistant secretaries, the Office of the Secretary of State, the Policy Planning Staff, and the Secretary of State himself.

Professor McCamy's study of the State Department shows it to be, contrary to popular impression, "young in age . . . new in experience." The important fact is, however, that this young, new personnel, whose center is a new air-conditioned building, is bound by traditional patterns of operations, by the policy heritage of the past, by a war record of ineffectiveness and lack of initiative, by declining prestige among other departments, and by adherence to a technique increasingly in disfavor. Notwithstanding these discouraging limitations, the essential task of the Department of State remains basically what it has always been. It is awesome and awe-inspiring. It is well calculated to give responsible State Department personnel chronic insomnia. The task of the department is nothing less than to try, until all efforts are proven in vain, to find a path through which the United States and the rest of the world can be led to security and peace.

► SELECTED BIBLIOGRAPHY

Increasing attention has been devoted since the war to the problem of the organization of the State Department and its place in the formulation and execution of American foreign policy. Graham Stuart's authoritative study, *The State Department* (New York, The Macmillan Company, 1950), emphasizes the historical development of the department's structure. The Task Force of the Hoover Commission presents more material on the operation of the department than does the commission's final report to Congress. The study of the Brookings Institution for the Bureau of the Budget places the State Department in the broader context of *The Administration of Foreign Affairs and Overseas Operations* (Washington, D.C., Government Printing Office, 1951). The report of Row, Ramspeck, and De Courcy, a State Department pamphlet, is entitled an *Improved Personnel System for the Conduct of Foreign Affairs*. The present scope of departmental plans for amalgamation of the two services can clearly be discerned in its publication, *Questions and Answers on Personnel Operations under the Secretary's Personnel Improvement Directive*. Contemporary organization of the department is contained in its telephone books, which diagram the organizational relations and list the various offices. Official descriptions of office functions are given in the *Manual of Regulations and Procedures* of the department. The Committee on Public Administration Cases made a study of the manner of origin and enactment of the Foreign Service Act of 1946. Much light is thrown on the prewar and wartime operations of the department by the two volumes of Cordell Hull's *Memoirs* (New York, The Macmillan Company, 1948) and by the three books of Sumner Welles: *The Time for Decision* (New York, Harper & Brothers, 1944), *Where Are We Heading?* (New York, Harper & Brothers, 1946), and *Seven Decisions That Shaped History* (New York, Harper & Brothers, 1950), particularly the last-named. Two excellent chapters on the department are to be found in James McCamy, *The Administration of American Foreign Affairs* (New York, Alfred A. Knopf, Inc., 1950), the second chapter on the department being based on an intensive study of departmental personnel. Further information on this subject may be had from close study of the *Biographic Register of the Department of State*. A satirical but withal informative chapter on the department ("Foggy Bottom") is included by Robert Allen and James Shannon in their *Truman Merry-Go-Round* (New York, The Vanguard Press, 1950). A more sober view of departmental difficulties on foreign policy is taken by Felix Morley in his lectures, collected and published under the title *The Foreign Policy of the United States* (New York, Alfred A. Knopf, Inc., 1951). A hard-hitting defense of Secretary Acheson is made by Elmer Davis, "The Crusade against Acheson," *Harper's Magazine,* March, 1951, and by McGeorge Bundy, *The Pattern of Responsibility* (Boston, Houghton Mifflin Company, 1952), while John Foster Dulles, *War or Peace* (New York, The Macmillan Company, 1950), contains the thoughts of the present Secretary of State on the course of American foreign policy.

CHAPTER EIGHT

REPRESENTATION OF THE UNITED STATES ABROAD

General Considerations • Development of the American Foreign Service • Career Problems in the Foreign Service • Nature and Operation of American Diplomatic Establishments • Multiple Representation of the United States Abroad • Selected Bibliography

Not the least result of the new role in world affairs which has been thrust upon the United States since 1945 is the confusion which commonly surrounds any discussion of the manner in which this country is represented abroad in its dealings with other governments. Time was, when the world was a simpler place in which to live, that practitioners in this field could be labeled *diplomats* and the process called *diplomacy*. These two words are no longer all-inclusive; they definitely ceased to be so in 1939 with the outbreak of World War II.

► GENERAL CONSIDERATIONS

DISTINCTIONS BETWEEN DIPLOMACY AND REPRESENTATION

Diplomacy now covers only part of the representation of one country's interests in another country; diplomats are no longer the only ones doing the representing. For purposes of this chapter, it seems advisable to define American diplomacy as the political form of representation carried out through American diplomatic establishments overseas. A diplomat is therefore a person operating from that establishment or as a formal member of a particular United States delegation to an international conference or organization, a person who is usually, but not exclusively, a member of the American Foreign Service. This definition excludes from the field of diplomacy two special kinds of operations: those undertaken by agencies of the government not actually assimilated into the formal structure of the American embassies or delegations; and special missions, also separate from the formal diplomatic establishment, which are sent abroad by, or at the direction of, the President of the United States.

Excluded by definition of the term "representative" as used in this chapter are both military government and intelligence personnel. The former certainly act on behalf of the United States in protecting American interests

310

and advancing American objectives; they do not, however, represent the United States in the classic sense since there is no government in the defeated country before whom to do the representing. Contacts between the various occupying powers, as in Germany and Austria, while constituting an important aspect of American foreign relations, are also excluded under this definition. The gathering of intelligence data in foreign countries likewise is not a part of American diplomacy, unless the officials in question, as is frequently the case, are a part of the formal diplomatic establishment. But even then the intelligence function is a separate story.

CAPACITIES AND REQUIREMENTS OF A DIPLOMAT

It would seem that in the very nature of things the diplomat must face two ways. His dual function, which is difficult to separate, is to represent the United States both formally and informally to another government, and also to represent the other government to the United States. The success of his mission depends on factors other than the degree of friendship existing between the United States and the government concerned. Rather does it depend on the extent to which he has correctly interpreted the foreign-policy position of his own country, both in general and with specific reference to the country to the head of which he is accredited, and also on the extent to which he has correctly reported back to the United States the motivations, goals, objectives, and present and probable policies of the government with which he is in regular contact. The nature of this dual role demands from the diplomat the quality of objectivity. For him to identify himself with either the advancement or the deterioration of relations with the country concerned would have the inevitable and disastrous consequence of blurring his vision and hindering the performance of his dual function. Frequently this identification is very difficult to avoid, particularly since both the United States and the other government wish to have a representative who is "sympathetic" to the country involved. By the legal device known as the *agrèment* the foreign government has the right to pass on a proposed American representative and can thereby assure at least the outward appearances of cordiality. Should an American representative become *persona non grata* to the foreign authorities, his recall can be requested and must be accepted by the United States. There still remains, however, a distinction between the formalities of diplomatic etiquette and the requirements of objectivity.

The representative functions of a diplomat may be divided into the symbolic, the legal, and the political. The diplomatic chief of mission in his person represents the head of his state. The practice of such symbolic representation, from which arose modern diplomacy, developed along with the growth of the nation-state system. Symbolic personification of the head of state accounts for the various privileges and immunities that attach to the person of the diplomat and to the establishment of which he is in charge. As a symbol the diplomat must spend a good part of his time participating in formalities, such as presenting his credentials to the head of the other state or calling on other diplomats, giving and attending large parties and receptions on patriotic and other ceremonial occasions. In himself he carries the prestige of the state and must therefore be the careful guardian of exact protocol. Until the Congress of Vienna settled the question of precedence, the diplomat had to be prepared to fight to maintain the prestige which attached to him in his symbolic capacity.

The diplomat also has legal obligations to perform, duties laid down by the laws and statutes of his own country to which international law and usage have given application abroad. In this guise he acts to protect American citizens, issues or denies visas and entry permits into the United States. Properly authorized, he can sign documents binding on his government, such as treaties and other undertakings. At international conferences his vote is legally that of his government. Finally, as political representative, the diplomat performs the twofold function mentioned above. He places before the state to which he is accredited the actions, policies, and intentions of his own government, and transmits to his government those positions which are conveyed to him by the responsible officials of the government to which he is accredited. It is his task to interpret those positions, to give them meaning which will guide the policies of his own government.

Harold Nicolson, out of his experience in the British Foreign Office, wrote in his book, *Diplomacy*: "These, then, are the qualities of my ideal diplomatist. Truth, accuracy, calm, patience, good temper, modesty and loyalty. They are also the qualities of an ideal diplomacy. 'But,' the reader may object, 'you have forgotten intelligence, knowledge, discernment, prudence, hospitality, charm, industry, courage, and even tact.' I have not forgotten them. I have taken them for granted."* Although published as recently as 1939, *Diplomacy,* read in 1953, seems to take on the quaint fragrance of an era long past. To be sure, Nicolson argues that the diplomat does not himself make policy, but only expresses the policy which is given him by his government. Even as a generalization, this does not seem to do full justice to the activity in which the diplomat engages, for policy itself can be shaped by the way in which it is expressed. As representative to his government of the views and intentions of the state to which he has been accredited, the diplomat has a good deal to say about the data and interpretations that form the indispensable groundwork of policy.

THE DECLINE OF DIPLOMACY

Even this slight amount of detailed attention to the proper qualifications of a diplomat appears to be overemphasis in a period characterized by the precipitous decline of diplomacy as an instrumentality of statecraft. At least six factors have been responsible for the present low esteem in which diplomacy now finds itself. One well-recognized factor is the development of

* Harold Nicolson, *Diplomacy* (London, Thornton Butterworth Ltd., 1939), p. 123.

mass and instantaneous communications. In the era of the telegraph, the wireless, the radio, and the telephone it is possible for a foreign office to give detailed instructions to its representatives overseas. This reduces almost to the vanishing point the diplomat's personal area of maneuver. His words and expressions, let alone his positions, cease to be his own, but become those of some anonymous drafting officer back home, who can and does lead the diplomat step by step through his negotiations. "You will seek an interview with the foreign minister and will say . . ."; these words are followed by the exact phraseology. Under modern conditions, there can be no doubt that every minute action and position of the diplomat is a national and not a personal one. This is not to say that so tight a checkrein is always kept, but the fact that modern communications make it possible to do so alters the nature of diplomatic representation. There should also be kept in mind the distinction between representation and negotiation. In the latter function the custom of Western countries is still to allow some leeway to their negotiators within broadly defined policy limitations. On the other hand, experience in dealing with the Russians has shown the West that Russian negotiators are completely at the mercy of their detailed instructions, from which they may not deviate without express permission.

A second factor in the decline of diplomacy is the rise of what is called "public diplomacy." The ideal of Woodrow Wilson, "open covenants openly arrived at," while not fully attained, is much closer than it was thirty years ago, and with its approach its disadvantages become ever more apparent. Conciliation, mediation, and compromise, some of the most important tools in the diplomatic kit for negotiations, become more difficult, if not actually impossible, to use when diplomats operate before the microphone or the television camera. Bargaining appears as the abandonment of a national interest. If it were not an interest, why was it expressed? If it were, why has it been given up? Any agreement is hard to arrive at when the diplomat finds himself taking an absolute, national position and directing his remarks not to other representatives, but to great, unseen, national and international audiences. Some postwar instances of public diplomacy, which is really not diplomacy at all, were the Security Council debate (with Mr. Malik in the chair) over the Korean war and the "deliberations" over the signing of the Japanese Peace Treaty, the details of which had already been worked out before the "conference" convened.

But the practice of public diplomacy arises out of something more fundamental than the mere change in the type of communications. The relationship between peoples and their governments, whether democratic or dictatorial, has also been altered profoundly. All governments must be alert as to the responses of the people to their policies. At any time, all the national resources, together with the lives of "civilians" and "combatants," may be thrown onto the scale of national power. Open diplomacy is thus one of several techniques which are not diplomacy at all in the old sense of representation and negotiation. Rather it is a procedure for augmenting national strength by increasing popular support for and identification with the government and at the same time influencing other governments and peoples. In this role open diplomacy becomes a part of ideological combat.*

For democratic states popular participation in and influence on government, combined with the existence of a set of common national values, has produced a sort of popular conscience and a general view of morality which does not always approve of classic diplomacy. Historically, diplomatic agreement has often been reached at the expense of various values, classes, interests, peoples, and even states when objectives deemed more important have been in view. Regardless of whether this process was "moral" or "immoral," it took place and enabled nations to reconcile their conflicting positions by the sacrifice of third parties. Such a procedure cannot so easily take place today. The change would be all to the good if there were one world-wide standard of morality, one system of values held in common by all peoples the world over. Unfortunately this is patently not the case. While philosophical systems have burgeoned, they have tended to become competitive and absolutist. Universalist ideologies—secular religions—tend to place upon diplomacy the insupportable burden of being guardian of conscience, donor of justice. Conflict between differing interpretations of these ill-defined precepts is magnified when absolutist ideologies are placed within the framework of the nation-state system, which operates on a theory of sovereignty and thus tends to equate values and ideals with the attainment of particular national advantage.

Diplomacy as a function was bound to decline as the international pattern changed from a multistate system to a bipolar world, where each of the poles represents a country with limited experience in the ways of traditional diplomacy. More will be said below concerning the development of the American Foreign Service, but one of the factors inhibiting its sound evolution has been the relative lack of need in the past for such an instrument. In the first chapter it was pointed out that after 1820 the United States embarked on a period of continental expansion, during which, with only a few exceptions, European relations were of minor importance. It is not much of an exaggeration to say that the United States during most of the nineteenth century used diplomacy scarcely at all, even in the affairs which brought it into contact with other states. For the most part, American objejctives, whether defined or implicit, did not require employment of that technique. The nineteenth century was a relatively peaceful one, and the United States had few if any national interests to protect in the arenas of power conflict outside the Western Hemisphere.

As a consequence Americans came to feel that the United States owed little if anything to the diplomatic technique of negotiation and compromise for regulating the behavior of states in the international environment. Moreover, the United States did not look with favor on compromise. Its aims were obviously legitimate and therefore must be accepted by other states, or they

* See Chapter Sixteen, "American Policy in the Battle of Ideas."

would not have been advanced in the first place. (A pale prelude to the Russian conception of diplomacy.) "You will, of course, impartially judge the questions that come before you for decision," Theodore Roosevelt told the American jurists attempting to arbitrate with the British the Alaskan-Canadian boundary. "In the principle involved, there will, of course, be no compromise," the President added. When the United States did become involved in world affairs, it found itself in a twentieth-century world of mass communications, public diplomacy, popular government, and absolutist ideologies. Without the heritage of diplomatic practice, American representatives became exponents of a "new diplomacy."

But the Americans were not the last on the scene. In Russia a small group known as Bolsheviks emerged from underground conspiratorial activity to control the largest state of the world. To the extent to which these new rulers understood the nature of the diplomacy practiced during the nineteenth and early twentieth centuries, they did not accept its principles. True, early Soviet pronouncements and behavior were sometimes in accord with accepted codes, but then it took some time to purge the Russian foreign service and replace its personnel with indoctrinated Communists. Chicherin, of the prerevolutionary school, was superseded, and even Litvinov in time became an anachronism, a dangerous cosmopolitan with an English wife. He was relegated to the limbo of abandoned Russian instruments, a deep, dark but not necessarily permanent limbo from which they might again emerge if Russian policy found them useful.

Diplomacy in its traditional sense is viewed from Moscow as a capitalist device for encircling and destroying the Soviet Union. The monumental Communist treatise on diplomacy bristles with such accusations, paralleled by assertions that the only true diplomacy is practiced by the Soviet Union. As a process of negotiation, the Russians regard diplomacy as little more than a technique for expressing positions and demanding their acceptance. Compromise is not unknown to the Soviet Union; it has reached agreements with other states and has even abided by some of them. But compromise is not viewed as a process for attaining a condition from which both parties to the agreement may benefit. Rather does it tend to be viewed against the background of recurrent conflict which is at the moment in either its fortunate or unfortunate phase for the advancement of Soviet objectives. In neither phase is diplomacy regarded as a regulatory device or as an instrument of statecraft which has much to contribute.

The ascendancy of the United States and the Soviet Union thus has meant the decline of diplomacy as it had been practiced within the European state system. The depreciation of the diplomatic currency by Soviet representatives has forced upon other countries, including the United States, methods of self-protection, including the retort in kind. Thus the United States, to whose innovations and practices of diplomacy the rest of the world would pay more attention were not more pressing problems originating in the East, has found itself defending, as against the Soviet Union, some of the ways of diplomacy as they were formerly understood and practiced.

Diplomacy and the diplomat still have a function to perform—in many respects, perhaps, a more important function, but one entirely different from that on which Mr. Nicolson's writings were based. What is this new role? How well is the United States equipped to play the new game, according to the vaguely discerned rules, for stakes higher than in any other period of its national existence?

► DEVELOPMENT OF THE AMERICAN FOREIGN SERVICE

THE PERIOD PRIOR TO 1924

The United States is the only major power in the world which separates diplomatic or "foreign service" from the general foreign office personnel. The separation is in large part due to the manner in which both the Foreign Service and the Department of State grew. Down to 1820 the nature of the new state's position necessitated a diplomacy which was clever and astute, albeit manned by only a few people with very limited funds at their disposal. In the few capitals at which the United States had accredited representatives, expenses were far beyond the appropriations allocated, so that chiefs of mission frequently had to spend large amounts of their own money to do their jobs properly. Mission chiefs were required, for example, to pay for stenographic services out of their own pockets, as well as to lay out sums to fulfill the ceremonial requirements of the offices. Under these circumstances only those with wealth could afford to enter the service of their country abroad, and even then people like Jefferson found themselves virtually bankrupt at the end of their tours of duty. While private wealth is not everywhere required today, it is still necessary to the largest diplomatic posts, such as London and Paris.

After 1820 two developments further weakened the Foreign Service. The first was the disentanglement of the United States from European affairs and the preoccupation of the nation with continental expansion. Representation of the nation abroad assumed a lower rank in the scale of values on the part of people with requisite qualifications. The second development was the enlargement in the number of contacts which the United States had with other countries, enlargement in quantity, not in importance. As a result, routine duties, primarily of a consular nature, began to occupy more and more of the representative's time. At first diplomats were expected to discharge these duties personally, although they were separable under international law. When other individuals were entrusted with them, they were permitted to extract fees for their services in lieu of salary. Not until 1855 was the consular service placed on a salary basis, and it remained separate, attracting a substantially different type of personnel, until the Rogers Act was passed in 1924.

Because the practice of diplomacy became less important in the national scheme of things, it fell a prey to the spoils system then being introduced into the national government. Says J. Rives Childs in his study, American Foreign Service:

> The diplomatic and consular posts abroad became, in effect, part of the sub-legal machinery of election. They were awarded in repayment for campaign contributions and the delivery of blocks of votes. . . . The high diplomatic posts were usually given to generous contributors and powerful politicians who wanted to enhance their prestige and satisfy the social ambitions of their wives. The consular posts were happy hunting grounds for the avaricious. The fees went into the Consul's pockets; at big posts such as Hamburg and London, the yearly plunder often exceeded the salary of the President of the United States. The less profitable consulates were usually given to lower-grade politicians and "wardheelers" whom the party in power wished to reward in some way, or remove from the scene.*

As a consequence of this practice a person who was empowered to act for and in the name of the United States might be colorful, awesome, or awful to the government to which he was accredited, but he was frequently not endowed with the qualifications for successful advancement of American interests, however limited they might be. Childs tells of the American minister to Persia, sometime during this period, who ceased to be invited to the home of an influential and cultured Englishwoman because, she said, "his aim was so bad when he spit tobacco juice that he was rapidly ruining her lovely Persian carpets and she did not think his company worth the sacrifice." And, more recently according to Childs, there was the chief of mission in a Latin-American country who "made a practice of walking around the house naked, continually trailed by a native girl bearing a tray of Scotch whisky, soda, and ice."† Additional evidence regarding the lack of a professional outlook in American diplomacy, the low caliber of personnel attracted to the Foreign Service, and the modest status of the United States in the world at that time is indicated by the fact that the first American ambassadors were not appointed until the second administration of President Cleveland.

The struggle to introduce quality and efficiency into the Foreign Service continued during the nineteenth century and did not reach fruition until the Rogers Act of 1924. One phase of the effort aimed at putting personnel under a merit system. The Act of 1856 provided for appointment to the consular service by the President on the recommendation of the Secretary of State after the latter had examined the qualifications of the applicant. Although legislation providing for a true merit system was defeated in 1895, President Cleveland enforced the principle through an executive order qualifying appointments on the basis of demonstrated fitness. Not until the administration of Theodore

---

* J. Rives Childs, *American Foreign Service* (New York, Henry Holt and Company, 1948), pp. 5–6. This and the following quotations are reprinted by permission of the publishers.

† *Ibid.,* p. 26.

Roosevelt, however, was a thorough effort at organization of the consular service made. By that time the United States, after its defeat of Spain, had become a major world power with expanded interests, greatly enlarged political commitments, particularly in the Far East, and a commensurately increasing world trade. The act of 1906 classified the various grades within the consular service and provided for inspection and checking of their offices. It was supplemented by an executive order prescribing appointment to the lower grades only after examination, and subsequent promotion dependent on demonstrated ability. The same principle of merited appointment was applied by President Taft to the diplomatic service below the top rank, likewise by executive order. Neither of these actions resulted in the introduction of a true merit system on a permanent basis. This development had to await the coming of World War I and the enactment by Congress of the Foreign Service Act of 1915.

Parallel to the struggle for a merit system was a drive to raise salaries and emoluments of office. The act of 1856 had divided the consular service into three classes; the first was to be paid by salary alone, the second permitted supplementary income through private occupations, and the third received only what fees could be extracted for services rendered. The same act established a salary scale for ambassadors and ministers which was to endure for ninety years, until the Foreign Service Act of 1946. While the salaries within the diplomatic service were probably adequate during the nineteenth century in terms of payment for work, they still did not take any account of related expenditures incurred in line of duty. No allowance for maintenance, entertainment, and representation were allocated either to diplomatic or to consular officials, although the effect of this neglect was felt primarily by the diplomats. The inevitable consequence of adding the criterion of independent means to the incompletely applied prerequisites of ability was to make of the diplomatic service a "rich man's club." When the United States finally got around to doing something about the organization of its Foreign Service in 1924, it had been a great world power for a quarter of a century, had fought and helped to win a war which left it with unchallengeable supremacy over the Western Hemisphere and the capacity to influence the behavior of states in Europe and Asia if it cared to exert itself.

FROM THE ROGERS ACT TO THE END OF WORLD WAR II

The importance of the Rogers Act of 1924 was fourfold. In the first place, it combined the diplomatic and consular functions, hitherto separate, into something which could justifiably be called a foreign service. It placed the merit system on a complete legislative basis, as regards both appointment and promotion of all personnel except ambassadors. Third, salaries at the lower levels of the consular and diplomatic services were raised, although the new levels were even then seen to be inadequate. Finally, a system of representation allowances was introduced which, although insufficient, particularly at the larger posts, nonetheless made a gesture in recognition of the principle that the duties of representation required expenditures other than those for just living and eating. For his efforts in securing passage of the act, Congressman John Jacob Rogers of Massachusetts has been called the "father of the Foreign Service."

The establishment of sound theories of organization was one thing; their translation into actual practice was another. In the two decades of development between 1924 and 1946 at least three factors operated to prevent the United States from emerging from World War II with a type of foreign service adequate to represent the nation in the entirely new international environment. The first was the quality of the personnel attracted into the Foreign Service. Between 1924 and 1931 it assumed a position on the scale of individual preferences about as low as that of the nineteenth century after 1820. America's was a business civilization, in outlook, in values, in accomplishments. Issues of foreign policy did not appear to have immediacy and importance in a nation consciously striving to limit its foreign commitments. The United States was on the road to what many economists solemnly described as perpetually increasing prosperity. Not only was more money to be garnered from careers outside the government, but greater prestige and status were attached to them as well. While the advent of the depression, followed by President Roosevelt's dynamic New Deal, changed many aspects of American internal life previously considered normal and permanent, foreign affairs still remained in the background until World War II began. By that time the pattern of American representation in terms of personnel had been fairly well set. Young men in search of a future found themselves in the army; older men with established reputations who desired to serve their country not unnaturally decided that they could contribute more in nondiplomatic fields, especially since the function of diplomacy seemed to have little to do with the overpowering urgency of securing military victory over the Axis Powers. While there were obvious exceptions to the foregoing generalizations, the quality of diplomatic representation had been set by the people who had entered the Foreign Service roughly twenty years prior to the event in question and had meantime risen to positions of authority and responsibility.

A second obstacle related to competency was the view which the Foreign Service had of its own job. The previous chapter pointed out the narrow way in which the State Department defined the field of American foreign policy and, consequently, departmental functions. The same remarks can as appropriately be applied to the Foreign Service, which, though separate from departmental service, did so much to stamp on the department its own view of its obligations. With manifest exceptions, personnel in the Foreign Service tended to maintain a restricted definition of foreign affairs and to view itself as a homogeneous and small group with interests, ideals, and experiences in common. (In this respect the Foreign Service resembled the officer corps of the peacetime American Army—a relatively small, easily recognizable group whose members were recurrently thrown into contact with one another at Army posts all over the United States and at the few assignments overseas, such as Panama and the Philippines.) Where this view was not in fact accurate in describing the attitude of individual Foreign Service officers, the fact that it was imputed to them by the public at large tended to determine the type of person who sought entrance into this narrow community. That this attitude toward foreign affairs did not accord with the needs of the United States before the outbreak of World War II, or with the new responsibilities thrust upon this country during and as a result of the war, helped to produce the third factor handicapping the growth of a national system of foreign representation.

No sooner had the Rogers Act established a supposedly unified Foreign Service than other agencies of the government began to intrude. First came the Commerce Department, which, under the leadership of Secretary Herbert Hoover, obtained Congressional authorization in 1927 for the establishment of a separate Foreign Commerce Service operating abroad. Then came the Agriculture Department, which was empowered by Congress in 1930 to organize its own Foreign Agricultural Service. In the same year the Secretary of the Treasury was authorized to appoint Treasury attachés for duty in foreign countries. In the middle thirties the Bureau of Mines of the Interior Department received equivalent authority and henceforth periodically dispatched its own emissaries to foreign countries. Other governmental agencies followed suit on an *ad hoc* basis.

This scattering of representation produced rivalry and duplication. While some of the representatives of other departments were nominally made part of the foreign diplomatic mission as attachés, they received orders from, and furnished information to, the agency which had sent them. Because they operated in technical fields long neglected by the Department of State, the importance of political control and unified responsibility was difficult to establish. Reports of special representatives which reached the Department of State only by courtesy of the other agencies not only had general informational value, but frequently provided material significant to policy formulation. In areas such as Latin America, where all the agencies of government were operating, foreign officials could be pardoned some confusion if they did not know whose voice on any particular issue was that of the United States. That the representatives of other agencies did not, for better or for worse, identify themselves with the Foreign Service and partake of its *esprit,* naturally added to rivalries and jealousies which found their way back home to influence the relations between the various organs of the federal government.

The Reorganization Act of 1939, sought and finally obtained by President Franklin D. Roosevelt, provided only a temporary solution to the problem. Foreign representatives of most of the other agencies were brought into a formal relationship with the diplomatic missions, which were in turn under the direction of the Secretary of State—a step toward the desirable goal of unity of representation. Immediately, however, World War II broke out, and its conclusion found the various diplomatic establishments more uncoordinated than ever. Before the principle of assimilation could be transferred into successful practice with respect to the Commerce and Agriculture Departments and the Bureau of Mines, other agencies sent their personnel abroad to undertake functions deemed by the agency itself or by the Foreign Service to be outside the scope of normal diplomatic activity. In addition to the various military services, foreign representatives came from the Labor Department, the Justice Department, and such new agencies as the Office of War Information, the Foreign Economic Administration, and the Office of the Coordinator of Inter-American Affairs. Their presence abroad focused attention on the existence of a dilemma which will be explored below in considering the problem of nondiplomatic representation. Whereas in December, 1939, there had been 5,080 American civilian employees in foreign countries, of which 4,236, or 83 per cent, were under the Department of State, by September, 1945, the number had grown to 389,328: 371,625 under the military departments, 10,936 under the Department of State, and 6,767 under other civilian agencies. Even excluding personnel under the military departments, the State Department's percentage had dropped to 62. Of the almost 11,000 employees in the Department of State, roughly half—almost the exact equivalent of the expansion from the 1939 figure—were in the Foreign Service Auxiliary, which had been created in 1941.

DEVELOPMENT OF THE FOREIGN SERVICE ACT OF 1946

It was obvious to all that the basis of the Foreign Service needed to be thoroughly reorganized after World War II. The question was: Who would do the reorganizing? At least five different groups of claimants entered the lists, each with its own ideas, some of which were shared by other groups, some of which conflicted. One group was composed of the executive agencies, other than the Department of State, which had interests and personnel in the field of foreign affairs. They were for the most part on the outside looking in (when the windows were not too steamed up) during legislative progress toward the Foreign Service Act. Another group was composed of congressmen interested in the problem. A special subcommittee of the House Foreign Affairs Committee had been appointed to draft legislation on the Foreign Service. But whose advice and counsel would it take? A third group was in the Bureau of the Budget, which thought that it had responsibility under the President for passing on proposed legislation before it was submitted to Congress, in order to check on both the organization and the policy matters involved. A fourth group consisted of State Department personnel, both at the lower levels and in the higher echelons, who would be affected by any provisions in the new act respecting amalgamation of the foreign and departmental services. Finally, there was the Foreign Service itself, which was quite accustomed to controlling its own destinies. The Foreign Service recognized the need for reorganization and legislative enactment, but felt definitely limited enthusiasm for most of the principles of "reform" which had been proposed.

Behind the scenes these groups cooperated, clashed, argued, evaded, and cajoled. Out of their interaction came the Foreign Service Act of 1946. Of the five groups mentioned there is little doubt that the last, the Foreign Service, left by far the greatest impact on the act. The original draft of the proposed legislation was prepared by Foreign Service officers. Criticisms of the draft came from other officers who felt that it had conceded too much to opponents of the Foreign Service's organization, although the intent had been merely to satisfy "outside" observers while preserving its essential homogeneity and separateness. The support of the Secretary of State was obtained for the draft even while officials of the department, the Bureau of the Budget, and other agencies were painstakingly preparing papers of analysis and suggestion. The sense of urgency felt by Congress for enactment of some legislation on the Foreign Service before adjournment gave a substantial advantage to the Foreign Service officers who had access to the Congressional subcommittee, while potential critics were successfully circumvented in both the drafting and the enacting stage of the act. Essentially, therefore, the Foreign Service Act of 1946 should be regarded as written primarily by and for the Foreign Service.

PROVISIONS OF THE FOREIGN SERVICE ACT OF 1946

The Foreign Service Act of 1946 is a lengthy and complex document, which attempts by statute to deal with all the details of diplomatic representation. As such it defies concise summary. For those interested in a career in the Foreign Service, careful study of the document in its entirety is essential. For those concerned with the major issues of American foreign policy in transition a statement of some of its principal features should suffice. These highlights concern the number of classes in the Foreign Service, the salaries of diplomatic representatives, the organization of representation, the supervision of the Foreign Service, and the process of advancement.

The number of classes within the Foreign Service was reduced from eleven to seven, of which one was the new class of career minister established by the act. The salaries within each class were raised to range from a low of $3,300 for the bottom of Class 6 to $13,500 at the top of Class 1, but no provisions were made for additional funds to meet differentials in costs of living at various posts or representation allowances. The salary of a career minister was set at $13,500, also, while that of a chief of diplomatic mission was to vary between $15,500 and $25,000, depending on the size of the post and whether its supervision were by an ambassador, a career minister, or other chief of mission.

More significant were provisions for the organization of the Foreign

Service. Five different types of personnel were recognized, with individuals able under certain circumstances to move from one classification to another in the course of their careers. At the top came the ambassadors and ministers, chosen by the President and subject to Senate confirmation. Also in this category was the career minister, chosen from the ranks of the Foreign Service officers. A second group comprised the regular officers of the Foreign Service within the various classes already mentioned. A new category was established, that of Foreign Service Reserve, which was to be composed of specialists in various technical fields. People outside the Foreign Service could be appointed within this classification to serve abroad for a four-year period and not to be eligible for consecutive reappointment. A fourth group was the Foreign Service Staff, whose personnel was to be of two sorts, those charged with administration and so-called housekeeping responsibilities, and those who were part of the permanent reserve of the Foreign Service. The fifth and final classification included alien clerks and employees, and consular agents appointed by the Secretary of State or the chief of mission acting in his behalf.

Directing the administration of the new system was the Foreign Service Board, which was to include representatives of the higher echelons of the Department of State and delegates from three other governmental agencies historically concerned with foreign representation: Commerce, Agriculture, and Labor. In actual operation the board depended much on the director general of the Foreign Service, who was himself a member of the Foreign Service. This post was a key point of control by the Foreign Service over its own affairs.

As a combined educational and training device the Foreign Service Institute was created. Successful candidates for the Foreign Service were to pass through the institute for preliminary indoctrination and orientation prior to their first appointment. The normal pattern also would find the officer returning to the institute for further training upon the conclusion of his first tour of duty abroad and before reassignment either to the department or to another foreign post. But the institute was intended to play a continuing role in the career of the officer. Composed of members of the department, of the Foreign Service, of other governmental agencies, and of academic people outside government service, it was designed to provide technical information, language instruction, and general political training at all stages of the officer's advancement. The Foreign Service Institute, when acting on a more advanced level, was to cooperate intimately with such other governmental training and educational centers, such as the Army War College.

Perhaps the most controversial feature of the Foreign Service Act of 1946 was the adoption of procedure similar to that of the United States Navy for the promotion-up or selection-out of personnel. The objective was manifestly to preserve room on the upper reaches of the ladder for officers whose ability was recognized, to ensure that no arbitrary or low ceiling was placed on their advancement by the clogging of the upper classes of the Foreign Service. Within the various classes, from the fifth to the second, it was therefore provided that individuals who remained eight years within a single class as a result of failure to receive a recommendation for promotion by Foreign Service boards were to be "selected-out" in order not to block the road for those coming along more rapidly from behind.

CRITICISMS OF THE FOREIGN SERVICE ACT OF 1946

The Foreign Service Act had been in operation scarcely two years when, after detailed study, the Hoover Commission issued some fundamental criticisms. One related to the continued separation of the Foreign Service from departmental personnel, a subject previously discussed.* Another concerned the diffusion of responsibility for administration of the Foreign Service, particularly the lack of clear authority by the Secretary of State as a result of the creation of the Foreign Service Board. The commission recommended abolition of both the board and the position of director general, a recommendation which forced the department to take steps, coincident with its hesitant approach to personnel amalgamation, to lessen the control of the Foreign Service as an autonomous, not to say independent, authority within the departmental organization.

Criticisms by the Hoover Commission were also leveled at the actual relationship between the Foreign Service Officers and the Foreign Service Staff and Reserve. The members of the Foreign Service Staff, it was found, were subjected to discrimination and handicaps in their careers by reason of their separate classification and the general view that their classification included only subordinate and menial positions. As for the Reserve, it was found that attainment by its personnel of the status of Foreign Service Officers was halting and unduly retarded. The Reserve, it was argued, was not set up to attract the best possible people for technical jobs, since most normal individuals were looking for careers and did not relish limited, nonrenewable appointments in a category manifestly inferior to the officer class. The commission also felt that in spite of the provisions of the act, too little attention was being paid to the principle of "lateral entrance" from outside the Foreign Service by properly qualified people into higher classes of the Service.

Additional criticisms of the Foreign Service Act, relating to the classification system and lateral-entrance provisions of the act, were made by the State Department's committee studying the problem of amalgamating the Foreign Service and the departmental personnel. This committee saw no reason for having Reserve and Staff systems separate from the general Foreign Service Officer category. With regard to the latter in particular, it found that procedures being followed in political, consular, economic, and public affairs programs were no different from those in the regular officer classifica-

---

* See Chapter Seven, "The Organization and Functions of the State Department."

tion. Regarding lateral-entrance provisions, the committee found that very few applications had been made and almost none accepted between 1946 and 1950. It concluded that "in this connection, there is little evidence that positive efforts have been made to attract top-notch Department and Foreign Service Staff and Reserve personnel to compete for lateral entrance into the Foreign Service Officer category."

Handicapped by lack of funds, as well as by disinclination and inertia, the Foreign Service was paying too little attention to the importance, which it had specifically recognized, of periodic and prompt reassignment of personnel from foreign posts to jobs in the Department of State and in other government agencies. On the last point especially very little had been done. In addition to financial reasons was the fact that most officers of the Foreign Service attached great value to tours of duty outside the country. Officers frequently found themselves with lower standards of living in Washington, where housing, food, and service were expensive, than at foreign establishments where income was augmented by cost-of-living and representation allowances. More important from a professional point of view was the feeling that time spent in the department was not an integral part but rather a hiatus in the advancement of an individual's career. This feeling was naturally reinforced by the continued separation of the Foreign and Departmental Services. Wrestling with this problem, the Department of State began, after the announcement of the findings of the Hoover Commission, a period of transition in the administration of the Foreign Service which promises to be a lengthy one. Begun under a Democratic regime, the transition is continuing under the Republican Administration.

Within the Foreign Service itself there has been additional criticism of one prominent feature of the 1946 act: the "promotion-up, selection-out" provision. Many believe that this principle adds significantly to the feeling of insecurity on the part of officers already heavily burdened with responsibilities, and that it places undue pressure on the various boards to promote. Resolution of the problem in either direction would be unsatisfactory, by placing officers in positions beyond their capacity or, alternatively, by losing altogether the contributions which they could make to the Foreign Service. It has been suggested therefore that the principle be modified to retain individuals whose ceiling of competence is reached below the top, but in a special category so that their cases would not recurrently come up for consideration along with those of aspirants still moving up the career ladder.

▶ CAREER PROBLEMS IN THE FOREIGN SERVICE

THE PROCESS OF RECRUITMENT

The quality of the diplomatic representation which the United States obtains is in large part determined by the screening process by which aspirants are selected for the Foreign Service. Candidates must pass a series of examinations ranking with the stiffest in the world. Those of a written nature are designed to test a variety of skills ranging from the general to the specific: proficiency in reading and writing at least one and preferably two foreign languages; ability to interpret figures and statistical tables and to absorb rapidly long and detailed documents; a knowledge and understanding of history, political science, and economics; skill and accuracy in written expression. The specific nature of these written examinations has varied from time to time at the discretion of the Board of Examiners. Of late, increasing emphasis has been laid on discovering intelligence, skill, and capacity for growth, rather than on an elephantine memory for esoteric facts and figures.

Once past the hurdle of written examinations, candidates must still undergo a limited but decisive test before a board which utilizes the techniques of examination and interview. The function of the board is to uncover the presence or absence of the intangible qualities which it believes are essential for successful diplomatists. As stated by the Board of Examiners, "the Oral Examination will be designed to determine the candidate's suitability for the Service in respect to character, personality, ability to profit from experience, and aural and oral proficiency in the use of Modern Languages."

There are many stories, some doubtless apocryphal, about this final oral examination. There is one about the examiner who was very deaf and relied on a large hearing trumpet. A candidate knew he was in serious trouble when, in the course of his answer, the examiner would remove the trumpet from his ear and lay it on the table, leaving the candidate to continue with full knowledge that nothing which he was saying could possibly be heard. Ambassador Beaulac tells of a candidate who expressed a desire to be sent to China on his first assignment but who, on questioning, revealed ignorance of the navigable distance of the Yangtze River and the Chinese name for a musical instrument. From defeat the candidate snatched victory by explaining that his choice of China indicated a preference, not a proficiency; the board could test the latter by questions on other countries. It did, and he passed. Another examinee, Beaulac relates, was not so fortunate after he had stated, in response to the board's invitation, his preference for initial assignment. Norway, he said, was too cold to suit him, while the tropics were too hot. He permitted the board to put in his mouth a desire for "something just in between" and failed.

This system of entrance requirements is designed for and actually attracts the exceptional college graduate. The average student in the average liberal arts college or university has very little chance of passing. Indeed there are frequent failures by the best graduates of colleges with the highest scholastic requirements. Candidates must usually resort to so-called "cram" schools, of which the Foreign Service School of Georgetown University is the best known. In this respect the American educational system differs profoundly from the British, which over the years has trained in the major universities limited numbers of students for the British Foreign Service. A study by Professor James L. McCamy indicates proportionately heavier recruitment to the American Foreign Service from the northeastern states than their population ratio to other sections of the country, a more substantial number being taken from the private rather than public high schools, and more from Harvard, Yale, Princeton, and Georgetown than from state-supported colleges and universities having much larger enrollment.

Do these selected people possess the skills best able to discharge the serious responsibilities placed upon them by the postwar position of the United States? There is no simple answer to the question. Diplomacy is a special technique; the nature of formal, diplomatic representation demands special qualifications which probably can be uncovered only by a board conducting an oral examination. At the same time, the decline of the prestige of the Foreign Service is not solely attributable to the decline of diplomacy as an instrument of statecraft. Criticisms from within the Foreign Service as well as from outside indicate that serious attention is being devoted to the problem of attracting the best minds as well as the best manners to represent the United States abroad.

The Foreign Service has justified cause for alarm in the declining number of applications during the postwar period. The figures are as follows: 1947—1,288; 1948—1,141; 1949—1,129; 1950—807; 1951—758, or a drop of over 40 per cent for the five-year period. Among the more obvious reasons for the increasing disinclination of Americans to enter their Foreign Service at the very time when talent was most needed were (1) the woefully inadequate recruiting system of the Foreign Service itself, which has done next to nothing to "sell" the college senior on the idea of representing his country abroad; (2) the impact throughout the Foreign Service of the irresponsible mudslinging indulged in by a few politicians; (3) the difficulty of the examinations; (4) the length of time between examination and appointment; and (5) the obstacles to rapid advancement in terms of both salary and job assignments. As a result of this decline in applications, the department has begun more determined efforts to inform college students of the opportunities in the Foreign Service and of the procedures which they must follow to enter it. Also students have been encouraged to apply for a limited number of "internships" in the Department of State, training positions which would familiarize them with the department and help them on the road toward careers in the Foreign Service.

PROMOTION IN THE FOREIGN SERVICE

Once the candidate has entered the Foreign Service and has his first assignment, his record begins as a dossier kept in the department. Materials in his personal file include special, unrequired reports which he has submitted on his own initiative, judgments on the quality of his routine reporting by department officers, and evaluations of his capacities by his superiors in the mission abroad. When he comes up for promotion, this dossier is read, along with those of other candidates, by a special board composed of departmental, Foreign Service, and public representatives, meeting with observers from other governmental departments. The judgment of this board is reached only after painstaking scrutiny by individual members, group discussion, and individual re-evaluation. The judgment is made on a comparative basis, depending on the number of promotions which can be made and the relative ability of all the candidates considered. As was mentioned above, the board must operate on the promotion-up, selection-out principle, which places an additional burden on their judgment.

This procedure has been criticized as placing an undue premium on the blank, clean record, rather than on one which reveals daring and imagination, qualities necessarily contentious, particularly in the young diplomat. It has been claimed that the frequently promoted officer is the careful officer, who as quietly and unobtrusively as possible sticks to his own job, "never volunteers," and avoids antagonizing his superiors or anyone who might at some time in the future become his superior.

While the board might indeed value carefulness and discretion above daring and imagination, while the dossier might be primarily the repository of derogatory remarks, this fault, if it is one, would seem to lie with the manner in which the system works rather than with the system itself. Doubtless some improvements can and will be made to ensure that the mechanics of promotion are as foolproof as possible. In the last analysis, however, promotion in the Foreign Service, like entrance into it, depends on the qualities of the individuals sitting in judgment on the candidates. It is the human factor which is all-important.

► NATURE AND OPERATION OF AMERICAN
DIPLOMATIC ESTABLISHMENTS

As of 1954 there were almost three hundred American Foreign Service offices. These fall into several categories. Of the formal diplomatic variety there are fifty-eight embassies and fourteen legations. The embassies are supposedly located only in the capitals of the larger and more important countries, but during World War II all United States missions in Latin America were raised to this status to indicate the closeness of cooperation which the government desired with its sister republics of the hemisphere. Over the embassies preside ambassadors extraordinary and plenipoteniary; over the legations, ministers entitled Envoys Extraordinary and Plenipotentiary. While the former are supposed to represent the person of the President and the latter not, the actual distinction is in size and importance of establishment. When there is no ambassador in residence or he is temporarily absent, a chargé d'affaires or a chargé d'affaires ad interim, as the case may be, heads the diplomatic post.

In the consular category are included fifty-two consulates general, one hundred twenty-seven consulates, and thirty consular agents. The differentiation again rests on the amount of activity taking place in the cities, apart from the capitals, where they are located. Consuls general, as their title implies, are in charge of the consulates general, and consuls or, in minor posts, vice-consuls, are in charge of the consulates. Final categories include seven political advisers' offices, in Japan and Trieste, and seven United States International Exchange Offices.

DIVISIONS OF A LARGE EMBASSY

The size of an establishment may vary from one person in the case of some minor consulates to upward of five hundred in such large posts as London and Paris. Normally the Foreign Service officer just beginning his career serves an apprenticeship in a small consulate before becoming part of the intricate machinery of a major embassy. A major embassy is run very much on the order of a Department of State in miniature. It has the same general subdivisions according to function: the consular, the administrative, the economic, the cultural and informational, and the political, of which the consular and political are the oldest. As the posts grew in personnel, administrative specialization was forced on the embassy. Administrative units of the Paris Embassy, mentioned by Childs in *American Foreign Service,* include the accounting unit, the code room, the mail room, the courier service, the telephone service, and the library. In addition to administrative management, organization, and planning, the Administrative Section has charge of the allocation and control of funds allotted to the mission, including the preparation and execution of the budget, personnel management, general administrative services, and security.

The duty of economic reporting was relatively simple in the past, being confined to technical studies and services for American businesses at home and abroad. With the increasing importance of economic techniques in American foreign policy, this division of the embassy expanded in scope and in members. Since the war it has had a close connection with political policies, concerning itself with the impact of a particular foreign economic policy on that country's over-all position in international affairs and with the economic effects which alternate courses of American statecraft might produce. Thus members of the Economic Section, in addition to promoting American business interests, are charged with reporting economic developments in such fields as agriculture, trade, transport, finance, and labor. They frequently participate in negotiations with foreign governments where the negotiations have direct economic relevancy—and few do not these days!

Only recently has the United States paid much attention to the cultural and informational aspects of American representation abroad.* There is much more to the cultural and informational work of the embassy than

* For detailed discussion of American informational policies see Chapter Sixteen, "American Policy in the Battle of Ideas."

explaining American policy informally and winning friends for the United States abroad. The Information Section may assist the chief of mission regarding press contacts and public relations. It may also participate in programs for the international exchange of persons. There is, furthermore, the reportorial function of diplomacy noted at the outset of this chapter. This branch is in part responsible for explaining to the Department of State the nature of foreign societies, the interaction between their component groups, the probable demands and limitations which the society will place on the foreign policy of the nation in question, and in consequence even the influence which particular American policies may be expected to have.

To meet the specialized needs of a large embassy a number of attachés have been assimilated into its structure. The Reorganization Act of 1939, previously mentioned, transformed the overseas representatives of the Commerce and Agriculture Departments into commercial and agricultural attachés who were to function under the direction of the ambassador. Others were added during the war: civil air attachés, labor attachés, legal attachés, and even petroleum attachés in posts where that subject was of special importance. Military and naval attachés, while also part of the embassy, have a different relationship to diplomatic representation and will be considered later.

CONTINUING IMPORTANCE OF THE POLITICAL UNIT

While other sections of the Embassy grew in numbers and importance, the political unit remained the center of foreign diplomacy. Personnel devoting their attention primarily to political affairs might in general be said to be performing one or a combination of the following tasks. The first is straight reporting of political developments in the country: the activities of the various parties, the latest pronouncements of the government, and so forth. Beyond this lies the problem of exploration and analysis. What do the latest developments portend? What clues can be obtained as to the probable next step of the government? Above all, how does the mass of information being channeled home to the State Department fit into a consistent, comprehensive picture of the state in question and its relations to the United States? Another function of the political division is that of maintaining contacts: contacts with private individuals who are citizens of the foreign state, with diplomats attached to other missions, with government officials; contacts at all levels from the bottom to the top, depending on the status of the officer in his own hierarchy. The purpose behind these contacts is not just to receive and pass along information or merely to perform the necessary ceremonial functions of a diplomat. The presence of embassy personnel— particularly of a large mission—is an integral part of the impression which other countries gain of the United States, an impression which this country naturally desires to be as favorable to the development of its own policies as possible.

Finally, the personnel of the political unit is constantly involved in negotiations with other representatives and with the government on matters small and large. Most of this negotiation is routine and technical, albeit of a political nature, and is handled from start to finish by the semianonymous secretaries of the embassy, dealing with people of comparable stature in other missions or in the foreign office. Even when matters of importance are up for negotiation, the chief of mission or his deputy chief frequently allows proceedings to be initiated down the hierarchical line, interposing himself only when the necessary spadework has been completed and the subject under discussion is ripe for successful conclusion. In instances where the chiefs of mission take a hand from the outset the help and frequently the actual presence of members of his Political Section are normal procedure abroad as in the Department of State, since on this section falls most of the detail of furthering the negotiations and of implementing their results.

Because of the mass of detail, both in reporting and in negotiation, which the personnel of the Political Section has to handle, specialization is inevitable. Specialization may be by area or by subject. A large embassy can be expected to have experts on the various geographical areas of most concern to the foreign office of the country in which it is located, experts who will report on policy toward those areas and discuss with foreign office representatives the policies of the United States and the country involved. Specializing by subject are embassy experts on the internal communist movement, national minorities, and so forth. For example, the American Embassy in Paris would be expected to have in its Political Section specialists on Franco-German relations, on the Communist and De Gaullist movements, and on French colonial policies, particularly in Algeria and Viet Nam. As with the Department of State itself, this specialization diminishes the further up the embassy ladder the individual Foreign Service officer climbs. Specialization, of course, is largely unknown at the smaller posts.

OPERATING PATTERNS OF A MISSION CHIEF

The successful chief of a large mission may conform to any one of four general administrative patterns. He can perform the ceremonial and formal representative functions of his office and leave the running of the embassy to his subordinates, usually the deputy chief of mission and the chiefs of the various sections. While this may be the popular impression of a model diplomat, one substantiated by Americans who have served their government in the past, this type is vanishing under postwar pressures. If he follows the second administrative pattern, the chief of mission views his task as primarily that of an administrator who is eternally vigilant to see that the members of his team work together smoothly and efficiently. The complexity of the large post makes this type desirable in limited numbers, and not infrequently the Department of State has such men of demonstrated administrative ability as roving trouble shooters to straighten out operations at various establishments.

In the third pattern, the head of mission can make a practice of delegating responsibility while keeping final authority in his own hands. He can run the embassy and be its chief while not interfering with his subordinates in the day-to-day performance of their duties. His presence will be felt, not only as administrator, but as final arbiter and decision maker on matters of importance. In large posts in countries where American relations are delicate and complex, this is the usual pattern of successful ambassadorial operation.

Finally, there is the ambassador who *is the embassy* in a very real sense, the man who runs the administrative side, and instead of delegating responsibility on matters of substance, performs most of the details of reporting and negotiation himself or at least keeps such a close watch on their progress that he can and does interject himself constantly. Of such a type was Ambassador Messersmith, lately retired from the Foreign Service. " 'Uncle' George," says Ambassador Beaulac, "was a meticulous worker who overlooked no details. He was the No. 1 letter writer in the service. He corresponded with a vast number of people on matters having to do with his mission as well as with other people's missions. His letters were long and frequently repetitious. He told me that he never had time to write a short letter. He detested telegrams because they weren't long enough. He believed that most telegrams were written not because the subject was urgent but because the telegram was the lazy man's substitution for a satisfactory report. . . . Serious and even grim, Messersmith had no hobby but his work. . . . The important problems of the Habana Embassy, except for sugar, he handled himself. He was a man of intense convictions who did not hesitate to change his mind. . . . Messersmith hammered away at every problem until it was solved. He never gave up. He never even relaxed. He complained continually about the delicate state of his health while doing the work of three men without apparent fatigue."* Spruille Braden, with whom Messersmith clashed over American policy toward Argentina and who left the Foreign Service at about the same time, was another indefatigable worker who kept all the lines of power, authority, and control of detail in his own hands.

THE PROBLEM OF PRESIDENTIAL APPOINTMENTS

The preceding pages have summarized the basis of operation of the American Foreign Service. But this is far from the whole picture of representation of the United States abroad. It was mentioned at the outset that the ambassador was the personal representative of the President. This fact has led American chief executives to take a hand in the appointment of men to the rank of ambassador, the latest example being that of President Eisenhower, who quite correctly regarded his ambassadorial appointees as important members of his new administration. Until it was removed by the Foreign Service Act of 1946, there was a statutory requirement that, upon

---

* Willard Beaulac, *Career Ambassador* (New York, The Macmillan Company, 1951), pp. 148–149. Copyright 1951. Reprinted by permission of The Macmillan Company.

being appointed ambassador, any officer must resign from the Foreign Service. This provision served to emphasize the intimate, political relationship between an ambassador and the President. The presidential power of appointment has been used on occasion throughout American history to reward worthy supporters of the President—party regulars, heavy contributors, and the like. In the past, the caliber of such men was apt to be low. Continual raising of the qualifications for ambassador has tended, however, to increase the ability of political appointees, to lower the ratio between political appointees and men in the career service, and to increase appointments of able men. At the present time a majority of ambassadors have had lengthy experience in the Foreign Service.

Despite any past abuses, there is much to be said in defense of the President's right to go outside the Foreign Service in naming his personal representatives to foreign posts. He may in this way be able to bring into the diplomatic arena men of the highest qualifications whose experience and stature have been gained elsewhere. Thus men with business experience have been selected for ambassadorships. Furthermore, it is frequently important that both the President and the foreign government know that the ambassador is in fact as well as in theory the personal representative of the President, that he speaks for the President, knows the mind and thoughts of the President, has access to him if need be; that he is, in other words, something beyond a civil servant, a single member of a complex bureaucracy. Finally, it is arguable with respect to even the most arrant political appointment that the man in question could do his country more good or less harm, as the case may be, by representing it in some far-off, not too dangerous country. Considerations such as these have governed ambassadorial appointments of the President at times. While the Senate has occasionally balked at particular nominees coming from outside the Foreign Service (Ed Flynn and Ed Pauley were examples), its proper inclination has been to respect the desire of the President to have a crony, a confidante, or a career man representing him personally abroad.*

► MULTIPLE REPRESENTATION OF THE UNITED STATES ABROAD

THE USE OF PERSONAL EMISSARIES

Presidential intrusion into the diplomatic process has not stopped with naming ambassadors. There has been increasing use made of the personal emissary who is outside the embassy framework. In part the practice arose from the magnified problems with which American foreign policy has to deal. Special problems occasionally seem more amenable to solution by special means. Thus first Patrick Hurley and then General Marshall were

---

* The appointment of Charles Bohlen as Ambassador to the Soviet Union is hardly an example of a presidential political appointment, although it does illustrate the inclination of the Senate to go along with the President in such matters. Bohlen was a Foreign Service officer with special knowledge of the Soviet Union.

sent to China to explore the possibilities of reconciling the Nationalist and Communist factions to a coalition government that could more effectively prosecute the war against Japan and, so it was thought, could prevent the slide of postwar China into chaos and communism. In part the practice has resulted from the increasing preoccupation of the President with matters of foreign policy. Unwilling or unable to delegate complete responsibility to his own Executive Department, he has taken matters into his own hands and has used a special envoy to project his own personality and ideas abroad. Thus Sumner Welles was sent on a tour of Europe in 1940 to explore and report personally to the President on the chances of peace.

In part the practice arose because of mistrust or antipathy by the President toward the State Department and the Foreign Service. President Roosevelt's hostility toward the department was well known. His attitude stemmed basically from his reaction to the type of personnel who composed the department, from the top to the bottom, and including especially the Foreign Service officers. In his book *Roosevet and Hopkins,* Robert Sherwood reports that "Hopkins told a friend that the President also asked him to have a look at the personnel in American embassies and legations and to report to him confidentially thereon. Roosevelt felt then [before the United States entered World War II] that there were individuals in the Foreign Service who were not entirely sympathetic to the policies of his administration, and as the years went by and he received reports from Hopkins and many others who traveled abroad, he became increasingly sure of it."*

On many vital issues Roosevelt wanted to be his own Secretary of State. He used Hopkins as his deputy: as his eyes, his ears, his voice, his reporter, his negotiator. Not only did President Roosevelt mistrust the motivations of the department and of its personnel; he also suspected the security of their communications during wartime. This led him to send his messages by way of Army or Navy channels, rather than through the department by diplomatic pouch and courier. He thus reinforced the effect of his intrusion into diplomacy by keeping the department ignorant of his intrusion, its extent, and direction.

The use of Hopkins as personal communicant between Roosevelt and Churchill during World War II is well known. When Hitler suddenly turned on the Soviet Union in June, 1941, pessimistic reports filtered back from American representatives in Moscow concerning the probable duration and intensity of Russian resistance. The problem was acute since there was no desire to waste American lend-lease supplies on a country about to capitulate. Hopkins was sent to investigate. On the basis of his optimistic report on the intentions and ability of the Russians to hold off the Germans, the decision was taken to admit the Soviet Union to the list of lend-lease recipients. After

---

* Robert Sherwood, *Roosevelt and Hopkins* (New York, Harper & Brothers, 1948), p. 233. This and the following quotations are reprinted by permission of the publisher.

the death of Roosevelt, President Truman sent Hopkins back to Moscow to secure the indispensable agreement on the Polish question without which the drafting of the United Nations Charter at San Francisco could not proceed. Hopkins took the assignment, notwithstanding his chronic illness, which was shortly to result in his death, and won Russian concession to the American viewpoint. There can be no doubt that Churchill and Stalin felt that in talking to "Lord Root-of-the-Matter," as the Prime Minister dubbed Hopkins, they were communicating with the President in a way which channels of normal diplomacy could not match.

The role of Hopkins in the Churchill-Roosevelt relationship was unique. During the war there took place, in Sherwood's words, "an informal, off-the-record but none the less official correspondence between the heads of two governments through a third party, Hopkins, in whose discretion and judgment each had complete confidence. Time and again, when the Prime Minister wanted to sound out the President's view on some new move, he would address a private cable to Hopkins saying, in effect, 'If you think well of it, perhaps you would ask our great friend for his opinion on the following proposal . . . etc.' Hopkins, having consulted Roosevelt, might decide that he did not 'think well of it' and would reply that this did not seem an opportune moment to submit the proposal. Or, if it were approved, Hopkins would reply, 'It is felt here that you should go ahead with your proposal to . . . etc.' "* Thus Hopkins was a presidential emissary whether or not he left the country or even the White House.

EFFECTS OF THE USE OF PERSONAL EMISSARIES

The advantages of having a personal emissary, apart from the formal diplomatic mission, are manifest. The President can keep more closely informed than is possible through departmental channels. He can more effectively control the execution of American foreign policy, with which he is charged by the Constitution. He can introduce speed and flexibility into a system inevitably slowed down and encumbered by detail. But it should be recognized that a price is paid for these advantages. One is the damaging effect on the ambassador of having most of the negotiations between the United States and the foreign government in which he is stationed conducted by people who are not part of the diplomatic establishment. Sherwood quotes a telegram which Ambassador Winant sent in 1943 to Harry Hopkins:

> During the past six months a situation has developed which has cut down my usefulness. I have had no business delegated to me as ambassador that could not have been done by an efficient Foreign Service officer. I have been by-passed constantly. I have had no contacts with the Prime Minister except on two occasions when he invited me to meet with him so that *he could bring me up to date on Anglo-American relations.* [Italics added.] Nine-tenths of the information I receive comes from British

---

* *Ibid.,* p. 269.

sources. Matters of serious importance relating to our foreign policy go to Mr. Churchill or Mr. Eden through other channels. Officials of the British Government have been friendly and frank with me but they are quick to appreciate when one in my position has been deprived of his authority. . . . There has been a whispering campaign in the past few months that I was to be relieved of my post and succeeded by Averell [Harriman], and yesterday I read in the London papers that I am to be succeeded by you. Such reports would do no damage were it not for the fact that you and Averell have done a considerable part of the exchange of communications that normally should be done by the Ambassador.

I think the President and Stettinius should know that no Ambassador can be an effective representative here in London unless he is given more information and support than I am receiving.*

The reply which Hopkins sent was equally revealing. It was four paragraphs in length—i.e., shorter than Winant's telegram. The first paragraph consisted of one sentence sympathizing with Winant and saying that he, Hopkins, would feel the same way under the circumstances. The second paragraph was longer. It denied that Winant was about to be replaced by anyone and stated that the President, the country, and Hopkins thought Winant was doing the best job of any American ambassador to Great Britain. (It would seem to have been a mistake, although indicative of his state of mind, for Winant to have interjected the personal note. It detracted seriously from the principle involved and gave Hopkins a loophole, which he used, to evade discussion of the principle.) The third paragraph was completely irrelevant, a one-sentence capsule of developments on the German-Russian front. Although Winant said he did not have access to much information, he undoubtedly knew as much as Hopkins was here reporting. The inclusion of this paragraph suggests that Hopkins was at a loss for words and wanted to pad the reply to a respectable length. The final paragraph expressed a desire to talk over the situation, a gesture made no doubt with full knowledge that such a talk could and would not take place. The message closed with an appreciation of Winant's work. "Buck up, old boy," Winant was being told, "things are tough all over." What was going to be done about the situation of which Winant complained? Nothing. Presumably Winant, having got the matter off his chest, was now supposed to go back to playing an obscure second fiddle to Lend-Lease Supervisor for Great Britain, W. Averell Harriman.

In addition to damaging the ego of the ambassador, other undesirable results are likely to follow when overseas representation is placed in other than embassy hands. A deleterious effect on the morale of the Foreign Service officers is inevitable. While some may have entered the Foreign Service looking for a good time traveling about in exotic foreign lands, the overwhelming

---

* *Ibid.*, pp. 754–5. The identity of the addressee is significant: the telegram was not sent to Winant's nominal superior, Secretary of State Cordell Hull, but rather to the man most likely to see that Winant's complaint reached the President.

majority are in search of a career which they have been led to expect is important to the national welfare. When duties which normally would fall to them go to others, not by any act of Congress or executive pronouncement, but by informal decision of a type and at a level impossible successfully to challenge, Foreign Service officers may in their frustration begin to regret the path they have chosen. One of the reasons for the growth of informal representation by the United States has been the belief that the Foreign Service could not adequately discharge the new responsibilities placed on this country in its foreign relations. But a solution by personal, *ad hoc* presidential appointments only aggravates the condition. Far from increasing the competence of the diplomats by broadening the pattern of their operations, non-embassy representation can have the opposite effect of relegating existing personnel to limited, subordinate responsibilities, even motivating some to leave the Foreign Service for other careers, and thus lowering the ability of the Foreign Service to recruit necessary skills and talents. Without any conscious intention of doing so, foreign governments may aggravate the situation. As Winant said, "they are quick to appreciate when one in my position has been deprived of his authority." Other governments will naturally channel the majority of their contacts and negotiation through American personnel who they feel truly represent the power and intentions of the United States. Thus the practice of non-embassy representation spreads, becomes self-perpetuating and difficult to abandon.

There are also the effects on American foreign policy to consider. One of the functions of the Department of State is to serve as a repository of information upon which qualified officials can draw. When the department is by-passed, that knowledge becomes diffused, difficult to locate. It may exist only in the heads of a few people whose tenure in office will not be endless. Thus the country found itself at a disadvantage in many concrete situations when death and ill-health removed President Roosevelt and Harry Hopkins from the White House. Their successors were not familiar with the background of current problems and frequently did not even know where to go for information to fill in the gaps. Secretary of State Byrnes wrote that he, despite his position as Secretary of State, had no inkling of some of the war-time arrangements made by the United States. Unlike Clement Attlee, who succeeded Churchill soon after the death of Roosevelt, President Truman had not been privy to the councils of President Roosevelt on many foreign-policy issues. Relatively fortunate were President Eisenhower and Secretary of State Dulles, both of whom had had experience in foreign affairs prior to their accession to office. But the country cannot rely on such happenstance for efficiency in foreign policy. By-passing the State Department through outside appointments places an additional burden on an already overladen chief executive. A President who wishes to manage foreign policy himself has the devices to do so. Another who wishes to delegate responsibility to his Secretary of State finds the department no longer able to function in the normal pattern. He must either permit a period of adjustment to take place, during which mistakes are made and opportunities missed, or find himself like his predecessor enmeshed in the details of foreign-policy execution. The alternatives are not very attractive in a period when any margin for error has largely vanished.

GROWTH OF MULTIPLE-AGENCY REPRESENTATION ABROAD

The problem created as a result of by-passing the State Department is not limited to the appointment of individuals. Under pressure of the immediate prewar and wartime emergency, which found the State Department woefully unprepared, various American agencies gained the right to autonomous representation abroad. This practice was maintained after the war when the United States was in the process of greatly expanding its foreign commitments.

A study undertaken for the Bureau of the Budget by the Brookings Institution found that "as of September 30, 1950 some 43 government departments, agencies or units were engaged in activities overseas, employing a total of civilian personnel, comprising both Americans and nationals of the various countries, of 74,879."* In addition to the diplomatic and consular activities of the Department of State alone, the Brookings study listed seven concrete programs in which agencies other than the State Department were participating: intelligence activities; economic aid programs in Western Europe, occupied areas, the Philippines, Korea, and "the general area of China" (southeast Asia and Formosa); mutual-defense assistance programs; educational exchange and technical cooperation programs; informational activities; administration of occupied areas; and the displaced persons program (since dissolved).

The postwar precedent for multiple representation was set with the decision to create a separate mission to Greece to administer the assistance program implementing the Truman Doctrine. So much friction developed between the diplomatic establishment of Ambassador MacVeagh and the mission of the late Dwight Griswold that both chiefs had to be replaced by one man in charge of all aspects of American relations with the Greek government. Nevertheless, the Greek precedent was followed by Congress, albeit over the strenuous objections of Secretary of State Marshall, in the establishment of a separate Economic Cooperation Administration. Later a different relationship to the diplomatic missions was created with the dispatch to Western Europe of staffs to supervise American military assistance under the North Atlantic Treaty. By 1950 these two groups were added to the military missions and personnel from the Agriculture, Commerce, Treasury, and Labor Departments.

The various agency representatives had little in common in the form of

_____

* The Brookings Institution, *The Administration of Foreign Affairs and Overseas Operations* (Washington, U.S. Government Printing Office, 1951), p. 244.

their relationships to the diplomatic missions. The Brookings study applied three criteria in an attempt to describe the varying relations: whether the technical personnel had been assimilated into the Foreign Service, whether they served on the staff of the chief of the diplomatic mission, and whether the State Department assumed part or all of the responsibility for the execution of the particular program. It found that overseas employees of some American agencies, such as those of the Labor Department, satisfied all three criteria, indicating rather complete integration with the diplomatic establishment. At the other extreme were the ECA personnel, who were separate from the embassies in all three respects. Some, such as the Military Assistance Advisory Groups, met the second and third, but not the first, criteria; some, such as those of the Institute for Inter-American affairs, and the Technical Cooperation Administration, only the third criterion; others, such as Treasury and armed service attachés, only the second. The Brookings study further observed that additional variations existed with respect to the line of communications which was followed and that individual embassies in some instances departed from the norm with respect to personnel of particular agencies.

To find any single solution to this administrative chaos has proved difficult. It seems fair to conclude, as did the Brookings Institution, that the least satisfactory relationship was that of the Economic Cooperation Administration missions. The size of their staffs, the breadth of their activities, the importance of those activities to the survival of individual foreign countries were factors that could not but aggravate the consequences of separation from the various diplomatic establishments. As the ECA developed, it began to add large-scale informational and exchange programs to its economic duties, while the economic duties themselves involved detailed representation and reporting. Larger ECA missions therefore came close to paralleling the work of the diplomatic establishments, and in some instances there was little doubt that the ECA assumed the greater stature in the eyes of officials of governments receiving large-scale assistance. The decision of Congress in 1951 to discontinue the ECA in favor of the Mutual Security Agency reduced somewhat the complexity of American overseas representation and opened the way for further examination of the most satisfactory relationship between specific missions and diplomatic establishments.

Three types of military personnel overseas deserve attention in a study of the problem of representation: the attachés, the missions, and the military assistance advisory groups. The military attachés are most closely assimilated into the diplomatic mission. While they are, of course, military personnel and not part of the Foreign Service, they are under the supervision of the chief of mission during their tour of duty. From him they receive political guidance and through him they report, both to the Department of State and to their own service headquarters in Washington. Their status is not much different, therefore, from that of labor or commercial attachés.

The military missions—including ground, air, and navy groups—have much more autonomy. Although their existence antedates World War II, particularly in Latin America, only in the postwar period have they come fully into their own as a result of the increased global military responsibilities of the United States. The agreement between the United States and the country desiring the mission may be negotiated under State Department auspices, but the selection of personnel is a matter for the Armed Forces to determine. Once stationed abroad, they report, not to the State Department or through the diplomatic mission, but direct to their parent agencies. If the reports are shown to the chief of diplomatic mission before or after they are sent, or reach the State Department at all, that procedure is not prescribed by the rules and regulations but rests on comity and practice, which may vary from country to country and from situation to situation. Likewise the heads of the military missions may take advice on matters of policy from the State Department representatives, and they frequently do. They are not required to do so, however, and when differences of opinion arise, as they have, they must be settled by negotiation between the representatives abroad or between the agencies at home. The relationship has more than a purely administrative significance.

The Military Assistance Advisory Group, set up under the Mutual Assistance Program, constitutes a special type of military mission. As described in the Brookings study, the MAAG is "headed by a high-ranking military officer, and a special assistant to the ambassador who is usually a senior Foreign Service Officer. The chief of the MAAG is designated by the Department of Defense, the special assistant by the Department of State. The MAAG's line of communication on policy matters is to the ambassador, beyond whom policy is determined in Washington. On military operational matters the line runs to the Department of Defense, both direct and, for NATO country programs, through the United States Military Representative or his Deputy in London (JAMAG). The MAAG is entirely separate from the military, naval, and air attaché sections of the embassy, because of a desire to avoid a possible unfavorable reaction on the part of foreign officials if military assistance were to be combined with what is generally regarded as an intelligence activity. The MAAG is divided into three sections corresponding to the three armed services, and there is usually one additional section concerned with administration."*

SOLUTIONS TO THE PROBLEM OF MULTIPLE-AGENCY REPRESENTATION

Both the Hoover Commission and the Brookings Institution wrestled with the problem of multiple representation, to which there are three significant aspects: the location of over-all authority as spokesmen for the United States, the relationships between the many agencies, in addition to the Department of State, which represented the United States abroad, and the

* Brookings Institution, *op. cit.*, p. 252.

responsibility for execution abroad of specific programs, such as economic and military assistance. Both studies agreed on the necessity of placing over-all authority in the chief of diplomatic mission. Said the Hoover Commission report on American foreign affairs in Recommendation 13: "The Chief of each United States foreign mission should be the responsible American spokesman for the area or country to which he is assigned. He should observe and counsel all United States activities therein, and he should be responsible for administration of his mission."* Said the report: "It is unworkable and dangerous . . . to have American spokesman and operators abroad dealing with foreign nations who are independent of the ambassadors or ministers and who are not responsible to them for supervision and coordination."† (It should be noted that the word "coordination" is a slippery one.)

The studies agreed that personnel of agencies, other than the State Department, which feel the need for overseas representation, should be under the direction of the Department of State and the chief of diplomatic mission during their period of service abroad. The Hoover Commission further stated that they should be "a part of the Foreign Affairs Service" and subject to return by the chief of mission, ratified by the Secretary of State, "for reasons related to improper deportment or for unsatisfactory work performance." Should these recommendations be carried out, all specialized personnel would have a relationship to the embassy similar to that of the Labor Department's representatives at the present time.

With respect to missions carrying out programs which are not under the jurisdiction of the Department of State, the Brookings Institution noted that "the existing organizational relationships between the military groups and the diplomatic missions at the posts abroad appear for the most part to be stable and satisfactory" and that consequently they should be followed in the case of ECA missions. The earlier recommendation of the Hoover Commission was apparently similar, but was stated more forcibly: the chief of mission should be "the ultimate authority with respect to foreign affairs aspects of program operations."

As part of its task of recommending measures for administrative re-organization,‡ the President's Advisory Committee on Government Organization, appointed soon after the election by President-Elect Eisenhower, came to grips with the problem of multiple representation of the United States abroad. The committee could draw on the studies of the Hoover Commission and of the Brookings Institution, whose conclusions have been mentioned above. The Advisory Committee's own recommendations, embodied in President Eisenhower's Reorganization Plans 7 and 8, simplified the relationship between the representatives of various agencies operating

* The Commission on Organization of the Executive Branch of the Government, *op. cit.*, p. 50.
† *Ibid.*, p. 51.
‡ For details as they affected the State Department, see Chapter Seven, "The Organization and Functions of the State Department."

abroad and the diplomatic mission by centralizing all information programs in the United States Information Agency and all economic programs in the Foreign Operations Administration. In addition, Reorganization Plan 7 abolished the Office of Special Representative in Europe, establishing in its place a new United States Mission to the North Atlantic Treaty Organization and to European Regional Organizations. The authority of the diplomatic mission in its dealings with the new North Atlantic Treaty Organization was strengthened by the precise statement of the Secretary of State's role in giving political guidance and in passing on appointments to the new agencies.* Even more explicit was the statement of the President, in sending the reorganization plans to Congress, that "each chief of diplomatic mission in each foreign country [must] provide effective coordination of, and foreign policy direction with respect to, all United States activities in the country."

Even should the foregoing recommendations be embodied by Congress in permanent legislation, certain serious difficulties would remain. Establishment of the principle of diplomatic supremacy does not, for example, change the fact that much of American policy is nondiplomatic and will continue to be so as long as East-West tension continues. Nondiplomatic activity abroad will normally be related to nondiplomatic agencies at home. The latter resist, and will continue to do so, any subordination of their responsibilities to the authority of the Department of State. Moreover, the right of the Secretary of State to give policy guidance and advice on appointments to other agencies operating in the foreign-policy field is far from subjecting those agencies to the overriding, final authority of the Department of State. This is a principle which Congress rejected once in establishing the Economic Cooperation Administration and rejected again in creating the Mutual Security Agency as successor to the ECA. The continuing conflict is over the extent to which the State Department should remain an operating agency. Secretary of State Byrnes, the Hoover Commission, President Eisenhower's Advisory Committee on Government Reorganization, congressmen, and many others have expressed the belief that the department should be a small, staff, planning agency, with others responsible for the execution of concrete programs. As the previous chapter pointed out, this distinction may be a valid one, but it makes difficult, if not impossible, the establishment in practice of the authority of the planner over the executor, when the plans to be executed are so large, cost so much money, and employ so many people. It must remembered that policy in large part grows out of day-to-day operations and becomes difficult to control when the decision maker is not also the executor.

It is apparent that public officials and others accepting the concept of a small State Department, pursuing primarily staff functions, also believe that separation of planning and operation is not only possible, but desirable, and that the Department of State, for various reasons, some theoretical, some practical, some objective, some subjective, should not have charge of most

* See Chapter Seventeen, "Western Europe and American Security."

of the activities involved in the conduct of American foreign affairs. So long as the bases of these judgments remain, so long as the bulk of American policy finds nondiplomatic expression, there will continue to be the same distinction in foreign representation between the diplomatic and the non-diplomatic types, with the former by tradition and theory having a monopoly of contact and negotiation with other governments, but with the latter carrying much if not the major part of the burden of representation and contact.

► SELECTED BIBLIOGRAPHY

Among the studies of diplomacy as a technique, those of Jules Cambon, *Le Diplomate* (Paris, Hachette, 1926), Sir Ernest Satow, *Guide to Diplomatic Practice* (London, Longmans, Green & Co., 1917), and Harold Nicolson, *Diplomacy* (New York, Harcourt, Brace & Company, 1939) stand out. Significant American studies include Hugh Gibson, *The Road to Foreign Policy* (New York, Doubleday & Company, 1944) and Walter Lippmann, *American Foreign Policy: Shield of the Republic* (Boston, Little, Brown & Company, 1942). Two excellent chapters in Hans Morganthau, *Politics among Nations* (New York, Alfred A. Knopf, Inc., 1948), are concerned with the subject of diplomacy. *Negotiating with the Russians* (Boston, World Peace Foundation, 1951), edited by Raymond Dennett and Joseph E. Johnson, contains the experience of Americans in specific negotiations with Soviet representatives. The contribution of Philip Mosely to the volume discusses "Some Soviet Techniques of Negotiation." In "Old Wine—Soviet Bottles," *World Politics,* January, 1950, Percy Corbett considers Soviet treatises on diplomacy. J. Rives Childs, *American Foreign Service* (New York, Henry Holt and Company, 1948), is a short treatment of the history of the Foreign Service, the organization and operation of a large embassy, and the changes made by the Foreign Service Act of 1946. The origin of the act and the method of its passage through Congress is examined by the Committee on Public Administration Cases. The Department of State's own publication, *The Foreign Service of the United States,* summarizes the history and status of the Foreign Service in the light of the 1946 act. Gordon Craig, "Promotion in a Career Service," *American Foreign Service Journal,* June, 1949, discusses the operation of the promotion-up, selection-out principle and gives suggestions for its improvement. Willard Beaulac, *Career Ambassador* (New York, The Macmillan Company, 1951), is an interesting account of a foreign service officer from entrance to ambassadorial appointment; see also Joseph C. Grew, *The Turbulent Era* (Boston, Houghton Mifflin Company, 1952). The chapter entitled "The Career Foreign Service Officer" in James McCamy, *Administration of American Foreign Affairs* (New York, Alfred A. Knopf, Inc., 1950), analyzes the personnel of the Foreign Service in terms of geographical background, education, experience, and the like. Three studies have contributed to an understanding of the present problem of organizing an efficient Foreign Service: the report to Congress in February, 1949, of the (Hoover) Commission on Organization of the Executive Branch of the Government, entitled

Foreign Affairs (Washington, D.C., Government Printing Office, 1949) and the Task Force Report on which that of the commission was based: H. H. Bundy and J. G. Rogers, *The Organization of the Government for the Conduct of Foreign Affairs* (Washington, D.C., Government Printing Office, 1949); the report to the Secretary of State by the Secretary's Advisory (Rowe) Committee on Personnel in August, 1950, entitled *An Improved Personnel System for the Conduct of Foreign Affairs;* and the report prepared for the Bureau of the Budget by the Brookings Institution, dated June, 1951, and entitled *The Administration of Foreign Affairs and Overseas Operations* (Washington, D.C., Government Printing Office, 1951), particularly Chapters II, VII, and VIII, on recent developments: "Representation in Foreign Countries," "Personnel Administration for Overseas Civilian Staffs," and "Key Elements of Administrative Doctrine for Major Governmental Units."

CHAPTER NINE

THE ROLE OF MILITARY INSTITUTIONS AND AGENCIES IN AMERICAN FOREIGN POLICY

► INTRODUCTION

Had this book been written in 1939 or even in 1945, it is quite unlikely that it would have included a separate chapter entitled "The Role of the Military." Beyond mentioning international wars in which the United States has participated and the use of military forces in conjunction with diplomacy, it would not have seemed necessary to discuss the way in which military personnel and agencies contribute to the formulation of foreign policy. But the military are now an integral part of the decision-making process, a change due to special factors which are to be discussed in the present chapter. The preceding pages have stressed the point that foreign-policy decision making in the United States must be viewed in terms of the revolution in the nature of American policy. The "new role" of the military is recent and may be characterized as one of the several "revolutions within a revolution" which have overtaken policy making since Pearl Harbor.

A whole generation of students have grown up for whom the identification of great military names—Marshall, Eisenhower, Bradley, and MacArthur—with important contemporary developments in American foreign policy is normal and natural. To them, the reminder that this is a relatively new experience may appear puzzling and the stress on the significance of the role of the military may appear to be somewhat unnecessary. However, by placing the new role of the military in its historical perspective certain trends and implications appear which might otherwise be lost. Nowhere is the complexity of the problems which confront America more clearly illustrated than in the realm of the military. The problems are essentially the same ones analyzed in previous chapters. It would be more exact to say *kinds* of problems, since

345

their substance may be quite different from situation to situation. Perhaps the best way to identify some of these kinds of problems is by asking questions:

1. How can the total strength of the nation be mobilized and utilized continuously for the preservation of national security without altering the form of government or having the mobilization actually interfere with the realization of objectives?
2. What is the balance between a military establishment sufficiently strong to protect the nation and yet not too strong to slip from the control of the civil leaders of government, the President and Congress?
3. What is the proper role of the military in the process of foreign-policy decision making and by what organizational devices can that role best be implemented?
4. What is the general impact upon foreign policy of military factors, decisions, and techniques?
5. What is the effect upon military policy and planning of technological and political factors?
6. What is the best way to organize the domestic military establishment for making and executing military policy?

Consideration of such questions leads directly to the kinds of problems alluded to: problems of effective decision making; efficient administrative organization; the cost of national security; discovery and use of appropriate foreign-policy techniques; the difficulty of maintaining partial mobilization in a political democracy; military planning under conditions of technological and political change; maintenance of the principle of civilian supremacy; the meshing of political objectives and military operations; the "unification" of the Armed Forces; the need for coordination of military and political aspects of foreign policy and of the impact of large-scale military organization on American society generally. This list suggests at once the range of complexity which is involved in a consideration of the new position of the military in the conduct of foreign relations. The importance of perspective should now be clearer; these are "problems" precisely because they have brought new choices, dilemmas, and unanswered questions to the American people. Many would not be problems in quite the same sense if America had had fifty years of experience similar to that of the past ten.

WAYS OF LOOKING AT THE MILITARY ESTABLISHMENT

There are four ways of thinking about the military establishment and all four are relevent, though not equally so, to the present study. First, it may be regarded as an important reservoir of national power, as the machinery through which American military power is mobilized and exerted. The Armed Forces are obviously a vital element in the nation's capacity to achieve objectives—capacity which is actual and potential. Second, it can be regarded as a decision-making organization, as a unit (or really a group of units) which makes and executes decisions. The administrative behavior of the

Armed Forces is just as crucial to national strength as the existence of tanks or divisions or strategic plans. Indeed, the latter factors depend upon the former. Furthermore, the manner in which the Armed Forces are organized and operate will be related to the nature of their impact on civilian agencies and policy making in general. Third, and probably most essential, the military establishment can be viewed as an integral part of the foreign-policy organization and decision-making machinery outlined in the preceding chapters. Finally, it can be thought of as one of several major agencies with responsibilities for administering foreign policy. Each of these four ways of looking at the military reflects a different purpose of study and therefore a different focus of interest and different choice of materials. Each suggests one aspect of the general relationship between military organization and foreign-policy analysis.

THE MILITARY AND THE ELEMENTS OF DECISION MAKING

Throughout Part I decision making has been the basic theme of analysis, the intention being to view the federal government and the political process as foreign-policy-making machinery. It seems logical to try to fit the military organization into this same frame of reference. The role of the military in foreign-policy formation may accordingly be analyzed with respect to the elements of decision making. What kinds of *authority and responsibility are formally allocated to* the military? What, in other words, are the tasks assigned by laws, decrees, orders, and administrative arrangements? What kinds of tasks have been assigned *informally*—that is, what functions, if any, are performed by the military without sanction of formal authorization? Such tasks may be classified here as those purely military but with foreign-policy implications and those more directly concerned with foreign-policy making and execution. Another element is *motivation*. What factors might be expected to motivate military personnel in carrying out their special tasks and in their general approach to foreign-policy issues? What kinds of *information* and what kinds of *analytical skills* do military officials or civilian heads of military agencies bring to the process? Do certain kinds of information and analytical skills come close to being a natural monopoly of the armed services or are they shared widely by other groups? Finally, how is *coordination* between the military and civilian agencies achieved? How are the services themselves *coordinated?* How do the military *communicate* with themselves, with the President, with the State Department, with Congress, and with the public? Tentative answers to these questions should help to describe the role of the military, to account for the behavior of the military in decision making, and to provide a sufficient basis for weighing certain issues which have arisen.

SOME PRELIMINARY DEFINITIONS AND DISTINCTIONS

Certain fundamental distinctions should be laid down here because they will have a bearing on the analysis which follows. *Military factors and values are one thing; military influence through advice from military personnel* is another. Hence military events, conditions, or considerations and the interpretations of these which may affect a foreign-policy decision are not the same as military officials having an influential voice in such a decision. In a loose sense, both represent influence; yet they are not necessarily synonymous. Nonmilitary officials may be guided by military values in their deliberations. Military advice is not the same thing as the exercise of authority by military personnel. This is the familiar distinction between policy-influencing and policy-making roles within the decision-making process. It is necessary to know whether influence on decision making is due to the acceptance of an interpretation of a problem or situation as authoritative or is due to the performance of an official function assigned to an individual. Often the two go together but not always. Furthermore, when the phrase "undue military influence" is employed, it should be made clear whether the word "influence" applies to the formulation of policy, to the execution of policy, or to a reversal of ends and means, i.e., military strength is an end in itself, valued for itself and not for what might be achieved by using it.

A distinction must also be drawn between *military implications* of political decisions and *political implications* of military decisions. There is more to this than merely saying they are opposite sides of the same coin. A military decision or question is one in which military values or criteria are actually, or are understood to be, dominant. That is, in deciding an issue or assessing a problem, the military aspects are singled out as having top priority or as being *the* focal point of interest. A political decision or question is one in which political values or criteria are primary. In both cases other kinds of values or criteria will probably also be involved. What happens is that the other values or criteria are given lower priority, are momentarily ignored altogether, or their possible sacrifice is accepted as a price for accomplishing something more strongly desired. It is probable that decision makers try to have their cake and eat it too. That is, in some cases, there is no intention to sacrifice one set of values for another but only to adopt different means to ends which remain constant or to postpone immediate ends until a later time. When decision makers speak of political or military necessities, it would appear to mean that certain situations, by definition, rule out the application of all sets of values but one. Regardless of the values or criteria which led to a particular decision or solution of a problem, the decision or solution will have *consequences*. The consequences may be anticipated or unanticipated. Even a *purely* military or political decision (one in which there seem to be *no other values or criteria involved*) may turn out to have nonmilitary or nonpolitical consequences or implications. As will be seen, it is very difficult to discover a military decision which has no political implications and vice versa. Nonetheless, it is essential to draw a distinction between the nature and combination of values which shape a particular decision and the kinds of consequences which may follow. The labeling of decisions (or policies) as "political" and "military" can be meaningful if it is made clear whether the ingredients or the results are being classified. After all, decision makers themselves employ the distinction and it is not very helpful to say that all political decisions in this day and age are military and vice versa. The latter statement is a quick way of calling attention to a general relationship which is important but which cannot be explored fruitfully until terms are more sharply defined.

A first step in this direction is to differentiate political and military aspects of foreign policy. An aspect of a policy, decision, or problem may refer to objectives and techniques; to rules for choosing among them on the basis of preference, efficacy, desirability, and so on; to factors or conditions; to the interests and attitudes of groups of decision makers. Thus a military aspect of a policy might mean its relation to, implication for, or impact on military plans and strategy, how the policy would be judged in terms of its military feasibility or potential military responses of other states; attitudes of the military group toward the policy or their interest in it; or the effect of the policy on the international balance of power. Naturally these are related and the distinctions tend to become blurred. Nevertheless, the differences are significant analytically. For example, a given policy may not involve a question of military feasibility but may have a bearing on the balance of power; or the policy may not affect existing military plans but may convince military experts that their future control over their own problems is affected.

Later the concept of the "military mind" will be treated more fully. Here briefly a distinction is in order between military mind and military attitude. They often go together; yet they are not necessarily identical. While the former term has many meanings, in essence it is employed to indicate the kind of thinking engaged in by military personnel—a pattern of thinking determined largely by previous training and a long career experience in military organization. Military attitude, on the other hand, seems to mean favoring military objectives, relying heavily on military techniques, and judging policies by military values. The military mind seems to be primarily an attribute of military personnel; the military attitude may be manifest in anyone.

Militarism—and its derived adjective "militaristic"—also has a range of meanings. When it is said that American foregn policy has become more militaristic or has become invested with a quality of militarism, all or some of the following may be implied: that the military power of the United States has been expanded greatly and at the expense of other forms of power; that an unhealthy reliance is placed on military techniques to achieve national security; that military officials have a relatively greater influence over the formation of foreign policy than have civilian officials; that foreign policy envisages aggressive goals or at least goals which can be justified only on a military basis; that decision makers tend to see all issues as military issues or tend to overemphasize the military aspect of policy problems; that military factors and conditions generally loom larger than formerly in the external setting.

WHAT IS MEANT BY "THE MILITARY"?

Having already used this shorthand term several times, it is advisable to be explicit about it. Any or all of the following may be referred to: first, the national security organization—the armed services from the Secretary of Defense down to military installations in outlying bases; second, the top military and civilian leaders whose positions of responsibility enable them to speak authoritatively for the armed services as a whole or for units thereof; and third, the values and attitudes characteristic of military officials and embodied in the organizational purposes of the military establishment. In sum, "the military" refers to a segment of the federal bureaucracy, to certain key specialists and officials, and to a set of ideas and purposes. The need for a shorthand expression opens the door to the dangers of stereotyping, that is, of assuming in advance that all military personnel think and act alike; that the military organization, viewed in the large, is completely homogeneous; and that military values are held with equal intensity by all members of the armed forces.* Such implications obviously are not intended here.

A NEW ROLE FOR THE MILITARY

It is the theme of this chapter that the military, as just defined, has a new role in the conduct of American foreign relations. The military, to put the matter bluntly, does have greater influence (in the broad sense) than has ever been true before. Furthermore, this is a most significant recent development which must be understood if the present foreign-policy process is to be understood. This development has introduced special problems. It has had a definite impact on the organization of foreign-policy decision making. Drawing together what has been said in preceding paragraphs, the new role of the military rests primarily on a larger peacetime military establishment, a greater functional importance of military techniques, an increasing relevance of military values, and enhanced prestige of military leaders. However, these factors in turn owe their existence and effect to the coincidence of still other factors including certain changes in the external setting.

► THE CHANGING ROLE OF THE MILITARY AND MILITARY FACTORS

TRADITIONAL RELATIONSHIPS BETWEEN MILITARY AND CIVILIAN GROUPS

Throughout much of the life of the American republic, civilian attitudes toward the military have been characterized for the most part by mistrust, by a rejection of the idea of a strong central government backed by military force, by a lack of respect for a military career, and by a conviction that the professional soldier possessed qualities of mind inimical to demo-

---

* See Burton M. Sapin, "The Role of the Military in the Formulation of the Japanese Peace Treaty," in Gordon B. Turner, ed., *A History of Military Affairs since the Eighteenth Century* (Ann Arbor, Mich., Edwards Brothers, 1952), III, 1011.

cratic traditions. The United States has had, nonetheless, its military heroes and has five times (usually following wars) elected military figures to the presidency. The attitudes above mentioned have been buttressed by a strong tendency toward pacifism. At the beginning of national existence, the negative nature of American foreign policy decreed that military values and armed force would not loom very large in considerations of national security. Almost complete freedom from fear of attack, since no strong nations abutted on any frontier, meant that effective arguments for a large military establishment were lacking. It should be noted, however, that these views did not apply to the Navy, which was given a prominent place in national policy during the nineteenth and early twentieth centuries. Agrarian interests particularly were opposed to a strong Navy, but the need to parry other maritime powers in the Mediterranean, in the Western Hemisphere, and later in the Pacific was overriding. Moreover, maintaining a Navy did not involve a great organization operating within a nation and thus constituting a potential threat to liberty. Until World War II, America did not have a large standing Army, and the Navy, though one of the largest in the world, never mushroomed into a huge administrative structure.

Throughout the years the military group has displayed certain attitudes toward civilians. Military leaders resented open civilian criticism, their generally inferior social position, and what they considered bungling, ineffective civilian decision making which neglected security questions until it was too late. As a result, the military tended to withdraw into its own world—the academy or the post. Aloofness from the public was tinged with disrespect for "the people." The military also tended to be quite nationalistic and generally to overlook the importance of nonmilitary considerations. The latter factor went hand in hand with deliberate avoidance of any involvement in politics or political issues. That national security rather narrowly defined should be dominant over all other considerations represented the military's general orientation toward foreign relations.

The principle of civilian supremacy over military functions and organization was firmly established in the Constitution. A civilian, the President, was made commander in chief. There were a number of other safeguards designed to limit the functions and power of the Armed Forces. First, a policy of keeping the size of the Armed Forces to a minimum. Second, reliance primarily upon a militia rather than on a standing army. Third, separation of the state militia from the professional army so that the militia could check attempted usurpation by the Regular Army. Fourth, Congressional control of appropriations for the armed services, with renewal required at least every two years. Fifth, the exclusion of army and naval officers from governmental positions other than military.

Functions of the military were restricted and precisely defined: to quell rebellion against the United States; to aid in bringing offenders against the United States to justice; to protect the United States from attack; to prosecute war declared by the Congress; and to serve as an instrument of foreign policy under the direction of the President. The traditional military organization (both Army and Navy) was small, highly professionalized and indoctrinated by narrow training at West Point and Annapolis, engaged mostly in routine operations, and remained isolated from the main streams of policy making. The enlisted service was scarcely representative of American society as a whole.

This general pattern of civil-military relationships was predominant from 1789 to 1941. There were exceptions, of course, but in the main, military personnel, values, and organization were of secondary status in American life and played a relatively minor role in the formation of American foreign policy. Militaristic influences which did seep into American policy came from civilian officials, jingoist newspapers, and interest groups such as the Navy League. Admiral Mahan—a sailor-scholar of substantial influence in the 1890's—was not typical of the military in general. No machinery was available for continuously mobilizing military advice at high levels of executive decision making.

Long before 1941, however, events and developments were undermining the traditional pattern.

RECENT EVENTS AND DEVELOPMENTS WHICH HAVE ALTERED TRADITIONAL CIVIL-MILITARY RELATIONSHIPS

It is not possible to give a complete history of how the military's role in foreign policy has been altered. It is possible, however, to list certain factors which will indicate the major reasons for the shift in the pattern discussed above. Some developments had their origin in World War I and the interwar period. World War I marked the first time a large "citizen army" was mobilized in the United States and sent abroad to fight. Reserve Officers' Training Corps units were set up in high schools, universities, and colleges. By 1941, 1,600,000 students had received some training. A number of Regular Army officers served in Citizens' Military Training Camps and in the state units of the National Guard. The number of veterans' organizations and service-motivated groups increased and their activities expanded during the twenties and thirties: the American Legion (1919), the American Military Institute (1933), the Air Reserve Association (1932), the Military Chaplains Association (1925), the Marine Corps Reserve Officers Association (1926), the U.S. Coast Guard Artillery Association (1931).* Under the Civilian Conservation Corps program over 3,000,000 young men came under the direction of some 10,000 regular and reserve officers of the military services. Recognition of the need for sound economic mobilization to back a major military effort was recognized in World War I, and led to the establishment in 1924 of the Army Industrial College to train officers in the problems of mobilization of the national economy.

---

* This is only a fragmentary list. See the *Army Almanac* (Washington, Government Printing Office, 1950), pp. 883–908.

During this period there were other forces at work which still tended to minimize the role of the military and to preserve the historic pattern of civil-military relationships. Chief among these was the fact of American detachment from the arena of world politics, already discussed in Chapter One. Congressional sentiment for neutrality was too strong to permit re-examination of the assumptions underlying military policy. As long as American policy was not based on a balance between capabilities and commitments, as was the case in the Pacific in the early years, military considerations could be played down.

World War II and its aftermath brought more fundamental changes and additional factors into operation. Again a mass citizen army was necessary. Officers trained in the naval and military academies were outnumbered by those who rose from the ranks or were processed through Officer Candidate School. Military leaders were given great prominence in the organization of government for war and their activities were widely publicized in the press. The total mobilization of the economy for a highly technological war required constant collaboration between top civilian administrators and top military officers. This contact was not always friendly, smooth, or effective, but the point is that for the first time the military group was thrown rudely into the political scramble and conflict, was called upon to participate in making tough decisions, and witnessed at firsthand the political confusion which accompanies a large-scale enterprise of government planning and public regulation. American generals did more than direct American armies; they commanded international armies and hence were compelled to carry on nonmilitary as well as military relations with allies. The functions necessary to the welding and strategic deployment of a three- or four-nation fighting force were diplomatic and administrative as well as military. Outstanding generals thus had a definite impact on the "foreign relations" of the United States. From another point of view, Americans got used to the idea of civilian activities taking second place to military requirements and to a complete reversal of the traditional priorities assigned to military and nonmilitary values.

Organizational changes also took place during World War II which were a direct consequence of the different role of the military. The Joint Chiefs of Staff was established and became the key military planning group. A Joint Strategic Survey Committee, one of several units created to assist the JCS, heralded a trend toward freeing senior officers representing all the armed services from daily administrative burdens in order to engage in strategic planning and discussion of international political questions having military aspects. In 1944, the State-War-Navy Coordinating Committee came into being for the purpose of enabling the Department of State to obtain systematic advice on politico-military matters and problems of foreign policy. Up to this time there had been no regular official mechanism for coordinating the actions of the three departments on matters of common interest to all of them. The international role of the military was further evidenced by the

Combined Chiefs of Staff made up of British and American military leaders. Barriers between the military and other groups in American society were weakened by the use of institutions of higher learning by the Armed Forces for training purposes. Hundreds of officers received graduate instruction in area study, public administration, and international politics in colleges and universities. The Armed Forces also made extensive use of social science techniques for pilot training and investigation of soldier attitudes and behavior.

Contrary to normal expectations, the postwar period did not bring a return of the military to its prewar limited role and isolated position. Except for a brief period immediately following hostilities when America demobilized, everything which happened was calculated to continue the trends noted above and to expand the functions of the Armed Forces. First and foremost were the implications of the basic decision of the United States to maintain peace by a commitment to use force against aggression and by providing military assistance to peace-loving friends and allies. The United Nations Charter, the Truman Doctrine, the Inter-American Treaty of Reciprocal Assistance, the North Atlantic Treaty, and the Mutual Aid Program all led to special activities squarely in the politico-military realm. All of them required military strength and all of them required the participation of the military in policy formation and execution. The deterioration of Soviet-American relations and the inability of the United States to alleviate the bipolar tensions have, of course, resulted in even greater reliance on national military power and regional alliances.

Second in importance was the decision for occupation of ex-enemy territory by the Armed Forces. It was originally anticipated that this would be a short job and would be primarily administrative in nature. Assuming that formal peace treaties could be negotiated quickly, the maximum length of occupation was expected to be two years. During this period the military would preserve order, help in reconstruction, and carry out clear policy directives handed down from the State Department and other civilian agencies. That both of these assumptions proved unrealistic goes a long way toward accounting for the relatively heavy and sometimes unintended influence of the military on foreign policy and relations. Evidence is overwhelming that the essentially nonmilitary tasks of occupation such as re-education and political purges of totalitarian groups in Germany and Japan were both unwanted and unsolicited by the Armed Forces. And certainly it is true that the military was badly prepared for these tasks. Occupation of enemy territories actually lasted five to eight years, a fact explained, obviously, by the confused state of the postwar world.

The acquisition of political functions via occupation duties was the result of a number of interrelated factors. The State Department let initial responsibility for occupation go to the military by deliberate choice, and many later political decisions fell to the military by default. Some short-circuiting of policy directives occurred because they were ambiguous or because communications among the agencies involved were faulty. In most cases something of the original flavor and intention of general policies is lost when they are translated into action in the field. There is an area of administrative discretion where additional choices are open. It was here that military biases and a low level of political sophistication were undoubtedly operative. Furthermore, several military leaders were inclined to exercise the full area of discretion available to them and to add to the area of discretion when they could do so. Vigorous military initiative appears to have been abetted by poor communications, slack controls by the State Department, and the division of labor between policy formulation and field operations to the end that often American policy was to all intents and purposes set by the army commanders. The Army, through General MacArthur, actually determined the course of Japanese-American relations. General Clay in Germany and General Clark in Austria were not as isolated from the center of decision making as General MacArthur was, but they too regularly performed political functions.

NEW TRENDS IN CIVIL-MILITARY RELATIONS

Events of the postwar period transformed the atmosphere which surrounded civilian-military relationships. The public grew to accept—and indeed to demand—a broader concept of national security which in turn required a central position for military power and a recognition of the need for military leadership. A combination of insecurity arising from the Soviet threat and the fabulous popularity and prestige of a quartet of five-star generals (Marshall, Eisenhower, Bradley, and MacArthur) resulted in a tendency to lean on military leadership. Acceptance of the key importance of military preparedness and the political character of mobilization of the free world paved the way for a continued extensive and socially approved participation of military leaders in public affairs which was unparalleled in any democratic nation. For many citizens the complexities of the postwar situation invited a reliance on a military solution, on the weapons which had brought victory in 1945.

Accordingly civilian groups and military groups were drawn more closely together. Contacts between the military and the rest of the population increased. Each became more exposed to the activities, views, pressures, and criticisms of the other. The military had to accept as normal a constant probing by the press, proposals for reforms by investigating commissions (e.g., the Eberstadt Commission, the Hoover Commission, the Doolittle Commission, the President's Advisory Commission on Universal Military Training, and so on), policy suggestions from veterans' groups and pressure groups, and the solicitations of occupied peoples. The public, on the other hand, was subjected to pressures from the military in the form of high-powered "public relations" and information activities calculated to sell the objectives of the armed services and to recruit personnel; it had to accept the spending of billions in the civilian economy, the carrying on of huge scientific projects in secret, and the establishment of permanent training bases; it was presented with the personal memoirs of distinguished generals, speeches and articles by active military officers, and the dramatization of military personnel and techniques. On the governmental level, contacts between Congress and the military were multiplied and changes in military organization represented an adaptation to new conditions.

The new environment of civil-military relations was marked by a decline in civilian mistrust or suspicion and by the discovery that civilian and military groups had problems in common. Civilian acceptance and allegiance both necessitated and permitted a new role for the military in American life. Hence the military rather drastically revised its official attitudes toward civilians and its view of its own role. By 1952, both civilian and military attitudes and relationships had undergone extensive alteration. To repeat, the change in pattern was both cause and effect; a cause of the new role of the military and an effect of conditions which either thrust new responsibilities on the military or made it easier for the military to assume them.

THE MAIN ELEMENTS IN THE NEW ROLE OF THE MILITARY

Certain conclusions clearly emerge from the impact of the foregoing events and developments. During the years since the end of World War II, the traditional position of the military has altered beyond recognition. Pushed out of its provincialism, the American military has become involved in a series of international experiments, the most notable of which are serving as the core of a United Nations police force in Korea and helping to build an international army within NATO. In the latter case, 185 Army, Navy, and Air Force officers are working with 223 officers from nine other nations in an integrated staff. Because the national military functions have expanded in the present kind of world, the range of opportunity for the armed services to affect the conduct of foreign relations and the nature of foreign policy is wide indeed. Perhaps the simplest method of illustrating the point is to ask in what ways the military can and does influence foreign policy in the broadest sense.

1. It is acknowledged both by military and civilian officials that the military can and must have *some* voice in the formation of foreign policy, especially those policies or issues which have military implications. As will be seen subsequently, there is not always agreement on the precise kind of voice the military should have, but there is no disagreement on the principle. Civilian officials solicit, and the military are not reluctant to give, their opinions on major foreign-policy decisions. The armed services took a leading part in the formulation of the European Recovery Program. President Truman announced in July, 1951, that on recommendation of the Department of Defense, the United States would go it alone to obtain naval and air bases from Spain because other members of NATO would not agree to the admis-

sion of Spain. In 1946, the proposal that the United States be given trustee-ship over the Marshall, Caroline, and Mariana Islands appears to have been the work of the Navy Department. Also in 1946 the Army and Navy favored an early Western Hemisphere defense pact regardless of whether Argentina agreed to certain political pledges. The Secretary of State disagreed but the military view prevailed. From 1947 to 1950 the State Department's attempt to open up the question of a peace treaty with Japan was in part frustrated by the opposition of the Defense Department. It is to be noted that the central position of the National Security Council and the JCS discussed in Chapter Six is indicative of the recognition given to the role of the military. On occasion high-level military personnel emerge as personal advisers to the President on national security problems.

2. Military officers increasingly have held important diplomatic posts, have engaged in special diplomatic missions, and have held what are normally civilian posts in the federal government. The wartime Chief of Staff, General George C. Marshall, became Secretary of State in 1947 and Secretary of Defense in 1950. Admiral Alan Kirk and General W. Bedell Smith served at different times as Ambassador to the Soviet Union. When General Mark Clark was nominated by President Truman to be Ambassador to the Vatican, the general made an interesting comment: "If I go, I will go as a military man in much the same status as General Walter Bedell Smith when he went to Moscow." Admiral Sherman, Chief of Naval Operations, before his death began the negotiations for bases in Spain. General Anderson (retired) was appointed General William Draper's deputy to assist in the coordination of military and economic aid to Europe. General Eisenhower's position as Supreme Commander of the Allied Powers in Europe from 1951 to 1952 was as much a diplomatic office as a military one because he was faced with the task of building a truly European army and a new staff organization for the North Atlantic Treaty nations. Although for General Eisenhower's successors, Generals Ridgway and Gruenther, the diplomatic task had been largely accomplished, the position of supreme commander still had political overtones. For example, General Ridgway put a narrowly military interpretation on his role and was publicly criticized by Europeans for doing so. It was alleged he ignored the psychological and economic issues raised by the NATO rearming program. General Kuter was chairman of the Civil Aeronautics Board and served as representative at the International Civil Aviation Organization. Colonel Byroade held the post of director, Bureau of German Affairs, in the State Department and is now Assistant Secretary of State for Near Eastern and African Affairs. At present, General Smith is Under Secretary of State. There appear to have been three possible reasons for the wide use of military leaders in essentially nonmilitary positions: first, President Truman and others argued that there was a dearth of technically qualified personnel who were *willing* to serve; second, as noted, the nation's outstanding military men had

attained enormous prestige, particularly abroad, and had gained extensive diplomatic or administrative experience during World War II which was timely
and valuable; and, finally, in view of the general political turbulence of the
postwar period in the United States, military appointees were on occasion
"safer" and less controversial than others. These reasons are not intended as
justification but only to suggest a connection between one facet of the new role
of the military and the existence of a combination of conditions. On a somewhat lower level, there has been a great increase in the number of military missions operating in foreign countries. Members in effect represent the United
States and function under rules of diplomacy. Here military and political activities certainly shade off into each other. The number of military attachés
abroad has increased. In 1948 there were 640 Army and Air Force personnel
on duty in fifty-nine countries and 120 Navy personnel in forty-three countries.

3. Military officers have increasingly lent their experience, prestige,
and *expertise* in support of foreign-policy programs. On the part of the officers themselves this can be intended or unintended, voluntary or involuntary.
Officers may feel compelled to do so or may willingly do so in order to serve
the Armed Forces. However this may be, it appears likely that the service
of General MacArthur as United Nations Commander in Korea (until his
removal) did much to convince doubtful citizens and congressmen that the
operation would be in excellent hands; a distinguished American general had
become associated with a crucial foreign-policy decision. General Marshall's
name is likewise connected with the beginning of the European Recovery
Program in 1947. When the hearings on the removal of General MacArthur
were held in 1951 and the bitter opponents of the Truman Administration's
foreign policy were vigorously pushing their case, it was the Joint Chiefs of
Staff and General Marshall as Secretary of Defense who carried the brunt of
the counterattack. This was a clear case of the nation's military leadership
rebutting not only General MacArthur's strong views on military strategy but,
more significantly, his interpretation of what the Far Eastern policy of the
United States ought to have been and should be. A distinguished commentator
put it thus: "To some critics it appears that the military prestige of distinguished officers is being borrowed by the civil authority which selects them
for preferment."* General Eisenhower, as the first supreme commander of
the forces of NATO, became identified with America's European policy. His
staunch advocacy of that policy by word and deed doubtless helped to create
popular support and to solidify the convictions of key members of Congress.
On May 3, 1952, General Eisenhower wrote a letter to the chairman of the
Senate Foreign Relations Committee, which was contemplating a cut in 1952
foreign-aid appropriations, to the effect that a substantial reduction might
menace the whole program. The chairman of the Joint Chiefs of Staff, General
Bradley, made several major addresses around the nation in 1951–1952

---

* Arthur Krock, New York *Times,* May 1, 1951.

which could best be described as foreign-policy statements. In fact, one of these, given at Chicago before the National Association of Radio and Television Broadcasters, was frankly headlined by the New York *Times* as "Text of Address by General Bradley on Foreign Policy of U.S."*

4. Among the most important expanded functions of the military is the administration or execution of foreign policy. Until 1949, when the primary responsibility for the administration of German affairs was taken over by the Bureau of German Affairs in the State Department, the Department of Defense (really the Army, the JCS, and the theater commanders) was in complete charge of all occupied areas. Even now the Department of the Army has important responsibilities because of the American armed forces still left in Japan and Germany. The point to be made here is that occupation functions plunged the military establishment into administrative problems for which it was ill prepared even though the State Department supposedly retained the responsibility for formulating policy. Military science is one thing, the art of government another. Not only were the lines of communication from decision to execution complex and often clogged, but the Army had to do things for which its traditional organization and methods were unsuited. The Department of Defense has primary responsibility for implementing the military aspects of the Mutual Security Act (and contributes personnel to the staffing of NATO). Another kind of administrative task is illustrated by the Korean conflict wherein the various American commanders are serving both American and United Nations objectives. Military experts represent the United States on various international military organizations—United Nations Military Staff Committee, the United States–Canada Permanent Joint Defense Board, the Inter-American Defense Board, and so on. For the foreseeable future at least, it would seem certain that much of the energy and resources of the military will be committed to the implementation of specific political decisions.

5. Since 1945 there have been numerous examples of what might be called gratuitous statements on foreign policy (or statements with political implications) by military leaders or civilian heads of military agencies. Such statements have usually not been cleared with the State Department or the President, nor duly authorized as part of the normal decision-making process, and may have serious repercussions. Among these would be classified the remarks of General MacArthur on American policy while he was still United Nations Commander. In a speech to be read in his absence and in a letter to the Republican leader in the House of Representatives he criticized that policy, advocating that the Korean war be carried to the Chinese mainland via air attacks and that aid be provided to Chinese Nationalist forces on Formosa. Secretary of the Navy Mathews in a public address in 1951 declared it might be necessary for the United States to wage "preventive war" on the Soviet

* New York *Times*, April 18, 1951, p. 8.

Union. At about the same time, General Anderson of the Air Force suggested much the same thing. In 1946 the Assistant Secretary of War for Air stated that the Air Force was an instrument of foreign policy and advocated a round-the-world "policy flight" of B-29's. As long as the basic characteristics of the decision-making process (see Chapter Three) remain as they are, it can be expected that this sort of thing will occur and will have domestic and foreign repercussions.

6. Naturally the military has a large voice in the preparation of the annual federal budget. This of course comprises a part of its responsibility for national security and may be regarded as primarily a military function. However, the military submits estimates as to the number of dollars to be spent on defense together with an itemization according to kinds of weapons and if this estimate is accepted, the military has thereby helped to determine how the total available national resources are to be applied to all foreign-policy objectives. One of the greatest sources of military influence is the fact that military budget requests are on the whole accepted by the President and Congress as authoritative.* The reservoir of national power is not unlimited; decisions must be made in terms of allocation of scarce means. Dollars spent on tanks cannot be spent on the Voice of America. Dollars spent on air power cannot be spent on Point Four. Steel required for the American military machine cannot be allocated to France or Britain. Demands for human resources —for troop replacements, for scientists, and for doctors—may conflict with other demands. Young men in uniform cannot farm or produce goods. Doctors are already in short supply in civilian life. The point is that military demands involve a shifting of the ingredients of power. If military demands are excessive in terms of available resources and needs, the nation may be seriously weakened. The economy may be dislocated if heavy armament demands are suddenly made. On the other hand, if military needs are under-estimated, the technology of new weapons is such it takes a long time to tool up for mass production. The military budget is, then, one of the crucial devices whereby the mobilization and use of national power is determined. One of the measures of the importance of the new role of the military is a comparison of the amounts spent on military and nonmilitary techniques of foreign policy.

7. In the course of the performance of military functions numerous things are said and done which affect American policy and foreign relations. An atmosphere of international tension may magnify an otherwise trivial incident into a matter of great significance. Major General Robert Grow, American military attaché in Moscow, was careless enough to allow his private personal diary to fall into Russian hands in 1952. The Russians photographed the document and made propaganda use of it. Among other things, several

---

* An exception would be the demand of President Eisenhower's director of the Bureau of the Budget that the 1953–1954 armed services budget be substantially reduced.

significant political facts were revealed: the general's secret dealings with other attachés, the kind of information America was seeking and from what sources, and the rift between Ambassador Kirk and General Grow. Tremendous embarrassment resulted for the United States, and future intelligence work in Moscow was placed in jeopardy. Another kind of example occurred when the American commander in Korea ordered a mass bombing of North Korean power plants along the Yalu River in order to apply pressure to the long-drawn-out truce negotiations. Within hours a serious debate developed in the British House of Commons between Prime Minister Churchill and the opposition party because of the extreme character of the move and the fact that the British were not informed of the bombing ahead of time. In another case, what must have been considered as a routine military release to the press in Korea had severe repercussions on the debate in Congrss over the whole Far Eastern situation. A subordinate military official told newsmen that twenty-five hundred Americans had been massacred in North Korean prisoner-of-war camps. The importance of this kind of military impact on foreign policy stems from an unavoidable truth about the contemporary world: there are few *purely* military decisions, functions, or situations.

8. Finally, the role of the military in the field of domestic policy has also expanded, as an indirect as well as a direct result of the foregoing considerations. In the field of education effects have been felt through the increase in the ROTC program, the establishment of special area and language studies, and draft policies. Passage of universal military training legislation would tend to augment this influence. Military officials affect the economic life of the nation through procurement pricing, choice of receivers of military contracts, renegotiation of contracts, and so on. Manpower policies, in which the Department of Defense has a voice, condition the size and distribution of the civilian labor force. Increasingly, officers of the armed services are placed on detached service with industry. Both the quality and the direction of scientific research have been affected by the military's vital interest in the development of atomic weapons. Topflight scientists have been called away from private industrial and university research laboratories. Freedom of research has been curtailed by the ban on the publication of many scientific papers, and a veil of secrecy has been drawn around projects of broad scientific interest.

The foregoing eight categories should be thought of as the principal forms in which military values and interests, military personnel in key positions, and military factors may condition the nature of American foreign policy and relations. The categories are related to each other. Thus because the military has been admitted to a central role in decision making, it is not strange that military leaders should become involved in publicly supporting certain policies. Because the military is engaged in administering foreign policy on a large scale, opportunities for political by-products are enhanced. Also, the categories are related to the changed conditions and relationships discussed earlier in the chapter. They define the major dimensions of the new role of the military. In the next section some problems which have resulted from these developments will be set forth.

► SOME PROBLEMS WHICH HAVE ARISEN FROM THE NEW ROLE OF THE MILITARY

The problems of concern here are actually components of a single large problem. Nevertheless, separate treatment of each one will convey the impression of complexity and many-sidedness.

CIVILIAN SUPREMACY

√ Serious, respected students of American institutions have seen in recent developments a threat to the principle of civilian supremacy. In certain cases, it has been felt, either the principle has been subverted or the way has been paved for its subversion. Walter Lippmann, speaking of the German policy of the United States as evidenced at the foreign ministers' meeting in London in June, 1948, said: "The prime mover of this German policy, though it was negotiated by the Ambassador in London, was General Clay, seconded by his immediate superiors in the Pentagon. . . . General Clay . . . has been a pro-consul, as respects the State Department very nearly an independent sovereign with whom the department could now and then negotiate, to whom it has never been able to issue orders." * William Hanlan Hale wrote in a similar vein: "From the start of the occupation it has been clear that the foreign offices of Great Britain and France, and not their military governors, determine their countries' policies in Germany. But General Clay stands out as a special case: since 1945 it has been unclear whether he or the State Department has the final word on what America does in and with Germany." † In the New York *Times* of August 1, 1948, General Clay denied the allegation that the State Department had never made policy in Germany but admitted that recommendations from his own staff along with those of State Department people in Berlin had played an important part. However, General Clay's opposite number, General Sir Brian Robertson received his instructions from the British Foreign Office after Cabinet-level decisions.

The year 1948 was a kind of high-water mark of alarm over the military's growing power and influence. Among the experts writing regularly in this field, a number pointed to the same set of danger signals: General Marshall was Secretary of State; Admiral Leahy was President Truman's personal chief of staff; General Smith was Ambassador to Moscow; the National Security Council (before changes in 1949) was dominated, at least numberwise,

---

* Walter Lippmann, "Today and Tomorrow," New York *Herald-Tribune,* July 26, 1948, p. 36.

† W. H. Hale, "General Clay on His Own," *Harper's Magazine,* December, 1948, pp. 89–90.

by the military—four to one; concerning Generals Clay, Clark and Mac-
Arthur it was felt that as administrators of policy in military government
they were also architects of it; and there were military missions in thirteen
South American nations. Furthermore, such unification as was achieved was
looked upon as strengthening the voice of the military. Military influence in
science and education was noted. A closer relation between the military and
industry was highlighted by new production contracts and by the fact that
several military leaders retired to executive positions in American business.
Public and Congressional opinion appeared to bow increasingly to military
leadership. A long battle to free the atomic energy program from military
control had just been fought and won. High-powered public relations staffs
were detected working skillfully for the armed services. Growing governmental censorship reflected a potential clash between the interests of security
and the ideal of a free press. Effective military-legislative liaisons sometimes
revealed a "military lobby" in Congress. All in all, the centralization of military power and the need to prepare for total war conceivably might give birth
to a "garrison state." Hanson Baldwin, with these things in mind, wrote:
". . . I say that the growing influence of the military in American life is dangerous to our democratic liberties."* Some years later another high point
of alarm emerged.

In 1951 the issue of civilian supremacy was raised dramatically by the
dismissal of General MacArthur. The actual shift in the United Nations command for the Korean conflict was a climax to a series of incidents in which
were revealed personal frictions, disagreements over military strategy and
foreign policy, repeated challenges to existing lines of governmental authority,
and poor communications between MacArthur's headquarters and Washington. In General Marshall's words, the whole affair could be characterized as
"the wholly unprecedented situation of a local theater commander publicly
expressing his displeasure at and his disagreement with the foreign and military policy of the United States." Apparently the JCS found the removal
necessary because, among other things, General MacArthur had in its view
flouted civilian authority and had violated the chain of command by going to
the public with his argument. He had set down his foreign-policy program in
an official letter to the Republican leader in the House of Representatives
and he had invited the enemy's field commander to negotiate with him on the
spot without prior consultation with Washington. During the long hearing,
General MacArthur defended himself by claiming freedom of speech and by
asserting that the JCS actually agreed with his views. He also emphasized that
a theater or a field commander must have complete command of even political
and social matters within his jurisdiction, although his sole objective is military victory.

No review of all the issues raised by the MacArthur case is possible

* Hanson Baldwin, "The Military Move In," *Harper's Magazine,* December,
1947, p. 481.

here. But there are two problems which are relevant to the issue of civilian supremacy. There seems little doubt that whether General MacArthur's for- eign-policy views are regarded as correct or not, he overstepped his purely military functions when he undertook to try to change the nation's foreign policy while still serving a command. The first problem, therefore, is this: How can civilian supremacy be maintained under conditions in which a mili- tary leader has gained sufficient political power to render him immune from civilian authority? President Truman apparently delayed a long, long time before he dismissed General MacArthur, who had built up a large following of citizens, newspapers, and civic and Congressional leaders. Before the re- moval, friends of General MacArthur in Congress threatened reprisal if the President acted. Now there is no question but that it would have been per- fectly proper for MacArthur to have resigned amidst all the fanfare he could muster in order to carry the fight on "the administration's foreign policy" to normal political channels. It is worth considering, however, what dangers are involved when a high military personage is able to usurp nonmilitary functions under circumstances where civilian checks are either absent or are weakened. A second problem grows out of the argument that the field commander must have complete supremacy. Even in wartime this arrangement may be risky unless the situation is such that only purely military decisions are presented for the commander to settle. One of the lessons learned in the North African campaign of World War II was that to settle political issues in a battle zone on the basis of military expediency—no matter how logical this seems—is to breed a legacy of factors which may affect final victory. The United States appears to have gone further than any other Western democratic nation in giving carte blanche to the field commander. British diplomats, for example, have much greater control over the politico-military decisions of British gen- erals. Justice William O. Douglas of the Supreme Court stated bluntly in a magazine of wide popular circulation: "The increasing influence of the mili- tary in our thinking and in our affairs is the most ominous aspect of our modern history." * By 1952 fear was being expressed that the Joint Chiefs of Staff had come to exert "undue power." Part of the fear of the JCS stemmed from organizational trends in which it appears that this body has been strengthened at the expense of civilian secretaries of Air, Army, and Navy. However, the JCS has also come into prominence because of the in- volvement of generals in partisan politics.

A subtle aspect of intentional or unintentional challenges to the su- premacy of civilian decision makers and nonmilitary values (and closely connected with the limits on the field commander or unified military agency) is illustrated in the testimony of General Van Fleet before the Senate Armed Services Committee in the spring of 1953. General Van Fleet, who com- manded the United Nations forces in battle in Korea, complained bitterly

---

* William O. Douglas, "Should We Fear the Military?—Yes," *Look,* March 11 1952, p. 34.

hat just when he had the enemy on the run he was hamstrung by truce nego·
tiations. He said bluntly that a clear military victory would have been possible
n Korea if only the political shackles on his operations had been removed.
His general position was supported by a letter from General MacArthur to
Senator Byrd and made public by the latter. Another kind of illustration can
be seen in the remarks of General Gruenther, SHAPE commander who
warned in a formal address in New York in October, 1953, that any peace
drive (there was considerable evidence that some general negotiations with
the Soviet Union might be under consideration) might tend to undermine the
defenses of Western Europe. The issue here is not the intention of General
Gruenther to carry out effectively his duties as NATO commander. Rather
t is the extent to which General Gruenther's judgment as a military officer
or as a military expert occupying a quasi-political role actually influences the
way people feel about the larger question of whether a nonaggression pact
between the West and the East is a good diplomatic move to make.

Some military leaders have been very self-conscious about limiting their
area of competence. In May, 1952, Admiral Radford—who later became
chairman of the JCS—said that the Navy had the capacity to blockade
Communist China, but added that the decision to do so was "beyond my
realm as military commander." Later on, in October of the same year while
on an inspection tour to Formosa as commander in chief of the United States
Pacific fleet, he said, "I have nothing to do with Government policy." Yet
Admiral Carney—who also later became a member of the JCS—is reliably
reported to have engaged in unauthorized talks with Italian officials over air
and naval bases in November, 1952. Though the admiral was commander of
the Mediterranean forces of NATO, it would appear that such talks should
have been opened by the State Department.

"GENERALS IN POLITICS"

This involvement has arisen in two ways. First, as an outgrowth of the
practice of using military leaders to win and sustain support for foreign policies, generals have been drawn into debate. General Bradley, who is personally devoted to the principle of military subordination in a democracy,
has made numerous speeches in which he has tried to explain strategy and
dispel misconceptions. While in most cases he was voicing military common
sense and was merely reiterating the foreign policy of the American government, in the political environment in which he spoke his remarks were interpreted as partisan appeals, particularly as the campaign year of 1952 grew
closer. The late Senator Robert Taft, a leading candidate for the Republican
nomination, bitterly criticized Bradley and declared that he had "lost confidence" in the Joint Chiefs and would replace Bradley if he were elected. On
April 26, 1951, he lashed out, saying the JCS "are absolutely under the
control of the administration" and that their recommendations "are what the
Administration demands they make." He further insisted: "I have come to

the point where I do not accept them (JCS) as experts particularly when General Bradley makes a foreign policy speech." Bradley's condemnation of the so-called "Gibraltar theory of defense" (based primarily on air power and sea power) was felt by Taft to be a partisan attack. Actually Taft made a campaign issue of military leadership. His own cause was being aided by retired and inactive generals. General Wedemeyer, an air-sea power advocate, headed a citizens-for-Taft committee and Brigadier General Bonner Fellers, also an exponent of reliance upon air power rather than land power in the defense of Europe, served with the Republican National Committee. General MacArthur—whose foreign-policy views and strategic thinking differed sharply from those of the government—openly supported Taft and was known to be his chief military adviser.

This kind of complication did not end with the election of a new administration. After President Eisenhower announced that the United States Seventh Fleet would no longer neutralize Formosa, Senator Hunt asked: "Were previous reports to Congress by Pentagon leaders their professional opinion, or were they colored by the opinions of the previous administration? Are the new policies a reversal of previous professional estimates or are they again reflecting the policies of the new administration?" In May, 1953, the President appointed an entirely new Joint Chiefs of Staff. While Senator Taft did not recommend the new members, it is known that he strongly approved —especially the chairman, Admiral Radford, whose general strategic views the senator shared.

Second, generals have been active in the quest for political office and have supported candidacies other than their own. Even while he was holding the post of NATO commander, General Eisenhower, through the efforts of his supporters, became a candidate for the Republican nomination for President. From the time of his removal as United Nations Commander in Korea and while still in uniform, General MacArthur made political speeches wherein he attacked the domestic and foreign policy of the administration and put himself very much in the presidential picture. He also gave the keynote speech at the Republican Convention in July, 1952. Thus two military leaders, not yet retired, were candidates for nomination to high office and were opposed or supported by civilians *and other military men* in an election year when military policy and foreign policy were sharp issues.

All this happened despite United States Army Regulations (600-10) in which members are forbidden to participate in "activity at political conventions or on political committees, the making of political speeches, the publication of articles or any other public activity looking to the influencing of an election or the solicitation of votes for themselves or others."

The participation of generals in American politics is not new; the names of Washington, Jackson, Harrison, Taylor, Peirce, Grant, Hayes, and Garfield are reminders of a long tradition. As Arthur M. Schlesinger, Jr., has pointed out, what makes the present situation unique is the fact that top military officials as a group are now accepted as authorities on broad matters of public policy, are admitted to the highest national councils, *and* are held accountable for their policy views. Generals have jumped or been dragged into the political arena, sometimes because of political motives, sometimes for other reasons. The military, even when it wishes to adhere to a narrow defini- tion of its functions no longer finds it possible, apparently, to give advice unobtrusively to decision makers. Military leaders have become decision makers and have ceased to be immune to political pressures. In a larger sense this change raises the issue of how far the cold war has made the nation de- pendent on military leadership, and of how adequate civilian leadership is.

But a more immediate issue is this: The responsible military leaders— regardless of who they are at a particular time—have a direct stake in the continuity of a minimum program for national security and in the avoidance of periodic upheavals of basic strategic concepts except where such is dic- tated by new conditions. Military planning must be long range, and necessary alterations in policy may not nicely coincide with party victories. These same leaders also have a natural concern that false military conceptions should not be permitted to circulate as part of the political coin of the realm. How can these various objectives be accomplished without immersing the military in politics and without stifling free public criticism? Moreover, the politicaliza- tion of generals has contributed to disunity and uneasiness among the profes- sional military group. The emergence of "Republican" and "Democratic" generals would have significant repercussions on the proper technical func- tioning of this group.

The pulls toward this latter situation are substantial. It is only natural that congressmen who have strong convictions on military economy, on the primacy of air power, on the necessity of strengthening the Western Hemis- phere before making sacrifices to European defense, and so on, will seek support and confirmation from respected military figures who in turn will deliberately "leak" information or talk in confidence without being willing to be quoted. Conversely, military leaders may try to seek support in Congress for policy views they would like to see become official. Hence military plans become election issues and military issues are discussed in terms of political objectives which have nothing to do with foreign policy. In an extreme situ- ation the electorate may in fact be choosing between two disagreeing camps of military planners. At the very least, military questions *may* not be analyzed on their merits.

THE "MILITARY MIND"

In view of everything which has been said so far in this chapter, it is not surprising that one problem which has emerged in the postwar era centers on the fear of a so-called military mind and its impact on policy making. The concept of the military mind has not been given precise definition. A few quotations will indicate the kinds of things meant by the term. Speaking of the military, Hanson Baldwin says: "Most of the men . . . are good public servants; many of them are exceptional. Collectively, however, they represent a pattern; they have in common the habit of command discipline and the mental outlook of military training—a tendency to apply in their thinking the yardstick of physical power. It is a pattern to be watched."* Justice Douglas argues that "the military mind is too narrow" by which he means that military education is too specialized and military techniques are too limited in terms of foreign-policy problems.† The military mind views world affairs solely from the perspective of preparedness for war and is generally opposed to public debate, dissent, and disagreement. Its response to social revolution is inappropriate. C. L. Sulzberger, after remarking that "there is popular suspicion of what is often referred to as the 'military mind,' " goes on to state that it involves formal rigid thinking and limited knowledge of social behavior generally.‡ Arthur Schlesinger, Jr., includes among the qualities of the military mind (a) the tendency to use military logic exclusively; (b) the propensity to see everything too clearly; and (c) the proneness to ignore ultimate values of a moral and spiritual sort.§ Referring to General Grant as President, John P. Marquand once wrote: "He was trained to be a soldier with a military mind and his deficiencies do not imply that a military mind necessarily unfits its owner to hold a high political office. Yet they indicate, perhaps, that the military mind does present its owner with specific handicaps which he must overcome in order to get on with the great mass of his fellow citizens, who have not been subjected to his disciplines and training. . . . All professional soldiers have similar attitudes and reactions unavoidably because they have the military mind." ‖ Finally, *Fortune* magazine has commented: "Our commanders have shown little talent for thinking beyond victorious force to the broad political situations. . . ."# It then went on to set forth the rules of American military thinking: first, a set of alternatives so completely explored that a course of action only has to be chosen; second, the devising of sweeping plans which are to unfold inevitably step by step; third, the mobilization of overwhelming material and the mounting of huge operations; fourth, neat solutions, either–or propositions. These rules seem to flow naturally from American industrial potential, the successful application of massive force to detailed plans, and the desire to conserve human life. However, *Fortune* finds pragmatic opportunism lacking in strategic planning and also alleges that military intelligence suffers from alternative optimism and pessimism regarding enemy strength and intentions.

These are quite typical interpretations of what is meant by "the military mind." The concepts seem to imply a combination of qualities which allegedly

* Baldwin, *loc. cit.,* p. 482.
† Douglas, *op. cit.,* p. 34.
‡ *New York Times Magazine,* June 1, 1952, p. 9.
§ *Reporter,* April, 1952, pp. 33–36.
‖ *New York Times Magazine,* March 30, 1952, p. 53.
Fortune, February, 1952, p. 93.

constitute a severe indictment of the intellectual capabilities of the professional soldier. Apparently the disabilities apply not only to purely military functions but particularly to the foreign-policy contributions of the military. The disabilities are due to training, to tradition, to experience, to the nature of military techniques and objectives, and to career membership in a highly bureaucratized organization. Concern over the nature of the military mind has increased because as military influence has increased, so has the opportunity for this type of thinking to shape foreign policy. Triumph of the military point of view—if this includes these qualities—might in itself comprise a retreat from civilian supremacy. Yet even when the principle is preserved, the effects of undue stress on military values must be guarded against.

The foregoing quotations stress certain attitudes, values, and perspectives deemed inappropriate for formulating and executing foreign policy. To summarize, the most serious criticisms of the military mind appear to be tendencies toward (1) rigidity in thought and problem analysis—the rejection of new ideas and reliance on tradition rather than on lessons learned from recent experience; (2) inadequate weighing of nonmilitary factors in military problems and inability to understand complex politico-military relationships; (3) an authoritarian approach to most social issues and situations accompanied by a disrespect and disregard for civilian authority; (4) insulation from nonmilitary knowledge or anything beyond what is narrowly defined as militarily relevant; (5) judgment of policy goals and techniques primarily in terms of military force and total victory from total war. Clearly these qualities would rarely be found completely dominant in any one military leader. Rather they typify collective attributes which are shared in at least a minimum degree by all military personnel. On this basis, military behavior can be explained and characterized.

The problem which arises from inappropriate habits of military thought is twofold: first, to minimize and counterbalance such habits in the training and organization of the military; and, second, to minimize the impact of such habits on the policy-making process.*

THE INEVITABLE AND COMPLEX MIXTURE OF FOREIGN POLICY AND MILITARY POLICY

It is all but impossible to make a neat separation between military and nonmilitary factors affecting foreign policy, between military and nonmilitary aspects of foreign policy, and between military and nonmilitary objectives and consequences. Earlier in this chapter distinctions like this were made—for good reason. Indeed, policy makers must make them too. It has become a truism to say that major decisions of foreign policy have military implications

---

* The authors do not imply that the foregoing analysis represents their personal convictions. Whether there is a typical set of mental characteristics which appear in most military policy-making personnel is a question which needs to be researched. That many outstanding commentators have reported and criticized such characteristics and their possibly adverse consequences for a sound foreign policy is in fact a part of the general problem being discussed here.

and that military decisions have foreign-policy implications. Sometimes both statements can be seen clearly in concrete situations; at other times it is difficult to tell where the political ends and the military begins.

The Korean conflict spotlights many of these difficulties. The decision to combat the invasion of South Korea was a political decision taken in the face of an earlier military decision that Korea was of small strategic significance—too small to commit extensive American military forces to its defense. Yet once involved, the commitment of American forces and their fortunes had serious results for the total military position of the United States—how many fighting divisions were left for other purposes, for example.

A political decision was made to "limit" the Korean action, that is, to free South Korea and crush the North Korean military effort without attacking Chinese territory beyond the Yalu River. This decision in turn affected the nature of the military campaign which could be waged. And in turn this affected the amount of pressure which could be brought to bear for a political settlement.

An age-old relationship between war and politics has been raised. Before Congress, General MacArthur declared: "War's very object is victory. . . . It is the object of war . . . to win victory and defeat the enemy at the earliest possible moment with the least losses to our own armies. . . ." Actually war is an extension of politics by more extreme measures. If political objectives are lost sight of, war becomes meaningless destruction—an end in itself. Past experience indicates that unlimited wars followed by total victory do not necessarily produce stable peace or the building blocks out of which to make a stable peace. Yet it was consistently argued by congressmen and others that the Korean policy was a "failure" because it was difficult to bring it to a satisfactory military conclusion—preferably a victory. The concept of limited war represented an attempt to control the impact of military techniques on political objectives, but the inner logic of military operations along with public expectations subjected the policy to misunderstanding and criticism.

Year-long truce talks between the United Nations forces and the North Korean Communist forces amply demonstrate the confused nature of the conflict. United Nations negotiators had to resist constantly the intrusion of political items into the truce agenda and it finally turned out that the issue of repatriation of prisoners could not be kept a military one. The issue soon emerged for what it was: a head-on conflict of values respecting the free political will of human beings and the worth of human life generally. Inadequate attention to the political nature of the Communist armed effort subjected the United Nations negotiators to considerable embarrassment when in May, 1952, a series of revolts by fanatical Communist prisoners in the Koje Island camp run by the United Nations forces disclosed bungling by American commanders. The revolts were obviously planned in such a way as to take the whole episode out of the realm of the military.

The nature of the relations between the American commander and the

United Nations during the Korean conflict suggests other political facets. General MacArthur was subject to severe attack by members of the United Nations who felt that he was ignoring their objectives and interests. It did not matter whether his military capabilities were superb or not, the judgment was largely political. In June, 1952, as mentioned before, General Clark, then commander, ordered bombing raids on power plants in North Korea along the Yalu River, the boundary between Korea and China. General Clark apparently considered this a military gesture without general significance for the Korean conflict but one which would put pressure on the Communist negotiators. However, France and Britain reacted at once, and criticized the bombing as a dangerous, unwise *political* act. Regardless of what General Clark thought he was doing, his decision was otherwise interpreted. Surprise was manifest on both sides: by the general that his move was thought to be political, by the British and French that the commander thought the bombing was a minor military tactic.

It might be thought that psychological warfare—inducing the enemy to surrender, disrupting his organization, and weakening his will to resist—is primarily a military function when geared to actual combat. Its purpose is of course military, but it may affect political objectives and, above all, it requires knowledge of the political values of the enemy. Psychological warfare in Korea has been slowly adapted to this broader end as knowledge has been gained of the enemy's attitudes. Psychological warfare has only recently been recognized as part of tactics and strategy.

The removal of General MacArthur represents another facet of the complexities of the Korean conflict. His military views, whether right or wrong, had definite political overtones. One of the primary reasons the JCS agreed to his dismissal was the realization that he was not in sympathy with the directives to end the war in Korea and as a consequence he might be responsible for grave misinterpretations of those orders.

There are other examples to illustrate the complicated intertwining of the military and the political. The Japanese Peace Treaty is one. From the military standpoint, an independent Japan looked like a "sitting duck" for Soviet military and political pressure. From the political standpoint, a reliable association with Japan could only be based on an agreement with a free nation. To the military, a free Japan might be drawn into economic relations with Communist China or might not be able to protect American military privileges granted by treaty. To the civilian policy makers, domestic unrest in Japan might jeopardize military rights unless a treaty of independence were negotiated. To the military, tangible assets were being gambled for intangible ones. To the others, a short-run policy might menace long-term American objectives. It is one thing to say that the civilian-political view should have triumphed. It is another to say that this was an easy choice or that it was clear how the interests of both could be equally protected.

Leaving the Korean war aside, another example can be seen in the task confronting General Ridgway, who succeeded General Eisenhower as Supreme Commander of NATO. He was confronted by an essentially political question —one that had to be decided eventually on the diplomatic level. The question involved how to command the Mediterranean area and how to link it to the defense of the Middle East. There were two opposing points of view which involved different conceptions of strategy and a struggle for command power. The British generally favored transferring Italy to the Central Command of NATO and establishing a separate command for Greece and Turkey directly under SHAPE. Such a move would reduce the size of the Southern Command under Admiral Carney of the United States. Admiral Carney was insistent that he continue to control the Southern Command, which included Italy, Greece, and Turkey. Under the circumstances, General Ridgway could scarcely view the deadlock as a purely strategic question. Mention of the North Atlantic Treaty Organization is a reminder of the political-military issues bound up with American aid to Western Europe. While military and economic aid do complement each other, they may also be rivals. One of the real dilemmas of American military and foreign policy has been this: Where should the relative emphasis be as between the two kinds of aid and what will be their effect on each other? The North Atlantic Treaty powers were trying rather desperately in 1952 to strengthen Western Europe militarily, particularly France, Resources diverted from this purpose and put into long-range economic recovery slowed up rearmament. On the other hand, too much rearmament might overburden the economies involved and set back hard-won recovery.

An excellent example of the difficulty involved in an artificial separation of the military and the political can be seen in the appointment of a political adviser to the United Nations Commander during the Korean truce negotiations. In April, 1953, Robert D. Murphy, retiring Ambassador to Japan and an old hand at advising military operations, was attached to the staff of General Mark Clark in order to help the latter "analyze and assess the implications" of the discussions. Hardly a day went by without some political matter arising. Unlike the Communists, the United Nations selected only career military men for armistice delegations. To take another example, the Congressional investigation into ammunition shortages during the Korean campaign (April, 1953) soon broadened out into a consideration of the political assumptions underlying the limited war concept, the roles of the JCS and the State Department, and the relationship between civilian secretaries and military officers in the Pentagon.

In view of the foregoing, it is instructive to compare the conclusions of Dr. Burton Sapin of Princeton University in his provocative and scholarly case study of the Japanese Peace Treaty. He argues that the important role of the military in this foreign-policy decision can be explained, for the most part, in terms of three factors: first, the control of occupation in Japan meant that the military built up knowledge and experience about Japan and there-

fore had definite ideas about Japan's future political status; second, the security aspect of the Japanese problem meant that Japan had to be kept on
the side of the free world because of the industrial resources and human
skills which the Japanese possessed; and third, the Korean war introduced a
natural military desire to preserve the maximum advantage in that conflict,
or, at least, to enable the military to maintain the Korean operation. Dr. Sapin
rightfully stresses that the crucial role of the Defense Department in the
development of the treaty, whether good or bad in itself, reflected "the sort
of situation in which the United States is operating today." He also stresses
that this recognition provides no neat formula for determining the desirability
of such a role.*

SECURITY PLANNING AND THE MILITARY APPROPRIATIONS

These examples point up another kind of problem. Apparently there
are inescapable value conflicts where political-military relationships are concerned: military and nonmilitary objectives conflict; military and nonmilitary
techniques either may be mutually exclusive or may reduce each other's
effectiveness; and different criteria of judgment lead to different views as to
the appropriateness of military versus nonmilitary approaches to policy issues
and as to the relative significance of military and nonmilitary factors. Risks
and consequences attach to all decisions. Political risks and consequences
attach to decisions in which military values and aspects are uppermost, and
vice versa. Implications of these comments can be seen in the case of security
planning which not only confronts the Defense Department with tough choices
and administrative problems, but constitutes one basic reason why the military cannot escape becoming involved in the political process. For military
policy in a sense must be confirmed or modified every time the federal budget
is acted upon by Congress. Military planners literally have to think at least
three years into the future on some budget items and on others even longer.
And they must also predict the kinds of problems which may arise in the
future. This projection is necessary of course because it takes from three to
eight years to get armaments from the drawing board into the hands of a
division in the field and to the fact that "guesses" must be made as to when
the international situation may deteriorate to the point where war is probable
and what type of war it will be. Further complications arise because technical
developments may render a multimillion dollar investment obsolete inside of
a year or two.

Then there is the factor of cost. It is well known that modern war is
expensive and is getting more expensive all the time. A jet fighter costs six
times more than an ordinary one. To increase the firepower of an infantry
division by 50 pr cent increases the cost from $19 million to $91 million.
One B-47 intercontinental bomber costs $3.5 million. And so on. Seventy-

* Sapin, *loc. cit.*, III, 1003–1014.

five million dollars may be required for the research and development of a new weapon, and $500 million to produce and maintain it. But the cost problem is not simply one of absolute amounts. Costs must be measured in terms of expected results, estimated enemy armaments, and general strategy. An armored division costs three times more than an infantry division, but is it three times as effective? With X number of dollars available, should more be devoted to air power or to naval power?

Military spending must be related to total national spending, and the impact of military spending on the economy must be estimated. What military planners think they want must be provided by industry. The following quotation from a report by the Industry Advisory Committee of the Munitions Board suggests another factor which complicates planning: "Procurement policies are determined by military programs which are fixed by national policy. Decisions of national policy are profoundly influenced by military implications of possible courses of political action. In the choice of military alternatives, considerations of logistic and industrial feasibility are controlling. In the last analysis, the factor of industrial feasibility is likely to assume a decisive role at all levels of action. Adequate methods for the reasonably accurate measurement of the industrial implications of a given military program or alternative programs do not exist." A perpetual hazard which hangs over all military planning is that after funds have been allocated and contracts agreed to and draftsmen have converted engineers' designs to production plans, something will happen to cut down or cut off the supply of a particular item. Yet too much military pressure on industry will overburden national resources and unstabilize production.

In view of what has been said it is not hard to understand the continuous fight over "economy" between the military and Congressional appropriation committees. On the one hand, Congress worries about losing control of the military budget, about waste and ruinous spending. On the other, the military worries about risks of attack and unpreparedness. Both worries are logical in the sense that they are based on interpretations of the responsibility of each and on real experiences. Fat and water have been found in military requests; so have wasted funds. The Armed Forces have undergone shortages in the Korean conflict. Trouble is compounded because it is difficult for either Congress or the military to be very specific or certain about what is meant by "ruinous spending" or a "level of preparedness which might invite attack" or "the minimum for national security." It is hard to decide how risky a "stretch-out" of aircraft production which, say, postpones a 130-wing Air Force from 1954 to 1955 or reduces the combat strength of the Air Force from 143 to 130 wings really is. When is the chronological point of maximum peril from the Soviet Union? Was it true in the summer of 1953 that it would take three years until the Russians would be capable of dropping hydrogen bombs? Civilian and military opinions within the Executive Branch do not always agree on the answers to such questions.

While it may be true, as Sir Winston Churchill is reputed to have said, that the military will fortify the moon if let alone, it is likewise true from the military's viewpoint that it dares not underestimate. Military leaders want the best equipment and it is logical for them to emphasize quantity. Four hurdles separate the Department of Defense military leaders from funds: the civilian secretaries, the Bureau of the Budget, the President, and Congressional committees. At any one of these points, nonmilitary values can and must enter in. Changes may come after the military leaders have established a set of assumptions concerning their needs. In 1952, the final estimate of the JCS for military funds for 1952–1953 was $71 billion. Secretary of Defense Lovett reduced this to $53 billion and the President on the Budget Bureau's advice reduced it to $52.1 billion. Congress finally granted $46.1 billion.

The problem of military vs. nonmilitary values with respect to defense spending was posed in graphic fashion in 1953 and 1954. President Eisenhower and his new Cabinet took over the reins of government convinced that the federal expenditures could be reduced, paving the way for a possible balancing of the budget and a reduction of taxes. In particular, "more defense for less money" became a slogan. It was soon discovered that there were limits to the reductions which could be made without jeopardizing fundamental objectives. On the one hand, reduction in defense expenditures—such as the $5 billion reduction in Air Force spending—raised the specter of increased military risk, while on the other hand, continued spending on a large scale for atomic defense might menace the nation's economy and bring political reprisals for broken promises. Shortly after the 1953–1954 budget was agreed to, the discovery was made that the Soviet Union had accomplished a hydrogen explosion—a fact which destroyed the assumption of United States superiority in, and invulnerability to, the most powerful atomic attack. This in turn raised anew the question of the appropriateness of the Air Force reductions and of the possibility of an atomic arms race. Representative W. Sterling Cole, chairman of the Joint Congressional Committee on Atomic Energy, said that it appeared to him that the alternatives had become "financial ruination" or "atomic devastation."

By the spring of 1954, some of the implications of the "New Look" in national defense became apparent. Further reductions in military expenditures for 1954–1955—particularly in Army combat manpower—seems to have been based on a calculated decision to increase the general military risk (or range of risks) confronting the nation in order to decrease the economic and financial risks. While there was no open debate on the new strategy implied in budget changes, members of Congress as well as military officials quietly expressed great concern over the reduction in expenditures.

Issues of this sort, to repeat, are complicated enough if all participants in decision making agree that the basic question is this: How much money can be effectively spent during what time period for a reasonable program of security in the atomic age? But when civilian and military disagree over enemy capabilities and over how military and nonmilitary values are to be applied to a given situation at hand, the issues become even more confused and difficult.

The foregoing considerations boil down to this: The question of force levels and weapon priority is no longer (if it ever was) a question which can be decided alone by military personnel, by civilian personnel in military agencies, or by the application of purely military criteria. There are also political, economic, technological, and psychological considerations connected with decisions on the size and balance of the armed services. Concentration on atomic weapons and strategic air power v. defense through balanced forces is not just an aspect of the controversy, say, between the Navy and the Air Force; it is discussed in and out of Congress too. The rapid growth of atomic and related weapons raises ultimately not only a moral issue but survival possibilities should another war come. Short of these are the cost element cited above and the technical aspects of feasibility of certain kinds of weapons for certain purposes. Time and again during the past three years, some national leaders (including General Omar Bradley when he was chairman of the JCS) have warned against public overconfidence from reliance on the atomic bomb to protect the nation. Other leaders have been concerned over the fact that the public generally is ignorant of atomic developments and their implications. Scientists like Dr. Ralph Lapp and Dr. Lloyd Berkner, themselves major contributors to the perfection of atomic weapons, have become alarmed over the tendency to put exclusive reliance on a single-weapon strategy.

These men do not oppose the concept of a strategic air command or the general assumption that quick, effective retaliation is a strong deterrent to an attacker. They do deny that the atomic bomb is the answer to all military exigencies and they fear that rigidity in military strength may force rigidities in foreign policy. Their argument is that continental defense—particularly civilian defense, which is not under control of the National Military Establishment—and a diversified offensive strength are necessary to avoid a military posture which invites enemy action.

It is not suggested here that scientists are, or should be encouraged in, second-guessing military experts. Rather, the conclusion is that the size and balance of the Armed Forces depend on choices which require social costs and risks, and that a rigid, inflexible military strength and strategy impair freedom of action in foreign policy.

A PERMANENT CITIZEN ARMY

With the expansion of both the size and the functions of the armed services have come problems the solution to which does not lie completely within the control of the military leaders. No longer can the Army, Navy, and Air Force rely exclusively on their own academies and training schools for sufficient manpower. In addition, the Army (and to a certain extent the other branches) is no longer an intimate professional group; it has become a mass enterprise, requiring impersonal techniques of management and control. One consequence of these two facts was bluntly put by Admiral Radford when he became chairman of the JCS: "A serious problem facing the new chiefs is that of improving morale in the service." There is recurring evidence that one of the reasons for low morale is the loss of a sense of belonging and purpose on the part of the rank-and-file servicemen. A second consequence concerns the attractiveness of a military career. More than ever before, the services need broadly educated officer material; yet their drawing power for permanent officers has declined to the point where top military management has frankly acknowledged a growing lack of confidence in military service as a worth-while and respected career. Increasingly frequent criticism of the "brass," constant controversy over fringe benefits, and the competition of private industry are the reasons most often cited for this condition. Not only are the Armed Forces not drawing as many future officers from the general population, but the percentage of re-enlistments among present officers has steadily declined. These two conditions and the consequences noted do not ease civil-military relations nor help the military discharge its new policy-making responsibilities more effectively.

CONCLUSION

The six problems—or clusters of problems—discussed in this section are components of one central problem: the proper role of the military in foreign policy and relations. Before turning attention to this, it is advisable to examine briefly the nature of the national security organization through which military policy is made and military functions are carried out. Problems of military organization and problems of the relations between the military organization and other parts of the decision-making structure are of course bound up with the new role of the military and the central problem of determining its proper role.

► THE NATIONAL MILITARY ORGANIZATION

An adequate description of the present organization of the Armed Forces would require a whole book. The present section will therefore attempt only to point out certain characteristics of the military establishment within the framework of analysis already employed. Of immediate concern is the Defense Department and its component units, since these are the chief mediums through which military decisions are made, through which military functions are carried out, and through which the role of the military in foreign policy is exercised. For convenience the omnibus structure which is the Defense Department can be referred to as the "national military organization" and will include everything from the Secretary of Defense on down to the remotest base in Alaska and the fighting ships at sea.

THE MILITARY BUDGET

Selected figures on military and related expenditures will reveal certain aspects of the military organization—its size, how dollars and productive effort are distributed among various defense functions, and target dates for the achievement of certain goals.

As already noted, the Eisenhower Administration reduced military spending for the 1954 fiscal year by some $2.3 billion from unexpended balances and $5.2 billion in new authorizations, making a total cash expenditure of approximately $43.2 billion for that year exclusive of Korean campaign costs and foreign military aid. Total expenditures (new plus previous authorizations) for the 1955 fiscal year were set at approximately $38 billion. With a new philosophy of "More Defense at Less Cost," it appeared likely therefore that annual military expenditure might level off at $37 billion or $38 billion after reaching close to $48 billion annually in 1952–1953. Even with these reductions, the annual military operation (again exclusive of foreign aid and the Korean struggle) was thus nine times the size of General Motors, a gigantic corporation. After it was confirmed that the Russians had exploded a hydrogen bomb, it was by no means certain that, after all the effort to reduce expenditures, additional billions would not be necessary for atomic production and defense against air attack. At any rate, by 1953 it was estimated that the total assets of the military organization were over $300 billion. Only a really substantial shift in the international situation could bring about an abandonment of programs to which Congress was thoroughly committed. Furthermore, the reservoir of unexpended yet authorized funds (estimated at $100 billion in 1952) would provide momentum for years to come. However, reductions in total military expenditures from the 1953 budget to the 1955 budget amounted to $5.5 billion.

The 1954–1955 military budget provides for the maintenance or achievement of the following kinds of objectives:

1. Total number of military personnel approximately 2,850,000 by July, 1957, but with 1,164,000 in the Army, 688,900 in the Navy, 970,000 in the Air Force, and 215,000 in the Marines as of 1955

2. An Air Force of 120 combat wings* by 1954 and 137 wings by 1957, with an over-all total of 22,900 aircraft by July, 1955

3. An Army of 17 divisions plus 6 drawn from 18 regimental combat teams by July, 1955

4. A Navy of approximately 1,078 active vessels of which some 400 are to be combat vessels, and an air arm of 9,940 planes as of July, 1955

5. A Marine Corps of 3 divisions and 3 air wings as of July, 1955

6. Organized Reserves and National Guard of approximately 950,000 men by 1954

---

* A wing may be 30 heavy bombers, 45 medium bombers, or 75 fighter planes.

7. Construction and maintenance of 250 bases in the United States and abroad—a continuation of a program begun in 1951 including $1 billion for secret air bases.

Naturally such figures must be approximate, but they do suggest a pattern of goals and proportions, especially when compared with prior figures. The total number of military personnel dropped between 1953 and 1955 were about 550,000, with the Army suffering the greatest loss in absolute numbers, the Navy next, the Air Force next, and the Marines last. In terms of dollar expenditures, the annual rate of new money for the Army was reduced from $17.4 billion in 1952–1953 to $8.2 billion in 1954–1955; for the Navy, from $12.5 billion in 1952–1953 to $9.8 billion in 1954–1955; and for the Air Force, from $17.5 billion in 1952–1953 to $11.2 billion in 1954–1955. Naturally, cessation of the Korean conflict in 1953 is reflected in these cuts. Thus the Air Force sustained by far the largest budget cut, which was reflected in a goal of 120 wings instead of 143 wings by 1954 as was originally decided on in 1951.

Even selected figures expressed more or less in round totals reflect certain choices. Though the Army lost heavily in combat manpower, the budget calls for greater expenditure on firepower (including, of course, atomic weapons) and a substantial reduction in "rear installations"—the army behind the one in the field. Similarly, though the Navy lost manpower, the number of combat vessels was not reduced, three supercarriers were begun, and increased funds were allotted for submarines and missile ships. Unlike the Army and the Navy, the Air Force (though reduced in total manpower in 1953–1954) will add steadily to its number of pilots—albeit at a slower rate than previously was the case. Emphasis has shifted from the quick build-up begun in 1951–1953 to a slower build-up with lower absolute goals. The 1953–1954 budget called for concentration on jet fighters and long-range bombers and for filling present wings to full combat strength.

From 1947 to 1951, only 20 per cent of the military budget went for hardware—for tanks, guns, ships, and aircraft. In the budget for 1952–1953, the amount increased to 50 per cent. Even more than 50 per cent of the 1953–1954 budget was expended on hardware. A smaller amount than in any year since 1950 was to be spent on manpower. After increasing from $800 million in 1950–1951 to $1.7 billion in 1952–1953, the expenditure for weapon research and development slackened off somewhat. By 1954, the monthly draft call was reduced substantially from the 50,000 level as a result of the Korean truce. Finally, though it is not included in the annual Armed Services Bill, the atomic energy program should be mentioned. In addition to the billions (approximately $6 billion) put into atomic research from 1940 to 1950, three major expansions of the program took place after the outbreak of the Korean conflict. The third one, begun in 1952, involved a five-year expansion totaling $6 billion. Expenditures on atomic developments were increased $600 million from fiscal 1954 to fiscal 1955.

THE DEFENSE DEPARTMENT

As is true of several other major agencies considered in an earlier chapter, the structure of the huge enterprise which is the Defense Department grew out of the National Security Act of 1947. Without in any sense attempting to summarize this major statute, it can be said that it was designed to take into account the drastic changes in the size, composition, and functions of the armed services which were due primarily to World War II and its aftermath. Accordingly, the National Security Act created an over-all administrative unit—the National Military Establishment consisting of a Defense Department which embraced the older Departments of the Army and the Navy and the new Air Force. The expanded role of the Joint Chiefs of Staff was formally recognized by making them the principal military advisers to the President and the Secretary of Defense. So far as policy making was concerned, the act was designed to "unify" the armed services under the Secretary of Defense acting as coordinator. Though he shared Cabinet status with the Secretaries of War, Navy, and Air Force, his powers were limited indeed. He could not order the individual armed services to do anything. His position was further weakened in comparison to the service secretaries by the fact that he had only three special assistants and a small office staff. Hence the Defense Secretary was handicapped by having inadequate information concerning the activities he was to coordinate and inadequate assistance in attempting to draw together diverse interests and objectives into a coherent security policy.

From 1947 to 1949, amidst a good deal of controversy over the new setup generally, and the role of the Defense Secretary in particular, the latter had to get along with limited and ambiguous power as well as a small staff. But in 1948 service rivalries had developed to the point where two formal conferences took place—the Key West conference of March, 1948, and the Newport conference of August, 1948. At these conferences, the Secretary of Defense, the three civilian secretaries, and the military chiefs of staff worked out a "division of roles and missions" among the armed services. Following this, the Secretary of Defense had the responsibility for policing the agreement; hence his role grew. In 1949, Congress recognized this and other developments by making substantial amendments to the 1947 act. The three service secretaries were deprived of Cabinet status, the Defense Secretary's functions were made more explicit, and he was given a larger staff. In addition, three assistant secretaries were provided for. By 1952, there were eleven boards, committees, and special offices operating at the staff level as against only four in 1947, and the personnel of the secretary's office numbered five times what it did at the beginning. Meanwhile, the Joint Chiefs of Staff were assuming the importance already noted, having direct access to the President with or without prior consultation with the Defense Secretary.

This capsule history indicates the changed and expanded role of the secretary and the inevitable pull toward centralization which results from a struggle to coordinate without sufficient power; moreover, the creation of units at the staff level furnished clear proof of the greater participation of military agencies in foreign-policy formation and execution as well as of a greater range of contacts between civilian and military policy makers. Also, by 1953 the Defense Department had grown to be unwieldy in the eyes of some observers, administrative costs had increased greatly, communications within the vast omnibus agency often failed (as in the case of Secretary of Defense Lovett's admitted ignorance of the Army's production difficulties which contributed to an ammunition shortage in Korea), civilian supremacy was jeopardized by organizational factors, and there were mounting criticisms of the JCS.

THE REORGANIZATION OF 1953

In his message to Congress which accompanied Reorganization Plan 6,* President Eisenhower emphasized three great objectives in the organization of national defense:

> [1.] There must be a clear and unchallenged civilian responsibility in the defense establishment. This is essential not only to maintain democratic institutions, but also to protect the integrity of the military profession.
>
> [2.] Effectiveness with economy must be made the watchwords of our defense effort. . . . To protect our economy, maximum effectiveness at minimum cost is essential.
>
> [3.] We must develop the best possible military plans. . . . They must incorporate the most competent and considered thinking from every point of view—military, scientific, industrial, and economic.

These objectives evidently motivated the President in recommending changes in the National Security Act. A close reading of the plan and the message also reveals that the President intended to accomplish such objectives by consolidating and strengthening the role of the Secretary of Defense. What started out to be a coordinating role with limited power becomes a frankly administrative and policy-making role under Plan 6. Apparently, the service secretaries are to be fully responsible for operations and are therefore to be less concerned with broad policy making. President Eisenhower gave Secretary of Defense Charles E. Wilson clear responsibility and authority for the total defense organization and for carrying out the reorganization. The lines of responsibility and authority run from the President through the Secretary of Defense to the secretaries of the military departments and to the military chiefs of staff. The Secretary of Defense can delegate to any officer or agency

---

* Reorganization Plan 6 of 1953 and the President's message were sent to Congress on April 30, 1953. Texts printed in the New York *Times,* May 1, 1953.

any of his functions, and he is the official directly responsible to the President for all that happens in the defense establishment. Contrary to previous arrangements, the Defense Secretary now designates (instead of the JCS) the military department to serve as executive agent in the case of a unified command (e.g., the Army for the Korean campaign) and the military commander of a unified effort reports directly to the secretary and acts only in his name.* In his message on Plan 6, the President said concerning this conception of the Defense Secretary Wilson's job, "I want all to know that he has my full backing in that role." The secretary also serves as a member of the National Security Council, the Defense Mobilization Board, and the North Atlantic Council.

To aid the secretary in providing unified, centralized, yet flexible policy leadership, most of the various staff boards, committees, and special offices which had grown up prior to 1953 were abolished and their functions transferred to six new Assistant Secretaries of Defense.† There now are ten assistant secretaries (which includes a general counsel with this rank) who are in charge of the following clusters of functions: Legislative and Public Affairs; Manpower and Personnel; International Security Affairs; Applications Engineering; Supply and Logistics; Properties and Installations; Health and Medical; Research and Development; and Comptroller. Each assistant secretary heads a staff unit. According to the President's order, these officials are to establish systems for obtaining complete and accurate information to support recommendations to the secretary but without imposing themselves in the direct lines of authority between him and the three secretaries of the military services. Under this arrangement, the Munitions Board, the Research and Development Board, the Defense Management Staff, the Armed Forces Medical Policy Council, the Military Liaison Committee to the Atomic Energy Commission, the Defense Management Council and Staff, the Defense Supply Management Agency, the Weapons Systems Evaluation Group, and the Military Traffic Service were abolished. This was clearly a move toward greater centralization and also toward possibly greater civilian control. Three-service boards or committees tended to permit logrolling among the services and military domination of policy making in certain instances. It is also clear that by increasing the number of assistant secretaries and giving them substantial freedom of operation, the President hoped to attain more flexible administration and to attract experienced executives into the government—all with a net reduction of total staff personnel.

---

* This was a revision of the Key West agreement referred to above.

† The secretary is, of course, given indispensable assistance by the Deputy Secretary of Defense, who also acts for, and exercises the powers of, the secretary during his absence and represents Defense on interagency groups. From time to time, the secretary may appoint special assistants to perform particular assignments. At the present time, there are two: the Director of Guided Missiles and the Director, Office of Public Information. Under the latter, all publications and information activities of the secretary's office and the separate military departments are consolidated.

UNITS CONCERNED WITH FOREIGN AND CIVIL AFFAIRS

General functions of the Department of Defense as they relate to the total foreign-policy-making process were discussed in Chapter Six. As already suggested, in addition to being responsible for maintaining and directing the Army, Navy, and Air Force (giant operations in themselves), the Defense Department carries on certain activities which clearly fall under the heading of foreign relations and diplomacy. Whereas formerly many of these functions were performed by separate offices and committees, the *Assistant Secretary for International Security Affairs* and his staff are now the chief policy-forming group. It is this official's primary responsibility to develop Defense Department views and positions with respect to the Mutual Defense Assistance Programs, North Atlantic Treaty affairs, United Nations affairs, the National Security Council, psychological warfare, international conferences, and politico-military matters generally. His staff is also responsible for the coordination of all Defense Department activities which fall under these headings. Whenever necessary, the assistant secretary or someone from his staff will represent, or arrange for the representation of, the Defense Department on interagency or international committees or organizations and provide policy guidance for such representatives.

It will be remembered that the Department of Defense has important operational responsibilities with respect to foreign military aid. It administers projects which involve shipment of finished components of military equipment to designated nations, training of foreign military personnel and additional financing for military production abroad. Until the reorganization of 1953 the top coordinating agency within Defense and which also represented Defense on the interdepartmental committee which made recommendations on the whole foreign-aid program was the Office of Military Assistance. This office also coordinated Defense Department foreign-aid activities with those of the State Department and what was then the Mutual Security Agency. The functions of the OMA have been taken over by staff members of the Assistant Secretary of Defense for International Security Affairs and the OMA is now under the supervision of this Assistant Secretary. Even under the new setup, it seems likely that program details have been left, as before, to the three separate armed services. To supervise the military assistance missions in various European countries, a *Joint American Military Advisory Group* has been established. Specific recommendations on military assistance programs for individual countries come from *Military Assistance Advisory Groups* attached to United States diplomatic missions.

American membership in the North Atlantic Treaty Organization has added further duties to the top-level staff of the Department of Defense. A military committee reports to the council and council deputies of NATO; the chiefs of staff of member nations constitute this committee. The real working agency is the *Standing Group,* which advises the deputies on strategic decisions and other military matters. American representatives on the Standing

Group are of course provided by the Defense Department. The Secretary of Defense is chairman of the NATO Defense Council. However, the Assistant Secretary for International Security Affairs must formulate the views of the Defense Department to be considered when position papers are being prepared for the United States representative on various NATO bodies; advise the Secretary of Defense on matters of interest to him which are before the NATO Council; and provide representatives from the Defense Department to interdepartmental committees considering NATO problems.

In addition, significant functions were performed by the Office of Foreign Military Affairs until the reorganization, the major ones having been to study problems before the National Security Council, to draft recommendations for positions to be taken by American representatives at international meetings, to make comments on day-to-day foreign affairs, to prepare Defense Department reactions to treaties and international agreements. The Office of Foreign Military Affairs was essentially a military agency dealing with those problems and issues in which political and military considerations merged. Accordingly, it helped prepare the Department of Defense for its negotiations with other governmental agencies and gave thought to the political implications of military policy or action. These functions are now performed by the Assistant Secretary for International Affairs and his staff.

The *Assistant Secretary of Defense for Research and Development* is concerned mainly with the status of scientific research as it relates to national security and with seeing to it that the needed research is completed. He and his staff must decide what weapon research needs to be done and must supervise the execution of projects in private and governmental laboratories. All this requires cooperation with representatives of the armed services, civilian agencies, industry, and science. Responsibility for procuring essential weapons and war material in the form and amount needed is centered in the *Assistant Secretary for Supply and Logistics,* who issues contracts for arms production and coordinates the stockpiling of strategic materials. Consequently, this official and the staff unit he directs participates in planning for industrial mobilization and maintains liaison with economic agencies such as the Office of Defense Management. Naturally these activities support the logistic and procurement duties of the JCS. The obvious importance of Congressional liaison and the many-sided interest of the Defense Department in pending legislature are reflected in the post of *Assistant Secretary of Defense for Legislative and Public Affairs.* Formulation and review of manpower policies is the task of *Assistant Secretary of Defense for Manpower and Personnel.* This involves, among other things, appraising the feasibility of strategic plans in terms of available manpower and limitations on the use of available manpower. Close contact is maintained with educational leaders, industry, and organized labor. Finally may be mentioned the *Assistant to the Secretary of Defense for Atomic Energy,* who is ordinarily the chairman of the Military Liaison Committee of the Atomic Energy Commission. His task is to establish and review policies on atomic energy within the Defense Department and to advise representatives of the department on external committees or agencies which deal with atomic energy problems.

The National Security Act of 1947 set up an *Armed Forces Policy Council,* members of which are the Secretary of Defense and the Deputy Secretary of Defense; the Secretaries of the Army, Navy, and Air Force; and the chairman and members of the Joint Chiefs of Staff. Intended to be primarily advisory, this group is not a decision-making body, but offers informal consultation to the Secretary of Defense on politico-military matters, administrative policy, and on matters to be considered by the National Security Council.

The operating departments within Defense—the Army, Navy, and Air Force—also reflect in their tables of organization the new roles and problems which have befallen the military. For the Army, the official most generally responsible for politico-military-economic affairs which affect this branch is the undersecretary. In particular he is concerned with international security policies and problems, civil affairs and military government, base rights negotiations, and civil defense. The undersecretary has a military assistant (at the rank of colonel) for politico-military affairs. The Assistant Secretary of the Army for Material has a Special Assistant for Foreign Military Aid who participates in the preparation of Army policy on the Mutual Defense Assistance Program. In the Office of the Chief of Staff for the Army there is a Chief of Legislative Liaison. In the Air Force, the Assistant Secretary for Matériel has a Deputy for Mutual Security Assistance Affairs and there is an Office of Legislative Liaison, with a director, deputy director, and assistant director, which handles everything but appropriations. At the operating staff level in the Air Force, the Deputy Chief of Staff (Comptroller) has an Assistant for Plans and International Affairs. So far as the Navy is concerned, all of these various politically oriented functions are apparently performed by the secretary and his executive assistants though no formal division of labor (as in the other services) is mentioned. All three services have separate Offices of Public Information.

THE JOINT CHIEFS OF STAFF

Technically speaking, the Joint Chiefs is a staff agency within the Defense Department. As such it is, in theory, no more and no less important than other units on this level. But for reasons suggested in Chapter Six, the JCS has emerged as a key military group whose influence transcends what the organizational chart implies. Reorganization Plan 6 significantly affected the functioning of this body. By 1953, there was criticism of the strategic and political views of the Chiefs. For one thing, they wore two hats in the sense that each was the leading military staff officer reporting to a civilian secretary and as a group they were major advisers to the President and the Secretary of Defense. Two allegedly disadvantageous consequences followed: first, as command officers, each member of JCS was burdened with daily administrative duties and detail work; second, when the Chiefs acted in their corporate capacity, the service secretaries might be by-passed or at least have difficulty controlling their military leaders. With the civilian Secretaries of War, Navy, and Air Force reduced below Cabinet status in 1949, and with the involvement of the Joint Chiefs in the vital controversies over the Navy–Air Force conflict, the MacArthur dismissal, and the Korean war policy, the service secretaries tended to be overshadowed. Moreover, the fact that the chairman of the JCS also tended to become a spokesman for all military personnel gave his words additional weight.

One of the objectives of Plan 6 was to restore the Joint Chiefs as a purely advisory and planning agency. Accordingly, the President relieved the members of all "time-consuming details of minor importance." As noted above, the power to designate the particular armed service which would act as executive agent in a unified operation was transferred to the Secretary of Defense. Although the President emphasized the "basic channels" of responsibility from himself through the Defense Secretary to the civilian secretaries and then to the military chiefs of staff, he specifically excepted the legal responsibility of the JCS to "advise" the President by the terms of the National Security Act of 1947. A second objective of Plan 6 was to improve the organization and procedures of the JCS. This was done by giving the chairman the power to "approve" the Joint Staff (210 officers assigned to aid the Chiefs in the performance of their duties) including their tenure. The chairman now also "manages" the staff, i.e., can give them orders. Third, the plan is intended to "broaden the degree of active participation of other persons and units at the staff level in the consideration of matters before the JCS and to bring to bear more diversified and expert skills." The President also directed the Chiefs to cooperate with other units in the Defense Secretary's office which dealt with budget, manpower, supply, and research matters and to invite civilian scientists and engineers to work from time to time with the Joint Staff.

Along with these changes, President Eisenhower and Secretary of Defense Wilson chose a "new team"—the membership of the JCS was completely changed even though the Navy representative (Admiral Fechteler) still had two years of his term left. The new chairman was Admiral Radford, who reputedly had played an extremely important part in the so-called "Revolt of the Admirals" against the Air Force B-36 program in 1949. Supposedly the new members came to their task without political strings and without substantial links to domestic politics of the past and therefore could take a "new look" at the Armed Forces. Hence in the summer of 1953, the JCS was asked to reconsider alternative strategic plans for war, the size and composition of the Armed Forces, weapon priorities, stockpiling practices, and production capacity estimates.

SOME MAJOR ORGANIZATIONAL ISSUES

Most large, complex organizations are more or less continually affected by tendencies toward and arguments for centralization or decentralization. The Department of Defense may be likened to a huge holding company engaged in such a wide variety of activities that its operations must be controlled by a complicated system of administration. Hence it is not easy to keep its functioning streamlined, coherent, and efficient. If decentralization is carried too far, inconsistency and halfhearted policy execution may result. If centralization is pursued too far, the organization becomes unwieldy because there are too many functions for all to be rigidly supervised from the top. The reorganization of 1953 raised in the minds of some experienced observers * a basic issue, namely, whether the United States defense establishment was drifting or being pushed into the Prussian type of general staff concept. So far as military organization is concerned, there are two quite different schools of thought. One adopts a single strategic concept, thus elevating one service and one weapon to top priority, with all decisions made by an all-powerful general staff not constituted by equal representation of the various military services. In this case, a high degree of centralization and lack of civilian supremacy go hand in hand. The second maintains a flexible strategy, relies on a multiple-service, multiple-weapon base, and combines civilian control with some degree of decentralization.

Appointment of Admiral Radford could be viewed as a move away from the one-weapon, one-service idea. And certainly President Eisenhower was preoccupied with the question of civilian control. However, it has been pointed out that the following factors may create opportunities for over-centralization and diminution of civilian control: the service secretaries are still downgraded, and under the reorganization more assistant secretaries are potentially interposed between them and the Secretary of Defense; the authority and influence of the chairman of the JCS may have been greatly enhanced by giving him opportunity to direct the Joint Staff. The latter could give the chairman a proportionately larger voice in the preparation of individual service plans, force levels, and budget estimates, thus making him in effect an unofficial superchief of staff.

Despite the interservice conflict which continues under less than complete unification, the military establishment does reveal attributes of a high degree of centralization. This fact is due to the gradual strengthening of the Joint Chiefs of Staff and the way it operates. One of the revisions in the National Security Act of 1947 made in 1949 provided that the chairman of the JCS was to inform the President "of those issues upon which agreement is reached. . . ." Papers submitted to the President or the National Security

---

* See, for example, Hanson Baldwin in the New York *Times,* "News of the Week in Review," May 3, 1953, p. 3; interview with Thomas Finletter, former Secretary of the Air Force, *U.S. News and World Report,* May 11, 1953.

Council are subscribed to unanimously and are not submitted otherwise. Often papers are routed through the Secretary of Defense; just as often the President may get advice directly from the chairman of the JCS, who then speaks as the one voice of the military establishment. It has been argued that this practice results in "too much synthesizing" so that the give-and-take and the fine points which enter into a recommendation are lost even if the chairman restrains himself from coloring a report. The President may therefore be deprived of the full advice of the individual chiefs of the separate services. Insofar as the connecting links between the President and the JCS by-pass the civilian secretaries the latter's dominance over military officials may be compromised. To the extent that the JCS is overworked, the amount, timeliness, and quality of recommendations may suffer. Centralization thus has its potential dangers as well as its obvious advantages.

The internal arrangements of the Department of Defense can be viewed in one sense as a reflection of the new role of the military and America's new international position. The military establishment has in fact acquired a complicated set of external relations, foreign and domestic. Certain organizational subdivisions, then, have resulted from the necessity to carry on such relations, and also affect the capacity of the Defense Department to carry them on effectively. Now and henceforth, the armed services must do the following kinds of things: advise (and consult with) many other federal agencies; make and sell plans to nonmilitary groups upon whom they are dependent for resources; carry on extensive day-to-day relations with Congress; grapple with the social implications of military activity at home and abroad; engage in research; handle pressures and requests from newsmen; and administer a vast civilian army. The chief organizational changes since 1947 have resulted in attempts to unify and coordinate the separate branches of the armed services, to provide advice to the Secretary of Defense on all of the various political aspects of military policy and operations, to enable the National Military Establishment to more effectively monitor its vast structure and varied activities, and to supply the Defense Department with adequate representation on interagency and international bodies.

Despite some evidence of increasing centralization of the military organization and despite recent reorganization, the Army, Navy, and Air Force are not unified in the strict sense. Recognition of the unification principle, along with the bestowal of equal status on the Air Force, was of course embodied in the National Security Act of 1947 after months of argument over the best way to integrate the nation's armed services to avoid duplication, conflict, and confusion. World War II experience demonstrated that some form of amalgamation was inevitable and necessary, but the services could not agree on a formula. The act of 1947 was a compromise, an unsatisfactory blend of a number of ideas current at the time. For two years an attempt was made to achieve unification under its provisions. As a result of the recommendations of the Hoover Commission in 1949, amendments were made which were aimed at strengthening the control of the Secretary of Defense over the policies of the three armed services. Since that time progress toward unification has been slow, though substantial gains have been made and the general situation is much better than in 1946 or 1947. During this period, the nation witnessed bitter disputes among the armed services. The effort to unify the services has left scars. Nor have unification and joint strategic planning at the JCS level removed sources of disagreement.

The point being made here is that at the present time there exist a struggle for power, a rivalry for funds, and honestly differing conceptions of strategy among the Army, Navy, and Air Force. It is easy to exaggerate the amount and the seriousness of these conflicts. It is easy, too, to mistakenly assume that only interservice rivalry is involved. In reality, since 1947 the relations between civilian secretaries and military officers and the relations between both of these groups and the President have also been involved. At one point it was Secretary of Defense Johnson vs. the Navy admirals (the so-called "Revolt of the Admirals" in 1949) when the former stopped construction of the 56,000-ton aircraft carrier. At another time, it was the admirals vs. President Truman over the decision to unify the services (1947). Even after organizational changes were set in motion by President Eisenhower in the spring of 1953, the Air Force bitterly and publicly criticized Secretary of Defense Wilson for the $5 billion cut in its budget.

There are several kinds of disputes which run continuously through interservice relations. The Navy challenges the Air Force's basic strategic concept of intercontinental bombing, scoring the B-36 as a "billion-dollar blunder." Furthermore, the Navy would like to control air operations over the oceans and has been fearful of cuts in Navy and Marine aviation funds. On the other hand, the Air Force has argued a minimal role for naval power in strategy and has insisted that money for giant carriers might be better spent on long-range bombers. The Army has emphasized the building up of a tactical air force while not entirely accepting the Air Force position as to the amount to be invested in long-range strategic bombing. The Army and Navy clung tenaciously to the "balanced forces" idea (roughly the same budget allotment for all three branches) until it was modified in the 1952–1953 allocations for military expenditures. The Army has disputed the Navy's control of amphibious warfare and the Army has tried to wrestle air support for ground troops away from the Air Force. There continues to be controversy centering on command over various new weapons such as guided missiles and over the assignment of targets. Bound up in such disagreements are certain larger questions: What kind of war shall we prepare to fight? What kind of strategy will provide maximum security? What kind of world do we want after a war?

To repeat, most of these issues remain. A shooting war in Korea, the personalities and the experience of Marshall and Lovett as Secretaries of Defense from 1949 to 1952, and the larger funds made available for the military have helped to pave the way for healing old wounds and welding the services into one team. The implications of the foregoing from the standpoint of foreign-policy analysis are worth noting. Rivalry for funds and divergent concepts of strategy are of course related to issues of organization—to the everyday meaning of unification, to the amount of autonomy for each branch, to how (and therefore what) decisions on military policy are made. Controversy may be an element of strength in the evolution of military policy but it may also be an element of instability or uncertainty. Probably under these circumstances the costs of military security will be greater, not just because of the tendency to appease rival claims on funds, but because concentration on one philosophy is improbable. Doubtless the operations of the foreign-policy decision-making process generally are further complicated to the extent that military policy in itself is uncertain. Moreover, if past practice is any criterion, the various branches of the armed services will continue to take their demands and policy views to Congress and to the public. The Navy and Air Force have been active since 1949 in building support for their respective positions among members of the Armed Services Committees in both houses of Congress. Finally, it is to be emphasized that the military organization cannot act as a cohesive, unitary group with all its strength mobilized on every policy issue against common "enemies," be they civilian executive officials or congressmen.

CONCLUSIONS

There are several obvious implications to be drawn from the foregoing birds'-eye view of the national military organization. First, the organizational highlights of the Defense Department represent in part accommodations to new and enlarged military responsibilities, to operations carried on abroad, and to a multiplication of contacts with other agencies in the government. Second, so vast is the National Military Establishment that the necessary points of coordination are very numerous and, in particular, the burdens on the secretary's staff units are very great. Third, most of the top-level administrative and policy-making roles in the Defense Department are filled by civilians. While this is, in theory, one of the safeguards for civilian supremacy, it is also true that these civilian officials are spokesmen for military values and functions. Furthermore, staff and operating units are either directed by or advised by military career officers. Fourth, the number of situations in the defense establishment where civilian and military experts must work together or where military experts are performing nonmilitary tasks has increased tremendously. Fifth, interagency collaboration in which the Defense Department participates takes place not only at the level of the secretary, deputy secretary, and assistant secretaries, but through countless committees and "work teams" comprised of representatives from staff and operating units. These considerations should be borne in mind throughout the next section.

grown in size, influence, and
position in the foreign-policy
formulation of foreign policy
s. This new role has raised a
ted earlier in the chapter. Thus
is really a cluster of problems:
military; State Department—
ps among the armed services;
aspects of foreign policy; the
reign military aid; the relation-
ific programs; the relationships
lations between the Department
eign policy aside from the State
n" and "relationships" is delib-
of the military are dependent
rganization are related to each
is related to the foreign policy
values and attitudes are related
the way military information is
inevitable relationships present

A proper role for the military will, in the view of the authors, be approximated when the defense organization successfully fulfills its various functions under the following conditions:

1. The maintenance of civilian supremacy. Civilian supremacy consists basically of the predominance of civilian authority in laying down the general lines of foreign policy and in devising a "grand strategy" for the preservation of national security. Such predominance would seem to rest upon several bases: ultimate decisions to be made by civilian authority; superior power and influence of civilian officials at every point in the decision-making process where the military participate; admission of military influence to decision making only through consultation and not by autonomous action of the military group. Clear allocation of power and responsibility between civilian and military officials and reliance where possible on qualified civilians for civilian positions are essential. Presidential decision on disputed lines of authority should be regularly relied upon and quickly forthcoming. It is particularly essential that where the military establishment administers foreign-aid programs or occupations, general policy directives from the State Department or the appropriate interdepartmental committees should truly limit the area within which the military exercises discretion. Attention must be given to appointment and promotion, budget control, civilian advisers, and departmental secretaries as effective checks on military activities and organization. Control of atomic energy and industrial mobilization should remain under nonmilitary agencies. Priorities to be given the possible value systems which may govern foreign policy should be determined by civilians; if military values are to supersede others, this decision must be made by civilian authorities. Civilian officials should insist on formulating a general political frame of reference within which military objectives are to be sought. Bids to extend military influence or for organizational changes which might so result should be resisted.

2. Minimization of the undesirable effects of the "military mind." To the extent that there are identifiable attitudes and intellectual qualities which are peculiar to military personnel (or in some cases manifest in civilian officials) and which are inappropriate to sound military policy and to the military contribution to foreign policy they should be either altered or quarantined. But first these pertinent intellectual characteristics must be defined and identified. As was pointed out earlier, the phrase "military mind" has many meanings. If it means a particular kind of perspective which is the result of specialized activity, then the military mind is one of a species which might also include a "State Department mind" or the "bureaucratic mind" generally. If it refers to the inappropriateness of techniques of military problem solving for political problems, then a different problem is involved. It is likely that whichever meaning is accepted, remedies or palliatives will be found in increased communication among civilian and military experts, broader training, insistence upon priority of nonmilitary values, and so on. Informed opinion is agreed that one serious manifestation of military habits of mind is the tendency to demand from civilian foreign-policy experts formulations which the military find congenial and understandable. Usually this takes the form of a demand for "clear" statements of policy or directives. The difficulty here is that clarity in this sense may not always be possible. A "clear" statement may be one in which subtle shades of meaning have been shorn off and which therefore does not truly express what the policy makers had in mind. Such a statement may have unforeseen consequences and may obstruct future action. At any rate, the decision as to what formulations are possible is not a military decision.

3. Maximum insulation of military officials from domestic politics. Hanson Baldwin and Demaree Bess disagree on the proposition that military officials should be insulated as far as possible from domestic politics. Baldwin argues: ". . . by the very nature of the American democracy, the military must not rise in public debate to engage in political argument. Under the American system, this is undeniably the prerogative of the President and of his civilian cabinet and assistants; it is not the duty, it is not even the right, of the military. . . . Theirs is not the job of public rebuttal or of public advocacy, even though they may be asked or even 'pressured' to so express themselves."* Bess, on the other hand, argues: "The good old American belief that professional military officers on active duty can and should be completely divorced from partisan politics no longer holds. Our military interests have become so intimately involved with other phases of national policy—and especially foreign policy—that no vigorous military leader can avoid taking a stand on these questions."† Baldwin's principle would seem to be sound according to traditional American concepts although Bess's judgment reflects current reality as was indicated above. There are three major reasons for "keeping the generals out of politics." First, the more military personnel become involved in partisan struggles, the more non-military values will tend to obscure their professional deliberations. It would be inadvisable to have military planning depend on whether this or that Congressional bloc would support a particular strategic plan—at least at the planning level. The difficulty is not that honest differences of opinion on strategy among civilian policy makers is undesirable, but that the use of military arguments for purposes which have little to do with military policy is likely to obscure issues and choices. Second, to the extent that military leaders become identified as Republican or Democratic, pro-administration or anti-administration, the value of objectivity and *expertise* is debased—*all* military advice becomes somewhat suspect. Third, and perhaps most serious, involvement in domestic politics makes it possible for military leaders to build enough political support outside the Executive Branch to make civilian supremacy more and more difficult.

 4. Consideration of military values, information and advice. As General Bradley has said, "The truth is that in these times of half-peace, half-war, neither the soldier nor the diplomat alone can lead the American people on a wise course of international action. Both voices must be heard. . . ."‡ If it is true that grand strategy is "that which so directs and integrates the policies and armaments of the nation that resort to war is either rendered unnecessary or is undertaken with the maximum chances of victory,"§ then the joint role of the civilian policy maker and the military expert is clear. To repeat, the intermingling of the political and the military aspects of foreign policy is inevitable. On the military side the role is *advisory* in that it is concerned with *feasibility,* not *desirability;* and *executive* in that it is concerned with implementation.

---

* Hanson Baldwin, "The Military Move In," *Harper's Magazine,* December, 1947, p. 481.

† Demaree Bess, "Are Generals in Politics a Menace?" *Saturday Evening Post,* April 26, 1952, p. 29.

‡ *Look,* March 11, 1952, p. 35.

§ Edward Mead Earle, as quoted in Chamberlain and Snyder, *American Foreign Policy* (New York, Rinehart & Company, 1948), p. 241.

In the performance of this role, sound military advice, accurate military information, and military values should be fed into the foreign-policy decision-making process *when and where appropriate*. Military advice is probably necessary at all stages of decision making but more so at some stages than others, depending on what is being decided. Military information so far as possible should not be "loaded" in an effort to strengthen the impact of military values on basic decisions. Accuracy refers not only to reliability under test, but also to the fact that a consensus of the best military thinking should undergird the analysis of such vital factors as the military plans and power of a potential enemy. Existence of widely varying, mutually inconsistent estimates of Russian strength, for example, constitutes in effect unreliable information—especially where conflicting opinions are claimed to be authoritative.

Appropriateness refers not only to the relevance of military values, information, and advice, but to the conditions under which these ingredients are considered. In general there should be consultation in situations where military factors must be considered and where the rules of consultation guarantee civilian supremacy. Thus the deliberations of a particular agency— say the National Security Council—would not be an appropriate place to inject military advice if the membership and operation of the agency gave the military group effective control over policy.

Finally, military advice as it comes to the civilian policy makers should have already built into it an accounting of social, economic, and political factors. These factors are bound up with military problems from the beginning. "Pure" military information and advice could hardly be accurate and sound and the missing elements would have to be inserted at the point where military and civilian consultation takes place. The weighing of social aspects must take place at all stages and in all branches of the decision-making process. As a matter of fact, the more the military gives attention to nonmilitary factors which affect its decisions and recommendations, the easier it will be to coordinate the military and civilian functions. Grand strategy requires the collaboration of two kinds of specialists, and one way of integrating perspectives is to have each gain some acquaintance with the problems of the other.

5. *Economical security through effective, efficient military organization.* There are several price tags on national security: dollars, resources, manpower, cherished values, and inconvenience—among others. When the costs of the military basis of national security are too great in terms of what is purchased, other needs and objectives have been sacrificed and influence of the military on national life is inordinate. Military values have then assumed an unintended priority. Money wasted on air bases cannot be spent on foreign economic aid. A military establishment which overburdens the economy reduces freedom of action and decision in nonmilitary matters. If the Defense Department is not effective, the success of foreign-policy implementation

may be jeopardized. If the Defense Department is organizationally inefficient it cannot collaborate usefully with other agencies. The whole point here is this: some of the preceding four conditions could be 100 per cent fulfilled and yet if the costs of military security were too high, if the use of military techniques were ineffective, and if the military establishment were inefficient, it could still be said rightly that the military was not performing its proper role in foreign policy. Congress appears to veer from one extreme to another. Sometimes large lump sums have been cut in a single afternoon from estimates which have taken months to prepare—amounts of half a billion or over. This is not to say that Defense Department estimates should never be checked carefully, but that blanket cuts should not become a substitute for probing the underlying issues. At other times congressmen will make headlines by attacking such items as $68 million worth of can openers, an investment in costly suspender buttons, a "luxury lodge" built for a general, and $45 million in too heavy overcoats—all pointing to "incredible waste." In many cases the charges turn out to be either false or misleading.* Effort spent on this sort of endeavor cannot be spent investigating the military's manpower policies (i.e., rejection of 4Fs), transport policy, and lack of unified purchasing—places where real savings might be made.

One could scarcely expect the above conditions to be *fully* realized. The brief listing may suggest one way of being concrete about the meaning of "the proper role of the military" and may provide a basis for evaluating the present role of military institutions, agencies, and personnel in the formation and execution of American foreign policy. Certain organizational features of the American system of government as well as factors in the external and internal setting of decision making are conducive to the maintenance of the conditions set forth, but others are not. What one can reasonably expect and what can be attempted is a balance in which the favorable conditions will generally prevail, thus ensuring a constructive role for the military but one which minimizes the dangers from swollen size and influence.

FACTORS WHICH CONTRIBUTE TO THE MAINTENANCE OF THE FOREGOING CONDITIONS

Congressional control of the military budget has tended to become weaker despite the creation of "unified" Congressional committees (the Armed Services Committee in each chamber replacing the old Military and Naval Affairs Committees as well as the armed services appropriations subcommittees). Attempts to exert normal legislative oversight over gigantic military appropriations have mostly taken the form of quibbling over details or arguing over basic concepts of strategy in terms of economy. On the other hand, Congressional investigating groups have proved very effective in ferreting out waste and prodding armament production. Technical federal budget procedures such as the "lump sum" appropriation, contingent funds,

---

* Milton Lehman, "The Watchful Congressmen and the Wasteful Army," *Reporter,* July 7, 1953, pp. 23–25.

and the privilege of item transfers within the military organization have further handicapped Congress. There are just three feasible approaches to the budget problem: change in the nation's foreign policy and hence in related military policies; the meat-ax technique of arbitrarily carving substantial amounts from military requests; and selective pruning by experts attached permanently to Congressional committees. Other things being equal, the latter would seem to be the best way.

But the budget problem ties in with other aspects of military-Congressional relations. Agreement on "grand strategy," estimates of enemy strength, and timing of armament build-ups will all tend to reduce the likelihood or necessity that partisan politics will distort legislative action. Concern over "ruinous spending" and anxiety over the hazards of predicting future military situations can at least be kept under control once certain basic factors can be taken for granted. Naturally this implies a minimum confidence and agreement between Congress and the military—a situation not easily arrived at or maintained. This is simply a specific phase of the more general problem of executive-legislative relations. Thus the relatively smooth, that is, cooperative, relationship between the Congress and the military establishment which might be expected to strengthen civilian control, promote legitimate Congressional oversight, and permit the performance of military functions without extraneous hurdles depends on the larger pattern of relations prevailing between the President and Congress. That several of the problems discussed arose between 1950 and 1952, a period of very disturbed executive-legislative relationships, is no coincidence. However, there are other prerequisites. Congress needs trustworthy information and a maximum frankness on the part of military leaders. By a similar token, unfortunate "security leaks" on the part of congressmen sitting in on executive committee sessions, leaks which arouse suspicions and reluctance, must be avoided.

Another factor is, of course, the President himself. According to the analysis of Chapters Five and Six, his leadership and action are crucial in shaping the allocation of power and responsibility in the Executive Branch and therefore he may influence the role of the military in foreign policy in several important ways. He may settle conflicts or break deadlocks as President Truman was called upon to do when he went to meet General Douglas MacArthur on Wake Island, October 15, 1950. He was accompanied by his special adviser on foreign affairs, by the Under Secretary of State; by the chairman of the Joint Chiefs, by the Secretary of the Army, and by the Ambassador at Large. The purpose of the conference was to settle American foreign policy in the Far East by bringing together high-level civilian and military officials. It was prompted by MacArthur's repeated public disagreements with Far Eastern policy.

There is nothing explicit in the Constitution to prevent the President from assigning foreign-policy problems to the military for solution, but to do so he would have to flaunt tradition. The point is that much depends on the relationship between the President and his military advisers, particularly the JCS. Unless the President shows restraint and some administrative skill he may consciously or otherwise allow the military greater influence than it is entitled to or make it difficult for civilian agencies (the State Department) to maintain their position of supremacy. Furthermore, his relationship to military advisers may evoke unfortunate responses in Congress. No one would seriously argue that the JCS ought to publicly challenge the judgment of the President, but it is also true that the President must try to protect his military advisers from attempts to involve them in politics. He can do this in part by being very sparing in his use of the members of the JCS as general policy spokesmen and by insisting that they stick closely to military issues. Presidential supremacy is not necessarily synonymous with civilian supremacy. The late President Roosevelt apparently was willing to grant great power to field commanders on the assumption that his would be the ultimate control. However, it did not always work out this way.

On lower levels the same thing is true: much depends on key personnel —their abilities, previous experience, and conception of the proper role of the military. Cases in point would be the Secretary and Deputy Secretary of Defense, the secretaries of the three services, civilian assistant secretaries, and advisers. No matter how good the system looks on paper, if civilian officials *within* the military establishment are weak, are uncertain of their roles, or become "captives" of the military, subordination of the latter in broad policy matters will be difficult to sustain. Upon these civilian officials also falls part of the burden of facilitating effective collaboration with other executive agencies and with Congress. Robert Lovett, Secretary of Defense from 1951 to 1953, was previously Under Secretary of State from 1947 to 1949 during which time he had teamed with Secretary of State George Marshall. At the same time, the Deputy Secretary of Defense, William Foster, had been a top official in the European Cooperation Administration. Under such circumstances the chances for smooth working relationships with other agencies are much greater and were so in fact during the period cited. Lovett had had long service in business and had been Assistant Secretary of War for Air from 1941 to 1945 so that military leaders had a respect for his technical knowledge. The attitude of military leaders themselves is important too. Both General Marshall and General Bradley had openly expressed convictions as to the necessity for the supremacy of civilian authority and apparently lived by these convictions in their association with the President and the Secretary of State.

Some of the conditions essential to a proper role for the military depend obviously on the organization and functioning of the Department of Defense. Unification of the armed services has made some progress. Undoubtedly Reorganization Plan 6 will tend to reduce waste, increase the effectiveness of military functions, and facilitate the development of sound military policies. And further progress would also lessen the chances of partisan politics being fanned by interservice rivalry and vice versa, particularly if the President, the Director of the Budget Bureau, and the Secretary of Defense work closely together. Beyond a certain point, however, unification might—unless balanced by similar developments elsewhere in the Executive Branch—represent a threat to civilian supremacy. One type of insurance against military tyranny is the fact that there is room for criticism and disagreement *within* the military organization. There is at least a possibility under the reorganization of 1953 that the relationship between the Secretary of Defense and the chairman of the JCS could become intimate enough to provide the secretary in effect with his own military staff—something now forbidden by the National Security Act.

The training of military leaders increasingly reflects the impact of the present role of military institutions in foreign policy and the new international position of the United States. The National War College, begun July 1, 1946, under the direct authority of the JCS, has been called "the highest level educational institution of the United States government." About one hundred of the best qualified, most promising officers of the Army, Navy, and Air Force (average age forty-two, average rank colonel and captain) together with similarly chosen officers from the State Department and other civilian agencies are thrown together in an advanced educational program. These officers live and work intimately with each other for a year, listening to lectures, attending seminars, doing research, drawing up reports, and trying to solve "problems" in small groups of six. Seminars and study groups are concerned with such subjects as basic factors in international relations, objectives and capabilities of states, politico-military aspects of national security, effect of atomic weapons on security planning, diplomatic history, and problems of American foreign policy generally. Several important purposes are served by this program. Officers from the various armed services share a common intellectual experience and learn to communicate with others under optimum conditions. Relationships between political and military factors are explored. State Department personnel work with military personnel on types of problems both must tackle together in the course of their regular duties. Since 90 per cent of the lecturers in the War College are civilians, it means that future policy makers of the Armed Forces are well exposed to nonmilitary points of view. The theory is that a new kind of officer is being fed into the military establishment.* There is good evidence that in the course of seven years a leavening influence has been gradually introduced into the higher echelons of military leadership. The same kind of training (in addition

---

* An excellent account of the program of the National War College and its results is to be found in John W. Masland, "The National War College and the Administration of Foreign Affairs," *Public Administration Review,* Autumn, 1952, pp. 267–275.

to regular military work) is being attempted at the Foreign Service Institute, the Naval War College, the Armed Forces Industrial College, the Command and Staff College (Carlisle, Pennsylvania), and the Air University at Maxwell Field.

In 1953, there were about 300,000 young men in the ROTC program in 372 American colleges and universities. With an average of 16 per cent of the curriculum devoted to military sciences the question has arisen whether the consequent loss of elective courses has deprived future officers of needed training in the social sciences and the liberal arts in general. At Princeton University an attempt is being made to meet one aspect of this problem through a military history course required of all ROTC students. This course stresses the political and administrative problems incidental to raising and maintaining a large military establishment in a democratic society, problems of coalition warfare, and the role of the military in the formation of foreign policy in war and peace.* Above it was noted that new units in the Department of Defense reflect the new role of the military. The extent to which these units can be staffed by officers trained in this way or to which these units can work with such officers in collaborating with civilian agencies will help determine whether the role is properly exercised.

COORDINATION AGAIN

In many respects, the most important factor in this whole situation is the one treated at length in Chapter Six, namely, coordination. Lack of coordination, in any of its several forms, seriously undermines the conditions requisite to a proper functioning of the military. Clearly coordination is required in order to establish a political frame of reference for evaluating and using military advice (i.e., a "grand strategy"); to correlate political and military aspects of foreign policy, including the economic and political effects of foreign military aid at home and abroad; and to integrate the attitudes and perspectives of military and civilian experts (i.e., the results of the military dealing with known quantities and aiming at concrete, well-defined goals). These coordinating processes are made possible by a number of devices and occur at a number of points in the system of activities by which foreign policy is made and executed. Aside from the President himself, who may act as coordinator, perhaps the most important agency is the National Security Council, already discussed. Its organization and working have been improved and the whole tone of military-civilian relations in the Executive Branch is affected by the Security Council's role. In 1948 one of the Hoover Commission Task Forces concluded that the inadequate top-level liaison between civilian and military policy makers was a menace to an effective foreign policy. While this menace has certainly been reduced, it is still possible for

* Gordon B. Turner, ed., *A History of Military Affairs in Western Society since the Eighteenth Century* (3 vols., Ann Arbor, Mich., Edwards Brothers, 1952).

the Security Council to slip into an improper role even though the former military numerical superiority of four to one has been abolished. Furthermore, an extension of the Security Council's functions to include supervision of the coordination of foreign-program operations and settlement of operations disputes would probably improve matters.

The general importance of interdepartmental committees must be re-emphasized. The crucial committee in terms of civilian-military relations, up until the reorganization of June, 1953, was the Mutual Aid Committee chaired by the State Department. This committee constituted a place where the military helped define foreign-aid policy although the State Department retained fiscal control of the military aid program; it was also a place where interrelationships between foreign economic aid and foreign military aid were considered. An interdepartmental committee, though assigned a critical role, is no automatic guarantee of effective coordination. As noted in Chapter Six there are actual and potential defects in the committee system, one of the chief of which is that the chairmen usually have no power to decide in case of a deadlock between two departments. Coordination at this level partly depends in turn on the existence of factors which make possible successful committee operation.

Military assistance programing requires coordination at other points, for the Defense Department acts as an operator as well as an adviser on broad policy. The European counterpart of the Mutual Aid Committee is the European Coordinating Committee. Each country which receives American aid has a "team" made up of United States officials from the State and Defense Departments and the Foreign Operations Administration—the chief of the Military Assistance Advisory Group, the ambassador, and a representative from the FOA. These teams prepare recommendations on the basis of a clear division of responsibility among military, diplomatic, and economic experts yet their deliberations must be integrated. Recommendations are screened by the European Coordination Committee and passed on to the Mutual Aid Committee. The ECC consists of a general from the American element at SHAPE, the United States military representative for military assistance to Europe (a general), a representative of the Joint American Military Advisory Group, the Deputy United States Representative on the North Atlantic Council (chairman), the United States Special Representative for Mutual Aid in Europe, and the United States Representative on the North Atlantic Defense Production Board. Obviously the purposes of the ECC are to coordinate the military, economic, and political aspects of the European defense effort by relating the work of American regional agencies in Europe and by making recommendations based on a study of the needs of individual countries. Needs must be assessed in terms of the actual military strength and production potential of recipient countries and the available United States resources made possible by the Military Assistance Program.

Economic aid to foreign nations must of course be calculated not only on the basis of normal peacetime criteria but also on the basis of the military program of the North Atlantic Treaty Organization.

Another point at which coordination of military and political aspects is required is NATO, for the simple reason that it is a political or diplomatic agency designed to carry out a regional security program of primarily a military nature. Thus the United States Deputy Representative on the NATO Council must have military advice, and the work of the NATO Council, SHAPE, and the Defense Board must be coordinated with the work of the European Coordinating Committee. It has become increasingly apparent that the job of the American commander of the NATO forces in Europe has heavy political overtones. General Ridgway, successor to General Eisenhower, in the summer of 1952 began to indicate that he no longer believed he could concentrate solely on the military side of his task. The American commander is inevitably dragged into political problems and is asked to take a stand on complicated European economic and social issues related to defense.

That foreign aid and NATO problems were not always properly coordinated under the above arrangements is attested to by the creation of a single United States mission to NATO and European Regional Organizations which now handles the needs of coordination in the field. This mission has replaced the European Coordinating Committee.

Occupation of ex-enemy territory has proved the most troublesome coordination point. The experience of 1942 to 1949 demonstrated the need for the State Department and the Defense Department each to be able to control certain aspects of policy in occupied territories. And it also demonstrated the difficulty of devising means for maintaining an effective relationship between the respective responsibilities of civilian and military agencies. Until 1949, the general pattern consisted of the Defense Department having principal responsibility for government and administration in Japan, Germany, Austria, and the Pacific islands placed under American trusteeship, subject to policy directives of the State Department. The State-War-Navy Coordinating Committee, predecessor to the National Security Council, was not able apparently to succeed in high-level coordination of foreign policy and occupation. Two major criticisms of occupation arrangements can be made: first, policy making was characterized by delay, and control of broad policy tended to slip, from civilian hands; second, execution of policy was hampered by the fact that from twelve to twenty civilian agencies might be operating in occupied territory without their status and relation to the field commander being clearly established. The general formula worked out in Germany after 1949 bestowed primary responsibility upon a high commissioner appointed by the State Department, leaving only police and military security functions to the Army. This appears to have been more satisfactory. However, the Supreme Allied Commander in Japan (an American general) remained a powerful figure with major responsibilities until the Japanese Peace Treaty came into effect in May, 1952. While immediate occupation problems have decreased, the experience in Korea (though at this writing occupation in the strict sense is not required because South Korea was "liberated") suggests that civil affairs planning and strategic planning are not yet well coordinated.

During a period of semimobilization, a great deal depends on the capacity of the Defense Department to decide on feasible production goals and to arrive at workable production arrangements with American industry. This involves cooperation among the JCS, the Munitions Board, the Office of Defense Mobilization, and individual firms. A Senate investigating committee reported late in 1952 that the military production program was lagging alarmingly. It appeared to the outside observer that one of the reasons lay in imperfect coordination among the agencies whose powers and facilities are necessary to meet huge armament goals. The committee was thinking seriously of recommending a "military production czar"—an admission of this conclusion.

Coordination is also achieved by a number of devices which may operate at all levels of the policy-making process. Perhaps the most customary technique is informal cooperation between "opposite numbers" in two departments, which does not depend on committee meetings or other formal opportunities but goes on continuously as the need arises. Another technique is low-level staff work, meaning collaborative planning below the level at which decisions are made. One advantage of this is that issues can be discussed or settled before a department publicly takes a stand from which retreat is difficult. Coordination is aided by the practice of regular and adequate reporting of Defense Department activities to civilian agencies and vice versa. Exchange of information should include "clearing" statements by officials of one department which affect the functions of other departments. Finally, educational programs which bring together civilian and military officers help to break down the barriers to fruitful collaboration. One of the obstacles to coordination is the great difference in interests and backgrounds between the two groups. Joint study and intellectual problem solving provide opportunities for understanding and surmounting these differences.

CONCLUSION

A proper role for the military establishment in the formulation and execution of American foreign policy depends on the approximation of certain conditions. The definition of this role must be related to the changing pattern of civilian-military relations, to consequent problems, and to the major characteristics of the present military organization. The "problem" boils down to the necessity for a sufficient realization of the enumerated conditions to make a proper role possible. No one factor or feature of organization is sufficient. Minimization of the dangers from military influence requires a number of safeguards.

► SELECTED BIBLIOGRAPHY

For a more detailed analysis of the problem of the role of the military, consult Burton M. Sapin and Richard C. Snyder, *The Role of the Military in American Foreign Policy*, Doubleday Short Studies in Political Science (New York, Doubleday & Company, 1954). A sound general study of the problem of civilian control of the military is Louis Smith, *American Democracy and Military Power* (Chicago, The University of Chicago Press, 1951). James L. McCamy, *The Administration of American Foreign Affairs* (New York, Alfred A. Kopf, Inc., 1950), pp. 227–270, is an excellent summary of the American occupation experience from the foreign-policy standpoint. Useful documents and essays are presented in Chapter X of L. H. Chamberlain and R. C. Snyder, *American Foreign Policy* (New York, Rinehart & Company, 1948). An excellent brief review of the civil-military relationship in policy formation is to be found in John J. McCloy, *The Challenge to American Foreign Policy* (Cambridge, Mass., Harvard University Press, 1953). The best detailed survey of the problem of Congressional budget control over military appropriations is Elias Huzar, *The Purse and the Sword* (Ithaca, N. Y., Cornell University Press, 1950). Alternative methods of coordinating the roles of the State Department and the Defense Department are discussed in the Brookings Institution, *The Administration of Foreign Affairs and Overseas Operations* (Washington, D.C., Government Printing Office, 1951), Chap. 5. Some of the larger issues raised by an expanded military establishment are analyzed in Jerome Kerwin, ed., *Civil-Military Relationships in American Life* (Chicago, The University of Chicago Press, 1948), and Harold D. Lasswell, *National Security and Individual Freedom* (New York, McGraw-Hill Book Company, 1950). Aspects of the MacArthur case are given lively, thoughtful treatment in Richard Rovere and Arthur Schlesinger, Jr., *The General and the President* (New York, Farrar, Straus & Young, 1951).

CHAPTER TEN

THE GENERAL ROLE
OF CONGRESS AND
ITS COMMITTEES

► INTRODUCTION

The reservoir of foreign-affairs powers available to Congress has already been discussed. This chapter will be concerned mainly with the various kinds of influences that Congress can bring to bear on foreign policy through the exercise of these powers, along with the factors internal to Congress itself which condition the exercise of its powers and hence determine the nature of its impact on the foreign-policy-making process as a whole. In this shift of attention from the Executive Branch, it is well to be reminded again that insofar as legislation is required, foreign-policy decision making should be viewed as a political as well as an administrative process. Congress adds another facet to the total system of activities whereby America interprets the international environment and arrives at a consensus on objectives to be pursued and techniques to be employed in foreign relations. This broad perspective is desirable because preoccupation with the President and executive agencies sometimes encourages the belief that Congress's role is of minor importance—being more or less "tacked on" to the foreign-policy-making process. Actually, the national legislature is a key link in the chain of democratic institutions. Congress is less important than the Executive Branch only in the sense that the latter has primary responsibility for the formulation of foreign policy and for the day-to-day conduct of foreign affairs. Congress's role is different but hardly less crucial in any ultimate sense. For the time being at least, it is advisable to abandon notions of innate Congressional inferiority and preconceptions as to what the role of Congress *should* be.

404

A FRAME OF REFERENCE FOR ANALYZING CONGRESSIONAL BEHAVIOR IN FOREIGN AFFAIRS

If Congress is regarded for analytical purposes as a single organizational unit, the scheme presented in Chapter Three provides a fruitful way of looking at the material presented in the present chapter. The powers and responsibilities assigned to Congress by the constitutional system are allocated *within* Congress among its various subunits just as were the powers and responsibilities of the Executive Branch. Powers and responsibilities are allocated between the House and the Senate, between the majority and the minority parties, among committees, and among leaders and officers in both chambers. In addition to the distribution of functions among those who play official and unofficial roles in Congress, the amount of control by Congress as an organization over the discretion of its individual members is important. Are allocations of power within Congress clear-cut or ambiguous, general or specific? Do they permit or encourage overlapping jurisdictions and do they operate to support a relatively centralized or decentralized decision-making process?

Next, the behavior of Congress can be viewed in the light of the factors which motivate its members, shape attitudes, prompt policy statements, condition committee activity, and influence voting. It is to be expected that Congressional mores and traditions, party considerations and requirements, conventional criteria of political success, the needs and values of the society or its various segments, and the life experience of individual members will all contribute to an explanation of motivation. Since Congress does not operate as an organic whole, the nature and degree of coordination among its various agencies and the way in which information and sentiments are communicated will affect the making of Congressional decisions. Of basic importance is the question of what kind of information Congress has at its disposal and what the sources of that information are. Along with its information must be considered Congress's capacity for policy analysis, these two ingredients comprising the intellectual process imbedded in decision making. Finally, it will be seen that policy selling and rationalization are applicable to Congress too. The manner in which policy decisions are sold in Congress, that is, the tactics whereby consensus is reached, is as significant as Congress's efforts to sell policy proposals to the public and to the Executive Branch. Together, these factors constitute the elements of Congressional decision making.

In addition, the criteria of effectiveness, responsibility, and maturity should be kept in mind as possible bases of judgment as to the way Congress performs its role in the total policy-making process. More particularly, the application of such criteria to the influence of Congress on foreign policy leads to queries concerning the adequacy of Congressional interpretations of the external setting, the logic of its judgments, the success with which it reflects the attitudes and values of the public at large, and the effectiveness of its enforcement of presidential responsibility. Again, it is not a matter of holding Congress to absolute standards, but of evaluating the degree to which

Congress has fulfilled its constitutional responsibilities and has made a constructive contribution to foreign-policy making, as well as of determining whether it does in fact add valuable ingredients of sound policy which cannot be expected from other governmental units.

Analysis of the executive organization for foreign-policy-decision making and execution indicates clearly that the present period of crisis has enormously complicated both the machinery and its operation. A frame of reference for the interpretation of Congressional behavior in foreign affairs would be incomplete if it did not also suggest that the crisis period has found the national legislature somewhat badly prepared for its great new burdens. Just as the whole executive mechanism for foreign affairs has had to be examined and modified in terms of developments since 1941, so Congress must now be seen as squeezed by, and reacting to, an extraordinary situation. Obviously, the policy-making machinery of Congress is only in small part designed specifically for foreign affairs, quite in contrast to the executive organization discussed above which, so to speak, specializes in foreign policy. Before World War II, Congress's increasing domestic burdens were already causing it to creak and groan its way through a mass of legislative business. While this fact is basis enough for understanding what Congress is up against in foreign affairs, it is also a warning that the new international position of the United States has far-reaching implications for the way Congress functions, and judgment of its present role in foreign policy should be affected accordingly. Some of the foreign-policy problems confronting Congress would be difficult in any case, but the question arises as to whether they are made more difficult by the manner in which Congress is organized and functions. For example, as indicated previously, foreign-policy issues are many-sided; each is really a cluster of problems only capable of being broken down in a very artificial sense. It then becomes important to know whether Congress has any organizational devices for looking at all the facets of an issue or problem. Though its techniques have not always succeeded, as appeared in the last chapter, the Executive Branch nonetheless has had to develop ways of merging the different aspects of foreign policy together at a high level in the decision-making process.

► SOME GENERAL CHARACTERISTICS OF CONGRESS RELEVANT TO FOREIGN POLICY

Before moving on to more specific considerations, it is quite essential to the purposes of this chapter, and to the three which follow, to mention certain features of Congress's organization, functioning, and general situation which have a bearing on its role in foreign policy. Such comments will provide some clues on the points suggested by the preceding frame of reference.

To begin with, there are at least three ways of looking at Congress. Congress represents interest groups and ideas. Congressmen speak for labor groups, business groups, farm groups, mining interests, bankers, stockmen, landowners, and so on, or see to it that their spokesmen are heard. They are brokers for private individuals and groups. They are also brokers for ideas and things—"economy," a large air force, anti-Communism, and the like. However, Congress is also a corporate body, with its own traditions and rules, and its behavior can occasionally be understood chiefly in these terms. Thus there will usually exist in Congress at any one time a fairly well-defined set of images of various individuals and agencies in the Executive Branch—a mixture of tradition and recent experience. So also will there be certain procedural requirements which tend to remain static through time and which are brought to bear on new members. Finally, Congress may be regarded as a microcosm of the American people, a mirror reflecting prevailing American attitudes. Congress may reflect—in composite form, of course—the fears, hopes, impatience, frustrations, and other temporary reactions characteristic of the public as a whole. Often these moods are fleeting, but they assume great significance if they happen to coincide with great legislative decisions. Congress is, then, representative and broker, an institution, and a random collection of average Americans.

It has become a settled interpretation of American government that the core of Congressional organization and procedure lies in its committee system. This is another way of saying that Congress does not operate as a unified body except for occasional full-dress debates and formal voting. To do its legislative business, Congress breaks up into smaller semi-independent units under powerful chairmen. Committee chairmen and ranking committee members constitute the power wielders in Congress apart from presiding officers, majority and minority leaders, and the heads of the policy committees of both parties. Inasmuch as committee assignments are on the basis of seniority, chairmen and ranking members are in fact only technically responsible to their party, to other officials of each chamber, or to the Congress as a whole. In addition, debate is relatively unlimited in the Senate and it is the privilege of all congressmen to introduce bills. The upshot is that individuals per se are very powerful in Congress. A senator or a representative, speaking only for himself, may under certain circumstances have far more influence on foreign policy than one would expect if he thinks of Congress as 535 members acting in a body. For some purposes and in some situations "Congress" means one person or a small group of persons rather than one chamber, or one party, or even a whole committee. Like all generalizations, this one is subject to qualification, but it is a significant aspect of Congressional behavior which must be remembered. The fact that such power may be in the hands of one representative of one voting district of one state or in the hands of one senator elected by a total of seventy thousand votes is worth noting.

Congressional individualism is intensified because members are probably on balance fairly free to exercise independence and initiative—at least with respect to issues which do not *directly* impinge on the interests of constituents or pressure groups and on which party leadership has not taken a strong stand. Dramatic outspokeness on major foreign-policy matters is often a quick, effective way to gain the political spotlight with minimum risk of offending particular people and groups. Although the two major political parties are very much involved in foreign-policy making in general, they do not function continuously and uniformly as checks on purely individual Congressional behavior. The parties themselves are fragmented in each of the two houses, being divided in turn into at least two and sometimes three informal groupings for voting and other purposes. In the Senate, the possibility of filibuster and an unwillingness to limit debate and to restrict speeches to specific issues at hand provide further opportunities for the expression of individual views or tactics. Congressional individualism has, among others, two consequences which are relevant for this study. First, it is sometimes difficult if not impossible to assign responsibility for Congressional action. To fix responsibility is not easy in the Executive Branch but the President is ultimately responsible, whereas Congressional responsibility cannot be clearly assigned to any single official, single party, or single group except in rare instances. Second, the prediction of Congressional behavior becomes at once more necessary and more difficult. Given the fact that Congress has the most complex legislative procedure in the world, individuals standing astride the legislative process at key points can upset the most carefully planned policy strategy or they can demand concessions for their acquiescence. It is easier to stall legislation than to pass it.

The role of Senator Taft in foreign-policy matters from 1950 onward testifies to the possibilities inherent in the American system. Whether because of intellectual conviction or because of political considerations, or some combination of the two, Taft became the chief spokesman for the opposition to President Truman's foreign policy until the Republicans won control of Congress in 1952. As a leading candidate for the Republican nomination, he helped to compose his party's platform. Even though defeated in his quest for the presidency, Senator Taft emerged as the most powerful figure in Congress. During the spring of 1953 and until his death in August, he was the chief ally of President Eisenhower in Congress and was informed and consulted with respect to all major decisions. For quite different reasons and with quite different results, Senator McCarthy was almost equally powerful. These two men were by all odds the two men in Congress most to be reckoned with on foreign policy and relations. They far overshadowed Senator Wiley, chairman of the Senate Foreign Relations Committee at least during the first session of the Eighty-third Congress.

The foregoing considerations help to explain the extremes of Congressional behavior. On the one hand, Congress may work very smoothly, getting much done without much waste motion; on the other hand, it may literally limp along for several months without passing one major bill. Debate may be reasonably full, germane, and contributory to sounder legislation. Another time debate may be scanty, lacking in focus, and without appreciable effect on legislation. It is the possibility that Congressional behavior may range at random between such extremes that makes Congress a somewhat uncertain element in the total decision-making process. The uncertainty is rarely deliberate in the sense that it is an objective in itself, and it is probably less the result of obstructionism than the result of the way Congress as an organization is structured and operates.

As is well known, Congress's work load has been increasing rapidly over a fifteen-year period. Both its organization and procedures were designed for an earlier day. Aspects of this problem can be seen in the work load of the individual congressman. There is general consensus that he is clearly overburdened. Estimates of the amount of time the average congressman spends on errands and services for his constituents run from 50 to 80 per cent. These requests can hardly be escaped since there is a well-established tradition that there are certain things a congressman must do. The average congressman probably receives not less than 250 letters a day and may receive up to 1,000 letters a day, all of which must be answered, to say nothing of phone calls and personal visits. Periodic visits home to find out what thousands of constituents are thinking are costly and time consuming. Talking to influential public figures takes another block of time. All these duties are over and above regular committe assignments and party activities. Much time has to be sacrificed to roll calls, during which the member must be present on the floor but cannot use his time profitably. One important committee membership, and many congressmen hold more than one, requires hours spent at hearings, committee meetings, drafting sessions, and personal investigations. Public functions must be attended and speeches given. Periodically, attention must be paid to securing re-election and repairing political fences.

This picture suggests that Congress, like the Executive Branch, suffers under its own set of pressures and distractions. One kind of pressure arises from trying to represent a heterogeneous constituency and to interpret special pleas and communications from it. In a sense, particularly in foreign policy, the congressman may be caught between the sentiments of interest groups and his view of the dictates of national interest, between what will conform to local and sectional attitudes and what the nation as a whole requires. He is subject to party considerations, to pressure from executive agencies, and to pleas from colleagues in Congress. He must constantly guard his own prestige and that of his committee. He is subject to exhortation by the President. Nor can he escape from many dilemmas and frustrations. If he tries to be completely independent in his thinking he may find himself politically ineffective. If he maneuvers his personal and organizational relationships in order to become effective he may have to compromise his views. If he concentrates on committee work, he may not have time to meet with individuals; yet if he does not attend to his Congressional duties his reputation may suffer and he may be denied patronage and access to influence. The congressman lives in a different kind of fish bowl, but a fish bowl it is, nonetheless.

Several conclusions follow from the foregoing discussion. The Congressional impact on foreign policy will be channeled through individuals and groups—either voting blocs, economy or nationalist blocs, a party, or a wing thereof—and any Congressional leadership will be exercised by such individuals and groups. It cannot be expected that Congress as an organic whole will exercise foreign-policy leadership. A pattern of frequent unexpected developments is characteristic of Congressional activities in general. There is always a potential tendency toward "negativism," inertia, and resistance to leadership. Responsibility for Congressional action is difficult to assign. The effectiveness with which Congress plays its role in foreign policy—whatever it is—will be conditioned in large measure by the relationship between the total legislative work load (including errands for constituents and private bills) and the way Congress is organized and operates.

▶ THE NEW ROLE OF CONGRESS IN THE FORMULATION AND EXECUTION OF FOREIGN POLICY

Historically, Congress has not played what could be described accurately as a well-defined role. Until quite recently, there has been no core of foreign-policy functions around which Congress could build a strong claim to deference and authority. On the whole, Congress played second fiddle—when it played at all. Congress has often aspired to more of a role than it has been able to achieve. Aspirations have come to the surface during occasional revolts against presidential leadership. The periods in which Congress's action or inaction with respect to foreign policy was crucial have been brief and widely spaced in time. Its impact has been sporadic and Congressional victory represented more often a check on the President than a presidential acceptance of the legislature's views. This is not to say that Congress has not been important. Indeed, one cannot fully understand the extent and use of presidential power without taking account of the nature and use of Congressional power, as will be seen in the next chapter. However it is generally true that until the middle 1930's Congress could not exercise regular leverage on the main direction of American foreign policy. This fact was due fundamentally to the kind of foreign relations America had and to America's position in world affairs. Furthermore, Congress's role was largely the Senate's role. The Senate, of course, has long insisted that it is a coordinate equal with the President, but was never quite able to make the contention stick. It did possess a continuing capacity to upset executive calculations, particularly with respect to treaties. In sum, Congress's role was essentially negative, sporadic, and opportunistic. Congressional action *affected* the President's foreign-policy behavior yet did not represent true initiative. Congressional criticism was unceasing, though the sting was mild because of the absence of effective sanctions.

For analytical purposes it is proper to say that since 1945 (the dating point is artificial in the sense that the forces which altered Congressional participation in foreign affairs were actually set in motion previously) Congress's role has become more important and has significantly extended. But it is necessary to be clear about what this means. It does not mean that Congress has suddenly acquired new powers. Nor does it mean only that Congress now does more often or more intensively what it did before. Developments have been such that *a greater number of the powers in Congress's constitutional reservoir have become relevant to foreign policy and Congress has a wider range of recurring opportunities to exercise those powers.* Major foreign-policy programs and major supports for national security require legislation. Only Congress can constitutionally assign national material resources to external objectives. Military, economic, and political techniques rest on *appropriations*. Once upon a time it was pleasant but not essential to have Congressional approval for foreign policy *after* its formulation. Now Congress *must be sold during* its evolution. Withal, it was evident by the Eighty-third Congress—despite the fact that the Republicans were in control of both branches for the first time in twenty years—that the legislature had reached the flood tide of assertiveness in the field of foreign relations.

The implications of this general point concerning appropriations are worth additional comment. On the military side alone, the new responsibilities of Congress are very imposing. In the first place, as was seen in the last chapter, military policy is one of the back doors to foreign policy. Congress exerts both direct and indirect control over military policy because it "raises and supports" the Armed Forces. In the second place, Congress has heavy responsibility to see to it that national security is purchased with minimum waste and that the principle of civilian supremacy is sustained. In the third place, Congress decides ultimately how national resources are to be distributed between military and nonmilitary means in foreign policy. In the fourth place, appropriations for the executive agencies engaged in policy making and execution give Congress an opportunity to influence organizational aspects of decision making. Congress may try to enforce its views both on *what* these agencies do and *how* they do it. As executive organization has grown more and more complex, this consideration has grown in importance.

Although more extensive legislative underwriting of foreign policy is perhaps the most crucial factor in the new role of Congress, it is not the only one by any means. As noted previously, American foreign policy is increasingly characterized by multilateral agreements inside and outside the United Nations. These must be approved either by the Senate or by both houses together. The tremendous power and initiative in the hands of the President and the Executive Branch have vastly complicated Congress's job of administrative oversight and enforcement of responsibility. This job was never easy and has become more vital as well as more difficult. It must be remembered that the executive bureaucracy has grown *in toto,* so that Congress has both a general task and one specifically directed to foreign-policy administration. Another reason for the enlarged role of Congress is that certain experiences during the period 1919–1941 taught the lesson that national security could be menaced when Congressional power was not properly integrated into the total decision-making process. The failure of the United States to join the League of Nations and the wrangle over neutrality legislation between 1935 and 1939 demonstrated that Congress's action or attitudes might be a controlling factor and that the day when Congress could be ignored with impunity had passed. From 1941 onward there has been explicit recognition in the Executive Branch of a necessity for broader participation by Congress.

What are some of the symptoms and results of the foregoing changes? Greater foreign-policy responsibilities have further taxed the already over-burdened resources of Congress. One of the more obvious contrasts between 1932 and 1952 is the greater proportion of Congressional energy in the form of hearings, debates, and investigations devoted to foreign-policy matters during the later year. Of 10,627 bills introduced in the first session of the Eighty-first Congress, 5,120 had foreign-policy implications direct or indirect. The State Department reported its interest in 657 of the bills, asking that Congress give high priority ratings to thirty legislative items and emergency ratings to ten.* Not only has foreign policy added to Congress's absolute burdens but it has confronted Congress with problems for which the domestic political process is not always appropriate. For example, rough-and-tumble Congressional criticism of a member of the cabinet, which might be expected as a normal byplay of the interaction of national political forces, has quite other consequences when it involves one of the country's primary spokesmen on foreign policy, such as the Secretary of State. It is usual for individual congressmen to act as sources of news for the press and for them to use the press as a device of policy strategy; on the other hand, congressmen now have access to information which should not become public knowledge.

Congress, for the reasons noted, now has a greater voice in the implementation of foreign policy and consequently has more opportunity to criticize implementation. However, it is in the area where means shade off into ends, and where discussion of means inevitably invites discussion of ends, that the door is open for Congress to shape policy goals. In other words, on numerous occasions Congress helps to *decide* foreign policy as well as to implement it. Often it appears that all Congress does is to hack away at the major policies which come from the Executive Branch, to take out bits and pieces from policies and make substitutions. But the impact of this process should not be underestimated. Congress can add overtones and interpretations to foreign

---

* H. H. Smith, "Reorganization, Senate Style," *American Foreign Service Journal,* June, 1949, p. 50.

policy which may vitally affect the way the world views American policy and which may measurably alter the actual operation of the policy. While the Executive Branch has lost none of its initiative, its legislative counterpart has gained initiative. Thus Congress was able in 1950 to include in a foreign-aid bill provision for a loan to Spain contrary to the express wishes of the State Department and the President.

There have been other results of Congress's new position in foreign affairs. One which is familiar enough is the use of foreign-policy issues for domestic or local political purposes. What is referred to is not legitimate, responsible criticism and discussion of alternatives, which is a fundamental duty of Congress. Rather it is the indiscriminate, irresponsible use of foreign-policy issues *for purposes having nothing to do with foreign policy per se* which has become increasingly frequent. Accusing the Secretary of State of being pro-Communist is apparently one of the ways of "getting votes back home." A most interesting development has been the meshing of Congressional politics and the politics of other countries. Earlier in this book it was stated that one of the pressures brought to bear on executive policy makers is the necessity of representing or interpreting the aims and interests of America's allies. It is too much to say that individuals and groups in Congress have become representatives of foreign interests in the literal sense. Nevertheless, the operations of the China Lobby* suggest something very close to this. A bloc in Congress has for several years argued for American support of an effort by the Chinese Nationalist Army (withdrawn to Formosa along with the Nationalist government) to recapture control of China. Another bloc has been sympathetic to the Franco regime in Spain. Still another bloc criticized Marshall Plan aid on the ground that it bolstered a socialist government in Great Britain. Similar in import is outspoken Congressional criticism of the domestic politics of other countries, particularly in connection with American aid abroad. Such communication is public and extradiplomatic.

Congressional groups also align themselves with opposing factions and points of view within the Executive Branch. A recent spectacular example was House Republican Leader Martin's solicitation of a letter from General MacArthur which advocated foreign-policy views contrary to those of the administration and at a time when the general was still United Nations Commander in Korea in 1951. During the hearings on General MacArthur's dismissal, most Republicans in Congress openly sided with his policy views. Congress may side with one agency rather than another as it did with the ECA in its conflicts with the State Department. Thus congressmen may "represent" administrative agencies or programs. The Air Force, for example, may have a more effective "lobby" in Congress than the Navy has.

Since 1945 more members of Congress have enjoyed practical experience in diplomacy through "field trips" than ever before in the nation's

* See Chapter Thirteen, "The Impact of Public Opinion and Interest Groups on Foreign Policy."

history. Senators have served regularly on American delegations to various United Nations agencies. In 1947–1948, the Herter Committee of the House of Representatives made its own on-the-spot study of economic conditions in Western Europe before the Marshall Plan was considered by Congress. Such experience has not been equally shared by all members of Congress, but it has been extensive enough so that Congress has directly and indirectly gained firsthand knowledge of what the diplomat is up against and what the external environment is like.

► CONGRESSIONAL ORGANIZATION FOR FOREIGN AFFAIRS

The foreign-relations power of Congress is divided unequally between the House and the Senate and is further subdivided within each. Because they are elected and organized differently, the two houses behave somewhat differently on foreign-policy matters.

THE PRE-EMINENCE OF THE SENATE

Tradition, plus the constitutional requirement for approval of nominations of diplomatic officials and policy-makers and for two-thirds approval of treaties, gives the Senate more leverage on foreign policy than the House enjoys. A greater degree of informality and less rigid control of debate in the Senate also enhance the opportunity for individual senators to wield influence. Treaties can be amended by a simple majority. Hearings on appointments can serve as occasions for debate on policies. It is probably true that the Senate looks upon itself and is looked upon by the Executive Branch as the chief Congressional watchdog of foreign policy. Relationships between the Senate and the Executive Branch are by and large more frequent and more regular in the field of foreign relations than in the case of the House. When three or four senators attack the Secretary of State or urge a reversal of American policy this is likely to be somewhat more significant than if three or four representatives do the same thing.

THE HOUSE OF REPRESENTATIVES

Actually, the expanded role of the House is synonymous with the larger role of Congress generally. An increase in the number of agreements submitted to both chambers, the more frequent the necessity for appropriations, and the desire for the broadest possible partisan backing for foreign policy have all contributed to make the House more than a silent, docile partner. The psychology of the House regarding appropriations differs noticeably from that of the Senate, certainly in foreign-policy matters. Often the House slashes large chunks from a foreign-aid program, apparently on the assumption that most of it will be restored first by the Senate and later by the action of the conference committee. It has been said that the House watches the purse while the Senate watches the President. However, in voting on the Mutual Security Act of 1953, the House wanted military aid to Western Europe contingent on the formation of a European Army but the Senate preferred to leave this to the President's discretion. The House Appropriations Committee seems to be more concerned with the details of expenditures than in policy objectives, more concerned with "efficiency" of operations than with the sum total of responsibilities which have to be met by an executive agency. In the summer of 1951, this committee cut 18 per cent from the State Department budget request, exhorting the department to improve the quality of its personnel and work instead of depending on quantity.

The House of Representatives does not, of course, confine its interest in foreign policy to appropriations. The House Foreign Affairs Committee passes on any legislation required to implement foreign policy. In February, 1951, 118 Republicans demanded that the United States concentrate its security in the Western Hemisphere. One year later, the entire House by a vote of 189 to 143 agreed to "direct" the Secretary of State to reveal full information on any agreements made by Truman and Churchill with respect to the troubled situation in the Middle East. Party cohesion is stronger in the House. Procedures are more mechanized and party leaders are more involved in strategy than in selling ideas. The result is that if the President's party controls the House, most big programs can be pushed through. Opposition to the Secretary of State or to his policies is more apt to be on a party or bloc basis rather than on an individual basis.

Strangely enough, despite the procedural strait jacket in the lower chamber, coordination between the Appropriations, Armed Services, and Foreign Affairs Committees is less effective than it is in the Senate. Three members of the Senate Foreign Relations Committee sit in when the Senate Appropriations Committee considers matters relating to foreign policy. Therefore, the possibility of an "appropriations revolt" is much greater in the House. In 1948, after the Senate Foreign Relations Committee and House Foreign Affairs Committee had approved the European Recovery Program, the House Appropriations Committee made a sizable cut in the agreed amount of American aid.

Periodically, the House makes a bid for a greater role in the treaty-making process. And periodically it shows its resentment at being treated as an inferior and at being left out of international conferences and the like. Beginning in January, 1944, various House leaders began to suggest that the House would be called upon to appropriate money on a large scale for foreign-policy purposes and that the peace treaties to follow World War II ought to be regarded as "agreements" so that the House could participate. On May 9, 1945, the Kefauver-Schwabe constitutional amendment, calling for treaties to be approved by a majority of the membership of both chambers, was introduced. The vote was 288 to 88 after an unusual two-day debate which received very little publicity. These were the chief arguments for the amendment: (1) it takes only a simple majority resolution of both houses to get into war, but a two-thirds vote in the Senate to make peace; (2) a treaty may supersede a law and thus the House can be deprived of its legislative prerogatives; (3) the House is called upon to appropriate money for treaties on which it had no voice; and (4) the two-thirds arrangement encourages the President to circumvent Congress. There is no evidence that the House has changed its mind, but before the amendment can be presented to the country, the Senate must act on it and that body's Judiciary Committee has so far refused to report the bill out.

THE IMPACT OF THE COMMITTEE SYSTEM

Congressional action on foreign policy is, of course, largely determined by committees. Hence the phrase "Congress and foreign policy" becomes "a small group of congressmen and foreign policy." There are fifteen standing committees in the Senate, nineteen in the House, and several special committees in each chamber as well as joint committees. Not all these committees have specific responsibility for legislation or other action bearing on foreign relations. In terms of major responsibilities, the most important committees are the Senate Foreign Relations Committee, the House Foreign Affairs Committee, and the Armed Services and Appropriations Committees of both House and Senate. Probably the bulk of Congressional activity is carried on by these groups. However, other committees also have foreign-policy functions. When tariff legislation is needed, the Senate Banking and Currency Committee and the House Ways and Means Committee must act. The subcommittee on Internal Security of the Senate Judiciary Committee is very much involved in foreign relations because it was established to administer the Internal Security Act of 1950, which was designed to protect the United States from subversion and which set up, among other things, immigration controls as part of that task.

It is unnecessary to catalogue the foreign-policy functions of all the committees. The point is that at least ten committees in each house have some such functions. Although major foreign-policy responsibilities are concentrated in a few committees, committee responsibilities are in fact divided. The existence of several committees which may pass judgment on foreign policy paves the way for fragmentation, rivalry, and duplication. There is no one agency through which Congress can gain a total view of foreign-policy problems. There is no one committee which coordinates the foreign-policy activities of all committees. Lack of coordination is always a possibility. The revolt by the House Appropriations Committee against the European Recovery Program in 1948 brought a bitter exchange between Senator Vandenberg, chairman of the Senate Foreign Relations Committee, and Representative Taber, chairman of the House committee. Both men were members of the Republican party, which controlled Congress at the time. Foreign-aid programs must run the time-consuming gamut of the Senate Foreign Relations Committee and the Senate Appropriations Committee as well as the House Foreign Affairs Committee and the House Appropriations Committee. Many important matters are gone over twice in the process. Division of responsibility among committees and its results are not confined to those with foreign-policy functions. As the line of demarcation between domestic and foreign policy has disappeared, a committee working almost exclusively on domestic matters may take action of prime significance for foreign relations. For example, a committee having jurisdiction over price control may by its action or inaction considerably raise the cost of items to be shipped through foreign-aid programs and thus cut down on the amount of foreign aid.

When discussing the committee system, one inevitably must pay attention to subcommittees. The reduction of the number of standing committees in both houses in 1946 and the steadily mounting legislative burden—particularly with respect to appropriations—have combined to enhance the significance of subcommittees. Much of the preliminary investigation and analysis is now done by subcommittees ranging from three to seven in number. Subcommittees are even more crucial in the appropriation process. One result of this factor is to magnify the influence of individuals. Another is that the State Department budget proposals may be screened—especially in the House—by two or three members who have had very little or no experience with foreign affairs or with the work of the department. It is unlikely that other members of Congress are going to pore through a thousand pages of testimony to check on the detailed recommendations of the subcommittee. Usually, the report of the Appropriations Committee (which in turn combines the reports of several subcommittees) is authoritative. As might be expected, there is a tendency for appropriations groups to regard the foreign-aid programs primarily as *spending programs* which require caution and scrupulous attention to detail. Thus the larger foreign-policy objectives are sometimes neglected; certainly little attention is paid to means-ends relationships, that is, to the adequacy of the money sought for the policy objective in view. Being relatively small (as well as for other reasons) the State Department budget appears to invite more significant slashes and much more questioning than the military budget. In 1949, the House Appropriations Committee added $800 million to the $45 billion military budget, yet cut $6 million from a State Department request of around $100 million. The appropriations process, which looms so large in foreign-policy decision making, transforms foreign-policy issues into purely budget issues to be decided by several small groups who may have had no experience in foreign affairs and who may not even know what the general objectives of the United States are.

Another result of the committee system is to buttress Congressional individualism by elevating committee chairmen and ranking members to positions of great power over the flow of legislation. Furthermore, the most powerful individuals ordinarily have two important committee assignments apiece. On this basis, one could at any one time list perhaps twenty members of each chamber who could bring extensive influence to bear on foreign policy. The chairmen of the Foreign Relations Committee and the Foreign Affairs Committee will, of course, be high among the leaders. But it is also possible for other single individuals, regardless of party controls, to attain leverage. For example, in the summer of 1951, Senator McCarran (Democrat, Nevada) was chairman of the afore-mentioned Internal Security Subcommittee and chairman of a subcommittee of the Appropriations Committee. The former had been conducting an inquiry into communism in the State Department and in the Voice of America program and the latter made recommendations on the State Department budget and the Mutual Security Program. So far as the State Department was concerned, Senator McCarran was more powerful than Senator Connally, who was chairman of the Senate Foreign Relations Committee.

Committee chairmen and ranking members arrive at their positions, as is well known, by operation of the seniority rule, not by virtue of party loyalty or expertness in a particular subject. Hence they have considerable independence and are not automatically under the discipline either of their party's leadership in Congress or of the President. Several weeks before the 1952–1953 Mutual Security Program was submitted to the Senate Foreign Relations Committee, its chairman, Senator Connally (Democrat, Texas), was announcing that the program had to be cut. This independence is all the more significant because of the control chairmen exercise over the legislative process. A chairman runs his own committee, decides on procedures, appoints subcommittees, controls hearings, can hold back a bill from the floor, and is often responsible for the strategy to be followed when a bill does reach the floor. The chairman is therefore a powerful figure.

Finally, the central role of the committee in the legislative process highlights the importance of the committee hearings which usually precede a committee's decision or report on some matter. Hearings are regarded as a primary source of Congressional information. Presumably hearings are supposed to supplement general debate by furnishing a place where analysis and clarification of issues is possible. Actually, hearings serve several additional functions not all of which necessarily contribute to sound policy decisions. They may serve to confirm a judgment the committee has already arrived at. They may constitute an uncritical attack on a policy idea or an executive official. Hearings serve to deliberately obscure issues, or they may function as a means of letting off steam without contributing constructively to the attainment of consensus.

THE SENATE FOREIGN RELATIONS COMMITTEE

The Senate Foreign Relations Committee is, on balance, the most important Congressional committee dealing with foreign affairs. It consists of thirteen members, seven from the majority party, six from the minority party. The chairman is one of the most influential members of the Senate. There is no better way to appreciate the functions performed by this committee than to review briefly its legislative history during the Eighty-first Congress (1949–1950). A total of sixty-seven treaties came before the committee; twenty-five, including the North Atlantic Treaty and the Charter of the Organization of American States, were approved. Other treaties ranged from a Convention for Safety of Life at Sea to an extradition agreement with South Africa, from an International Wheat Agreement to a Claims Convention with Panama. Most of the twenty-five which were approved involved highly technical economic and scientific problems. Thirty-six bills and resolutions were processed by the committee and enacted by the Senate. These treaties, bills, and resolutions dealt with mutual defense, economic assistance, strengthening of the United Nations and implementation agreements made under United Nations auspices, the Inter-American System, commercial and consular treaties, fisheries conventions and legislation, bridges and boundary legislation, international meetings, exhibitions and games, claims and other financial arrangements, and international commodity arrangements. In addition, the committee conducted a special investigation into disloyalty among State Department employees and drafted a bill providing for reorganization of the State Department, which was accepted by the Senate. The bills and resolutions finally reported out were culled from 118 referred by the Senate and 32 by the House. During the two sessions of the Eighty-first Congress, the committee passed upon 1,049 nominations, including 53 ambassadors, the United States high commissioner to Germany, the members of delegations to the General Assembly of the United Nations, the ECA administrator, and the Secretary of State.

To do all this required 175 meetings of the full committee, 105 of which were in executive (secret) session. At various times, 19 subcommittees were established to handle particular legislative business, each of which held its own meetings. The special State Department investigation took five months, including thirty-one days of hearings, and the North Atlantic Pact hearings consumed sixteen working days. There were only two items on the two-year agenda which required hearings and activities over and above regular committee and subcommittee meetings at which recommendations were discussed and reports drawn up. Fifteen meetings of conferees from the Senate Foreign Relations Committee and the House Foreign Affairs Committee to iron out differences on bills and resolutions took place and five joint meetings of the two bodies were held for such purposes as discussing the European Recovery Program or listening to the Secretary of State.

Clearly an immense amount of work is handled by the Senate Foreign Relations Committee, especially when one realizes that there are only thirteen members to share the load and that members have at least one other important committee assignment. Throughout the eighteen months preceding the adjournment of the Eighty-second Congress in 1952 the committee had more measures before it, held more meetings, and spent more hours on foreign-policy matters than in any other comparable postwar period. In the course of two sessions, each member can normally expect two or three subcommittee assignments and on at least one he will be chairman. By 1950, both the number and the complexity of the items of business which come before the Senate Foreign Relations Committee had so increased that the chairman announced in April that the committee had been organized into eight permanent subcommittees in order to facilitate consultation with the State Departmen—another aspect of the committee's work. There is almost daily informal contact between the committee members and staff and the Department of State. During the Eighty-first Congress, the Secretary of State appeared formally seventeen times, and the Defense Secretary, the ECA administrator, and officials of the State Department talked to the committee on numerous occasions. During the Eighty-second Congress, the Secretary of State appeared fourteen times in a consultative capacity and eight times as a witness on pending legislation in addition to meeting informally with the chairman and ranking committee members. The new subcommittees more or less correspond to the oganization of the State Department: United Nations Affairs; Economic and Social Policy Affairs; Far Eastern Affairs; European Affairs; Near Eastern and African Affairs; American Republics Affairs; Public Affairs; and State Department Organization. Each member serves on two of the consultative subcommittees. Not only is the whole scheme designed to facilitate regular contacts with the Executive Branch; it also represents a recognition that no one member can become reasonably well acquainted with all the ramifications of foreign policy with which the committee deals. Under this arrangement, a member has a chance more or less to specialize in two areas and to have his other subcommittee assignments geared into these areas. When the full committee meets, the members of the permanent subcommittees are better able to contribute special knowledge to the issues at hand. Two majority party members and one minority party member compose the subcommittees except for the United Nations and European Affairs, on which party representation is equal. The subcommittees meet irregularly but at least once monthly with the Assistant Secretary of State who is in charge of their subject areas as well as with other appropriate officials when their presence is required. The subcommittees are not, of course, simply legislative committees. They are also consultative and are designed to keep the members of the larger committee better informed of what is going on. While he was negotiating the Japanese Peace Treaty, John Foster Dulles (then holding the rank of ambassador) met nine times with the Far Eastern Subcommittee.

In addition to its functions of processing treaties and preparing legislation, the Senate Foreign Relations Committee serves as an overseer of certain programs authorized by Congress. Regular periodic reports are received from the Foreign Operations Administration on the foreign-aid program and from the State Department on such matters as United States participation in the United Nations and international information activities. The committee is also a fruitful source of special studies and other documentary materials. One of its functions is to educate the Senate and to provide information gathered and processed under the supervision of the Senate.

THE IMPORTANCE OF ITS CHAIRMAN

The chairman of the Foreign Relations Committee holds one of the most prestigious positions in Congress. Because of the nature of the committee system all chairmen are powerful, but the Foreign Relations Committee probably ranks close to the top in respect and influence in the Senate. A series of distinguished Senators have occupied the office—Sumner, Lodge, Borah, Sherman, Stone, Pittman, and Vandenberg. Combining the constitutional rights of the Senate with vigorous personal leadership, Borah and Sumner could brag that under them the Foreign Relations Committee was almost a separate department of the government on an equal footing with the presidency. Quite apart from the rules of the Senate and personal initiative, the chairman is powerful because he can smother treaties and bills or see that they are reported unfavorably or in changed form. He can push treaties and bills through the legislative mill with skill and precision or he can mismanage them. He appoints subcommittees and their chairmen. He usually has direct access to the President and to the Secretary of State. In the last analysis, however, the chairman's behavior will reflect at least in part his conception of the office and any individual ambitions he may have. Senators Pittman (1934–1940) and Connally (1940–1946; 1948–1952) seem to have regarded themselves primarily as Congressional leaders for the administration, although the latter became increasingly independent toward the end of his tenure. Lodge and Borah appear to have been vigorously independent of presidential influence regardless of whether their party was in power or not. Doubtless there are limits to the extent to which the chairman can exercise his own initiative, and his power is certainly not absolute. But without his support the sponsors of a treaty or a bill would find it exceedingly difficult to obtain Senate approval. In March, 1952, it was known that Chairman Connally favored a reduction in the foreign-aid program for 1952–1953—he had said so publicly. President Truman took unusual steps: he made two special pleas to Congress and one over a national radio and television hookup. It seems unlikely that such pressure would have been necessary if the Foreign Relations Committee chairman had been enthusiastically in favor of the program as submitted.

The chairman's influence will depend, too, on the respect accorded his tactics and views. During the period of his chairmanship, 1946–1948, Senator Arthur Vandenberg (Republican, Michigan) enjoyed a prestige among his colleagues in the Senate which not even a Borah or a Lodge surpassed. Vandenberg earned this position in part by a dramatic reversal of his own views on foreign policy. From one whose outlook on the world and America's place in it was rather provincial and somewhat in the isolationist tradition, he became a foremost interpreter of what the new international situation meant to American policy. There is ample evidence that Vandenberg's change enabled many others to change without losing face and without feeling they had "sold out" to Rooseveltian views and Democratic pressure. The fact that Vandenberg was a Republican was crucial. The bipartisan collaboration which was worked out after 1945 owed much to Vandenberg's energy, vision, and leadership. Because Vandenberg was the kind of man he was and because he demonstrated a remarkable capacity to learn quickly and to throw off outmoded views, his personal contribution to American foreign policy was great indeed. During his chairmanship and later when he was ranking member, his leadership strengthened the committee and, most important, strengthened the relationship between the Congress and the Executive Branch. At a time when America had to make far-reaching decisions, Vandenberg supplied an element of integration which counteracted the natural tendency of Congress to fragment in the face of great issues and which provided a rallying point for positive, majority views so that negative, minority views could be seen in proper perspective. The example of Senator Vandenberg strongly suggests the significance of the personal qualities and role definitions of the key figures in the legislative process.

COMMITTEE PROCEDURE

A brief résumé of the legislative history of the North Atlantic Treaty will illustrate some aspects of the way the committee attacks major issues. After many months of diplomatic negotiation, the Secretary of State met with the committee in executive (secret) session on February 18 and March 8, 1949. On March 18, the treaty provisions were made public. Sixteen days of hearings began on April 27, during which time about one hundred nongovernment witnesses were heard in addition to the Secretary of State and other executive officials. The committee held executive sessions again on June 2 and 6 and on the latter day the treaty was reported to the floor of the Senate with a unanimous recommendation. On July 5, the Senate began sixty-three hours of debate in which thirty-one senators spoke for and twelve senators spoke against the treaty. The Senate passed the treaty on July 21, 1949, by a vote of 82 to 13.

There are several features of this procedure which should be noted. First, it took nearly six months to obtain approval after the legislative machinery had been set in motion. Without necessarily subscribing to a "speed for the sake of speed" argument, it may be queried whether this much time was really required. Time-consuming habits and practices which do not add to the richness of debate or soundness of decision may be costly to the nation's diplomacy. Second, the device of executive sessions enables the committee to have access to information for its own deliberations without that information becoming public knowledge. Third, the hearings—which take up 1,270 printed pages—did not change the committee's mind but did probably clarify certain issues surrounding the treaty, a fact which is generally true of most hearings. Fourth, when the committee sent the treaty to the Senate floor, its recommendation for approval was accompanied by a comprehensive report which set forth an official interpretation of the provisions of the treaty and which remains authoritative. This report states not only the reasons why the committee approved the treaty but explains also what the committee thought it was doing when it decided to adopt the foreign policy embodied in the alliance.

THE ROLE OF THE COMMITTEE

Analysis of the role of the Senate Foreign Relations Committee is not complete with a statement of what it is supposed to do and what it does do and how. Certain patterns in its activities and certain consequences of such patterns must be mentioned. On the basis of observations of, and inferences drawn from, its actions and methods since 1945, the committee can be said to fulfill the following functions (in addition to those already mentioned as its specific tasks). First, it has more continuous contact with the Executive Branch on matters of foreign policy than any other Congressional unit. While there are, obviously, other contacts between the two branches, it is the committee's liaison which is the core of the relationship. Second, insofar as coordination takes place within the Senate and between House committees and Senate committees it would appear to rest in large part on the efforts of the Foreign Relations Committee. In some instances the committee can and does exert initiative toward coordination. In others it must work through party leaders and the officials of each chamber. The central function of this committee with respect to coordination derives from a combination of its prestige, power, and superior knowledge—the latter particularly. It knows or should know more than any other committee about what is happening and what is about to happen. But the task of coordination is not easy because of the formal and psychological barriers between the upper and lower houses, because of committee rivalry, and because of the burden of legislative business. Third, to the extent that foreign-policy leadership is possible in Congress, this committee (assuming a strong chairman) provides it. Leadership is used here in two senses: to mean tactical efforts on behalf of executive policy recommendations, and to mean the offering of alternatives to executive proposals. When the committee offers neither kind, there is, to all intents and purposes, no leadership in Congress at all. Fourth, the committee is a most self-conscious guardian of Congressional prerogatives in general and of senatorial prerogatives in particular. Except when it responds once in a while to partisan pressure, the House of Representatives is on the whole less inclined to get aroused over alleged presidential usurpation.

Fifth, the Foreign Relations Committee has paid particular attention to the United Nations, to ways of strengthening it, and to the problem of making American policy consistent with United Nations obligations. It was Senator Vandenberg who in 1947 insisted upon an amendment to the Greek-Turkish

Aid Act (legislative embodiment of the Truman Doctrine) which would cancel the American program if it was contrary to United Nations interests and policies. During the Eighty-first Congress, the committee devoted much of its time to hearings on various resolutions pointing toward strengthening the United Nations and achieving an eventual world community. When the North Atlantic Alliance was up for consideration, it was the committee which insisted on a full airing of the relationship between that alliance and the United Nations Charter. Sixth, the committee has capitalized on its power to approve presidential nominations. As a result of recent reorganizations in the Department of State there are upward of thirty top policy-making officials subject to senatorial approval. Representation in the United Nations required sixty-five actions by the committee in the Eighty-first Congress. In addition, the committee acts on ambassadors, ministers, envoys, and lower-ranking diplomatic officers. Hence there are more appointments than ever before which are policy making in function or are closely related to it. Since 1945 in particular, there has been a pronounced tendency to broaden the term "qualification for office" to include the holding of particular views on policy and to subject nominees to close questioning on their past and, if possible, future policy views. Therefore the nomination of a top-level official *may,* and recently often has, become the occasion for policy review and argument. The public hearings held on Dean Acheson in 1949 were the first ever held on a nomination for Secretary of State. Much of the cross-examination centered around Acheson's views toward the Soviet Union and on American policy toward the Soviet Union. The nomination of Spruille Braden as Assistant Secretary of State in 1946 and the 1951 nomination of Philip Jessup to be a member of the American delegation to the United Nations, provided other occasions on which the committee has taken advantage of the opportunity to criticize individuals and policy in general. Hearings on nominations cease to be perfunctory and almost become special investigations. If, as is often the case, an official has served in a number of positions, the commitee can try to hold him accountable for previous actions. By the time Ambassador-at-Large Philip Jessup was appointed to the United Nations delegation in September, 1951, he had already been subjected to cross-examination in connection with "charges" brought by Senator McCarthy and in connection with several investigations into China policy. After commenting frankly on what it thought of Jessup's qualifications, the committee refused to act on his nomination to represent the United States at the General Assembly.

Clearly, professional competence is not the only thing the committee is interested in; it wants to know what nominees think about foreign-policy issues and what role if any they have played or intend to play in the development of certain policies. This view gives the committee an opportunity to state some of its own policy views publicly, to issue warnings to the Executive Branch, to try to bind a nominee to certain broad lines of policy, and to punish officials for what the committee regards as "mistakes." Finally, the committee is able from time to time to make substantive contributions to the negotiation of treaties. Ranking members helped draft the North Atlantic Treaty before it was presented for processing by the whole committee. At the insistence of the committee, for example, the phrase, "such action as it deems necessary," was added to Article 5 (quoted on page 163). One of the important functions of the committee is to issue reports on bills and treaties submitted to the Senate which stand as part of the official interpretation by the latter.

THE HOUSE FOREIGN AFFAIRS COMMITTEE

As the House of Representatives has become more important, so has its Foreign Affairs Committee. In the Seventy-third Congress (1932–1933), the committee reported out nine minor public bills, none of them concerned with major foreign-policy matters. In the first session of the Eighty-first Congress, the same committee reported out fifty bills and joint resolutions, held 138 hearings, heard 340 witnesses, and approved an expenditure of $7 billion for foreign affairs. But it would be a mistake to assume that the House Foreign Affairs Committee is as powerful in foreign affairs generally or is as important in the House as the Senate Foreign Relations Committee is in the Senate.

For many years, assignment to the House Foreign Affairs Committee was not sought after. Domestic matters were paramount and the committee had no special duties like those of its Senate counterpart. House procedures thwarted any initiative it might have. It had no regular contact with the State Department. Certain aspects of foreign affairs were considered not to be within its jurisdiction: economic aspects, immigration, and regulation of foreign commerce. Until World War II the committee let itself be guided by the wishes of the State Department. It had no special sources of information which would enable it to develop initiative and leadership. The result was that the committee did not attract superior personnel, did not train experts in foreign affairs, and generally reflected House apathy. Beginning in 1945, this picture has gradually changed. The committee is no longer regarded as a "dump heap where service was a chore rather than a privilege." In recent years, a deliberate attempt has been made to appoint experienced congressmen with an interest in foreign policy to the committee, which has shown definite signs of initiative, and has demanded more equal treatment at the hands of the Senate and the State Department.

However, the House Foreign Affairs Committee does not have as proportionately great command over foreign-policy matters in the House as the Senate Foreign Relations Committee has in the Senate. The committee in the House can be more easily by-passed. The Ways and Means Committee, the Banking and Currency Committee, the Armed Services Committee, the Appropriations Committee, even the powerful Rules Committee are all potential rivals. Nor has the Foreign Affairs Committee been able to coordinate the different groups in the House which impinge on foreign policy. For example, consideration of the Point Four Program in the Eighty-first Congress was divided between the Foreign Affairs Committee and the Banking and Currency Committee.

The House Foreign Affairs Committee is also organized on a division of labor basis except that it has eleven regional subcommittees which do not parallel as closely the structure of the State Department as do those in the Senate Foreign Relations Committee. For some legislative matters special subcommittees are employed. As is true of all House committees, the Foreign Affairs Committee is larger than its counterpart in the Senate—sixteen Republicans and fourteen Democrats (June 1954). Aside from the differences noted above, both committees employ the same procedures.

CONGRESSIONAL STAFFING FOR FOREIGN AFFAIRS

Exceedingly important aspects of the organization of Congress are the specialized staffs available to it in various areas of public policy. So far as foreign policy is concerned, the staffs of the Senate Foreign Relations Committee and the House Foreign Affairs Committee together constitute the core of experts. The committee in the Senate has a chief of staff, two staff associates, and eight clerks, while the committee in the House has a staff administrator, a committee clerk, three staff consultants, and four staff assistants. In addition the personal staffs of senators and representatives who have served long periods on the two committees can be considered a part of the reservoir of experts. Compared to that of the Executive Branch, Congress's staff help is obviously nowhere near as large numerically. The quality of its work is therefore significant.

The tasks performed by these staff personnel are indispensable to the operations of the two committees. They check for accuracy and soundness the foreign-policy studies which accompany proposals from the Executive Branch, prepare independent studies, aid in the exploration of policy alternatives, arrange hearings, provide quick, unbiased information for committee members, and help prepare questions to be asked of witnesses at hearings. When a committe comes to draft its final report on a measure, its staff takes primary responsibility for drafting. Executive-legislative collaboration also takes place at the staff level. Here the duties of staff members include arrangement of meetings between congressmen and executive policy makers, the preliminary convass of issues and problems, the relay of information, and some attempts to reconcile differences.

Another source of expert advice and information is the Library of Congress's Legislative Reference Service, which has a foreign-affairs research section. Personnel are available for regular assignment to standing committees and for assignment to special committees. The chief contribution of the Reference Service is to provide scholarly independent studies which the committee staffs do not have time to prepare.

When it is recalled that information and analysis are the ingredients of the intellectual process of decision making, the importance of the staff function is clear. Congressional competence in foreign-policy matters rests in part on these committee staffs. Busy committee members could not get along without them. In a sense, the staffs act as extensions of the congressmen's minds, making possible an *expertise* which would otherwise be lacking. Above all, the staffs provide a certain psychological security for committee members, who need not be entirely dependent on the Executive Branch for facts and interpretation. It is generally agreed that staff performance in foreign affairs has greatly improved in recent years. A high-water mark was reached in 1948, when Congress mobilized a total staff of thirty persons to work on the European Recovery Program. This group was made up of the permanent staffs of the Senate Foreign Relations Committee and the House Foreign Affairs Committee along with the staffs of two special committees. Congress thus prepared its own estimates of the needs of European nations. Senator Vandenberg paid high tribute to the staff work when he introduced the Foreign Assistance Act.

►HOW CONGRESS INFLUENCES FOREIGN POLICY

Congress influences foreign policy in a variety of ways—partly because Congress has several important facets, as noted, and partly because of the number of opportunities and techniques available to it. The way Congress employs these techniques indicates its actual role and may also indicate the role to which Congress aspires. The influence Congress exerts is in terms of its formal functions, but its manipulation of techniques may reveal the trial and error by which Congress is seeking to establish a certain kind of relationship with the Executive Branch. This process is of paramount interest in a period of transition. Not all influences are equally important nor are all techniques equally effective. A speech is usually not as important as a resolution; a resolution is not as important as a statute. A cut in appropriation is more likely to be effective than a hearing; the vote is more influential than the debate which preceded it. However, the key to importance will be found in the particular situation and in the intentions of Congress. Most Congressional influence is intentional, yet some is unintentional. It seems improbable that Congress really intends to create anxiety among America's friends in Western Europe. Some of the anxiety undoubtedly stems from the fact that many Europeans accept what Congress says and what it does as equally influential. Moreover, Congress may affect the nation's political and strategic position in the world by acts which ostensibly have nothing to do with foreign policy, namely, domestic policies.

CATEGORIES OF CONGRESSIONAL INFLUENCE

1. Congress may exert influence on policy formulation or decision making within the Executive Branch. This may be accomplished by legislating

administrative arrangements. Thus in 1951, because it disliked what it thought was too much contol of that committee by the State Department, Congress abolished the International Security Affairs Committee, an interdepartmental body for coordinating foreign-aid programs. Since Congress deals with the executive hierarchy at all levels from the President down to bureaus, offices, and divisions, it can influence the decision-making process at any level. Congress is known to trust some agencies and not others, to favor some, to oppose others, to regard some as closer to it than to the President. Congress may try to channel the advice the President gets on certain matters. For example, in its resolution of April, 1951, on the "troops to Europe" issue, the Senate requested that the Joint Chiefs of Staff approve any attempt by the President to send more divisions to Western Europe. Influence on executive decision making can also be brought to bear through the creation of a Congressional "climate of opinion" which must be taken into account. A series of speeches, pointed questions, a resolution—all may express approval or disapproval of an action taken or contemplated. In December, 1951, Senator Smith of the Senate Foreign Relations Committee succeeded in obtaining a pledge from members of the American delegation to the United Nations Assembly that they would not advocate or favor admission of Communist China to the United Nations. After the MacArthur hearings and the investigations of Communism in the State Department, it is doubtful whether any executive policy maker would have dared recommend the recognition of Communist China. A concurrent resolution was passed on May 15, 1951, stating that "the Congress of the United States hereby requests and urges that the General Assembly of the United Nations take action leading to the placing of an embargo on the shipment of arms, ammunition, and all other materials which might add to the warmaking potential of Communist China." Rumblings of protest and warning, especially at budget time (January to April), do not *compel* the executive policy makers to do one thing rather than another, but it inevitably forces them to think about legislative strategy and the risks attached to ignoring Congressional views.

Congress may use other tactics growing out of its legitimate powers to affect the internal arrangements and rightful functions of the Executive Branch as well as the execution of foreign policy. In connection with his many investigations (including trade with Communist China) in the spring of 1953, Senator McCarthy succeeded in doing the following things: he forced the State Department to reverse three directives within ten days; he announced a voluntary pledge from the owners of 295 Greek vessels to stop trading with China; and he pried loose secret directives to the Voice of America. When Charles Bohlen, the top expert on the Soviet Union was nominated to be ambassador to the Kremlin, Senator McCarthy and others raised a storm of protest, claiming that Bohlen's role in the negotiation of the Yalta Agreement and his identification with the Truman-Acheson foreign policy disqualified him. The small group of critics also charged that the FBI file on Bohlen revealed he was a "poor security risk." Though Bohlen was eventually confirmed by a wide margin, Secretary Dulles had to describe Bohlen as a mere reporter, not a policy maker. Given Congressional pressure on the question of subversion, the security officers of the State Department and other agencies concerned in foreign policy now have a key voice in the *assignment* of personnel and in *promotions*—both of which may involve judgments on the policy views of particular persons. Shortly after his appointment as Security Officer of the State Department, it was clear that Scott McLeod was in close contact with certain senators and had discussed personnel issues with them. Such straws in the wind suggest that possible Congressional influence over "who decides what" can extend beyond mere approval of nominees for office.

2. Congress may directly participate in a policy decision through an international agreement or a legislative act. Both foreign-policy objectives and techniques can be affected this way. In most cases, Congress is called upon to implement policy presented by the Executive Branch without basically altering that policy though the consequences of the implementation may turn out to be serious in their own right. Congressional insistence on a mandatory loan to Spain as part of the foreign-aid program exemplifies Congressional addition of an item neither the President nor the State Department wanted. The overall program was left intact. Congress may uncover an aspect of policy which executive policy makers have ignored. Such was the case when the Senate argued successfully for an amendment to the Greek-Turkish Aid Bill (1947) which would take account of the interest of the United Nations.

When a foreign-policy measure is fed through the legislative process, new or different interpretations may be attached to it and perhaps even new meanings. In the course of arriving at a consensus on a given policy, Congress will develop certain expectations concerning the policy and its objectives. Thus it might be said that as the Marshall Plan was finally approved by Congress in 1948 it had more of an anti-Russian flavor than it did when it came from the Executive Branch. The report of the Senate Foreign Relations Committee on the North Atlantic Treaty, already mentioned, constitutes part of Congress's interpretation of what the treaty means. This interpretation can never be completely overlooked because it will condition the way Congress judges the consequences and future development of the policy.

Another kind of legislative impact is exemplified by the McCarran-Walter Immigration Act of 1952, which constitutes a revision of all previous legislation covering the admission of aliens into the United States. Generally speaking, the act makes entry into the United States much more difficult at a time when population pressures are mounting in parts of Western Europe. The burden of proof is on an alien to make a case for his entrance by demonstrating that an American citizen can employ him. Directed at preventing the entrance of subversive persons and enemy agents, the law denies admission to anyone who belongs in any country to a political party which has advocated the forceful overthrow of the government in the United States. This provision of course makes it possible for ex-Nazis and Falangists to enter but keeps out ex-Communists. The act also affects the crews of foreign ships each time they touch American ports; they must submit to questioning and receive special permits for layovers. For these and other reasons, a flood of formal protests descended upon the State Department after the act went into effect. Despite criticisms and pleas by President Eisenhower, Congress showed little inclination to modify its action. As an important gesture in a concerted campaign of psychological warfare, President Eisenhower asked Congress to admit 240,000 refugees from behind the iron curtain over and above regular immigration quotas which might be admitted in two years. Congress allowed him 217,000.

3. Congress may influence the implementation of foreign policy and national security through control over appropriations. Here is a direct technique of censure and disapproval inherent in the right to determine the size of appropriations and to direct the spending of funds. Because appropriations must be renewed annually, Congress has a recurring opportunity to check the amount *and* the objectives of foreign-policy expenditures. Both amount and directions for spending may affect the success or course of the policy without having explicitly altered the goals involved. For several years (1949–1952) Congress steadfastly refused to appropriate anywhere near what the State Department requested for political and psychological warfare. The same was true of President Truman's Point Four Program. In 1951, the House of Representatives made a 10 per cent reduction in the appropriation for American participation in the United Nations after the United States had already made its pledge to the United Nations budget. At the same time, Civil Defense appropriations were slashed from $535,000,000 to $65,000,000 and the National Science Foundation from $14,000,000 to $300,000. Congress certainly influenced the effectiveness of aid to Western Europe by requiring that 50 per cent of all goods shipped from the United States be carried in American ships. One of the really important devices Congress can use for enforcing its policy ideas on the Executive Branch is the "foreign-policy rider"—the attaching of directives to appropriations bills, even to bills having nothing to do with foreign policy per se. A classic example is the so-called Kem amendment to the third supplemental appropriation bill, which denied American aid to any country exporting militarily useful products to the Soviet Union or its satellites. President Truman signed the bill but made a public statement, saying "It is . . . a major piece of legislation affecting our foreign policy, but it was never considered by the House Foreign Affairs Committee or the Senate Foreign Relations Committee." Implementation can also be affected by investigations and by periodical review of reports to Congress. Discretionary decisions at various steps in the execution will be influenced by expectations as to how Congressional committees will react. It seems likely that new programs and foreign-policy techniques are somewhat handicapped for this reason.

For as long as foreign aid continues, Congress will have the last word on the total amount to be spent. Beginning in 1952, an economy-minded legisature reduced the estimates of the Executive Branch by much more than oken amounts. The sequence of events in 1953 is instructive. As one of his ast official acts President Truman recommended a foreign economic and military aid budget of $7.6 billion. His successor, President Eisenhower, felt his amount could be pared considerably and finally submitted a request for $5.4 billion in new money—representing his conviction of an honest minimum. On June 10, 1953, the Senate Foreign Relations Committee reported a Mutual Security Bill totaling $5.3 billion. The next day, the House Foreign Affairs Committee reported a bill providing for $4.99 billion (a cut of half a billion over the President's original request) and also providing that one half of the amount specified for military aid to Europe be conditional upon the formation of a European army. On June 19, 1953, the House quickly passed this bill. After a debate lasting a week or so, the Senate accepted the $5.3 billion total recommended by its committee. The discrepancy between the two versions of the 1953–1954 Mutual Security Act was resolved in conference, the compromise amount being $5.1 billion in addition to an authorized but unspent balance from the previous year. However, whether one half of the European military aid was to be withheld pending the formal establishment of a European army was left to the discretion of the President at the behest of the Senate conferees. When it came to an actual appropriation, further cuts were made. On July 18, the House Appropriations Committee agreed to recommend a total amount of $4.4 billion—a cut of over $600 million in the new funds voted in the authorization bill. A week later the Senate Appropriations Committee approved $4.5 billion in new money. Again the new measure went to conference and the compromise was $4.5 billion. On August 3 the final bill went to the President, giving him over $900 million less in new cash than he asked for. While it is difficult to say precisely what difference the reduction would make in the actual aid program, it is clear that the foreign-aid program would have to be trimmed below what could be purchased by the President's minimum.

4. A favorite technique of Congress is the resolution. Though not binding on the President in any legal sense, resolutions serve several purposes: to warn executive agencies, to express Congressional interest in certain kinds of foreign-policy problems, to prod the executive, to bestow *prior* approval of a contemplated step by the Executive Branch, and to bestow approval *after* an executive agreement or other policy move has been made. The resolution passed by the Senate in April, 1951, after it had approved the sending of American troops to Europe under the Atlantic Alliance, was in one sense a warning to the President to consult Congress in the future when any further action under the treaty might involve the constitutional prerogatives of Congress. Recently a number of Congressional resolutions have expressed interest in world government and in the unification of Europe. Resolutions have exhorted the United Nations to take a firmer stand toward Communist China.

In some respects Congressional initiative is best expressed via resolutions. Resolutions of this type may reflect either a feeling that the President is too slow or a desire to show that Congressional cooperation will be forthcoming if a certain course of action is followed. On March 15, 1943, Senators Ball, Burton, Hatch, and Hill introduced a resolution that "the United States take the initiative in calling meetings of representatives of the United Nations for the purpose of forming an organization of the United Nations" which would have, among other attributes, the power to preserve peace by force if necessary. On September 21, 1943, Representative Fulbright introduced into the House a resolution "favoring the creation of appropriate international machinery with power adequate to establish and to maintain a just and lasting peace. . . ." On November 5, 1945, Senator Connally introduced a resolution that the United States "join with free and sovereign nations in the establishment and maintenance of international authority with power to prevent aggression and to preserve the peace of the world." The latter two resolutions were passed by overwhelming majorities and put both houses on record in advance as favoring the membership of the United States in the kind of international organization which emerged from the San Francisco Conference of 1945. The possibility of the League of Nations experience repeating itself was thus minimized by prior acceptance of a general policy *in principle.* Impetus for the North Atlantic Alliance came initially from a paragraph in a resolution introduced by Senator Vandenberg in June, 1948, which urged the President to enter into negotiations leading to a regional security pact. On June 3, 1953, the Senate attached a "manifesto" to a United Nations appropriations bill declaring Communist China should not be admitted to the world body.

5. Hearings, reports, debates, and individual speeches also influence foreign policy. During the face-to-face exchanges in hearings, spokesmen for the Executive Branch gain some impression of what aspects of a policy seem to bother members of Congress. They are able to determine what the mood of Congress is, what its limits of tolerance are for certain actions. They are also called upon to "explain" policies and in the course of explaining they may shape the meaning of these policies. Such techniques also influence executive policy making in a roundabout way. Sometimes suspicions and other reactions abroad which result from activities in Congress that may domestically be brushed off as "part of the game of politics" turn out to have a rather significant impact on America's foreign relations. During the successive years of foreign aid, congressmen periodically "advised" Europe to arm itself and to reform itself and to help itself—a practice which caused considerable resentment abroad. The two great debates in 1950–1951—"troops to Europe" and MacArthur's dismissal—partially shook Europe's confidence in American policy simply because histrionics and verbal fireworks obscured a large area of agreement. In February, 1951, Senator Connally, chairman of the Senate Foreign Relations Committee, bluntly called upon France to contribute its share to European defense instead of expecting so much from the United

States. Another type of influence was exemplified when a Senate Agriculture subcommittee's investigation of coffee prices ended with a recommendation for close scrutiny of American loans to coffee-producing nations and for cessation of ECA coffee purchases until coffee prices came down. This action not unnaturally upset Brazil and thirteen other coffee-producing nations.

President Eisenhower's decision in February, 1953, to deneutralize Formosa by withdrawing the American Seventh Fleet from its task of preventing an armed engagement between the Chinese Nationalist forces and the mainland of China touched off a series of statements and a lively debate. After a secret conference with the admiral of the Pacific Fleet (Radford, later chairman of the Joint Chiefs of Staff), the chairman of the House Armed Services Committee, Representative Dewey Short, proposed a naval blockade of the China coast and reported that the admiral was called home to discuss this possibility with the White House. Then Senator Wiley, chairman of the Senate Foreign Relations Committee, said that the President's decision opened the way for bombing railroads on the Chinese mainland. Senator Knowland, chairman of the Republican Policy Committee, endorsed the blockade idea and hinted at a more aggressive Far Eastern policy. The late Senator Taft, then the most influential member of the upper chamber, insisted the United States was at full war and urged both a blockade and a bombing of continental China. These and other remarks quickly raised expectations and alarms among the public and among rank-and-file members of Congress. It was then necessary for Secretary of State Dulles and General Bradley, then chairman of the Joint Chiefs of Staff, to make disclaiming statements and to insist that no such moves were in fact calculated. Senator Wiley said later he was just thinking his own thoughts out loud. Senator Knowland said it was all part of the "war of nerves" against the enemy.

Later on in the spring of 1953, an unusual and bitter exchange between Senator McCarthy and Clement Attlee, leader of the British Labor party, took place. Mr. Attlee had aroused the senator's ire by some blunt comment on the American Constitution and the conduct of foreign affairs; when he replied he addressed the British parliamentary figure as "comrade" and warned the United States could "go it alone" if its allies were not more reasonable. Senator McCarthy's Republican colleagues were somewhat shocked by all this and Senators Wiley and Smith of the Senate Foreign Relations Committee felt that McCarthy's injudicious remarks had hurt the United States regardless of who was right or wrong. France came in for more criticism when in July, 1953, a staff report of the Senate Appropriations Committee declared France was "constitutionally incapable of balancing her budget" and was using American aid as a substitute for higher taxes.

Examples of this sort could be listed indefinitely. What do they suggest as to the Congressional impact on foreign policy? First, it is through these mediums—direct face-to-face exchanges in hearings, in committee, subcommittee, and staff reports, in debates, and in isolated individual utterances—

that pressures for "statements," "facts," and "commitments" are applied to the policy makers in the Executive Branch. Such pressures may result in limitations on policy formulation or in speeding up the policy-making process. In extreme cases, action may be forced, though not on Congress's own terms. Second, the State Department and other agencies may use these devices as ways of informing or persuading Congress. Often a senator or a representative will act virtually as a spokesman for the Secretary of State on a particular issue. Again, there may be close cooperation in the issuing of reports which serve as a basis for Congressional thinking. Third, expressions of Congressional viewpoint not incorporated in formal resolutions, statutes, and appropriations function as predictors of future behavior, just as the debate over foreign aid in 1953 portended the end of a large-scale program. Fourth, clarification (in many cases a new or different interpretation of action already taken) may result—either directly from Congressional statements or indirectly from executive responses to Congressional statements. Finally, and most important, the examples cited represent activities which become the basis for interpretations by foreigners. Lacking sophistication in their understanding of American politics, even astute observers abroad sometimes accept as authoritative that which is not necessarily authoritative at all. Furthermore, isolated acts in Congress may collectively contribute to the formation of general evaluations of the character of American foreign policy.

CONGRESSIONAL INVESTIGATIONS

Special investigations, whether carried on by *ad hoc* or by standing committees, have become steadily more important as a method whereby Congress influences the formulation and evolution of foreign policy. One reason for this trend is the general increase in the number of investigations. Between January 3, 1951, and March 22, 1952, the Eighty-second Congress authorized 225 separate inquiries over and above normal legislative and appropriations requirements. About $3.5 million was appropriated. As of April 1, 1953, the Eighty-third Congress had authorized $3 million. The traditional purpose of investigations has been to accumulate facts and information on which to base legislation. Usually, the inspiration for investigations comes, not from either branch of Congress as a corporate body, but from private interest groups, personal interests of members of Congress, normal committee activity, or considerations of party strategy. Until recently, it was generally agreed that investigations had relatively slight influence on the *content* of foreign policy despite great fanfare and public attention. Perhaps the outstanding probe before World War II was the Nye Committee's $135,000 effort to determine how America got involved in World War I, an investigation authorized in order to lay the basis for neutrality legislation. It would not appear, however, that the voluminous record of that investigation had much direct effect on the legislation. Moreover, the Nye Committee carried on a jurisdictional rivalry with the Senate Foreign Relations Committee. Other foreign-affairs investigations have suffered from inadequate preparation and have been badly conducted. Bias and minority distortions have minimized their usefulness.

While recent special investigations have not accompanied all the bills and treaties affecting foreign policy and foreign relations, they have emerged as an integral part of Congress's role in the field of foreign policy. Special investigations focused on the firing of General MacArthur, and on alleged Communist sympathizers in the State Department, eventually managed to touch on substantive issues such as policy toward Communist China, toward the Soviet Union, and toward Western Europe, and on aspects of policy formation such as the roles of specific individuals and the roles of specific agencies. A review of the records of the House Un-American Activities Committee, the Senate Subcommittee on Internal Security, the subcommittee of the Senate Foreign Relations Committee which investigated the State Department, and the joint Senate Armed Services—Foreign Relations Committee which held hearings on General MacArthur's dismissal would show that in one degree or another the major problems of postwar American foreign policy were spotlighted.

There is no doubt that the special investigation backed by Congress's imposing power is one of the most potentially useful techniques Congress has. Indeed, without this device Congress would find it difficult to legislate effectively. Information is an essential ingredient in decision making, and investigations can be a direct, efficient way of gaining access to it. Furthermore, investigations present a natural temptation for the congressman in that they offer both a scalpel and a blunt instrument for going after the Executive Branch. The general veil of secrecy and obscurity which often surrounds the decision-making activities of the Executive Branch, along with its other natural advantages, in foreign affairs make public exposés an attractive weapon. Theoretically, a properly conducted investigation could be not only a source of information for Congress but a means of enforcing presidential accountability as previously defined.

Unfortunately, however, inappropriate procedures can thwart the attainment of these purposes, and other purposes may be intruded that are not really germane to foreign-policy formation. Searching for scapegoats, accumulating campaign fodder, building political reputations, and augmenting a party's legislative strategy may all be legitimate objectives within the general political system, but they may also mitigate against the use of investigations as a constructive Congressional technique. Little is gained if Congress merely tries to prove the validity of a judgment already made. Bringing unsupported charges directly or by innuendo against individuals and agencies in the Executive Branch, and identifying error in judgment with treason both tend to undermine public faith and create an unfavorable environment for policy making. To pin the blame for alleged policy mistakes on single individuals when decision making is obviously a group process does little to expose fallacies in the thinking of the Executive Branch or to improve the decision-making process. Hostile cross-examination and verbal jousting are not necessarily fruitful ways of re-examining foreign policy.

As investigations have grown in number and as the psychological impact of the Soviet challenge has been intensified, alarming abuses have become more frequent. Congressional immunity has helped to open the door to violations of constitutional rights of witnesses. Regarding their effect abroad, Senator Lodge said: "The repercussions from the present investigation into disloyalty charges are such that it would not be right for me to disregard the mounting damage which is being inflicted on the position of the United States abroad. . . ."* Abuses have ranged from assumption of guilt till proved innocent to assumption of guilt by association, from badgering of witnesses to defamation of character. Dr. Edward U. Condon, director of the National Bureau of Standards, was accused before the House Un-American Activities Committee of being the "weakest link' in the nation's security chain. This turned out to be absolutely untrue, but proof was months in coming and the eventual clarification received no headlines comparable to those accorded the original charges. Dr. Condon's case was not an isolated exception. Not only was America criticized abroad, but indiscriminate charges during investigations drove competent personnel from the government and undoubtedly handicapped recruitment.

No adequate discussion of the general problem of Congressional investigations can be undertaken here. It must be emphasized, however, that as Congress's role in foreign policy has expanded, investigations have become more important for two reasons: more investigations focused nominally on domestic matters eventually impinge on foreign affairs *and* more investigations are directly concerned with foreign-policy issues. The abuses mentioned above suggest a Congressional dilemma: How can subversive influences on foreign-policy formation be weeded out without jeopardizing individual rights at a time when all that America stands for is on trial? Another set of problems arises from the necessity to make investigations fruitful in terms of Congress's foreign-policy functions. They are costly in both time and money. By 1952, investigations had become sufficiently numerous to raise the question whether Congressional energies were not being unduly diverted from more important legislative business. No one has ever estimated how much investigations cost the executive agencies in time spent on the preparation of reports and on the witness stand. Such considerations are not valid, however, if the results actually strengthen Congressional participation.

The results of investigations are likely to be fragmentary and uncertain; in other words, the influence exerted by Congress through this medium is uneven. Hearings on the dismissal of General MacArthur were long and costly

* Henry Cabot Lodge, *New York Times Magazine*, April 4, 1950, p. 12.

and it is difficult to see what Congress gained that could not have been gained by other means or by an investigation of Far Eastern policy per se. There was not even a final formal report issued by the investigating group. One of the central issues involved was the role of the military in the formation of foreign policy; yet this issue was not probed with any thoroughness. It has been alleged that because of the revelations of the MacArthur hearings, the administration's policy toward Communist China "hardened." There is some question whether this change was not already under way because of the Korean conflict. Nevertheless it seems likely that the combined effects of the MacArthur hearings and the investigation of the "troops to Europe" issue did clear the air somewhat and did temporarily reduce the range within which the administration could alter American security policy in Europe and in the Orient.

The eighteen-months inquiry into the activities of the Institute of Pacific Relations might have yielded useful knowledge about the impact of private research groups on the information and analysis of the State Department and other executive agencies. Whatever else may be said about the final report on the Institute of Pacific Relations, it did not accomplish much in this direction. On the other hand, it would be unfair to say that nothing constructive results from these investigations. Often an exposé will spur the executive agencies to action or provide them with a basis for action. Often things which should be out in the open are revealed only through Congressional effort. The revelation of the $2 billion in trade carried on between various Western allies of the United States and Communist China during the Korean conflict perhaps gave the United States a strong talking point in its attempt to reduce the possibly harmful effects of such trade even though the revelation came only just prior to the signing of a truce. In May, 1953, a Senate Armed Services subcommittee reported that a shortage of ammunition in Korea had contributed to the loss of American lives. Substantial blame was placed upon Defense Department organization. Apparently these findings were not unrelated to a speed-up of reorganization in the military establishment.

Unfortunately not all the results of Congressional investigations are intended or anticipated. In addition to the grave problem of the rights of witnesses alluded to above, the probing of executive agencies may paralyze or disrupt the administration of foreign-policy programs. For example, as the result of a strong protest from Senator McCarthy, whose Permanent Investigating Committee was conducting a search for waste, bad management, and subversion in the International Information Program of the United States, the State Department forbade the Voice of America to use quotations from Soviet-endorsed writers in its propaganda broadcasts. On February 19, 1953, in direct response to Congressional disclosures and criticism, the department rescinded an order of February 3 which permitted the staff of the Voice to quote Communist writers or Communist-sanctioned writers in an effort to show the people behind the iron curtain that their leaders were insincere, inconsistent, and had not fulfilled their pledges. The new order in effect crippled the ideological division of the Voice of America, which had developed an impressive program in forty-six languages of convicting Soviet leaders, including Stalin, by their own utterances. Henceforth no writings of "Communists, fellow-travelers, et cetera" could be incorporated in foreign broadcasts except when quotations appeared in "reputable news agencies and newspapers." The same order also removed "controversial" books from the shelves of United States information libraries abroad. After considerable argument and confusion both inside the State Department and in the press, the order of February 19 was finally "clarified" by an order of March 18, which relaxed the restrictions on the use of Communist materials. But in the meantime several harmful by-products had resulted. The ideological warfare as carried on through short-wave broadcasts was severely curtailed and uncertainty about the whole program grew out of charges and innuendos by Senator McCarthy and others that some of those making policy decisions for the Voice were "soft" toward Communism. Disagreements over policy internal to the Voice were intensified and made public at a time when the administration had avowedly stepped up its psychological warfare. Morale of officials in the whole international information program visibly declined. Foreign newspapers used the withdrawal of controversial books from United States libraries to allege abandonment of freedom of ideas. Most observers familiar with the information program in general, and the Voice of America in particular, were agreed at the time that a responsible, quiet investigation was necessary and should lead to changes. However, the way in which the investigation was conducted and the consequences it produced resulted in over-all harm to the national interest.

CONCLUSION

Congressional influence on foreign policy is exerted through the various channels mentioned above. It is really a series of influences which comprise the total impact of Congressional behavior. That impact can be characterized in a fivefold manner. First, Congress adds a time factor to policy formation. When Congress can or must exert its power and influence, policy development takes longer. Second, Congress is a constant source of pressures and irritants for the Executive Branch, and the necessity for working out strategies with respect to Congress eats into the policy-making resources of executive agencies. Third, Congress may stimulate or accelerate or alter a course of foreign policy but, generally speaking, it does not originate policies or trends in policy. Fourth, Congress does not directly alter major foreign-policy goals and techniques except by grafting on its own ideas, but it indirectly influences goals and techniques by controlling the amount of national resources to be committed and by setting the conditions of expenditure. Fifth, Congress adds an element of uncertainty to America foreign policy.

► FACTORS WHICH CONDITION CONGRESSIONAL
  THINKING ABOUT FOREIGN POLICY

It was noted earlier that several kinds of pressures operate on the congressman. This point is part of, but not identical with, the larger question of what shapes the average congressman's views about foreign policy. There are, of course, a number of influences which overlap, and which vary in intensity from one individual to another, and in significance from one issue to another. However, patterns of Congressional thinking on foreign policy do develop—majority and minority patterns. The patterns have consistency and persistency. One speaks of the "isolationist" pattern which dominated Congress from 1935 to 1941. In 1952, one could detect the formation of an "economy group" which seemed bent on cutting down all types of foreign-aid appropriations and the military budget. By 1953, a strong "nationalist" type of thinking had emerged. Such patterns usually transcend party or regional considerations but may be rooted in them.

One set of influences is comprised of the individual congressman's personal values and beliefs—what have been called his private preferences.* These will be influenced by his life experience, his ambition, his religious affiliation, his education and training—in short, his personality and character as of a given moment. Like everyone else, the congressman in the course of his lifetime acquires many common-sense rules for interpreting events and people as well as principles which he applies as criteria of judgment. Furthermore, the Congressman has objectives, particularly political ones which may condition his behavior. Obviously, when party and regional ties are weak, such influences will be relatively strong.

Another set of influences interlocks with the first: the ideas of the external setting held by the congressman, which must be reconciled with and judged by his values and beliefs. In other words, the congressman will make up his mind by going through an intellectual process which weaves together policy recommendations, information, and analysis of information—the same ingredients characteristic of the executive decision makers. There are some differences between the two. Ordinarily, Congress is not confronted by a range of separate alternatives; rather, it has the opportunity of accepting, rejecting, or modifying a particular formulation of foreign policy. Moreover, the congressman's information differs in nature and quantity—it is generally less detailed and there is less of it. Finally, the analysis or interpretation of information by Congress is probably less sophisticated on the whole than that of the policy makers in the Executive Branch.

It was observed previously that an elaborate system of information collection is available to the Executive Branch. What are the congressman's

---

* Robert Dahl, *Congress and Foreign Policy* (New York, Harcourt, Brace & Company, 1950), Chap. 1.

sources of information concerning the external environment and the desires of his constituents? Among the unofficial sources are other congressmen, contacts in executive agencies, influential friends, and non-governmental leaders with whom informal relations are maintained. Information and viewpoints from these sources are unofficial in the sense that they represent the private assessments of the individuals involved, are usually not quotable, and are not common knowledge. The average congressman has many such contacts, some more significant to his thinking than others. Persuasion in Congress is accomplished more on the basis of friendship and trust than is usually realized and may have little or nothing to do with party affiliation or official status in Congress. Congressmen also exploit contacts in the Executive Branch. Such activities may range from genuine attempts at self-enlightenment to embarrassment of the administration by quoting it against itself without mentioning any names. Apparently executive officials willing to "leak" information to congressmen can be found for almost any issue. There are, in addition, sources within Congress itself: special committee reports, studies made by the Legislative Reference Service, and official statements by Congressional leaders, particularly key chairmen and the chairmen of the party policy committees. If the congressman has the time and the inclination to read them there are several foreign-policy background studies issued each session ranging from 25 to 150 pages in length and dealing with various subjects ranging from Soviet treaty violations to the operations of the Voice of America. The statements of Congressional leaders would appear to be very important sources of information. Leaders are of two types for present purposes: first, those whose generally great prestige and influence in the national legislature carry over into foreign-policy issues; second, those whose previous special experience in foreign affairs qualifies them to be listened to with respect. Short of continuing first hand experience of confidential sources of information in the Executive Branch, both types must depend on the general sources mentioned above. Thus the difference between them refers rather to the way a leader's interpretation is received than to his sources.

Of extreme importance are the commercial mediums—the newspaper, periodicals, and other mass communications. Probably the average congressman relies most heavily on the newspaper or radio for his impressions of what is going on in the world. Editorials of respected newspapers are regarded as reliable sources of information on the state of public opinion—an indispensable ingredient in the congressman's world of reality. Weekly news magazines supplement the data supplied by newspapers. So far as the mass commercial mediums are concerned, the congressman's reading habits are not much different from those of other Americans. The pictures of external events and conditions which the mass mediums present to the congressman are pretty much the same pictures presented to the whole population. A fourth source is the Executive Branch itself—official reports and statements from responsible decision makers. Information from executive agencies is channeled most prominently through the State of the Union address by the President, special messages, the annual budget, and testimony before committees in closed or open session. These are perhaps the more obvious channels. Congressmen may write letters to the Secretary of State and other officials and receive authoritative replies. Informal yet official consultation is another method by which information is exchanged. The latter is more common than is realized although little publicity surrounds it. Opinion leaders constitute another potential source of interpretations of reality. In this category fall influential columnists like Walter Lippmann, Hanson Baldwin, James Reston, and the Alsops, also nongovernmental experts in foreign affairs including individual scholars and research organizations, and spokesmen for powerful interest groups. Information from such sources flows through public hearings, mass mediums, and private consultation. Interest groups should be considered as information sources because in addition to selling policies they are also, implicitly or explicitly, trying to sell their views of factual conditions and situations.

A NOTE ON THE ROLE OF CONSTITUENTS

Constituents have their own views of foreign affairs and these too constitute information for the congressman. Letters and telegrams from constituents are therefore another source of information. Congressmen sift and evaluate such communications. Apparently nearly a third are deemed to be "inspired" by certain groups, that is, they are not the result of spontaneous action by separate individuals. Also, it is generally felt that a large proportion of the letters a member of Congress receives in a year are written by chronic letter writers—a small segment who write at the drop of a hat, so to speak. Hence letters which come from unfamiliar names and are individualistic in the sense of not betraying a pattern of inspiration are more likely to be effective. Special attention is usually paid to letters from prominent constituents. Public opinion polls are leaned upon heavily. However, most congressmen, if they were frank about it, would probably admit that they rely on a kind of "intuitive feel" which is composed partly of impressions picked up by face-to-face contact and from respected informants. The role of constituents depends in large measure on the congressman's interpretation of *his* function. For the rest, it is a matter of whether the constituents do in fact attempt to bring pressure on the congressman which he will recognize as valid. While constituents *can* so influence Congressmen, they do not in fact do so very often except on a limited group basis. Coupled with the lack of a clear definition of the congressman's function—Does he lead or follow? Does he represent in the literal sense?—all these facts combine to mean that in foreign affairs the elected representative of the people has a fairly wide latitude.

Theoretically, the congressman-constituent relationship is a vital link in the democratic system. Presumaby, congressmen are responsible to the voters. As noted in a previous chapter, elections are one of the devices by which responsibility is enforced. Thus the representative and the senator are held acountable every two and six years, respectively. In between those periods, accountability appears to rest primarily on the individual congressman's interpretation of his role, on how much he wishes to discover the will of his constituents and how skillful he is at detecting the feelings and preferences of constituents and projecting them into the legislative process. How accurate is the congressman's information concerning (a) the content of his constituents' views—the pictures *they* have of the external setting; and (b) their values? When a senator says his constituents no longer trust the Secretary of State, regard the Soviet Union as being on the verge of declaring war, and are hostile to continued foreign aid, how accurate are these statements? To the extent that constituents' interpretations are inaccurate or are unverifiable by the congressman the possibility exists that Congressional action will be irresponsibe. This is another problem which goes beyond foreign policy, but the relationship between the congressman and his constituents ties in closely with one aspect of Congress's general role in foreign affairs.

The congressman's constituents must be regarded as more than the voters of a particular election district. Any constituency will have influential individuals and economic interests which the congressman feels bound to listen to if he is to fulfill his duty and stay in office. A good many of the conditions attached to foreign-aid programs find their source in the fact that there is a farm bloc in Congress, a cattle bloc, a shipping bloc—in other words there are congressmen who serve as spokesmen for economic groups. Regardless of whether over-all foreign-policy needs require it, particular economic interests must be recognized. A primary example is the American tariff, which represents a series of needs being protected by legislation which importantly affects American foreign relations. Ethnic and religious groups may be vocal and powerful enough to persuade the congressman to see foreign-policy issues their way.

SECTIONAL ORIENTATIONS

An obviously significant component of the constituent-representative relationship rests on the fact that there are types of thinking about foreign relations generally and reactions to specific foreign policies which can be identified and partly explained in terms of roughly sectional or regional forces. One of the most pertinent features of the Eighty-third Congress (1953–1954) was the degree of control exercised by senators and representatives from Midwestern states: thirteen of nineteen key chairmanships in the House and nine of fifteen in the Senate. Republican senators from the Midwest outnumbered their Northeastern colleagues by nineteen to seventeen, and in the House Midwestern representatives outnumbered Northeastern representatives by ninety-five to eighty. In the Senate, the Foreign Relations, the Banking and Currency, Government Operations, Interior and Insular Affairs, and Rules and Administration were chaired by Midwesterners. Now it is alto-

gether too easy to slip into an assumption of a simple one-to-one relationship between geographical representation and foreign-policy views. In the
absence of sufficient and reliable evidence, what can be said is that, by
and large, Midwestern congressmen and senators *tend* to exhibit the following patterns of thought: first, an uncompromising, black-or-white view
of the actions of other states; second, a generally unsympathetic attitude
toward Great Britain; third, a suspicion of the worst of foreign diplomats;
fourth, a feeling that the United States has done more than its share of
checking aggression and that European nations will take all the United
States will give without being properly grateful; fifth, a conviction that thrift
is just as applicable to foreign affairs as to the family budget; and sixth, a
skepticism of the strength and resolve of Western Europe. Both in their utterances and in their voting, Midwestern members of Congress more often express this constellation of values. In other words, such inclinations are more
characteristic of them than of members from the West, South, and the Northeast. Accordingly, it is not surprising that the strongest sentiment in favor of
economy in foreign aid and of a more vigorous policy in Asia was to be
found in the Midwestern group of the Republican party. Some observers were
prone to label this "isolationism" or the "new isolationism," but these are
possibly misleading labels. It would appear, rather, that the dividing line was
not on the basis of involvement vs. withdrawal but on the amount and nature
of accommodation to the interests and desires of America's allies. The thought
patterns listed above suggest that the Midwestern legislators were much less
inclined to tolerate foreign influences on decision making in the United States
and were impatient with alleged restraints of membership in the United
Nations.

A recent study bears out this general point. For the period 1935–1941,
members of Congress from the Northeast voted most consistently internationalist regardless of which party was in control. Republican and Democratic
representatives from the Great Plains states (Wisconsin, Minnesota, Iowa,
North and South Dakota, Nebraska, and Kansas) opposed so-called internationalist policies, voting against foreign loans, increased armed strength,
and modification of neutrality laws and did so against the advice of party
leaders and the official party stand.*

A NOTE ON THE SOURCES OF CONGRESSIONAL INFORMATION

Unlike the Executive Branch, Congress does not and cannot control
most of the sources of its information. Congress cannot really do much about
poor newspaper reporting, about distortions in the other commercial mediums,
or about the analytical capacity of its friends and influential advisers. On the
whole, Congress has to take its information where it can find it. This is another way of saying that Congress does not have a well-developed machinery

* George L. Grassmuck, *Sectional Biases in Congress on Foreign Policy* (Baltimore, Johns Hopkins University Press, 1952), Chap. VII.

under its control for providing it with information relevant to foreign policy. Because the Executive Branch has its own facilities, it has an independent basis for evaluating other sources. Congress has no such guide against which it can check unofficial sources, mass mediums, views of opinion leaders, and so on. Furthermore, the multiplicity of sources adds to the chances of confusion, of sources competing with each for attention and acceptance. They may also tend to cancel out each other's influence. It is not easy for the executive decision maker to acquire complete, reliable information; yet he has available the results of skilled and specially trained reporting which can be quietly pondered. The congressman, on the other hand, is subject to literal bombardment by many pictures of reality.

Clearly the wide range of sources suggests that not all congressmen will have equal access to them. All congressmen will not have equally effective confidential sources in the Executive Branch. Not every congressman will attend all important hearings or read committee reports and studies. Not all will have opportunities to consult regularly with the executive policy makers. Not all congressmen will be equally interested in foreign affairs. Consequently, there will normally be an uneven distribution of information among individual members. This fact will explain why some congressmen are regarded by their colleagues as experts. It will also explain—partially—the existence of voting blocs which transcend party and sectional lines. Such blocs reflect a lack of a common body of information. But the more significant point is whether there is adequately distributed throughout Congress that minimum of information necessary for sound decisions. In turn, this will depend on the availability of a minimum of information and upon the adequacy of communications within Congress. One method of communicating a minimum level of information is through open, well-focused debate. Another is the circulation of brief documents which most congressmen are willing and have time to read.

Congress inevitably leans heavily on executive sources of information. The level of Congressional judgment will depend in part on the communication of information to those members with particular responsibilities for foreign policy—the Senate Foreign Relations Committee and the House Foreign Affairs Committee. Another link in the communications network requires that these committees circulate information to other committees whose actions may impinge on foreign-policy matters. Often different committees acting on common policies are not acting on the basis of the same information. For many congressmen, the internal sources of information are the most crucial, but these, it must be recognized, depend on the other sources.

CONGRESSIONAL PSYCHOLOGY AND FOREIGN POLICY

Thus far in noting briefly the factors which influence Congressional thinking and behavior with respect to foreign policy, social values, personality, and sources of information have been mentioned. Other factors have to do with the way a congressman's views are shaped by his membership in Congress as an organization—by Congressional values, traditions, and previous experiences. Only a few can be suggested here. For one thing, Congress probably experiences certain frustrations in its dealings with foreign affairs. In fact its normal frustrations appear to be intensified in the case of foreign-policy decisions. First, there is the feeling that the United States is already half committed when a proposal reaches Congress. Senator Vandenberg once said, "Congress does not enjoy original jurisdiction in foreign relations. . . . We come in, usually at the 11th hour when our choice is the lesser of two evils. . . . As when we have been asked, upon other occasions, to declare war, the fact is that by the time these issues reach us for ultimate conclusions, we are heavily precommitted. . . ." John Foster Dulles, when he was a member of the Senate, spoke of the North Atlantic Pact in these terms: "You are dealing with a situation where there is a Pact which has been heralded all around the world, which has been signed with solemnity by the representatives of twelve nations . . . there is an accomplished fact of which we have to take cognizance." Often, then, after haranguing the administration and fate itself, Congress grants close to what is asked for because it cannot afford the risk of noncompliance. Second, Congress feels somewhat inadequate in the face of the information and policy-selling techniques which are considered the monopoly of the Executive Branch. An important hearing confronts Congress with a solid line-up of prestigious figures from executive agencies armed with experienced counsels and information which is not common knowledge. The result is a feeling of being overwhelmed and a suspicion that executive spokesmen are holding back relevant data in order to retain an advantage. Third, Congress appropriates billions for foreign-policy and national security purposes without as much assurance that it knows what the money is buying as it has in the case of domestic programs. Since 1945 groups of congressmen and subcommittees of the two foreign-affairs committees have made more frequent visits abroad, but for the most part members are not able to see foreign policy in action. Committee staffs are too busy to make detailed investigations. Congressmen therefore have to trust newspaper reports, executive statements, and sometimes offhand interpretations of friends. In such circumstances, a straight economy argument carries more weight than it would if a relatively large number of congressmen had firsthand knowledge of how money was being spent abroad.

Fourth, Congressional psychology is conditioned by the long-standing gulf between the legislative and executive branches—a problem to be further explored in the next two chapters. This is, of course, a large matter to generalize about and has many facets. There is, for example, the kind of minimum, ever-present distrust of the President—a factor which is related to the others. To the extent that the President exerts vigorous leadership in foreign affairs it becomes more difficult for Congress to avoid playing a negative, unsatisfying role. The mere existence of divided responsibilities suggests to

Congress that it must criticize, must oppose regardless of how it does so. The reservoir of potential hostility always remains, but its expression depends on issues and trends. Some congressmen oppose the President because of genuine convictions, some for party reasons, some for the sake of personal political ambition. More important, however, are the generalized attitudes toward the President which can be activated at any particular time. These become institutionalized in the sense that it can be assumed that in one degree or another all congressmen share them simply because this is one requirement or by-product of membership in the national legislature. In addition to the latent distrust of presidential power, there is the common notion that administration spokesmen always ask for more than they expect to get. Another is the notion that briefs for foreign-policy proposals—especially the very lengthy ones—are *too perfect*. There must be *something* wrong with them. Yet another is that bureaucrats are interested primarily in their own careers and livelihood.

Finally, "politics" enters the Congressional psychology on foreign relations. The range of possibilities is wide indeed. Party membership as a factor will be treated later, but two revealing examples of the influence of politics in general can be taken from recent Congressional history. Both relate to the presentation of a $7.9 billion foreign-aid program to Congress in January, 1952. Senator Connally of Texas, chairman of the Senate Foreign Relations Committee, immediately announced his opposition publicly in no uncertain terms. Normally, Senator Connally, as a member of the President's party and chairman of the committee, would be expected to offer his criticisms privately and more or less to lead the measure through the hearings and the Senate debate. As it turned out, Senator Connally was facing a hard fight for re-election in Texas and was under heavy attack there because of the foreign policies of the Truman Administration. Furthermore, general opposition on the part of representatives and senators to foreign-policy spending appeared to arise from the fact that the billions asked for would produce no tangible results for constituents to whom an appeal for votes had to be made a few months later. From the standpoint of the average congressman the necessity of making an acceptable legislative record was probably a much more immediate issue than the Communist threat to Western Europe, especially when it could not be proved definitely that a cut in the program would result in measurable harm. Such a statement imputes no bad faith to congressmen; rather, it emphasizes that continuance of membership periodically becomes the frame of reference within which policy problems are viewed.

► CONGRESSIONAL WEAKNESSES IN FOREIGN POLICY

Clearly Congress exerts strong influence on major foreign-policy decisions and the conduct of foreign relations generally. What factors tend to work against the effective discharge of Congressional powers and responsibilities? The following brief list of disabilities is derived from the nature of Congressional organization and procedure. Individual weaknesses are of course interrelated and are not all equally apparent at all times. One of the significant things to be said about Congress is that one never knows when its weaknesses will be crucial. Some seem to be permanently built into all Congressional policy making.

NO CLEAR DEFINITION OF CONGRESS'S ROLE

Strangely enough, though the functions performed by Congress appear to be quite specific, Congress as a corporate body has not precisely defined its role in foreign-policy making. It has not consciously adopted a set of rules for guiding its conduct in foreign affairs and for evaluating its contribution to foreign-policy making. One result is that Congressional behavior fluctuates between two extremes. At one extreme, Congress sets its sights too low. It quibbles over details instead of concerning itself with policy alternatives. Thus its role is essentially negative. At the other extreme, Congress tries to do too much—it overreaches itself and tries to do things it ought not to do. The first is characteristic of foreign-affairs appropriations including the military. The second is characterized by the grafting of recommendations, accepted without proper exploration, onto executive proposals. Where Congress's role actually falls between these extremes will depend less on the nature of foreign-policy problems *per se* than on other factors such as the pressure of domestic legislation, the views of a few key figures, political requirements, and so on. Foreign-policy decisions are basically different in nature from domestic decisions if for no other reason than that the former involve less familiar phenomena and carry more risks. Yet Congress goes about its foreign-policy business in substantially the same way that it does domestic business.

DIFFICULTIES IN COORDINATION

Given the way Congress is organized and operates, it is exceedingly difficult for Congress to command what might be called a "whole picture" of foreign-policy problems and developments. The limited Congressional resources devoted to foreign policy are partially wasted in duplication between House and Senate and between committees in each chamber. Even more serious, however, is the fact that crucial relationships are often missed by Congress simply because committees and subcommittees deal with separate aspects whose connections are nowhere evaluated. There is no one body in Congress which examines all the things Congress does in the perspective of general American foreign policy. Nor does Congress as a whole do this. Thus until recently Congress has not balanced American resources against American foreign commitments made since 1945. Inconsistencies in foreign policy can often be traced to this source. One committee makes its decisions on the assumption that the export trade of Western European nations will improve while another votes "peril-point" clauses in tariff legislation to permit the

United States to withdraw from trade agreements if certain domestic manufacturers are hurt by foreign competition. One committee grants aid to Europe in a way calculated to provide goods at the lowest price, but another insists that half of all shipments be made in American ships, whose freight rates are higher. Lack of coordination adds to the time Congress takes to act. Differences in foreign-policy thinking on the part of appropriations groups and others dealing with foreign policy are never really reconciled. Nor is it systematically possible to integrate the views, interests, and contributions of the "impetuous newcomer"—the House—and those of the Senate.

After one committee has given lengthy consideration to a piece of foreign-policy legislation, it may be referred to another committee. In May, 1952, after the Senate Foreign Relations Committee had reported out a foreign-aid bill, it was sent to the Armed Services Committee. This practice may not only delay action but may also result in the application of new values that are not properly related to the previous values which entered into the legislation. For example, the Foreign Relations Committee may feel that a minimum of military aid is an absolute minimum political requirement, while the Armed Services Committee may feel that this amount is too great in view of the needs of the domestic military establishment. Here are two different sets of paramount values which may not be reconciled, if at all, until floor debate is in progress, at which time reconciliation may be difficult. At one time in April, 1953, the Senate had three committees investigating the International Information Program.

RELATIVELY INFERIOR INFORMATION AND ANALYSIS

While Congress's information has improved in quality and quantity and while one would not expect Congress's resources to be as extensive as those of the Executive Branch, there is room for further improvement.* Congress, and particularly its key committees, could be kept better informed by executive agencies. Chairman Connally of the Senate Foreign Relations Committee complained in January, 1951, that he did not know the United Nations was going to vote on a "cease-fire" order for the Korean conflict. Instances of this sort happen frequently. But the more important information is that required by Congress in order to make its own decisions. On balance, Congress is too dependent on sources not under its control.

Congress needs information about external conditions: Are the French able to contribute substantially to their own rearmament? If so, how much? Congress needs information about the most effective foreign-policy tech-

---

* It is true that the increase of investigations has yielded to certain individuals in Congress a great deal of information about technical operations in the foreign-policy area such as the Export-Import Bank. It is also true that in August, 1953, some eighteen subcommittees were scheduled to go abroad to study the foreign-aid program, military bases, refugees, and international trade. Twenty-one Democrats in the Senate under the leadership of Senator Hill of Alabama have established a "night school" to which various experts are invited to lecture on vital issues after the business day is done.

niques: What are the potentialities of Point Four? Congress needs information about the consequences of various policies: What will be the effect of military rearmament of Western Europe? Moreover, Congress needs information which is nonpartisan, comprehensive, objective, and expert; in other words, from its own point of view, competent and trustworthy. Finally, such information needs to be widely circulated in Congress, not kept in the exclusive possession of a few. During March, 1952, a bipartisan group of twenty-five senators (over a fourth of the Senate) declared its intention of trying to get the Senate to establish a temporary "non-partisan, Hoover-type, survey commission" which would study the relations of the United States with its North Atlantic allies. A study of this magnitude would be too large for the committee staffs and the Legislative Reference Service to handle. Congress does not make maximum use of its existing research and analysis facilities, but at the same time it needs additional facilities.

BY-PRODUCTS OF THE PARTY SYSTEM

The problem of party politics in foreign policy will be treated in the next chapter. Several other Congressional weaknesses are related to the absence of genuine responsible party government in the American political system, that is, the absence of centralized, disciplined parties capable of enforcing minimum allegiance by members to party policy. Instead of getting a real party split on foreign policy, splinter groups and blocs develop, all powerful enough to obstruct but none capable of offering leadership either on behalf of executive policies or alternative policies. It is exceedingly difficult to obtain clear majority and minority policies in Congress because no groups can, over any substantial period of time, speak authoritatively for the two points of view. The result is that clear alternatives are rarely presented. Individual preferences and sets of minority preferences are overrepresented. Interest groups find it relatively easier to influence foreign-policy legislation partly because the congressman is not protected by his party and partly because there is not always an incentive to vote with the party. One reason why positive leadership by Congress in foreign affairs is hard to generate lies in the nature of the American party system. Even though the committee chairmen, policy steering chairmen, floor leaders, and influential individuals are all of the same party, there is no guarantee they will function as a team. In the second session of the Eighty-second Congress it was difficult to find more than three or four senators who would provide legislative leadership on the 1952–1953 foreign-aid appropriation.

THE LEVEL OF DEBATE AND DISCUSSION

Five kinds of beneficial effects might be expected from an adequate full-dress debate on foreign policy, adequacy being defined in this case as a time allotment befitting the importance of the subject and a relatively high degree of logical analysis and knowledge directed to the subject: (1) the more expert congressmen pass on information and analysis to their colleagues; (2) the fears and desires of the general public are recognized and incorporated into or taken notice of in the deliberations; (3) alternatives are weighed and consequences explored in some detail; (4) the general public is thereby informed; and (5) the basis of a national consensus is identified, made explicit, and adopted by Congress. For a variety of reasons, general debate in Congress does not really perform these functions; if they are performed it is by committees or other devices which are little publicized and involve only a handful of legislators. Apparently Congress itself often does not regard debate as very important; it usually competes with committee hearings and investigations and is inhibited by various rules. As a deliberative body the House of Representatives hardly exists. The Senate devotes more time to debate; nevertheless, Congress as a whole gives a relatively small fraction of its working hours to it. During the first session of the Eighty-first Congress, 2,563 bills were enacted after 704 hours of debate in the House and 1,145 hours of debate in the Senate. Allowing for the fact that many bills are passed without discussion, not much time is left to be prorated among important bills. Furthermore, there is no "germaneness rule," which means that speeches and argument do not have to be directed to the subject at hand; members can arise and talk about almost anything. Consequently, precious hours are eaten up by irrelevant discussion. There appears to be no effective substitute for general debate; yet Congress seems unable to select a limited number of policy issues a year to allot as many hours to them as necessary, and to keep discussion relevant.

PROCEDURAL COMPLICATIONS

Previously it was remarked that the Congressional impact on foreign-policy making is characterized in part by time implications and uncertainty. In turn, these factors are traceable to Congressional procedures. These procedures were laid down in an era when Congress's responsibilities and work load were much less heavy. Few changes have been made since. Congressional procedures have therefore become an important source of delay, irresponsibility, irrationality, and, in some cases, impotence. It is not necessary to argue that Congress ought to make crucial decisions overnight—indeed existing rules of procedure permit Congress to legislate without adequate consideration—to recognize that the delay in the North Atlantic Treaty, Point Four, and military aid during early 1949 weakened somewhat the full effect of those policies in the existing context of international diplomacy. The twenty-eight steps which comprise the legislative process permit at various points delays which have little to do with the substance of policies. In March, 1952, Congress shelved a Universal Military Training program by a complicated parliamentary maneuver in which the merits of the proposal were never really at stake. Time taken for roll calls alone adds up to more than ten per cent of the total spent on legislation. Improved methods for recording votes would free time for debate and other functions vital to sound policy.

The world's most complicated legislative procedure can be very cumbersome—with serious results in terms of Congressional effectiveness. First, Congress cannot act quickly enough and therefore loses even limited control over how problems and issues are shaped for decision. Second, Congress cannot always select the really important issues and devote the requisite time and resources to their consideration. Third, Congress often finds it easier to refrain from legislating than to legislate, easier to legislate *any* bill rather than one rationally calculated to achieve stated aims. Fourth, Congress often finds itself incapable of overseeing the tremendous expenditures of the Executive Branch.

This last point suggests that procedural disabilities of Congress are particularly significant in the matter of the federal budget and control over appropriations. The appropriations process allows policy decisions to be made via riders attached by a small minority of Congress without review by Congress as a whole. Since there is no single federal budget evolved by Congress, items cannot be seen in relationship to one another and there are several opportunities for irresponsible action. Again, one need not go so far as to argue that all appropriations should be approved or that budget cuts are wise, but only that where budget changes involve policy changes they should be submitted and debated as such. The absence of a presidential item veto and the separation of authorization and appropriations make possible the smuggling of substantive decisions into columns of figures. Congress seems also to be in an undesirable position with respect to the military budget, which now runs annually between $40 billion and $65 billion. Staff shortages and the difficulty of getting all the relevant facts make it almost impossible for Congress to eradicate many existing administrative practices and inefficiency. As remarked earlier, the tendency to concentrate on details may result in a partial forfeit of Congressional influence over national security policy through relative neglect of such questions as stockpiling, strength of the Air Force, and mechanization of the Army. A subcommittee dealing with military appropriations may have only a two-man staff. In addition, it has to examine nonmilitary appropriations. Except for special investigations, Congress relies mainly on information supplied by the armed services. A fruitful evaluation of the military budget requires a high capacity for interpreting figures and asking the right questions. Staff shortages, time pressures, and the necessity to perform services for constituents reduce Congressional capacity in these matters.

SHORTCOMINGS OF HEARINGS AND INVESTIGATIONS

Mention of procedural difficulties is a reminder of the special importance of procedure in hearings and investigations. Procedure is crucial here because the way hearings are conducted largely determines their usefulness. Bearing in mind the scarce resources of Congress, the results of hearings and investigations measured in terms of money and time invested will depend on whether Congress obtains new information, adds to its capacity for policy analysis, provides a real opportunity for alternative policy views to be heard, uncovers implications of policy proposals previously ignored, and is able to exercise a responsible check on the Executive Branch. Although procedures are standardized to the extent that a list of witnesses drawn up by the committee testifies and is cross-examined by members of the committee all under the control of the chairman, who greatly influences the day-to-day business, what actually happens and the spirit and thoroughness of the proceedings vary widely. Hearings and investigations range from very good to very bad. But it is more serious that there is no guarantee beforehand that an important foreign-policy issue will be handled well. Congress has no code to regulate this aspect of its work, and weaknesses are tolerated apparently on the assumption that some good is bound to come out of it all.

Contrary to the general view, not all hearings and investigations hear all sides of an issue or hear all persons who might have insights or information to contribute. During the hearings on military aid to implement the North Atlantic Alliance, not one single witness was heard in opposition. In the case of the Atlantic Alliance both sides were heard amply; yet the regular members of the Senate Foreign Relations Committee had issued favorable comments prior to the hearings and tended to ask the witnesses questions designed to elicit responses which would confirm their own views. Two nonmembers of the committee perhaps did more to clarify certain issues by their line of questioning than any of the members. When the Japanese Peace Treaty was up for consideration in February, 1952, only a small number of witnesses were called—called quite suddenly, thus making it impossible for some to appear—and not one domestic economic group which might be expected to have some interest in trade arrangements was questioned. To the extent that hearings and investigations are contrived to prove or confirm a previous judgment they are not serving Congress to full advantage.

A small group of its members sitting down with executive decision makers should provide a unique opportunity for Congress to probe the way in which policy formulations are arrived at and to ascertain the soundness of policy judgments. To do this is not easy and to do it well requires that personal vituperation, scapegoating, and overdramatizing must be kept to a minimum. When hearings and investigations become three-ring circuses, serious purposes are jeopardized and individual rights are menaced. With policy issues so intertwined with issues of loyalty, it is particularly essential not only to protect the constitutional rights of witnesses but to ensure an atmosphere in which governmental and nongovernmental personnel who have something to give to Congress will do so with confidence and candor. Through faulty procedures or the absence of proper regulations, Congress has sometimes seriously erred on both counts. Badly managed hearings also distort public opinion and undermine public confidence. Highly publicized investigations which stress personalities and "charges" are not likely to clarify foreign-policy issues. The fact that many committees fail to issue brief, official statements of what Congress learned in particular investigations further encourages the public to take a cynical view of all investigations or to be confused as to their results.

► WHAT CONGRESS CONTRIBUTES TO FOREIGN POLICY

These weaknesses can be viewed as factors which tend to restrict and minimize Congress's potential positive contributions to foreign-policy formation. That these weaknesses have been manifest from time to time is a point that must enter any evaluation of Congress's role. But it does not follow that they are inevitable or that Congress can add no elements of strength to foreign-policy decision making. Most of the weaknesses will be found to have opposing points of strength, both in Congress and in the policy-making process as a whole. Filtering foreign-policy proposals through the Congressional mill takes time and may take too much time, but it may also result in a series of advantages. First, there is a check against too much haste in the Executive Branch. Major foreign-policy programs carry a heavy price for being hastily launched. Second, when the executive policy makers present their formulations to Congress, they are compelled to retrace the intellectual process through which they arrived at the policy and to justify it to people whose approach may be somewhat different. Mistakes can be caught, as was seen earlier in the chapter. Implications can be spelled out. Assumptions can be questioned. Clarification of objectives can be demanded. Third, Congress can give voice to national needs and interests of which the executive may be ignorant or may have deliberately ignored. Congress may tend to "over-represent" group and subnational views; nevertheless these are part of the national interest and should be given proportionate weight. Furthermore, in the American system the cooperation of functional groups—labor, business, agriculture—is necessary for the implementation of foreign-policy programs which draw on national skills and resources. Congress also reflects the preferences of the general public. Fourth, the area of agreement underlying a foreign policy ought to be wider and more solid after Congressional action is taken. If Congress's representative functions are adequately fulfilled, a large majority support for a policy should provide it temporarily, at least, with truly national underwriting. Fifth, Congressional debates and hearings can be a primary source of information for the general public. Beyond the pros and cons of argument, some sense of the complexity of the problems and the nature of the external environment can be conveyed.

Another kind of contribution Congress can make is to encourage the Executive Branch to improve its decision-making procedures. Congress financed the famous Hoover Commission study in 1948–1949 and enacted legislation based on the commission's recommendations which improved the organization of decision making. Unification of the Armed Forces and the establishment of the National Security Council would have been unlikely without Congressional support. Congress can, of course, go too far in trying to lay down detailed rules for administrative agencies, with the unfortunate results noted elsewhere. Nonetheless, Congress can push for broad reforms and can provide the authority required for major alterations of the functions of executive agencies. This is an important part of Congress's primary task of keeping the exercise of presidential power responsible and effective.

Perhaps the major Congressional contribution lies in the provision of the sinews of foreign policy—the imposing economic and military tools and techniques of American statecraft. Since 1945, Congress has appropriated, with considerable generosity, billions for foreign aid, has underwritten the reconstruction of the military establishment, has supported America's disproportionate share of United Nations expenditures, and has approved a system of American alliances. To the extent that the imposition of conditions on foreign aid has been desirable, Congress has been somewhat more diligent than the Executive Branch in exploring and insisting upon such conditions. At the same time, Congress has been less enthusiastic about cultural programs and psychological warfare and technological help to backward areas.

These positive contributions, mentioned only briefly, are implicit in the earlier account of how Congress influences foreign policy, as are Congressional weaknesses. Weakness and contributions obviously depend on certain conditions. So does the new role toward which Congress is moving.

► CONCLUSION

This is a transition period for Congress as well as for the Executive Branch. Not only can Congress now exercise more power over foreign policy; it is apparently self-consciously seeking a role wherein it can influence policy in the early stages of development and therefore be in a position to help determine end results. In other words, Congress appears to want an affirmative role, one which does not leave all the initiative to the President. Much of the maneuvering Congress has done in the postwar years can be interpreted as a kind of trial-and-error approach to finding ways of exercising more initiative. Whether Congress succeeds in achieving this type of role or not, it will still be able to exert tremendous power and influence over foreign policy for reasons noted earlier in the chapter.

The rationality, responsibility, and consensus with which Congress exercises its power, the amount of initiative it is able to achieve, the maximization of its contributions, and the control of its weaknesses will all depend significantly on certain conditions—in the present instance, conditions internal to Congress itself.

A fundamental factor in this connection is that Congress has been reluctant to reform itself, to adapt its organization and procedures to its contemporary problems. What reform there has been has come very slowly and has been piecemeal. The Reorganization Act of 1946 was the first "major" reform effort in twenty-five years. While needed changes, such as reducing the number of committees and strengthening staff arrangements, were enacted, many needs were left untouched. Some provisions of the 1946 act were never carried out, the single budget, for example. This legislation came after Congress had made a thorough study of itself, but it only partially reflected the conclusions of the study. Since 1946, some congressmen, writers, and scholars have periodically criticized the most obvious of Congressional defects and have suggested modifications in organization and procedures. The criticisms have in the main come from friends of Congress, from those who are convinced that a strong, effective Congress is essential to democratic government.

Actually, Congress has not evaluated itself in the light of its new responsibilities in foreign affairs. There is abundant evidence that most senators and representatives want a vigorous, positive, leadership role for Congress in relation to foreign policy and there is abundant evidence that most of them realize that Congress needs to reform itself. However, as a corporate body, Congress seems unable to gain any leverage on its own operations. It is too simple to say there is no will for reform. It is more like a vicious circle—the very things which need reforming prevent the beginning of reform. Congress has not seen clearly the implications of its disabilities for the role in foreign policy to which it aspires.

This is not the place to review the suggestions which have been made for improvements in Congress, but some general points can be suggested for the purpose of highlighting those weaknesses of Congress which seem to be strategic for foreign-policy formation:

1. Congress must somehow reduce its work load so that more time of individual members can be spent on vital legislative business.

2. The allocation of foreign-policy powers and responsibilities should be more centralized so that Congress is better able to offer consistent judgments and to exercise coherent leadership. The number of committees dealing with foreign-policy matters should be reduced.

3. Coordination would be improved by creating a joint Senate-House Foreign Relations Committee, by joining the appropriations process with the authorization process in the case of foreign-policy legislation, and by creating majority and minority policy committees consisting of the chairmen and ranking members of committees.

4. Irresponsible individual and minority action could be reduced by eliminating the seniority rule and strengthening party discipline.

5. Congressional competence would be improved by choosing chairmen and committee members wherever possible on the basis of knowledge and experience.

6. Congressional communications could be enhanced by more full-dress germane debates on basic foreign-policy issues in both houses and by joint investigations.

7. Congress's representative function could be made more effective by providing more time and better techniques for analyzing public preferences.

8. The information and analysis available to Congress would benefit in quantity and quality by improving investigative procedures, by making more use of independent research facilities, by increasing committee staffs, and by having members of Congress serve temporarily in executive posts where they could observe directly foreign-policy making and the administration of foreign affairs. Improvements of this kind would touch most of the weaknesses noted above and would probably secure a more continual and uniform Congressional contribution.

Conditions within Congress are not the only ones to affect its general role and the nature of its influence on foreign policy. The way the Executive Branch performs its foreign-policy functions is an important factor. Blunders, confusion, lack of leadership on the part of the President can make Congress's task more difficult and can tempt Congress into a role it is incapable of performing. The strategy employed by the President and the Secretary of State may also call forth unfortunate responses from Congress. On the other hand, the weaknesses of Congress affect the behavior of the Executive Branch and may make it difficult to carry out successful policies. In short, neither the role of the President nor that of Congress can be fully understood without an analysis of executive-legislative relations. To this attention is now turned.

► SELECTED BIBLIOGRAPHY

The best single volume on Congressional participation in the making of foreign policy is Robert Dahl, *Congress and Foreign Policy* (New York, Harcourt, Brace & Company, 1950). An entire issue of the *Annals* of the American Academy of Political and Social Science, September, 1953, is devoted to Congress and foreign policy and is valuable because of the extensive expression of views by leaders of the House and Senate. Useful readings and documents are conveniently grouped in L. Larry Leonard, *Elements of American Foreign Policy* (New York, McGraw-Hill Book Company, 1953), pp. 155–190, and L. H. Chamberlain and R. C. Snyder, *American Foreign Policy* (New York, Rinehart & Company, 1948), Chaps. 4, 5. W. Y. Elliott, *et al., United States Foreign Policy* (New York, Columbia University Press, 1952), Chaps. 4 and 11, consists of a suggestive analysis of weaknesses and recommendations for reform. An excellent summary of Congressional behavior with respect to the North Atlantic Treaty is contained in pages 382–413 of S. Bailey and H. Samuel, *Congress at Work* (New York, Henry Holt and Company, 1953). F. Rigg's *Pressures on Congress* (New York, Columbia University Press, 1952) is a case study centering on repeal of the Chinese Exclusion Act.

CHAPTER ELEVEN

EXECUTIVE-LEGISLATIVE RELATIONS AND THE PROBLEM OF A BIPARTISAN FOREIGN POLICY

Introduction • Patterns of Executive-Legislative Relations • Some Characteristics of the Foregoing Patterns • The Significance of Legislative Procedures and Strategies • Sources of Difficulties in the Foregoing Patterns • Nature of the "Problem"

► INTRODUCTION

The nature of the American political system is such that great emphasis must be laid on the importance of the relationship between the executive and legislative branches of the federal government. Much has already been said directly or indirectly about this relationship. In the chapter on decision making, the reader was reminded that Congressional behavior may become a significant aspect of the setting or environment in which executive policy makers must formulate foreign policy. Constitutional allocation of power and responsibility has been analyzed and some of its consequences suggested. It has been shown that the powers of the President and Congress are partly independent (legally speaking), yet in practice may conflict or may veto each other; that some powers cannot be fully exercised except in collaboration; and that the two sets of powers are not always clearly defined. Two chapters have been devoted to the actual role of the President and Congress as well as to their differing interpretations of their own and each other's proper role. Enough description of the internal organization of the two branches has been provided to indicate the ways in which reciprocal influences have been felt and the ways in which organizational factors determine what may be called loosely executive and legislative behavior. Knowledge and understanding of this sort is a necessary underpinning for the analysis of the basic relationship which is the chief concern of this chapter.

Naturally the consequences which flow from the "separation of powers" have long interested as well as worried students of American politics. Prior to the revolution in American foreign policy, however, separation of powers and checks and balances were relevant mainly because of the constitutional rule requiring a two-thirds approval in the Senate for all treaties. Not that this was of small significance, for there has been a rather steady stream of

457

unflattering comments directed at the Senate by strong Presidents who found their plans thwarted by "that stubborn, willful little group of men." The now classic example of the failure of the League of Nations Covenant and the Versailles Treaty to pass the Senate is of course cited as the most costly casualty of the forced collaboration between President and Congress imbedded in the constitutional system. Nonetheless, the fact that the relationship between the two branches has recently become the vital link in the decision-making process arises from America's new international responsibilities in general and from the new role of Congress in particular. Therefore the separation of powers as both phenomenon and problem is being re-examined in the light of developments since 1939. The executive-legislative relationship is substantively more important and also subject to greater critical evaluation.

It is probable that most readers of this book will have, consciously or otherwise, personal views as to the respective contributions and performances of Congress and the President. Some will tend to have a more favorable image of, and greater faith in, Congress, while others will feel similarly about the President. Political emotions being what they are, it is easy to let reactions against a particular President color attitudes toward the presidency in general. On the other hand, it is easy to accept the cynical image of Congress. The danger from such tendencies lies in the possible distortion and oversimplification of the executive-legislative relationship which may result. To avoid this possibility and to achieve better understanding of this fundamental relationship the reader should resist the temptation to prejudge either element in the equation.

It has been convenient up to this point to simplify things by referring to *the executive-legislative relationship*. This phrase is deceptively simple. It really covers a whole *set of relationships* or a *set of processes*. Also included in the phrase are the complex factors which affect the relationships or processes and the interwoven problems which appear to result. A fruitful definition of the problem of Presidential-Congressional relations in foreign-policy making is only possible when the simple formulation is abandoned. At the risk of apparent repetition it will be useful to pause for a brief summary of the major patterns of executive-legislative action and interaction in the field of foreign policy. These patterns grow out of the separate and joint exercise of the powers described in Chapter Four and out of the attempts of one branch to protect itself against what it regards as the illegitimate exercise of power by the other branch. The latter includes, of course, reciprocal attempts to influence the exercise of power.

▶ PATTERNS OF EXECUTIVE-LEGISLATIVE RELATIONS

1. Treaties and the two-thirds rule. International agreements embodied in formal treaties bring the President and the Senate together in a special relationship. Ordinarily, legislative action is taken on the basis of majority vote. Treaties are an exception—two-thirds of the Senate members present must concur. Thus, opposition votes are worth about twice as much as favorable votes. And there hangs over every treaty the possibility that seventeen Senators representing a twelfth of the population may cause its defeat. Short of complete rejection, the Senate may amend a treaty, add a formal reservation which requires renegotiation, add a declaration or qualification which does not require renegotiation, send the treaty back to the President for changes, pigeonhole the treaty in committee, or issue a report which stands as Congress's authoritative interpretation of the terms.

2. *Executive agreements*. Another pattern consists of an international agreement which is negotiated by the President and approved by a majority of both houses of Congress. Majority approval may be expressed in the passage of a legislative act authorizing the President to negotiate executive agreements under certain conditions without their having to be referred back to either the House or the Senate, i.e., the Reciprocal Trade Agreements Act of 1934. As noted in a previous chapter a joint resolution (not a statute) supported by both houses may signify prior Congressional approval on an *ad hoc* basis. For example, in 1943, Congress adopted the so-called Green-Sayre formula recommending that the President pledge American participation in the United Nations Relief and Rehabilitation Administration by executive action alone. Either regular legislation or a joint resolution may express approval *after* an executive agreement has been negotiated. As also noted earlier, non-self-executing executive agreements always require some sort of Congressional action. Self-executing agreements—those not requiring appropriations or statutory changes—may or may not be accompanied by Congressional action.

3. *Senate approval of nominations*. In a very real sense, the President finds his policy-making activities severely handicapped if the Senate does not approve his nominations for certain key posts. A Presidential appointee must be acceptable to the Senate as whole for his policy ideas and abilities and especially to the two senators from his home state. The latter consideration, of course, represents "senatorial courtesy."

4. *Legislation*. Perhaps the most complicated pattern of all is the full-scale legislative process which literally takes months, involves more than the House Foreign Affairs Committee and the Senate Foreign Relations Committee, and results in the commitment of billions of dollars to foreign-policy objectives. The Economic Cooperation Act of 1948 (the Marshall Plan) is an outstanding example. Far from being an unusual action, the necessity for annual appropriations to sustain the military establishment and the foreign-aid program means that the legislative pattern has become a regular feature of foreign-policy making.

5. *Continuous communications*. There are several typical patterns of consultation which are potentially regular in the sense that they can be carried on by Congressional and executive officials who are responsible in some way

for the conduct of foreign affairs. Thus any edition of the Legislative History of the Senate Foreign Relations Committee will contain the phrase: "Members of the committee and the committee staff are in almost daily communication with officers of the Department of State." Contacts of the House Foreign Affairs Committee are also regular but somewhat less numerous. It is likely that, on the whole, committee staffs actually carry on much of the oral and written communication. Executive policy makers are in steady contact with other Congressional committees as well. The annual budget requires that State Department officers and others concerned with foreign policy appear before the Appropriations Committee of each house and before each Armed Services Committee too. For obvious reasons, these more regular contacts do not take place at the level of secretary, under secretary, and assistant secretary, although the new regional subcommittee set up in the Senate Foreign Relations Committee has probably increased the Congressional contacts of the assistant secretaries in the State Department. Normally, spokesmen for these officers or officials who are immediately below them in the hierarchy draft replies to letters, prepare information papers, and talk to individual congressmen. Included in the regular type of communication are weekly meetings held at the White House between the President and House and Senate leaders where crucial foreign policy issues may be discussed.

6. *Discontinuous communications.* The Secretary of State appears before the Senate Foreign Relations Committee whenever it is deemed necessary. Such sessions may be open or closed and may include the whole committee or a subcommittee. He will appear before other groups as the occasion demands. Presumably he will answer queries put to him in writing from time to time by individual members of Congress. The secretary may invite a number of Congressional leaders to an informal conference. Below the level of secretary, numerous luncheons are held at which members of Congress and their staffs discuss foreign affairs with State Department personnel. On particular matters, the President may call an *ad hoc* White House conference of Congressional leaders—the chairmen of the foreign affairs committees, the majority leaders, and the chairmen of the policy committees—to meet with his foreign-policy advisers, including the Secretary of State.

7. *Investigations.* Another facet of executive-legislative relations is represented by special investigating committees, *ad hoc* investigations by regular committees and by permanent groups created for purposes of overseeing the Executive Branch. Potentially, any issue can be brought under investigation, any executive official may be called. Obviously, the purposes of investigation are fundamentally different from the routine contacts, say, of the Senate Foreign Relations Committee and the State Department. The spirit of these contacts could properly be described as "Congress *and* the President" or "the legislative *and* executive branches" whereas during investigations it may be "Congress *versus* the President."

8. *President and Congress: the bureaucratic relationship, the constitu-*

tional relationship, the party relationship, and the psychological relationship. This brief review of patterns of executive-legislative relationships in the national government would not be complete without a reminder of some rather obvious points. Because the terms "President" and "Congress" may refer to several aspects of the role and conduct of each, the patterns noted should be viewed as expressing more than one *kind* of relationship between the two branches. "Bureaucratic relationship" suggests that subunits of the two branches may be closer to each other than to the larger organization of which each is a part. Contacts at the "bureau-committee level" may be handled as much by permanent civil servants or staff personnel as by executive political appointees and members of Congress. Such relationships may be highly formalized in the sense that they differ markedly from the highly volatile, more politically sensitive relationships. It is of course a well-known fact that subunits of the Executive Branch complicate executive-legislative interaction by making their own special appeals to Congress regardless of presidential policy and by becoming special targets of Congressional wrath.

That the general relationship can be viewed as primarily constitutional is also quite clear. Thus the President's annual message, the veto, the hearings, the passage of bills, executive prerogatives, and so on—all these reflect the constitutionally prescribed relationship in the broadest sense. Other phenomena can be explained only as consequences of the President's being the party leader. His actions will have one kind of effect on congressmen who are members of his party, another kind of effect on members of the opposition party. If the President's party is the majority party he has a certain leverage over the majority leaders. Clearly the attitudes and behavior of the minority party toward the President cannot be accounted for solely by the constitutional rivalry imbedded in the separation of powers.

While the bureaucratic, constitutional, and party components of the relationship are vitally important, there is another aspect best (though crudely) identified as "psychological." It will be necessary to return to this point later, but suffice it here to remark that the President's personality and his personal treatment of congressmen may be just as important. Both the President and Congress can do things independently which are well within their constitutional rights yet which psychologically affect their relationship. Congressmen have been known to badger a President until some sort of response was elicited which, though justified perhaps, had more serious repercussions by putting the President in an unfavorable light generally. Presidents have been known to make blunt comments about individual senators and representatives which not only have been resented but have stimulated resistance to policies. These examples point toward the familiar concept of mood. Various possible moods may characterize executive-legislative relations— trust, permissiveness, frustration, hostility, and so on. Closely allied to mood will be prevailing images held by a particular President and a particular Congress of each other. Mutual images will consist of a set of estimates and expectations. Over a period of four or eight years, Congressional veterans and the President get to know each other pretty well. With experience come estimates of each other's aims, ways of thinking, role definitions, margins of tolerance, and vulnerabilities. Reciprocal expectations of behavior are based, of course, on formal factors, such as party organization and constitutional requirements. Nevertheless, expectations are also based on the behavior of individual human beings as perceived by those who come in contact with them.

► SOME CHARACTERISTICS OF THE FOREGOING PATTERNS

VARIETY WITHIN THE PATTERNS

As long as the federal government continues to function, these basic kinds of patterns will continue. Within them, however, a wide variety of action and conditions of action is possible. The Versailles Treaty (including the League of Nations Covenant) and the North Atlantic Treaty were both examples of the exercise of the treaty-making power. There the similarity of the two cases ends. The former failed; the latter succeeded. Unlike the Versailles Treaty, the North Atlantic Treaty grew out of close collaboration between the State Department and the Senate Foreign Relations Committee. Beginning with the Vandenberg Resolution (which in effect invited the Executive Branch to negotiate such a treaty along certain broad lines) of June, 1948,* the committee actually helped to draft the provisions. As Chairman Connally put it, the Secretary and Under Secretary of State were the chief architects and the committee provided the stone and mortar. It is doubtful that the Senate knew what was in the Versailles Treaty or was asked about its views before the final draft was formally submitted. Furthermore, there were warnings of rejection long before the final vote was taken. The famous Kellogg Pact of 1928 was also a product of close consultation, whereas the Petroleum Agreement with Great Britain in 1945 was finally withdrawn after bouncing back and forth several times between the Senate and the Executive Branch.

Historically, the relationship between the Secretary of State and the Senate has varied. Secretary John Hay virtually shunned the Senate Foreign Relations Committee. On the other hand, Elihu Root attended so many meetings he was looked upon almost as a regular member. During his term of office, a particular secretary may vary the pattern. For example, Secretary of State Acheson met for two hours in May, 1950, with the Senate Foreign Relations Committee, briefing the members and soliciting comment and advice prior to sailing for top-level diplomatic discussions with France and Great Britain. At other times, Acheson was accused of being stand-offish.

---

* Senate Resolution No. 239, 80th Congress, 2nd Session.

MULTIPLE MEANINGS OF "CONSULTATION"

It is very important to note that "consultation" or "collaboration" between the executive and legislative branches has several meanings. Whether one speaks of the President and the whole Congress, the President and Congressional leaders, or the State Department and the Senate Foreign Relations Committee, the alternate terms refer to at least five different actions: (1) informing or briefing by executive policy makers before a decision is made or immediately thereafter but before public announcement (briefing often includes reporting on the progress of policies and sketching in critical situations where no policy has been formulated); (2) discussion among members of the two branches in which Congressional ideas on policy problems are expressed and in which presidential experts clarify their views; (3) meetings whose purpose is to sell policies already decided on and to convince Congressional leaders that they should support these policies on the floor of the Senate or the House; (4) actual participation by Congress in the drafting of treaties, agreements, and foreign-policy legislation other than by adding riders or qualifying resolutions; and (5) performance of joint functions incapable of being carried out by the President or Congress acting separately—appointments, war making, and so on.

When members of Congress are asked to serve (in effect) as diplomatic representatives of the United States at international conferences it is, of course, an example of collaboration. Though a long-standing practice, multilateral diplomacy is now much more frequent. More than one purpose can be served by appointing congressmen members of American delegations to conferences. It can serve to underline two-party unity behind a given policy, as was true when Senator Connally (Democrat) and Senator Vandenberg (Republican) both attended the first session of the United Nations Assembly. It is also a way of feeding back to Congress firsthand information not processed by executive agencies and of training foreign-policy experts within Congress. Attendance at a conference which may yield a treaty is also a way of enlisting able champions when the treaty comes up for debate in the Senate. Senators Lodge and Underwood performed this function after participating in the Washington Naval Conference of 1921; the vote on the naval convention was close but the two senators' roles were crucial. Republican President Hoover sent Democratic Senators Reed and Robinson to the Naval Conference of 1930; the forthcoming treaty was accepted without partisan struggle. No implication is intended that this is an infallible device. Occasionally, Congress has ignored such gestures and gone its own way regardless. The point here is that, once again, within a given pattern of executive-legislative interaction variation is possible.

CHOICES DETERMINE VARIATIONS WITHIN PATTERNS: PRESIDENTIAL TACTICS

Another basic characteristic of the foregoing patterns is that the particular variation which a pattern takes is the result (usually) of someone's deliberate choice. Thus the President is always confronted by alternative answers to the question of how he will handle Congress. Will he ask Congressional approval and collaboration regardless of the price? Will he act as though Congress is his constitutional coordinate or subordinate? Where he is not required constitutionally to do so, will he "consult" Congress anyway? Will he try to "manipulate" Congress by his special access to the press and public opinion? Will he address a special message to Congress or not? How will he react to Congressional demands that he release information?

Some of these points can be illustrated by reference to the first months of the Eisenhower Administration in 1953. The choices which President Eisenhower made as to how he would handle his relations appear to have rested on certain assumptions: Congress is the coordinate equal of the Executive Branch in the formation of national policy; head-on clashes with Congress ought to be avoided if at all possible because the slight majority held by the Republicans required strict party unity on major issues; Congressmen can be "reasoned with," and if they were made aware of the real nature of complex problems, agreement was possible; and engagements in "personality clashes" are fruitless and dangerous. Acting on these assumptions, the President tried to forestall constitutional opposition by welcoming Congress to equal status, made a frank appeal for party unity—by which he meant (apparently) *all* members and *all* policy views—and held successful, frequent White House breakfasts and luncheons at which frankness was the order of the day. In his press conferences, the President refused to discuss Congress or individual congressmen, turning questions into their most general form and answering in terms of "principles." Direct, all-out appeals to Congress were used sparingly. On certain issues in the first session of the Eighty-third Congress, the President took a firm stand: the nomination of Charles Bohlen to be ambassador to the Soviet Union, foreign-aid appropriations, and the military budget. Staff opposition to the Reciprocal Trade Agreements Act was handled by a request for a temporary extension and a pledge of a thorough study by a bipartisan commission.

Even where apparently the President *must* go to Congress he still has choices open to him. He may decide to cast an international agreement in the form of an executive agreement instead of a treaty, thus by-passing the two-thirds vote in the Senate. If his powers alone are sufficient to carry out the provisions, both houses may be by-passed. Should he desire majority Congressional support for an executive agreement, he may seek it before or after he signs the agreement for the United States. Under certain circumstances, the President may appoint a foreign-affairs advisor or diplomatic representative known to be opposed by the Senate without the approval of the latter body. Such a person can either be appointed to his personal staff or be given an interim status (while Congress is not in formal session).

What factors condition presidential choices? The nature of the subject matter of a policy or agreement will be one consideration. Usually *pure* executive agreements have been avoided on those subjects in which Congress is deemed to have a strong interest and clear constitutional powers, i.e., regulation of foreign trade and economic policy generally. On *minor* problems the President may be more willing to gamble on by-passing Congress. Since 1945, no *major* foreign-policy move has been incorporated in an international agreement which was not submitted to Congress. Of great influence will be the President's assessment of the *risk* involved in substituting a pure executive agreement for some other form. Risk is measured in terms of whether the President thinks he can carry out an agreement once made public and in terms of whether Congress may reverse the policy embodied in an agreement by subsequent contrary legislation. The prevailing political climate may make it impossible for the President to run the risk of a sharp Congressional debate on a particular matter. When time is precious, the President may feel it is not in the nation's interest to permit a long debate in the Senate alone or in both House and Senate. Unless Congressional procedures are reduced to a farce, even a very rapid legislative action takes time, more time than would be the case with a pure executive agreement.

Regardless of these conditions, there may be situations where the President is compelled to enter into an agreement on his sole responsibility and without Congress's being formally notified or where he feels relatively safe proceeding on his own. The first is illustrated by acts of the President as commander in chief in carrying on a war or laying the basis for immediate postwar arrangements. A typical instance of this type is the so-called Yalta Agreement of 1944, discussed earlier. The second includes those cases where the President had adequate, clear statutory authority. Franklin Roosevelt's famous Destroyer-Bases Agreement of 1940 was justified by the Attorney General on the ground that there were statutory provisions permitting the President to dispose of military items under specified circumstances.

▶ THE SIGNIFICANCE OF LEGISLATIVE
PROCEDURES AND STRATEGIES

Discussions of executive-legislative relationships and the varied patterns associated therewith usually neglect the impact of procedures and leadership in Congress itself. The passage of a major piece of legislation is a complicated business indeed. This is not the place to recite the familiar steps involved, but it should be noted that here, too, choices which have nothing to do with the substance of policy, and which are obscured from all except the most experienced observers, may in fact determine the success of a treaty or the content of foreign-policy bills. The reader will recall that in the general chapter on decision making the point was made that legislative strategy was one of the factors affecting the decisional activities of the Executive Branch. Before a policy is presented to Congress, an estimate has to be made of Congressional mood, and decisions must be taken as to how much information is to be revealed, the best time to proceed, and which Congressional leaders are to be entrusted with responsibility on the floor of each chamber. Several examples of the effects of executive strategy have been cited, among them the Military Aid Bill of 1949 (implementation of the North Atlantic Treaty), which suffered delays and modifications because of mistakes in strategy made by executive officials, particularly with respect to revealing the number of troops intended for Western Europe.

Once a bill or a treaty is in the Congressional mill, so to speak, the strategy employed for it becomes even more important. Strategy failures by majority leaders may be due to lack of clear explanation of the various objectives and provisions of a measure or to the desultory nature of attempts to convince those members who are "on the fence." America's refusal to join the World Court during the interwar period is generally regarded as a costly mistake in diplomacy to be attributed to unfortunate workings of the two-thirds rule in the Senate. When the final vote was taken on the issue in January, 1935, the resolution to join lost by seven votes. At the time it was known that there were fifteen members of the Senate who were not committed yet were favorably disposed. Apparently they shifted to the opposition at the last minute. Close study of strategy reveals that the Democratic members of the Senate Foreign Relations Committee did not function as a united group and that the chairman did little to rally support among the uncommitted. On balance, it seems reasonable to suppose that neglect lost the measure. At other times it may not be a failure to rally votes, but maneuvers on the part of the Rules Committee in the House, which permits sabotage (at least temporarily) of measures which seem otherwise certain of acceptance. The lukewarm reception which first greeted the "aid to underdeveloped areas" program (Point Four) seemed due in part to the failure of administration spokesmen in Congress to explain the true nature of the proposal. In May, 1952, 103 Democrats were absent from the floor of the House of Representatives when a proposed cut of $1.7 billion in the foreign-aid program was up for consideration.

► SOURCES OF DIFFICULTIES IN
THE FOREGOING PATTERNS

If the American political process on the national level always worked smoothly and with reasonable speed, was subject to a minimum of conflict, kept within the bounds of accepted rules, and resulted in rational action, this chapter could end here. By this time, however, experts and citizens alike have become sensitized to the possibilities of trouble inherent in executive-legislative relations. Customarily, the "separation of powers" is offered as *the* explanation. Apart from the fact that this abstraction is rarely broken down into concrete terms, it is too simple. The multiplicity of interrelationships outlined above point logically to potential sources of difficulty and to certain recurrent problems.

THE TWO-THIRDS RULE

One of the primary targets of criticism is the two-thirds rule, which grants a special power to the Senate and thereby to the states. It can be argued that the provision has outlived its usefulness and that the conditions which led to its acceptance in 1787 have long since disappeared. There appears to be no sound reason now for endowing the states as such with this privilege. The Senate is no longer a small body and it does not function in close personal collaboration with the President, as intended in 1787. Operation of the rule opens the door to possible minority or individual dictation which may or may not coincide with regional or state interests. Reservations can be added to treaties by a simple majority vote, thus permitting blackmail by those whose votes are crucial. Another indictment against the two-thirds provision is that the new role of the House of Representatives makes it unfair that the Senate alone act on commitments which the House may have to support with appropriations, a consequence which deprives the House of a rightful voice. Finally, it is argued that the existence of the two-thirds requirement continually tempts the President to attempt to by-pass the Senate by the use of executive agreements. Opposition to the rule has become more or less symbolized in the defeat of Woodrow Wilson on the old League of Nations and as the time approached for peacemaking after World War II American statesmen expressed concern lest the same fate overtake efforts to build a new international organization.

On the other hand, it can also be argued that fears over the harmful impact of the two-thirds rule are largely unfounded and that there are positive advantages to its continuation. Eighty per cent of all treaties have been approved without far-reaching changes and only sixty out of more than two thousand treaties have been completely rejected.* Only twelve treaties failed to gain the requisite two-thirds majority from 1860 to 1933, and of these only two were of great importance. While this is all true, it ignores the fact that some treaties are never submitted, and unwanted modifications on others are accepted in order to avert failure on the final vote. Yet the requirement of an extraordinary majority in the Senate can be looked upon as a greater guarantee of consistency in foreign policy than a simple majority. A simple majority may constitute a hollow, temporary victory. There is ample evidence that, both at home and abroad, Senate acceptance of a treaty is regarded as more binding on the nation than an agreement backed by a majority of the two houses. Because more members must be convinced, a clear, firm basis of agreement must be established.

* D. F. Fleming, *The Treaty Veto in the American Senate* (New York, G. P. Putnam's Sons, 1930).

Though the general public seems to favor a change and though the House of Representatives has repeatedly attempted to introduce a constitutional amendment, it is unlikely that the two-thirds rule will be abandoned. Books and articles devoted to critical analysis of foreign-policy making in the United States continue to recommend unanimously that the present requirement be changed. So far, the Senate Judiciary Committee has refused to report out proposals for amendment. Recently the Senate not only has shown no disposition to relinquish its privileged position but has shown renewed interest in protecting the prerogatives of the states from inroads via the treaty power. In February, 1952, fifty-six senators urged an amendment to protect the rights of American citizens from international agreements such as the Human Rights Convention, the International Freedom of Information Compact, and the Genocide Pact.

At any rate, the employment of certain carefully planned techniques of executive-legislative collaboration since 1934 has enabled the American people to join an international organization (1945) and to initiate a Western alliance (1949)—both tremendous departures from traditional policies—without the unfortunate consequences predicted from the operation of the two-thirds provision. Nonetheless, as long as the rule prevails, a great deal will hinge on the continued success of such techniques. That the anticipated difficulties did not seriously handicap postwar foreign policy is due in great part to the so-called bipartisan foreign policy to be discussed later.

INTERNATIONAL AGREEMENTS AS A VEHICLE OF PRESIDENTIAL POWER

The availability of the pure executive agreement as a means of by-passing Congress and as a means of exercising powers the President alone possesses can be productive of trouble too. As noted in previous chapters, the powers of the President as commander in chief loom very large. During the postwar years, Congress became increasingly sensitive on the subject of "secret commitments" (real or alleged) entered into by the President. In June, 1948, Resolution 213 was introduced in the Senate "calling on the President for information concerning the Potsdam Agreements . . ." particularly on *undisclosed* obligations to which the United States is committed. It was not acted upon because the State Department complied with the request. After President Truman had held talks with Prime Minister Churchill in January, 1952, the House of Representatives passed a resolution to the effect that the Secretary of State transmit to the House of Representatives at the earliest date, full information with respect to any agreements, commitments or understandings which might have been entered into by the President and the Prime Minister of Great Britain in the course of their conversations.* The Senate Foreign Relations Committee qualified its acceptance of the Japanese Peace Treaty in March, 1952, by declaring that nothing in the treaty or the advice and consent of the Senate to its ratification implied

---

* New York *Times*, February 21, 1952, p. 6.

recognition by the United States of the provisions regarding Japan which favored the Soviet Union and which were contained in the so-called "Yalta Agreement."*

The proposed Bricker amendment was discussed as a constitutional issue in Chapter Four. It seems reasonable to suppose that the substantial support for the proposal manifest in the Senate was due in part to the general intention to recapture some of the ground allegedly lost to the President during the period 1939 to 1952. One clear aim of the amendment is to redress the balance of power between Congress and the President—at least so far as treaties and agreements are concerned. Regardless of the merits of the legal argument made on behalf of Senator Bricker's campaign, many of his colleagues had by 1952 become alarmed at what they thought were real and potential abuses of both treaties and pure executive agreements. An important issue here is the degree of freedom to be left to the President in the negotiation of international agreements concerning matters which fall within the purview of the several states or which would otherwise be beyond the jurisdiction of the federal government in the absence of such agreements. The Legal Adviser of the State Department reported that twelve of twenty-three treaties approved by the Senate from January to July, 1953, would have been affected if the Bricker Amendment had been in force: an agreement with the Bonn government pertaining to the validation of West German bonds; an agreement giving the members of NATO jurisdiction over crimes committed by the Armed Forces of any other member within their borders; a set of two agreements covering the status of the international military headquarters of NATO and the status of NATO officials within the territories of member states; treaties of friendship, commerce, and navigation with Israel, Denmark, Greece, and Japan; less comprehensive treaties with West Germany, Ethiopia, Finland, and Italy. Under the Bricker Amendment, certain provisions of all these would have required majority approval of all forty-eight state legislatures.

CONTROVERSIAL NOMINATIONS

It has been noted that Congress (the Senate really) now takes more than a routine interest in appointments to the State Department policy-making echelons and to the key posts in the diplomatic service. Trouble can arise if the Senate does not agree with the policy views of these nominees. On occasion the President can temporarily by-pass the situation through the use of special agents—a device which may itself bring more trouble than it is designed to avoid. Congress from time to time vehemently criticized certain policies of Franklin Roosevelt because Harry Hopkins (whose appointment was never submitted to Congress) was deemed to be the conceiver and executor of those policies.

The Bohlen case (his nomination was submitted in March, 1953), al-

* New York *Times,* March 20, 1952, p. 1.

ready cited previously, is an excellent example of the kind of difficulty which can arise when the exercise of a legitimate function is pushed beyond customary expectations. Before the episode was over, although Mr. Bohlen had obvious qualifications as a Russian expert, the Secretary of State felt called upon to reduce the role of ambassador to the Soviet Union to that of a mere observer, the President had to throw all his influence behind the nomination, and two members of the Senate were permitted to examine the security files on Mr. Bohlen—the latter an executive preserve hitherto jealously guarded by the President. After trying vainly to find the nominee a "poor security risk," the anti-Bohlen forces in the Senate seized upon the accusation that Mr. Bohlen had been present at the "infamous" Yalta Conference and therefore was disqualified for the post. If this argument were accepted, the practice of having a permanent corps of career diplomats would be impossible.

LEGISLATIVE MISTAKES

So far as the ordinary legislative process is concerned, the kinds of difficulty which may emerge are fivefold: first, the administration (the President, the State Department, and so on) may not keep a sufficiently close check on the committee chairmen and majority leaders responsible for the floor strategy of foreign-policy bills; second, unnecessary delays may weaken the government's position in diplomatic negotiations; third, lack of coordination within Congress may consume executive resources (the time and energy of key officials) which might be devoted to more constructive purposes; fourth, conditions and objectives are grafted onto foreign-policy proposals, not on their merits but because Congressional organization and procedures exaggerate individual and sectional influences; and fifth, proposals may come from the Executive Branch without sufficient accompanying clarifications as to their meaning or legislative priority.

COMMUNICATION FAILURES

Ultimately, as many sources of difficulty may arise from the state of communications between the President and Congress as there are patterns of communication. And the problem of communications is closely linked to the psychological relationship between the two branches. From the point of view of Congress, the feeling of "good communications" seems to rest not just on the sheer number of contacts but on the substance or satisfactions derived from them and particularly on the nature of high-level contacts. It takes relatively little, apparently, to create a mood of "poor communications." Thus an off-the-record discussion between the Secretary of State and the Senate Foreign Relations Committee may be reported as "unsatisfactory." Or the State Department may make an important announcement which catches the committee by surprise. Occasionally, the State Department may ignore hints and suggestions from Congress.

Difficulties of communication become very acute when the two branches begin to joust with each other via the newspapers. This communication through a third party is a procedure at best fraught with mischief. Hot words make good copy and soon both sides are responding to paraphrases or quotations of what each actually said. Words are normally subject to more than one meaning and, in the absence of face-to-face contact wherein intervening questions can be asked, emotion rather than reason may become the basis for choosing one word rather than another. During the first phase of the so-called "great debate" on foreign policy in late 1950 and early 1951, President Truman and Senator Taft carried on a bitter duel in the press over the extent of the President's power. Not once did the two meet personally. It took several weeks to establish the true position of each after a series of misunderstandings. The possibility that ill-considered sentiments will be exchanged in the press is enhanced by the fact that whether the President or Congress is the principal source of foreign-policy news will seriously affect the balance of power between them. Certainly long-range verbal battles can temporarily poison the relationship. Such may be the case even when communications between committee staff and executive agencies are on the whole satisfactory.

INVESTIGATIVE ABUSES

In the chapter on the State Department it was made clear that routine and special investigations can disturb executive-legislative relations. It was pointed out that the systematic exposure of individuals, documents, and plans during the period 1940 to 1952 sapped the department's resources, shattered the morale of personnel, and left behind a reservoir of ill feeling. This is not to say that Congress had no right to investigate or that these particular efforts were unjustified, but only that certain consequences were forthcoming. Nor was the unfortunate aftermath confined only to the department; many congressmen were disappointed or shocked by what they thought was a calloused indifference to the revelations of the investigating groups. As is well known, Congressional investigations probably as a general rule create a certain minimum of ill will but some may produce overreactions.

The varied activities carried on by Senator McCarthy and his investigating staff illustrate not only the adverse effects of unrestrained inquiries upon the morale and effectiveness of executive agencies, but also the fact that the long arm of Congress can reach into the proper domain of executive officials. Senator McCarthy attempted—with more than a little success—to force decisions on the State Department with respect to trade with Communist China, to tell the Voice of America what it could and could not broadcast, and to render immune from duly constituted authority in the State Department those employees who cooperated with his committee. And in April, 1953, the Senator announced that he had "negotiated" an agreement with the owners of 295 Greek vessels in which the latter promised not to trade with Communist China.

PARTY FACTORS

Finally, the possible patterns involved in the party relationship may be cited as a serious source of difficulty. By this time it has become a perennial horror of American politics that in close national elections, one party may capture the presidency and the other Congress, or that between presidential elections the majority party may lose control of either or both of the two houses. Under these circumstances, the President has the initiative; yet he lacks the degree of control or influence he has over Congressional leaders when they are members of his own party. The President may not be in a very strong position even if his is the majority party if the margin is so small that a handful of turncoats may turn the tide. Conceivably, the President might have a safe majority without necessarily being able to influence key committee chairmen. When any of these situations prevails, a whole range of disturbances is possible, from hostility to stalemate to Congressional supremacy for a temporary period. More will be said later concerning the nature of party government in the United States and its relation to foreign-policy formation.

This brief summary of the sources of difficulties implicit in the patterns of relationships between the President and Congress should provide a basis for formulating a definition of the multisided problem of the actual or potential "gulf" between the two branches. Obviously the relationship between the President and Congress cannot be explored unless the possible meanings of "relationship" between the President and Congress are kept in mind.

▶ NATURE OF THE "PROBLEM"

There appears to be no good reason to review here the many theories and diagnoses focused on the way the President and Congress do or should relate themselves to each other in the American political system. Writers have differed, sometimes widely, in their conception of the "problem." Nor is this the place to argue the case for presidential supremacy or for Congressional initiative. The primary concern at this point is to make clear the various component elements of the problem—in effect to specify the *problems* which make up the problem. When the difficulties noted become chronic and substantially affect the policy-making process, problems emerge. As suggested elsewhere, the American people have lived since the founding of the Republic under threat of deadlock and open warfare in policy making at the national level. Now the threat is more acute because of the new role of Congress, because of the greater consequences of the exercise of normal presidential powers, and because major policies require the united action of more members of Congress and the Executive Branch than at any time in the nation's history.

OVERLAPPING JURISDICTIONS AND IMPRECISE ALLOCATION OF POWER AND RESPONSIBILITY

The problem here is fundamentally this: When either the Congress (or any part of it) and the Executive Branch (or any part of it) acts alone as a decision-making unit, or when both comprise a single decision-making unit, how does the distribution of authority and influence between them affect the conditions under which action takes place? Previously it was suggested that what each branch can do or cannot do and the circumstances under which the two must or should act together are not always clear either by an appeal to the written rules or to precedent. Precise delineations between presidential and Congressional powers were rejected in favor of a situation in which each could watch or check the other if necessary. Several consequences follow. A straight power conflict is always possible and could result in deadlock. Actually, this has not happened—at least not to the extent of paralyzing the government. However, short of such a development, there is need for continual accommodation of the rival claims to prerogative as well as a kind of running quarrel over the interpretation of constitutional prerogatives. Closely bound up with the question of power—the legal right to take certain kinds of actions and to be obeyed—is the question of role in a somewhat larger sense. Certain things are expected of each branch and have developed on the basis of precedent. Congress is expected to hold the exercise of presidential power responsible. The President is expected to take the initiative in the formulation of foreign policy. Part of the problem arises, then, from the way in which these expectations are fulfilled, from the interpretation placed on Congress's role by Congress itself and by the President on his role. What follows is that Congress does not always accept the President's interpretation, and vice versa. Strong Presidents, favored by a talent for leadership, by opportunity, and by crisis have been inclined to put a broad interpretation on the proper role of the chief executive and to take full advantage of the advantages natural to initiative. Congress has, from time to time, asserted and made good its own claim to initiative. Congress has occasionally gone beyond legitimate legislative oversight and usurped functions belonging to the President. When this happens, Presidents have been known to try to "punish" Congress by an appeal to public opinion. Therefore, each branch is engaged in constant interpretation *and* defense of its prerogatives. Always in the background is the question of the nature of the partnership when the two act together. Strong Congressional leaders—chiefly the foreign-affairs leaders in the Senate—have usually insisted that they were "coordinate equals." Presumably such leaders have been insisting that Congressional participation in foreign-policy making was a matter of constitutional right, not presidential tolerance.

That Congress must enforce presidential responsibility adds further complications. Regardless of the prescribed separation or sharing of powers, Congress delegates power to the President and therefore becomes the principal in the principal-agent relationship which constitutes the responsibility equation. One never hears of the President enforcing Congressional responsibility because delegation can never run that way; Congress has need of an executive, not the other way round. Thus if Congress had no unique powers of its own, it still would have to keep the President "honest," i.e., compel him or his staff to act *when* action is necessary, and to act *within* the grant of power made. Potential conflict is implicit in any custodial arrangement because the two elements in responsibility are heavily judgmental and the equation runs only one way: the principal is much better able to punish the agent than vice versa.

MALDISTRIBUTION OF INFORMATION AND CAPACITY FOR POLICY ANALYSIS

The agent in this case is no ordinary agent. The Executive Branch bases *its* conception of *its* own role (power and function) on the fact that by and large it possesses superior information and superior capacity for evaluating information and for proposing effective courses of action. In other words, the presidency possesses more, substantially more, rationality. Naturally the tendency is to stress this. Congress, on the other hand, stresses the responsibility requirements which inhere in the oversight of administration. Therefore the problem of executive-legislative relations may be posed as presidential possession of rationality versus Congressional enforcement of responsibility; the Executive Branch distrusts legislative rationality and the legislature distrusts executive restraint.*

Here is an important clue to the different perspectives of the policy-making process held by official participants and therefore to conflict. The term "rationality" as used in this connection can be equated with the criterion of effectiveness. It is an implicit and explicit assumption of many agencies in the Executive Branch that Congress is not capable of an accurate appraisal of the external setting and of devising courses of action calculated on the basis of such an appraisal. Congress not only denies this but is convinced that presidential agencies have an innate tendency to overstep the bounds and hence can be contained by institutional devices such as budget control, statutes, and formal constitutional provisions.

Several factors are interwoven here which carry the problem beyond this formulation. In the first place, regardless of how Congress's role is defined, it requires a high level of information. Lacking its own sources, it is generally dependent on executive sources. Although Congressional committees have staffs which prepare studies or can draw on the resources of the Legislative Reference Service, and although individual congressmen in-

---

* See Robert Dahl, *Congress and Foreign Policy* (New York, Harcourt, Brace & Company, 1950), Chap. 10.

creasingly go abroad for firsthand observation, it is still true that the amount of information needed for conducting foreign relations in general and for Congress's contribution to policy in particular far exceeds the amount drawn from such sources. Furthermore, Congress needs information not just for its action on the substance of policy but in order to enforce presidential responsibility. For this reason, Congress may want to know things which it would otherwise not need to know. To ensure that the President acts when he is supposed to and within the limits of his grant of power, Congress (in theory) needs to know what problems confront the nation and what the Executive Branch intends to do or has done about them. Since Congress's view of what is fitting for it to know is not automatically satisfied by the flow of information from the executive agencies which gather that information, Congress most of the time requests, demands, pries, begs, and borrows in an effort to satisfy its needs. One of the significant indexes of legislative-executive tension is the frequency and intensity of demands for information by Congress and its attempts to exploit other sources.

Of course such efforts are often resisted by the Executive Branch because there is disagreement over how much Congress needs to know and because presidential agencies seek some protection from the upsetting scrutiny of the public eye, i.e., probings which go beyond enforcement of responsibility and become "meddlesome" without being helpful either to the agencies or to the constitutional system.

The complications do not end here. Considerations of security—the withholding of information valuable to potential enemies—enter into the picture. In case certain data are in this category, are they to be refused to Congress? While Congress and the President might disagree as to what constitutes "classified" information, the decisions rest with executive agencies because planning, intelligence, and confidential negotiation are under their control. During a period of cold war, with enemies pretty well defined, the pressure to narrow down the number of persons who share "top-level secrets" increases. At the same time Congress's anxiety becomes intensified. Thus the problem becomes the need to know vs. the need for secrecy. The Executive Branch asks: "How much confidential data must be released to Congress? To which key committees and members? Congress asks: How much is being hidden from us under the cloak of security requirements?

To push complications even further, one consequence of the maldistribution of information between groups or individuals is the emergence of the expert-layman relationship. In general, there is little doubt that the relative lack of information puts Congress in the role of the layman vis-à-vis executive experts. It is a well-known fact that in certain circumstances people—including congressmen—develop antipathy for certain kinds of experts. The line between expert-worship and expert-distrust is a thin one indeed, and distrust may emerge when the layman suspects that superior information is being used to justify expanded power or is being used to cover up poor judgment. On both counts Congress is sensitive. Yet superior information does constitute a great advantage in any decision-making system and ordinarily to him who knows the situation falls the initiative. Hence even when Congress has doubts it must yield unless it has a counter set of "facts" to offer. One result of this situation is the setting up, occasionally, of rival sources of information. Rival sources may be internal to Congress, nonofficial, or even within the Executive Branch itself. There appears to be a persistent tendency to cancel the effects of testimony of executive officials by the testimony of other executive officials. When this happens, an argument over which is authoritative ensues. In the last analysis the President can decide, but Congress meanwhile receives fuller information because the Executive Branch will attempt to refute the testimony of witnesses which Congress regards accurate.

Information and capacity for analysis are linked. Here too an imbalance prevails if one separates the right to interpret information *per se* from interpretation based on specialized training, experience, and analytical skills. In this sense, the advantage lies with the Executive Branch. Not all Congressional interpretations of international events are unsound nor are all executive interpretations automatically sound. At best, the congressman experienced in foreign affairs is a lay expert—a cut above the layman without experience. The point can be put in this way: Who is best qualified to judge the significance of a revolt in Bolivia? A member of the Senate Foreign Relations Committee, a member of the Division of Latin American Republics in the State Department, or the staff of the embassy in the Bolivian capitol? Can the experienced congressman correctly interpret the implications of the New Soviet Five-Year Plan for future arms production in the Soviet Union? There is a whole range of analytical problems which require a technical competence which is largely a monopoly of presidential agencies.

It is one of the alleged attributes of the expert that in regard to his specialty the impact of emotion or inappropriate criteria on his awareness of facts and on his estimates is held to a minimum. Executive distrust of Congressional capacity for policy analysis is based in part on the conviction that issues are obscured and estimates are imperfect because of the level of intellectual skill which congressmen can bring to bear on technical information. Executive judgments, on the other hand, may be advanced or accepted as authoritative because, presumably, they result from a special kind of thinking. Furthermore, it is argued, most congressmen lack sufficient firsthand experience to "make sense" of unfamiliar social phenomena and the intricacies of diplomacy.

The imbalance in the distribution of information and capacity for policy analysis between the two branches becomes a problem to the extent that it shapes the feelings of Congress and the President concerning their mutual relationship in general. From it stem suspicions over the validity of judgments.

Efforts to redress the balance may be resisted, may result in wasteful duplication, and may intensify the disagreement over roles.

MOTIVATIONAL DIFFERENCES WHICH AFFECT THE FOREIGN-POLICY BEHAVIOR OF THE TWO BRANCHES

In the light of the analysis in the two previous sections, it is evident that there are compelling reasons why the "psychology" of the two branches with respect to foreign policy is basically different. Differences in role, in amounts and sources of information, in intellectual skills, and in experience help to explain why the orientations of Congress and the President differ— why they do not think and feel similarly about the same policy issues. As noted in other chapters, the pressures on each are different too, as well as the factors they must weigh in reaching decisions.

To these considerations can be added an obvious yet significant fact: Congress must provide the material bases of foreign policy, and the Executive Branch must execute programs and strategies. Congress realizes that administering policy often results in the making of policy or, to put Congress's fear another way, that execution of policy involves further choices which may have a considerable effect on original intentions. The final concrete product after the translation of generalized policy declarations into specific acts may or may not truly reflect Congress's wishes. The possibility that it may not accounts for much of the anxiety among legislators, anxiety which sometimes seeks an outlet in an overzealous intervention in the purely administrative activities of presidential agencies. On their side, these agencies feel that they cannot carry out policies effectively if at every turn they are hamstrung by "meddling" congressmen. The problem is this: Where does legitimate Congressional insistence upon the integrity of declared policies end and destructive oversight begin?

It is, of course, also well known that in terms of the way in which the American system actually works, the respective constituencies of the President and Congress are different. The President regularly alleges, and there is some basis for it, that he represents and speaks for the whole nation, for the majority regardless of how they are distributed throughout the country: he is the one nationally elected figure. Congress, on the other hand, represents regions, voting districts, states, and various groups. Congress's political support is fragmented and the lower house is subject to re-election every two years. On balance, it is probable that the President and the executive agencies are more insulated against direct, continuous pressure from organized groups. In view of all this, it is not surprising that the two branches disagree over which best "represents" the nation. To the extent that Congress and the President do actually represent different aspects of the nation, respective attitudes on foreign-policy problems are different. A stress on unity is a familiar theme of presidential leadership, whereas Congress is constantly sensitized to the diversities of American society.

Friends and allies may be looked upon, to repeat a point made earlier, as constituents of the President and the Secretary of State. The allies are more directly aware of the impact of Congressional foreign-policy utterances than are the legislators themselves. Much time is spent by American diplomats and other officials explaining or explaining away things which happen on the domestic political scene and which have overtones for, or potential influence on, the nation's foreign relations. Congress is seldom inhibited by the requirements of diplomatic protocol or subtlety, one reason being that individual members seldom have to confront in person puzzled or angry foreign representatives. Many executive experts are as close to other governments as they are far from domestic groups, whereas the converse is true of Congressional leaders.

Worthy of notice, too, is the fact that although in the Executive Branch the officials of concern here do nothing else but work on aspects of foreign relations, congressmen vote on domestic as well as foreign policy and serve on committees which handle both. The former do not normally think much about domestic policy unless their problems demand it. The latter, naturally, are more inclined to associate the two spheres in their thinking. One consequence of this is that Congressional consideration of foreign-policy issues is likely to reflect values and pressures which may enhance conflict with executive experts.

COORDINATION

Enough has been said about the meaning of coordination and its role in decision making to render unnecessary anything more than an assertion of its obvious importance in executive-legislative relations. Insofar as joint approval of the two branches is required for certain foreign-policy actions, a minimum of coordination is indispensable. A complete breakdown of coordination would mean that no action could take place. Unless the legislative process breaks down entirely, a minimum of coordination will be present. Since communication and coordination are so closely linked, the former will also be present. Complete failure of communication and coordination between the President and Congress is not the chief problem, although this is always a possibility. Rather, the problem lies in the consequences of different degrees of communication and coordination. Earlier in this chapter the range of difficulties which can arise from faulty executive-legislative communication was set forth. Some of these help to create ill feeling, suspicion, or confusion. But the most fruitful way to view this aspect of the many-sided problem under discussion is to ask what purposes in the joint decision making of the President and Congress in foreign affairs are to be served by keeping lines of communication "open" and "satisfying" and by "effective" coordination.

The purposes may be listed as follows: first, to keep within reasonable limits the *time* required for legislative underwriting of foreign policy; second, to prevent the intrusion of values into foreign-policy decisions which are inappropriate to the subject matter, i.e., to control the price of support and compromise so that objectives agreed to by both branches are not defeated; third, to curtail possible misunderstandings by careful use of words and by candid exploration of alternate meanings of decisions arrived at; fourth, to avoid situations and periods where the two branches are working at cross-purposes; fifth, to ensure that the intellectual ingredients of decision making (information and capacity for policy analysis) are so distributed that each branch can properly play its role (however defined) and without having to compete wastefully for intellectual resources.

A sixth point can be singled out for special comment. It has already been remarked that the essence of coordination is the "integration of perspectives"—meaning, essentially, the acceptance by two or more persons, groups, or organizational units of a common definition of a problem. It has also been remarked that the two branches have distinctive contributions to make to the foreign-policy decision making process. Congressmen bring to bear on decisions the preferences and feelings of various segments of the public (its representative function) and the executive officials bring to bear a high degree of *expertise*. Under a democratic system both are essential. The two quite different contributions may be viewed as merging in the decision-making process. Though it is difficult to imagine an exact balancing, neither should dominate a particular decision. Perspectives, of course, also include the factors mentioned in the previous section.

A coordination between the President and Congress which brought about a perfect integration of perspectives would find a common definition of the problem to be solved, an acceptance (after scrutiny) of the formulation of alternatives (goals and means) by the executive agencies, an agreed analysis of the consequences of alternatives, and the application of precise, agreed values in order to determine the choice. Such a condition is not arrived at automatically or even easily and depends upon open communications and give-and-take argument. Neither is perfection to be expected. The point is that in the sense defined, the perspectives of the executive and legislative branches must undergo *some* integration or action is unlikely. Naturally, the blend of perspectives may vary widely *and* may consist of one side accepting the other's.

Finally, another reminder. For convenience, it has been necessary to speak as though "Congress" and "the President" were homogeneous, monolithic units. Actually within each, as we have seen, there is a separate problem of coordination. Therefore the nature and degree of coordination *between* will depend significantly on coordination *within*. The more difficult coordination is within a unit, the more difficult it will be between units. No student of American national government can long forget that each branch tries, for certain purposes, to manipulate or "use" the other. Success of such tactics is linked to the state of unity within the branch. Integration of perspectives requires that there be authoritative perspectives to integrate. Because the state of unity or internal coordination is so fluid, the problem of executive-legislative coordination is not easy and is always changing.

PARTY POLITICS AND EXECUTIVE-LEGISLATIVE RELATIONS

The nature of the American party system tends to contribute to this fluidity. Even so, parties do obviously represent a cohesive element within Congress and even within the Executive Branch; moreover, parties may comprise a bond between the two. But the lack of responsible parties in American politics certainly affects the impact of the executive-legislative relationship on the formulation and execution of foreign policy. Because of factors already touched upon, the President lacks what might be called "party control" over key members of Congress and committee chairmen, and majority leaders similarly lack control over their own members. In the absence of true central control of party candidates and of effective sanctions over their behavior after election, the leeway for individual senators and congressmen to flout party leadership proportionately increases. Not only does the nature of American parties prevent their serving as a positive cohesive link between the President and Congress, but party politics are permitted to become a more disruptive force than otherwise might be the case.

There may be at times genuine differences of opinion between the Republicans and the Democrats on substantive issues of foreign policy, and individual members of Congress may be motivated to act in foreign affairs by other than narrowly partisan considerations. The problem under discussion here, however, is behavior which is primarily motivated by values which have nothing to do with foreign policy yet which weaken executive-legislative coordination in this area. Acting on partisan impulses, a small group in the Senate can defeat a treaty. Enough members of his own party may refuse to support a presidential foreign policy to cause its demise. An individual congressman may embarrass the President and the nation by irresponsible statements. In an off-year national election, candidates of the President's own party may run on platforms which stress opposition to the existing foreign policy. Investigations conducted for partisan or purely individual reasons may undermine morale and weaken policy execution despite the fact that the President's party is the majority party. Members of the minority opposition may engage in irresponsible activity at the same time that their leaders are "cooperating" with the majority party. Thus party politics may be a direct cause of "poor" executive relations—meaning that the party's interests or an individual's place in it are given priority over teamwork. Party politics may be an indirect cause of poor relations—meaning that party customs fail to prevent irresponsible action and to limit the excesses which result from legitimate Congressional pursuits. One need not argue that parties can offer nothing constructive to the policy-making process or that there is no party control at all involved in the executive-legislative relationship. Rather the argument is that one answer to the nature of the relationship—particularly when disruption occurs—must be sought in the nature of American political parties.

FLUCTUATION OF CONDITIONS UNDER WHICH FOREIGN POLICY IS MADE

The final "problem within a problem" follows logically from the others and from what was said in the previous section. To the extent that foreign policy must be decided on the basis of executive-legislative collaboration, it is subject to widely varying conditions the impact of which on policy varies. Variation is possible between relatively rigid Congressional control and broad executive freedom, between temporary deadlock and the "honeymoon" period following the election of a new President, between noisy argument and quiet discussion, between great activity and almost no activity. All this spells uncertainty. No one has yet discovered a particular set of conditions which will automatically sustain a durable, smooth, mutually satisfying relationship. The appearance of indefinite cycles and phases complicates the decision-making process and renders uncertain the prosecution of programs already adopted. From the standpoint of the Executive Branch, the proper exercise of its responsibilities rests on a prediction of the possible conditions (and their effects) which may prevail. To be sure, officials on the executive side can exert some control on the equation, but the very essense of the President-Congress relationship is that it is badly structured in the foreign-policy realm at this stage in the nation's history. Estimates are difficult and may have unforeseen consequences. If the executive underestimates what is possible, uses caution, and proceeds slowly, valuable time may be lost. If the executive overestimates, defeat may be risked or the price of forced victory may be reflected in hostility on later issues.

CHAPTER TWELVE

EXECUTIVE-LEGISLATIVE RELATIONS AND THE PROBLEM OF A BIPARTISAN FOREIGN POLICY (*Continued*)

Some Conditions of Effective and Responsible Interaction between the President and Congress • Responses Which Tend to Undermine Harmonious Interaction • "Bipartisan" Foreign Policy—an Adaptation to the Need for Harmonious, Effective, Responsible Interaction • The Problem of Executive-Legislative Relations Reconsidered • Conclusion • Selected Bibliography

Having established the complex patterns of executive-legislative relations and having defined the problems which flow from the separation of powers, the analysis can be carried a step further. To highlight the adaptations which have been made to the problems cited and to provide a backdrop for a brief review of various proposed "solutions," two questions must be asked: What are the conditions of a harmonious, effective, responsible interaction between the President and Congress? What factors tend to undermine such conditions? After some tentative answers to these questions have been stated, an extended discussion of "bipartisanship" will be in order. Finally, the whole problem of executive-legislative cooperation will be reconsidered in terms of typical proposals for improvement.

It should be remembered at this mid-point that these two chapters attempt simultaneously to describe and to analyze an important aspect of foreign-policy decision making in the United States *and* to focus attention on a crucial problem area. The two purposes are related because diagnosis of the problem can be no more adequate than the analysis of the process or system to which it is related. If one is interested primarily in the improvement of relations between the President and Congress, four possibilities are open: to alter in some way the patterns described above and thus to eliminate difficulties and weaknesses; to correct one or more of the six sources of difficulties which inhere in the patterns; to remove the occasions for hostile and mistrustful responses by each branch; and to develop adaptive devices which enable the participants to "live with" the situation at minimum cost in time, resources, and sound policies.

▶ SOME CONDITIONS OF EFFECTIVE AND RESPONSIBLE INTERACTION BETWEEN THE PRESIDENT AND CONGRESS

Studies of the American political system usually discuss the over-all relationship between the President and Congress in terms of conflict and cooperation—the more of one, the less of the other. According to this formulation, the existing state of affairs with respect to the patterns discussed in the last chapter can be located somewhere along a continuum ranging from total conflict to total cooperation. The total relationship is then said to be more cooperative or more conflicting, as the case may be.

Without entering into a lengthy semantic argument, one can recognize several objections to the cooperation-conflict frame of reference. Cooperation is not easy to define; it may mean a number of things including complete capitulation of one of the parties to a relationship and "bribed interdependence" wherein there is reluctant joint action because the parties to the relationship find it impossible to do without each other. In other words, cooperation does not necessarily connote a healthy relationship. On the other hand, conflict is not always harmful—it depends on what kind it is and how it is controlled. To eliminate all conflict of values between the President and Congress would be to eliminate some vital intellectual ingredients from the policy-making process. Another objection to labeling the total relationship between the branches as "cooperative" or "conflicting" is that important differentiations are swallowed up. For example, there may be open opposition to a presidential nomination placed before the Senate Foreign Relations Committee; yet at the same time the committee's staff and representatives of the State Department may be working closely on the text of a treaty. Either label—"cooperative" or "conflicting"—may obscure significant actions and conditions which do not conveniently fit. If an attempt is made to define those labels in terms of the number of "defeats" sustained by the President or gained by Congress, analysis is reduced to scorekeeping. Not only does this help transform policy making into a contest between adversaries, but it tends to focus attention only on the dramatic episodes. Not that such are insignificant, but the dramatic quality may be superimposed by the treatment given in newspapers and by the hot words of officials uttered on the spur of the moment. Furthermore, the judgment of what is a defeat will differ, depending on the criteria employed. A defeat of a foolish policy might well be a victory for the system even though one party was successfully opposed.

Accordingly, perhaps it is more rewarding to think of the conditions of effective and responsible interaction between the executive and legislative branches along the lines suggested in other chapters. Thus the precision and clarity of powers and functions, appropriate motivations, open communications, adequate information, and required intellectual skills properly applied to policy problems would become foundation stones. To find out whether the conditions of decision making will permit or do permit effective and responsible interaction, it is necessary to know the rules by which the participants guide their behavior: How are roles interpreted and what agreed limits, if any, are placed upon expanded interpretations? What kinds of acts are regarded as hostile, as violations of the requirements of the system? What kinds of behavior and conditions produce frustration and anxiety on the part of the participants? What, if any, are the rules for settling conflicts within the decisional system—conflicts of role interpretation, conflicts of value, and conflicts of perspective? What kinds of strategies and tactics— legislative, presidential, policy selling—tend to facilitate or block the inter- action process? Answers to these questions are to be found ultimately in a factual examination of the American foreign-policy-making system. It will be helpful, too, to bear in mind the distinction between major and minor decisions or policies, and between policy as rules and policy as action. In general, it can be argued that the national security depends heavily on the success with which major decisions are made and clear, agreed guides to future action are evolved.

In the best of all possible worlds, the decision-making process would result in rational action (effective policies) responsibly arrived at and would always manifest a mature response to the external environment. The decision- making system could hardly meet these standards unless relations within the system met the same criteria—that actions of congressmen and executive offi- cials are rational in terms of the purposes of the system, that their behavior constitutes a mature response to the requirements of the system, and that the various responsibility equations (Congress and the voters, committees and the total membership of Congress, Congress and the President, among presidential agencies) are preserved. Thus the three criteria—effectiveness, responsibility, maturity—would be met both in the way action was taken and in the sub- stance of the action itself. If these conditions were to prevail, it would not necessarily mean that the difficulties and problems outlined above would dis- appear, although some might. Rather, it would mean that these difficulties would be held within narrower limits. Hostility, frustration, and mistrust would be kept to a minimum in order that disagreements could be explored calmly and on their merits. Self-restraint would be exercised in order to allay suspicions as to motivations. Rules and standards would be worked out care- fully so that disputes could be subjected to impersonal settlement. The decision-making system would be constantly examined for trouble spots and for possible improvements.

Interactions under these conditions would be reasonably harmonious and certainly effective. Difficulties inherent in the two-thirds rule, presidential agreements, approval of nominations, legislative strategy, communications, investigations, and party politics would be partially eliminated, and if they did arise would not be permitted to undermine responsible, rational action. The potential conflict of roles between the President and Congress would be circumscribed by a more precise allocation of powers and functions. Rules would be devised for handling the consequences of overlapping jurisdictions. Organizational reforms would be carried out with role requirements in mind. A periodic review of the general role of each branch in view of changed conditions would take place. Coordination would permit complete identification, integration, and reconciliation of the different perspectives and values held by each. Presidential and Congressional decisional units would have free access to information and analytical skills adequate and appropriate enough to enable functions to be performed effectively. Party disagreements would consist of honest differences of opinion mobilized for presentation by party leadership, and foreign-policy issues would not be subordinated to a struggle for power and prestige. Finally, uncertainties concerning behavior in the two branches would be reduced through a stabilization of expectations which would minimize guesswork in the employment of strategies of action.

In actuality these conditions are rarely approximated. However, it is revealing to compare the real and the ideal as a basis for describing and assessing the existing system. Discrepancies between what is and what might be and some of the reasons for the discrepancies have already been presented.

The difficulties and problems cited are intensified by certain emotional responses on the part of members of Congress and officials of the Executive Branch which reflect as well as create disharmony, mistrust, frustration, and hostility. What are the typical stimuli which seem to produce these reactions? It goes without saying that the responses cited below relate back to the patterns and consequences discussed in Chapter Eleven.

► RESPONSES WHICH TEND TO UNDERMINE HARMONIOUS INTERACTION

CONGRESSIONAL RESPONSES

1. A week after hearings by the House Armed Services Committee on unification in the spring of 1950, Admiral Denfield was fired as Chief of Naval Operations. The committee said: "The removal of Admiral Denfield unquestionably tends to intimidate witnesses from the Executive Branch. It greatly aggravates the ever-present difficulty of obtaining uninhibited testimony upon which to base legislative decisions." Nearly three years later Senator McCarthy insisted successfully that a State Department employee be reinstated to a position from which he was demoted after testifying for the senator's investigation of the way the department had handled its loyalty and security problems. In recent years, Congress has repeatedly attempted to lay hold of departmental files containing information allegedly needed to carry

on investigations. President Truman (1945 to 1952) refused to open security and loyalty files and withheld a secret diary kept by Secretary of Defense Forrestal. In general, Congress resents executive hampering of investigations. President Truman never quite lived down his phrase "red herring" concerning Congressional charges of Communist infiltration in the State Department.

Frustration in this connection is compounded by the fact that several important executive agencies must perforce carry on their activities in secret— the National Security Council and the Central Intelligence Agency. Hidden behind the doors of the latter are operations of vital significance for national security, i.e., estimates of Soviet capabilities and intentions, operations of which Congress supposedly can have no knowledge. There were indications in 1953 that Congress was growing weary of the arrangement.

2. Whatever else may be said about budget procedures (weaknesses of Congress with respect to the federal budget have been commented on in another chapter), Congress tends to feel overwhelmed by the strategy and tactics of presentation utilized by the Executive Branch. As is well known, the budget is an enormous document—the 1952–1953 version weighed 5¾ pounds, consisted of 1,316 pages, and asked for $85.4 billion. Thousands of budgeteers in many executive offices work all year round on segments of the final product; millions of man-hours go into its preparation. Roughly five hundred experts in the Bureau of the Budget alone work not only on amounts but on the manner of presentation. During testimony, graphs, charts, models, and special reports bombard the handful of congressmen (plus their small staff) whose task it is to make some sort of judgment on the wisdom of the amounts requested. Disregarding for the moment the question of whether executive officials do deliberately try to "fool" Congress, the effect of the appearance of bureau heads from the White House, the Pentagon, and other agencies has been described by Congressman Scrivner (Republican, Kansas, a member of the defense subcommittee of the House Appropriations Committee): "Every time a bureau or department chief comes before us to present his little segment of this program, he has with him anywhere from nine to seventeen assistants, ranging all the way from majors up to three-star generals. . . . There we are, seven of us on our side of the table, with two assistants, and there they are on the other. . . . It makes us feel many times absolutely futile and helpless."* Furthermore, Congress appears to believe that executive agencies automatically ask for more than they really need. Every request is suspect; yet Congress is frustrated by a lack of means to prove conclusively that its suspicions are in fact justified.

3. Congress lives in apprehension that the President or his staff will commit the national legislature to a policy *in advance* of Congressional discussion or knowledge. While the North Atlantic Alliance was being hammered out during 1948–1949, the State Department announced the amount

---

* Quoted in Douglas Cater, "The Power of the Purse and the Congressman's Plight," *Reporter,* December 11, 1951, p. 26.

of arms aid requested by America's future allies and revealed the total amount to be submitted to Congress. The proposal for military aid was definitely linked to the treaty. A bitter outburst in Congress resulted. Leaders protested that an attempt was being made to commit Congress in advance by grouping the two measures. On another level, Congressional leaders of both parties grew increasingly critical of the so-called secret provisions of the Yalta Agreement (the United States, the Soviet Union, and Great Britain) as difficulties in Far Eastern policy intensified after 1950. It will be recalled that on several occasions Congress has demanded to know the content of personal discussions between the President and ranking diplomats of other states.

4. After Congress has agreed to the general outlines of a policy or a program of action, bungling or, from Congress's viewpoint, deliberate sabotage at the implementation stage prompts hostility and tempts Congressional meddling in purely executive functions. A prime example is the series of Congressional attacks on the United States Information Program, particularly the Voice of America. From 1950 onward, the Program was condemned as poorly planned, mismanaged, and ineffectual. Senator McCarthy's investigation in 1953, in the eyes of most competent observers, was carried to the point where the Voice of America was almost paralyzed. In other words, Congressional frustration has some roots in the fact that to implement policy is often to remake policy. In 1950, the House Appropriations Committee accused the President of "thwarting a major policy of Congress" by impounding funds appropriated the previous year for the maintenance of a 58-group Air Force.

5. Impatience with executive experts and diplomats also arises from what Congress considers to be "soft" handling of friends and allies. An outpouring of billions, in Congress's eyes, justifies the expectation, even requires, that the recipients will be willing to take advice from the United States and show their appreciation. Members of the Executive Branch allow gratitude to be forgotten and fail to insist that advice be accepted by friends and allies.

6. Obviously Congress does not like to be "left out" of important decisions—a corollary of disliking to be committed in advance. Perhaps this is the most chronic, deep-seated source of ill feeling. It applies to all basic decisions, not just to those involving the powers of Congress. Both houses were resentful when the President decided to commit American troops to the defense of Korea without adequate prior consultation or even formal notification afterward. In particular, Congress's own foreign-policy experts—the key committee chairmen—dislike to have their associates read about developments in the papers. When the Korean cease-fire proposal to Communist China was announced in January, 1951, Senator Connally (chairman of the Senate Foreign Relations Committee) publicly told the State Department he wished it would stop making major decisions without consulting his committee.

7. Though heavily dependent on executive sources for much foreign-policy information, Congress does not always trust administrative communiqués on foreign affairs. Often Congress suspects that executive officials are attempting to make their case in advance by encouraging public attitudes which will make it difficult for Congress to reject their interpretation of a problem or an issue. Sometimes this resentment centers on the President himself, who may take his case directly to the people via radio or television in an effort to create pressure behind Congress, so to speak. More often, however, resentment is caused when executive agencies employ press agents and public relations counsels to "explain" their programs and to build public support. Periodically, Congress tries to eliminate the funds which sustain such tactics, but without much success. Not only does Congress resent the use of these facilities in attacks on its membership; it worries over the very fine line between "information" and "persuasion." The former is essential to democracy, the latter converts various executive groups into lobbyists who bring their own special pressures on Congress.

EXECUTIVE RESPONSES

1. Presidential frustration arising from the crucial position of the Senate has been a prominent feature of foreign-policy making since the day George Washington vowed never to appear before the Senate again to discuss a treaty. Republican and Democratic Presidents alike have chafed under senatorial delays and refusals. Naturally, this has led to presidential outbursts on the competence, good sense, and character of members of the upper chamber. After the Senate had refused to approve a protocol he had arranged with Santo Domingo, Theodore Roosevelt in 1905 said: "The Senate is wholly incompetent to take such a part." When the Senate blocked a bill to arm merchant vessels, Woodrow Wilson made his famous declaration that "a little group of willful men, representing no opinion but their own, have rendered the great government of the United States helpless and contemptible." In 1951, President Truman bemoaned the fact that it sometimes takes the Senate "a year to be prompt." During the early days of President Eisenhower's administration the Senate took over three weeks to confirm the appointment of Mr. Charles Bohlen as Ambassador to Moscow.

2. It ought to be evident by this time that it takes a great deal of effort to mobilize the Executive Branch behind an important policy. Then, after months or even years of labor to get a proposal before Congress, it is possible that parliamentary maneuvering may result in shelving it without the merits of the proposal ever being at issue. Such was the case in March, 1952, when a confused parliamentary situation in the House of Representatives killed a universal military training plan for eighteen-year-olds. The President and his staff are always at the mercy of procedural bungling on the floor of either house. In August, 1949, when the State Department was seeking the means to use economic and arms aid with respect to the rapidly deteriorating situa-

tion in China, the House Rules Committee blocked consideration for reasons which apparently had little to do with the actual contents of the legislation.

3. A significant source of executive annoyance with Congress is the legislative rider, referred to earlier as a Congressional tool for influencing foreign policy. Commenting bitterly on House Resolution 3587 (interim) Deficiency Appropriation Bill, President Truman said on June 2, 1951: "This rider—Section 1302—makes broad and sweeping changes in our procedures for restricting trade between the free world and the Soviet Union and its satellites. It is thus a major piece of legislation affecting our foreign policy, but it was never considered by the House Foreign Affairs Committee or the Senate Foreign Relations Committee."*

4. During the past four years, to a degree never previously matched, executive officials have resented certain by-products or accompaniments of legitimate Congressional investigations. From the viewpoint of these officials, they have been subjected to irresponsible, libelous, personal attacks far beyond policy disagreements or even incompatibility on personality grounds. Under the cloak of Congressional immunity, key members, in public and private hearings and press releases, have made accusations to which no real answer was possible. Secretary of State Acheson was once characterized by Senator McCarthy as "the elegant and alien Acheson—Russian as to heart, British as to manner."† General George Marshall (who served as both Secretary of State and Secretary of Defense) was once characterized in the following fashion by Senator Jenner: "He not only is willing, he is eager to play the role of front man for traitors. The truth is that this is no new role for him, for General George C. Marshall is a living lie."‡ Continuous slander not only puts top-level decision makers under terrific pressure but tends to undermine public confidence in them and to reduce their effectiveness in dealing with other countries. Given the great increase in the number of Congressional investigations, executive officials must spend more and more time testifying, thus reducing the time and energy available for regular duties.

5. As already mentioned, a favorite technique of Congress is to pick out certain officials or factions within the Executive Branch and to use their statements, policy views, and influence as techniques for weakening the solidarity of the Executive Branch or the President's leadership. It becomes very difficult for decisions to be adhered to and for cooperation to be effective if Congress sides with a minority group in the Executive Branch in such a way as to alter power relations within that branch. Whatever the merits of General MacArthur's military and political judgment, it became increasingly harder for President Truman and the Joint Chiefs of Staff to retain their rightful control over policy after a large segment of Congress embraced the general as "theirs." When the Bureau of the Budget after long study and consultation

---

* New York *Times*, June 3, 1951, p. 12.
† *Ibid.*
‡ *Ibid.*

decides on a certain appropriation for the Air Force, it is upsetting to have Congress yield to the pleas for a substantial increase above that amount. There have even been cases where Congress has encouraged a revolt against executive order. Disgruntled officials whose recommendations have been rejected by the President or some other superior make welcome spokesmen for Congressional viewpoints. The President is more or less continuously threatened by the possibility of embarrassment of this sort.

6. Since 1948, representatives and senators have traveled extensively abroad—sometimes on government business, sometimes not. Irritation and harm to the activities of the policy makers may result. Unwise statements made while abroad may require months of careful repair work. Such was the case when Senator Thomas, traveling in Europe in 1947, called the Swedes "ingrates." Globe-trotting legislators often bombard embassy staffs with requests for special favors and services of all kinds. Occasionally American diplomats are embarrassed by the attempts of visiting legislators to by-pass the diplomatic establishment and to discuss policy matters with the heads of states. Thus certain United States Senators talked directly to General Franco of Spain about a possible loan without first clearing their plans with the American embassy in Madrid.

7. A basic handicap in the discharge of executive responsibilities is the problem of predicting Congressional reactions and voting line-ups. Apparently it is almost impossible to predict (within a reasonably small margin of error) *who* in Congress will oppose a foreign-policy measure, *how* intense their opposition will be, what *form* it will take, and what *strategies* will be most effective in overcoming it. Further complications arise when there is a small number of senators who aspire to important roles in foreign policy and when the numbers of Republicans and Democrats are very close. In November, 1950, two years after the election of Democratic President Truman, there were forty-seven Republicans (counting five who might bolt the party) and forty-nine Democrats (of whom twelve might oppose the administration). In January, 1952, the number of anti-Truman senators was fifty despite a nominal superiority of Democrats. President Eisenhower confronted a Senate of forty-eight Democrats, forty-seven Republicans, and one Independent in 1954. Under these circumstances, the President must usually count on a temporary coalition of four or five groups around a solid core of regulars in either house. This same coalition might not, however, be possible for the next issue. The matter of individual opposition is even more difficult. Certainly President Eisenhower and Secretary of State Dulles were not able to anticipate the last-ditch opposition of Republican Senator McCarthy to the nomination of Charles Bohlen as Ambassador to the Soviet Union.

GENERAL CONDITIONS AFFECTING RESPONSES

Needless to say, whether these responses are held to a minimum or are intensified depends on certain conditions. Ordinarily reactions of the foregoing sort are less serious during the "honeymoon" period—immediately after the national triumph of a new President and his party. Toward the end of a given President's administration when it is unlikely he will or can seek re-election, intensification is to be expected. A crisis period may put such a premium on executive leadership that usual reactions are submerged by others which sustain quick, harmonious action. On the other hand, when a turning point is reached, when past courses of action are being re-examined, negative responses may be intensified. The climate of public opinion also enters in. A mood which favors either presidential dominance or Congressional resurgence will probably result in increased hostility because the behavior patterns which produce adverse reactions are normally typical of attempts to expand the role of one branch or to maintain the *status quo* in the face of pressure for change. Finally, it is obvious that manifestations of hostility and frustration will be related to the key personalities involved. If the handful of key figures in executive-legislative relations concerning foreign policy do not get along well together or dislike each other personally, antagonisms latent in the system will be accentuated.

► "BIPARTISAN" FOREIGN POLICY—AN ADAPTATION TO THE NEED FOR HARMONIOUS, EFFECTIVE, RESPONSIBLE INTERACTION

One of the most significant recent developments in the processes of policy formation is the so-called "bipartisan" foreign policy. This development appears to be an outgrowth of the peculiar characteristics of the American political system which have already been mentioned—separation of powers, joint exercise of powers by the President and Congress, and Congressional organization and procedures. Thoroughly mixed in with these features are the organization and operation of the two major parties. One adaptation to the latter in the area of foreign-policy making has been "bipartisanship" which is, accordingly, part and parcel of the larger problem of legislative-executive relations as outlined.

THE ROLE OF PARTIES GENERALLY

Before discussing the origin and nature of the bipartisan approach, it seems desirable to say something about the general connections between the party system and foreign policy. Numerous allusions, direct and indirect, to this subject have been made at various points in previous chapters. The key to a brief set of reminders concerning the role of parties lies in the realization that many kinds of reality are implied in the term "party system": The national party as a vehicle of nomination and election, a loose coalition of factions and state organization formed for limited purposes such as formulating platforms and electing a President and a Vice-President; all the state and local units whose interests and problems may be quite different from those of the national organization—it is here that the control over senatorial and Congressional nominations rests; the party leaders who comprise the administration under the direction of the head of the party, the President; the party members who occupy the key roles in Congress, presiding officers, floor leaders, and others; the party as a set of values and interests which influence the judgment and behavior of individual members; the party as a voting bloc of varying periods of duration on a varying range of policies; and, finally, the party as a vehicle of personal ambition and achievement.

The President is, of course, the national party chief, and what he says and does has great weight and can certainly influence the fortunes of individual members of his party. Yet the efforts of strong Presidents like Woodrow Wilson and Franklin D. Roosevelt to intervene in local elections or to purge undesirables or to ensure a majority of support in Congress have not been successful. Nor can the President control nominations. In off-year Congressional elections, the President's majority is more likely to be weakened than strengthened. Party leaders in Congress have little control (in the strict sense) over individual members. Committee chairmen can, if they wish, function independently of both the President and the majority leader. Revolts against the party leadership can occur and it is seldom that a near unanimous party vote can be "delivered" for major measures. It is also probably true that the election of most representatives to Congress is not affected by foreign-policy issues in any significant way. On balance, it can be argued that the real disagreements over foreign policy have been not so much partisan as regional, economic, or broadly ideological. That is, party values in the narrow sense compete with the preferences of a particular body of constituents, with economic interests which need protection, and with the cluster of personal values (views of the external setting, and the like) held by the individual congressman or senator. Obviously, loyalty to a party position is a crucial factor for some members of Congress under some circumstances. Existing evidence, however, does not entirely support the general proposition that party affiliation is a dominant source of values and inspiration.

Given the events from 1950 onward, which culminated in the bitter foreign-policy fight in the 1952 presidential election, it may seem an exaggeration to state that, all things considered, parties as such have played a relatively minor role in the formation of policy. Until quite recently, foreign-policy issues have been of direct prominence in few national elections. The long predominance of domestic problems, rivalry between President and Congress, personal political conflicts, and unique wartime situations have all conspired to prevent the evolution of a clear pattern of Republican or Democratic foreign policy. Despite changing party control over the years, consistent lines of policy were developed until the outbreak of World War II. Party platforms, when they have dealt with foreign policy, have not—again, until recently—revealed any clear tendency for national conventions to serve as vehicles for the clarification and consolidation of coherent party stands.

Most of the votes in the Senate on major policies during the past decade have revealed clear two-party backing: joining the United Nations, 89 to 2; the Mutual Security Act of 1951, 61 to 5; the Mutual Security Act of 1952, 64 to 10; the Japanese Peace Treaty, 66 to 10; the agreement on relations with Germany, 77 to 5—to name only a few of the recent ones. Furthermore, the vote on other major issues reveals that where a majority of each party voted on each side of an issue, the measure would not have passed had not a minimum number of the opposition party voted in favor. An example was the loan to Great Britain in 1946, when the vote in the House of Representatives followed this pattern: Democrats, 157 for, 32 against; Republicans, 61 for and 122 against. Hence if 34 more Republicans had voted against, the bill would have failed. Another example was the House vote on the Greek-Turkish Aid Bill in 1947 (the Truman Doctrine): Democrats, 160 for and 13 against; Republicans, 127 for and 94 against. Now while it is accurate to say that the Democrats were more solidly in favor of this action than the Republicans, nevertheless a truly Republican vote (i.e., 90 per cent of the party, say) would have caused defeat. During President Eisenhower's first six months he could thank the Democrats for his victories in twenty-three of thirty-one situations where presidential aims clashed with the Congressional sentiment as expressed by a majority of his own party. It is generally agreed that solid Democratic support saved the foreign-aid program from further cuts in June, 1953.

This kind of occurrence can be partly explained by the fact that behind the party labels are voting blocs which cut across Republican and Democratic categories. Over a period of time (assuming no change in the President) most members of Congress can be classified into three general groups in terms of whether they support or oppose the administration on foreign-policy issues always, most always, or occasionally. To take another approach, potential voting blocs can be sorted out on the basis of a crude nationalist-internationalist split. Here one might expect to find a relatively small number voting consistently for and against the main lines of American policy in the postwar period. A larger number would fall into the internationalist category (including probably more Democrats than Republicans at this writing) though differing with the more consistent group in opposing at least some measures and standing for different emphases—such as favoring a more vigorous Far Eastern policy and less concentration on Europe. A fourth group would be made up of those voting against most measures which could be called internationalist except for the NATO program and limited foreign aid. These groups, of course, might be related to the twofold ideological split within each party— the more liberal and the more conservative. In turn the ideological split is related to regional, economic, and population factors.

Despite the implication of the foregoing that it is difficult to isolate neatly something called "party influence" in the formation of foreign policy, a number of connecting links and correlations can be pointed out. In 1954 it was possible to say, for example, that a *plurality* of Republicans *tended* to be more skeptical of the possibilities for a genuine defense community in Western Europe and to be more restricted in the amount of American accommodation to the wishes or needs of friends and allies which they thought was necessary. A *plurality* of Democrats appeared to feel otherwise. Again, a *majority* of Republicans wanted the President's power to lower tariffs under the Reciprocal Trade Agreements Act curbed, while a *majority* of Democrats did not. By the use of explicit criteria and voting statistics one can demonstrate that Democrats have been less "isolationist" and less "nationalist" in their preferences for various policies than have the Republicans in given time periods. It is also easy to establish that a majority of one party or the other voted yea or nay on particular bills. Such tabulations and correlations do not, of course, prove that votes were cast primarily because of loyalty to a party line.

Party spokesmen in Congress—the presiding officer, the majority and minority floor leaders, policy committee chairmen, regular committee chairmen—may declare an official position on particular foreign-policy issues. Individual members may regard themselves as bound by these views and by the views of the President if he is of their party. Obviously intraparty decisions on leadership roles and committee assignments have had a direct influence on the way policy issues have been handled and on whether key posts are occupied by members with one kind of approach to foreign policy or with one set of values rather than another. In individual cases the fact that a senator comes from a state where ethnic minorities are important in the vote may heavily influence the stand he takes on immigration matters or on general policy relating to particular foreign countries. Senator Ferguson of Michigan (up for re-election in 1954) probably had in mind the Polish districts of the industrial areas of his state when he took a leading role in denouncing Mr. Charles Bohlen's "connection" with the Yalta Agreement, one provision of which allegedly "sold out" Poland to the Soviet Union.

From the President's point of view the frequent shakiness of his majority in Congress may confront him with an important choice in strategy. On the one hand, by treating Congress very carefully and by making concessions he would otherwise not make, he can try to preserve his narrow voting margin intact. Or he may seek more freedom by reliance on a two-party coalition, which is less fragile—at least on larger questions. That he must pay a price in either case is due less to the separation of powers than to the nature of the party system.

Nothing said thus far should be construed as a denial that the parties as presently constituted cannot act as cohesive forces for certain purposes. From 1950 onward, the Republicans in both houses appeared to follow a consistent, well-disciplined campaign to discredit Secretary of State Acheson and many of his policies and to turn certain foreign-policy issues into political liabilities for the Truman Administration. As the 1952 national election moved nearer, the Republican leaders were calculating every move in terms of whether it would strengthen their presidential campaign. Also during this period, 118 House Republicans took the rather unusual step of signing a resolution declaring that the United States should concentrate on hemisphere defense and pay less attention to more far-flung arrangements and in January, 1952, 38 Republican senators declared they had completely lost confidence in Dr. Philip C. Jessup, President Truman's interim appointee to represent the United States on the Security Council.

While very few national elections in the nation's history have turned primarily on foreign relations, elections can actually and potentially affect foreign policy in several ways. Perhaps the most important effect is the possibility of paralysis of foreign-policy decision making during the campaign and during the eighty-six days between Election Day and the inauguration of a newly elected President—a situation which is likely to prevail whether debate over foreign-policy matters has been sharp or not. It is probably not an exaggeration to say that it was in part because of the exceedingly lively nature of the 1952 presidential election that certain decisions with respect to the North Atlantic Treaty Organization and the European Defense Army had to be postponed from June, 1952, to February, 1953. During the fall of 1952, debate on the Korean and Tunisian questions in the General Assembly of the United Nations came to a standstill because authoritative statements of American policy could not be obtained just before, and even some weeks after, the election. A campaign sometimes compels or tempts a President to be less than frank with the general public or, on the other hand, he may make campaign promises which circumstances may not let him keep. In 1940, the world was at war but America was still technically neutral. The risk was great that President Roosevelt would have been denounced as a warmonger if he revealed all he knew or if he attempted openly to lead public opinion. There may also be a temptation for the President to create, by shrewd statecraft, the illusion that he and his party are indispensable.

THE PROBLEM OF PARTY POLITICS AND FOREIGN POLICY

Everyone agrees that foreign policy is weakened if it becomes a "political football." Why is this so? The chief danger of election campaigns and other manifestations of partisan activity is that values appropriate to foreign policy are pushed aside in favor of the quest for power or the pursuit of objectives which have nothing to do with national security. Things are said and done *solely* for their effect on personal and party political fortunes. Support for policy becomes precarious. Criticism becomes irresponsible. When Congress and the presidency are controlled by different parties, executive-legislative conflict is usually aggravated.

The problem created by party politics is threefold: first, a minimum continuity in policy is required despite possible overturns in the House and Senate every two years and in the presidency every four years; second, national unity in a time of crisis is an obvious necessity; yet unity must not be allowed to snuff out healthy responsible opposition and argument in the policy-making process; and third, opposition and argument should not be carried to the point where needless uncertainty makes it difficult for other nations to deal with the United States. Former Secretary of State James F. Byrnes had these troublesome dilemmas in mind when he said: "Twice in a generation doubt as to American foreign policy has led other nations to miscalculate the consequences of their actions. Twice in our generation that doubt as to American foreign policy has not brought peace but war."* He was referring, of course, to the eventual involvement of the United States in two world wars when some of the belligerents based their policies on the assumption that America would stay out.

ORIGIN AND EVOLUTION OF BIPARTISANSHIP

Although the conduct of World War II quickly became a two-party enterprise with prominent Republicans Knox and Stimson serving as Secretaries of Navy and War, respectively, the real impetus toward bipartisanship came with the realization that recurrence of such events as the unfortunate demise of Woodrow Wilson's League of Nations proposal and America's failure to participate in the building of peace after victory had to be avoided. Costly mistakes on both sides of Capitol Hill had been responsible. Early in the war, Secretary of State Cordell Hull began regular discussions with members of Congress on postwar foreign-policy problems. Throughout 1942 and early 1943, leading members of the Senate Foreign Relations Committee and the House Foreign Affairs Committee from both parties met with the secretary and other officials of the State Department for briefing and to discuss the broad outlines of postwar policy. On March 16, 1943, two Republican senators (Ball and Burton) and two Democratic senators (Hill and Hatch) introduced a resolution asking that the United States take the lead in calling meetings to form an organization of the United Nations. The Fulbright Resolution (House Concurrent Resolution 25) was passed by the House on September 21, 1943. After several outstanding public speeches during the summer of 1943 on the Ball-Burton-Hatch-Hill Resolution, the Senate passed the Connally Resolution (Senate Resolution 192 as amended) on November 5, 1943—the vote being 85 to 5. Both the Fulbright and the Connally Resolutions were passed after days of discussion and both put the members of the two major parties in each house squarely on the record as favoring *the idea* of participation in an international organization. In March, 1944, Secretary Hull appointed a bipartisan Congressional committee to aid in drafting a Charter to be considered at the Dumbarton Oaks conference of the Big Four powers—China, Great Britain, the Soviet Union, and the United States. Key members of both parties comprised the American delegation to the United Nations Conference of May, 1945, which approved the present Charter. In

---

* Address at the American Club, Paris, France, October 3, 1946.

une, 1945, the United States Senate accepted, by a vote of 89 to 2, the participation of this country in a new international organization which had far
more power than the rejected League of Nations.

Meanwhile bipartisanship was developing in other ways. Prior to the real
heart of the presidential campaign of 1944, Secretary Hull met with John
Foster Dulles, foreign affairs adviser to Republican candidate Thomas Dewey.
They agreed that the future peace was "a nonpartisan topic." Mr. Dewey suppressed whatever desire he may have had to make campaign capital out of
foreign-policy issues. Though not quite as effective, a similar agreement (tacit,
probably) appears to have held for Mr. Dewey's candidacy in 1948. During
a period when the Democrats dominated the presidency, Republicans attended
the Mexico City Conference of 1945, the first meeting of the Council of
Foreign Ministers in September, 1945, the Moscow Conference of 1946,
and sessions of the United Nations General Assembly. By early 1949, bipartisanship had become a well-established tradition. Blair Bolles was able to
write: "A large portion of the record of the United States in international
relations since it accepted in 1945 a position of leadership in peacetime world
affairs is the fruit of the bipartisan system."[*]

Several things are worth noting at this point. It is hardly possible to separate bipartisanship and executive-legislative collaboration in general; Democrats might as easily have defeated the United Nations Charter. The approach,
which originated in the desire to avoid Woodrow Wilson's plight and particularly to minimize the role of foreign-policy issues in presidential elections,
was later broadened to include other purposes. During the period of its development, 1942–1948, the Democrats were continuously in control of the executive, the Republicans intermittently in control of Congress.

THE MULTIPLE MEANINGS OF "BIPARTISANSHIP"

Thus far it has been assumed that the meaning of the term "bipartisanship" is simple and commonly agreed upon. Such is not the case, however.
Verbal expressions as well as the actual consequences of the approach indicate
that at least six different interpretations of the term are current.

1. Consultation between the Executive Branch and party leaders. This
would appear to be the core concept, as it were. Yet the questions *who?
how? when?* have been answered in various ways. It is generally assumed
that the initiative for bipartisan consultation rests with the Executive Branch.
If so, *with whom* must the President or the Secretary of State consult? At
various times and on various issues, both the number and the constituency
of the group consulted have been different. Practice indicates that the ranking
members of the Senate Foreign Relations Committee are basic to any consultative system—this would include, of course, the chairman and the senior
minority party member as well as two or three others from each party

---

[*] Blair Bolles, "Bipartisanship in American Foreign Policy," *Foreign Policy
Reports,* January 1, 1949.

selected for their judgment, prestige, or experience. When the House is in cluded, the same would hold for the House Foreign Affairs Committee Senator Taft once used the phrase "the responsible representatives of th Republicans in Congress." This is, notably, an ambiguous phrase, but it als suggests that the above group may be inadequate. Hence a second layer o Congressional officials may be involved: the majority leader or floor leader i each house, the whips, and the chairmen of the respective party Polic Committees. To this might be added the President of the Senate and th Speaker of the House, along with the chairmen or ranking members of certai relevant committees such as Armed Services, Appropriations, and Judiciary The outer layer of consultees has consisted of rank-and-file members of bot parties chosen, perhaps at random, for meetings at the White House or lunch eon with the secretary.

Thus there is a list of potentially "key figures" in Congress whom th Executive Branch may consult. And the corollary is that a principle of rep resentation is at work here. The leaders of the minority party must in effec represent the interests of their party. Not all the key figures in the develop ment of bipartisan collaboration have been in Congress and not all Con gressional leaders have always been included or have regarded themselves a bound by their colleagues who have been included. John Foster Dulles and Governor Dewey played leading roles, though neither was a Congressiona leader. Senator Taft, always a powerful figure, apparently played a minor role until Senator Vandenberg fell ill in 1950.

What does "consultation" really mean? Again, several answers are to be found in practice. As noted earlier in this chapter, it may mean *to inform* members of the minority party in advance of an action or in advance of news releases; *to listen* to their ideas and arguments at some point in the development of policy; *to take advice* by conceding modification of policies already pretty well formulated; *to engage in joint policy making*. In addition there are a variety of mechanisms through which each kind of consultation might be facilitated—briefing sessions, informal luncheons, executive sessions of committees, verbal and written, regular conferences, and so on. When Senator Johnson, Democratic floor leader, announced in February, 1953, that his party would cooperate to carry on a bipartisan approach "as soon as the machinery for such consultation is established," he did not specify what this might be.

Naturally enough, the Republicans during the years 1942 to 1948 and particularly since 1948 have insisted on a concept of bipartisan consultation which would fully admit them to the policy-making process. Both Senator Vandenberg (often called the real architect of the bipartisan approach) and Senator Taft agreed on this. Speaking of the Military Aid Bill in September, 1949 (when the Democrats controlled the Senate), Vandenberg said, "I think it is important that the public should know that the bill, as finally recommended by [our] committee, is a complete revision in all major aspects of the orm urged by the administration."* He also cited the development of the North Atlantic Alliance in 1948–1949 as a classic example of consultation n which the leaders of both parties actually helped draft treaty provisions. Senator Taft argued in March, 1950, that "to be bipartisan, there must be real consultation on policies *before* they are adopted, with the responsible representatives of the Republicans in Congress. . . . It . . . is *not accomplished* by the appointment of an individual Republican to executive office as a roving ambassador. . . ."† (He was referring to the appointment of John Foster Dulles as policy adviser to Secretary of State Acheson.) Senator Ives (Republican, New York) has also argued: ". . . Republicans should be given a voice at the *inception* of policies and should not be just in the position of being asked to approve and ratify something which the administration has worked out on its own."‡

2. *Exclusion of certain issues from presidential campaigns.* Generally speaking, the attempt to excude foreign-policy issues from political campaigns by means of an agreement between the candidates of two parties is done in order to prevent foreign policy from becoming a major campaign issue and to control criticism of the incumbent party in the interests of unity. There has been some difference of opinion as to what these inhibitions mean in practice but the objectives in the elections of 1944 and 1948 were clear. The Republicans in these two cases received confidential information via conferences in return for their restraint.

3. *Enduring support of policies after debate and normal constitutional processes.* Presumably a policy which has evolved laboriously through long executive and legislative processes, particularly when it is finally sealed by a substantial majority in the Senate, may be regarded as having a solid consensus to support it. Bipartisanship has come to mean a tacit pledge that settled areas of policy shall not be "unsettled" by capricious partisan attack. Unsettled areas of policy are obviously not included under this aspect, nor is criticism of the implementation of settled areas of policy.

4. *Bipartisan voting.* The phrase "bipartisan foreign policy" also refers to the degree of two-party support for policies on which Congress has an occasion to vote. A measure which would not pass on the basis of the majority party vote alone may be termed "bipartisan." Or a measure may be termed "bipartisan" if a majority or more of each party supported it. For eleven key foreign-policy issues in Congress from 1945 to 1948, support was overwhelmingly bipartisan—84 per cent of full two-party support.

5. *Elimination of purely partisan considerations in reaching agreement.* Secretary of State Hull, who began two-party consultation, thought that controversy and criticism between parties was permissible "provided the critic honestly bases his argument on his conception of our national interests; but

---

* Quoted by Arthur Krock, New York *Times,* July 6, 1951, p. 22.
† New York *Times,* March 22, 1950, p. 10.
‡ New York *Herald-Tribune,* March 20, 1950, Section 2, p. 1.

it is inadmissible to inject advantages of party or of person in foreign policy."*
Senator Vandenberg was fond of the word "unpartisan" and used it to
characterize the European Recovery Program. Five Republican representatives
in the House in July, 1948, stated: "We wish to do our part in determining
a foreign policy which is not a Democratic policy or a Republican policy
but an American policy."† Senator Smith (Republican, New Jersey) once
remarked "We want a part in framing policy, in the setting up of an all-
American policy."‡ The word "nonpartisan" has also been employed. Whatever the semantic differences here, two distinct notions are implicit in the
terminology and are rarely separated. One refers to a policy which is, so to
speak, a joint product of both parties and therefore cannot be claimed by
either as its triumph or contribution and cannot be criticized by either party
in connection with efforts to discredit the other in the eyes of the voters.
Presumably such a joint policy is less likely to become a political football. The
other notion is that of a policy which embodies *the national interest* as something quite different from a mere adding up of particular interests expressed
by the parties. One use defines bipartisan policy in terms of the way it is
reached; the other defines bipartisan policy in terms of the values and preferences which underlie it.

6. *Appointment of minority party members to responsible policy-making
roles.* The practice of appointing prominent senators to be delegates to international conferences goes back a good way, but in recent years it has been
followed much more extensively and with much greater consequences. In
addition, a new practice of appointing minority party representatives to permanent policy advisory posts in the State Department has grown up. Before
he became Secretary of State in January, 1953, the career of John Foster
Dulles, leading Republican expert on foreign affairs after World War II,
illustrates both developments. He attended the Dumbarton Oaks Conference
in 1944, and the San Francisco Conference of 1945 and was a leading member
of United States delegations in 1946, 1947, 1948, and 1950. In this capacity
he helped formulate American policy in the General Assembly of the United
Nations. Mr. Dulles also attended the first session of the Council of Foreign
Ministers in 1945. President Truman appointed him adviser to Secretary of
State Acheson in April, 1950. A few months later he took on the heavy
responsibility of negotiating the Japanese Peace Treaty.

Former Republican Senator Cooper of Kentucky was appointed to serve
under a Democratic administration as special adviser to Secretary of State
Acheson. In 1950 Senator Lodge (Republican, Massachusetts) served on the
Administrative and Budgetary Committee of the United Nations. Former
Republican Senator Warren Austin served as United States representative on

---

* Quoted in Blair Bolles, "Bipartisanship in American Foreign Policy," *Foreign
Policy Reports,* January 1, 1949, p. 2.
    † *Ibid.*
    ‡ New York *Herald-Tribune,* July 12, 1950, p. 10.

the Security Council and head of the United States mission to the United Nations from 1947 to 1952. At present, one Democrat and one Republican are appointed in alternate years from the Senate and House to serve on the delegation to the General Assembly. Senator Vandenberg not only went to the San Francisco Conference but also attended the second and third sessions of the Council of Foreign Ministers in 1946.

AGREEMENT AND DISAGREEMENT OVER THE NATURE OF BIPARTISANSHIP

To the extent that bipartisanship in foreign policy has been accepted as "good and right" by the public and the politicians, it is not a simple, well-defined thing; it is a mixture of several ideas and objectives. And it is impossible to tell at this time whether a new permanent practice has been added to policy making or whether the approach is another makeshift device for minimizing certain difficulties in specific situations. Agreement is lacking as to the character of a truly bipartisan policy. Certainly there is no agreement as to the range of foreign-policy topics and problems to be covered. Should short-term tactics and execution of policy be subject to this approach? Should all foreign-policy actions which can be taken by the executive be included as well as those requiring Congressional approval? Neither is there any agreement as to the institutional implementation required for bipartisan policy. Finally, though bipartisan collaboration has involved the acceptance of inhibitions in legislative and political conduct, there has been no real codification of the rights and duties appropriate to the majority and minority parties.

Despite the ambiguities and disagreements, there is a threefold common core of agreement: first, bipartisanship is expressed in a sharing of power and responsibilities between the major parties and between the executive and legislative branches; second, the aim of bipartisanship is a minimum harmony, unity, and consistency in foreign policy; third, the basis of harmony, unity and consistency, is agreement on fundamental principles and objectives.

BIPARTISANSHIP IN PRACTICE

The effort to take politics out of foreign-policy making yielded positive results during the period 1942 to 1948. The very least one can say is that there was a significant coincidence between the conscious attempt to reduce capricious party conflict or maneuvering and the fact that at no time during this period could it be said that the chief executive really lacked solid two-party support for major developments in foreign policy. However, after 1949 the bipartisan approach was in for rough going. There were always pressures at work against complete use of the approach and against its complete success. The election of 1952 grew out of and symbolized a serious breach between Congress and the President and between the two parties on certain important foreign-policy issues.

Although foreign policy was not a key topic in the 1948 election, the bipartisan tradition did not prevent Governor Dewey from appealing to blocs of voters on China policy and on the disposition of former Italian colonies in the peace settlement, nor did it prevent President Truman from appealing to them on the Palestine problem. During the 1948 campaign there was sharp criticism of President Truman's methods and efficiency which by implication included foreign affairs. In August, 1950, shortly after American intervention in Korea, four Republican members of the Senate Foreign Relations Committee issued a public statement charging bungling in Europe and Asia and expressing resentment at the Vandenberg-Dewey-Dulles policy of keeping politics out of the 1948 campaign.

In 1948 (the Eightieth Congress) the Republican party controlled both houses. Despite the fact that the European Recovery Program was a bipartisan triumph, individual Republicans occupying key positions continued to attack the program and to delay appropriations. A particularly bitter argument took place between Chairman Vandenberg of the Senate Foreign Relations Committee and Representative Taber, chairman of the House Appropriations Committee, over the latter's attempts to slash ERP funds. At the same time influential figures such as Senators Taft, Gurney, Wherry, and Brooks and Representatives Knutson and Mundt did not regard themselves as bound by the bipartisan cooperation of other Republican leaders. Senator Gurney spearheaded an eventually successful effort to appropriate a loan for Franco's Spain after that nation had been deliberately omitted from ERP.

As a matter of fact, certain areas of foreign policy have been excluded, by accident or design, from bipartisanship in any of its facets as described above. The Reciprocal Trade Agreements Act—foundation of economic foreign policy since 1934—was subject to increasing Republican opposition after the war. At various times when the act came up for renewal—1945, 1948, and 1951—Republican attacks were strong and the act survived by a straight party vote with only a small margin. Such subjects as support of a new Jewish state in Palestine, Latin-American policy generally, refugee questions, and China policy were all outside the bipartisan framework and this fact was openly recognized by the Republican leadership. The Republican party did not as a party attack these areas of policy but they were "fair game" in a sense that European policy and United Nations policy were not.

Perhaps the most serious breach in bipartisan coverage was Far Eastern policy in general, exclusive of the Japanese Peace Treaty. Republican leaders were very critical of administration efforts to mediate between Chiang Kai-shek and the Communists in 1947. After the Communist triumph in 1949 criticism mounted. The nation entered the Korean conflict without any real consultation with Congressional leaders of either party, partly because there was not sufficient time. In July, 1950, Senator Taft condemned this omission and said, "We haven't had a truly bipartisan foreign policy in the Far East such as we have had in Europe. . . ." With the removal of General MacArthur as United Nations Commander, the whole China-policy issue came to a head. During the lengthy hearings in the spring of 1951, the Republicans were on the offensive and the Democrats in Congress and the President were on the defensive. The momentum gained by the Republicans carried over into the precampaign days of 1952 and into the campaign itself.

Regardless of considerable evidence that the Republicans were not unaware of developments of American policy toward China, it is a fact that whatever that policy was it had not been the recognized product of close collaboration between the two parties in Congress as were the United Nations Charter, the European Recovery Program, and the North Atlantic Alliance. There is no point here in reviewing the partisan argument over who was to blame for the course of events in China or for the failure of the bipartisan system. But several other comments are in order. China finally fell into Communist hands in 1949, a time when the bipartisan machine was out of order. Senator Vandenberg was ill. Mr. Dulles was running for the Senate in New York. After his surprise victory in 1948 President Truman tended to neglect the minority party in Congress. Attempts to revive the system in the spring of 1950 by appointing Mr. Dulles and Mr. Cooper to the State Department and by offering renewed consultation had not fully succeeded on the outbreak of hostilities in Korea in June. Meanwhile Senator Taft more or less succeeded to Vandenberg's leadership and his increased interest in foreign affairs resulted in even greater opposition to the administration. He let it be known—as has been stated—that the Dulles appointment did not wholly meet the requirements of bipartisan collaboration.

THE PRESIDENTIAL CAMPAIGN OF 1952 AND ITS AFTERMATH

Both sides agreed that the "Korean problem" was the chief issue of the election. The Republicans launched the bitterest, most thorough attack on an administration's foreign policy since the debate over American intervention in World War II which had taken place two years before Pearl Harbor. Focusing its attack on the general area of Far Eastern policy, the Republican party argument ran along these lines: (a) the incompetence, mistakes, and improvisation of the Democratic leadership made the military effort in Korea necessary, i.e., the withdrawal of American troops in June, 1949, the neutralization of Formosa by the Seventh Fleet, and Secretary of State Acheson's definition of the "defensive perimeter" of the United States to exclude Korea as an *invitation* to the Communists to attack; (b) once in the conflict, the administration was unable or unwilling to win a decisive military victory and unable to negotiate an honorable peace—the South Koreans had not been sufficiently armed, military commanders had been hamstrung by civilian authorities in Washington, and Communist strength had been underestimated; (c) a "soft" Democratic policy toward the Communist world, as exemplified by Yalta, Potsdam, and the sell-out of Chiang Kai-shek, had resulted in the Berlin Blockade, the fall of China, and the loss of initiative to the Soviet Union and its satellites. Candidate Eisenhower urged more emphasis on the Far East (a neglected area of foreign policy), promised he would go to Korea to get a firsthand impression, urged "positive" policies to help "liberate" nations dominated by the Soviet Union, and generally promised a new, dynamic foreign policy to replace the negative, worn-out policy of the incumbents. Eisenhower also said, "It is not possible to have continuing cooperation on the administration basis of heads they win and tails the Republicans lose." He branded himself a "Vandenberg Republican" willing to revive and extend the bipartisan foreign-policy approach.

President Truman and Governor Stevenson (the Democratic candidate) answered these charges by pointing to the actions taken to check the thrust of Soviet power and ideology beginning with the Truman Doctrine of 1947, and by insisting that entrance into the Korean conflict had actually thwarted aggression. The Republicans were accused of advocating policies which would result in expansion of the Korean fighting into a full-scale war with China. Stevenson charged Eisenhower with pure vote-getting strategy in saying he would go to Korea, and with misleading the people into believing there was a magic formula for solving the Korean problem. The Democrats denied that their policies delivered China into Communist hands, saying that only military intervention in China could have saved the Nationalist forces. Secretary of State Acheson carefully pointed out that in the speech defining the "defensive perimeter" of the United States he had been specifying what this country would defend as it would its own territory, and he accused Eisenhower of omitting other sentences in which he stated clearly that if other areas (outside the perimeter, i.e., Korea and Formosa) should suffer aggression the entire civilized world under the United Nations Charter was determined to protect them. Eisenhower was quoted as favoring military withdrawal from Korea when he was chief of staff and also as believing the Russians only wanted cooperation in 1945.

All this debate to the contrary notwithstanding, it would be a mistake to give the impression that there was a complete breach over foreign policy. Generally speaking, of course, the Democrats were inclined to exaggerate their triumphs and ignore their mistakes while the Republicans were inclined to exaggerate the nature of changes which could be made in present policies and to capitalize on factors over which the Democrats had no control. The Democrats were inclined to stress the "national" nature of policies while the Republicans refused to accept the notion that to criticize was unpatriotic. However, Stevenson and Eisenhower agreed on many things—the need for allies, the need for continued American support of European unity and a European army including a Franco-German military partnership, the need to stay in Korea and to try for an honorable peace, the undesirability of expanding the Korean war. The Republican candidate actually criticized more what the Democrats had not done and appeared to be saying that many policies were satisfactory but not pushed far enough. A good many skilled observers felt, on balance, that the main differences were over details and methods, not principles. Which party could do it better? seemed to be the question.

The nomination of General Eisenhower was heralded as a triumph for the wing of the Republican party whose general philosophy of foreign affairs came closest to that of the Democrats. Leaving aside the extreme positions taken in the heat of a campaign, it is probably true that Eisenhower's identification with NATO and the bipartisan base of European-policy generally kept differences over foreign policy within much narrower limits than would otherwise have been the case. Since John Foster Dulles was the chief architect of the Republican foreign-policy platform, another link with established policies was present. It was possible nearly a year after the campaign to remark on how few *basic changes* had taken place after the bitter conflict over foreign policy carried on simultaneously with a costly military action.

Once again some qualification is necessary. As suggested, bipartisanship itself became an issue. The Democrats were accused of leaving the Republicans out of Far Eastern policy formation and then blaming the latter for mistakes while claiming as triumphs policies which were developed on a collaborative basis. On the other hand, the Democrats argued that the Republicans had ample time and opportunity to offer alternatives (which they did not do) and took full advantage of hindsight to criticize irresponsibly. It is also true that Eisenhower's emphasis on Asia, his remarks on "liberating" satellites, and his failure to comment in detail on Europe tended to undermine the confidence of America's European allies in the continuity of American policy and in the self-restraint they had come to feel were essential to successful American leadership.

DIFFICULTIES AND POSSIBLE DANGERS IN THE BIPARTISAN APPROACH

With the foregoing as background, it is possible to mention briefly some of the problems which have accompanied bipartisanship.

1. The lack of agreed definition of the working arrangements of bipartisanship means that a device which was designed to minimize irritation actually may become a source of irritation. The majority party and the Executive Branch in a sense never know when their obligations have been discharged. In November, 1950, after listening to repeated Republican complaints, Chairman Connally of the Senate Foreign Relations Committee denounced their claims as unreasonable. Although Democratic Senators Johnson and George of the Senate Foreign Relations Committee were "informed" of President Eisenhower's decision to "deneutralize" Formosa, Senator Humphrey protested that the Democrats might be asked to rescue Republican policies in which they had no voice. Largely unanswered is the crucial series of related questions: How many and who of the minority party should the President consult with and under what kinds of circumstances?

2. In the absence of real party discipline, it is never entirely certain whether the agreement of the minority party's foreign-policy leaders will be sufficient to prevent irresponsible attacks and successful inroads on genuine biparty policies. Even in the heyday of bipartisanship, a small group of power-

ful senators and representatives consistently behaved as though no holds were barred. This is not to say that maverick opposition is not kept within more satisfactory bounds, but it does prove that bipartisanship is limited in its effectiveness.

3. Closely linked to the previous point is the question whether foreign-policy differences are really party differences. While on occasion they are, it appears that on the whole internal differences of viewpoint within a party may be just as serious as those between parties. If the leadership and majority of each party could reach agreement, dissonant elements in each party may still have more in common with each other than they have with their own group. The legislative history of the Reciprocal Trade Agreements Act shows that when the two parties are completely in disagreement with each other and solidly in agreement within themselves, bipartisanship tends to be unworkable. If there is substantial agreement both within and between parties, bipartisanship is unnecessary. Consultation and negotiation are essential when there are internal differences but the party as an organized political force may not truly reflect those differences. In other words, can bipartisanship as it has developed in practice accurately and effectively take account of the shifting coalitions which transcend party labels?

4. Experience with bipartisanship raises the question whether it is an equally good technique or set of techniques for all kinds of foreign-policy problems and issues. Some of the many possible reasons for the breakdown over China policy have been referred to, but it is also worth noting in addition that the most conspicuous successes claimed for the bipartisan approach have been in cases where the end product of the policy-making process was a treaty or a concrete long-range program such as foreign aid. Examples, of course, are the North Atlantic Alliance and the Marshall Plan. The essence of these policies consisted of drafting clauses and appropriating definite amounts of money. On the contrary, the China problem—developing piece-meal as it did from 1945 to 1950—required negotiating with other nations, reacting quickly to events as they occurred, watchful waiting, dealing with problems in which the United States lacked control over relevant factors, and formulating general ideas which might be appropriate in guiding more specific decisions. The latter kind of problem is rather difficult to handle via bipartisan consultation, hearings, and so on. Had a decision been sought for a Pacific NATO or Aid Program it would have been different.

5. Bipartisanship is dependent—heavily dependent—on leadership. It is no routine compliment to equate successful bipartisanship with the leadership of the late Senator Vandenberg. From January, 1945, to shortly before his death in 1951, the Republican senator from Michigan made a major contribution both to the substance of policy and to its process of formation. On January 10, 1945, Vandenberg made a significant speech which marked the end of a slow change of mind which finally converted him from an isolationist into a stalwart supporter of "maximum American cooperation" to maintain

world peace. He became an outstanding Congressional expert in foreign affairs and renounced further political ambition to make a career out of his work on the Senate Foreign Relations Committee. It is difficult to overestimate how much of the solid partnership between Congress and the Executive Branch and between the two parties was due to his painstaking formal and informal persuasion and discussion. His prestige and influence depended on more than seniority—many senators have attained that without at the same time acquiring such eminence. Vandenberg's conversion to "internationalism" was well known—it was slow, thorough, and realistic, hence commanding of respect. Less convinced groups in the Republican party could support him without fear of "wild-eyed idealism." Naturally, his experience as a long-time isolationist gave him shrewd insight into the kinds of opposition certain senators might feel toward the "new" foreign policy and therefore made him a formidable debater. Vandenberg was an outstandingly popular senator of his day; not a little of this popularity was based on his understanding of his colleagues and of what it meant to be a senator. Not only did he treat fellow senators with respect and affection even when he disagreed basically with them, but he did the same with executive officials. The Secretary of State knew that "amicable disagreements" with Vandenberg were possible and that relations with him would not be impaired by disputes.

Senator Vandenberg represented a type of leadership essential to bipartisanship—he gave up presidential ambitions, he acquired practical knowledge of foreign affairs, he could convince his colleagues. On the other hand, the fact should be noted that the "architect of bipartisanship" was in turn partly dependent on the way he was treated by the administration and by the majority party leaders. The cooperation extended to him by the State Department and the President helped to enlarge his opportunity to exercise leadership. Vandenberg complained openly when the Democrats changed the ratio of party members on the Senate Foreign Relations Committee from 7 to 6 to 8 to 5 because he felt it would weaken his position in the Republican party.

The availability of John Foster Dulles was another factor in the leadership requirement of bipartisanship. Dulles, being a man of long experience in international law and diplomacy, had different qualifications from Vandenberg's. He was held in high esteem by most Republican leaders and in equally high esteem by the Democratic administration.

6. Finally, it remains to raise a different order of questions about bipartisanship. "The purpose of bipartisan collaboration in foreign policy is not and should not be to circumvent democratic control of foreign policy, but to promote effective democratic participation in shaping that policy. Its purpose is not to eliminate public discussion or criticism, but rather to render our foreign policy less vulnerable to criticism in democratic debate"—so writes Benjamin Cohen.* After several years of the bipartisan system, some com-

---

* Benjamin Cohen, "The Evolving Role of Congress in Foreign Affairs," *Proceedings of the American Philosophical Society,* October 25, 1948, p. 215.

mentators began to wonder whether a part of the price for rendering foreign policy less vulnerable to partisanship is not a reduction of public debate and a blunting of critical analysis. General discussion in Congress serves the two-fold purpose of informing the public and of permitting expression of a wide range of public preferences. True, there were two "great debates," one on Far Eastern policy and one on the President's power to send troops to Europe, but the first was not covered by bipartisan agreement and the other was a constitutional issue. If bipartisan policy making tends to shift decision to a relatively few key figures in Congress, does this not make the process more obscure? Does it still ensure that all major alternatives will be considered? To the extent that bipartisanship results in the effort to neutralize or to check possible opposition, do minority views get overrepresented? Suppose a prominent, influential senator has a particular view of foreign policy, i.e., he believes more in self-help than in allies. Under a bipartisan system does this view command greater attention than if it were competing openly with other ideas? Is private consultation among leaders equal to real debate? During the critical months of 1946, Prime Minister Clement Attlee of Great Britain permitted a full-dress debate on his government's policy in Germany. Early in 1946, the foundations of a bipartisan, revised American policy toward the Soviet Union were decided on without any thorough debate in Congress or anywhere else. In 1948, Senator Vandenberg indicated that he was unwillingly silenced on the Palestine issue. Putting American foreign policy beyond controversy seems, in principle, to be logical and desirable; yet much would seem to depend on whether debate has been merely discreetly hidden or whether it has really been suppressed.

Moreover, should the President or the Secretary of State be held responsible for decisions or limitations or suggestions which they feel they have to accept during the "infighting" of two-party cooperation? To put the matter another way, should the opposition party be given *both* the opportunity to help decide and the opportunity to criticize final results? These two questions relate, of course, to the problem of responsibility. Conceivably, a bipartisan system which hamstrings the executive while simultaneously permitting maverick revolts and criticism might enhance tendencies toward irresponsibility.

It is generally assumed that unanimity in a political context is superior to a normal majority as a basis of consensus. Does bipartisanship result in a policy based on the lowest common denominator? Satisfaction is taken in the fact that the vote in the Senate on the United Nations Charter was 89 to 2. Would 90 to 1 have been even more satisfactory? Did this vote predict more unity among citizens than would have prevailed had the vote been 65 to 26? Would a stronger charter have been desirable at the risk of a smaller majority? Did the procedures of bipartisanship produce the nearly unanimous agreement or merely reflect what was already true?

In earlier chapters, flexibility and boldness were set forth as necessary qualities of executive action in foreign affairs. Does the requirement of consultation with the bipartisan coalition reduce the possibility of such action? There is considerable evidence that the bipartisan leaders of 1948 quashed a contemplated move by President Truman in October of that year to send Chief Justice Fred Vinson on a special "mission to Moscow." Regardless of the merits of the plan the implications of the outcome are clear.

SUMMARY

When all is said and done, peculiarities of the American political process probably make some kind of bipartisanship inevitable. Possibilities of obstructionism are too great to be ignored, and this is one way of limiting them. Clearly, under the American system the administration cannot compel the opposition to "put up or shut up." At the same time, however, bipartisanship has its own intrinsic difficulties and is dependent for its effectiveness on favorable conditions. Bipartisanship thus can be characterized as an adaptation to meet certain potential weaknesses in the American system, an adaptation whose effectiveness may be decreased by the existence of other weaknesses.

► THE PROBLEM OF EXECUTIVE-LEGISLATIVE RELATIONS RECONSIDERED

The dimensions of the problem of executive-legislative relations ought by now to be clearly established. If there has seemed to be undue emphasis on the difficulties involved, this is only a reflection of the actualities of the American governmental system, and it should not be interpreted as an effort to exaggerate troubles at the expense of the virtues of the system. No understanding of how foreign policy is made in the United States is possible without the kind of detailed analysis suggested above. Treatment of the problem has often been oversimplified: one factor or a set of related factors is said to be *the* cause of the "gap" between the two branches and a "solution" is recommended accordingly. Many writers tend either to understate the problem or to regard it as hopeless until the whole system is rebuilt. But it can and should be readily acknowledged that with all its complications and potential disorders, the system does result in decisions and policies, many of them sound and effective. It should also be admitted that the system exacts a price and is fraught with danger.

It would appear that some of the difficulties mentioned can be minimized, i.e., the frequency of their occurrence and their seriousness can be curtailed; and that some will have to be accepted as more or less permanent disabilities requiring adaptations. Without presuming that completely harmonious, effective, responsible interaction is possible, an effort can be made to establish bases or conditions for executive-legislative relations which are *more harmonious, effective, and responsible than not*. Whatever "solutions" or "improvements" or "adaptations" or "devices" are employed, the proper role of both the President and Congress must be preserved. As stressed in previous chapters, each has a unique contribution to make to the policy-making process, each has functions the other could not satisfactorily perform or even perform at all. Either must be able to use appropriate tactics and strategy to protect its role from encroachment by the other. One set of criteria for judging solutions to the problem is, then, the probable effect upon the legitimate role of the two branches and their capacity to defend themselves. The discussion of the roles of the two branches presented earlier included a statement of their weaknesses. Obviously, improvement or remedy of such weaknesses will contribute to an easing of the difficulties which may arise in the mutual relationship.

If the analysis of the nature of executive-legislative relations is reasonably accurate, it follows that, while there is need at present for role clarification, no exact blueprint is possible, first, because the power of each branch cannot be precisely defined to fit every occasion; and second, because the conditions under which each perform its functions change often enough so that in *some aspects* the roles require constant redefinition.

PROPOSALS FOR SOLVING OR AMELIORATING THE PROBLEM

The enlarged significance of foreign-policy issues has, of course, intensified the search for fundamental alterations which might conceivably eliminate the dangers and pitfalls inherent in the separation of powers. Many general suggestions that have been made without foreign affairs particularly in mind would certainly affect them. Some are so unlikely to receive serious consideration in the foreseeable future that they need not be mentioned in any detail. Thus it is highly unlikely that the tenure and method of electing the President and Congress will be basically changed so as to create a parliamentary system similar to Great Britain's.

1. One group of proposals concerns the formal machinery of executive-legislative consultation. A favorite theme here is the establishment of some sort of joint executive-legislative foreign-policy council. This might be accomplished in a number of ways. A separate body might include the President, the Secretaries of State and Defense, the director of the Foreign Operations Administration, the director of the Central Intelligence Agency, the chairmen of the Congressional foreign-affairs committees plus their ranking minority members, majority and minority leaders, and party Policy Committee chairmen. Or the Cabinet might be reconstituted to permit the attendance of leading members of a joint Congressional committee on foreign policy. Alternatively, members of such a Congressional committee might be permitted to sit from time to time with the National Security Council. Clearly there are a variety of possible methods for creating an executive-legislative foreign-policy consultative body. All share a common feature: recognition of the necessity of high-level consultation by creation of a formal body requiring regular meetings. It is noteworthy that several of these proposals contemplate the creation of a joint House-Senate committee on foreign affairs or at least

a national security committee for each chamber consisting of representatives and senators from committees which have a substantial interest in foreign affairs. Closely related is the proposal for executive-legislative investigating commissions consisting of distinguished citizens and private experts appointed by the President as well as members of both parties from Congress. The purpose would be to avoid the disadvantages of regular investigations which are often partisan and careless of sound procedures.

An outstanding instance of the latter type of device is the so-called Randall Commission created by President Eisenhower to review the nation's economic foreign policy. Of the seventeen members, seven (including the chairman, Clarence Randall, chairman of the board of Inland Steel Company) were appointed by the President and five members each from the Senate and House were chosen by leaders of the two parties. The Congressional members represent not only the two major parties, but extremes of views on the tariff and other economic questions. Among the citizen members, finance, labor, industry, business, and the university are represented.

2. In February, 1953, Walter Lippmann called for policy leaders from the Executive Branch to cooperate in a "question and report period from the floor of Congress."* Long recommended by Senator Kefauver and others including many previous Presidents, this proposal would mean a return to the practice of the First Congress— a practice dropped shortly thereafter. Though obviously full of pitfalls from the executive point of view, this procedure would have the advantage of answering Congress's chronic complaint about lack of information. Regular question-and-answer periods would provide ample opportunity for congressmen to ask *directly* about matters troubling them and to receive answers without the press or other congressmen acting as intermediaries. It might also mitigate Congress's attempts to rival the President as a source of news because, when replying, an executive officer would be speaking simultaneously to the whole Congress and to the whole United States.

3. In recent years, political scientists and other students of American government have debated the desirability of responsible party government for the United States. The arguments against the present party system are familiar enough: lack of discipline diminishes party cohesion and the capacity of the party to fulfill campaign promises; the two major parties are loose coalitions which unite only for election purposes: party leaders are not able to speak for their parties or keep members in line for Congressional voting; because the two parties must build the broadest base of public support they come to stand for so much that policy differences between them are obscured and thus genuine alternatives are seldom offered; under present conditions, it is very difficult to determine whether the election of one party represents a true expression of the preferences of a majority of the American people. Truly responsible party government (as in Great Britain, for example) would doubt-

* In his syndicated column, New York *Herald-Tribune*, February 2, 1953, p. 30.

less require constitutional changes but, whatever the merits of this kind of proposal, it appears unlikely to happen. However, short of this, various changes could be made which might strengthen the party system: (a) A genuine national party leadership responsible to the rank-and-file membership would have the power to speak authoritatively for all members, to call *annual* conventions to formulate policy, and to veto state and local party activities and candidates. Presumably this would require full control of patronage and campaign funds by the central leadership. (b) The leadership of each party would consist of a single spokesman (the party leader) and a small executive council comprising key party officials from both the executive and legislative branches. (c) The national party organization would be aided by an enlarged research staff which would help to create a sound factual basis for policy recommendations. (d) To buttress these changes, Congressional rules would have to be changed. Most important to the strengthening of the party system along the lines suggested would be abolishing both the seniority rule for determining committee assignments and the filibuster.

It is argued that this kind of strengthening of the party system would provide sufficient incentive and discipline to foster the development of a single, authoritative party viewpoint on major issues; to provide coherent, effective leadership in Congress for a President's program regardless of whether it was eventually doomed to defeat or not; and to prevent irresponsible minority party criticism. To reduce the system would not, it is argued, suppress differences of opinion but would confine them (until reconciled) to intraparty discussions outside Congress and would keep them responsible. Interparty differences would be genuine and clearly identified and, once reconciled, would become the basis of a consensus which could not be upset by any group within either party. Whatever the viewpoint of either party, it would tend to be a national viewpoint and would also tend to control the impact of subnational pressures which so often unsettle Congressional relation with the President. It is also argued that responsible parties would narrow the range of circumstances where bipartisanship was necessary and would render two-party agreement more durable.

4. Quite independent of proposals to alter the nature of political parties, strengthening of the bipartisan approach has been recommended as a way of "living with" the splintering of parties, the lack of party responsibility and disciplines, minority veto, and the tenuous coalitions required for successful legislation. Specific proposals on bipartisanship do not really go beyond the characteristics already cited; bipartisanship is a recommended solution as well as a set of practices. On the basis of the analysis above, it would appear, however, that as the approach is defined, its effectiveness depends largely on a number of conditions which are not directly controllable through bipartisanship itself, including presidential leadership and the personal qualities of the key Congressional figures involved in collaboration. The more that parties

represent real foreign-policy differences instead of comprising labels which conceal differences based on other criteria, the more chance there is that bipartisanship will prove durable. But even if these conditions are taken for granted, the basic need, if there is to be continued satisfactory bipartisanship, is a "theory" accepted by the participants. There must be agreement on the following points: the kinds of foreign-policy matters to be included—day-to-day decisions, long-range planning, commitments (executive agreements and treaties), techniques which necessitate use of Congressional powers, and so on; which leaders of the majority and minority party in Congress are to be consulted by the Executive Branch (Should there be a set number or should it vary with the problem?); a definition of "consultation" (Does it mean "inform," and if so, when? Does it mean receiving "advice," and if so what is the status of it? Does it mean joint policy making?); the conditions under which the participants in the bipartisan system are to vary; and what mechanisms are appropriate in cases where consultation may legitimately mean several different things. In the absence of such agreements, the rules and procedures of bipartisanship tend to be renegotiated each time a new occasion arises. A codification would probably reduce some of the friction which bipartisanship has generated in its short lifetime.

Proposals of the foregoing types are classified as institutional because they usually require new machinery or a modification of old machinery, and because they imply some sort of recognized agreement, whether written or unwritten. It is relatively easy to propose changes like these; however, in the last analysis their merit must rest not on the mere fact that they provide opportunity for effective executive-legislative interaction but on whether they actually take into account the complexity of the "problem" as defined, whether they could survive certain conditions which would still prevail, and whether they would help eliminate the factors tending to undermine harmonious, responsible collaboration.

LEADERSHIP, ROLE INTERPRETATION, AND PERSONALITIES

Regardess of the merit of formal proposals, and ignoring basic alterations in the constitutional system, executive-legislative policy making will still depend very much on factors which cannot be legislated or automatically created by formal arrangements. These factors are customarily designated as psychological. They will call to mind certain determinants of the decision-making process discussed earlier: roles and the interpretation of roles, motivations, intellectual skills and analysis, communication, and strategies of action—particularly as applied to the leaders in both branches.

There is no substitute for strong motivation to take an appropriate course of action. Senator Vandenberg was so strongly motivated to work for bipartisanship that competing motives (i.e., ambition to be President) were overcome and his energies could be devoted exclusively to it. Both President Truman and President-Elect Eisenhower were motivated to "ease" the transfer of power from Democrats to Republicans after November 8, 1952, and before January 20, 1953. During this period, there were numerous high-level talks involving not only the two highest figures but the Secretaries of Defense and State and their designated successors, and representatives from the Budget Bureau and Mutual Security Agency. President-Elect Eisenhower kept silent on foreign-policy issues to avoid further embarrassment to the administration. Outwardly, at least, the transfer of power appeared to be orderly and effective —somewhat contrary to common expectations. While there was no institutional provision for this kind of thing, both sides were motivated to do it out of concern for possibly harmful effects from an awkward feature of the American system.

Senator Connally (Democrat, Texas), who in effect succeeded Vandenberg when he became chairman of the Senate Foreign Relations Committee in January, 1949, was not as strongly motivated in the cause of bipartisanship as was Vandenberg; in fact, he personally alienated many Republicans whose cooperation was essential, particularly Senators Vandenberg and Taft. Senator Connally's conception of his role as chairman of this key committee permitted him to feud openly with the President and the State Department. Mention of the Senate Foreign Relations Committee recalls that the personality of the chairman has been a vital factor in defining not only the role of the committee but that of the Senate as a whole. The strong men in this role— Sumner, Lodge, Borah—have all been ambitious men who put the Senate's coordinate position ahead of peaceful relations with the President. Others put service to the administration ahead of protecting the Senate's rights and interests. It requires an unusual combination of traits to do both. As noted, Senator Vandenberg seemed to have come closest to this idea in recent years.

Although Senator Taft did not become chairman of the Senate Foreign Relations Committee when the Republicans organized Congress in January, 1953, he did become *the* leader of the Senate and, for the most part, of Congress as a whole. Taft had lost his last chance at the presidency to President Eisenhower and the two men had fought bitterly for their party's nomination. The senator suppressed his personal feelings and the temptation to take advantage of the President from his impregnable position in Congress, while the President was magnanimous in victory and went out of his way to build a strong working relationship with his former antagonist. Whatever their private emotions, the two men collaborated effectively because each had the will to do so. There was no public agreement between them on foreign policy, but until his illness forced his retirement from Senate leadership, Senator Taft exerted his great influence on behalf of most of the major policies on which the administration wanted Congressional action. There is little doubt that Senator Taft's untimely death weakened one of the effective links between the two branches. Not only were Taft's skills and experience missing, but his successor, Senator Knowland, was not as powerful a figure. This circumstance tended to diffuse power in the Senate, thus making the President's task more difficult. The significance of Senator Taft's power for the President could be seen in the different results when Taft either supported or deserted the latter's interests. The majority leader brought the Bohlen issue to the floor despite the bitter opposition of Senators Bridges and McCarthy, and victory resulted. On the other hand, Taft finally lost interest in the resolution on Russian treaty violations and the resolution died without being brought to a vote. The whole point is that the President has to decide whose roles and capacities are essential and then has to establish a workable personal relationship with those persons.

Self-restraint does not arise from institutional forms but institutional forms can result in the creation of circumstances which call it forth and which help preserve it when it appears as a personal quality in the men whose actions affect executive-legislative relationships. It has already been remarked that one of the pre-eminent characteristics of the American system is the range of pressures to which executive officials are subject. Pressure often kills self-restraint. At the same time self-restraint is an attribute of personality. Whether it is manifest in the right men at the right time is a matter of accident. A short temper and a sharp tongue may be accompanied by admirable traits, but when they are manifest on both sides of the executive-legislative equation, trouble is inevitable. The feud between President Truman and Senator Taft (1949–1952) was in part a personal one—the two men did not like each other—and hence it was characterized by bitter remarks uttered in moods of rage and pique. There were, of course, other facets of the conflict but the lack of self-restraint certainly intensified it. President Truman accused the senator of the crassest kind of political ambition and Taft once exclaimed about Truman: "He seems to have gone completely off his head."*

A previous section outlined executive and legislative responses to situations and actions which tend to undermine harmonious relationships between the two. No great wisdom is required to see that self-restraint judicially exercised would tend to decrease the number and intensity of these responses. Irresponsible statements and actions by individual members of Congress, investigative abuses, and so on—all these are subject to restraint. The Congressional attack on Secretary of State Acheson (1950–1952) proceeded to the point where even the Democrats in Congress regarded him as a political liability—a vicious circle which helped to reduce the secretary's effectiveness as a spokesman for the United States. So anxious were certain Congressional Republicans to discredit what they called Truman-Acheson policies that they carried the fight into the early days of the Eisenhower Administration by attempting to block the appointment of Charles Bohlen (a Foreign Service

* New York *Herald-Tribune,* April 20, 1952, p. 1.

career officer) as Ambassador to the Soviet Union. The battle was eventually lost but meanwhile a significant delay was imposed and Mr. Bohlen's prestige was not enhanced.

As to the President, self-restraint is part and parcel of his capacity for leadership. He must decide when and how to retaliate for the use of Congressional weapons against him, his office, and his program. Choosing when to fight is an important presidential judgment. If he fights on small issues he may dissipate his strength for bigger ones. If he has to draw up all his heavy artillery he may pay too high a price for victory, leaving behind a reservoir of ill will which will affect the next issue. On the other hand, if the President does not retaliate at the right time or if he deliberately avoids a showdown with Congress he may find that his power has been circumscribed and that his ability to take the initiative in foreign policy has been limited.

The President's exercise of self-restraint will depend on his personality and also on how he defines his role—a point discussed at length earlier. President Eisenhower deliberately adopted the view that getting along with Congress was one of his primary tasks. He apparently believed that the initiative for a satisfactory relationship rested with him and that Congress must be treated as a friend rather than an enemy. Therefore at a time when a high degree of cooperation could be expected automatically, he went out of his way to guarantee such cooperation. To begin with, his philosophy permitted a wide tolerance of Congressional acts, regardless of what he personally thought or how they affected his role. During his first ninety days in office, the following events occurred: Secretary of State Dulles was accused of overruling the State Department's security officer; the President's personal choice for Ambassador to the Soviet Union, Charles Bohlen, was charged with being a party to the "soft" Truman-Acheson policy toward the Soviet Union and therefore of being unqualified; Senator McCarthy, who led the attack on Bohlen, appeared to usurp executive functions when he obtained, independently and using his own staff, a pledge from Greek shipowners not to trade with Communist-controlled countries; Congress would not or could not agree on a simple resolution condemning Soviet abrogation of postwar international agreements and releasing the United States from obligations based on such agreements; when the President announced the deneutralization of Formosa as a somewhat dramatic indication of a new foreign policy, certain vocal congressmen kept pressing their questions on the Secretary of State until the latter was forced to admit, bit by bit, that the move did not represent very much of a change; finally, a move to restrict the President's long-standing power to negotiate international agreements was pressed in the form of the Bricker amendment. All this despite the fact that the Republicans had come to power on the surge of a great popular majority for Eisenhower and despite the new President's avowed admission of Congress to a coordinate policy-making role. In other words, a quite different kind of leadership from that of former President Truman did not completely eliminate embarrassment and setbacks for the Executive Branch. Nevertheless, the philosophy of executive-legislative relations embraced by Eisenhower perhaps may be credited with keeping adverse possibilities within limits.

Because President Eisenhower so explicitly stated his philosophy of executive-legislative relations, a good deal of attention was centered on the results of the philosophy in action. The episodes mentioned above were regarded by some critics as full-scale defeats and were cited as horrible examples of what happens when the President acts with "restraint." Delicate handling of Congress was interpreted as a failure of leadership. It was argued that the President's refusal to condemn publicly certain acts of his own party members only encouraged irresponsible behavior. In particular, these critics noted that after Senator McCarthy had usurped executive authority by "negotiating" (this was the senator's word) an agreement with Greek ship-owners and had generally made the Department of State appear somewhat ineffectual, he escaped a direct personal rebuff by the President. Instead, the senator and the Secretary of State issued a joint statement in which the word "negotiation" was conspicuously absent and in which both agreed that international agreements were the sole prerogative of the Executive Branch and that pertinent information in the possession of Congressional committees would be relayed to the proper authorities in the proper way. This was thought to be a "moral victory" for Senator McCarthy, one which he later tried to expand by publicly inviting employees within the executive branch to pass on to him rather than to their superiors any information regarding possible violation of security regulations.

Whether one agrees that the President stored up trouble for himself by such tactics depends in part on how strong he feels about the particular issue and about the particular senator, but it also depends on whether he would agree with President Eisenhower's interpretation of his over-all position vis-à-vis Congress. He was almost totally dependent on the Republican leadership in Congress because of his own lack of experience and because the members of his top administrative team were new to their jobs. On the crucial issue of foreign aid, for example, the President's staff had only three months in which to prepare estimates and then he had to rely almost completely on three men —General Gruenther, Commander of NATO forces, Secretary of State Dulles, and Director of Mutual Security Stassen. By this time Congress had many experts on foreign aid and in all probability knew more than the President's spokesmen. Many of the older hands in the foreign-aid program could not be sent to Congress as star witnesses because they were identified with the Truman Administration. In the face of a slight Republican majority the President also knew he wanted support for touchy issues—the admission of over-the-quota refugees from iron-curtain countries and a reduction of the Air Force budget. He was rewarded in both cases, though he asked for 240,000 refugees within two years and Congress approved 214,000 within three years. By June, 1953, even with Senator Taft withdrawn from active leadership, the President could insist successfully that a Senate rider to a United Nations appropriations bill declaring the United States should leave the world body if Communist China were admitted be killed.

This is not to suggest that President Eisenhower's tactics were right or wrong. Rather it is a reminder that judgment in these cases depends on whether the observer regards a particular issue as major or minor, on whether he feels that the President made things easier or harder for himself in other Congressional encounters, and on whether individual cases should always take precedence over the general relationship the President is trying to establish.

President Eisenhower's techniques for dealing with Congress highlight another point. General Persons, who for ten years had represented all three military services in Congress, was added to the President's immediate staff as expert in executive liaison. There were much more frequent *ad hoc* meetings with members of both houses than had been true during the previous two years. Above all, the President made an effort to establish a sound working relationship with Senator Robert Taft of Ohio—the man he defeated for the Republican nomination. It is generally agreed that Taft's leadership and influence in the Senate were crucial. Senator Bridges (president pro tempore of the Senate), Senator Knowland (chairman of the Republican Policy Committee), Senator Wiley (chairman of the Senate Foreign Relations Committee), and Senator McCarthy (chairman of a special investigating committee) were all key figures, but Taft's position was central. To repeat, the influence of key leaders like Taft cannot be explained solely in terms of official roles. Therefore, purely formal arrangements or mechanisms will not necessarily include all the key figures. Senator McCarthy, for example, achieved an influence far beyond his official rank in the Senate.

In addition to the personal relations on the presidential level (including the President's immediate staff), it is particularly important that the chairmen of the key committees, their staff chiefs, and the Assisant Secretary of State for Congressional Relations be able to get along together. Rivalries among committees and committee staffs are institutional in large part, but good personal relations and the will to cooperate can help overcome lack of coordination.

The kinds of factors suggested in this section are a reminder that changes in rules, in ways of doing things, and in organization will not inevitably produce desired reform. On the other hand, formal factors can supplement psychological factors and can create situations in which personality traits are rendered less significant. Suppose one postulates overweaning individual influence in the Senate as a possible disruptive element in executive-legislative collaboration. Three "solutions" may be proposed. First, to elect, or to hope to elect, senators having a high sense of responsibility so that the individual power will not be abused. Second, to reduce the scope of individual influence by, say, abolishing seniority. Third, to establish indirect safeguards to limit the impact of individual influence by devices such as bipartisanship. Much the same arguments would hold for other sources of difficulty.

CORRECTION OF INTERNAL WEAKNESSES IN BOTH BRANCHES

This is an appropriate place to remind the reader that the internal weaknesses of Congress and the Presidency are relevant to a discussion of solutions and palliatives with respect to the problem under consideration. Internal improvements of the types suggested in Chapters Six and Ten have nothing to do with the separation of powers per se—which is one more indication that executive-legislative relations are affected by other than purely formal, constitutional considerations. Not a little of the dissatisfaction felt in Congress over presidential policies in recent years has been due to organizational arrangements which allegedly produced "bad" policies and faulty execution. It is not a matter of whether Congress is entirely right, but of the organizational conditions under which Congress has confidence that it has received true consensus of executive thinking arrived at by sound procedures. What is Congress to make of several different estimates of Soviet capacities and intentions emanating from executive agencies? And what of the contradictory statements on the atomic position of the United States? Does this promote trust? To reverse the matter, which voice or set of voices in Congress is to be taken as authoritative? How much confidence can the executive agencies have when long negotiations with the Senate Foreign Relations Committee are upset by the Appropriations Committee? The point is that better coordination within each branch might enhance the possibility of effective interaction between them.

Regardless of whether one is prepared to say that the efforts have been significant and the results extensive, reorganization of the Executive Branch *in the area of foreign affairs* has taken place on a rather imposing scale. Beginning with changes in the State Department in 1938 and proceeding through successive changes in that agency culminating in 1949, through the National Security Act of 1947 (including amendments) and the Hoover Commission recommendations in 1949, and on to the Eisenhower reorganization plans of 1953, alterations have been made in the organization for the formulation and execution of foreign policy. On the other hand, Congress— with one notable exception—has undergone only one limited reorganization (1946) and this was not primarily directed at the foreign-policy problems with which it is concerned. The exception tends to prove the present contention: the creation of specialized subcommittees of the Senate Foreign Relations Committee, which paralleled the organization of the State Department, appears to have facilitated communication and coordination between the committee and the department.

The adoption of enforceable rules to curb the abuses of investigations by

Congressional committees might eliminate many of the sources of confusion, bitterness, and mistrust. One of the useful by-products of successful committees such as the Herter group, whose penetrating preliminary research on European recovery problems preceded the adoption of the Marshall Plan in 1948, has been to raise the level of intellectual competence which congressmen can bring to bear on foreign-policy issues. Such examples, though unfortunately limited, suggest that side shows, time wasting, and vendettas against executive personnel are not inevitable. Leaks from secret sessions which may embarrass the nation can be avoided by stricter rules.

For a number of years executive officials have been accustomed to clearing public speeches with the President or the Secretary of State. A joint House-Senate foreign-policy committee might have as one of its functions the clearance of formal communications by members of Congress. In view of the fact that individualism is probably an enduring characteristic of Congressional procedures, some effort might be made to prevent irresponsible or injudicious statements which can be mistaken as authoritative by decision makers in other nations. Perhaps, too, budget procedures can be altered to permit Congress to discuss the assumptions, objectives, and time strategies embodied in annual estimates. Some progress has been made in freeing committees from imprisonment in details. An omnibus national security budget might enable Congress to grasp the large issues, including civilian control of the military.

So far as the presidency is concerned, the changes instituted by President Eisenhower in 1953 could potentially remove several targets of Congressional criticism. Presumably the President's staff position has been improved and the National Security Council has been strengthened. Apparently the handling of the problem of security risks is less vulnerable to the sensational probing by Congressional groups. Temporarily, at least, the Joint Chiefs of Staff has been depoliticalized. The Voice of America has been reorganized. An attempt has been made to restore the State Department to its pre-eminent position.

Beyond this there are three possibilities which might strengthen executive-legislative relations. First, the control of public utterances by the administration's foreign-policy leaders could be tightened. The "Tower of Babel" effect noted in Chapter Three tends to provoke an identical echo in Congress. Second, now that there are a large number of executive officials who are concerned with aspects of Congressional liaison, a composite picture of the general state of affairs prevailing in the legislative body ought to be available to the President. Up to now, certain presidential blunders could be explained only in terms of ignorance of events which later turned out to be vitally important to presidential plans. Third, the activities of Vice-President Nixon during 1953 indicate that this office might loom larger in executive-legislative relations. Mr. Nixon is generally credited with persuading Senator McCarthy to withhold a letter he was about to send to the President which would have opened up the whole question of the government's policy on trade with Communist China in a very awkward fashion.

► CONCLUSION

It is clear that there is no one institutional device, no one strategy, no one attitude, no one basic reform that will guarantee protection against the possible consequences of patterns of executive-legislative interaction. There is no major formula for solving the "problem." Harmonious, effective, respon‑sible interaction appears to rest on a number of conditions, factors and choices.

Furthermore, the problem involves much more than the separation of powers and formal constitutional considerations, and it arises on more occa‑sions than when the President asks Congress for money, goods, and support. It also arises when there is need for self-restraint on both sides, particularly when Congress has to be patient because positive action is not possible. The statement that leadership is one of the prerequisites of effective interaction is incomplete: responsible leaders *in both branches* are essential. No President can do it all alone, and no Congressional leaders can overcome executive fumbling.

Different strategies may produce equally successful results, but poor strategies, the lack of strategy, the presentation of an inadequate or unclear case by executive agencies, and so on, threaten trouble. The successful cases of collaboration usually rest on the painstaking work of many key officials— they didn't just happen. So complex have the two organizations become, so complex the subjects with which they are jointly dealing, that policy cannot— like Topsy—just grow.

Perhaps it is not amiss to end this chapter on a note of irony. As Harold Stein has remarked, "Never in the history of the Republic has foreign policy been so dependent on congressional action as it was during the administration of President Truman; and no President has had more success in securing favorable congressional action than Mr. Truman in spite of constant attack on him in Congress, in the newspapers, and among the public, and even though his chief lieutenant, the Secretary of State, was being vilified as none of his predecessors had been for a hundred years or more."* This is a warning against predictions that the system will not work and against oversimplified explanations of why it does.

► SELECTED BIBLIOGRAPHY

D. Cheever and H. F. Haviland, Jr., *American Foreign Policy and the Separation of Powers* (Cambridge, Mass., Harvard University Press, 1952), is a carefully prepared historical review of executive-Congressional relations combin‑ing summaries of epochs and detailed cases; it is excellent supplementary reading for the preceding two chapters of this book. Chaps. 4 and 11 of W. Y. Elliott.

---

* Harold Stein, "Foreign Policy and the Dispersion of Power," *Public Adminis‑tration Review,* Summer, 1953, pp. 196–197.

et al., United States Foreign Policy: Its Organization and Control (New York, Columbia University Press, 1952), presents a vigorous criticism of the present system by a Woodrow Wilson Foundation Study Group of which Professor Elliott, McGeorge Bundy, Don K. Price, Harry D. Gideonse, Arthur Schlesinger, Jr., and George F. Kennan were members; included also are recommendations for drastic changes of the sort omitted here. Chapters 3, 4, 7, 8, 12, 13, 14, of Robert Dahl, *Congress and Foreign Policy* (New York, Harcourt, Brace & Company, 1950), analyze in more detail various points treated above. Some of the effects of presidential-Congressional relations on foreign policy are discussed by B. Bolles in "President, Congress and Foreign Policy," *American Perspective,* March, 1949. Though somewhat dated, T. Finletter's *Can Representative Government Do the Job?* (New York, Harcourt, Brace & Company, 1945) is a stimulating study of the problem of collaboration between the President and Congress. The following discuss the treaty-making process and the two-thirds rule: K. Colegrove, *The American Senate and World Peace* (New York, The Vanguard Press, 1944); R. J. Dangerfield, *In Defense of the Senate: A Study in Treaty-Making* (Norman, Okla., University of Oklahoma Press, 1933); D. F. Fleming, *The Treaty Veto of the American Senate* (New York, G. P. Putnam's Sons, 1930) and *The United States and the World Court* (New York, Doubleday & Company, 1945); and W. S. Holt, *Treaties Defeated by the Senate* (Baltimore, The Johns Hopkins Press, 1933). *International Executive Agreements: Democratic Procedure under the Constitution of the United States* (New York, Columbia University Press, 1941) by W. McClure is a standard work on executive agreements and the constitutional problems they raise. A good brief account of the early development of bipartisanship is contained in B. Bolles, "Bipartisanship in American Foreign Policy," *Foreign Policy Reports,* January 1, 1949. A stimulating argument, pro and con, over the merits of bipartisanship is carried on by Willmore Kendall and others in "Is the Bipartisan Policy Democratic?" *American Perspective,* Spring, 1950.

CHAPTER THIRTEEN

THE IMPACT OF PUBLIC OPINION AND INTEREST GROUPS ON FOREIGN POLICY*

The Nature of Public Opinion • The "Roles" of the "Publics" • The Roles of Organized
Interest Groups • The Roles of Community Leaders • Decision Makers as Opinion Leaders,
Opinion Gauges, and Lobbyists • Summary Comment on the Roles of the Publics •
Selected Problems of Public Opinion and Foreign Policy in a Democracy • Persistent
Dilemmas of Democratic Foreign Policy • Selected Bibliography

No nation in the world pays greater deference to something called
"public opinion" than does the United States. In no nation does "pressure
politics" occupy a more central place in the governmental process. These
phrases refer, of course, to a range of factors which influence the formation
and execution of public policy in general and foreign policy in particular,
namely, the politically significant values, attitudes, and activities of private
individuals and organized groups.

Logically, the phenomena subsumed under the heading of public opinion
belong in a chapter on American society which attempts to outline some
of the social factors which have a direct or indirect bearing on the nation's
foreign policy and external relations. Obviously the formation and significance of opinion as well as the action of organized groups cannot be ex-

---

* The authors decided not to base this chapter on an analysis of the latest public
opinion polls and surveys available because such material would be largely dated by the
time the book was published. Furthermore, emphasis on polls and surveys may distort
the true scope of the general topic treated here. Even with extensive tables and charts,
the fundamental questions remain: What does the data mean and what conclusions can
be drawn from them? These questions refer not only to what can be predicted with respect
to public conduct, but to how data relate to policy formation. Illustrations for some of the
major points made in the chapter can be found in the following sources: reports of Gallup
and Roper polls in leading newspapers; quarterly summaries (discontinued in 1952) in the
Public Opinion Quarterly; Public Opinion 1935–1946 prepared by Mildred Strunk under
the editorial supervision of Hadley Cantril (Princeton, N. J., Princeton University Press,
1951); and Chapters 44–51 of T. A. Bailey, *A Diplomatic History of the American People*
(New York, Appleton-Century-Crofts, Inc., 1950), which draws heavily on recent polls.

plained without reference to the nature of a particular society. But in view of the necessity to provide a more specific discussion of this one social factor, it has seemed more satisfactory to wait until the formal governmental machinery had been described and the policy-making officials had been identified. Having established a crude scheme for understanding foreign-policy decision making, this question can now be asked: What is the relationship between public opinion and group politics on the one hand and the formation of foreign policy on the other? This question can be refined somewhat in terms of the earlier analysis of the nature of decision making. Decision makers may be conceived of as carrying on their deliberations in a setting—one aspect being termed the "internal" to point up clusters of domestic as distinct from foreign social forces and conditions—which may directly or indirectly affect their behavior. Thus limitations arise from the internal setting. Individuals and groups try to influence the decision makers. The decision makers will be relating themselves and their task to the internal setting. Therefore the question becomes this: In what ways and under what conditions does the public become part of the setting of decision making, thereby in effect participating in policy formation without having official status in the governmental system?

Having said that the primary purpose of this chapter is to suggest some of the more important links between public opinion and foreign-policy decision making and having discussed the latter in Chapters Three through Twelve, it is necessary to clarify the ambiguous phrase "public opinion." It will be found that public opinion is not a single well-defined force nor does it have a single well-defined impact. Given the nature and complexity of the decision-making structure and the number of possible processes through which foreign policy evolves, it is clear also that there are many places and times at which public opinion might make itself felt.

Before proceeding, some of the reasons why the significance of public opinion is now universally taken for granted ought to be stated briefly. First, a revolution has taken place in the Western world since the turn of the nineteenth century which has changed diplomacy from an art practiced largely in secret to an art practiced increasingly under public scrutiny. International relations, for better or worse, have become "democratized." This trend has, of course, coincided with the spread of democratic institutions and values. Mass communications and extended news coverage have at once informed the people and made them curious about the activities previously the exclusive concern of kings, foreign ministers, and little-known civil servants and diplomatic experts. Second, there has been a great change in the number of citizens affected by major foreign-policy decisions, particularly those requiring a substantial commitment of human and nonhuman resources. Therefore, in the absence of complete dictatorship the support of those who supply the underpinnings of foreign policy is required. Third, there has been an increase in the number of people who are politically consequential, that is, who have sufficient leverage on the political process to have their specific needs and interests taken into account. The more power is diffused in a society the greater the number of individuals and groups who may at any one time and on any one issue possess a potential check on public policy making. Fourth, in a democracy, government needs discriminating rather than blind support for the objectives of foreign policy. Hence, a consensus based on free discussion must be worked out. Furthermore, government is constantly justifying itself to the people it serves. Finally, public opinion is a potent factor in foreign policy because decision makers behave as though it were. Washington officials, no matter what their place in the policy-making process and for different reasons, live in a psychological atmosphere in which public opinion is a kind of invisible specter—always present, uncertain, and threatening. But to Washington officials public opinion is also something to be manipulated, to be controlled if possible. The elaborate mechanisms connected with both these reactions are revealing.

► THE NATURE OF PUBLIC OPINION

In order to set the stage for the later attempt to assign reasonably clear roles to something more than vague forces, certain explicit definitions are in order. This may be done by examining the two elements of the phrase, first "public," then opinion.

THE "PUBLIC"

Three kinds of publics can be distinguished for purposes of analysis:

1. The *mass* public—the great body of citizens, the unorganized, undifferentiated adult population whose feelings and views are measured by and reflected in polls, surveys, votes, letters, and so on
2. The *attentive* public *—roughly 5–10 per cent of the mass public who, because of their individual intellectual activities, take a continuous interest in foreign affairs, are aware of all major issues, and are, comparatively, the best-informed citizens
3. The *effective* public †—those individuals and groups who are the nation's opinion leaders because they strongly influence, as well as articulate and represent, the opinions of the mass public and because they have various types of access to the policy-making process and to policy makers

---

* This suggestive concept originated with Gabriel Almond. Any student of public opinion and foreign policy owes a substantial debt to his *The American People and Foreign Policy* (New York, Harcourt, Brace & Company, 1950).

† It is to be noted that this formulation differs from Almond's, which employs the term "elite"; the authors have elected to avoid what they regard as certain difficulties and misconceptions attached to the term.

In turn, the effective public must be thought of as having four components:

    a. *Organized groups*—the hundreds of organizations which are politically active whether solely dedicated to foreign-policy objectives or not

    b. *Mass communication leaders and mediums*—newspapers, radio, television, and periodicals of large circulation; editorial writers, news analysts, and specialized commentators

    c. *Teachers, clergy, nongovernmental foreign-policy experts,* including the staffs of those professional journals which are read by particular segments of the attentive public

    d. *Community leaders*—individuals who influence opinion even though their social positions or professional affiliations do not endow them with this special right or privilege

These categories are obviously crude and overlapping. A teacher, for example, might be considered a member of both the attentive and the effective publics. Or, within the effective public, a single individual might be a member of an organized group and also function as a teacher. A number of combinations are possible on the basis of this sort of labeling. But the chief advantage of the breakdown is to make the point that the public is not a homogeneous force and to set the stage for later statements concerning the role of public opinion in foreign policy. When it is possible and useful to make generalizations which hold true more or less for all the categories, use of the term "general public" is appropriate so long as the distinctions are remembered.

One important use of a concept of multiple publics is to indicate that the process of opinion formation and influencing foreign policy is quite complicated. It is not just a matter of a mystical relation between government officials and the mass of citizens, between leaders and followers. The public is a creature of many parts whose behavior and significance vary widely. Therefore, while there is something called the "general public" as defined above, it must be said that it is constantly changing, depending on specific foreign-policy issues and circumstances. Publics are forming and re-forming. Probably the attentive stratum remains a kind of permanent nucleus. However, kinds of publics form for kinds of issues. The public for a major issue differs from the public for a minor issue. A general policy issue may have a different public from that of a specific policy issue. Foreign-policy objectives may interest a different segment of the general public from that interested in foreign-policy techniques. At any moment in time or on any one problem, the questions are these: What is the nature of this particular public? How have its different segments responded? Apparently, while there is a role for the public generally, that role is partially defined by the roles of its various segments. The question of the size, composition, and behavior of the various potential publics for foreign policy is obviously related to the question of consensus. Consensus must underwrite nearly all phases of foreign policy; yet the nature of the consensus will depend in part on the kind of public which has formed or which can be formed.

"OPINION"

Opinion may be defined as an attitude toward or reaction to particular questions, issues, events, or circumstances, usually repeated through time and conditioned by a psychological process in which the perceptual basis of the attitude or response is conditioned by certain factors. Elements which may go into the formation of an opinion may be roughly summarized as follows: Responses are functionally selective for the individual, that is, he will perceive external phenomena in terms of his psychological world and certain features of the external environment may not "exist" for him at all. The images of reality held by the individual—what the world looks like to him after he has selected those phenomena psychologically relevant for him; cultural values, folkways, and central ideas which affect in some degree every member of a society—these orientations are built into the individual and become for him "unconscious cues"; knowledge, information, and rational thought—all contribute to the formation of an opinion.

Opinions are not all of a piece. At least some distinctions must be noted here. Opinions may be structured or unstructured—a structured opinion meaning that the individual already has a frame of reference and a set of cues he regards as reliable before an event or issue comes to his attention. An unstructured opinion is one where the individual has no familiar intellectual apparatus to guide his response; he may have information but he uncertain of his judgment. An opinion may be casual, off the cuff, and momentary, or it may be carefully thought out and settled in the individual's mind. The intensity of opinions varies widely from passive acquiescence to willingness to sacrifice. Having a viewpoint is one thing; translating into any type of action is quite another. Nor is a "vague feeling" the same as a definite conviction. Opinions may be expressed or unexpressed. True attitudes may be deliberately suppressed or there may be no opportunity for expression. Likewise, expressed opinions may be effective or ineffective—a man sitting before his own fire with profound convictions is not to be compared with the activities of the woolgrowers in successfully pleading with a Congressional committee for a higher tariff on imported wool. A person's attitudes may be held in general, focused on abstract rather than specific, concrete issues and events. One may be opposed to warlike moves in general yet support such moves in real situations, or one may hold certain ideas but not make the connection with existing phenomena which relate to them.

THE CONCEPT OF MOOD*

The foregoing discussion suggests that public opinion may not always be expressed in a yes-or-nor response to a specific question. To probe the underlying factors listed above and to call attention to less well-structured aspects of public attitudes, a concept of mood may be helpful. Mood is best defined as consisting of psychological states, such as awareness, rejection,

---

* See Almond, *op. cit.* pp,. 9–14, 53ff.

dependence, and involvement, and also generalized feelings about the external relations of the nation. Mood thus is characterized by inclinations and reactions, by tendencies and responses. Mood will be determined by a range of potentially effective stimuli—some within the individual or group, such as unconscious cues or frustration of aims; others in the external setting, such as crisis or threats.

To be more specific, the public (this word is used in the broad sense) mood with respect to events and policies can be deduced as more or less one of involvement or noninvolvement, optimism or pessimism, tolerance or intolerance, and certainty or uncertainty. Noninvolvement suggests that support for established official policy would be less vocal, active, or enthusiastic, that responses to changes in policy would be essentially negative, that fewer organized groups would be active, that there would be more "don't know" responses on polls, and so on. A high degree of involvement would imply the opposite, including a primitive awareness of responsibilities, fear, and watchful waiting. An optimistic mood would be one in which a favorable interpretation is placed on the results of policy, expectations for new actions would be high, and peace and security are felt to be achieved or susceptible of achievement. Pessimism would involve judgments of policy failure and expectations of unwelcome developments. Trust would be associated with optimism and mistrust with pessimism. If the mood of the general public is tolerant, it might be expected that new, untried courses of action would not be rejected or resisted without a proper trial, that national sacrifice would be accepted if not welcomed, that the whims and caprices of other nations would be taken for granted, and that unclear consequences of policy and slow progress would be borne with patience. Intolerance might take many forms, including hostility and opposition to the acts of other nations. Finally, an uncertain mood would be one in which most members of the public do not possess clear rules for interpreting events and policies—in short, there is conjecture about what is going on and why. While there might be identifiable mood concerning specific policies or actions—particularly in a case like the Korean campaign—it is more likely that mood is centered around a cluster of problems or around the nation's relations with others, or around basic possibilities such as war and peace.

SUMMARY

It has been argued that the "public" has segments and groupings with differential functions, status, knowledge, interests, influence, and degrees of organization. It has also been argued that "opinion" embraces more than a snap response to a poll or a letter to a congressman. Attitudes are formed by processes in which social and psychological factors are operative. Opinions can be classified in terms of the process through which they are formed—in response to emotion or as a result of rational thought and in terms of their consequences, that is, whether they are recorded and lead to action. Mood can be derived from evidence of attitudes and responses—alternative states of mind and generalized feelings about foreign relations and foreign policy.*

► THE "ROLES" OF THE "PUBLICS"

It follows from what has been said above that the analysis of the impact of public opinion on foreign policy must rest on an assumption of several publics having different effects upon policy making. These publics are constituted in different ways, their moods and attitudes are arrived at through different processes, and they are related to each other and to the decision makers. Therefore the general links between public opinion and foreign policy should be conceived of in terms of sets of relationships, a series of processes, the performance of roles or functions, and channels of communication.

THE MASS PUBLIC

The role of the mass public is, on the whole, more indirect than direct, more general than specific, more negative than positive, and more passive than active. This segment of the public is unorganized and hence most of the time can bring pressure directly only by letters and telegrams. Apparently the mass public helps to set outer limits for foreign policy. Its moods tend to affect the tempo and degree of basic changes in foreign policy. No group of policy makers can afford to be too far out of line with the permissiveness or tolerance of the mass mood. The overwhelming sentiment of the citizens of the United States in the late 1930's was against any deep involvement in the developing conflict in Europe—a fact which certainly slowed down the reorientation of American foreign policy under Franklin D. Roosevelt. And it seems highly unlikely that the decision makers would ever adopt ends and means which violated in any real sense the common values held by the majority of the adult population.

Mass moods and opinions must first be expressed, then identified, and after that admitted to the policy-making process. While one hundred million citizens might unanimously agree on a course of action, if this were unknown to the decision makers or were ignored by them it would matter little. No impact of this kind of social fact on foreign policy is possible unless and until the decision makers take it into account. Essentially what takes place is an *assessment* of various kinds of evidence: opinion surveys, an election, letters to newspapers, the White House, congressmen, or the State Department. Expressions of this kind prove very little in and of themselves; they must be *interpreted*. Groups of policy makers have different ways of collecting and evaluating such data. On the one hand, the State Department, as noted in Chapter Seven, has an Office of Public Affairs with a Division of Public

---

* A good example of this is E. Roper and C. Crusius, "What Americans Think When They Think about the Peace," *Saturday Review,* June 6, 1953, p. 7— a discussion of the public mood concerning international cooperation and organization.

Liaison devoted to a rather elaborate opinion analysis operation which includes all the mediums of communication. On the other hand, the individual senator or representative may simply count the pro-and-con letters from constituents and come to a crude judgment about the public mood in his state or district.

Regardless of whether the collection and interpretation of data are carried out according to reliable methods or not (and this is an important point in itself), the crucial question is how seriously the estimates of mass mood and opinion are taken by, say, the State Department. A related question is this: Are these estimates taken more seriously than estimates of the moods and opinions of organized groups and recognized opinion leaders? Except where major decisions are involved it is likely that mass opinion serves more as a guide for the conduct of policy makers toward the unorganized public than as a specific directive for foreign policy—that is, estimates may reveal ignorance, apathy, lack of understanding, rising impatience, and so on, which have to be "corrected."

Among the kinds of evidence taken into account by the decision makers are the estimates made by appointed and self-appointed spokesmen for the mass public. These estimates are of course based in turn on evidence of some kind—intuitive feeling, personal contacts, unusual sources of information, and the like; nevertheless, these are accepted by the decision makers as evidence. Spokesmen, in the sense implied here, range from political officials who are not in the national government to community leaders, and from prestige figures to authorities on certain subjects. The mass public in effect helps to create such spokesmen through elections, through grants of respect and deference, and through becoming enthusiastic readers and listeners.

An estimate of the mass mood or opinion may prompt the policy makers to take steps which they feel will conform to the values and needs of the people. For example, it is probable that one reason for negotiating the Korean armistice in 1953 was a conviction among the decision makers that the public was rapidly becoming intolerant of additional expenditures of men and matériel in this way. In this case there may be a direct connection between a condition assumed to prevail among the unorganized public and the choices of top-level officials. Or the mass public may be persuaded to support the aims of opinion leaders and organized groups who have access to the policy-making process. To the extent that mass support increases the chances that policy makers will consider the demands of private leaders and groups, it can be said that the impact of the mass public is indirect.

Policy makers, working directly on the mass public or indirectly through opinion leaders, are constantly attempting to prepare citizens for new policies and to "sell" policies currently before the nation for adoption. President Franklin D. Roosevelt's major addresses on the new international position of the United States from 1937 to 1941 undoubtedly helped to pave the way for a policy of international cooperation which was a radical departure from previous isolationism. For several weeks before the San Francisco Conference of 1945 the nation was blanketed with a campaign on the provisions of the proposed United Nations Charter. Any issue of the State Department *Bulletin* will reveal the public addresses of the Secretary of State and other top officials designed to "sell" proposed policies or justify those adopted. Through periodic press conferences policies and developments are explained to the mass public. During the past dozen years the State Department has developed a rather vast domestic information program. One aspect of the role of the mass public is to be defined in terms of these official efforts to "inform" and "justify."

THE ATTENTIVE PUBLIC

Much the same analysis would hold for the role of the attentive public but with some important additions. It is quite probable that this core public is relatively more influential because its interests and activities are not confined to general questions and major choices. Normally, it is the attentive group which is subject to special appeals by segments of the effective public, particularly the opinion leaders and organized movements. This fact, together with their possession of more detailed information and superior interpretive capacity, explains why these members of the unorganized public participate more fully in the discussion of competing policy alternatives. The citizen who is in the attentive public because he obtains more information than is normally available in the mass mediums of communication and because foreign-policy problems are for him an intellectual hobby is, in all likelihood, a member of the public which forms around *any* foreign-policy issue. In all probability these are the people who read *The Reporter, The Nation, The New Republic, Harper's Magazine, The Atlantic Monthly, Foreign Affairs, World Politics,* the Foreign Policy Association *Reports,* and newspapers whose coverage of international politics is thorough, i.e., the *New York Times* or *The Christian Science Monitor.** Some citizens must be counted among the attentive public because they comprise the clientele of organized groups who take a special interest in particular policies. Thus the manufacturer of shoes becomes a member of the attentive public where import duties are concerned—he has more information, he has more specific ideas about what he does and does not want, and he is more involved than most of the mass public would be. Other citizens can be counted in because their attention is aroused by a group whose purpose is to mobilize active support for "sound" policies. Actually, the membership of the League of Women Voters can be regarded as a component of the attentive public. It would seem reasonable to suppose that these kinds of citizens have a greater grasp of the details and subtleties of foreign policy, enter into genuine discussion of alternatives, and are more active generally in the sense that they are more likely to attend meetings, to

---

* This is a suggestive, not exhaustive, list.

support the policy recommendations of various groups, to vote on issues and to express themselves in written communications to officials.

COMPARISON OF MASS AND ATTENTIVE PUBLICS

Both the mass and the attentive publics are unorganized, though both are subject to the leadership of the effective public—opinion leaders, mass mediums, groups, and so on. Both play the same general kind of role. If both are considered as a reservoir from which the particular public for particular issues is drawn, however, the attentive citizens are much more likely to become part of a public on a wide range of issues. It can be argued too that the moods and attitudes of the attentive public are better structured and therefore are not subject to extensive fluctuations in the short run. This is partly due to the fact that its members are much less dependent on the mass mediums. Because its interest appears to be more sustained, the attentive public does not swing sharply from involvement to withdrawal. Nevertheless, this group is not immune to cycles of opinion, to feelings of optimism and pessimism or tolerance and intolerance, and to ideas which may be fashionable at the moment.

THE ROLE OF THE EFFECTIVE PUBLIC

As defined above, the effective public is comprised of opinion leaders and organized groups—persons who, because of their social position, their control over the flow of information, their organizational backing, and their access to officials, exert a strong influence over public moods and attitudes and also over foreign-policy making. Clearly the unorganized publics—mass and attentive—cannot act continuously in the usual political sense. Beyond voting and letter writing, unorganized citizens are more or less dependent on the effective public to act for them and to provide cues and information. The individual member of the mass public cannot become a news gatherer, nor can the attentive citizen become an expert researcher in the field of foreign affairs. Therefore, the enormous significance of the role of the effective public lies primarily in the dependent status of other segments of the general public. While there are, as pointed out above, direct links between decision-making officials and the unorganized publics, perhaps the most important links are indirect, with the various components of the effective public acting as intermediaries. In this sense, these elements perform specialized functions on behalf of both government and the great body of citizens.

1. Mass communications. The average individual has to depend on newspapers, radio, television, and mass periodicals (*Life, Newsweek, U.S. News and World Report, Time,* various Sunday supplements are examples) for factual information concerning what is going on in the world and what the government is doing about it. Perhaps the primary role of the mass mediums—so called because they are giant, mechanized enterprises engaged in the mass production of "news" which reaches millions simultaneously—is to provide a record of events together with some cues for interpreting the events, i.e., whether they are to be regarded as good or bad, threatening or nonthreatening, and so on. The unorganized public (both mass and attentive) must rely on these media for its "images of reality," i.e., for the ingredients which comprise its mental pictures of events, conditions, and trends outside the United States and foreign-policy decision making in Washington. Included in the basic information are, of course, reports on what other Americans, individuals, and groups are thinking and doing about foreign affairs.

News is not just presented—either it is interpreted for the reader or he is supplied with cues for his own interpretation in a number of ways, some subtle and indirect, some obvious and direct. Usually the connection between "reporting" and "editorializing" or between presenting the news and making some judgment about it is so intermixed that the reader is unaware of the connection or its significance. Public moods and attitudes are conditioned by interpretive cues supplied in the very process of reporting and presenting as well as by a clearly differentiated accompaniment of reporting and presenting. Interpretation becomes involved immediately at the point where news happens and is first gathered—from among all the possible facts comprising an event the reporter or foreign correspondent selects a story or selects from certain ones to include in his report. As these stories and accounts come in to the big wire services (Associated Press, United Press, International News Service, and so on) further operations are performed. The material is "processed," which is to say edited and re-composed for sending out to the newspapers that subscribe to the service. Occasionally, news stories sent in by correspondents may be "killed" or, in Washington, the staffs of the wire services may decide something is unworthy of attention. At the newspaper itself, there are further opportunities for interpretation. Not everything which comes in can be printed; limited space dictates the need for choices. Editors can decide to feature something—give it added significance by the way it is presented in the pages of the newspapers. Over a period of days the newspaper may decide to push a certain story or related stories. Whether a story is given a headline, the wording of the headline, the wording of subheadlines —these factors will condition the image passed on to the reading public. Stories may be relegated to the back pages, headlined in small type, or omitted entirely.

In addition to interpretive cues supplied in this way, editorials and special commentaries provide direct interpretations of factual information. Editorials represent, usually, a consensus of the views of the newspaper's policy makers and experts and may be run on the editorial page or on the front page next to an important story. Distinguished foreign correspondents and reporters who submit signed articles and commentators who write regular columns which are syndicated in hundreds of newspapers play a great part in the opinion-forming process. The Alsops, Walter Lippmann, Hanson Baldwin, James Reston, Elmer Davis—to name a few—carry special weight with readers. Radio and television's outstanding commentators also fall in this class. Editorials and the views of commentators perform several functions for the unorganized publics: to attach "meanings" to events, conditions, and "policies in action" in terms of certain values—an explanation of the "news behind the news" and the connection between present or past events and existing policies; to voice criticism of official foreign policy and to present alternatives; to explain and "sell" official decisions after they have been made; to fill in relevant background data omitted from news stories; and, finally, to promote public interest in, and awareness of, significant foreign-policy issues. Widely respected foreign-affairs experts who have access through the written or spoken word to large audiences stand in a special relation to the attentive public. It is not too much to say that the followers of, for example, Walter Lippman constitute a whole segment of that public. These persons look to him for cues which in turn structure their moods and attitudes.

Mass communications, then, inform and persuade with varying degrees of success and with differential effects. Persuasion is a subtle process and it should perhaps be noted that people can be influenced without really knowing it; also, they can be influenced by the "aids" consciously selected and provided by editorial and expert commentary. However, while facts and interpretations of fact comprise the raw materials of public moods, attitudes, and opinions, the actual structure of the latter is never wholly due to the content and techniques of the mass mediums. Other social forces are operative. The average adult citizen's responses to the communication stimuli will also be governed by his previous experience, his general orientations toward his environment, his social status, his education and training, his group memberships, and his party affiliation. Each person brings to his exposure to mass mediums some perspectives relevant to public affairs as well as tendencies toward receptivity or resistance to certain kinds of stimuli. Perception is always selective; therefore something must condition whether and to what extent individuals will permit information on foreign affairs in the mass mediums to penetrate their consciousness and whether and to what extent individuals will be receptive to cues. It is well known that the foreign policy and external relations of the nation are simply not in the range of perception of some segments of the mass public. Some of these are heavily exposed to mass mediums but reject this category of information. Others similarly exposed absorb the information but reject the cues; indeed, they purposely avoid having opinions. Another group may be termed the "valley people," the people who avoid, deliberately, the mass mediums and, in fact, all contacts beyond the narrow psychological limits of their own individual lives; the "mountains" which bound the valley cut off communication with events and people about which the inhabitants of the valley apparently care nothing. Certainly a sizable segment of the mass public has only limited perspectives on the "outer world" of foreign policy. All this is only to suggest that the fact that there are millions of newspaper readers and radio listeners in the United States is no reason to assume that the standardized information on foreign policy has an equal impact on all. Probably it is much safer to assume a common store of information only among the attentive public. Members of the mass public are much more dependent on communication opinion leaders for simple cues which guide their feelings and probably accept these cues much more uncritically than does the attentive public. In the case of the attentive public, not only is there less dependence for cues on the mass communications but the members do *not* respond mostly on an emotional level. Such cues tend to be "accepted" by the attentive public after some rational thought and tend to influence opinions more than mood.

THE PRESS AND FOREIGN-POLICY DECISION MAKING. So far as government officials—the decision makers in both branches—are concerned, the mass communications serve several basic functions epitomized by the activities of the nation's press. First, as they go about the business of reporting to their readers, the members of the newspaper profession also play a key role in keeping government responsible to the people at large. The nature of the responsibility process has already been discussed, as has been the significance of the President's relations with the press. Responsibility cannot be enforced unless at least two conditions are met: exposure of the actions of government officials, and provision of opportunity for criticism and non-official comment on accepted and contemplated policies. Much depends on the skills of the "Washington press corps" in ferreting out accurate information from high and low levels of policy making, where all kinds of resistance may be met. Much also depends on the capacity and willingness of the press to open its facilities to all kinds of criticism (provided it in turn is responsible)—even that which is repugnant to editorial views. Actually, the press brings criticism to bear on national policies in two ways, each equally important. Editors and commentators, functioning as opinion leaders, address themselves to the government through the mass mediums, *and* the press acts as a channel of communication for other opinion leaders and groups who rely on press facilities for access to policy makers and other segments of the public. Thus the press itself criticizes and acts as a medium for other critics.

Shading off from expression of criticism and from the exposure of things hidden from public view is another function: the press attempts faithfully to reproduce for the public the "great debates" on foreign policy held in Congress and in the Executive Branch. The task of the press goes beyond the dramatic aspects of such events. Out of the torrent of words, the clash of personalities, and the interesting sidelights must be distilled the policy alternatives, values, and interpretations of reality which are subject to controversy. Since the great majority of the unorganized public cannot attend the debate personally and do not read the *Congressional Record,* they are dependent on the mass mediums for accurate presentation of the issues. On the occasion of the presentation of alternatives being considered by the decision makers, the various publics are stimulated to express preferences for one alternative or set of alternatives and to present fresh alternatives. Letters and telegrams are sent to representatives, senators, the President, the State Department, and editors of newspapers and news magazines. Public opinion polls can be taken on the assumption that more people have become psychologically involved and have more factual knowledge than would be true in the case of less dramatic, less publicized, less crucial matters. Usually a "great debate" will have the effect of reviving dormant ideas which have not entered into official consideration or of causing new approaches to be considered in a more favorable atmosphere. The great debates on "troops to Europe" and the removal of General MacArthur produced a resurgence of so-called "isolationist" thinking assumed to have been stifled by the developments from 1945 to 1950. One net effect of this function is to broaden the internal setting in which decisions are finally taken and to activate the public, which eventually becomes involved in a foreign-policy issue.

A third, and very significant, function of the press is to serve as a source of reliable information and interpretation with respect to public moods and opinions. Editors and commentators are at once important indexes of opinion and authoritative judges of opinion trends. Press leaders have special access to other opinion leaders in local communities and in Washington. But from the standpoint of the State Department it is probable that newspapers and other communications are relied on as guides to the moods and opinions of the unorganized public, particularly the mass public. The leading public opinion polls are syndicated and printed in various mediums.

Another function performed by the press for policy makers is the collection of information. In addition to the dependence of Congress, the foreign-affairs agencies of the Executive Branch also rely on the published and unpublished materials gathered by foreign correspondents. Though the Central Intelligence Agency, the Defense Department, and the State Department have their own special sources, the press services may have different and sometimes superior sources. At any rate, analyses of public opinion, events, and conditions abroad prepared by the private press constitute a vital part of the information which decision makers have at their disposal.

The government must be in more or less constant communication with all the publics; this is accomplished by the performance of press functions as noted above and, of course, through the use of the mass mediums by the decision makers. Speeches and press conferences fall in this category. Closely related to this is what has been called the function of the "trial balloon." There may be several purposes involved in the use of the press for exploratory activity: to ease the public into a gradual acceptance of something which might come as a great shock if presented too suddenly; to obtain a preview of possible reactions of public opinion at home and abroad, including the degree of opposition to a proposed course of action; to smoke out the views of other decision makers or to otherwise influence their behavior. On February 25, 1953, President Eisenhower announced to the press that he would talk to Stalin at any reasonable place if it would help to ensure peace, *adding* that the American people must desire such a talk and that America's allies must have full knowledge of its agenda. This was an example of a direct, obvious kind of trial balloon.

Another kind is accomplished by the following procedure. A high-level, responsible official will call leading reporters together for an off-the-record "briefing." Certain policy matters are explained fully but the reporters are told that they cannot attribute the story to this particular official or to any other or any agency. Under these circumstances, the White House can always deny anything which is printed. An example of this technique occurred in April, 1953. After Secretary of State Dulles held such a meeting a story was widely circulated to the effect that the United States was considering agreeing to a dividing line across the "waist" of Korea and truce talks were resumed. The story was denied by the White House, which said that the "administration has never reached any conclusion that a permanent division of Korea . . ." was desirable. James Reston, distinguished reporter of the New York *Times,* calls this the "government art of denying the truth without lying." It should be noted that this role of the press puts the professional newsman in the position of deciding whether to suppress news or to run the risk of being repudiated by government officials whose word must be taken as authoritative. However, the necessity for trial balloons is well established. After trying to confine themselves only to carefully policed official releases, the American delegation to the San Francisco Conference of 1945 finally had to establish a "Calculated Leak Office."

No discussion of the role of the press would be complete without mention of the impact of press functions which are considered undesirable by the policy makers. Needless to say, public revelations during delicate negotiations can play all kinds of mischief. In their efforts to get a story and to expose decision making to public view, the members of the press may defeat the legitimate aims of officials and provide a propaganda advantage for other nations. In March, 1953, when the British Foreign Minister, Anthony Eden, and several other high-ranking Britons were in the United States for top-level economic and financial talks, American newsmen were not briefed in advance and could obtain no story from the American participants. The British team talked freely, with the result that a story was printed suggesting that President Eisenhower had had to intervene to soften the attitude of those negotiating for the United States. In addition, the British viewpoint was much more thoroughly and sympathetically presented. These reports adversely affected the position of the Treasury and State Department officials representing the United States. The press revealed the deneutralization of Formosa in February, 1953, before the President could communicate officially with Congress. When some papers drew their own inferences from the move the official denials and explanations which had to be made had the effect, taken in conjunction with other factors, of narrowing the desired scope of the decision and of reducing its psychological impact.

That the press acts as a communicator among decision makers has been emphasized at several points in this book. Communication via the newspapers is communication, to be sure, but it is quite different from face-to-face discussion in private. Many foreign-policy issues receive entirely different treatment within the Executive Branch, depending on whether an individual official or a group of officials "tries the case in the press." Many plans get smoked out before they are ready for public discussion. The thoroughness and effectiveness of the press also constitute a potential inhibition on decision making because the development of a policy is rarely undertaken unless early revelation can be tolerated.

To conclude, mass communications serve a cluster of public opinion functions. Essential services are performed, separately, for both the general public and the government. The core of the mass mediums—the national press —acts as a vital set of channels which join the various publics and the policy makers.

2. Teachers and clergy. Two groups of opinion leaders must be commented on briefly because of the position of social influence each occupies. Not only because of obvious sanctions available to them but because of the prestige they enjoy, teachers and clergy have a continuous, direct opportunity to shape citizen moods and attitudes. As individuals performing social roles, the two groups chiefly influence the mass and the attentive publics. Regardless of whether they try consciously to affect foreign-policy judgments, their functions are such that some impact is inescapable. So far as public opinion *in general* is concerned, studies indicate a clear correlation between education and religious affiliation on the one hand and the nature of opinions on the other.

It seems reasonable to assume that, apart from whatever specific advice on specific policies they might give, teachers and clergy have an opportunity to shape moods and attitudes in the following ways: (1) Teachers and clergy supply information—additional to that supplied in the mass mediums—or remind listeners of what they already know. When current events are taught in secondary schools or when specialized courses are given in college, the student is usually exposed to a wider range of information. Sermons may also add to the store of knowledge possessed by the churchgoer. (2) When teachers and clergy devote themselves to questions of public policy, they are in the process alerting some of their listeners to those questions, they are adding those questions to the range of things perceived by their listeners. (3) They suggest appropriate values for governing choices. The clergy naturally tend to stress the application of religious values to the judgment of events and policies. Teachers may stress democratic values or analytical values, such as adequate information, "thought" rather than "emotion," careful assessment of all relevant factors, and so on. (4) To the extent that these two groups of opinion leaders participate in the "great debates" on foreign policy it is probable that students and congregations are more likely to be exposed to discussion of several alternatives or at least to alternatives not adequately treated in the mass mediums.

If this is a fair projection of the possible kinds of influence that teachers and clergy may have, their importance is obvious. For they contribute, actually or potentially, unique qualities to opinion formation. It is their recognized function to teach. Teaching foreign policy per se may be a negligible part of all teaching, but the perspectives and knowledge gained from school and church will be among the factors which condition the general orientation of citizens toward the foreign relations of the nation.

NONGOVERNMENTAL EXPERTS. One subcategory of teachers deserves special mention—the various academic specialists and scholars whose interests, formal training, or experience comprise an *expertise* in the general realm of foreign policy. This group would include social scientists, historians, and area experts, most but not all of whom hold positions on college and university faculties. As recognized intellectual leaders, they influence other teachers, advanced students, and segments of the attentive public through their books and articles in scholarly journals. This group is singled out not only because its members are opinion leaders as are teachers generally but because they serve as expert consultants to the government. Through them the official policy makers can supplement their own intellectual resources. Foreign-policy consultants may actually hold official posts in the State Department or other agencies on a temporary basis, they may serve on presidential commissions, or they may be called in singly or in groups for a few hours or a few days of discussion with government policy makers. It therefore seems permissible to consider them as representatives of a highly specialized segment of the effective public. As America's international position has become more complicated, the outside consultant has been used more frequently and, presumably, has had some influence on decision making.

Another reason for mentioning the expert-scholars who advise the government is that their values and perspectives are likely to be substantially different from those of reporters, editors, commentators, political leaders, organized groups, the clergy, and so on. The views and perspectives of expert-scholars are also likely to be different from those of the official decision makers. For one thing, the professional scholars usually have no ax to grind, no special cause to plead, and usually do not represent any particular group. Hence they can attack an issue on "its merits." If they have spent their intellectual life working with materials related to foreign policy or living and observing in certain key areas of the world, they presumably have developed special insights that are based on a desire for knowledge for its own sake and are unaffected by political considerations. Their opinions are less susceptible to the pressures which affect policy makers. For another thing, expert-scholars are perhaps more inclined to take a larger view of a problem and therefore to ask more questions which may be relevant but ignored by self-interested parties. On occasion, outside experts may possess technical skills not present in the personnel of the decision-making organization.

The contribution of these experts to the decision-making process is varied. Ordinarily it is not information or data per se which the government needs, their sources being, on balance, superior to private sources. Rather, what may be needed is a trustworthy interpretation of conditions, events, or the policies of other states. This will be especially true where the policy makers are confronted with unforeseen developments or new factors concerning which experience is lacking. Experts are also asked for their judgment on possible courses of action and on the probable consequences of proposed courses of action. The policy makers may want a reliable check on their estimates or they may desire an expression of preference by experts because no official preference or agreement exists or is possible. Finally, the consultation of outside experts may be a legitimate tactic employed by decision makers to forestall opposition in Congress or among segments of the general public and to buttress the arguments for policy programs.

Though it is almost impossible to document the precise impact of individual outside experts on specific policies, it is possible to cite certain aspects of foreign policy on which they have been consulted extensively and on which government's *expertise* was something less than adequate at particular moments during the past fifteen years. Perhaps the first large-scale use occurred during the years 1942 to 1945 when economists, political scientists, historians, international lawyers, and area specialists were enlisted in the task of preparing the groundwork for the new postwar international organization and for postwar American foreign policy generally. For this purpose, consultants were brought into the State Department on a per diem basis to draft memoranda and to participate in discussions. As the Soviet Union emerged more and more as the prime factor in postwar world politics, a handful of Russian experts largely drawn from research enterprises at Columbia and Harvard and from a small number of other faculties were consulted. Similarly, as the Far East, particularly China, became more and more unsettled and required new policies, a relatively small number of experienced scholars familiar with the region and its problems were called upon for advice. The whole postwar foreign-aid effort, together with complex problems of economic development in certain areas and of dollar balances in Western Europe, required the insights and competence of economists.

▶ THE ROLES OF ORGANIZED INTEREST GROUPS

It would be manifestly impossible in the space available to list and describe the relevant activities of the hundreds of organized groups which are periodically or continually active with respect to foreign policy. America is, par excellence, a nation of groups—groups of varying degrees of organization, purposes, and social significance. All the diversity of American life is reflected in economic, political, ethnic, religious, and social groups. These have different purposes and are more or less highly organized. Regardless of whether groups are effective or not, have huge financial resources or not, have a large membership or not, or pursue narrow or broad interests, all have this much in common: they claim to speak officially and authoritatively for a sizable, important segment of the unorganized public whose interests are the nation's interests or they claim to have special competences (information or technical skills or both) pertinent to foreign-policy formation and execution. This section will attempt to suggest the typical kinds of groups and kinds of purposes they may have, their access to the policy-making process, and the functions they perform.

There are three noteworthy reasons why more groups are more continuously involved in attempts to influence the decision makers. First, the fact that major foreign policies are legislated is an open invitation to pressure groups to plead their causes on very familiar grounds. Second, major foreign policies—such as the Mutual Security Program and the peace treaties—may affect most economic groups; the broader foreign-policy issues become, the more they will attract approval or disapproval. Third, the more technical foreign-policy programs and their execution become, the more likely it is that the government will have to rely on private groups, i.e., atomic physicists, engineers, industrialists, labor leaders, and so on, for specialized help.

MAJOR TYPES OF GROUPS INTERESTED IN FOREIGN POLICY

A review of the organizations which testify on policy legislation such as lend-lease, the British loan of 1946, the Mutual Security Program, and the Reciprocal Trade Agreements Act provides an excellent roster of the group structure which impinges on foreign relations. Economic groups include the National Association of Manufacturers, the Chamber of Commerce of the United States, the American Farm Bureau Federation, the Congress of Industrial Organizations and the American Federation of Labor, the American Tariff League, the American Paper Institute, the United States Steel Corporation, the American Mining Congress, the National Dairy Union, and many others. Some fifty economic groups have opposed the renewal of the Reciprocal Trade Agreements Act. Important social groups include the American Legion, the Daughters of the American Revolution, the Navy League, the American Veterans Committee, the National Federation of Women's Clubs, Rotary International, the Kiwanis, and the Lions. The National Council of Churches of Christ, the Roman Catholic Church, and the Zionist Organization illustrate powerful religious groups. Professional groups which exert significant influence are the League of Women Voters, the United Nations Association, the Foreign Policy Association, the Brookings Institution, the Council on Foreign Relations, the American Bar Association, the National Education Association, and the various institutes of international affairs. On occasion, economic, social, professional, and even religious groups will form coalitions—as in the case of the Committee for Support of Marshall Plan Aid and the Nation-wide Committee of Industry, Agriculture, and Labor on Import-Export Policy.

Though they are not as highly organized, this list must of course include the ethnic minorities which are so characteristic of American society. There are some thirty distinct nationalities represented; moreover, approximately 25 per cent of the population have either been born abroad or have parents who have been born abroad. Many of these ethnic groups retain European languages (German, Italian, Polish, French, and Swedish), have their own newspapers, and maintain strong contacts with members of their families still living outside the United States. Many have their own churches or are affiliated with powerful church organizations. As might be expected, viewpoints of these ethnic groups tend to form around immigration issues and around the particular relationships between the United States and the nations of their origin. Normally, ethnic factors operate in Congressional and presidential elections where a concentrated Jewish, Polish, Italian, or Irish vote may turn on a foreign-policy issue. For example, in New York City the Jewish vote is so important that on matters concerning the country of Israel the administration in power will pay close attention to the possible effects of its actions on that vote. In October, 1953, rumors were circulating that United States aid to Israel might be cut off because of recurrent border incidents in which Arabs and Israelis were involved. The Republican candidate for Mayor of New York was summoned to Washington to talk to Secretary of State Dulles and returned to New York with the declaration that aid to Israel would *not* be discontinued. Ethnic minorities also have national spokesmen (i.e., the American Polish Association) who in effect lobby in Washington and who presume to speak for blocs of individuals though the latter are not, strictly speaking, members of an organization.

Among the organized interest groups must be counted the two political parties, insofar as this means the National Committee of each and the state and local units of each. National Committee members and the state and local leaders are not official decision makers on the federal level, and hence can be considered part of the effective public for purposes of analysis. Even the national convention can be considered a possible source of pressure on decision makers through the discussion of platforms and candidates. In between times, the National Committee and the state and local units become involved in foreign policy whenever by-elections or trends in voter opinion turn on such issues. If nominees in Congressional elections can be aided by a presidential speech or other tactic, the party organization will so request. The opposition party, outside the official governmental structure, may also act as an organized pressure. Adlai Stevenson, defeated Democratic candidate for President in 1952, became spokesman for his party and after a trip around the world in 1953 made proposals to President Eisenhower to which the latter listened at a White House conference. Mr. Stevenson was not speaking as an ordinary citizen but as a titular party leader who had received over twenty-five million votes. Another reason for including the two parties in this list is that studies have shown a definite correlation between party affiliation (among the mass of voters) and foreign-policy attitudes. This means that many citizens take their cues for reactions to various issues from what is understood to be the party position.

ACCESS TO DECISION MAKING

Representatives of organized groups have several ways of influencing the legislative aspect of foreign-policy decision making. They testify at hearings and investigations, may help draft legislation, may help committee staffs collect information, and may persuade individual congressmen to act in their behalf. Opportunities to influence policy within the Executive Branch are equally numerous. Departments hold hearings too—as exemplified by the Trade Agreements Committee, which attempts to discover how proposed tariff reductions will affect various producers and sellers. Many consultants who serve executive agencies in some expert capacity really represent private groups. As noted previously, presidential commissions are often composed of distinguished leaders from business, finance, labor, and agriculture and presumably one of the purposes of forming such a commission is to tap the judgment of men who can speak authoritatively for typical large groups. Advisory groups and committees also prepare special reports to serve as a possible basis for decisions. In addition to these points of access in the Executive Branch, the demands of pressure are formally evaluated by the Division of Public Liaison in the State Department.

The foregoing are what might be termed institutionalized channels of information and persuasion joining the internal setting and the decision-making process. But the values and opinions of organized groups may also be fed into decisions via the motives of the decision makers themselves. It was commonly acknowledged early in the Eisenhower Administration that the key posts were deliberately filled by business leaders. To some extent these leaders share the values of important segments of business and therefore to that extent those segments are "represented" in official counsels. One value which was frequently expressed by the new administration and which was expressed in defense planning was a balanced federal budget, assumed by businessmen outside government as a primary condition for a sound economy. In this case, values absorbed by the decision makers as a result of their group affiliation or social role *before* they became officials tend to influence their policy judgments. Such values have become in effect an integral part of the intellectual process of individual decision makers. On the other hand, group values can be reflected in policy because of the estimates and expectations of the decision maker—estimates of the strength and soundness of group demands and expectations concerning the consequences of recognizing or ignoring such demands. In this case, the decision maker does not necessarily share the group values but allows them to sway his judgment.

THE PURPOSES FOR WHICH ACCESS IS USED

1. Groups urge values on the unorganized public and the decision makers. The articulate groups which partially make up the effective public espouse competing formulations of the national interest, that is, they attempt to define the values (wants and needs) which should guide the selection of specific policy alternatives. Closely related to formulations of national interest is the attempt to identify certain situations confronting the nation as threatening or as demanding action. An excellent example of the offering of competing values and interpretations of events can be seen in the period 1935 to 1941. On one side were such groups as the National Council for Prevention of War, the Women's International League for Peace and Freedom, and the America First Committee. Though their motives differed a great deal, these groups acted as a powerful lobby in favor of neutrality and noninterventionism. Their leaders did not regard the deteriorating situation in Europe as a threat to the United States, did not want America to support one side or the other after World War II broke out, and put peace above all other values. Opposed to this general orientation were the Committee to Defend America by Aiding the Allies and the Fight for Freedom Committee, both of which embraced groups which had fought for revision of the Neutrality Act and which advocated all aid to the Allies short of war. This lobby viewed the European conflict as of grave interest to the United States and argued that an Axis victory would have consequences far worse than giving up peace temporarily to guarantee an Allied victory. A sort of latter-day version of the Committee to Defend America is the Committee on Present Danger, a group of fifty leaders from business, industry, communications, and education which formed in 1950 to stimulate awareness both in Congress and among the mass public of the threat of Communism to the nation's security.

In 1954, two general value conflicts among organized groups could be sensed. One concerned the amount of accommodation the United States should make to the demands and desires of nations with whom cooperation is essential. In a sense this could be termed a nationalist-internationalist split or, as some viewed it, a self-interest–moral principle split. But these formulations are somewhat misleading. The basic conflict seemed to be over the extent to which the United States should allow continued foreign aid to displace certain other goals such as a balanced budget and income tax reduction, over whether to risk defeats in the United Nations, over whether to go along with certain United Nations programs such as Technical Assistance and UNESCO educational efforts if this meant giving up an American national program of aid to underdeveloped countries and control of materials used in public schools. This same kind of conflict had been crystallized around the Korean campaign, where the United States had borne the brunt of the effort yet had to pay attention to the attitudes of other members of the United Nations involved in the conflict. From 1951 onward, the American Legion, the Veterans of Foreign Wars, and the Daughters of the American Revolution have rather consistently argued for a restricted interpretation of how much the United States should sacrifice its control over its own actions. Other groups, the League of Women Voters, for example, have argued that it is in the self-interest of the United States to accommodate itself to the legitimate needs of friends and allies and to live with the possible inconveniences of joint diplomacy.

Related to this kind of split is one which focuses on economic foreign policy. Some organized economic groups (to be mentioned below) feel strongly that the national interest is best served by protecting the domestic producers—anything which decreases the market for them hurts the whole country by weakening its productive capacity. On the other hand, other economic pressures insist that the interests of a few producers must be sacrificed to the larger national interest, which is to provide additional markets for those nations which have been aided by billions of American dollars to increase production but find themselves denied a market in the United States. Imbedded here is not only a different interpretation of national interest but a different view of the relative importance of a sound international economy and how it is to be achieved.

As Professor Almond* has pointed out, there is a fairly solid group consensus on certain basic ideas despite the fact that the conflicts noted run beneath the surface of agreement and flare up on specific issues. Naturally there are qualifications and differences of emphasis, but the consensus now appears to include resistance to all forms of Communist expansion, participation in alliances and other security arrangements which are costly and require global planning, and dedication to an eventual international order which embodies at least the core American political values.

2. *Groups urge the acceptance of general and specific objectives.* One major function of organized groups is to build support for particular policies among the mass and the attentive publics. Since on important issues there is likely to be some opposition, one result may be competitive discussion of alternatives. It is generally agreed that organized groups do not create opinion because original stimuli come to the unorganized public from the mass mediums and opinion leaders. Rather, groups tend to make vocal, to clarify, and to crystallize opinion. Several examples will illustrate the point here. When President Truman announced the nomination of an ambassador to the Vatican in November, 1951, Protestant organizations carried on a nationwide campaign among fifty million of their members and generated sufficient opposition to compel withdrawal of the nomination. The Zionist Organization spearheaded the campaign to build public support for a change in govern-

---

* Almond, *op. cit.,* Chap. 8.

ment policy toward the conflict between Palestine and the Arab states in 1947–1948 and, later, to prepare the way for a favorable reception of the new state of Israel. In both cases, the foreign policy of the United States embraced the objectives desired by Jewish organizations, although powerful forces, including the oil companies with substantial holdings in the Middle East, were opposed to American support of the Jews in that region against the avowed aims and interests of the Arabs. The League of Women Voters is given a large share of the credit for mobilizing effective public backing of the loan to Great Britain in 1946. One of the most powerful group of influences in the field of postwar foreign policy was the China Lobby—an organization of nearly four thousand Chinese with forty-five local offices in the United States which preserved and augmented the great affection for China already held by church groups and which received open support from prominent members of Congress. This lobby helped to maintain a steady flow of aid to the Chiang Kai-shek government ($5 billion from 1937 to 1951) and to preserve a favorable image of the Kuomintang leader in the face of mounting evidence that all was not well with the Nationalist regime. Even after this regime moved to Formosa, the China Lobby succeeded in affecting public opinion to the extent that a calm, rational re-examination of American policy was rendered exceedingly difficult.

After the Eisenhower Administration had announced a philosophy of "trade not aid" early in 1953, a drive began to make the objective of American economic foreign policy the protection of the domestic market. The Nation-wide Committee of Industry, Agriculture, and Labor on Import-Export Policy (representing independent oil producers, the coal industry, pottery and glass plants, woolgrowers, cotton manufacturers, the dairy industry, the lead and zinc miners, leather processors, hatmakers, nut growers, cattlemen, fisheries, and the clock and watch manufacturers) was created to wage a public campaign in behalf of higher tariffs and import quotas. The American Tariff League and the National Labor-Management Council on Foreign Trade Policy worked closely with this committee. Ranged on the opposite side of this issue, working for a continuance of so-called liberal trade policies, were the National Foreign Trade Council, the Detroit Board of Commerce, the Committee on Economic Development, the National Association of Manufacturers, and the United States Chamber of Commerce. There was a vigorous, lengthy argument as a result of this joining of a very specific issue of economic policy. Both inside and outside Congress, the split between groups was wide, thus indicating that circumstances could produce a severe breach in the economic aspect of the foreign-policy consensus.

3. The impact of groups on the conduct of foreign policy. One of the most significant developments in the postwar period has been the enlarged role of labor groups in foreign policy. Under the Foreign Assistance Act of 1948 the employment of two labor advisers by the European Cooperation Administration was required and from then on organized labor representatives held advisory posts. In addition, a corps of labor experts operates as part of the diplomatic establishment in twenty-three foreign capitals. The American Federation of Labor substantially influenced policy execution in Germany when it successfully argued for postponing the dismantling of a few German plants "to provide time for the gradual re-employment of thousands of workers whose jobs would have been affected." Secretary of State George Marshall went so far as to suggest in the summer of 1948 that Clinton Golden of the CIO be appointed Ambassador to France. Even though the Eisenhower Administration was dominated to begin with by business leaders, the need of experts from organized labor will continue by virtue of the general significance of trade unions in European politics and in view of the expansion of the labor movement in all countries.

The Association of Atomic Scientists—through their *Bulletin of the Atomic Scientists,* through opinion leaders, and by direct pressure on decision makers—has tried consistently for several years to counterbalance what it regards as an overemphasis on atomic weapons in national security planning. In February, 1953, Clarence Francis of the General Foods Corporation headed a group of fifty-five businessmen and financiers who comprised eleven teams which eventually visited fourteen countries and reported back to the director of the Mutual Security Agency on ways of improving the foreign-aid program. The American Association of University Women has aided in an exchange program through which women from Germany and Japan came to the United States to live for a specified period of time. From early in 1952 onward, a committee of the American Bar Association took the leading role in agitating for a constitutional amendment to curb the President's treaty-making power and actually drafted the resolution which was later sponsored by Senator Bricker.

Economic groups have succeeded in persuading congressmen to add riders and amendments to appropriations bills which increase the cost of foreign-policy techniques and intensify adverse reactions abroad. Three such examples may be mentioned here: first, the "Buy American Clause"—foreign bids for the supply of goods and services under all the foreign-aid programs must be 25 per cent below American bids; second, Department of Defense money cannot be spent "for the procurement of any article of food, clothing, cotton or wool . . . not grown, reprocessed, reused, or produced in the United States or its possessions. . . ."—a provision which naturally applies to overseas forces and therefore deprives certain nations of a potential market and the American taxpayers of possible savings; and third, 50 per cent of all goods shipped to foreign ports under the aid programs have been carried in American vessels. The concerted attack by the American Legion on Secretary of State Dean Acheson in August, 1952, is a reminder that groups may attempt —and occasionally with some success—to undermine public confidence in a top-level policy maker.

4. Groups participate in the making of foreign policy. Groups may be invited, in effect, to become participants in policy formation. An example of this is a technical matter such as the tariff, where affected interests are asked to discuss specific rates with a Congressional subcommittee or the Trade Agreements Committee. Another entree to policy making is provided by advisory commissions and committees where several major groups are usually represented. While the United Nations Charter was being hammered out by the State Department in 1944 and early 1945 the major types of groups were heard regularly on a kind of committee basis, a procedure which was more than *pro forma*. A third way for an organized group to become part of the decision-making process is through special reports and other research activities which may be accepted as a basis for official decisions. Thus, because of its memorandum on the subject prepared with government encouragement under its War and Peace Studies Project, the Council on Foreign Relations is generally credited with influencing President Roosevelt's 1940 decision to include Greenland within the scope of the Monroe Doctrine.

One of the most celebrated cases involving the role of a private research group occurred in 1950–1952, after Senatory McCarthy attacked the Institute of Pacific Relations as a victim of Communist infiltration and charged that the Institute's publications reflected a Moscow line.* His main point was that the China policy of the United States had been subverted by Communist influence exerted through the IPR. The story of the charges made against this research organization, the long investigation by the Senate Internal Security Subcommittee, and the final committee report are too long and complex to be reviewed here. One facet of the story is relevant and that is the question of the relation between the IPR and the decision makers. As an organization of scholars, the Institute published two journals, the *Far Eastern Survey* and *Pacific Affairs,* some 220 books dealing with the politics, economics, and diplomacy of the Far East, and numerous data papers prepared for national and international conferences. But the charges that the Institute allegedly controlled or unduly influenced the Far Eastern foreign policy of the United States arose fundamentally from two circumstances. During the critical war and postwar periods when China and other areas of the Far East were in process of violent flux and when American policy became inadequate and groping, the nation had only a handful of qualified experts on this area, most of whom knew each other intimately and most of whom were associated with the IPR in one way or another. Those of this group who became decision makers kept up their close personal relations with the others. In addition, as might be logically expected, the IPR was called upon to supply specialists from time to time. Owen Lattimore, later himself a controversial figure, became the personal representative of President Roosevelt to Chiang Kai-shek. During World War II, prominent government officials asked to be delegates

---

* Hearings on the IPR were held from July 25, 1951, to June 20, 1952, by the Internal Security Subcommittee of the Senate Committee on the Judiciary. A final report by the full committee was issued July 2, 1952.

to international conferences sponsored by the Institute. There is also a record of telegrams and other messages exchanged between officials concerned with Far Eastern matters and officers of the research body.

It is very important to note, however, that there has been no convincing evidence presented that the IPR was an action group in the same sense as others discussed in this section or that it advanced a particular, coherent Far Eastern policy. Rather it would seem logical to assume that the effective influence, if any, arose from the existence of a small intellectual community of experts (some in government, some not, but all experienced in the ways of Chinese politics especially) who shared common information about this vital area and also shared a professional judgment as to the assumptions upon which a sound policy would have to be built. Now this sort of relationship can give rise to a situation in which the orientations of policy makers can be conditioned by an outside organization; nonetheless, this is a long way from saying that the decision makers took their policy ready-made from a private agency. From one point of view, the whole furor over the Institute of Pacific Relations is a classic example of how motivational tendencies of decision makers may be partly explainable by their previous professional experience and group affiliations, especially when the latter continue after an official position has been accepted. From another point of view, the case illustrates the likelihood that organized group influences will be enhanced when the supply of some skill or competence is scarce and the government must rely on private sources.

5. *Groups educate and inform the other publics.* Mention of the Institute of Pacific Relations is a reminder that certain highly significant organized groups discharge an essentially educational and informational function directed toward both the unorganized publics and the opinion leaders. Outstanding examples are the Foreign Policy Association, the Council on Foreign Relations, the Brookings Institution, the National Planning Association, the Carnegie Endowment for International Peace, and the League of Women Voters. Through their publications these organizations provide the members of the attentive public and opinion leaders (teachers, clergy, and nongovernmental experts) with more information, better analysis, and somewhat different bases for judging policy issues than is normally true of the mass mediums.

While their purposes and techniques differ, all such organizations share a common interest in presenting a maximum amount of objective information and in helping citizens to think clearly and constructively about foreign-policy problems. When they do take a stand on a particular issue it is usually in the interest of "sound" policy or in the interest of the whole nation as distinct from any of its parts. Perhaps the most "activist" of the groups listed is the League of Women Voters (which in a sense is typical of several powerful women's organizations such as the General Federation of Women's Clubs), which issues *The National Voter* twice monthly as a guide to its 100,000 members and 750 local leaders. This newsletter discusses major issues before

Congress or being considered in the Executive Branch and informs the membership of the stand taken by the national organization on specific policies. The League also urges its local affiliates to stimulate letters to Congress on pending matters.

The League through its local discussion groups, the Council on Foreign Relations through its study groups in key cities, the Foreign Policy Association through its World Affairs Councils, and the Carnegie Endowment through its conferences attempt to crystallize opinions and to train opinion leaders. In some cases, public meetings open to all citizens are held to clarify issues and debate alternatives. In other cases, the aim is to create an attentive public which will bring direct pressure on the government. Or an effort is made to equip local community leaders with the necessary information and analysis so that they in turn may lead the rest of the citizens. There are both formal and informal relations between these groups and the decision makers. Often the government will request their cooperation in a program to inform the unorganized publics concerning a problem or to solicit support. An outstanding example of this was the concerted campaign of some ninety groups to inform the public at large of the provisions and significance of the United Nations Charter in 1945.

► THE ROLES OF COMMUNITY LEADERS

Community leaders on the state and local level are apparently a significant element of the effective public. Though their official positions and group affiliations are certainly relevant, their prestige also appears to be built on social position, community service, and personal popularity. At any rate, community leaders play a twofold role. First, what such men think is accepted by the national decision makers as a reliable clue to what the mass thinks or would think if issues were widely discussed. Therefore a special attempt is made to find out what the moods and attitudes of selected individual community leaders are. Second, community leaders may be recruited as opinion leaders to help spread information and build support for existing policies. Occasionally foreign-policy matters become explosive local issues as in the case of the use of UNESCO reading materials in public schools. On such occasions, the community leaders (apart from the teachers and the clergy) may become stabilizing and mediating influences. This is particularly true when organized groups attack the other opinion leaders because of their ideas and teaching practices.

► DECISION MAKERS AS OPINION LEADERS,
   OPINION GAUGES, AND LOBBYISTS

Top-level executive decision makers, from the President down to the assistant secretaries, naturally exercise a great influence over public moods and attitudes. Direct appeals are made to mass audiences which are designed to "sell" policies already decided upon, to prepare the way for contemplated policies, and to inform concerning significant events and trends. These officials achieve their purposes through attempts to control what is said—information —and how it is received by listeners or readers—cues for interpretations. It is a mistake to assume that the dramatic, well-publicized speeches and press conferences of the President and Secretary of State exhaust the significant occasions on which decision makers act as opinion leaders or engage in exchanges which affect public opinion.

In all executive agencies the functions of the press secretary, the information officer, and the public relations counsel (some have all three or some combination of them) have assumed major proportions and attest to the complex daily relationships with all segments of the public. Groups demand to be heard and the press demands news. The information officer and the public relations expert not only provide factual materials but are also engaged in a goodwill operation. It is vitally important that the President, the Secretary of State, and other ranking officials have a "good press" because the public image of such officials influences the way their words are received. Through interviews and written replies to questions, decision makers are engaged in a rather constant give-and-take over the meaning of policy. Private groups try to expose policy actions they do not like or try to attain a favorable interpretation. Decision makers have to conceal some things and see to it that correct interpretations are given the released information. Hence a continual struggle.

This particular aspect of the total public opinion relationship in a democracy is a vital one. It takes place at many points. Therefore there are many potential trouble spots and there may be competing versions of events and policies. Sometimes inconsistencies and confusions arise because policies are unclear or are not clearly understood or because one agency disobeys the rules on the timing and content of announcements. At other times, an agency or an executive group may in effect be conducting a campaign in behalf of its aims as against other executive groups. The Air Force, for example, has public relations experts and information officers who have access to the press to plead their case to the public and to Congress. Executive groups may operate to all intents and purposes as lobbies and thus try to enlist the support of other groups—preferably organized groups with influence in Congress.

Congressmen act as opinion leaders too. Perhaps their versions of policy may differ from those of the Executive Branch. Senators and representatives, through their questioning of the Executive Branch, increase the information available to the general public and their comments may well affect the public "image" of policy-making officials. There seems little doubt that sustained Congressional criticisms of Secretary of State Dean Acheson (1949–1952) did much to render him a political liability—which means that the leaders of the Democratic party felt that many voters would vote against the party on the secretary's account. Members of Congress are on the whole closer to organized groups than are executive officials and pride themselves on their ability to translate the preferences of the general public into policy. It is also probably true that most congressmen are closer to the unorganized publics than is the average top-level executive policy maker, despite the President's capacity to make a personal appeal. Members of Congress not only act as opinion leaders and communicators of public moods and opinions, but are often regarded by executive decision makers as accurate gauges of private group and individual feelings on foreign-policy questions. Thus Congress estimates the public and the Executive Branch estimates Congress. To the extent that the State Department or any other agency receives its impressions of the views of the general public through Congress instead of directly through polls and surveys, the public will have a relatively greater influence because of the sanctions available to Congress.

► SUMMARY COMMENT ON THE ROLES OF THE PUBLICS

It would appear from the previous section that the relationship between foreign policy and public opinion involves a number of agencies—public and private—a number of processes, and a number of lines of communication. In other words, there are several interrelated functions and processes. Opinions are being formed and re-formed. Moods which transcend particular policies are developing and changing. Information and cues to interpretation are being communicated from group to group, from group to individuals, and from the governmental to the private level. Images of policies and policy makers are being formed. Judgments are being made. Estimates of feelings and attitudes are prepared. Decisions are arrived at based partly on expectations concerning possible public sanctions.

There are direct relations between government and the unorganized publics. There are indirect relations in which the effective publics mediate between the unorganized publics and the government: groups speak for the unorganized citizens and groups act on behalf of the government to promote support for policies and to communicate information. There are direct relations between the organized groups and their clientele—the members of the attentive and mass publics who subscribe to group values and group aims or who receive their additional information from such groups. Opinion leaders provide direct cues to the unorganized population. Organized groups and opinion leaders make demands on the decision makers, support the decision makers, and expose decision-making activities. Among the effective publics there are conflicts and rivalries that determine the limits of consensus and that determine which demands will be most effective.

In conclusion—and in general—the publics do not initiate foreign-policy actions; rather, they affect the direction and tempo of policy and its administration. Debates over values and policy alternatives are carried on among the publics and affect decision making. Despite serious conflicts, actual and potential, there is at any one time (except a period of rapid change) a substantial consensus and minimum public support. Segments of the general public have major roles in the collection and circulation of information and not all that is to be known about foreign policy circulates equally among all elements of the public. Important limitations on the freedom of choice of decision makers arise from the moods and opinions of the unorganized publics and from the sanctions and influence possessed by the organized publics and opinion leaders.

▶ SELECTED PROBLEMS OF PUBLIC OPINION AND FOREIGN POLICY IN A DEMOCRACY

As has so often been true of the other problems discussed in this book, the problems discussed below are really clusters of problems and are interrelated. Persumably, one of the fundamental intentions of the American political system is to yield effective governmental policies democratically. Preserving the national security in a democracy is not easy. In fact, the necessity of carrying on complex external relations puts a severe strain on the political institutions of a democratic society.

THE PROBLEM OF RELIABLE AND ADEQUATE INFORMATION

Free circulation of free information is a prime requisite of democracy. An "informed public" is necessary to provide support for accepted policies, to keep government responsible, and to make possible a constructive role in policy making. Without proper information, the general public can hardly act wisely. If there are to be opinions and moods and actions they must be about something. Generally speaking, the various publics need five kinds of knowledge or information: (1) events and problems relevant to foreign relations—in both the internal and external settings; (2) policies and policy alternatives; (3) the consequences of various alternatives and the results of past policies; (4) background data necessary to relate events, conditions, and policies; and (5) appropriate values for judging policies and choosing among alternatives. Government officials and professional political scientists do not all agree on what the general public—particularly the unorganized publics—*can* know and *should* know, but they do agree that minimum information is required. The questions of what information should be given to what segments of the public, who is to provide such information, i.e., what private and governmental agencies, and how it is to be communicated are being constantly argued about and temporarily answered. It is a basic fact to be well remembered that information on foreign policy is not and cannot be equally distributed throughout American society: some citizens know nothing and some government officials know everything; the unorganized publics know less than the organized; some groups know more than others; opinion leaders are usually well informed; and the mass mediums have unusual access to information, not all of which they reveal. Maldistribution of information is not in itself a disadvantage or a problem: it all depends on the consequences for democratic values and for policy formation.

Reliable opinion surveys regularly reveal among the mass public a significant proportion of "I don't knows." Generalizing from a number of polls, it is clear that anywhere from 20 to 33 per cent of the adult population are almost totally unaware of current international events and cannot answer such simple factual questions as "Where is Formosa?" "Who is Marshal Tito?" A majority of the unorganized publics, while not completely lacking in this kind of information, nonetheless are hazy on the details of major policies and trends. Thus 58 per cent are aware of the "cold war," but cannot spell out the real differences which separate the United States and the Soviet Union. One third of the voters did not know that Dean Acheson was Secretary of State. Only 5 per cent can identify the Point Four Program. Over one third know little about the foreign-aid program. While 65 to 75 per cent have opinions—that is, can and will answer questions—yet only 25 per cent are reasonably well informed on both policies and events.

Ignorance is not confined to the less educated or to the unorganized publics. Even citizens with college degrees have shown surprising gaps in information. Organized groups may be extremely uninformed on everything but their own narrow concerns. Lack of precise information is also accompanied by vague impressions and misconceptions. A large percentage (79) have heard about Communists in the State Department and 64 per cent have heard that Europe is not doing all it should to help itself. Such impressions may become the basis of firm judgments. After the long hearings on the Institute of Pacific Relations during which the charges against Owen Lattimore were featured, a majority of graduate students in a leading university thought Lattimore was Assistant Secretary of State—a post he never had held, to say nothing of holding it while under attack. The mass public apparently shares a number of misconceptions about the hydrogen bomb, chief among which is that it is a miracle weapon which unaided can win a war.

There are several possible reasons for the persistent and substantial lack of information on the part of the general public. First, the information is available, i.e., it circulates effectively and accurately via the mass mediums, books, and reports, but is rejected by the individual for psychological reasons or for other reasons does not alter his views. Second, the information is available but does not circulate effectively and accurately. Third, information is deliberately withheld at some point in the various possible communication channels. The latter two points will be touched on below. As to the first reason, it might be remarked that from the logical premise of the need for an informed public it is often reasoned that more information better communicated will lead to sounder and more extensive public participation. However, studies have demonstrated that most citizens lack a meaningful context within which to consider factual information, that a certain percentage of the population are chronic know-nothings and reject all stimuli beyond a narrow psychological universe, that people tend to select information which is congenial to their prior attitudes, and that individuals tend to interpret the same facts differently. This suggests that new or additional information is very important but is no guarantee of improvement in the quality of thought.

THE PROBLEM OF CENSORSHIP AND CONFLICTING SOURCES OF INFORMATION

At one of the critical points in the communication process involving public opinion, namely the relationship between the press and the government, a real threat to the circulation of vital information has arisen. After discovering that a very large proportion of secret information was being published in newspapers and "slick magazines," President Truman on September 25, 1951, issued an executive order requiring the security or information officers of all government agencies to employ the standardized procedures of the State Department and the Defense Department for separating security from non-security information. In effect, the order made one person in each agency responsible for deciding what information was to be regarded as vital to national security and whether it was to be classified as restricted, confidential, secret, or top secret. The general purpose of the order was "to keep security information away from potential enemies." Its more specific purpose was to assure that information affecting national security—particularly military secrets—would be protected when it became necessary for agencies other than the Defense and State Departments to share this information. On numerous occasions it has been found that military officers had protected a secret with great care only to find that some other executive agency such as the Atomic Energy Commission or some congressman had given the information out for publication. Even the Security and Exchange Commission—an unlikely agency to possess military secrets in a normal situation—has access to industrial production plans because it cannot permit new stock issues for plant expansion without knowing how the new facilities are to be used. The Department of Agriculture, which is engaged in research on bacteriological warfare, is another example.

In a letter which accompanied his order, the President insisted that the new regulations must not be so administered as "to withhold nonsecurity information or to cover up mistakes made by any official or employee of the Government." Further, the President wrote, "I wish to urge upon every department and agency head conscientious adherence to the spirit and letter of these regulations in the interest of safeguarding the national security on the one hand, and the protection of the public's right to information on the other hand."* Discussing the new order with reporters, the President was frank to recognize the dangers inherent in it and argued that the situation had gotten so out of hand that something had to be tried, at least experimentally. He promised quick action in the event of abuses brought to his attention. But

---

* New York *Times,* September 26, 1951, p. 5.

the nation's press was unanimously disturbed over the order and was not entirely satisfied with the President's clarification after the order was issued. The reaction of the American Society of Newspaper Editors was summarized in this statement: "We strongly oppose an executive order which formally designates each head of a Government agency an authority to classify information as injurious to national security, without definition of what breaches national security, and without appeal or review. We feel that the net effect of this executive order would be to formalize the suppression of much news to which the public is entitled."*

Newsmen were also concerned because it has become increasingly difficult, from their point of view, to identify what the President called "responsible officials qualified to judge" the relationship of information to national security. The executive order obviously multiplied the number of points at which such judgments must be made and irresponsible censorship could occur. In the absence of a formal system for reviewing the decisions of individual security officers and in the absence of clear definitions, it was felt that the "natural tendency" of bureaucrats to deny information would be intensified. In cases of doubt, the issue would be resolved in favor of suppression. "Overclassification" is the source of constant complaint by reporters; "underclassification" is the source of great fear on the part of high-level officials who are entrusted with the nation's security.

Several years after President Truman's controversial order, and with a new administration in power, the problem was still very real. In April, 1953, the American Society of Newspaper Editors was complaining that some actions of the Eisenhower Administration "have seemed fearful of public knowledge." Newsmen noted that with a few exceptions members of the Cabinet were holding fewer press conferences than had been true under the Truman regime. Scientists of the stature of Dr. Ralph Lapp and Dr. Lloyd Berkner were condemning the secrecy surrounding atomic weapons as depriving the public of information without which they could hardly think constructively about national security. A tremendous study of civilian defense and American vulnerability to atomic bombs called "Project East River" resulted in ten volumes of careful findings, the seven most significant of which were kept secret. And yet also in April, 1953, Secretary of Defense Wilson, professing alarm over the reports of weapon developments and high-level policy discussions which crept into the newspapers, ordered a crackdown on press releases.

The absence (or impossibility) of a clear, enforceable policy of censorship concerning "security" information not only has the consequence of needless suppression of information but also results in surprises and confusions. In 1950 the rift which had existed for months between General MacArthur on the one hand and the State and Defense Departments on the other was

---

* New York *Times,* September 30, 1952, p. 6.

suppressed, only to have the story hit the public as a great shock. After the Soviet Union was reported to have discovered how to detonate a hydrogen bomb (October, 1953) a series of confusing statements emanated from Washington. The director of the Office of Defense Mobilization issued a report which said: "Soviet Russia is capable of delivering the most destructive weapon ever devised by man on chosen targets in the United States."* Following this, the Defense Secretary said, "It will be perhaps three years before they [the Russians] have a reasonable number of bombs and airplanes that could deliver them. . . ." † From the chairman of the Joint Congressional Committee on Atomic Energy came this statement: "We need more civil defense, more continental defense, and since we are a God-fearing people, I hope a prayer. I think the condition is that desperate." ‡ He also called for an expenditure of $10 billion a year on continental defense. The Secretary of Defense said he could not spend more than $500 million. While the secretary was trying to keep things in perspective, the Civil Defense Administrator was predicting a dire fate for the United States. The recently resigned chairman of the Atomic Energy Commission had already asserted that within one or two years the Russians could destroy the United States. President Eisenhower, annoyed by this confusion of tongues, ordered that henceforth all statements were to conform with the decisions of the National Security Council or be cleared with the White House.

Five examples can be cited in the growth of secrecy: the increase in executive sessions in Congress; the almost total reliance on official releases from executive agencies and refusal to brief reporters in off-the-record sessions; the impounding of official records or the refusal to keep any records; the enlargement of military security; and the refusal of returning diplomats to talk to reporters—a regular source of news from abroad in bygone days. The last-named development is traceable in part to Congressional investigations. On top of it all, censorship in all but a few foreign nations has exceeded all expectations.

THE PROBLEM OF INTEREST, INVOLVEMENT, AND CAPACITY FOR ANALYSIS

Even if the optimum information were perfectly communicated to all publics, there would remain additional conditions for their effective, constructive participation. Taking the public as a whole (including all categories) it would appear that other attributes are desirable in addition to the possession of facts: sustained interest or psychological involvement—particularly on the part of the unorganized publics; a capacity to interpret events and policies in a meaningful context and to perceive relationships between events and policies; a capacity to weigh alternatives against a clear set of values; an ability

---

* Cited by James Reston in the New York *Times,* October 7, 1953, p. 4.
† *Ibid.*
‡ *Ibid.*

to control the impact of generalized feelings upon judgments and choices between specific policies and to be patient in the face of subtle developments and disappointments; an awareness of the legitimate interests of other nations; a desire to act with self-restraint and reasonable expectations; the willingness to choose and support capable leaders; and the willingness to learn from past mistakes.

Apathy and withdrawal are strong tendencies among the mass public. In the absence of crisis or major issues, the pull toward what has been called "privatism" is strong indeed. Many citizens feel acute helplessness in the face of complicated issues and decision-making processes. Foreign-policy matters have to compete for the attention of busy individuals with limited energy and capacity for concentration. Unless a person's educational training and community agencies buttress involvement in foreign affairs, there is a tendency to concentrate energy on those factors which make immediate personal demands. Attention is further discouraged by the circumstance that the citizen either is left out of any significant debate—as in the case of the North Atlantic Treaty and the Japanese Peace Treaty—or finds it difficult to discover what alternatives are really at stake.

Except perhaps for the attentive public, unorganized citizens are not consistent in their views and are not skilled at interpreting correctly American policies and the policies of others. Polls have shown that a sizable group does not think that the Russian-American conflict is ideological—a view that could arise only from a serious misconception concerning Soviet behavior. Polls also reveal that many Americans look upon the foreign-aid program as sheer generosity rather than enlightened self-interest, that they see no connection between repayment of loans by foreigners and the height of the American tariff, and that they see no contradiction between believing the United States should not intervene in the domestic affairs of other nations and being in favor of propaganda and foreign-aid programs.

Certain characteristics hold true in general of all publics. One concerns cycles of opinion. To take one example, American opinion toward the Soviet Union from 1917 to 1954 went through at least five distinct phases corresponding more or less to the periods 1917–1921, 1921–1929, 1929–1939, 1939–1945, 1946–1954. During this time opinion ranged from tolerance to intolerance, from friendship to hostility. It is not necessary to review these periods to make several points. First, such changes do, of course, take place in response to the altered behavior of a foreign nation—in this case the Soviet Union, whose conduct in 1954 was in marked contrast to its conduct in 1925 or 1935. Second, attitudes toward the Soviet Union were conditioned in part by events in the United States, by the depression of 1929–1933, which permitted a quite different evaluation of the relations with the Soviets which would be satisfactory and of the Soviet anticapitalist economy. Third, changes in attitudes toward the Soviet Union took place during a thirty-five-year period on the basis of inadequate knowledge and without a commonly accepted frame of reference for the interpretation of Soviet behavior ever emerging. There is considerable evidence that there was a sizable discrepancy between actual changes in Soviet goals and motives and the changes in American attitudes. This is what is meant by an unstructured opinion—one in which a relatively small change in behavior produces a relatively large shift in opinion.

Instability of mood (distinct from cycles of opinion) can be the decision makers' nightmare. Sudden shifts in tolerance, involvement, hope, and expectation which stem from generalized feelings rather than from rational judgment can paralyze foreign-policy planning or may force undesirable limits on the government. For example, in 1953 there developed a noticeable feeling of doubt and impatience over the United Nations. This appeared to permit attacks on the international body that were sufficiently numerous and serious to alarm officials.

PROBLEMS ARISING FROM FASHIONS IN IDEAS, CLICHÉS, AND STEREOTYPES

First to be noted are certain intellectual fads which prevail from time to time among the various publics, particularly the opinion leaders in mass communications and education. There are several manifestations of this. After World War I began a whole series of interpretations as to why America had entered or "been dragged into" it. In more or less chronological order, the various theses explaining America's involvement despite a declared intention of remaining neutral were these: (1) the success of British propaganda; (2) American investment in Allied nations was more substantial than in Germany and foreign trade with the Allies was essential to American economic well-being; (3) the munitions makers acting nationally and internationally conspired to push America into war for the sake of huge profits; and (4) America entered the conflict of her own free will because British victory was less intolerable, represented less of a threat to long-range interests, and would establish a balance of power the United States could probably live with in peace.

The point here is not that it is bad per se for a nation to go back and re-examine its past conduct or to have wide differences of opinion over the reasons for it; rather, the question is, What effect does the re-examination have on current policy formation? It so happens that the events of the middle 1930's prompted the American people to ask themselves about World War I and why neutrality had failed. One of the most famous Senate investigations of all time, the Nye Committee's investigation of the munitions industry, helped confirm a conviction among opinion leaders that America was more or less duped into World War I and that America could have and should have kept out. At a time when the fundamental assumptions underlying American foreign policy were being destroyed, a readjustment to new conditions was partially paralyzed by a particular set of ideas held by a sufficient number of leaders.

Another and more serious manifestation concerns the estimation of the national power of other states. Fads tend to focus around degrees of overestimation and underestimation. On the basis of what is now known, the national power of Germany and that of Japan were miscalculated in recent years. German strength, when Hitler began his moves in 1934 to establish predominance, was overestimated and reactions to German behavior were influenced thereby; the blackmail was more effective because it was deemed to have more power behind it than it did. Later, German invincibility became almost a myth. Japanese power in the last stages of World War II was over-estimated, as was the fanatical behavior of Japanese soldiers; thus the way was paved for decisions having far-reaching political consequences. In the case of the Soviet Union, the public has swung from underestimation in 1940 to overestimation in 1952. The exaggeration of present Soviet strength is accompanied by an underestimation of Russia's future potential.

What have been called fashions in ideas are related to the policy making process and affect decisions. Once again the point is not that ideas change or that to err is not human. The point is that while a particular estimate of national power prevails, contrary evidence is either ignored or misinterpreted. When the estimate changes it is not usual that a middle ground is reached; more often the other extreme is embraced. Now it should be added that competing estimates of Soviet power, for example, circulate regularly among the publics and among officials too. Ordinarily one general estimate will be authoritative in the sense that most commentators, scholars, and other opinion leaders accept it and employ it.

Clichés and stereotypes are also characteristic of public opinion—not the only characteristic, be it emphasized, yet sufficiently persistent to be discoverable at any moment in time. There is a natural tendency even among the well educated, the well informed, and the expert to simplify the complex political phenomena. It is when simplification slips over into oversimplification that important effects on the content of opinion and the nature of public discussion are to be noted. This is expressed in the use of shorthand terms which convey part but not all of the truth and in the use of phrases which indiscriminately type certain kinds of conduct, whether or not such conduct is in fact similar. Oversimplification is also expressed in phrases which presumably have a strong emotional appeal without having much concrete meaning. "Appeasement," "Reds" or "Commies," "power politics," "aggressive," "peaceloving," "peace with honor" and many others have been common currency for a decade. As just stated it is the consequence of their circulation which is significant. An example or two will suffice. "Appeasement" loomed large when Soviet-American relations became hostile and when Soviet foreign policy was deemed to threaten world peace. It loomed large in this context because of the remembrance of Hitler's successful blackmail of Europe during the period 1933–1939 and because of an unwillingness to make concession to Russia which might turn out similarly. In public debate over the proper policy toward Russia, "appeasement" apparently embraced any concessions under any circumstances. If this were maintained to its logical conclusion, no

eaceful settlement of the Soviet-American conflict would be possible short
f complete capitulation on all issues by Russia. If, on the other hand,
appeasement" were limited to mean concessions from weakness without adequate counterconcessions (really blackmail), the way would be open to dis-
uss the possibility of making concessions from strength with equal concessions
n return. Europe, for better or worse, made concessions to Hitler from
weakness. The United States was hardly in the same position vis-à-vis Russia
fter 1948. Widespread use of this phrase did much to snuff out proposals
or legitimate concessions for the purpose of relieving Soviet-American
ensions.

PROBLEMS OF THE DIVISION OF LABOR AMONG THE PUBLICS

The core of the analysis in this chapter, it will be remembered, was based
on the assumption that there are several publics and actual roles in foreign
policy somewhat peculiar to each. It was also argued that there are a set of
complex relationships joining the publics to each other and to the decision
makers. Therefore the effectiveness and soundness of public participation appear to depend basically on the performance of certain functions and on the
preservation of communication lines. Some of the problems mentioned above
grow directly out of weaknesses or failures in the performance of the mass
mediums, opinion leaders, and organized groups.

Though government censorship can be and is an important limitation on
the amount and quality of foreign-policy information available, it is obviously
possible for the mass mediums—particularly the newspapers—to decide in
effect on what the reading public shall know. During 1952–1953, radio news-
casts and newspapers carried noticeably less news on the United Nations—a
fact which might be related to decline in public enthusiasm. Newspapers
sometimes fall into the habit of printing "all the news that fits the pattern,"
i.e., the pattern of what has been regarded previously as significant. During
the years of American occupation of Germany there was singularly little news
from Germany which ran counter to the assumption that democracy was well
on its way in that country. The rather idealistic image of Chiang Kai-shek and
the long-time affection for the Chinese people as well as wishful thinking
probably helped prevent the American mass mediums from giving the public
a full report on the crucial social changes going on in China after 1939 and
especially after 1945. Since 1945, there has been a reduction of foreign
correspondents from two thousand seven hundred to three hundred and only
in Britain, France, Italy, Germany, and Japan are the news services fully
staffed on a regular basis. Mass communications may also manifest bias, sen-
sationalism, and uniformity. To the extent that this is true several of the
basic conditions for sound mass opinion will be weakened.

To repeat, the unorganized publics are incapable of initiative and integrated leadership in the field of foreign policy. They are dependent on the
mass mediums for information and for cues to interpretations of the external

setting. They are heavily dependent on the opinion leaders and certain groups for supplementing the information available in the mass mediums, for providing instruction on sound policy analysis, for making clear the policy alternatives established by the government, for reviewing arguments pro and con and for insisting upon diversity of viewpoint. This places an enormous responsibility on the schools, the churches, the community leaders, and the respected commentators. The success with which various roles are carried out in the processes whereby opinions are formed and communicated depends ultimately on the social institutions which embody various functions.

Do enough Americans receive a sufficient education? If the mass public cannot perceive relationships between policy and policy, and between policy and event, is the nation's intellectual training for citizenship at fault? If the citizens feel that foreign affairs are so complicated that they ought to be "left to those who know," where did this attitude come from and what factors reinforce it? If opinion leaders exhibit intellectual habits inappropriate to constructive leadership, why are they leaders and what is the check upon them? Why are small groups able to dominate, on occasion, the moods and opinions of the unorganized public without being challenged effectively by individual leaders or by other groups? Why did the United States get caught with so few Far Eastern experts in the postwar period? How can fallacious reasoning and insufficient evidence be accepted without question? These questions, the answers to some of which are obvious, suggest how deep the explanation must go when the problem of public opinion and foreign policy is fully opened up.

Up to a point, organized groups make an indispensable contribution to opinion and policy formation, as has already been noted. However, groups can be guilty of bias, parochialism, and selfishness. While it is unfruitful to divide all groups into good and bad, selfish and unselfish, the consequences of group behavior for effective decision making can and should be judged. Except for the groups having an avowed educational purpose, it is unlikely that individual organized groups can exert integrative leadership. Each seeks to press its claims with respect to values and objectives, each may have its own peculiar view of appropriate ends and means in foreign policy. Many groups are taking a more and more active role in foreign affairs without having even the level of expert advice they have on domestic policy. The proliferation of organized groups makes for overspecialization and often a Tower of Babel in which a clear formulation of major alternatives is impossible. Economic groups are capable of such sustained pressure on an issue as to distort its over-all aspects. Examples cited earlier show that all sorts of concessions to group demands can be logrolled into foreign-policy legislation. One very significant question raised by recent developments is this: Can the give-and-take between groups interested in affecting legislation and the compromise between lobbyists and legislators—both recognized as legitimate (within imits) in domestic matters—be tolerated on the basic programing of national security?

The minimization of these difficulties would seem to depend on several factors. First, the self-restraint referred to earlier applies to groups as well as to the unorganized public. Though this is not a quality inborn in interest groups, one function of opinion leaders is to remind such groups of their wider social responsibility. Second, a strengthening of Congress and the party system increase resistance to group demands which cannot be deferred to except by sacrificing the majority view or basic values. Third, the formation of group coalitions around central issues might counteract overspecialization and parochialism and allow for a sharp posing of alternative views. In particular, coalitions of the educational groups might prevent excesses of distortion and judgment. Fourth, since organized groups appeal to the attentive and mass publics, it is necessary that the latter receive an adequate presentation of the government's position and other information through the mass mediums. Fifth, the more substantial the capacity of the unorganized publics for policy analysis, the more unlikely it is that organized groups can "sell" their special aims without opposition.

THE PROBLEM OF THE "PROPER ROLE OF THE PUBLIC IN THE FORMATION OF FOREIGN POLICY"

The thorny problem of the "proper role of the public in the formation of foreign policy" is at least susceptible of clearer analysis in the light of this and other chapters. Four types of argument are usually made: the public, or the common man, is the final, most trustworthy arbiter of policy; it does not matter what the public thinks, policy responds to other forces; even if it were desirable, it is not possible to create enlightened, effective public opinion; finally, real decisions must be made by the "elites"—elected representatives, experts, and interested groups. Interwoven with these is a controversy over whether "open diplomacy" is possible or desirable. Antagonists can usually be grouped according to whether they espouse "elitist" theories or not and according to whether they are optimistic or pessimistic about the capacity of political man to be rational, to be educated, and to be responsible.

By-passing such considerations for the moment, what can be said on the basis of the preceding distinctions and descriptions? It seems clear that the general public—including its four segments—*cannot be a policy maker in the strict sense;* that is, the initiative and leadership must rest largely with official decision makers. This would be true even if the United States could be converted into a huge town meeting—there would still have to be responsible officials. But the general public can and must *participate* in policy making through the impact of its value orientations, through saying yes or no to basic choices (i.e., joining the United Nations or the Atlantic Alliance) which have consequences for the whole society, and through exercising a check on undesirable actions already taken. Participation occurs by means of a variety of *direct and indirect representations.* The various publics are represented differently—which is to say they may have a different kind of impact on policy and this impact may be *registered* in different ways. In form (if not in substance) a democratic foreign policy implies that *at the point of decision* the rights and contributions of the various publics will have been, or are, freely and accurately represented by responsible officials and agencies. From issue to issue, from action to action, the *degree of direct general public participation* will vary, and so will indirect participation. Similarly, the degree of direct and indirect participation among the various publics will vary. Obviously, in some cases, *over*representation of one segment of the public may result in *under*representation of another. Aside from democratic values (representation as a good in itself), one primary aim of public participation is to provide *stable, rational support for foreign policies* once they are agreed upon. Much cynicism revolves about the role of the unorganized public. And yet on big issues, on appropriate issues, conditions are present which make direct soundings of the mass opinions feasible: mass communications can inform the people, issues can be stated simply, and reliable survey techniques can offer a method of estimating the consensus.

The failures, misconceptions, and conditions which tend to undermine a proper role for the general public and which tend to make foreign policy undemocratic have already been suggested in the problems discussed above and in other chapters. The role of the public must, of course, be considered in the light of the chief characteristics of foreign-policy decision making in the United States. The processes and lines of communication described in this chapter offer many opportunities for possible breakdowns, short circuits, and errors: Congressmen may lose touch with sentiment at home. Minority influences may temporarily triumph within Congress. Partisan struggle may obscure issues. Senators and representatives may overrepresent groups as distinct from the mass. Rivalry between the President and Congress may multiply the number of authoritative statements bombarding the public and may create competitive appeals from the government which are confusing. Lack of coordination within the Executive Branch may result in conflicting interpretations of policy. The President's failure to reach the mass public may strengthen the organized publics. Public opinion experts in the State Department may err in their estimates or ignore segments of the public. Such propositions could be repeated at great length.

▶ PERSISTENT DILEMMAS OF DEMOCRATIC FOREIGN POLICY

It remains now to mention very briefly certain dilemmas from which there seems to be no easy escape. These are situations or conflicts which apparently a democratic system must learn to live with.

THE GOVERNMENT'S RIGHT TO SUPPORT V. MANIPULATION

On the one hand, the public is dependent on the government for information and official interpretation. The government also needs support. But a logical extension of the methods it uses for these legitimate purposes may put it in the position of being able to "manipulate" the public. This can become a very complicated issue when it is realized that in an age of psychological warfare, it is increasingly difficult to distinguish statements designed to fool or unnerve an enemy from statements designed to inform the people. The issue is not entirely solved by having a free and responsible press because the government still must use the mass mediums to create a favorable atmosphere for its operations.

SECRECY AND SECURITY V. FREE INFORMATION

The dilemma posed by security controls is as difficult as any America now faces: how to maintain intact the constitutional guarantee of freedom of press and to assure the flow of information to the democratic citizen while at the same time preventing the acquisition of vital secrets or other data by a potential enemy. Most government officials would admit that the general public cannot have full understanding without a fairly full disclosure of facts; yet those are precisely the facts the administration would not like an enemy to have. For example, the American peoples were confronted by hard choices in 1954 respecting continental defenses and balance of armed forces. The ability of the United States to prevent or survive a major war depends in part on the size and nature of the atomic stockpile—information the Soviets would doubtless like to have. Similarly, military planning depends on a knowledge of what areas the government will defend against attack; yet it would be unwise to reveal this in advance. Thus far, no one has discovered a satisfactory formula for drawing the line in such cases.

EFFECTIVE LEADERSHIP V. FRANKNESS

Closely related to the problem of security controls is the question concerning whether and to what extent the leaders of a democracy can take the people into their confidence and listen to their wishes during a period of national crisis. This issue grew specifically out of President Roosevelt's leadership during the trying period when America was moving toward World War II. There appears to be general agreement that Roosevelt, "when confronted by an apathetic public and a critical foreign menace, felt compelled to deceive the people into an awareness of their peril."* Some political scientists argue for a literal democratic foreign policy with all its risks. They would choose an absence of deception and possible harm to the nation rather than deception and national preservation. These experts say the fact that Roosevelt was

---

* Thomas A. Bailey, *The Man in the Street* (New York, The Macmillan Company, 1948), p. 11.

largely correct is irrelevant. They hold that the responsibility of the leader is that he follow the will of the people, not that he follow his own convictions as to what national security requires. They believe that to withhold information from the electorate, on the ground that it is incapable of making a correct decision, sets up a vicious circle in which the very conditions necessary for adequately preparing the public are lacking. Others, taking the opposite view, feel that the President in a time of crisis is acting as the representative of the people and that eventual redress is available. Even so, they argue, the President has a duty to preserve the nation which transcends his duty to be frank. At any rate, any President is likely to find himself in a position of having to deceive the people for their own good, not knowing whether history will find him guilty of undemocratic or treasonable conduct.

It is often said that democracy requires open diplomacy and that open diplomacy is a contradiction in terms, or that democracy and secret diplomacy are incompatible. Unless one insists that quick decisions and some secrecy *in principle* violate democratic values, this particular formulation of the secrecy dilemma can be shown to be artificial. Day-to-day responses to a changing international situation (especially if war is imminent) are not easily reconciled with leisurely debate and referendum, but there are other ways in which a policy can be representative. Furthermore, a fundamental distinction is necessary here between a policy decision and international negotiation of a decision. The public should have information pertinent to basic decisions. The carrying out of policy is a matter for technicians, and often secrecy in diplomatic intercourse is useful and required. Because a decision is made in public is no guarantee it is democratic and because a decision is made in secrecy is no reason to believe it must be irresponsible or illegal.

FOREIGN V. DOMESTIC PUBLIC OPINION

Official decision makers—particularly those in the Executive Branch—not only have to function under the sometimes unpredictable pressures from their own people but have to take account of an international public as well. Totalitarian states can usually insulate their policy makers from both sources of opinion. Democratic states are caught both ways, for the requirement of representation of public views at home is accompanied by a need to pay a decent respect to the opinions of friends and allies. If the two sets of publics were independent of each other the problem would be somewhat simpler. However, it is almost impossible for decision makers to address words to one without being heard by the other. What must be said to one audience for purposes of clarification or pacification may alienate the other audience. At the present time the American Congress and the American public are economy-minded, a fact which necessitates cuts and talk of cuts in foreign aid. But Western European nations interpret this as an indication of possible American withdrawal. When United States officials reassure the Europeans, segments of the American public interpret this as a breach of commitment.

These selected problems are not cited to stress the difficulties of democracy. Rather, the point being made is that even if all the conditions for intelligent, stable, effective public participation in foreign-policy making were present, some continuing troubles would remain.

► SELECTED BIBLIOGRAPHY

The best general study on the subject of this chapter and essential supplementary reading is Gabriel Almond's *The American People and Foreign Policy* (New York, Harcourt, Brace & Company, 1950). Two earlier studies of value are L. S. Cottrell and Sylvia Eberhart, *American Opinion on World Affairs in the Atomic Age* (Princeton, N. J., Princeton University Press, 1948) and *American Attitudes toward Russia* (Ann Arbor, Mich., University of Michigan, Survey Research Center, 1948). T. A. Bailey, *The Man in the Street* (New York, The Macmillan Company, 1948), is an interesting brief historical survey of persistent trends in public thinking about foreign relations. L. H. Chamberlain and R. C. Snyder in *American Foreign Policy* (New York, Rinehart & Company, 1948), Chaps. 12 and 14, present a wide selection of readings on the role and influence of public opinion and pressure groups. *Public Opinion and Foreign Policy* (New York, Harper & Brothers, 1949), by Lester Markel and others, is a conventional study by recognized experts of public opinion as an instrumentality of American foreign policy at home and abroad. E. E. Schattschneider, *Politics, Pressures, and the Tariff* (New York, Prentice-Hall, Inc., 1935), is a classic study demonstrating certain kinds of influence by pressure groups on economic foreign policy. Various writers discuss the proper role of the general public in the making of foreign policy decisions in a symposium, "Can Foreign Policy Be Democratic?" *American Perspective*, September, 1948. The possible relationship between parties and foreign-policy attitudes is explored by G. Belknap and A. Campbell in "Political Party Identification and Foreign Policy," *Public Opinion Quarterly*, Winter, 1951–1952. Chaps. 3, 4, 5, 6, and 9 of D. Perkins, *The American Approach to Foreign Policy* (Cambridge, Mass., Harvard University Press, 1952), explore the social foundations of basic American attitudes toward foreign relations generally.

► PART TWO

POSTWAR AMERICAN
FOREIGN POLICIES

CHAPTER FOURTEEN

THE POSTWAR INTERNATIONAL ENVIRONMENT

Introduction • Changes in the State System • The Situation of Bipolarity: Absence of a Mediator • American-Soviet Relations • Influence of Technology • Role of Ideas • Changes in Governmental Form • Economic Dislocation • Weakness of International Regulatory Mechanisms • Conclusion: The Problem of the Assessment of Soviet Behavior • Selected Bibliography

► INTRODUCTION

Earlier chapters of this volume have emphasized the fact that special circumstances of the nineteenth century enabled the United States to grow to a powerful nation without any real understanding of the international setting —the interaction of states—in which it was growing and without engaging in the difficult, complex task of analyzing its own internal capabilities, its capacities for influencing that environment in order to promote American interests. The entanglement of the United States in World War I did not succeed in awakening the United States to a clear comprehension that the responsibilities attendant upon the possession of national power could no longer be avoided. It was only at Pearl Harbor that the tragic truth, already learned by Czechoslovakia, Poland, Norway, Denmark, Belgium, Holland, Yugoslavia, Albania, and Greece, was finally brought home to this country—that it takes only one to make a war, that no state, particularly one so rich and powerful as the United States, can attain security without sacrifice and effort on its own part. In the holocaust of war the American people and their government saw demonstrated the unsoundness of three of their traditional, interrelated beliefs. They found that responsibility concomitant with influence could not be avoided with impunity, that use of American capabilities to influence the international environment was a necessity and a responsibility, not merely an evil to be eschewed wherever possible, and that, as a result, neutrality by decree could not keep any nation out of war, especially not a large nation with world-wide interests and influence.

The United States, then, was prepared after World War II to accept

571

some of the implication of the new position in the international firmament to which victory had raised it. But, as subsequent chapters in this section will examine in detail, this acceptance was still limited in many respects, and, furthermore, was based on assumptions about the nature of the postwar environment, many of which became demonstrably false within the first two years after 1945. The world in which the United States was finally willing to play a role commensurate with its power was a world in which the pattern of state interaction was being radically and rapidly altered through the introduction of many new and unique factors into an equation already cloudy and difficult for statesmen to read.

▶ CHANGES IN THE STATE SYSTEM

THE ELIMINATION OF GERMANY AS A STRONG POWER

As a result of military power mounted by a global coalition, two of the stronger component units in interstate relations—Germany and Japan— were eliminated. Upon the formation of the German Empire in 1870, the former agglomeration of German principalities became the greatest state in Europe. Bismarck, the Iron Chancellor, made Berlin the center of European diplomacy, wresting the leadership away from Paris and London. Although its belated arrival on the world scene and the nature of its continental position precluded the establishment of an empire rivaling those of Britain and France in size and importance, Germany had become by 1914 a nation whose interests and power reached round the world. Its temporary eclipse after 1918 came only after four years of fighting against most of the major nations of the world, with the declining Ottoman and Austro-Hungarian empires as its only allies. Without the timely entrance of the United States, furthermore, it is doubtful if Great Britain and France could have held Germany to anything more than a stalemate, which would have left Germany as the arbiter of the destinies of Europe.

The interlude based on the Versailles Treaty was but a brief one. The arrangements set up by that treaty depended for their perpetuation either on the willingness of the Allies to enforce on Germany the details of the peace settlement (a willingness which they did not exhibit after 1923) or on the voluntary acceptance by Germany of its diminished, artificial status (a course of action which most German groups were never prepared to accept and which was denounced finally with the selection by Hindenburg of Adolf Hitler as Prime Minister in 1934). Against a resurgent, expansionist Germany, Europe in 1939 was weaker than it had been in 1914. The second defeat of Germany was longer delayed than the first and demanded a far greater price, not in lives alone (in fact some countries, such as France, lost fewer men in World War II than in World War I), but in economic, financial, political, social, and ideological disruption. The margin of Allied victory was even smaller. The entrance of the United States, while again decisive, did not result in German defeat until three and a half years later, as compared to nineteen months in World War I.

At the end of World War II Germany as a state was gone, the Thousand Year Reich obliterated by bombs; complete occupation and unconditional surrender left no German government with which to negotiate or on which to impose a treaty. The Allies—Great Britain, France, the Soviet Union, and the United States—were now sovereign in Germany, legally as well as in fact. There was general agreement, furthermore, that the elimination of Germany as an important component of the community of nations would not this time be temporary. When a new German government was permitted to re-enter the international system, it would be one representing a power base drastically reduced geographically, economically, and militarily, and would confront a world organization prepared, as the League of Nations was not, to maintain this reduced status. The peace of the world seemed to require assurance that Germany should never again recover enough freedom of action to serve as a hair trigger setting off global conflict.

There was still substantial uncertainty, however, as to what the future role of Germany in Europe would be even though that nation had apparently been destroyed. Could Germany again become dangerous? Was it still capable of rising Phoenixlike to new heights from the ashes of defeat? The French certainly would have answered yes. Were the people of Germany capable of reformation? Could they be set once more on the paths of righteousness which, once trodden, would make it safe for Germany's erstwhile enemies after a short time to open the door for international participation to a new nation with diminished but still important power and responsibility? Some Americans and many Englishmen thought so. Or was Germany so badly defeated, so devastated by bombing that a limited, tough occupation would accomplish its permanent removal as a factor of power to be reckoned with, regardless of what the Allies did or did not do after the withdrawal of their troops? Some who observed in 1945 the heaps of rubble that had been large German cities were convinced that this was so. The implications of Germany's defeat for United States policy will be explored more fully in Chapter Seventeen, "Western Europe and American Security," but it should be noted at this point that the dominant American mood was one of uncertainty mixed with optimism. While the future would bring developments unforeseen in 1945, the wartime coalition which had defeated the Axis Powers could, it was evidently felt, solve in cooperation and harmony any new problems which might arise. Fervent wishes fathered happy thoughts; a world worn by the worst war in history hoped an era of prolonged peace, plenty, and progress was at hand.

THE ELIMINATION OF JAPAN

On the other side of the world another formerly prominent actor on the international scene had been removed, with consequences likewise difficult to forecast. It was apparent before World War II that the success of Japanese aggression depended to a far greater extent than that of Germany on the possession of regional preponderance of power. Hitler's Axis partner could not be considered a world power in the same sense as Germany. In addition, Asia historically had exerted far less influence on the international environment than Europe. Therefore the defeat of Japan seemed to presage far less readjustment in the pattern of interstate relations.

On the other hand, as has been pointed out in an earlier chapter, the advent of Japan to major rank at the end of the nineteenth century and its immediate entrance into competition with rival *Western* imperialisms in the Far East meant that the Western state system had become in fact global in its extent. Although this fact was unrecognized at the time, although Great Britain and the League of Nations were still unprepared to recognize it in 1931 and 1937, Pearl Harbor finally demonstrated unequivocally that security was indivisible, that a deterioration of relations in one part of the world, signalized by an upset balance of power and moves toward state expansion, caused the foundations of all other states to tremble. Except for a very brief historical period of little more than a decade (1919–1931), Japan had never been assimilated into the heretofore wholly Western community of nations.

After World War II, however, it was clear that the problem ignored in preceding decades—the assimilation of Asiatic nations, of which Japan was only one, into the international system of states—would now have to be successfully solved. What did this process of assimilation entail for American power and responsibility? Could it be undertaken at all without Japanese participation? If not, on what basis could and should Japan be accepted as a part of the new structure?

THE CHINESE QUESTION MARK

The postwar international environment in the Far East was further complicated by uncertainty as to the status of China. China had been practically isolated from the West since 1937, when Japan resumed its Asiatic aggressions begun in Manchuria in 1931. This isolation, together with the Japanese occupation of much of China, made it difficult for statesmen to forecast the role which China would play once Japan had been removed from the scene. The defeat of Japan left the Nationalist regime of Chiang Kai-shek weak, worn by eight years of struggle from a geographic base of limited productive value. At the same time, the very elimination of Japan increased immeasurably the relative power and importance of China and created opportunities for Chinese influence throughout Asia unparalleled since the intrusion of Western states into the area. But in order to realize these opportunities Chiang had to replace former Japanese power with his own and to unify the country under his leadership, as he had been in the process of doing when the Japanese struck. While Chiang's chances seemed good at the end of World War II, there was still the problem of the Chinese Communists, about which the United States knew very little. Could the Communists be induced to compromise their basic differences with the Nationalists? If not, could Chiang defeat them and confine them to a small, unimportant area of China, as he had in the nineteen twenties?

THE NEW POWER OF THE UNITED STATES

Not only had two formerly prominent figures disappeared in the postwar scene, but also two other actors who had hitherto moved about in the wings were now rushing toward or being pushed into positions front and center. American statecraft after World War II was prepared to accept the dual proposition that international politics was power politics and that the United States, possessing power, could not avoid participation and responsibility. This was a new position in American foreign policy and one which contrasted markedly with the repudiation a generation earlier of Woodrow Wilson's attempt to lead the United States into a position in accord with its capabilities. The effect of previous denials of the possession of power and of policies based on power was to lead to mistaken estimates by other states of the real strength of the United States. Hitler, like the Kaiser before him, gambled on American weakness and inability to translate its potential strength into military might in time to do its allies any good. Hitler, like the Kaiser, was disastrously in error. When President Roosevelt called on the nation to produce fifty thousand planes of all sizes and types, even as the German *Wehrmacht* was sweeping through Holland, Belgium, and France, his speech was denounced by Charles A. Lindbergh as "hysterical chatter." There were many Americans prepared to agree at that time that the United States would not, should not, and certainly could not fight Germany, Italy, and Japan all over the world at the same time. As Robert Sherwood points out in *Roosevelt and Hopkins,* Lindbergh himself later aided in testing some of the more than 300,000 war planes which the United States subsequently produced. As for munitions, the United States was in 1944 turning out as much as Great Britain, the Soviet Union, Germany, and Japan all together. Winfield Rieffler remarks, in an understatement, that this quantity "was still considerably less than could have been extracted from American industrial economy."*

The United States became in fact the "Arsenal of Democracy." *But* it raised a huge army of millions of men besides. *And* it equipped that army, not once, but many times as older weapons became spent or obsolescent. *And* it transported that army to invasion sites in North Africa, Europe, Oceania, and on the Asiatic mainland. *And* it simultaneously continued to furnish its allies with material which in Russia's case alone was estimated to equal about 10 per cent of that country's own military production. And, finally, while Americans after Pearl Harbor were disabused of the impression that the United States could gain victory over the Axis with its left hand while engaging in golf matches with its right, the sacrifices of the domestic civilian economy

---

* Winfield Rieffler, "Our Economic Contribution to Victory," *Foreign Affairs,* October, 1947, p. 95.

remained slight. Studies have shown that Americans on the average were better fed and better clothed during the war than they ever had been before, and even before the war they had been the best fed and best clothed people on earth. American wealth, real and not inflated, continued to rise to a national productivity figure in 1945 twice that of 1929.

While United States economic might at home was growing, its soldiers overseas reversed the role of the United States in the earlier anti-German coalition of 1917. Then the United States had been a junior partner, a "Johnny-come-lately" to a functioning business. Now the United States was the executor of an estate whose assets had largely been exhausted, many of them dissipated without tangible result, an estate on the verge of bankruptcy. From North Africa to Nagasaki the United States led the way to victory. If Americans are wont as a result to duplicate the Russian contention that they won the war all by themselves, there is, if not justice or entire truth, at least some substance to their boast. All too well did the rest of the world know that there was a new "superpower" in the international environment, one whose strength was greater than that of any power ever known. In its economic production and in the distribution of its Armed Forces it covered the earth. Was this not to be, as Henry Luce argued, the American Century?

FATE OF SMALL STATES

As the strong grew stronger, the weak grew weaker, many in absolute as well as in relative terms. What was to become of small states? Time was when their own determined effort had been enough to thwart the aggressive designs and hired mercenaries of far larger nations. Time was when they could tip the scales of the balance of power one way or the other by the addition or subtraction of their own power, when their bargaining position was so strong that they could exact concessions from all suitors. But if Holland, Denmark, and the rest could not survive the blitzkrieg, how could they count any longer in a world perpetually threatened by a supercolossal blitzkrieg? Did their very existence henceforth depend not at all on what they themselves did, but on decisions reached in faraway capitals, decisions over which they could hope to exert no influence? Did not their self-preservation depend on the self-abnegation of the new giants in an environment where humility and restraint were, to say the least, extremely rare? Or was there a possibility that they might yet play a significant role through their influence in an international organization powerful enough to enforce its decisions even against the newly great powers of the world?

ROLE OF THE MIDDLE POWERS

Uncertainty also surrounded the role which the so-called "middle powers" might play in the postwar environment. These countries were of two types. Some, like Britain and France, had a long history of past greatness, but entered the postwar period greatly weakened. But weakened how much? Was France now to play a bit part indefinitely, while Britain remained one of the "superpowers"? On the other hand, there were some countries, like Canada and Australia, which emerged from the conflict with a relatively improved status. Even Brazil claimed in 1945 to be one of the middle powers, the fifth or sixth greatest in the world, and its neighbor to the south, Argentina, while scoffing at Brazilian pretensions, put in its own bid for recognition. The question of the power and role of the middle powers became increasingly acute as tension grew between the United States and the Soviet Union. With sufficient strength nations of this class could perhaps serve as mediators between the two giants, or, failing that, declare themselves out of any conflict between the two, relying on their own strength and solidarity to command respect for their position.

► THE SITUATION OF BIPOLARITY:
ABSENCE OF A MEDIATOR

Both Great Britain and France did in fact aspire to the role of mediator, and individuals and groups in both countries still hope that their nations may yet be able either to perform this function or to keep entirely aloof from the East-West power struggle. One of the issues on which the British Labor party conducted its successful campaign of 1945 was that Socialists could more readily than the Conservatives form a bridge of understanding between capitalist America and Communist Soviet Union. Earlier, at the San Francisco Conference, where the Charter of the United Nations was adopted, representatives of a predominantly Conservative British government seemed at times to be attempting to act as mediators, justifying their *political* in-between position in terms of the *geographical* in-between position of the British Isles and the British Empire with respect to the United States and the Soviet Union. In the 1950 British elections Winston Churchill sought to turn the Labor claim of 1945 back upon his opponents by demanding yet another effort, led by Britain, to solve the East-West deadlock. As late as 1953 Churchill seized the initiative by suggesting that the time was ripe for a meeting of the leaders of the Big Four—the United States, Britain, France, and the Soviet Union. Neither effort to assert British leadership in international diplomacy was successful. The Laborites won the election of 1950, and representatives of the three Western powers suggested a meeting, not of the Big Four leaders, but of their deputies, with an agenda fixed in advance, a suggestion received coldly by the Soviet Union. British weakness had made it impossible for that nation to play an independent role on the world stage. A later chapter will discuss in detail this decline of British power and its consequences for American foreign policy.

From across the English Channel came a wail over the dire consequences of national impotence.* In an article entitled "Can France Again Be a Great Power?" André Géraud, whose writings under the name of Pertinax are well known on both sides of the Atlantic, declared:

> League of Nations or United Nations notwithstanding, the influence which any nation commands is in relation to the amount of physical force it can gather. France's weakness offers a danger not only to the French people, but to the world at large. . . . The history of the 40 very full years prior to the French disaster can be cited to prove that French diplomacy, despite some glaring defects, has on the whole been more far-seeing and better able to perceive the trend of European events than the British and the Americans. . . .† All through 1945 and 1946, and so far in 1947 it seems true that not a single international discussion on German affairs has led to the adoption of a French proposal of importance. M. Bidault has kept on enunciating French policy in a somewhat professorial tone, above the din of controversies. Seldom has anyone found it worth while to return a full answer. . . . This painful state of affairs is resented by any French Minister awake to the contrast with a past not so remote. . . .‡ They [the French] see Americans and Britons err consistently in their judgment on French and German affairs. They are afraid lest the problems of Russian affairs do not find the Anglo-Saxon leaders sufficiently experienced and surefooted. It is natural that Frenchmen should have to play second fiddle to the great virtuosi of the day; the trouble is that they can hardly follow the virtuosi's reading of the score.§

If the somewhat mystical program of Charles de Gaulle is capable of rational explanation, it would seem to include the desire to lead France not only to a position of effective opposition to Communists, foreign and domestic, but also to increased independence from American power. Many Frenchmen who do not follow De Gaulle agree that the great dependence of France on the United States is a necessary evil which should be eliminated as soon as possible.

The same debility has been exhibited by other powers which aspire to the middle rank. Canada and Australia have undoubtedly exerted greater influence than ever before both inside and outside the British Commonwealth, but like the parent, the offspring have found themselves definitely arrayed in one of the two world-wide coalitions. China, for which great things were planned in American thinking about the postwar world, was so far from greatness under Kuomintang leadership that its huge continental mass fell

---

* See the 25th Anniversary number of *Foreign Affairs,* October, 1947.

† Is this saying very much?

‡ This is perhaps somewhat exaggerated.

§ André Géraud, "Can France Again Be a Great Power?" Reprinted by permission from *Foreign Affairs* (New York, October, 1947, pp. 28–29). Copyright by Council on Foreign Relations, Inc.

easily into Communist hands, which have taken it definitely (irrevocably?) into the Soviet camp. Brazil has still remained the land of a tomorrow which never seems to dawn, a country plagued by poverty, bad climate, disease, and a remote geographic position. Nor has Perón's Argentina done much better in its efforts to achieve diplomatic importance, despite its recurrent denunciation of the "twin imperialisms" of communism and North American capitalism. Perón's bid for recognition through his announcement of the successful harnessing of atomic energy "by a new process" provoked more skeptical amusement than serious attention throughout the world.

AMERICAN ATTITUDES TOWARD THE SOVIET UNION

"Bipolarity" has therefore become the novel feature of the postwar international environment. The augmented power of the United States and the Soviet Union, the increasing disparity in strength between these two and the small states, and the failure of the middle powers to achieve sufficient strength for a truly independent policy have resulted in a division of the world into two great spheres of influence with the middle ground, the no man's land, between them rapidly vanishing. Neither of the two superpowers desires this uncomfortable situation; it is dangerous to both of them as well as to the allies and followers in each camp. It means the loss of much of the margin for error that formerly existed in diplomacy. To make a wrong guess, to take one false step may now mean destruction, not decades or years hence, but tomorrow.

In 1945 it was still far from clear that the world political situation was rapidly assuming this pattern, that the United States and the Soviet Union were in fact face to face without intermediate buffer zones and mediating forces. And insofar as direct dealings between the two nations were concerned, there was still considerable optimism among Americans that the wartime coalition could be continued, that the many problems of peacemaking could be handled by concerted policy or at least by consistent, if separate, policies. If there was skepticism in Washington over the possibility of postwar American-Soviet friendship, little of it was transmitted to the American people, who were, after all, hardly in the mood to assess correctly the many danger signs already apparent to professional eyes. Twice within a quarter of a century the two countries had fought on the same side against Germany (albeit briefly in 1917). There was no popular disposition to underestimate the heroic deeds of the Red Army and its contribution to victory over Hitler. In fact, there was a tendency to contrast to the disadvantage of the United States, Britain, and France the halfhearted efforts of these states to keep Hitler in check with the strong stand on behalf of collective security against Nazism which had been taken by the Soviet Union through the League spokesman, Westernized Maxim Litvinov, from 1933 to 1939. The Nazi-Soviet Pact? Might not that have been a smart move by Stalin, a defensive move, taken in the knowledge that the Western powers were trying to turn Hitler toward the East, a purchase of time to prepare for the inevitable conflict?

Some Americans turned back to examine the scanty history of American-Russian relations and purported to find therein that, in the words of one of them, "our traditional friendship has not been based upon sentiment and casual gestures of good will, but upon each nation's realistic appraisal of its own national interest. The record is a reasonably consistent one from the days of our early cooperation in defense of freedom of the seas to those of our united action against the menace of Fascism."* It is now clear that, whatever generalities may be ventured concerning the Czarist period, the adjective that most closely characterizes the course of American-*Soviet* relations is "hostile." While there have been fluctuations, as in the dealings of any two states, wholehearted amity, trust, and understanding have never been present. Indeed, these qualities have hardly epitomized Soviet dealings with any nation on earth, large or small.

From 1917 to 1945 American-Soviet relations passed through five distinct phases: first, the period immediately preceding the Bolshevist seizure of power and the succeeding Civil War; second, the period of nonrecognition, from 1920 to 1933; third, the years from President Roosevelt's recognition to the Nazi-Soviet Pact of August, 1939; fourth, the period of that pact, which lasted until Hitler's attack on the Soviet Union in June, 1941, and included the Russo-Finnish War; finally, the Lend-Lease period of 1941 to 1945, ending with the surrender of Germany and the abrupt termination of Lend-Lease by President Truman.

► AMERICAN-SOVIET RELATIONS

EARLY BOLSHEVIK PERIOD

Wilsonian America welcomed the overthrow of the Czar and the advent of Kerensky. This event made more palatable United States entrance into World War I on the basis of a crusade by democratic governments against tyranny and absolutism. The United States wanted to believe in Kerensky's stability and in the continuance of Russian belligerency against Germany. It was easy, therefore, to underestimate the dangers of Bolshevism. Ambassador Francis cabled that "extreme socialist or anarchist named Lenin making violent speeches and thereby strengthening government; designedly giving him leeway and will deport opportunely." Credits and cash were put at the disposal of Kerensky to enable him to stay in the war, but soon Kerensky was gone and the "extreme socialist or anarchist" had taken over.

Even then it was not believed that the Bolsheviks could last long. The

---

* Foster Rhea Dulles, *The Road to Teheran* (Princeton, N. J., Princeton University Press, 1944), p. 261.

United States, which had recognized Kerensky six days after the Czar's abdication, wanted no part of Lenin and his crowd. If unrecognized, he might go quietly but, quietly or not, he would go. Russia was in a state of unparalleled turmoil, with Reds, Whites, Czechs, Germans, Ukrainians, and what-not fighting obscure battles in obscure places for obscure purposes. It was in this situation that the Allies intervened, against the wishes of the American government, which disregarded the erstwhile Ambassador Francis' plea that "the only way to end this disgrace to civilization is for the Allies immediately to take Petrograd and Moscow." Reluctantly, to protect its own interests in a chaotic situation, to aid the evacuation of the embattled Czechs fighting their way across Asia in one of the longest military marches in recorded history, to prevent the Japanese from seizing Russian Manchuria, the United States dispatched a force of about eighty-five hundred men to that area. Thus was founded the Soviet legend that its post–World War II rival had at an earlier time *led* Allied efforts to overthrow the Leninist regime.

There is little doubt that determined British and French intervention in the Murmansk and Crimean areas of European Russia could have disposed of Lenin. But while Western intervention was tangible enough and definitely hostile to the Soviets, the powers could not agree on a concerted effort of sufficient strength to destroy Bolshevism. Other matters, seemingly more important, occupied their attention, and in the early days of the Russian Civil War it looked as though the Whites could beat the Reds without a great deal of outside assistance. In the summer of 1918 Germany launched its final offensive, which came all too close to succeeding. After the defeat of Germany came months of negotiation, culminating in the Versailles Treaty. The time had passed for successful Western intervention in the Russian Civil War. Instead the Western powers adopted the policy of isolating the "running sore" of Bolshevism from Europe by a string of small states tied to the West. Europe would proceed, as it had recurrently in the past, without Russia.

NONRECOGNITION PERIOD

After the end of the Russian Civil War and the withdrawal of the interventionist forces, the United States continued its nonrecognition policy. This policy had a solid basis in self-interest, whatever might be said for it in terms of international law. The new Soviet government left no doubt concerning its hostility toward the United States and all other bourgeois, capitalist nations. It foresaw the day when such nations would topple into Communist hands, and it tried to hasten the triumph of the "international proletariat." National Communist parties were formed in many countries, usually out of dissident socialist, anarchist, or syndicalist groups, and publicly paraded their primary allegiance to the Comintern, centered in Moscow. The United States did not escape the efforts of these groups to foment unrest and strife, although the burgeoning prosperity of the twenties and the lack of class consciousness of the American people made their attempts difficult and largely unproductive. Then, too, the Soviet Union had repudiated the debts of the Czarist regime and was confiscating foreign property, including that of Americans. While little could be done to protect such property inside Russia, nonrecognition gave American courts the legal stand from which to nullify the effects of such decrees inside the United States.

Throughout this period Americans evinced considerable interest in what the Soviets were up to. Absence of trustworthy, firsthand reports did not prevent readers from making their choice between articles entitled "Red Poison" and "These Charming Russians"; "Russian Nudists" and "Puritan Bolsheviks." A few American businessmen, responding to Soviet overtures, established mutually satisfactory contacts with the new regime. Trade between the two countries, always small, reached a figure in 1928 more than double that of 1913. Americans participated generously in the relief program organized by Herbert Hoover during the Russian famine of 1922, a famine brought on by the effects of the Civil War and by the all-out efforts of the Soviets to collectivize Russian agriculture and to eliminate elements hostile to their control. As a result of these and other factors, the groundwork for re-establishment of diplomatic relations had been laid by 1933. By that time most of the other major countries had already taken this step, some more than a decade previously. Debt repudiation had not affected the United States as seriously as it had such countries as France, nor was the step any longer a novel or a unique one. As the depression grew, other countries much closer to home arbitrarily canceled public and private obligations. The passage of time likewise had taken the edge off property confiscation as an issue. Some companies had made their own settlements, and others had given up. The depression itself provided an argument for recognition. As trade levels fell precipitously, it made less and less sense to place obstacles in the path of what little commerce might be found.

Then, too, the Soviet regime obstinately refused to topple. The transition from Lenin to Stalin was made with remarkable smoothness, and the latter fastened his own interpretation of Communism on the Russian people without their resorting to revolution. In the international ramifications of Stalinism, as they were then understood, there lay another reason to re-establish relations. The failure of international Communism under the Comintern's control to achieve any lasting successes outside Russia combined with the Stalin-initiated first Five-Year Plan to give the impression abroad, carefully fostered by official pronouncements, that the Soviet Union was turning from unattainable world revolution to building "socialism in one country." Coincidentally, the Soviet Union, alarmed by the obvious threat of Hitler, was ending its enforced and self-imposed isolation from the League of Nations. In fact, the Soviet was taking the lead in trying to make of that organization the instrument of true collective security that the French had envisaged a decade earlier.

To other governments, as well as to the newly installed Roosevelt Administration, it appeared that Russia would be a valuable partner in frustrating German revisionism in Europe and Japanese aggression in Asia.

AMERICAN RECOGNITION OF THE SOVIET UNION

Recognition was accorded the Soviet Union in an exchange of notes dated November 16, 1933, between Franklin Roosevelt and Maxim Litvinov. The Soviet government promised "to respect scrupulously the indisputable right of the United States to order its own life within its own jurisdiction in its own way and to refrain from interfering in any manner in the internal affairs of the United States, its territories or possessions" and to refrain from "any agitation or propaganda having as an aim the violation of the territorial integrity of the United States, its territories or possessions, or the bringing about by force of a change in the political or social order of the whole or any part of the United States, its territories or possessions."* While under the aegis of the "popular-front" dictate, American Communists seemed to follow this agreement, but it cannot be said that any respectable group in the United States welcomed the dubious support of this minuscule agglomeration of esoteric misfits. Additional agreements related to the freedom of worship for Americans within the Soviet Union, most-favored-nation treatment, and the settlement of claims, which last was never worked out between the two countries. In summary, it may be said that the United States was recognizing belatedly an undoubted though unwelcome fact and that the Soviet Union was permitting this country to do so. While recognition undoubtedly improved official relations between the two governments, those relations never reached a level of cordiality. Any basis for solid rapport was lacking. The United States took no part in League activities; the American mood, as reflected in the Neutrality Acts, was to stay aloof from European quarrels then growing in intensity. Soviet trade provided no path to prosperity; in fact, commercial conflicts probably bulked larger than the value of the trickle of goods which traveled to and from Russia.

AMERICAN-SOVIET RELATIONS: 1939–1941

Any easing of tension between the two nations came abruptly to an end by three events in 1939. The Soviet Union allied itself to Germany, which most Americans regarded as the greatest menace to world peace. This agreement allowed Hitler to destroy Poland and then to turn the full weight of his *Wehrmacht* on Britain and France, countries which most Americans regarded as their friends and protectors of world peace. The Soviet Union then attacked Finland, little Finland, peace-loving Finland, democratic Finland, debt-paying

---

* Letter of Maxim Litvinov to President Roosevelt, November 16, 1933. Quoted in Robert Strausz-Huppe and Stefan Possony, *International Relations* (New York, McGraw-Hill Book Company, Inc., 1950), p. 758.

Finland. Speedily relations between the United States and Russia sank to the lowest point since 1920. This assault was as brutal as any of Hitler's, and Americans reacted accordingly, though official policy never came as close to war as did that of Britain and France, which planned to send an expeditionary force to fight with the Finns. While the Finns won every battle in the American newspapers until they suddenly lost the war, Americans equated the two dictators in the strange alliance as major enemies of all that this nation held sacred (even though they were not yet prepared to fight for it). In this period the House of Representatives failed by only three votes to cut off appropriations to maintain an American ambassador in Moscow, just as it failed by one vote to end the Selective Service Act, on which American military power was being built.

THE WARTIME COALITION

No sooner had Americans discovered where Stalin stood than their discovery was outmoded by the German attack on Russia of June, 1941. This event caused much soul-searching in the United States. If Stalin was as bad as Hitler, did he deserve any lend-lease assistance? If, as American experts were daily reporting, Germany could defeat Russia within four (six, ten?) weeks, would not American aid be a waste of money which would be better used to accelerate American rearmament or enlarge shipments to Britain? The decision of the Roosevelt Administration was taken quickly (although supplies did not start to reach Russia in any quantity until March, 1942) and was based on the realistic premise that the major job at the time was to help anyone who would help defeat Hitler. In this the American President was perfectly in accord with the British Prime Minister, which doughty anti-Communist did not hesitate to welcome Stalin as a member of the anti-German coalition into which the Russian ruler was so rudely flung by Hitler's greatest mistake. The Anglo-American-Soviet alliance can therefore be said to date from June, 1941, athough it was not until six months later that the United States became a full belligerent and not until January 1, 1942, that the United Nations Declaration, the only formal agreement including all three powers, was signed.

It is beyond the scope of this chapter to present in detail the twists and turns of American-Soviet relations during World War II. Major John R. Deane, who ought to know, has described it as "the strange alliance," and every year of postwar perspective adds to its strangeness. Liaison between the two armies was virtually nonexistent. The United States was not privy to Soviet battle plans, nor was it in a position to make accurate assessments of Soviet capabilities as the battle lines swept east and west across most of European Russia. Conversely, there was much that the United States did not wish to tell its new ally, information both military and political. Separate wars were fought on separate fronts, and the aloofness of the Russian ally was heightened by the growing intimacy of Anglo-American relations. It should be remembered that it was not until the end of 1943, two years after the United States entered the war, that the first meeting of the heads of the three states was held—at Teheran, Iran.

WARTIME DISPUTES WITH RUSSIA

Nonetheless, there was never much secret about what the Soviet Union wanted. It wanted lend-lease supplies in large quantities and the establishment of a second front in Europe. On both counts it was to be disappointed. British demands, the build-up for the European invasion, the tortuous routes to northern and southern Russian, and the shortage of shipping space combined to make it impossible for shipments to reach expected levels. Also, the Soviet Union refused to regard any Western military action except invasion across the English Channel as a second front: not the landings in Africa in 1942, nor the invasion of Italy and the removal of Mussolini's government in 1943. On both issues Russian representatives perforce accepted delays; they could not do otherwise. But meantime two myths were being built in Russia that were to emerge full-blown after the end of hostilities: Soviet military equipment alone turned back the German onslaught; the Red Army alone defeated Hitler's *Wehrmacht*. Both myths provided foundations for the postwar policy of hostility toward the United States and other Western powers consciously adopted by the Kremlin.

Other discernible causes of the postwar poisoning of American-Soviet relations lay in the political sphere. As soon as Stalin was relatively sure that the key points of Russian defense—Leningrad, Moscow, and Stalingrad— would not fall to Germany, that is, early in 1942, he evinced a plain desire to discuss details of the peace settlement for Europe. Such a frame of mind accorded with British predilections, but hardly with American. It became established American policy not to discuss in any detail future arrangements in Europe and to hold the British to this line, although sometimes with only limited success, as when the British and the Russians arranged for the division of influence in the Balkan countries. American reluctance to discuss postwar settlements apparently stemmed from a number of factors: lack of leadership and a tendency to avoid decisions on the part of a President already overworked on military matters; fear that detailed arrangements might produce dangerous disaffection among the American people, particularly among minority groups; weakness of a State Department inadequate in either quality or quantity of personnel to undertake the necessary planning; unwillingness to negotiate with the Russians until American and British armies were firmly established in Europe; and, finally, uncertainty over the role which the United States could and should play in Europe after the defeat of Hitler.

While these arguments against making decisions early in the war regarding the postwar settlement may be appreciated, even in retrospect, they did not convince former Under Secretary of State Sumner Welles, who makes clear that the postponement caused serious delays in American planning for the settlement which had to come some time, and that the inevitable result was piecemeal negotiation on a variety of separate but related issues, none of which were viewed in their proper perspective as part of a general pattern of postwar objectives. Other chapters will discuss in detail the decisions which were reached during the war on such subjects as Eastern Europe, Germany, and the new international organization. However, two summary points should be mentioned here which vitally affected the postwar environment in which the United States and the Soviet Union found themselves face to face.

VAGUENESS OF WARTIME AGREEMENTS

In the first place, negotiations undertaken during the war generally resulted in statements of agreement so vague that they concealed actual disagreements and set the stage for future disputes between East and West. Stalin is said to have remarked at Teheran that he would make Russian intentions known "at the proper time." From the Western point of view the "proper time" can be argued to have been during the war itself, when the Soviet Union was dependent on lend-lease assistance and anxious for the beginning of the invasion of Europe across the English Channel. In retrospect it becomes clear that Russia intended to extend its influence as far West as possible and certainly intended to play a dominent role in Poland and the Balkans. In both areas Soviet policy was soon shown to be at variance with the milder forms of influence which the West expected of the Soviet Union and to which it thought its Eastern ally committed. Failure to obtain a clear picture of Soviet intentions through hard-and-fast agreements made during the war may not have lost Eastern Europe to Russia, since Russia would have been there with troops in any case while the Allies were far away. But it did mean that such actions as the arrest of London Polish leaders, the speedy demise of the London Polish government, and the flagrant intervention to impose the Groza Communist government on Rumania were viewed as isolated occurrences instead of being recognized as a consistent effort at Soviet political aggrandizement.

Second, and more specifically, the impasse over Germany, to be discussed in the chapter on Western Europe, had its origins in this same failure of East and West correctly to evaluate each other's objectives. To the Soviet Union, American evasions on the subject of what was to become of Germany looked like sinister preparations for German recovery, particularly when the United States neither accepted Soviet reparation claims on Germany nor produced the reconstruction loan desired by the Russians as a substitute for or possibly an addition to reparation claims. To the Americans evasions came naturally since there was no agreement in the United States on what a German policy should be and, indeed, no thorough exploration of the implications of the various proposals being blithely bandied about by Treasury, State, War, and White House. The point should not be overlooked that American indecision over Germany, unwillingness to accept or reject the proposed Russian loan, plus the abrupt ending of Lend-Lease immediately after the defeat of Germany may have had much to do with the Kremlin's determination to shift Russian policy from one of negotiation and compromise to one of adventurous aggression and intransigence. This is in no wise to say that the United States is mostly to blame for the increasing tension between East and West, but only that certain policies and lack of policies on the part of the United States alerted the Kremlin to the incompatibility of Russian and American objectives even while the United States continued to hope that an avenue toward accommodation could be found.

▶ INFLUENCE OF TECHNOLOGY

Calculations concerning the power and behavior of states in the postwar international environment have been made increasingly difficult by the addition of new factors to the equation and by changes in the old ones. One such change is in the relationship of technology to modern war. Between the seventeenth and twentieth centuries methods of warfare remained fairly well fixed and hence well known. To be sure, the American and even more the French Revolutions had introduced the concept of the popular army and the *levée en masse*. Even with this change, however, war was a phenomenon, fought with limited objectives for a limited and specifically definable time span. Wars had beginnings and ends; in between, the energies of the entire population were not primarily related to the pursuit of military objectives. The armies of the American Civil War were the largest engaged in combat during the nineteenth century, even including the long, intermittent struggles between Great Britain and Napoleonic France. While the nature of war had changed considerably from the period of Italian city conflict, when a fortified town could surrender without battle if clearly outmaneuvered by its enemies, the other extreme of unremitting, total, last-ditch warfare was still far in the future.

Already the twentieth century is approaching this extreme. In its first fifty years technology has added more weapons revolutionizing the nature of warfare than appeared in the preceding three centuries put together. Before military science could digest the implications of the submarine, the repeating rifle, the tank, and the airplane were thrown into the fray to upset calculations even further. The lessons about war supposedly learned in the course of the four years from 1914 to 1918 had to be unlearned in 1939 and 1940. Conclusions concerning the all-conquering nature of the blitzkrieg drawn by such experts as Lindbergh likewise were falsified during the Battle of Britain and the defenses of Leningrad, Moscow, and Stalingrad. The second struggle against Germany made it apparent to all that war was now approaching the ultimate with respect to objectives, involvement of the civilian population, and commitment of national resources and finances. Still obscure, however, were the implications of this knowledge for relations between national societies.

Then, at the very end of World War II, came the atomic bomb, the most powerful and the most revolutionary implement of warfare the world had yet seen. Hardly had people learned to live in full appreciation of its existence—if not to understand its meaning—when portents of even more deadly weapons, such as hydrogen bombs, bacteriological preparations, and globe-encircling bombing planes, began to appear. It seemed as though war had become a battle of laboratories and designing boards, a race to produce a new invention before it should be rendered obsolescent by its successor. We are told that a comparison between the atomic bomb exploded over Hiroshima and those now entering the nation's stockpiles is roughly equivalent to a comparison of the first horseless carriage with the modern streamlined automobiles now jamming the nation's highways. Production of the hydrogen bomb makes the same comparison applicable to the difference between the H-bomb and its puny predecessor, the improved A-bomb.

ATTITUDES TOWARD THE ATOMIC BOMB

What are the consequences for international relations of the technological impact on warfare? The confusions and contradictions which appear in attempts to answer this question can be illustrated by the rapid changes in responsible, intelligent American thinking about the atomic bomb. In the initial shock and horror at the destruction wrought at Hiroshima and Nagasaki, many Americans felt that such things could not be, that safety from the atomic bomb demanded an extreme solution of some sort, whether by world government, or by taking the Russians into our confidence as rapidly as possible, or both. But when President Truman abruptly refused to tell the Russians first and negotiate afterward, when the dream of world union vanished, sober second thought ensued. The Russians were daily becoming more menacing; their violations of wartime pledges multiplied; yet something deterred them from full-scale aggression in Europe. Could it be the American monopoly of the atomic bomb? Perhaps it was a good thing to have the bomb after all. Maybe it was just as well that the Russians in the United Nations were being obstinate concerning the American plan for international control. Probably it would be years, if ever, before the Soviet Union discovered this highly valuable "secret." This was the period when the bomb was labeled "the absolute weapon."

Echoing the words of the 1945 Truman-Attlee-King pronouncement, the collaborating members of the Yale Institute of International Studies stated: "No adequate defense against the bomb exists, and the possibilities of its existence in the future are exceedingly remote. . . . It is precisely this ability to absorb punishment, whether one is speaking of a warship or a city, which seems to vanish in the face of atomic attack. . . . Superiority in numbers of bombs is not in itself a guarantee of strategic superiority in atomic bomb warfare."*

But the Russians did make and explode an atomic weapon. The monopoly was lost. Did this mean that within the very near future the two nations would be equal in power because of the possession of an "absolute" weapon, only limited numbers of which were necessary for victory? American thinking veered off on another tangent. Perhaps the weapon was not so absolute as had previously been thought. Some interpreted the technical studies made in Germany and Japan by the Strategic Bombing Survey to mean that the damage done by one or more atomic bombs could be measured and hence was limited and, still more important, that the new bomb did not and could not cause much more damage than mass raids with so-called "conventional armaments." After pleading guilty to an earlier, mistaken opinion, one of the authors of *The Absolute Weapon* continued in an article in *Foreign Affairs†* to stress the point that ratios in the supply of bombs possessed by the United States and the Soviet Union were still important and would remain so for an indefinite period, that there could be substantial, if not completely adequate, defenses in terms of retaliatory power, interception of atomic bomb carriers, plant dispersal, and so on.

The concept of defense through threat and ability to retaliate was in itself new, since the ability to retaliate implies that the country will survive the first sneak attack from the enemy, a possibility which at first had seemed remote. Moreover, it was possible that large cities might have far greater absorption power than originally believed. Proper construction of buildings could shield many from exposure; the weapon might not detonate right on the target; and the morale and discipline of the people might enable them to keep things moving after the attack had passed. The dispersal of lines of communication, production facilities, governmental apparatus, mechanisms of retaliation could ensure survival of the first blow, and even of the second, third, and fourth, while the United States carried out its own counterattack on the enemy.

The historical perspective of armament development likewise helped to push the atomic bomb into the category of limited weapons effective in limited situations. Even more destructive than the atomic bomb were the hydrogen or "hell" bombs and other "fantastic weapons" which United States (and Russian) technicians were developing. On the other hand, the destructive powers of "conventional armaments," constantly augmented in quantity and quality, were actually approaching that of the first atomic bombs, while the latter were already obsolete. An additional source of comfort in the loss of a monopoly once deemed so important derived from the unsuitability of the

---

* Bernard Brodie, ed., *The Absolute Weapon* (New York, Harcourt, Brace & Company, 1946), pp. 28, 29, 46.

† Bernard Brodie, "The Atomic Bomb as Policy Maker," *Foreign Affairs,* October, 1948, pp. 17–34.

atomic bomb in many tactical situations. The experience in Korea and the planning of European defense seemed to show that traditional modes of warfare could survive the addition of one more weapon, however revolutionary it might at first have appeared to be.

Thus within the space of five short years prolonged practical discussion of what the atomic bomb meant in the daily lives of the people had had its inevitably calming effect. The horror of last night had become the reality of daylight, and in so doing lost much of its horror. From *No Place to Hide* and "a choice between the quick and and the dead," the people of the United States were turning to *What to Do When an Atomic Attack Comes.* "What to do" appeared to be to avoid getting hit, to remain calm, to help others, and to trust the governmental organization. Perhaps it is in the nature of the human animal not to be able to stare at destruction for any long period. The last war showed the toughness and the will to live of people for whom there seemed to be no rational reason for continued existence.

The important point regarding the limited experience of living with the atomic bomb is that people cannot attain any objective comprehension of the international environment in which they live. Their view becomes warped by judgment based on incomplete evidence, judgment based on irrational fear or equally irrational hope. So popular conclusions as to the nature of the new implement of war were based, not on knowledge of the facts, plus cold calculation, but on deductions from two explosions during wartime and on what people wanted to believe. It was a situation in which even the expert, like the man on the street, was unable to divorce himself completely from his hopes and his fears. One fact is sure: the implication for international politics of the atomic bomb and of its successors, the hydrogen bomb and other weapons, will somehow be fitted into the reckonings which statesmen have to make about their own and their adversary's power. It is possible that only when it is too late may we awake to find that the first, instinctive reaction of dread and horror was the correct one, that although this view arose out of ignorance and fear, it was more in accord with the reality of man's new relation to his environment than the sober reflections of men writing later, men who could not bear to think of their civilization as doomed.

▶ ROLE OF IDEAS

The atomic bomb is all too tangible and real. It has upset the political balance of state relations and raised the question of whether the concept of war itself may not be outmoded. Intangible, but equally real, is the surprising strength shown by ideas and clusters of ideas known as ideologies, which also have troubled the sleep of statesmen seeking for clues to order and stability. Disturbing to Western leaders has been the shift of the democratic ideology from an offensive to a defensive position. It had seemed to the nineteenth and early twentieth centuries that the idea of popular sovereignty, bringing with it improvement in man's dignity and comfort, would shortly triumph throughout the world, or at least in "advanced," "civilized" countries. During World War I a disintegrating Austro-Hungarian Empire was given an extra push by Woodrow Wilson's masterful and timely espousal of the principles of freedom and self-government. But with the end of the "war to end war" the world was still not safe for democracy. It had in fact become even more unsafe. Old ideas that had served as foundations for the Western state system could hardly hold their own against the new rallying cries of fascism and communism. Both of the totalitarian ideologies made effective use of internal subversion to destroy their enemies. Hitler's rantings at "Herr" Benes incited the Germanic Sudeten minority to defiance of governmental control. Part of the explanation for the collapse of France, where few Germans lived, was the corrosive fear of the French that they had no chance of winning, combined with the soul-destroying doubt in many French minds as to whether their own government was worth fighting for.

FASCISM AS AN IDEOLOGY

As an ideology fascism lagged behind communism in mass appeal. Fascist theory, such as it was, became more highly developed in Italy than in Germany, but in both countries it was clearly tailor-made to cloak the aggressions of two tyrants bent on carving out for themselves as large empires as possible. It was only to be expected that the aftermath of war should leave scattered traces of fascism in defeated Germany and in such other regimes as Franco's Spain and Perón's Argentina. These diverse remnants cannot rightly be dignified as an ideology, however, since they do not comprise a fully formulated, theoretical concept of government so much as techniques adopted by individuals to perpetuate their own control. Furthermore, the appeal of fascism is now definitely national, not universal. This is not to say that danger does not lurk in totalitarianism of the right, either in the threat which one nation with such a government might pose to the cooperative efforts of the rest of the free world, or, and perhaps more important, through belief by people in other countries that American policies are bent on fostering regimes indistinguishable from those which came so close to destroying Western civilization.

COMMUNISM AS AN IDEOLOGY

By contrast, communism appears in the postwar environment as much more potent in appeal and scope than fascism ever was. Backed by the increased strength of the Soviet Union, communism is not as easy to combat as its erstwhile partner of the right. Fascism, particularly as exemplified by Hitlerite Germany, could be condemned in the nations of the West as anti-humanist. Far from being the "Wave of the Future," it all too frequently appeared in the guise of tribal paganism and barbarism. Now the Soviet Union, after an embarrassing lapse of two years, 1939–1941, and a brief period of partial cooperation, 1941–1945, is busy at the old stand, attempting to "sell" the idea that fascist brutality is indigenous to the social, economic, and political order of the Western nations, that the only distinction between its allies in Word War II and its German enemy is one of degree, and that that degree is ever diminishing.

In peddling this program, communism is not limited to any special race or ethnic group; it is truly totalitarian in its scope and in the geographic area to which it may be applied. The communist movement does not depend on any particular governmental structure, or on financial and moral support from small minorities within each country; it can be a minority, underground group devoted to subversion and sabotage or an accepted political party appealing to the broad mass of the people. It appropriates for its own the very terminology of the West: sovereignty, popular rights, liberty, equality, and democracy.

Thus the Soviet Union has at its disposal new techniques of foreign policy wholly alien to the traditional, a pattern of devices that can be used in ever-shifting forms depending on time and place. The battle of ideas and ideologies is an integral part of the cold war. The United States has been forced by the aggressiveness of the other superpower to add a new dimension to its own foreign policy also and to develop for itself a system of techniques as flexible as those of the Soviet Union. A later chapter in this section will be devoted to this problem, the role of ideas in American foreign policy.

► CHANGES IN GOVERNMENTAL FORM

Alterations in the form of government follow naturally in the wake of war. Equally naturally, their extent tends to vary directly with the intensity, scope, and duration of the conflict. By the first two of these criteria the six years of World War II produced changes far more extensive than any other war, and it should be remembered that Spain had been experiencing war and its aftermath for sixteen years and that Asia had been in the midst of the turmoil caused by Japanese aggression for over twenty.

It is clear that changes in forms of government caused by the last war have not as yet run their full course in many parts of the world. This fact complicates the formulation of long-range American foreign policies. Is the objective of the United States to maintain the present order wherever it is found, even if the forces making for rapid change have not had their full impact? Or does this country propose to support only the particular types of changes which it feels will produce an international environment most conducive to its own and world security? If so, what specific American policies can aid in attaining this end? Meantime the Soviet Union stands to gain merely from the continuance of chaos and confusion, and has the comfortable alternative of perpetuating changes for their own sake or of using an emergent pattern of government to increase its own influence. The United States, on the other hand, cannot afford the luxury of such an irresponsible position. It must peforce try to develop and foster in its external relations a type of world order in which Americans and other peoples of diverse cultures will want to live.

► ECONOMIC DISLOCATION

A final factor that has been intruded into the calculations of statesmen is the seemingly irreparable economic dislocation caused by World War II. Here war has magnified a problem the outlines of which were distinguishable earlier. During the nineteenth century it appeared that mechanical inventions applied to industry and agriculture had made it possible to increase the production of goods and food at a rate faster than the growth of the world's population. Increased communications, by rail and steamship, combined with increasing trade between nations to distribute these goods and food. Certainly the distribution was not even: in any particular country some people were rich while others were poor, and in the world generally some nations were rich while others were poverty-stricken. Nonetheless economists now labeled "classical" could argue with cogency that continuation on the same path of progress would eventually lead all nations and peoples, not to equality perhaps, but at least to bearable and rising standards of living.

The great depression of the nineteen thirties, followed so soon by the great war of the forties (How much of a causal relation was there between the two?), demonstrated to the world that there was no necessary correlation between the total productive capacity of the world and the standards of living which the peoples of the world can enjoy. In combating the depression, many nations had recourse to economic devices aimed at controlling and channelizing trade in order that national advantages could be realized at the expense of other members of the international "community." Gone was the self-restraint necessary to abide by the theory that for one nation to profit others must be permitted to do so also. World War II administered a *coup de grâce* to existing systems for the allocation of goods and services within many countries, and to the international trade pattern which the nineteenth century had evolved. Economic power became more fully mobilized than ever before in the interests of national survival, and from the attendant dislocations, changed but not lessened by the demands of the cold war, the world has not as yet recovered.

The result has been well-nigh universal acknowledgment that the so-called "automatic" mechanism of the "market" cannot be relied upon to result in the production of commodities most needed and their distribution to people who most needed them at prices which they could pay. Under national as well as international pressure more and more countries have adopted measures of controlling their internal economies for such diverse ends as domestic social welfare and military strength, sometimes seeking to reconcile these seemingly conflicting objectives within the same program. Many countries have had no experience with and felt no consequent sympathy for the theories and practice of international specialization which the nineteenth century had worked out This was true of the newly emergent states of Asia and the underdeveloped countries of continental Europe. Particularly to countries producing raw materials, the path of progress toward economic power and stability seemed to lie in "hothouse," artificially stimulated industrialization, whether or no the capital or natural resources for a modern complex economy were present They therefore adopted nationalistic economic measures and pressed at international conferences for what they regarded as a more equitable price and quantity relationship between their exports and the consumer and producer goods which they were required to import.

POPULATION AND PRODUCTIVITY

In view of the adverse conditions of national production and international trade which the war had left, experts began to re-examine previously accepted concepts of population growth and natural resources supply. They found that under conditions which had become chronic during the twentieth century much of the world was overpopulated. Even worse, these overpopulated areas were the very ones where the rate of increase was continuing high and where the difficulties of adjusting population to land resources, either through limitation of the former or more scientific utilization of the latter, were the greatest. Resources were being exhausted not only in the underdeveloped areas, but in the countries with more advanced economies as well. A time seemed near at hand when some of the vital foundations of modern society would approach exhaustion.

Remedial measures were difficult to apply. Conservation for future generations ran up against the demands of contemporary utilizers or, as in the United States, against traditional patterns of exploitation carried over from an era when resources had appeared inexhaustible. International cooperation to achieve efficient use of resources which were most plentiful appeared almost utopian when measured against the heightened nationalism which had all but destroyed the concept of common obligations and responsibility by states as members of an *economic* as well as of a political world community. Proposals to limit population growth ran into widespread ignorance and religious opposition in underdeveloped areas and were difficult to apply in countries still in the throes of postwar ferment. They were also opposed by regimes only too well aware of the relation of numbers to national strength.

DISPARITY OF WESTERN AND SOVIET TRADE PRACTICES

Once again the Soviet Union deliberately added a further disturbing element to an already unbalanced situation. In its state control over production and distribution Russia had far surpassed Germany, not to mention such other countries as Britain and France. Soviet trade practices of the twenties and thirties indicated that, while total Russian involvement in the international commodity exchange was not large, that country was prepared to dump its products on the market below cost if necessary and to resort to all the devices of bilateral bargaining from which it could derive advantage. During and immediately after the war, economic experts wrestled long with the problem of whether state-controlled economies could be fitted into a framework of multilateral trade operating under so-called liberal principles. Even as the non-Soviet nations attempted unsuccessfully to adopt such a pattern among themselves, the Soviet Union gave its familiar negative answer to the question of Russian participation. Instead it has used its economic power as one of many devices for cementing its hold on the satellite nations of Eastern Europe. Even should the rest of the world somehow manage to restore some semblance of prewar trading conditions, therefore, it would still be confronted with the necessity of deciding how freely trade could be carried on with the Soviet bloc by Western states and individuals.

For the United States, as a later chapter will make plain, there exists serious contradictions between economic courses advocated by various domestic groups, and an additional disparity between official postwar economic foreign policy and the political necessity of winning allies in the cold war with the Soviet Union.

► WEAKNESS OF INTERNATIONAL REGULATORY MECHANISMS

Devices for international control have not been effective in bringing order to the world environment in which national states must live. Whereas the mechanisms potentially available to an international organization are more powerful and can be made effective over a wider area than ever before— perhaps for that very reason—nations have been loath to accept their general application on behalf of the world community. Still apparent is the disillusionment of Western peoples and their leaders, who believed that the end of the war would see a new era in which international organization would command a respect and prestige never before attained.

International law, flaunted by the Axis Powers, and apparently incapable of bridging the gap between the technical and the political fields, seemed about to derive new strength from its application below the impersonal state level to the conduct of individuals, as exemplified by the theory and conduct of the Nuremberg Trials. Additional strength appeared to derive from the association of legal principles with a world political organization having a new structure more attuned to the facts of international power than was the League of Nations. Diplomacy, the third regulatory mechanism, also seemed on the verge of greater effectiveness through its divorce from the stilted nomenclature, procedures, and controls characteristic of the eighteenth century, and its transference into an open, frank, sharp instrument for the mitigation and settlement of conflicts between peoples.

It will be the purpose of a later chapter to trace in detail the frustration of these hopes for an effective regulation of state behavior and the attendant adjustments necessitated in the foreign policy of the United States.

► CONCLUSION: THE PROBLEM OF THE ASSESSMENT
   OF SOVIET BEHAVIOR

While knowledge about the Soviet Union is great enough to preclude the formation of policy purely on the basis of stereotypes, it is still not sufficient for reasoned analysis and successful prognostication concerning probable future Russian behavior. There are formidable barriers to the collection of the type of data the United States requires. One handicap is the deliberate shroud of secrecy woven by the Russian government. Since 1946 the Soviets have systematically destroyed contacts between West and East which might have permitted the former to learn something about the latter. Those Westerners, such as foreign diplomats, who cannot be excluded altogether, find their movements in the Soviet Union handicapped, guided, and under surveillance, their attempts to approach Russians other than their formal, foreign-office counterparts frustrated and set at naught by the feeling deliberately instilled in the average Russian that it is unwise if not dangerous to talk to foreigners. Beginning in the thirties, the Soviet government has clamped a progressive blackout on statistics, so that production figures, budget expenditures, and the like, cannot with any degree of accuracy be measured from abroad. Furthermore, the Soviet statistics which have appeared are obviously unreliable. Much to the annoyance of Western economists, the Soviet Union does not hide its intention to use facts and figures as instruments of propaganda—not as measures of Soviet strength so much as actual contributors to that strength. The prodigious efforts in the United States and elsewhere to determine conditions in the Soviet Union have been of great value, but the energy expended per fact obtained and analyzed is extremely large.

Obviously it is of the utmost importance for the United States to know as much as possible concerning Soviet interpretations of the international environment, since upon this interpretation is based Soviet foreign policy. Soviet foreign policy in turn goes far toward determining the international environment, in the light of which American foreign-policy decisions must be made. Only by being able to estimate with some degree of accuracy the probable course of Soviet policy can the United States government interject any element of foresight into its own decision making and thus hope to avoid the manifold perils inherent in improvisation.

Because of the complexity of the international environment, some features of which have been discussed in the course of the present chapter, it is all the more important that policy makers avoid the ever-present temptation to adopt a one-track, cause-and-effect interpretation. In the field of international politics it is difficult to trace any single "effect" to any one "cause" when both are bound up in a pattern of complex interaction involving multiple ingredi-ents. Part of the rigidity and irrationality so apparent in Soviet policy certainly is attributable to just this point: that the rulers of the Kremlin attempt to deal with their international environment in terms of simple, limited hypoth-eses, any one of which may have an element of reality, but which do not collectively encompass all observable data. Into the same error American statecraft cannot afford to fall. Success can be found only in a pattern of policy fully as complex and delicate as the environment it seeks to manipulate.

► SELECTED BIBLIOGRAPHY

The element of power in international politics has been discussed by most writers in the field. In addition to Nicholas J. Spykman, *America's Strategy in World Politics* (New York, Harcourt, Brace & Company, 1942), see Hans Mor-genthau, *Politics among Nations* (New York, Alfred A. Knopf, Inc., 1948), and Harold and Margaret Sprout, eds., *Foundations of National Power* (New York, D. Van Nostrand Company, 1951). On the decline of Europe and its importance for the United States, see Hajo Holborn, *The Political Collapse of Europe* (New York, Alfred A. Knopf, Inc., 1951), William T. R. Fox, *The Super-Powers* (New York, Harcourt, Brace & Company, 1944), and the same author's "American Foreign Policy and the Western European Rimland," *Proceedings* of the Ameri-can Academy of Political and Social Science, January, 1948. Details of the power developed by the United States in World War II can be found in Winfield Rieffler, "Our Economic Contribution to Victory," *Foreign Affairs,* October, 1947; the War Records Section, Bureau of the Budget, *The United States at War* (U.S. Government Printing Office, 1946), and Office of Defense Mobilization, *Man-power Resources for National Security* (U.S. Government Printing Office, 1954). Features of bipolarity are suggested in Arnold Wolters, "The Role of Power and the Role of Indifference," and Maurice Ash, "An Analysis of Power, with Special Reference to International Politics," both appearing in *World Politics,* October and January, 1951, respectively. Also, Thomas A. Bailey, *America Faces Russia* (Ithaca, N. Y., Cornell University Press, 1950); Crane Brinton, "The Last Hege-mony," *Virginia Quarterly Review,* Winter, 1951; and William T. R. Fox, "Recon-ciliation of the Desirable and the Possible," *American Scholar,* April, 1949. Changing attitudes toward the atomic bomb may be discerned by consulting John Hersey, *Hiroshima* (New York, Alfred A. Knopf, Inc., 1946), Dexter Masters and Katherine Way, eds., *One World or None* (New York, McGraw-Hill Book Company, 1946), Bernard Brodie, ed., *The Absolute Weapon* (New York, Har-court, Brace & Company, 1946), Bernard Brodie, "The Atomic Bomb as Policy Maker," *Foreign Affairs,* October, 1948. In later chapters discussing the subject in more detail will be suggested additional material on the role of ideas, the appeal of communism, and the breakdown of international mechanisms in the security field. The course of American-Russian relations through history has been studied by Foster Rhea Dulles, *The Road to Teheran* (Princeton, N. J., Princeton University Press, 1945), and William A. Williams, *American-Russian Relations* (New York, Rinehart & Company, 1952). Of especial importance in the study of Soviet behavior is X, "Sources of Soviet Conduct," *Foreign Affairs,* July, 1947; Historicus, "Stalin on Revolution," *Foreign Affairs,* January, 1949; George Kennan, "America and the Russian Future," *Foreign Affairs,* April, 1951; Nathan Leites, *The Operational Code of the Politburo* (New York, McGraw-Hill Book Company, 1951); Legislative Reference Service, Library of Congress, *Tensions within the Soviet Union* (Washington, D.C., Government Printing Office, 1951); C. Groves Haines, *Threat of Soviet Imperialism* (Baltimore, The Johns Hopkins Press, 1954); former American Ambassador to Russia Walter Bedell Smith, *My Three Years in Moscow* (Philadelphia, J. B. Lippincott Company, 1950); Barrington Moore, *Soviet Politics: The Dilemma of Power* (Cambridge, Mass., Harvard University Press, 1953); Waldemar Gurian *et al., The Soviet Union, Background, Ideology, Reality* (South Bend, Ind., University of Notre Dame Press, 1951); Harold Lasswell, " 'Inevitable' War: A Problem in the Control of Long-Range Expectations," *World Politics,* October, 1949; Edward Crankshaw, *Cracks in the Kremlin Wall* (New York, The Viking Press, 1951); G. L. Arnold, "Stalinism," *Political Quarterly,* October–December, 1950; W. G. Carlton, "Is Communism Going Nationalist?" *Virginia Quarterly Review,* Spring, 1951; Ruth Benedict and Margaret Mead, "Child Rearing in Certain European Countries," *American Journal of Orthopsychiatry,* April, 1949; R. J. Tarn, "Continuity in Russian Foreign Policy," *International Journal,* Autumn, 1950; Margaret Mead, *Soviet Attitudes toward Authority* (New York, McGraw-Hill Book Company, 1951); Geoffrey Gorer, *The People of Great Russia* (London, Cresset Press, 1949); Irving Goldman, "The Psychiatric Interpretation of Russian History," *American Slavic and East European Review,* October, 1950.

CHAPTER FIFTEEN

EVOLVING PATTERNS OF ECONOMIC FOREIGN POLICY

Ingredients of a Successful Economic Foreign Policy · Interaction of Domestic and Foreign Economic Policies · Viewpoints regarding American Economic Foreign Policies · Historical Landmarks in American Economic Foreign Policy: 1930–1951 · Conclusions · Selected Bibliography

The case for a special chapter on economic measures in a book devoted to postwar American foreign policy can be simply stated. Upon the strength of the United States depends the continued freedom of non-Soviet areas of the world. In turn American leadership depends, not only on the guns, ships, and planes which it can produce, but on the deterrent effect that economic power in the United States and, through American aid, in the hands of its allies can wield. American policy makers are forcing upon the Kremlin the disturbing knowledge that if it unleashes another world war, the economic strength of the forces of freedom will be capable of translation into military might so formidable that any initial victories of aggression will ultimately disappear in disastrous defeat. If analysis of the economic ingredient of American foreign policy is therefore indicated, its close scrutiny is further necessitated by the startling and rapid changes which have taken place in American economic policy in the last two decades, with respect both to the concrete instruments used and to the theories underlying their selection.

▶ INGREDIENTS OF A SUCCESSFUL ECONOMIC FOREIGN POLICY

POSSESSION OF POWER

A successful American economic foreign policy would seem to depend on three ingredients: the possession of economic power, a willingness to use it, and the choice of the appropriate instrument to express that power in the international environment. About the first criterion there can be little doubt. As was mentioned in the preceding chapter, the United States in 1944 turned out military material roughly equal to that of its two principal allies and its two main enemies and this sum was only a fraction of what "total" mobilization could have wrung from the economy. Its production effort, partial though it was, plus the absence of war damage, made the United States after 1945 the greatest economic power in the world. Various standards of measurement support this conclusion. Its products of mine, soil, and industry were the most sought after by the other nations of the world. Its goods were desperately needed if the other countries were going to recover from the war and their peoples attain a semblance of their prewar living standards. That the United States is the source of approximately half of the world's exports is no accident.

And the obverse side of the coin is equally revealing. Other nations in general can attain economic viability only by greatly increasing the sale of their products to each other and by penetrating the American market. The American market looms large, since United States consumption through a national market comprises roughly half the world's total. To sell to the United States is therefore the equivalent of entering a market area equal to all the rest of the world combined. In financial terms reaching this market is even more crucial than its size would indicate. With one or two minor exceptions, the American dollar is the only "hard" currency that any country has been able to establish and maintain since the war. Dollars earned by exports to the United States therefore place in the hands of other countries the power to buy anywhere else in the world products needed for their national economies. Because the United States is unwilling to contemplate the use of its financial resources indefinitely into the future for outright subsidies to the economies of other countries in a foreign counterpart of the "pump-priming" days of the New Deal, ways must be found of bridging this so-called "dollar gap" by methods other than military mobilization. The crux of the problem is whether the United States is to open this, the greatest market, to the world's goods. The standard of American living, the highest in the world, creates demands for varieties and quantities of products sufficient under conditions of stability to assure in large measure the economic viability of the non-Soviet world, on which American prosperity and security in turn depends, provided that an import psychology, implemented by concrete measures, can be created and maintained, a formidable proviso for a traditionally protectionist country.

WILLINGNESS TO USE POWER

It is not safe to assume, however, that the possession of economic power is the same thing as the possession of an effective economic foreign policy. Like other components of national strength, the effectiveness of the economic instrument depends, as has just been indicated, on a willingness by the government to use it to advance national interests. Two important implications lie in this statement. First, there must be a clear national recognition of the need to translate economic strength into a coherent foreign economic policy. Such a recognition has finally come to the United States after American wartime assumptions of limited postwar international responsibility were proved false in all quarters of the globe. A conscious decision to conduct economic policy, as distinct from economic relations, has few historical roots in the

United States. Only when the depression of the thirties forced it to, did the United States begin the painful process of formulating an economic policy that was something more than a collection of heterogeneous enactments, decisions, and pronunciamentos.

Second, a willingness to use economic power implies a degree of systematic government planning historically rare in this country and, whether for sound or unsound reasons, still anathema to large and important segments of the populace. Such governmental initiative further entails a reversal of the view held during much of American history of the proper role for government to assume in its foreign economic operations—advancement and protection of private business, agricultural, and investment interests *at their behest*. This is not to say that measures to these ends should no longer be taken or that the groups just mentioned should not profit thereby. What is indicated is the paramount test of whether the national community in general is being aided, whether, that is, the governmental initiative in all types of foreign relations, including the economic, that is now essential in a world of conflicting, mobilized nation-states results in policies which benefit the United States directly. Certain of the difficulties of applying this test will be pointed out below in discussing the intimate connection between foreign and domestic, between general and particularistic economic foreign policies.

CHOICE OF INSTRUMENTS TO EXPRESS POLICY

There are all too many examples of states with both power and inclination to use that power which have nonetheless compiled dismal records in economic foreign policy because they have failed in the third ingredient for success—the choice of the proper instrument to express policy. This matter of instrument selection is far from being as simple as it sounds. The twentieth century has rapidly evolved economic mechanisms of such complexity that their arrangement in a productive pattern is difficult. The pattern chosen by decision makers is furthermore greatly influenced by domestic demands and expectations that may be radically divergent from the officially interpreted exigencies of the international environment.

Because power, however, great, is never total, another variable must be added to the equation: the decreasing intensity of effect which particular economic policies can have as the geographic distance increases from the United States. But geographic distances in turn may not correspond with cultural, political, and ideological distances, all of which are inextricably involved in the conduct of economic relations with other countries. Thus it is clear that inherent in the choice of productive economic policies are calculations as to time, as to space, and as to locality of effect. Some measures, excellent in themselves, may be premature in the situation at any given moment, while hindsight recurrently demonstrates that the opportunity for the successful employment of others has passed. Measures highly effective in the Caribbean and Central America may lose most of their potency in the

Far East, where countries, even in a shrinking world, are still far away from the United States. Or the variable may be the type of culture, the form of government, the interrelation of ideas held by other peoples. Moreover, the proximity to the Soviet Union of particular countries may negate economic measures which would be successful if the countries were not under immediate threat of communist expansionism. All these factors must be borne in mind by decision makers intent on augmenting the impact of American economic foreign policy. What combination of instruments available to the United States can produce the best results in an international environment where the United States finds itself unable to do everything for everybody, at the same time?

▶ INTERACTION OF DOMESTIC AND FOREIGN ECONOMIC POLICIES

One of the criteria involved in the choice of economic measures was mentioned as the reciprocal influence between decision making in foreign relations and domestic demands and expectations. The interrelationship of foreign and domestic conditions results in the inseparable connection of international and national policies. There has in the past been a tendency to draw an artificial line between domestic and foreign economic policy, allowing many Americans to believe that it is entirely feasible to pursue one kind of objective at home and quite another abroad—that there is in fact no connection between domestic conditions and policies and the direction or success of American external policy. This artificial division may be made as a result of ignorance, of mere wishful thinking, or of a lack of coordination between policy makers who individually know better but whose responsibilities are incompletely defined or outright inconsistent. The fallacy is perpetuated by writers for whom the task of examination and analysis is thereby greatly simplified.

At the expense of additional complexity, therefore, this chapter will at its outset indicate a few of the many facets of the interrelationship between domestic and international policies in the economic field. Seven points will be discussed: the historic demands of protectionism, the pressure of private interest groups, a tradition against domestic economic controls, the requirements of military mobilization, the presence of partisan domestic politics, the difficulties of executive-legislative relations, and the obstacles to effective coordination within the Executive Branch of government. With regard to each some examples of consequences for foreign policy will be cited.

HERITAGE OF PROTECTIONISM

This country grew to greatness under a philosophy that its burgeoning industry was entitled to an initial advantage if not a practical monopoly in the American market. As the number of industrial establishments increased in quantity and variety, ever-new elements of protectionism were added. Even after the United States had attained formidable industrial strength, the benefits of protection were continued. They were also extended to agricultural activity, which was growing apprehensive as its percentage of the total national product began to decline. Demands of specific interest groups did not alone account for this steady trend; there was also an intangible philosophy of the United States as a producing economy. Never in the course of its history did this country subscribe to the thesis of import freedom which Great Britain so long supported; rather did its methods more closely approximate the Continental view, especially the German. It is a matter of considerable irony that the American government, which has pressed measures for liberalizing trade upon Western Europe and which after the war led the efforts for the adoption of an international trade charter, should at the same time have to contend with the arguments of small, undeveloped states that the precedent of American protectionist experience should serve as a guide for their own actions.

Nor has assistance to industry and agriculture been the only element of domestic protectionism which has affected American foreign policy. American unionism came to feel that its own interests were promoted by high tariffs which would prevent a "flood" of "cheap" imported goods made abroad by "substandard" labor, goods which, by selling at a lower price in the United States than those locally produced, would drive local manufacturers out of business and thus deprive American wage earners of jobs. The sense or nonsense of this argument in general economic terms was considered highly irrelevant. Also, at the turn of the century, American labor began to demand another form of protection: against wholesale immigration of peoples who would depress the national wage scale by accepting work at less pay, people, moreover, who were indifferent to union organization for the attainment of higher wages and shorter hours. While labor was not the only group advocating drastic immigration barriers, its conception of its own interests was reflected in the restrictive immigration statutes which followed World War I. The discriminatory aspects of this legislation poisoned American relations with China and Japan, and the legislation itself has made it difficult for the American government to admit refugees in any quantity to the United States.

The practice of agricultural protectionism likewise deserves elaboration. Domestic price-support programs which bear little relation to world prices reflected an undergirding philosophy, quite apart from the political pressures of particular groups involved, that American agriculture as a way of life should be perpetuated. Protection of agriculture made it difficult to write meaningful trade agreements with such agricultural states as Argentina, complicated the task of placing needed commodities in the hands of our foreign allies at prices they could afford to pay, introduced an aura of schizophrenia into simultaneous American policies of liberalizing trade practices while defending international agricultural commodity agreements, government purchase programs, agricultural import quotas, and the like.

PRESSURE BY PRIVATE GROUPS

A second facet in the relationship between domestic and foreign policy, one that is characteristic of the functioning of American democracy, is the use of pressure by private groups to gain government definition of their own particular interest in foreign and domestic policy as the national interest. Such a stated congruence of the particular and the general may be justifiable in instances where the entire nation gains through promotion of the advantages of certain private individuals and groups. But at other times the connection is obscure, if in fact it exists at all. It can, for example, be argued that national security and economic interest were promoted by government support of private investment in such areas as the Caribbean through diplomatic practices which were sometimes exceedingly forthright. The success of American silver interests in influencing government policy, which in turn had a profound effect on other countries like Mexico and China, is likewise well known. More recently, Congressional enactment of import quotas on dairy products caused ramifications in American foreign relations, being at least partially responsible for the delay at Geneva in granting to the United States permission to withdraw trade concessions to Czechoslovakia. Recent investigations into lobbying activities by various groups in Washington make it unnecessary further to belabor the point that not infrequently other countries gain the impression that American foreign economic policies are nothing more than an extremely unstable, composite result of pressure by private interests aiming at the identification of their own welfare with that of the nation as a whole.

TRADITION AGAINST GOVERNMENT ECONOMIC CONTROLS

While the United States has never had an economy completely free from government regulation, and now exhibits, under pressure of international events, an increasing amount of political control, the basic philosophy remains one of opposition to federal "intrusion." Popular and Congressional support of this philosophy, as advanced by such business groups as the National Association of Manufacturers, influenced the decision after World War II to abandon precipitously the national wartime price-control structure. (One of the factors in the appointment of Julius Krug to succeed Harold Ickes as the Secretary of the Interior was the record of the former in liquidating the War Production Board within a few months after the end of the war—an unparalleled achievement for a government bureaucrat.) As a consequence of removing the control lid, prices of American goods rose. Foreign governments as well as American citizens paid more for items in the American market in a competitive situation where the demand ran far ahead of the supply. Latin-American nations still have not forgotten that the almost unique dollar balances they had accumulated during the war bought far less both in quantity and in quality than they had been led to expect. For the

British the uncontrolled rise of American prices reduced the effectiveness of the American loan by roughly a third.

REQUIREMENTS OF MILITARY MOBILIZATION

One of the pressures on the American economy during the Korean war arose from the requirements of military strength in terms of both men and materials during a period of partial mobilization. At the same time that the United States armed itself, it wished to promote the rearmament of its friends, especially in Western Europe. But rearmament of the non-Soviet world placed the nations in competition for scarce raw materials and finished products. Part of that competition was initially reflected in cut backs of civilian production in certain lines, but the effect was international as well. Some countries complained that after June, 1950, the United States so far outbid them in the scramble for resources related to rearmanent that their own efforts were handicapped. Others—raw material producers—were also unhappy, in their case because the virtual monopoly position enjoyed by the United States enabled this country to use its purchasing power to keep prices from going still higher or even, in the case of tin, to beat down the price. So serious were the international repercussions of American economic policies directed toward rearmament that intergovernmental arrangements had to be worked out for the purchase and allocation of available resources. Only when the period of military stalemate was reached did these pressures on the American and the free-world economies begin to abate.

PRESENCE OF PARTISAN DOMESTIC POLITICS

It should be clear from what has already been written that the connection between international economic policy and domestic partisan politics is frequently very close. During most of the period when techniques of economic foreign policy were changing, the Republican party was out of executive office and only once had organized the Congress. As is the case of all "outs" trying to become "ins," the Republicans attempted to take advantage of economic issues where they could find them. General questions which seemed suitable for exploitation included the concept of governmental economic regulation, referred to above, the size and duration of foreign-aid programs, and expanding, oppressive bureaucracy. In particular cases Republican opposition was manifested in arguments and votes against every measure of economic foreign policy from the Reciprocal Trade Agreements Program through the British Loan and beyond. When the Republicans took over the Executive Branch of the government after the 1952 elections, they found that the party's tradition of opposition was difficult to change into positive leadership in the foreign economic field. In the absence of party coherence and discipline, this meant that Congressional support from the Democrats was necessary to ensure the continuance of the Reciprocal Trade Agreements

Program and the maintenance of foreign-aid programs on a decreased but still effective scale.

EXECUTIVE-LEGISLATIVE RELATIONS

The attempt to arrive at coherent, stable economic foreign policies thus involves such other problems as bipartisanship, the relations between the executive and legislative branches of government, and the effectiveness of intra-executive coordination, which subjects are more fully explored in other chapters. Executive-legislative conflict over economic policy is further illustrated by the development of the Charter for the International Trade Organization. Efforts to this end were centered during and immediately after the war in the Department of State. While frequent publicity enlightened the public on the progress being made along the arduous path from national drafts to a definitive document adopted by international conferences, the policy remained an executive one in general and a State Department responsibility in particular. Little effort was made to gain prior agreement from Congress, Congressional committees, or individual congressmen before the proposals were submitted to other governments. Quite apart from the disparity between the principles laid down in the charter and the practices which postwar conditions forced upon individual nations, this lack of commitment by influential congressmen to the charter prevented its adoption by the United States. While the time for ratification came and went, the Executive Branch did not even submit the charter to the Senate.

COORDINATION WITHIN THE EXECUTIVE BRANCH

American advocacy of liberal trade principles also highlights the difficulty of coordination within the Executive Branch of the government. In the early days of the Food and Agriculture Organization, American delegates, who were employees of the Department of Agriculture, advocated specific international policies, such as commodity agreements, which appeared highly inconsistent with the liberal trade proposals even then being prepared by their colleagues in the Department of State. Controversy between Congress and the Executive Branch also attended the initiation of the European Recovery Program as a result of Congressional insistence that the program should be administered by an agency other than the State Department and, furthermore, that the personnel of the ECA should be recruited wherever possible from sources other than the State Department.

▶ VIEWPOINTS REGARDING AMERICAN
ECONOMIC FOREIGN POLICIES

The complexity of the relationship between domestic and foreign policy in the economic field which has been indicated in the foregoing pages should be borne in mind as we turn to discussion of particular economic techniques. So elaborate is the pattern of economic instruments which the United States has evolved that it can most clearly be considered from four different points of view: first, the general *type* of policy exemplified; second, the nature of the machinery involved in the implementation of policy; third, the relationship of the countries affected to the United States; and, fourth, the various philosophies lying behind the particular policies adopted.

POLICIES CLASSIFIED BY TYPES

Among the bewildering number of specific economic techniques, four general types can readily be discerned. The first involves a number of policies having to do with the control or promotion of trade. Into this category fall such instruments as the Geneva Agreements on Tariff and Trade, the International Trade Organization, and the Reciprocal Trade Agreements Program. Also included are bilateral purchase agreements, commodity agreements, and import quotas.

The second type involves government action regarding investments abroad. It would include such official acts as the British Loan, assistance which the United States has given to the stabilization of other currencies, the International Bank, and the International Monetary Fund. Advocacy of the enlargement of the area of private investment, which has continued since the end of the war, belongs in the second category, as do concrete policies adopted to this end, including integral parts of the Point Four Program.

Activities, either governmental or private, directed toward the relief of foreign peoples, the rehabilitation of their countries, and the recovery of their national economies comprise the third type of economic policy. In this area the United States has written a long and expensive record of public action since the end of World War II, although similar policies, mainly under private impetus and direction, appeared, of course, far earlier in American history. It can indeed be argued that this category includes, by implication if not directly, most of American international economic activity since World War II, because the United States has gradually become committed to the proposition that the recovery of the non-Soviet world is essential to the attainment and maintenance of United States security. Specific measures would certainly include American participation in the United Nations Relief and Reconstruction Agency, the European Recovery Program, and many of the elements in the assistance program for Greece (but not that for Turkey).

The fourth type of economic activity has become increasingly important as the cold war with the Soviet Union has developed in intensity. It is the pattern of policies clearly designed to develop military power. While it must be granted that the distinction between economic and military objectives is frequently elusive, a distinction between the third and fourth categories does assist in classifying many recently adopted programs. For example, aid to Turkey, unlike that to Greece, had the clearly defined purpose of improving Turkish military ability to resist possible Soviet aggression. Also the clear intention of Congress, translated into official policy by the ending of the Economic Cooperation Administration and the initiation of the Mutual Security Agency, was the subordination of further assistance to European economies to the exigencies of European military rearmament. As an ensuing chapter will show, the priorities were thereby reversed in the relationship between economic and military objectives which had been established at the start of the European Recovery Program, and which had been later reasserted with the adoption of the initial program of military aid under the North Atlantic Treaty.

POLICIES CONSIDERED BY THE MACHINERY INVOLVED IN THEIR IMPLEMENTATION

The classification of foreign economic policies according to the nature of the machinery employed can most easily be visualized as a series of four concentric circles. The largest is made up of the more or less world-wide international agencies in the economic field in which the United States, by reason of its power and influence, plays an important part. The next largest circle would include regional agencies, still international in their scope, but geographically restricted. A still smaller circle would enclose policies of a bilateral variety, involving the United States and one other country only. The fourth and smallest circle represents unilateral action: legislative enactments, action by executive agencies, and by advisory groups of the American government. Falling within all four of these circles are activities which, while private in their initiation and control, directly affect the total economic foreign policy of the country.

International economic agencies have proliferated since World War II. In addition to the United Nations Relief and Rehabilitation Administration and the International Bank and Fund, which have already been mentioned, a partial listing would include the Geneva Agreements on Tariffs and Trade, the prospective International Trade Organization, the Food and Agriculture Organization, the International Labor Organization, the Economic and Social Council of the United Nations, with such subsidiary organs as its commissions for Europe, the Far East, and Latin America. While these last named are regional in their scope, the close affiliation they maintain with the world organization makes them more properly included in the international category. Moreover, their world rather than regional orientation is indicated by the development within the various geographic groupings of separate economic devices which have taken concrete organizational form, principally agencies for Latin America and Western Europe.

The Organization of American States has its own Economic and Social Council, whose terms of reference prescribe cooperation with, but clear separation from, the various organs of the United Nations. The various pacts with formal or informal American affiliation which form the basis for the cooperation among the states of Western Europe have important economic ingredients. The Organization of European Economic Cooperation, the European Payments Union, and the Schuman Plan do not include the United States but exist solely because of measures of American economic foreign policy. At the 1951 Ottawa meeting of the foreign ministers of the Atlantic Pact nations great attention was paid to the second article of that primarily military instrument. This article states that "the parties will contribute toward the further development of peaceful and friendly international relations by strengthening their free institutions, by bringing about a better understanding of the principles upon which these institutions are founded, and by promoting conditions of stability and well-being. They will seek to eliminate conflict in their international economic policies and will encourage economic collaboration between any or all of them." In implementing these clauses the twelve nations joined, under the leadership of American, British, and French representatives appointed for the purpose, in examining the economic impact of Western European rearmament plans and, conversely, the contribution to military power on the Continent which each national economy might be expected to make. It may confidently be forecast, therefore, that the North Atlantic Alliance itself will have important economic subdivisions belonging to this second, regional category of international agencies.

Many of the policies falling in the classification by type explored above —tariffs and trade, investment, relief and reconstruction, economics and military are bilateral in nature. Indeed a subsequent chapter will argue that, for the relationship of the United States to the other American republics at least, the multilateral organization merely sets the stage and provides the framework within which particular bilateral policies operate. Much of the impetus toward bilateral economic measures arose from the failure of the multilateral organizations to acquire the power and competence necessary to perform the tasks assigned to them. The high expectations regarding the effectiveness of multilateral organizations were based on a lack of understanding of the real nature of the postwar international environment: underestimation of the economic requirements of the nations of the world, overestimation of the degree of Soviet cooperation, as well as failure to see the limitations inherent in any structure including representatives of many nations. As the international picture became more clear, the United States turned to such bilateral measures as the 1946 loan to Britain, the program of assistance to Greece and Turkey, and many others.

Although many bilateral economic instruments were created because no other course was possible, there is a special utility in this type of machinery, since it allows more flexibility as to timing, scope, and duration. For example, it was easier to satisfy British financial requirements through a direct multi-billion dollar loan, and at the same time ignore Latin-American desires for more funds at easier terms, when the decision was implemented on a bilateral basis than it would have been had the two demands been considered concurrently within an international organization. Bilateral machinery also permits greater direct influence by the United States on the individual state concerned than would result from multilateral arrangements, however much the latter may in fact depend on the resources of the United States alone. This desire to project American influence directly in the matter of relief and rehabilitation was a fundamental factor in the decision to abandon national support of UNRRA over the protests of some influential, individual Americans, including UNRRA Director Fiorello La Guardia. Increasing hostility between the two postwar giants, the United States and the Soviet Union, plus general pessimism concerning the possibility of bridging the gap, led both sides to rely increasingly on bilateral instruments for economic policy, a trend which contributed to the deterioration of the few remaining multilateral organizations in which both countries participated, such as the Economic Commission for Europe. At many points Congress took the lead in pressing for adoption of the bilateral approach.*

There is no sharp dividing line in practice between the unilateral and the bilateral implementation of economic policy. By unilateral machinery is meant action by any of the many governmental agencies which operate in the foreign economic field and the specific enactments of Congress with respect to national economic policy. The Reciprocal Trade Agreements Program, for example, rests on legislative statute as a unilateral policy, while its implementation depends on bilateral negotiation. Technical Assistance Programs likewise rest on unilateral expressions of policy, although their mode of implementation differs. The Export-Import Bank, an autonomous agency within the Executive Branch, has been granted authority to loan substantial amounts abroad as part of over-all American economic policy.

It can readily be seen that the decisions taken by these national agencies frequently depend for their implementation on other, bilateral agreements and arrangements. The connection between the two types of instruments may therefore be close; one may be the source of initiation of the other. This is not true in all cases, however. The European Recovery Program, also a unilateral policy, has close connections, not primarily with individual Western European countries, but, as a result of the insistence of the United States from the outset, with the regional group known as the Office of European Economic Cooperation. Similarly the development of the Technical Assistance Program is not based solely on bilateral agreements, but also involves intimate relations with such regional agencies as the Latin-American Economic and Social Council, and with such world institutions as the United Nations Economic and Social Council and the International Bank. In each case the pattern of cooperation depends on the requirements of each specific project.

Only an extended exploration of American foreign economic policy, one beyond the scope of this chapter, could include the diverse activities of

---

* Chapter Twenty, "The Place of International Organization in American Foreign Policy," discusses in more detail the relationship between the bilateral and the multilateral types of organization, emphasizing the difficulties which the use of the former entails for the development of the latter.

private American individuals and groups which affect official economic policy. Nonetheless their direct influence on official policy should be recognized in this discussion. This influence can readily be seen in the following illustrations. It was extensive private investment by Americans in Western European countries after World War I, particularly in Germany, which, by materially promoting German recovery, enabled the rickety structure of reparations, war debts, and intra-European financial arrangements to hold up as long as it did. The widespread default by Latin-American governments on loans made by private Americans contributed to the coolness between the United States and many countries in that area during the early thirties and led directly to the substitution for private loans of United States governmental loans and credits made through the Export-Import Bank. The Foreign Bondholders Protective League, a private organization in the United States, is still working in close harmony with the Department of State to recover by formal settlement some of that defaulted investment.

Groups of private individuals have played a substantial role in the development of technical assistance to underdeveloped areas by aiding foreign governments in drawing up projects, by providing personnel to administer them, and by searching out the fields in which private and governmental investment can cooperate in economic development. The activities of the American Red Cross in devastated areas such as Korea likewise directly affect both the choice of national economic policies for the range of possible alternatives and the over-all success of American policy with respect to the countries.

One final example: The United States government has played an important part in the creation of the new state of Israel from the Palestine mandate. It was the first government to recognize the *de facto* existence of Israel as a politically independent entity. At the same time, it must be acknowledged that the economic difficulties of Israel would be much greater if not completely insurmountable were it not for financial assistance given by millions of private Americans. The interest which public officials have manifested in this private venture is evidence of recognition that without this vital financial support the national stake which the United States has in the preservation of Israel, as part of a general policy looking toward a new foundation for Near Eastern stability, would be seriously in jeopardy.

POLICIES CONSIDERED BY RELATIONSHIP OF THE COUNTRIES AFFECTED TO THE UNITED STATES

United States foreign economic policy can also be discussed from the point of view of the relationship between the United States and the countries which the policy is designed to affect. Four general relationships, each with several subgroupings, exist in the present international environment. There are, first of all, the formal allies of the United States: to the south, Latin America; to the north and east, the expanding community of the North Atlantic powers, within which a number of national groupings are evident;

to the west, the nations of the Far East now allied to the United States—Australia, New Zealand, the Philippines, and Formosa. Beyond the allies which the United States has managed so far to attract are the nations of the "in-between" world. This group comprises most of the Near East from Iran in the north to Egypt and Saudi Arabia in the south, and most of the Far East, from India through Indonesia. There would appear to be a rather tenuous dividing line both politically and ideologically between these first two groups of countries. Individual states in the third category may also fall within one or both of the first two. But for economic as well as for other reasons, it may be desirable to differentiate as a third group the former enemies of the United States—Germany, Italy, and Japan. Finally, there are the new "enemies" of this country, the Soviet Union and the countries which have been brought into its orbit—the satellites of Eastern Europe and the China of Dictator Mao Tse-tung.

While there must obviously be variations in economic policy to fit national requirements within each of the afore-mentioned groups, there are nonetheless general distinctions between them with respect to the pattern of economic policies considered most likely to promote the objectives of the United States. The policies being employed at any particular time, therefore, depend on the requirements of the countries within the group and also on the degree of intimacy between the group and the United States. These two criteria, which American policy makers must always bear in mind, may produce similar policies for two groups even though their relationship to the United States is by no means congruous. Thus, Latin America, an area in which most of the countries are allied by choice or by necessity with the United States, needs from the United States many of the same things as do the nations of the Near East, which fall into the "in-between" world category. Furthermore, because American involvement with Latin-American affairs antedated that with the Near East, many of the policies which were originally developed for the former have been applied to the latter. Technical assistance in economic development is one example; granting of loans and credits is another.

These superficial similarities in techniques applied, however, should not obscure the fact that there are profound differences in the nature of Near Eastern and Latin-American social, political, and economic institutions and also great variations in the all-important strategic distance between the two areas and the Soviet Union. If another war is avoided, there may be time for cooperative efforts directed toward modernizing and stabilizing Latin-American economies to bear full fruit. Even disregarding the explosive factor of Arab nationalism, which may make the Near Eastern area more resistant to cooperation with the West, the time factor is far different. The ever-present threat of the Soviet power in that area forces American policy makers to give priority to the economic and military type of policy over such other types as the financial and measures of rehabilitation and recovery, although the latter may well in the long run be more conducive to the maintenance of American interest. Under other circumstances the shortsighted intransigence of the ruling Iranian groups in declining proffers of American aid would have meant the breaking of most economic relations between the countries. But the nearness of the Soviet Union and the weakness of Iran has forced the United States to continue its active interest and its search for formulas which can reconcile Iranian and Western objectives without playing into Soviet hands.

Economic policies affecting the Western Europe allies of the United States and the former enemy states of Germany, Italy, and Japan will be discussed in detail in subsequent chapters dealing with postwar American relations. However, the changes which have taken place in the economic aspects of these relations should be mentioned here. With respect to Western Europe, the first recognition that American assistance was needed found expression in loans and credits, notably the $3.75 billion grant to Great Britain. But even before the loan had been exhausted, the slowness of Western European recovery, measured against the increasing hostility manifested by the Soviet Union, produced a shift in American policy from use of a purely financial technique to the far more comprehensive approach involved in the European Recovery Program. With the advent of the ERP the relationship of the United States to Western Europe became profoundly altered. The British Loan had been sold as "good business" with a trustworthy friend, as a grant which not only would be repaid with interest but would produce conditions in England enabling that country to remove many of its trade restrictions, thus benefiting the United States a second time. Now the ERP proposed to *give* Western Europe almost twenty billion dollars, not because the United States would get this huge sum back with interest, not even primarily because American exporters would profit from the transaction, but because the *political* structures of Western European nations needed a massive economic transfusion.

But before this new policy was ended, another shift took place. By 1950 the primary objective was no longer economic recovery, but rather the creation of military potential and military power in being. It may be expected that this new pattern, when carried to completion, will cost the American taxpayer, not to mention the citizens of Western Europe, more than did either the loan or economic recovery policies. To shift from a financial approach to a policy of reconstruction to economic and military policy and all in four years is rapid transition for any country. From fiscal interest to economic interest to military involvement in Western Europe is a correspondingly great alteration in the Americans' view of the requirements of their national security.

Another change fully as dramatic as those outlined above has taken place with respect to policies toward the defeated members of the Axis. The initial presumption was that occupation of Germany and Japan was to be punitive in character. This policy entailed heavy expenditures to support

American troops and also to undertake the necessary, but limited, rehabilitation of the countries themselves. Basically the expenditures were for the purpose of controlling countries which had all but succeeded in permanently upsetting the stability of the world. However, with respect to Germany first and later Japan, three different but related complaints soon began to be voiced by various groups in the United States: first, that the occupation was costing the United States too much money; second, that the reduction and maintenance of German and Japanese economies at an artificial level made little sense from an economic, humanitarian, or ideological point of view; third, that the economic recovery of both countries was necessary to the recovery of other nations in the area.

These pressures, coinciding with the collapse of the anti-Axis wartime coalition, produced drastic changes in policy. A new objective appeared— to increase the economic power of Germany and Japan in order that they might assist other nations in the area and also be better able to resist the pressure of the Soviet Union and of international communism. The logical fruition of this later policy was the rapid advancement of the two countries toward full sovereignty and their consequent treatment by the United States more and more on the basis of equality. In fact, in many respects the prior relationships have been reversed; from being supplicators for relief and assistance, both Germany and Japan have become the supplicated, actively wooed by American statecraft to become allies of the United States against the Soviet Union.

In the case of Italy the transition of Western policy from control to cooperation was the same as for Germany and Japan, but took place considerably earlier. Before the end of World War II Italy had worked its way from a position of defeated enemy to "co-belligerent" against Germany. The conclusion of a peace treaty, in which the Soviet Union joined, raised Italy another notch. By its participation in the European Recovery Program and the North Atlantic Pact the status of Italy again improved, this time to full membership in the anti-Communist family. Such a position was of course incompatible with the restrictions which the peace treaty had placed on Italy, and it was therefore no surprise that the Western countries late in 1951 removed these symbols of inferior status from their own legal and political relationships with Italy.

Against its new enemies the United States has gradually mobilized the entire arsenal of economic weapons available to it. The crucial decision in this respect was not taken in Washington at all, but in Moscow, when the Soviet Union decided that it would not participate, and would not permit any of its satellites to participate, in the European Recovery Program. Earlier the United States had abandoned UNRRA, partly because such a large proportion of that agency's funds, most of which came from this country, was going to help Russia and the Eastern European countries.

Two negatives—no relief, no reconstruction for the Soviet sphere—did not, however, make a positive. The United States soon began to do what economic damage it could to its new enemies. Gradually economic ties between the Soviet bloc and the West were allowed to lapse or were broken off. The American Congress joined with agencies of the Executive Branch in scrutinizing the pattern of American trade in order to cut down as much as possible on materials sent to the Russian bloc. At first the criterion for this restriction was the strategic nature of the goods themselves, their usefulness for Russian and satellite military power. As with the historical development of the definition of contraband in case of actual war, however, there was found to be no clear distinction between materials directly translatable into military power and those which merely increased the over-all strength of the Soviet Union. Inevitably demands were heard that as little as possible of *anything* should be sent to the Russian sphere or bought from Eastern Europe, the Soviet Union, and China. The decision to restrict East-West trade was taken with full knowledge that Soviet retaliation could make more difficult the acquisition of materials needed for American rearmament.

This economic warfare between the two superpowers involved, of course, the allies of each. There were many products, principally but not exclusively raw materials, that Western Europe needed and could most easily acquire from the East, while on the other side of the iron curtain lay an important traditional market for Western European goods. Furthermore, both Western Europe and the United States were pressing hard for the former to acquire non-dollar sources of imports which could relieve the strain on that precious currency. However, for direct American trade Soviet-controlled areas had never bulked large, and the United States was not losing much by abandoning trade contacts altogether. The result was, if not a direct clash of interest between the United States and the countries of Western Europe, at least the appearance of a different scale of priorities with respect to trade policy. Western European countries, while anxious not to increase the aggressive power of their Soviet neighbor, argued the importance of Eastern trade to their own recovery, and consequently sought a restricted definition, in terms of both quality and quantity, of what constituted dangerous exports. But in its drive to reduce to a minimum East-West trade, particularly Western exports, the United States held the ace. This country supplied Western Europe with goods directly and with dollars to buy other goods. It could and did argue that goods obtained with American dollars should not pass through Western European hands to the East. The United States could further demand, with the ultimate sanction of being able to cut off further aid, that goods produced in Western Europe should not be shipped East, since the entire Western European economy was dependent on American assistance. When the outbreak of war in Korea demonstrated that international communism was prepared to commit acts of military aggression where it felt there was a chance of quick, cheap success, Congress became impatient with the laborious, incomplete attempts by executive agencies to hold down trade with America's enemies. On its own, Congress set up as prerequisite to continued assistance a requirement for certification by all countries being aided that exports in critical commodities had been eliminated or that a specific exception had been granted by the National Security Council. Thus the President has been forced to give publicity to Western trade with Communist countries by declaring publicly that American security demands continued aid to particular Western nations in spite of their trade with the East. A rough balance has therefore been struck between the minimum trade desired by the United States and the maximum sought by American allies, a balance wholly satisfactory to neither side but one which enables the close economic and military cooperation to continue.

Elimination by both the Soviet Union and the West of the economic ties holding together a divided Europe has naturally had serious consequences for United Nations activity. At its Geneva headquarters one of the subsidiary organs of the Economic and Social Council, the Economic Commission for Europe, has recurrently discussed, among other problems, ways of accomplishing precisely the reverse of the objectives of the United States and the Soviet Union; i.e., how to increase total intra-European trade. Each side has accused the other of having flung the first stone. An aura of unreality has surrounded the work of the commission, whose representatives in other capacities have been hard at work to frustrate the commission's objectives. Trade between Western and Eastern Europe has been almost totally a function of bipolar conflict. There are still a very few countries, such as Sweden and Switzerland, which have stood apart, and trade between the two Europes has not altogether ceased. Rather it has been carefully planned and controlled in quantity, type, and direction for the noneconomic purpose of political warfare. As an example, after the death of Stalin, the Malenkov regime, as part of its peace offensive, began to use the Economic Commission for Europe as a platform on which to argue for greater East-West trade even in terms which would benefit the West more than the Soviet Union.

POLICIES CONSIDERED BY THEIR UNDERLYING PHILOSOPHIES

A fourth way in which measures of economic policy may be classified is according to the philosophy or general purpose which appears to lie behind them. Three should be listed. The first may be labeled the general international approach, a long-range philosophy of what we would like the world's economic interrelationships to look like. By way of example, the United States has since 1933 devoted considerable energy to promote the proposition that trade between countries should take place on more "liberal" lines, free from the nationalistic strait jackets which have hampered it. Other elements in this general philosophy are positive values placed on the development of other national economies. Retarded states, it is declared, should be helped toward a more complex and productive pattern. All states should be guided toward the kind of pattern which the United States believes it represents, namely, a free economy run by private individuals for their own profit.

The second philosophy might be called that of specific internationalism. It includes a cluster of ideas following one general theme: that the economic power of the United States should be used in support of the position which the United States has assumed in the international environment; that the purpose of policy is to aid and reward the friends of the United States, to influence and convert the waverers, to punish and subdue the nation's enemies.

There is perhaps in practice some limitation on this philosophy in that a friend irrevocably committed to support the American position has thereby lost some trump cards to use in claiming a reward for his faithfulness. Also some friends are more important to the United States than others and therefore seem to deserve more substantial recognition. In discussions of the British Loan, Great Britain was portrayed as a trustworthy friend of the United States, meriting assistance because its postwar weakness was in part attributable to having fought two years alone against the common enemy. On the other hand, Mexico, which also had done what it could to aid the United States and whose problems were fully as great as England's, was worthy of some help but not as much because, after all, where else could Mexico go? And anyway, Britain was much more important as an ally of the United States. The arguments over economic aid to Marshall Tito were focused on the question whether the Yugoslav leader could thereby be tied to the Western camp or was in fact, as some claimed, a wolf in sheep's clothing who would take what he could get and then at a propitious time return to the Soviet wolf pack.

The third philosophy, while closely related to the second, may be labeled that of national advantage. The function of foreign, like domestic, economic policy, according to this approach, is to attain the maximum national advantage for the United States in relation to other countries of the world. Assistance to friends, influence of waverers, punishment of enemies, all must always be judged by national policy makers against this standard: Do the particular policies concretely increase the power, prestige, and position of the United States as one of many sovereign entities operating in a world without effective supranational authority and therefore dependent in the last analysis upon its own resources? Achievement of greater degrees of national prosperity, indefinite expansion of exports, and opening of markets to private investment are some of the objectives which would seem to be consistent with this philosophy of national advantages.

While some specific economic policies may be in line with all three of the general philosophies outlined above, more often than not concrete measures can be seen as embodying one philosophy. The British Loan is an example of three-level consistency. It was supposed to make it possible for Britain to enter wholeheartedly into international, liberal trade arrangements which the United States was then promoting (philosophy one, above). The loan was also a measure of aid to an ally (philosophy two). Finally, to convince economic nationalists the administration stressed the concrete benefits which would accrue to the United States from the loan, such as the interest rate, more exports to Britain (philosophy three). But increasingly since World War II, with the declining hopes of achieving a peaceful, united, democratic world, American economic measures have perforce been based on the specific international philosophy of aiding friends, influencing waverers, and punishing enemies. Restricting trade with Communist countries, for example, is inconsistent with the achievement in the near future of worldwide liberal trade patterns and undoubtedly affects adversely the standard of living of peoples under Communist control. Such restrictions, however, are clearly motivated by the determination to accomplish the more limited international aims of weakening the East during the period of the cold war. Likewise have nationalist economic measures been adopted by the United States notwithstanding their effect upon international objectives. Some examples are limitation of imports to protect American producers, restrictions on the operation of the Reciprocal Trade Agreements Program, provisions for the use of American ships to carry products shipped abroad under assistance programs. Had proposals by individual Americans to enforce the abandonment of British socialism and French *dirigisme* as prerequisites for United States aid been adopted, national advantage might thereby have been gained, but only at the expense of the goals of the second philosophy—that of strengthening our specific international position.

The value of classifying the manifold economic policies of the United States according to the basic philosophy which underlies them lies in the assistance which such a system renders to clarity of thinking about foreign policy in general. Neither individual Americans nor the United States government gains by self-deception or by attempts to delude others into believing this country is acting, say, in accordance with the first philosophy when its real, if perhaps unrecognized, objective is to maximize national advantage. The emphasis on promoting private investment in the Technical Assistance Program may be an example of such confusion between the objectives of the first and third philosophies. On the other side of the ledger, delusions also persist. There is a notorious tendency for other countries to look upon the United States as motivated solely by philosophies two and three, usually by three alone. Hypocrisy and deception are attributed to American pretensions that their motivation is in reality philosophy one, the requirements of the general international community. Such cynicism and resultant hostility pain the United States, which, perhaps to a greater degree than true of most other countries, desires to be well thought of abroad. Students of foreign policy should recognize that at any one time the United States is seeking to do several things, not all of which it can accomplish, and some of which are inconsistent with others. Hypocrisy will be less easily attributable to the United States if Americans themselves are aware of this inevitable inconsistency.

VALUE OF THE FOUR CLASSIFICATION SYSTEMS

It should be possible to classify any particular economic policy which the United States has in its arsenal according to the appropriate subdivision within each of the four categories which have been set forth. Most of these policies have already been mentioned for purposes of illustration, but some test should be made of the way in which the classification procedure works. At the 1951 Atlantic Pact Conference at Ottawa the United States accepted a policy of purchasing in Western Europe military items for the common defense. This can be classified thus: (1) by type: economic and military; (2) by machinery of implementation: regional; (3) by area affected: Western European allies; (4) by philosophy: specific international. The much-criticized loan made to Poland in 1946 by the Export-Import Bank can be described as follows: (1) by type: financial and investment (possibly relief and rehabilitation); (2) by machinery of implementation: unilateral; (3) by area affected: what the United States then thought to be the in-between world; (4) by philosophy: general international. The ending of trade concessions with Czechoslovakia by the United States, after permission had been obtained from the other participants in the Geneva Agreements on Tariffs and Trade, would fall into the following subdivisions: (1) by type: tariffs and trade; (2) by machinery of implementation: bilateral within an international framework; (3) by area affected: the new enemies of the United States; (4) by philosophy: the specific international one of punishing America's enemies.

The employment of this descriptive system is useful in the following ways. First, it reveals American economic foreign policy in all its complexity as any single classification system cannot. Most frequently economic foreign policy is described either in terms of historical trends or by reference to the geographic area affected. Neither pattern does justice to the full array of policy alternatives available to American statecraft at any particular moment. Second, in addition to indicating the complexity of American economic policy alternatives, the classification system serves to reveal more clearly the extent of the influence which the United States has acquired, both absolutely and relatively, as a result of two world wars, the gradual recognition of this power by the American government, and the increasing determination of the United States to mobilize economic weapons for the attainment of national objectives. Use of this system thus highlights the contrast between contemporary conditions and two previous periods of American history: the era before the Civil War, in which the position of the United States in the international environment was one of weakness; and the interwar period, in which the United States had power but failed to admit the fact and to use its power to advance national interests. The system here presented can be used precisely to show the shifting patterns of policy, the breadth of some, the restricted nature of others, the inconsistencies of several, and the alteration in objectives which has taken place in the economic foreign policy of the United States since World War II.

▶ HISTORICAL LANDMARKS IN AMERICAN ECONOMIC FOREIGN POLICY: 1930–1951

THE SMOOT-HAWLEY TARIFF

There are at least ten landmarks that have appeared in the course of economic policy over the past twenty years. The first was the Smoot-Hawley Tariff of 1930, the highest tariff in American history and one which revealed all the dangers of a legislated tariff, inevitably based on the aggregation of private interests rather than on the requirements of the United States and the American people as importers and consumers. An observation made twenty years earlier could appropriately be repeated: "Practically everything necessary to existence comes in free: curling stones, false teeth, sea moss, canary bird seeds, stilts, skeletons, leeches. The new tariff bill puts these familiar commodities within the reach of all." (Exception: in 1930, some of these items were made subject to duty.) No fewer than thirty-three countries protested President Hoover's signing the bill, while twenty-five retaliated with tariffs of their own.

THE RECIPROCAL TRADE AGREEMENTS ACT

The Smoot-Hawley Tariff substantially promoted the growth of nationalistic controls throughout the world. But it also produced a reaction in the form of the Reciprocal Trade Agreements Act of 1934 and the continuing attention thereafter by Secretary of State Cordell Hull to the negotiation of bilateral reduction in trade barriers. In fact, the Trade Agreements Program occupied such a prominent place in Hull's view of the international environment that it almost seemed to be presented as a panacea for all the ills of the world.

THE EXPORT-IMPORT BANK

The third landmark was the establishment in 1934 of the Export-Import Bank. Originally there were to be two institutions, one to promote with the newly recognized Soviet Union, the other mainly to provide indirect assistance to American producers by loaning money, primarily to Latin-American countries, so that they could buy from the United States. From these relatively limited beginnings the bank has expanded, especially since World War II, in the size of its operations and their geographic scope.

LEND-LEASE

In 1941, however, the bank proved incapable of coping with the problem of assistance to the group of nations which the United States was coming to regard as protecting American as well as their own interests in fighting Hitler's aggression. By the Lend-Lease Act (a fourth landmark), as implemented in the Master Agreement with Great Britain, the United States partially reversed its policy of loaning money at rates of interest to beleaguered governments with the expectation of financial profit. Article 7 of the agreement went further in laying the groundwork for American postwar proposals for the liberalization of trade—a continuance of the trade agreements philosophy—by committing both countries to the proposition that the final settlement of lend-lease accounts should not burden commerce between the two countries and should include "provision for agreed action . . . open to participation by all other countries of like mind, directed to the expansion, by appropriate international and domestic measures, of production, employment, and the exchange and consumption of goods, which are the material foundations of the liberty and welfare of all peoples, to the elimination of all forms of discriminatory treatment in international commerce, and to the reduction of tariffs and other trade barriers. . . ."*

THE BRITISH LOAN

Part of the money loaned to Great Britain by the Financial Agreement of 1946 was to be used to settle its lend-lease account, but the objective of this fifth landmark in economic policy was to put America's wartime ally on its feet. The occasion was utilized, moreover, to renew the commitment of Great Britain to United States trade principles. Part of the "purpose of the line of credit" was "to assist Government of the United Kingdom to assume the obligations of multilateral trade, as defined in this and other agreements." Specifically Great Britain agreed to "complete arrangements as early as practicable and in any case not later than one year after the effective date of this Agreement, unless in exceptional cases a later date is agreed upon after consultation, under which immediately after the completion of such arrangements the sterling receipts from current transactions of all sterling area accounts . . . will be freely available for current transactions in any currency area without discrimination; with the result that any discrimination arising from the so-called sterling area dollar pool will be entirely removed and that each member of the sterling area will have its current sterling and dollar receipts at its free disposition for current transactions anywhere." †

UNRRA

The loan to Great Britain stands midway between two other economic landmarks. In retrospect it can be seen as a transition from general aid for a war-devastated world to specific assistance for America's most valuable allies, the countries of Western Europe. Even before hostilities had come to an end, the United States had taken a leading part in the formation of the United Nations Relief and Rehabilitation Administration, later affiliated with the United Nations Economic and Social Council as one of several specialized

---

* Quoted in Ruhl Bartlett, *Record of American Diplomacy* (New York, Alfred A. Knopf, Inc., 1950), p. 647.
 † *Ibid.*

agencies. Although Congress at times was embarrassingly tardy in appropriating money for the American quota to UNRRA, American dollars comprised about three quarters of the total $4 billion spent by the agency to the end of 1946. Strenuous diplomatic efforts had been made, principally in Latin America, to induce other nations to fulfill their obligations, until the United States itself decided to abandon UNRRA in favor of fitting relief and rehabilitation into an evolving pattern of techniques to support emerging political objectives throughout the world.

THE EUROPEAN RECOVERY PROGRAM

Two years after the British Loan and the decision to end UNRRA came the European Recovery Program, proposed by Secretary of State Marshall first as a theoretical possibility, later made concrete through British and French initiative. While the proposal in its American origin and in the first European conference was definitely open to Soviet participation, it is doubtful that Congress and the American people would have unhesitatingly committed themselves to the spending of billions of dollars for assistance to foreign countries within a framework which included the Soviet Union and its satellites, especially since Congress had just rejected the same principle as embodied in UNRRA. Though it was not presented primarily as a cold-war measure, therefore, the existence of the cold war was the dominant factor in the enactment of the first foreign-aid bill.

AGREEMENTS ON LIBERAL TRADING PRINCIPLES

Only the passage of time can produce the perspective necessary to assess definitively the relative importance of the many postwar enactments in the economic field. As East and West raced toward complete deadlock, the number of American economic measures multiplied. While Congress was debating the European Recovery Program, the years of diplomatic effort spearheaded by the Department of State apparently came to fruition in the signature, at the end of the long and frequently bitter Havana Conference, of the Charter of the International Trade Organization. This conference had been preceded a year earlier by an equally long meeting at Geneva, which had produced the General Agreement on Tariffs and Trade. While the United States made substantial modifications from its original position, the signing of both documents by other nations was in itself a significant tribute to American power and determination. The General Agreement involved the United States and twenty-two other trading countries, with several others adhering later. The signators represented three quarters of the world's trade and committed themselves to modifying trade barriers affecting two thirds of their imports—one half of the world's trade totals. The first trade modifications went into effect in 1948, and subsequent meetings produced still further reductions. Only one Soviet satellite, Czechoslovakia, was party to the agreement, which was signed just one month after the successful Communist coup. But by the end of 1951 that country also had been excluded from trade concessions so far as the United States was concerned.

The General Agreement on Tariffs and Trade was designed to constitute a specific foundation for the International Trade Organization, the charter of which was signed at Havana. There the United States made further modifications in its original proposals in order to placate countries with underdeveloped economies, with exchange difficulties, or with preferential tariff systems. The charter itself was a lengthy document of some nine chapters, comprising one hundred articles. The first three chapters recorded the fashionable devotion of the signators to full employment, high levels of economic activity, stimulation of private and public international investment, and promotion of economic development. Written largely at the insistence of the underdeveloped nations, these chapters contained, however, no clues as to how these highly desired ends were to be attained.

The next three chapters of the charter laid out a pattern of strong statements in favor of liberal trading principles, leaving at the same time loopholes for the exploitation of national exceptions. The principles included the lowering of tariff barriers on a multilateral basis through application of the most-favored-nation clause in its unconditional form, the elimination of trade preferences, the outlawry of discriminatory practices, and the banning of "invisible" tariffs which nullify commitments, such as revaluation of goods being imported and intricate customs procedure. A dim view was also taken of the import quota system as the basis of trade discrimination, of exchange controls, and of subsidies. Countries with state trading systems were to operate them on a nondiscriminatory basis, following as nearly as possible procedures used in countries whose private importers and exporters are motivated by considerations of profit. Commodity agreements were to be restricted, both in type and in time, to surplus commodities and to periods of distress, with participation open to consuming nations as well as to producers. This principle represented a partial and temporary victory for the International Trade Organization Charter over the Food and Agriculture Organization.

While exceptions to the afore-mentioned principles were provided, the purpose of the International Trade Organization, as established in Chapter Seven of the charter, was to see that the exceptions remained just that and did not themselves become rules barring the achievement of further trade liberalization. In general the ITO was to have the right, in addition to carrying on the informational and service functions normally provided by all international unions, to investigate complaints, to examine the degree to which states were fulfilling their obligations, and to pass on requests for departures from the trade principles agreed to. Ultimate authority in instances of disagreement between member states or between members and ITO was to be the International Court of Justice.

The International Trade Organization has not come into formal existence. When the United States, moving spirit and arbiter of the ITO's destinies, permitted it to be known in 1951 that the charter would not be submitted to Congress (where its fate was doubtful, to say the least) the ITO passed at least temporarily into the limbo of forgotten dreams, a casualty of the cold war. The prodigious labors of the framers of the charter should not be regarded as having been totally in vain, however. The preceding General Agreement on Tariffs and Trade still stands, not as a formal organization, but as a series of bilaterally implemented measures within a multilaterally accepted framework.

The importance of the General Agreement lies in the obligation which signatory nations have assumed not to increase arbitrarily and suddenly their trade barriers. It has introduced a much-needed element of stability into an otherwise chaotic international trading system. Furthermore, if anything approaching a stable and peaceful international environment is ever achieved, further steps can then be taken toward the development of international trade according to a multilateral pattern. Something like the charter will then be needed to supervise compliance with assumed obligations. While very far from perfect, a long way from ideal, the charter is a great advance over anarchic practices of preceding decades and provides an indication of what can be achieved and the paths which future efforts should follow.

POINT FOUR—TECHNICAL ASSISTANCE

In his inaugural address of January 20, 1949, President Truman said:

> *Fourth,* we must embark on a bold new program for making the benefits of our scientific advances and industrial progress available for the improvement and growth of underdeveloped areas. . . .
>
> The United States is pre-eminent among nations in the development of industrial and scientific techniques. The national resources which we can afford to use for the assistance of other people [are] limited. But our imponderable resources in technical knowledge are constantly growing and are inexhaustible.
>
> I believe that we should make available to peace-loving peoples the benefits of our store of knowledge in order to help them realize their aspirations for a better life. And, in cooperation with other nations, we should foster capital investment in areas needing development. . . .
>
> With the cooperation of business, private capital, agriculture and labor in this country, this program can greatly increase the industrial activity in other nations and can raise substantially their standards of living.
>
> Such new economic developments must be devised and controlled to benefit the peoples in the areas in which they are established. Guaranties to the investor must be balanced by guaranties in the interest of the people whose resources and whose labor go into these developments.
>
> The old imperialism—exploitation for foreign profit—has no place in our plans. What we envisage is a program of development based on the concept of democratic fair-dealing. . . .

Democracy alone can supply the vitalizing force to stir the peoples of the world into triumphant action, not only against their human oppressors, but against their ancient enemies—hunger, misery, and despair.

Although the principal ingredients of what came to be known as the Point Four Program had, with the exception of private investment, for more than a decade formed an integral part of United States economic cooperation with the other American republics, the President's public enunciation of a "bold new program" captured the imagination of American and foreign peoples. Carefully prepared pronunciamentos began to issue from the State Department regarding the meaning of the new plan, both for underdeveloped areas and for American administrative practices. Little of this effort captured the imagination of Congress, however. By trimming requests for funds to implement the Point Four Program, Congress has doomed it to a halting, piecemeal approach considerably short of "bold." Nonetheless, the continuing need of influencing waverers in the in-between world makes Technical Assistance Programs one of the foundations of United States economic foreign policy.

The concept of Point Four itself is a bifurcated one. In addition to unilateral programs administered by the United States in cooperation with the underdeveloped country involved, the American government provides funds for programs adopted by the United Nations. Thus is implemented President Truman's statement that "this should be a cooperative enterprise in which all nations work together through the United Nations and its specialized agencies wherever possible." * Technical assistance under the United Nations has been handicapped by the inevitable delays in decision and implementation by a large, international body and also, until 1953, by the stubborn refusal of the Soviet Union to contribute to this work, despite its initial support of the theory of technical assistance by the United Nations. As the United Nations develops skill and experience in this complex field, however, the United States will stand to gain increasingly by its bifurcated approach. National programs can be geared to the changing, specific requirements of over-all American economic foreign policy at the same time that the United Nations and the American position therein are strengthened through multilateral administration of other technical assistance programs.

THE 1951 FOREIGN AID BILL

The final landmark which will be discussed briefly is action taken by Congress when passing the 1951 foreign-aid bill and the coincident Ottawa Conference of Atlantic Pact representatives. The product of these two deliberations, although they approached a common problem from almost opposite directions, was to fuse economic and military techniques, at least insofar as Western Europe was concerned. Congress in effect decided that the basic criterion for American assistance should henceforth be the establishment of

* Quoted from the famous "Fourth Point" of President Truman's Inaugural Address, January 20, 1949.

military power in Continental Europe. At the same time, Western European countries, which had had clear indication previously from American representatives that such would be the future direction of American policy, hastened to present at Ottawa all possible arguments against permitting military requirements to endanger the substantial economic progress which had been made under the European Recovery Program. In the light of the Ottawa discussions, the ensuing NATO Conference in Lisbon attempted to set realistic rearmament goals which would endanger as little as possible the delicate economies of the various European countries.

The dilemma defies complete solution, as a subsequent chapter will point out.* Atlantic Pact countries cannot maintain present living standards and the present slow rate of advancement toward independently viable economies and at the same time reach the goals for military strength which have been set. This means that both the United States, which wants to see the latter, and Western Europe, which wants to maintain the former, must constantly measure the reciprocal impact of economic and military techniques in order to prevent Western Europe from being either so weak as to invite Soviet aggression or so hollow behind the armored shell that Communist termites could destroy the entire structure by boring from within.

► CONCLUSIONS

Anyone considering the development of American foreign economic policy in the postwar period should beware of too-glib generalizations concerning trends and emerging patterns. Because policy in this as in other respects is still in transition, the analyst in the future, say fifty years hence, will be better able to perform the task of evaluation and interpretation. But such postponement would not be of much use to the contemporary student, attempting to thread his way through the maze created by the interaction of policies and external and internal events. What follows, therefore, is a suggestive and highly tentative summary of the major aspects of the present pattern.

SHIFTS WITHIN EACH OF THE CLASSIFICATION SYSTEMS

There seem to be discernible shifts within each of the four classifications of economic foreign policy outlined earlier. With respect to type of policy, the present pattern reveals the subordination of tariff and trade, financial and investment, relief and rehabilitation policies to the exigencies of the economic and military situation as interpreted in Washington. American relations with Western Europe have followed this trend all the way to its logical conclusions, but the same evolution may also be seen, perhaps less advanced, in Latin America. At the 1951 meeting of foreign ministers in Washington eco-

---

* See Chapter Seventeen, "Western Europe and American Security."

nomic aspects of North American–Latin American relations were considered in the light of the strategic, military issues arising out of the cold war, post-Korean variety. In the Far East, American economic measures are fast becoming part of the effort to establish and hold a line against Communist imperialism. Asian countries comprising that line (Viet Nam, Formosa, South Korea, the Philippines, Japan) stand higher on the priority list than those further to the rear (Indonesia) or unwilling to become part of the line at all (India). The steady deterioration of East-West relations has forced upon the United States a search for effective weapons to combat international communism *now*, not at some indefinite time in the future.

A change has also taken place in the type of machinery used to express American economic foreign policies. Immediately after World War II writers purported to see an "internationalization" of techniques which formerly were unilateral or bilateral. Certainly this was the presumption behind the creation of the many multilateral organizations for which all-inclusive membership was anticipated, such as the International Trade Organization, the United Nations Economic and Social Council, and the International Bank and Fund. But here also the refusal of the Russians to play the game according to the new rules had a profound effect. The chapter on international organization details the rapid retreat of the Soviet Union from participation in world institutions which has taken place since 1947. This is not to say that these institutions no longer serve a useful purpose; but that they were created to operate in an international environment that does not at present exist. There remain many functions which they can perform under present conditions; their maintenance is highly desirable against the day when international stability may be restored without war; and they are increasingly being fitted into the world-wide coalition of anti-Soviet states. However, after 1947 the United States gave higher priority to bilateral and unilateral machinery, and since 1949 it has paid increasing attention to the possibility of relating bilateral and unilateral instruments to existing or emerging regional groupings.

With regard to the areas which American economic policy is designed to affect, it is clear that Western Europe, including Germany, now holds first place. This emphasis is due not only to the paramount strategic importance of Western Europe to American security, but also to the fact that in this area the United States can operate with maximum advantage. In terms of strategic location, the so-called "neglect" of Latin America, constantly decried by our Good Neighbors, is both understandable and justifiable. It was to diminish this feeling of neglect and at the same time to gain information to balance, if possible, Latin-American needs and desires with United States capabilities and intentions that the Eisenhower Administration sent Milton Eisenhower on the "grand tour" of the other American republics in 1953.

In terms of the difficulties of operation it must be recognized that the United States suffers considerable handicaps with respect to both the Near and Far Eastern in-between world. In the Near East a long history of disinterest and noninvolvement leaves gaps in knowledge and a continuing scarcity of contacts which, when combined with significant strategic geographic distance, makes difficult the discharge of the greatly enlarged commitments implicit in the policy of containment. In the Far East the United States has also enlarged its commitments, often without consciously realizing their implication and at times without having either the national will or the ability to make good on them when challenged. Here also the strategic geographic distance is great, and the result—an Asia "out of control"—has forced the United States to reformulate its objectives and policies, including economic ones. While this painful process was taking place, the Truman Administration, as did the administration of Franklin Roosevelt during World War II, maintained a steady "Europe-first" attitude, even against savage domestic criticism.

This criticism was doubtless responsible in part for the election of Eisenhower and a Republican administration. But, while taking into account changing Far Eastern requirements resulting from the Korean truce, the new administration has been careful to reassure Western Europe that the bases of America's world strategy were not being altered. In Western Europe itself American economic policy makers are besieged with claims and counterclaims for first attention, since it is all too well recognized that the United States is unwilling and unable to do everything for everybody. The European pulling and hauling for lead place finds Great Britain arguing its superior power and global interests, France its key position in Western European defense, West Germany its proximity to the East-West, cold-war line, Italy the magnitude of its problems, Belgium the greater success of its national efforts, and so on down the line. Reconciliation of competing demands upon the United States continually challenges the machinery of the North Atlantic Pact and places heavy burdens on interagency coordination within the American government.

The final trend which deserves notice concerns the philosophy underlying economic policy. There seems to be a movement away from the extremes of general international goals and national advantage toward the attainment of specific international objectives by rewarding friends, influencing waverers, and punishing enemies. This trend is not consistent or complete, and will not become so. Strong groups still adhere to the two other philosophies, and the interrelationship of the three is obviously intimate. It should be noted in this connection, however, that the exigencies of trying to attain specific international objectives in an international environment characterized by extreme bipolarity have deprived the traditional concept of "intervention" of much of its meaning. This is especially true with respect to economic policy. The disparity in strength between the two superpowers and the rest of the countries in the world and American and Soviet mobilization of all available instruments of statecraft against each other have resulted in the definition of intervention as what the United States does that another state does not happen to approve. Some measures adopted by the United States involve intrusion which America's allies resent, such as the announced intention, since abandoned, of the European Cooperation Administration to dictate financial policies and productive techniques in Western European countries. However, the record of the ECA shows that many activities now welcomed by the Western European countries would have been permitted in earlier eras only under duress. The accomplishments of American missions in such countries as Greece and Italy further support the contention that intervention cannot at present be defined in any commonly accepted legal terminology. To the Soviet Union the term means one thing; to Latin America, quite another; to Western Europe, seeking desperately to augment its power against the Russian threat, a third; to the nations of the Far East, yet a fourth; and so on.

The fact that so many countries have ceased to quibble over the definition of intervention suggests that the related concept of "sovereignty" is losing some of its clarity and needs to be redefined in the light of the twin developments of international institutions and East-West cold-war techniques.

THE COST OF AN EFFECTIVE ECONOMIC FOREIGN POLICY

How much has its postwar economic policy cost the United States? This question cannot be answered with any degree of precision because of the intricate relationship, previously noted, between domestic and foreign policies, because of the blending of economic and other techniques, because of the lag between appropriation and expenditure, because of the existence of so many international mechanisms in the economic field. Cost components which would have to be added together would certainly include the following: American contributions to UNRRA, to the International Bank, and to the International Fund; loans and credits to Great Britain, China, and other countries bilaterally arranged; costs of the activities of the Export-Import Bank; the European Recovery and Greek-Turkish Programs (only part of the latter); portions of expenditures by the Mutual Security Agency; the Technical Assistance Program and related efforts of the Institute of Inter-American affairs; possibly part of the American contributions to the United Nations, the Organization of American States, and some of their subsidiary agencies; sums going for commodity and stockpile purchases undertaken primarily for foreign assistance; special relief grants to such nations as Yugoslavia and India.

How can the cost of economic warfare against Eastern Europe and the Soviet Union be measured? Or the cost of efforts that went into the formulation of the International Trade Organization? What about such activities as the International Labor Organization? Or those of the International Civil Aviation Organization? During the more than five years of its existence the Lend-Lease Administration supplied the United Nations fighting the Axis with goods totaling over $49 billion. It can conservatively be estimated that this figure, an integral part of the cost of World War II, will be surpassed by

American efforts, in cooperation with an overwhelming majority of the peoples and governments of the world, to win a peace which will bring the Four Freedoms closer to realization.

▶ SELECTED BIBLIOGRAPHY

Many of the reports issued by the United Nations have a direct bearing on American economic foreign policy. Special reports cover particular commodities, geographical areas, and individual countries. Also to be noted are reports of the United Nations Economic and Social Council, its Economic Commission for Europe, and affiliated specialized agencies, such as the Food and Agriculture Organization and the World Bank. The official history of UNRRA is a three-volume work headed by George Woodbridge, *History of UNRRA* (New York, Columbia University Press, 1950). For postwar American trade policies with special reference to the International Trade Organization consult the United Nations Conference on Trade and Employment, Final Act and Related Documents (Washington, D.C., Government Printing Office, 1949), and W. A. Brown, Jr., *The United States and the Restoration of World Trade* (Washington, D.C., The Brookings Institution, 1950). The State Department has also put out much material on the ITO in the form of special memoranda and articles in its *Bulletin,* among them, "Expanding World Trade—U. S. Policy and Program," "Twenty-five Questions and Answers on the Proposed International Trade Organization," "The International Trade Organization—Key to Expanding World Trade and Employment," Clair Wilcox, "The American Trade Program," State Department *Bulletin,* February 16, 1947. Other State Department publications on commercial policy include "Commercial Foreign Policy of the United States" and "Commercial Treaties and U. S. Economic Foreign Policy" (Washington, D.C., Government Printing Office, 1950). Another article by Clair Wilcox on the ITO appeared in *Foreign Affairs,* April, 1949, "Promise of the World Trade Charter," while other commentaries on the same subject were Percy Bidwell, "The United States and the International Trade Organization," *International Conciliation,* March, 1949; Harold H. Hutcheson, "The United States and World Trade," Foreign Policy Association *Reports,* January 1, 1950, and Harry C. Hawkins, *Commercial Treaties and Agreements* (New York, Rinehart & Company, 1951). For details on the progress of the European Recovery Program see the periodic publications of the ECA. In 1950, when the transition from economic to military recovery was altering the ERP, Howard Ellis and the research staff of the Council on Foreign Relations issued *The Economics of Freedom: The Progress and Future of Aid to Europe* (New York, Harper & Brothers, 1950); the Brookings Institution brought the record up to date in *American Foreign Assistance,* by William Adams Brown, Jr., and Redvers Opie (Washington, D.C., The Brookings Institution, 1953). The Technical Assistance (Point Four) Program is discussed by the State Department's *Point Four* (Department of State Publication 3719) and subsequent memoranda on the same subject. Two issues of the *Annals* of the American Academy of Political and Social Science, those of March and July, 1950, were devoted to technical assistance. See also the Brookings Institution, *Major Problems of U. S. Foreign Policy, 1949–1950* (Washington, D.C., The Brookings Institution, 1949); John Adler, "The Underdeveloped Areas: Their Industrialization," Pt. III, Memorandum 31, March 31, 1949, of the Yale Institute of International Studies; Peter G. Franck and Dorothea Franck, "The Implementation of Technical Assistance," *International Conciliation,* February, 1951; Robert Mack, *Raising the World's Standard of Living* (New York, Citadel Press, 1953), and Walter Sharp, *International Technical Assistance Programs and Organization* (Chicago, Public Administration Service, 1953). A more popular account, stressing the opportunities for American business, is Willard Espy, *Bold New Program* (New York, Harper & Brothers, 1950). Three reports to the American government on the organization of its foreign economic programs are, in the order of their appearance, that of Gordon Gray, *Report to the President on Foreign Economic Policies* (Washington, D.C., Government Printing Office, 1950); that of the International Development Advisory Board, headed by Nelson Rockefeller, *Partners in Progress* (New York, Simon and Schuster, 1951), and that of the Brookings Institution, *The Administration of Foreign Affairs and Overseas Operations* (Washington, D.C., Government Printing Office, 1951), especially Chapter IV. Organizational problems are also treated in comprehensive yet readable fashion by Wallace Parks, *United States Administration of International Economic Affairs* (Baltimore, The Johns Hopkins Press, 1951).

CHAPTER SIXTEEN

AMERICAN POLICY IN THE BATTLE OF IDEAS

Objectives of a Policy of Persuasion • Objects of a Policy of Persuasion • The Necessity for an American Ideological Policy • Bases of the Appeal of Communist Propaganda • Formulating an American Ideology: Difficulties Involved • Techniques for Expressing an American Ideological Policy • Governmental Organization for Ideological Policies • The Place of an American Ideological Policy • Conclusion • Selected Bibliography

The techniques which states employ to attain their objectives run a lengthy gamut from negotiation and compromise, the task of traditional diplomacy, to coercion and compulsion by economic and military means, which may be indistinguishable, except in legalistic technicality, from outright, formal warfare. Somewhere in between the two extremes fall ideological policies, which, as will be seen, are usually used in conjunction with other techniques, all aimed at the same general objective. Thus the United States, on behalf of the United Nations, was attempting to negotiate a truce in Korea at the same time that American troops were fighting limited military actions along the Korean front and American ideological policy, in an effort to persuade the peoples of Asia of the justice of the United Nations cause, was continuing to emphasize the aggressive actions of Communist China.

It can be seen that an ideological policy goes beyond the normally rapier-like thrusts of diplomacy and, while it may involve subversion, does not use the blunter instruments of coercion and compulsion. Between diplomacy and overt coercion lies a large area of maneuver within which propaganda, while at times approaching one extreme or the other, still rests its emphasis on persuasion of the propaganda's recipients.

► OBJECTIVES OF A POLICY OF PERSUASION

Both the elements of persuasion and the characteristics of the recipients require further examination. Like diplomacy, propaganda seeks to convince other peoples or governments of the truth of either one or both of two basic points: that the present course of the other nation's foreign policy is wrong and dangerous; and that an alternative policy is possible and will be productive. The policy of the other country may be declared to be wrong because it will not attain the objectives desired, because it is in conflict with basic moral principles (wrong in the ethical sense), or because it represents a falsification of the wishes and expressions of the people. Thus the Russians may be told that their foreign policy will not lead to their government's stated objectives of peace and prosperity. Russian (and American) foreign policy is declared in the ideological battle to violate the most fundamental precepts of nature and morality: Communists enslave peoples; Americans prepare an atomic war. Or, finally, Russian (and American) people are told that they had better look more closely at their country's behavior in international affairs because it does not conform to their manifest needs and desires: each government, says its opponent, talks to its citizens of peace and plenty but actually prepares for war and destruction.

Moreover, says the ideological policy aimed at persuasion, the present policy is not only wrong, it is dangerous. Here propaganda approaches the field of coercion. If pursued further, the argument goes, the present course will bring ruin to the government and its people. The United States, declared the Russian delegates to the assemblage signing the Japanese Peace Treaty, is preparing the foundation for a new world war in the Pacific, and it is the "duty" of the Russians to "warn" the nations of the dire consequences of American foreign policy. The United Nations commanders pointedly state that if the Chinese do not keep the truce in Korea and instead renew operations, their armies will be destroyed and Manchuria probably bombed.

The coin of persuasion, however, has two faces. The black side of present policy is contrasted with the rosy prospect if only another course were followed. If you should die now, says an insurance salesman to the head of a family, your wife and children would be in desperate straits. But if you sign this attractive policy, both you and your family would be taken care of in any eventuality ("death" is usually not mentioned). American "atom diplomacy," says the Kremlin, will plunge the world into another war. But there is no need for such tactics. "Coexistence," Stalin and Malenkov have remarked at strategic intervals, is not only possible; it is the way of ensuring world peace and stability. If the Russians manifest a desire for peace by deeds as well as words, says the United States, a settlement is still possible.

Two elements are usually presented with regard to the alternative policy the propagandist is promoting. The course now being pursued is not immutable; the alternative is possible. Also this alternative, unlike the present policy, is attractive; it leads to desirable goals for the nation concerned and for the rest of the nations with which it comes into contact. Throw off the yoke of fascism, the Allies told the Italians: it has been done before; you can do it. Once done, there will be an end to the war Mussolini dragged you into, a war you can never win, and Italians will be free.

► OBJECTS OF A POLICY OF PERSUASION

INDIVIDUALS AND THE MASS

The messages contained in an ideological policy are obviously tailored to fit the recipients. Whereas diplomacy of necessity deals with affairs between governments, propaganda aims not only at governments but at the people behind the governments as well. This focus of mass persuasion exists whether the political institutions are democratic, monarchical, fascistic, or communistic. Its rationale lies in the twentieth-century relationship between governments and peoples. Most of the population of the world lives under irresponsible rulers, but this is far from saying that these rulers are *unresponsive*. In a sense dictatorship demands more of its citizens than does democracy. It has more powerful weapons of persuasion and coercion at its command. Yet while it devotes maximum effort toward gaining acceptance for the course it wishes to follow, the totalitarian regime must still take careful account of the wishes and demands placed upon it by the people, even if it chooses not to satisfy them or cannot satisfy them. Simply to ignore their existence is to place a perilous strain even on a dictatorship. That both fascism and communism are acutely sensitive to this intimate relationship is evident from the record. Since taking power, Soviet rulers have been telling their people that things are better than they were under the Czars and they will get even better as time goes on. Does the United States have the atom bomb? So do we, and we shall have atomic energy and many other things, Molotov reassures the anxious Russian people. Trust in me and follow me, orated Hitler to the Germans, and you through your Fuehrer will put an end to your humiliation and second-class status; Germany will enjoy unequaled prestige, power, and prosperity in Europe. Similarly, democratic governments must be responsive as well as responsible. The American government, like the British, the French, and other democratic regimes, tells its citizens through speeches, pamphlets, and books that American foreign policy is their foreign policy, created for their benefit, aimed at the objectives which they have chosen. This is the internal face of official propaganda, whose purpose it is to achieve a maximum effect in foreign policy by increasing and maintaining popular identification with the regime in power.

If the propagandizing state approves of another government's foreign policy, well and good. It may direct the bulk of its ideological fire elsewhere, or it may attempt to support that government in its relationship with its citizenry. The latter is a very delicate task, since people resent anything that can be labeled "foreign intervention" even though the purpose is to strengthen the existing government. But if the propagandizing state wishes to change a nation's foreign policy, one way is to weaken and if possible destroy popular identification with the regime. The United States tells the Chinese and the peoples of Eastern Europe that the governments now holding power in their countries are not their own, but Soviet-inspired and Soviet-directed toward Soviet aims. The overwhelming majority of the American people want peace, say the Soviets, but their rulers, in an unholy alliance with Wall Street, follow the path toward war. Americans have nothing but friendly feelings for the Russian people, declares the MacMahon Resolution, adopted by Congress, but unfortunately the Soviet rulers will not permit this friendship to exist. Without it there may be conflict, fomented by the Kremlin. If the identification between peoples and government is weakened, the latter will find it more difficult to pursue the same, objectionable policies. Policies may be modified or changed out of fear that alienation of popular loyalty will either destroy the government altogether or at least prevent the mobilization of power behind official foreign-policy objectives.

A successful ideological policy, however, aims at more than just driving a wedge between people and their government. It must be aware, as anyone familiar with public opinion is aware, of the gradations of prestige and influence which exist among people in a society. Rather than directing messages indiscriminately at all Rumanians, Poles, or Chinese, say, the United States may seek to alienate from their government particular individuals or groups of Rumanians, Poles, or Chinese whose opinion carries weight among their countrymen. One such individual with prestige and influence may be more important than a thousand undifferentiated citizens who are convinced that the government is bad but have neither the knowledge nor the power to act. Propaganda therefore seeks to create, augment, and support institutions and groups outside the governmental apparatus which can successfully compete for the loyalty of people. If this process can be pushed far enough, the government may find itself in an insecure position, its power diminished, its appeals for support ignored. Obviously this policy is easier to follow in democratic and semidemocratic systems which are by definition pluralistic. In contrast, communism aims at a monolithic structure of society, with the state directing and controlling every institution and group with which the individual can possibly identify himself. That this aim is easier to posit than attain is clear from the periodic purges that take place in Eastern Europe precisely for the purpose of eliminating any nationalistic or Western influence which may compete successfully with the Sovietized government for the loyalty of the people.

From what has been said, it should also be clear that external propaganda which takes full advantage of the stratification of opinion approaches the technique of subversion. In inviting people of power and influence to attract around themselves and their institutions support for antigovernmental thought and action an outside state is inviting them to commit treason. Hesitantly, erratically, and reluctantly the United States government has been forced to broaden its definition of what constitutes subversion and treason from the actual use of violence to overthrow the government to include also teaching of violence as a doctrine. Totalitarian states have gone all the way down this road. Treason for them may consist in listening to a foreign broadcast, in talking with foreigners, in reading foreign literature, in knowing too much about foreign countries. The aim is, as the Chinese have put it, "brainwashing," cleansing the mind of any ideas which may compete with the message the government wishes to impose on the people.

There is great similarity between the methods of the foreign and the domestic propagandist. Such organizations as the American Meat Institute, the National Association of Manufacturers, the Congress of Industrial Organizations not infrequently take full pages in newspapers to present their cases directly to the reading public. At the same time they attempt to persuade and influence the so-called leaders of public opinion, who may be more adept at garnering mass support than they or who as individuals may have greater weight with the government than either the organizations concerned or the indistinguishable mass of citizenry. And the same bifurcated approach is followed by departments of government to gain sympathy and support from both the unidentifiable American and the prominent individual. No sinister connotations necessarily attach to these efforts, which arise from recognition of the potential power to be gained by directing both mass and individual opinion.

So does official propaganda for foreign consumption seek to use mass and leadership opinion in other countries, sometimes with significant results. Prior to 1940 Germany employed a mixture of attraction and threat to exploit the divergencies in French and other national societies to the point where unified resistance to aggression was impossible, a precedent which the Soviet Union now seeks to emulate. In France, Communist techniques include subversion but go far beyond that in efforts to persuade both the average Frenchman and individual Frenchmen with prestige and influence that they and their country stand to gain, if not from outright identification with Soviet policy in international affairs, at least from maximum separation and independence from the goals and policies being followed by the United States. The aim is threefold: to build up sufficient pressure to alter French policy, or, failing that, to make impossible the successful implementation of present policy, or, best of all and probably unattainable, to bring about not only a change in government policy but a change in the personnel of government as well. The French Communists would thus like to change French policy away from rearmament; if this is impossible, to prevent the attainment of rearmament goals; or, as a maximum, to force their way back into the government.

FOREIGN GOVERNMENTS

The foreign government itself may be the object of an ideological policy. Here, as in the case of mass appeals, the approach may be both general and specific. Efforts at persuasion may be directed at the entire structure of government in the hope of altering the end product of the decision-making process, no matter where the power of decision may lie. This may be characterized as the buckshot or broadside technique. It presumes, for the sake of propaganda policy, that there is something called the "government" over and apart from the individuals who compose it. This presumption may be substantially correct in the case of such totalitarian regimes as the Chinese and the Russian or such personalized dictatorships as Franco's and Perón's. In democratic states and even in some totalitarian regimes, however, the locus of power over foreign-policy decision may be readily identifiable in terms of a particular bureau, a department, a group of individuals, or even a single person. In these instances a specialized appeal may alter governmental policy or make more difficult continued pursuit of the present course by helping to produce and strengthen divergent views and divided counsels within the political structure.

Again there is a helpful analogy in domestic practice. Investigation of lobbying activity has shown that various organizations direct their appeals both to congressmen en masse as equal members of a branch of government and to individual congressmen whose positions give them particular power in the functioning of that body. Once again, there is nothing insidious in the obvious recognition that persuasion of fifty freshmen representatives or a dozen freshmen senators may, while undoubtedly desirable, be far less important than persuasion of, say, the head of the House Rules Committee or the chairman of the Senate Armed Forces Committee. All congressmen are subjected to pressure, but the pressure varies with the position and prestige of the congressman concerned. And the same may be said of the Executive Branch of government. Presentation of one's case to the President himself may be less productive than persuasion of the individual, well down in the bureaucratic hierarchy, who is responsible for letting the particular contract, establishing the price ceiling on the obscure product, admitting applicants to veterans' benefits, and so on ad infinitum.

Distinguishing different focal points in the decision-making process and attempting to bring pressure to bear upon them may be exceedingly difficult in the case of totalitarian states such as the Soviet Union. Even in this extreme, however, the same general principles apply. For years students of Soviet policy have thought they discerned a basis for differentiation within the top command itself with respect to influence over decisions taken in the name of the state. With the death of Stalin, Malenkov has been faced with what may be a long struggle to shape the machinery and personnel of Soviet government to his own ends. Periodic purges in Stalinist Russia and the elimination of Beria and his followers by Malenkov would indicate the existence of disagreements over objectives, policies, and tactics. It therefore becomes of crucial importance to learn as much as possible about the few individuals involved— their background, their motivations, the rules they follow. Granted that the present rulers in the Kremlin understand only the language of power, that language is capable of subtle inflections. Can members of the Soviet regime be convinced, no matter what they may say publicly for domestic or foreign consumption, of the simple proposition behind present American foreign policy: that while the United States will not tolerate and will resist with all possible force further Soviet aggression, this country does not itself aim at an aggressive war to destroy the Soviet state; hence that Russia may remain communist if its rulers abandon their external threats against the peace of the world.

As one moves outward from the center of Communist control, the area of maneuverability for ideological policy increases. In Eastern Europe purges of elements opposed to communism and later purges of those who conducted the first purges indicate profound disagreements and hostilities within those "People's Democracies." Here American propaganda stands to gain much from a combination of attempts at blanket persuasion that the present policy of those governments is wrong and dangerous while an alternative policy is possible and productive, combined with specific, varied appeals calculated to influence particular potential dissidents.

► THE NECESSITY FOR AN AMERICAN IDEOLOGICAL POLICY

The United States has had little experience with ideological policies. Throughout much of its history it believed that the illustrious success of its dramatic experiment in popular government would induce the peoples of Europe to abandon their monarchs and follow the American example. Wilson's use of propaganda against the Central Powers in World War I represented no permanent change in United States policy. In fact, its subsequent return to isolation implied that this country did not care what other nations did or did not do or what type of government they had. The result of previous neglect of the techniques of propaganda was that the United States during World War II had to create from scratch instruments for ideological warfare and frequently had to improvise ideological policies as well. The speed with which these instruments were abandoned or cut back after the defeat of Germany and Japan once again implied that the United States had no intention of making ideological techniques a basic part of American statecraft.

But a new crisis arrived with the breakup of the wartime coalition. Russia's return to its historic attitude of hatred for the West posed immediate problems for the United States and for other countries outside the Soviet orbit. Ignoring Soviet propaganda blasts was not enough. Nor was purely negative rebuttal effective. Such a defensive attitude enabled the Russians to maintain the initiative, to keep the West off balance by lightning shifts in the propaganda barrage. Today it might be "atomic diplomacy"; tomorrow, the efforts of Western imperialists to keep Asian peoples enslaved by "capitalistic colonialism." Domestic and international experience was proving that the sober truth hardly ever catches up with the big lie. While one charge was being refuted, another was being added to it, so that in the end a tissue of lies and distortions could masquerade as a comprehensive indictment. If the nations of the West were to continue to hold the support of their own peoples (remembering that every fourth Frenchman and Italian was a Communist), strengthen the lines of cooperation among themselves, and influence the behavior of the in-between world always suspicious of the West, they also had to learn to make effective use of ideological techniques.

The burden of formulating a positive propaganda policy lay heaviest on the United States by reason of its enforced leadership of the non-Communist countries. A new ingredient had to be added to the arsenal of American statecraft, new in scope and in potential impact, one which could heighten the effectiveness of other policies, whether diplomatic, economic, or military.

In formulating a successful policy the United States was confronted with a complex task. Intensive efforts had to be made to analyze the opposing propaganda of the Soviet Union and to understand the basis for the appeal of communism both in general terms and in a specific time-space context. For too long the American government acted as though Soviet propaganda was so palpably false that all that was needed was to get across the truth to the reasonable people in other countries. Only after thorough analysis of the irrational as well as the rational attractions of Communist propaganda could the broad lines of an American ideological policy be formulated, with the dual objective of counteracting Communist propaganda and winning converts for the foreign policy of the United States. Furthermore, in expressing an American ideology constant attention had to be devoted to the nature of American society and American institutions, which set limits to what the United States can say abroad and to the impact of what it does say. Next the proper mediums of expression for its messages had to be chosen. Finally, the policy of persuasion had to be brought into the most efficacious relationship with other techniques of American foreign policy.

As Edward W. Barrett, former Assistant Secretary of State for Public Affairs, makes plain in his authoritative book, *Truth Is Our Weapon,* the task before the United States after the breakup of the wartime coalition was to "start over" on an ideological policy, to build the machinery anew for the expression of that policy, to persuade Americans that the use of ideological techniques was not a panacea for settling the cold war but an important ingredient in a coordinated, effective American foreign policy. Thorough examination of all these problems is beyond the scope of this chapter, but certain elements and implications of each can at least be suggested.

▶ BASES OF THE APPEAL OF COMMUNIST PROPAGANDA

What do we know or think we know about the appeal of communism to peoples outside the reaches of the Red Army, to people, that is, who have a degree of freedom of choice to accept or reject ideas? Since the Soviet Union put its propaganda machine into high gear after the war, this question has been examined by government agencies, by private research groups, by writers seeking to tap the popular market for material on communism and Russia. It is well at the outset to distinguish between the mass of people in other countries and the elite cadre that heads the national communist movements. The latter, in accordance with communist dogma, is small in all countries, infinitesimal in some. Although this "hard core" can under some circumstances be cracked or even split apart, the main task of American propaganda is to construct an appeal persuasive to those who follow or could be made to follow the dictates of the dedicated few fanatics. What makes others ready to accept this leadership, even against the strong, traditional motivations of nationalism, patriotism, and respectability?

ANTICOLONIALISM

One successful element in Soviet propaganda directed at the people of the Near and Far East is the powerful appeal of anticolonialism. This is wrapped up in a tidy package labeled "Sovereignty, Independence, and Freedom." Such slogans have for some time struck a responsive chord among colonial nations, but the response has been quickened since the war by the conjunction of three factors, all of which will receive further attention in a later chapter dealing with the Far East. The first is the increasing weakness of the colonial powers of Western Europe, which emerged from World War II both unable and unwilling to restore and perpetuate their old relationship to dependent areas. The second is the unprecedented experience which parts of Asia, notably Malaya, Indo-China, and Indonesia, enjoyed in the direction of their own affairs under the Japanese occupation. The third is the ignorance and lack of experience of these formerly colonial peoples with imperialism, Soviet-style, which enables the rulers of the Kremlin to equate anti-imperialism with anticolonialism and anti-Westernism. Natural advantages accrue to a state outside the colonial area, seeking to unseat the power of the nations which for centuries had assumed responsibility for its control.

DISINHERITED CLASSES

The nature of the communist appeal to dependent peoples suggests two further groups potentially sympathetic to this siren song: disinherited classes and downtrodden economic groups. The former, whether they be racially, ethnically, socially, or religiously distinct, are not participants in the direction of their government; rather are they the outcasts, the discriminated-against, and the subjects of governmental control. If their unequal lot is accepted passively and submissively, as is true of many Indian groups of Latin America, communism falls on barren ground. With some groups, however, this is not the case. They form the chronic revolters, the exponents of native nationalism, continuously seeking recognition and expression for their own goals and values, striving to achieve a status in the community and in the nation better than that they are now obliged to accept. To these groups communism speaks of the dignity of man, of equality based upon value and service to the community rather than upon sterile, legal formulas, such as popular vote, legislative initiative, and so on. Present also are undertones suggesting supranational cooperation possible among good communists. Included at this point is the tale of beautiful brotherhood among the various nationalities comprising the Soviet Union. (Evidence suggests that this tale is a fable, but the legend may be just as persuasive as the truth.)

THE ECONOMICALLY OPPRESSED

To the economic groups at the bottom of the economic ladder communism makes much the same appeal. In Marxist terms it points to the discrepancy between productive efforts of this group and their reward. This philosophy of anticapitalism is based on the argument that managerial, entrepreneurial, financial groups are oppressive, predatory, parasitic on the economy, that they are the *causes* of the unsatisfactory condition of the downtrodden classes. The parasitic economic oppressors, it is argued, can and should be eliminated, as has been done in the Soviet Union. This communist appeal is still effective regardless of the fact that the Marxian analysis of the two-class conflict is fundamentally faulty and that in the Soviet Union a governmental bureaucracy now performs, with less regard for personal welfare, much the same functions as those of the eliminated capitalist classes.

These three appeals have enabled the propaganda of the Soviet Union to appropriate the very word "democracy" for its own use. This arrogation would be amusing were it not so dangerous. It has frequently confounded American negotiators who thought they knew what the word meant and who thought it meant the same thing at all times and in all places. What the Soviet Union has done is to define the word in economic and social terms and to deny the validity of the political and legal concepts of Western democracy which evolved during the eighteenth and nineteenth century. To those who are informed about the Soviet Union it is clear that communist tyranny begins by sacrificing the political and legal elements of democracy in order to perpetuate or even magnify pre-existing social and economic disparities. This truth, however, is hidden from depressed economic and social groups, which either have had no experience with the political connotations of Western democracy or have seen Western democracy operate against them.

COMMUNISM AS A WAY OF LIFE

Perhaps most fundamental is the appeal of communism to individuals and to groups as a way of life. This new way of life posits values and goals which are claimed to be greater and of more importance than those previously subscribed to by the individual. It is an uncomfortable but undeniable fact that in the twentieth century the individual in many parts of the world finds it impossible to attain his aspirations through his own efforts. Communism invites him to surrender, to abandon his unequal struggle against forces which he cannot hope to control and instead to submerge himself in another way of life which can provide relief from unbearable tension and frustration. Such submergence entails relief from responsibility, an "escape from freedom" into a totalitarian system in which the individual can accept direction from above instead of attempting to make decisions for himself.

In such Western nations as France, Germany, and Italy this appeal finds response among those for whom the enlargement of individual responsibility has brought troubles and defeats instead of rewards. "This generation of Americans," said President Franklin Roosevelt in 1936, "has a rendezvous with destiny," but where doubt and fear of the nature of that destiny exist, the possibility of totalitarian control appears. Both Hitler and Mussolini based their case for leadership on the chaotic situation in which Germans and Italians found themselves as a result of the failure of "decadent democracy," from which, they continued, only totalitarian government, commanding full and undeviating loyalty of the people (as a mass, not as a collection of individuals) could rescue them. Most of the world, moreover, has not participated in Western democratic evolution. For many peoples "freedom" in the Western sense is strange, unprecedented, and unwelcome.

Two Russians have well expressed the mood which communism seeks to exploit. Wrote Dostoyevsky (before the 1917 Revolution): "Man is tormented by no greater anxiety than to find some one quickly to whom he can hand over that gift of freedom with which the ill-fated creature is born." Simonev, one of the Soviet writers best known in the West, said: "If you ask me what the Soviet system has done for the writer, I should answer that, first of all, it has erased from his inner self all sense of loneliness, and given to him the feeling of complete and absolute 'belonging' to society and the people."

As a way of life, communism, like fascism, offers not only an escape from an unequal struggle, but also the positive hope that, contradictory as it may sound, the individual in giving up his burden of decision may find through his submergence in the group and his unquestioning obedience to authority the only avenue for the fulfillment of his own values and goals. You by yourself cannot attain these ends, says communism, but you as a member of an all-powerful movement may reach them in the future. "There'll be pie in the sky bye and bye," although the recurrent postponement of Utopia may place it beyond the experience of one or more generations. The potency of this appeal is revealed in the personal histories of Arthur Koestler and Richard Wright, contained in the book *The God That Failed.* For both, the economic forces unleashed by the depression proved too great to meet, and so they sought relief from responsibility in association with a movement which purported to have all the answers. The economic pressures of two decades ago have been replaced by the equally real economic effects of the most disastrous war in history and the psychological tensions and fears of a world seemingly incapable of recovering its sanity. Monolithic dogma, which provides answers to problems in all aspects of an individual's relation to society, may present large initial attractions to people who have never known freedom and to people for whom freedom was not enough.

► FORMULATING AN AMERICAN IDEOLOGY:
   DIFFICULTIES INVOLVED

How can the United States formulate an ideological appeal best calculated to meet and defeat communism in the market place of ideas? It does little good, as implied above, to emphasize only the power of the United States. Those squeezed between the two superpowers are only too well aware of the existence of power and of the fact that it lies outside their control. It is natural if, under the circumstances, they fail to make the rather sophisticated distinction between the facts of power and the goals and uses to which it is put. Says François Mauriac, French novelist and philosopher: "It is not what separates the United States and the Soviet Union that should frighten us, but what they have in common. These two technocracies that think themselves antagonists are dragging humanity in the same direction of dehumanization."

It was the United States, after all, which for most of its own history recurrently equated power with evil, "power politics" with the forces of darkness. Beyond the point of showing that the objectives of the United States have a possibility of attainment, it does little good to boast about newly found national muscles. As the distinguished French teacher and journalist Raymond Aron put it: "Europeans know that they are living under the guns and you [Americans] are not. They know that their lands may very well be your battlefields. If you are fair, you will agree that that is a grim prospect, and the longer you delay making it clear to them that you know it and this knowledge is an inherent element in your strategic plans, the longer it will be before they are persuaded to drop their reluctance and accept American leadership." *

It may also come as something of a shock to some Americans that successful persuasion cannot be expressed solely in terms of the superiority of American society and institutions. Because our society has so obviously progressed further than any other in the development of marvelous mechanisms, there is a natural tendency to identify what the United States stands for with a television antenna on every house, a freezer in every kitchen, two cars in every garage. In its early form the propaganda of the United States was all too prone to emphasize the unparalleled economic level attained by the American people. The values of many foreign peoples, growing out of civilizations far older than the American, are nonmechanistic in conception. Conscious of their inability to attain the fancy trimmings of consumer products arising out

* Raymond Aron, "America and the Mind of Europe," *Saturday Review of Literature,* January 13, 1951, p. 12. This and the following quotation are reprinted by permission.

of scientific discoveries over the last half century, these peoples—whether or not they are merely manifesting defense mechanisms—tend to deprecate the material aspects of civilization in what appears to be an emphatic last-ditch stand for old values. In this regard it matters not whether the people in question are the ruling clique of Latin America, the feudalistic rulers of the Near East, the newly emergent groups of India and the Far East, or the peoples of Western Europe. Undoubtedly there is a lot of "sour grapes" in their attitudes. If pressed in logical argument (often difficult to do) they would probably admit that they do want the accouterments of American civilization but only on their own terms and adapted to their own way of life.

Raymond Aron states the problem thus:

> When they [Europeans] see the tin can replacing home cooking, Coca Cola substituted for the noblest product of the soil (I mean of course wine), the taste-destroying refrigerator threatening the extinction of the earthen cellar, they grow properly alarmed. And having before them the incontrovertible evidence that man's scientific ingenuity has outrun his good sense, they lay all the blame for the deplorable results of technology at your [the Americans'] door and look upon you as a nation of robots, yourselves standardized and feverishly intent upon introducing standardization into the farthest corners of the earth.*

The warning is plain that too much emphasis on the transmission of American technology will encounter resistance, perhaps irrational, but in any case the result will be the defeat of propaganda attempts. The danger is that the Soviet Union, by way of contrast, will be able to identify itself with the many nations whose people lag behind American mechanical standards. You and we, say the Russians, don't have these things; *we* don't like them. On the other hand, communism offers not only the intangible advantages of preserving traditional values, but also a way in which the wondrous things produced by Americans can ultimately be attained. Manifestly this line of argument is both inconsistent and false, since communism does destroy traditional values and cannot rival the American standard of living. These flaws may be unknown, however, and, if revealed, may merely aggravate the tendency of peoples caught between the United States and the Soviet Union to resist the ideas that both are trying to sell.

Nor can a successful ideological policy be based on the example of American political institutions. There is a persistent tendency for Americans to identify democracy as periodic elections, a two-party system, a bicameral legislature, and an independent judiciary; in short, as a political machine that is built and set in motion and thereafter runs itself. This is a comforting view; it enables Americans to overlook their own shortcomings. But it is dangerous. It facilitates Soviet appropriation of the word "democracy," a process which was previously described. It is also erroneous. In its Balkan policy

---

* *Ibid.*, p. 15.

after the war the United States pressed far more for the trappings of political democracy than for its social and economic prerequisites. The same fault can be found in some more recent assessments of the state of democracy in other areas. In plain fact one country may be a democracy without many of these devices and be well on the road toward democracy with none of them, while another country whose constitution is closely modeled after that of the United States may be tyrannically ruled. As former Secretary of State Acheson pointed out, democracy is a continuing process toward political maturity; it does not emerge full-blown. What counts is the direction in which a particular government is moving and the progress which it is making.

The response of other peoples confronted with the equation of the ideals of the United States with its political institutions is likely to be almost wholly negative. American political institutions are *sui generis;* they are too difficult to follow. Furthermore, they are too disruptive of existing systems. The destruction of old and traditional processes may create such a chaotic situation that it would be difficult to replace them with anything, let alone with democratic procedures. The Latin-American Indian under Spanish rule was in most localities not free. Now the constitutions of most American republics prescribe his political and judicial equality, but the theory is frequently disregarded in practice. For the old system in which the Indian was protected in his inferior status has been substituted a relationship in which he may have little or no protection.

The other negative response, indicated by the example just given, is that there is disparity between *American,* as well as foreign, democratic political theory and actual practice, that Americans take the shadow of *Democracy* for the substance of democratic procedure. In truth the disparities are there, have always been there and available for inspection, both foreign and domestic. In contrast to the black curtain of Soviet secrecy this constant scrutiny remains the best defense for the United States: we are aware that our progress toward maturity is not complete; our many faults and shortcomings are receiving continuing, corrective attention; in fact, we lead the way in this process of self-examination.

Danger also lies in identifying the American ideological message with American economic institutions: private enterprise, production for profit, private control over distribution, and the rest. Little of the world outside the United States is capitalistic; little evidence exists that other peoples yearn for capitalism, however much they may want what American capitalism can produce. Such identification may lead to popular confusion in the economic field comparable to the political confusion noted above. Americans may assume that a Britain under socialism could not be a dependable friend and ally of the United States because its economic system had been deliberately made different; or that Argentina and Spain, which possess many capitalistic attributes, are *for that reason* dependable.

The impossibility of persuading other peoples to choose the American

rather than the Soviet side simply by holding up the United States as a pattern to be slavishly imitated has forced ideological policy makers to the more difficult task of drawing up and evaluating appeals which can have effect on particular peoples in particular areas. As formulated by the United States Advisory Commission on International Information, "the foreign policy of the United States must be based on three universal cornerstones: The first is the Principle of Self-Determination. The second is the Fact of Interdependence of all peoples. The third is a deep and abiding faith in mankind under God."*
Founded on such principles, American ideological appeals can stress their objectives in terms of national independence and individual freedom. Reiteration and implementation of these messages in varying forms in various areas serve to confront the Soviet Union on grounds of its own choice, but grounds on which it labors under many serious handicaps.

NATIONAL SELF-DETERMINATION

In accenting national self-determination the United States has tapped a current far stronger than communism in many areas. Since the beginning of the nation-state system, nationalism as a concept has had an attraction for peoples which has held its own against all competitors. While the pull of international communism is undoubtedly strong, there is no indication that it, any more than international socialism, international theology, or any other universalist movement, can overcome the appeal of national self-determination. Arguments on behalf of nationalism do not mean, and have not been construed to mean, support of the aggressive, disruptive type of nationalism which has tended to make the word itself one of opprobrium. Rather, American pronouncements seek to demonstrate the ability of states to engage in measures of vital, far-reaching, and intimate cooperation, while each member retains its own national identity, its own pattern of relationships among its peoples, and its own structure of value and goals. This emphasis can be seen in the increased effort to give meaning to practical measures of intra-European cooperation through policies initiated and wholeheartedly accepted by the states of Western Europe themselves.

Emphasis on national independence also lessens the disadvantages of American statecraft in the Far East. Earlier chapters have pointed out that anticolonialism and anti-imperialism were among the strongest elements in the American political tradition. Even after 1898, when the policy of the United States approached that of power without responsibility, its anticolonial attitude remained. When the weakness of Great Britain and other Western European powers thrust responsibility on the reluctant United States, policy wavered between adherence to the old attitudes and recognition of the reality that European positions in the Far East offered convenient foundations for an anti-Soviet containment policy. Nonetheless, as a subsequent chapter indi-

---

* *Ibid.*

cates, European weakness, Asiatic determination, and Russian expansionism have made it possible for the United States to return to advocacy of national independence without giving thereby too much substance to Russian charges of hypocrisy. This suggests the need for emphasis on the separateness of American policy from those of its Western European, colonial allies, especially since those allies are themselves anxious to be relieved of a relationship both costly and embarrassing. Nor would an ideology of anti-imperialism indicate any change in the basic American decision to give priority to European security. Quite the contrary. It would enable the West to place increasingly on the Soviet Union the inevitable disadvantages of seeking to dominate an area "out of control," while simultaneously adopting techniques to make that domination as difficult as possible.

That this theory does in fact motivate Washington policy makers is attested to by considerable evidence. Carefully, cautiously, obscurely, behind the diplomatic scene, the United States sought to bring the Netherlands around to a point of view which would satisfy the demands of Indonesian nationalism while at the same time giving promise of a new relationship which would salvage some Dutch pride, not to mention some Dutch economic and commercial interests. While forced to take a more and more open stand with the French, American policy coupled its support with pressure on the French to implement its promises of freedom to Viet Nam. If the Viet Minh forces are ever defeated, the relationship of Viet Nam to France might speedily become similar to that now existing between Indonesia and the Netherlands. Imperfect though it has admittedly been, the half-century record of the United States in the Philippines is concrete evidence that an Asian people can be aided by a Western country in the development of its own free institutions.

Most powerful of all, perhaps, is the challenge which the United States could throw out to Communist China. Following the theory laid down in the beginning of this chapter, ideological policy makers could contrast the self-destructive, paralyzing policy of China's present rulers in following the dictates of the Kremlin with the possible, productive policy to be found in freedom from the Soviet Union and in concrete manifestation of goodwill toward the West. From this goodwill, tangible benefits could flow to the people of China which far outweigh those which the Soviet Union can offer, not the least of them being the ability of the Chinese to work out their own development in their own way. The beginnings of such an ideological policy were in fact made by Secretary Acheson by reason of the infusion of the "China issue" into domestic American politics and the intervention of the Chinese Communists in Korea. It cannot yet be said whether conditions will permit resumption in the near future of propaganda techniques designed to split the Chinese-Russian axis.*

---

* For further details on this point see Chapter Eighteen, "Bases of American Foreign Policy in the Far East."

One of the incalculable assets of Marshall Tito's Yugoslavia for American policy lies in the fact that its continued existence falsifies Soviet claims and lends substance to those of the United States. After World War II, communism's first approach to Eastern Europe was national, seeking, so said its propagandists, friendship for the Soviet Union, but not dictation by the Kremlin, not communization. Each country was to be encouraged to develop its own institutions in its own way. Tito's break with the Cominform, reinforced by the positions taken by both sides, demonstrates that Soviet protestations were a sham temporarily assumed in order to fashion the instruments of control which would communize Eastern Europe at a rate and by means arbitrarily determined from Moscow. On the other hand, the carefully worked out support which the United States and the West have given Tito indicates a relationship which does in fact as well as in theory permit, encourage, and protect national independence within the framework of cooperation for mutual benefit. While Tito has been given food, tools, and military equipment, at no time has he been asked by the United States to alter the nature of his regime or to support the international objectives of his benefactor (although he has found it in his own interest to make gestures in both directions).

INDIVIDUAL FREEDOM

The related appeal on which American techniques of persuasion can be based is the value of individual freedom, but freedom carefully endowed with social and economic meaning as well as with political connotations. In this direction United States policy has gradually matured under pressure of the communist appeal mentioned earlier and in response to the actual needs of other nations outside the Soviet orbit. Their situation has been well summarized by a Latin-American diplomat in words applicable to other areas as well:

> It is not possible to pretend that the people of today, who are in need and who suffer, will risk their lives to stop an extra-continental invasion, military or ideological, in defense of a pseudo-democratic system to which they have been sacrificed as victims. Any change for them is better; they live at the bottom. They have nothing to lose, and although they may not believe at heart in the suggestive propaganda of Communism, they feel full well that any change could not be worse. . . . Many times I have been surprised to see barefoot country people, undernourished, living in huts without floors, and sleeping in beds without mattresses, cross themselves upon the mention of Communism, demonstrating thus their incompatibility with the Soviet ideology. I believe that if I were in their place, I would most probably be a convinced and recalcitrant Communist, because this is the doctrine that attacks the system in which this unhappy mass of humanity so miserably floats—the hungry peoples of Latin America.

Or as an American observer graphically phrased it, "The word [for most Latin Americans] was not 'Red.' It was 'Poor.' "*

The words quoted suggest not only the importance of careful correlation of such policies as the Mutual Security and Technical Assistance Programs with efforts at persuasion, but also the need for a fundamentally different approach toward Europe and Asia, between *status quo* and change. An appeal to Western Europe may mean something if stated in terms of reconstruction and conservation. Our allies may be willing to accept the idea that tomorrow will not be worse than yesterday or the day before yesterday, because they had something yesterday. The glory, prestige, and power of Western Europe is, historically speaking, only recently departed. Outside Western Europe, however, an appeal in the name of reconstructing or preserving something may be worse than useless when non-Europeans yesterday and today had nothing. Tomorrow must be better than today and not a mere return to yesterday if converts are to be won and the dynamic appeal of communism successfully counteracted.

Communism deliberately sets out to destroy the *status quo;* American agreements and policies aimed at bolstering it cannot be effective in the great part of the world that detests and fears the *status quo.* "We welcome and encourage change where it is in the direction of liberty and democracy," declared former Secretary Acheson, and the United States has shown itself† willing to implement policies to that end, notably the Technical Assistance Program. It would be truly ironical if this country, which did not grow to its present greatness by championing the *status quo,* were now to become frightened and confused by twentieth-century change merely because it is not entirely pleasant, not entirely orderly, its course not entirely foreseeable. A "Hold-Back-the-Dawn" technique may, with the full power of the United States behind it, be successful in a good many cases over the short run. The success will in most instances, however, be illusory, unable to prevent violent, unchanneled, uncontrollable change when the dikes of the *status quo* are finally broken.

As in the case of national independence, so with individual freedom, the Soviet Union offers a target that is difficult to miss. For the Soviet Union, as noted above, *offers* economic freedom and betterment in return for control and submergence of the individual. In practice the Kremlin takes the latter without making good on the former. Its slave-labor camps, the periodic purges wherever its power reaches are dramatic proof of the taking. On the other hand, aggressive international communism cannot live up to its ideological offer of economic improvement; rather does it consume masses of people, as

---

* Milton Bracker, "Beneath the Ferment in Latin America," *New York Times Magazine,* February 13, 1949, p. 50.

† Address to the Pan American Society of the United States, September 19, 1949, contained in *Strengthening the Forces of Freedom.* Department of State Publication 3852, p. 180.

did Hitlerism, to provide fuel for its further adventures against the peace and freedom of the world. The United States can and does contrast this awful picture with its own ability, through technical assistance, loans, credits, grants, and the rest, to help other peoples to improve, to *change* their present lot, while at the same time enlarging, not restricting, the area of individual liberty.

► TECHNIQUES FOR EXPRESSING AN AMERICAN
   IDEOLOGICAL POLICY

The preceding pages of this chapter have been devoted to the basic premises on which the message of persuasion of the United States is or can be based, as well as to the theory of its content. A full presentation of the actual content of the many and varied mediums of communication is a task too large for this chapter. But it is possible to classify and describe briefly the tools available to express American ideology abroad. They may be divided into four general categories: (1) persons, (2) the written word, (3) the spoken word, and (4) the visual message.

EXCHANGE OF PERSONS

The first category consists of the international exchange of persons, originated by the State Department's Division of Cultural Relations in 1938. Until the end of World War II the program was mainly confined to Latin America, but since then it has been broadened to cover most of the noncommunist world. The annual number of exchanges has now reached 7,500 under Congressional authorization provided by the Information and Educational Exchange Act of 1948 (the Mundt-Smith Act). In general the exchange program operates at two levels, the cultural and the scientific. Cultural interchange aims to bring to the United States for limited periods of time present and potential leaders in other countries—students, teachers, lecturers, labor leaders, and so on—primarily but not exclusively those who hold no official governmental position. In return Americans of equivalent status are sent to other countries to study, teach, and observe. The main direction, however, has been inward toward the United States. In administering cultural exchange the Department of State has followed a provision of the 1948 act by entering into contracts with such private agencies in the field as the Institute of International Education, and by cooperating with other private groups where the latter so desire.

After the war, strenuous efforts were made to include the Soviet Union and its related countries within the program. A few exchanges took place before the breakdown of East-West communication in 1947 and 1948. Even while shutting off travel to the West, the Soviet Union did agree in principle to such exchanges, but never got around to implementing its decision; then it neglected to reply to American overtures; finally it rejected them out of hand with an accompanying barrage of propaganda against all Western influences in the Soviet Union.

Manifestly the theory behind cultural exchanges is that more and more people with influence in other countries will learn more and more about the United States; that increased knowledge will lead to increased understanding, which will promote greater friendship, ending in increased cooperation on the national level. At any point this fine theory may break down in practice, either for the other country involved or for the United States. The rapidity with which the program has developed and the fact that cultural interchange has always taken a back seat to the more dramatic, controversial Voice of America have resulted in a neglect of the essential analysis which ought to accompany the exchange of persons. Just what groups in countries X, Y, and Z have the most influence over government policy? Are they amenable to influence in this manner? Should it be the policy of the United States to cultivate them or not? While the impact of limited stays in the United States on private individuals has been favorable, what effect have their visits had on government policy? Can the effect upon government policy be increased by bringing to the United States prospective future leaders rather than those of established status and mature years? So far cultural exchange appears to be operating on the nonselective principle of the more, the merrier.

Exchange of persons on the scientific level forms an integral part of the program. Here there is a significant movement both from and to the United States. Exchanges of this type are obviously closely related to other, non-ideological techniques of American foreign policy. The intent may not be so much to instill a favorable orientation toward the United States as to prepare the groundwork for and implement specific aspects of cooperation in the economic, administrative, or military fields. Ideological overtones may exist, however, as illustrated by the exchange of military personnel between the United States and other countries. Particularly among unstable, underdeveloped nations the armed forces hold the key to power. Inculcation of American military practices may not only be part of cooperation for security, but may aim at transmission of such democratic ideals as civilian supremacy and the professional, nonpolitical role ideally played by a military establishment within a national community.

THE PRINTED WORD

The United States deals so heavily in persuasion through the printed word that space permits little more than an indication of the scope of this medium. Before Congressional attacks and reduced funds forced a disorderly retrenchment, American information centers numbered about 150. They had the support of the United States governmental and private sources, and frequently their operation was actively aided by the local government involved. It has been estimated that the United States Information Service (USIS) offices annually produce and distribute five hundred million pamphlets, booklets, posters, and the like. Increasing emphasis has been placed on supplementing openly labeled United States material with indirect propaganda. Material has been made available to local newspapers, magazines, and other agencies, which they can use under their own auspices, thus avoiding domestic irritation at a barrage of paper identified as originating in the United States. So successful have been efforts at distributing American printed material that Soviet-dominated nations one by one have taken steps to eliminate USIS activities.

While much more could be done through concentrated effort, the United States now provides some assistance to private individuals and publishers undertaking to reach foreign markets. The American government has also purchased reprint rights to American books and magazine material in order to make them available to peoples of other countries under the imprint of their own nation, rather than that of the United States. It was estimated in 1951 at the height of the American information program that 2,000,000 copies of books and magazines were issued in 23 foreign languages. Finally, the American diplomatic establishment and other official groups sometimes sponsor special magazines for foreign circulation. The outstanding example was *Amerika,* which was forced to suspend publication in July, 1952, after the Russians had taken steps to prevent its reaching the newsstands.

The device of the printed word has obvious possibilities, limitations, and dangers. Its persuasive effect depends on literacy, a prerequisite not attained by large percentages of the people in many countries. It also depends on widespread circulation. American libraries and American embassies and consulates are naturally located in large metropolitan areas, which may be effectively cut off from easy communication with the hinterland. Local newspapers and magazines may suffer from the same distributive difficulties. It would furthermore appear that persuasion through this medium is limited both socially and economically to strata in other countries which may possess great power and influence, but which do not comprise the bulk of the population. People making use of this type of information, even if it is readily available, come usually from groups above the bottom of the social hierarchy. Its potential influence would therefore seem to be selective rather than inclusive.

Finally, care and alertness must constantly be exerted in this field so that governmental relations are not jeopardized. Persuasion by use of the printed word is highly vulnerable to hostile government action, as experience with communist control devices illustrates. Even countries in the "in-between" or "allied" worlds may resent being flooded too openly with American printed materials of various types. Any consequent positive impact on the people may be more than offset by the official hostility incurred. In this sense, this mode of persuasion is necessarily limited to selective private and general governmental categories of recipients, mentioned earlier. Assistance to national sources of information (newspapers and magazines), while indirect and perhaps not approaching outright subsidy, affords an opportunity to avoid nationalistic charges of "cultural imperialism."

THE SPOKEN WORD

By far and away the most glamorous example of the medium of the spoken word is the Voice of America. Here are propaganda and ideological warfare in the open; over the Voice the United States continuously blasts the pretensions of the Soviet Union and states the case for the Western superpower. As a device it is deceptively simple, being capable of almost unlimited expansion in three directions: areas reached, time allocated per area and country, variety of program put on the air. Notwithstanding Congressional reluctance to appropriate funds in the amounts requested, the Voice of America has become a substantial enterprise. In 1951 thirty-eight short-wave transmitters were sending programs from this country, in addition to the booster stations overseas set up to speed the messages to their varied destinations. Over a hundred individual programs in fifty different languages were broadcast, and additional facilities were leased in Great Britain, Western Europe, and Latin America. This effort was still far less than that of the Soviet Union and recognizably inadequate to reach the many peoples and countries the United States wanted to reach at the right time and with the right message.

Use of this medium is inherently simple in the sense that ideology is expressed and the problem of reception permitted to take care of itself. But it is precisely at this point that questions arise: What about reception? Behind the iron curtain and in the Soviet Union the Voice is but a whisper in the darkness. Former Assistant Secretary of State Edward Barrett has estimated that the Russians are spending more in their attempts to jam American broadcasts to Russia and its satellites than the United States is spending in making the broadcasts. But not only is the "Golden Throat" at the mercy of hostile government measures, such as prohibitions against listening, jamming, confiscation, and control of the distribution of short-wave sets, and so forth. It is also limited because of the small number of people who have short-wave radios, who can tune in the Voice of America, and who care to listen to its broadcasts. These elementary prerequisites eliminate most of the people in the rest of the world, and an especially high percentage in the allied countries of Latin America, the in-between world of the Near and Far East, and the hostile world of China. As in the case of the written word, the audience for the Voice would seem to be restricted to a relatively small number of recipients and to those from selected groups, although word-of-mouth communication may enlarge the audience to a size difficult to measure.

This is not to say that the coverage of the Voice should be curtailed. In fact, in communist-controlled areas it is about the only way in which the American message can penetrate. But because the device is selective, maximum attention ought to be devoted to making its appeal most effective. So far, however, the main emphasis has been on sheer volume: the number of broadcasts, the number of languages, the total hours broadcast. Merely to have a broadcast heard by foreign audiences is in itself obviously only a minor part of the propaganda objective. It is far more important to understand which groups and classes are actually reached and what their positions are in various national societies, to discover the programs to which they are most receptive, and to judge the relative impact on them of direct propaganda pronouncements as against factual reporting or programs of higher entertainment content.

Efforts to circumvent some of the problems of limited reception—in addition to the use of booster stations and increases in the number and strength of transmitters—can be and have been made. Possibilities include transcribed or "canned" broadcasts and indirect use of national radio facilities. The former can be prepared in the United States, transmitted to American diplomatic establishments overseas, and there made available to local stations and national foreign networks. The advantage of such an arrangement lies in the preference of radio listeners for local stations rather than short-wave reception directly from the United States. With respect to support of national broadcasts, whether in the form of lease of time, provision of material, financial aid, or some other device, the same caveat applies as in the case of American assistance to national newspapers and magazines. The tolerance for American-originated words may well be limited, even when these words, as would seem desirable in the case of recordings, are mainly documentary, factual, or entertaining, without direct propaganda overtones. Assistance that turns into support, which in turn is transmitted into subsidy, approaches the area of subversion. Although the Germans followed this course in Latin America, both in regard to newspapers and radio stations, the United States must be more self-restrained and circumspect in order to avoid inconsistency between American actions and the picture of the United States it is desirous of presenting.

THE VISUAL MESSAGE

Visual persuasion is fancy terminology for the use of various types of motion pictures. The types vary by content: entertaining, documentary, technical, and scientific; and by source: governmental, private and nonprofit, and private for profit. In this medium also attention must be directed to the nature of the reception. Government-sponsored motion pictures have been relatively few in number, with some documentary and more technical and scientific. There are obvious barriers to encroaching on the Hollywood monopoly of "entertainment," however much that locality may choose to abuse the term. Films of outright propaganda do not fit as readily into the American conception of its ideological policy as they did in the case of Germany or do now in the Soviet Union. Government-sponsored films of the "documentary" type, such as "The Negro in American Life" and "The Outline of American History," emphasize what the United States is like rather than what other peoples should do to help this country.

The production of scientific motion pictures has obvious usefulness in connection with other aspects of American cooperation, as under the Technical Assistance Program. Other governments and peoples have exhibited great interest in such films, and they have the advantage over all other aspects of persuasion previously considered in that they can reach the broad mass of foreign populations. With a few portable generators, screens, and projectors the United States has reached far into the jungles of the Amazon to find a large and receptive audience. Illiteracy is no barrier, as it may be for the written word. Indeed, the size of the audience—now estimated at more than four million persons a week—compared to the limited original cost has led the State Department to pay increasing attention to the two steps between production and viewing. Film libraries in the various consulates and embassies have been augmented, and the growth in the number of mobile units has permitted the distribution of the films outside the immediate metropolitan confines where most American embassies and consulates are located. The nature of the audience indicates the desirability of such efforts. Not only are peoples in the larger communities more sophisticated and demanding of entertainment, hence less desirous of imbibing documentary or scientific information, but their sources of entertainment are also comparatively large and varied. Governmental efforts cannot and in most instances should not attempt to compete with private initiative. On the other hand, peoples in remote areas provide audiences which normal mediums of entertainment cannot profitably reach. It is in such localities that the spread of technical information in fields of agriculture, health, and sanitation is most needed.

The problem of coordination between the various agents of persuasion will be dealt with below, but it should be noted here that the relationship is most complex in the fields of the radio and the motion picture. The government produces some films of its own. Some it transmits to other countries through the American embassies, others through nondiplomatic American agencies operating overseas, still others through private channels of distribution. Privately maintained film libraries in the United States make motion pictures available to the American government for circulation abroad. Finally, while Hollywood has its own vast network to reach the foreign market with its product, it has also helped with the distribution of films in which the government has had an interest, has produced others for government circulation, and has provided the government with its own pictures in cases where the United States believes their showing in foreign countries would serve some productive purpose. For example, documentaries in the main are produced in Hollywood on official order or, after their privately initiated production, are circulated at the suggestion of the government through official or private channels. There is a further, recognized interest on the part of the government in seeing that foreign countries do not go too far in cutting, restricting, or eliminating altogether local distribution of privately produced American films.

► GOVERNMENTAL ORGANIZATION
FOR IDEOLOGICAL POLICIES

The many facets of the propaganda technique present difficult problems of coordination, particularly for a democratic state only recently committed wholeheartedly to the delicate art of ideological persuasion. Problems of coordination, in the search for a consistent, effective national policy, exist on at least three levels: within the various agencies of the government, among those agencies, and between the United States and its establishments overseas.

At least four governmental agencies have been engaged in what can loosely be called propaganda work: the Defense Department, the Central Intelligence Agency, the Mutual Security Agency, and the State Department. The activities of the first two bear an obviously close relationship to "black" propaganda, which includes subversion on the one hand and intelligence collection on the other. Informational programs of the MSA were substantial in both Western Europe and the Far East. Within the State Department itself informational and ideological programs have followed the divided pattern between the geographic and functional units discussed in the earlier chapter on the department. The functional aspects have been under the general direction of an Assistant Secretary for Public Affairs. Part of this office has been specifically in charge of the International Information and Educational Exchange Program, which includes the Voice of America, Exchange of Persons, Libraries and Institutes, Motion Pictures, and so on. In addition, there have been attached to each of the component parts of the regional bureaus public affairs officers whose stated task it has been to provide a two-way channel between the functional and the geographic units: advising the former on State Department policies toward particular areas, advising the latter of the best mediums and techniques for gaining foreign acceptance of those policies.

Interdepartmental coordination has taken place through at least two agencies. One organ was the Inter-Departmental Committee for Cultural and Scientific Cooperation, which had representatives of nearly two dozen executive agencies meeting under the chairmanship of the State Department member. Its purpose, as implied by its title, was to make as effective as possible the machinery for the exchange of persons in cultural, political, and scientific fields. The more important instrument of coordination has been the Psychological Strategy Board, which is a purely advisory committee. This board, like the Central Intelligence Agency, was charged with reporting to the National Security Council "on its evaluation of the national psychological operations, including implementation of approved objectives, policies, and programs by the departments and agencies concerned." While the board has had a director from time to time, he was not himself a member of the board, which was composed of representatives of the State Department, the Defense Department, and the Central Intelligence Agency, with a delegate from the Joint

Chiefs of Staff sitting in. The staff of the board was kept small, and most of the professional personnel assigned to it were in the actual employ of one of the three afore-mentioned agencies. The board's frame of reference and its staff reflected a deliberate policy decision that operation of American ideological policy should rest with the various executive agencies rather than with a separate unit of government. A very important corollary to this was the view that an ideological policy must for maximum success be integrated with other American foreign policies, not conceived and executed as a separate and distinct entity.

This problem of coordination in the formulation and execution of American ideological policies was inherited by the Eisenhower Administration from its predecessor. After detailed study of existing machinery and of proposals which had been made by such groups as the Hoover Commission and the Brookings Institution, the President's Advisory Committee on Government Organization recommended, as one of the plans to reorganize the government's Executive Branch, the establishment of a United States Information Agency. This agency would take over informational activities of the State Department, the Mutual Security Agency, and the Technical Cooperation Administration, except that responsibility for the exchange of persons would remain with the Department of State.

While the United States Information Agency would be autonomous, it would be closely linked with both the Department of State and the President's Office. The proposed reorganization stated that the new agency would receive full guidance on American foreign policy from the Secretary of State, who would also "control the content of a program setting forth official United States positions for use abroad" as well as "advise with the President concerning the appointment and tenure of the director." In the administrative hierarchy the agency would be a subsidiary of the National Security Council, reporting to the President through that council. Since the Psychological Strategy Board had occupied the same position and supposedly had served to coordinate ideological policies, it was no surprise when the President's Committee on International Information Activities recommended a few weeks after the proposed reorganization was made public that the Psychological Strategy Board be abolished and an Operations Coordinating Board be established inside the National Security Council instead.

THE PROBLEM OF COORDINATION

Readers of the preceding chapters on United States government organization in the field of foreign policy will be wary of accepting the proposals outlined above as definitive answers to the problem of arriving at an effective American ideological policy. Much of the clamor for a separate agency to administer information programs has arisen as part and parcel of a continuous Congressional attack on the State Department. It has been not only the ineffectiveness of the department and the hostility of some of its personnel which has prevented the development of American policy in this field. The tardiness with which Congress admitted that any propaganda at all was needed, the pinch-penny manner in which it reluctantly doled out money, the hysterical and baseless charges which some of its members hurled at the information program have stunted the growth and warped the techniques of American ideological policy. Removing control from the State Department and raising the new agency to a position closer to the White House, a position, moreover, that may be partially covered by the cloak of secrecy which enshrouds the National Security Council, may result in discouraging attacks on this aspect of American foreign policy. But improvement in coordination ultimately depends less on the establishment of a new agency than on the relationships which that agency has with others which must carry on American overseas operations. These can only be worked out over a period of time under presidential direction and with the cooperation of personnel at all administrative levels in all the agencies involved.

A second problem of coordination that will continue to exist is that involving the relations between agencies in Washington and personnel connected with the various American establishments overseas. In no field of American foreign policy, the ideological included, can personnel abroad be permitted to operate without close policy guidance from Washington. Without such guidance, particular programs in particular areas may conflict with one another, thus defeating the objectives of American foreign policy. On the other hand, as this chapter has shown, ideological programs must have great flexibility and subtlety in order to be successful. These qualities can only be instilled by personnel actually on the spot, by people who know the intricacies of the local setting in which they work and the special requirements for successful persuasion which must be met. This suggests that any agency in Washington which is concerned with ideological policy must constantly bear in mind the admittedly narrow distinction between well-conceived, long-range planning and detailed, day-to-day execution. To the extent to which it facilitates such planning, the proposal for an Information Agency tied directly to the organization charged with the formulation of American foreign-policy objectives, the National Security Council, represents an advance over previous organizational patterns. However, flexibility in implementation of broadly based ideological policies can only be attained as the United States gains experience in this field and as the use of ideological techniques comes to be accepted by the American people and their representatives as an important and permanent part of American foreign policy.

▶ THE PLACE OF AN AMERICAN IDEOLOGICAL POLICY

What can the United States legitimately expect in the way of results from its ideological policy? There is perhaps a danger that Americans will seek more than is attainable in the way of conversion. Some may insist that "who is not for us is against us," and that those who are for us must follow the United States without deviation or criticism. But in the long run no profit is to be gained from blind obedience by other countries to American leadership or from the policy of certain Latin despots who would avoid international criticism of their regimes by wrapping themselves in the American flag and professing to be more pro-American than the Americans. It is, after all, the Soviet Union, not the United States, which seeks complete domination over all countries within range of its influence.

Far from expecting complete, unquestioning devotion, the United States should not even anticipate full appreciation of its prodigious efforts on behalf of the free world. In his brilliantly written, if somewhat superficial and exaggerated study, *The American People,* British anthropologist Geoffrey Gorer purported to find that

> in every one of these reports [on foreign cultures], no matter how technical . . . there was a paragraph on the attitudes of the natives toward the principal occidental countries, and without exception these paragraphs stated that of all the countries America was the most loved, the most admired, the most trusted. It didn't matter how small and obscure these peoples were, how little experience they had had with Americans or even, as in the case of some Micronesian Islanders, if they had had none at all, this paragraph had to find a place. To read of a people to whom such sentiments were not ascribed would, it would appear, be as damaging to one's self-esteem as to be faced by an unsmiling shoeshine boy or a silent bartender.*

The same point is made in more sober fashion by Former Assistant Secretary of State Edward W. Barrett, who writes in *Truth Is Our Weapon:* "It is nonsense to pretend, as some do, that all the existing doubts and dislikes could be cured by a 'bold information program.' Some of the difficulties are little short of inevitable. No nation which achieves enormous power can expect to be loved at the peak of that power. It can win respect and perhaps even some trust, but not love." †

There is equal danger for the United States, in the naïve belief that all it needs to do in order to win the "battle for men's minds" with the Soviet Union is to give the lie to Soviet falsehoods, tell the truth (although not always the whole truth) about the United States, and concentrate on getting the truth to other peoples. "This propaganda," said President Truman about Russian activities, "can be overcome by truth—plain, simple, unvarnished truth—presented by newspapers, radio, and other sources that the people trust. . . . If they are given the true facts, these falsehoods become laughable instead of dangerous." ‡ Similarly Ralph Block wrote in the State Department Bulletin:

* Geoffrey Gorer, *The American People* (New York, W. W. Norton & Company, 1948), p. 228.

† Edward W. Barrett, *Truth Is Our Weapon* (New York, Funk & Wagnalls Co., Inc., 1953), pp. 196–197.

‡ New York *Times,* April 21, 1950.

"A correct understanding and the true facts would supplant vague or incorrect understanding and international distortions; and other people and governments would be influenced by true understanding to think and act in ways conducive to acceptance of United States standards and interaction with them."*

Notwithstanding the fact that the intensification of American propaganda efforts began in 1950 under the appealing slogan "The Campaign of Truth," the basic trouble with this stupendously simple concept is that it is misleading and incomplete. In the first place, there is no guarantee that a foreign people barraged with propaganda from all sides will choose our particular brand. In the second place, even if they do choose the brand labeled "American," there is no guarantee that this choice will be anything more than a passive, intellectual agreement that, yes, the Soviet Union is lying, deceitful, dangerous, and yes, the United States is truthful, trustworthy, and beneficent. It is what comes next that is of crucial importance; the gap between persuasion and action must somehow be bridged.

Both of these points have been succinctly stated by Professor Paul Linebarger, an expert on psychological warfare. "It can be argued that most of the approaches used by the Voice of America are reasonable, that this reasonableness is supported by American opinion, and that both our governmental propaganda and our domestic opinion are incorrect because they are based on the belief that people anywhere choose sides because of the rational merits of the case."† But, continues Professor Linebarger, "it can be argued very pointedly indeed that opinion *as opinion* has never mattered in the history of the world and never will. Opinion becomes significant in human action only when it is transformed into action. As long as the Americans want people to be verbally on the democratic or United Nations side they are likely at the most to get verbal approval. . . . Yet we might find that when the day of battle came most of that 90 per cent would willingly fight against us, because American propaganda had never told people what to do, never asked for them to act."‡

Another pitfall in the path of a successful ideology lies in the dichotomy between the demands for conservatism at home and dynamism abroad. As the United States approaches maturity, it naturally exhibits less tedency to question, alter, or change basic institutions and social relationships which have so successfully borne the test of time. If this "American system" is not for export, neither should the values and goals which it expresses be at the mercy of external ideological exigencies. This interaction between domestic and foreign affairs runs through all problems connected with American foreign policy.

---

* Ralph Block, "Propaganda as an Instrument of Foreign Policy," United States Department of State *Bulletin,* XXII, No. 572 (June 19, 1950), p. 987. The same argument is made by Barrett, *op. cit.*

† Paul M. A. Linebarger, "The Struggle for the Mind of Asia," *Annals* of the American Academy of Political and Social Science, 278 (November, 1951), p. 33.

‡ *Ibid.*

Persuasion of foreign peoples and governments, however, demands in some instances and in many areas of the world the advocacy of policies of change and development. Only through considerable adroitness will it be possible for Americans to be conservatives at home in the nonpolitical sense of the word, while at the same time being reformers abroad. That this balance is possible is conclusively demonstrated by the accomplishments of the European Recovery Program in Western Europe and the potential effect in underdeveloped areas of the Technical Assistance Program.

► CONCLUSION

The intent of this chapter is threefold. In the first place, it sets forth in theoretical fashion, with concrete examples, what an ideological policy consists of and what such a policy can and cannot be expected to accomplish. Therein it is made plain that propaganda must be combined with other techniques of statecraft. By itself it can accomplish little. On the other hand, other approaches, whether economic, political, or military, are weakened if they are not accompanied by a campaign of persuasion which seeks to hold the allies that the United States has, attract others now outside either camp, and make it as difficult as possible for the Soviet Union to maintain its grip on the peoples now within its orbit.

In the second place, the chapter shows some of the ingredients that go to make up an effective American ideological policy. Certain difficulties inherent in the position of the United States, combined with historic inexperience in this field, make the formulation and execution of such a policy a formidable task. Nonetheless it is possible to discern the outlines of an appeal which would strike at communism at its weakest points, and this appeal has steadily taken on shape and substance since American preoccupation with the problem began in earnest in 1948.

Finally, attention has been directed to the machinery through which the United States seeks to transmit its message to other governments and other peoples. Undeniably much remains to be done before that machinery can be perfected, not the least of the tasks being that of convincing the American people and their Congress that an ideological policy is worth while and deserves continued, adequate financial support. There are, furthermore, limits to what can be done with each part of that machinery, limits which this chapter has explored. The search for the most effective combination of message and machinery cannot be expected to end until the constant, unremitting tension which characterizes American-Soviet relations has itself receded. However, if the limited experience of the few postwar years can justify cautious optimism over American advances in the economic and military phases of its foreign policy, so also can it be concluded that the United States has made substantial progress toward developing an ideological policy appropriate for the international atmosphere in which it must live.

▶ SELECTED BIBLIOGRAPHY

Among the books which consider the problem of American propaganda against the background of experience gained during World War II are Paul Linebarger, *Psychological Warfare* (Washington, D.C., Infantry Journal, 1948), and Daniel Lerner, *Sykewar* (New York, George W. Stewart, Inc., 1949). The implications of propaganda policies for domestic institutions are explored in volumes by Fredrick Irion and Leonard Doob, both entitled *Public Opinion and Propaganda* (New York, The Thomas Y. Crowell Company, 1950; and New York, Henry Holt and Company, 1948). Because of the recency of American postwar concentration on the formulation and execution of an ideological policy, little material has as yet appeared in print which bears directly on the subject, with the outstanding exception of Edward W. Barrett, *Truth Is Our Weapon* (New York, Funk & Wagnalls Company, 1953). The United States Advisory Commission on Information, appointed by the President, reported on the then existing stage of the American propaganda effort in *The World Audience for America's Story* (Washington, D.C., U.S. Government Printing Office, 1950). Ralph Block, Assistant Secretary of State Edward Barrett, and William Johnstone have all written for the Department of State *Bulletin* on American ideological policies; the first two articles appeared in the issue of June 19, 1950, and were entitled "Propaganda as an Instrument of Foreign Policy" and "U.S. Informational Aims in the Cold War," respectively, while Mr. Johnstone's article, "Our Answer to the Big Lie," was contained in the March 5, 1951, issue. An address by President Truman to the American Society of Newspaper Editors, "Going Forward with a Campaign of Truth," was printed in the May 1, 1950, issue of the *Bulletin*. Isabel Carey Lundberg considers the ideological importance and implications of American foreign policy in "World Revolution, American Plan," *Harper's Magazine*, December, 1948. Frank Tannenbaum argues that an American ideological policy closely related to traditional American ideals and values is both possible and necessary: "The American Tradition in Foreign Relations," *Foreign Affairs*, October, 1951. Parts of the Brookings Institution report, *The Administration of Foreign Affairs and Overseas Operations* (Washington, D.C., Government Printing Office, 1951), are concerned with the informational and exchange programs of the government. Three articles of the November, 1951, issue of the *Annals* of the American Academy of Political and Social Science concern ideological foreign policy: Richard Becker, of the State Department, "Truth as a Weapon of the Free World"; Paul Linebarger, "The Struggle for the Mind of Asia"; T. V. Smith, "The Ideological Strength and Weakness of the American Position." An extremely timely and useful summary of the status of American ideological policy at the end of 1951 was made by Anthony Leviero in a series of six articles appearing December 10–15, 1951, in the New York *Times*. Raymond Aron in "Does Europe Welcome American Leadership?" and Arthur Koestler in "Appalling Alternatives" discuss dangers and opportunities for American propaganda in the special issue, January 13, 1951, of the *Saturday Review of Literature* entitled *America and the Mind of Europe*.

WESTERN EUROPE AND AMERICAN SECURITY

The United States formally entered World War II because it was attacked. Many months before Pearl Harbor, however, the Roosevelt Administration, supported by a majority of the Congress and of the American people, had committed itself to the proposition that this country could not permit an Axis victory. Decisions taken in support of this proposition make it difficult to date precisely the practical involvement of the United States in the war. Was it when overage destroyers were traded to Great Britain for base rights in the Western Hemisphere? Or when the Lend-Lease Act made America the "arsenal of democracy"? Or when American naval vessels began to convoy merchant ships crossing the North Atlantic and engaged in combat with German submarines? Or when President Roosevelt signed the Atlantic Charter, the sixth point of which spoke of the "final destruction of Axis tyranny?"

In reply to Roosevelt's handwritten copy of Longfellow's poem "Sail on, O Ship of State," Prime Minister Winston Churchill had said to the President, "Give us the tools, and we will finish the job." But of course Great Britain could not finish the job alone; it could barely hold off the Nazi hordes assembled on the European coast to invade England. Even when Hitler drew Russia's millions into war against him, the Continent was still his, and there was no way for Britain to re-enter and defeat the latest aspirant to Continental hegemony, as Wellington had done a century earlier. It was going to take more than the "tools" which a nonbelligerent United States could give to another power; it was going to take a fully mobilized America, with its energies directed to war, its equipment in the hands of its own Army, Navy, and Air Force, to destroy the German mastery of Europe.

Colonel Charles E. Lindbergh, idol of the twenties said, "There is no Ghengis Khan or Xerxes marching against our Western nations. This is simply

663

one more of those age-old struggles within our own family of nations."* Hitler would have wanted the American people and their government to agree with the "Lone Eagle's" analysis, but they did not. To an extent not matched in 1917 Americans accepted the thesis that there was a direct connection between their own security and the achievement by Germany of hegemonical status in Europe. Until the United States entered the war fully, only Great Britain and the Soviet Union could contest that status and ultimately defeat it. Therefore, both were fighting for American objectives in continuing in the war; both needed and were entitled to American support. After the United States actually entered the war, all three powers in the coalition were pursuing the same war aim: the final, irrevocable destruction of Nazi Germany.

▶ PRELIMINARY ESTIMATES CONCERNING
POSTWAR EUROPE

The way in which the United States entered the anti-Axis coalition is extremely important since it determined in large part the course of postwar policy. Unlike 1917, the United States was determined in 1941 that American security should not again be endangered by events in Europe and to that end planned the complete defeat of the one country capable at the time of threatening that security. Because German victory was so close in 1941, the United States had to create a military power far greater than that mounted in 1917. This power was translated into action only when its allies were near to defeat, and therefore gave to the United States the leadership in the war against Germany's west flank. In 1917 Pershing had successfully resisted the amalgamation of American with British and French troops fighting in Europe. In 1941 there were no British or French troops fighting in Europe. France was defeated; Britain alone could not re-enter the Continent. The inevitable consequence was the entrance of American power into Europe from the west as Russian power appeared from the east. In the hands of two non-European powers lay the future of a continent for centuries accustomed not only to working out its own destiny, but also to imposing its will on most of the rest of the world. From the nature of the struggle and from American attitudes toward it, then, it was clear that there would be a definite postwar commitment by the United States toward future European stability.

AMERICAN VIEW OF A LIMITED EUROPEAN COMMITMENT

But how extensive and of what duration was to be that commitment? The answer depended on three factors: the postwar strength of the Soviet Union and the course of that country's policy; the ability of Great Britain, France, and the other countries in Western Europe to recover, not their former position, but sufficient strength to maintain their own domestic

---

* This excerpt from a Lindbergh speech is contained in Edward R. Murrow's provocative record "I Can Hear It Now" (New York, Columbia Records Inc.: No. ML 4095, 1948).

viability and a preponderance of power over a prostrate Germany; and finally, the way in which the United States interpreted the warranty it had issued. Because the first two factors were misinterpreted, the third was posited in a limited, short-run fashion which all but destroyed Western Europe before the postwar transition period was over.

The fact that the American commitment was thought of as limited was not remarkable. Besides being based on the presumed ability of Europe to organize its own affairs, it arose out of a historical reluctance to become embroiled in the conflicts of that unhappy Continent at all. Although the flourishing of Axis aggression had wrought a great change in American attitudes, under the leadership of the Roosevelt Administration, it was by no means certain that a full-scale commitment of unlimited duration would prove acceptable to Americans, even if necessary. Great care had to be exercised that the United States not create in Europe, as it had in Asia, a dangerous disparity between what it stated to be its objectives and the scope of the policies it was prepared to adopt to see them attained.

Thus President Roosevelt in August, 1941, wished to avoid any specific mention in the Atlantic Charter of a postwar world organization. Thus the President later told Stalin that American troops would not be used for international enforcement action in Europe. Thus the duration of American occupation of Germany, once "unconditional surrender" had been accomplished, was originally conceived as very short, perhaps only two years. At the end of that time, the postwar transition would presumably be at an end. Western Europe, particularly France and Britain, would be able to protect themselves against an enfeebled, perhaps dismembered Germany. From that point on, American undertakings for the maintenance of security would be the general ones arising out of membership in the United Nations Organization, obligations of the same type as those incurred by all other members. As in Asia, so in Europe, security would be largely self-operating, based on the interaction of national states with about the same strength and motivations they had traditionally had. The one important change would be the removal of Germany in Europe—matching the removal of Japan in Asia—from an important place in the state system.

SUPPOSITIONS CONCERNING EUROPEAN POLICIES OF THE SOVIET UNION

Just as there was to be a limit to American power entering Europe from the west, so was Soviet power entering from the east to be limited. American suppositions arose from basic premises concerning Soviet capacities and Soviet intentions. In discussions with British and American leaders the Russians had made much of the internal devastation wrought by the German armies. The figures concerning lives lost, peoples uprooted, establishments and homes destroyed, communications broken, crops and livestock ruined were almost beyond the West's comprehension. How could a state survive, let alone continue a dynamic, aggressive policy after undergoing such an experience? Figures were used both statistically and emotionally to bolster Soviet claims to reparations from Germany and the Axis satellites, and also to make a case for separate White Russian and Ukrainian representation in the United Nations. To the West the logical conclusion was that Russian energies would for some time to come be concentrated on problems of reconstruction, not only on the resettlement of peoples, the resumption of agriculture and industry, but also on the re-creation of the hold which the Soviet system had previously had on the Russian people. Only at its peril, the West believed, could the Kremlin neglect the re-establishment of national control in favor of external adventures.

While Soviet policy would be limited by decreased Russian capacities, it would certainly reflect the motivations and concepts of the Soviet leaders. The West was aware of its ignorance on this score, an ignorance built up over decades of Soviet isolation from the European and the world community of states. But to the West there seemed signs indicating that postwar Russian behavior might follow the normal pattern of "national" states, rather than the revolutionary dictates of international Bolshevism. From its entrance into the League of Nations until it was excluded from the Munich settlement, the policy of the Soviet Union had apparently been directed toward genuine collective security and cooperation with the West against Germany. Even in the period of the Nazi-Soviet Pact, Russian objectives appeared to be the maintenance of neutrality and the expansion of state frontiers into areas previously held or coveted under the Czars. The precipitous German incursions into Russia had accelerated the trend toward nationalism. Hindsight makes it easy to see that the objectives and means posited by communist dialectic had not so much been abandoned as put into cold storage, but this was not recognized at the time. Joseph Stalin rallied the people as Russians, not as communists, to defend their fatherland, their soil, against the invaders. His speeches were collected and published under the suggestive title, "The Great Patriotic War of the Soviet Union." Other nationalistic devices to bolster the people in their ordeal were also employed. The church was given more freedom, and church leaders responded with prayers for victory. Enhanced prestige was accorded to the Russian army, now viewed as an army of a nation-state, not as an instrument for Bolshevik revolution. Revised historiography emphasized the continuity of the state with the past, with such despised leaders as Catherine and Peter. Amidst all this the Comintern, the central machinery for controlling communist parties abroad, was abolished, and everywhere in Europe those parties, reversing the stand they had held before June, 1941, took the lead in national resistance to Germany.

ACCEPTANCE OF SOVIET PRIMACY IN EASTERN EUROPE

As in Asia, so in Europe, did it seem that Russian objectives were limited, legitimate, and easily satisfiable. Accordingly arrangements for future territorial settlement in Eastern Europe were made by Churchill and Roosevelt in the expectation that they would make possible the speedy disposition of German, Italian, and Austrian problems by ensuring a continuance of the wartime coalition. The Versailles Treaty had contributed to the fragmentation of Eastern Europe through the breakup of Austria-Hungary and the reconstitution of Poland. National antagonisms among the small states prevented the growth of any cooperation in the political and economic sphere which might have protected them against the revival of German and Russian power. French alliances with Poland and the Little Entente could provide no lasting substitute, since France was unable to contribute much to the viability of these countries. Central and Eastern European ties with France further detracted from efforts toward regional cooperation, particularly since both Hungary and Bulgaria, which occupied pivotal positions, were regarded as enemies by reason of their affiliation with the Central Powers during World War I.

German revival and the remilitarization of the Rhineland isolated Eastern European countries from the West and opened them to German expansion. When Italy was brought into the Axis and the Soviet Union, first excluded, was invited to share in the spoils, the fate of Eastern Europe was sealed. By 1939, nations in the jaws of the Nazi-Soviet nutcracker had lost what little economic freedom and diplomatic maneuverability they had previously enjoyed. They were confronted with the unpalatable alternative of fighting and being destroyed (Poland, Yugoslavia, Greece) or of joining the Axis as very junior partners (Hungary, Rumania). The end effect was the same.

It was inevitable that with the removal of German penetration into Eastern Europe, Russian influence would be substituted. But what was that influence to mean, and what were to be its geographic limits? It was this question that the West sought to settle during World War II. The first step was taken by the British, who, over the protests of Secretary Hull, came to an agreement with the Soviet Union that would exclude Greece from the Soviet sphere and divide Yugoslavia into areas of British and Soviet influence. When Churchill was unsuccessful in obtaining American agreement to the invasion of Europe through the Balkans, it was certain that the closing days of the war would find the Red Armies already in control of most, if not all, of the countries assigned to the Soviet sphere.* The Russian declaration of war on Bulgaria in the closing hours of Axis resistance indicated Soviet determination to be the final arbiter of Eastern Europe by virtue of its military occupation of that region. In this way its position was bolstered even before the fall of Germany. As each of the Axis satellites was knocked out, arrangements called for setting up an Allied Control Commission. One had been established in Italy, but because that country was a field of British and American military operations, the commisson was dominated by the two Western powers. Similarly, with the Red Army in Bulgaria, Hungary, and Rumania, a

---

* It is quite probable that the Russians would have been there even if the British and Americans had landed in Greece and Yugoslavia.

Russian was chairman of each Control Commission, leaving Allied "control" over the new occupiers more theoretical than real.

YALTA DECLARATION ON LIBERATED EUROPE

Thus wartime activity made it certain that the Soviet preponderance of power in Eastern Europe would be continued into the peace. At the same time, Great Britain and the United States wished to see this "preponderance" defined so as to leave domestic political and economic institutions of each country for its own determination. This position they attempted to attain in the only way possible in the absence of British and American armed forces— by negotiation and written agreement. Accordingly, at Yalta the Big Three agreed upon the Declaration on Liberated Europe. By its signature, the Soviet Union specifically accepted "a principle of the Atlantic Charter—the right of all peoples to choose the form of government under which they will live—the restoration of sovereign rights and self-government to those peoples who have been forcibly deprived of them by the aggressor nation." Nor was Russia to be the sole interpreter of the way in which this principle would be followed. There must be set in motion, read the Declaration, "processes which will enable the liberated peoples to destroy the last vestiges of Nazism and Fascism and to create democratic institutions of their own choice." Accordingly, "the three governments will *jointly* assist the people in any European liberated state . . . to form interim governmental authorities broadly representative of all democratic elements in the population and pledged to the earliest possible establishment through free elections of governments responsive to the will of the people. . . ." These commitments were spelled out in detail regarding Poland and Yugoslavia. All three powers were bound "to *consult together* on the measures necessary to discharge the joint responsibilities. . . ."*

► FALSITY OF AMERICAN WARTIME ESTIMATES

RUSSIAN VIOLATION OF THE YALTA DECLARATION

Returning from Yalta, Churchill declared of the Russians: "Their word is their bond. I know of no government which stands to its obligations even in its own despite more solidly than the Russian Soviet Government." The distinguished British leader was whistling in the dark. Less than six months later the Russians, at Potsdam, were being asked to consent to a reorganization of the governments of Bulgaria, Rumania, and Hungary. In the interim the West had been given a foretaste of Soviet tactics when Andrei Vishinsky appeared in Bucharest to deliver the ultimatum that the "broadly representative" Rudescu regime must be replaced by one dominated by Groza, a Communist. All that the Soviets would agree to at Potsdam was a revision of the government according to "agreed procedures." There was no such revision. By the time the peace treaties were signed with the Axis satel-

---

* Italics added.

lites, it was clear that Russian ambitions in Eastern Europe were neither as legitimate nor as easily satisfiable as the West had thought. The guarantees contained in the peace treaties with respect to human rights and the fundamental rights of speech, press, religion, and political association were only of legalistic interest. Protest over their violation could not reverse the trend toward Soviet domination.

There was a fundamental quarrel in semantics involved in the struggle over Eastern Europe. The West thought words meant what they commonly had meant, while the Russians declared with Humpty Dumpty that they meant whatever they said they meant. To the West, Allied "assistance" meant cooperation with the local authorities; to the Russians it meant dictation. To the West "concert" of policy meant consultation before the event; to the Soviet Union it meant *ex post facto* acceptance of Russian action taken. A "democratic" government meant a communist one to the new occupiers, while the phrase "vestiges of Nazism and Fascism" was interpreted to apply to all nonsupporters of the new government. This logic therefore prepared the way for the application of "fundamental freedoms" only to non-Fascist organizations, i.e., Communist and Communist-allied groups.

By 1947, Soviet behavior in Eastern Europe had made it abundantly clear to the United States that the first presumption on which a self-operating system of European stability was supposed to function was false. Far from being anxious to withdraw from Europe and concentrate on domestic reconstruction, the Soviet Union was consolidating its power as rapidly as possible behind the iron curtain. Some kind of European balance could still have been struck if there had been substantial power remaining in Western Europe. But not only was the Soviet Union far stronger and more expansive than had been believed, but the main powers of Western Europe, Great Britain and France, were far weaker. Both, in fact, were not far from collapsing. American power in Europe had also been greatly weakened through precipitous demobilization, which had reduced United States troops in quantity and quality.

LONG-TERM BRITISH WEAKNESS

Elements in the decline of British and French strength were recognizable as early as the end of the nineteenth century. As was pointed out in an earlier chapter, Great Britain had long since lost the ability to maintain the balance of power in Europe and to protect by itself its interests in Asia. Fortunately, its victory in World War I had enabled Britain, prior to 1939, to maintain the illusion and practice of power without possessing, as in the preceding centuries, the components of power. Its Continental rival, Germany, had been defeated and did not recover its former position until 1936. Abdication of responsibility by the United States thrust the burden of diplomatic leadership on Britain by default. The withdrawal of Russia from the world scene and the lengthy period of internal preoccupation of the Soviet revolutionary regime made it possible to ignore the potential strength of that land giant.

In the Far East there was a hiatus in Japanese expansionism between 1920 and 1931, and only in the late thirties did Japanese ambitions expand from China to cover the entire Far Eastern area. Only when Britain was called once again to thwart the German drive for European hegemony were its real weaknesses brought into the spotlight. They were then seen to embrace most of the components of national power: demographic, economic, military, and political.

For Great Britain World War II had indeed been a war of survival, into which all its resources had been poured. After the fall of France the British had confronted Hitlerite Germany alone for a year, until the Soviet Union was dragged reluctantly into the struggle. The British, in Churchill's picturesque words, had "held the fort alone till those who hitherto had been half-blind were half-ready." In numbers the British were at a disadvantage of about two to one. In military equipment they had entered the war with a sad lack of preparation. Not until 1936 had the bumbling Conservative government taken the first steps toward rearmament. Pacifism had penetrated deep into the British mind, finding expression in Labor's contradictory program of supporting the League system of collective security, while maintaining as low a level of armament as possible. Only a few Churchills cried in the wilderness as British leadership undermined the Versailles settlement, even after the advent of Hitler, by its naval agreement of 1935, by its refusal to oppose the German occupation of the Rhineland or the *Anschluss* with Austria, and by its final betrayal of France's eastern ally, Czechoslovakia, at Munich.

Had Britain had available the relative power it possessed in the eighteenth and nineteenth centuries, its mistaken policies might have been serious but not disastrous. In an era of total war, however, Britain's formerly strategic position was all but lost. Large armies with the latest destructive devices could, as the Germans showed, overwhelm whole countries in a matter of days. While the Channel was still too wide a ditch for Hitler to jump in the face of the magnificent British air defense, the time was long past when the British fleet could surround the Continent and slowly strangle the enemy by a tight economic blockade.

In fact, it was Britain which was slowly being strangled. The ability of the British industrial economy to sustain modern warfare for long periods had been falling relative to that of Germany and the United States since the turn of the century. Coal production in the eight postwar years 1921–1929 exceeded the prewar level only once, whereas Germany produced more in every year save that of the Ruhr invasion, and France after 1924 surpassed its prewar figure. Problems of British production placed a greater strain on British trade, which failed after World War I to recapture the markets it had formerly held. Ability to pay for necessary imports of foodstuffs and raw materials was further hampered by the declining position of the world's goods carried by the British merchant marine and by the liquidation of British overseas investments. Seventy per cent of the holdings in the United States had been sold during World War I, and evidence presented by Secretary of the Treasury Henry Morgenthau, Jr., at the Congressional Lend-Lease hearings in 1941 indicated an almost total inability of the British to finance American-produced war material which was needed to hold off the German armies.

POSTWAR BRITISH WEAKNESS

Great Britain emerged at the end of World War II, as twenty-five years earlier, a victor over Germany. Some American observers professed to find a still-powerful Britain, one of the "super powers," an equal "partner for peace." The sad fact, however, was one of insolvency. Britain was not able to recover by its own efforts from the effects of the war; far less was it able to maintain the imperial, world-wide commitments of a super power. Punctilious exactitude in Washington regarding the letter of the Lend-Lease Act stopped the vital flow of American goods immediately after the surrender of Japan. At the very time materials were most needed for reconstruction a lapse of several months ensued before so-called "pipeline" products (on order but not delivered) were permitted to leave the United States for Britain. Another few months passed before the "loan" of $3.75 billion was passed by the Congress, the first substantial reversal of earlier American expectations regarding limited European commitments. On top of all these difficulties a winter of unparalleled severity all but stopped the wheels of British industry for four vital months. In the words of journalist and radio commentator Howard K. Smith: "If the blizzard had not brought Britain to her knees, something else would have. But the blizzard dramatically highlighted the perilously slim margin on which Britain was living."

Unable to reconstruct the center of its power, Great Britain perforce abandoned the positions which that power had hitherto maintained. In Asia, India, Ceylon, and Burma were freed willingly but also of necessity by a Laborite government, which was promptly accused by the Conservative Opposition leader of "clattering down" the British Empire. In the Near East, Great Britain decided it could not hold onto Palestine against the clamors of both Jews and Arabs. But most dramatic of all was the announcement that Britain no longer could support with its armed forces the shaky Greek government against the communist-led EAM, or National Liberation Front.

By 1947, the year of decision, for the United States in Europe, it was clear that Great Britain was not one of the superpowers. Just what position Great Britain could assume, however, was still uncertain. Some British voices, like the *New Statesman and Nation,* were beginning to speak of the British Isles as another Denmark or Switzerland, a small, weak country which should declare itself out of the East-West conflict. American military observer Hanson Baldwin claimed that Britain was "tied—inevitably—to the United States," while Howard K. Smith called Britain "in effect a senior satellite of the United States."

BASES OF POSTWAR FRENCH WEAKNESS

It took the blizzard of 1947 to reveal the full extent of British weakness. That France was no longer the foremost military power on the Continent had been evident at least a decade earlier, when the French government permitted Hitler, to the latter's surprise, to march unopposed into the Rhineland. Commonly forgotten in the hopeful days of national regeneration in 1945 was the depth of the cleavage existing between Frenchmen, an internal condition which frustrated all attempts by political and economic institutions to restore any semblance of France's former greatness.

At first it had appeared that the Fourth Republic would be able to solve the problems which had defeated the Third. Of these problems, the multiplicity of parties and the many ephemeral political alignments, which led to continued governmental instability were serious but only surface manifestations. Behind them lay deeper rooted social, economic, and ideological factors. The very idea of a republic had never found universal acceptance in France, much less the idea of a democracy. Antirepublican forces continued to agitate the French scene and achieved a temporary triumph in the Vichy regime. Although the Third Republic became politically identified with the middle and peasant classes, their political control was recurrently threatened by the economic and financial power retained by smaller, undemocratic groups. This meant that the Third Republic, in the governments of which the large Radical Socialist party was most prominent, could not effect many of the reforms necessary to solidify social and economic democracy in France. Failure to do so was made more serious as time passed by the growth of industrial labor groups which, in France as elsewhere in the Western world, were beginning to demand effective political and economic participation in the life of the nation. Thus the basic elements which maintained the Third Republic were threatened both from above by groups unwilling to surrender the power which had historically been theirs, and from below by emergent groups wishing to move ahead with changes which had been posited as far back as 1870.

The inability of the numerous French governments between the two wars to take the many necessary steps of social, economic, and financial reform necessary for continued political health was a reflection of the basic weakness and uncertainty which was responsible for the defeat of France. Parties of the extreme right were antirepublican in orientation; for them the political changes involved in the initial creation of the Third Republic had been too great. The parties of the center and left-center were involved in the defense of the political institutions of 1870 but were unable to agree on the economic measures of the twentieth century. For the left, working for economic and social reform, the problem was whether the necessary measures could be taken within the bourgeois framework of the Third Republic. The Communists answered no; the Socialists yes, provided that these measures should have priority over the exigencies of national strength in foreign relations. Repeatedly the French people voted for reform; repeatedly French cabinets between elections moved toward the right. The mere perpetuation of government became an art, an end in itself, inviting the manipulator and the opportunist, à la Pierre Laval. Bureaucracy burgeoned while government languished.

This lack of common identification with a single set of political and economic institutions was deepened by the Vichy regime and the civil war which it entailed. The experience of the first two postwar years showed that the Fourth Republic could not alter the situation. After the nonparty regime of General de Gaulle, who resigned because his arguments for a stronger executive were not accepted, French government speedily reverted to the old prewar pattern. Until De Gaulle formed his own Rally of the French People, for which he claimed a status above party, the Communists were the largest group in France and, as shown by the 1951 elections, still commanded the loyalty of more people than any other party. As leaders of the resistance, the Communists had contributed much to French discipline in the period of their cooperation in political responsibility. In 1947 they were forced into opposition, driven by the exigencies of serving a foreign master who no longer wanted to see France revive. The three groups of the center—the Radical Socialists, the MRP (Mouvement Républicain Populaire), and the Socialists —could agree on little else but the necessity of preventing the Republic from being submerged under the waves from either the left or the right.

By continuous participation in cabinets which could not cope with inflation, wages, or the rising cost of living, the Socialists forfeited much of the popular basis of their strength. The Mouvement Républicain Populaire, a Catholic party of liberal orientation, lost almost half its strength to the De Gaullists in 1947 and became embroiled with its political partners in the generations-old issue of anticlericalism. Radical Socialism, the conservative center of the Third Republic, was by default of other leadership thrown into positions of political responsibility on the same negative platform that it had supported ever since the end of World War I—the defense of the Republic, as a political system, against its enemies, foreign and domestic. To this banner rallied enough of the right to enable France to limp from crisis to crisis. By 1947 a dramatic contrast was already evident between French ineffectiveness in the face of the severe problems left by the war and the Spartan measures of survival being taken by the British Labor government.

Whereas some question still remained concerning the future role of Britain, there was little question concerning France. Continuation of French democracy depended on outside assistance; there was no area of maneuver for France between the giants of the East and West. Despite the deluded cries of the Communists and the "neutralists," the nation of Louis XIV and Napoleon depended for its recovery and continued safety on American, not French, policies.

► ORIGINAL OCCUPATION POLICIES IN GERMANY AND THEIR BREAKDOWN

The unexpected dynamism of Soviet behavior met the unexpected weakness of the West in Germany. The inevitable result was a reversal of the original American presumptions concerning postwar policy toward that country. Plans made during the conflict called for four-power *cooperation* (after a place was found for France) in the treatment of Germany. The essentials of that treatment were to be negative; things were to be done to Germany, things which the Germans would not like and which therefore would have to be extracted by a harsh occupation.

Germany itself might well be dismembered. Roosevelt, Churchill, and Stalin were in agreement that Germany would have to be broken up into a number of different states, although British and American advisers were openly dubious of the plan. Nonetheless, it was agreed at Yalta that the deputy foreign ministers, with headquarters in London, should formulate concrete plans in order that the three governments might "take such steps, including the complete disarmament, demilitarization, and the *dismemberment* of Germany as they deem requisite for future peace and security." In the actual discussions of the deputy foreign ministers, dismemberment assumed such a low priority that ways of effecting it were never considered. And when, on the collapse of Germany, a new surrender document was prepared by SHAEF, dismemberment was not included at all. The unconditional surrender of the German armed forces enabled the Allies to issue a proclamation on June 5, 1945, assuming sovereignty over Germany. Again dismemberment was not mentioned, although the assumption of full powers would have enabled the occupying nations to do anything they wanted, if they could agree to do anything at all. Premier Stalin formally interred dismemberment as an objective, after the West had tacitly abandoned it, with his famous statement that "the Soviet Union . . . does not intend to dismember or destroy Germany. . . ." It remained for the breakdown of the Four-Power Allied Control Commission in Berlin to effect the division of the defeated enemy into two parts: the American-British Zones, to which the French Zone was later united, and East Germany, controlled by the Soviet Union.

If there were to be one Germany for occupation purposes, at least it was to be so weak a Germany that it never again could menace the peace of the world. Reparations were to be exacted in substantial amounts, on behalf of the neighbors who had suffered at Hitler's hands, although the total remained to be determined. The Soviet Union put in a claim to $20 billion, half for itself, half for its East European partners, and Roosevelt said that this figure could be "used as the basis of discussion." Ever afterward Russian official policy interpreted these words as agreement, although anyone familiar with domestic American politics would recognize the familiar device of putting off decision on an issue with respect to which there was no agreement, while at the same time avoiding outright repudiation of the idea. The payment of reparations through removal of productive facilities from Germany and through shipments out of current production was to keep German resources from being directed toward national recovery. The German economy was to serve the revival of Germany's victims, while being itself kept weak.

How weak? The plans of Secretary of the Treasury Morgenthau, which were accepted by Roosevelt and Churchill at the second Quebec Conference in 1944, were very specific:

> The industries referred to in the Ruhr and in the Saar would therefore be necessarily put out of action and closed down. It was felt that the two districts should be put under somebody under the World Organization which would supervise the dismantling of these industries and make sure that they were not started up again by some subterfuge.
>
> This program for eliminating the war-making industries in the Ruhr and in the Saar is looking forward to converting Germany into a country primarily agricultural and pastoral in its character.*

THE ORIGINAL DIRECTIVE—JCS 1067

Even after the State and War Departments, with the active assistance of Harry Hopkins, had induced President Roosevelt to reverse his position on the Morgenthau Plan, Allied thinking on Germany's economic future remained highly punitive and dominated by the idea that the peace of the world depended on keeping Germany weak for generations to come. The original directive from the Joint Chiefs of Staff to the Commander in Chief of the United States Forces of Occupation (the famous JCS 1067 sent to General Eisenhower) had this to say in its economic part: "Except as may be necessary to carry out these objectives [occupation and control of Germany], you will take no steps (a) looking toward the economic rehabilitation of Germany, or (b) designed to maintain or strengthen the German economy." This general statement was spelled out somewhat in subsequent paragraphs concerning the German standard of living: "You will estimate requirements of supplies necessary to prevent starvation or widespread disease or such civil unrest as would endanger the occupying forces. Such estimates will be based upon a program whereby the Germans are made responsible for providing for themselves out of their own work and resources. . . . You will take no action that would tend to support basic living standards in Germany on a higher level than that existing in any one of the neighboring United Nations. . . ." The same heavily punitive note ran through the Potsdam Declaration on Germany of July, 1945, the conferees including practically verbatim the last sentence of JCS 1067 quoted above.

---

* Memorandum quoted in *The Memoirs of Cordell Hull* (New York, The Macmillan Company, 1948), p. 1610.

Further agreements among the Allies related to economic control and deconcentration of industry. JCS 1067 specifically mentioned the prevention of research "which has been connected with the building of the German war machine" and the prohibition of production of "iron and steel, chemicals, non-ferrous metals (excluding aluminum and magnesium), machine tools, radio and electrical equipment, automotive vehicles, heavy machinery and important parts thereof" except for the purposes of attaining general occupation objectives. There was the further and very flat statement: "It is the policy of your government to effect a dispersion of the ownership and control of German industry." The Potsdam Agreement with respect to industrial production was somewhat weaker, mentioning control and restriction of "metals, chemicals, machinery and other items." On the subject of breaking up industrial combines and reorganizing the German economy, however, the Potsdam conferees agreed on harsh and unequivocal paragraphs. "At the earliest practicable date, the German economy shall be decentralized for the purpose of eliminating the present excessive concentration of economic power as exemplified in particular by cartels, syndicates, trusts, and other monopolistic arrangements. In organizing the German economy, primary emphasis shall be given to the development of agriculture and peaceful domestic industries." (These are echoes of the Morgenthau Plan.)

Original Allied plans naturally called for complete demilitarization, but this was only one aspect of what was to be a thoroughgoing reorganization of German society. War criminals were to be tried, and, in the words of the Potsdam Agreement, "Nazi leaders, influential Nazi supporters and high officials of Nazi organizations and institutions and any other persons dangerous to the occupation or its objectives shall be arrested and interned." Lesser figures, whose membership in Nazi groups was more than nominal, were to be removed from their positions and replaced by others more trustworthy. The judicial system was to be reorganized and German education controlled to "eliminate Nazi and militarist doctrines and to make possible the successful development of democratic ideas." With respect to German re-education, JCS 1067 had been more specific than the Potsdam Agreement, providing for the reopening of schools only after the Nazi teachers and tainted textbooks had been eliminated. These brief quotations make plain the original intention of the Allies to pull out Nazism from German society by the roots and to undertake the stupendous task of replacing that odious authoritarian system with a new, purged, cleansed, and peaceful order.

BREAKDOWN OF FOUR-POWER AGREEMENT DESTROYS ORIGINAL OCCUPATION OBJECTIVES

Success in the treatment of Germany according to the original intentions of the Allies depended, as did the success of the United Nations, on the continued cooperation of the United States, Great Britain, France, and the Soviet Union. From the very outset that essential cooperation was difficult. Although the Potsdam Conference had succeeded in laying the groundwork of basic principles to guide the Allied commanders in Berlin, including a formula for reparations shipments from the Western Zones to the Soviet Union, France had not been a participant at the conference and hence did not feel bound by the principles there agreed to, although France was now to be accorded a position equal to that of the Big Three in Berlin. The result was that the first few months of the formal occupation were marked by French intransigence, against which Allied control almost broke down. General Clay has stated that during this period he and the British representative were more frequently in agreement with the Russian than with the French delegate.

But it was the Russians who finally caused the collapse of the occupation machinery. As the efforts at four-power control over Germany continued from Berlin, East and West were moving further apart on German questions as they were on all other matters basic to a lasting settlement of the war. The Russians, frustrated in their attempts to obtain Allied agreement to their demand for $10 billion in reparations, began to use East Germany to obtain the reparations without Allied agreement. Because they wished to cement their control over East Germany the Soviets refused to treat Germany as an economic unit as prescribed at Potsdam and failed to carry through agreed-upon shipments to the Western Zones. At the same time the Russians were making free use of the currency plates given them by the Allies to print occupation marks for their area of Berlin without rendering any account of the amount printed.

The United States led the three Western powers in what retaliatory measures lay at their disposal. They could at least cease to abet the Russians in their unilateral extraction of reparations from Germany by halting shipments authorized by the Potsdam Agreement from the Western zones. This they did. Likewise the United States could and did take preliminary steps leading toward a union of its occupation zone, first with the British, then with the French Zones. From these steps emerged the West German Federal Republic, although at the time of the Anglo-American zonal merger it had been explicitly stated that the merger was to be limited to economic matters. When the currency reform was finally put into effect for the Western areas of Berlin, the financial ground was cut from under the Russian occupation mark. These last two measures—the organization of the West German state and the Berlin currency reform—led the Soviet Union to drastic steps aimed at forcing the West from Berlin, which was in the heart of the Eastern Zone. Upon institution of the blockade in 1948, East and West, facing each other across the narrow dividing line in the German capital, were but one step from war.

By 1947, then, it had become clear that the problem of the postwar treatment of Germany could not be solved by the four occupying powers acting in concert. While some of the specific reasons for the breakdown of the Control Council in Berlin have been given in the preceding paragraphs, the basic cause was that neither East nor West was willing to follow the Potsdam philosophy that Germany should be punished as severely as possible. East and West began to bid for German support against each other. In other words, both Soviet and Western policy ceased to treat Germany as an end in itself and now sought to use Germany toward an entirely different end: victory in the cold war. Against this background of competition for German support, the meetings of the Allied foreign ministers at Moscow and London in 1947 had no hope of reaching a settlement. In fact, it became apparent that the Soviet Union was using the gatherings as it was using international meetings of the United Nations: not for the purpose of negotiation and compromise, but to reiterate vituperative charges against the West and attempt to arouse world opinion (in this case German opinion) against Britain, France, and the United States.

The United States, beginning with Secretary of State James Byrnes's speech at Stuttgart in 1946, likewise was bidding for German support. Denazification programs, more detailed and thorough than those of any of the other four powers, removed many Nazis from important political and economic positions but had not begun to accomplish the large task originally envisaged when they were turned over to the Germans to administer. With respect to economic policy a more profound change took place. Once Americans began to manifest concern over whether the Germans lived or starved to death, systematic reduction and control of the German economy to the agricultural and minor-industry level envisaged in JCS 1067 was impossible. Congressional complaints that the occupation was costing too much reached sensitive ears in Berlin. German economic revival became ever more imperative as the rest of Western Europe failed to recover and as German cooperation with the West rather than the East was sought. Deconcentration of industry, which had never assumed a top place in General Clay's priority of objectives, achieved some notable results, particularly in the early period, but, like denazification, was never carried to the lengths originally intended at Potsdam. To the West, faced with obvious Soviet intentions of spreading communist influence as far as possible in Europe (even the blindest could hardly ignore the coup in Czechoslovakia of February, 1948), a place had to be found for the recently defeated enemy. That enemy had to be made a partner, and the obvious price of abandoning all the original occupation objectives short of accomplishment was deemed by American policy makers to be well worth paying.

▶ SUMMARY OF STAGES IN AMERICAN POSTWAR RELATIONS TOWARD EUROPE

The translation into national policy of the recognized relationship between American and Western European security can be traced through several, frequently overlapping stages. Beginning under the concept of limited commitment previously mentioned, the United States gradually assumed responsibilities of leadership supported by power. The various way stations in the transition may be identified as multilateral relief, bilateral and multilateral finance and trade, bilateral economic assistance, leadership in multilateral economic cooperation, bilateral military assistance within a multilateral framework, beginnings of multilateral military cooperation under American leadership. This list reveals the original reliance on traditional techniques, a subsequent shift to economic measures on an unparalleled scale, and a further shift to unprecedented military policies. As the complexion of American relations toward Western Europe has become more clearly delineated, a basis for some deductions as to the possible future course of events has become possible.

ECONOMIC POLICY: THE CONCEPT OF RELIEF AND REASONS FOR ITS ABANDONMENT

The United States took the initiative in establishing the United Nations Relief and Rehabilitation Administration in the midst of the war. Endorsement by Congress made it possible for UNRRA to begin its activities with an original capital of $2 billion. Because the United States contributed 72 per cent of UNRRA's funds and 90 per cent of the goods it distributed, the agency from beginning to end was, despite representation of forty-four nations, substantially an American enterprise. It reflected the original American conception of limited commitment, with heavy emphasis on the relief of peoples in newly liberated countries. Rehabilitation meant "assistance in the resumption of urgently needed agricultural and industrial programs and the restoration of essential services." The presumption was that the need for this emergency organization would be over soon after the war itself was ended. Actually UNRRA was terminated by the American announcement in December, 1946, that it would withdraw from participation, but the American decision was based only in part on the argument that the job of UNRRA had been accomplished.

Although the American representative to the United Nations, Adlai Stevenson, told the other countries that few of them would need relief aid in 1947 and that in small amounts, the fundamental motivation behind the shift in American policy was political. The operations of UNRRA were nonpolitical in the sense that the criterion of need was the sole one applied. But because it was inevitably dealing with governments, UNRRA could not avoid embroilment in international politics. Most of its assistance in Europe went to the liberated countries of Eastern Europe, especially to Czechoslovakia, Poland, and Yugoslavia, and to the Soviet Union. As it became clearer that the Soviet Union was bent on bringing those nations into the Soviet orbit, it appeared that American assistance was facilitating the Russian task at the very time the United States government was protesting Soviet policies. Regardless of the humanitarian axiom that "hungry peoples have no politics," this discrepancy made no sense to Congress and to the State Department. For the

State Department, Secretary Byrnes declared: "I should say that it is our position that whatsoever the United States does in the way of relief should be done by the United States unilaterally. We want to give aid as the United States and not as a member of an international organization."* To put this idea even more bluntly, the United States wanted to use its economic power as a political weapon to reward its friends and punish its enemies, and it had no friends among the governments of Eastern Europe.

John C. Campbell concluded from the UNRRA experience: "Thus the shadow of diplomatic conflict with the Soviet Union during 1945 and 1946 beclouded American idealism and chilled our enthusiasm for unselfish giving."† The cloud and chill came from the frigid blasts of the "cold war."

FAILURE OF NORMAL AGENCIES IN AN ABNORMAL SITUATION

Part of the reasoning behind the ending of UNRRA was that established international agencies should take over the job of reconstruction now that the problems of relief had been declared satisfied. These agencies were of two types: those concerned with loans and those concerned with trade. Reliance on them would have the dual effect of channeling American relationships to Europe through the traditional routes of finance and trade, while restricting that contact mainly to the countries of Western Europe, which were becoming more clearly identified as friends and supporters of the United States in the growing diplomatic combat with the Soviet Union. There were, first, the International Bank and the International Fund, both loosely affiliated with the United Nations under terms leaving them practical autonomy. Behind these agencies was the Export-Import Bank for the granting of national loans, supplemented by such special credits as Congress might see fit to vote. In the field of trade, the State Department was relying heavily on its proposals for an International Trade Organization to bind the nations of the world to liberal practices which would maximize mutual benefits accruing from the interchange of goods. Finally there was the United Nations Food and Agriculture Organization, whose special field of operations is indicated by its title.

The difficulty with the machinery mentioned above was that it did not bridge the gap between the discontinuance of emergency relief and the beginning of reconstruction. The purpose of these particular agencies was to permit financial relations between states to operate with less friction than in the past, once the nature of those relations had been defined for the postwar period. The International Monetary Fund was thus designed to assure the stability of national currencies against short-run crises. The insistence on devaluation by the French and later the British merely highlighted the fact that the Monetary Fund could not operate in the hectic, postwar period of adjustment between

---

* Cited by John C. Campbell, et al., The United States in World Affairs, 1945–1947 (New York, Harper & Brothers, 1947), p. 335.
    † Ibid., p. 338.

national financial structures. In March, 1946, the National Advisory Council on International Monetary and Financial Problems declared that "the International Bank will begin lending operations in the latter half of 1946 and . . . during the calendar year 1947 the International Bank will assume the primary responsibility for meeting the world's international capital requirements that cannot be met by private investors on their own account and risk."* Subsequent events proved this statement of the NAC palpably erroneous. Notwithstanding the fact that the International Bank was intended to promote reconstruction as well as development, it was still a bank, prepared to *loan* money at interest where the applicant was a good credit risk. In the unstable world of 1947 there were only a few good credit risks, and most of them did not want or need loans from the International Bank. Like the Monetary Fund, it could operate only when some order had been brought out of the postwar chaos. The orderly trickle of its disbursements could not of itself end that chaos.

As was developed more fully in an earlier chapter,† the proposals for an International Trade Organization permitted national deviations from liberal practices during the exceptional, transitional period. Unfortunately for the ITO its definition of the "exceptional" far too closely approximated the actual state of postwar economic relations between nations which showed few signs of being limited and transitional in time. Because most nations found it impossible to accept the obligations of the Charter of the ITO, the tariff reductions under the accompanying General Agreement on Tariffs and Trade could not alone solve the principal problems arising among the world's major trading nations. The premise, based on prewar experience, had been that trade policies affected political relations. While this premise was still potentially accurate after 1945, it was obscured by the severe impact of political conflict on international trade relations.

Efforts of the Food and Agriculture Organization to cope with the maldistribution and pricing of agricultural commodities likewise ran up against the overshadowing specter of political conflict, which diminished the willingness of individual members to make commitments to an international organization whose primary motivations were nonpolitical. FAO director Norris E. Dodd declared late in 1951 that the member nations of the organization had failed to attain one tenth of the goals they had set for themselves five years earlier, that member countries had made recommendations to themselves and each other but had not then carried them out.

Western European needs became acute, therefore, before the period of reconstruction. Normal lending practices could not solve them on an international level, nor, as it proved, could national loans by the United States do so. The Export-Import Bank was a novice in the field of reconstruction; its previous activities had been confined mainly to the Latin-American area,

---

* Quoted in *ibid.*, p. 374.

† See Chapter Fifteen, "Evolving Patterns of Economic Foreign Policy."

whose countries had received roughly two thirds of its disbursements. Its loans were granted usually for a fifteen- to twenty-year period, carried a 3 or 4 per cent interest rate, and were specifically tied to the purchase of American goods to be transported, wherever possible, in American vessels.

After the war the focus of the Export-Import Bank shifted from Latin America to Europe. Between June, 1945, and December, 1946, it loaned almost $2 billion to European countries, all but $102 million going to Western Europe. But even as the loans were being made, it was becoming ever clearer that the bank's facilities could not be adequate for the reconstruction problems faced by Western Europe and that the needs of that area were not primarily for tied loans at all, whether made by the United States directly or by international agencies which were largely American-supported. When the bank announced at the end of 1946 that "it must bring to an end its program of emergency reconstruction credits," it was saying in effect that, despite increased funds allocated to it by Congress, assistance to Western Europe must take another form.

SHIFT TO DEVICES OF SPECIAL ASSISTANCE: THE BRITISH LOAN

Already the United States had gone outside the mechanism of the Export-Import Bank to meet the urgent requirements of Great Britain. The special loan to Britain of $3.75 billion signalized the transition of the United States from its presumption of limited commitment met by traditional policies to embarkation on the untrodden path of large-scale assistance to support Western Europe as an ally indispensable to American security. The loan to Britain was unprecedented in size; its rate of interest was low (2 per cent), possibly lower than the cost of the money to the American treasury. Interest payments could be waived by agreement when the British got into difficulties. On the other hand, the money was loaned, not granted outright as the British had wished, and the sum was smaller than British officials had hoped for. The arrangement carried with it obligations on the part of Great Britain to make sterling convertible into other currencies, thus relating the loan to simultaneous American efforts toward free trade.

The Congress of the United States took seven months to appropriate the money. The delay reflected substantial Congressional fear and opposition concerning the new path taken by American foreign policy. The administration laid heavy emphasis on the normal, financial aspects of the transaction. "It is not a pension, gift, or handout of any description, whatever," declared Secretary of State Dean Acheson. "It is an investment in the future," an investment made because it would be profitable to the United States as well as to Britain. But the real nature of the commitment being made could not be totally obscured. Although the administration carefully avoided drawing direct anti-Soviet implications, there were others inside and outside Congress who were not so reticent. Winston Churchill at Fulton, Missouri, had, in the presence of President Truman, sounded the alarm at Soviet behavior and called for a close association of English-speaking peoples. Senator Vandenberg, powerful exponent of Congressional cooperation in official American foreign policy, had told the Senate, "If we do not lead . . . some other great and powerful nation will capitalize our failure and we shall pay the price of our default." It was not difficult to penetrate the Senator's circumlocutionary description of the Soviet Union, nor was Senator Barkley's pronouncement any less clear! "I do not desire, for myself or for my country, to take a position that will drive *our ally* into arms into which we do not want her to be folded"; nor Speaker Rayburn's; "I do not want *Western Europe, England, and all the rest,* to be pushed further into and towards an ideology that I despise. I fear if we do not cooperate with this *great natural ally* of ours, that is what will happen." In the final analysis it was the hardening of American policy toward the Soviet Union and the determination to keep Western Europe out of the clutches of that power which made possible the loan to Great Britain. ·

APPROACH TOWARD UNLIMITED COMMITMENT: THE TRUMAN DOCTRINE

That even the loan of unprecedented sums of money would not be enough, to place Western Europe on its feet became dramatically apparent early in 1947. Far from advancing, recovery was coming to a halt, one of the factors being the severe winter previously mentioned. The American government was involved in leisurely consideration of the European crisis and what the United States ought to do next when the British announced their withdrawal from Greece. There was nothing surprising to Washington in the fact of withdrawal. British commitments were being reduced wherever possible throughout the world, but the directness and timing of the announcement forced the American hand. The result was a request by President Truman for Congressional appropriations to assist both Greece and Turkey.

The implications of the British and American actions went far beyond the geographical confines of two small Mediterranean countries. The manner in which the British abandoned a Greek government they had done so much to sustain in its civil war, coupled with the form in which the President presented his request to Congress, forced American consideration of the entire problem of the role that the United States would have to play in Europe and of the policies which would make that role effective. The presidential message of March 22, 1947, to Congress bluntly stated for the first time the clear opposition of the United States to the Soviet Union and the inability of any machinery other than national action to thwart Soviet ambitions. "Totalitarian regimes," said the President, "imposed on free peoples, by direct or indirect aggression, undermine the foundations of international peace and hence the security of the United States. . . . The United Nations and its related organizations are not in a position to extend help of the kind that is required. . . . I believe that it must be the policy of the United States to support free peoples who are resisting attempted subjugation by armed minorities or by outside pressures." It should be observed that while appropriations were requested only for Greece and Turkey, the language of what came to be known as the Truman Doctrine was not confined to any individual countries or to any one region. If the subjects of the contemporary Greek and Turkish regimes could be characterized as "free peoples," the words might logically be interpreted as being synonymous with "noncommunist." If this were the case, then *any* noncommunist regime in danger of losing its identity under external or internal pressure fell into the category of nations whose security was intimately connected with that of the United States.

THE MARSHALL PLAN FROM PROPOSAL TO POLICY

There was a lapse of only three months between the promulgation of the Truman Doctrine and the significant speech of Secretary of State Marshall at Harvard University.* The obvious intent of the secretary was to find for the more advanced, less immediately threatened nations of Western Europe a suitable formula that would permit expression in concrete American policies of the same general security relationship that had already been acknowledged in Congressional debates over the British loan. The question was to decide which American policies would be most suitable for the special problems involved. For Greece and Turkey the answer was military and economic assistance under direct American supervision. Particularly in Greece, time would not wait for the United States to see whether or not the Communist-led EAM forces could be defeated by the Greek government acting alone. In Western Europe the problem was greater in its scope but less immediate in its urgency. After the failure of the foreign ministers in April, 1947, to reach agreement over Germany, United States policy could not delay in the hope of East-West *rapprochement* that might never come. In France the estrangement of the Soviet Union meant that its largest single political party, which might at any time attain power, legally or illegally, was devoted to objectives diametrically opposed to those of the West. The same was true in Italy, although here the Christian Democrats had an edge over the Communists. In both France and Italy Communists had been members of the governmental coalitions, making it impossible for those countries to devote their efforts to anti-Soviet policies, however necessary such policies might be to the security of Western Europe. As already mentioned, Great Britain, while not teetering on the edge of Communist submergence, had been sliding down the slippery path of economic weakness toward national bankruptcy.

Several points in Secretary Marshall's address are worth noting in an

---

* Secretary Marshall's idea had been foreshadowed by Under Secretary Acheson's address delivered a month earlier in Cleveland, Mississippi, presumably as a trial balloon to test public opinion.

examination of the changing relationship of the United States toward Western Europe. No concrete program was outlined. "Any government willing to assist in the task of recovery," said the secretary, "will find full cooperation on the part of the United States." Certain conclusions followed logically. American cooperation would not be expressly limited to any particular type of government. The enemy was not the Soviet Union or even international communism, but "hunger, poverty, desperation, and chaos," which were hindering European countries in attaining stability. Nonetheless, "governments, political parties, or groups which seek to perpetuate human misery in order to profit therefrom politically or otherwise will encounter the opposition of the United States." Cooperation, then, was to be economic and not military, as befitted the needs of Western European countries. Upon those countries rested the initiative for primary harmony among themselves in the working out of programs of national recovery which would promote rather than handicap the recovery of the entire region.

Above all, the speech of Secretary Marshall pointed the way toward abandonment of the measures which had proved ineffective: multilateral agencies affiliated with the United Nations, and bilateral loan arrangements between the United States and individual recipients.

Two further developments were necessary before the European Recovery Program could emerge as an effective instrument for the promotion of Western European security against the Soviet Union: the elimination of the Soviet Union itself from the program, and the establishment by Western Europe of an organization adequate to administer the Program.

It may be doubted whether the American Congress, or the American government for that matter, after having cleared UNRRA out of the way, would have reacted warmly to the re-entrance of the Soviet Union and Eastern Europe as beneficiaries of American assistance. Fortunately for American decision making, the Soviet Union took itself and its satellites out of the picture. Russia did accept the invitation of Bevin and Bidault to discuss ways of taking up the United States offer, and no less than eighty-nine Russians made the journey to Paris with Foreign Minister Molotov. The size of the Russian delegation indicated serious attention to the future course of Soviet policy in the light of the potentially vast expansion of American economic assistance to Europe. Molotov speedily made it clear, however, that his country would only consent to accept American aid on its own terms, terms which violated the basis of Marshall's proposal. Each country, said Molotov, should draw up by itself a list of its own requirements, and American funds and goods could be used as each country saw fit. European cooperation such as the British and French foreign ministers envisaged would open the door to American imperialism and would violate national sovereignty, a concept to which the Soviet Union devoted a lot of words.

Germany should not be included in the program because that defeated enemy was subject to the jurisdiction of the Council of Foreign Ministers. When Bevin and Bidault showed no signs of accepting propositions which would have killed all chances of American assistance, Molotov and his followers left for Moscow, but not without sounding an ominous warning to the West of the dire consequences of their course.

Britain and France were now free to go ahead without the embarrassment of Soviet participation, yet without the responibility for having themselves slammed the door on Russia. Twenty-two countries were invited to another conference for the purpose of setting up a "committee of cooperation." Fourteen accepted; the eight within the Soviet orbit hesitated until word was received from the Kremlin. Some of the eight, such as Hungary, Finland, and Czechoslovakia, had strong traditional trade ties with Western Europe and desperately needed the kind of aid which Russia could not give. Would they nonetheless have to refuse? They would. The Russian response to the Western invitation was to force them all, even Czechoslovakia, to decline and instead to strengthen their ties with the Soviet Union through the subsequently established Cominform. In retrospect it was clear that the Russians felt they could not risk the effect upon Eastern European countries of large-scale American assistance, which would turn their economic faces toward the West.

Between July and September, 1947, the European nations outside Soviet control intensively studied ways of making maximum use of American aid. They were under pressure of two sorts. Time was of the essence; the situation in most countries was daily worsening. Delays in order to perfect machinery might be fatal. On the other hand, the machinery had to be sufficiently in evidence to satisfy the American requisite of cooperation. While United States representatives did not participate officially in this second conference, they did advise Europe as to what proposals the prospective benefactor would be likely to accept. The conferees were told that the first figure of $29 billion to be spread over a four-year period was far too large, that the United States would like to see determined efforts to balance the individual national budgets, and that the device of the customs union to facilitate intra-European cooperation should be explored. The document as finally presented to Secretary Marshall was two volumes in length and emphasized not only what Europe needed, but also what Europe was going to do to help itself and precisely how, with American assistance, the cooperating countries would, by 1952, have placed themselves on a sound economic footing.

THE FOREIGN ASSISTANCE ACT OF 1948

By the time President Truman signed the Foreign Assistance Act on May 3, 1948, several points about the new American relationship toward Europe had been made plain. Congress was in no mood to accept a four-year commitment in terms of specific appropriation and was clearly of a mind to terminate American aid at the end of the period, that is, in 1952. The test of European self-help was to be constantly applied; the United States wanted the initiative in recovery to remain with the cooperating countries themselves. Congress also insisted that this country benefit in more direct, tangible ways than merely by contribution to Western European revival. Recipient nations were to turn over strategic materials needed for the American stockpile. At least half of tthe American goods were to be transported in American ships, and the Economic Cooperation Administration was to purchase surplus agricultural products in the United States wherever possible. While the enemy was still defined as "hunger, poverty, desperation, and chaos," the connection between these conditions and the spread of communism was made far more explicit. Wavering congressmen, fearful of the billions to be granted to Europe, were brought into line by the anticommunist appeal, while conditions attached to the Foreign Assistance Act, some of which have just been mentioned, purchased the support of still others acutely sensitive to the political pressure of special-interest groups.

Although the American Congress moved with unaccustomed speed, considering the extent of the change it was making in traditional foreign policy and the fact that the Republicans controlled both legislative branches, European need could not wait for passage of the Foreign Assistance Act. The situation was particularly desperate in France and Italy, where recovery was lagging and the governments had recently taken the bold step of eliminating the Communists from political, executive positions. The administration accordingly requested emergency appropriations, which Congress passed under the Interim Aid Act, authorizing the immediate expenditure of almost $600 million, mostly for food, fertilizers, and fuel.

Another delay occurred between the passage of the Foreign Assistance Act and the actual initiation of operations by the Economic Cooperation Administration. It was probably lengthened by the determination of Congress to vent its displeasure with the State Department through the establishment of a separate agency to administer funds for Europe. The new agency was discouraged by legislative statute from employing officials already working in the government, which meant that, instead of an organization built around the nucleus of people who had already spent much time in planning the ERP, personnel had to be recruited almost from scratch. Therefore, Western Europe lived from hand to mouth for roughly eighteen months after the original address of Secretary Marshall until American assistance could turn the tide of oncoming economic chaos.

ACCOMPLISHMENTS OF THE EUROPEAN RECOVERY PROGRAM

The manner in which United States grants were spent during most of 1947 and 1948 magnified even more the accomplishments of the European

Recovery Program, once it got under way. The meaning of the administrative techniques employed is explored in another chapter, concerned with changing American economic foreign policy. By the end of 1950, however, unparalleled expenditures had brought results which approached even the optimistic bases on which cooperative efforts of Western Europe were begun. This is revealed in the two tables, prepared by Brookings Institution, which follows:

AMERICAN ECONOMIC ASSISTANCE TO WESTERN EUROPE
(In Millions of Dollars)

July 1, 1945—September 30, 1950

Country	Before ERP Period	During ERP Period	Total
Austria	299	440	739
Belgium-Luxembourg	222	464	686
United Kingdom	4,179	2,402	6,581
Denmark	16	190	206
France	2,119	1,854	3,973
West Germany	992	2,074	3,066
Greece	583	622	1,205
Iceland	—	112	112
Italy	1,099	1,000	2,099
Netherlands	365	767	1,132
Norway	39	194	233
Sweden	1	80	81
Trieste	13	23	37
Turkey	29	230	258
Other ERP countries	2	27	29
Unallocated ERP countries	158	256	414
Totals	10,116	10,735	20,851

SOURCE: The International Studies Group of the Brookings Institution, *Current Issues in Foreign Economic Assistance* (Washington, The Brookings Institution, 1951), p. 73.

Revealed in this first table is the fact that for both Great Britain and France economic assistance given before the beginning of the European Recovery Program exceeded, by a substantial sum in the case of Britain, that actually disbursed under the Program itself. On the other hand, Germany, which had hitherto received less than $1 billion, more than doubled its portion. The special problem of Germany in connection with Western European economic and military cooperation will be considered in detail below. Britain, France, and West Germany together received almost three fifths of the total assistance given under the European Recovery Program, a total of more than $6.25 billions.

PRODUCTION AND COMPARATIVE PER CAPITA INCOME

Country	Coal (millions of tons)	Crude Steel (millions of tons)	Per Capita Income (dollars)
United Kingdom	18.3	1.4	773
Western Germany	9.2	1.1	320
France (incl. Saar)	5.4	0.9	482
Belgium-Luxembourg	2.4	0.6	582
Italy	—	0.2	235
Netherlands	1.1	—	502
Soviet Union	21.0	2.1	308
United States	46.0	7.4	1,453

SOURCE: The International Studies Group of the Brookings Institution, *Current Issues in Foreign Economic Assistance* (Washington, The Brookings Institution, 1951), p. 79.

AMERICAN PRESSURE FOR "INTEGRATION" AND "UNIFICATION"

It was apparent from the outset of the European Recovery Program that if the goal of a self-sustaining Western European economy were to be reached by the conclusion of the program in 1952, unparalleled efforts in economic cooperation had to be made by the countries involved. As the program developed, therefore, increasing attention was devoted by the ECA to this objective. The United States had magic words for its goal. They were "integration" and "unification." Just what they meant was frequently in doubt both in this country and in European nations, some of which, like Great Britain, were noticeably reluctant to take steps which they felt might endanger their own national efforts.

It is the "policy of the people of the United States to encourage the unification of Europe," declared Congress in the Foreign Aid Act of 1948. On his return from Europe in the Fall of that year Administrator Paul Hoffman reported that "the long-range goal I put before the OEEC was the effective integration of the economy of Western Europe—the building of a single market of 270 million consumers, in which quantitative restrictions on the movement of goods, monetary barriers to the flow of payments and eventually all tariffs should be permanently swept away."

Some important implications followed from this goal which the United States had set for Europe. To accomplish it or even to make substantial progress toward it would necessitate a far more positive, active role on the part of the United States in the area than had previously been envisaged. Measures would have to be carried out in day-to-day operations which would render meaningless the traditional legalistic distinction between "intervention" and "nonintervention." If national rights guarded for centuries by European states were to be broken down, there had to be a degree of sustained participation on the part of American officials in many aspects of European state policy unparalleled in the relations between modern large states and reversing altogether the relationship between the United States and Europe prevailing during the nineteenth century. The other side of the coin, which Congress was conspicuously reticent about examining, was the obligation of the United States to buy more of what Europe produced at the same time that Europe was being encouraged to get along with far fewer imports from the United States. Paul Hoffman maintained that private capitalism could make this adjustment. Secretary Acheson said that government assistance to individual American establishments might be necessary. Whether political conditions would permit either development remained uncertain.

EUROPEAN EFFORTS AT ECONOMIC COOPERATION

The accomplishments of the ECA naturally fell far short of European integration, but a beginning was made. The Organization for European Economic Cooperation (OEEC) was forced, in spite of the reluctance of some of its members, to accept the responsibility for collective recommendations concerning the allocation of assistance. A more tangible result was the establishment, after considerable negotiation, which included pressure from the United States, of a strengthened European Payments Union, an improvement over earlier efforts in that it "provides for a multilateral, rather than a bilateral settlement of payments within the area; it is free from some of the rigidities and inflexibilities inherent in the earlier system's advance calculations of bilateral trade balances; the fact that the surplus and the deficits are to be settled, not by gifts, but by gold or dollar payments and credit provides great incentives for creditors to increase imports and debtors to increase exports; and it does not rely completely on United States dollar assistance, as had the earlier plans, and so is capable of functioning after ECA aid ceases."* So far the Payments Union has been able to survive serious strains created by rapid fluctuations in the credit-deficit position of some of its members, notably Great Britain and West Germany, the chronic deficit position of France and Italy, and the continuing strong creditor position of Belgium. Part of the agreement setting up the Payments Union was aimed at promoting more liberal trading principles among the participants. Clauses, albeit with exceptions, provided for the elimination of discriminatory national trade measures and the progressive removal of import quotas. The schedule for the freeing of imports was met, but it did not take account of the frequently substantial imports on government account.

Other plans for economic integration among restricted numbers of Western European countries remained mostly on paper. The date for completion of the Benelux economic union was postponed until January 1, 1951, and then postponed indefinitely, the conflict being too great between the con-

---

* International Financial Section, *Survey of United States International Finance* (Princeton, N. J., Princeton University, 1950), p. 267.

trolled economy of Holland, with a soft currency, slow recovery, little unemployment, and the relatively free economy of Belgium, with a hard currency, rapid recovery, and considerable unemployment. The French Economic Council disapproved of, and the French Assembly did not ratify, the Franco-Italian agreement of March, 1949, which had called for a customs union between the two countries to be accomplished by 1950. The French, who were anxious to push off for multilateral settlement many of the economic problems with which they could not cope themselves, were unwilling to aid in the bilateral solution of problems connected with Italian unemployment and a low standard of living. By far the most ambitious and far-reaching proposal on the economic level was the Schuman Plan for the integration of Western European and West German coal and steel industries. More will be said about this plan below in connection with the problem of West Germany, but the plan itself, which was finally put into operation early in 1950, was potentially far broader than the two products directly involved, in that an organization was established which could serve as a basis for Western European pooling of other industrial and agricultural products and also for any political federation which could later be achieved.

NONECONOMIC ACCOMPLISHMENTS OF THE ECA

The main accomplishment of the Economic Cooperation Administration lay in the amount of goods it distributed and the production increases it generated. As the Foreign Assistance Act anticipated, most of the goods came from the United States, the dependence being heavier for industrial than for agricultural commodities. Although by 1950 neither industrial nor agricultural production had reached the goals set by the program, the production of coal had almost reached the 1937 level and steel production had exceeded the 1938 figure. Total industrial production exceeded the 1938 level by almost a quarter, an increase of almost one half over 1947. Agricultural production reached 103 per cent of the prewar average, and Western European dependence on overseas food sources was approaching the prewar figure of 34 per cent. By 1950 it was predicted that *if nothing intervened* the over-all goals of the program would be realized, on schedule, by 1952.

What did intervene, of course, was the Korean war, but before turning to the impact of military considerations on the relationship of the United States to Western Europe, something should be said about the noneconomic, less tangible accomplishments of the European Recovery Program. These included enabling Western European governments to maintain an anticommunist position, the economic integration of West Germany into the program, and the evolution of successful techniques for American cooperation with governments in vastly differing internal and external conditions.

Although Communists had been pushed out of the French and Italian governments in 1947, there remained the danger that the objectives of American assistance could be thwarted either by Communist capture of political power or by internal sabotage. In both countries economic and social conditions made the Communist appeal attractive to the voters. France, however, notwithstanding chronic cabinet collapses, was able to postpone any national election until the summer of 1951, when the beneficial impact of the Recovery Program was at its height. In Italy the elections of 1948 were fought largely on the issue of American assistance. With Ambassador Dunn ostentatiously emphasizing grain deliveries from the United States and with adroitly timed proposal that Trieste be returned to Italy, enough support was engendered to enable the coalition organized around the Christian Democrats of De Gasperi to hold the Communists at bay. In both countries Communist-organized strikes and demonstrations were aimed at slowing national recovery efforts, although they were masked as protests against low wages and rising prices. The Communists in France retained their grip on the large industrial trade unions, but the willingness of the government, especially of Socialist Interior Minister Jules Moch in the crippling strikes of 1948, to take strenuous measures prevented the strikes and demonstrations from achieving their *political* result. They did, however, lay the groundwork for further manifestations of labor discontent by making plain the inability of the French government to maintain economic recovery and to satisfy the legitimate grievances of the workers at the same time. Inevitably weakened in the process was the popular appeal of French socialism as a reformist movement. In Italy, also, a government which found it difficult to remove the basic causes of *economic* unrest, at least was successful in preventing the Communists from turning unrest into political channels for their own benefit.

West German participation in the European Recovery Program was part of the conscious effort by American occupation authorities to reverse the original, punitive objectives in favor of rapid rehabilitation of Germany as an economic and political entity. This decision was in turn based on a fusion of three ideas: that agreement with the Russians on any basis satisfactory to the West was impossible, that German economic recovery was indispensable to the recovery of Western Europe, and that the American taxpayer, now being asked to assist Western Europe, should be relieved of some of the burden resulting from a punitive German occupation. The consequence was that West Germany was made a member of the Marshall Plan even before the creation of the political apparatus of the West German state. This development cast General Clay in the interesting, if somewhat anomalous, role of German advocate in the deliberations of Western European governments, competing for a share of the resources to be made available by his government even against the recommendations made by his nominal superiors in Washington. As a consequence of the re-entrance of a truncated Germany into Western European economic affairs, both McCloy, Clay's successor, and Secretary Acheson were in April, 1950, officially calling for *full* West German integration into Western Europe.

THE SCHUMAN PLAN

No clearer example can be cited of the intimate connection between economics and politics than the French proposal known as the Schuman Plan. At all stages in the postwar period the French had given strong indication of their fear of what a revived Germany might mean to the security of France, whether Germany were inside or outside the formal framework of economic cooperation. It was the same old fear, kept alive by the national memory of three invasions within three quarters of a century, that twice as many Germans as Frenchmen (an equal number if only West Germany were counted) and an overwhelming German economic power, even without Alsace-Lorraine and the Saar, could add up to renewed German domination over Western Europe. At the same time, France could do nothing on its own to remove this potential threat. France well knew that the United States could, and quite probably would, create a strong West Germany regardless of the attitude of France. Nor was the French government able to take effective national action which would raise its own relative power. The solution which France found to its distressing dilemma was contained in two brilliant diplomatic suggestions. The first, made by Foreign Minister Robert Schuman in the spring of 1950, was a proposal "to place all French and German steel and coal production under a common high authority in an organization open to the other European countries." The second, which will be discussed later in this chapter, was to merge German troops into a European international army.

President Truman called the Schuman proposal "an act of constructive statesmanship," and a publication of the State Department quoted Schuman's hopeful words on the consequent impossibility of another Franco-German conflict. But what, exactly, was the plan, and to what other countries would it apply? To the British it was so vague as to be nebulous, but seemed probably to envisage precisely the type of privately powered international cartel in which no Socialist government would want to take part. Hence Great Britain politely declined to participate, thereby arousing the ire of American congressmen, who had little sympathy with socialism anyway. Italy and the Benelux countries met with French and German officials for months before the plan emerged as a fifty-year treaty signed on April 19, 1951, and was put into formal operation sixteen months later, in August, 1952, although the coal-steel "pool" itself was not formally initiated until February, 1953. The clauses of the treaty revealed a succession of elaborate devices to regulate coal and steel production, beginning with a Higher Authority and including a Consultative Committee, on which employers, unions, and workers were to be represented, a political Assembly and Council, and a Court of Justice to adjudicate complaints. Full pooling of the steel resources of the signators could only come gradually upon the successive solution of such complex problems as the high cost of Belgian coal, the relationship of Britain to the plan, and the determination of a status satisfactory to both France and Germany for the valuable Saar territory.

If the appeal of the plan to the five Western European countries was the fear of German power and a desire to harness it to their own welfare, the appeal to West Germany was the interest in taking one more step on the rapidly shortening road toward the recapture of national sovereignty. Concretely, the plan was viewed as a device to eliminate the International Ruhr Authority, which under the Occupation Statute was setting limits on steel production and hampering the complete return to industrial control of the Ruhr titans who had so willingly cooperated with the Hitler regime. It is clear, therefore, that there was a direct connection between the Schuman Plan and the increasing American efforts to gain German *military* cooperation in Western Europe. If the Ruhr industrialists, who never liked the decartelization elements in the Schuman Plan anyway, could gain their freedom from the Ruhr Authority without any such new commitments, why should Germany ratify the treaty at all? Acceptance of the plan by West Germany hence stood as a tribute to the power and adroitness of the Adenauer government in winning out over pressure from the right and opposition from the supernationalist Social Democratic party of Kurt Schumacher.

► MILITARY POLICY: THE TRANSITION FROM ECONOMIC TO MILITARY ASSISTANCE

Before the European Recovery Program was a year old, the United States took a further step in support of the thesis that American security could be maintained only if Western Europe remained out of Soviet hands. Economic assistance could bolster national governments against communism striking from within and was indispensable to the attainment of strength to resist external aggression. But to counteract Soviet expansionism there had to be military power in Western Europe. Events of 1947 and 1948 brought home to the West the decidedly uncomfortable fact that should the Russian and satellite armies decide to march, there was little to prevent them from reaching the English Channel. The weakness of Western Europe in the military field might provide an invitation to Soviet aggression which would plunge the world into another global catastrophe.

Nor was the danger of such aggression considered remote. As has been mentioned earlier, the Soviet answer to Allied moves to create political institutions in West Germany was a blockade of Berlin which brought the world to the very brink of war. Soviet aircraft menaced Allied planes flying the narrow "corridor of freedom," while Soviet power completely isolated on the ground the tiny area of Berlin, set in the middle of the Russian occupation zone. Even before the airlift demonstrated that Berlin could, contrary to Soviet and some Allied expectations, last through the winter, Czech

Communists had seized control of their government under the benevolently watchful eye of the Kremlin. At the same time, in the Far East, Chiang's armies melted away, despite $2 billion in American economic and military assistance. China was passing into Communist hands without any direct participation by the Russians at all. To the anxious West it looked as though the next Soviet move, one which the West was powerless to thwart, would be to concentrate its power in Europe and take as much as possible of that already divided continent in its communist grasp.

After the creation of the West German state the United States faced the problem of finding means of continuing and augmenting its contribution to the maintenance of Western European security, since the movement of Germany toward national sovereignty necessarily lessened the ability of the United States to express its power directly in Germany either to keep the Germans in line or to confront Soviet positions in the Eastern Zone. A way therefore had to be found to show both Western Europe and Russia that the revival of Germany was part of an increased rather than a decreased responsibility in Europe. A solution involved three coordinate measures: (1) military assistance to Western Europe, (2) augmented direct American power in Europe, and (3) closer affiliation of West Germany with the other countries in the area. The instrument devised was the same as had been applied to the Western Hemisphere in the Rio Treaty, a regional security pact declared to be compatible with the United Nations, one which would specifically define the military commitment of the United States. Foundation for such a move had been laid in Europe by the Brussels Pact of March, 1948, which, in turn, had been founded on the Anglo-French Treaty of Dunkerque, and in the United States by the ratification of the Rio Treaty and the adoption by the Senate of the Vandenberg Resolution. So far as these measures were related to the concept of international organization in American foreign policy they will be examined in a later chapter.* But the question here is this: What did they mean in the relationship of the United States to Western Europe?

THE NORTH ATLANTIC PACT

Negotiations which began in Washington in the fall of 1948 culminated in the signing of the North Atlantic Treaty by representatives of twelve countries in April, 1949. The ceremony was not without its ludicrous overtones— the band present for the occasion included among its selections "I Got Plenty of Nuttin' "—but the basic mood was one of solemnity. The activating clause of the treaty was the one-sentence first paragraph of Article 5: "The Parties agree that an armed attack against one or more of them in Europe or North America shall be considered an attack against them all; and conse-

---

* Chapter Twenty, "The Place of International Organization in American Foreign Policy."

quently they agree that, if such an armed attack occurs, each of them, in exercise of the right of individual or collective self-defense recognized by Article 51 of the Charter of the United Nations, will assist the Party or Parties so attacked by taking forthwith, individually and in concert with the other Parties, such action as it deems necessary, including the use of armed force, to restore and maintain the security of the North Atlantic area."

Article 6 went on to make clear that the treaty would operate, not only with respect to the home territories of the signatory states, but also in case of attack "on the Algerian departments of France, on the occupation forces of any Party in Europe, on the islands under the jurisdiction of any Party in the North Atlantic area north of the Tropic of Cancer or on the vessels or aircraft in this area of any of the Parties." The inclusion of part of Africa and of Italy in the North Atlantic might be stretching the definition of that term slightly, but no one considered such details of any importance.

On the surface the treaty appeared fairly clear and precise, but before Senate ratification had been accomplished that body had had over three months to explore all its terminology. What concerned the Senate most was whether the treaty deprived Congress of the right to declare war. In actuality the very nature of modern conflict had already removed that right, making a declaration of war a formality, as the attack on Pearl Harbor had demonstrated. Totalitarian nations did not abide by the amenities of following a formal diplomatic warning by declarations of mobilization, then by declarations of war, and finally by attack. The attack came first. However, Secretary Acheson, already far from enjoying universal popularity in Congress, could not tell the Senate that in clinging to its cherished prerogative it was clinging to an anachronism. Instead he called on his dexterity as a lawyer to reassure the Senate that the only commitment being made was to "restore and maintain the security of the North Atlantic area." Just how that was to be done would still be determined by the government of the United States, its executive and legislative branches. At this point Western Europeans unacquainted with American political processes must have wondered whether they had any American commitment at all, should the United States seek to use the large escape hatch contained in Article 5.

On July 21, 1949, four important votes were taken on the treaty. One was an amendment introduced by Republican Senator Watkins, specifically denying any obligation on Congress to declare war if a treaty-member were attacked; another, also by Watkins, denied any obligation on the United States to use its armed forces without the express approval of Congress. Both were overwhelmingly defeated by votes of 87 to 8 and 51 to 11, respectively. Included in the minority was only one Democrat, Senator Glen Taylor, the vice-presidential nominee in 1948 of Henry Wallace's Progressive party. The third amendment, defeated 74 to 21, with three Democrats on the losing end (Byrd, Johnson of Colorado, and Taylor) would have denied any obligation by the United States to provide military aid to Western Europe. On the treaty itself 82 voted for ratification, 13 against, including Democrats Johnson and Taylor. Republican opposition included Donnell, who had led the fight on the treaty, Floor Leader Wherry, and Senator Taft, previously regarded as the Republican spokesman on domestic issues, but with the continuing illness of Senator Vandenberg, increasingly outspoken on matters of foreign policy.

IMPLEMENTATION OF THE NORTH ATLANTIC TREATY

What Americans said the treaty meant was obviously of less importance than the meaning given to it by concrete American policy. Implementation of the agreement by the United States since 1949 has taken five significant forms, three involving further extended debate in Congress. The government took steps to increase American military power in the United States, a movement that attained the level of partial mobilization after the Chinese intervention in Korea in November, 1950. While the eyes of the American people were fixed on the actual fighting in Korea, the administration repeatedly made it clear that heavy pressure by General MacArthur and others would not alter the priority of concern with Western European security.

Of the other four measures taken under the pact, two involved direct American participation and two the rearmament of the countries in the area. Congress was prepared to agree to the dispatch of further American divisions to augment those stationed in West Germany, although it was not willing to give the Executive Branch carte blanche to raise the number of American soldiers in Europe to any size that military authorities might desire. There was, on the other hand, virtually unanimous enthusiasm over the nomination of General Eisenhower as head of the North Atlantic Treaty Organization. Notwithstanding his reputed presidential ambitions, the Columbia University president enjoyed highest esteem in both the Democratic and Republican camps. The new commander of the North Atlantic Pact forces lost no time in throwing the full weight of his power and prestige behind the effort to translate paper obligations of the signatory states into military strength in being. His determination to execute the job entrusted to him and his quiet optimism that the job of defending Western Europe in Western Europe actually could be done acted from the first as a source of inspiration on both sides of the Atlantic in the dark days of Korean catastrophe.

The North Atlantic Pact provided both the occasion and the machinery for the development of large-scale military assistance to Western Europe. Even before the ink was dry on the treaty, the administration asked Congress to pass on requests submitted by the pact countries. As the votes on treaty amendments given above indicate, the legislative body was prepared, albeit belatedly, to accept this interpretation of America's obligation. The first installment on account was authorized on September 29, 1949, although military material did not begin to reach Western Europe in quantity until the spring of 1950. In granting military assistance, both Congress and the Executive Branch made it plain that there was no substitute for Western European rearmament. As in the case of the European Recovery Program, primary responsibility rested upon the nations of the area themselves. The United States was willing to aid and cooperate only in an undertaking that would be a collective responsibility.

EFFECT OF THE NORTH ATLANTIC TREATY ON EUROPEAN ECONOMIC RECOVERY

Serious problems were created by the intrusion of military considerations into the economic relationship between the United States and Western Europe. At first, Congress had declared that it "recognizes that economic recovery is essential to international peace and security and *must be given clear priority.** If these words were meant as something more than soothing sirup to American antimilitarists and European "neutralists," they carried the implication that this country intended to rearm itself and Western Europe while at the same time continuing to promote European production and consumer standards of living.

Until 1950 the essential impossibility of doing everything at once was obscured by heavy American purchases in Europe for its own rearmament and the delay of Western European countries in taking national measures to increase their own military strength. After November, 1950, however, a clear priority began to emerge which was the direct opposite of that contained in the Congressional pronouncement just quoted. Henceforth economic policies would be considered in the light of the overriding objective of rearming Western Europe, not only with American-produced equipment, but, more important, by the conversion of European production facilities to fulfill military demands. The shift in the relative priority of economic and military techniques was made explicit by Congress in passing the 1951 multibillion-dollar overseas aid bill. Congress cut a quarter of a billion from the amount requested by President Truman for continued economic assistance to Europe, and the final amount, $1,022,000,000 was roughly one fifth of the $5,072,-476,271 appropriated for military aid. Creation of the Mutual Security Agency as successor to the Economic Cooperation Administration demonstrated that henceforth the primary purpose of economic aid was going to be the support of the program for the rearmament of Europe.

As they attempted to rearm, America's European allies came face to face with an extremely uncomfortable predicament from which there were in theory only three escape routes. Individual countries could export more to the United States and buy far less, using the gain to help finance their arms production. It appeared that, short of drastic change of American import

---

* Quoted by Richard C. Stebbins, et al., *The United States in World Affairs, 1950* (New York, Harpers & Brothers), p. 123.

practices, exports to this country from Western Europe could not by individual or collective national effort be pushed much beyond the level attained with ERP assistance, particularly in a period that would demand reallocation of their own resources from the export market to meet rearmament requirements. Reduction of imports, on the other hand, would have an immediate, damaging impact on domestic standards of living and quite probably on national production levels as well.

A second way out would, in theory, be a decision by the countries of Western Europe to maintain standards of living at the levels attained, holding fast to economic recovery before undertaking rearmament. This was the course advocated by Aneurin Bevan in Britain and "neutralists," Communists, and others in France. It would result in failure to achieve the military strength on which the North Atlantic Treaty Organization was predicated, and would, instead, perpetuate conditions conducive to communist aggression. Thoroughly implemented determination to pursue this course could only result in destroying the presumptions on which the North Atlantic Pact was based, and could thereby lead the United States to reduce and perhaps to eliminate both economic and military assistance.

Finally, Western European governments could tighten the belts of their people once more, sacrificing the domestic economy to military exigencies. This avenue toward security was naturally unwelcome to countries which had just begun to see the delayed dawn of recovery from the ravages of the worst war in history. To follow it would demand not only a high degree of national morale, but also stable, efficient, and determined governments. It would require mutual understanding on both sides of the Atlantic: in America, understanding of the sacrifices of peoples whose standard of living, partially revealed in income figures listed above, was already far below the American level; in Europe, understanding that the fault, after all, did not lie with greedy American desires to achieve hegemony over half the globe but rather lay at the doors of the Kremlin, which definitely wanted hegemony over as much of the globe as possible.

CORRELATION OF MILITARY AND ECONOMIC PROGRAMS

At the Ottawa meeting of the North Atlantic Pact countries in 1951 Western European representatives presented for joint consideration their dilemma and the unattractive nature of any one of the three solutions mentioned above. Out of the discussion came several decisions, all based on acceptance of the fact that the problem would continue to be present so long as American and Western European rearmament continued. W. Averell Harriman, the director of the Mutual Security Agency, and a limited number of representatives from the Western European countries on whom the military burden fell most heavily were charged with the task of assessing European needs in the light of rearmament commitments. The job would be in the nature of a continuing audit of capabilities and requirements, on which the United States could base a flexible program of military and economic assistance.

The United States, further, appeared willing to transfer funds appropriated within the limits set by Congress from the military to the economic category and to give priority insofar as possible to types of military assistance which would place dollars in the hands of Western European countries. Finally, it was recognized that, while each cooperating country must bear a just share of the burden, it was almost impossible to make hard-and-fast commitments as to the military strength which could be attained over a three-year span. From this fact the logical conclusion was drawn by those most concerned with the creation of a European army: that greater emphasis should be placed on fulfillment of limited, early goals within the first year as the indispensable foundation on which to base effective plans for later buildup.

Further efforts were made to cope with these unprecedented problems at the meeting of the NATO Council of Foreign Ministers in Lisbon in February, 1952. A definite commitment to create *present* military power rather than paper divisions for future delivery was contained in the announcement that "the NATO nations agreed to provide approximately fifty divisions in appropriate conditions of combat readiness . . ." by the end of 1952, an increase of some twenty divisions over those then available to General Eisenhower. As was apparent from the statement, however, General Ridgway, successor to the Republican presidential candidate, would not find all fifty divisions at his beck and call on December 31, 1952. The Lisbon conferees also formally approved two related projects: the creation of an integrated European army (the European Defense Community) and West Germany's association with it in a status of recovered sovereignty.

No sooner had the definite NATO goals been announced than the countries of Western Europe on which the strength of the organization depended began to experience not unexpected difficulties in fulfilling their commitments. The strength of national economies and the stability of individual governments varied from country to country. Economic pains forced Churchill's British government to announce that national rearmament programs would have to be stretched out over a longer period than originally contemplated. No one was more pleased to hear this than Labor-rebel Aneurin Bevan, who had resigned from Attlee's government after telling his prime minister that rearmament could and should be diminished. In France a precariously poised right-of-center coalition pressed hard for increased American assistance to the tune of $625 million, which the French thought had been promised them at Lisbon. Without this aid, the French argued, their financial situation would continue to deteriorate and France's rearmament schedule would of necessity be revised. In Italy, where the government appeared to be in a stronger position than in France, a gravely weak domestic economy made doubtful any substantial military contributions over and above the strengthening of Italy's security position in the Mediterranean and in relation to Central and Eastern Europe.

► RELATIONSHIPS OF EUROPEAN COUNTRIES
TO THE COLD-WAR LINE

In part, variation in the ability of various European governments to cooperate in mutual defense arose from their fundamentally different relationships to the East-West cold-war line. This factor complicated the task of the North Atlantic Treaty Organization in arriving at basic military plans that would be both effective and acceptable to all the partners. Brief attention should therefore be given to the positions of Great Britain, West Germany, France, Spain, Yugoslavia, Greece, and Turkey.

BRITISH POSITION WITH RESPECT TO EUROPE

Great Britain has always been a part and yet not a part of Europe. The essential ambiguity of its relationship was deepened as a result of World War II. On the one hand, the ability of modern warfare to overwhelm entire countries in a few days had reduced the English Channel to a small ditch, too wide for Hitler to cross but not wide enough to prevent vast physical destruction throughout England. Western European weakness in the face of the Soviet challenge necessarily entailed increased involvement of England in Continental security. The time was gone, never to return, when Britain could retire from Europe into "splendid isolation" and from its insular position manipulate for its own purposes the European balance of power. Britain was now an inextricable part of that balance and would be courting prompt destruction if its side of the scales should become outweighed.

On the other hand, Britain's very weakness drew the home isles away from the Continent toward closer relations with the Empire and the Commonwealth. For all its diminished state, Great Britain was still the center of a world-wide system, which was incapable of precise definition, but nonetheless involved obligations and responsibilities far from Europe. Metropolitan France could focus on itself all the overseas empire, but this policy was manifestly impossible for Great Britain, which was only the senior partner in a commonwealth of sovereign, independent states. Thus Britain found the balance between European and global commitments delicate to maintain. This fact lay behind the manifest British reluctance to enter fully into cooperative measures in Europe: its early resistance to the European Payments Union, its flat refusal to join the Schuman Plan, its limited commitment to the projected European Defense Community, and its progressive cooling toward any Western European political union. Great Britain, by reason of power, position, and responsibility, demanded for itself a special relationship to Europe and to the United States. There was little reason to believe that the demand would be ignored in the United States, despite American annoyance at its ally's heel dragging on measures for European "integration." For the United States Great Britain was the number one ally against the Soviet Union, not only in Europe, but wherever Soviet power was confronted.

REARMAMENT OF WEST GERMANY

This chapter has recurrently emphasized the fact that recovery by Allied-occupied West Germany of increasing freedom was inevitable, once recogniton had been given to the twin factors of Western European weakness and Soviet expansionism. The culmination of this movement was reached with open, official American discussion of German rearmament after months of veiled hints and ambiguous denials. Said John A. McCloy on September 4, 1950: "In some manner, in some form the Germans should be enabled, if they want to, to defend their own country. It seems so difficult to say to these people that you can't share in the defense of your country if you're attacked. If that sounds like rearmament [what else could it have sounded like?] then it's rearmament."*

By the time McCloy spoke almost all of the original American policies in Germany had been abandoned short of accomplishment. Decartelization and deconcentration of industry had never gone very far or enjoyed more than lukewarm support in the higher echelons of General Clay's command. Many of the Nazis who had been uprooted and penalized under "traffic court" procedure, and many others who had never been touched, were back at work at the same old stands: in industry, in education, in the legal system, in the government bureaucracy. In October, 1951, Chancellor Adenauer admitted that 134 officials of his Foreign Ministry had been members of the Nazi party. At about the same time Otto Dietrich, former boss of the Nazi press, openly reappeared as an editor of an official trade publication in Düsseldorf. German "democracy," Adenauer style, left much to be desired by Western standards. It was even doubtful how long the wily leader could hold his own against even more extremist, nationalist, antidemocratic elements. High officers of Hitler's armies, including those in the late Fuehrer's Elite Corps, were openly creating veterans' organizations. The Socialist Reich party, which the West German government formally repressed, had won suffcent support to demonstrate the attraction for the Germans of a program strikingly similar to that of National Socialism. Now demilitarization, the one original occupation objective which had been accomplished, was to be undone.

It was against this background that the second brilliant stroke of French diplomacy was made (the first being the Schuman Plan referred to earlier). The French well knew that they could not hold back German rearmament indefinitely against the exigencies of military weakness in other Western European countries and the consequent pressure exerted by the United

* New York *Times,* September 5, 1950, p. 1.

States. On the other hand, France was naturally unwilling to permit the kind of all-out, no-strings-attached rearmament of Germany which could only place the perennial enemy once again in the position of being able to dominate Western Europe. The French proposal, made by René Pleven, was that small German units be assimilated into a European army after this army had actually come into existence.

The Pleven Plan, adhered to with tenacity by French negotiators, was enough to stop in their tracks plans for immediate German rearmament when the question was first officially raised at a meeting of the West's Big Three in Washington in November, 1950. Britain was cool to the plan, the Americans noticeably hostile. The French persisted. Adenauer, as he had done so often in the past, took advantage of the situation to place all three occupying powers on the defensive. If the West wanted German rearmament, Germany would be happy to oblige, *provided* that there be a virtual ending of the occupation and resumption by West Germany of sovereign status. But the price of any such change in the status of Germany, said the French, had to be ratification of the Schuman Plan as well as the implementation of the Pleven Plan. Otherwise it was a certainty that the Schuman, and perhaps both plans, would be lost.

Thus were the three elements intertwined: a European army, a merger of West European steel-producing facilities, and the resumption of full sovereignty by Germany. It took a year to convince the United States that the three were truly inextricable, a year of French persistence and Adenauerish mixture of bluster and conciliation, plus an opportune invitation from communist East Germany to discuss unification of all Germany. This last move the West could not tolerate, nor was Adenauer, whose Christian Democrats, unlike the German Socialists, were principally a West-zonal party, much more anxious that the merger take place, particularly if the three Western powers would give him what he wanted.

From the mélange, after many months of tortuous negotiation, there came two agreements as significant as any signed in the postwar period. The first was a collection of five documents aimed at the creation of the European army (called the European Defense Community) and its close association with the North Atlantic Treaty Organization. Involved in this arrangement were the Benelux countries (the Netherlands, Belgium, and Luxembourg), Italy, France, and West Germany. The Defense Community Treaty was to be of fifty years' duration, a normal, arbitrary limit for such instruments. The international army was to be composed of contingents assigned by the member states, would wear a common uniform, and be subject to the command of the North Atlantic Treaty Organization. As in the case of the Schuman Plan, however, the Defense Community had its own supervisory instrumentalities: a Council of Ministers composed of representatives of the six signators; a Commissariat, which was an executive organ of nine members serving six-year terms, supposedly supranational in the sense that it was not directly responsible to any government, charged with organizing and administering the forces of the Defense Community, but not, as noted above, with their actual, military command; an Assembly, temporarily the same body as that provided under the Schuman Plan, but, when made permanent, to constitute "one of the elements of an ultimate federal or confederal structure founded on the principle of separation of powers and entailing a system of bicameral representation"; and a Court of Justice to settle disputes. Obviously the Defense Community Treaty would be in full operation, not when the states composing the Defense Community had ratified the treaty, but only when an international army had actually been brought into being and when Western European unity had made the difficult transition from dream to reality.

But in the meantime the importance of the treaty lay in the avenue it provided for the rearmament of West Germany and its association with the North Atlantic Treaty Organization. The other five signators were already NATO members, but the decision not to admit West Germany to full participation led to additional organizational and administrative problems. To meet them four other documents were signed, along with the Defense Community Treaty. The first was a protocol providing for reciprocal assistance between Great Britain and the Defense Community. The second was a protocol to the North Atlantic Treaty extending that treaty's guarantees to the Defense Community, a provision referring only to West Germany, since the other states involved were already covered; the third, a protocol by the Defense Community reciprocating the guarantees to the North Atlantic Treaty members. Finally, there was a statement by Secretary of State Acheson and Foreign Minister Eden designed to relieve the fears of the French that West Germany, once in possession of its sovereignty, might turn against the Defense Community. The United States and Great Britain, reads the declaration, would regard any threat to the integrity or unity of the European Defense Community as a threat to their own security and would maintain in Europe "such forces as they deem necessary and appropriate to contribute to the joint defense of the North Atlantic area."

Intimately related to the documents involving the European Defense Community were the contractual arrangements signed by the representatives of the United States, Great Britain, and West Germany. When put into operation, they would change the status of West Germany from that of occupied country to participating member of the free world. As the official summary states, this transition was a complex process, a fact which is reflected in the number and length of the contractual agreements. The drafting of these agreements required great care and skill, since they were not and could not be a peace treaty definitively liquidating the war. Germany was still divided and no one wished the division to be permanent. Moreover, West Germany was on the very frontier of the East-West conflict and, so long as it was in this position, would need direct military assistance in the form of foreign troops, formerly occupying forces, now defenders of West German

reedom. The contractual arrangements therefore had to deal with this three-
old problem: the sovereignty of West Germany, the division of Germany,
and the maintenance of non-German forces on West German soil.

The Convention on Relations between the Three Powers and the Federal
Republic provided for the freedom of West Germany, limited only by specified
rights reserved to the former occupying powers. The Occupation Statute was
o be repealed (making necessary additional conventions mentioned below);
the Allied High Commissions and Land Commissions were to be abolished
and future relations were to be conducted through ambassadors. For its part
he Federal Republic agreed to conduct its affairs in conformity with the
Charter of the United Nations, even though it could not become a member
of that organization so long as the Soviet Union possessed a veto. The
reserved rights of the three powers concerned the stationing of troops, the
declaration of a state of emergency in all or part of the Federal Republic, the
protection of the position of the three nations in Berlin, in which the Federal
Government was to assist, and the conduct of negotiations leading to the
reunification of Germany.

The Convention on the Settlement of Matters Arising Out of the War
and the Occupation could be only provisional in nature because the three
powers had no authority to negotiate any definitive peace treaty with Germany. This convention of twelve articles contains clauses on such technical
subjects as Germany's prewar external debt, restitution of foreign property
rights, and the waiver by Germany of claims growing out of the war and
occupation, all conventional clauses in peace treaties. Another article leaves
open the subject of reparations for later determination, when and if a peace
treaty is negotiated. Finally, this convention incorporates pious statements
by West Germany on two basic objectives of the occupation: deconcentration
of industry, and compensation for Nazi victims. With regard to the former
the convention noted that "the Federal Government has many times declared
its support for the program of deconcentration to destroy excessive concen-
trations of economic power." In the chapter on compensation the Federal
Republic assumed undertakings "in line with the unanimous declaration of
the Bundestag of the 15th October, 1951, concerning the need to make moral
and material amends to the victims of Nazi persecution." The official summary then adds, blandly, "This is a problem peculiar to Germany." While
there is no doubt concerning the fact that the West German state has undertaken these obligations, the fact that it has also recovered a substantial
measure of sovereignty removes the ability of the former occupation powers
to force any German government to fulfill them. There is little foundation for
optimism that deconcentration of industry or compensation for the victims
of Nazi persecution will be carried out in a manner deemed satisfactory to
the Western democracies.

The Convention on the Rights and Obligations of Foreign Forces and
Their Members in the Federal Republic is composed of fifty articles and two

annexes. In them are spelled out the details governing the relationship between the Western forces and the West German state, including provisions of materials, goods, and services, the protection of German labor employed by the Western forces, and the respective jurisdictions of foreign military and German civil legal tribunals.

The Finance Convention is one of the major links between the contractual agreements on the one hand and the European Defense Community and the North Atlantic Treaty Organization on the other. French, Belgian, and Luxembourgian forces stationed in West Germany are to become forces of the Defense Community. More important, the West German state assumes the triple commitment of contributing financial support to the Defense Community, to foreign forces stationed in its territory, and to its own rearmament.

Additional letters forming a part of the contractual agreements concern such details as Control Council legislation to continue in force after the ending of the occupation, radio frequencies, and private, prewar obligations of Germany. Finally, one of the letters confirms the understanding by the four signators that the new arrangement "does not constitute recognition by the Federal Republic of the present status of the Saar." Thus one of the most thorny of Franco-German issues, one which inevitably will affect the ability of Western Europe to achieve security on the basis of the interlocking agreements discussed in this chapter, still remains to be settled by two governments, neither of which can well afford to abandon the claims it has made to jurisdiction over that valuable area.

FRENCH ATTITUDES TOWARD WESTERN EUROPEAN SECURITY

For France, as this chapter has indicated, the necessity for rearmament merely added one more to a whole string of seemingly insoluble problems. To put forth the effort required to meet its obligations in Western European defense would jeopardize the progress made by France under the European Recovery Program. Not to do so would weaken French prestige, already badly shaken, and its claim to leadership in land defense and to coordinate naval responsibility with Great Britain in the Mediterranean. Rearmament before the delicate adjustment of Germany's economy with that of Western Europe had been consummated under the Schuman Plan would increase the potential superiority of the historic enemy's economy. To neglect military power when German rearmament was seemingly but a matter of time would raise again the specter of military inferiority. France had pushed hard for a political union of Europe as a way of surmounting its own national poblems, but the European Assembly and the Council of Europe would for a long period to come be only a gathering of state representatives; the barrier of sovereignty would have to be broken first through other devices.

France was engaged in a war in Indo-China, a war widely unpopular among Frenchmen, but one from which it could not extricate itself without irreparable damage to its prestige and without creating precedents of weakness which would invite further colonial revolt, notably in North Africa. The struggle against Asiatic communists had already weakened the ability of France to fight against European communists, foreign and domestic. The National Assembly elections in 1951 had returned the central coalition to power, thwarting the bid of General de Gaulle and alienating some Frenchmen from the Communist party. Would that coalition be able to hold France to rearmament schedules after the great bulk of Frenchmen felt the pressure on an already unsatisfactory standard of living? If the struggle against the Soviet Union entered the military phase, would French power be thrown unreservedly into the battle or would it be 1940 all over again, a divided people magnifying their own weakness? Succeeding coalition governments could only clutch at anything that promised to lighten the international burden on France. German rearmament could be delayed by the addition to the European Defense Community Treaty of French protocols which encumbered the process of ratification. Further negotiations with Indo-Chinese states could be undertaken in the hope that they would lead to more active native participation in the war against the Viet Minh. Appeals could be made to the United States for greater but vaguely defined assistance in the same war. Above all, French governments could see signs in the internal struggles of Communist-dominated Eastern Europe and in those of the Soviet Union itself that the Russian menace to Western Europe was abating, that further East-West negotiations might prove successful and thereby relieve France of many of its rearmament requirements.

POSITION OF SPAIN

Soviet expansionism and American policy had forced France to accede to the revival of the feared neighbor to the east; likewise they forced France to contemplate the rehabilitation of the detested neighbor to the south. The bases of the burgeoning American rapport with Franco deserve some examination. They exemplify the difficulty of determining *national* interest or *national* policy. The startling change in official relations with the erstwhile pariah was caused by the shift in the internal balance of conflicting forces within the United States under pressure from external events. Hostility to the little dictator was based on the totalitarian and oppressive nature of his regime and his collaboration with Hitler during World War II. Nor was it forgotten that Franco owed his power to German and Italian intervention in the Spanish Civil War. Anti-Franco policy was supported by both American labor organizations—the Congress of Industrial Organizations and the American Federation of Labor—which pointed to the Spanish dictator's persecution and suppression of labor groups and individuals in that unhappy country.

A position of opposition to Spanish fascism had seemed for years relatively stable in the upper branches of the State Department and in the White House. "You cannot have an intimate working partnership with such a regime in the economic field and in the defense field," declared Secretary Acheson on May 11, 1949. On January 19, 1950, the secretary was writing to Senator Connally that "it is difficult to envisage Spain as a full member of the free Western communities without substantial advances in such directions as increased civil liberties and as religious freedom and the freedom to exercise the elementary rights of organized labor." When the United Nations resolution, recommending the discontinuance of official relations with Spain, was repealed (with the support of American representatives) President Truman announced he would be in no hurry to send an ambassador to Spain. After the refusal of the Export-Import Bank to consider a loan to Franco, the President declared his personal opposition to such a loan. Even when the Congress authorized the granting of more than $62 million to Spain, Truman stated that executive implementation would not come for some time, if ever.

And yet the United States and Spain moved ever closer together. Why? For one reason, the Defense Department had never been impressed with the politico-ideological motivations of the anti-Franco policy. As problems of military security grew in importance, so did the weight of the Defense Department argument. Persistent and powerful support for *rapprochement* existed in Congress, to be seen especially in the efforts of the nominally Democratic Senator Pat McCarran to gain diplomatic recognition and then money for Spain. In addition, the administration stalwarts like Senator Tom Connally did not seem to be of exactly the same anti-Franco mind as Acheson and Truman. The Spanish loan, first denied by the Export-Import Bank, then narrowly defeated in Congress, finally passed. President Truman's stated denial of intention to implement the loan provisions contrasted with the actual utilization of the money by Spain soon afterward.

The long step toward American-Spanish accord was made in the summer of 1951 with the conclusion of negotiations by Admiral Sherman for American economic and military assistance to Spain in return for base rights in that country and its Mediterranean islands. The arrangement was made without any of the political or economic prerequisites mentioned by Secretary Acheson. Even before the Sherman agreement, the Spanish foreign minister had interpreted the reversal of American policy this way: "The great American nation seems to have been chastised by the fact that its last disillusionment [the sacrifice of Spain to appease Russia] has been marked in red with the young blood of its soldiers." Spain's "heroic crusade against Communist barbarity" had been vindicated. The West had come to the belated recognition that the elements in Spanish administration which it had deemed objectionable were in fact necessary to defeat communism.

Despite the protracted delay in entering upon full military and economic cooperation, the American-Spanish accord meant the *de facto* inclusion of Spain in the Western European security system, even without formal membership in the North Atlantic Treaty Organization. The rationale had been purely military. Spain had more to contribute in the way of manpower and defense installations than its highly unsavory regime could subtract. The economic cost of making that military contribution effective would be high, but the money would be well spent. Other European countries might feel uneasy, but their dependence on American dollars and American equipment left them little room for effective objection. Gone was any hope that Franco could be forced to reform or would be replaced altogether. Possibly economic assistance would still result in some alleviation of the sorry lot of the Spanish people.

YUGOSLAVIA'S RELATIONSHIP WITH THE WEST

Yugoslavia presents the other side of the Spanish coin. The break with the Cominform by Marshal Tito, once the shining jewel in the Kremlin crown, opened great opportunities to the West, provided, of course, that the break was permanent. Retrospective research uncovered a story of suspicion, mistrust, and conflict dating back to the early days of World War II, when the Soviet Union refused to aid Yugoslav Communists in any tangible manner. Cominform policy seemed to exclude Yugoslav reconciliation on any terms other than the humiliating, abject confession of heretical error so familiar to renegade Communists. The strong Marshal, whose own efforts had largely freed his country from the German yoke before the arrival of Russian troops, not only showed no signs of knuckling under, but actually had the temerity to claim that *he,* not the Kremlin or the Cominform, was the true Marxist and it was others who were the renegades. Moreover, in the months following the rupture, Yugoslav foreign policy moved from cautious abstention on issues of East-West conflict to carefully explained support of many elements in the American position.

If the United States were sufficiently adroit, the anti-Soviet coalition could be strengthened in a number of respects. A strong Yugoslavia would constitute a formidable barrier to further communist penetration of Southern Europe. Italian Communists, like their French comrades, would be isolated from direct contact with the source of their inspiration. The position of the Allies in the Mediterranean would be made more secure, and in the Adriatic also. Nor were these negative advantages without their positive counterparts. Officially friendly relations would demonstrate to Asiatic as well as to European peoples that it was not the United States which insisted on rigid orthodoxy as the price for cooperation—that governments of the left as well as of the right could find a place in the non-Soviet system compatible with the retention of sovereign power to determine their own political, economic, and social institutions. For Eastern European countries suffering under the increasingly constricting yoke of Soviet exploitation, Yugoslavia could serve as a shining beacon in the darkness, an indication of what could happen if they too could find their way out of the toils. And Yugoslavia could provide a base for the penetration of Titoism through the iron curtain. Purge upon purge in the satellite countries demonstrated that there were many in Eastern Europe who were nationalists first and Soviet serfs second. Rising discontent in Eastern Europe and the internal struggles of the Soviet Union could serve as a spur for national Communist leaders, an opportunity for cautiously expanded independent action with the ultimate goal of Tito's Yugoslavia before them. National communism in Eastern Europe was not, of course, the goal of American policy for that area, but certainly any weakening of Soviet power would be a gain for the West.

Slowly and carefully, for, when all was said and done, Tito was still a Communist and a dictator, United States policy moved to exploit its opportunities. Economic assistance was made available, not only from the United States proper but also in the form of a loan by the World Bank. An inspection tour by General Collins was the prelude to an agreement which would place American military equipment in the hands of Tito's army. An effectively outfitted Yugoslav striking force would give pause to Soviet satellites, Hungary, Rumania, Bulgaria, and isolated Albania; in addition it might be one more weight in the scale of deterence to Soviet aggression elsewhere. On his part, Tito took steps to make his regime more acceptable to the West, without weakening the bases of his own control. As with Spain, however, whether Yugoslavia could be formally affiliated with Western European defense was another question, the answer to which might be considerably delayed.

CHANGING POSITION OF GREECE AND TURKEY

Already Yugoslavia's separation from the Cominform had brought, if not friendship, at least considerable diminution in tension between that country and its neighbors already in the Western camp—Italy and Greece. For the latter this development meant that, after the end of the civil war, the way was cleared for expansion of the machinery of the North Atlantic Treaty Organization to include both it and Turkey. Both openly desired membership, Turkey feeling that it would be only deserved reward for military support of the United States and the United Nations in Korea. Further advantages to inclusion would be the facilitation of cooperation throughout the entire Mediterranean area and the formal warning to the Soviet Union that aggression against either country would automatically involve the full-scale retaliation by Western Europe and the United States. At the 1951 meeting of Atlantic Pact countries in Ottawa it was accordingly decided to amend the pact by individual consent of each member so that Turkey and Greece could be included.

ENLARGEMENT OF THE NORTH ATLANTIC PACT

Admission of Greece and Turkey made the "North Atlantic" Pact just a title, and a misleading one at that, for a primary instrument in a coalition which aimed at the containment of the Soviet Union everywhere in the world. American membership related the pact to defensive arrangements in the Far East which are discussed in another chapter. British participation entailed an Anglo-American cooperation which was global in its extent

Adherence of France and the Benelux countries, particularly if reinforced by a fully integrated West German state, ensured that the original objective of the pact—the security of Western Europe—could never be lost sight of. Italian and Greek membership symbolized the extension of the security system along the southern flank of Europe, in the Mediterranean. Finally, Turkey was to be the link between Western Europe and any security system which the West could negotiate with the countries of the Near East. Difficulties with explosive nationalism, anti-Westernism, Israeli-Arab hatred might indefinitely delay the construction of an orderly multilateral arrangement. They could not, however, obscure the interest which Turk, Arab, Israeli, Briton, and American had in common: to prevent encroachment on the Near East by the dangerously nearby Soviet Union.

► SELECTED BIBLIOGRAPHY

The yearly course of American policy with respect to Europe can be followed in pertinent portions of the annual volumes written by members of the Council on Foreign Relations, *The United States in World Affairs* (New York, Harper & Brothers, published annually). Among the best surveys of postwar European conditions are Theodore H. White, *Fire in the Ashes* (New York, William Sloane Associates, 1953) and Crane Brinton, *Temper of Western Europe* (Cambridge, Mass., Harvard University Press, 1953), while Hajo Holborn places *The Political Collapse of Europe* (New York, Alfred A. Knopf, Inc., 1951) in historical perspective. Varying approaches to European unity are considered by Barbara Ward in *The West at Bay* (New York, W. W. Norton & Company, 1948) and in *Policy for the West* (New York, W. W. Norton & Company, 1951); by Paul Reynaud in *Unite or Perish* (New York, Simon and Schuster, 1951); and by Paul Hoffman, *Peace Can Be Won* (New York, Doubleday & Company, 1951). European political organization is detailed by Frederick Schuman, "The Council of Europe," *American Political Science Review,* September, 1951. Comprehensive coverage is given to the European Recovery Program in Howard Ellis, *The Economics of Freedom* (New York, Harper & Brothers, 1950), and ECA accomplishments are assessed in Princeton University's International Finance Section's annual *Survey of United States International Finance.* Some studies made of the operations and implications of the North Atlantic Pact include Eugene Emons, "Politico-Military Aspects of Western Defense under the North Atlantic Pact," *Air University Quarterly,* Fall, 1950; Ernest Block, "European Rearmament and United States Foreign Aid," *Review of Politics and Statistics,* November, 1950; "NATO and World Peace," *Annals* of the American Academy of Political and Social Science, July, 1953; Blair Bolles, "The Armed Road to Peace," Foreign Policy Association Headline Series No. 92, March–April, 1952; and Drew Middleton, "NATO Changes Direction," *Foreign Affairs,* July, 1953. *The Saturday Review of Literature* has devoted two special issues to *The United States and Britain* and *The United States and Europe.* The same broad relationship is treated by

Saul Padover, "America and Europe," *Social Research,* December, 1950, and by some contributors to the Winter, 1951, issue of the *Columbia Journal of International Affairs,* entitled *American Foreign Policy.* Among the early postwar attempts to evaluate the position of Great Britain were Percy Corbett, *Britain, Partner for Peace* (New York, Harcourt, Brace & Company, 1946); Crane Brinton, *The United States and Britain* (Cambridge, Mass., Harvard University Press, 1945); William T. R. Fox, *The Super-Powers* (New York, Harcourt, Brace & Company, 1944); an Anglo-American conference report written by Henry Roberts and Paul Wilson, *Britain and the United States,* published for the Council on Foreign Relations by Harper & Brothers, 1953; the Royal Institute of International Affairs, *British Security* (London, Royal Institute, 1946). Two later studies by the Royal Institute should also be noted: *Defence in the Cold War* (London, Royal Institute, 1950) and *United Kingdom Policy* (London, Royal Institute, 1952). Edward Meade Earle has edited the offerings of many contributors in *Modern France* (Princeton, N. J., Princeton University Press, 1951) and Donald McKay considers *The United States and France* (Cambridge, Mass., Harvard University Press, 1951) against a predominantly historical background. From time to time *Foreign Affairs* has presented articles on French developments; and the Royal Institute has published Dorothy Pickles, *French Politics* (New York and London, Royal Institute, 1953). Lucius Clay gives an account of his stewardship in *Decision in Germany* (New York, Doubleday & Company, 1950) and a further look at American policy in the same country in *Germany and the Fight for Freedom* (Cambridge, Mass., Harvard University Press, 1951). The occupation period is also treated by Edward H. Litchfield, *et al.,* in *Governing Postwar Germany* (Ithaca, N. Y., Cornell University Press, 1953). A slightly different view is given, with special emphasis on economic policy, in James Stewart Martin, *All Honorable Men* (Boston, Little, Brown & Co., 1950); for denazification policy see Ira Hirschman, *The Embers Still Burn* (New York, Simon and Schuster, 1949). Both Neumanns, Sigmund and Franz, incline toward pessimism regarding German political institutions, the former in *Germany,* one of the Headline Series of the Foreign Policy Association, No. 82, July–August, 1950, and the latter in *German Democracy, 1950,* a pamphlet in the International Conciliation Series, May, 1950. A more optimistic tone is found in James K. Pollock, "The First Year of the Bonn Government," *Journal of Politics,* February, 1951, while Arnold Wolfers argues for the speedy rearmament of and granting of sovereignty to Germany in *Germany—Protectorate or Ally?* issued by the Yale Institute (now the Princeton Center) of International Studies. Drew Middleton, whose dispatches in the New York *Times* detail day-to-day developments, also has written an excellent account of American occupation policy to 1949 in *Struggle for Germany* (Indianapolis, The Bobbs-Merrill Company, 1949).

CHAPTER EIGHTEEN

BASES OF AMERICAN FOREIGN POLICY IN THE FAR EAST

Introduction: Beginnings of American Involvement in Asia • Traditional Politics • American Wartime Estimates of Postwar Conditions • Falsity of American Assumptions regarding Postwar Conditions • New American Techniques to Meet the Unforeseen Situation • Summary • Selected Bibliography

In considering the bases of American foreign policy in the Far East, attention will be focused on three large interrelated areas: Southeast Asia, China, and Japan. The first is now emerging into national sovereignty; the second has recently changed the directors of its sovereignty; while the third is in the process of recovering its sovereignty. With respect to American relationship to the Far East, four questions must be answered. What were the traditional techniques employed by American statecraft? What was the wartime estimate of postwar developments in the Far East, the presumptions on which future policy was to be founded? What has happened to this estimate in each of the three areas? And finally, in the light of changed circumstances, what appear to be the instruments now available to American statecraft, and how are they being employed?

► INTRODUCTION: BEGINNINGS OF AMERICAN INVOLVEMENT IN ASIA

The traditional techniques for the expression of American foreign policy in the Far East were evolved after the middle of the nineteenth century and were elaborated as a result of the direct commitment to Guam and the Philippines assumed upon victory over Spain. Interest, supported by active policy, thus antedated by almost a century any comparable relationship to Europe. This historical disparity may help to explain, if not make more rational, the contemporary American phenomenon of the isolationist-interventionist. His existence may be traced back at least as far as the beat-Japan-first—in opposition to the official policy of beat-Germany-first—argument during World War II. He now would lessen and weaken American commitments to Western European countries, while at the same time he would incur graver obligations in support of Chiang Kai-shek's Formosa Nationalists. Behind his view lies the time-hallowed tradition of involvement in Asia, beginning with American traders, continuing through Commodore Perry's intrusion into Japan, and emerging full-blown in McKinley's self-asserted divine guidance in holding onto the Philippines.

► TRADITIONAL POLITICS

ABSENCE OF RECOGNIZED SECURITY INTERESTS

In spite of its Pacific possession, American policy was not predicated on the existence of direct security interests in that area which this country was willing and able to defend. As General MacArthur stated—in his unread message to the Veterans of Foreign Wars in 1950—prior to World War II "the western strategic frontier of the United States lay on the littoral line of the Americas with an exposed island salient extending out through Hawaii, Midway and Guam to the Philippines. That salient was not an outpost of strength but an avenue of weakness along which the enemy could and did attack us." Contrary to the implication of the general's statement, however, there was nothing peculiar or nefarious about this "avenue of weakness." Great powers, of which the United States was definitely one after 1898, are frequently in the position of not being able to defend themselves, their possessions, and their allies in all places at the same time. Portions of their strategic interest may be vulnerable to attack by another great power or even by a smaller state with local preponderance of strength. Nations in this situation rely on the over-all strength at their disposal to discourage attack or to retrieve their positions ultimately should an attack be made. This was certainly the case regarding German possessions outside Europe in 1914 and many British possessions in the Far East in 1940. Such was the position of the United States in 1898.

A peculiarity of American policy, however, lay in the fact that after 1898 the United States chose for the most part to refrain from any commitment to defend its possessions. It did not have to fight for them in World War I because German power was rapidly removed from the scene, and, more important, because the expansionist power in the area, Japan, fought on the Allied side as payment for the right to acquire German holdings and in return for Allied recognition of its special interests with regard to China. As has been pointed out in an earlier chapter, the United States maintained a low degree of military effectiveness in the area after 1918. It did not build its naval power to the strength authorized by the Washington Treaty and kept Guam and the Philippines in a state of virtual disarmament. When Japan renewed its aggressive policy against China in 1937, it had attained a preponderance of power later demonstrated to cover most of the Far Eastern area. The Western European powers and the United States were too involved in the consequences of their comparative weakness toward German expansion to be able to reverse the deteriorating Pacific situation. When World War II called the United States to the defense of its possessions, it was unable to hold them against Japanese power.

Hand in hand with the absence of military strength to defend American holdings went a refusal to make any military commitment to defend a balance of power among Asiatic nations. As will be discussed below, American policy in Asia utilized the balance of power technique, but the United States was not prepared to support that technique with military force, although the maintenance of a balance of power was essential to the attainment of American objectives in the area. Consequently, by the time the United States was forced to fight in 1941, all semblance of the previous balance had disappeared, and Japanese power, from its base in North Asia, was erupting into Southeast Asia.

This lack of support for an Asiatic balance of power was typical of American foreign policy throughout the world. Unwittingly the United States believed in the balancing of European and Asiatic power, but traditional American statecraft denounced the term itself and not infrequently reiterated its determination to do away with the concept forever. For example, the attainment of a hegemonic status by any European nation would do great, perhaps irreparable, damage to the security position of the United States. This country has in fact fought two world wars to prevent that dire possibility from occurring. However, it entered both wars so late that hegemony in Europe had all but been attained, and it did not include the restoration of a balance of power among its war aims.

USE OF COMPETING COLONIAL IMPERIALISMS

The first of the traditional techniques of American policy in the Far East may therefore be said to be conscious and unconscious avoidance of the use of direct military power. The second, also involving an unconscious choice, was the use of competing colonial imperialisms to open up the Asiatic mainland to trade and investment. Although the American objective was definitely economic, nonimperialistic, and even had anti-imperialist undertones, the United States was quite willing to profit from the imperialist techniques of others. What it wanted was an opportunity for *American* as well as European commerce. When Japan refused to admit trade, the United States threatened force. When European nations used force in China, the United States did not scruple to reap the commercial advantages therefrom.

For the most part, with Japan the exception, the United States did not wish to engage in the dirty job of wresting from the hapless East the original commercial concessions. Such activity would have involved a direct commitment larger than the United States cared to make, an overt use of force which was abhorrent to its piously expressed principles. The United States did want the China trade, however; in fact, it became more and more fascinated by that elusive will-o'-the-wisp. The two American policies designed to attain these objectives were the most-favored-nation formula and the Open Door. Both were "me-too" policies, by which the United States, frequently with the encouragement of China itself and later of Great Britain, asked for all the commercial advantages the other powers fought for. Since the United States did not believe in using force and would not make the commitment necessary to get its own exclusive sphere of influence, it naturally did not wish other powers to do so.

In the colonial area of Southeast Asia the United States was quite willing to see the establishment and maintenance of Western imperialism if it were permitted as a consequence to develop its own economic interest. This passive assent, of course, directly contradicted the American anti-imperialist ideology discussed below. In China, competing imperialisms left room for American commercial policy to assert itself so long as the imperialisms were really competitive and did not agree on partitioning China and so long as there were enough nations present in China to prevent any one of them from grabbing all the spoils.

BALANCE OF POWER TECHNIQUE

Because the American technique for the attainment of economic objectives was frequently followed unwittingly and because it ran into difficulties in the twentieth century for lack of force to back it up, the technique was not recognized for what it truly was—a balance of power policy designed to prevent the domination of the area by any one state, whether it be Britain, Russia, Germany, or Japan. For the United States it was an ideal type of balance, one in which this country was not involved. In this respect the situation was analagous to Britain's nineteenth-century relationship to the Continent. But Great Britain, except when directed by misguided statesmen, actively held the balance by being willing in the final analysis to use its power on one side of the scale or the other (perfidious Albion). The United States did not possess comparable power nor was it willing to use what it had to preserve the balance. Instead it relied on diplomatic expression and moral preachment, weak reeds indeed. In this context the Open Door notes of Secretary of State John Hay may be viewed as a diplomatic device for attaining economic objectives without any commitment of power. The Open Door notes were only partly successful, and that to the precise extent to which they were in accord with the purposes of the competing imperialisms of the time.

BALANCE OF POWER TECHNIQUE: THREATENERS OF THE BALANCE

The chief threats to the balance came from Russia and later from Japan. Against both American policy *without* power was arrayed. Great Britain could have been a greater threat at an earlier time when American definition of interests had not been so clearly established. Britain, however, for its own reasons preferred to see in China nonexclusive spheres of interest, a view which coincided with American objectives. After Japan's active entrance on the scene, its actions, such as detaching Korea from sovereignty ties to China, the Sino-Japanese War, and the 1902 and 1905 alliances with Britain, were at first viewed by the United States as welcome frustrations of the ambitions of Russia, which was then regarded as the chief threat to the balance of power. Japanese policies therefore seemed to redound to the advantage of the other powers, including the United States. Japan was believed to be more like the West in its institutions, its pattern of development, its economic objectives than either the weak, inscrutable China or the monolithic, glacialistic Russia. Superficially also Japan seemed to have the same geopolitical relationship to the Asiatic mainland that Britain did toward Europe—an energetic, rapidly industrializing, commercial state anxious to prevent any threatening hegemony on the continent it faced.

In actuality Japan wished merely to prevent Russian hegemony in order to substitute its own, a policy which Great Britain could not follow in Europe after it had been thrown out in the fifteenth century. As Japan's real intentions became clear with its steadily expanding influence, the United States was forced to reconcile two policies it had been pursuing: that of the Open Door, with its corollary of preserving Chinese territorial and administrative integrity, on the one hand, and that of passive support of the imperialism that had opened up China in the first place, on the other.

To preserve some semblance of the former the United States had to admit the continuance of the latter, although imperialism on the mainland ceased to benefit this country in the twentieth century as it had in the nineteenth. In the Root-Takahira and Lansing-Ishii Agreements America gave executive recognition to the special relationship of Japan to northern China. However, the United States was able in return to tone down the Twenty-one Demands, particularly the abandonment of the infamous fifth group, which would have established Japanese tutelage over all of China. The 1922 Washington Naval Conference was hailed at the time as a skillful formula to give Japan security in its home islands without power enough for external aggression, especially since Japan had supposedly renounced aggression in signing the Nine-Power Treaty guaranteeing the independence of China.

Events of the ensuing two decades served to demonstrate, however, that the balance of power in the Far East did not depend on solemn diplomatic covenants, but rather on the inclination and ability of a number of states to limit each other's interests. Japanese military action in Manchuria in 1931 had a long history of peaceful and not-so-peaceful penetration behind it and could not be stopped by Britain and France, whose power was declining; by Germany, which had been forcibly excluded from the area; or by Russia, which was preoccupied with consolidation of the Communist regime. It can be seen, therefore, that the inexorable course of events after the turn of the century finally left the United States alone to face Japan if America wished to preserve the principle of the Open Door, which had been developed as the best defense of its economic, humanitarian, and ideological interests, against the savage, determined, powerful imperialism which threatened to engulf all the Far East.

IDEOLOGICAL TECHNIQUE

Traditional American foreign policy had a substantial moralistic content, and one can discern in the relations of the United States with the Far East an instance of the successful use of the ideological technique. The governments and peoples of Asia were constantly reminded of the friendship the United States felt toward them and the lack of territorial ambitions which made that friendship genuine. These statements were convincing because in truth it was no part of American objectives to attain political or economic domination. Its commercial policies were pursued without thought of using trade as a forerunner of the flag.

An anti-imperialist tradition was deeply rooted in the United States, a tradition which found its strongest manifestation in Asia even after the defeat of Spain made the United States itself an imperialist power. Originating in a revolt against its own colonial overlord, the United States henceforth carried its messages of freedom wherever its foreign relations reached. To Western European countries the American proclivity for pointing out the right, the moral path has been highly irritating. Witness the famous Churchillian response to American goadings on the subject of India: that he had not become the King's First Minister to preside over the dissolution of the British Empire. To some weak peoples in the Western Hemisphere—such as the Cubans and Panamanians—American moralistic expressions have at times seemed to be outright hypocritical. With all its irritating innuendoes of superiority, with all its discrepancy between preachment and practice, the anti-imperialist tradition nevertheless gained friends for the United States in Asia.

When this country declared its unwillingness to use the peoples of Asia as pawns to American ends, it was willing to *write* a long record to that effect in an effort to get other powers to follow its example. Thus this technique favored the rapid development of independence and national sovereignty throughout the Far East, even in the Philippine Islands. Its strength was the strength of weakness. Its persuasiveness was dependent on the absence of, and disinclination to use, American national power. But at the same time the absence of power behind its moralistic policies enabled other countries not so dedicated to place their strength athwart American policy.

It should further be remembered by way of footnote that American friendship to the peoples of Asia, unwillingness to use them as means to its own ends, encouragement of their national independence did not apply to unfortunate Asiatics who sought or gained admission to the moralistic United States. Asiatics were barred by discriminatory, highly offensive immigration legislation. Once in the United States they were denied equality of economic opportunity, freedom to attain an education, and ultimate equality in the administration of justice (i.e., the shipment of West Coast Japanese and Nisei to detention camps in World War II). Apparently the United States wanted its friends to stay at more than arm's length and not raise embarrassing questions about racial equality (as Japan attempted to do at the Versailles peace settlement).

MESSIANICAL TECHNIQUE

Accompanying its anti-imperialistic policy and carrying some of its overtones was the cultural and messianical activity of many private American citizens. While the United States as a government opposed the forceful instrusion into the Far East of Western nations, many of its citizens felt a compulsion to enlighten and instruct the peoples of Asia. In the religious field Asiatics were to have conferred upon them the benefits of Christianity; they were to be rescued from the hell of heathenism. Two things need to be said about this American missionary urge. It is possible to ridicule it by contrasting Christianity with the far older religious beliefs which had found roots in Asia. It is possible to scorn the superior righteousness inherent in the principle that any one religion contains a monopoly of truth, and that truth must be made to prevail over error. Whatever justification this criticism may have, however, it neglects the very real accomplishments of the messianic conveyor outside the narrow area of theology.

For Western missionary activity was great in the cultural and technical fields as well as in the religious. Schools were established fostering education from the primary grades through colleges and universities. Standards of health and sanitation were raised in the never-ending fight against pestilence and disease. Missionaries were teachers and sanitary engineers as well as propagators of the gospel. When pestilence, disease, and starvation continued to ravage overpopulated, undernourished lands, financial assistance from Americans was requested and the appeals were heeded. Communist China unwittingly pays great tribute to missionary activity in its persecution of Western theologians, who brought friendship and help to Asia, together with Western ideas of all kinds.

Emphasis is placed on the role of American theologians because it was unique. Their success in winning friends for the United States was dependent upon the very absence of American national power and official propaganda. This country did not discourage missionary work, but it did not undertake to direct it or to give it strong political implications as did the French, Spanish, and to a lesser extent the German governments. Official American policies made clear that the flag did not follow the missionary any more than it followed trade.

American reaction to the incident of the Boxer Rebellion serves as an illustration of the messianical and ideological technique in foreign policy. When the Boxers, encouraged by the Manchu empress, ravaged, murdered, and pillaged the property and persons of foreigners, including missionaries, finally isolating foreign establishments in Peking, the United States sent about five thousand troops to join the fourteen thousand sent by other powers on a punitive and relief expedition. The American government, however, claimed only $25 million of the $333 million indemnity levied on China. Seven years later it remitted almost $8 million and in 1924 returned an additional $6 million. Some of the money was used by China to assist the study of Chinese scholars in the United States.

DEPENDENCE OF TRADITIONAL TECHNIQUES ON BALANCE OF POWER AND ABSENCE OF UNITY

This brief exploration of the traditional techniques of American statecraft in the Far East suggests that their success was dependent on two factors largely unrecognized at the time. The first was the presence in the area of a balance of power. With its deterioration and ultimate destruction went a consequent decline in American success. A continuing cause of American difficulties in Asia was the failure to date of efforts to restore the balance of power destroyed by Japan. The second factor was the lack of national unity and power in the area, except for Japan. The mainland of Asia was a power vacuum, an arena of struggle between, and conquest by, outside nations. In this respect Asia differed greatly from Europe and led to a consequent difference in American policy between positive entanglement in the former and negative aloofness from the latter. While the power of European countries relative to that of the United States rapidly declined after 1900, enough power remained to make American statecraft wary and desirous of adhering to historical precepts against meddling. In contrast, the situation in Asia invited meddling, even of the unconscious variety frequently found in American policy, because Asia *could* be used as an *instrument* of policy. When the United States pronounced itself in favor of national development of China, it meant the development of enough power to resist further imperialism but not enough to shut Westerners out and to make China an aggressor itself rather than the object of aggression.

Lack of unity arose from the age-old weakness of China. Chinese nationalism was a good thing so long as it was not too successful. Thus the remarkable upsurge of China between 1926 and 1931 under the leadership of the Kuomintang and Chiang Kai-shek threatened to destroy the second unrecognized basis of American policy: the absence of power on the Asiatic mainland. Because this upsurge also threatened the penetration policy of Japan, the Japanese embarked on aggression to bring weakness again to China and in so doing upset the first foundation of American policy: the balance between competing nations in Asia. Once more China seems to be growing in unity and strength, this time under Communist domination. Once more American interests are threatened, and more seriously than ever before. But that gets us ahead of the story. The fact of an Asia weak, disunited, and the subject of competing, outside influences explains the seeming paradox of far greater American involvement in Asia at the time that Europe posed the greater danger to American security. Once again the American isolationist-interventionist is seen to be following historical practices in a situation to which they were no longer applicable.

► AMERICAN WARTIME ESTIMATES OF POSTWAR CONDITIONS

During World War II American statecraft had to engage in the risky practice of making educated guesses as to what the postwar Asiatic scene would look like after the defeat of Japan. Naturally these estimates were for the most part not publicized, but because they became the bases of policy immediately after September, 1945, they can be deduced with some accuracy. This detective work will provide answers to these questions: What did the United States plan to do in Asia after 1945? Why could it not do what it originally thought possible? What changes in policy have been and should be made to meet the new situation, so different from the wartime prognosis?

ESTIMATES OF SOVIET POSTWAR BEHAVIOR

Important estimates were made concerning the Soviet Union, China, and Southeast Asia. Delusions about the nature of the Soviet Union were prevalent and, for that matter, are with us still. It was discovered by a process of historical exigesis that Russian ambitions in the Far East were limited, as legitimate under the circumstances as those of any other country, and hence easily satisfiable. If suspicion arose that Russian ambitions were perhaps somewhat different, there were always wartime declarations of the Soviet government to lull Americans. Had not Stalin himself said that the Chinese Communists were not Communists at all and that only Chiang could govern China after the war? Had not Madame Chiang publicly paid tribute to Soviet aid to the Nationalists as being greater than that of any other country, the United States included? Had not the Russians, while helping Chiang, kept aloof from the isolated Yenan group which persisted in calling itself communist, neither recognizing nor assisting it?

THE YALTA DEAL

Cautious diplomacy should be prepared for more than one eventuality, and American diplomacy thought it was being cautious with respect to the Russians. Soviet aid was needed, so said the highest military authorities, in the war against Japan. A price would have to be paid for that aid. Most of that price seemed legitimate and was to be taken from Japan, which had taken it originally from China. *But if the price were not legitimate, or if it were just the prelude to further, illegitimate demands, why the Soviet Union had the power to take what it wanted anyway.* In return for Soviet denunciation of its neutrality treaty with Japan and entrance into the war after the six months' wait for the denunciation to become effective, the United States and Great Britain agreed to hand over Outer Mongolia, the Kurile Islands, and the southern half of Sakhalin. A joint Chinese-Soviet company was to administer the Chinese-Eastern and the South Manchurian Railroads, recognizing Chinese "full sovereignty in Manchuria" and at the same time the "pre-eminent interests of the Soviet Union." Russia's lease to Port Arthur was to be "restored" and Dairen "internationalized, the pre-eminent interests of the Soviet Union in this port being safeguarded." President Roosevelt agreed to help Marshal Stalin, on his request, to obtain the concurrence of Chiang Kai-shek. He thus provoked a rising tide of posthumous criticism on the ground that he was enforcing the alienation of rights and territories which did not belong to America or to America's enemy, but rather to an American ally.

Chinese representatives subsequently agreed in Moscow to the Yalta arrangement. How could they do otherwise? It was not Roosevelt but Stalin who held the high cards. American and British statesmen shared a sense of satisfaction with the agreement as a *limiting* factor circumscribing Soviet ambitions. Russia would not settle for less and might take more. Who would prevent it? Now, after Yalta, if the Soviets went on to take more, as they did, they at least were doing so in direct abnegation of their recorded word. In the absence of power and willingness to use it in the area, diplomatic sanctions inscribed on paper were better than nothing at all.

RUSSIAN ISOLATION AND THE PRIMACY OF EUROPE IN RUSSIAN CALCULATIONS

There was some evidence in addition to historical analogy and Stalinist pronouncements to support the American belief that Soviet ambitions in the Far East were limited. It was widely believed in the United States that the terrible destruction wrought in Russia by Nazi armies would necessitate years of reconstruction and would give Russian policy a domestic focus such as it had had in the decade following the Russian Civil War. This belief was strengthened by Soviet statements stressing the magnitude of the effort necessary to restore the country.

Indications seemed to point to a European focus for Russian policy, which for centuries had swung back and forth like a pendulum between East and West. From Europe had come Hitlerite Germany, which had been so close to defeating Russia and unseating its government. It was going to take the combined efforts of the four principal members of the United Nations to prevent a recurrence of that threat. Soviet desires to alter the prewar map of Europe were known and generally accepted. There was no reason why smaller states in Central, Eastern, and Southeastern Europe should not be friendly to the Soviet Union in a desirable shift of orientation away from Germany. Agreements had been reached on most of the preliminary problems of Europe, including the establishment of four-power control over Germany. Implementation of the agreements would require the cooperative efforts of the United States, Britain, France, and Russia. For

Russia there seemed more than enough to tax its postwar resources without attempts to grab in the Far East more than had already been granted. Consolidation of existing positions rather than advancement to new positions seemed to be indicated.*

WARTIME ESTIMATES CONCERNING CHINA

Wartime estimates of the future course of China posited a continued and rapid increase in national strength. During the twenties Chiang had brought to China greater unity than it had known for ages. While Japanese armies had overrun much of the country, driving the Nationalists away from the coasts into less productive holdings, Chiang was still the undoubted leader of China with a reputation enhanced rather than diminished by his continued refusal to bow to Japanese might. His patriotic devotion China's allies were now to crown with success. To be sure there were the Communists in far-off Yenan, who seemed to be fighting the Japanese with even greater effectiveness as the war wore on. Chiang was so distrustful of the Communists that he was maintaining large armies to blockade their area in violation of the agreement both had made to cooperate against the invader. But while the Communists were a problem, that problem, it was generally believed, would be solved either by their amalgamation with the Kuomintang or by their liquidation through military action similar to that two decades earlier. The former course would be preferable, since it would prevent even a short civil war, and would result in broadening the base of popular representation on which the Nationalist regime rested. Americans were well aware that reform was needed in the Chinese government; many American criticisms paralleled those by the Yenan group. The chief obstacle to further Chinese progress was therefore deemed to be the military one of keeping China in the war at all. When General Stilwell wanted to force reform on the "Peanut" and make him pay more attention to the Japanese and less to the Communists, Roosevelt promptly acquiesced in Chiang's request for Stilwell's recall, substituting an American general of positive, Nationalist sympathies. For the United States the predominant objective was to keep the Nationalists in the war against Japan. Since Chiang naturally wanted help with a minimum of advice on matters deemed his sole concern and since there was not to be much American aid available anyway, that was the way the game had to be played.

CHINA AS THE KEYSTONE OF ASIATIC SECURITY

By reason of its postwar growth in power China would, it was thought, replace aggressive, defeated Japan as the keystone of security and stability in the Far East. There was consequently some logic in granting to *any* Chinese government the same special position on the Security Council of

---

* For detailed discussion of wartime agreements regarding Eastern Europe and their flouting by the Soviet Union, see Chapter Seventeen, "Western Europe and American Security."

the United Nations as that to be held by the United States, Great Britain, France, and the Soviet Union. Such a position would reflect both encouragement and prophecy as to China's postwar role in the Far East. The final implications of the Chinese position-to-be would be compelling on whatever Chinese government might emerge, forcing it to adhere to an independent national policy which would benefit the United States.

The ambiguities of the American role in China, the rapid disintegration of Nationalist power on the mainland, and the Chinese Communist intervention in Korea have obviously brought drastic changes in American policy, which will be explored below. It is still to early to say with certainty, however, that the American prognosis of Chinese independence from foreign domination as a consequence of an increased national power will not in the long run prove to have been correct.

WARTIME ESTIMATES OF SOUTHEAST ASIA

With regard to Southeast Asia, the wartime estimate assumed the resumption of colonial administration, but of a new type, one willing and able to conduct the area through a swift and orderly transition to national independence. Perhaps it was the historic lack of direct American responsibility in Southeast Asia which blinded Americans to the fact that two potentially incompatible policies were being simultaneously proposed for the area: a philosophy of anti-imperialism, which had found new strength during the war in the speeches of Henry Wallace, Roosevelt, and others, and the necessity for continued friendly relations with the colonial powers of Western Europe—Britain, Holland, and France.

The orderly transition to independence which was posited would permit the three nations close but indirect influence. In each instance, it was believed, the mutual interests of the emerging nation and of the former ruler would be best served by continued "cooperation" (tutelage) in economic, security, and possibly even political affairs.* The pattern which was anticipated followed closely the projected course of American policy toward the Philippines. These islands wanted their independence; they represented a security commitment which had proved difficult to discharge; and they were a threat to certain domestic economic interests. It was therefore to the benefit of both the United States and the Philippines that their relationship be changed from American control to one of close cooperative partnership in the postwar world.

ECONOMIC VISIONS

Political stability throughout the Far East, which constituted the underlying premise of the wartime estimate, would open up attractive vistas of

---

* American thinking treated India as a special case, separate from the colonial area of Southeast Asia, advocating immediate, untrammeled independence for the entire subcontinent.

substantial United States trade expansion in accordance with the liberal principles even then being formulated by the State Department. In other words, economic gains would follow naturally from the political stability which the United States believed would follow the war. There would be little need for separate techniques to gain economic, as distinct from political, objectives. Moreover, the other traditional techniques of friendship, cultural influence, and so forth, would likewise be useful in the postwar situation.

PILLARS OF FAR EASTERN SECURITY

Security in the area, it was believed, could be maintained with a minimum of direct American involvement. It would rest on three pillars. The first would be the existence of stable, strong nations in the area itself: China, India, and Australia. Maintenance of security would also be the responsibility of the colonial countries, which would be in the process of building a new relation toward Asia. Finally, there would be the world-wide security machinery of the projected United Nations Organization, based on unity of the Big Three.

ORIGINAL OCCUPATION OBJECTIVES IN JAPAN

The potential fly in this smooth soothing sirup was deemed to be the one country which for half a century had devoted its increasing energies to upsetting the balance of power. The problem of Japan was to prevent that country from ever becoming a threat, and the various aspects of presurrender policy were directed toward that end. Reparations were to be exacted to pay for the damage Japan had done and to increase the rapidity of reconstruction on the part of the recipients. Japan was to be deprived of all but its home islands, both as a measure of justice—to show that aggression did not pay—and to remove springboards to any future expansion. Economic policy was to be so executed that Japan could not by its preponderance of economic strength manipulate the rest of the Far East to its own advantage. To achieve these objectives a precarious balance had to be struck between three elements. The first was a Japanese domestic standard of living adequate to remove that nation from American relief rolls and adequate to enable Japan to aid, through mutually beneficial trade, the advancing economies of other countries in the area. But, second, Japan must not have sufficient strength to renew its economic aggression.* Third, a political reorganization would be put through which would remove from power the economic, military, and political groups which had formerly united behind an aggressive policy. By their democratization Japanese political institutions would be so reconsti-

* Granted that it was theoretically possible to endow a country with a satisfactory domestic standard of living, with enough economic strength to engage actively in international trade, without at the same time making it possible for that country to become a potential threat to world peace and security, no such balance was ever reached for either Japan or Germany.

tuted that these objectionable elements could never again return. Once purging measures had been taken—and they would not take very long—the new Japan could be safely admitted to the international community as a minor participant in the new system for Asiatic stability.

▶ FALSITY OF AMERICAN ASSUMPTIONS REGARDING POSTWAR CONDITIONS

If the wartime assumptions are viewed in the light of the actual course of postwar events, it becomes clear that their falsity was manifested throughout the Far East at about the same time. The principal actors—the Soviet Union, China, and Southeast Asia—stubbornly refused to behave after the war as American statecraft believed they would.

SOVIET ENTRANCE INTO THE PACIFIC WAR

One of the unstated assumptions about the Japanese future was that it would be determined almost solely by the United States, that the delicately balanced apple cart would not be upset by intrusion of outside influence. Even before the war was over, however, the Soviet Union declined to limit its role to an off-stage noise. Subsequent research has shown that the Kremlin did not want Japan to quit before Russia could get in its own licks. The Soviet Union thus refused in February, 1945, to mediate between the Japanese and the Allies, as the former had proposed. Further overtures were made by Japan at the time of the Potsdam Conference. From the Soviet viewpoint they were well answered by the Potsdam Declaration, which threatened the "annihilation" of Japan unless its government "proclaim now the unconditional surrender of all Japanese forces." The net effect of Japanese approaches had been to show Russia that it had better get into the war in a hurry while there was still a war to get into. It is therefore probable if speculative that Russia would have entered the war to protect its own interests even without the Yalta request by the United States and Great Britain.

The sudden denouement of the war further threatened Soviet ambitions and as a result forced the Soviet Union to the essentially ludicrous policy of continuing to fight an enemy who had already capitulated. The first atomic bomb was dropped by the United States on August 6 and the second on August 9. Russia declared war on Japan on August 8, six months to the day after its denunciation of the neutrality treaty, and began its offensive August 9. Japanese willingness to surrender was transmitted through the Swiss government the very next day, and by August 14 agreement on the condition of that surrender had been reached. The war was over for everyone except the Russians. They continued their advance through Manchuria, issuing military communiqués speaking of the "heroic deeds of our brave Far Eastern warriors" and the "fanatic resistance of the Japanese." Not until

August 20 did the Soviet Union issue its own separate demand to the Japanese to surrender, and three days after this carried out the "daring" air occupation of Dairen and Port Arthur.

Obviously what the Soviet Union was attempting to do was to provide by its actual participation in the war a foundation which would justify equality in the future control of Japan. To this end Molotov had on August 10 proposed to Ambassador W. Averell Harriman that the Soviet Union land troops on the Japanese home islands to participate in the surrender. Harriman's response was that the proposal was an insult to the United States, which had fought Japan for four years compared to Russia's two days. Molotov also wanted agreement on the appointment of General Vasilovsky as Commander in Chief in Tokyo with rank equal to General MacArthur's. This proposal Harriman characterized as nonsense. Confronted with American determination, Molotov capitulated and accepted the designation of General MacArthur as Supreme Commander of the Allied Powers.

The Soviet Union had lost the first round of its fight to enter Japan on an equal footing, but there was some compensation. Acquiescence in General MacArthur's administration in Tokyo solved the relationship of a controlled Japan to North Korea and Manchuria to Russia's advantage. The Soviet Union's activities in these two areas on the Asiatic mainland were outside the purview of the United States. Russia was able to arrange matters there to suit itself.

ESTABLISHMENT OF THE FAR EASTERN COMMISSION

Having failed to gain an equal role in the occupation for General Vasilovsky, the Soviet Union next tried to reduce General MacArthur's position to that of figurehead by advocating the establishment of a Far Eastern Control Commission, which would determine occupation policy in the same way that the other Control Commissions functioned for Germany and Austria. Secretary of State Byrnes later acknowledged that "we were placed in an embarrassing position" when confronted at the London meeting of foreign ministers in September, 1945, with Soviet insistence. The embarrassment arose because Russia was supported by Britain and Australia, to both of which countries it looked as though MacArthur intended to go it alone in Tokyo. Under the circumstances, the secretary was forced to follow what later became the familiar Russian tactic of the stall: the item of a Japanese Control Commission was not on the agenda; the American delegation had to consult the occupation authorities (MacArthur) before preparing its position and was thus not ready to discuss the matter.

Between that September meeting and the December meeting in Moscow the United States brought Great Britain around to its view that, while there would have to be a commission, there should be no *Control* in it. Consequently when the commission started its meetings in Washington in February, 1946, it was under terms of reference requiring "respect of existing control machinery in Japan, including the chain of command from United States Government to Supreme Commander and the Supreme Commander's commission of occupation forces." In simple language this meant that directives were to be transmitted through the United States to be executed by an American-controlled occupation. In the absence of any directives, the occupation was to continue its functions. Since the United States had acquiesced to a Soviet demand that decisions of the eleven-member commission be by majority vote, including the concurrence of the Big Powers, no directions displeasing to the occupation authorities could be passed unless there was disagreement between MacArthur and the State Department.

While the commission from time to time issued general directives, the crucial focus of Japanese control was in Japan, in the establishment of the Supreme Commander. The Soviet Union, naturally wishing to participate in the decision making where it actually existed, volunteered to contribute twenty thousand troops to the occupation forces. MacArthur rejoined with a threat to resign if the offer were accepted, but his job was safe on this score. There was no one in Washington who wanted any such number of Russian troops in Japan. Russia then sought to make of the Allied Council for Japan a supervisory instrument of MacArthur's policies, but the council, as established, had no veto power over SCAP and was in fact rarely consulted on anything. It served instead as observer for the member governments and as advisers to them, not to MacArthur.

RUSSIAN EFFORTS TO FRUSTRATE AMERICAN OCCUPATION POLICY

All the efforts of the Soviet Union to intrude its direct power and influence into postwar Japan were thus turned aside. There was nothing left for Russia but resort to more indirect tactics in efforts to frustrate the course of American occupation policy. For example, Russia pressed hard for a definition of war criminals that would include the Emperor, members of his court, heads of principal industries, political leaders, and most of the government bureaucracy. Its position on this score found some support among such Asiatic nations as China and India, but did not result in broadening the scope of the trials and purges. The effect of accepting the Soviet definition would, of course, have been to have made political and economic stability impossible. In the ensuing unrest greater opportunities would then have existed for the Japanese Communist party to seize or be elected to power.

Stirring up trouble for the conservatively oriented Japanese government was one of the primary objectives of Soviet policy. Its propaganda center was the Russian Embassy, which early in the occupation was five times as large as any other embassy in Japan. A guerrilla warfare raged between the embassy and SCAP, with the latter taking more and more direct measures to curb the activities of the former. A Russian spotlight always played on the many legitimate Japanese grievances, such as the low standard of living, poor labor conditions, and inadequate housing, in efforts to make common cause with the people against the alleged failure of political democracy in Japan. With hundreds of thousands of prisoners of war, the Soviet Union was able to introduce some Communist agitators into Japan. It used repatriation machinery to return first Communists and favorably indoctrinated prisoners, leaving many prisoners to languish indefinitely in Russia.

As direct Soviet influence waned with the years of occupation, the Japanese Communist party did a left-about-face, paralleling the shift in tactics by national Communist parties the world over. In 1945 statements of the party had emphasized its lack of contact with the Russians and the need for democracy in the Western sense of the word in Japan. "Direct liaison with the Soviet Union will harm rather than assist our movement. . . . We are aiming at the early establishment of a democracy in its real sense . . . democracy in the American way."

The failure of the party to achieve any notable successes in Japan, the widening split between East and West, the establishment of the Cominform, and finally the war in Korea pushed the Japanese Communists into a campaign of subversion and sabotage. On January 6, 1950, Communist leader Nosaka was denounced by his colleagues as "anti-democratic, anti-Socialist, anti-patriotic, anti-Japanese," terms which the Russians had also applied at one time or another to many East European Communists. Nosaka's response was the typical and revealing obeisance to the changed line. "We must," he said, "fulfill the historic mission *assigned* to the Japanese Communist Party in the *international* movement." There is, in addition, evidence that the Japanese Communists were informed in advance of the North Korean attack and of the assistance to be rendered by the Chinese Communist armies, and were instructed to assist the venture by sabotaging any aid given the South Korean government by the Allied occupation forces.

In retrospect it can be seen that the persistent Soviet ambitions in Japan went far beyond any legitimate objective of division of responsibility among the members of the wartime coalition. They were part and parcel of a concerted, consistent policy of expansion of power felt throughout the world. As such they falsified an important assumption of American policy and proved to be one of the major determinants of the change in American thinking about the future role of Japan, which will be examined later in this chapter.

FAILURE OF CHIANG'S LEADERSHIP

Just as wartime estimates of Russian behavior proved incorrect, so did those concerning Chinese unity and progress under Chiang Kai-shek. The basis of the undoubted failure of American policy in China was that the United States found itself inexorably committed to the losing side of a revolutionary situation. Secretary of State Acheson placed primary responsibility for the loss of China on the nature of Chiang's leadership: ". . . The failure of their [the Chinese people's] government to respond to their needs, its ineptitude and blindess destroyed all their confidence and support. The Nationalist Government was overthrown in China not by force of arms. It collapsed from its own inherent weakness and the withdrawal of the people's support. The Communists won by default, not by what they offered. They employed the well-known Communist technique of probing for weakness and, on finding it, exploiting it to the full. . . . The revolutionary movement in China, which began a half century ago as an expression of the aspirations of the Chinese people, has been captured, for the present, by the Communists."*

Presumably the Secretary did not intend to minimize altogether the onward rush of Communist military forces, aided and abetted by Nationalist weakness and by the alienation of the loyalty of the Chinese people. A seeming *non sequitur* also exists between the statements that the Communists did not win by what they offered and that they now control the revolutionary movement. The secretary undoubtedly was alluding, as he later did explicitly, to the discrepancy between the Communists' *program to attain power* and the *actual ends to which they used power*.

If the Chiang movement at its outset was both revolutionary and nationalist, able at one stage to all but liquidate the Communists, what had happened to it? The answer, "inherent weakness and the withdrawal of the people's support," gives rise to further questions of *why*. In addition to faulty policies of the Chiang regime itself, it might be suggested that the causes of Chiang's ultimate failure lie in the ingredients of the revolutionary situation existing in China at the end of the war. During the course of his eight years' resistance to Japan, the political basis of Chiang's support had dramatically shifted. Thrown back to the west, Chiang had lost touch with the peasantry, with the commercial class of the east coast, and with much of the industrial class as well. Most of the roots of the clique around him did not reach down to the Chinese people at all. As a consequence, the claim of Chiang to be the center of national unity, of patriotic identification was seriously weakened.

In the second place, ferment and conflict continued throughout the substantial part of China occupied by Japan. The Japanese could not bring stability, law, and order; patriotic resistance to the conquerors took the inevitable form of maximimizing chaos. In other words, a condition favorable to revolution existed over much of China before the war ended. This situation became explosive when the Japanese withdrew and was aggravated by the sudden manner in which they withdrew. At one historical moment Japanese armies were spread out over the expanse of China; the next moment they were gone, leaving behind only a vacuum of power to be filled.

---

* Address before the Commonwealth Club of California, San Francisco, California, March 15, 1950. Quoted in *Strengthening the Forces of Freedom,* Department of State Publication 3852, p. 140.

Finally, in contrast to the known corruption and ineptitude of the Nationalists, there were ignorance and doubt about the true nature of Chinese Communism. This doubt existed not only in the minds of Western statesmen, largely cut off from contact with Yenan, but in the minds of the Chinese people as well. By espousing popular measures of reform, by emphasizing the minority of Communist participation in local and regional government, by ostensibly basing their regime at the outset on a peasantry, neglected and persecuted by the Nationalists, the Communists were able to forge powerful attractions for the masses of the Chinese people, or at least to assure their sympathetic neutrality in the civil war to come. They were further aided by the appeal of promises not at the time proven false over those of the Nationalists which had repeatedly been falsfied.

DILEMMA OF AMERICAN POLICY IN CHINA

The foregoing elements in the revolutionary situation placed American statecraft in an almost impossible situation. Traditional diplomatic practice favored continued relations with the legitimate government of Chiang. The United States desired Chinese political stability and orderly development and was prepared to continue substantial economic support to those ends. Legal and political friendship for the Nationalists had been further cemented by common membership in the wartime coalition. In this relationship the United States suffered from a guilt complex for having been compelled to deny China most of the assistance it had requested during the war. This feeling reinforced American determination to help the Nationalists fill as quickly as possible the vacuum left by the Japanese surrender and evacuation, aid which placed American policy and American troops squarely in the middle of the ensuing conflict.

At the same time that the United States was favorably inclined toward the Nationalists it recognized the symptoms of that regime's increasing debility. To arrest Chiang's decline, above all to make it possible for him to consolidate once more his power over China, American advisers made repeated suggestions for modification and improvement in the structure of his government. They believed a compromise could be reached with the Communists which would end the civil war. Despite the impressive, if temporary, progress made by General Marshall, compromise was inherently impossible between the two antagonists, each with its own military organization, its own bases of support, its own memory of past decades of conflict, and its own belief in ultimate complete victory. Chiang was unwilling to weaken his own control through compromise, especially since he was aware that refusal would not mean the end of American support. Far from using this highly potent sanction, the United States actually increased its aid in the days immediately following the Japanese surrender. This country provided a ferrying service for Chiang's troops, holding Manchurian positions for their arrival, and furnishing staff advice to his armies and equipment to his men. The

American aid which made Chiang less amenable to pressure also increased the intransigence of the Communists. They saw a mediator who urged compromise while assisting one of the contestants. What more, Mao felt, could the United States do against him if he refused to make concessions? By continuing the civil war, on the other hand, Mao could place the United States in the unflattering role of a foreign imperialist aiding a puppet government and thereby strengthen his own appeal to three basic Chinese attitudes: anti-imperialist, anti-Nationalist, and anti-Western.

While the United States ultimately cut off military aid to Chiang when it became clear that he had lost the civil war, this country had been unwilling to take this drastic step earlier as a means of forcing Chiang to accept its suggested compromises. The United States was likewise unwilling, *even if it had been able,* to go to the other extreme, as some prominent Americans advocated, and grant Chiang the all-out, unconditional assistance which would have brought him out on top. Instead the United States did just enough to enable Chiang to lose the Chinese mainland with the maximum turmoil and the greatest possible recrimination from *both* sides.

FALSIFICATION OF AMERICAN ASSUMPTIONS CONCERNING SOUTHEAST ASIA

Even while wartime presuppositions about Russian behavior and Chinese developments were falling apart, American assumptions concerning the future of Southeast Asia were also proving to be fallacious. The Western European nations had far greater difficulty than had been anticipated in reasserting their control over their colonies. The defeat of Holland and France and the narrow margin of British survival had practically destroyed their ability to exert power in the Pacific. The weakness of the home base of all three countries proved to be deeper and of longer duration than America had thought, and their retarded domestic recovery made them unable and unwilling to maintain overseas commitments as extensive as in the prewar period. Moreover, the colonial countries, under pressure of wartime idealism and American attitudes, had changed their own conception of imperialism. Instead of control responsible solely to their own dictates, they now spoke of "guidance," of "assistance" to native populations. In addition, therefore, to economic weakness there was also a patent lack of determination on the part of the colonial powers to reassert control in the old pattern. (The Dutch constituted a possible exception. They wanted to re-enter Indonesia early and with force, but were prevented by the British and Americans from doing so.)

The weakened Western colonialism was contrasted with the stronger, more intransigent nationalism on the part of Southeast Asia's inhabitants, a development which had been fostered, in part consciously, by the Japanese. "Asia for the Asiatics" had become a reality during the defeat of the white man. While Japanese control was nowhere regarded as a permanently adequate substitute, the Japanese had placed Asians of some countries in administrative positions far higher than those reached under Western rule. As a result, native nationalists, gaining experience in leadership as collaborators, were ready to take power as insurrectionists upon the defeat of Japan.

As in China, the way in which defeat came to Japan helped to create a revolutionary situation. After the surrender, but before the colonial troops could reach the scene, a vacuum of power was created, into which rushed native forces armed with Japanese equipment.

The prewar fabric of relations between the West and Southeast Asia had thus been broken on the military and political levels. The same was true of the economic ties between the Asiatic exporters of primary goods and the Western consumers. This relationship was basically exploitive and antinationalist in the view of the Asians, who were determined to have an end to it. When the West talked of greater economic development, there was no meeting of minds, because Southeast Asia was thinking of a different kind of development. Dissatisfaction on the economic issue caused the nationalists to lay the entire blame for the condition of the area at the door of their former rulers. It could be theoretically demonstrated that both Latin America and Southeast Asia, as underdeveloped areas, stood to gain most by a continued international division of labor and liberal trade principles. But neither the Southeast Asians nor the Latin Americans cared to listen. To meet this new situation successfully would have required that the United States reverse its previous policy and discard its wartime assumption of continued noninvolvement. In the crucial two years after the war the United States was not ready to take such a step. After the surrender of Japan, it did consent with some reluctance to transport colonial troops back to their former territories under the rationale of disarming the stranded Japanese soldiers. Little more was the United States willing to do. The same rationale could conceivably have justified the full commitment necessary to reassert colonial control, but any such policy would have gone against previous American practices and violated traditional anti-imperialist attitudes as well. These colonies, Americans felt, should be independent soon; if the nationalists showed enough power to force an advancement in the date, far be it from the United States to try to resubjugate them.

APPEALS OF COMMUNISM IN SOUTHEAST ASIA

In this chaotic situation the revolutionary appeal of international communism flourished. The important components of that appeal were national, economic, social, and racial. Communism could support national independence and anti-Western imperialism, since the peoples of the area had not had any experience with the harsh, Russian-style imperialism. Its economic appeal attacked colonial exploitation and was successful in setting up a double standard which seemed completely illogical to the West. The Russians were not prepared to take *any products* of the area; hence they were not exploitive. They were unable to put *any investments* into the area; hence they were not imperialistic. On the other hand, Western nations were damned if they didn't and damned if they did. If they did not freely give large sums of money with no strings attached to foster economic development, they were accused of reneging on earlier, roseate promises. If they did attempt to grant loans and credits, whether private or governmental, they were accused of continuing old-fashioned colonial exploitation. The irresponsible luxury of noninvolvement, which had formerly been enjoyed by the United States, had now passed to the Soviet Union.

Against the Western desires for political stability, communism matched a social appeal for a changed order of society. This new order was not communistic—most national leaders in the first years after the war wanted no part of communistic social organization—but was directed against the very social groups deemed parasitic by both communists and nationalists: the entrepreneurs, the "capitalists," the commercial classes, and so on. These were the functions formerly monopolized by the Westerners (and the Chinese); hence the social message of communism merged with its racial appeal. The national leadership in the newly independent countries was to be nonwhite, antiwhite. To be sure, it might be drawn from a wafer-thin crust of native intelligentsia and might include many Moscow-trained elements. But at any rate the old slogan of "Asia for the Asiatics" was to be vindicated; administration was to be native and nationalist, not white and Western. On this issue, the Soviet Union was able to make capital of its Asiatic character, and of the inclusion in the Union of many non-European races, ethnic groups, and cultures, particularly since Asians were largely ignorant of the brutal Russification campaigns even then being carried on by the Soviet government.

COMMUNIST CONTROL OF NATIONAL MOVEMENTS

Where national movements in Southeast Asia were unsuccessful, as in Malaya and Indo-China, steadily increasing Communist control became discernible. As they did in Eastern Europe, Communists aimed at the capture of coalition regimes so that the other cooperating elements could neither break away nor exert any influence on policy. This meant domination of the institutions of decision making, which in Southeast Asia are often separate from the ostensible "government." For example, Dang Xuan Khee, alias Truong China, who returned to Viet Nam from Moscow in 1947, rose to be the principal political power, with General Ho Chi Minh relegated to the status of attractive nationalist figurehead. The infiltration of nationalist Indo-Chinese armies resulted in Communist direction of the only effective fighting force opposing the Western countries. But combined with tightening Moscow control has been continued espousal of originally sponsored measures of reform. Consequently the non-Communist nationalist can find no alternative between allegiance to the West and following the Communist line. The absence of many of the ingredients of a modern, complex society tightens the dilemma. Where there is no history of individual freedom, no experience with democratic procedure, no concept of the Western meaning of private property, no burgeoning middle class, it has proved possible for Communists to draw a rigid line between the "we" of nationalism and the "they" of colonialism.

PRESSURE OF COMMUNIST CHINA

Following the defeat of Chiang on the mainland, international communism had made use of China in a variety of ways. In such areas as Viet Nam active Chinese military intrusion has galvanized General Ho and his followers into greater activity. There is evidence that the Chinese Communists have outfitted Viet Minh divisions with equipment, mostly of United States manufacture, which was captured from the Nationalists, and that they are running training camps in China for Viet Minh soldiers.

The Chinese Communists have also begun to direct to their own ends the organization of overseas Chinese, which had previously been controlled by Chiang. Both groups wish to use these organizations for the same purposes, to increase Chinese influence in Southeast Asian areas where Chinese form a significantly large minority. Complete Communistic control over Chinese merchants, financiers, and traders will be extremely difficult, but the tradition of nationalistic orientation is there to aid, especially when buttressed by blackmail extorted from Chinese with relatives in Communist hands in China.

International communism also gains greatly from the shining precedent of a successful revolution brought to fruition under Communistic auspices. A united, dynamic, expansionist China exerts pressure on the peripheral regions which is difficult to resist. So long as Mao and Malenkov see eye to eye, the latter stands to benefit.

After the Chinese accepted a truce in Korea, the French, with good reason, felt that one result would be the intensification of Chinese aid to Viet Minh and possibly the ultimate intrusion of Chinese forces in such numbers as to make of the area another Korea. Under the circumstances the French have asked for assurances that the United States would throw its full weight against outright Chinese invasion of Viet Nam. The American response was an attempt to build a collective security system for the South Pacific, a system which would avoid the necessity of unilateral American military action unwelcome alike to the American people and to many of America's allies.

WEAKNESS OF THE "MIDDLE GROUND" IN ASIA

As has been seen in the case of Japan, *nationalist* communism has become increasingly difficult. The various local parties have been brought into harmony with the policies of the Soviet Union through greatly strengthened doctrinal and organizational ties. The consequence of the widening breach between the United States and the Soviet Union has been tragic for groups, peoples, and ideas caught in between. In Southeast Asia, where nationalism fights imperialism, it is the Soviet Union which fights the United States, in the same way that a corrupt Iranian parliament fights the British oil companies. The middle ground vanishes beneath the feet of those who would stand upon it; there is no other conflict.

India is a living example of this vanishing middle ground. At the 1947 Asian Conference in Delhi, Prime Minister Nehru proclaimed: "We represent the ancient civilization of the East as well as the dynamic civilization of the West. Politically we symbolize in particular the spirit of freedom and democracy which is so significant a feature of the new Asia. Asia under India's leadership is reclaiming its place in the world's councils, asserting for the first time effectively her right to demand from the West in Asia the standards the West has taught Asia." The basic principles of India's foreign policy were to be support of the United Nations in action against aggression; but alignment with neither the Eastern nor the Western bloc; but moral support of Eastern nationalism and anti-imperialism.

The tragedy of India's middle position is that while much of what Nehru says is true, particularly the last statement quoted, other truths make that position increasingly untenable. India has patently not been able to lead Asia, not only because much of Asia is still a battleground, but because Indian statesmen have not been able to solve the grievous internal problems which continue to make such leadership impossible. Support of nationalism and anti-imperialism has meant support of Chinese communism in its efforts to gain Western recognition and a seat on the Security Council. But Chinese communism has turned on its supporter without warning in its invasion of Tibet, while international communism regards India as a country ripe for agitation and infiltration. India has been willing to stand with the United Nations against the North Koreans, but the Chinese intervention forced it to choose between this principle of collective security and its announced support of the "New China." The policy which India followed—i.e., abstention—was the equivalent of a declaration that aggression should be fought *only* when it was a small conflict which did not involve any major powers on either side. It was not an Indian policy, operating from a middle ground, which brought the truce talks in Korea, but the power and determination of the United States and the United Nations. As anti-imperialism grows ever closer to militant, Communist expansion, moral support becomes incompatible with any middle ground; in truth the middle ground, unfortunately, has all but disappeared.

► NEW AMERICAN TECHNIQUES TO MEET THE UNFORESEEN SITUATION

In the Far East the postwar period has seen the triumph of communism in China, the expansion of Soviet policy and objectives in Manchuria, Korea, and Japan, and the sweep of militant nationalism in Southeast Asia from Malaya to Indo-China. To meet these developments, unforeseen by American wartime prognosticators, United States foreign policy has had to jettison most of its traditional techniques and engage in the painful process of evolving new ones adequate to meet the danger to its interests. By 1953 most of the newly adopted techniques were apparent. They may be divided into the following categories: direct military commitment, indirect military commitment, international cooperation, economic assistance, and ideological weapons. Do they hold out the possibility of forging in the Far East a new stable system productive of the kind of peace the United States desires, or can they at best only prevent further deterioration in the area?

DIRECT MILITARY COMMITMENTS: KOREA

Since 1947 the United States has expanded its direct military commitment, a trend in striking contrast to traditional practice and wartime estimates. Since the attack of North Korean forces on the South Korean republic in June, 1950, American troops under United Nations auspices have been engaged in the difficult task of maintaining on the Asiatic mainland itself a friendly foothold free from Communist contamination. While the decision of the United States to go to the aid of South Korea was taken for reasons far broader than the protection of its own national security, the strategic location of the divided country should not be overlooked. Directly across the Tsushima Strait from the southern end of Korea lies the Japanese island of Kyushu, while the main island of Honshu is only a comparatively short distance across the Sea of Japan. All of Korea in the hands of a powerful, expansionist enemy would pose a grave threat to the American-Japanese position. The northern frontier of Korea is equally important. It lies directly adjacent to Manchuria, at the juncture of Chinese and Soviet territory. Viewed from Peking or Moscow, a Korea in the hands of a Western enemy would invite attempts to split the two allies, to stir up trouble in a Manchuria whose ultimate control has not yet been decided, and thus to magnify any difficulties arising between the two friends.

Once the North Korean aggression began, neither East nor West could view with equanimity the unification of the country by one side or the other. Each committed enough military power to prevent this from happening, but neither was willing or able to throw into the conflict the great numbers of troops necessary to gain complete victory. The inevitable result of such a situation was a stalemate, reached, significantly enough, at a line in very close proximity to the thirty-eighth parallel, which formerly divided Eastern-orientated North Korea from Western-orientated South Korea. Whether the stalemated armistice can be transmuted into a peace which will satisfy the strategic concepts of the major powers engaged is still uncertain.

DIRECT MILITARY COMMITMENTS: JAPAN

Another direct security commitment was formalized when the Japanese Peace Treaty became operative. Under the terms of the treaty the United

States retains rights to bases on the Japanese home islands in dramatic recognition of the new situation attained by Japan between 1945 and 1951. For these bases are manifestly not designed to protect international peace *against* Japan but rather symbolize the usefulness of the country in protecting international peace against the Soviet Union and Chinese communism. It should further be noted that these are not United Nations bases held by the United States, or held on behalf of the United Nations by a Japan admitted to membership in that organization. Since the United Nations contains representatives of communist countries, including the leader of world communism, and it would be unseemly, inappropriate, not to mention ineffective, to have United Nations supervision over bases potentially directed against one or more of its members. American possession is further evidence of the leadership which the United States is now exerting in the Far East on behalf of all the noncommunist countries in the area. On the same day—September 8, 1951—that the Japanese Peace Treaty was signed, Japan, through its signature to the Security Treaty consented to the continuance of American forces in Japan. The arrangement is stated as "provisional" pending the acquisition by Japan of enough power to defend itself alone or the attainment of enough stability in the Pacific to make unnecessary the continued presence of American forces. In addition to protecting Japan and the general security in the Far East, American troops may help, "at the express request of the Japanese Government to put down large-scale internal riots and disturbances in Japan caused through instigation or intervention by an outside Power or Powers."

DIRECT MILITARY COMMITMENTS: THE PACIFIC ISLANDS

As early as 1947 the United States indicated its desire for rights on former Japanese islands over and beyond the League mandates which Japan had seized from Germany. This contemplated expansion of American military power included the Ryukyu, Bonin, and Volcano Islands. The fifteen Bonin Islands lie south of Japan and have a land area of only forty square miles. The Ryukyu Islands encircle the eastern side of the China Sea between Japan and Formosa and include Okinawa. Secretary of State James Byrnes said in his book *Speaking Frankly,* "I see no objection to Japan's keeping the Ryukyu group north of Okinawa. From Okinawa south, it is my hope that the islands will be placed under a United Nations trusteeship. *For sentimental reasons,* the United States will want a trusteeship interest in Okinawa."* The United States now wants the Ryukyus, including Okinawa, for definitely other than sentimental reasons.

Article 3 of the Japanese Peace Treaty reads: "Japan will concur in *any* proposal of the United States to the United Nations to place under its trusteeship system, *with the United States as the sole administering authority,*

---

* James F. Byrnes, *Speaking Frankly* (New York, Harper & Brothers, 1947), pp. 224–225. Italics added.

Nansei Shoto south of Sofu Gan (including the Bonin Islands, Rosario Island, and the Volcano Islands) and Parece Vela and Marcus Island. Pending the making of such a proposal and affirmative action thereon, the United States will have the right to exercise all and any powers of administration, legislation, and jurisdiction over the territory and inhabitants of these islands, including their territorial waters."* The final sentence makes it clear that American possession of the islands in question will continue should any hitch arise in the United Nations over the proposal for a strategic trusteeship.

The disposition of the Ryukyus, Bonins, and Volcanos therefore follows the pattern laid down earlier with respect to the former Japanese-mandated islands, the Marshalls, the Marianas, and the Carolines. The Navy Department wished after the war to retain these islands for the United States outright, a plan that was certainly in derogation of the rights the United Nations had inherited from the League. The Navy, however, continued adamant until Secretary Byrnes was able to demonstrate that American military authorities could do under a strategic trusteeship everything they wished to accomplish by outright annexation.

Agreement on this issue cleared the way for submittal to the United Nations on November 6, 1946, of the American plans for the islands. Here additional difficulties were encountered. Molotov had previously argued with Byrnes that the Soviet Union should be considered within the Charter's definition of "states directly concerned" and hence should have the right to review the American proposal. Byrnes's reply, as he reports it, was a highly successful example of diplomatic pressure and blackmail. "While it could be assumed," he told Molotov, "that we would stand by Mr. Roosevelt's promise [for Soviet acquisition of the Kuriles and southern Sakhalin] . . . we certainly would want to know, by the time of the peace conference, [with Japan] what the Soviet Union's attitude would be toward our proposal for placing the Japanese mandated islands under our trusteeship."† The thinly veiled warning was effective, and in the Security Council the Soviet delegate supported the American position in view of the "incomparably greater sacrifices" of the United States, as compared with those of other powers, in the war with Japan. (The Soviet Union was to forget its recognition of the facts very soon and to claim that Russia alone had won the war in Asia, as it had in Europe. But this was before the cold war had begun in earnest.) The United States for its part accepted two Russian proposals for inclusion in the agreement: the omission of the provision for administration of the islands as an "integral part of the United States," and the addition of the word "independence" to the list of objectives sought for the islanders.

Objection to the American trusteeship was by no means confined to the Soviet Union. At the outset Great Britain and Australia wanted the United States to delay its proposal until negotiation of a Japanese peace treaty.

* Italics added.
† *Ibid.,* p. 221.

At one point the discussion became so acrimonious that American delegate Warren Austin threatened to withdraw the draft entirely, having the United States to rule the islands by right of conquest. Bowing to the inevitable, the Security Council on April 2, 1947, approved American trusteeship over the former Japanese mandates, a land area of 846 square miles, with a native population of about 48,000.

MILITARY COMMITMENT TO THE PHILIPPINES

The final direct military commitment of the United States was made in the Philippine Islands. Again the strategic location is important. Stretching along the South China Sea from Borneo and Celebes on the south, north almost to Formosa, the Philippine Islands are in a position to exert air and naval pressure on Malaya, Siam, Indo-China, Hainan, Formosa, and part of the South China coast, and, conversely, to prevent the eruption into the Pacific of power generated within that area. Although most aspects of the American relationship to the newly independent Philippine Republic fall into other than military categories and will be discussed later, arrangements have been made under a bilateral security pact for the retention of key bases by the United States, from which island security can be safeguarded and, more positively, influence directed outward toward the Communist-controlled mainland.

INDIRECT MILITARY COMMITMENTS: KOREA

Except for troubled Korea, the direct military commitments which the United States made were with regard to off-shore positions and did not of themselves constitute an adequate foundation for containing Asiatic communism. This situation necessitated further emphasis on *indirect* military commitments, which, while more complete geographically, were also, with one or two exceptions, to areas off the coast of Asia. The first of these was to the Republic of Korea. Before the attack by North Korea was launched, American advisers and military equipment had been furnished to Syngman Rhee's army, but as military leaders have since testified, the assistance was limited by the fear that it would be South Korea which would do the attacking. From June, 1950, until the signing of the armistice in July, 1953, the South Korean forces fought along with the United Nations troops, and during the protracted truce talks assumed responsibility for more than half the battle line. However, even after the truce was signed, American military assistance continued to be necessary.

JAPANESE ARMED STRENGTH

When General MacArthur, prior to his removal, was queried as to what amount of armament was needed by the Republic of Korea, his reply was, in effect, a plea to give a higher priority to the requirements of the

Japanese National Police Reserve. Paramilitary training of this reserve was carried on for some time under the auspices of SCAP, making the transition from police force to army fairly simple after the entrance into force of the Japanese Peace Treaty. Although the question of German rearmament has attracted far greater public attention, the rearmament of Japan represents the same and as great a reversal of the original premises on which occupation policy began. An article in the new Japanese constitution, allegedly constructed in General MacArthur's headquarters, unequivocally renounces war forever, but this is not being construed to mean that Japan shall not have the wherewithal to make war.

The rationale of the United States, accepted by its allies, is reflected in the Japanese Peace Treaty and in the Security Pact, signed the same day by the United States and Japan. In Article 5 of the Peace Treaty Japan expressly accepts obligations under Article 2 of the United Nations Charter to settle its international disputes by peaceful means and to avoid the threat or use of force. On their part the other signators "recognize that Japan as a sovereign nation possesses the inherent right of individual or collective self-defense referred to in Article 51 of the Charter of the United Nations" and that Japan may voluntarily enter into collective security arrangements. Japanese freedom to enter such arrangements would seem to have been substantially modified by the provision in the Security Pact that for its duration Japan "will not grant, without the prior consent of the United States of America, any bases or any rights, powers, or authority whatsoever, in or relating to bases or the right of garrison or of maneuver, or transit of ground, air or naval forces to any third power." In signing the pact both Secretary Acheson and Premier Yoshida clearly forecast the day of revived Japanese military power. "The United States," said Acheson, "believes that Japan . . . will in due course increasingly assume responsibility for its own defense against aggression . . .," while Yoshida declared that "it has always been my conviction that Japan, once she regains liberty and independence, must assume *full* responsibility of safeguarding that liberty and independence."

Several other points about the treaty are significant for the question of Japanese rearmament. Unlike the treaties negotiated with Italy and the Axis satellite states, no express limitation is placed on the various components of any future Japanese armed force. Reference to specific articles of the United Nations Charter suggests that, after the entry into force of the Peace Treaty, Japanese entrance into the United Nations will be smooth. It is only to be expected, however, that such an attempt would be blocked by yet another blackball cast by the Soviet Union, a nonsigner of the Peace Treaty. Mention in that treaty and in the Security Pact of "collective" security and self-defense indicates that the contribution to be made by Japanese rearmament goes far beyond the negative, if important, one of protecting the islands against external attack. The way, in fact, is opened toward making Japan, rather than China, as had earlier been envisaged, the Asiatic bulwark of security and stability for that area.

Presumably Japan's choice in the matter of rearmament, assuming that it ever had any, has been made. Certainly the limited Japanese public opinion that is regarded as responsible has increasingly favored some kind of national armed force, particularly since Chinese intervention in Korea has brought communist power so close to the home islands. Statements by American officials have furthermore made it clear that the United States will not alone do the job of protecting Japan. As in the case of Western European countries, so has Japan been told that the price of American military assistance is "continued and effective self-help." Japan apparently no longer has the option of defenselessness, nor would American security interests in that dangerous arena of combat be best served thereby. The relations between the United States and Japan since the signing of the Peace Treaty are based on the premise that mutual security requires Japanese national rearmament, American military assistance, and the retention of American bases in Japan.

INDIRECT MILITARY COMMITMENTS: THE PHILIPPINES

In addition to formalizing arrangements for United States bases, the mutual assistance treaty with the Philippine Republic provides for American military equipment and staff advisers to the Philippine Army. Aid from the United States will serve a dual purpose. It will, it is hoped, permit the Philippine government to put an end to the Hukbalahap trouble, which has been sapping national strength since the end of the war. The Huks participated in national resistance to the Japanese but continued their guerrilla activities after the war in order to force on the government extensive measures of economic reform. Confined mainly to the peasantry, the movement has become increasingly militant and closer to communism in its orientation as efforts at forcible repression have failed. Beginning with the Philippine Military Assistance Act, passed by Congress in 1946, the United States has been strengthening the military power of the government, although, as will be seen, it has been recurrently critical of Philippine reluctance to adopt measures of reform which could accomplish a considerable abatement of internal tension. If and when strife in the Philippines is ended, a well-armed and -equipped Philippine army could contribute substantially to its own defense against potential external aggression.

INDIRECT MILITARY COMMITMENTS: FRENCH INDO-CHINA

On the Southeast Asiatic mainland the United States has undertaken an ever-widening indirect military commitment to aid the embattled French in their war against the Viet Minh. French involvement in Indo-China has been sapping French strength in Europe, upon which the success of the North Atlantic Pact depends. Since 1945 about a quarter of a million troops and more than ten thousand officers have participated in the war, the number of dead and missing exceeding twenty-five thousand. The commitment of approximately two hundred thousand men, of which half are from metropolitan France, has seriously affected the ability of France to fulfill its rearmament goals in Europe.* Despite determined efforts to raise native Viet Namese armies, senior and staff officers are almost all French. To the direct military drain must be added the incalculable effect on recruitment in France of military-leadership material capable of bringing back the French army from its 1940 depths to some pale semblance of its former greatness. In economic terms the effort has meant the expenditure since 1947 of sums which the French estimate to have been equal to or greater than American assistance to France under the European Recovery Program and its successor, the Mutual Security Program. Again the indirect effects should be kept in mind: serious internal political divisions over a "colonial" war, delayed domestic recovery, incomplete reconstruction of industry, aggravated financial instability, and continued inability and unwillingness on the part of France to adopt the fundamental measures of administration and reform necessary for permanent economic health and viability.

As the war has dragged on, the French have tended increasingly to argue that they are fighting America's battle for the containment of communism. Cogency is lent to this proposition by the threefold nature of communist control over national independence movements mentioned earlier: capture of national coalitions by communist elements, use of Communist China as a threat and instrument of penetration, and strengthening of doctrinal and organizational ties to the Kremlin. Since the United States has reversed its traditional view of commitments in the Far East, it has accepted the French view of its responsibility in Indo-China. Visits of leading Frenchmen to the United States and of Americans to France have provided occasions for reiterating the statement that the French battle in Viet Nam is an integral part of the free world's self-defense against expansive international communism. Even before the North Atlantic Council meeting of 1952 issued a declaration in this sense, the United States had begun to back the French with military assistance which has increased to equal roughly two fifths of French expenditures.

American aid is, finally, based on the somewhat shaky premise that the regime of Bao Dai, former nationalist, erstwhile collaborator with Japan, now collaborator with France when he can spare the time from the haunts of Hong-Kong, the resorts of the Riviera, and the spas of Switzerland, represents an acceptable alternative to Ho Chi Minh's increasingly militant communism. Following the agreement of March 8, 1949, between the French and Bao Dai, the latter's "government" was recognized by the United States and other coun-

---

* The Indo-Chinese war inevitably affects French attitudes toward Western European defense, the rearmament of Germany, and the association of Great Britain with the European Defense Community. For details see Chapter Seventeen, "Western Europe and American Security."

tries. While France granted the pudgy "emperor" more concessions than it had been willing to give Ho in 1946, there are still some important strings attached to the attractive-sounding "independence within the French Union." The Indo-Chinese army is to have only French advisers and French equipment (possibly via the United States), and the French are to retain bases in the country with the sole right to determine the number of troops to be stationed there. Viet Namese foreign relations are to be "under the direction and within the responsibility of the Government of the Republic of France." French citizens alone of all foreigners are to have a status of legal extraterritoriality in the country: the right of trial in special mixed courts under the presidency of a Frenchman. Economic ties are to remain close. Viet Namese currency is to remain within the franc bloc, and no alteration in the status of French enterprises is to be permitted without the consent of France.

The French have been under considerable diplomatic pressure to make concessions which would weaken national resistance, and the 1949 agreement was the result. Despite the deliberate policy of holding governmental portfolios open for the nationalists, the concessions have proved to be inadequate. The Bao Dai regime may be acceptable to the West, but the ruler's past history and personal character have not endeared him to his countrymen. Under the exigencies of war, which finds the Viet Minh still in control of substantial portions of the country, the arrangement for future independence is necessarily less real than the present military operations of the French. What the nationalists, controlled by the communists, want is not membership within the French Union but the end to all ties to France. For its part, France has already spent more on the war in Indo-China than the territory is worth economically. It continues to fight because it does not know how to stop, because its prestige as a great power will not permit surrender, and because victory for the Viet Minh will prove an attractive precedent, tempting other parts of the empire, particularly restive North Africa, to do the same. The United States wants France to win and is willing to help because it does not want to see French prestige weakened in Europe or French strength diminished elsewhere in the empire; but above all because the United States does not want to see communism, an instrumentality of Russian national power, extended further on the Asiatic mainland.

INDIRECT MILITARY COMMITMENTS: NATIONALIST CHINA

The North Korean attack, followed by the Chinese Communist intervention, has brought a substantial change in official policy toward Chiang, although administration spokesmen have been bashful about admitting it. The present relationship is one somewhere between an indirect and a direct military commitment. Prior to June, 1950, American military training was being given to Chiang's forces on Formosa, along with the substantial economic aid without which the exiled regime could not have endured. Officially, however, the American attitude was that, while it would of course not like to see the island fall to the Communists, they were welcome to attempt the difficult job if they had a mind to. The eruption of war in Korea changed all that. President Truman's decision to aid South Korea included announcement of the dispatch of an American fleet to maintain the *status quo* in Formosa. While Chiang expressed dissatisfaction over his consequent inability to attack the mainland, the real result of American action was to keep the Communists off the island.

As the war in Korea continued, and particularly after the large-scale intervention of Chinese Communist troops, American attitudes toward Formosa changed from a negative unwillingness to let the island fall to the Communists toward a more positive view. General MacArthur had long been arguing that Formosa was an indispensable link in the American security system in the Pacific. The Defense and State Departments now agree with him. American aid in large quantities, initiated in the fiscal year 1950–1951, and supervised by United States military, naval, and air missions, has made an arsenal of the island, has immeasurably increased the fighting effectiveness of Nationalist troops, and has enabled Chiang to carry out measures of administrative reform which make his regime more acceptable to the native Formosans and more impressive to foreign observers.

While the military commitment of the United States is therefore substantial, and its indirect ramifications are vast, Chiang, Americans of all shades of opinion, and presumably Chinese Communist leaders agree that perpetuation of the present situation is impossible. What is to become of Formosa and Chiang? Can Chiang's American-trained, American-equipped army conquer the great bulk of China by itself? Few believe so. Is the Nationalist leader to be ferried to the mainland by American vessels, a beachhead established by American guns, an invasion launched by American arms and armies? Some would have it so, but they are not now in control of American policy, and the adventure on which they would launch Chiang and the United States looks desperate indeed. Are the Communists to be permitted to make an attack on Formosa now that a Korean truce has been arranged? Few would agree. American thinking on the subject of containment has hardened policy to a point where further Communist expansion would be met with force. Is the island of Formosa, which was to be taken from Japan and returned to China under World War II arrangements, now to be separated from China and placed under United Nations mandate? State Department policy has seemed at times to lead in that direction. But who is to have the mandate, or is Formosa to be independent, a minute Nationalist territory? Other countries, including allies of the United States, do not wish to involve the United Nations in any such arrangement or to undertake the type of guarantee necessary to keep Chiang indefinitely in control of Formosa. It is safe to say that these questions will bedevil statesmen and trouble the peace for some time to come. With the conclusion of the truce in Korea these questions become compelling. But a solution that will preserve peace, satisfy American security interests, and be acceptable to American, European, Nationalist, and Chinese Communist opinion is not as yet in sight.

MILITARY COOPERATION

A third technique of American policy, in addition to direct and indirect military commitments, is cooperation with independent nations for the maintenance of security in the Pacific. It will be remembered that American wartime estimates envisaged these independent countries as forming one of the three pillars of Asiatic security, and believed that they could fulfill this function alone. They have not been able to do so, and now the United States has placed its power behind them to this end.

On September 1, 1951, the United States signed a treaty of mutual defense with Australia and New Zealand. Article 4 of the treaty contained the operating clause, stating that "each party recognizes that an armed attack in the Pacific area on any of the parties would be dangerous to its own peace and safety and declares that it would act to meet the common danger in accordance with its constitutional processes. . . ." It should be noted that the terms of the pact were far less precise than those of the North Atlantic Treaty, with its "attack on one is an attack on all" formula. Furthermore, no specific commitment existed, following the North Atlantic wording, "to restore and maintain the security of the North Atlantic area." The pact may be regarded in part as an attempt to broaden the international base of security arrangements in the Pacific and in part as the price the United States was willing to pay to get Australia and New Zealand to sign and ratify a Japanese peace treaty which would contain no barriers to the revival of Japanese military power, perhaps even to the extent which had enabled Japan only a decade earlier to extend its control uncomfortably close to the two Pacific members of the British Commonwealth.

The implications of the pact for cooperation between Australia and New Zealand, members in the British Commonwealth of Nations, on the one hand, and the United States, an ally of the center of that commonwealth, on the other hand, should not be missed. It was widely felt during the war that one consequence of the decline of British power in the Pacific would be the closer association of Australia and New Zealand with the only remaining nation able to promote their security. The difficulty which the United States has had in redefining its objectives in the area, as well as the reluctance of the two countries involved to take any steps which might give the appearance of weakening their Commonwealth ties, has delayed the formal fruition of the new relationship.

ECONOMIC COMMITMENTS

By way of contrast to expanding military techniques, the traditionally primary weapon, economic commitments, have come to occupy an increasingly secondary position. At least three separate techniques now being used fall within this general category: purchase agreements, economic assistance, and the Point Four Program. All offer great potentialities which so far have not been realized.

Turmoil in Asia, following on the heels of war, resulted in the general failure of the area to resume its former place in world trade as a supplier of raw materials. Under the pressure of war, the old trade patterns were replaced by purchase agreements to secure the needed products from other areas—such as Latin America and Africa—and by the development of national sources, either natural, substitute, or synthetic. Even so, there is still a need in the West for such Asiatic products as tin, rubber, and tungsten, which the East under stable conditions could supply at prices considerably lower than its wartime competitors. The United States government has entered the scene with purchase agreements to help meet the requirements of its partial mobilization. This large demand has combined with unrest in the raw-material-producing countries to bring about a price pattern that is highly unstable and considerably speculative. As a consequence, little real and lasting assistance has filtered down to the native grower, laborer, and producer, although large profits have been made in some instances.

It must be recognized that the new pattern may prove to be fundamentally different from the old, even if Asiatic production of raw materials is resumed at prewar levels. The continuing weakness of the Western European colonial countries and the unparalleled economic strength of the United States have resulted in the replacement of the political control of the former by the economic power of the latter. While the United States is willing to pay good money for what it gets, its action in the case of tin prices illustrates a reluctance, not felt by Western European countries in the past, to support artificial prices created by a sellers' market and maintained by a restrictive international producers' cartel.

Direct assistance to Asiatic governments was mainly under the supervision of the European Cooperation Administration and its successor, the Mutual Security Agency before the incorporation of the latter into the Foreign Operations Administration. With such supervision the programs have been closely related to the security objectives of the United States. Thus substantial assistance has gone to both Formosa and the Viet Nam. To Formosa was allocated almost $100 million annually since 1951. In Viet Nam, American personnel have attempted, wherever possible, to work directly with the native Viet Namese, Cambodians, and Laotians, rather than through the French officials, irritating as this may be to the *amour-propre* of the French. To make sure that the natives distinguish between the United States and France in this area, economic assistance has gone hand in hand with American information programs.

ECONOMIC AID TO THE PHILIPPINES

By reason of its special relationship, the United States has so far given special economic attention to the Philippines. Indeed, the period of formal Philippine independence began with concomitant American recognition, embodied in the Rehabilitation Act of 1946, that the United States was under special obligation to assist the recovery of the islands from the effects of the war and to give them a good start on their new road. Charges have been made by Filipinos that this obligation was not fully honored by the United States. Certainly the Philippine government has not made the most efficient use possible of the funds granted it. At the request of the Quirino Administration, the Bell Mission was sent from the United States to survey conditions and make recommendations. The result was a frank report that minced no words. Philippine policy was found to be deficient in at least five respects. There was still widespread corruption in government. The tax structure was totally inadequate and, worse, placed the heaviest burden on those with low incomes. Although foreign-exchange control of a sort existed, it permitted the import of unnecessary luxury items which in turn led to high profits by speculators and to the export of capital. The remaining capital sources were low and, instead of going into productive investment, were being used for speculation, especially in real estate. Although one of the crying needs of the country was for agricultural diversification and increase in agricultural production, far too little had been attempted and even less had been accomplished.

Many of the same charges could be leveled at other governments in so-called underdeveloped areas, particularly in Latin America. As any government would be, the Philippine administration was outraged at the undiplomatically presented truth, especially when it was made public for all to read. A source close to the President issued a written communiqué which was vitriolic: "Filipinos, there is no question, are inefficient all right—even in their grafting—due no doubt to the simple lack of sufficient experience. With more time and greater chances they will yet show that they can equal or even surpass the stink familiar and now taken for granted in Washington and such very proper, exemplary centers of power, prosperity, and culture."* When the explosion had blown itself out, however, the Philippine government indicated its willingness to take the steps recommended by the Bell Mission as prerequisites to further American aid. So long as the Philippines remain so strategically important to the United States, mutual interest would dictate economic as well as military cooperation.

TECHNICAL ECONOMIC ASSISTANCE

Assistance of the type envisaged by President Truman's Point Four Program has been slow in materializing, as have similar efforts under the International Bank and the United Nations. Here again studies have been made, some agreements have been reached, and some money has been appropriated, although a lag between appropriation and disbursement has existed. Difficulty naturally arises in cooperating on long-range development in areas such as Malaya, Indo-China, and even Indonesia, where the essential prerequisite of a military decision has not been reached. But more of the trouble lies in the

* New York *Times,* July 9, 1950, p. 1.

complex nature of the area and of the tasks to be undertaken. Certainly the concept of economic progress which would bring higher living standards and better health to overpopulated countries with impoverished, undernourished, disease-ridden, short-lived people is a noble one worthy of the humanitarian interests of the United States. This objective is also firmly grounded on national self-interest. But basic understanding of modern economic operations is even more lacking in much of the Far East than it is in the Near East and in Latin America, and the instillation of fundamental knowledge takes time. The alteration in traditional beliefs and cultural patterns basically antithetical to economic progress takes even longer.

Furthermore, since it is government-to-government in direction, technical assistance to be effective must be channeled through Asiatic regimes both willing and able to employ the techniques involved. Not only is the ability in many instances lacking, but there is a natural hostility by reactionary as well as Communist-controlled regimes to engage in programs which, by their very nature, alter and perhaps destroy the bases of their power. To elude any native governmental obstruction and at the same time to maximize the economic impact of the assistance programs, American teams of experts, particularly in the fields of health and sanitation and of agricultural productivity, are kept small and wherever possible work on a decentralized level with localities and with individuals. Finally, the connection between technical assistance and private capital investment has unfortunate connotations to nationalist governments now engaged in a struggle to free themselves from the vestiges of Western imperialism, of which exploitation by capital is regarded as one. This is not to say that these formidable obstacles cannot and should not be overcome. Recognition of their existence, however, should counsel patience regarding short-term results. In the parlous state of Southeast Asia, short-term successes must be achieved by the use of other American techniques or there will never be a chance for Point Four to attain the long-range possibilities inherent in it.*

IDEOLOGICAL TECHNIQUES

It was pointed out at the beginning of this chapter that traditional American foreign policy in the Far East carried a high moralistic content and that frequent use has been made of ideological techniques to maintain and advance American interests. Against many handicaps, of which the domestic ones are far from insignificant, the State Department has attempted to carry on from this same platform, particularly with regard to China. The intent has obviously been to open up divergencies between Chinese and Soviet objectives, into which American policies can drive wedges deep enough to diminish the threat of expansionist international communism. Speeches by State Department officials and by American representatives at the United Nations have accordingly

---

* For a more complete discussion of technical assistance see Chapter Fifteen, "Evolving Patterns of Economic Foreign Policy."

rung the changes on two basic questions: Who is the imperialist in Asia? Who stands for peace and freedom? The Chinese Communists during the civil war accused the Nationalist regime of being a puppet in the hands of the United States. Now the shoe is on the other foot. Communism, says the United States, is an alien dogma fastened by force on the Chinese people by those who would serve other masters, the rulers of the Kremlin. One of the best examples of the ideological approach are the speeches made during 1949 and 1950, prior to the outbreak of the Korean war, by the then Secretary of State Dean Acheson.

Who is the friend of the Chinese people? "So far as we are concerned," said Secretary Acheson, "we know that we are interested in the peoples of Asia as people. We want to help them as people. We do not want to take anything from them for ourselves. We do not want to deny them any opportunity, any freedom, any right. We do not want to use them for any purpose of our own." On the other hand, "can the Chinese people fail to observe that, whatever may be the promises for the future, under the terms of the treaty and agreements recently concluded in Moscow, the USSR has special rights in China which represent an infringement of Chinese sovereignty and which are held by no other power? It is Soviet Russia which, despite all the tawdry pretense of the treaty terms, occupies the role of empire builder at China's expense." *

The United States has given and is prepared to give real aid to China; the Soviet Union takes much out of China with one hand and returns a pittance with the other. ". . . Soviet Russia has promised to return certain Manchurian property but not the industrial equipment robbed by the Red Army in 1945. Is this aid? Is it even a belated admission of a theft which deprived not only China but all of Asia of some two billion dollars worth of productive capacity? . . . Soviet extends to China a three-hundred-million-dollar, five-year credit at an interest rate of one percent yearly. . . . [Because of the ruble's revaluation] the Chinese people may find Soviet Russia's credit to be no more than forty-five million dollars per year. They can compare this with a grant—not a loan—of four hundred million dollars voted by the American Congress to China in the single year 1948." †

Such statements could constitute potent propaganda, since they are basically consistent with the facts. That the ideological weapon has so far produced no *discernible* results is due to factors other than the phraseology of the American message. For one thing American opinion at all levels has been and is now split on what course to pursue toward Communist China. Many have attacked State Department policy since 1945 as too soft and have advocated such stringent measures as a tight economic blockade to cut down China's war potential. Others, including the State Department, which has to deal with American allies who have recognized the Communist regime, would

---

* *Strengthening the Forces of Freedom,* p. 145.
† *Ibid.,* p. 147.

confine a blockade to a lengthy list of strategic materials. The question of the proper China policy is directly related to the serious domestic issue of the extent of subversive infiltration into American decision-making agencies. As a result, Asiatics have good reason to suspect that the United States speaks to Asia with many voices, no one of which represents a united governmental or popular opinion.

Unofficial and official divisions within the United States have thus blunted America's ideological weapon. But dullness has also been caused by the serious deterioration of the situation in Asia since 1950. Domestic reasons lay behind the refusal of the United States in 1949 to recognize the palpable fact that Mao controlled the mainland of China. American delegates therefore denied the Communist regime the right to a seat on the Security Council of the United Nations, clinging to the fiction that Chiang's delegates still represented something more than the small, offshore island of Formosa. Communist intrusion into the Korean conflict and its assistance to the Viet Minh naturally hardened American determination not to allow an aggressor to enter an organization devoted to the maintenance of international peace and security. So long as the possibility of further Chinese aggression exists, the United States will naturally take the lead in keeping trade with China at a low level, particularly with regard to products which could add to the Chinese war potential.

The point of the above paragraphs is the simple one frequently overlooked: the ideological technique can be successful only when it is fully consistent, not only with the facts, but also with the other techniques simultaneously employed.* The new definition of United States security interests in the Far East has led to military, economic, and other policies which have directly intruded American power into the area, with consequently great effect on every one of the countries involved. The policies adopted to protect these expanded security interests are sharply at variance with the ideological protestations being made at the same time. To the peoples of Asia, both the United States and the Soviet Union appear as intruders, whose pressure they would like to avoid. Some prefer one intruder to the other, but the unfortunate meaning of the cold war is that while the present split between East and West continues, neither side will watch with equanimity while the other's power fills the vacuum which is the Far East.

► SUMMARY

Through no fault of American policy most of the Asiatic continent is beyond the reach of American influence, and this at the very time in American history when the security of the nation is most intimately connected with Far Eastern events. It must further be admitted that the expansive revolutionary pattern so destructive to American influence has not yet been halted.

---

* This point is spelled out in more detail in Chapter Sixteen, "American Policy in the Battle of Ideas."

The United States will continue at a disadvantage until this comes about, for the course of postwar relations with China demonstrates the extreme difficulty, if not the impossibility, of American identification with revolutionary, nationalist movements. The inevitable consequence of the development of the United States to great-power status and the nature of its domestic political, economic, and social institutions have been to orient its policies in the foreign field toward stability, order, and evolutionary change within a legal framework. The United States was not itself born in this manner, nor were these its early objectives. They are not now, unfortunately, the objectives of much of the rest of the world, into which the Western state system is seeking to bring stability and order. Full recognition of American disadvantages in a revolutionary situation should lead the United States toward a formulation of policies which do not attempt the impossible. At the same time, it should lead to increasing emphasis on those techniques of policy which may initiate evolutionary change and development, such as the Technical Assistance Program, which may ultimately help to produce the type of stability which the United States seeks.

With most of the mainland beyond the reach of its influence, the United States has had to strengthen its policies for the maintenance of military security in the remaining area. Such measures, however, are essentially negative. The positions which have been attained since 1947 by direct and indirect commitment and by military and economic assistance do not, and in themselves cannot, reverse the unfavorable situation. This proposition would remain true even if, as seems increasingly unlikely, all of Korea should be freed and the French should win complete victory in Indo-China. Despite the claims of Chiang and his American supporters, the United States government has so far wisely recognized that Formosa is not a springboard from which American influence can leap once more into Asia, but rather the wobbly end of a long buccaneer's plank which Chiang has been forced to walk. In reversing its policy toward Japan, the United States, as in Germany, is taking a calculated but enforced risk that a revived and strengthened former enemy can be transformed into a faithful friend. Even should this gamble turn out to have been a shrewd one, Japan, like Formosa, cannot serve as a base by which American influence can reintrude onto the mainland. The best that can be expected is that a new Japan can contribute materially to the retention of what areas still remain out of Communist hands.

DISADVANTAGES OF THE SOVIET UNION

The preceding section presents the dark side of the picture. Americans viewing it have been tempted to reach the unhappy conclusion that what is dark for the United States is inevitably rosy, permanently rosy, for the Soviet Union. While the cold war has destroyed the middle ground and Russia has filled much of the vacuum left by waning Western influence, it cannot be assumed that this substitution is going to be immutable. Indeed, a persuasive case can be made for the argument that the disadvantages of the West in Asia are about to be inherited by the Soviet Union. These disadvantages may be stated as economic, geographic, social, demographic, and ideological.

The economic problems of underproduction, overpopulation, and disease frustrate efforts at their solution by the countries themselves. With the maximum amount of Western assistance these problems would still remain for a long time to come. It is this liability which has now been inherited by Chinese and Soviet communism. The Chinese begin with few tools other than determination. The Russians have been unwilling and unable to approach a solution to their own economic problems and tend always to place first emphasis on what they can get out of an area, not what they must put in. This exploitative relationship has already caused trouble for Russia in Eastern Europe. There is less to exploit in Asia, but the assistance of the Soviet Union has so far been, as former Secretary Acheson stated, small and substantially spurious. Given a hundred years of control, these economic liabilities might be overcome, but the liabilities themselves may ensure that the period of control is considerably less than a hundred years.

Geographically, the disadvantage of the Soviet Union may be stated in military terms as the overextension of lines. It is cold comfort for the one in retreat to contemplate this extension of the enemy's influence, but the fact remains that the thousands of miles between Moscow and Peking are in strategic terms much greater than the thousands of miles between San Francisco and New York, or between New York and Paris. Geographic remoteness places a great burden on the techniques by which control is consolidated. When the problems of the area are added, these techniques may break down altogether. In repudiating the Chinese Communists during the war, Stalin may, among other things, have been voicing a recognition of the Kremlin's geographic limitations. The Chinese Communists had to win the civil war themselves; the continued necessity of self-reliance may breed independence of policy, however often it is camouflaged and denied by the whitewash of mutual admiration that always accompanies Communist pronouncements concerning various members of the family. Whitewash cannot hide the fact that since the death of Stalin Mao's position in the hierarchy of international communism has improved. As the struggle for power within the Soviet Union continues, Mao becomes the primary spokesman for communism in Asia. Once this position has been assumed, it will be increasingly difficult to relegate China's dictator to the role of junior partner in the Far East.

Communism posits the destruction of the capitalistic organization of society as found in Western Europe and the United States and its reconstruction along entirely different lines. Theoretically the new basis is to be the proletariat, the working class, but, as exemplified in the Soviet Union, the new elite was composed of the managerial class, the bureaucracy, and, most recently, the military. In this way power was consolidated in a country in theory not ready for a communist revolution. There is even less in Asia with which to create this social reorganization, whether the new order is stated in theory or described in fact. To all intents and purposes there is no proletariat, no managerial class, no bureaucracy, and, except in China, little formal military establishment. There is, outside of China, no peasantry in the European sense.

All this would suggest that extreme sensitivity and adaptiveness on the part of communism will be necessary to take advantage of what social institutions can be manipulated. Before and during the civil war this seemed the path that Mao was following. But at this point a horrible dilemma appears. If a form of social organization which differs from classical communist theory develops, the consequent society will not be communistic, even as interpreted by the Kremlin, and will be less amenable to policies of a communist nature. If the puristic theory is followed in practice, the attempt to fashion a communist society where none of the ingredients exist may very well fail and destroy the communist leaders in the process. Confronted with this dilemma, international communism has invariably chosen the second course—in Eastern Europe, and now, apparently, in China. The difficulties inherent in this choice have led to an inexorable process of "national deviation" on the part of those Communists who failed to create communism out of the whole cloth. With their periodic purging, control from Moscow has tightened. When added to other ingredients, this may make a boiling cauldron of Chinese-Russian relations.

Not only are the Asian people, newly merged in the communist orbit, far removed geographically from the Kremlin and depressed by hitherto insurmountable economic problems, but in numbers they far exceed those of Soviet Russia. Granted that communism has always been a minority movement and that it has been able to fasten control on large numbers of people, there may well be a limit to the minority-majority relationship which will be reached in Asia. Communism, even if successful in remaining in the saddle, may be given a different policy direction, particularly in external relations, by the demands of its captive peoples. Even Soviet policy has not been able to operate in complete separation from the views of its Russian subjects. Indeed, official propaganda, often with a note of desperation, has claimed identification between government policy and popular desires. Some congruence must also exist for Asians, with their own problems and their own historical memory. How big a tail can the Russian dog wag before he drops from exhaustion?

One of the major communist techniques to overcome the aforementioned liabilities has been the use of ideological weapons. Heavy emphasis is laid on hatred of the Western "enemy" (e.g., the present Chinese Communist campaign) and on common identifications under the tent of international communism. Active hatred of the enemy would seem to depend on the continued proximate presence of that enemy to lend substance to the cries of "Wolf, wolf!" The Western "wolves" are now largely gone from the mainland. A successful policy of containment that frustrates the expansiveness of communism generated by hate campaigns may go far toward falsifying the campaign itself, hardening the cynicism of the people to continued calls to action which achieves no noticeable result apart from failure to cope with the far more pressing problems of economic subsistence.

How long can a common view of the world and of Asia's place in the communist scheme of things be maintained in an area that has few Marxists and fewer Stalinists? Once the pattern of identifications begins to shatter, all sorts of outside, extraneous views enter to complicate the problem of communist control. Building and maintaining this unitary pattern is already proving difficult in Eastern Europe and may in the long run be impossible. Although Asia's experience with the West has been more limited and far more limited and far more unhappy than that of Russia's European satellites, it is *Asia's* civilization which is at stake, a civilization far different and far older than Russia's.

Former Secretary Acheson has said of the peoples of Asia: "We do not want to use them for any purpose of our own." What the United States does desire is to prevent their use by the Soviet Union. Herein lies the great distinction between American and Soviet policy, because Russia *does* want to use the people of Asia for its own purposes, has attempted and will continue to attempt to do so. The purposes of Russia are not the purposes of Asia, if the foregoing analysis is correct. If American policy remains clearly grounded in this conviction, if a necessarily expanded direct security commitment is never taken as an objective in itself but solely as a means toward the maintenance and expansion of Asia's own freedom, then it seems reasonable to expect long-range progress and ultimate success in the attainment of the real objective of American Far Eastern policy: a system of peace on which can be founded continued betterment in the conditions of the peoples of Asia.

► SELECTED BIBLIOGRAPHY

The history of American-Russian relations in the Far East can be traced in Pauline Tompkins's book of that title (New York, The Macmillan Company, 1949) and also in the two volumes of David Dallin, *The Rise of Russia in Asia* (New Haven, Conn., Yale University Press, 1949) and *Soviet Russia and the Far East* (New Haven, Conn., Yale University Press, 1948). Among the significant volumes on the area as a whole which have been published since the war are Owen Lattimore, *Situation in Asia* (Boston, Little, Brown & Company, 1949); George B. Cressey, *Asia's Lands and Peoples* (New York, McGraw-Hill Book Company, 1951); Henry Maurer, *Collision of East and West* (Chicago, Henry Regnery Company, 1951); Harold Vinacke, *The United States in the Far East* (Stanford, Calif., Stanford University Press, 1952); and Lawrence Rosinger and associates, *The State of Asia* (New York, Alfred A. Knopf, Inc., 1951). American policy in general and in detail before World War II is discussed by A. Whitney Griswold in *The Far Eastern Policy of the United States* (New York, Harcourt, Brace & Company, 1938); also John Fairbank, *The United States and China*

(Cambridge, Mass., Harvard University Press, 1948); and the publication of the Department of State entitled *United States Relations with China* (Department of State Publication 3608). Sections of the book by former Secretary of State James Byrnes, *Speaking Frankly* (New York, Harper & Brothers, 1947), concern wartime and immediate postwar negotiations with the Soviet Union. Arguments concerning the proper future course of American policy after the Chinese Communists seized control of the Chinese mainland are to be found in such works as Edwin O. Reischauer, *Toward a New Far Eastern Policy,* one of the Headline Series of the Foreign Policy Association, No. 84, November–December, 1950; in two articles by David Rowe, author of *China among the Powers* (New York, Harcourt, Brace & Company, 1945): "Where Do We Stand in Asia?" *Virginia Quarterly Review,* October, 1949, and, with Nathan Leites, "The Choice in China," *World Politics,* April, 1949; and in Gerald Winfield and John Fairbank, "What Can the United States Do in China?" *Foreign Policy Reports,* March 15, 1949. A special issue of the *Saturday Review of Literature* for August 4, 1951, containing articles, among others, by Carlos Romulo, Harold Isaacs, and U. K. R. V. Rao, was devoted to *The United States and the Challenge of Asia.* Material on the rise of Chinese Communism is found in Harold R. Isaacs, *The Tragedy of the Chinese Revolution* (Stanford, Calif., Stanford University Press, 1951); Conrad Brandt, Benjamin Schwartz, and John K. Fairbanks, *A Documentary History of Chinese Communism* (London, George Allan & Unwin, Ltd., 1952); Werner Levi, *Modern China's Foreign Policy* (Minneapolis, University of Minnesota Press, 1953); and Frank Moraes, *Report on Mao's China* (New York, The Macmillan Company, 1953). Two important articles by H. Arthur Steiner discuss the organization and objectives of the Chinese Communists: "The People's Democratic Dictatorship in China," *Western Political Quarterly,* March, 1950, and "Mainsprings of Chinese Communist Foreign Policy," *American Journal of International Law,* January, 1950. Sources of special reference to Southeast Asia include Lennox Mills, *The New World of Southeast Asia* (Minneapolis, University of Minnesota Press, 1949); C. Du Bois, *Social Forces in South East Asia* (Minneapolis, University of Minnesota Press, 1949); Phillips Talbott, *et al., South Asia in the World Today* (Chicago, University of Chicago Press, 1949); Philip Thayer, ed., *South East Asia in the Coming World* (Baltimore, The Johns Hopkins Press, 1953); Virginia Thompson and Richard Adloff, *The Left Wing in Southeast Asia* (New York, William Sloane Associates, 1950), and the same authors' "Empire's End in South-East Asia," No. 78, 1949, in the Foreign Policy Association's Headline Series. Victor Purcell discusses *The Chinese in Southeast Asia* (Toronto, Oxford University Press, 1951); and Milton Sachs, "The Strategy of Communism in Southeast Asia" in *Pacific Affairs,* September, 1950. Among the many assessments of American occupation of Japan and the possible course of that country are M. Macmahon Ball, *Japan—Enemy or Ally?* (New York, The John Day Company, 1949); Russell Brines, *MacArthur's Japan* (Philadelphia, J. B. Lippincott Company, 1948); Ernest Reischauer, *The United States and Japan* (Cambridge, Harvard University Press, 1950); Robert B. Textor, *Failure in Japan*

(New York, The John Day Company, 1951); Hugh Barton, ed., *Japan* (Ithaca, N. Y., Cornell University Press, 1951); and Edwin O. Reischauer, *et al., Japan and America Today* (Stanford, Calif., Stanford University Press, 1953). Paul Langer and Rodger Swearingen write of the special problem of "The Japanese Communist Party, the Soviet Union, and Korea," in *Pacific Affairs,* December, 1950. The Department of State's *Korea, 1945–1948* (Department of State Publication 3305), describes conditions between the end of the war and the North Korean attack, while another pamphlet entitled *The United States Policy in the Korean Crisis* is a compilation of documents of the first days following the outbreak of war. House Report No. 2495, 81st Congress, 2d Session contains *Background Information on Korea.*

CHAPTER NINETEEN

AMERICAN SECURITY IN THE WESTERN HEMISPHERE

Introduction: Beginnings of the Pan American Union • The Security Area: Multilateral Instruments • The Economic Area: Multilateral Instruments • The Political Area: Multilateral Instruments • Conclusions • Selected Bibliography

By 1953 the relationship among the twenty-one American republics had evolved to a point where the appellation "system," already in use for many years, has some degree of accuracy. Periodic attempts had been made during the nineteenth century to establish a confederation, league, or union among the Latin-American republics, but all had come to naught, although conferences were held for that purpose in 1826, 1848, 1856, and 1864. Continuity of organization may be said to have begun with the 1889 meeting initiated by the United States and attended in Washington by all the then independent countries except the Dominican Republic. It was this conference which established the Commercial Bureau of the American Republics, later called the International Bureau, and in 1910 given its present name, the Pan American Union. Periodic international conferences of the American states were held, usually at five-year intervals, except for a thirteen-year gap between 1910 and 1923 occasioned by World War I. In addition, many special meetings and congresses were convened on specific subjects of common interest.

► INTRODUCTION: BEGINNINGS OF THE
PAN AMERICAN UNION

The Pan American Union from the time of its establishment has constituted the core of what organization existed, in spite of the fact that it rested on the resolution of a conference rather than on a treaty. Although the form of the Union changed and the scope of its activities broadened widely, its status up to 1945 remained comparable to that of typical bureaus attached to any of the international unions that proliferated during the nineteenth and early twentieth centuries. Originally restricted to the "prompt collection and distribution of commercial information," the Union soon became the collating and publication center for all technical information important to the American republics, and in addition served as the organizer and secretariat for the formal conferences and for many of the special meetings.

At first the Pan American Union, like the bureaus of other international unions, was under the supervision of the host nation, the United States Department of State. In time, however, a Governing Board was established, on which all the American governments had right of representation regardless of whether or not they were recognized by the United States. The Union was specifically barred, however, from taking any hand in "political" matters, and this prohibition reflected the lack of any sense of community either among the American republics themselves or between them and the United States.

FACTORS HINDERING THE GROWTH OF AN INTER-AMERICAN COMMUNITY

After World War I the barriers of mutual suspicion, hatred, and distrust were heightened by many factors inherent in the then existing relationship. With few exceptions, the Latin-American countries revealed a uniform lack of maturity in their social, economic, and political institutions. Rare was the government which was based on the freely given support of the people. Revolutions, *coups d'état,* and uprisings caused rapid changes of regime except where a strong man, on the order of the Venezuelan Gómez or the Mexican Díaz, held the country in a tight, personal grip. Under such circumstances the growth of a meaningful inter-American organization was difficult.

Nor were the Latin-American countries agreed on much save their dislike for the United States. Eighteen were theoretically Spanish in heritage and culture, but with an admixture of Indian and mestizo ranging from an insignificant percentage in the case of Argentina and Uruguay to a majority in the case of Mexico, Guatemala, Ecuador, and Peru, among others. The largest state, Brazil, had been controlled by Portugal, and the small island of Santo Domingo was divided between the Spanish-speaking, racially mixed Dominican Republic and the French-speaking, Negro Haiti.

Feuds, jealousies, and outright wars were not uncommon between these diverse countries. To cite some examples: Nicaragua, El Salvador, and Honduras quarreled over the Gulf of Forseca; Nicaragua and Costa Rica over the area of the projected interoceanic canal; Colombia and Peru over Leticia; Peru and Ecuador over the latter's boundary; Peru, Chile, and Bolivia over the sea-access of which Bolivia had been forcibly deprived; and Bolivia and Paraguay over the Chaco. Brazil and Argentina were rivals for economic and political influence in Paraguay, Bolivia, and Uruguay. A series of overlapping confused conventions, treaties, and other agreements which theoretically bound the Latin-American nations to resort to various measures for the peaceful settlement of disputes were enthusiastically signed and rarely ratified by all countries. This legal floriation was comparable to the development of European arbitral devices and was almost equally powerless to prevent or to settle conflict.

After World War I most of the Latin-American countries entered the League of Nations, and some, such as Argentina, played a significant role in that organization. This action was in direct contrast to the attitude and position taken by the United States. During the heyday of the League, 1920 to 1933, therefore, some other American governments tended to place their obligations to the League above any interest in a purely regional grouping and to oppose developments in the Western Hemisphere which might tend to weaken the world organization. This was particularly true of the larger states of South America, such as Argentina, geographically removed from the influence of the United States.

Even more serious differences with the United States existed. In a utopian brotherhood the lion lies down with the lamb, but in the reality of interwar hemisphere relations the North American lion seemed willing enough to do so on his own terms, while the Latin-American lamb was naturally chary of accepting any such invitation. The nadir of trust and understanding was reached at the Sixth International Conference of American States in 1928, at which Secretary of State Hughes defended the two American practices most bitterly resented by Latin Americans. He maintained the right of his government under international law to intervene, as it had been doing, in most of the countries of the Caribbean area. To be sure, these interventions were not for the purpose of political or territorial aggrandizement, but the attendant long-term fiscal and economic tutelage by the United States aroused Latin-American wrath.* The secretary also bluntly refused to permit the conference to discuss American tariff policy, which other republics, led by Argentina, claimed, with considerable justice, was depriving them of markets in the United States while adding to the power of that country to export to others products for which the importers could not easily pay.

The reversal of previous United States policies, the progressive collapse of the League structure, and the erratic but discernible progress of Latin-American governments toward maturity made possible the rapid development of inter-American organization after 1933. Much of the newly added structure remained on an informal basis until after World War II. Foreshadowed by the undertakings agreed upon at the special Mexico City Conference in 1945, the principal features of the system were delineated in the security and administrative fields at the 1947 Conference on the Maintenance of Continental Peace and Security, held at Rio de Janeiro, and the Ninth Inter-American Conference, convened the next year in Bogotá. What, then, is the essential nature of this Inter-American System, and what is its relation to the facts of international power?

---

* More detail on United States Caribbean policy may be found in Chapter One.

RECONCILIATION OF SOVEREIGN EQUALITY WITH DISPARITY OF POWER

The system itself may be viewed as a highly successful technique for reconciling two contradictory ideas. The first of these is the theory of state sovereignty, which is expressed in foreign relations as the juridical equality of states large and small. Sovereignty is a difficult concept to define with any precision or pretense to universal applicability; rather does it frequently appear as a group of ideas not always mutually compatible. In its internal application sovereignty implies the undivided authority of the government over persons and property within its jurisdiction, although not infrequently that authority may be claimed in theory and subordinated in practice to the power of another state. With regard to the relations between states, the doctrine of sovereignty declares that states are equal with respect to their rights under international law no matter what their relative size and strength may be. Since international law confers but few self-operating rights, sovereignty permits the denial by a government of any other authority legally capable of controlling its commitments and obligations. Upon the state alone supposedly rests the power to decide whether or not to undertake commitments, the extent of those commitments, and whether or not at any point it shall honor them. International law, being based on the concept of sovereignty, may be broken by a particular state, but such action, while illegal, may not be legally repaired by force exercised upon a state without its consent. Obviously this anarchic aspect of sovereignty is fundamental to the international instability in which the world lives and is highly incompatible with the development of effective international organization. Reconciliation of sovereignty with international action lies in the theory that a state may voluntarily consent to a diminution of its sovereignty, if all other states do the same, thus preserving the juridical equality in status, and also in the argument that there is a fundamental difference between the legal and political aspects of state relations.

As applied to the Western Hemisphere, sovereign equality means the noncoercion of a small country, such as Paraguay, by a large one, such as Argentina, and the right of both to be the final and sole judges or the extent to which they will enter upon obligations involving one another.

Part of the difficulty of defining state sovereignty is due precisely to the second fact inherent in the Inter-American System: the profound and immutable disparity of power. Regardless of the legal equality of El Salvador and the United States, the national strength of the latter gives it preponderance over the former and the rest of Latin America, as well, albeit in varying degrees. This preponderance cannot be evaded. It exists, whether the United States chooses to translate it into foreign policies or not. The actual process by which foreign policies are decided and implemented must always take place under conscious or unconscious influence of the vast differences in power. It is a tribute to the degree of effective inter-American organization which has been attained that its growth has coincided, not with an abatement of the power differential, but rather with a substantial increase.

RESPONSIBILITIES ENTAILED BY THE POSSESSION OF POWER

The possession by the United States of disproportionate power gives rise to two sorts of responsibility which are often difficult to reconcile. The United States has a primary responsibility to exercise its power to protect the national interest and attain the objectives of the country, however they may be defined. It was this primary, unilateral type of responsibility which the United States assumed after the Civil War when it began an increasingly effective defense against foreign intrusion into the Western Hemisphere in accordance with the Monroe Doctrine, originally enunciated forty years earlier. Onto the shoulders of no other government or group of governments can this type of responsibility be shifted. Its discharge, moreover, grows daily in importance and complexity with the alteration of three interacting variables: the absolute increase in the national strength of the United States; the still greater increase in the disparity of power, not only between the United States and Latin America, but between the United States and the other nations of the world; and finally the demands made by the people of the United States on their government.

But the increasing power of the United States and its disparity with that of Latin America has given rise to a second responsibility—to the peoples and governments of the other American republics. This concept is difficult to define in such terms that it does not seem a rationale for imperialism. Particularly is this true because of the theses which have been advanced in the past, such as the Roosevelt Corollary to the Monroe Doctrine. The talk of unilateral responsibility is but a convenient peg on which to hang various interpretations of the type of responsibility mentioned in the preceding paragraph. Latin-American governments and peoples with good reason resent any presumption of right by the United States to be arbiter of their destinies. It was recognition of the first type of responsibility and blindness to the second which led the United States down the interventionist road. Increasingly since 1933, however, the government has come to realize that its decision making must be influenced, not alone by a concept of *national* interest in the narrow sense of the term, but by the wishes, goals, objectives, and attitudes of Latin-American peoples and governments, as they define and present them. To disregard Latin-American wishes or to arrogate to the United States the right unilaterally to determine what they ought to be would tend to blur the distinction essential to American foreign policy between the Latin American–United States relationship and that of Eastern Europe with the Soviet Union.

As will be pointed out in more detail in the course of this chapter, reconciliation of national and Latin-American interest is frequently difficult and sometimes impossible. It is complicated by the undoubted fact that Latin-American desires, goals, and objectives are at times mutually inconsistent and change rapidly within a single government, between various governments, between the peoples of one nation and their government, and indeed between peoples in one country. Recognition of the difficulty in interpreting and discharging this type of responsibility is no excuse, however, for denying its existence and abandoning the effort. It will remain so long as the Latin-American nations form an important but weak part of the world system.

THE PROBLEM OF MULTILATERALIZATION OF THE MONROE DOCTRINE

The pattern which inter-American organization has gradually evolved to reconcile the theory of state sovereignty with the facts of international power within the hemisphere may be viewed as a series of concentric circles, ranging outward from the unilateral relationship through the bilateral to the multilateral. As the system has acquired focus and broadened in scope, an evolution in policy has been discernible outward from the unilateral (United States foreign policy action) to the multilateral (cooperation among all the American republics). While this shift is indispensable to the formation and operation of any multilateral organization, the absence of a true world or regional government means that the shift can never be complete: unilateral policy will always be important and fundamental. Thus it is generally in the interests of the United States to foster and accelerate this shift toward multilateral action, but at the same time American policy makers must not thereby be blinded to the basically unalterable distribution of power remaining constant during the process.

Delusion regarding this fact is easy and fairly prevalent among writers in the field. Ever since the Eighth Inter-American Conference in 1938 provided a framework for consultation in the event of actual or threatened aggression from outside the Western Hemisphere, some Americans have been alluding to the "inter-Americanization" of the Monroe Doctrine. With each elaboration of procedure the Doctrine has once again been declared inter-Americanized or multilateralized until the apogee reached in the Rio Treaty of 1947. In sober fact, however, the Monroe Doctrine has not been in the past, is not now, and can never in the foreseeable future be inter-Americanized in the full meaning of the term. It is still the United States which can, if it will, prevent the further colonization by European powers, bar transfer of existing colonies from one titleholder to another, and frustrate extra-hemisphere conspiracies to attack any of the American republics.

Transfer of responsibility without power is either meaningless or dangerous. In the case of the Inter-American System such transfer is said to have taken place either by those who delude themselves that "wishing will make it so" or by those who would use the supposed existence of a multilateral responsibility as a shiny façade to mask policies they advocate. Both groups are dangerous to the rational determination and execution of American foreign policy. The error of the first is the error of unrealistic idealists and utopians adrift on the dark waters of international politics. Unacquainted with the facts and implications of power, they would desire not to be contaminated by knowledge. People of this group helped to "oversell" the United Nations to the American people and as late as 1947 continued to speak of the United Nations as the first line of American security (meaning the only line). Some would will a world union, a world federation, or what have you, into being according to a blueprint of organization, simple or complex—a world union which naturally would only act in the interests of the United States. Dreamers are valuable to any society, provided only that their dreams are placed in the proper perspective.

At the other extreme are those whose realism takes the cynical form of seeking to create the semblance of multilateral organization behind which the United States can implement unilateral policies, or an organization of such flexibility that it can be manipulated to the shape and direction desired by this country. People in this group also speak of the inter-Americanization of the Monroe Doctrine. What they mean is that a gaudy gesture has been made to Latin-American sensibilities and now the power of the United States can safely venture forth, clothed in the shiny raiment of selfless leadership. President Theodore Roosevelt was franker when he spoke of the unilateral action of the United States in "the exercise of an international police power," but he was talking of the same relationship as are modern "realists": responsibility by right of power solely to the national interest of the United States and denial of the existence of responsibility to Latin-American peoples and governments. It is just this type of hypocrisy which the Soviet Union constantly charges as characteristic of American dealings in international affairs. Perhaps the charges will have proved valuable if they maintain the United States in a state of constant alertness to the implications inherent in its relations with the other American republics.

The principal areas of concern to the Inter-American System are the strategic, the economic, the political, and the ideological. Within each the narrowing relationship of multilateral to unilateral may be discerned. Examination of the three types of relationship in each of the four areas serves to define the position and role of the United States in the Western Hemisphere.

► THE SECURITY AREA: MULTILATERAL INSTRUMENTS

At the special Conference on Problems of War and Peace, held in Mexico City in February and March, 1945, the American republics signed the Act of Chapultepec, Part II of which bound them, "following the establishment of peace," to "consider the conclusion in accordance with their constitutional processes, of a treaty establishing procedures whereby . . . threats or acts of aggression against any American Republic . . . may be met. . . ." The conference had taken place outside the framework of the Pan American Union and was limited to states "cooperating in the war effort" in order to exclude by defintion an Argentine regime which was providing substantial aid and comfort to the Axis. However, Argentina was asked to accede to the Final Act and by its signature gave one more promise of abiding by the obligations of a Good Neighbor. This promise was honored no more

than others which it had made on such matters as eliminating Axis espionage
agents and sequestering and liquidating Axis assets in Argentina.

Under these circumstances the State Department policy makers, Byrnes,
Braden, and Briggs, were unwilling to negotiate a treaty of collective security
either without Argentine participation or with the presence of representatives
of the Perón regime. Theoretically the impasse was between all the other
American republics, including the United States, and Argentina. Actually the
United States, forcefully led by Spruille Braden, engaged in a diplomatic duel
to gain Argentine compliance. The duel was lost when the publication of the
Blue Book, labeled "Consultation among the American Republics with Respect to the Argentine Situation" (actually the compilation solely by the
United States of documentary proof of Argentine-German wartime collaboration), did not prevent the election of Juan Domingo Perón to the presidency
and the consequent legitimatization of his government. If the treaty was to be
negotiated one party had to give ground. Under heavy fire from many sources,
including such influential participants in bipartisan foreign policy as Senator
Vandenberg, it was the United States which abandoned its original position
and accepted some token gestures of Dictator Perón as evidence of his good
faith. After several postponements, therefore, the Inter-American Conference
for the Maintenance of Continental Peace and Security convened at the Quin-
tandinha Palace outside Rio de Janeiro on August 15, 1947.

The only item on the conference agenda was the conclusion of the treaty
forecast by the Act of Chapultepec. Argentina made three serious efforts to
weaken the pact, only one of which was partially successful. On the other two
issues its delegates, when outvoted, abandoned their country's everyone's-out-
of-step-but-me attitude and with good grace bowed to the will of the majority.
Although Argentina signed the Rio Treaty, it was not until three years later
that President Perón was able to ram ratification through the Perónista-
dominated legislature.

Condemning the use of war in terms reminiscent of the Kellogg-Briand
Pact, the American republics agreed to settle peacefully all disputes by procedures already a part of the inter-American system before submitting them
to the United Nations General Assembly or the Security Council. To meet
an armed attack taking place within the security zone surrounding the
hemisphere or within a territory of an American state a definite procedure
was established. Because such an aggression against one state was recognized
as an attack upon all, each of the other states undertook to assist the country
attacked until collective assistance could be organized. If the act of aggression was by an American state, it might be ordered by the rest acting
together to suspend hostilities under threat of sanctions for noncompliance.
Collective action by the American republics was to be taken by a meeting
of foreign ministers and ranged from a recall of representatives through
economic sanctions to actual military force. Decisions in these matters were

to be taken by a two-thirds vote and were to be binding on the minority as well as the majority, except that no country could be made to participate against its will in military sanctions.

Precedent existed for the security zone of the Rio Treaty in the large area of neutrality hopefully declared by the American republics at Panama in 1939 and rejected by both Axis and Allies. Unlike the latter, however, the new zone stretched from pole to pole and included a fair chunk of Antarctica within its confines. Its Pacific periphery covered the Galápagos Islands, possessions of Ecuador on which the United States was permitted to establish a wartime naval and air base for the defense of the Panama Canal, the Aleutian Islands, and Alaska, but not the Hawaiian Islands. In the east the line was drawn between Greenland and Iceland, thus embracing Canada and Greenland, nonsignators to the treaty, within the security system.

During the deliberations over the treaty Argentina had wished to limit collective action to attack by a non-American power, relying on peaceful procedures alone to settle inter-American disputes. Meeting failure in this, Argentina next proposed that, as had been the case in the old League Council, decisions to apply sanctions against aggression be unanimous. In favor of a simple majority action was Uruguay, whose 1935 proposal for collective intervention in internal affairs on specified occasions had elicited much comment but little support outside the United States. Both propositions were voted down in favor of the two-thirds rule mentioned above.

In its third attempt at modification, however, Argentina was more successful. Its proposal to exclude from collective action attack upon forces of the American republics stationed outside the zone (i.e., United States forces) led to sharp exchanges between the Argentine delegate and Senator Vandenberg. The senator was forced to admit that procedure would be different in the event of aggression taking place outside the zone. Presumably the difference lies in the agreement in one article to assist an American state resisting aggression before the foreign ministers made a decision, whereas according to another article of the treaty in the event the attack were not an armed attack or took place outside the security zone, such a decision would be awaited before any action was taken. It is not inconceivable that the foreign ministers, in dealing with the latter situation, could apply the same sanctions as in other attacks, thus making the distinction one of promptness of assistance.

Surface indications are that the Rio Treaty provides a multilateral security system within the Western Hemisphere. Despite polite bows in the direction of the United Nations and assertions of compatibility with its articles, the American republics are claiming the right to settle their own disputes, to repel by themselves aggression against them while keeping the United Nations informed of their progress. Primacy of the regional arrangement over the world organization, made possible by Article 51, which had been forcefully advocated at the San Francisco Conference by the Latin-American countries, is protected by the right of veto of the United States in the Security Council. As Senator Vandenberg declared in urging ratification of the pact, "the jurisdiction of the 'region' will cease whenever—but not until—'the Security Council has taken the necessary measures to maintain international peace and security' as required in its Charter. I underscore 'necessary' measures." The American republics themselves are placed in a position of being able to decide when, if ever, the jurisdiction of the Security Council is to be accepted.

In completeness of coverage also the Rio Treaty gives the impression of multilateralization of security arrangements. *"Every* controversy which may arise between them" is to be settled. There is to be no time gap between attack and collective enforcement action, since every state is to take "immediate" measures to fulfill its obligations, although the principle of sovereignty makes it the judge of what constitutes fulfillment. Hostile action which is not outright armed aggression may be dealt with on appeal of the allegedly injured state. The equality of states is recognized in the provision of one state, one vote. Unlike the League of Nations and the United Nations, no one recalcitrant nation can block collective action. For diplomatic, economic, and miiltary sanctions only a two-thirds majority of the ratifying states is necessary, and the Organization of American States may, upon application, convene the collective Organ of Consultation by an absolute majority vote.

Without in any way deprecating the importance of the Rio Treaty— which is great—it should be made clear that the theoretical multilateralization of security is belied by the facts. Nothing in the provisions of the Rio Treaty has removed or can remove the primacy of responsibility for the defense of the Western Hemisphere from the government of the United States. That responsibility, as has been said before, is not absolute, but is commensurate with the preponderance of power in the hands of this country. The Latin-American republics cannot by themselves resist aggression originating outside the hemisphere, which aggression, of a direct, military nature, has become increasingly improbable. The Germany Navy did propose an offensive operation against South America in the early stages of World War II, but Hitler vetoed the idea. Any nation, including the Soviet Union, which had attained such tremendous military power that it could successfully translate it into force three thousand miles across the Atlantic and Pacific would thereby be able to overwhelm the military establishments possessed by, or possible of creation in, Latin America. Strategic geography furthermore places greater priority on the defense of North America and the Caribbean area, where the power of the United States is most evident. Latin America, even under the terms of the Rio Treaty, remains primarily dependent on the North American member to deter aggression, acting either in the name of the Inter-American System or on its own outside that System.

The voting procedure theoretically makes it possible for the smaller nations to bind the United States against its wishes to take all contemplated collective action to deter aggression except the use of its own armed forces. But how is this conceivable in practice? Two types of situations might be envisaged: A two-thirds majority of the Latin-American republics wishes to take action, but, either before the Organ of Consultation meets or during its deliberations, this majority learns that the United States is opposed and is prepared to carry its opposition through to a negative vote. Recognizing its present and future dependence on American power, the majority probably will not bring the issue to a formal vote. This is the most probable outcome. Alternatively, the majority, possibly led by a nation such as Argentina, which would relish the opportunity of placing the United States in an embarrassing position, could press the question and receive its mandate to act under the System. Such a course, were the United States determined in its opposition, would actually go far toward destroying the Inter-American System, its economic and political aspects along with its security. Indeed the relationship between the United States and the small countries of Central America and the Caribbean is so close as to render extremely difficult the mustering of any such two-thirds majority.

BILATERAL SECURITY ARRANGEMENTS

Consideration of the implementation of the strategic concept established for the Inter-American System in the Treaty of Reciprocal Assistance requires the transfer of attention inward from the multilateral to the bilateral and unilateral circles. In this field the substantial cooperation developed during and after World War II has been almost entirely on the bilateral basis of agreements negotiated individually by the United States with other American republics. Agreements which have been made cover three types of military cooperation: the transfer to Latin America of United States arms and equipment, the training in Latin America and in the United States of Latin-American military personnel, and the provision of army, naval, and air bases. Shortly after the war the State, War, and Navy Departments joined in presenting for Congressional consideration proposed legislation entitled the Inter-American Military Cooperation Act, under which the United States government would be permitted to transfer arms to other American republics. Despite repeated introduction, the bill was not passed, both because of the preoccupation of Congress with other matters and because some representatives were justifiably fearful of the effect that augmented military establishments would have on Latin-American peace and stability. The act was defended by its sponsors as enabling Latin-American countries to fulfill their obligations under the Act of Chapultepec, whose provisions roughly paralleled those later embodied in the Rio Treaty, and the United States to that end sold limited amounts of equipment under the authority of surplus property legislation. Authority for further transfers was contained in omnibus military-aid legislation passed by Congress in 1951. Convenient multilateral sanction for continued arms shipments was contained in Resolution III, entitled "Inter-American Military Cooperation," which was signed in April, 1951, at the fourth meeting of the foreign ministers. The resolution called on the American republics to "strengthen those of their armed forces best adapted to the collective defense" and to "cooperate with each other in military matters."

Notwithstanding this resolution and references in it to the Inter-American Treaty of Reciprocal Assistance, the pattern of relationship involved in the provision of military equipment clearly remains bilateral. To be sure, the Charter of the Organization of American States, adopted at Bogotá, provides, in addition to the continuance of the wartime Inter-American Defense Board, for an Advisory Defense Committee "composed of the highest military authorities of the American States participating in the Meeting of Consultation . . . to advise the Organ of Consultation on problems of military cooperation that may arise in connection with the application of existing special treaties on collective security." Little more than formal similarity to the arrangements under the North Atlantic Pact exists, however. So far as defense of the Western Hempishere is concerned, the United States considers individual Latin-American requests within the overall strategic requirements of the area *as it has conceived them.*

The same pattern exists in the case of military training and bases. Individual United States training missions are now stationed in all the American republics, some countries having three—army, navy, and air. In addition, two bilateral boards, Brazilian-American and Mexican-American, have been continued from the war period. United States missions were placed at the request, sometimes American-inspired of the country receiving them, and were designed in some instances to replace ousted Axis military representatives. Members of Latin-American military establishments are brought to this country for further training under arrangement with the United States by the country concerned. Any comprehensive program of training which exists is American in conception and execution, although inter-American organs such as the Defense Board have placed themselves on record as favoring it. A very real connection can be readily seen between American missions and the transfer of military equipment. Such equipment is needed to fulfill the mission's training function and, if not forthcoming, might cause the restive Latin-American country to seek other supplies and possibly other advisers. This at any rate is the rationale advanced by Army and Navy spokesmen for the continuance of arms transfers in quantities subsantial in comparison with the area's prewar armament level.

During the war the United States maintained troops at bases in Latin America, reaching from Mexico to Uruguay. These establishments had the threefold purpose of protecting the Panama Canal (over one hundred were located in Panama alone), of repelling any aggression directed at the continent, and, in the case of Brazil, of serving as links in the air-ferrying service of planes, parts, and equipment to North Africa. Permission for these bases was bilaterally negotiated, with the result that arrangements varied from exclusive operation, as in the Galápagos, to landing rights on fields built and maintained by the American republic itself, as in Uruguay. In returning the bases to their owners after the war, the United States also secured in some cases agreement for their maintenance in total or partial state of readiness and for American reoccupation in event of another conflict. Should war break out once more, these valuable protective installations would in all probability be again opened to American forces in bilateral implementation of a multilateral resolution adopted by the United Nations, the Organization of American States, the Inter-American Defense Board, and other agencies.

UNILATERAL SECURITY RESPONSIBILITIES

Implicit in the bilateral pattern is the unilaterally assumed responsibility of the United States. Its operation may be seen to fall into at least four categories. Multilateral resolutions approved general military cooperation between members of the Inter-American System. Negotiation by the United States with separate countries has delineated that cooperation. The government of the United States alone has made the requisite decision on the amount and the nature of military equipment it would and could offer Latin-American states. That government alone decides which bases it requires for the defense of the hemisphere, their state of readiness, and the number and character of American troops to be stationed thereon. Behind such decisions is the conception which the government has of the demands of its own security, which in turn implies both strategic and tactical decisions it alone must take. Any comprehensive military plan involving the Western Hemisphere is only partially sketched out to Latin-American representatives, although it involves definition of the role which each American republic is expected to perform within it. For the other American republics hemisphere defenses is of primary importance, but the United States has many serious commitments outside the hemisphere which command a higher priority. Those commitments, such as the North Atlantic Pact and action on behalf of the United Nations in Korea, have been unilaterally assumed. They imply a size, balance, and deployment of Armed Forces of the United States which are bound to have a profound effect on the Inter-American System, yet the Latin-American countries naturally have no voice in the determination of the nature of the United States military establishment.

Finally it should not be forgotten that within the hemisphere itself lie areas in which United States action is unilateral. Puerto Rico, the Virgin Islands, the Panama Canal Zone, the Guantánamo naval base—all are important to hemisphere security. Latin America was not consulted when these defense points were acquired, nor has it been consulted regarding their disposition. Its preponderance of power inevitably places on the United States alone the responsibility for hemisphere defense.

► THE ECONOMIC AREA: MULTILATERAL INSTRUMENTS

The economic aspects of the Inter-American System have a direct bearing on military security. Once again multilateral organizations are found, the principal one being the Economic and Social Council, established in the Bogotá Charter as successor to the wartime Financial and Economic Advisory Committee. According to that charter the council "has for its principal purpose the promotion of the economic and social welfare of the American nations through effective cooperation for the better utilization of their natural resources, the development of their agricultureand industry and the raising of the standards of living of their peoples. To accomplish this purpose the Council *shall:* a) propose the means by which the American nations may give each other technical assistance in making studies and formulating and executing plans to carry out the purposes referred to in Article 26 ['. . . strengthen their economic structure, develop their agriculture and mining, promote their industry and increase their trade'] and to develop and improve their social services. . . ." A parallel council was also established under the United Nations to make studies and recommendations for that body along the same lines.

Acting under the inspiration of President Truman's Point Four Program, the Inter-American Economic and Social Council passed in February, 1950, a lengthy and detailed resolution calling for the establishment of a Coordinating Committee on Technical Assistance under the chairmanship of the Secretary General of the Organization of American States and having a membership drawn from the Pan American Union and "cooperating inter-American" specialized agencies, of which there are many. The committee was to make studies, determine priorities among various projects within general limits laid down by the council of the Organization of American States, allocate funds to various inter-American agencies from an account contributed by all the American republics, establish liaison with the United Nations and with appropriate administrative divisions of member governments, and act as a clearinghouse for information. The same resolution called for the formulation of "one coordinated program of technical assistance" for the hemisphere as a whole.

The Coordinating Committee on Technical Assistance began operations in June, 1950. This committee, after considering projects submitted, gained approval by the Economic and Social Council of a schedule for 1951 calling for the expenditure of an amount equivalent to roughly $2.5 million allocated to some thirty-seven projetcs, which had been arranged within three broad "priority" divisions. The fourth meeting of the foreign Ministers recommended that "during the present emergency period, preference among economic development projects should be given in the following order: projects useful for defense purposes and projects designed to satisfy the basic requirements of the civilian economy; projects already begun, the interruption of which would entail serious losses of materials, money, and effort; and other projects for economic development."* It is as yet too early to determine what role either multilateral agency, the Economic and Social Council or its subsidiary, the Coordinating Committee on Technical Assistance, will actually play in the related fields of technical assistance and economic development.

In addition to the Economic and Social Council, an integral part of the *Inter-American* System is the grandiose document known as the Economic Agreement of Bogotá, embodying in forty-three articles "the desire of the American States to maintain, strengthen and develop in the economic field and within the framework of the United Nations the special relations that unite them. . . ."

A formidable documentary basis has therefore been constructed for multilateral operation of economic relations among the American republics. The essential test of its efficacy lies in the answer to this question: Does the Inter-American System plan the economic development of Latin America and of the United States, stabilizing national price levels and currency ratios, allocating resources among the various countries, and administering their distribution? Despite many resolutions of the fourth meeting of the foreign ministers dealing with these subjects, the manifest answer is no, no more than the Economic and Social Council does throughout the rest of the world on behalf of the United Nations. No such activity would be permitted by the United States even in the unlikely event that the other twenty countries should agree, and the Latin-American ECOSOC has been too realistic to try to take such action.

BILATERAL ECONOMIC CONFLICT: INCOMPATIBILITY OF INTEREST

Notwithstanding the fact that the Latin-American ECOSOC has seized upon the idea of technical assistance, economic relationships remain bilateral in two respects and unilateral in that the United States retains the unhampered ability to enter upon commitments and to discharge them in its own fashion. The bilateral relationships derive from the fact that Latin America as a whole may be considered as arrayed against the United States in terms of what it wants from this country and what the United States is prepared to grant in return for what *it* wants. This conflict was well exemplified in the Economic Charter of Bogotá previously alluded to, the articles of which attempted to balance the conflicting objectives of both parties. In spite of the substantial ingenuity of the drafters, about two dozen reservations to the agreement were entered, including two by the United States. As seen in the charter and other pronouncements and actions, what Latin America wants is large-scale gifts, loans, and credits to aid its economic development. To this end it wants guarantees of access to raw materials and finished products at

---

* Art. XII, *Proceedings, Fourth Meeting of Consultation of Ministers of Foreign Affairs* (Washington, Pan American Union, 1951), p. 250.

nonfluctuating, reasonable rates. And withal it wants to retain the right to such nationalistic devices, fiscal and commercial, as it may see fit to adopt. Above all, it wants to raise its *want* to the level of a *right*. Article 3 of the charter speaks of the *"principle* of facilitating access, on equal terms, to the trade, products, and means of production, including scientific and technical advances, that are needed for their industrial and general economic development . . . [and the American republics] *resolution* that, as a general policy, there should be taken into account the need to compensate for the disparity that is frequently noted between the prices of raw materials and the prices of manufactured products, by establishing the necessary balance between them." (The United States entered a reservation to the second clause above.) Article 28 went even further in proclaiming that "the States a) recognize that they are *committed* to cooperate with one another, by all appropriate means, so that their economic development shall not be retarded but rather accelerated as much as possible. . . ."

The same emphasis on assistance as a matter of right appeared in the economic resolutions adopted by the fourth meeting of the foreign ministers. In Resolution XII on "Economic Development" the American republics declared that "the economic development of underdeveloped countries should be considered as an essential factor in the total concept of Hemisphere defense." Accordingly ". . . the American Republics *shall supply,* subject to the provisions of Resolution XVI [on "Allocations and Priorities"] the machinery, mechanical equipment, and other materials needed to increase their productive capacity, diversify their production and distribution, facilitating in appropriate cases financial and technical cooperation in carrying out plans for economic developments."* The resolution was based on drafts submitted by a number of the American republics, notably Bolivia, Mexico, and Chile. The words quoted bear close resemblance to the original Chilean proposal.

What Latin America wants from the United States expresses the first bilateral relationship. By way of contrast, what the United States wants from Latin America is primarily the raw materials essential to the development of its full economic power to meet the challenge posed by the Soviet Union. It would like to see the economic development of Latin America along lines which it deems economically sound and which will thereby promote the stability of the area. It would finally like to see Latin America abandon or modify its nationalistic devices so that trade might be broadened, United States private investment encouraged, and American businesses located in Latin America secure from arbitrary, discriminatory, and confiscatory policies.

While an article of the Economic Charter of Bogotá speaks of the indispensability of industrialization, "particularly that of those States which have not succeeded in fully utilizing their natural resources," the adjective "sound" is made to precede "industrialization." While another article advocates the continuance "in appropriate cases" of government or inter-govern-

---

* Italics are the authors'.

mental credits, the same article continues that "sufficient economic reasons shall exist for the particular purposes to be served by such credits, and the projects to be undertaken shall be adapted to local conditions and be able to survive without the need of excessive protection or subsidy." Succeeding articles recognize the importance of private capital investment, provide that it "shall receive equitable treatment," free from "unjustified, unreasonable or discriminatory measures that would impair the legally acquired rights or interests of nationals of other countries in the enterprises, capitals, skills, arts or technology they have supplied" (reservations by Mexico and Guatemala), and specify that "the States shall take no discriminatory action against investments by virtue of which foreign enterprises or capital may be deprived of legally acquired property rights, for reasons or under conditions different from those that the Constitution or laws of each country provide for the expropriation of national property. Any expropriation shall be accompanied by payment of fair compensation in a prompt, adequate and effective manner" (reservations by Mexico, Guatemala, Ecuador, Argentina, Honduras, Cuba, Venezuela, and Uruguay).

The same proximity of Latin-American and United States economic desires is found in the resolutions of the fourth meeting of the foreign ministers. In the resolution on economic development previously cited, the paragraph immediately following that concerning the supply of equipment was taken from the original United States draft and mentions as one of the purposes of financial and technical collaboration "encouraging the investment of public and private capital." Resolution XIII on the production of strategic raw materials is in accord with United States objectives in stating "that the American Republics should adopt in their respective countries practical and feasible measures for increasing the production and processing of basic and strategic materials required for the defense emergency. . . ." The next paragraph, however, comes not from the United States but from a Latin-American draft. By it the American republics *"undertake* a) to accord one another . . . the priorities and licenses required to obtain necessary machinery and material to increase the production, processing, and transportation of these necessary basic and strategic materials."

It would not be too much to say that the Economic Agreement of Bogotá and the resolutions of the fourth meeting of the foreign ministers have left the discrepancy of interest between the United States and Latin America where they found it. Latin America still awaits in vain for assistance on the scope of the Marshall Plan—i.e., billions in gifts. The United States meets with little success in modifying Latin-American fiscal and economic practices and has not succeeded in opening Latin-American gates substantially to its private capital. Requirements of mobilization have placed a further strain on the already unsatisfactory economic relationship. Augmented demand has raised the price of strategic raw materials, making some Latin-American suppliers happy. On the other hand, the United States has taken measures of its own and collectively with Great Britain and other members of the North Atlantic Pact to limit this price rise, and even, as in the case of tin, to effect a price rollback. The United States also participates in international arrangements for the allocation of scarce raw materials in order to limit competition which results in price increases. Latin-American views of this situation are reflected in numerous resolutions of the fourth meeting of the foreign ministers, one of which calls for Latin-American representation on all international bodies dealing with the allocation of raw materials. Latin America also has inserted into the inter-American record its opinion that prices of manufactured goods needed for its development should be kept to reasonable levels and Latin America assured, as part of the collective security effort, of an adequate supply of these goods.

BILATERAL AND UNILATERAL ARRANGEMENTS

Economic conflict involves not only the bilateral relationships between the United States and Latin America, but also the unilateral decisions on the part of the North American government. As in the case of military agreements, the United States has negotiated and continues to negotiate individually with other American republics such matters as purchase contracts, commercial treaties containing clauses on private investment, and technical assistance treaties. If the United States cannot get Latin America to accept its interpretation of what Latin America wants and should have, neither does the United States intend to accept the blanket thesis of what it *owes* Latin America. In the resultant standoff on trade, investment, and basic economic philosophies, the United States remains free, as it must, to allocate its economic resources as it sees fit. Since its resources are not unlimited, a scale of priorities must be arranged between domestic requirements and those of foreign areas: Europe, the Near East, the Far East, and Latin America. For obvious reasons Latin America does not rate very high in this scale of priorities, nor is the distribution of United States materials within the Latin-American allocation as heavy on the side of economic development and industrialization as some Latin Americans would wish. In fact, Latin America may stand fairly close to the bottom of the scale, and there is little that the other American republics can do about this, to them unfortunate, unilateral determination.

▶ THE POLITICAL AREA: MULTILATERAL INSTRUMENTS

Peaceful coexistence of twenty-one independent states is difficult to arrive at and maintain. Particularly is this true where there exists no special similarity in geography, ethnic and racial composition, social and economic institutions, cultural heritage, and political government, and where the practical hegemony of one state extends over half of the others. The term "Latin America" is deceptive in that it covers a bewildering variety of cultures and societies in the nineteen individual countries. In size they range from half a continent (Brazil) to the equivalent of one of the small American states (Uruguay, Haiti, El Salvador, Costo Rica, Panama). In location they are found in all climates from the temperate through the tropical to the frigid arctic south. In racial composition they are white, Indian, mestizo, and Negro, with most countries being an amalgamation of all these elements. In political systems they include an advance social democracy from which the United States might learn much (Uruguay), tyrannical personal dictatorship (that of Trujillo in the Dominican Republic being the outstanding example), and dictatorship approaching the European, fascistic model (that of Perón). In economic development they run the gamut from the complex industrial type similar to that found in the United States to backward agrarian communities typical of those of the Near East and the Far East. While eighteen speak the same language (Spanish), their cultural heritage from Spain is by no means uniform. In addition Brazil is Portuguese-speaking and Haiti, French.

Under such circumstances the stage of international political cooperation reached in the Western Hemisphere is analogous to the dog that could walk on two legs: the wonder is not that he does it imperfectly but that he does it at all. After the slow evolution from 1890 to 1933, a rapid development took place between 1933 and 1942, and spectacular progress was made between 1945 and 1949. The result is a form of international organization which goes far beyond that attained by the League of Nations or the United Nations. In view of their accomplishments and the hope of more to come, the American republics were naturally reluctant to subordinate their system at San Francisco to the as-yet-unproved United Nations. The subsequent deterioration of United States–Soviet Union relations, with its attendant negation of many features of the United Nations Charter, has fully justified Latin-American fears. In their political relations they look primarily to the Inter-American System as it has been embodied in the Charter of the Organization of American States, signed at the Ninth Inter-American Conference at Bogotá, Colombia, in 1948.

PROVISIONS OF THE BOGOTÁ CHARTER

The Bogotá Charter is a highly elaborate instrument of eighteen chapters, comprising 112 articles. As had become their somewhat bewildering habit, the delegates collected in the charter many of the sentiments subscribed to in earlier meetings. Thus both Article 5 and Article 24 assent that an act of aggression against one is an attack upon all. Article 15 reiterates and even broadens the concept of nonintervention first laid down in the Seventh Conference fifteen years earlier.

During the war the Emergency Advisory Committee for Political Defense had adopted the principle of collective consultation among the American republics prior to recognition of revolutionary regimes in order to limit the possibility of successful subversion by Axis agents. The occasion for the committee's resolution was the overturn of the Peñaranda regime in Bolivia, which had placed in positions of authority persons suspected of German sympathies. Consultation had preceded recognition of other Latin-American governments, but the Bolivian case was the only one where collective non-recognition was used as a weapon to bring about changes in a nation's leaders. After the war, the Uruguayan government, with Péron's Argentina decidedly in mind, proposed that a common standard of human rights be determined and that the American republics consider common action against governments which did not measure up to it. The Uruguayan "initiative," as it was called, was in line with precepts then being followed at the Nuremberg Trials and would have opened the door to intervention in the internal affairs of a country, not by one nation alone, but by the entire inter-American community. The United States, which obviously would have borne the brunt of leadership in any such collective action, was at the time itself embroiled with Argentina. Therefore the State Department authorities, Byrnes, Braden, and Briggs, welcomed the Uruguayan suggestion with undiplomatic alacrity. Most of the other American republics, however, felt misgivings and hostility. Many had followed the policies of the Committee for Political Defense reluctantly, some not at all! most did not wish to express too much hostility to another, and large, Latin-American country; a majority felt that a dangerous precedent might be set, leading to United States intervention closer to home under the cloak of inter-American sanction.

In its draft charter for consideration at the Ninth Conference, the Pan American Union reflected the wishes of the majority in a proposed article restating the principle of nonintervention. Article 15 of the charter, as adopted, went even further than the original draft of the Pan American Union. It reads: "No State or *group of States* has the right to intervene, directly or indirectly, for any reason whatever, in the internal or external affairs of any other State. The foregoing principle prohibits not only armed force but also any other form of interference or attempted *threat* against the personality of the State or against its political, economic, and cultural elements."* It is quite apparent that this provision is so broad as to be meaningless. Almost any action of a country in international affairs, particularly that of a large and powerful country like the United States, can be found under this definition to infringe upon the affairs of another country. Trade practices, immigration laws, preclusive or even negotiated purchases, general pronouncements on freedom—in short almost anything the United States does or does not do in its Latin-American relations could, by applying the yardstick of Article 15, be construed as intervention. Given such an article in the basic charter of the American republics, what actually constitutes intervention can only be determined by concrete United States policy and Latin-American reaction thereto.

* Italics are the authors'.

Going on from the declaration of principles, the charter prescribes the organs of the Inter-American System. Some are not radically changed from before, others are placed on a permanent basis, and still others are brought into a better-defined relationship with the system. These organs are stated to be (1) the Inter-American Conference, (2) the Meeting of Consultation of Ministers of Foreign Affairs, (3) the Council, (4) the Pan American Union, (5) the Specialized Conference, and (6) the Specialized Organizations. As their names imply, the fifth and sixth instruments just listed are conferences and organizations dealing with technical matters of concern to the inter-American community. Although they are to cooperate with appropriate agencies of the United Nations, "the Inter-American Specialized Organizations shall preserve their identity and their status as integral parts of the Organization of American States" (Article 100). As in security matters, the primary responsibility of Inter-American organs for economic and cultural cooperation is to the hemisphere rather than to the world system.

It had been the original intention of the American republics immediately after World War II to hold some kind of meeting of their delegates every year. Reflecting this desire, Resolution IX of the Mexico City Conference had called for a full-dress conference of American states every four years and a meeting of the foreign ministers every year in which the conference did not convene. The charter returns to the earlier conception in both cases. The Inter-American Conference is declared to be the "supreme organ of the Organization of American States" and is charged with decisions as to the "general action and policy of the Organization" (Article 33). It is scheduled to meet every five years, with special meetings or other changes in the date to be made with the approval of two thirds of the American republics. The meeting of the foreign ministers is to convene solely for the consideration of urgent business when requested by one nation and so voted by a majority of the American republics. Obviously the most urgent business which could occupy the meeting would be the calling into operation of the defense treaty to meet actual or threatened aggression. Such a meeting may be called by the Council of the Organization, the former Governing Board (Article 43), and its deliberations have the assistance of an Advisory Defense Committee (Article 44) composed of the "highest military authorities of the American States participating in the Meeting of Consultation" (Article 45). This Advisory Defense Committee is to convene only when the meeting of the foreign ministers takes place (Article 47) or when given specific projects and reports on which to work (Article 48).

What was formerly the Governing Board of the Pan American Union has been separated from that body under the charter and has become the Council of the Organization of American States. The council is to have a chairman, also is elected for one year and, like the vice-chairman, is not immediately eligible for re-election (Article 47). At Mexico City an attempt had been made to have only special delegates accredited to the Governing

Board, instead of adding another task to those of the ambassadors accredited to the United States government. This attempt had failed through inaction on the part of most of the American republics, probably, in some instances, because it involved what seemed an unnecessary increase to a small national budget. The charter, therefore, wisely provides (Article 118) that the council representatives shall be "especially appointed . . . with the rank of Ambassador," but the job may be given "to the diplomatic representative accredited to the government of the country in which the Council has its seat" (i.e., the United States).

The council is designed to serve as a continuous, coordinating agency for the Inter-American System and is assisted in its work by three bodies. Of these, the Inter-American Economic and Social Council, already mentioned, has twenty-one members, one for each of the American republics. In the case of the other two assisting organs to the council, however, the very important principle of limited representation is adhered to. The Inter-American Council of Jurists, the number of which is not specified, is to appoint as its permanent committee (Article 68) the nine members of the Inter-American Juridical Committee (Article 69), which was established as the Neutrality Committee at the Panama meeting of the foreign ministers in 1939. Similarly, the Committee for Cultural Action is to have five members appointed by the Cultural Council (Article 76). The functions of both committees are self-evident.

The Pan American Union is described in Article 78 of the charter as the "General Secretariat of the Organization" and as such has been given the responsibility of providing from its various divisions the secretaries for the three councils described above (Article 88), while the assistant secretary general is to serve as secretary of the council itself (Article 86). Reflecting the desire to see the Union less in the shadow of the United States, all the delegates at Mexico City agreed that the secretary general was to be appointed for ten years and made ineligible for reappointment, and was not to be, as formerly, a citizen of the United States. This provision has been embodied in the charter (Article 79). With the death of Dr. Leo Rowe in 1947 the post passed for the first time to a Latin American, Dr. Alberto Lleras of Colombia.

Provisions for ratification and entry into force of the charter follow those of the defense treaty. Both are to become operative with the deposit of ratifications by two-thirds of the American republics and both may be denounced by any state on two year's notice, after which time both instruments remain in force for all other American republics. Pending ratification by the requisite number of states, however, the charter is to remain provisionally operative.

Also overhauled and clarified by the Bogotá Conference was the confused machinery for the peaceful settlement of disputes, which had long been the subject of overlapping resolutions and conventions. Assembled under the title *Pact of Bogotá* are all means of peaceful settlement, ranging from good offices to arbitration. Ratifiers of the treaty bind themselves "to refrain from the threat or the use of force" and "to use the procedures established in the present treaty, in the manner and under the conditions provided for. . . ." However, a reservation by Argentina expressly nullifies the binding effect of arbitral and judicial decisions so far as that country is concerned. Also, the United States delegation unhappily was forced to follow the Senate in its conditional acceptance of the International Court and in addition maintained in its reservation the right of diplomatic protection, which seemed weakened by an article of the treaty.

EVALUATION OF THE INTER-AMERICAN SYSTEM

One searching for traces of order in international relations cannot but applaud the efforts of the Bogotá delegates. It is too early as yet to appraise the operation of the political system, although, as will be considered in more detail below, it has already been applied to good effect in the settlement of the Costa Rican–Nicaraguan and Haitian–Dominican Republic controversies. So far as the United States is concerned, we may pose the question whether its role in the Inter-American System has been satisfactorily determined by the machinery which has now been created. While noting the vast improvement over the past two decades, an objective answer would have to be largely negative.

Certainly one of the tests of a fully functioning international organization is the supremacy of the collective will over that of any one member. Difficult as it may be for Soviet propagandists to believe, the United States since 1933 has taken the lead in attempting to develop the independence of the Inter-American System from its own control. The State Department drafted the initial proposals to this end, many of which were embodied in a resolution adopted at the Mexico City Conference. American initiative was present in the removal of the formal barrier to the political competence of the Pan American Union. American delegates did not oppose proposals to relocate the Union itself or to hold meetings of such integral parts of the system as the Governing Board (the council of the Organization) in capitals other than Washington. The United States heartily approved of the rotation of the offices of the secretary general and chairman of the council. It was not the fault of the United States that the principle of special, *ad hoc* delegates to the council was not accepted.

CAUSES OF LACK OF FREEDOM OF THE INTER-AMERICAN SYSTEM

All the afore-mentioned devices look toward increasing the independence of the Inter-American System from United States influence, and as more experience accumulates for the operation of the charter, evidences of this trend may be seen in practice. Technical and administrative devices, however, cannot be expected to alter substantially the facts of international life which must constantly frustrate the development of true independence. As mentioned at the outset of this chapter, the disproportion of power in the hands of the United States continues to grow, and the consequent responsibility cannot be abdicated. On the organizational level a recurrent problem arises. Let us suppose, as has repeatedly happened, that the State Department becomes aware of a problem which affects the United States and some or all of the other American republics. It would like the Inter-American System to consider possible courses of action and consequently requests formally or informally the opinion of Latin America. The other American republics are at once placed in an embarrassing position. Should they express an opinion and find the United States on the opposite side of the fence, they might be humiliated by having to adapt or reverse their attitudes. For some countries the opposite is true: they want to know where the United States stands in order to oppose the Colossus of the North. In any case, the response to a State Department inquiry might well be the polite, lengthy evasion for which diplomacy and the Spanish language are so well suited. Perforce the State Department on many problems is placed in the position of having to exert what some of its members now choose to call "leadership," and the Inter-American System follows along behind. Out of this unfortunately unalterable relationship arises a temptation for the United States to avoid the delay while the machinery of multilateral organization goes round and round, and instead to by-pass the system through resort to informal diplomacy of a bilateral nature. Unused machinery rusts, and rust has been found on many cogs of the Inter-American System.

Responsibilities of the United States to countries and organizations outside the Western Hemisphere also make difficult the development of inter-American freedom from United States control. The regional organization is not and cannot be consulted on many United States commitments which in the present state of the world are vital to United States security. A serious dilemma is thereby created. Upon the foundation of inter-American friendship and understanding rests much of the ability of this country to aid free nations elsewhere. Furthermore, the Western Hemisphere, or part of it at least, would constitute the final bastion of United States security. However, because it is beyond the capacity of the United States to give every nation in the world what it wants, this country must give priority to its commitments outside the hemisphere at the expense of Latin-American wishes and demands. The net effect of the situation is to tie the Inter-American System to the course of extrahemispheric events over which twenty Latin-American republics have little or no control. This course may be distasteful to Latin-American countries, mindful of their ardent wooing by the United States in the years immediately before and during World War II, but to the United States no other course is possible. It was to reassure Latin America that it would not be more neglected in the future than in the past and to make that neglect as palatable as possible that President Eisenhower sent his brother on a good-will tour of the hemisphere soon after the Republicans took office.

In spite of the inter-American "friendship and understanding" mentioned above, there is an irreducible balance of Latin mistrust and suspicion arising from the awareness of their own weakness and the remembrance of past ways in which the United States chose to employ its power. In truth, the American republics would prefer that they and their system were free from the United States altogether; that they cannot be inevitably gives rise to frustration and irrationally motivated expressions and policies. Latin-American countries, therefore, can be expected to take alarm at any signs that their North American Good Neighbor is rethinking the related concepts of intervention and nonrecognition, as is demonstrated by the provisions of the Bogotá Charter previously cited. They may be expected to continue economic practices which the United States politely points out make no sense by either Latin-American or United States standards. It is the frustration attendant upon incompletely realized nationalism which is at issue. When Secretary of State Acheson declared the adherence of his government to the purely factual tests of recognition—actual control of territory and willingness to discharge previously accepted international obligations with the understanding that recognition so determined is not necessarily the predecessor of intimate cooperation—Latin-American leaders might be pardoned some skepticism. They saw a different practice followed for almost a year in the case of Nicaragua; they were acquainted with the policy that Secretary Byrnes followed toward the Balkan satellites of the Soviet Union; above all, they looked at the policy of the United States toward Communist China. Statesmen of the democratically orientated Latin-American countries continue to see, even if the United States denies it, the connection between recognition and cooperation as exemplified by Juan Perón, Chiang Kai-shek, and Francisco Franco. Latin-American dictators see that the United States can say one thing and practice another. Today they are safe; future *caudillos* might not be similarly blessed. That the United States has acted in the past and does at times still act arbitrarily and unilaterally accounts for only part of the suspicion and mistrust. The power of the United States may cause it to act in an offensive manner with impunity at any time; individually or collectively Latin America cannot say it nay.

THE SPECIAL DIFFICULTY OF ARGENTINA

The difficulties inherent in the position of a great power capable of exerting varying degrees of hegemony and control over twenty other countries reach their highest pitch in the relations of the United States to Argentina. Argentina, even more than the United States, is a doubtful partner in the Inter-American System, and the basis of the doubt is geopolitical. This fairly large state is located at the opposite end of the hemisphere from its more powerful neighbor. Because of the existence of surrounding small states which are distant from the United States, Argentina is able to exert a good deal of ✓ local influence. Added sources of trouble are a competitive agricultural system, profound political differences, and a fancied cultural superiority on the part of Argentina. Argentina seems destined to continue its role of rival in inter-American affairs. What Argentine leaders would like to do, what they have since 1936 periodically attempted to do, is either to warp the framework of inter-American relations into an anti-United States instrument or, failing this, to keep the system as weak as possible. Thus prior to the 1942 conference Argentina sought to mobilize the surrounding states in support of its opposition breaking relations with the Axis Powers. Thus Perón successfully strove to interpret United States distaste for his aspirations as unwarranted intervention in domestic national affairs, feared by many other American republics. Thus Argentine delegates tried to weaken the Rio Treaty of Reciprocal Assistance and Perónistas in the legislature delayed its ratification. Against these efforts may be measured the laudable success of the United States and most of the other American republics in preventing the attainment of either Argentine objective. When embroiled with Argentina, the United States has insisted that the essential quarrel was between the community of American republics and the lone recalcitrant. To a substantial degree this position has been in accord with the facts, and the fruits of the Good Neighbor policy may be seen in the substantial acceptance of a premise which earlier would have been laughed out of court.

There remains every advantage to American statecraft in using the formal framework of the Inter-American System wherever applicable to its relations with Argentina. That country will then be faced with the unpalatable alternative of modifying its practices to bring them into line with those of the other American republics or of seeing most of Latin America, together with ✓ the United States, collectively arrayed against it in order to attain the type of inter-American community which the overwhelming majority desires. The ironic truth is that so long as Argentine recalcitrance exists, posing as it does economic and political threats to its neighbors, the United States stands to win friends and influence people throughout Latin America.

► CONCLUSIONS

The progress made by the Inter-American System in recent years demonstrates the old adage that more flies can be caught by honey than by vinegar. Latin America has by no means forgotten the vinegarish actions of the United States in the past, but it has responded to the honeyed words and supporting deeds of the Good Neighbor over the last two decades. In the Rio Treaty the American republics have implicitly admitted the necessity of United States leadership in maintaining the security of the hemisphere and have agreed in advance to cooperate to the best of their ability. Whether this document will stand an actual test by a powerful aggressor cannot be stated with certainty, but the large measure of support won, at an economic price to be sure, during World War II, and the fact that the only potential threat for a long time to come is that of the detested Soviet Union are powerful arguments for the efficacy of the Rio Treaty.

More surprising, perhaps, is the acceptance in both the Act of Chapultepec and the Rio Treaty of the position that sanctions by less than unanimous vote could be levied against an *American* state guilty of aggression. This decision had to be taken in the full knowledge that it involved endorsement of the use under certain circumstances of United States power against a Latin-American country. Already the United States has played a prominent part in application of the inter-American machinery to settle by mediation disputes between Caribbean and Central American countries. Reading the record of the Organization of American States in both the Costa Rican–Nicaraguan and the Haitian-Dominican disputes, one is impressed by the determination of the Inter-American System to avoid the diplomatic brush heavily laden with whitewash in favor of clear, forthright statements apportioning censure for actions by the disputants. Here also limited experience may justify only guarded optimism as to the ability of the System to cope with disputes involving states other than those small ones directly in the shadow of the power of the United States.

In addition to the ability of the inter-American machinery itself to act, stress must again be laid on its importance in providing the indispensable multilateral framework behind which necessary bilateral and unilateral measures may be taken by the United States. No blank check has been given; none has been requested. However, prior indication of a willingness to cooperate on matters of mutual concern has made possible a degree of understanding in areas ranging from the technical through the economic to the military which could hardly have been dreamed of before 1933. In order for that understanding to continue to flourish, the formulators of United States policy must place a decided premium on flexibility of technique, while not expecting an optimum result. The United States, for example, cannot expect love and affection from Latin America nor even a rational response to all its overtures. Small people do not love a giant living in the same house, even if he is not, as the British writer J. B. Priestley claimed, "whimsical" and "drunken." Particularly do small people not love a giant who has what they want and to whom they are always in debt of one kind or another.

Because change characterizes all political life, Latin-American included, the United States must make clear by deeds as well as by words that it has no devotion or commitment to any particular *status quo* in the other American republics. That includes all types of *status quo,* of which the political is only one, racial-ethnic relationships, social, and economic being others. In promoting economic development through credits and technical assistance, the United States is directly encouraging certain types of change. Inevitably these changes will have profound effects upon the nature of Latin-American society, indications of which may already be seen. Such changes will ultimately reach the present ruling elites in Latin-American countries, altering the bases of their power and causing shifts in their political institutions. Although it is easier to deal with stable governments in the anticommunist line-up, even if they are dictatorial in character, any such hold-back-the-dawn technique, while possibly effective in the short run, may over a longer period cause more drastic disturbances from pent-up, dynamic forces.

These considerations suggest that, within the severe limitations dictated by its power position, the United States has a responsibility to the global requirements of its foreign policy, and to Latin Americans as well, to make clear on all suitable occasions its position in favor of Latin-American-originated political maturity. As sociologist W. Rex Crawford expressed it: "Freedom and democracy remain words to conjure with in Latin America. Few are those who dare to speak up in the literature and philosophy, that in Latin America are so close to politics, for any ideal other than the generous one of humanity and democracy. If countries are defined by the goals they set themselves, our neighbors are democrats."* Latin-American nations have placed themselves on record in resolution after resolution as seeking democracy. Economic development does not necessarily lead to popular and responsible government, but it is in the best interest of the United States to encourage such a trend. This course would entail careful disassociation, within the requirements of diplomatic etiquette and partnership in the Inter-American System, from the petty tyrants who seek to wrap themselves in the United States flag and to be more American than the Americans in their eagerness to enlist in the anticommunist crusade. It also means positive encouragement for governments that are seeking to remove the many obstacles that have obstructed the path toward democratic practice. To do less would not only deny the faith that Americans themselves seek to live by, but, whatever may be the exigencies of American foreign policy in Europe and Asia, might well weaken the basic security position of the United States within the Western Hemisphere.

► SELECTED BIBLIOGRAPHY

Recent studies on United States relations with the other American republics are few. Samuel F. Bemis, *The Latin American Policy of the United States* (New York, Harcourt, Brace & Company, 1943), treats the subject historically and ends with 1942. Dexter Perkins, *The United States and the Caribbean* (Cambridge, Mass., Harvard University Press, 1947), and Arthur Whitaker, *The United States and South America: The Northern Republics* (Cambridge, Mass., Harvard University Press, 1948), both in the Harvard Series on American Foreign Policy,

---

* W. Rex Crawford, "Pathology of Democracy in Latin America, A Sociologist's Point of View," *American Political Science Review*, March, 1950, p. 147.

are useful, if brief, popular discussions focused on a few countries. A useful documentary collection is James Gantenbein, *The Evolution of Latin American Policy* (New York, Columbia University Press, 1950). Lawrence Duggan, *The Americas* (New York, Henry Holt and Company, 1949), and Ernest Guerrant, *Roosevelt's Good Neighbor Policy* (Albuquerque, N. M., University of New Mexico Press, 1950), concentrate mainly on events since 1933, with the former providing a broader, nonpolitical framework. On relations during World War II, see Edgar Furniss, "American Wartime Objectives in Latin America," *World Politics*, April, 1950. A pioneering attempt to view Latin-American relations from the vantage point of international politics was Nicholas Spykman, *America's Strategy in World Politics* (New York, Harcourt, Brace & Company, 1942). An opposite point of view in many respects may be found in Carlos Davila, *We of the Americas* (New York, Ziff-Davis Publishing Company, 1949). An excellent geographic treatment is provided by Preston James, *Latin America* (New York, The Odyssey Press, 1942). Economic problems are discussed in such works as George Wythe, *Industry in Latin America* (New York, Columbia University Press, 1949); Simon Hanson, *Economic Development in Latin America* (Washington, D.C., Inter-American Affairs Press, 1951); and that by the United Nations, *Economic Development in Latin America and Its Principal Problems* (United Nations Publications 1950, II, G. 2). George Soule, David Efron, and Norman T. Ness, *Latin America in the Future World* (New York, Rinehart & Company, 1945) is mainly concerned with wartime conditions in Latin America and with the development and possibilities of United States cooperative programs. A symposium in the *American Political Science Review*, March, 1950, gives historical, political science, economic, and sociological interpretations of the "Pathology of Democracy in Latin America." For the relationship of the United States to the Inter-American System, see Edgar Furniss, "Recent Changes in the Inter-American System," *International Organization*, September, 1948, and "The U.S., the U.N., and the Inter-American System," *Political Science Quarterly*, September, 1950, by the same author.

CHAPTER TWENTY

THE PLACE OF
INTERNATIONAL
ORGANIZATION IN
AMERICAN FOREIGN POLICY

The United Nations six years after the San Francisco Conference is not the organization which the member states thought they were joining when their delegates signed the Charter on June 26, 1945. The altered aspect of the successor to the League of Nations has in part resulted from the way in which the Charter itself has functioned. The behavior in the United Nations of all the members—small countries, middle-sized powers, the United States, and especially the Soviet Union—has also had an important effect. Most fundamental of all have been the changes in power relations among states, over which the United Nations has been able to exert little control. What, then, has happened to the United Nations, and what is the present place of international organization in American foreign policy?

► INTRODUCTION

FAILURE OF PREVIOUS INTERNATIONAL POLITICAL ORGANIZATIONS

Operations of an international organization include technical, administrative, and informational aspects. The organization ultimately stands or falls, however, on its ability as regulator of state relations to avoid and settle conflicts, that is, on its operations at the political level. After the Napoleonic Wars a rudimentary form of international organization was developed in the Council of Europe and the Holy Alliance, which had interlocking directorates.

These groupings of the main European powers of the era fell apart over the divergent views of revolutionary change held by Great Britain on the one hand and by Austria and Russia on the other. Under Bismarck's leadership a new Council of Europe was created after the unification of Germany. Although this council was able for a time to reconcile the conflicting interests of the larger and smaller nations in the Balkans, the unity of the limited membership was broken by the evolution of hostile systems of alliances—the Triple Alliance and the Triple Entente—with no area of maneuver between them. On the same rock foundered the League of Nations, the first truly world organization in terms of membership and purported jurisdiction. In the technical, administrative, and informational fields the League performed invaluable services. It might be performing them yet except for its impotency in the face of conflict among the major powers and between large and small states. It was this failure and the memories which crowded the halls of Geneva that determined the drafters of the United Nations Charter to begin anew.

THE PARAMOUNTCY OF SECURITY

There is of course a direct relation between security and functional and technical organization. Recognition of this fact has led to elaboration in the United Nations Charter of provisions designed to mitigate the sources of conflict, whether they be economic, social, or ideological. The very existence of the organization can contribute further to the avoidance or settlement of conflict by diplomatic means. The organization provides a meeting place, a trained secretariat, even in some instances a mediator to smooth over tensions before they reach a breaking point or to resolve by *informal* means antagonisms between states. Later in this chapter the success of the United Nations in this respect will be examined.

Any organization that wishes to endure, however, must do more than discuss the sources of conflict, do more than seek the avoidance and settlement of disputes by diplomacy. The sources are Hydra-headed; some may be alleviated, mitigated, even removed. Others remain, and still others appear. Conflict will continue long after the nation-state system has been discarded; it will remain so long as peoples have contact with peoples. Likewise, diplomacy had been at work to avoid or settle conflicts for centuries before formal international organization came into being. International organization can assist the work of diplomacy, but it is not essential to it—witness the overwhelming preponderance of diplomatic discussion which still takes place outside the United Nations.

SECURITY STRUCTURE UNDER THE UNITED NATIONS

International organization, as exemplified by the Charter of the United Nations, imposes on the parties to the international disputes a prescribed code of conduct. Local resources for settlement, including the facilities of regional groupings, are first to be exhausted. Under United Nations jurisdiction, modes of pacific settlement may be prescribed, which run the gamut from conciliation through mediation to arbitration and adjudication. The hope of the United Nations, as of all other organizations, is that this machinery can settle disputes before actual hostilities have broken out or can restore peace after it has been ruptured. The power of the organization depends ultimately, however, on its willingness and ability to impose effective sanctions on a transgressor. Knowledge that these sanctions will be applied may serve as a deterrent to unilateral, forcible national action, but the sanctions must in fact be potent enough to frustrate an aggressor determined to flout the stated will of the community of states. As did the Covenant of the League of Nations, therefore, the United Nations Charter permits the application of sanctions of both an economic and a military nature and commits the members to follow policies in this regard laid down by the organization.

► EFFORTS TO IMPROVE LEAGUE MACHINERY

MEMBERSHIP

The drafters of the Charter were determined to avoid the manifest flaws in the League machinery for the maintenance and restoration of international security, flaws which had led to the destruction of the League in the holocaust of World War II. One defect related to the inclusiveness of membership. In contrast to League experience, both the United States and the Soviet Union were participants in the United Nations from the start. Indeed the United States took the lead in preparatory arrangements from the outset, beginning with the Declaration of the United Nations, signed on New Year's Day, 1942. This reversal of American attitude was made possible by the Pearl Harbor attack, which pushed the country formally into the war. As late as the preceding August President Roosevelt had felt compelled by his interpretation of American public opinion to postpone any commitment to a world organization. At the Argentia Conference, where the Atlantic Charter was signed, in place of the words "effective international organization" which the British delegates proposed, the Atlantic Charter's sixth point said merely that the two countries "hope to see established a peace which will afford to all nations the means of dwelling in safety within their own boundaries, and which will afford assurance that all the men in all the lands may live out their lives in freedom from fear and want."

Notwithstanding its vagueness as to the machinery for maintaining peace, the United Nations Declaration was important as a part of the connective links which led from the wartime coalition to the San Francisco Charter. For with the United States in the war, American officials began work on a new structure to replace the League, thus reversing the neutrality-based position of the President. But the United States went even further in seeking actively an agreement by the Soviet Union that it would join a world organization after the war. First the Russians signed the United Nations Declaration; then in October, 1943, Secretary of State Cordell Hull (who had never been in an airplane before) at the age of seventy-two journeyed to Moscow for the purpose of discussing problems of war and peace with the British and Soviet foreign ministers. One of the products of the Moscow Conference was the Declaration on General Security, in the fourth point of which the three representatives agreed that "they recognize the necessity of establishing *at the earliest practicable date* a general international organization, based on the principles of sovereign equality for all peace-loving states and open to membership of all such states, large and small, for the maintenance of international peace and security." At the Teheran Conference of November, 1943, the Soviet commitment was renewed. Thus by the time the three powers gathered at Dumbarton Oaks, in August, 1944, there could no longer be any doubt that one of the primary weaknesses of the League, abstention by the United States and the Soviet Union, was not to be duplicated in the prospective United Nations Organization.

LOCATION OF THE UNITED NATIONS IN NEW YORK

A further gesture to American and Soviet membership was the removal of the site of the world organization from Geneva to the United States. This change was favored by the United States and supported by the Soviet Union. The new location of the United Nations symbolized the declining power of Europe and the fact that this was not to be primarily a piece of machinery established by, directed by, and operated on behalf of the states of Europe. The old League had summarily expelled the Soviet Union for its attack on Finland, although it had previously failed to take such drastic action (or any action at all) in the case of Japan's attack on Manchuria, Germany's invasion of the Rhineland, Austria, Bohemia, Moravia, and so on, or Italy's attack on Albania. *Amour-propre* would not permit the Soviet Union to return to the scene of its humiliation. It was further felt that American public opinion, still believed to be receptive to the siren calls of isolation, would be more interested in, hence more favorably inclined toward, an organization located in its midst, even if, as it turned out, the voices emanating from the United Nations had to compete with the din created by the world's greatest city.

RELATION TO NONMEMBERS

Another ambiguity in the League Covenant had been its relationship to countries which were not members of the organization. Article 17 provided that nonmembers of the League, if involved in a dispute, would be "invited to accept the obligations of membership." If they should refuse, "the Council *may* take such measures and make such recommendations as will prevent hostilities and will result in the settlement of the dispute."* The italicized word clearly indicates the permissiveness of the League's jurisdiction. Language of the United Nations Charter is not at all equivocal. Article 2, Para-

---

* Italics added here and in the following brief quotations from the Charter.

graph 6, reads: "The Organization *shall ensure* that states which are not
Members of the United Nations act in accordance with these Principles so far
as may be necessary for the maintenance of international peace and security."
As Goodrich and Hambro, authoritative annotators of the Charter, comment,
this provision would seem inconsistent with the generally acknowledged principle of international law that treaties cannot bind third parties without their
consent. Whereas the articles of the League concerning the maintenance of
security had dealt with disputes among members (*vide* Articles 12, 13, 15,
16), both Chapter VI and Chapter VII of the Charter, dealing with "pacific
settlement of disputes" and "action with respect to threats to the peace,
breaches of the peace, and acts of aggression" respectively, contain articles
(34 and 39) giving the Security Council power to investigate "*any* dispute,
or any situation which might lead to international friction or give rise to a
dispute" and to "determine the existence of *any* threat to the peace, breach of
the peace, or act of aggression. . . ."

A disgruntled member of the League could withdraw if he wished after
the expiration of two years' notice. No right of withdrawal is written into the
Charter, although official records of the San Francisco Conference recognized
that such a right existed for any member "if its rights and obligations as such
were changed by Charter amendment in which it has not concurred and which
it finds itself unable to accept." * The practical impossibility of amending the
Charter make such an eventuality extremely remote.

ABANDONMENT OF THE RULE OF UNANIMITY

One of the improvements in the Charter over the Covenant of which the
drafters were produest was the abolition of the requirement of unanimity
before the United Nations could take action to maintain peace. It was naturally expected that unanimity among all the members of the General Assembly
would be virtually impossible to obtain and would also prove difficult in the
more restricted Security Council. League provisions had left the members
free to take such action as they deemed fit if the Council could not reach
unanimous agreement. Even if the League Council were able to reach a decision, interpretations of the League Covenant by its members had weakened
that organization still further by making each member the final and sole judge
of the manner and degree to which it chose to fulfill its obligations. The improvement over the League machinery which the framers of the Charter
devised was contained in Article 27, Paragraph 3, which provided: "Decisions
of the Security Council on all other matters [excepting 'procedural matters']
shall be made by an affirmative vote of seven members [out of eleven] including the *concurring* votes of the permanent members. . . ." The manner in
which the Security Council has operated in practice has resulted in lowering
still further the majority necessary for action by permitting a permanent

---

* Cited by Leland M. Goodrich and Edvard Hambro, *Charter of the United
Nations, Commentary and Documents* (Boston, World Peace Foundation, 1949), p. 21.

member to be absent or to abstain on questions without interpretation of such procedure as a vote against the contemplated action. This practice has been followed on several occasions by all permanent members, including the Soviet Union, although it does not seem in accord with a literal construction of the Charter.

POWERS OF THE COUNCIL IN MATTERS OF SECURITY

The cumbersome machinery of the League was further streamlined by removing from the General Assembly the power to deal with matters affecting peace and security. In the words of Article 24, "In order to ensure prompt and effective action by the United Nations, its Members confer on the Security Council *primary* responsibility for the maintenance of international peace and security, and agree that in carrying out its duties under this responsibility the Security Council acts on their behalf." Only the Security Council can take *action* which is binding on all states in the United Nations. The General Assembly was to be permitted to *talk* about matters of security, as indeed they may talk about anything, but they were restricted to making recommendations and these only if the Security Council were not considering the question or if it explicitly requested the Assembly's opinion. These were provisions in the Charter as originally drafted; elaborations which subsequently broke the exclusiveness of the Council's jurisdiction will be discussed later in this chapter.

ROLE OF THE PERMANENT MEMBERS

The hierarchy of power contemplated by the Charter ran from the General Assembly to the Security Council and finally to the "'permanent members" of the Council. The League of Nations had also had members with the right to sit permanently in the Council. This was, however, only a right of representation and most emphatically did not carry with it any individual power to block Council action, since that power was possessed equally by all Council members. The United Nations Charter proceeded to give to the permanent members the power which the framers felt was equivalent to their position in the world in the provisions of Article 27, part of which was quoted above. Although denunciation of the so-called "veto" right began almost as soon as knowledge of it seeped out, the reasoning behind the voting formula is still difficult to refute. The strength in the hands of each one of the great nations was such that attempts to coerce any one of them would inevitably involve the United Nations in another world war, which the organization itself might well not survive. The right of one of these major nations to vote against measures of coercion directed at itself was merely a realistic reminder that almost any one of the Big Five could back its intransigence with such force as to deter most members of the United Nations from the contemplation of sanctions against it.

The unanimity formula, however, was to be definitely restricted. It was not to apply to any recommendations which the Council might make under

Chapter VI looking toward the pacific settlement of disputes in which a major nation was involved. Nor was it to apply to so-called "procedural matters" coming before the Council.

Perhaps it is necessary to remind Americans that their delegates were as united in their support of this right of veto as were those of the Soviet Union, although the latter had argued originally for an even broader interpretation. Joined by Great Britain, both countries stood firm at San Francisco against all assaults by middle and small states on their privileged position. The admission of France and China to the same status as that of the three superpowers, and the exaggerated Soviet view of what constitutes a question susceptible of veto should not blind students of international organization to the basic facts of power politics. The League, confronted by the defiant aggression of major states in the pre–World War II period, was powerless to protect the victims. Had the League chosen to push the issue in the case of Japan, Germany, Italy, or Russia to the logical ending—the application of complete economic and military sanctions—either one of two results, both disastrous to the League, would have occurred. Either the transgressor would have succeeded in his aggression before the sanctions took effect, and the League, as in the case of Ethiopia, would have been forced to the humiliating position of acknowledging its failure; or else, as the sanctions became effective, the League would have become involved in the very world war it was supposedly created to prevent. The new distribution of power arising from World War II increased the impotency of any international organization to take forceful action against any one of the major powers. It seemed to the drafters of the Charter that they were giving the new machinery a chance for life by recognizing its limitations in advance, rather than by waiting for the disastrous discrepancy between pretension and practice to appear at some critical time in the future.

▶ AMERICAN AND SOVIET DELUSIONS
ABOUT THE UNITED NATIONS

MISCONCEPTIONS IN THE UNITED STATES

At the outset of the chapter mention was made of the fact that none of the three categories of states—small, middle, and large—actually participated in the same organization that their dreams and beliefs had conjured. Of no country was this more true than the United States. Because of fear as to what the American people and their representatives in Congress might do to the Charter, a veritable wave of propaganda and influence was generated on behalf of American membership in any new world organization. Even as official executive commitments in this direction were becoming more precise, widespread efforts were mobilized to avoid duplication of the fate of the Treaty of Versailles. The Republican party, bemused by the energy of Governor Dewey of New York and the public reversal in attitude of Michigan's distinguished Senator Vandenberg, was induced to follow the path laid down by the rather vague Mackinac Resolution. So long as President Roosevelt's hand was firm, the Democratic party, which had proved in the decade of the thirties to be far less isolationist than the Republican, was certain to favor participation by a heavy majority.

Both branches of Congress also went on record, the House by passing the Fulbright Resolution in September, 1943, the Senate following two months later with the Connally Resolution. The former was a short, simple document endorsing "the creation of appropriate international machinery with power adequate to establish and maintain a just and lasting peace" and "participation by the United States therein through its constitutional processes." The Senate had been invited to concur in the House resolution, but that august body, and particularly the distinguished Texas senator, who headed its Foreign Relations Committee, preferred not to associate itself with the junior branch, which would have less authority in the field of foreign policy anyway. The resultant Connally Resolution repeated verbatim the wordage of the Moscow Declaration quoted above, but went on to make two points crystal-clear. The first was that this new organization was to be one of "free and sovereign nations," the second that "participation by the United States therein" meant that the instrument must be a treaty submitted to and ratified by the Senate.

Another device utilized to gain Congressional support for American membership in the United Nations was consultation on the part of the executive with representatives of both parties in Congress. This consultation had been going on for some time before Dumbarton Oaks and resulted in the sending of senators and representatives as part of the American delegation to the San Francisco Conference. Between the conclusion of the Dumbarton Oaks meeting and the ratification of the Charter, efforts to ensure American support reached a crescendo. The American people and their Congress could hear anything about the United Nations that they wanted. The United Nations was to provide relief from "power politics"; it was a security system in which the United States could trust; it was the first line of defense of the United States. On the other hand, the freedom of the United States was not one whit impaired; its sovereignty was still retained; its domestic institutions, however they might be defined, were intact from legal or political interference; indeed the United States could still retreat to its old position if the venture in international cooperation proved to be a failure. If the Charter was all things to all men, no wonder the Senate ratified it with only two dissenting votes. No wonder such confusion attended the attempts at popular explanation of the Charter that only one person out of three had even a rudimentary knowledge of how the organization would work.

SOVIET VIEWS OF THE UNITED NATIONS

Postwar evidence suggests that the Soviet Union was also deluded as to the nature, scope, and development of the United Nations it was joining. The organization the Russians wanted was, in fact, little more than an elaboration of the wartime coalition of the Big Three. Military and political decisions had been made by the Big Three in the course of the struggle against Germany without any consultation with the very junior partners of the United Nations. This system would, the Russians thought, be continued into the peacetime era. The function of the organization would hence be twofold. It would facilitate meetings between the heads of the three states or their deputies, a definite improvement on the hazardous, haphazard arrangements previously prevailing. Participation of the other nations of the world would be for the purpose of accepting the measures previously worked out by the Big Three. Great-power agreement was essential in the Soviet view, but agreement of a particular sort. It would be the result of diplomatic consultation, not of common acceptance of binding rules of conduct laid down in advance. Power was its own law; the Three could do what they could agree to do.

Nor was it necessary to have agreement on all points affecting every part of the globe. This was the rock on which other alliances had smashed. Harmony among the great powers would be preserved by reason of there being as few issues as possible to create disharmony. Each of the Three would be responsible for the functioning of his own particular sphere of influence: the United States in the Western Hemisphere; Great Britain in the Dominions and Western Europe; the Soviet Union in Eastern Europe. Together the Three would administer Germany and Japan, and cooperation of a diplomatic, not a legal, variety would be needed only should issues arise affecting the relation of one sphere of influence to another, or with respect to issues created in areas where there existed no preponderance of power of any of the Three.

The preceding paragraph is a formalization and clarification of a Soviet viewpoint which was never fully expressed, but which seems implicit in its behavior since 1939. It should be remembered that the Soviet Union had hardly come to terms with Germany when it began to press for a division of various nearby areas between them. The advancement of what seemed to Hitler to be exaggerated ambitions had been one reason for his turning on Russia less than two years after the German-Russian accord was reached. The Soviet position taken during the war on such issues as the veto power and the granting of big-power status to France and China is perfectly consistent with the purpose of the United Nations as the Russians envisaged it. Also accounted for is the apparently paradoxical scorn on the part of Soviet delegates for certain small countries while at the same time they loudly proclaimed Russian support of the principle of sovereign equality of states. Small countries, according to Russian views, are contemptible when they get in the way of the big powers. Particularly is this true of small states in the American-British "spheres" which try to hold the Soviet Union to account for what goes on in its own "sphere." The function of these small states is to agree with arrangements made for them. In fact, they could be made to agree if the big powers responsible for their behavior desired to take the necessary action.

Therefore either Honduran protests at Soviet actions are inspired by the United States, which is a hypocritical procedure, or else the United States cannot control Honduras, which is dangerous weakness menacing the peace of the world. The principle of sovereign equality of states is interpreted to mean that no state is accountable for its actions to aught save its own ability and strength. Thus there is no "right" on the part of the United Nations to do anything respecting the Soviet Union; there is only gracious permission granted by that sovereign state to an organization of its own creation.

SIMILARITY OF RUSSIAN VIEWS TO ROOSEVELT'S INITIAL POSITION

Not only was this the limited type of organization which Stalin wished to join, but this was essentially the type he thought he was going to join after his discussions with President Roosevelt at Teheran. There the American leader outlined the proposals which had been developed within the State Department. As Sumner Welles, who was for a time heading this work, has stated: "The members of the State departmental committee were almost unanimously of the opinion that any new world structure should be based on *regional organizations* similar to the Organization of American States.* Each regional organization would periodically elect representatives to sit in a superior executive council to which *supreme authority* would be delegated by all the members of the United Nations. This executive committee was to be composed of eleven members, seven to be elected by the regional organizations, and the remaining four to be delegates of the United States, the Soviet Union, Great Britain, and China.† These four were to have permanent seats."‡

Welles goes on to say that the veto right envisaged by the committee was far more limited than that which actually emerged from the San Francisco Conference. (There is no doubt also that the Americans did not think their proposals would result in an organization operating in the way the Soviet Union wished, but the important point at this juncture is not the American but the Soviet interpretation.) As propounded by Roosevelt to Stalin at Teheran, the organization would consist of an assembly, holding its periodic meetings in various places, and an executive committee to deal with all *nonmilitary* matters. Stalin then asked the crucial question concerning this committee—in Sherwood's paraphrase: "whether this committee would have the right to make decisions which would be binding on all the nations." To which Roosevelt's reply, although labeled "indecisive" by Sherwood, seems clear enough: "He [Roosevelt] did not believe that the Congress would permit the United States to be bound by the decision of such a body. He said that the Committee would make *recommendations* for settling disputes with the

* Can one detect here the influence of Welles himself, who was a prime proponent and had had great experience with the workings of the Inter-American System?
  † France was not included.
  ‡ Sumner Welles, *Seven Decisions That Shaped History* (New York, Harper & Brothers, 1951), pp. 184–185. Reprinted by permission of the publishers.

hope that the nations concerned would be guided thereby."* One can almost see Stalin losing interest in any such committee.

The power of the organization was to be vested in the "Four Policemen" —the United States, Britain, Russia, and China. Again Stalin immediately got down to brass tacks. How would Europe regard Chinese participation in enforcement action in that area? Wouldn't a European committee of Britain, Russia, and the United States be better? Roosevelt: Congress would not agree to such a limited committee which "might be able to compel the involvement of American troops." Stalin: But the Four Policemen concept would require American troops overseas. Roosevelt: "He had only foreseen the sending of American naval and air forces to Europe and that any land armies needed in the event of a future threat would have to be provided by Britain *and the Soviet Union*."† This was exactly the type of answer best calculated to fit into the Soviet preconception of the functions of the new world organization.

Belief that the American proposals were consistent with Soviet thinking must have been strengthened by the ensuing discussion of the enforcement action to be taken by the Four Policemen. Although Sumner Welles refers to "the President's blunt statement . . . that the chief threat to the future peace of the world would be aggression by a majorpower,"‡ it would appear from Sherwood's account that the "major power" in mind was a state whose strength lay somewhere between that of a small country and that of the Big Three. "There seems to be no evidence," says Sherwood, "of any discussion of the possibility that the offending aggressor might be one of the Four Policemen." § This attitude was the same one adopted by the Sovet Union, as well as by the American participants in the Dumbarton Oaks Conference, and was embodied in the United Nations Charter.

▶ CHANGES IN THE ORGANIZATION WROUGHT
    BY SMALL AND MIDDLE POWERS

That the United Nations did not turn out to be the organization which the Soviet Union thought it would be is primarily attributable to the determined action of such small and middle powers as the Latin-American states and Australia. Indeed it is difficult to see just how Roosevelt and the State Department hoped to obtain the consent of the rest of the world to the proposals they originally had in mind. After Teheran American thinking begaı to recognize the importance of creating the type of international organizatioı acceptable to the fifty-odd other nations as well as to the Big Three. Sumnet Welles has sharply criticized the failure of the State Department, after he

---

* Robert Sherwood, *Roosevelt and Hopkins* (New York, Harper & Brothers, 1948), p. 785. This and the following quotations from the Sherwood book are reprinted by permission of the publishers.
    † *Ibid.,* p. 786.
    ‡ Welles, *op. cit.,* p. 190.
    § Sherwood, *op. cit.,* p. 786.

departed, to consult Latin America prior to the Dumbarton Oaks Conference. Such a procedure, of course, could not be followed, since it would have been deeply offensive to the Soviet Union to have the United States even appear to place higher priority on Latin-American consultation than on obtaining its agreement. Nor would Russia have liked the appearance of the United States at Dumbarton Oaks with the pressure of twenty countries behind its position, particularly when those countries, in the Soviet view, did not have power enough to merit consultation at all.

When the other American republics, assembled at the Mexico City Conference, did see the proposals, they had grave reservations. In their comments, presented at Mexico City and later at San Francisco, the Latin-American countries wanted to limit the veto power, to enlarge the power of the General Assembly, to extend the jurisdiction of the International Court, and to specify in more detail the principles on which the world organization was to be based —in sum, to curtail the overwhelming power of the Big Three, Four, or Five, the very idea which had formed such an integral part of the original American and Soviet concept.

It is clear that the majority of the small states, joined by such other countries as Australia, wanted to see in the new international machinery formalized, adequate procedures to protect themselves from the consequences of their weakness, weakness which had constituted an invitation to German and Russian aggression and which, relative to the power of the United States and the Soviet Union, the war had only increased. The full measure of protection which they sought was not and indeed could not be embodied in the Charter as finally adopted at San Francisco. They did, however, obtain alterations in the draft which later developments proved to be most significant. These were, first, the broadening of the right of Assembly discussion; second, the reversal in relationship between regional groupings and the United Nations; and, third, the modification of the veto right. Other changes were the elaboration of the first chapter on purposes and principles, the designation of the Economic and Social Council as a "principal organ" of the United Nations, the formulation of the clauses on trusteeship, and the enlargement of the definition of "domestic jurisdiction."

INCREASE IN THE DISCUSSION RIGHTS OF THE GENERAL ASSEMBLY

The stress which the proposed world organization laid on the virtually exclusive jurisdiction of the great powers over the maintenance of security led the other states to look most carefully at the clauses relating to *their* body, the General Assembly. They found the Dumbarton Oaks draft deficient in this regard. It had granted the Assembly the "right to consider the general principles of cooperation in the maintenance of international peace and security . . . to discuss any questions relating to the maintenance of international peace and security brought before it by any member or members of the Organization or by the Security Council. . . ." At the suggestion of the smaller states an article was introduced ahead of the phraseology just quoted, which said that "the General Assembly may discuss *any questions* or *any matters* within the scope of the present Charter or relating to the powers and functions of any organs provided for in the present Charter. . . ." Article 10 thus laid the groundwork for the unlimited right of talk possessed by the Assembly. It also explicitly enabled the Assembly to examine, if not to correct, the operations of all other United Nations bodies, including the Security Council itself. That domain of the great powers was not to prove sacrosanct to criticism.

RELATION OF REGIONAL GROUPINGS TO THE UNITED NATIONS

In Chapter Nineteen on United States security in the Inter-American System, mention was made of the success attendant upon the efforts of Latin-American and other countries to get into the United Nations Charter Article 51, the "self-defense article," which freed the operations of their regional arrangements from prior jurisdiction of the Security Council. The Dumbarton Oaks proposals, presented at San Francisco, had contained a section on regional arrangements which was attached to the chapter on United Nations enforcement action. This section was made into a separate chapter. It provided for regional groupings consistent with the Charter, for encouragement by the Security Council of pacific settlement of disputes on the local level prior to their submittal to the United Nations, and for utilization of the regional group by the Security Council for enforcement action, provided that no enforcement action should take place "without the *authorization* of the Security Council."

These clauses (Articles 52–54) are still in the Charter, but their clear implication of the superiority of the United Nations over the region with respect to combating aggression is reversed by Article 51, which provides a foundation for the claims to compatibility with the United Nations of the Inter-American System, the Brussels Pact, the North Atlantic Treaty Organization, the Pacific Pact, the Arab League, and so on, and therefore deserves to be quoted in full:

> Nothing in the present Charter shall impair the inherent right of individual or collective self-defense if an armed attack occurs against a Member of the United Nations, until the Security Council has taken the measures necessary to maintain international peace and security. Measures taken by Members in the exercise of this right of self-defense shall be immediately reported to the Security Council and shall not in any way affect the authority and responsibility of the Security Council under the present Charter to take at any time such action as it deems necessary in order to maintain or restore international peace and security.

Under Article 53, if the Security Council refuses to authorize regional action, or if it is deadlocked, or if a big-power veto is entered, no action is to take place. Article 51 not only permits a regional group to go ahead on its own in such cases, but also permits it to take action prior to any decision at all by the Security Council and to continue its measures until the positive decision of the Council declares that peace and security have been restored. The same "inherent right" attaches to individual, unilateral state action, about which the Dumbarton Oaks draft had been altogether silent. If Article 51 is truly concerned with an "inherent right" within the full meaning of the term, there would appear to be no way short of declaring such action to constitute in itself a breach of the peace, for the Council to stop regional or individual action which it might deem inappropriate or dangerous.

VOTING PROCEDURE

Most of the fire of the small and middle powers at San Francisco was directed at the voting procedure in the Security Council. After persistent efforts to get discussion of the question had failed, a large group of delegates drew up twenty-two questions which were designed at least to gain elucidation as to what the formula meant. The Big Three refused to answer and in addition stated that the text could not be changed. The United States, Britain, and the Soviet Union were not going to join an organization in which there was no veto. On the other hand, there was real danger that the smaller states would not care to participate actively in an organization dominated by the great powers under a voting procedure seemingly capable of any construction the latter might wish to make of it. The deadlock was broken on June 7 with the issuance of a statement of the Four Sponsoring Governments (the Big Three plus China) that "no individual member of the Council can alone prevent consideration and discussion by the Council of a dispute or situation brought to its attention. . . ." This statement meant that the veto could not be extended to include the Security Council's agenda. The framers of the Charter had provided that there was to be no right of veto over measures of pacific settlement recommended by the Council under Chapter VI of the Charter. Definition of the voting procedure in this way did not represent as much of a modification as the small states had hoped for. On the other hand, it was more than the Soviet Union had earlier been willing to grant and more than its later actions indicated it was prepared to see embodied in United Nations practice.

THE DOMESTIC JURISDICTION CLAUSE

Before considering the weakening of the United Nations with respect to its ability to preserve international peace and security, one more change made at San Francisco should be noted. This relates to the domestic jurisdiction of states and was proposed by the major powers with the support of Australia. The comparable clause in the Dumbarton Oaks proposals had applied only to the pacific settlement of disputes. At San Francisco the major powers felt that broadening the potential scope of the world organization, particularly with respect to economic and social matters, demanded an equivalent clarification in the domestic jurisdiction provision. This clause was accordingly taken out of Chapter VI and placed in Chapter I on purposes and principles (as Article 2, Paragraph 7). It reads: "Nothing contained in the present Charter shall authorize the United Nations to intervene in matters which are essentially within the domestic jurisdiction of any state or shall require the Members to submit such matters to settlement under the present Charter. . . ." The United Nations, however, was still to be free to apply enforcement measures to maintain international security

The balance of authority between the state's internal sovereignty as guaranteed by Article 2, Paragraph 7, and the powers of the United Nations as contained in its Charter can only be determined by the practice followed in each case. A great deal obviously hinges on the nature of the problems which arise and the power of the states involved. Questions such as immigration and trade practices are protected by this clause. On other matters, such as non-self-governing territories, human rights, and overturn in national regimes, the United Nations has succeeded in gaining the power of discussion and the power of recommendation. When the Netherlands claimed that its "police action" in Indonesia was a matter solely for internal Dutch determination, the Security Council, without passing directly on the relevance of Article 2, Paragraph 7, took positions obviously based on its power to act.

The scope of matters which a state can claim to be exempt from United Nations discussion, recommendation, and action is determined by political, not legalistic, considerations. Can the state itself veto Security Council action or get a great power to do so on its behalf? Can the state muster enough votes in the General Assembly, in the Economic and Social Council, in the Trusteeship Council, or in other organs to gain acceptance of its definition of what constitutes exclusive, domestic jurisdiction? These would appear to be the questions on which depend the balance between national sovereignty and international organization.

The attachment of the United States to the domestic-jurisdiction formula may be seen in the Senate's reservation to its agreement to submit "legal" disputes to the International Court of Justice: that the disputes shall not concern matters "essentially within the jurisdiction of the United States of America *as determined by the United States of America*."*

► CASE STUDIES OF THE RELATION BETWEEN UNITED
NATIONS FAILURES AND LACK OF GREAT-POWER
HARMONY

With all the changes, elaborations, and amplifications embodied in the Charter of the United Nations as finally produced by the San Francisco Conference, the abilty of the world organization to maintain international peace and security still rested where it always had: on the harmony of the great powers. Although the Preamble of the Charter began, "We the *Peoples*

* Cited by Goodrich and Hambro, *op. cit.*, pp. 480–481.

of the United Nations," this was to be no world government, as was made abundantly clear in Article 2, Paragraph 1: "The Organization is based on the principle of the sovereign equality of all its Members." When translated into the field of international politics, this meant the sovereignty of states strong enough to gain respect for it. World War II had so widened the disparity in state power that only three nations—the United States, Great Britain, and the Soviet Union—would, it was thought, have this power after the war. British weakness, of longer duration and greater extent than had originally been anticipated, further restricted to two—the United States and the Soviet Union—the number of powers whose agreement was a prerequisite for successful international organization.

The manner in which the two giants participated in the world organization both helped to cause and was in turn affected by the increasing split between East and West. As outlined in preceding chapters, wartime American suppositions about postwar Soviet behavior in Europe and Asia proved inaccurate. As each Soviet move provoked an American response, to which there was a Soviet counterresponse, it was inevitable that the resultant cold war, which found the two at loggerheads all over the globe, should have repercussions in the halls of the United Nations. Simultaneously it became apparent that the Soviet Union was intent on forcing upon the United Nations its own interpretation of world organization. Russian policies motivated by the determination that the United Nations should not be permitted to act in the increasing number of cases on which there was no great-power agreement contributed in turn to heightened international tension. The United States also resorted to counter-measures which by 1953 had substantially altered the focus and activity of the United Nations.

The consequences for international organization of the East-West split may be traced with regard to each of the following basic issues with which the United Nations was confronted from the very first day of its existence: arms for the United Nations international police force, control of armaments, control of atomic energy, nonpolitical cooperation, and universality of the world organization. In each of these fields the failure of the United Nations has reflected the basic conflict in American-Soviet relations and at the same time has significantly worsened those relations.

FAILURE TO CREATE AN INTERNATIONAL POLICE FORCE

In order for United Nations enforcement action against an aggressor to be effective, superior power must be available to the international community. Under the League Covenant the individual states bound themselves to carry out decisions of the Council but only to the extent which they themselves might determine. In practice the League applied economic sanctions only once, and then incompletely, and military sanctions not at all. While unwilling to move all the way to an international police force, the framers of the Charter established under Article 43 and 45 a procedure whereby the members *in advance* would have troops and planes available for use by the Security Council. The joker in the procedure was that agreements regarding these forces also had to be negotiated in advance.

By the middle of 1947 it had become apparent that the Military Staff Committee, established on February 16, 1946, by the Security Council, was not going to be able to conclude any such agreements. While the representatives on the committee were in accord on many obvious points, no decision could be reached on the nature or size of contribution which the permanent members should make, the numbers to be contributed by other countries, the location of the international units, or the provision of bases for the Security Council. The Soviet Union, usually alone, contended that each of the permanent members should contribute exactly the same number and type of forces, thus limiting them to the lowest common denominator: i.e., the portion of the British army, or the amount of Chinese ground equipment, navy, and air force which those respective governments saw fit to volunteer. The Soviet Union also wished to restrict the forces to locations within the contributing country, while the other committee members wished permission for advance bases to be written into the agreements. All in all, it was clear that the Russian delegates wanted the forces available to the United Nations to be as small and widely separated as possible and probably wanted no internationally controlled army at all. The failure of the Military Staff Committee's efforts also had the effect of destroying Article 45, which, as a gesture to the enthusiasts of air power, had provided for "immediately available national air force contingents," if the agreements contemplated by Article 43 could be negotiated.

The framers of the Charter had not wished the organization to be without power to enforce its decisions in the interim before the activation of Article 43. In Chapter XVII, hopefully entitled "Transitional Security Arrangements," had therefore been placed Article 106, which gave to the signers of the Four Nation Declaration in Moscow (the United States, Great Britain, the Soviet Union, and China) plus France the right to consult among themselves "with a view to such joint action on behalf of the Organization as may be necessary for the purpose of maintaining international peace and security." Here was a provision granting the permanent members of the Security Council practically a blank check to enforce peace all over the world, with no accountability to the United Nations if they could agree. But they could agree on little, and on nothing at all concerning joint military action.

LIMITATION OF ARMAMENTS

A very significant change had taken place in the thinking of statesmen on the subject of disarmament. National leaders of the nineteenth and early twentieth centuries, particularly in the United States, were convinced that armaments led to war, that the quality of armaments was related to the destructiveness of the war, and that any peace system must therefore rest on successfully implemented measures of disarmament. While the Atlantic Charter spoke of the "crushing burden of armaments," it had become abundantly clear by the outbreak of World War II that the foregoing propositions were all true, but contained only part of the truth. It was equally true that disarmament of peace-loving states could be dangerous, that even general limitation of armaments could leave in the hands of a potential aggressor a tempting initial advantage in attacking first. All attempts of the League to cope with the highly technical as well as political problem of just how to attain disarmament had led to failure with respect to land and air forces. Therefore the framers of the Charter chose to place their emphasis on the "control" and "regulation" of armaments rather than on their limitation.

The only place where "disarmament" is mentioned at all is in Article 11, giving the General Assembly the right to discuss the "principles governing" disarmament and to make recommendations thereon. While the first session of the General Assembly did avail itself of this right, its resolution of December 14, 1946, placed responsibility for the implementation of plans for disarmament where it belonged—on the Security Council. That body, declares Article 26, "shall be responsible for formulating with the assistance of the Military Staff Committee . . . plans to be submitted to the Members of the United Nations for the establishment of a system for the regulation of armaments." No such plans have been forthcoming, since the Commission on Conventional Armaments, established for this purpose by the Security Council, became involved in the same old chicken-egg relationship question as had the League: Which comes first, disarmament (regulation of armaments) or security? The logical answer of *both* really means *neither*. In its report of August 12, 1948, the commission sadly concluded that "a system of regulation and reduction of armaments and armed forces can only be put into effect in an atmosphere of international confidence and security," which in turn could only be created by imlpementation of Article 43, conclusion of a German and a Japanese peace treaty, and effective control of atomic energy. Everything was related to everything else.

One more effort to obtain disarmament under the United Nations was contained in the proposal of the United States, Great Britain, and France submitted to the November, 1951, meeting of the General Assembly. The proposal was undoubtedy motivated by other reasons, in addition to the simple desire to reduce armaments. Western initiative was a psychological blow in the atmosphere of the cold war, designed to take the play away from the Soviet Union, which for years had had a working monopoly on the "disarmament" cry. Allies of the United States greatly feared that a small "incident" might set off a war which would utterly destroy them and continued to exert what pressure they could on the United States to make further attempts to reach a settlement with Russia. Other members of the North Atlantic Pact, furthermore, were searching desperately for a way out of the dilemma of military weakness and the economic gains produced by the ECA vs. military security at the sacrifice of those gains.

There were few grounds for optimism that the dismal record of the United Nations in the disarmament field would be reversed as a result of the three-power proposal. Atomic and conventional armaments were considered as one problem, a concession the United States had for some time indicated it was prepared to make to the Soviet Union, but the two essential features of the American atomic energy plan were retained: progressive stages in the divulgence of information and an effective international inspection. If the Soviet Union were now ready to change its position on both points, signs were not apparent.

CONTROL OF ATOMIC ENERGY

While the failures to implement Article 43 and the regulation of armaments were taking place in relative obscurity, full limelight shone on the attempts of the United Nations to wrestle with the problem created by the discovery that action of certain atoms could be harnessed within a bomb casing and released over a target area. Bernard Baruch told the Atomic Energy Commission, established by the General Assembly but responsible to the Security Council, that "we are here to make a choice between the quick and the dead. That is our business. . . . If we fail, then we have damned every man to be the slave of Fear. Let us not deceive ourselves. We must elect World Peace or World Destruction."*We hope that the American delegate was wrong in his heartfelt, impassioned words, because the effort has failed. Has World Destruction then been elected?

The trouble was partly that the United Nations was never designed to deal with such a problem as atomic energy. Furthermore, neither the United States nor the Soviet Union, especially the latter, behaved as though it believed the words of America's prominent elder statesman. To control atomic energy adequately demanded changes in the Charter which would have made of the United Nations a truly supranational authority in this field. As the applications of the new source of power, both military and economic, inevitably proliferated, the United Nations would, by reason of its primary authority, be transformed into a world government. There could be no veto in the Security Council to hamper its inspection of atomic facilities in various countries. Adequate control, ran the initial argument of the United States, could only be ensured by direct United Nations supervision over atomic energy from the mine through the plant product. None of this was the Soviet Union prepared to accept, although its position changed from time to time and at one point appeared to approach the proposals of the United States. For its part, the United States was not prepared to change its proposals to

---

* Cited in *International Control of Atomic Energy: Growth of a Policy,* Department of State Publication 2702, p. 138.

any great extent, although outside observers did not believe that the original suggestions provided the only conceivable way the problem could be solved. Nor was the United States prepared to give up its atomic stockpile in advance of the *implementation* of an agreement. Neither was it prepared to give up final and complete determination of what constituted completion of the various stages toward an effective system of control. And who can say that the American Executive Branch, Congress, and the American public would have themselves been willing to accept the United States plan even had the Russians suddenly agreed? This question became increasingly uncertain as the estrangement from the Soviet Union widened into hostility and conflict. Russian intransigence fortunately spared the United States the unwelcome decision as to whether or not to recognize its own child.

From the first, regulation of the atomic bomb and regulation of the so-called "conventional armaments" were intertwined. The Soviet Union never tired of claiming that the two problems should be considered together. On the surface this proposition seemed reasonable. There was also considerable logic in the contention of the United States, however, that separation was necessary and that control of atomic weapons should be given priority because the contemplated control mechanism was unique in the annals of international organization and without its adoption the regulation of other implements of war was hopeless. Endless discussion in the Atomic Energy Commission demonstrated that international control of atomic energy was unattainable too. The overwhelming majority of the commission was prepared to accept the essentials of the American plan, as were the great majority of the Security Council and General Assembly members. Russia and its satellites were not. Although the Assembly told the commission to keep on working when it reported its deadlock and although President Truman removed one source of Soviet complaint by indicating American willingness to merge the two problems, the Soviet Union only hardened its stand.

REASONS FOR RUSSIAN INTRANSIGENCE ON ATOMIC CONTROL

Suspicion has grown since 1947 that the Russians, despite their willingness to palaver endlessly and even to come up with "new" proposals from time to time, never had any intention of accepting an effective mechanism to control atomic energy. Why? At the outset the Soviet Union, having no bomb, was negotiating from weakness, a position no great state, and especially Russia, has ever relished. As pointed out above, the setting of various stages at which the United States would divulge information left this country free at any point to quit and keep its bombs. This was a question of mutual trust in international politics, always ticklish to maintain between any two sovereign states, and impossible between the United States and the Soviet Union. The Russians must have felt that any system of control would place hostages in the hands of the West for Soviet good behavior on other issues. The Russians were aware that their behavior would not be classified as "good" by the "capitalist enemies."

Even after the widely awaited atomic explosion showed the world that Russia had been able to produce (and far earlier than the West had thought possible) at least one bomb, Soviet attitudes did not change toward the heart of the American plan—a system of adequate, if ill-defined, international inspection. Inspection meant the entry into the Soviet Union of United Nations agents. There they might uncover economic and industrial facts which Russia was carefully concealing. (The Kremlin is wont to classify as secret practically everything connected with its national strength, particularly production figures and available resources.) Westerners might also be able to document and give widespread publicity to the inadequacies of the Soviet civilian economy: the production of consumers goods, their distribution and price, housing, and so on. The degree to which that totalitarian state relies on police-control methods shocking to Westerners might be uncovered. The length to which the Russian rulers have gone since 1946 to root out of Soviet society all traces of Western ideas indicates a fear that contact between Russian citizens and the West may weaken or undermine altogether the enforced identification of Russians with the Soviet system.

Finally, the Soviet Union regarded the veto as an essential part of the Charter, the basis of its participation in the international organization. It was unalterably opposed to the total abandonment of this principle in questions involving atomic energy control. As the endless discussions unwound, the matter of a veto seemed irrelevant in case the United Nations confronted a determined violator. American insistence on this point was unnecessary. To the Russians it looked as though the United States wanted to change the Charter by a procedure not originally contemplated, to make of the United Nations an entirely different organization from that which they had joined. To observers, puzzled by the adamant American attitude on a nonessential point, the basic Soviet determination to avoid atomic control was concealed behind its logical opposition to removing the foundation of great-power participation in the United Nations.

RELATIONSHIP OF FUNCTIONAL TO POLITICAL COOPERATION

The philosophy lying behind Soviet foreign policy has destroyed one of the fondest and most persistent beliefs regarding world organization: that elaboration of functional, technical, nonpolitical cooperation would lead to effective international organization on the political level. The theory behind this belief looked fairly persuasive until the Soviet Union arrived on the scene. Mutuality of interest between states is easiest to find in the nonpolitical fields. Cooperation takes the form of regulation of necessary day-to-day operations for the benefit of all. Practice in such regulation develops successful techniques for coping with more perplexing problems of a political nature. The nineteenth century saw constantly increasing world interdependence on the functional level as exemplified by many international unions, some of which had real control over state action. The League of Nations further enlarged these activities, introduced some integration, and aligned many with the League itself. Under the Charter of the United Nations functional organization has become almost all-embracing: financial (International Fund and Bank), economic (Economic and Social Council, its affiliates, and the International Labor Organization), legal (International Court), cultural (UNESCO), and many others.

But the simple and tragic fact is that there appears to be an insuperable hurdle between functional and political cooperation, a hurdle heightened by deliberate Soviet policy. Mutuality of interest permits functional organization without disturbing concepts of national sovereignty. Effective political control does not. Political conflict, not cooperation, has been an inherent aspect of national sovereignty from the beginning of the state system. Political conflict has unfortunately become imbedded in the minds and hearts of men, as the Preamble to UNESCO recognizes. People and their governments, in case of political incompatibility, have so far preferred to see functional cooperation destroyed rather than to yield the sovereign right of conflict to effective political regulation.

All this is discouraging, but the Soviet Union has gone further. Whereas most of the Western world has been attempting with considerable success to remove more and more aspects of state relations from the dangerous political field, the Soviet Union has done just the reverse. It has adopted as a basis of policy a definition of political relations so all-inclusive that it encompasses almost the entire functional field as well. For this reason Soviet nonparticipation in the functional aspects of United Nations activity is virtually complete: it is not a member of the International Civil Aviation Organization, UNESCO, or any other of the "specialized agencies" of the United Nations except the World Health Organization. Its belated participation in the Trusteeship Council illustrates its willingness to join only if the political benefit is obvious and the potential regulation of its own untrammeled sovereignty small. Russian practice makes every political conflict reverberate throughout the entire functional field. It admits of no such thing as technical representatives, experts uncontrolled by their governments. Does the Soviet Union believe Nationalist China no longer entitled to United Nations membership? Then Russian representatives walk out of *every* group in which there is a Chinese member, walk out with a maximum of fanfare and insult. Under these conditions the inevitable consequence has been the failure of functional cooperation to contribute to the alleviation of political tension.

ADMISSION OF NEW MEMBERS

Political conflict has made it impossible for the United Nations to attain the universality originally contemplated. One state, Spain, was branded at

San Francisco as an international pariah and was barred from the gates of the United Nations. Even though Western attitudes toward Franco have changed, under American pressure, from hostility to uneasy tolerance, the technicalities of admission will continue to operate against his regime. Article 4 of the Charter says: "Membership in the United Nations is open to all other peace-loving states [other meaning in addition to the "original" members] which accept the obligations contained in the present Charter and, in the judgment of the Organization, are able and willing to carry out these obligations." The addition of the expression "peace-loving" to the normal requirements followed the Moscow Four Power Declaration, later embodied in the Dumbarton Oaks proposals. Although Paragraph 2 of the same article makes the General Assembly responsible for the final decision on applications, it can only act "upon the recommendation of the Security Council." A two-thirds majority of the Assembly is necessary, but the prior consideration in the Security Council has been construed as a matter of "substance" and hence subject to the veto.

The Soviet Union's definition of "peace-loving" has led it to veto the application of states with regimes it happened not to approve. This has resulted in the rejection of Eire, Portugal, Jordan, Finland, Italy, Ceylon, Nepal, South Korea, and Austria. For its part, the West has been chary of admitting former Axis satellites which have now come under Communist control: Bulgaria, Hungary, Rumania, and Albania. It also views with suspicion the claimed "independence" of the Mongolian People's Republic. From time to time the General Assembly has put what pressure it can on the Council, via recommendations and requests for reports, but this effort has been in vain. Equally unavailing was an advisory opinion handed down by the International Court of Justice at the request of the Assembly, stating in essence that a member should not be guided by political considerations in passing on applications, because they were not expressly incorporated into Article 4 of the Charter. Only a logrolling enterprise would seem capable of breaking the deadlock—a "you-vote-for-my-applicant-and-I'll-vote-for-yours" procedure. This was proposed in 1946 by the United States and rejected by the Soviet Union. Three years later it was suggested by the Soviet Union and turned down by the United States. Meanwhile fourteen states have been kept cooling their heels in the vestibule of the United Nations; only eight (Afghanistan, Iceland, Siam, Sweden, Pakistan, Yemen, Burma, and Israel) have been accepted.

► RESULTS OF THE EAST-WEST DEADLOCK

STRENGTHENED REGIONAL ORGANIZATIONS

The distintegration of the wartime coalition and the attendant inability of the United Nations as originally conceived to cope successfully with problems basic to world security have forced development of international organ-

ization in two different directions, one a retreat from world to regional organization, the second the adaptation of the Charter to meet the new crisis.
Although progress has been made along both lines, neither can prove an
adequate substitute for the great-power harmony on which the United Nations
was founded.

It will be remembered that strengthened regional groupings formed a
basic part of original State Department thinking, whereas the Dumbarton
Oaks proposals clearly relegated them to a position subordinate and sub-
servient to the contemplated universal association. A retreat from the second
positon was then made by the inclusion in the Charter of Article 51, which
has been used as the jusification of all later regional arrangements. Of these
the most important are the Organization of American States, for the United
States and Latin America; the Brussels Pact, the North Atlantic Treaty
Organization, and the Council of Europe, for Western Europe, Great Britain,
and the United States; the Arab League, for countries in the Near East with
the exception of Israel; and the proposed Middle East Command, for this
entire area. Because the basic motivation and operation of these systems are
political and not organizational, their detailed consideration has fallen naturally in the chapters which deal with American foreign policy in the
special areas involved. Relevant here are implications which these arrangements may reveal about the scope of international organization and American
attitudes thereto.

The fundamental question about all these groupings is whether they are
international organizations on a regional basis at all or merely elaborate
alliances directed at one of the two superpowers. Let us grant at the outset
that the distinction may tend to blur and become indistinct, that we are
dealing here not with two separate categories but with a continuum, one end
of which can be labeled "international organization" and the other "simple
alliance." To locate the approximate position of each grouping on the continuum at least three tests should be applied: Are there mechanisms for
peaceful settlement *among* the members? Does the grouping include legal,
social, economic, in other words functional and technical, aspects of cooperation, as well as measures for common security? Does the extent of great-
power participation give these organizations a distinct orientation in the
bipolar framework?

THE ORGANIZATION OF AMERICAN STATES

If these three criteria are applied, the Organization of American States
comes closest to the international organization end of the continuum. It is by
far the largest grouping, encompassing twenty-one states and what is pop-
ularly, though not technically, known as a hemisphere. While the security
aspects are basic and anti-Soviet motivations apparent, methods of peaceful
settlement are far from absent. Indeed, as an earlier chapter mentioned,
problems arise because those methods are so elaborate, so plentiful, so prone
to overlap. Even when one takes into account the poor ratification record of

many American republics, especially Argentina, it still remains true that procedures exist for the pacific settlement of disputes between members within the system, that the members are bound to follow those procedures, and that of recent times they have been applied. United States participation undoubtedly entangles the Organization of American states to some extent in East-West conflict, but the elaboration over some fifty years of methods of cooperation in a wide range of functional and technical fields give it a substance and direction distinct from present world political situations. If the Soviet Union did not exist, or if it and the United States were on the friendliest of terms, the Organization of American States would still exist with much the same structure which it has at present.

THE ARAB LEAGUE

The Arab League is in some respects similar. It was formed before the establishment of the United Nations, with the signing of the Arab Pact on March 22, 1945, by Egypt, Syria, Lebanon, Jordan, Iraq, Saudi Arabia, and Yemen. From the first its activities also were directed toward political objectives: freedom of the area from the vestiges of Western colonialism, and prevention of a Jewish state in Palestine. The former objective still motivates the words and deeds of some of its members, but the latter has revealed its basic direction and demonstrated its weakness. Article 6 of the Arab Pact calls for the convocation of the Arab Council should aggression occur or be threatened. Decisions of that council shall be unanimous, but majority decisions are binding on those states which supported them.

The test of the Arab League was Israel. Aided no little by British advice and equipment and by the manner in which Britain chose to terminate its physical occupation of the Jerusalem mandate, the Arab League undertook to suppress the new Jewish state by attacking it from three directions simultaneously. Not only did the Arab League fail to defeat Israel; it could not hold even those portions of the mandate originally marked for the Arabs in the partition plans. The only success was attained by King Abdullah's Jordan Legion, equipped, trained, and advised by the British. The effect of the Palestine fiasco was to weaken the Arab League seriously, to bring to the surface the many social, economic, political, dynastic, and religious conflicts that exist between its members. In most of the countries it caused grave internal unrest, including coups, revolutions, and assassinations. In this atmosphere the Arab League, originally oriented almost solely along nationalist and security lines, has not developed the other aspects of cooperation which would place it close to the international organization side of the spectrum.

THE MIDDLE EAST COMMAND

In late 1951 the United States, Great Britain, and France put forth an ingenious plan for a Middle East Command, designed to embrace, in addition to themselves, several countries which were members of the Arab League, as well as Israel and Turkey. As its name implies, the purpose of the Command was to "assist and support the states willing to join in the defense of the Middle East and to develop the capacity of each to play its proper role in defense of the area as a whole against outside aggression." If it ever comes to fruition, the proposal will clearly be in the nature of an alliance rather than a regional organization. The Command, say the three initiating nations, "will not interfere in problems and disputes arising within the area," such as the continued Arab hostility toward Israel. While the possibility of decreasing peacetime responsibility of the three outside powers is mentioned, present conditions place such developments in the remote future. The rejection of the plan by Egypt and its opposition by Syria and Iraq, all of which are more interested in seeing the removal of Western influence rather than its perpetuation by such devices as a Middle East Command, make it possible that some countries in the area, such as Turkey and Israel, will eventually join in cooperative security arrangements, while others will remain aloof. The result would be to drive a deep wedge into any truly regional international organization. Motivations behind the suggestion were the effective enrollment of the area as part of the global containment of the Soviet Union and the search for a formula that would maintain Western leadership to that end.

EUROPEAN REGIONAL ARRANGEMENTS

Arrangements among the European states and with the United States are bewildering to a student of organization by reason of their varying functions and membership. In the economic field, there are, in addition to bilateral agreements, the small Benelux Union, the sixteen-member Organization for European Economic Cooperation, and the relationship to the United States via the Economic Cooperation Administration. In the realm of military security are the Brussels Pact, the North Atlantic Treaty, and, via the United States Mutual Defense Assistance Act, a relationship to such outside countries as Greece, Turkey, Iran, the Philippines, Nationalist China, and South Korea. In the field of political organization is the Council of Europe.

Division of function is notoriously obscure. The Brussels Pact, for example, although primarily a security alliance, contains clauses on economic and social cooperation, while the political Council of Europe has undertaken consideration of both economic and military problems. The welter of arrangements and the variety of national relationships obscure several important conclusions. There has been a steady progression toward clearly defined military cooperation. The United States has become more and more deeply involved in the organizational relationships. The West German state has likewise entered more and more closely into European affairs. There has been a tendency for arrangements to expand their geographic frontiers far beyond the European confines. The arrangements themselves contain important aspects of true international organization which have to date, however, not developed very far.

The development of military cooperation, on the other hand, has been rapid. Whether it has been rapid enough to maintain the security of Western Europe is not as yet clear. Only a year passed between the signing of the Dunkirk Treaty and the signing of the Brussels Pact. The latter was effected in March, 1948, and had undoubtedly been hastened by the Communist coup in Czechoslovakia the preceding month. A year later the North Atlantic Treaty negotiations came to fruition in Washington. By 1951 the organizational principles of that treaty had begun to emerge, although detailed cooperation between national armed forces in various theaters and in various battle mediums lagged behind. The long debate which preceded a direct United States commitment of American contingents and the limitation of that commitment was exasperating to those who scanned the black international skies and saw the flashes of lightning and heard the rolls of thunder which they felt were preludes to a deluge. Viewed in historical perspective, however, against deeply imbedded American attitudes toward Europe, the reversal of traditional policy was startling in its speed.

The involvement of the United States in European organization was both economic and military, and had political overtones as well. It was the United States which urged the establishment of machinery for the formulation of plans for *European* recovery, in place of uninational competitive economic measures. The United States, without fully understanding the obstacles, implications, and terminology, has favored more and more European "unification" and "integration" in order that the best use might be made of American aid and of Western European resources. Thus the United States looks with interest on the plans for and operations of political organization in Europe. The occupation policies of General Clay and Mr. McCloy emphasized the Western ties of the West German State through its entrance into European economic organization and, ultimately, into the military organization as well.

Finally, the dependence of Western Europe on the United States has resulted in the expansion of its organizational ties. To the extent that Great Britain participates, its ties with the Commonwealth bring British dominions all over the world into close relation to Western Europe. The OEEC, because of its function in the disbursement of ECA funds, has included Greece and Turkey. The North Atlantic Pact includes Iceland, not considered a part of Europe for other purposes; Portugal, which is not in the North Atlantic and not a participant in European economic cooperation; Italy, which by definition is in Western Europe, but is not in the North Atlantic either; and Greece and Turkey, which are closer to the Near East than to the North Atlantic. It is possible that as plans for the defense of Western Europe proceed, Spain and Yugoslavia, both of which claim consideration by reason of their strategic locations, will ultimately be more intimately connected with the formal military framework of NATO.

Regional organization with purely Western European membership has also made great strides. The partial opening of the Coal-Steel Pool and the proposal for a European Defense Community have inevitably led to plans for a European political community which would have supranational powers, as the Council of Europe does not, and which would, at the outset, be composed only of the members of the Coal-Steel Pool and Defense Community —i.e., West Germany, France, Italy, Belgium, the Netherlands, and Luxembourg. When and if such a political community emerges, international organization in Western Europe will have reached a very advanced stage, since blueprints call for the endowment of the central authority with broad powers over economic, military, and political matters. To date, however, the obstacles to such a community remain formidable. In additon to the reconciliation of differences between the potential members, principally those between France and West Germany, the obstacles include the indefinite degree of participation of Great Britain, continued economic and military dependence by the area on the United States, the explosive question of German unity, and the position of Western Europe in the East-West cold war. But the dream of a European Union is an old one; it has been given new vitality by the contemporary state of international tension, which finds the states of Western Europe powerless to control their own destinies. Too short a time has elapsed since organizational structures began to floriate in Western Europe after World War II to justify the pessimistic conclusion that the difficult transition, previously noted, between functional cooperation and effective political organization cannot be made in this area.

► EFFORTS TO STRENGTHEN THE UNITED NATIONS

THE INTERIM COMMITTEE OF THE GENERAL ASSEMBLY

At the same time that the retreat from the Charter through the large doorway of Article 51 has been taking place, efforts have been made, led by the United States, to transform the United Nations itself into a more effective organization for the maintenance of security. Since the Soviet Union's veto power has nullified the clauses of the Charter giving predominant responsibility to the Security Council (with the exception of the Korean case to be considered in a moment), attention has been directed toward enlarging the competence of the veto-free General Assembly. Although suggestions along this line had been made as early as 1945, the first concrete steps were taken when the General Assembly in November, 1947, acted on Secretary of State Marshall's proposal and established its Interim Committee or Little Assembly. There was ample justification in the Charter for such a move. Article 22 empowered the Assembly to create "such subsidiary organs as it deems necessary for the performance of its functions." As defined by Articles 11, 13, 14, and 35, those duties included "the general principles of cooperation in the maintenance of international peace and security," the promotion through studies and recommendations of "international cooperation in the political field," the recommendation of "measures for the peaceful adjustment of any situation . . . which it deems likely to impair the general welfare or friendly relations among nations," and the consideration of "any dispute, or any situation" brought before it by a member or a nonmember state.

Each member had the right to representation on the Interim Committee, whose function, as its name implies, was to maintain general supervision over the international scene while the Assembly was not in session. The Assembly, in establishing the Interim Committee, called specific attention to the fact that both organs were barred from consideration of any dispute of which the Security Council was "seized" (graphic phraseology meaning "to have on the agenda"). Notwithstanding its undoubted legality under the Charter, the committee was violently attacked by Soviet representatives, who saw in it, and correctly so, an attempt to evade the Security Council veto, while the United States welcomed the committee as a device by which it could direct attention to the corrosive consequences of Soviet behavior inside and outside the United Nations. Naturally the Soviet Union and its satellites had nothing to do with the committee. The boycott had the advantage of freeing the committee from the filibustering and red tape usually attendant on Soviet participation in a minority position on any body. On the other hand, the express limitations of the Charter inevitably prevented the committee from doing more than gathering information and attracting attention to dangerous situations; in other words, it pursued the same line as that enforced on the General Assembly itself.

"UNITING FOR PEACE" RESOLUTIONS

The Interim Committee was but a prelude to further American proposals made to the General Assembly in the fall of 1950. The Soviet-sponsored attack on South Korea had alarmed the world over the possibility that the impotence of the Security Council would encourage Russian as well as small-power aggression. To be sure, the self-imposed absence of the Soviet delegate fortunately permitted the Security Council to mobilize the United Nations under American leadership for the defense of South Korea, but there was no belief that this self-defeating Russian policy would be repeated in any future emergency A determined effort was accordingly made in the "Uniting for Peace" Resolutions to lay the groundwork for Assembly action to maintain security.

The second and third resolutions were concerned with the failure of the Security Council. The second made the gesture of recommending implementation by the Security Council of the appropriate articles of the Charter regarding the provision of armed forces for the United Nations. The third recommended to the Security Council that it discuss collectively "or otherwise" the problems hampering the activities of the United Nations for the maintenance of international peace and security, and that it report the results of these discussions to the General Assembly.

Because the functioning of the Security Council was not likely to be fundamentally affected by Resolutions B and C, more importance attached to Resolution A. In it a rationale for elarged Assembly competence was first set forth. Primary responsibility for maintaining peace and security, said the resolution, still rests with the Security Council. But the inaction of that body does not relieve the members of the United Nations of their responsibilities under the Charter in this field. Hence, if the Security Council did not function in the face of aggression, the General Assembly could act immediately if in session, and if not in session might be convened at the call of *any* seven members of the Security Council. To keep the Assembly informed, a fourteen-man Peace Observation Commission was established for the two years, 1951 and 1952, which by a two-thirds vote of the Assembly or its Interim Committee could go to the scene of trouble if the state concerned invited or accepted its presence.

Finally, a way around the block to armed forces for the United Nations was apparently found in Article 51. Members of the United Nations were asked to keep a portion of their armed forces available for collective action and to report their size and composition to the General Assembly's Collective Measures Committee. Should the members desire advice on this score, a Military Experts Committee was established.

The important implication of the General Assembly's Resolution A is that it and not the Security Council can become the enforcement agency for world organization. In case of aggression the General Assembly need not wait for the smaller body to deliberate and be stymied by Russian vetoes. The Assembly itself may meet, hear firsthand reports by the aggrieved state and by its own committees. If measures of pacific settlement which it recommends fail or are already too late, it may invoke the inherent right of individual or *collective* self-defense. It can call on individual states or groups of states to take military action on behalf of the world organization with armed forces which those members have stated are available for such a call. And all this it can do, not by unanimous vote, as had been required in the League Assembly, not with concurrence of the permanent members, as in the Security Council, but by a two-thirds vote of the international community provided only that seven of the Security Council agree to a meeting of the Assembly if it is not already in session.

REVERSAL IN IMPORTANCE OF THE SECURITY COUNCIL AND THE GENERAL ASSEMBLY

Soviet vetoes—close to sixty in 1954—plus the determination of other United Nations members, as exemplified in the proposals just mentioned, not to permit Russia to halt altogether the work of the international organization in the political field of maintaining peace and security have had the effect of drastically altering the procedures and relationships contemplated by its framers. Specifically, the hierarchy of responsibility and influence, previously running from Assembly to Security Council, has been reversed. Already the Security Council has declined strikingly in importance as a place of meeting for the great powers. Whereas the Council met no fewer than 168 times in 1948, with agenda full of new and old problems, only 42 meetings were held in 1952. In 1953 the nadir of Security Council activity was reached— six meetings on only one question, the selection of a successor to Trygve Lie, and ended with Soviet agreement to the nomination of Dag Hammarskjold. Only restored harmony of the major powers, prerequisite to Security Council action, will permit that body once again to seize the initiative and discharge the responsibility placed in its hands by the Charter.

► EFFICACY OF THE UNITED NATIONS IN VARIOUS
TYPES OF POLITICAL CONFLICT

The deleterious effects of extreme bipolarity on the security functions of the United Nations can further be brought out by consideration of the effect of United Nations action on various types of state conflict. For purposes of this discussion all nations other than the Big Two are considered small states. Though this is still an oversimplification which does an injustice to the remaining strength of such middle- and lower-middle-class powers as Great Britain, France, and Canada, World War II and developments since have narrowed the gap between small and middle powers so far as their ability to affect their own destinies are concerned. Five categories of states may be envisaged: small states in which neither the United States nor the Soviet Union has interest and influence (SS); small states within the American sphere (SSUS); small states in the Soviet sphere (SSUSSR); the United States; the Soviet Union. Eleven types of state conflict involving the four state types are possible: between small states in which neither great power has influence (SS-SS); an uninfluenced small state and one in the American sphere (SS-SSUS); an uninfluenced small state and one in the Soviet sphere (SS-SSUSSR); an uninfluenced small state and the United States (SS-US); an uninfluenced small state and the Soviet Union (SS-USSR); a small state in the American sphere and the United States (SSUS-US); a small state in the American sphere and the Soviet Union (SSUS-USSR); a small state in the American sphere and one in the Soviet sphere (SSUS-SSUSSR), a small state in the Soviet sphere and the Soviet Union (SSUSSR-USSR); a small state in the Soviet sphere and the United States (SSUSSR-US); the United States and the Soviet Union (US-USSR).

ARAB-ISRAELI CONFLICT

Two of the three successful efforts of the United Nations in the field of international security fall into the first category of conflict listed above: between small states uninfluenced by either great power. This situation approximately describes the conflict between Israel and the Arab League, although labeling United Nations action in Palestine as a success is perhaps stretching the meaning of the word. Israel was created and maintained by the force of its own arms, not by United Nations assistance. The attainment of the ambiguous cease-fire status was made possible by the revealed weakness of the Arab League and by the willingness of the stronger Israeli forces to halt before all possible land had been captured. Although the cease-fire as yet has not been transformed into any permanent settlement, nonetheless the United Nations did help to keep the conflict localized, did mitigate its ferocity, did hasten the end of active fighting, and does help to maintain the uneasy truce. Its contributions, therefore, may be regarded as substantial, if not determining.

DUTCH-INDONESIAN CONFLICT

The three-year period of intermittent Dutch-Indonesian fighting falls into the same category, since the Netherlands, while subjected to pressure of a diplomatic nature from the United States, could not at the time have been regarded as within the sphere of American control. In this case also the United Nations success was limited. It did not prevent the resumption of fighting after truce lines had been established, nor did it dictate the final relationship worked out between Holland and its former colony. Steady and unremitting pressure by the United Nations, however, probably did help to induce the Netherlands not to engage in the type of effort now being undertaken by the French in Indo-China. Therefore the world organization again contributed substantially to the form, extent, and promptitude of Indonesian independence.

DECLINE OF OTHER TYPES OF CONFLICT

The inevitable consequence of the growing hostility between the United States and the Soviet Union has been to enlarge the scope and intensity of spheres of influence of each great power. Therefore the situation just considered, in which conflict exists between small states within *neither* sphere, is a declining phenomenon. The same may be said of the second and fourth types of conflict: between an uninfluenced state and a state in the American sphere, and between an uninfluenced state and the United States. Here the disposition of the great power involved may be to encourage United Nations mediation, but the chances are remote that the small state concerned will in actual fact be outside the sphere of either great power. Perhaps the present conflict in Iran also illustrates the tendency of both the uninfluenced small state and the one in the American sphere (no derogation of Great Britain is intended in this purely schematic presentation) to rely on modes of settlement outside the machinery of the United Nations.

TYPES OF CONFLICT IN WHICH THE UNITED NATIONS IS INEFFECTIVE

While it is conceivable that the United Nations might attempt to take action in the case of a small, uninfluenced state involved in conflict with a small state in the Soviet sphere or with the Soviet Union itself, its chances of success are remote unless it wishes to run the risk of a world war. There would appear to be little likelihood of a repetition of the 1946 Iranian-Russian case, which may also be called a United Nations success. The Soviet Union thought it was running little risk in supporting the "autonomy" of Azerbaijan and was surprised at the concern showed by the United Nations in keeping the item on the Security Council agenda even when requested by *both* parties to the dispute to forget the whole affair. The Soviet Union withdrew its troops from Iran because the potential losses seemed greater than the immediate gains. Duplication of the incident is unlikely, because the Soviet Union now knows that such action can result in a world conflict which it so far seems desirous of avoiding.

This leaves six types of conflict in which the United Nations system of maintaining security is likely to be ineffective. Conflict between the United States and the Soviet Union cannot be resolved by the forceful interposition of the world organization, and the same is true for a small state in the sphere of one of the great powers conflicting with one of the Big Two. In the case of the United States, that country sometimes does and sometimes does not choose to use the facilities of the United Nations, but in any event the machinery invoked would not include internationally organized force. Conflicts within the sphere of influence of each of the Big Two are to be settled by the regional group itself, and not by the United Nations. Thus the Haitian-Dominican dispute went to the Organization of American States; and the Cominform, backed by Soviet power, has shown itself capable of enforcing order between the satellite states of Eastern Europe, with the significant exception of Yugoslavia, which was cast by the Kremlin into the outer darkness, there to wander ever closer to the pole of American power and influence.

▶ IMPORTANCE OF THE UNITED NATIONS IN AMERICAN FOREIGN POLICY

It may be seen in this chapter that international organization has undergone considerable change since 1945. In evaluating its place in present American foreign policy the transition from the initial viewpoint, "How can the nations of the world cooperate to establish and maintain peace?" to the new focus, "How can the *free* nations of the world cooperate to forestall communist aggression?" must be constantly borne in mind. The approach to the first question calls for techniques primarily nonmilitary in nature: diplomatic, legal, organizational, economic, sociological, and the like. The transition to the second question places ever greater emphasis on measures directly related to military security. The first thing to be said about the present place of international organization in American foreign policy, therefore, is that it has a smaller and less important place than was contemplated during the wartime planning period or in the years preceding disillusionment with the goals and motivations behind Soviet policy.

Although voices are still heard, urging that the United Nations should lead to world government, they are being lost in the din created by those who are either disillusioned with international organization altogether or who would shape the United Nations into an instrument to tighten the world-wide anti-Soviet coalition. Senator James Eastland of Mississippi wanted the United States to withdraw from the United Nations if Communist China should be admitted. Senator Pat McCarran was in more of a hurry, urging that the United States "pull out of the U.N. while there is yet time to save this country." Other voices in Senate and House have urged the United States to "go it alone." Proposals that no American be permitted to work for the United Nations unless he had been cleared by the Attorney General were viewed in United Nations headquarters as less an attempt to tighten American security controls than part of a deliberate campaign to force the United Nations to locate itself elsewhere.

Such counsels, even when coming from Congress, do not represent the official policy of the American government. But the relationship of the government to American public opinion and its leaders makes it increasingly difficult in the present international climate for the United States to rely to any greater extent on international machinery for the attainment of its own security. When former Secretary of State Marshall appeared before a Congressional committee considering amendments to the Charter and argued against such proposals on the grounds that the present Charter was the best one obtainable under present circumstances, a lay paraphrase of his testimony might have run thus: "The United Nations may not be very much, but it is better than nothing, and the United States is stuck with it for a while."

DEVELOPMENT OF ADMINISTRATIVE RELATIONS

It may at first seem paradoxical, but it is nonetheless true, that the decline of the United Nations as a security organization has seen the coincident increase in American administrative energies devoted to discharging efficiently the complex lines of relationship between the government and the United Nations. The United Nations and its specialized agencies held 428 major meetings in 1949 with approximately six thousand individual sessions. United States representatives at these sessions had to be ready to state, if necessary, the official position of the American government.To make certain that as wide a consensus as possible is reached between the State Department and the twenty-four other agencies of the American government intimately concerned with this country's participation in various phases of international organization a pyramidal structure has gradually been developed. This structure contains, said a staff assistant to the Assistant Secretary of State for

United Nations Affairs, "a broad basis for the purpose of securing as many points of view as possible, exchanging ideas and information and hammering [out] our final policy recommendations; a system of screening, reviewing, and channeling, to secure responsible approval of the tentative policies and, where necessary, reconciliation with positions taken in other situations; and, finally, a point of departure at which the official sanction of the Government can be granted so that the representative at the other end of the line may be assured that he speaks with the final authority." Sometimes this system breaks down or is by-passed completely, as, for example, when the American delegation at the United Nations was placed in the embarrassing position of having to admit ignorance of United States *de facto* recognition of Israel several hours after announcement of the step had been made in Washington.

The focal point of communication between the government and the American delegations to international organizations and conferences, including the United Nations, is the State Department's Bureau of United Nations Affairs. The bureau contains five offices, which have a total of 120 officers, the largest group of which is in the lowest rank: Dependent Area Affairs, International Administration and Conferences, United Nations Economic and Social Affairs, and United Nations Political and Security Affairs. It is significant that over 40 per cent of the officers are concentrated in the one entirely administrative office—the Office of International Administration and Conferences—mainly in its Division of International Conferences. This leaves a total of only seventy officers in the policy-planning offices of the bureau, and many of them, of course, fulfill primarily administrative functions. It is further significant that the size of the bureau has remained fairly constant over the past three years, with the emphasis, in fact, being placed on the reduction rather than the expansion of staff. From 1947 onward the main improvement has been, not in the employment of additional officers, but rather in the development of more efficient administrative practices.

Two factors account in large part for the increased attention to administrative relationships. The first arises from the United Nations itself as a going concern. Notwithstanding the paralyzing effect which Soviet policy has had on much United Nations business, the mere survival of the organization for six years has inevitably resulted in the increased bulk of activity noted above. A Senate committee investigating the internal operations of the United Nations tabulated the steadily increasing expenditures of that body, exclusive of emergency relief programs and special activities as follows: 1946—$19,390,000; 1947—$27,901,969; 1948—$38,387,531; 1949—$42,575,-368; 1950—$44,520,773.

The second factor is the changing focus of American foreign policy generally since 1945. The assumption of the responsibility attendant upon its new power position has meant increased activity in all fields of foreign relations, a development which has been reflected in domestic policy as well.

American policies carried on outside the United Nations, including those regarded as primarily domestic, have had a profound impact on this country's relationship to the United Nations. Obvious examples are the national rearmament program, economic aid to Western Europe, procurement of material stockpiles, and the development of technical assistance under President Truman's Point Four Program.

IDEOLOGICAL USE OF THE UNITED NATIONS

The breakdown of American-Soviet relations has forced the United States to utilize the United Nations as an instrument in the cold war. This change in the American view of the role of international organization from being an end of policy to being the means to some other end is highly important and can be expected to continue so long as the present impasse remains. When Vishinsky, Gromyko, and Company first began to use the meetings at Lake Success as occasions for vitriolic attacks on the West, the countries outside the Soviet sphere were stunned. The initial reaction was that this was some underhanded way of wringing new concessions to the Soviet Union. The response therefore followed the Biblical injunction: "A soft answer turneth away wrath, but grievous words stir up anger." American representatives rather prided themselves on not descending to the level of debate reached by the Soviet, but, instead, on keeping their own statements and replies factual and mild, albeit firm. The hope behind this policy still was that when the thunder and lightning had subsided, agreements could be reached.

When American statesmen concluded regretfully that the Soviet Union was not using diatribe merely as a prelude to compromise, United States policy shifted. Soviet representatives were in fact speaking not to their primary antagonists at all, but with a mixture of threat and cajolery were attempting to weaken the support of the West by countries allied to it, to keep "neutral" nations out of the Western camp altogether, to tie the Soviet satellites closer to the Kremlin by filling in details of a picture of Western warmongering, and to maintain the sole identification of the Russian people with a Soviet state which was protecting them from attack. The United States finally concluded that it had to engage in this war of words or run the risk of seeing the war won by default. Discussion in the United Nations was one of several means used to counteract the picture of the West drawn by the Russians, and to seize the initiative wherever possible so as to place the onus of blame for world insecurity where it properly belonged. In this exchange other nations of the free world have joined, as have the Russian satellites, so that the rigidity of debate in the United Nations reflects the rigidity of organization of a bipolar world. "Neutrals" have had to jump one way or another; those which, like India, attempt to continue an "on the one hand . . . but then on the other" view end up by straddling issues, avoiding decisions, by compiling a record of increasing inconsistency.

Examples abound of the use of the United Nations by the United States as a platform for ideological warfare. Two may suffice here: first, the heated attacks by the American delegate, Warren Austin, in August and September, 1950, on the actions of the North Koreans and on the source of their inspiration, the Soviet Union; second, the declaration by Secretary Acheson before the 1951 Paris meeting of the General Assembly that Communist China follows a line of international conduct so low that it would take considerable improvement to raise it to the general level of barbarism. It may be that the point of diminishing returns has been reached by American tough talk of this nature when used for the purpose of cementing relations with allies which are one and all fearful of a third world war. There have been indications that other countries have asked the United States on occasion to moderate its language, particularly when the Soviet Union was thought to be on the verge of making some conciliatory gesture. But it should be remembered it is the United States, not America's allies, which has the responsibility of leading the free world. Also it is true that American, like Russian, statements are directed at the domestic, national audience as well as at the leaders of other countries.

THE UNITED NATIONS AS AN EXAMPLE IN COOPERATION

However, the use of the United Nations as an ideological medium by the United States is not limited to verbal approaches. The United States and the other nations of the West have directed their ideological policies to make the United Nations appear as an example of free world cooperation against the dark picture of Soviet domination. This is a delicate policy to pursue successfully. Great care must be taken to play up the prestige of the United Nations, to avoid pressure on other countries to "vote right," to emphasize the practical ways in which the United Nations can contribute to international security through its functional aspects, to see that other members besides the United States play significant roles in the deliberations of the organization, however tedious adherence to parliamentary rules may be at times. Even Soviet and satellite delegates are permitted their rambling rantings virtually unchecked. As in the United States Senate, invocation of cloture may do more harm than good. These are sovereign nations, says the United States, freely cooperating for their mutual benefit. If the Soviet Union cares to join in the activity, it will be welcome.

THE UNITED NATIONS AS AN ANTI-SOVIET COALITION

At the same time, however, that American policy is directed at making the United Nations a showcase of free-world cooperation, the same organization is used as an integral part of the world-wide anti-Soviet coalition. The United Nations can perform this function either in its own right or by serving as multilateral sanction for bilateral or unilateral American action. In both cases extreme caution must be exerted to give the minimum of plausibility to the contentions of Soviet propaganda that the United Nations is but a tool in the hands of American warmongers. This contention can be falsified, but a delicate touch is needed, since the basic fact remains that the United Nations is being used as a means to an end to be attained under the leadership of the United States.

The creation of the General Assembly's Interim Committee and the Uniting for Peace Resolution, both discussed above, were designed to improve the effectiveness of the United Nations in the types of disputes in which it has hitherto proved virtually impotent: those to which the Soviet Union or one of its satellites is a party. While the provisions for collective action against a great power or a small one protected by a great power may be inoperative, the Assembly now has the power of investigation and recommendation, flounting of which by Russia will enable the rest of the world correctly to assess the blame for disturbances of the peace, a considerable ideological advantage for the West. The presence of Soviet and satellite delegates in the United Nations is also of advantage in this connection. Their blunt efforts to disorganize and frustrate international machinery contributes to the unity of other states in their opposition to such actions. Confronted with the Soviet danger, constantly reminded of its existence by the Soviet representatives themselves, other nations are under pressure to reconcile their differences, which otherwise would lead to conflict and disunity among the members of the Western coalition.

THE UNITED NATIONS AS SANCTION FOR AMERICAN POLICIES

The use of international organization to sanction national policies of the United States was pointed out in the chapter dealing with American relationships toward the Inter-American System. We now see the same policy evident in the United Nations. One example has been the skillful use of United Nations machinery in the Korean affair. The resolutions of the Security Council adopted in June, 1950, provided the necessary authorization for the United States to undertake the defense of South Korea. Since that time American commanders have operated under the aegis of the world organization, but the real lines of communication have run through Washington. The contributions made by other members of the United Nations to the action, while militarily small, have, however, been symbolically important as a demonstration of the collective nature of the undertaking. Somewhat more clumsy was the use of the trusteeship clauses of the Charter to sanction American retention of strategic bases in the Pacific. The rationale in this case is a compound of two elements: theoretical jurisdiction of the United Nations over national policy in the trusteeship agreement, and operation of the bases to enhance the international security to which the Charter is devoted. A final illustration is the use of the United Nations Economic and Social Council to provide a channel through which the United States makes technical assistance available to underdeveloped nations at the same time that other aid is granted on a bilateral basis.

While it is obviously not always possible or desirable to seek multilateral endorsement for bilateral or unilateral policy, American statecraft should not neglect the technique merely because it is cumbersome or because the habit of national action is more deeply ingrained than the comparatively recent experience with international mechanisms. It must also be recognized that the domestic pressure of chauvinism is not infrequently exerted upon the Executive Branch of government by private or legislative groups that incorrectly feel that American prestige suffers when United States leadership and direction is obscured. It was awareness of the value of the United Nations to this aspect of American foreign policy which led the late Senator Vandenberg to add an amendment to the Greek-Turkish aid bill providing that American assistance would cease whenever the General Assembly or the Security Council should determine that it was no longer necessary, and that the United States would not use its veto power in the latter body to frustrate a majority decision. In consideration of the North Atlantic Pact, both before Congress and the United Nations, official spokesmen were careful to emphasize its compatibility with the letter and spirit of the Charter. This policy was successful in eliciting from Secretary General Trygve Lie a statement to the same effect.

THE UNITED NATIONS AND REGIONAL ARRANGEMENTS

These considerations point to the importance of the United Nations as a cover for regional arrangements and as a link between them. While the weaknesses of the United Nations in the security field have caused the proliferation of such groupings, the latter are no substitute for the former. The whole in this case is immeasurably greater than the sum of its various parts. Without Article 51 and the ensuing chapter the United Nations might well have broken down completely against the determination of various states to work out among themselves measures of mutual security unattainable under the world organization. On the other hand, Article 51 is not designed as an escape hatch from which world responsibility is evaded under the guise of regional protection. No permanent satisfaction can be found in this direction, and the net effect would be to divide the world into two hostile and ultimately warring systems of alliances.

Division of power is inherent in the postwar situation. The policies of the Soviet Union have forced the free world to ally itself closely for common protection. Division has gone far, but so long as the regional groupings are related to the United Nations in fact as well as in theory, not only can they function more efficiently in their relationship one to another, but they can contribute as well toward protecting the development of universal world organization. So long as the latter remains as a bridge and a link, the security position of the few states not included in any regional system may be serious but not hopeless. Such states are then enabled to play an important and constructive role in world organization as diplomatic bridges between East and West.

THE UNITED NATIONS AS LINK BETWEEN EAST AND WEST

Negotiation between the West and the Soviet Union has for four years been all but fruitless. This does not mean, however, that the avenues to such negotiation must be needlessly sealed, unless indeed the West is prepared for a third world war which Russia might lose but which democratic civilization could not win. If the United States is prone to feel that negotiation, Russian style, is fruitless and time wasting, it has constantly to bear in mind that for the overwhelming majority of states the alternative is infinitely worse. So many of the normal lines of communication with the Soviet Union have been severed, usually at the Eastern end, that greater weight attaches to the few that are left. The United Nations is one.

International facilities can function in any of three ways, one of which was suggested above. A member of the United Nations not directly attached to either side may serve as a channel through which contact is established. This it may do either on its own initiative or at the suggestion of one of the major antagonists. Such an operation, be it noted, may and probably does have little to do with the formal relationships delineated by the Charter. Two outstanding examples, both of which proved futile, were the attempt of the Argentine representative to use his position as chairman of the Security Council to formulate a settlement to the Berlin blockade acceptable to the United States and the Soviet Union, and the recent persistent effort of Indian spokesmen to find a common ground on which the West and Communist China could meet.

Another way in which the United Nations can serve as a channel of communications is through the nonnational personnel of that organization. It was former Secretary General Trygve Lie's dynamic decision that his office, unlike the comparable one under the League, should have a responsibility and jurisdiction of its own arising from its relationship to the Charter and apart from its obvious connection with the member states. In fulfillment of this conception of his role, the Secretary General did not hesitate to intrude his office into Security Council and Assembly procedure, by suggesting items for inclusion on their agenda or by taking a personal hand in the course of the discussion. Lie also rode the circuit on behalf of the United Nations to investigate personally whether and in what manner his office might contribute to the relief of international tension. Such positive approaches inevitably aroused the irritation of both East and West, but Western recognition of the value of his function was indicated by American insistence over the opposition of the Soviet Union and its satellites that he not be forced from his position. Likewise, when Lie finally resigned, the Western powers were determined that a man of equal stature should occupy the post of Secretary General. The acceptance by the Soviet Union of Dag Hammarskjold meant that the important functions of the office would be performed by a citizen of one of the few countries left which has not as yet become formally engaged on one side or the other of the East-West conflict. Thus the office of Secretary General will continue to be open as a meeting ground of the opposed factions, a place where contact can be maintained and proposals exchanged out of the limelight that focuses on all formal United Nations gatherings.

Finally, the halls or councils of the United Nations may be used for direct approaches from one side to another. Informal negotiations between Philip Jessup and Jacob Malik prepared the way for the agreement which lifted the blockade of Berlin, the most dangerous threat to world peace arising between 1945 and the outbreak of the Korean war. Truce talks between the antagonists in Korea grew out of proposals made by the Soviet representative. In order to make direct negotiations possible the Russians abandoned, at least temporarily, the farcical contention that the Chinese had only volunteers in Korea and that the Soviet Union had no responsibility or control at all over events taking place in that divided country. Bombast, diatribe, and vituperations, and the pitiless light of publicity which focuses on the United Nations certainly make more difficult direct approaches and fruitful negotiation between East and West. The record proves, however, that such approaches are possible even under trying conditions. Elimination of the facilities which make them attainable could only aggravate the international insecurity in which all nations of the world now find themselves.

► CONCLUSION

In his testimony before the House Foreign Relations Committee in 1953 Henry Cabot Lodge, Representative of the United States to the United Nations, thus summed up the value of the United Nations to the United States and its place in American foreign policy.

> Many persons had the idea at the end of World War II that the United Nations would be an automatic peace producer—that a few gifted lawyers scattered around the world would draft a charter, that this charter would be ratified by the nations, that a handsome building would be erected, and that then the world would have an automatic device for peace. The truth is that there is no automatic device for peace. If the United Nations is as automatic as a burglar alarm, it is doing well. But what happens after the bell rings is up to the members, and you will get results solely in proportion as you contribute.
>
> For Americans the United Nations is not only a place to promote peace. It is the greatest single place in which to develop partners who, valuing their own freedom, will fight to defend it wherever it is attacked, and thus, on a basis of mutual respect, help us in our struggle to survive. The United Nations is primitive; it is evolutionary; it has not brought— and will not bring—the millenium. But it is useful; its cost is small; it is

an intelligent first step; it stands between us and international anarchy. It thus stands between us and World War III or the extinction of human freedom—or both.

▶ SELECTED BIBLIOGRAPHY

The following are some of the general books on international organization, with special emphasis on the United Nations: Clyde Eagleton, *International Government* (New York, The Ronald Press Company, 1948); Leland Goodrich and Edvard Hambro, *Charter of the United Nations: Commentary and Documents* (Boston, World Peace Foundation, 1949); Werner Levi, *Fundamentals of World Organization* (Minneapolis, University of Minnesota Press, 1950); L. Larry Leonard, *International Organization* (New York, McGraw-Hill Book Company, 1951); Eugene Chase, *The United Nations in Action* (New York, McGraw-Hill Book Company, 1950); Norman Bentwich and Arnold Martin, *Commentary on the Charter of the United Nations* (New York, The Macmillan Company, 1950). Also see Leland Goodrich's bibliographical article on "International Organization," *World Politics,* April, 1951. A more specialized subject is treated in exhaustive detail by Hans Kelsen in *The Law of the United Nations* (New York, Frederick A. Praeger, Inc., 1953); Hans Morgenthau, *Politics among Nations* (New York, Alfred A. Knopf, Inc., 1948) contains two excellent chapters on international law and international organization. For details of American planning of the United Nations Charter consult the three works of Sumner Welles: *The Time for Decision* (New York, Harper & Brothers, 1944), *Where Are We Heading?* (New York, Harper & Brothers, 1946), and *Seven Decisions That Shaped History* (New York, Harper & Brothers, 1950). Additional material may be found in Robert Sherwood, *Roosevelt and Hopkins* (New York, Harper & Brothers, 1948); Cordell Hull, *Memoirs* (New York, The Macmillan Company, 1948); and Ruhl Bartlett, ed., *The Record of American Diplomacy* (New York, Alfred A. Knopf, Inc., 1947). Details of negotiations over atomic energy are contained in two reports by the State Department: *Atomic Energy: Growth of a Policy* (Department of State Publication 2702), and *Atomic Energy: Policy at the Crossroads* (Department of State Publication 3161). The quarterly *International Organization* publishes articles, summaries, and documents on the working of the United Nations, its affiliated agencies, and other international organizations. See particularly the issue of May, 1951, which contains articles by W. T. R. Fox, Benjamin V. Cohen, and Alexander Rudzinski on "The United Nations in the Era of Total Diplomacy," "The Impact of the United Nations on United States Foreign Policy," and "The Influence of the United Nations on Soviet Policy," respectively. In the same magazine for August, 1950, Lincoln Bloomfield discusses "the Department of State and the United Nations." Other significant special studies include the sharply critical account by John Maclaurin, *The United Nations and Power Politics* (New York, Harper & Brothers, n.d.); the Royal Institute of International Affairs, *Documents on Regional Organizations outside Europe* (London,

Royal Institute of International Affairs, 1950); Stephen Schwebel, *The Secretary General of the United Nations* (Cambridge, Mass., Harvard University Press, 1952); Eduardo Jimenez de Arechaga, *Voting and Handling of Disputes in the Security Council* (New York, Carnegie Endowment for International Peace, 1950). The Committee on Expenditures in the Executive Departments, United States Senate, reported on *The Internal Operations of the United Nations and Certain International Organizations in Which the United States Participates,* published as Volume V of *United States Relations with International Organizations.* D. F. Fleming summarized the record of "The United States in the United Nations" in an article for the November, 1951, issue of the *Annals* of the American Academy of Political and Social Science, entitled *The Search for National Security.*

INDEX

INDEX

INDEX